bei Suche bitte eingeben:

Titel:
Frauen und Gesundheit

M.

Claudia Fuchs
Heiningerstr. 11
66798 Wallerfangen
Tel.: 06837 / 1074

Claudia Fuchs
2001

D1752791

Frauen und Gesundheit
– Ethnomedizinische Perspektiven –

Women and Health
– Ethnomedical Perspectives –

Zeitschrift für Ethnomedizin • hrsg. von der Arbeitsgemeinschaft Ethnomedizin e.V.

Journal for Ethnomedicine • edited by the Arbeitsgemeinschaft Ethnomedizin

Sonderband / Special Volume 11/1997

Frauen und Gesundheit
– Ethnomedizinische Perspektiven –

Women and Health
– Ethnomedial Perspectives –

Herausgegeben von

Christine E. Gottschalk-Batschkus,
Judith Schuler
und
Doris Iding

im Auftrag der
Arbeitsgemeinschaft Ethnomedizin

VWB – Verlag für Wissenschaft und Bildung

Zum Titelbild:
Frau aus Papua Neuguinea mit Gesichtstätowierung.
Die Gesichtstätowierungen stammen aus dem Initiationsritual der Mädchen
und stellen auch ein Schönheitsideal dar.

About the Frontcover:
Woman from Papua New Guinea with face tatoo.
Tha face tatoo is used in the initiation rites of the girls
and represents also a beauty ideal.

Die Deutsche Bibliothek – CIP-Einheitsaufnahme

[Curare / Sonderband]
Curare. Sonderband. - Berlin : VWB, Verl. für Wiss. und Bildung
Früher Schriftenreihe. - Früher Verl. Vieweg, Braunschweig, Wiesbaden
Reihe Sonderband zu: Curare

11. Frauen und Gesundheit. - 1997

Frauen und Gesundheit : ethnomedizinische Perspektiven = Women and health / hrsg. von Christine E. Gottschalk-Batschkus, Judith Schuler und Doris Iding im Auftr. der Arbeitsgemeinschaft Ethnomedizin. - Berlin : VWB, Verl. für Wiss. und Bildung, 1997
(Curare : Sonderband ; 11)
ISBN 3-86135-563-9

Verlag und Vertrieb:
VWB – Verlag für Wissenschaft und Bildung, Amand Aglaster
Markgrafenstr. 67 • D-10969 Berlin • Postfach 11 03 68 • D-10833 Berlin
Tel. +49 [0]30 251 04 15 • Fax +49 [0]30 251 04 12

Herstellung:
GAM-Media GmbH, Berlin

Copyright:
© VWB – Verlag für Wissenschaft und Bildung, 1997

Frauen und Gesundheit - Ethnomedizinische Perspektiven
Women and Health - Ethnomedical Perspectives

Herausgegeben von
Christine E. Gottschalk-Batschkus, Judith Schuler und Doris Iding
im Auftrag der Arbeitsgemeinschaft Ethnomedizin

Inhalt / Contents

A. INHALTSVERZEICHNIS DER BEITRÄGE
   CONTENTS OF CONTRIBUTIONS..6

B. VORWORT UND DANKSAGUNG
   PREFACE..11

C. BEITRÄGE
   CONTRIBUTIONS

   1. Frauengesundheit im Kulturvergleich
      Women and Health in transcultural Comparison
      a) Afrika / Africa...13
      b) Asien / Asia...113
      c) Südostasien und Ozeanien / Southeast Asia and Oceania.............133
      d) Nord-, Mittel- u. Südamerika, Karibik /
         North-, Middle-, Andine America, The Carribbean.....................147
      e) Europe / Europe..185

   2. Frauengesundheit in der Interdisziplinären Diskussion
      Women and Health as Diskussed by Different Disciplines......................207
   3. Zentrale Themen
      Central Issues
         Schwangerschaft und Geburt / Pregnancy and Delivery...................279
         Menstruation / Menstruation...335
         Genitalbeschneidung / Female Genital Mutilation.........................341
         Migranten und Flüchtlinge / Migrants and Refugees......................367
         AIDS..401
         Psychische u. Psychiatrische Störungen/Psychiatric Disorders..........409

D. AUTOREN UND HERAUSGEBER DIESES BANDES
   AUTHORS AND EDITORS OF THIS VOLUME......................................437

E. KEYWORDREGISTER (deutsch) 445

F. INDEX OF KEYWORDS (english)..447

C. Inhaltsverzeichnis der Beiträge
Contents of the Contributions

1. FRAUENGESUNDHEIT IM KULTURVERGLEICH
WOMEN AND HEALTH IN TRANSCULTURAL COMPARISON

a) AFRIKA / AFRICA

Preparation of Rural Adolescent Girls to Adulthood in Fitche District, Ethiopia
Wie Mädchen in ländlichen Gegenden auf das Erwachsensein vorbereitet werden (Distrikt Fitche, Äthiopien)
K. Weldemichael Afework, Edmund J. Kayombo & Armin Prinz 13

Das Leben der Frau in arabisch-islamischen Ländern. Betrachtungen eines Frauenarztes
The Life of Women in Arabic Countries. A Gynaecologist's Point of View
Wilhelm Föllmer 21

Women and the Political Economy of Traditional Medicine in Kenya: A Historical Perspective
Frauen und die politische Ökonomie traditioneller Medizin in Kenia. Historische Aspekte
Peter Mwangi Kagwanja 29

Bori - Der Körper spricht
Bori - The Body is Speaking
Herta Maria Nöbauer 39

The Role of Ethnomedicine in Promoting the Health of Women in Kenya
Die Bedeutung der Ethnomedizin für die Förderung von Frauen- Gesundheit in Kenia
Wilson Nyaoro 45

***Kanyalen*, eine Frauenmaske**
Kanyalen: A Womens' Mask
Kirsten Langeveld 53

The Missing Component in Family Planning in Tanzania
Der fehlende Faktor in der Familienplanung in Tansania
Edmund J. Kayombo, K. W. Afework & Armin Prinz 61

Health Definitions of Women in a Low-Standard Settlement of Dar Es Salaam, Tanzania
Gesundheitsdefinitionen von Frauen in einem ärmeren Stadtquartier von Dar es Salaam, Tansania
Brigit Obrist van Eeuwijk 71

Socio-Cultural and Environmental Factors in Maternal Health in Nigeria
Soziokulturelle und Umweltfaktoren mütterlicher Gesundheit in Nigeria
Josephine Nkiru Alumanah 79

The Precarious Health Situation of African Women South of the Sahara
Die schwierige gesundheitliche Situation afrikanischer Frauen südlich der Sahara
Martin W. Bangha 85

Women have an Edge over Men on Traditional Medical Practice (TMPc) Knowledge: The Assumption versus the Field Situation
Frauen haben einen Vorteil gegenüber Männern in Bezug auf Wissen über traditionelle Medizinpraktiken: Die Annahme und die Wirklichkeit
Musingo Tito E. Mbuvi 97

The Interrelationship between Health- and Nutritional Status for Girls, Mothers and Grandmothers
Wechselbeziehungen zwischen der Gesundheits- und Ernährungssituation von Mädchen, Frauen und Großmüttern
Veronika Scherbaum...103

b) ASIEN / ASIA

"Pro Aama" - Psychosocial Situation of Women and Children in Nepal
Die psychosoziale Situation von Frauen und Kindern in Nepal
Georgia Friedrich & Murari Prasad Regmi...113

Munda Women (India) and Health Care
Munda-Frauen (Indien) und Gesundheitsversorgung
Peter Paul Hembrom...123

Skin Care and Herbo-Mineral Beauty Aids in India
Hautpflege und Kosmetik aus Kräutern und Mineralien in Indien
Shashi B. Vohora & Divya Vohora...125

c) SÜDOSTASIEN UND OZEANIEN
SOUTHEAST ASIA AND OCEANIA

Neue Wege in der Gesundheitsvorsorge für die weibliche Maori-Bevölkerung Neuseelands
New Initiatives from Maori Health Groups for Indigenous Women in Aotearoa, New Zealand
Christine Binder-Fritz...133

Mutterschaft und Behinderung in der matrilinearen Kultur Palaus
Motherhood and Disability in the Matrilineal Culture of Palau
Evelyn Heinemann...141

d) NORD-, MITTEL- SÜDAMERIKA UND KARIBIK
NORTH-, MIDDLE -, ANDINE AMERICA, THE CARRIBBEAN

Frauen und Gesundheit im aktuellen kulturellen und sozialen Kontext Lateinamerikas
Women and Health in the Actual Sociocultural Context of Latinamerican Societies
Angelika Denzler...147

The Role of Women in the Traditional and Modern Peigan / Blackfoot Community
Die Rolle der Frauen in der traditionellen und modernen Peigan / Blackfoot-Gemeinschaft
Sybille Manneschmidt & Reg Crowshoe..157

Arbeit, Ethnizität und Gesundheit in Brasilien -Das Beispiel der Afro-Brasilianerinnen-
Employment, Ethnicity and Health in Brazil -The Case of Female Afro-Brazilians-
Chirly dos Santos-Stubbe..163

The Two Sides of the Moon. Fertility of Wayana Indian Women and their Crops in the Guyana Amazon
Die beiden Seiten des Mondes. Fertilität der Indianischen Wayana Frauen und die Gewächse im Guyanischen Amazonengebiet
Britta Veth..175

e) EUROPE / EUROPE

Was verstehen spanische und deutsche Frauen unter Gesundheit? Subjektive Gesundheitskonzepte im internationalen Vergleich
How do Spanish and German Women interpret Health? Lay Health Concepts in Transcultural Comparison
Petra Scheibler..185

Ein Schlüssel zur Frauengesundheit: Hebammenbetreuung in acht europäischen Ländern
A Key to Women's Health: Midwivery Care in Eight European Countries
Beate Schücking..193

Die Rolle der Frau als Heilerin und Hexe in Europa zwischen 1100 und 1800
The Role of Women as Healers and Witches in Europe between 1100 and 1800
Doris Iding...199

2. FRAUENGESUNDHEIT IN DER INTERDISZIPLINÄREN DISKUSSION
WOMEN AND HEALTH AS DISKUSSED BY DIFFERENT DISCIPLINES

Women and Suicidal Behaviour in the Ccontext of a Psychiatric Hospital Ward
Frauen und Suizidverhalten im Kontext einer psychiatrischen Einrichtung
David Aldridge...207

Die Bedeutung der melodischen Improvisation für Brustkrebspatientinnen während ihrer frühen rehabilitativen Phase nach einer Mastektomie
The Meaning of Melodic Improvisation for Beast-Cancer Patients During Early Rehabilitation after a Mastectomy.
Gudrun Aldridge..217

Einschneidende Maßnahmen - Schönheitschirurgie und Geschlechterverhältnisse in der westlichen Medizin
Cutting in Measures - Cosmetic Surgery and the Relationship Between the Sexes in Western Medicine
Angelica Ensel...231

Körperlichkeit von Frauen in der Konsum- und Leistungsgesellschaft und der Zusammenhang zu Essstörungen
Corporeality of Women in a Consumer- and Achievement Oriented Society and its Correlations Towards Eating Disorders
Tine Eschertzhuber..235

Frauen und umweltbedingtes Krankheitsgeschehen. Ergebnisse einer Sozialökologischen Untersuchung
Women and Environmentally Induced Development of Diseases
Gerhard Grossmann..243

The Impact of Religion on Women's Mental Health
Religion und die psychische Gesundheit von Frauen
Annie Imbens-Fransen..249

Hidden carers - Die besondere Rolle der Frau in der Gesundheitsselbsthilfe
Hidden Carers - The Central Role of Women in Lay Health Care
Petra Scheibler & Annette Schmitt..257

Übergänge im Frauenleben - Medikalisierung und Stigmatisierung durch die westliche Medizin
Rites of Passages in Female Sexuality: Medicalization and Stigmazitation in Western Medicine
Eva Schindele...263

Geburt als Initiation der Frau oder wie ging es zu, dass Athene dem Zeus aus dem Kopf entsprang?
Birth as Rite of Passage for Women or how Athene came out of Zeus' Head.
Sigrid Weiß...269

3. ZENTRALE THEMEN
   CENTRAL ISSUES

SCHWANGERSCHAFT UND GEBURT
PREGNANCY AND DELIVERY

Folk Customs, Beliefs and Traditional Curing Methods of the Period between Conception and Weaning in Hungarian Peasant Communities
Volksbräuche und traditionelle Heilverfahren von der Empfängnis bis zum Abstillen in ungarischen bäuerlichen Gemeinschaften
Peter Babulka & Ágnes Pataki...279

Schwangerschaft als Risiko - Zur Entwicklung der Schwangerenvorsorge in Ost- und Westbezirken Berlins
Pregnancy as Risk - The Development of Prenatal Care in Districts of East- and Westberlin
Elke Barbian & Inez Werth..287

Wendepunkt Geburt - Unvereinbarkeit von Frau- und Muttersein als Gesundheitsrisiko in westlichen Industrieländern
Turning Point Birth - The Incompatibility of Being a Mother and a Woman as a Health Risk in Western Industrial Countries
Joachim Bensel & Gabriele Haug-Schnabel..293

Hebammenwesen im Andenraum. Eine Form des weiblichen Schamanismus?
Midwives in the Andean Communities, A Form of Female Shamanism?
María Ofelia Burgos Lingán..303

Teenage Pregnancy as an Issue of Gender Violence: The Case of Zimbabwe
Schwangerschaften von Jungendlichen als ein Thema der Gewalt zwischen Geschlechtern: Der Kasus Zimbabwe
Caroline Hof & Annemiek Richters...313

Frauengesundheit und Geburtssysteme
Women and Health and Birth Systems
Liselotte Kuntner..321

Die Veränderung des Körperbildes in der Schwangerschaft
Body Image Changes during Pregnancy
Claudia Offermann..329

MENSTRUATION / MENSTRUATION

Blutspuren. Das Tabu Menstruation im westlichen Kulturkreis
Traces of Blood. Menstruation as a Taboo in Western Cultures
Marie-Therese Karlen..335

GENINTALBESCHNEIDUNG
FEMALE GENITAL MUTILITATION

Female Genital Mutilitation in the North of Burkina Faso
Genitalverstümmelung von Frauen im Norden Burkina Fasos
Karl L. Dehne, Jürgen Wacker, Jean Nadembega & Roselyne Ira...341

Beschneidung von Mädchen und Frauen - Über die Schwierigkeit, Traditionen zu verändern
Female Genital Mutilation - About the Difficulty to Change Traditions
Friederike Schneider...355

MIGRANTEN UND FLÜCHTLINGE
MIGRANTS AND REFUGEES

Arbeitsmigrantinnen in der Bundesrepublik - Kulturspezifische Gesundheits-/Krankheitskonzepte
Female Labour Migrants in Germany. Culture Specific Concepts of Health and Illness.
Giselind Berg......367

Aspekte der gesundheitlichen Versorgung türkischer Migrantinnen in Deutschland
Aspects of the Health Care Situation of Turkish Migrants in Germany
Matthias David, Theda Borde, Emine Yüksel & Heribert Kentenich......373

There will Always be Sadness in Our Home The Consequences of Sexual Violence Towards Female Refugees, Identification and Treatment.
Die Konsequenzen sexueller Gewalt an weiblichen Flüchtlingen, Identifikation und Behandlung
Mia Groenenberg......379

The Health of Refugees: Are Traditional Medicines an Answer?
Gesundheit von Flüchtlingen. Ist traditionelle Medizin eine Lösung?
Barbara E. Harrell-Bond & Wim Van Damme......385

Migration to Multicultural Australia: Its Impact on the Self-Care of Women
Übersiedlung in ein multikulturelles Australien: Die Auswirkung auf die Selbstversorgung der Frauen
Elvia Ramirez & Shane Taylor......393

AIDS

Women and AIDS in Uganda and the Future of Ethnomedicine
Frauen und AIDS in Uganda und die Zukunft der Ethnomedizin
Kabahenda Nyakabwa......401

PSYCHISCHE UND PSYCHIATRISCHE STÖRUNGEN
PSYCHIATRIC DISORDERS

Women and Epilepsy: Psycho-Socio-Economical Problems of Female Epileptics and their Attitude towards Epilepsy
Frauen und Epilepsie: Psychologische, gesellschaftliche und wirtschaftliche Probleme von Epileptikerinnen und ihrer Einstellung zur Epilepsie
Yonas Bahire Tibeb......409

Challenges for Adequate Ethnomedical Contributions Towards Addressing Depression in Contemporary African Women: An Educational Psychological Perspective
Forderung nach adäquaten ethnomedizinischen Beiträgen im Hinblick auf depressive Erkrankungen bei afrikanischen Frauen heute: eine bildungspsychologische Perspektive
Hannah I. Carew......415

„Ukonjwa wa fikira mingi" - Psychische Störungen, psychosozialer Kontext und subjektive Krankheitskonzepte bei ostafrikanischen Frauen
Depressive Symptoms, Psycho-Social Risk Factors and Subjective Explanatory Concepts in East African Women
Heike Dech, Joyce Nato, Horst Haltenhof & Wielant Machleidt......425

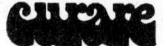

Vorwort
Beate A. Schücking

Frauen und Gesundheit - in industrialisierten Ländern ist dies eine „Qualverwandtschaft" geworden: obwohl alle sozialen Parameter hier günstige Bedingungen für ein Maximum an Gesundheit gewährleisten, zuverlässige Familienplanung, gute Ernährung und gesicherte Lebensumstände den meisten Frauen zu einer hohen Lebenserwartung verhelfen, sind sie immer noch das „schwache Geschlecht". Sie gehen häufiger zum Arzt, erhalten dort mehr Medikamente und andere Verordnungen, sie suchen zusätzlich auch außerhalb der etablierten Medizin Hilfe; kurz, sie sind die besten Kundinnen jeder Art von Gesundheitsversorgung, und das von der Pubertät bis ins Greisenalter. Ihre physiologischen Normalzustände (wie z. B. die Schwangerschaft oder das Klimakterium) werden zusätzlich medikalisiert, mit dem Ergebnis, dass die für Frauen aufgewandten Beträge im Gesundheitswesen ständig expandieren.

In dieser Situation ist das Vorhaben des hier vorliegenden Bandes, ethnomedizinische Perspektiven zur Frauengesundheitsthematik aufzublättern, von besonderem Interesse. Wo lassen sich gleiche Problemmuster erkennen - wo ähnliche Umgehensweisen? oder doch ganz andere Wahrnehmungen auf dem Hintergrund ethnischer Tradition? Wie ist es mit der Selbstbestimmung der Frauen jeweils bestellt? Dieser Sonderband der Curare versammelt Beiträge aus unterschiedlichsten Fächern, aus verschiedenen Kulturen und Zeiten. In seiner Interdisziplinarität repräsentiert er den Stand der Frauengesundheitsforschung; die hier vertretene Vielzahl von Autorinnen und Autoren ebenso wie der thematisch vertretenen Regionen wurde bisher noch in keinem Curare-Sonderband zuvor erreicht. Die breite internationale Palette macht neugierig und regt zu Vergleichen an. Vielleicht lassen sich die von der Weltfrauenkonferenz in Peking 1996 formulierten Forderungen nach gleichberechtigter und angemessener, akzeptabler und verfügbarer Gesundheitsfürsorge für alle Frauen als roter Faden in einigen Beiträgen aus sehr verschiedenen Regionen erkennen - als Frage, die Maori-Frauen mit Deutschen, Afrikanerinnen mit Latinas verbindet.

Den Herausgeberinnen ebenso wie ihren Helferinnen und Helfern ist zu danken für ihr großes Engagement in der Zusammenstellung dieses Frauenforschung ebenso wie Gesundheitswissenschaften und Medizin bereichernden Bandes.

Osnabrück, im Juli 1997   Beate A. Schücking

Preface
Beate Schücking

Women and Health - nowerdays there is a painful affinity between these topics in industrialized countries: Although the social parameters on the whole ensure conditions favorable to good health and life expectancy of the majority of women is usually high due to reliable family planning, good nutrition, and secure living conditions, women are still called the „weaker gender". They consult doctors more frequently who provides them with more drugs and other prescriptions than male patients, and they also seek help in addition to orthodox medicine; in a word, from puberty to old age, women are excellent clients of any kind of health care. Furthermore, their normal physiological conditions such as pregnancy or menopause are medicalized, with the result of constantly increasing expenses for them in the field of health services.

In the face of this situation, the aim of the present volume to show ethnomedical perspectives on the topic of women´s health, deserves particular attention. Where can similar patterns of a problem or analogue handling or, on the contrary, totally different perceptions against the background of ethnical tradition be recognized? How does self-determination function in each of the ethnic groups concerned? The special issue of the periodical *curare* contains articles from completely different fields, from different cultures and times. By its interdisciplinary approach it represent the latest development of research on women´s health. Never has a special issue of *curare* presented articles by so many authors and dealt with so many regions. The international range of this volume serves to arouse curiosity and to prompt comparison. Perhaps the call for equal, appropriate, acceptable and available health care for women all over the world, as formulated by the Women´s World Conference at Peking in 1996, can be seen as the leitmotif of some of the articles from very different regions - as a central issue which unites Maori, German, African, and Latina women.

The editors and their assistants deserve praise for their enormous efforts to compile this volume which will enrich women´s studies as well as health science and medicine.

Osnabrück, in July 1997   Beate A. Schücking

Danksagung

Zunächst bedanken wir uns sehr herzlich für die tatkräftige und ausdauernde Unterstützung in allen Computerfragen, Konvertierung- und Lesbarkeitsproblemen bei Dr. Marc Batschkus und den Mitarbeitern des Instituts für Medizinische Informationsverarbeitung, Biometrie und Epidemiologie (IBE) der Ludwig-Maximilians-Universität München. Ohne sie wären wir der Flut verschieden beschriebenen und formatierten Disketten aus aller Welt nicht Herr geworden.

Wir danken Fau Ute Iding-Doll und Frau Claudia Buckels aus dem Übersetzungsbüro EXPRESS-TEXT für ihre professionellen und ehrenamtlichen Übersetzungsarbeiten. Es trafen teilweise abenteuerliche Briefsendungen ein, wie z.B. ein brüchiges Papierröllchem vom anderen Ende der Welt, das durch ein Schnürchen zusammengehalten war. Beim vorsichtigen Auseinanderrollen rieselte Staub und Sand aus der Sendung. Auch diese wertvollen Informationen, die in dieser Sendung enthalten waren, konnten die Damen in ein korrektes Englisch verwandeln.

Auf Papier bzw. Diskette brachte uns ein fleißiger Mitarbeiter, Herr Sebastian Raith, zahlreiche Manuskripte. Es sei ihm für seine Flexibilität und Durchhaltevermögen gedankt.

Und schließlich ließ sich in der Schlussphase der Vorbereitungen Frau Ulla Schuler noch für die letzten eiligen Übersetzungen gewinnen. Sie ermöglichte es, dass das Manuskript schlussendlich vollständig und rechtzeitig an den Verlag geschickt werden konnte.

Herzlich danken wir auch allen unseren 47 Autorinnen und 23 Autoren für die gute Zusammenarbeit, die rasche Bearbeitung von Korrekturen und ihre Geduld mit uns Herausgebern.

An unseren Lesern liegt es nun, für die Frauengesundheit auf dieser Welt die Verhältnisse ein Stück weit zu verändern.

München, im August 1997   Die Herausgeberinnen
Christine E. Gottschalk-Batschkus, Judith Schuler und Doris Iding

Preparation of Rural Adolescent Girls to Adulthood in Fitche District, Ethiopia
Wie Mädchen in ländlichen Gegenden auf das Erwachsensein vorbereitet werden (Distrikt Fitche, Äthiopien)

K. Weldemichael Afework, Edmund J. Kayombo & Armin Prinz

Abstract: This paper presents result of study conducted in Fitche district, from March 1996 to July 1996. It examines how rural adolescent girls are prepared to adulthood. The study found that girls in rural area learned from their mothers on domestic chores. Most of the rural girls stated that they knew nothing at all about menses and never got any knowledge on the hygiene of menstruation. The study noted that due to restriction of parents to their daughters to socialise with boys, there was „telefa" (kidnapping) and rape. It was found at rural area that virginity is very relevant at marriage. Female circumsision was reported as an important for a woman to be accepted in the community. Parents reported that they didn't advise their daughters on puberty, menses and sexuality. Further more, they showed that they were responsibile for the daughters marriage. The paper recommends parents should change some tradtional beliefs which have negative impact to the adolescent girls. The school committee, district counsel, women organization and community as a whole should try to end up „telefa", rape, female circumcission and provide family life education.

Zusammenfassung: Der vorliegende Beitrag berichtet über eine Studie, die von März bis Juli 1996 im Fitche Distrikt durchgeführt wurde. Untersucht wurde, wie heranwachsende Mädchen in dem ländlichen Gebiet auf das Erwachsenendasein vorbereitet werden. Die Studie ergab, dass Mädchen in ländlichen Gebieten von ihren Müttern lernen, die häuslichen Arbeiten zu erledigen. Die meisten Mädchen gaben an, gar nichts über Menstruation zu wissen und nie über Menstruationshygiene aufgeklärt worden zu sein. Die Studie stellte fest, dass es, weil die Eltern ihren Töchtern den Umgang mit Jungen verbieten, zu "telefa" (Entführung) und Vergewaltigungen kommt. In ländlichen Regionen spielt die Jungfräulichkeit bei der Eheschließung eine bedeutende Rolle. Die Beschneidung (Zirkumzision) der Mädchen gilt als wichtige Voraussetzung, um von der Gemeinschaft akzeptiert zu werden. Eltern berichteten, dass sie ihre Töchter nicht über Pubertät, Menstruation und Sexualität aufklärten. Außerdem bekundeten sie, dass sie für die Verheiratung der Töchter zuständig seien. Der Beitrag empfiehlt, dass die Eltern einige traditionelle Einstellungen ändern müssten, die einen nachteiligen Einfluss auf die heranwachsenden Mädchen haben. Das Schulkomitee, der Rat des Distrikts, die Frauenorganisation und die Gemeinde sollten gemeinsam versuchen, der "telefa", der Vergewaltigung und der Beschneidung ein Ende zu setzen und eine Erziehung zum Familienleben zu bieten.

Keywords: Ethiopia, adolescents, menstruation, kidnapping, family life education, Äthiopien, Adoleszenz, Menstruation, Entführung, Erziehung zum Familienleben.

Introduction

Young people ages 10 to 19 number more than 1 billion, comprise nearly one-fifth of the world population, and are growing in number. Virtually all of this growth is occurring in developing countries, with sub-Saharan Africa leading the way (MCCAULEY 1995). In the world as a whole, the number of young adults is expected to grow to more than 1.2 billion in 2010 (UN, 1994). All cultures recognize and mark the transition from child to adult (WHO 1977). The concept of this transition as a life stage, however, did not exist in developed countries until the late 1800s and early 1900s (HARARI 1993, JUSTER 1987). The World Health Organization (WHO) has defined adolescence as the progression from appearance of secondary sex characteristics (puberty) to sexual and reproductive maturity; development of adult mental process and adult identity; transition from total socioeconomic dependence to relative independence (WHO 1985). This process of development requires proper preparation of adolescence to adulthood. The aim of this paper is to present the findings of an assessment study on preparation of rural adolescent girls to adulthood. Special emphasis is given on the cultural aspect to wards virginity, sexuality and marriage. It is also intended to explore the interaction of information between parents and daughters.

Methods

The study was conducted in the rural communities of Ethiopia, in Fitche district, Oromia region from March 1996 to July 1996. The village was located 105 kms from Addis Ababa, and 10-25 kms from the principal road to the scattered villages. The total population of the villages was approximately 4000. The majority ethnic groups were Oromos, whereas the minority were Amaras. The study used a purposive sampling to enroll study subjects. It involved in-depth interview of adolescent rural girls, focus group discussion (FGD) of rural, suburb girls and boys, and a separate focus group discussion with mothers and fathers of adolescent girls whom were interviewed. In the rural area, 6 in-depth interview were conducted for girls, 2 FGD with illiterate and literate girls respectively, one FGD with illiterate mothers and fathers respectively, and one FGD for illiterate and literate boys respectively. In the suburb area, there were 3 FGD with girls and two FGD for boys. A total of 51 girls, 30 boys, 12 mothers and 10 fathers participated in the FGD. The age of the girls ranged from 13-18 years while the age of boys was 14-19 years (Table 1).The mothers ranged from 26 to 48 year. Two mothers were remarried after divorce and the rest were in first marriages. Whereas, the age of the fathers ranged from 35 to above 55 years. Two men were remarried and the rest of men were in the first marriages. The women were house wives and the men were farmers. In addition the study had an in-depth interviewed with indigenous women and man of whom were aged more than 70 years. The indigenous woman was widowed and the man was a bedridden patient. All participants of the FGD have an average of 6 children. In general, the groups are relatively homogenous with regard to age, gender, social status and knowledge. This facilitated individuals to feel more free to participate than in heterogeneous groups, since those with higher status tend to dominate the discussion. The information were collected by using Audio recorder in Amharic language and one FGD was conducted in Oromiffa. The information was checked by replaying the cassettes before transcription. After that, all the collected information was transcribed first to Amharic and then to English. The result is presented below.

Table 1. Distribution of adolescents by sex and education

Grade	Girls	Boys	Total
Illiterate	15	7	22
3-5	7	6	13
6-8	9	5	14
9-11	20	12	32
Total	51	30	81

Results

The majority points of the discussion were on the preparation of adolescent girls to adulthood. The emphasis was on menstruation, puberty, sexuality, virginity, relationships with a boy friend, marriage and interaction of information with parents related to upbringing of adolescents to adulthood. The majority of rural adolescent girls came from farmer families and seven parents of the daughters partially served the orthodox church. Most of the parents in the suburb were employed in government jobs and private small scale business. Girls in the rural area assisted their mothers with household tasks such as fetching water, backing „injera" (Ethiopian bread), cooking, cleaning house and the compound, gathering firewood washing clothes and child care. On the other hand, girls in the suburb assisted their mothers only when necessary, as there was a maid employed to do the household tasks. The majority of girls initiated their menses at the age of 15 and some of the remaining at the age of 14. All girls mentioned that the signs of puberty were the onset of menarche, enlarged breasts and increasing weight. Most of the rural girls stated that they knew nothing at all about menses before the onset, while some of the girls from the suburb reported they had heard from school and friends, but had no details. Many girls described their feeling on the onset of menses. A rural girl stated that, „I was very shocked and wept as nobody made me familiar", another one said, „ I heard when my friends were talking. I was very shocked when I started menstruating. But I have never talked to any body as it is „newer" (not accepted norm) sharing ideas on such issues in my village". In both groups, except one suburban girl, girls never got any knowledge on the hygiene of menstruation. The major points related with marriage were discussed: 1. initiation of marriage by parents; 2. interference by parents; 3. outcasting; 4. consensus validity and culture. Surprisingly, all the rural girls declared that virginity is very relevant to maintain marriage; and breaking marriage is a common phenomena if the girl was not found to be virgin at the wedding night. They explained that until recently the virginal status of the bride at marriage was confirmed by the public display of her blood following the first intercourse. Beside to this, in the suburb, this real tradition of expecting virginity at marriage is likely to disappear due to the interaction between suburb and urban people. However, it was learned that the best men of the groom sing to declare the bride was

virgin by showing a placebo to the public display for the sake of the tradition.
1. Initiation of marriage by parents: In the rural, the study found until recently marriage was initiated by parents. The girl never knew her groom, but she was aware of the wedding day and sometimes she may be informed about the groom. Before the agreement of the marriage, both side of parents investigated and cleared any kind of blood relationship by their own patrilineal and matrilineal up to seven generation to avoid interrelative marriage due to religious believe.

   Four types of union were recognized as „marriage" by girls. These were civil, religious, customary unions and „telefa" (kidnapping or abduction). Most rural people lived together under religious and customary type of marriage. The first three were legally accepted in the country. The last, „telefa" of the girl with or without her consent was illegal. The consent of the girl was obtained, if she initially agreed with the boy and if her parents rejected the request.
2. Interference by parents: It was reported that the interference of parents was mainly related to the initiation of marriage. The boy's parents and relatives recommended that he should marry someone, who is accepted „yechewa lij" (in the sight, character and status of the parents) . When their son agreed, they sent elder men (respected by the community) to the girl's parents for request of marriage .
3. Outcasting : FGD participants indicated that a person may not be expected to marry if he/she was from another a socially unacceptable group like „budda" (evil eye) „ketkach" (black smith), „shekla serri" (potter), „komata" (leper) , or „baria zer" (descendents of slave).
4. Consensus validity and cultural role: The study was informed that in most cases, if the girl knew her groom, she avoided him and vise-versa, due to cultural reasons. It was unacceptable for the future bride/groom to have any communication.

From the Focus group discussion, it was hypothesized that there are three types of girls with regard to attitude of virginity and initiation of marriage (see schematic presentation).

The schematic presentation:

1	2	3
Traditional Orthodox	Traditional Conservative	Traditional Liberal

1. Traditional orthodox - this type of girls accepted virginity as an honor to herself, her family and marriage initiation by family as traditionally recommended; did not accept sexual intercourse before marriage.
2. Traditional conservative - accepted virginity as an honor and welcomed marriage initiation by family and „teleffa"; did not accept sexual intercourse before marriage.
3. Traditional Liberal - accepted virginity as an honor and welcomed marriage initiation by family and „telefa". In addition they accepted sexual intercourse before marriage.

The continuum presents three major groups and the third group was often seen in the suburb. The distinction demarcation between the first two categories was insignificant. Given that there were very strong traditional sanctions (may assume that they will lose social value and this was also pointed out during the FGD), it would appear that a large majority would be in the „traditional orthodox" category in the rural, but at the suburb a substantial majority would be in the „ traditional liberal" group.
Some of the statements of each group is shown below:

Traditional orthodox group:
A girl said that it was very disgraceful and „newer" (unacceptable), to lose virginity before marriage. It was her „glory and honor". Having sexual intercourse before marriage cannot be thought of. It was a disgrace. Another said „marriage should be initiated by parents" as it is their responsibility.

Traditional conservative:
This group accepted marriage initiation by both parents and also „teleffa". The major reason for accepting the latter is the agreement made by the two partners as stated by one of the rural girls. Some other rural girls also supported this view. A 16 old year girl said „ it was „kal" (promise); it must be respected . „Kal" or some also called it „kal kidan". To keep her kal kidan, she deliberately agreed with him, so that he may kidnap her". They also reported that sex would happen in few cases. However, sex before marriage was not accepted by this group.

Traditional liberal:
A 15 year old girl from the suburb stated that „women who are educated and have their own job would often initiate their marriage without interference from their parents". Another girl from eleventh grade said „sex before marriage is acceptable and will help both partners to know each other". This group was predominately seen in the urban area. This group did not agree with the initiation of marriage by families, but accepted it to conform with the traditional concept and to gain consensus validity in the community. One girl said, „marriage is not initiated based on one's interest. It is the family which is the sole decision maker. I do not agree with this but failure to accept it will result in the rejection by my parents and the community". The other pointed out, marriages that were initiated by parents tend to have more conflicts and physical violence. As a whole, major points of discussion of rural and suburb girls are summarized in Table 2 below.

Table 2
Summary notes on sexuality by gender expression

Variable	Rural girls	Suburb girls
Menstruation	Most of them were frustrated and wept at the first „show".	The same.
Belief of menstruation	May be massive, if a girl eats „karia" (pepper), warmth by being close to the fire, eating very hot food.	Not pronounced.
Belief to lose virginity	Carrying heavy weight & jumping.	The same.
Place and time of encounter	Holidays at the church, wedding places (singing & dancing), school, fire wood, „sindedo" (thick plaiting reed), dry cow dung collection & fetching water of encounter	The same and „lekso" (condolence)
Traditional practices	All practiced biting their breast by „yewha inat" (Water Strider „Gerrie" or Water Boatman „Corixidae"?) to make the breast bigger.	Most of them practiced.
	Most of them practiced „ters nekesat" (tatooing of the gum) for beauty and stopping of gum bleeding. of childhood.	All practiced.
Condition of initiating relationship	Most of the time by force and in few cases love.	By love & in few cases by force.
Partner	Often not expected to have boy friend & is called „kenfer wedaj" (friend of the lip).	Accepted; is called a boyfriend.
Premarital sex	Is highly condemend and unacceptable & considered as highly damaging to the reputation of the girl and her family.	In most of the girls accepted for sustaining relationship.
Marriage partner	in most cases chosen and pre-arranged by parents	Girls chose, agree & conform for the tradition by parents

Consequences of premarital sex	pregnancy, abortion, suicide, death, migrating to unknown place due to fear of being stigmatized by the community and punished by parents.	STDs, AIDS, pregnancy, abortion & conflicts with parents.
Problem encountered by participants	marriage by will of parents, rape, dropping of schools due to fear of „telefa", no free time for studying due to domestic jobs.	rape, no recreation places.

Attitude of boys puberty and sexuality

The boys discussion concerning issues of sexuality were fairly brief and to the point, in contrast to the discussion conducted with the girls. The majority of boys noticed „onset of puberty" at the age of 13-14. As the signs of puberty were mentioned hair at facial and genital area, wet dreams, „buger at the face" (acne), aggressiveness, disobedience to parents, and initiating relationships with girls. The source of information for both rural and suburb boys was friends, tales, over hearing gossip and school education. A few students from the suburb supplemented that with video sex films and books. All boys, except 5 practiced sex at an average age of 14. The first encounter for the majority of boys were prostitutes and for three other boys were housemaid girls at their home. The rural boys mentioned the reason for initiating sex with prostitutes was to the impossibility of having sex with girls in the rural areas before marriage and the cost of some prostitutes was affordable to them. Whereas the suburb boys said that girls give many appointments until they agree for sex. Both groups of boys were given no advice on puberty and sex from their parents. The only advice that they got from their parents was a warning advise not to have bad friends and relationship with girls that may spoil the future life. Some of the parents also warned them not to initiate sexual relationship due to „yezemenu besheta" (the current disease „AIDS"). The rural boys were also advised to learn the farming work of their father to replace them. Among 18 rural boys, only one boy said at present that he has a girl friend. While three out of 12 boys from the suburb each had a girl friend, two boys have two girl friends each and the rest had none. Both rural and suburb boys reported that some girls at the suburb initiated sex, while the rural girls were still very orthodox and refused any kind of sexual relationship. Most of the boys believed that a man must experience sex for the preparation of the wedding night to be capable of deflowering the bride. In contrast to this group, five boys stated that both should avoid any kind of extramarital sex and be virgin at marriage in the church. Many of the participants strongly stated that in the absence of virginity, they beat and return the bride to their parents. Some of them may accept as a virgin in the presence of love.

Consequence of premarital sex (Table 2) did not bother most of the suburb boys. They considered that as the responsibility of their partners. In contrast to their ideas, the rural boys mentioned at an early age marriage and conflict among parents when they did not agree for the marriage. Only a small minority of both groups mentioned and worried about the risk from Sexually transmitted diseases and AIDS.

Parents experience on their adolescents stage and preparation of their daughters to adulthood

It was learned that all women took the „yewha inat" (Water Strider „Gerrie" or Water Boatman „Corixidae"?) to bite their breast between age of 8 to 10. They were informed about the „yewha inat" from their friends and practiced when they went to fetch water. All the mothers reported that during their childhood about puberty, menstruation and sexual issues were not oriented, which was the same even to the fathers. Six women were informed about menses not explicitly by their friends after the on set of menstruation. Four women were married at an early young age (8-11 years) and initiated their menses after the marriage. They were told by their husbands that menstruation occurred every month to a women up to death. The remaining two women got an information from their mother and sister respectively after the menses onset. The majority of them considered that menstruation as a secret matter and made a woman unclean. Therefore, they hid the occurrence from any body. It appears that this culture has been inherited by their daughters of not telling their parents about their initiation. It was found that virginity was given special importance for marriage. All women and men were virgin at marriage. The indigenous woman said, that when she had married, a woman called „dengetur" (lady of the bed chamber) checked her whether she was virgin. She advised her about sexual relationship with the groom and traditionally the bride during wedding night did not accept and go to bed „willingly". The dengetur was responsible to convince and was the first to inform the best men of the groom of the bride being virgin by showing the blood sheet after being deflowered. If the bride was not virgin, the „dengetur" can be punished by being beaten together with the bride. The groom gave the bride „yetesebre dabo" (a broken loaf of bread) to carry to her parents as a symbol that she was not virgin. The groom might ask her parents to refund him the amount of money invested to the marriage. Mothers reported that the accompaniment of the bride by „dengetur" was not practiced during their time of marriage. They also stated that they were not checked for being virgin. Virginity was assumed to be mandatory to be married. Since being not virgin, the girl was punished by her parents or/and the groom and this made few girls to migrate to unknown place before or after the marriage. It was shown that at former times parents made decision for their daughters whom to marry. For example, the study found eleven mothers were married their husbands whom were decided by their parents, as well as their respective husbands. The only women from the suburb who divorced and remarried said that she married both men by her agreement. In the case of fathers also parents were responsible to recommend them with whom to be married. Both mothers and fathers reported that they did not have any kind of communication before the marriage.

The mothers reported that at present, some girls after they started to go to school, they did not accept some of their advise and argued about it. For example, girls do not accept the advice of avoiding hot (sharp) foods, „karia" (pepper) which cause to initiate menstruation before the time and making the menses massive and excessively heavy job which was the reason to rupture the hymen. On the other hand, the illiterate girls accepted what they were told by their parents. It was reported that the reason for refusal of their advice was an impact of the education rendered by schools. For this reason some parents preferred not to send their daughters to school.

The mothers educated their daughters on all domestic chores a women supposed to do. They reported that they never advised their daughters on menstruation, puberty and sexual issues, as were done to them by their parents. Whereas, the men during discussion, they showed that to advise about menstruation was the responsibility of mothers. Both, parents said that when they were aware that their daughters had reached adulthood, they restricted and controlled their daughters not to go alone at a far distance. They, further warned them not to have any kind of relationship with boys, which could be the cause to spoil their future life. They called attention to their daughters „semachenen indatatefu" (not to be blackened their names) due to premarital sex in the community. They informed them by giving an example of a girl in the village or in the country who became a „woman" and ruined her reputation and as well of her parents in the community. The men also supplemented that whenever they saw their daughters talking with unknown person, they whipped and barred them not to go out from the house without their permission. In general the parents' expression, fell within the traditional expectation that their daughters must be virgin before marriage, and they should have to accept the person they chose them for marriage. Mothers as well as fathers stressed in the discussion, that if their daughters become against their will, they may „inregmalen" (curse them). Additionally mothers reported that they advised their daughters before marriage, how to be good woman to the husband. That means, to be a trustful wife and to treat in a good manner the relatives of the husband. The men mentioned that they followed and controlled if their daughters were circumcised at the expected time. They reported that the reason for circumcision was that, uncircumcised women was sexually powerful like a „weifen" (bull) than a man. Traditionally, uncircumcised woman in their community was considered like an insult.

Discussion

Preparation of adolescents to adulthood involves parents, community, schools and policy makers. This study showed that the majority of adolescent girls at the rural and as well as at the suburb were not got information on puberty and sexuality. For example, the shown fear of menstruation and the reported practices of „yewha inat" for making the breast big indicates that they were ignorant of the physical body change of adolescent girls. The bigness of the breast noted might be a result of inflammation due to being bitten by „yewha inat". In general, from the observation of the rural site and discussion of parents, we found that girls should stay with their mothers and learn domestic chores, while boys stay with their fathers at the field and learn man's work. Such a similar belief on upbringing of adolescents in Africa showed by other researchers (SCHLEGEL 1995, KAYOMBO 1992, DONALD 1986).

The study that all girls initiated their menses at the age of 14-15 years is the same with urban study finding in Addis Ababa (AFEWORK 1995). In contrast with this finding in many developed and developing countries, girls initiate their menses earlier at the age of 12.5 years in America (Forrest 1993, Winter 1982) and Kenya 12.9 years (GYEPI-GERBRAH 1985). The reason for earlier menarche in girls are not well understood and most of the change might be attributed to better health and nutrition (FORREST 1993, GYEPI-GERBRAH 1985, WINTER 1982). Whereas the majority of boys in the study noticed the „onset of puberty" between 13-14 years; and some of the body physical changes with deviant characters. This finding is underscored with other findings that occurred during puberty age (SENANAYAKE 1990, WINTER 1982, BARRY 1996). The on set of menstruation almost to all girls as well as to their mothers was a confusing and even frightening experience. Above all they never got any knowledge on hygiene of menstruation. There is a common belief to girls to hide menstruation and considering a menstruating woman is like unclean due to religious believe. It was further noted that there was an information gap of parents whose responsibility to inform the adolescents about puberty in general.

This study has shown three types of girls according to the attitude of virginity and initiation of marriage. Even though at present most of the rural girls are traditional orthodox groups and substantial suburb girls are with traditional liberal groups, as time goes, we expect that due to the interaction of rural and urban most traditional orthodox groups will change to traditional liberal groups.

The advice and rendered care of the bride by „dengetur" in former times which was not reported at the time of mothers and adolescent girls indicate the change of culture due to interaction of rural and urban people. It is a common believe of parents considering sexual issues as a privet and secret among married couples only. OLAYINKA (1987) has shown that sexuality is regarded in Africa as a gift to be used for procreation of human species and any public display of sex related feeling is seen as a debasing this gift. Premarital sexual activity for rural and suburb girls is strictly condemned before marriage by parents. In many parts of developing countries, as well as in this rural site virginity is mandatory for marriage (AHMED 1992, ENEL 1992). Parents indicated that they keep their daughters in a strict surveillance and advise them to avoid over exercise, like jumping and excessively heavy work in order to prevent the accidental rupture of hymen, which was the same shown by DONALD (1986). To substantiate this argument, we got two girls at the rural site who were dropped out from the school due to the fear of parents from „telefa". The above mentioned strictness of parents to rural girls and rendering a warning and fearful advice and sometimes even punishment by parents was not for the girls health, but to maintain parents social status in the community for proper bringing up the daughter at marriage.

Both rural and suburb girls reported that, didn't initiate sexual intercourse due to shyness related to sexual issues. But during the discussion of both rural and suburb boys indicated that some suburb girls were open to „romantic" love with premarital intercourse. On the contrary both groups of boys informed that the rural girls were very orthodox and refuse any type of relationship related to sexual intercourse. The statement of the boys about the suburb girls is supported by a finding from a study conducted in the urban slum community which showed that out of 540 unmarried female only 20 were virgins (AFEWORK 1995). During FGD, parents reported that they expect boys to be virgin at marriage and this norm was strictly enforced in former times (Donald 1986), however most of rural and suburb boys in this study had sex with prostitutes. This is likely to subject adolescent boys to risk of acquiring Sexually transmitted diseases (STDs) and Acquired immunedefficiency syndrome (AIDS). The overall „sexual cultural" by adolescents may be viewed as a complex interplay of traditional sanctions and modern expectations. It was observed that the rural girls used three hours to go and return to school on foot and there might happen on the way rape and telefa. As indicated in the study the common way of initiating relationship by boys was force, parents should have to understand that girls may lose virginity not on their will. Parents through school committee, district council, farmer organization should try to find solution to end the prevailing rape and „telefa". The reason pointed by fathers about female circumcision it raises doubts. As shown by HOSKEN (1979) in Ethiopia, the practice of female circumcision was to reduce sexual sensitivity of women, so that they do not dominate the man in sexual performance. In addition, female circumcision was to maintain virginity as was in Sudan and Egypt (HOSKEN 1979). The most disturbing issues, some of the problems encountered by rural girls and the fate of the victims of sexually abused girls and related consequences, while the young boys are not worried about such problems is also a series concern. On the other side the inability of most rural parents to understand the problems of girls and the expectation of parents from their daughters to respect the tradition is an issue discussed and find optimal solution.

Conclusion

The noted ways of up bringing of adolescents in this study do not equip adolescents to tackle some consequences mentioned by participants of the FGD. For instance, marriage by the will of parents, outcasting to exclude marriage request, reservation of parents to render advice to adolescents on puberty, sexuality and sever punishment due to misbehaviour which may be a result of ignorance need to be changed. The deaf ear and closed eyes of the community at the village level and district council on the noted rape, „telefa" and circumcision which are a common problems of the country in the name of culture have a series side effect to adolescent girls need to be addressed adequately from the village level to the national at large. Even though this paper is addressing to adolescent rural girls at Fitche district, Ethiopia, but adolescent as a whole is a world wide problem which needs be studied carefully in different communities with reference to the cultural systems. Social groups, such as schools, youth organizations, women organization, parenthood association, farmer organization, religious bodies and overall policy makers should work together in finding a sustaining solution for ending the noted problems of adolescents. For example, family life education, should be designed to meet all aspect of the youth. The planning and implementing should include parents, teachers, religious bodies, health personnel and lawyers. Emphasis should be given to positive cultural practices and safe awareness with respect to the present health problems.

References

AFEWORK K.W, D.TESFAYE ,K. MESFIN., F.WORKNEH, A.PRINZ. 1996. *HIV infection among the residents of urban slums of Addis Ababa:* presented on Österreichiscen Gesellscaft für Tropenmedizin und Parasitologie.

AHMED S.A., H.M. KHEIR. 1992. Sudanese sexual behaviour, sociocultural norms and the transmission of HIV, In *Sexual behaviour & net working: Anthropological and sociocultural studies on the transmission of HIV* editedby TIM DYSON, pp. 303-314, International Union for scientific study of population (IUSSP) Liege.

BARRY H III., A. SCHLEGEL. 1984. Measurements of adolescents sexual behaviour in the standard sample size of societies. *Ethnology,* 23: pp 315-329.

DONALD N.L. 1986. The emerging adolescent. In Wax and Gold: Tradition and Innovation in Ethiopian culture, pp. 95-147. The university of Chicago press, Midway reprint edition.

ENEL C., G.PISON. 1992. Sexual relations in the rural area of Mlomp (Casamance, Senegal). In *Sexual behaviour & net working: Anthropological and sociocultural studies on the transmission of HIV* edited by TIM DYSON, pp. 249-267, International Union for scientific study of population (IUSSP) Liege.

FORREST, J. D. 1993. Timing of reproductive life stages. in *Obstetrics and Gynecology* 82(1): pp. 105-111. July.

GYEPI-GARBRAH, B., D. J NICHOLS, G. M. K KPEDEKKPO. 1985. *Adolescent fertility in sub-Saharan Africa: An overview.* Boston, Pathfinder Fund, (Mimeo), p.57.

HARARI, S .E. and VINOVSKIS. 1993. Adolescent sexuality, pregnancy, and childbearing in the past. In: *The politics of pregnancy : Adolescent sexuality and public policy.* Edited by LAWSON, A. and D. L., RHODE, pp. 23-45. New Haven, Connecticut, Yale University Press.

HOSKEN F.P. 1979. *The Hosken report, Genital and sexual mutilation of females.* Women's International Network News/ 187 Grant ST, Lexington Mass. 02173 U.S.A.

JUSTER, S.M. and M.A VINOVSKIS. 1987. Changing perspectives on the American family in the past. *Annual Review of Sociology* 31: pp. 193-206.

KAYOMBO E.J., I.N. SEMALI. 1993. *Attitudes and knowledge on sexuality among teenagers and related traditional and cultural factors. A case of Dare-Salaam.* A consultant report submitted to center of African studies - Nairobi

MCCAULEY A. P., C. SALTER, KIRAGU K., SENDEROWITZ J. 1995. *Meeting the Needs of Young Adult* Maryland: Johns Hopkins School public Health, Population Information Programme, Population Reports Series M. Number 41 Population Reports.

NTOZI, J.P.M. 1990. *Preliminary Tables of Adolescent fertility Survey in Masaka District,* Unpublished Manuscript, Makerere University, Kampala.

OLAYINKA K. 1987. Sexuality and circumcision. In: *The circumcision of women: A strategy for eradication.* pp. 37-39 first published by Zed Books, London & USA.

SCHLEGEL A. 1995. A cross-cultural approach to adolescence. In *Journal of the Society for Psychological Anthropology,* ETHOS, Edited by SCHLEGEL A., 23 (1) pp: 15-32.

UNITED NATION (UN). 1994. Department for economic and social information and policy analysis. Population division. *The sex and age distribution of the world populations:* The 1994 revision. New York, UN, (ST/ESA/SER.A/144), 858 p.

WINTER, J. S. D. 1982. Nutrition and Neuroendocrinology of puberty. In: *Adolescent nutrition.* Edited by WINICK, M., p3-12. New York, John Wiley & Sons,.

WHO. 1975. *Pregnancy and abortion in adolescence:* Report of a WHO meeting. Geneva, WHO, (WHO Technical Report Series No. 583).

WORLD HEALTH ORGANIZATION (WHO). 1977. *Health needs of adolescents.* Geneva, WHO, (WHO Technical Report Series No. 609) 54 p.

Das Leben der Frau in arabisch-islamischen Ländern. Betrachtungen eines Frauenarztes
Women's life in Arabic Countries. A Gynaecologist's Point of View
Wilhelm Föllmer

Zusammenfassung: Das soziale Umfeld der arabischen Frau wird durch den Koran bestimmt; der Ehemann ist erziehungsberechtigt. Die Einengung ihrer persönlichen Freiheit führt nicht selten zu psychischen oder psycho-somatischen Störungen. Von Geburt an ist das Mädchen zweitrangig gegenüber dem Knaben und wird entsprechend behandelt. Jungfräulichkeit ist Voraussetzung für eine standesgemäße erste Ehe. Die Verheiratung erfolgt daher vor oder mit der ersten Menstruation. Die erste Schwangerschaft tritt bei diesen „Kindfrauen" in 60% im ersten Ehejahr auf. Geburtsverletzungen sind häufig, da geschulte Hilfe fehlt. Die Kinderlosigkeit ist ein bedrückendes Schicksal für die arabische Frau.
Die Gesundheit der Frau in subtropischen oder tropischen Gebieten ist besonders gefährdet, wenn eine Schwangerschaft auftritt. Bei der Therapie darf dann keine Rücksicht auf den Föten genommen werden, um das Leben der Mutter zu erhalten. Es bestehen große Unterschiede zwischen modernen und traditionellen islamischen Staaten, zwischen Großstadt und Landbevölkerung. Die Emanzipation der Frau hat in den Großstädten moderner islamischer Staaten begonnen. Berufsausbildung macht die Frau frei von der Unterwürfigkeit gegenüber dem Mann.

Abstract: The social environment of the Islamic woman is determined by the Koran; the husband is entitled to be her educator. The limited freedom causes often psychical or psychic-somatical disturbances. A girl is less estimated than a boy and is correspondingly treated. Virginity is the condition for a marriage in accordance to her rank. Therefore, the first marriage will happen before or with the first menstruation. The first pregnancy takes place in 60% of those „children-women„ during the first year of marriage. Injuries by the delivery happen frequently because of lack of skilled assistance. Sterility is a depression destiny of an Islamic woman. The health of women with tropical or endemic diseases is especially endangered when a pregnancy will happen. The therapy has to be performed to protect the life of the mother regardless of the health of the child. There are great differences between the modern and the traditional Islamic states, between the population of a large city and of rural areas. The emancipation of women started in large cities of modern Islamic countries. The education in a profession deliberates the women from the resignation to the man.

Keywords: Islam, psychosomatische Störungen, arabische Länder, Muslemic Siciety, psychosomatic disorders, arabic countries.

In den islamischen Ländern, besonders in den strikt traditionellen, wird das Schicksal der Frau weitgehend durch die Vorschriften des Korans bestimmt. Dort heißt es:
> „Die Männer sind die Verantwortlichen über die Frauen, weil Allah die einen vor den anderen ausgezeichnet hat und weil sie von ihrem Vermögen hingeben. Daher sind tugendhafte Frauen die Gehorsamen und die (ihrer Gatten) Geheimnisse mit Allahs Hilfe wahren. Und jene, von denen ihr Widerspenstigkeit befürchtet, ermahnt sie, lasset sie allein in den Betten und straft sie, wenn sie euch dann gehorchen, so sucht keine Ausrede gegen sie, Allah ist hoch erhaben, groß." (SURE 4:35).

Der Mann ist also der Erziehungsberechtigte gegenüber seiner Frau und kann sie auch strafen. Damit ist die Stellung des Ehemannes als Patriarch festgelegt.

Wohl ist es der Ehefrau möglich, sich von ihrem Manne scheiden zu lassen, allerdings erst nach einem durch die Verwandten versuchten Versöhnungsversuches, der erfolglos war. Geschieht die Scheidung auf Wunsch der Ehefrau, ohne dass ein Verschulden des Ehemannes vorliegt, so ist die Frau verpflichtet, die „Morgengabe", die meist den Eltern gegeben wurde, zurückzuzahlen. Den ärmeren Frauen und solchen ohne Berufsausbildung ist das nicht möglich. Sie müssen sich in ihr Schicksal ergeben, sind dem Manne völlig ausgeliefert. Depressionen, Hysterie und andere psychische Reaktionen sind daher nicht selten. Aber schon von Geburt an ist das Mädchen einem psychischen Druck ausgesetzt, denn die Geburt einer Tochter wird als ungerecht empfunden:
> „und wenn einem von ihnen die Nachricht von (der Geburt) einer Tochter gebracht wird, so verfinstert sich sein Gesicht, indes er den inneren Schmerz unterdrückt.
> Er verbirgt sich vor den Leuten ob der schlimmen Nachricht, die er erhalten hat. Soll er sie trotz der

Schande behalten oder im Staube verscharren?
Wahrlich übel ist, wie sie urteilen!" (Sure 16: 59-60)
Trotz der Ermahnungen des Propheten werden Knabengeburten noch immer höher geschätzt, da sie die soziale Sicherheit für die Eltern bei Krankheit und im Alter darstellen. Das „soziale Netz" des Staates ist in diesen Ländern noch wenig geknüpft.

So ist zu verstehen, dass die kleinen Mädchen schon von früh an einem ständigen psychischen Druck ausgesetzt sind in dem Bewusstsein, sie seien minderwertiger als Knaben. Sie werden sich daher widerspruchslos allen Anforderungen unterziehen, die an sie gestellt werden.

Schon frühzeitig müssen sie Hausarbeiten verrichten und die jüngeren Geschwister betreuen. Durch die ihre physische Substanz überschreitenden Belastungen, kommt es nicht selten zu Veränderungen am Knochenskelett. Das wird oft noch begünstigt durch unzureichende und unzweckmäßige Ernährung, die arm besonders an tierischem Eiweiß ist. (In Libyen bei der ärmeren Bevölkerung 10,4 g täglich nach FAO Studien) (Abb. 1)

Die erhaltene Jungfräulichkeit ist Voraussetzung für die erste Eheschließung. So werden die jungen Mädchen schon vor oder mit der ersten Periodenblutung, spätestens im ersten Jahr der Geschlechtsreife verheiratet. (Tab. 1).

Sie haben gewöhnlich wenig Einfluss auf die Wahl des Bräutigams. Nicht selten ist er älter und die Braut ist oft nicht die erste, die einzige Ehefrau.

Zwar gibt es den Brauch, dass sich Braut und Bräutigam kurz vor der Hochzeit – die Braut meist das erste Mal unverschleiert – allein gegenüber stehen, der Bräutigam der Braut ein Glas Mandelwasser als Heiratsantrag anbietet und die Braut die Möglichkeit hat, das Mandelwasser abzulehnen und damit auch den Bräutigam. Das ist praktisch unmöglich, da die ganze Familie der Braut Vorwürfe mit entsprechenden Folgen machen würde.

In der Hochzeitsnacht muss dann „Blut fließen"

Telefonischer Anruf einer Araberin: „Können Sie bitte sofort kommen, um eine Patientin anzusehen? Es ist dringend!" Haus im arabischen Viertel der Großstadt, Erdgeschosswohnung, überall eine dämmerige Beleuchtung, die Einrichtung dem arabischen Mittelstand entsprechend.

Eine Anzahl heftig diskutierender Menschen in der Wohnung. Ich erfahre, dass es die Familie des Bräutigams und die der Braut ist, die auf das Ergebnis des ersten ehelichen Zusammenseins gewartet

Abb. 1
Lybisches Mädchen beim Wasser holen (Foto: Wilhelm Föllmer)

	– 6 Mon.	– 12 Mon.	– 18 Mon.	– 24 Mon.	– Mon.	Grav. ohne Periode	Keine Angaben
(a)	1	6	6	19	3		
(b)		1	7	3			
(c)			1	1			
	1	7	16	27	4	4	3

(c) Periode während des Stillens aufgetreten, weitergestillt

Tab. 1
Wie viele dieser Frauen hatten ihre erste Periode, nachdem sie abstillten (a), und wie viele stillten ab, nachdem die erste Periode aufgetreten war (b)

hatten. Als die Mütter des Jungen Paares nach genügend langer Zeit das Schlafzimmer des Brautpaares betraten und das Ehebett begutachteten, war keine Spur von Blut zu entdecken. Sofort erhob die Mutter des Bräutigams den Verdacht, dass die Braut nicht mehr unberührt gewesen sei. Heftige Vorwürfe waren die Folge. Die Eheschließung, vor allem der Ehevertrag, in dem die Brautgabe und die Rechte der Frau festgelegt sind, wurden in Frage gestellt. Ich sollte nun den Streit schlichten und wurde in das wenig beleuchtete Schlafzimmer des Brautpaares geführt.

Die junge Braut völlig verschüchtert, der noch junge Bräutigam unsicher-befangen. Unter diesen Umständen sollte ich feststellen, ob der Hymen schon früher verletzt worden war. Ich hatte meine arabische Krankenschwester Kheria und auch Instrumente mitgenommen. In Gegenwart der beiden Mütter des Brautpaares wurde die Untersuchung durchgeführt. Der Hymen war unverletzt, etwas dehnbar. Ich konnte sagen, dass nicht immer beim ersten Zusammensein bei einem solchen Befund die Verletzung des Hymen eintreten müsse. Eine gewisse Erleichterung trat bei der Brautmutter ein. Dann kam mir der Gedanke, den Bräutigam in Abwesenheit der Mütter zu fragen, ob überhaupt das Zusammensein mit seiner Frau stattgefunden habe. Nach einigem Drängen kam die schamhafte Antwort: „Nein, es hat nicht geklappt!" Als ich dies den Familien mitteilte, völlige Umkehr der Stimmung. Die Brautfamilie triumphierte. Ich verließ schleunigst das Haus, um mich den überschwenglichen Dankesbezeugungen der Brautfamilie zu entziehen.

Nicht selten kommen Mütter mit ihren kleinen Töchtern zum Arzt und sagen: „Meine Tochter hat einen Unfall gehabt. Würden Sie nachsehen, ob nichts verletzt wurde." Der Arzt muss dann wissen, dass nachgesehen werden soll, ob der Hymen intakt ist.

Aus dieser ganzen Situation heraus wird bei verletztem Hymen der Arzt nicht selten gebeten, eine Hymenplastik vorzunehmen. Schwieriger ist für den Arzt die Entscheidung, wenn bei intaktem Hymen eine Schwangerschaft eingetreten ist.

Ein 15 jähriges Mädchen wird von den Eltern zu Verwandten in die Stadt gegeben, um ihre Ausbildung zu beenden. Nach einigen Monaten kommt die Mutter mit ihrer Tochter in die Sprechstunde, da Regelstörungen eingetreten seien. Die Untersuchung ergibt: Intaktes Hymen und eine Schwangerschaft im 5. Monat. Der vermutliche Vater ist der Ehemann der Tante, der sich mit dem Mädchen „beschäftigt" habe! Jetzt wurde von der Mutter die Bitte ausgesprochen, die Schwangerschaft durch Schnittentbindung zu beenden und den Hymen zu erhalten, da sonst das Schicksal des Mädchens deprimierend sei. Es wurde dann die Schnittentbindung, aber erst 14 Tage vor dem errechneten Geburtstermin vorgenommen und ein gesunder Knabe entbunden. Er sollte bei entfernten Verwandten aufwachsen. Die Mutter würde sagen, dass die Tochter an einem Tumor operiert worden sei. Der Hymen war intakt.

Diese Verhältnisse sind Folge der Geringschätzung der Individualität der Frau. Sie werden als Objekt und nicht als Subjekt gewertet. Die arabischen Männer vertreten häufig noch die Auffassung, dass Frauen dazu da seien, dem Manne zu dienen und Kinder zu gebären.

Bis vor nicht allzu langer Zeit bestand bei den Eltern in Libyen auch die Auffassung, dass Schulbildung für ein Mädchen nur hinderlich sei, um eine gute Ehefrau zu werden. Das änderte sich aber, als junge Libyer zur Weiterbildung nach Amerika oder nach England gingen und Ausländerinnen als Ehefrauen mit nach Hause brachten. Sie hatten erkannt, dass gebildete Frauen bessere Ehepartner sein konnten. Der „Heiratswert" der Mädchen mit Schulbildung nahm daraufhin zu; die Eltern schickten vermehrt die Töchter zur Schule und jetzt besteht offiziell Schulpflicht auch für Mädchen.

Die soziale Stellung mit ihren seelischen Spannungen und psychischen Belastungen wird sich nur für d i e Frauen ändern, die durch Schulbesuch und anschliessender Berufsausbildung nicht mehr bedingungslos dem Manne ausgeliefert sind. Eine gesunde, den Verhältnissen angepasste Emanzipation ist dadurch in manchen modernen arabischen Staaten schon zu beobachten.

Wurde die Ehe geschlossen, so begann bei diesen „Kindfrauen" die erste Schwangerschaft bei 86,6% innerhalb von 12 Monaten, bei 60,6% schon innerhalb der ersten 6 Monate nach der Eheschließung.

Die Schwangere wurde von der Familie beraten und die Entbindung fand im Kreise der weiblichen Angehörigen der Familie unter Betreuung durch eine „weise Frau" statt. Die tatsächlichen Kenntnisse über den normalen und pathologischen Geburtsverlauf sind bei den „weisen Frauen" äußerst gering. Komplikationen werden nicht rechtzeitig erkannt. So sind bei der Einlieferung im Krankenhaus Befunde zu beobachten, die in Deutschland kaum mehr gesehen werden: wie verschleppte Querlage mit oder ohne Armvorfall, eingekeilter kindlicher Kopf bei Missverhältnis zwischen Kopf und Beckeneingang mit abgestorbener Frucht, wodurch sich anschließend große vesico-vaginale und recto-vaginale Fisteln ausbilden. Unvollständig entwickelte Beckenendlagen. Geburtsverletzungen der Vagina oder Dammrisse bis 3. Grades sind nicht selten und bleiben meist unversorgt. Das Schicksal all dieser Frauen ist bedauernswert, wenn sie nicht entsprechende ärztliche Hilfe finden.

Ist die Entbindung glücklich überstanden, so folgt eine Schwangerschaft der anderen. Da in den arabischen Ländern - im Gegensatz zu anderen afrikanischen Ländern - der Ehemann nicht verpflichtet ist, sich von seiner Ehefrau fern zu halten, würden Entbindungen und erneute Schwangerschaft in kurzen Abständen aufeinander folgen. Um Mutter und Letztgeborenes vor Schaden zu bewahren, hat der Prophet dafür den Rat gegeben, das Letztgeborene für 2 Jahre zu stillen, da während der Zeit des Stillens eine Schwangerschaft nicht eintreten würde. Es ist erstaunlich, dass nur durch Beobachtung diese Erfahrung gewonnen wurde, deren Richtigkeit durch Veränderungen im Hormonhaushalt heute bestätigt werden kann. Untersuchungen in Libyen zeigten, dass diese Methode der „Familienplanung" mit Erfolg angewendet wurde (Tab. 2).

Trotzdem machen die Frauen zahlreiche Schwangerschaften durch, ca. 8 ausgetragene Schwangerschaften im „Durchschnitt" neben erfolgten Fehlgeburten. Die Frauen fühlen sich verpflichtet möglichst viele Kinder, möglichst viele Knaben zu gebären, da die frühkindliche Sterblichkeit hoch ist und 1958 etwa 48% und jetzt noch ca. 30% im Durchschnitt beträgt. Kinder sind aber die „Sozialversicherung der Eltern bei Krankheit und im Alter".

Durch Senkung der „frühkindlichen Mortalität", durch das Bewusstsein der Mutter, dass fast alle Kinder am Leben bleiben, kann den Frauen die Verpflichtung genommen werden, so viele Schwangerschaften durchzumachen. Eine „Familienplanung" hat ja der Prophet selbst empfohlen. Es ist im Islam zur Erhaltung der Gesundheit der Mutter auch erlaubt, die Befruchtung, die Vereinigung von Samenzelle und Ei zu verhindern, so dass auch eine moderne Familienplanung möglich ist. Eine Schwangerschaftsunterrbrechung lehnt der Islam jedoch strikt ab.

Es ist überhaupt erstaunlich, dass der mütterliche Organismus, der durch mangelhafte und unzweckmäßige Ernährung sich im Eiweißdefizit befindet, trotzdem in der Lage ist, das Eiweiß für den Aufbau des Föten und für die Milchproduktion immer wieder bereit zu stellen. Das reduzierte Geburts-

Monate vor 1. Menstruation					Monate nach 1. Menstruation					
36–24	24–12	12–6	6–3	3–1	1–3	3–6	6–12	12–24	24–36	36–x
2	6	10	5	8+1[1]	15	4	17	19	8	5
			13+1[1]		19					
		23+1[1]			36					
	31+1[1])				68					

[1]) Schwangerschaft ohne Periode.

Tab. 2
Verteilung des Heiratstermins in Beziehung zum Eintritt der ersten Menstruation.

gewicht des Kindes mit 3000 g ist auf diese Mangelsituation zurückzuführen. Der Gesundheitszustand der Mutter würde sich also bei Einschränkung der Schwangerschaften bald so bessern, das sie ihren Aufgaben als Erzieherin der Kinder und als Hausfrau gerecht werden könnte.

Die Senkung der frühkindlichen Mortalität hat sich die WHO mit dem MCH (mother and child health)-Programm zum Ziel gesetzt. Mütter- und Säuglingsberatungsstellen vermitteln den Frauen vor allem Kenntnisse für die Zubereitung einer gesunden und ausreichenden Ernährung und für die Säuglingsbetreuung. Durch die eintretenden Erfolge wird sich der Gesundheitszustand der Kinder und der Frauen und damit ihr Lebensschicksal allmählich bessern.

Ist innerhalb des ersten Jahres der Ehe eine Schwangerschaft nicht eingetreten, so wird der Rat der weisen Frau und schließlich der des Arztes gesucht. Sind mit den diagnostischen Maßnahmen und einer unter Umständen vorgeschlagenen Operation Kosten verbunden, so treten Probleme auf, wenn die Frau kein eigenes Vermögen besitzt, um die Arzt- und Operationskosten zu bezahlen. Der Ehemann wird sich, wenn er die Kosten tragen müsste, überlegen, ob er mit dem Betrag nicht das Brautgeld für eine andere Frau bezahlen könnte. Die Frau wird dagegen alle ihre Ersparnisse einsetzen, um schwanger zu werden. Dabei liegt ihr nichts an einer wissenschaftlich fundierten Diagnose, sondern sie möchte ein Kind haben und ist bereit, sich allen Untersuchungen und Behandlungen zu unterziehen, denn das Schicksal einer kinderlosen Frau ist deprimierend. Ist der Mann bereit, sie weiterhin zu behalten, so wird sie zur „Dienenden" für alle weiteren Ehefrauen, für die ganze Familie. Sie wird sich oft darin fügen, denn die bei der Frau nachgewiesenen Sterilität ist ein Scheidungsgrund für den Mann.

Wie auch früher in Deutschland kommt das Ehepaar zum Arzt und der Ehemann erklärt: „Herr Doktor, meine Frau bekommt keine Kinder!" Fragt man ihn nach seiner Zeugungsfähigkeit, so ist er fest davon überzeugt, dass es an ihn nicht liegen könne, denn „alles sei bei ihm in Ordnung." Er ist dann kaum zu überzeugen, dass eine Untersuchung seiner Samenflüssigkeit notwendig ist, da ja auch Veränderungen der Samenflüssigkeit des Mannes Ursache der Kinderlosigkeit sein kann. Gegen eine solche Untersuchung sträuben sich aber viele der Ehemänner, da ihre männliche und soziale Anerkennung bei einer festgestellten Zeugungsunfähigkeit sehr leiden würde. Da es auch für die Frau ein Scheidungsgrund wäre, so wollen sie es gar nicht wissen. Da sich solche Ehepaare deswegen nach einiger Zeit trennen und dann andere Partner heiraten, so werden sich schließlich die, die fruchtbar und die, die unfruchtbar sind, zusammenfinden. Auf jeden Fall muss sich der Arzt bei der Diagnosenstellung sehr diplomatisch verhalten und, wenn möglich, die „Schuld" der Kinderlosigkeit auf beide Partner verteilen.

Wie wichtig für eine Frau es ist, nachzuweisen, dass sie empfangen kann, erlebte ich bei einer Patientin, die wiederholt Fehlgeburten durchgemacht und kein lebendes Kind hatte. Sie hatte alle abgegangenen Foeten in Spiritus aufbewahrt und die Gläser demonstrativ auf einen Schrank aufgereiht. Bei einer erneuten Schwangerschaft kam sie in meine Klinik. Es bestand eine Schwäche der Cervix, des Verschlussapparates des Uterus, wodurch es jedesmal zum vorzeitigen Fruchtabgang gekommen war. Mit einer entsprechenden Behandlung bis zum Ende der Schwangerschaft wurde dann ein gesundes Mädchen geboren. Die Freude war trotzdem geteilt, da es ja kein Knabe war.

Das Auftreten einer sekundären Sterilität, d.h. dass nach der ersten Entbindung keine Schwangerschaft mehr eintritt oder nur noch Fehlgeburten folgen, ist bei der mangelhaften „Geburtshilfe der weisen Frauen" nicht selten. Auch diese Frauen werden an Ansehen verlieren und darunter leiden.Ebenso können andere Störungen durch eingetretene und nicht versorgte Geburtsverletzungen vorhanden sein, die ihre Rolle als Frau beeinträchtigen. Die Tätigkeit des Arztes kann bei solchen Patienten sehr dankbar sein. Um solche Schäden durch Entbindungen bei den Frauen zu verhindern, sollten in diesen Ländern genügend Hebammen ausgebildet werden, die in der Lage sind, eine normale Entbindung zu leiten und pathologische Verläufe zu erkennen, um die Patientinnen rechtzeitig in die Klinik einzuweisen. Dazu sind nicht Hebammen mit dem hohen englischen Ausbildungsstandard erforderlich, sondern „community midwifes", Gemeindehebammen, ausreichend, deren Ausbildung kürzer und der Schulbildung angepasst ist. Außerdem wären diese Hebammen mit der nicht-klinischen Arbeit zufrieden.

Die Hygiene im Genitalbereich wird von der arabischen Frau sorgfältig beachtet. Dazu gehört zum Beispiel, dass alle Schamhaare durch Zupfen sorgfältig entfernt sind. Auf Befragen wurde lächelnd gesagt, dass dadurch auch das „Zusammensein" intimer sei. Tägliche Waschungen sind vorgeschrieben, besonders auch nach dem Verkehr, wobei auch die Vagina mit Wasser und Seife gereinigt wird. Infolgedessen verliert die Scheideninnenhaut ihre sonst typischen Eigenschaften. Ausfluss ist selten bei den

Frauen zu beobachten. Als Gynäkologe kann man immer wieder feststellen, dass dieser Bereich vorbildlich gepflegt ist.

Der allgemeine Gesundheitszustand ist bei den meisten der verheirateten arabischen Frauen der ländlichen Bevölkerung reduziert, denn sie leben in ständigem Eiweißdefizit. Fleisch ist teuer und wird ein Mal in der Woche gegessen. Milch und Eier werden gemieden, da sie bei dem heißen Klima als Krankheitsüberträger bekannt und gefürchtet sind. So besteht die Nahrung aus billigen Mehl- und Teigwaren und Gemüse, das allerdings durch langes Kochen arm an Vitaminen ist. Schließlich besteht der Brauch, dass die Männer zuerst allein essen und Frauen und Kinder mit dem zufrieden sein müssen, was die Männer übrig lassen. Häufige Entbindung und Mangelernährung führen bei den Frauen zu ausgeprägten Anämien, die kritisch werden können, wenn eine weitere Schädigung des Blutbildes durch Erkrankungen wie Malaria, Bilharziose, Hakenwurm- oder Ascarisbefall hinzutritt.

Aber schon eine neue Schwangerschaft kann zu schweren Komplikationen führen, da z.B. in Libyen bei der einfachen Bevölkerung der Brauch besteht Holzkohle gegen die in der Schwangerschaft auftretenden Magen- und Darmbeschwerden einzunehmen. Die Patienten bieten dann das Bild einer schweren Schwagerschaftstoxikose. Vorsichtige Bluttransfusionen und eine entsprechende Therapie könnten diesen Zustand bald bessern, aber die Bevölkerung der arabischen Länder lehnt Bluttransfusionen häufig strikt ab. Es besteht der Glaube, dass durch eine Blutübertragung besondere verwandtschaftliche Bindungen mit entsprechenden Verpflichtungen entstehen und außerdem auch charakterliche, seelische Eigenschaften übergehen würden. Ich verlor eine etwa 25 Jahre alte Patientin nur durch die Weigerung der Angehörigen, dass eine Blutübertragung durchgeführt wurde.

Immer wieder zeigt sich, wie wichtig - auch für Menschen, die nicht Lesen und Schreiben können - eine einfache, aber kompetente Gesundheitsberatung und -Schule ist. Die meisten Frauen sind bildungs- und lernfähig und an allen Fragen der Gesundheitspflege sehr interessiert.

Reist eine Touristin in einem islamischen-arabischen Land, so wird sie kaum etwas von diesen Problemen der Frauen erfahren. Einmal sind sprachliche Barrieren vorhanden, zum anderen lernt sie das Land aus der Perspektive des 5, 4 oder 3 Sterne Hotels oder eines Clubs kennen und mit organisierten Omnibusfahrten zu den Sehenswürdigkeiten des Landes. Mit der weiblichen Bevölkerung wird sie kaum in Berührung kommen, das tatsächliche Leben der Frauen nur selten kennen lernen.

Trotzdem wird sie feststellen können, dass große Unterschiede schon im äußeren Erscheinungsbild zwischen moderner Großstadt und traditioneller Landbevölkerung besteht. Schließlich sind große Unterschiede in der Stellung der Frau in der Gesellschaft zwischen den einzelnen islamisch-arabischen Ländern vorhanden.

Ich hatte Gelegenheit, mit einer jungen Tunesierin mich über Frauenfragen wiederholt zu unterhalten. Sie war Verkäuferin in einem Teppich- Andenkenbasar in einem 5 Sterne Hotel in Port el Kantaoui, war verlobt und wollte bald heiraten.

Sie sagte mir: „In Tunesien sind die Frauen schon mehr und mehr emanzipiert. Der Staat hatte noch unter Burghiba, dem ersten Präsidenten in Tunesien, die Einehe eingeführt und schon dadurch die Stellung der Frau als Ehefrau erheblich gefestigt. Jetzt können auch die jungen Mädchen selbst die Schule wählen, die sie besuchen möchten und dann auch ihre Berufsausbildung bestimmen. Sie sind auch nicht mehr zu Hause „eingesperrt", sondern dürfen mit ihren Freundinnen allein in die Stadt gehen, um Besorgungen zu machen oder sie dürfen auch zusammen Sport treiben. Die Verschleierung, wie z.B. in Libyen üblich, gibt es in Tunesien nicht mehr (Abb.2).

Darin irrte sie sich allerdings, denn bei einem Besuch im Landesinnern konnte ich wiederholt Frauen sehen, die den Barakan trugen.

Als ich sie danach fragte, erklärte sie mir „In traditionellen Familien kann das noch Brauch sein, aber die Allgemeinheit der Frauen ist dazu nicht verpflichtet.

Die einzige Einschränkung der persönlichen Freiheit, die noch besteht, liegt darin, dass für eine Reise ins Ausland, die die Frau allein unternehmen möchte, das Einverständnis des Vaters oder des Ehemannes im Pass eingetragen sein muss. Aber welche Frau will schon allein ins Ausland reisen!? Jedenfalls kann sich in Tunesien jede Frau kleiden, wie sie will und sich frei bewegen, ohne irgendwie belästigt zu werden."

Auf einer Einladung einer angesehen, reichen tunesischen Familie fand ich das bestätigt. Bei den Damen war letzte Pariser Mode bis zum Minirock zu bewundern. Als ich einen der Gäste, einen gut aussehenden, etwa 40 Jahre alten Tunesier, nach der Emanzipation der Frau in Tunesien fragte, meinte

Abb. 2
Barakan in Lybien (Foto Wilhelm Föllmer).

er lachend: „Die ist bei uns leider schon viel zu weit fortgeschritten!"
Eine gesunde Emanzipation der Frau entwickelt sich jedenfalls zusehens in den modernen arabisch-islamischen Ländern, und macht die Frau frei von der deprimierenden Unterwürfigkeit gegenüber dem Mann. Die Frau ist in diesen islamischen Ländern ebenso glücklich oder unglücklich in ihrer Ehe wie eine Frau in Deutschland.
Allerdings ist der Gegensatz zwischen den einzelnen arabisch-islamischen Ländern und ihren Bevölkerungsteilen noch immer außerordentlich groß und Rückschläge sind möglich, wenn religiöse Fanatiker die Regierung übernehmen.
Neben diesem sozialen Umfeld, das die Gesundheit der Frau erheblich beeinträchtigen kann, ist sie durch endemische und Tropenkrankheiten wie z.B. Malaria, Amöbiase, Bilharziose, Hakenwurm- und Askarisbefall besonders gefährdet, da sie alle zu ernsten Komplikationen bei Eintritt einer Schwangerschaft führen können. Hier sei nur kurz auf die Malaria und Amöbiase eingegangen.
Bei einer Bevölkerung, die in einem Gebiet mit endemischer Malaria lebt, ist die akute Malariainfektion mit ihren typischen Erscheinungen nur im Kindesalter zu finden. Bei älteren Kindern und Erwachsenen entwickelt sich eine gewisse Immunität. Die subjektiven Erscheinungen sind dann so gering, dass die Frauen ihre tägliche Arbeit verrichten können. Tritt eine Schwangerschaft ein, so können in der zweiten Hälfte schwere zerebrale Erscheinungen auftreten, die als Eklampsie nicht selten verkannt werden. Auch können durch die Anstrengung der Geburt, dem Blutverlust und die Laktation akute Symptome mit Fieberschüben ausgelöst werden. Wo die Malaria nicht endemisch ist/ können die Fieberanfälle zur Fehldiagnose Puerperalfieber, auch Pyelitis führen.
Eine Holländerin war niemals in den Tropen gewesen. Auch Tripolis in Libyen gilt als malariafrei. Sie kommt mit einer Fehlgeburt im 5. Monat in die Klinik und hat anschließend Fieberanfälle, die ein Puerperalfieber vermuten lassen. Im Fieberanfall wurde Blut abgenommen und wegen der vergrößerten Milz auch auf Malariaparasiten untersucht. Der Test war positiv. Durch entsprechende Behandlung kam es zur prompten Entfieberung.
Die weitere Nachforschung ergab, dass in der oberen Etage des zweistöckigen Wohnhauses ein älterer britischer Kolonialoffizier wohnte, der eine schwere Malaria durchgemacht hatte. War er der Infektionsherd?
Durch Attacken mit hohem Fieber kann es zu Fehl- oder Frühgeburten kommen. Aber auch eine mehr schleichende Einwirkung auf den Föten und seine Entwicklung kann eintreten, da die Erythrocyten, die bei einer Malariaerkrankung zu 60-90% von Parasiten befallen sind, zur normalen

Sauerstoffversorgung des Föten nicht mehr ausreichen.

Die WHO hat große Anstrengungen unternommen, durch die Bekämpfung der Anopheles-Mücke die Malaria in Nordafrika zu beseitigen. Trotzdem wird es für eine Europäerin ratsam sein, ein solches Land während einer Schwangerschaft nicht aufzusuchen oder bei Beginn einer Schwangerschaft bis zu ihrem Ende zu verlassen. Denn die Unschädlichkeit der Medikamente, die zur Prophylaxe und Therapie der Malaria erfolgreich eingesetzt werden, für den Foeten ist noch nicht sicher erwiesen.

Anders bei der einheimischen Bevölkerung, wo die Gesundheit der Mutter über den Wert des Kindes geht. Hier wird der Arzt über die Anwendung frei entscheiden.

Die Amoebiase ist in den subtropischen und tropischen arabischen Ländern weit verbreitet. Sie tritt auch bei der Europäerin selten als akute „Amöbenruhr" auf, sondern verläuft gewöhnlich mit uncharakteristischen Darmsymptomen als subakute oder chronische Form.

Immer ist der Darmtrakt geschädigt, es besteht eine subakute oder chronische Colitis. Durch die dabei veränderte Darmflora ist auch die Bildung der B-Vitamine gestört. So kann es während der Schwangerschaft, die mit einem erhöhten Vitamin-B Bedarf einhergeht, zu einem bedrohliche Vitamin-B-Defizit kommen.

Auch hier stehen wirksame Medikamente zur Verfügung, die alle Nebenwirkungen haben und deswegen während der Schwangerschaft mit Bedacht eingesetzt werden sollen. Oft ist aber der Gesundheitszustand der einheimischen Frauen durch die gestörte Ausnutzung der Nahrung so reduziert, dass Rücksicht auf die Frucht nicht möglich ist.

Mit den beiden Beispielen sollte nur gezeigt werden, welchen besonderen Gefahren die Frau bei bestehen einer Erkrankung durch den Eintritt einer Schwangerschaft in diesen Ländern ausgesetzt ist. Immer wieder zeigt sich dabei auch, wie wichtig die Schulung der einheimischen Frauen in allgemeiner und persönlicher Hygiene, in der einwandfreien Zubereitung der Nahrung und in allgemeinen Gesundheitsfragen ist. Nur durch die Hebung ihres Gesundheitszustandes kann das Schicksal der arabischen Frau in den traditionellen islamisch-arabischen Ländern verbessert werden, nur dann kann eine gesunde Emanzipation in diesen Ländern einsetzen.

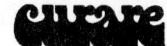

Women and the Political Economy of Traditional Medicine in Kenya: A Historical Perspective
Frauen und die politische Ökonomie traditioneller Medizin in Kenia. Historische Aspekte

Peter Mwangi Kagwanja

Abstract: Medical systems, owing to the social aetiology of disease and ideological nature of therapy, mirror class and gender relations in society. Traditional medical systems so not only bespeak the unequal gender relations in patriarchal societies, but are themselves steeped in unequal relations with bionedical system within the context of the capitalist world system. This article undertakes a historical and theoritical analysis of women's role in traditionalmedical systems in Kenya. Focussing on pre-colonial and post colonial societies, it rqaues the unequal gender power relations have their corollary in unequal access to medical knowledge and services. Trends towards professionalization and incorporation of indigenous medical systems into the biomedical regime has on the whole deepened the marginalization of women's health affairs.

Zusammenfassung: Wegen der gesellschaftlichen Ätiologie von Krankheit und wegen der ideologischen Natur von Therapie spiegeln medizinische Systeme die Klassen- und Geschlechterbeziehungen in der Gesellschaft. Traditionelle medizinische Systeme lassen nicht nur die ungleichen Beziehungen zwischen den Geschlechtern in patriarchalen Gesellschaften erkennen, sondern sind selbst von ungleichen Beziehungen zum biomedizinischen System im Zusammenhang des weltweiten Kapitalismus durchdrungen. In diesem Beitrag wird die Rolle der Frauen in traditionellen medizinischen Systemen Kenias historisch und theoretisch analysiert. Mit scharfem Blick auf die prä- und postkolonialen Gesellschaften wird argumentiert, dass den ungleichen Beziehungen zwischen der Macht der Geschlechter ein ungleicher Zugang zu medizinischem Wissen und Service entspricht. Die Trends zu Professionalisierung und Einbindung der heimischen medizinischen Systeme in das biomedizinische Regime haben insgesamt die Marginalisierung der Frauen-Gesundheitsversorgung verstärkt.

Keywords: Africa, Kenya, women, traditional medicine systems, political economy, history, Afrika, Frauen, politische Ökonomie, Geschichte, traditionelle Medizin, Kenia.

Women's participation in traditional medical systems, as physicians and therapy - seekers, is passionately interlinked with the basic ingredients of power, privileges and hence on, domination which underpin class societies like Kenya. Owing to the acclaimed social aetiology of disease and ideological nature of therapy, medical systems are, invariably, repositories of social values, power, and privileges as well as mechanisms of control. Beyond their inherent concern with mundane issues of health, medical regimes, as JUDITH LASKER (1977) avers, „serve non-medical goals of a society's dominant groups" and, therefor, mirror the prevailing class and gender relations in society. Nonetheless, issues of gender power relations within traditional medical systems have not received adequate attention in the international struggle for the liberation and empowerment of womenfolk.

The political economy approach to the study of medical systems in general, and traditional systems in particular, is inspired by perspectives: the marxist and „world systems" variants of political economy. (The Marxist perspective has tended to stress the historical context and social aetiology of health care and, the ideological nature of medical knowledge (TAYLOR & RIGER 1985; WAITZKIN 1979; MORSY 1990:33). On the other hand, dependency of „world system" theorists, as is their wont, link the problems of health, including the mal-distribution of modern medicine and the ghettoizaton of traditional systems, to the same socio-economic determinants that cause the underdevelopment of Third World societies (WALLERSTEIN 1979; NAVARO 1981; 1986). SOHIER MORSY (1990: 34) credits the dependency perspective with the extension of primary considerations to the very relations between biomedicine within the global capitalist political economy has tended to determine the fortunes of traditional systems.

In the light of this, the general proposition for the mix of traditional and modern medicine is viewed with profound suspicion of political economic and cultural hegemony of the latter. The trend towards „professionalization" of traditional medical systems and their gradual incorporation into the official health system has sounded the death knell for their autonomy.

In this chapter we undertake a historica lanalysis of the patterns of women's participation in traditional medical systems in Kenya within the wider context of capitalist development. Three argument are presented here. First, women's participation in traditional medical systems cannot be extricated from the theoretical debate on patriarchy and matriarchy in African societies. The traditional division of labour as wess as control over knowledge in the medical field echo this relationship. Thus, women play a central role in the „primary health care„, to use a modern phrase, and in domestic nutrition, hygiene, material health and child-care. With few exceptions, women are peripheralized in specialized practice herbalism, bone-setting, surgery, divination and so on-, which offer prospects for accumulation of wealth and augmentation of power and prestige.

Second, the advent of colonialism exposed women to a deteriorating disease environment, and itself created political, economic conditions which undermined women's health. Women were not only excluded from the benefits of western medicine, they were also caught in the social and religious crossfire between the latter and traditional medicine.

Third, the professionalization and qualitative expansion of traditional medical systems in post independence era has augured wess for the improvement of rural women's helth, but their under representation in traditional practice has heralded their marginalization in the benefits for professionalization. Incorporation of Traditional Birth Attendants (TBAS) into the national health systems raises critical questions on the prospects of their power and autonomy.

Women and Traditional Medical Systems: Some Theoretical and Analytical Issues
Discussion on the inherent gender power relations in traditional medical systems dovetails into the debate on patriarchy and Matriarchy in African societies. It is asserted that historically, European societies have been patriarchal (totalitarian male rule and oppression of women) and in contrast, Africa is the cradle of matriarchy (a pro-female, mother-focused society) (DIOP 1989). Using the example of the Igbo of Midwestern Nigeria, OKONJO (1979: 45), contrasts the „dual sex" and „single sex" African and European societies, respectively. He posits that in „dual sex" Africal societies, each sex manages ist own affair and women's interest are represented at all levels. On the contrary, in European „single sex" system „status - bearing roles are pre-dominantly the preserve of men... women can achieve disinction and ricognition only by taking on the roles of men in public life and performing them well".

Matriarchal ideological structures have, however, been weakened, and perhaps supplanted by centuries of contact with patriarchal Islamic and European structures (DIOP 1989). In The River Between, the Kenyan novelist, Ngugi Wa Thiono, alluding to the ancient legend of he female leader, Wangu Wa Makeri, captures the infiltration of patriarchy into the kikuyu society as follows: Long ago women used to rule this land and ist men. They were hash and men began to resent their hard hand. So when all the women were pregnant, men came together and overthrew them (1965: 15)

Matriarchal ideological structures were gradually overlaid with patriarchal ideology. This largely explains the inherent ambivalence in the perception of pregnancy (and menstruation) as both a symbol of female potency on the one hand, and veritable moments of vulnerability and impurity on the other. Manopause is considered by the kikuyu as a stage of ritual purity when women can assume roles such as midwives, healers or ritual leaders.

This also underpins teh powerful community-based pronatalist pressre that prevades almost all kenyan communities. J. S. MBITI (1969: 110-11) observes that „Lunhappy is a woman who fails to get children, for whatever qualities she might possess this failure to bear children renders her a dead-end of a human life on both the geneological line and her own line since nobody from her blood will remember her and keep her in a constant state of personal immortality when she dies".

Childlessness, even where it is a fault of the husband, is considered as an irreparable humiliatio for a women. Ist often interpreted as a breach of taboos and customs of her side. In contrast, social power and prestige of a woman are measured by the number fo children she bears; her status is further enhanced if she prolifically produce male offsprings.

Pronatalist pressure was based of acute need for labour, in the absence of technology in a labour intensive agrarian economy. It was also sustained by the precarious African ecology of disease and high mortality rate caused by numerous epidemics. The weight of the latter point can be appreciated if one considers that in the pre-colonial era, and the first phase of colonialism, Africa's population declined of stagnated. Between 1750 and 1850, for instance the continents population constituted mere 13 per cent of the total world population. This declined from 11 percent in 1800 to 8 per cent by 1900 (UNITED NATIONS 1973: 32). The countervailing argument is that among the hunter-gatherer communities such as the Okiek and Dorobo, where demand for labour is not acute, such pronalist pressure is minimal. To that end, Collier and Rosaldo argue that „motherhood and biological reproduction are far less central to the cultural conceptions of the female status than are women as sexual beings" (in BROWNER & SARGENT 1990; 219).

Cultural institutions and practices such as polygemy wife-inheritance, levirate mittiage and early (forced) marriages, witch are now recast and demonized as health risks to wonem, were basically sustained by this desire to procreate. Division of labour and knowledge specialization in medical systems conform to the perceived centrality of women in reproduction. While all children's diseases, all obstetrics, all of the „everyday" complaints are handled by women, particularly the elderly women, surgery, bone-setting, and special diagnostic and therapeutic problems are handled almost exclusively by men.

Women accumulated enormous knowledge in edible medical vegetation and other material medica related to nutrition. From the extensive research that has been done on communities in Western Kenya -Lou, Abaluhya, Kalenjin and Teso - it is clear that women had deep knowledge of the nutritional and medical value Gynandropsis Gynadra (spider weed), Solanum Nigrum (Black Nightshade), Vigna Unguiculate, and C. Olitarius (KOKWARO 1976; KANGETHE 1987; OPOLE 1991). Gynandropsis, for instance, was prepared in a variety of ways to cure scurvy, relieve aching eyes, cure ailments of both protein and vitamin deficiency syndromes associated with marasmus of kwashiakor. In addition, it was fed to lactatic mothers and pregnant women to make them healthier and to reduce dizzy spells (OPOLE 1991). At a more specialized level, traditional midwives possessed a good understanding of jundamental obstetric and pediatric principles. Lou midwives give herbal medicine to lessen labour pains, hasten birth, expell retarted placenta, to reduce post-partum abdominal pains, and to aid breast-milk production. When a baby lies in a wrong position, either squatting of feet first these midwives are adept at identifying and correcting the anomaly during antenatal visits or during birth (KAWANGE 1995: 85). OtherAfrican midwives also had drugs that can induce abortion in teh first three month of pregnancy and in Uganda, and area where there is a hith incidence of dystocia (retarded labour), the midwives have priparations within stimulate uterine contractions. Bantu midwives used Indian hemp during labour for ist sedative properties (FITCH 1983). It was also common practice to expose newborn babies and infants to the sun for a period each day, which almost wiped out the occurrence of rickets.

But when it came to surgery in meternal issues, where it occured, men appear to have predominated. This is confirmed by the case of the male surgeons of Bunyoro - Kitara, Uganda who performed the widely discussed caesarean poerations (FITCH 1983). Similar caesarean operations are not recorded in Kenya, exept in relation to female circumcision whrer women were the surgeons. In a number of cases, women could handle complex therapeutic problems, particularly where they had herbal skills. Among the Marakwet of the Rift Valley, herbal practice was done by women (chepkerichin), but herbal knowledge could be passed to those men woh failed beget children (and thus to keep wives). (KIPKORIR & WELBOURN 1973). Among the kikuyu, only men could become diviners and herbalists (Andri Ago), but occasionally a woman could bi possessed by magic, thereby becoming a diviner and herbalist (LEAKEY 1977:1152). If such taditional practises as removal of lower teeth, tattooing of the body, and piercing of ears among some Kenyan groups have been fought from a medical front (they can cause wound sepsis and cross infection), female circumcision has drawn the ire of ist opponents as the most potent vestige of patriarchal ideological stricture on the right of women. JOMO KENYATTA (1978) avers that circumcision, both male and female, was „the condition sine qua non of the whole teaching of tribal law, religion and morality" on which traditional medical systems were based. The cultural explanation for this practice, most especially excision an infibulation, is that it curbs sexual promiscuity by reducing the pressures in sexual intercourse and protects parents against societal reprisals. Those opposed to circumcision often concedes that male cicumcision was medically friendly to women particularly in the context of widespread polygamy, wife inheritance and levirate marriages. kirya argues that „women.. who engage in regular sexual contacts with circumcised men are less likely to develop cancer of the cervix than those who are in regular contact with uncircumcised men" (1989:111). On the other hand, clitoridectomy is said to contribute to childbirth complications due to fibrosis around the birth canal and even cause deaths of initiate as a result of uncontrolled bleeding or secondary infections. But the debate goes beyond these medical concerns. Female circumcisions is potrayed as a selfish way of viewing life on the part of men who want to enjoy themselves while rducing women to tools (KIRYA 1989:107). To thst end, the human rights discours os invoked and imported into the circumcision saga. CORINNE KRARTZ

(1994:341), however, vehemently objects to the treatment of the rite as the same phenomenon in all places or ist definition as Genital mutulation. She posits that the anti-circumcision campaign is not free of propagandistic and sensational images intended to mobilize political action. Undestanding the reasons why females present themselves for circumcision, and ist implications for power and prestige in society, are germane to the unravelling of this problem. To a rural female kenyan, female circumcision is not so much a violation of her human rights, as an augmentation of her social standing, power and prestige. Here lies the dilemma.

Women, Traditional Medicine and the Colonialism Society
In HARTWIG and PATTERSON`S (1978:4) incisive declaration, „the unhealthiest period in African history was undoubtedly between 1890 and 1930". This period which ovelaps with the advent and consolidation of colonialism in Kenya, has been pquated to the Black Death, „the cataclysmic pandemic that ravaged Europe in the fourteenth century" (ZELEZA 1993:41). Colonialism, in ARNOLD`S damning words (1988:4), „was a major health hazard for indigenious people,„ thanks to population disruption, adaptations to new productive activities, contact with foreigners, and „an outbreak of biological warfare on a vast scale" (FORD 1971: in ZELEZA 1993:41) that it set in motion.

Intrusion of non-African epidemics and transmission of previously localized diseases in Kenya led to a deterioration in the ecology of disease, weakened people`s immunity, and overstretched traditional therapeutic systems. The painfully slow penetration and maldistribution of Western medicine as well as its insensitivity and hostility to traditional therapeutic systems hardly helped the situation. Kenyan woman were not only the Cinderella of colonial health policy but also the principal victims of the deteriorated disease environment. Suffice it to say that the negative effects of colonial land, agriculture and migrant labour policies on helth, dood production, nutrition and hygiene are well documented (BECK 1981; BOWLES 1979; ARNOLD 1988; PATTERSON & HARTWIG 1978). But colonialism impact on womens´s health has not been clearly focused on. The system of labour migration´s precipitated acute cases of malnutrition among women and children who were horded in marginal and unproductive land, and left at home by the menfolk. Aside from their reproductive role, women became the producers of over 90 per cent of food to supplement the meagre wages men were paid in the capitalist sector. These wages (which stood at & 13 per annum for most of the colonial period) wrer inadequate to buy soap, install windows in huts, and to provide lighting and sanitation needs. Thus respiratory diseases as well as cholera and diarrhoea among rural women and children attained epidemic proportions. Overcrowding in unhygienic huts by polygamous and large families in order to escape hut tax also took ist toll on women health. Finally, cash crop production undermined traditional food crops.

In his withering condemnation of the wholesale introduction of monocultural maize production, BOWLES (1979:203) has noted that: „maize is not only protein deficient but also, as compared with sorghum and millet, lack in calcium, iron, phosphorus, thiamine, riboflavin and niacin, the last defiency being primaryly responsible for pellagra....."

The colonial medical system was grossly understaffed, underfinanced and skewed in flavour of the burgeconing urban enclaves, and basically served the needs of administrators, settlers, missionaries and their families. The vast majority of the population continued to rely primarily on traditional forms of healing (BECK 1981:10). Besides the colonial states reluctance to train African paramedical staff to serve rural areas, or to built health centres instead of grandiose urban - based hospitals, its financing of health services declined from $ 250,000 in 1931 to $ 200,000 in 1934 (Beck, 1981:23). ARNOLD (1988:4) has perceptively observed that the benefits of Western medicine arrived late in the colonial era and even then it was barely adequate. After the Mau Mau war, spending on African health shot from $ 360,000 in 1945 to $ 2,602,832 in 1962 much of it devoted to preventive activities. Health centres grew from nil in 1946 to 140 in 1962. The relationship between traditional medical systems and biomedicine, the latter engaged in an implicit alliance with the colonial state, was adversarial. Under the instigation of missionaries, the veritable crusaders of Western medicine and its cultural and ideological accompaniments, the colonial state hurtled down on the heads of traditional healers the notorious Witchcraft ORDINANCE (1925), which legistlated a jail term not exceeding five years to traditional physicians „suspected of witchcraft; The ordinance was, effectively used as a structure on traditional healers scope of operation. It has since   hang over their heads like the sword of Demoes (NYAMWAYA 1995:34-35). GREUNBAUM (1981, in MORSY 1990) is apt when she concludes that bio-medicine served an important political role.

As major consumers of taditional medicine and pillars of its social and religious framework, women were caught in the cross-fire of the cultural and political conflict between the latter and bio-medicine, which was spearheaded by christian missionaries.

On remarkable event is the female circumcision controversy between christian missionaries (Dr. Arthur and Dr. Philip), and the leadern of th Kikuyu Central Association (KCA) in the 1930's. While these missionaries from the Church of Scotland Mission cited health reasons, their aim of breaking the magicol-religious basis traditional medicine and of establishing the universalitiy and hegemony of Western medicine are unmistakable. This evident scramble for womenfolk fitted traditional patriarchy and colonial „patriarchy" both of which recognized the centrality of women's supplort for their survival. Missionaries, who provided better health care than the state and industry combined, were perhaps more vitriolic and vociferous than the colonial administrator in their opposition to traditional medicine. The state ded not ban female circumcision but only introduced resolutions intended to reduce the operation to minor incision, ad to have it performed by trained women with some knowledge of asepsis. Between 1914 and 1931 only 56 persons were convicted on issues of female circumcision, most of whom were fined small amounts of money (BECK 1981:22). The colonial state considered traditional healers, not as subsidiaries or supplement to the paucity of modern medical services, but as significant aspects of African rural life. The co-estence of bio-medicine and ethnomedicine wasw acepted as inevitable by both medical officials and administrators from the1930s. Nevertheless, unlike in India, where practioners of Eyurvedic, Siddha and Unanni Medicine were at liberty not only to practice but also to develop associations and schools, in Kenya traditional medicine was accorded low status, and ghettoized, and encumbrances put on the path of its development. The state was not keen on incoporating aspects of traditional medicine into bio-medicine. Female birth attendants continued to attend to all children's diseads, all obstetrics, and gynecological problems, with little or no assistance or collaboration with formal health practitioners. But they did not prevent their patients from consulting biomedical doctors in hospitals or health clinics.

The failure of biomedicine to penetrate and establish its hegemony and monopoly in rural areas bespeaks the inability of colonial capitalism to subdue or to fully incorporate traditional cultures into the web of capitalist social relations.

Nevertheless, biomedicine continued to serve as a symbol of power, prestige, and hence, domination and to be skewed in favour of a small urbenized and privileged section of society. The vast bulk of women, who continued to rely on traditional therapeutic systems, subsisted on the fringes of the emergining class society.

Women Utilization of Traditional medicine in the post colonial Era

Kenya's multifarious helath structure fits in the following general characterization of the Third World model by LAST (1990: 360):

(1) a relatively weak and underfinanced system of hospital medicine, largely urban centered, staffed by doctors (nationals and foreigners) trained to different countries; (2) a legal system that privileges that hospital system yet is unable, in practical terms, to outlaw any alternative; (3) a very large number of local practitioners of traditional medicine bonesetter, midwives, barber-surgeons, and so forth who have always tried to meet the health needs of the community; (4) a wide spectrum of modern alternative therapies, alongside a market in medical drugs imported, sometimes unmaked and instuctionless, from all over the world; and (5) a population that is dispersed and often difficult of access yet has high rates of morbidity and mortality.

Its declated official health policy is to provide „health for all„, but in practice assess to modern medicine, which consumes 5.4 per cent of the total national expenditure remains a preserve of less than a fifth of the population (25 million) very much like the situation in colonial days (WORLD BANK 1995). 75 per cent of the total health personnel live and work in urban areas; 57 per cent of Kenya's households travel over 6 kilometers to teh nearest heath centre. The ratio of health centres to teh population which rose from 1:200,000 to 1:50,000 between 1963 and 1995 is still a far cry from the governments target of 1:20,000. 60 percent of health services in the formal sector are provided by the Government, through the ministry of Health, and 40 percent by Non-Governmental organizations. Nevertheless, there services have not eschewed the main constraints of biomedicine in Third world countries: inaccessibility in terms of physical distance and cost; shortage of drugs and equipments; inability to treat certain diseases impersonal care (that is, between medical staff and patients, and patients expectations of instant cure (IDRC 1980).

The vast bulk of women have not only been excluded from th esymbols of power and privilege associated with access to modern medicine but have been ravaged by indigenous diseases as well as new ones like venereal diseases and HIV/AIDS in the ever precarious disease environment. For every 1 man infected with AIDS, there are 4 women. Maternal mortality rate oscillates between 200 and 600/100,000. 1 out of every 20 girls is under the threat of death due to haemorrhage, infection, obstructed labour and unsafe abortion. Abortion cases account for 1.3 pertcent to 4 per cent of total admissions to Kenyan hospitals and 13.4 per cent - 51.6 per cent of all gynaecological admissios to hospitals, thus making abortion the single-most lethal killer of Kenyan mothers.

Moreover, women are still victims of increasing incidence of rape, violence and medically risky cultural practices such as widow inheritance, child (early) marriage (often forced), and female circumcision. According to one source, 50 per cent or a total of 6,300,000 Kanyan frmales still undergo female circumcision (TAUBIA 1995: 25). Female curcumcision is on the decline in urban areas, but it still goes strong in rural areas of Rift walley, Norht-Eastern and other provinces, where females between 8 and 13 years under go this ancient rite.

Specific services targeted at women in the formal medical sectors such as maternity serveces and maternal/child Health (MCH) clinics, have hardly resolved the crisis of health among rural women. MCH/Family plannilng services are essentially structured to serve children with some allowance for accompanying mothers. Consequently, the only women served in the MCH/FP clinics are those in the reproructive age and specifically on ante-natal of with contraceptive problems. 68 per cent of MCH/FP services are in the Government sector and have suffered from the management crisis, lack of funds, and corruption, which have became the hallmark of the post colonial state.

Dissatisfaction with modern medical services has brought Kenyan wome nto the hearth of traditional medicine. To be sure, this is not and isolated development: between a quarter to one fifth of the people in the scandinavian countries, particularly Norway, now utilize alternative medicine - acupuncture, homeopathy and chiropractic (CHRISTIE & SANDBERG 1989). This is not only a response to the inherent inadequacies of modern (western) therapeutic modalities, but also to their commodification and exposure to extreme laissez-faire marketism in recent years.

The exact proportion of Kenyan population who utilize traditional medicine is not clearly established. This is because people are unwilling to admit openly that they consult traditional healers; large proportion of Western educated elite and christian convert use it descteetly. Moreover, there is dearth of statistical information becarse most traditional physicians do not keep records. Two researches carried out in the 1976-79 period indicate that 17 per cent of 2.6 million people who sought nonlicensed treatment obtained it from traditional healers (see table I).

Traditional medicine has also proliferated and grew in popularity amon the urban poor. A study carried out in the sprawling Mathare valley of Nairobi in the 1980s reveals that there was one traditional healer to a population of 847, a very high patronage by all standards (GOOD 1980)

This patronage of traditional medicine has increased with the increasing specte of poverty, rising cost of drugs and removal of government subsidies on medical services as a result of Structural Adjustment Programme (SAPS). The basically urbanized Asian immigrants in Kenya continue to rely on Ayurveda, yoga, Unanni and Siddha, largely for cultural rather than economic reasons. The inter-relationship between the latter and African medical systems is not clear, nor is the level of utilization of Asian traditional therapies African population.

Although, as usual, statistics on women's utilization of traditional medicin are not forthcoming, it is clear that their patronage is higher than that of men. Statistic from one „professional" herbal clinic the Karati Rural Service Centre (CRSC) tends to confirm this (see table 2). Of a total of 18,720 patients treated at the KRSC clinics, the vast majority were women.

Women continue to rely on traditional birth attendants for their obstetric, gynecological and children's diseases. 80 percent of all births in th country are handled at home by traditional midwives rather than trained workers in maternity hospital wards (SINDIGA 1995: 6). Wheras 90 percent of pregnant. Women receife at least one antenatal cheking, only 46 per cent of birth are assisted by trained per-

Table 1
Percentage Distribution of Household Members in Kenya Receiving Non-institutional Treatment by Province

	Coast	Eastern	Central	R.Valley	Nyanza	Western	National figure
Shop	74.7	67.0	35.7	46.0	56.3	57.6	57.6
Self medication	2.4	20.1	60.0	42.5	19.8	21.9	25.6
Traditional medicine	22.3	11.6	1.2	10.3	16.7	16.9	13.9
others	0.6	1.3	3.1	1.2	7.2	3.6	2.9
Totals	100	100	100	100	100	100	100

Source: Republic of Kenya: The integrated Rural Surveys 1976-1979
Nairobi: Central Bureau of statistics, 1987 P 62

Table 2
KRSC patient attendance 1984-90

Year	1984-85			1987-88			1989-90		
Clinic	male	female	total	male	female	total	male	female	total
Nairobi	1878	2491	4369	789	1102	1891	-	-	914
Nyeri	-	-	-	1303	959	2262	-	-	748
Meru	-	-	-	200	350	550	-	-	430
Nyanhururu	480	553	1003	250	370	620	-	-	597
Kinangop	1566	1867	3433	518	572	1090	-	-	437
Kericho	-	-	-	520	550	1070	-	-	600
Total			8805			7483			3726

Source: Githae, 1995-57
NB. Each of the clinic was operated once a week

sonnel (ROGO 1996: 71).

In her illuminating study of ethnomedical therapies in maternal and child health among the rural Luo, KAWANGO notes that „TBAs are preferred over hospital-trained midwives not only because of thier accessibility, affordability and good personal relations, but also because of their apparently sound knowledge in maternal child health care (1995-85).

Traditional Medicine, however, continues to be enmeshed in a legal, cultural and religious conflict with biomedicine and repressed by the state. As WANDIBBA (1995) observes in regard to the Luhya of Western Kenya, traditional healers" are consulted either openly of sectetly depending on the ecucational status, age and/or resigious affliation of the client. Old men and women with no or low formal education consult diviers openly whilst young people with high educational levels tend to do so sectetly..."

Thus the „professionalization" fo herbalism is partly intended to liberate traditional medicine from these ideological strictures imposed on it by decades of conflict with biomedicine.

Women and the Professionalization of Traditional Medical Practice

Since the late 1970s, the professionalization of inddigenous medical practice has become a crucial issue in teh global medical agenda. The initiative has come from the World Health Organization. Since the World Health Assembly (WHA) in 1977, the WHO has encouraged its member states to organize their traditional practitioners. The Alma Ata Conference recommended that government give priority to utilizing traditional medicin in national drug policies and regulations this was reaffirmed at the 40th World Health Assembly in May, 1987 (AKERELE 1987).

According to LAST (1990: 350) the raison d'etre for the WHO policy lies in its global medical agenda and an international disease environment rife with new epidemics which have become veritable drains on national resources: „With the much proclaimed target of health for all by the year 2000, the shortage of medical manpower in the present period of economic crisis in teh Third World is so acute that medical practitioners of all kinds are potentially acceptable rectuits to national health services. Add to the extra demand on recources posed by the AIDS epidermic, and issues such as the training and licensing of auxiliary practitioners came to the fore as mattersof urgency".

The Kenya government has taken its cue. Its 1979 National Divelopment Plan acknowledged the pivortal role of traditional medecine in teh national health system and undertook to further research in traditional therapies, and to integrate certain cdres of traditional sector practitioners such as midwives into teh Government health institutions in the rural areas (KENAY 1979: 136). It encouraged the formation of associations of traditional healers. Two associations were formed: the Umoja Wa Waganga Wa Mitishamba (Union of herbalists) and Association of African Traditional Medical Practitioners of Kenya. In its 1989-1993 National Development Plan, the government stated that these associations: Will facilitate the gathering og necessary information for the use, developments and appropriate adaptation of traditional diagnostic, therapeutic and rehabiltative control technologies that will become part and parcel of formal medical research and of the Primary Health Care Programme (KENYA 1989: 244).

Professionalization of herbalism, as SWIDERSKI (1995: 50) argues „has the advantage of bringing traditional healers out of the social ad religious conflict with biomedicine into the role it can play in a specific national medical system." Moreover, it can give traditional healers access to educational facilities, funds and emable them to collect fee from patients with national healthcare system. The KRCS, cited earlier, is a typical case of modernization of traditional mecical practice throuh the use of biomedical methods ad procedures such as empirical research into herbs, establishing herbal tree nursaries, employing university trained researchers ad clinicians, and keeping proper records (GITHAE 1995: 59-63).

In that regarden, Kenyan traditional medical practitioners have taken the path already taken by Chiropractors in the United States, Homeopaths in Britain, Naturopaths in Germany, and Ayurvedic doctors in India. This, however, requires large amunts of money, a relative high edducation which most ordinary herbal illiterate practitioners do not have. Due to heavy capital investment involved in the professionalization; it is only logical that they raise their fees.

This may cut off majority of rural poor, thus defeating the very objective of the rehabilitation of rtaditional practice. Already, ‚professional' herbalism hs began to acquire an elitist tinge. Associations of herbalists charge as much as Ksh. 1,000 (or US $ 20) which is beyond the reach of poor herbal practitioners.

On another note, the professionalization of traditional practice has largely augmented the status of male traditional practitioners. This is largely so because special diagnostic and therapeutic problems such as surgery, bonesetting, divination, dentistry, and so forth are handled almost exclusively by men. Although the prospects of proessionalization of traditional midwifery along the lines of obstetrics, gynecology, paediatrics ad counselling on general health matters are undoubtedly good, few women have ventures in this direction.

The Governmentof Kenya and a number of Non-Governmental Organizations, notably AMREF and UNICEF, are in the forefront of integrating traditional midwives into the official health structures. This has taken the form fo organizing seminars and workshops to train TBAS. Older and basically illiterate practitioners consider these siminars and workshops as unsuitable to them; their school like nature have only benefited the young, literte TBAS. Thus most older TBAS are profoundly skeptical as to whether there is anything new they still need to learn.

The professionalization of TBAS has taken the firm in one word corporation of these practitioners into the primary health care system. To that end, a national curriculum, together with teaching aids and charts, have been published and launched (KENYA 1991a 1991b). Criticisms to this process hinge on the issues of autonomy and power or traditional midwives. As SINDIGA et. al (1995) perceptively observe, „it appears that TBAS are made to work as functionaries of the biomedical establishedment essentially to reduce the number of cases going to the hospital ad making referrals of complicated cases and are thus likely to their status in their communities in the process of incorporation in official healthcare".

In the same token, Mc CORMACK (1986: 154) aptly remarks that. „They (TBAS) will be the bottom of the bureaucratic heap, poorly paid or asked to work free, given least prestige, the last to be supplied with drugs ad in service training". They are therefor, no better than appendiges of the extension worders of the Ministry of Halt (LAST 1986: 3). The natural trend that can quarantee the autonomy and prestige of TBAS is collaboration rather than incorporation into official health. This requires that the two systems make appropriate referrals to one another on routine basis.

The benefits to accrue from this arrangment include the pugrading of the skills of TBAS regarding such issues as hygiene, ad imbuing biomedical workers with cultural sensitivity.

The problem of incorporation of indigenous medical practice as a whole into biomedicine through professionalization is firmly situated in the wider global agenda of the latter to bring traditional praaactice under ist heel. WHO`s patronage has served mainly to encourage national ministries of health to icorporate traditional healers into the hospital-based profeesions, offering them retraining and a minor role in state health services (LAST 1990: 352; SARGENT 1996). In a word, the universalization or even internationalization of indigenous medical workers call into question the practitioners autonomy it has been averred that international congresses, to which healers are often invited, have tended to be dominated by professionals froml biomedical fields intent on incorporating them into their own universal systems any traditional expertize that is available (LAST 1990 : 352). As MORSY (1990) further argues, underlying the general proposition for a mix of traditional and modern medicine is an agenda of incorporating the former into the political economic arena and cultural hegemony of biomedicine.

At the extreme, traditional medical practitioners might eventually play second fiddle in the internationaalization of medical knowledge where they will identify herbal medicine and ist sources which will aid the international search for an assmbly of herbal drug. Operating within a fluid and larsely, non-legal and non-institutional framework, these herbal experts are likely not to benefit from the international systems of intellectual property whilst their acknowledge will be commoditized and may find ist way into the drug market monopolized by biomedical practitioners.

References
AKERELE, O. 1987. „The Best of Both Worlds: Bringing Traditional Medicine Up to Date" *Social Science and Medicine* 24 No. 2: 177 -181.
ARNOLD, D., (ed). 1988, *Imperial Medicine and Indigenous Societies.* Manchester : Manchester University Press.
BECK,A. 1981. *Medicine, Tradition and Development in Kenya and Tanzania 1920-1970.* Massachusetts.
BOWLES, B.O. 1979. „*Underdevcelopment in Agriculture in Colonial Kenya: Some Ecological and Dietary Aspects*"in B.A. OGOT (ed.)
BROWNER, C.H. and F.S. SARGENT. 1990, „*Anthropology and Studies of Human Reproduction*" in JOHNSON and SARGENT (eds)
CHRISTIE, V.M. and E. SANDBERG. 1989. „*A Dialogue Between Practitioners of alternative (traditional)Medicine and Modern (school) Medicine in Norway*" Paper to the Eleventh Internaional Coference on the Social Science and Medicine. Leeuwenhorst Congress Centre, the Netherlands 24-28 July.
DIOP, C.A. 1989. *The Cultural Unity of Black Africa: Domains of Matriachy and Patriarchy in Classical Antiquity,* Karnak House, London
FITCH, C.S. 1983. „*The African Background of Medical Science*" in SERTIMA (ed).
GITHAE, J.K. 1995. „*Ethnomedical Practice in Kenya: the Case of the Karati Rural Services Centre*"in SINDIGA et, al. pp 55-63.
GOOD, A.M. 1980. „Tehnomedical Systems in Africa and the LDCs: Key Issues for Geographers" in M.S. MEADE (ed.), *Conceptual and Methodological Issues in Medical Geography.* Chapel Hill: University of North Carolina pp. 93-116.
HASKIN, M.J. and E.G. BAY (eds) 1976. *Women in Africa: Studies in Social and Economic Changes.* Stanford University Press, California.
IDRC. 1980. *Taditional Medicine in Zaire: Present and Potential Contribution to Rural Halt Service,* Ottawa IDRC
JOHNSON, T.M. and C.E. SARGENT. 1990. (eds) *Medical Anthropology: Contemporary Theory and Method.* New York: Preager
KANGETHE, L. 1989. „*Indigenous Vegetation in Kenya*"A Paper Presented at Workshop on Values of Indigenous Vegetation. KENGO. Nairobi.
KAWANGO, E.A. 1995. „*Ethnomedical Remedies and Therapies in Maternal and Child Halt Among the Rural Luo*". in SINDIGA et. al.pp 80-93.
KENYA, GOVERNMENT. 1979. *Development Plan, 1979 - 1983* Nairobi; Government Printers.
---. 1991. *National Curriculum For Traditional Birth Attendants.* Nairobi; Ministry of Health in conjunction with Who and the Government of Belgium.

---. 1991. *Traditional Birth Attendants. Guide.* Nairobi: Ministery oh Health and WHO. Kenya Office.
---. 1989. *Development Plan 1989-1993.* Nairobi: Government Printers.
KEYATTA, JOMO 1978. *Facing Mount Kenya:* Nairobi : Heinemann Educational books.
KIBWANA, K. (ed.). 1995. *Women and Autonomy in Kenya: Policy and Legal Framework.* Nairobi: Claripress.
KIPKORIR, B.E. and F.B. WELBORNE. 1973. *The Marakwet of Kenya: A Preliminary Study.* Nairobi: East African Publishing House.
KOKWARO, J.O. 1976. *Medicinal Plants of East African.* Nairobi. East African Publishing House.
LAST, M. and G.L. CHAVUNDUKA (eds). 1986. *Professionalization of African Medicine.* Manchester: Manchester University Press.
LASKER, JUDITH 1977. „The Role of Health Services in Colonial Rule: The Case of the Ivory Coast,,, *Culture, Medicine and Psychatry,* 1:277-97.
LEAKEY, L.S.B.. 1977. *The Southern Kikuyu Before 1903* Vol. I, II, III, London: Academic Press.
MAC CORMACK,C.. „*The Articulation of Western and Traditional System of Health Are"* in LAST M. and G.C. CHAVUNDUKA (eds.).
MBITI, J.S. 1969. *African Religions and Philosophy.* London: Heinemann.
MORSY, SOHIER 1990. „*Political Economy in Medical Anthropology"* in JOHNSON and SARGENT (eds.)
NAVARO, Vicente 1986. *Crisis, Health and Medicin: A Social critique.* London: Tavistock.
NYAMWAYA, D.O.. 1995. „*A Case for Traditional Medicine in Official Health Services: Flogging an Dead Horse?"* in SINDIGA et. al. (eds).
OGOT, B.A. (ed.) 1979. *Ecology and History in East Africa:* Nairobi: Kenya Literature Bureau.
OKONJO, K. 1976. „*The Dual- Sex Political System and Country Politics in Midwestern Nigeria"* in HASKIN and ONGONGA J.J. and G.R. GRAY (eds). 1988. Proceedings of the 3rd Professors World Peace Academy, East Africa Regional Conference held in Mombasa, Kenya- September.
OPOLE, M.. 1991. „*Women Indigenous knowledge Base in the Translation of Nutritional and Medical Values of Edible Local Plants in Western Kenya"* in KWESI PRAH. (eds) pp. 81-96.
PATTERSON, K.D.S. and HARTWIG, G.W. 1978. (eds). *Disease in African History. Durham:* Duke University Pr.
PRAH, K. K.(ed). 1991. *Culture, Gender, Science and Technology in Africa.* Windhock: Harp Puplucations.
PRESS IRWIN. 1980. „Problems in the Definition and Classification of Medical Systems" *Social Science and Medicine* 14B:45-57.
ROGO, K.O.. 1995. „*Summary of Research Findings on Women and Health in Kenya: Developing an Action Agenda".* In Kibwana.
RUBEL, A.J. and M.R. HASS. 1990. „*Ethnomedicine"* in JOHNSON and SARGENT (eds) pp 115-158.
SERTIMA, I.V. (ed.) 1983. *Blacks in Science: Ancient and Modern.* New Brunswick and London: Transaction Books.
SINDIGA, I., C.N. CHACHA and M.P. KANUNAH. (eds), 1995, *Traditional Medicine in Africa.* Nairobi: East African Educational Publishers Ltd.
------.et al. 1995. „*The Future of Traditional Medicine in Africa"* in SINDIGA et.al (eds) pp. 175-183.
SWIDERSKI, R.M.. 1995. „*Building Confidence in Traditional Healers"* in SINDIGA et.al. (eds.) PP 40-54
TAUBIA, NAHID. 1993. *Female Genital mtilation: A Call for Global Action.*
TAYLOR, REX.. 1983. *The Second Sickness: Contraditions of Capitalist Health Care.* New York: Free Press
------. and A. RIEGER. 1985. „Medicine as social Science: Rudolph Virchous on the Typhies Epidemic in Upper Silesia". *International Journal of Health Services* 15(4) 547-59. United Nations (1973) Determinants.
UNITED NATIONS 1973. *Determinants and Consequences of International Demographic, Economic and social factors.* New York: United Nations.
WAITZKIN, H.. 1979. „The Marxist Paradigm in Medicine" *International Journal of Health Services* 9(4)683-99.
WALLERSTEIN, I.. 1979. *The Capitalist World Economy: Essays.* New York: Cambridge University Press.
WORLD BANK. 1995. *World Development Report.* Oxford: Oxford University Press.
ZELEZA, P.T.. 1993. *A Modern Economic History of Africa,* Vol.I. Dakar: CODESRIA Books Series.

Bori - Der Körper spricht
Bori - The Body is Speaking

Herta Maria Nöbauer

Zusammenfassung: Der vorliegende Artikel überprüft die rituellen Praktiken von Bori, die Hausa-Frauen anwenden, um mit sozialer, politischer und persönlicher Not fertig zu werden. Dabei gehe ich von einer Kritik an den westlichen therapeutischen Diskursen aus, die aufgrund der hierarchischen Opposition von Körper und Geist/Subjekt und Objekt eine universelle Norm der Psychologisierung von Not annehmen. Mit Bezug auf die Medizinanthropologin Scheper-Hughes stelle ich die Frage, ob Bori-Frauen für die Lösung ihrer Nöte „somatische" Taktiken den „psychologischen" vorziehen. In der Umkehrung der Frage Foucaults nach jenen Körpern, die eine muslimische Gesellschaft wünscht, erkunde ich die Lebensformen, die unfruchtbare leibhaftige Frauen brauchen. Ich komme zum Schluss, dass Bori einen Rahmen mit vorwiegend „somatischen" Lösungstaktiken darstellt. Dies ist offensichtlich Resultat aus den differenten Vorstellungen und Wahrnehmungen des Körpers in der muslimischen und nicht-muslimischen/traditionellen Gesellschaft und drückt sich vor allem durch eine unterschiedliche Bewertung von „Hitze" aus: im Rahmen von Bori darf der Körper „überkochen".

Abstract: This article will examine the ritual practices of Bori which are applied by Hausa women to cope with social, political and personal distress. I start from a critique of the Western therapeutic discourses which - as a consequence of the hierarchical opposition of body and mind/subject and object - are based on the assumption that distress exclusively can be solved by psychological tactics. In accordance with the medical anthropologist Scheper-Hughes I will investigate whether Bori-women prefer „somatic" tactics rather than „psychological" ones to deal with distress. Inverting Foucault's question about the kind of body desired in a Muslim society I will ask which ways of life infertile women as embodied persons need.
I come to the conclusion that Bori represents a scope with predominantly „somatic" tactics. Obviously resulting from the different conception and perception of the body by Islamic and non-Islamic/traditional society this difference is expressed mainly by a different appraisal of „heat„: in Bori the body may „boil over".

Keywords: Hausaland, Bori-Frauen, rituelle Praktiken, Körper-Geist-Hierarchie, Körpervorstellungen, Hausaland, Bori-women, ritual practices, body-mind-hierarchy, conceptions of body.

Zur Themenstellung

Ausgangspunkt des vorliegenden Artikels bilden philosophische Reflexionen, die Erkenntnis nicht auf abstrakte Begriffsbildungen der Cogito stützen, sondern in denen Erfahrung im Kontext historischer Bedingungen zum zentralen Element wird. Für eine kritische Medizinanthropologie scheint mir daher eine Auseinandersetzung mit der neu aufgenommenen Rezeption der Phänomenologie Merleau-Pontys und bestimmten feministischen Annäherungen an die Dialektik des Subjekt-Objekt-Verhältnisses und die Körper-Geist-Beziehung sinnvoll. Beide Sichtweisen zielen auf Versuche ab, historisch starr gewordene, hierarchische Dualismen aufzuzeigen.

„Auf diese Weise ist der Leib Ausdruck der gesamten Existenz, nicht als deren äußere Begleiterscheinung, sondern weil sie in ihm sich realisiert. Dieser inkarnierte, „verkörperte" Sinn ist das zentrale Phänomen, dessen abstrakte Momente Leib und Geist, Zeichen und Bedeutung sind." (MERLEAU-PONTY 1966:198)

In feministischer Lesart honoriert Isabell Lorey das Sujekthafte des „Leibes" damit, dass sie mit diesem alle im Fleisch materialisierten Konstruktionen meint. Im Gegensatz dazu bezeichnet sie mit „Körper" den sozial konstruierten Körper. Sie kritisiert daher berechtigt, dass nach wie vor unberücksichtigt bleibt, dass selbst entschleierte Konstruktionen im Fleisch sitzen, eben weil sie sich materialisiert haben. (LOREY 1993:10-23).

Ein solches Verständnis von Leib erlaubt in neuer Perspektive eine ethnologische Annäherung an ein konfliktträchtiges Phänomen wie Besessenheit durch Geister, um das sich Frauen mit zum Teil unheilbaren Problemen konzentrieren. Darauf basierend können auch ethnologische und im speziellen therapeutische Diskurse über den Bori-Kult der Hierarchisierung überführt werden, denen eine ausschließliche Psychologisierung von Konfliktlösungen und in der Folge eine mehr oder weniger ausgeprägte, implizite oder explizite Verobjektivierung und Minderstellung des Körpers eigen ist.

In vergleichbarer Weise formulierte Scheper-Hughes für die Kritische Medizinanthropologie ein Körperverständnis, das sie als „Gewebe des Austauschs zwischen den ‚drei Körpern'" beschreibt: dem repräsentierenden sozialen Körper *(body social)*, dem kontrollierenden politischen Körper *(body politic)* und dem selbst-bewussten, individuellen und existentiellen persönlichen Körper *(body personal)* (SCHEPER-HUGHES 1994:231).

Die Entstehungsgeschichte eines synkretistischen Kultes wie Bori scheint auf vor-islamische Zeit zurückzugehen, seine weitere Entwicklung aber steht in engem Zusammenhang mit der Islamisierung des Hausalandes. Diese fand ihren gewaltvollen Höhepunkt Anfang des 19. Jahrhunderts („Heiliger Krieg„). Von da an begannen orthodoxe (Fulani-) Muslime Bori als Ausdruck volkstümlichen Wissens zum Feindbild zu stempeln. Umfassende Islamisierung aller Lebensbereiche und muslimische Machtmonopolisierungen drängten Bori an den gesellschaftlichen Rand. Die Lebensweisen der Frauen (vor allem auf dem Land) werden nach wie vor von islamischen und lokalen nicht-islamischen Mustern bestimmt. Bori-Frauen sind, obwohl muslimisch, traditionellen Institutionen verpflichtet. Sie setzen sich in erster Linie aus Erstfrauen, „freien Frauen" *(karuwai/zawarawa)* und jenen Frauen, die die Seklusion verweigern, zusammen. Sie sind jene Frauen, welche an den Grenzen der gesellschaftlichen Ordnung die Grenzen geschlechtsspezifischer Normen überschreiten (dürfen).

Für das Gros der weiblichen Bori-Adepten bestehen ihre Probleme in der Erfahrung von Unfruchtbarkeit und als Folge davon ihrer Abweichung von der den Frauen zugeordneten Norm der ausschließlichen Rolle als Ehefrau und Mutter. Gesellschaftliche Marginalisierung ist die direkte Konsequenz solcher Abweichung. Aus dem Umgang von leidenden Subjekten miteinander als Kult-Anhängerinnen und mit ihrer Situation der Abweichung soll versucht werden, einen Zusammenhang zwischen eigenständiger Körper-Sprache und Gesellschaftskritik herzustellen. Ausgehend von SCHEPER-HUGHES' (1994:236; 238) Kritik an einer in unseren westlichen Gesellschaften universell angenommenen Norm der Psychologisierung sozialer und politischer Not und der daraus abgeleiteten Oppositionierung von psychologischen und somatischen Lösungstaktiken stelle ich die Frage, ob und inwieweit in der Gesellschaft der Hausa soziales und politisches Elend eher „psychologisiert" oder eher „somatisiert" wird. Neben dieser berechtigten Kritik an eurozentristischen Standards geht es mir im vorliegenden Artikel mit der Verwendung dieser Termini nicht um eine Kritik des Oppositionspaares „psychologisch" versus „somatisch„, sondern um das Hinweisen auf Synonyme, die Differenz und Hierarchie ausdrücken. Dabei ist, wie ich behaupte, eine hierarchische Bewertung nicht nur den ethnologischen Diskursen, sondern auch den muslimischen Vorstellungen von Körper und Person inhärent.

Motiv des vorliegenden Aufsatzes bildet die Umkehrung der Foucault'schen Frage nach jenen Körpern von Frauen, die eine muslimische Gesellschaft wünscht, in die Frage nach den Lebensformen, die vor allem unfruchtbare und daher leidende, dabei aber höchst aktive Frauen-Körper, brauchen.

Welche Frauen-Körper wünscht die muslimische Hausa-Gesellschaft?

Das stratifizierte und nach Geschlechtern getrennte Sozialleben der Hausa charakterisiert eine ausgeprägte Disziplinierung und Kontrolle. Selbstkontrolle stellt das Fundament schlechthin des moralischen Systems dar (SCHMOLL 1993:207). Disziplinierung und Kontrolle kennzeichnen daher auch gerade die körperlichen Prozesse und Praktiken der Hausa. Ja, Gesundheit wird erst durch die konstante Kontrolle und Balancierung der diversen körperlichen und umweltbedingten Prozesse hergestellt. Diese Prozesse fassen die Hausa vorwiegend in thermale und flüssige Begriffe. Primäres Ziel stellt die Ausgewogenheit von „Hitze" und „Kälte" im physischen wie moralischen Sinne dar. Aber auch die Vorstellung und Bedeutung der Flüssigkeiten (Wasser, Urin, Blut, Schleim; Milch bei gebärenden Frauen) durchdringt die Konstruktionen von Gesundheit auf der personalen, sozialen und kosmologischen Ebene (MASQUELIER 1994:40). Unfruchtbarkeit, unter der eine große Zahl der Bori-Adeptinnen leidet, wird demgemäß mit Trockenheit und Dürre assoziiert.

Da der Einfluss des Islam auf das traditionelle Körper-Verständnis und die traditionelle Medizin unleugbar stark ist, fällt eine klare Unterscheidung zwischen traditionellen und muslimischen Vorstellungen schwer. Derlei Unterschiede lassen sich erst in rituellen Körperpraktiken fest- und einschreiben.

Die Machtkämpfe zwischen Bori-AnhängerInnen und Muslimen um die Kontrolle des Körpers durchziehen sämtliche rituelle Praktiken (Namensgebungszeremonien, Hochzeiten, Begräbnisse). Trotz eindeutiger Dominanz islamischer Praktiken existieren aber auch unadäquate Verhältnisse zwischen diesen und den traditionellen Konzeptionen von Person und Kosmos (MASQUELIER 1994:27).

Muslime protestieren nicht gegen unsichtbare Geister, die integraler Teil der traditionellen Bori-Kosmologie sind, sondern unterdrücken die Praxis der Geisterbesessenheit mit ihren Implikationen von Unbescheidenheit und Mangel an Kontrolle über körperliche Prozesse. Ihr Angriff gilt der leib-haftigen Hingabe an Geister, weil der Körper, der als Ort für Geister dient, sich der Kontrolle durch Muslime entzieht. Mit Foucault können wir antworten, dass Bori-Adepten aufgrund differenter Körperpraktiken eine eigene Vorstellung von Kontrolle und damit eine eigene Definitionsmacht über ihre Körper auszeichnet. Wie Masquelier zeigt, verbindet Bori die Person kontinuierlich mit einer umfassenden kosmologischen Realität und besteht auf deren symbiotische Beziehung. Im Gegensatz dazu zielt der Islam mehr auf ein abgegrenztes, unabhängiges Selbst (MASQUELIER 1994:35). Islamische Hegemonie geht demnach auch aufgrund ideell differenter Ritualpraktiken durch die Körper hindurch. Darauf werde ich weiter unten nochmals eingehen.

Zentrales Moment in den menschlichen Beziehungen bildet *kunya* (wörtlich: Scham, Bescheidenheit) - ein Konzept, das einerseits bestimmte Beziehungen tabuisiert und andererseits „kühlende" Bescheidenheit des Kopfes *(kai)* sich selbst und anderen gegenüber auferlegt. So ist es für eine Mutter beispielsweise verboten, das erstgeborene Kind (vor den Augen anderer Personen) zu berühren oder zu umarmen oder es beim Namen zu rufen. Kunya bezeichnet auch die „kühlende" Selbstkontrolle „überhitzter" Emotionen. Zu diesen zählen der Ausdruck von zu viel Freude, Liebe, Begehren, Neid, Eifersucht, Wut, Sorgen ebenso wie Schmerzen während der Geburt oder Hunger.

Die anzustrebende Balance der humoralen Kräfte von „Hitze" und „Kälte" ist nur im Kontext von *lafiya*, der Auffassung der Hausa von Gesundheit zu verstehen. Diese bezeichnet vollkommenes körperliches, geistiges und soziales Gleichgewicht (FLEISCHER 1977:113). In der Assoziation mit tatsächlichem und metaphorischem Kochen repräsentiert Feuer neben Macht(verlust) auch Leben und Vitalität und dient auch als zentrale Metapher für das Verhältnis in einer Ehe und für die Reproduktion. Für Frauen gelangt „Hitze" besonders dann zu Bedeutung, wenn sie während einer Schwangerschaft das Kind im Bauch „kochen,", bis es reif zur Geburt ist. So verursacht nach Meinung der Hausa die „Hitze" im Bauch der Mutter die roten Flecken auf dem Körper eines Neugeborenen. Entsprechend muss eine Frau nach der Geburt den Hitzeverlust durch heiße Bäder und „heiße" Nahrung (vor allem scharfe Gewürze) ausgleichen (MASQUELIER 1994:38). Ebensowenig geziemt es sich für eine gebärende Frau, ihren Schmerzen Ausdruck zu verleihen. Üblicherweise bringt sie ein Kind alleine zur Welt, die Hebamme und andere Frauen tauchen erst nach dem unmittelbaren Geburtsvorgang auf. Hunger zu zeigen ist nur Kindern erlaubt, weil diese noch nicht über genügend Selbstkontrolle verfügen. Für Erwachsene gilt die Einhaltung einer Etikette, die auf „kühlender Bescheidenheit" beruht (SCHMOLL 1994:206f). Den Inbegriff von zu viel „Hitze" innerhalb der häufig praktizierten polygynen Ehestruktur stellt die eifersüchtige Mitfrau *(kishiya)* dar. Selbst wenn sie sich aufgrund ungleicher Behandlung durch den Ehemann sehr verletzt fühlen, ziemt es sich für Hausa-Frauen nicht, ihre Eifersucht zu zeigen.

Unfruchtbarkeit hat nicht nur folgenschwere Auswirkungen auf die ökonomische Absicherung von Frauen, sie bildet für beiderlei Geschlechter auch häufig den Grund für Scheidung, die auch für Frauen relativ unkompliziert durchzuführen ist. Eine unfruchtbare Frau erfährt neben ihrem Schuldgefühl oft auch die Ablehnung nicht nur durch den Mann, sondern auch durch dessen Verwandte. Teilweise wird die Frau aus diesem Grund sogar psychisch und physisch misshandelt (KLEINER-BOSSALLER 1993:97).

Die hauptsächlichen Ursachen von Unfruchtbarkeit erklären die Hausa neben anderen (vgl. FLEISCHER 1977) zumeist in Störungen der sozialen Beziehungen. Vorwiegend werden dafür Konflikte zwischen Mitfrauen und deren Manipulationen verantwortlich gemacht, aber auch Malams oder Medizinmänner können „böse Medizin" produzieren, die Unfruchtbarkeit hervorruft. Eine weitere und im Kontext von Bori entscheidende Ursache für Unfruchtbarkeit beiderlei Geschlechts können bestimmte Geister bilden. Bei deren Intervention wenden sich die betroffenen Frauen an die Bori-Heilerinnen um Medizin. Gerade gegen Unfruchtbarkeit werden alle traditionellen und modernen Therapien angewandt (FLEISCHER 1977:51f.).

Welche Lebensformen brauchen leib-haftige Bori-Frauen?
Wann und ob kranke Frauen dem Kult beitreten, entscheiden regional variable Faktoren. Grundsätzlich differenziert wird, dass entweder ein Krankheitsprozess eine Frau dazu bewegt oder zwingt, sich in den Bori-Kult initiieren zu lassen oder aber die Geister durch matri- oder patrilineare Erbfolge weitergegeben werden.

Erfolgt der Beitritt über einen Prozess der Krankheit, stellt der sehnliche Wunsch nach Initiation in den Kult auch eines der beiden Kriterien dar. Krankheit als das strafende Signal der Götter wird in ihrer ganzen Tragweite positiv angenommen. So wird die Allianz mit den Göttern wiederhergestellt und die Person geheilt. Entscheidend ist, dass nur eine Frau, die sich den Beitritt wünscht, auch als Heilerin tätig werden kann. Einen nicht unwesentlichen Beitrag für einen derartigen Wunsch einer Frau kann ihre Freundschaft zu einer bereits initiierten Bori-Frau leisten. In solchen Fällen wird deutlich erkennbar, dass Krankheit nicht unbedingt eine direkte ursächliche Wirkung auf den Beitritt ausübt, sondern über eine „positive Flucht in die Krankheit" ein Vehikel zum Kult gesucht wird.

Das zweite Kriterium für einen krankheitsbedingten Beitritt bildet die unerwünschte Betroffenheit. In diesem Fall zwingt der Leidensdruck eine Frau dazu, sich in den Kult initiieren zu lassen. Diese Adeptin übernimmt eine „reduzierte" Form der Inkarnation, um die Verbindung mit den Göttern wieder aufzunehmen und praktiziert daher nur die notwendigsten und verpflichtenden Bori-Riten (MONFOUGA-NICOLAS 1972:291;194).

Frauen müssen demnach zunächst erkranken bzw. den umfassenden Vorstellungen von Gesundsein widersprechen, wenn eine Affinität zu Bori hergestellt werden soll. Somit wird Somatisierung zur notwendigen Voraussetzung für den Kultbeitritt und erscheint Krankheit als aktive Körperpraxis. Da der persönliche und soziale Leidensdruck unfruchtbarer Frauen enorm ist, bildet Bori ein geradezu ideales Forum der Umpolung der (Selbst-)Wahrnehmung ihrer leib-haftigen Existenz, ihres Ansehens und Versöhnung mit ihrer neuen Identität und den Göttern. Diese Aussöhnung findet durch und mittels ihrer Körper, die sie den Göttern hingeben, Ausdruck.

Um ein klareres Verständnis der Unterschiede der rituellen Körper-Praktiken bei Muslimen und Bori-AnhängerInnen herstellen zu können, erscheint es mir notwendig, einige Erklärungen zum traditionellen Begriff der Person abzugeben. *Jiki,* der fleischliche, sinnliche Körper, existiert in Beziehung mit *kurwa,* dem unsichtbaren, flüssigen Doppel einer Person und *rai,* der Lebenskraft. In besonderen Situationen kann sich das Doppel vom Körper, so speziell nach dem Tod, loslösen, sofern es nicht unter Einhaltung spezifischer Rituale zusammen mit dem Körper verabschiedet wird. Spätestens beim Tod einer Person wird unter Berücksichtigung der rituellen Praktiken die Beziehung zwischen *jiki, rai* und *kurwa* als einheitlich deutlich. Das besondere Zusammenspiel zwischen *jiki* und *kurwa* ermöglicht das Phänomen der Inkorporation. Der Körper bildet eine energetische Substanz, dessen bestimmte Teile auf ein anderes Individuum Einfluss ausüben, wenn dieses Körperteile zu sich nimmt. Dieser Prozess der Bezauberung bedeutet demnach sich zu transformieren und auf unbewusste Weise mental das Abbild dieses Anderen zu werden (DIAWARA 1988:69-71). Ein schweres Doppel kann sich auf natürliche Weise gegen Geister schützen, ein leichtes hingegen bedarf besonderer Schutzmaßnahmen. Das Doppel ist lediglich bestimmten Initiierten und den Geistern zugänglich. Krankheit wird in solchem Verständnis durch das Vertauschen von *kurwa,* das durch den Einbruch eines Geistes hervorgerufen wird, verursacht. Zeichen für die Anwesenheit eines Geistes sind lokalisierbare Beschwerden. Eine solche Vorstellung über das Zusammenwirken von *jiki* und *kurwa* erklärt die Notwendigkeit besonderer Rituale sowohl für Körper als auch Doppel. Das Schwinden dieser traditionellen rituellen Praktiken bezeichnen die Bori-AnhängerInnen denn auch als primäre Ursache für die gegenwärtige Bedrohung ihrer körperlichen Integrität durch sichtbare und unsichtbare Kräfte.

Bori-Kontrollprozesse sind ähnlich den islamischen Ritualpraktiken in thermische Begriffe gefasst, unterscheiden sich aber von zweiteren durch eine wesentlich umfassendere kosmologische Einbindung. Da erst entsprechend ausgeprägte Hitze das Herabsteigen der Geister ermöglicht, ist die Kontrolle des Feuers, das in jeder Person brennt, wesentlich. Jedoch wird genau diese auf sehr differente Art durchgeführt. Reale und metaphorische Hitze spielen in Bori-Praktiken eine große Rolle, um die Reinheit und Reife der Teilnehmerinnen zu fördern. So wird die Initiation *(girka)* als ein rituelles Kochen aufgefasst: *„Aka girka ta"* meint wörtlich „man kochte sie". Das Forum, in dem die Bori-Zeremonien abgehalten werden, muss durch Musik, Tanz, Parodie und Rivalität aufgeheizt werden, passives Beobachten der Zeremonien lässt den Ort kalt. Dieses Zusammenspiel zwischen menschlichen Körpern und ätherischen Geistern stellt für Muslime eine große Bedrohung dar. Genau hier manifestiert sich meiner Ansicht nach auch der gravierendste Unterschied zwischen Bori-Ritualen und muslimischen Ritualen: Bori-Kontrolle bezieht „Hitze" mit all ihren körperlichen Sinnlichkeiten mit ein - der Körper darf „überkochen" -, während muslimische Kontrollprozesse „Hitze" und deren körperliche Entsprechungen ausschließen. Muslimische Selbstkontrolle zielt unter Ausgrenzung der mit ihren „überhitzten"

Emotionen verbundenen Körperpraktiken „direkt" auf die „kühlenden" Effekte ab.

Wenn MASQUELIER Bori als einen „genuinen Körper des Wissens, dem sich jede/r in Zeiten von Krisen zuwenden kann," versteht (1994:23), erlaubt dies die Folgerung, dass der (ausgegrenzte „überhitzte,") Körper in genau diesem Rahmen die Möglichkeit findet, nicht nur Rebellion oder Protest gegen sozio-politische und ökonomische Krisen, Zwänge und Unterdrückungsmechanismen zu symbolisieren und repräsentieren, sondern darüber hinaus selbst zum Präsentierenden und Sprechenden wird. Wie historisch für Bori nachvollzogen werden kann, besteht ein Zusammenhang zwischen der Heftigkeit einer Krise und dem Auftauchen neuer Geister sowie der Eigenschaften bestimmter (neuer) Geister. In solchen Krisenzeiten, in welcher keine andere oder wirksame Art des Protests verfügbar ist, schaffen heilende Institutionen wie Bori zusammen mit somatischen Taktiken „Waffen der Schwachen".

Wie SCHEPER-HUGHES betont, drücken leib-haftige (embodied) Personen durch ihre Körper komplizierte, widersprüchliche und feindliche Gefühle aus, wodurch sie soziale Not sichtbar machen. Darüber hinaus unterlaufen sie aber auch auf subversive Art die Oppositionierungen von Geist und Körper, Kultur und Natur und Persönlichem und Sozialem (1994:232).

Die Macht von Bori wurzelt in der „Intentionalität" der rituellen Praxis und in der Berührung zwischen Leibern und Göttern. Die Formulierung einer „somatischen Lösungstaktik" (SCHEPER-HUHGES 1994) erscheint mir daher zwar mit Einschränkung im medinzinanthropologischen Vergleich brauchbar, trifft aber als Begriff nicht den leib-haftigen (embodied) Sinn von Bori.

Es mag eine gewagte, aber konsequente Behauptung sein, dass in Krisen geratene unfruchtbare Frauen über Bori nicht nur eine Neubewertung ihrer sozialen Position, sondern auch eine andere Selbstwahrnehmung erfahren, für die Bori das Forum darstellt, die „verkörperte" Person anzuerkennen. Oder umgekehrt: erst die Vorstellung einer „verkörperten" /leib-haftigen Person (embodied person) ermöglicht eine Institution wie Bori.

Die Tendenz, soziales und politisches Leiden eher zu „somatisieren" denn zu „psychologisieren,", scheint demnach auch in der Hausa-Gesellschaft von jenen sozialen Gruppen wahrgenommen und ausgedrückt zu werden, die einerseits nicht-muslimischen und dominierten Vorstellungen verbunden sind und andererseits jenem sozialen Geschlecht, nämlich Frauen, die „doppelt" dominiert sind, angehören.

Schlussfolgerung

Im Rahmen ethnologischer Zugangsweise und Aufbereitung von Phänomenen, die uns mit Körper und Körperpraktiken konfrontieren, halte ich eine Reflexion über unsere eigenen, d.h. westlich geprägten Konzeptionen von Körper und Wahrnehmung notwendig. Nur über diese kann sich eine Anerkennung kulturell reicher Lösungsstrategien und Kommunikationsformen entwickeln, wie das auch SCHEPER-HUGHES fordert (1994:238f). Ein genaueres Nachdenken über das Sprechen über Körper und der Körper betrachte ich als einen adäquaten Ansatz dafür, wachsamer für Möglichkeiten der Übersetzung von differenten Vorstellungen über Körper zu sein.

Die Notwendigkeit solcher Reflexion wird zugleich aber auch gerade durch die in den Wissenschaften gültigen Paradigmen eingeschränkt und erschwert. Die den Sozialwissenschaften inhärente Tendenz zur Abstraktion und den Naturwissenschaften vorzuwerfende Neigung zu biologischem Reduktionismus hemmen eine Neuorientierung um unsere leib-haftige Existenz beträchtlich. Das soll nicht grundsätzlich pessimistisch stimmen, wie das etwa URSULA SHARMA resümmiert (1996:262). Denn wie vorwiegend feministische und poststrukturalistische Theorien in den vergangenen zwanzig Jahren zeigten, braucht es eine umfassende Kritik von Denk- und Machtstrukturen der „main-stream„-Wissenschaft, um historisch starr gewordene Maximen zu verändern. Gerade für eine Disziplin wie die Medizinanthropologie könnte es eine besondere Herausforderung darstellen, eine dergestaltige Neuorientierung zu forcieren.

References

DIAWARA, I. 1988. Les cultes de possession avec transes au Niger. Cahiers de Sociologie économique et culturelle. *Ethnopsychologie* 9:67-79.

FLEISCHER, L. 1977. *Zur Rolle der Frau in Afrika. Heirat, Geburt und Krankheit im Leben der Hausa-Frauen in Nigeria.* Bensheim.

KLEINER-BOSSALLER, A. 1993. Zur Stellung der Frau in der Hausagesellschaft: ein brüchig GEWORDENER Konsens. In *Muslime in Nigeria. Religion und Gesellschaft im politischen Wandel seit den 50er Jahren.* Edited by J. ABUN-NASR, pp. 83-

126. LIT Hamburg.
LOREY, I. 1993. Der Körper als Text und das aktuelle Selbst: Butler und Foucault. *Feministische Studien* 2:10-23.
MASQUELIER, A. 1994. Lightning, Death and the Avenging Spirits: Bori Values in a Muslim World. *Journal of Religion in Africa* 24/1:2-51.
MERLEAU-PONTY, M. 1966. *Phänomenologie der Wahrnehmung.* Berlin.
MONFOUGA-NICOLAS, J. 1972. *Ambivalence et culte de possession. Contribution à l'étude du Bori Hausa.* Paris.
SCHEPER-HUGHES, N. 1994. Embodied Knowledge: Thinking with the Body in Critical Medical Anthropology. In *Assessing Cultural Anthropology.* Edited by R. BOROFSKY, pp. 229-242. McGraw-Hill New York, St. Louis.
SCHMOLL, P. 1993. Black Stomachs, Beautiful Stones: Soul-Eating among Hausa in Niger. In *Modernity and Its Malcontents. Ritual and Power in Postcolonial Africa.* Edited by J. COMAROFF and J. COMAROFF, pp.193-220. Univ. of Chicago Press Chicago and London.
SHARMA, U. 1996. Bringing the Body back into the (social) Action. Techniques of the Body and the (cultural) Imagination. *Social Anthropology* 4/3:251-263.

The Role of Ethnomedicine in Promoting the Health of Women in Kenya
Die Bedeutung der Ethnomedizin für die Förderung von Frauen- Gesundheit in Kenia

Wilson Nyaoro

Abstract: Women's multiple roles and responsibilities in the society expose them to myriad health risks that are poorly understood. Modern health care initiatives have not effectively addressed the health needs of women. Such initiatives are usually characterised by a number of problems which include, inter alia, inefficacy, inaccessibility, and dangerous side-effects. Based on these observations, this paper calls for the revitalization, strengthening and development of ethnomedical systems and their integration into modern health care systems. From a long-term practical experience and knowledge, ethnomedicine has been found to be cost-effective, efficacious, accessible and reliable. It has minimal or no side-effects; effective in its healing properties; and, uses a holistic approach to the treatment process. Drawing from practical experience and using selected examples of medicinal plants in Kenya, this paper discusses issues on the health status of women and the curative nature of medicinal plants. In conclusion, the paper reiterates the effectiveness and appropriateness of ethnomedicine as a primary health care system and the need for further research on the various elements of ethnomedical systems within different cultural landscapes.

Zusammenfassung: Durch die Vielzahl der Rollen, die Frau in der Gesellschaft in Kenia spielen und durch die Verantwortung, die sie zu tragen haben, ist die Frau einer Menge gesundheitlichen Risiken ausgesetzt, die nur schlecht verstanden werden. Moderne Gesundheitspflegeprogamme haben diese gesundheitlichen Bedürfnisse der Frauen nur am Rande und dadurch bedingt unwirksam angesprochen. Solche Programme werden normalerweise von vielen Problemen einschließlich Unwirksamkeit, Unzugänglichkeit und gefährlichen Nebenwirkungen charakterisiert. Auf diesen Beobachtungen basierend, ruft dieses Referat zur Wiederbelebung, Stärkung und Entwicklung von ethnomedizinischen Systemen und ihrer Integration in moderne gesundheitliche Pflegesysteme auf. Durch langjährige und praxisorientierte Erfahrung wurde bewiesen, daß Ethnomedizin kostenrentabel, wirksam, zugänglich und zuverlässig ist. Es hat geringe, bzw. keine Nebenwirkungen; es besitzt wirksame Heileigenschaften und basiert auf einem ganzheitlichen Ansatz für den Behandlungsvorgang. Dieser Text führt ausgewählter Beispiele in bezug auf praktische Erfahrungen und Anwendung von Heilpflanzen in Kenia auf. Außerdem werden Fragen/Themen besprochen, in denen es um die Gesundheitszustände von Frauen und die heilsame Wirkung medizinischer Pflanzen geht. In der Zusammenfassung betont das Referat die Wirksamkeit und Angemessenheit von Ethnomedizin als primäres Gesundheitsversorgungssystem und die Notwendigkeit, weitere Forschungen über die unterschiedlichen Elemente in ethnomedizinischen Systemen innerhalb verschiedenen kulturellen Hintergründen durchzuführen.

Abb. 1
Local Name: Ober (Luo), Botanical Name: Albizia coriaria (Foto W. Nyaoro)

Keywords: Kenya, Women, Safety, Conceptualisation, Significance, Cost-effectiveness, Kenia, Frauen, Sicherheit, Konzeptualisation/Vorstellung, Bedeutung, Konstenrentabilität.

Introduction

„Herbalism is as old as man himself; it is not only the oldest of the healing arts, but still the safest-entirely free from the side-effects which render so many man-made drugs more dangerous than the disease ... "
(LAW 1970:7)

The history of ethnomedicine is as old as human history. It owes its origin in antiquity. In early civilizations, food and medicine were intimately linked, and many plants were eaten for their health-giving properties (THE BROCKHAMPTON LIBRARY 1996:5-7; GENDERS, 1975:11-31; COON, 1974:15-24). The medicinal properties and effects of herbs and other medicinal plants are well known because for centuries such plants were the only medication known to mankind. Their application for internal and external uses has always been a major factor in the practice of medicine. However, with advances in medical science and technology, conventional medicine rose in popularity, sending the practice of ethnomedicine into decline. Despite this, the modern medicine reaches out to only roughly 15-20% of the population in developing countries (WHO, 1991:1-2). In rural areas ethnomedicine continued to thrive in local folklore, traditions and practices. In such situations, many people still turn to herbal remedies which have been used and approved by their own parents, grandparents or even great grandparents. The more natural appearance of medicinal plants has led to its growing support and popularity (BLACKWELL 1990:1-32; THOMSON AND WILLIAM 1978:1-16). Furthermore, scientific research into medicinal plants and their active ingredients has confirmed the healing power of plants and enlarged the range of medicinal plants currently in use. Today, ethnomedicine continues as an effective and more natural method of treating and preventing illness.

As noted above, public interest in ethnomedicine has increased over time, particularly over the last two decades. This resurgence of interest away from synthetic drugs to medicinal plant drugs can also be partly attributed to possible side effects; inaccessibility of modern health care facilities in terms of physical distance, cultural barriers and monetary cost; bad publicity; and, public mistrust of the modern medical and pharmacological industries. WHO (1991:3) observes that the last two decades have seen considerable growth in popular, official and commercial interest in the use of traditional practitioners and their remedies. Indeed, for the majority of the world's population these have been, and in many instances are still, the only forms of medical care readily available (IDRC, 1980:1-40; HYMA and RAMESH 1994:65-137).

There are many other reasons for the increasing popularity of ethnomedicine in developing countries. The economic crises and political disruptions have often led to severe shortages of certain modern drugs which are often imported, thus forcing the affected people to make use of ethnomedicine whether or not this is government policy. This has, in some cases, resulted in increased quackery and charlatanry. In addition, the means and resources to be used in bringing modern medicine and health care services to local populations often do not exist. The recurrent and capital costs of expanding modern health care based on western models of development to reach rural populations are enormous and are therefore beyond the reach of most developing countries such as Kenya. Thus, ethnomedicine provides an alternative medical paradigm especially for women who form the majority of the vulnerable groups of the society.

The Concept of Ethnomedicine

Ethnomedicine (EM) is the sum total of all the knowledge and practices, used in diagnosing, preventing or eliminating a physical, mental or social disequilibrium which rely exclusively on past experience and observation passed on orally from generation to generation in unlettered societies (WHO 1991:3-4; KOKWARO 1993:1-2; AYENSU 1978:2-11). According to HYMA and RAMESH (1994:65-66) an ethnomedical system may be defined "as comprising the acquired knowledge, resources, organization, behaviour and strategies (traditional and scientific, indigenous and imported) that a community or society utilizes for individual or collective well-being". Thus, it may be seen as evolving from a popular view of the world and life which incorporates theories and accepted explanations of the nature and causes of illness and the appropriate and expected remedies. In view of these observations, it can be argued that ethnomedical system is strongly influenced by social and cultural factors and by interpersonal relations

(HYMA and RAMESH 1994:65-137; WARREN et. al. 1995:1-27).

Ethnomedicine is a holistic medical discipline based on an extensive and comprehensive spoken and written knowledge foundation with established benefits for treatment and prevention of disease and maintenance of positive health utilising natural products from local medicinal plants. Ethnomedical system is holistic in the sense that it views man in his totality within a wide ecological spectrum and emphasizes the view that ill health or disease is brought about by an imbalance or disequilibrium of man in his total ecological system and not only by the causative agent and pathogenic evolution (OKOTH-OWIRO 1994:33-57; WHO 1991:3-12). Ethnomedicine should be viewed as the sum total of practices, measures, ingredients and procedures of all kinds which from time immemorial had enabled mankind to guard against disease, to alleviate his sufferings and to cure himself (KOKWARO 1993:1-9). The whole theory of healing by medicinal plants is based upon the art of helping the human body to build up its own natural defences and restore good health, mankind's natural birthright, by natural and wholesome methods (LAW 1970:7-104). This is because of the realization that the human body contains within itself the power to heal. Ethnomedicine introduces internally or externally substances which will build the body up, restore its natural functions and strengthen its natural defences.

Scholars, various ethnic groups, individuals and health practitioners and professionals have used different terms for ethnomedicine. These include folk-medicine, native-medicine, herbal medicine, traditional medicine and botanic medicine. However, whatever term is used, it must be recognized that ethnomedicine reflects the socio-cultural and religious structures of the indigenous societies from which it developed, together with vast amounts of knowledge of values, behaviour and practices representing the wisdom of centuries of experience encompassed in folk traditions (GOOD and KIMANI 1980:301-309; OKOTH-OWIRO 1994:33-57; WARREN et. al. 1995:5-23). Ethnomedicine may therefore be considered as a solid amalgamation of dynamic medical know-how and ancestral/ spiritual experience (KOKWARO 1993:1-13; IWU 1993:1-7).

In Kenya, the development of ethnomedicine is based on the principle which holds that such medicine must be developed in a holistic framework and in the context of the culture of the particular indigenous community, trying to adjust to changing circumstances and times (ONIANG'O 1987:1-15). The system is therefore not static but a dynamic one. It should be further noted that Kenya has a large number of ethnomedical systems which came about as a result of high ethnic diversity of the resident population. It is important to recognize that every culture has its own characteristic traditional health care system. The foundational theories, concepts and principles upon which indigenous health science is based are different from the western medical science. However, KOKWARO (1993:1-3) argues that irrespective of ethnic diversity, all ethnomedical systems in Kenya are composed of a number of basic elements 'which include, inter alia: a collection of beliefs, myths, customs and rites; a body of traditional healers/traditional health care specialists;family groups with significant knowledge in the prevention and cure of illnesses, where women notably plays a significant role; a collection of plant, animal, and mineral resources with characteristic preventive and healing properties; and, an epistemological body concerning spiritual connection with nature and mankind's spiritual selves which involves living a virtuous life and the maintenance of a continual and harmonious relationship with the gods.

The traditional systems of medicine are based on the conceptual framework of the mind, body and their interaction in dynamic terms whose interaction produces the psychosomatic entity or person (FRATKIN 1975:1-61). Traditional health practices are part of a cultural identity. It is to witness the past, to know the present, and to analyze the future. The forces which create an enabling environment for traditional health practices to function are partly based on spirituality, the wholeness of the person, the maintenance of balance, and harmony with habitat and nature. The practice of traditional medicine therefore strengthens and reinforces family and community connections. Thus, the traditional healer usually re-establishes the patient's lost harmony which in turn determines the very survival and perpetuation of the society.

Health Status of Women
The health status of women, particularly in the developing countries like Kenya, has become a major concern. Women's multiple roles and responsibilities in the society expose them to myriad health risks that are poorly understood. Current estimates indicate that more than 500,000 women die annually during pregnancy and childbirth, while many more are disabled (LEWIS and KIEFFER 1994:122). The

root causes of poor reproductive health include: inadequate education; poor nutrition and poor general health status; overwork; early marriage and childbearing; violence against women; female genital mutilation; low social, economic and legal status; and, lack of control of resources and little or no role in decision making. Until recently, maternal and child health care initiatives and programmes have tended to focus on children and on reduction of infant mortality. Such initiatives and programmes fall under the general rubric of `safe motherhood' and include such activities as increased access to family planning, pre-natal and post-partum services; training of traditional birth attendants, nurse-midwives and other health workers to improve the safety of childbirth; immunizations and improved drug supply strategies; nutrition and health education campaigns (LEWIS and KIEFFER, 1994:122-137). However, health is increasingly being recognised as a matter of family and holistic concern. It is now realized that healthy women are a crucial component in the health of nations.

The reasons for this shift in focus can be understood in relation to central role of women in bearing and raising children and because of the tremendous vulnerability of women and children to morbidity and mortality during pregnancy, childbirth and infancy. Pregnancy and lactation tax heavily on a woman's health. It should be further noted that risks to women's health are intimately linked to the quality of life and to the relationship of women to their economy, society and culture. The adverse effects of development on women, on the one hand, and the centrality of women's roles in economic development (as in the case of agriculture and other business enterprises) on the other, have been documented and acknowledged by practitioners, activists and renown scholars.

The health needs of women go beyond mother-and-child needs and include pre-reproduction and post-menopause needs. This is because of the realization that a significant and growing proportion of women's life time and activities occur outside of the arena of reproduction. The current health care initiatives have generally failed to consider non-reproductive aspects of the status of women's health before, during, after or outside of the child-bearing experience. Nor do they consider the complex of social, cultural, physical, spiritual and economic issues involved in the way women carry out their productive and reproductive lives. Based on these observations, it can be argued that there is urgent need to adopt a broad definition of the concept of `safe womanhood' in which safe motherhood is central but not sufficient. Furthermore, the health needs of women must include social equality, reproductive rights and political participation. These are needed not only for general health reasons but also to enable women to escape abuse, exploitation and infections such as HIV/AIDS and other venereal diseases (PHILLIPS and VERHASSELT 1994:1-32). It is therefore imperative that the focus of international, national and local concern must be expanded to include the quality of women's life during the entire life cycle within a context that addresses physical, mental, spiritual, social, cultural and economic health. Perhaps, this can only be achieved through the promotion and integration of ethnomedical practices in the conventional medical systems in Kenya.

Ethnomedicine and Women's Health

The recent upsurge of interest in local traditional medicine in Kenya is partly attributable to the successes obtained in curing almost all diseases and the realization that it is an effective, safe, reliable and cost-effective means of primary health care system. Traditional medicine has been described as one of the surest means to achieve total health care coverage of the population using acceptable and economically feasible methods. The cost of consulting a western style doctor and the price of medication are usually beyond the means of most people. Ethnomedicine is locally available at low cost with the advantage of local knowledge of indigenous treatments. Nearly all of the medicinal plants/herbs the local populace requires for the most common illnesses can be grown in their own gardens or flourish abundantly in nature. Ethnomedicine is not only cheaper, accessible and older than other forms of medicine, but also safer because it has minimal or no side-effects. It is not only very effective but also very quick acting; however, some long standing conditions will take longer to clear up. It has also been realised that ethnomedicine can cure certain diseases which can not be cured by the western medicine. In the absence of modern health facilities and drugs, as in the case of most rural areas, traditional medicine play a significant role in promoting the health of women.

One of the most important features in herbal medicine is that the herbs, as used by traditional healers, are living. They contain the enzymes which are the living part of the cells; chlorophyll which has the property of forming blood, especially in combination with vitamin A; and hormones, vitamins and extremely valuable mineral salts such as nitrogen, iron, potash and other ingredients that are necessary for absolute health (LEYEL no date:1-297). It is these features that have made ethnomedicine to have enormous potential for the promotion of health status of the vulnerable groups of the human population, particularly the women.

Women in their reproductive period especially when pregnant or lactating are particularly vulnerable. They are vulnerable to illhealth arising from injury, disease, nutritional deficiencies and social pressure. Women are therefore characterised by a number of reproductive health problems which include: complications of pregnancy and childbirth; unwanted or poorly timed pregnancy, including adolescent pregnancy; sexually transmitted infections(STIs), icluding AIDS; infertility; other diseases of the reproductive system, including reproductive tract infections, cancers, and menstrual disorders. Traditional medicine plays a significant role during pregnancy and every community in Kenya has particular herbs and treatment procedures for various ailments. The herbs take care of the common ailments during the mother's pregnancy such as nausea, anaemia, infections in the mother, complications and pain during labour and delivery etc. Certain herbal remedies can be used to increase and improve lactation after the baby's birth. Traditional medicine can be used for the treatment of menstrual disorders or irregularity, nervous conditions, acupuncture for excessive bleeding, and regulation of menstrual cycle. Acupuncture has been found to be a great pain reliever for prolapse of the womb and can be used as a sedative.

In some communities, hormonal deficiencies in women have been cured by traditional medicines where modern medicine cannot always help. There are proven traditional cures for many sexually transmitted diseases, sterility and problems with the cervix. In addition to these disorders, ethnomedicine has been used in Kenya to treat the women's general health before, during and after pregnancy. Although there are traditional methods for birth control, these are not used extensively in the Kenyan context. This is partly because of the cultural stigma attached to the number of children one has.

There are a myriad of medicinal plants, some of which are still in experimental states. The medicinal plants discussed below (for more information see KOKWARO 1972:1-95 and KOKWARO 1993:1-244) therefore only form the tip of the ice berg.

Selected Medicinal Plants found in Kenya and their Uses

BOTANICAL NAME: Acacia lahai
LOCAL NAME: ALAKTAR (Luo)
MEDICINAL USES: Bark is used to clear toxaemia of pregnancy and bowels.Bark is also used for the treatment of skin eruptions in children.

BOTANICAL NAME: Albizia coriaria
LOCAL NAMES: OBER (Luo), OMUBELE (Kakamega)
MEDICINAL USES: Bark is used for the treatment of menorrhagia, threatened abortion, and post-partum haemorrhage. Roots are used for the treatment of venereal diseases.

BOTANICAL NAME: Carissa edulis
LOCAL NAMES: KIKAWAM MUKAWA (Kamba), OCHUOGA (Luo)
MEDICINAL USES:Used for lower abdominal pains when a woman is pregnant. In addition, it is used for indigestion; roots together with other medicinal plants is used for treating chest pains; and, root decoction is also used for malaria.

BOTANICAL NAME: Cassia abbreviata
LOCAL NAME: MSOKO (Taita)
MEDICINAL USES:Mainly used by women with uterine problems. A decoction of the roots cures fever or malaria, stomach troubles, gonorrhoea, pneumonia and uterus and chest complaints. A mixture of the bark, cattle urine and water is usually boiled and used as a purgative.

BOTANICAL NAME: Clausena anisata
LOCAL NAMES: KISIMBARI (Kakamega), MATATHI (Kikuyu), MJAVIKALI

MEDICINAL USES: Pounded roots in the form of soup is usually given to the pregnant woman to drink so as to facilitate or make delivery easy. The woman is also supposed to drink the soup two days after having given birth to cleanse the uterus of blood. Root decoction may be taken by women to hasten lactation after childbirth. Root decoction also form an effective cure for headache, malaria, influenza, indigestion and syphilis. Twigs are usually used as tooth-brushes and are believed to cure toothache.

BOTANICAL NAME: Gynandropsis gynandra
LOCAL NAMES: AKEYO (Luo), LISAKA (Bunyala)
MEDICINAL USES: Roots are boiled and the decoction is drunk to facilitate childbirth, for stomach-ache, and for the treatment of conjunctivitis and severe infection by threadworms. The young softer leaves are pounded and the resulting liquid is usually used to treat aching ears. It is said that the same liquid can be used to treat ears, nostrils and eyes in cases of epileptic fits.

BOTANICAL NAME: Heliotropium subulatum
LOCAL NAME: EBONYO or KAMOTHINE (Turkana)
MEDICINAL USES: Used as a medicine for post-parturition diseases in women.

Abb. 2
Local Name: Kuogo (Luo), Botanical Name: Lannea stuhlmannii (Foto: W. Nyaoro)

BOTANICAL NAME: Hypoestes aristata
LOCAL NAME: TURKWOT (Kipsigis)
MEDICINAL USES: Boiled in water and used for diseases of the breast. Roots chewed as a remedy for coughs, colds, and sore throats.

BOTANICAL NAME: Hyptis pectinata
LOCAL NAME: OLUWO CHIEL (Luo)
MEDICINAL USES: Leaves of this plant mixed with those of Chenopodium opulifolium and Leonotis nepetifolia can be pounded, mixed with water and drunk by women having pain during menstruation. The plant can also be used to treat diseases such as congestion of the lungs and stomach pains.

BOTANICAL NAME: Lannea stuhlmannii
LOCAL NAME: KUOGO (Luo)
MEDICINAL USES: A decoction of the bark is taken as a remedy for headache and for stomach pains. It is also given to pregnant women to relieve abdominal pains and a poultice of the leaves is applied to the abdomen to hasten childbirth.

BOTANICAL NAME: Phus vulgaris
LOCAL NAMES: AWAYO, SANGLA MODONGO (Luo), MUTHIGIO (Kikuyu)
MEDICINAL USES: Roots mixed with other plants are usually given to expectant mothers to facilitate delivery. It may also be used for infertility problems. In addition, extract from the boiled fruits is taken to stop diarrhoea; stems are boiled and liquid applied to wounds; the powdered root is mixed with gruel and drunk for gonorrhoea; and, leaves are used for the treatment of haemorrhoids.

BOTANICAL NAME: Piliostigma thonningii
LOCAL NAMES: MULAMA (Kakamega), MUREMA (Kikuyu), OGALO (Luo)
MEDICINAL USES: An infusion from the roots is drunk to stop prolonged menstruation in women, as a remedy for colds in the chest, and as a cure for venereal diseases. The green and dry leaves are used as a cure for stomach pains and snake bites respectively. The bark is chewed to relieve coughs, colds and chest pains. The plant juice can be used to treat gonorrhoea, or used for fresh cuts to stop bleeding and numb the wound. A root decoction may be used to stop haemorrhage and miscarriage in women.

BOTANICAL NAME: Rhynchosia hirta
LOCAL NAME: NYATIK-OTENGA (Luo)
MEDICINAL USES: Used to secure a quick and painless delivery or for the removal of a retained placenta. Roots are used for the treatment of bilharzia, stomach troubles and as a purgative.

It was extremely difficult to limit my choice to plants which appear in this paper. There are so many other valuable indigenous medicinal plants (which can be used to promote the health of women) in addition to the ones described in this paper that I feel I have only scratched the surface of this fascinating but vital subject.

Conclusions
In view of escalating costs of modern health care systems and services and the recognition of health as much more than the absence of illness, the adoption of ethnomedical systems which are based on the people's practical experience and knowledge have been found to be more appropriate in the promotion of the health of women. The experience in Kenya has shown that ethnomedical system is cost-effective (since it uses local resources); safe (with minimal or no side effects); effective and 'quick acting'; and, uses a holistic approach to the treatment process.

Based on the aforementioned observations, it is recommended that 'selected' ethnomedical systems should form an integral part of national health care policy. Rural, Urban and Peri-urban health initiatives and programmes need to recognize and draw on the contribution of traditional health care services. Such initiatives should promote local self reliance in health care by using skilled local traditional medicine practitioners. There is also need to develop and strengthen legal and institutional framework in order to support and promote the operations and practices of ethnomedicine. Financial and technical support should be provided to develop and strengthen the knowledge or epistemological components of ethnomedical systems. This will ensure the perpetuation of such knowledge and sustainable development of traditional health care services.

Research on medicinal plants should be intensified at three levels. Firstly, botanical gardens and research institutes should be encouraged to collect, classify, and grow the known medicinal plants to assure the authenticity of the materials being used by local ethnomedical practitioners. It is often very difficult for one to be absolutely sure which plant species form the active ingredients of a particular traditional drug. Secondly, pharmacologists and biochemists should be encouraged to analyze the chemical composition of medicinal plants that are already documented so as to ascertain and extract the active ingredients of the plant species that seem to have great potential in the formulation of new effective drugs. Such studies will help eliminate those plants that are of little medicinal value and encourage the promotion of those species with high potential. Thirdly, there is need for continuous exploration and experimentation of medicinal plants that have not been identified and whose medicinal values and uses are not well understood.

Kenya has great potential for the development of ethnomedicine. There are numerous medicinal plants/herbs, some of which have not yet been documented. Locked away in the cells of many of these plants are some of the world's greatest natural medicinal chemicals. Their ethnomedical values and potentials, especially for the promotion of women's health, are enormous. Perhaps only time will tell.

Caution:

This paper will not enable you to become a herbalist or ethnomedicine specialist but it will enable you to appreciate the potential of medicinal plants in safely and effectively alleviating many common ills, pains and suffering especially among women. Never, and I repeat, never use medicinal plants as described in this paper unless so advised by a qualified practitioner of ethnomedicine. Just as one should not take patent medicines without a prescription, ethnomedicines should be taken under the direction of an experienced practitioner. Like with all medicines, incorrect dosages of medicinal plants can be dangerous and even fatal.

Acknowledgements

The author wishes to thank members of staff of Kirstenbosch National Botanical Gardens(Cape Town) and United Nations Environment Programme (Nairobi) for providing the necessary information requested for reference and which formed the basis of the preparation of this paper. It is also noted with appreciation the cooperation of Traditional Medicine Practitioners visited during the research period. The author is deeply indebted to Belinda Allan for her confidence in the ability and professionalism of the author. Special thanks also go to Doris Iding and Christine E. Gottschalk-Batschkus and the other members of the Society for Ethnomedicine for their tireless efforts in making the final publication of this paper a success.

References

AYENSU, E.S. 1978. *Medicinal Plants of West Africa. Reference Publications,* Inc.,Michigan.
BLACKWELL, W.H. 1990. *Poisonous and Medicinal Plants.* Prentice-Hall, Inc., New Jersey.
COON, N. 1974. *The Dictionary of Useful Plants: The Use, History, and Folklore of more than 500 plant species.* Rodale Press, Emmaus.
FRATKIN, E.M. 1975. *Herbal Medicine and Concepts of Disease in Samburu.* Unpublished Seminar paper No. 65, University of Nairobi.
GENDERS, R. 1975. *Herbs for Health and Beauty.* Robert Hale and Co. Ltd., London.
GOOD, G.M. and KIMANI, V.N. 1980. " Urban Traditional Medicine: A Nairobi Case Study." *East African Medical Journal,* Vol. 57, Number 5, 301-316.
HYMA, B. and RAMESH, A. 1994. Traditional Medicine: Its extent and Potential for Incorporation into Modern National Health Systems. In: PHILLIPS, D.R. and VERHASSELT, Y. 1994. *Health and Development.* Routledge, New York.
INTERNATIONAL DEVELOPMENT RESEARCH CENTRE (IDRC) 1980. *Traditional Medicine in Zaire: Present and Potential Contribution to the Health Services.* IDRC, Ottawa, Canada.
IWU, M.M. 1993. *Handbook of African Medicinal Plants.* CRC Press, Inc., Florida.
KOKWARO, J.O. 1993. *Medicinal Plants of East Africa.* Kenya Literature Bureau Nairobi, Second Edition.
KOKWARO, J.O. 1972. *Luo-English Botanical Dictionary of Plant names and uses.* East African Publishing House, Nairobi.
LAW, D. 1970. *Herbs for Cooking and for Healing.* W. Foulsham and Co. Ltd., New York.
LEWIS, N.D. and KIEFFER, E. 1994. The Health of Women: Beyond Maternal and Child Health: In: PHILLIPS, D.R. and VERHASSELT, Y. (eds.) 1994. *Health and Development.* Routledge, New York.
LEYEL, C.F..no date. *Green Medicine.* Faber and Faber Ltd., London, pp. 1-297
ONIANG'O, R.K. 1987. *Traditional Care for Pregnant Women in Selected Communities in Kenya.* Unpublished report, Kenyatta University, Nairobi.
OKOTH-OWIRO, A.. 1994. Traditional Health Systems: Issues and Concerns. In: ISLAM, A. and WILTSHIRE, R. (eds.) 1994. *Traditional Health Systems and Public Policy: Proceedings of an International Workshop* , Ottawa, Canada, 2-4 March 1994.
PHILLIPS, D.R. and VERHASSELT, Y. 1994. Introduction: Health and Development. In: PHILLIPS, D.R. and VERHASSELT, Y. (eds.)1994. *Health and Development.*Routledge, London.
THE BROCKHAMPTON LIBRARY. 1996. *Book of Herbal Remedies.* Brockhampton Press, London.
THOMSON, M.D. and WILLIAM, A.R. 1980. *Healing Plants: A Modern Herbal.* McMillan, London.
WARREN, D.M.: SLIKKERVEER, L.J. and BROKENSHA, D. 1995. *The Cultural Dimension of Development: Indigenous Knowledge Systems.* Intermediate Technology Publications, London.
WORLD HEALTH ORGANIZATION(WHO)1991. *The World's Women 1970-1990: Trends and Statistics.* United Nations, New York.

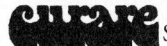

Kanyalen, eine Frauenmaske
Kanyalen: A Womens' Mask
Kirsten Langeveld

Zusammenfassung: Der Tod eines Babys verursacht in jeder Familie in der Welt großes Leid. In Afrika ist dieses Problem weitverbreitet, denn die Säuglingssterblichkeit ist hier viel höher als auf anderen Kontinenten. - In der Diola-Gemeinschaft in der Casamance im Süden des Senegals ist das *kanyalen*-Ritual eine Antwort auf das Problem. Es wurde zum Schutz der Frauen und ihrer Nachkommenschaft gegen die bösen Kräfte eingerichtet, von denen man glaubt, dass sie das Übel verursachen. In diesem Beitrag möchte ich versuchen darzulegen, dass dieses Ritual als ein Maskenritual betrachtet werden kann. In der Diola-Gemeinschaft treten während der Riten verschiedene Masken auf, die im allgemeinen Männern gehören und von ihnen getragen werden. Im Gegensatz zu den Männermasken wird die *kanyalen*-Maske lebenslang getragen. Das Tragen dieser Maske geschieht nicht immer freiwillig. Obwohl die Männer und islamischen Befürworter versuchen, das Fortbestehen des *kanyalen*-Rituals zu verhindern, lassen die Frauen es nicht dazu kommen. Denn dieses Ritual ist eine wichtige Institution zur Statuserhaltung der Frau.

Abstract: The death of a baby causes in every family in the world a great grief. In Africa it is a widespread problem since the death rate of babies is much higher than on other continents. In Diola society a group that lives in the Casamance the southern part of Senegal the answer to this problem is the *kanyalen* ritual. It is created to defend the woman and her spouse from evil forces, who are believed to be the cause of her burden. In this contribution I would like to explain why this ritual can be considered as a mask ritual. In the Diola society several masks perform during rituals. In general men own these masks and are the performers. Unlike the mens' masks, the particular *kanyalen* mask is almost always worn for a lifetime and is also not always voluntarily. Although men and islamic predecessors try to restrain the persistence of the *kanyalen* ritual, women will not allow this to occur. For this ritual is an important institution to maintain the status of women.

Keywords: Kulturelle Anthropologie, West Afrika, Frauen, Fruchtbarkeit, Masken, Cultural Anthropology, West-Africa, Women, Fertility, Masks.

kanyalen: Die maskierte Frau.

„Mein *kanyalen*-Name ist Djacumba, das bedeutet Sau. Warum die Frauen diesen Namen ausgesucht haben? Weil es eine Sau kalt lässt, ob ihre Kinder sterben oder nicht."

Mit verbitterter Miene erzählt hier eine Diola-Frau aus Diatock, einem Dorf in der Basse-Casamance im Senegal. Eine senegalesische Frau mit dem Schicksal,

Abb. 1
An *Kanyalen* woman „en face".

mehrmals hintereinander ihre Kinder kurz nach der Geburt verloren zu haben, bleibt nicht unbeachtet. Verschiedene Gruppen geben ihr einen besonderen Status, die Diola nennen sie *anyalen,* die Manding *dimbaya* und die Wolof *yalodal* (eine Frau, die über das Verlieren von Kindern Bescheid weiß) oder niawle (niaw heißt wörtlich 'hässlich'). Kanyalen, die Masken-Institution als kulturelle Antwort auf das vorzeitige Kindersterben bei den Diola im Boulouf-Gebiet und in Ziguinchor, der Hauptstadt der Region, ist Gegenstand dieser Untersuchung. Hier wurden auch zwei weitere Gruppen mit herangezogen, die Manding und Bainouk. Diese Untersuchung wurde finanziert von der Niederländischen Stiftung für Tropenforschung (WOTRO). Die Feldarbeit fand mit Unterbrechungen zwischen 1992 und 1996 statt. Die Diola leben im Süden Senegals, in der Casamance, dem fruchtbarsten Gebiet des Landes. Die Abstammung der Diola verläuft patrilinear. Die Ehe ist exogam, und dort, wo die Dörfer islamitisch sind, ist Polygamie akzeptiert. Das Leben von Mann und Frau spielt sich in getrennten Welten ab. Nach dem Initiationsritual, *bukut,* das in jeder Generation einmal stattfindet, werden die Jungen zum Mann. Die Mädchen werden zur Frau, wenn sie verheiratet sind und Kinder zur Welt gebracht haben. Für die Diola-Frau ist die Fruchtbarkeit bestimmend für ihren Status. Eine unfruchtbare Frau muss damit rechnen, verstoßen zu werden. Der Zugang zu den Frauenriten wird ihr verweigert. Bei einer Frau, die mehrmals hintereinander ihre Kinder vorzeitig verliert oder Fehlgeburten hat, wird diagnostiziert, dass ein böser Kraft hier die Hand im Spiel hat. Deshalb wird sie die *kanyalen*-Maske (anyalen ist das Singular, bunyalen das Plural, die Institution heißt *kanyalen,* siehe auch JOURNET 1991) tragen müssen, und das Ritual wird zu ihrem eigenen Schutz in oder außerhalb des Dorfes in die Obhut anderer Frauen, eines Mannes oder einer Masken-Gesellschaft genommen.

In den bisher erschienen Publikationen wurde die *kanyalen*-Institution sporadisch erwähnt (siehe auch FASSIN 1987:55. WEIL 1976 übersieht sie), aber nicht als Maske erkannt, obwohl sie alle Eigenschaften einer Maske aufweist. In großen Teilen Afrikas ist eine Maske ein effektives Abwehrmittel gegen böse Mächte, je nach Art und Ernst des Bösen wird eine spezielle Maske eingesetzt. Will man den Begriff Maske definieren, gilt es nicht nur die Gesichtsbedeckung und das Kostüm in Augenschein zu nehmen, sondern die Gesamtheit des Glaubens mit dem damit verbundenen Gebrauch der Maske. Für den Träger einer Maske ist es wichtig, dass seine Identität den bösen Geistern verborgen bleibt. Das bedeutet übrigens nicht immer, dass das Gesicht des Trägers auch tatsächlich nicht zu erkennen ist. Manche Diola-Masken tragen überhaupt kein Kostüm, sie tanzen nachts, damit niemand weiß, wer sich hinter der Maske verbirgt. Auch bei den Diola treten die Masken auf, um die Menschen gegen böse Kräfte zu schützen. Wenn mit der Maske die ganze Gemeinschaft beschützt werden soll, bleibt die Identität des Maskenträgers allen außer den Mitgliedern der Maskengesellschaft und fast immer den Frauen und Kindern, verborgen. Soll die Maske den Träger selbst beschützen, dann versteckt sie die Identität des Trägers. So tragen z.B. die Jungen vor und während des Zirkumzisionsrituals, dem *bukut,* Masken zum Schutz gegen böse Kräfte.

Die *kanyalen*-Maske wurde als Schutz für diejenigen Frauen geschaffen, die Schwierigkeiten mit der Fortpflanzung haben. Man überlässt sie nicht ihrem Schicksal, sondern behandelt sie so, dass sie sich lebenslang von den anderen Frauen unterscheiden. Ihre Beschützer geben ihr und ihrem Baby während des Initiationsrituals zur *anyalen* einen neuen Namen, der alte wird „begraben". Diesen neuen Namen behält die Frau nun als Zeichen ihrer Identitätsveränderung für ihr weiteres Leben, damit der böse Geist sie nicht entlarven kann. Da sie ihr Leben lang gefährdet sein wird, trägt sie die *kanyalen*-Maske auch lebenslang. Wie jede Maske muss auch die *anyalen* während Festlichkeiten ein besonderes Kostüm tragen und darin auftreten und tanzen. Und wie jede andere Maske ist die *kanyalen*-Maske oft die Antreiberin, und speziell von dieser Maske verlangt man ein possierliches Gehabe. Die Alltagserscheinung der *anyalen* ist nicht selten miserabel, auch das ist ein Mittel, die bösen Geister zu verscheuchen. Wie zu allen Diola-Masken gehört auch zur *kanyalen*-Maske eine orale Tradition. Die *anyalen* komponiert und singt ihre eigenen Lieder, die meistens ihr Schicksal beschreiben. Während des Initiationsrituals bekommen die *anyalen* und ihr Kind Amulette umgehängt, und außerdem erhält sie ein Amulett, das sie zum Schutz für sich und das Kind immer bei sich tragen muss. Das kann ein Stock oder eine halbe Kalebasse sein, beide sind mit Kaurimuscheln und Perlen verziert. Manchmal werden auch Amulette im Zimmer der Frau versteckt. Die *kanyalen*-Maske ist eine typische Frauenmaske, die nie von Männer getragen wird. Obwohl die Männer verschiedene Masken haben, gibt es darunter keine, die unmittelbar mit der Fruchtbarkeit des Mannes zusammenhängt. Daraus lässt sich schließen, dass die Männer die Lebenserhaltung der Nachkommenschaft nicht zu ihrer Verantwortlichkeit zählen.

Wohl kann die *anyalen* sich in die Obhut eines Mannes mit religiöser Funktion oder einer von einem Mann getragenen Maske begeben und hat so als unvollwertige Frau leichter Zugang zu der Männerwelt als die anderen Frauen. Trotzdem oder vielleicht gerade deshalb entsteht bei den Männern Widerstand gegen die *kanyalen*-Institution. Wie sich noch heraus stellen wird, gibt es für die Frauen jedoch bisher noch keinen Grund, diesem Widerstand der Männer nachzugeben.

Die *kanyalen*-Maske.

Wie wichtig Gebären und Geburt im Leben einer Diola-Frau sind, wird deutlich, wenn beides oder eins von beiden nicht normal verläuft. Eine unfruchtbare Frau ist keine vollwertige Frau, was innerhalb der Frauenwelt bedeutet, dass sie in manchen Dörfern von den Riten um die Frauengeheimnisse ausgeschlossen wird. Die Frau, die vorzeitig ihre Kinder verliert, nimmt eine besondere Stellung ein. Im Gegensatz zur unfruchtbaren Frau hat sie Zugang zu den Frauenriten. Die Nachkommenschaft ist in der Diola-Gemeinschaft keine individuelle sondern eine gemeinschaftliche Angelegenheit. In den verschiedenen Dörfern des Boulouf-Gebietes und in Ziguinchor sind es im allgemeinen die Frauen, die darüber entscheiden, ob eine Frau eine *anyalen* wird, was durchaus plausibel ist, denn sie tragen ja die Verantwortung für die Nachkommenschaft. Wenn eine Frau längere Zeit nicht schwanger ist oder überhaupt noch keine Kinder hat, sprechen die anderen Frauen sie daraufhin an. Eine Frau, die aktiv Schwangerschaften verhütet, wird in dieser ruralen Welt als abweichend angesehen, sodass die Frauen manchmal versuchen, sich heimlich Verhütungsmittel zu beschaffen.

Eine Frau, deren Kinder vorzeitig sterben, wird nich ohne weiteres eine *anyalen*, dazu bedarf es eines Initiationsrituals. Obwohl mit dem Begriff *kanyalen* überall das selbe Problem gemeint wird, ist die Behandlungsweise im einzelnen in den verschiedenen Dörfern unterschiedlich. Fassin berichtet, dass auch eine unfruchtbare Frau eine *anyalen* werden kann, das ist im Boulouf-Gebiet nicht gebräuchlich (FASSIN 1986:55). Die Frau kann selbst entscheiden, eine *anyalen* zu werden, aber in den meisten Fällen tut sie das nicht, es geschieht überraschenderweise. Die für sie verantwortliche Gruppe von Frauen nimmt sie unter falschem Vorwand mit in ihren neuen Wohnort. Wenn die Entscheidung einmal getroffen ist, muss die Frau die *kanyalen*-Maske tragen, auch gegen ihren eigenen Willen.
Meine Assistentin erzählte:

„*Riz N'Diaye schimpfte gewaltig, als es ihr klar wurde, dass sie eine* **anyalen** *werden sollte. Drei Tage aß sie nicht, dann akzeptierte sie es.*"

Ist der Entschluss einmal gefasst, eine Frau zu einer *anyalen* zu initiieren, wartet man mit dem Ritual meistens bis das Kind geboren ist. Fassin berichtet, dass der Moment des Umzugs an einen anderen Ort von dem Grund abhängt, weshalb die Frau eine *anyalen* wird. So wird eine Frau mit Fehlgeburten zu einer anderen Zeit den Wohnort wechseln, als eine Frau, die viele Kinder verloren hat (FASSIN 1987:60-61). Diese strengen Regeln konnten bei dieser Untersuchung nicht festgestellt werden.

Dass es sich wirklich um eine Statusveränderung handelt, macht das Initiationsritual der Frauen in Kandiou deutlich. Nach dem Ritual zur *anyalen* ist die Frau wie eine 'Wiedergeborene'. Die drei Phasen, die zu einer Statusveränderung gehören, wie van Gennep und Turner (VAN GENNEP 1960 und TURNER 1969) es beschreiben, nämlich Trennung, Marginalität oder Liminalität und Inkorporation, sind auch bei dem *kanyalen*-Ritual deutlich zu erkennen. Das besondere ist, dass die *anyalen* in der zweiten Phase, der Liminalität, bleibt und in ihr inkorporiert wird. Die kennzeichnende Symbolik der Liminalität wie Turner sie darstellt (TURNER 1974:94-106) trifft für die kanyalen-Maske zu.

Eine liminale Person fällt aus dem Rahmen von Gesetz und (Rang)ordnung einer Gesellschaft und ist von anderen liminalen Personen nicht zu unterscheiden. Sie trägt wenig oder keine Kleidung, benimmt sich unterwürfig, gehorcht widerstandslos und akzeptiert Strafe (TURNER 1969:95).
Ein Informant aus Kandiou berichtet:

„*Die Frauen sind zusammen und die Frau ist nackt wie ein Neugeborenes. Sie tanzt und läuft im Kreis herum. Dann setzt sie sich bei ihren Kleidern auf die Erde. Mit einem Amulett, das sie von nun an immer bei sich tragen wird, wird sie eingeweiht, die Frauen berühren ihren Rumpf damit. Die Frau streckt ihre Arme vor sich aus, eine andere Frau stellt sich auf ihre Füße und zieht sie hoch. Wie einem Kind zieht man ihr die Kleider an.*"

Eine andere Version des Initiationsrituals, die ein Informant aus Ziguinchor mitteilte, ist weitaus rigoroser:

„*Die* **anyalen** *wird geschlagen und ausgeschimpft, dass sie alles auffisst und kein Kind hat. Zum Schluss* *der Zeremonie muss sie aus einer Schale essen, in die man alle möglichen Gerichte geschüttet hat, manchmal sogar mit Sand vermischt."*

Die Initianda wird "wiedergeboren". Sie bekommt einen anderen Namen und wechselt zeitlich ihren Wohnort und bekommt hier fiktive Eltern. Während der Initiation gibt man ihr ein Kostüm, das sie bei Riten oder Zeremonien tragen muss. Dann muss sie auch tanzen und singen. Sie trägt die *kanyalen*-Maske, die ihre "alte" Identität verbirgt, und weil die Mutterschaft eine lebenslange Aufgabe ist, wird sie diese Maske auch lebenslang tragen. Fassin berichtet, dass die *anyalen* ihren alten Status wieder erhält, sobald sie zu ihrem Ehemann zurückgekehrt ist (FASSIN 1987:64). Davon weicht die im Boulouf-Gebiet und in Ziguinchor erhaltene Information ab. Hier behält eine *anyalen* diesen Status ihr ganzes Leben.

Das Tragen der *kanyalen*-Maske ist bei weitem folgenschwerer für die Trägerin als es die von Männern getragenen Masken sind, weil sie ihr Leben entscheidend ändert. Die von Männern getragenen Masken beschützen die anderen, und ihre Träger bleiben verborgen. Die *kanyalen*-Maske beschützt ihre Trägerin, deren Identität bekannt ist, und widerspiegelt die eingeschränkte Kraft ihrer Mutterschaft; ihr Erscheinen muss possierlich sein. Das Tragen dieser Maske gibt nicht nur ihren niedrigeren Status wieder, darüber hinaus handelt es sich um Inversion, ihr Verhalten ändert sich, sie benimmt sich so, wie es sich für eine normale Frau nicht gehört. - Die *anyalen* kennt zwar das wichtigste weibliche Geheimnis, das Geheimnis des Gebärens, aber sie gehört nicht vollständig zur Frauenwelt. Sie partizipiert an den Frauenritualen, aber durch ihre Maske betont sie ihr Anderssein. Oft haben die anderen Frauen sie zu dem Tragen dieser Maske verpflichtet, um ihre abweichende Stellung zu unterstreichen. Die *kanyalen*-Maske widerspiegelt in extremer Form ihre Situation. Während eines Zeitraums von zwei Jahren wird sie buchstäblich von ihrer Gemeinschaft isoliert, und sie wird mit Hilfe anderer Frauen alles daransetzen, um ihre Kinder am Leben zu erhalten, damit sie wieder in ihre eigene Familie und Gemeinschaft zurückkehren kann. - Der niedrigere Status der Frau weist noch ein weiteres Merkmal auf: sie kann niemals anderen ihre Dienste verweigern, auch nicht, wenn es sich um Personen handelt, die jünger sind als sie selbst, etwas, das in normalen Verhältnissen ungebräuchlich ist. Im Grunde gehört sie ihr Leben lang zu der Generation der unverheirateten Mädchen. - Bei Tänzen und Festen erwartet man von ihr das Gehabe und Auftreten eines Clowns. Ihr neuer Vorname weist indirekt auf ihre Situation hin und ist gleichzeitig denigrierend. Manchmal ist es eine Markenbezeichnung oder der Name einer Institution, jedenfalls ist es ersichtlich kein gewöhnlicher Vorname. So kann sie z.B. *Woulo* heißen, was Hund bedeutet, oder *Sotiba* nach einer Textilfabrik in Dakar. *Domoro* heißt, "du isst und du kriegst kein Kind", was unmittelbar zum Ausdruck bringt, wie man über eine Frau denkt, die keine Kinder hat. Aus alledem lässt sich schließen, dass die Reproduktion einer Nachkommenschaft für die Aufnahme der Frau in die patrilineare Gemeinschaft unabdingbar ist. Bleibt diese Bedingung unerfüllt, wird der Aufenthalt der Frau in der Familie des Ehemannes problematisch.

Die *anyalen* wird nach der Geburt ihres Kindes zwei Jahre nicht in ihrem eigenen Haus wohnen. Manchmal zieht sie in ein anderes Dorf oder eine andere Stadt, meistens nur in ein anderes Viertel. Sie bekommt fiktive Eltern, bei deren Familie sie wohnt und deren Nachnamen sie annimmt. Außerdem wird sie oft unter den Schutz einer Gruppe von Frauen gestellt, die an Stelle ihres Ehemannes die Verantwortung für sie übernimmt. Sie darf ihre eigenen Kleider nicht zum neuen Wohnort mitnehmen, was noch einmal ihre Identitätsveränderung betont: ihre alte Kleidung gehört zum Status einer normalen Frau. In Thionck Essyl trugen die *bunyalen* der beiden vorigen Generationen leere Reissäcke oder braun gewordene Moskitonetze. Die *bunyalen* der letzten Generation brauchen keine hässlichen Kleider mehr zu tragen, wohl aber Kleider, die sie von den anderen Frauen unterscheiden; meistens tragen sie alltags nur Ketten als Kennzeichen einer *anyalen*. Eine Informantin aus Thionck Essyl berichtet, wie es einer *anyalen* vor zwei Generationen noch erging:

„*Trug eine **anyalen** ein schönes Kleidungsstück, dann spuckten die anderen Frauen oder schneuzten sich die Nase darauf, weil eine **anyalen** hässliche Kleider tragen muss.*"

Eine *anyalen* hat weder das Recht noch einen Grund, attraktiv auszusehen, denn sie erfüllt ja gemäß dieser Tradition nicht die ihr von Natur aus obliegende Pflicht. Eine weitere Erklärung, die die Frauen selbst geben, hängt mit ihrem Glauben an böse Geister zusammen. Auch eine Frau, die keine *anyalen* ist, darf sich nicht auffallend kleiden oder angenehm riechen, denn das könnte böse Geister anziehen. Auch wenn die *anyalen* heute keine Lumpen mehr zu tragen braucht, so wird sie doch zu Riten und Festen nie die Uniform ihrer Mitbewohnerinnen tragen (Bei den Diola-Frauen trägt bei Festlichkeiten jede Generation eine Uniform, *asobi* genannt, die die Grenzen zwischen den Altersgruppen markieren.).

Die *bunyalen* eines Dorfes tragen während der Feste und Zeremonien alle das gleiche Kostüm.

Das Amulett, das die *anyalen* bei der Initiation erhält, muss sie immer bei sich tragen. Oft ist es ein mit Kaurimuscheln und Perlen verzierter Stock. Manchmal bekommt sie eine halbe Kalebasse, deren Rand ebenfalls mit Kaurimuscheln und Perlen verziert ist. Man glaubt, dass dieses Amulett der Wächter über die Seele des Kindes ist, und dass das Kind zu sterben droht, wenn die Frau das Amulett verliert. Ohne Stock oder Kalebasse kann die Frau keine Kinder gebären. Außerdem beschützt dieses Symbol die *anyalen*. Ein Informant, der die Zirkumzision der Jungen ausführt, erklärte:

„Die Kaurimuscheln schenken der Frau Schutz und Glück. Sie hat auch genau die Form des weiblichen Geschlechts. Die Kraft der Kaurimuschel ist eine weibliche Kraft."

Der Stock der *anyalen* hat manchmal deutlich eine Phallusform; der Informant fügte hinzu:

*„Der Stock ist das Symbol der Fruchtbarkeit, der Reife und des männlichen Geschlechts. Die Frau kann auch einen Strumpf nehmen und ihn so formen, dass er wie das männliche Geschlecht aussieht. Beim Tanzen hängt sie ihn sich um und zeigt ihn den Frauen und rät ihnen, sich vorzubereiten. Wenn die **bunyalen** sich so benehmen, hilft Gott ihnen, und sie werden Kinder kriegen. Die kleine Kalebasse steht für das weibliche Geschlecht."*

In diesem Zusammenhang ist ein Zitat aus meinem Tagebuch erhellend:

*„Eine Gruppe von Frauen war mit Hirsestampfen beschäftigt. Eine **anyalen** bat mich um meinen Rock. Ich bat sie, mir ihren Wickelrock zu geben. Daraufhin löste sie ihren Wickelrock, und es entstand eine große Hilarität. Sie trug nämlich keine Unterwäsche. Zuvor hatte sie meine Assistentin gefragt, ob wir auch große Geschlechtsteile mitgebracht hätten, ihre eigenen seien nämlich sehr klein."*

Die *anyalen* bezeichnet ihre Genitalien als klein, um damit anzudeuten, dass sie wie eines kleines Mädchen ist. Mit den Symbolen des Stocks für das männliche und der Kalebasse für das weibliche Geschlecht wird die prokreative Kraft der Genitalien vergrößert. In den untersuchten Fällen erhielt die *anyalen* eher einen Stock. Wahrscheinlich macht es nichts aus, ob ein Stock oder eine Kalebasse als Amulett gewählt wird, da es sich um gleichwertige Symbole handelt. Journet beschreibt, dass die *anyalen* in ihrem Forschungsgebiet beides, Stock und Kalebasse bekommen. Meine eigenen Untersuchungen ergeben, dass die Diola-Frauen den Stock, die Manding-Frauen die Kalebasse bevorzugen (JOURNET 1991:28).

Obwohl der Stock ein Phallussymbol ist, will das nicht heißen, dass das Tragen der *kanyalen*-Maske eine Geschlechtsumkehrung bedeutet. Eher ist anzunehmen, dass damit eine Verbindung zum Ehemann hergestellt wird, von dem die *anyalen* für zwei Jahre getrennt leben muss. Weil analysiert die *kanyalen*-Institution als eine Institution, die bei Teilnahme zur Geschlechtsumkehrung führt (WEIL 1976). Das wird für sein Forschungsgebiet, die Manding in Gambia, zutreffen. Im Boulouf-Gebiet verhält es sich nicht so. Hier benimmt sich die *anyalen* abweichend, aber das wird nicht als männliches Betragen angesehen, sondern als unerwachsen. Es ist das Benehmen einer misslungenen Frau. Man könnte sie als ein drittes Geschlecht bezeichnen, denn in der *kanyalen*-Maske ist sie weder Frau noch Mann. Die *anyalen* beschreibt in ihren selbstkomponierten und gesungenen Liedern oft ihr Schicksal, wie z.B. eine Frau aus Kandiou:

„La mère ehheoha, elle a perdu ses enfants (3x)
Si elle parle les gens sont derrière lui,
Les gens disent que je suis mauvaise pour cela elle a perdu
ses enfants.
Les gens parlent derrière moi, ils ne parlent pas face à
face.
Les gens parlent du matin au soir.
Entré, ses frères ont demandé, elle est malade, comment ça
va avec elle?
Elle dit, qu'elle ne fait rien dans la maison
Elle n'a pas des enfants, elle n'a rien.
On peut lui faire passer par le bac à Affiniam, elle peut
rester là-bas parce qu'elle n'a rien.
Sa mère aussi demande ce qu'elle fait,
Elle dit qu'elle ne fait rien parce qu'elle n'a rien
Elle peut lui faire passer par le bac, et la laisser là-bas."

Im ersten Lied wird die Kritik ihrer Umgebung ausgesprochen, dass sie ihrer Aufgabe als Frau nicht gerecht wird. Im zweiten Lied wird ein Bild skizziert von einer nutzlosen Frau die nichts zu tun hat und nichts besitzt, also eigentlich keine Frau ist, und dass sie besser das Haus verlassen sollte, wie es die *anyalen* auch wirklich tut. Erklärt wird das damit, dass sie den bösen Kräften entfliehen muss. - Der Text ihres dritten Liedes klagt den Mann an: in einem anderen Gebiet, in Fogny, östlich von Kandiou würden die Männer besser funktionieren. Eine solche Beschuldigung kann nur in einem Lied ausgesprochen werden, niemals könnte sie ernstlich in der Öffentlichkeit besprochen werden. Die Diola sind der Auffassung, dass Fruchtbarkeitsprobleme zur Domäne der Frau und nicht der des Mannes gehören. (Siehe auch JOURNET 1991).

> „Les hommes ne vont pas l'amour bien comme là-bas à Fogny
> Parce que à Fogny on prend le tabac et ils partent chez les femmes.
> Les hommes ne vont pas l'amour avec le tabac c'est à Fogny qu'ils vont cela (3x)."

Wird die *anyalen* von einem Geist verfolgt, 'isst' sie selbst das Kind oder 'essen' andere es 'auf'? Der Glaube an Hexerei ist unter den Diola weit verbreitet. Trotz Islam und Christentum gehört hier die Hexerei zum täglichen Leben. Man versucht, sich mit allen möglichen Mitteln dagegen zu schützen. Unglück, Krankheit und Sterben werden fast immer mit Hexerei erklärt. Man kann die nächsten Angehörigen oder die Nachbarn der Hexerei beschuldigen. Das geschieht nicht öffentlich, man flüstert es hinter dem Rücken der Hexen, der *alupout asai* oder *aboudia asai* wie sie in Diatock genannt werden. Man glaubt, dass diese Hexen die Seele einer Person "aufessen". Es kommt nicht selten vor, dass eine der Ehefrauen eines Mannes beschuldigt wird, das Motiv kann sicher die oft unter einander herrschende Eifersucht sein. Das Glück, viele Söhne zu haben, weckt oft den Neid der Ehefrau, die nicht so viele Söhne hat, und diese wird dann der Hexerei angeklagt, wenn es der ersteren nicht so gut geht.

Neben dieser Erklärung des vorzeitigen Kindersterbens durch Hexerei gibt es in den verschiedenen Dörfern noch ganz unterschiedliche Erklärungen. In Diatock meint man, dass die Frau einen zweiten Ehemann hat in der Gestallt eines Geistes, eines *djin*, der aus Eifersucht auf den Ehemann dessen Kinder tötet. Oder man versteht das Kindersterben als Racheakt einer verstorbenen Person an einer Frau, die sie im Leben nicht gut versorgt hat. Diese Person reinkarniert im Kind und stirbt vorzeitig. Eine Frau kann auch ihre Kinder verlieren, weil ihre Eltern oder die Eltern ihres Mannes ein Tabu verletzt haben. Die Frauen, die eine *anyalen* in ihren Schutz genommen haben, konsultieren einen Marabut oder jemanden mit einem 'doppelten Blick', *apakena asai* (Diatock). Dieser Weise kann die Ursache für das vorzeitige Sterben ihrer Kinder sehen. Manchmal wird eine *anyalen* öffentlich angeklagt, ihre Kinder selbst 'aufgegessen' zu haben, so z.B. in Thionck Essyl, wo ein Marabut einer *anyalen* diese Schuld zuwies. Die Frau leugnete, und erst nach langer Zeit konnte sie ihre Beschützerinnen davon überzeugen, dass sie keine Hexe war. Wird eine Frau dieser Form von Anthropophagie bezichtigt, muss sie das Dorf verlassen, weil man befürchtet, dass sie auch andere Kinder "aufessen" könnte. In Diatock gab man der *anyalen* nicht die Schuld am Sterben ihrer Kinder, aber sie hatte die Konsequenzen zu tragen. Dies geht aus folgendem Zitat hervor:

> „Früher wurde in Diatock die anyalen von den Frauen geschlagen, die sie beschützten und verantwortlich für sie waren. Man glaubte, dass die Seele des Kindes in der Frau war, und dass es immer dasselbe Kind war, das wiedergeboren wurde. Man schlug die Frau, um das Kind zu strafen."

Oft werden die Dinge, die heute noch geschehen, so erzählt, als ob sie der Vergangenheit angehörten, weil es negative Handelsweisen betrifft und man sehr wohl weiß, dass Außenstehende sie missbilligen werden. Ein andere Erklärung lautet, dass das Kind stirbt und reinkarniert. Um das feststellen zu können, wird ein Ohrläppchen des gestorbenen Kindes penetriert. Seine Leiche wird schlecht behandelt und statt in ein Leichentuch in ein gewöhnliches Tuch gewickelt. Die Frauen meinen, dass das Kind, wenn es reinkarniert, nicht mehr sterben wird, weil es nun deutlich ist, dass der Geist des Kindes schuld ist. Obwohl im allgemeinen der Mann nicht öffentlich als Schuldiger für das Kindersterben genannt wird, erzählten die Frauen in Thionck Essyl, dass auch ein Mann es verursachen kann; wenn er z.B. ein Tabu verletzt hat, werden seine Söhne sterben und seine Töchter am Leben bleiben.

Auch wenn eine Frau zunächst akzeptiert, eine *anyalen* zu werden, kann sie sich entschließen, die Maske abzulegen. Denn man achtet sehr wohl auf die Effektivität der *kanyalen*-Maske. In Diatock sagte eine Frau, die zehn Kinder zur Welt gebracht hatte, die alle gestorben waren:

> Ich hätte es schon akzeptiert, eine **anyalen** zu sein, und hätte auch die Aufgaben erfüllt und die Tänze aufgeführt, wenn ich gesehen hätte, dass das Erfolg gehabt hätte. Aber es hat an dem Sterben meiner

Kinder nichts geändert, deshalb habe ich es aufgegeben.
Zwar nannte sie sich selbst keine *anyalen* mehr, aber sie blieb vage darüber, ob die anderen ihr diesen Status noch zuerkannten. Ihr Ehemann hatte sie uns als *anyalen* vorgestellt. Jedenfalls war es für sie selbst klar, dass diese Rolle für sie keinen Sinn mehr hatte.

Umgekehrt kommt es aber auch vor, dass eine Frau, die in erster Instanz nicht geneigt war, eine *anyalen* zu werden, diese Maske mit voller Überzeugung trägt, wenn sie sieht, dass ihre Kinder nun am Leben bleiben.

Islam

Obwohl die *Kanyalen*-Institution dem Glauben an böse Geister und Hexerei entspringt, also zur traditionellen Religion gehört, hat sie sich trotz der Anwesenheit des Islam erhalten können. Es verhält sich sogar so, dass der Marabut bei den Problemen der *anyalen* mit einbezogen wird. Die Initiation findet bei einem Heiligtum, *ukin,* statt. Vor der Initiation fragen die Frauen bei der Suche nach der Ursache des Übels oft einen Marabut um Rat, denn er kann die Ursache für das vorzeitige Kindersterben sehen wie *apakena asai* (Diatok), jemand mit einem "doppelten Blick" auch. Der Marabut kann für die *anyalen* eine Medizin zubereiten, mit der sie sich waschen muss, um sich gegen die böse Kraft, die sie angreift, zu wappnen, oder er gibt den Auftrag, ein Tier zu opfern oder Geld für ein Opfer zu bezahlen. Eine Frau, die ihre Kinder verliert, kann die Verantwortlichkeit für ihre Beschützung auch einem Marabut übergeben. Aber der Marabut verlangt Geld für die Medizin, das sie oft genug nicht hat. Sie ist auch im materiellen Bereich auf die Unterstützung der anderen Frauen angewiesen.

Manche islamitischen Regeln lassen sich nicht gut mit der *kanyalen*-Institution vereinbaren. Ein Marabut verlangte z.B. von einer Frau, nur die islamitische Heilmethode anzuwenden. Trotzdem initiierten die Frauen sie zur *anyalen*. Der Marabut war nicht damit einverstanden, dass die Frau tanzte. Die Frau tat es aber doch, "um sich bei den Leuten wohlzufühlen". Sie bekam von den Frauen eine Kalebasse, auch das war nicht im Sinne des Marabut. Diese Frau nennt sich nicht eine *anyalen,* wird aber von den anderen Frauen als solche behandelt. Während Festlichkeiten wird sie mit ihrem *anyalen*-Namen angesprochen und zu den anderen *bunyalen* gesetzt. - Es ist aber auch möglich, dass ein Marabut aufträgt, eine Frau zur *anyalen* zu initiieren. Wie erwähnt kann er eine Frau auch der Hexerei bezichtigen, eine schwere Anklage, die Frau wird alles daransetzen, um die für sie Verantwortlichen vom Gegenteil zu überzeugen.

Die *kanyalen*-Gesellschaft

In Ziguinchor gibt es eine große *kanyalen*-Gesellschaft, die unter der Leitung einer Präsidentin vorsteht mit altersbedingter Hierarchie. Jedes Stadtviertel hat seine eigene Gesellschaft. Man kann die Gesellschaft mieten, z.B. wenn Leute für den Reisanbau gebraucht werden. Außerdem kommt die Gesellschaft zusammen, wenn eines ihrer Mitglieder ein Fest feiert. Journet berichtet, dass eine *anyalen* in der Stadt strenger behandelt wird als im Dorf. Im Gegensatz zu dem, was Fassin für Pikine (Dakar) beschreibt, sind in Ziguinchor die Rituale noch genau so wichtig wie in den Dörfern (JOURNET 1991:29 en FASSIN 1987:64-67). In den untersuchten Dörfern ist die *kanyalen*-Institution nicht straff organisiert. In Kandiou haben die Frauen einen heiligen Ort, *fudiodiaf,* zusammen mit den Frauen des Dorfes Djendjelate, das einen Kilometer von Kandiou entfernt liegt. Hier werden die Frauen zu *bunyalen* initiiert. Die *bunyalen* treten während Festlichkeiten zusammen auf und essen zusammen von den anderen Generationsgenossinnen getrennt. (Es ist üblich, dass während der Rituale oder anderer Zusammenkünfte jede Generation zusammen isst). - In Diatock treffen sich die *bunyalen* zur Hochzeit eines ihrer Kinder. Sie tanzen und beten zusammen für das Brautpaar. Die Initiation zur *anyalen* findet in Heiligtümern, *touba* und *adjarimandjor,* statt, die auch für Männer zugänglich sind. - In Thionck Essyl gibt es offiziell keine *kanyalen*-Organisation, aber man kann diese Frauengruppe zur Arbeit auf dem Feld mieten, in gewisser Hinsicht kann man also auch hier von einer Gesellschaft sprechen. Warum gibt es in der Stadt im Gegensatz zum Dorf eine echte *kanyalen*-Gesellschaft? Oder bezeichnet man sie im Dorf nur nicht als Organisation, obwohl es offensichtlich Organisationsformen gibt? Vielleicht hängt das zusammen mit dem wachsenden Druck, den die Männer ausüben, um die *kanyalen*-Institution abzuschaffen. Solange die Frauen in den Dörfern behaupten, dass es gar keine Organisation gibt, können die Männer weniger dagegen opponieren. In der Stadt spürt man diesen Druck nicht so, weil die Gruppe der Frauen viel größer ist.

Kanyalen und die Männer
Ist die Frau einmal zur *anyalen* initiiert, ändert sich ihr Verhältnis zu ihrem Ehemann einschneidend. Er hat ja keine Machtbefugnis mehr über sie , wenn sie das Haus verlassen hat. Das heißt aber nicht, dass er nicht auch die Initiative ergreifen könnte, seine Frau diese Maske tragen zu lassen. Wenn die Frau nach Verlauf zweier Jahre wieder zu ihrem Ehemann zurückkehrt, wird ein mit einer Hochzeit vergleichbares Fest veranstaltet. Es hat den Anschein, als ob der Mann eine neue Frau heiratet, sie bekommt neuen Hausrat und neue Kleider. Denn sie ist ja jetzt eine *anyalen,* hinter ihrer *kanyalen*-Maske bleibt ihre alte Identität verborgen. Wie aus einem der zitierten Lieder einer *anyalen* ersichtlich ist, können auch die Ehemänner als Ursache des Übels verantwortlich gemacht werden.

In manchen Fällen legt eine *anyalen* nach dem Tod ihres Mannes die Maske ab. Eine Erklärung hierfür könnte sein, dass hier der Mann der Verursacher des vorzeitigen Kindersterbens war. Denn im allgemeinen bleibt die Frau auch nach dem Tod ihres Mannes eine *anyalen.* Zwar kann sie keine Kinder mehr bekommen, aber man glaubt, dass auch ihre Enkel noch von dem bösen Geist bedroht werden können, es sei denn, die Schuld hat beim Mann gelegen, dann verschwindet mit seinem Tod auch die Gefahr für seine Enkel. Auch das Mutter-Sohn-Verhältnis wird durch die *kanyalen*-Maske beeinflusst. Der Sohn erhält einen *anyalen*-Namen und darf an Festen der *bunyalen* teilnehmen. So tanzte der Sohn einer verstorbenen *anyalen* auf einer Hochzeitsfeier im Kostüm einer *anyalen*. Ein Mann kann eine *anyalen* unter seinen Schutz nehmen, z.B.wenn er ein bestimmtes Amt bekleidet, oder einen heiligen Wald besitzt, die Zirkumzision der Jungen ausführt oder ein Marabut ist. In diesen Fällen kann er auch bei der Initiation der *anyalen* anwesend sein. So laufen also verschiedene Linien von der Männerwelt zur Frauenwelt. Warum wollen die Männer in Thionck Essyl dann, dass die Frauen die *kanyalen*-Maske abschaffen? An erster Stelle werden wirtschaftliche Argumente angeführt. Die Initiation koste zu viel Geld, und auch sei die Medizin für die Frauen, die sich dafür verbürgen, zu teuer. Nach Meinung der Männer sollten die Frauen das Geld anderweitig ausgeben. Sie selbst müssen auch eine große Summe bezahlen, wenn ihre Frau eine *anyalen* ist. Bei ihrer Rückkehr nach zwei Jahren muss der Ehemann genau so viel ausgeben, wie bei einer neuen Heirat (siehe auch JOURNET 1991:33). Die Frauen in Thionck Essyl haben vorläufig nicht vor, die *kanyalen*-Institution aufzugeben. Sie glauben an die Effektivität der Maske. Eigene Kindern erhöhen ihren Status im Haushalt, ohne Kinder haben sie kein Mitbestimmungsrecht. Diejenigen Frauen, die eine *anyalen* in ihren Schutz nehmen, übernehmen für zwei Jahre die Machtbefugnis des Ehemannes über diese machtlose Frau, um dafür zu sorgen, dass auch die *anyalen* wieder Nachkommen bekommt. Obwohl sie dazu verurteilt sein wird, ihr weiteres Leben die Maske zu tragen, droht ihr, wenn es ihr gelingt, ihre Kinder am Leben zu erhalten, kein Ausschluss aus der Gemeinschaft wie es der unfruchtbaren Frau geschehen kann. Die Frauen haben die *kanyalen*-Maske also geschaffen, um die Macht der Prokreation in ihren Händen zu halten, und aus Solidarität mit denjenigen Frauen, die Schwierigkeiten mit der Prokreation haben. Es ist eine traditionelle Institution, die sich schlecht mit dem Islam in Einklang bringen lässt, und das ist ein Grund mehr für die Männer, diese Institution abschaffen zu wollen. Sie sähen es lieber, dass ein Marabut die Frauen heilte.

Es gibt noch eine weitere Erklärungsmöglichkeit für den wachsenden Widerstand der Männer gegen diese Institution: Wie Journet beschreibt, dürfen sich die Männer von einer *anyalen* nicht scheiden lassen. (JOURNET 1991:38). Die Männer möchten wohl auch die Macht der Frauen als Gruppe einschränken. Und eine Gelegenheit, das zu erreichen, ist der Kampf gegen die *kanyalen*-Maske.

References
FASSIN, D. and IBRAHIMA BADJI. 1986. Ritual buffoonery: a social preventive measure against childhood mortality in Senegal. *The Lancet* january 18:142-143.
FASSIN, D. 1987. Rituels villageois, rituels urbains. La reproduction sociale chez les femmes joola du Sénégal. *L'Homme* 104 oct.-déc.:54-75.
GENNEP, V. 1960. *The rites of passage.* Routledge and Kegan Paul.
JOURNET, O. 1981. La quete de l'enfant. Représentation de la maternité et rituels de stérilité dans la société Diola de Basse-Casamance. *Journal des Africanistes* 51 fasc.1-2:98-115.
JOURNET, O. 1991. Un rituel de présrvation de la descendance: le kanyaalen Joola. in *Grossesse et petite enfance en Afrique noire et à Madagascar.* Edited by DOMINIQUE DESJEUX, pp. 19-39. Editions L'Harmattan Paris.
TURNER, V. 1969. *The Ritual Process.* Routledge and Kegan Paul.
WEIL, P.M. 1976. The state of life: food and female fertility in a West African society. *Africa* 46-2: 182-195.

The Missing Component in Family Planning in Tanzania
Der fehlende Faktor in der Familienplanung in Tansania

Edmund J. Kayombo, K. W. Afework & Armin Prinz

Abstract: Less than 8% of people living in south of the Saharan countries are using the modern contraceptives. Factors which account for low use of modern contraceptives are inadequate of contraceptives, lack of competent personnel for providing the services and political will. Cultural component does not feature much as a factor of low users of contraceptives. This article shows there is a missing component (cultural component) in family planning in Tanzania. It traces cultural component in FP programmes in Tanzania from 1959 up todate. It shows only 11% of women in Tanzania are using modern contraceptives and 42% of these women are in Dar-Es-Salaam and in some regions have between less than one to one percent of the total users. The most commonly used contraceptive is pill (87%). The article shows the major weakness of Tanzania FP is to neglect the cultural component and the traditional methods used for FP. It further shows various traditional methods used for FP in Tanzania from time immemorial and are possible being used by regions which have low users of modern contraceptives. The paper calls for scientist and researchers to identify the traditional methods used for the FP and assess them in terms of effectiveness and safety. Those found effective with insignificant side effects should be encouraged to be used so as to supplement the reported inadequacy of the modern contraceptives. It strongly argues there is no way developing countries can improve the health well being of the families, enhance quality of life, promote economic growth and overall social development without incorporating FP programme.

Zusammenfassung: Weniger als 8 Prozent der Bevölkerung der Länder südlich der Sahara benutzen moderne Kontrazeptiva. Für diesen geringen Verbrauch moderner Kontrazeptiva verantwortliche Faktoren sind die Unzulänglichkeit der Verhütungsmittel, Mangel an kompetentem Personal für das Versorgungsnetz und fehlender politischer Wille. Die kulturelle Komponente spielt für die seltene Anwendung von Verhütungsmitteln keine große Rolle. Der vorliegende Beitrag zeigt, dass ein fehlender Faktor (kulturelle Komponente) in der Familienplanung in Tansania besteht. Die kulturelle Komponente in den Familienplanungsprogrammen in Tansania von 1959 bis heute wird dargestellt. Die Untersuchung zeigt, dass nur 11 Prozent der tansanischen Frauen moderne Verhütungsmittel benutzen, von diesen 42 Prozent in Dar-Es-Salaam leben und in einigen Gegenden höchstens bis zu einem Prozent der gesamten Nutzerinnen. Das am häufigsten benutzte Kontrazeptivum ist die Pille (87 Prozent). Der Beitrag zeigt, dass die größte Schwäche der tansanischen Familienplanung darin besteht, dass die kulturelle Komponente und die traditionellen Methoden der Familienplanung vernachlässigt werden. Außerdem werden verschiedene traditionelle Methoden der Familienplanung aufgezeigt, die seit undenklichen Zeiten in Tansania angewandt werden und für Regionen geeignet wären, in denen moderne Kontrazeptiva wenig benutzt werden. Wissenschaftler und Forscher sind vonnöten, um die traditionellen Familienplanungsmethoden zu identifizieren und ihre Wirksamkeit und Sicherheit zu beurteilen. Die Anwendung der als wirksam erkannten Methoden mit unbedeutenden Nebenwirkungen sollte propagiert werden, um die erwähnte Unzulänglichkeit moderner Kontrazeptiva zu kompensieren. Ohne die Einbeziehung von Programmen zur Familienplanung, so das strenge Fazit des Berichts, haben Entwicklungsländer keine Möglichkeit, den Gesundheitszustand der Familien zu bessern, die Lebensqualität zu fördern, wirtschaftliches Wachstum und die gesellschaftliche Entwicklung insgesamt zu steigern.

Keywords: Africa, Tanzania, Family planning, Contraceptives, Traditional medicine, Afrika, Tansania, Familienplanung, Verhütungsmittel, traditionelle Medizin.

1. Introduction

Africa South of Sahara has been observed to have less than 8% users of modern contraceptives (BRYANT 1994, KAYOMBO 1995a). DESTLER et al (1990) and KELLER et al (1989) have shown that, it is in the first stage (Emergent) of growth of (FP). But African governments South of the Sahara have accepted FP in 1970's and some countries have integrated in maternal and child health care (BRYANT 1994, MINISTRY OF HEALTH 1989). Why should be such low percentage users of modern contraceptives?

MINISTRY OF HEALTH (1989), MASTROIANNI (1990) BRYANT (1994), and KAYOMBO (1995a) have shown that, there has been scarcity of contraceptive materials, lack of competent personnel for FP services and as well as political will to implement the FP programmes. But, fewer users of modern contraceptives in African countries south of Sahara cannot be explained only by lack of availability of contraceptive, competent personnel and political will, but as well as how safe, effective and acceptable are these contraceptives within cultural, social and ethical frame work of individual. Again why emphasis is only to modern contraceptives and not to the traditional ones which had been used from time immemorial (HIMES 1963, MOLNOS 1973, ROBERTSON 1990)?. This calls another important valuable which is not always discussed adequately and that is the cultural components and in particularly, the traditional methods of birth control in African countries, South of Sahara and its impacts in family planning programmes.

Family planning (FP) in this article, is defined as process which enable the couple, individual to plan when one or the couple wishes to conceive, and be full aware of the responsibility in doing so, and the methods which are health and cultural accepted in the community of achieving this goal are available and accessible. Whereas, Cultural components in this article involves traditional beliefs, taboos, age at marriage practice of child births and methods of birth control. It also include value of the children, social structures and traditional health care system. All these interact with each other and make the individual to behave in the expected way of the community in all aspects of life in the community, otherwise the individual may be seen as a transgressor of the norms of community. As shown by MASTROAIANNI (1990), ROBERTSON (1990) COEYTAUX (1987) and MOLNOS (1973) cultural component has an important role in promoting FP programme in any community. This article traces cultural components, particularly traditional methods of birth control and their impact in FP in Tanzania mainland.

2. Status of FP in Tanzania Todate

Tanzania is in East Africa and is composed of Tanzania Mainland and Zanzibar and Pemba Islands. Tanzania mainland has a total population of 27 million people (estimated from 1988 Population Census) with growth rate of 2.8%. Family Planning programmes (FPPs) in Tanzania Mainland is divided into three major periods: the initial stage (1959-1973), integrated family planning programme and maternal child health care (1974-1984) and National Family planning: Plan for Operation (1983-1993) the programme which is still taking place todate.

The National Family Planning Programme (NFPP): Plan for operation (1983-1993) was designed after evaluating the past trend of FPPs from 1959-1983. The overall goal of the NFPP was to promote FP and protect health and nutritional status of family health especially the mother and children. The broad objectives was to raise contraceptives acceptance from about 7% to 25% by 1993. To implement the programme, six alternatives strategies for delivering of this FP were suggested. The first alternative was community based distribution (CBD) of contraceptives whose objectives was to utilize non prescription of contraceptives like condoms, foams, spermicides and others.The second, was integrated FP approach whose objectives included tackling several problems which were interlinked. The third, was integrated FP with other primary health care (PHC) programmes.The fourth approach, was counseling on clients who were in need of FP. The fifth alternative approach, was to see FP as a social problem and hence it involved every body in the community, and the sixth alternative, was social mobilization and advocacy for FP strategy to the public in general.

Out of six alternatives, only two approaches are being implemented. These are community based distribution (CBD) approach which is now being implemented in Bagamoyo districts in coastal region, and it is reported to be doing well (NATIONAL FAMILY PLANNING and AMREF 1992). The other one is integrated FP approach, which is being implemented in Kilimanjaro region and it is reported that it has increased the acceptance rate of contraceptives in both rural and urban centres by almost 50% from the previous programmes (NATIONAL FAMILY PLANNING and AMREF 1992).

All these programmes together have increased an awareness on the need of FP services; and more than 70% of Tanzania population know more than one modern method of FP (MINISTRY OF HEALTH 1989, NGALABA et al 1993). Recent studies show about 11% women are using modern contraceptives (NGALABA 1993, KAYOMBO 1995a) and about 30% of the unmet needs of FP (VOGEL 1993). The most commonly used contraceptives are pills (87%), loop (3%), condom and Depo provera (2% each) and whereas spemicides is approximately half percent (TANZANIA 1992, NGALABA et al 1993) (see fig.1 and 2). TANZANIA (1992) has further shown there are other methods used by people for birth control, but were not spelt out. It is perhaps sterilization, injectables, vasectomy, norplant and etc. But it is not likely to be the traditional methods because the users are more than the ones stated (KAYOMBO 1992, SAFE MOTHERHOOD WORKSHOP 1992).

Evaluating the type of contraceptives used in Tanzania, one could be tempted to think that the programmes of FPPs are targeting to women only, as FP is their business. For example, examining fig. 1 one could expect to see the condom users to be increasing with time as a measure for preventing unwanted pregnancy and AIDs, whose prevalence rate is 3% (WORLD BANK 1992). But in contrast, only very few men are using condoms; as opposed to Taiwan where condom users are increasing with time (FREEDMAN et al 1976). The type of contraceptives used in Tanzania are also noted in other countries, South of the Sahara (KAYOMBO 1995A, BRYANT et al 1994). The contraceptives used in FPPs in Tanzania (and as well African countries South of the Sahara) suggest that FPPs managers appear to be stereo type of thinking that man does not care about FP. Otherwise one could note an increasing use of male oriented contraceptives such as condoms and vasectomy.

Decision and action to use contraceptives in many communities involves individuals, couples, families mother in-laws aunts and even peer group (KAYOMBO 1990, COOPERATING AGENCIES TASK FORCE 1989, UNITED NATIONS (UN) 1984). Again researchers in Africa about FP, show men often know more about contraceptives and may have favorable attitude towards use of contraceptives (BRYANT et al 1994). Furthermore it has been observed in African countries man have the decision power in households economies (MCCAULEY 1994) and half of reproduction equation are men. All these aspects are not featuring well in FPPs in Tanzania. Thus, it is being argued here that FPPs should address to these aspects as well and men should be targeted in FP programmes.

Looking at FP in Tanzania again, it appears the programmes aims to fulfill demographic and environment objective which is to limit population growth at any cost. It seems that infertility is not a problem. But studies on population are estimating that about one in ten couples are involuntary infertile, and in some areas where population growth has been most dramatic, infertile is also endemic occurring in as many as 20% couple (MASTOIANNI 1990). The author of this paper has met several women in Tanzania going to various healers in search of getting traditional medicine so that they can have a baby and some have been successful, after failing to get such services from formal hospitals. It follows then, to promote FP in any community, it should satisfy the unmet needs such as to assist the needs of couple or individual who wants to have a baby.

Furthermore, it has been observed that, belief system which women and sometimes man have internalized in their mind, carry certain number of children of both sexes whom they want to be born (KAYOMBO 1995A, BRYANT et al 1994). Therefore, these women continue bearing children regardless of information on the control of fertility. These kind of people need to be identified when attending MCH clinic, and effectively counseled on the side effect of continual child birth. In addition, FP service providers should be cautious on the negative attitude towards certain medical procedures which sometimes are unnecessary such as pelvic examination may deter, otherwise motivated people from seeking FP. Again some clients need privacy or confidentiality at FP clinics particularly on issues of reproduction (in most African countries human reproduction issues are not spoken openly) (Aferwork et al forthcoming), competent counselors, friendly personnel and opportunity on informed choice about contraception.

Moreover, examining fig. 2, most of continuing users of modern contraceptives are from Dar-Es-Salaam city (42%). It is likely that even in other regions of Tanzania most of modern contraceptives users are urban population. In some regions like Kagera, Rukwa, Tabora and Mara (see fig. 2.) the modern contraceptives users are between less than one to one percent of total users of contraceptives. However, examining family size in these regions is between 6-5 person per household, whereas the National average is 5 people per household. In Dar-Es-Salaam, on the otherhand, family size is 4.3 (1988 Population Census, NGALABA et al 1993). It can be argued that, definitely this people are using certain forms of contraceptives for birth control, otherwise the family size would be remarkable high (more than seven people) in region which do not use the modern contraceptives. But what methods do they use to control births other than modern contraceptives?

3. The missing component in FPPs in Tanzania
FP is a process which has been practiced from time immemorial and is coined in the cultural system in any community (MOLNOS 1973, HIMES 1963, ROBERTSON 1990 GRANT 1992). Thus, for effective FPP,FP managers have to go to people in their respective communities and establish what they do, know, think and believe about FP and marry this with whatever the FPP managers think about FPP in the community.

But ‚examining all FPPs in Tanzania together one could note that, the cultural component which is supposed to link with other components in FP such as economic, health facilities, technology for FP and political involvement was not included. Managers of FP in Tanzania appear to assume that there were no traditional FP methods. But, records show before introduction of modern contraceptives, child spacing was 2-3 years (SWANTZ 1966, MOLNOS 1973). MOLNOS (1973) has also pointed out that, frequent births were seen as „animal like". The wide range of child spacing were guided by beliefs, taboos which were interwoven in the cultural system of the community, and every body involved in reproduction were to adhere to these restrictions. The wide child spacing was also noted in all countries South of the Sahara (MOLNOS 1973). The child spacing noted before introduction of modern contraceptives in Tanzania (and south of the Saharan countries) suggests that these people were aware of Malthus theory that, too great a population endangered survival of people in the community

In addition, to belief and taboos, there were traditional gadgets which were used to control births. For example, SWANTZ (1966), KAYOMBO (1992) and SAFE MOTHERHOOD WORKSHOP (1992) have pointed out that, one method which was used as control birth was a string which had two knots in which medicine were tied into it. It was to be worn by women on waist with one of the knots in front and the other behind and was to be removed when individual or couple wanted to have a baby. The string was carefully kept to be used again after delivery. Again, SAFE MOTHERHOOD WORKSHOP (1992) reported that, in some tribes if a woman became pregnant before time allowed, she could take an oral medicine which arrested the growth of foetus until time for her to conceive was ready. Similar method was reported by SWANTZ (1966) among the Wanyamwezi in Tabora region.

Again, KAYOMBO (1992) has shown that one healer in Dodoma region dispensed concussion to child bearing women for birth control. The concussion was to be drunk for three days immediately after menstruation period. While taking the drug, the women should abstain from sexual relation. Concussion used as a method for birth control has also been reported by RAUM (1967) among the Wachagga, SAFE MOTHERHOOD WORKSHOP (1992) around lake Victoria Zone, SWANTZ (1966) and IBRAHIM (1967) among the Wanyamwezi of Tabora region. Furthermore, Safe Motherhood workshop has shown among the Wachagaa, women married to brothers tried to regulate times when they should have babies so that one group of women could provide services for the one who has just delivered. Women also were able to prevent unwanted pregnancies by taking herbal medicine.

The author of this paper while in the field study in Mbeya rural districtin1990, the headmistress of one primary school told him that many primary school girls in her school were involved in premarital sex but she did not had problem of pregnancies as in other primary schools in the region. The author attempted to inquire from the TBAs who were his study population, if their were any medicine given to adolescence to prevent any unwanted pregnancies. At first, TBAs resisted, but through discussion of various gynaecological problems they handled in the study area, it was learnt that, adolescent girls were given medicine to prevent from unwanted pregnancy. It can be argued thus, pre introduction of modern contraceptives,these people had their preventive techniques to prevent the unwanted pregnancy. The herbs which have been used since time immemorial are likely to have an effective remedy for contraception.

Besides, providing FP for limiting births in traditional health care system, they also assisted the individual or the couple who did not have a baby and wanted to have a baby by the use of herbal medicine (HERDBERG et al 1982). They also provided herbal drug to individual or couple who had only one sex of their children to have the alternative sex as well, and treated gynaecological problems. HERDBERG et al (1982) and MBURA et al (1985) have shown various medicinal plants used in traditional health care system for treatment of gynaecological problems, sexual transmitted diseases and infertility. For example, HERDBEG et al (1982) have shown that „Mtogo" (Diplorhynchus welwtitschii) medicinal plant, its stem is used to treat fluidity of semen, whereas „mtopetope" or „mbokwe" (annona senegalensis latifolia) is used to treat sterility and produce lactation. Again, they have shown „mfume" (sterculia cfr appendiculata K) and „mnyakun" (conmiphora pugnensis) medicinal plants are used to treat excessive bleeding during menstruation.

There are many medicinal plants used in traditional health care system which are interwoven in the culture of the community. Looking in the traditional FP services, one can note that it was a complete set which satisfies both needs for those who want to have children and the sex preference and those to limit birth control and as well as for reproduction of health care. This might be one of the possible explanation why more than two thirds of world child bearing women prefer to deliver at home with the assistance from traditional health care providers, particularly the TBAs (KAYOMBO 1995B, BRYANT et al 1994, COSMINSKY 1983). It is likely that TBAs are also providing traditional FP services.

These methods used for contraception in Tanzania are also reported in various countries in the world (MOLNOS 1973, HIMES 1963, ROBERTSON 1990, GRANT 1992) . For example, the Cherokee Indians of North America used herbal remedies for contraception purposes (ROBERTSON 1990). The Guyana and Martinique used solution consisting of Lemons juice and an essence derived from Mahogany husky (ROBERTSON 1990). As argued by GRANT (1992), most methods of regulating fertility are controlled by women and communicated intergenerationally and through midwives or other female healers and herbalist. GRANT (1992) has also shown, many Third World Women today continue using indigenous methods of birth control passed on through female support network, especial those transmitted by their own mothers and grandmothers. It is likely that these methods are being used today in Tanzania (and some other African countries) by regions who had fewer users of modern contraceptives, hence they require an assessment in terms of effectiveness and health side effects. It has to be noted many women are suspicious with modern contraceptives and hence refuse to risk injury for the sake of reputed enhanced effectiveness of commercial methods (GRANT 1992). They would prefer to use the known traditional methods for FP services.

The botanist, pharmacist, anthropologist and medical doctors should look at traditional methods used in FP and see how they can be incorporated in the present FPPs. For example, after identification of botanical names of medicinal plants used for FP, treating gynaecological problems, their toxicity level could be checked through literature search by the use of Botanical Abstract Index or NAPLALET or screening the medicinal plants in laboratory to determine the active ingredients and toxicity level. The medicinal plants which have positive effect in FP and had no significant health side effects to users should be encouraged to be used, while further studies are being carried in identified medicinal plants to determine the active ingredients. Besides the medicinal plants, other methods used in traditional FP should be evaluated and see their effectiveness in birth control. The effective materials and medicinal plants could supplement the reported unmet needs of FP in Tanzania and other parts of the world.

It has to be noted that the unmet needs of FP would increase global as an impact of promotion on use of modern contraceptives which is being carried world wide. More than half of supply of modern contraceptives in developing countries is funded by donors. According to CONLY et al (1993) and MASTROIANNI (1990) it is likely that in some years to come, funding from donors may be limited. It is thus being argued here that special emphasis should be looking on traditional methods and modifying them where necessary to fit to the present situation of FP. These will reduce too much reliance on imported knowledge of FP and other health problems in detrimental of traditional medicine and its resources. Furthermore, it has to be noted that modern knowledge on contraceptives are often imposed and inflexible. Some modern contraceptives had been reported to have serious side effect to users (FORSTER 1978, BUSTAN et al 1993, AKHTER et al 1993).

4. Conclusion

The article has shown the cultural component in FPPs in Tanzania was not included. Similar problem is noted in other countries South of the Sahara which have lowest number of modern contraceptives users (KAYOMBO 1995A, BRYANT 1994). But for an effective programme on FP it should include the cultural component which have to link with other components such as economic, health facilities, technology involved in FP and the political component .When these are in balance are likely to promote users of FP services. It has to be noted that not only providing convenient, high technical quality is important, but also overcoming the political, social, informational, psychological and administrative barriers that keeps away people from using contraceptives or that make difficult for them to use FP effectively (MASTROIANNI 1990 BRYANT et al 1994). Furthermore, traditional methods which have been used from time immemorial are continual being used today in many developing countries (GRANT 1992, MASTROIANNI 1990 KAYOMBO 1992), and hence need to be researched and see in what ways can be incorporated in NFPPs.

It is to be noted that, if cultural component is included in FPP has significant effect to users. For example, in Tunisia it has been reported that the national FP (ONFP) was able to provide more comprehensive reproductive health care in one hospital by stressing the cultural significance of the 40th day postpartum, the end of seclusion for mothers and the new borne. ONFP designated the 40th day for follow up and made available of neonatal, postpartum and FP services to women in a single clinic. In 1987, study showed that 83% of new mothers turned for the 40th day check up. Of these 56% began using FP methods (COEYTAUX 1989). The approach now is being expanded to the entire country.

All in all, research programmes on FP should asses whether clients are receiving the intended level care and what impact this has in both short and long run. Effort is required by researchers, the government, non government organization to look in detail on the traditional methods used in FP and see their effectiveness. Furthermore there is a need to look into all customs and try to find the rationality behind of using these traditional methods for FP and link with the health of the baby and the mother. Above all, researchers should try to find proper methods both traditional and non traditional of FP, which are culturally accepted and affordable and these should be promoted at any cost to everybody. Emphasis should be given to the traditional ones because, Tanzania has the resource and what is needed is to exploit this resource for the health of the mother, child and the whole nation at large. There is no way developing countries can improve the health well being of the families, enhance quality of life, promote economic growth and overall social development without incorporating FP programme.

References

AFEWORK, K.W., et al. (forthcoming)Preparation of rural adolescent girls to adulthood in Fitche disrict, Ethiopia, In: *Women and Health*, Edited by GOTTSCHALK-BATSCHKUS et al. VWB Berlin,Germany.

ARKHTER, H et al 1993. Five -Year Clinical Evaluation Norplant Contraceptives Subdermal Implants in *Bangladesh Acceptors Contraception* 47:569-582.

BRYANT, ROBEY M. A, PHYLLIS TILSON PIOTROW and CYNTHIA SALTER 1994. *Making Programs Work Maryland:* Johns Hopkins School public Health, Population Information Programme, Population Reports Series M. Number 12 December.

BUSTAN, M. N. 1993 Oral Contraceptive Use and Breast Cancer in Indonisia *Contraception*, 47, 241-249.

COEYTAUX, F. 1989. Celebrating Mother and Child on the Fortieth: The Sfax Tunisia Postpartum Program. *Quality/Candid/ Qualite* 1: 1-24 March.

CONY, S. R. and SPEIDEL, I. J.1993. *Global Population Assistance. A Report Card on Major Donor Countries* .Washington D. C. Population International.

COOPERATING AGENCIES TASK FORCE 1989. *Informed choice: Report of Cooperation Agencies Task Forces*, P 34. Baltmore ,Maryland: Johns Hopkins School public Health, Health Centre for Communication July.

COSMINSKY, S.1983. Traditional Midwifery and Contraception. In *Traditional Medicine and Health Care Coverage* Edited by R. H. BANNERMAN, JOHN BURTON and CH'EN WEN-CHIEH pp. 142-162 WHO Geneva.

DESTLER, H. , H. LIBERI, D. SMITH, J. and STOVER, I 1990. P*reparing for the twenty -first century. Principles for FP services Delivery in the Nineties.* pp. 60 . Washington D . C. United States Agency for International Development office of Population. November.

FREEDMAN, R. and BERELSON, B. 1976. The record of FP programme. *Studies in Family Planning* 7(1) January pp. 1-40.

FORSTER , G. M and B, G, ANDERSON. 1978. *Medical Anthropology* New York Willey.

GRANT, N .1992. *The selling of Contraception* Ohio State University Press Columbus.

HERDBERG, I et al 1982. Inventory of Plants used in Traditional Medicine in Tanzania. 1. Plants of Families of Acanthaceae - Cucurbittaceae. *Journal of Ethnopharmacology* 6 pp. 29-60.

HIMES, N. E. 1963. *Medical History of Contraception* New York Gamut Press Inc.

KAYOMBO, E. J. 1989. *Traditional Cultural Influence Health its Role in Modern Health Care. A case of Tanzania* A paper Presented to a Seminar of Women and Health Safe Motherhood Initiative maternal Mortality Morbidity in Tanzania 13th-14th November.

_____1990. *Traditional Health Practices Beliefs Taboos as they Affect Community* A paper Presented to Women and Health Workshop on Traditional Health practices Mombassa Feb. 12-24.

_____ 1992. *Distribution of Traditional Birth Attendants and Herbalist in and Singida Regions.* A consultant Report Submitted to Director of AMREF and The National Family Planning Programme in Tanzania.

_____1995a. Legalizing Abortion and Its Health Implications in African Countries .In *Disasters, Accidents ,Violence and Health in Africa* Proceedings of Joint TPHA 12 th Annual and ESCAPHA 2nd Biennial Scientific Conference on October 25th-29th .Edited by J. Z. KILLEWO ARUSHA. Tanzania.

_____1995b Traditional Birth Attendants (TBAs) and Maternal Care in Tanzania. In *Political Economy of Health Care in Sub-Saharan Africa.* Edited by EZEKIEL et al University of Illinois Arbana Chapter 9.

IBRAHIM R. G.1967. *The people of Great Unyamwezi Tanzania* International African Institute London.
KELLER, A., SEVEREYNS, P. KNAN and DODD, N. 1989. *Towards Family Planning in the 1990s.* A review and Assessment. International Family Planning Perspective 15(4) pp. 127-135.
MASTROIANNI, L 1990 Forward. In *An Illustrated History of Contraception.* Edited by ROBERTSON W. H. 1990 The Parthenon Publishing Group. pp. 11-13 New Jersey USA.
MCCAULEY, A. P., ROBEY, B., BLANK, A. K. and GELLER, J. S.1994. *Opportunity for Women Through Reproductive Choice.* Baltmore Maryland: Johns Hopkins School public Health, Population Information Programme, Population Reports Series M. Number 12 June.
MBURA, J. S .I.; H. N. MGAYA and H. K., HEGEN HOUGEN 1985. The use of oral herbal medicine by women attending Clinic in Rural and Urban Areas Tanga District *East African Medical Journal* pp. 541-544.
MINISTRY OF HEALTH 1988 *The National Family Planning Programme: Plan for Operation* Dar-ES Salaam Government Printers.
MOLNOS, A.1973. *Cultural Source Material for Population Planning in East Africa* Vol. III EAP Nairobi.
NATIONAL FAMILY PLANNING and AMREF 1992. National Family Planning and AMREF: *Research Proposal "Expanding Health and Family Planning delivery System Using Traditional health care Practitioners."*
NGALABA, S., S. H. KAPIGA, RUYOBA, I., I. TIES BOERMA 1993. *Tanzania Demographic and Health Survey 1991/1992.* Bureau of Statistics Planning Commission Tanzania Dar-Es-Salaam.
RAUM, O. F. 1967. *Chagga Childhood* OUP
ROBERTSON W. H. 1990. *An Illustrated History of Contraception* The Parthenon Publishing Group New Jersey USA
SAFE MOTHERHOOD WORKSHOP 1992. *Workshop Report on Safe Motherhood* Initiative in the context of Continuing Health Practices in Tanzania. University of Dar-Es-Salaam. 13th-14th June.
SWANTZ, L. M. 1966. *Religious and magical Rites of Bantu Women in Tanzania* M. Phil Thesis Helsinki
TANZANIA 1992. *Health Statistics 1990.* Bureau of Statistics President's office Planning Commission Dar-Es-Salaam.
UNITED REPUBLIC OF TANZANIA 1988 *Population Census Preliminary Report* Bureau of Statistics Ministry of Finance Economic affairs and Planning Dar-Es-Salaam.
UNITED NATIONS (UN) 1984. *Programme of Action of Conference :* Note by Secretary General pp. 83
VOGEL, D. USAID/Tanzania (Response to Questionnaire) December 6 quoted BRYANT, ROBEY M. A, PHYLLIS TILSON PIOTROW and CYNTHIA SALTER 1993. *Making Programs Work.* Baltmore Maryland: Johns Hopkins School public Health, Population Information Programme, Population Reports Series M. Number 12 December
WORD BANK 1992. *Tanzania AIDs Assessment Planning Study 1992* Washington D. C.

Appendix

CONTINUING ACCEPTORS OF FAMILY PLANNING FROM 1983-1989

Year	Pill	Loop	Condom	Depo-Sperm	Others	Total
1983	51752	1843	1277	1569	393	56834
1984	54946	1826	1653	1064	1347	60836
1985	99952	2459	720	890	2244	106265
1986	76565	2387	857	1306	4194	85309
1987	127785	3058	1480	2103	9219	143645
1988	44087	2396	2704	1337	1293	51817
1989	113825	5091	3844	5616	15292	143668
Total	568912	19060	12535	13885	33982	648374

Source: Tanzania 1992. Health Statistics; 1990 Bureau of Statistics President's Office, Planning Commission Dar-Es-Salaam Tanzania (This data has been used in drawing fig. 1 by using percentage)

REGIONAL DISTRIBUTION OF TANZANIA MAINLAND OF CONTINUING USERS OF FAMILY PLANNING

Region	Pill	IUD	Condom	Depo-Sperm	Others	Total	%
Arusha	5207	106	112	11	58	5494	5
Coast	7071	49	40	69	8	7236	8
DSM	33332	1820	319	1235	2230	38935	42
Dodoma	3231	1	42	15	21	3311	4
Iringa	1496	40	124	32	188	1877	2
Kagera	160	1	1	1	546	709	0.01
Kigoma	1639	22	17	5	373	2056	2
Kilimanjaro	3418	218	56	112	194	4053	4
Lindi	963	6	45	10	7	1031	1
Mara	493	15	48	6	1	562	0.6
Mbeya	3632	138	84	21	97	3972	4
Morogoro	3081	35	93	39	126	3374	4
Mtwara	4672	29	10	50	241	500	5
Mwanza	1964	22	37	29	18	2068	2
Rukwa	632	52	107	61	1	859	0.9
Ruvuma	3571	22	12	159	140	390	4
Shinyanga	1947	46	158	56	483	2692	3
Singida	3456	9	67	8	41	3577	4
Tabora	81	8	0	0	1	89	0.01
Tanga	2323	9	55	101	57	2544	3

Source: Tanzania 1992 Health Statistics; 1990 Bureau of Statistics President's Office, Planning Commission Dar-Es-Salaam Tanzania

Note:
1. DSM= Dar-Es-Salaam
2. The Regional Distribution of Continuing Users of Contraception is based on Seven years(from1983-1989) average.
3. This data has been used in drawing fig. 2.

Fig. 1
Continuing Acceptors of Family Planning from 1983-1989

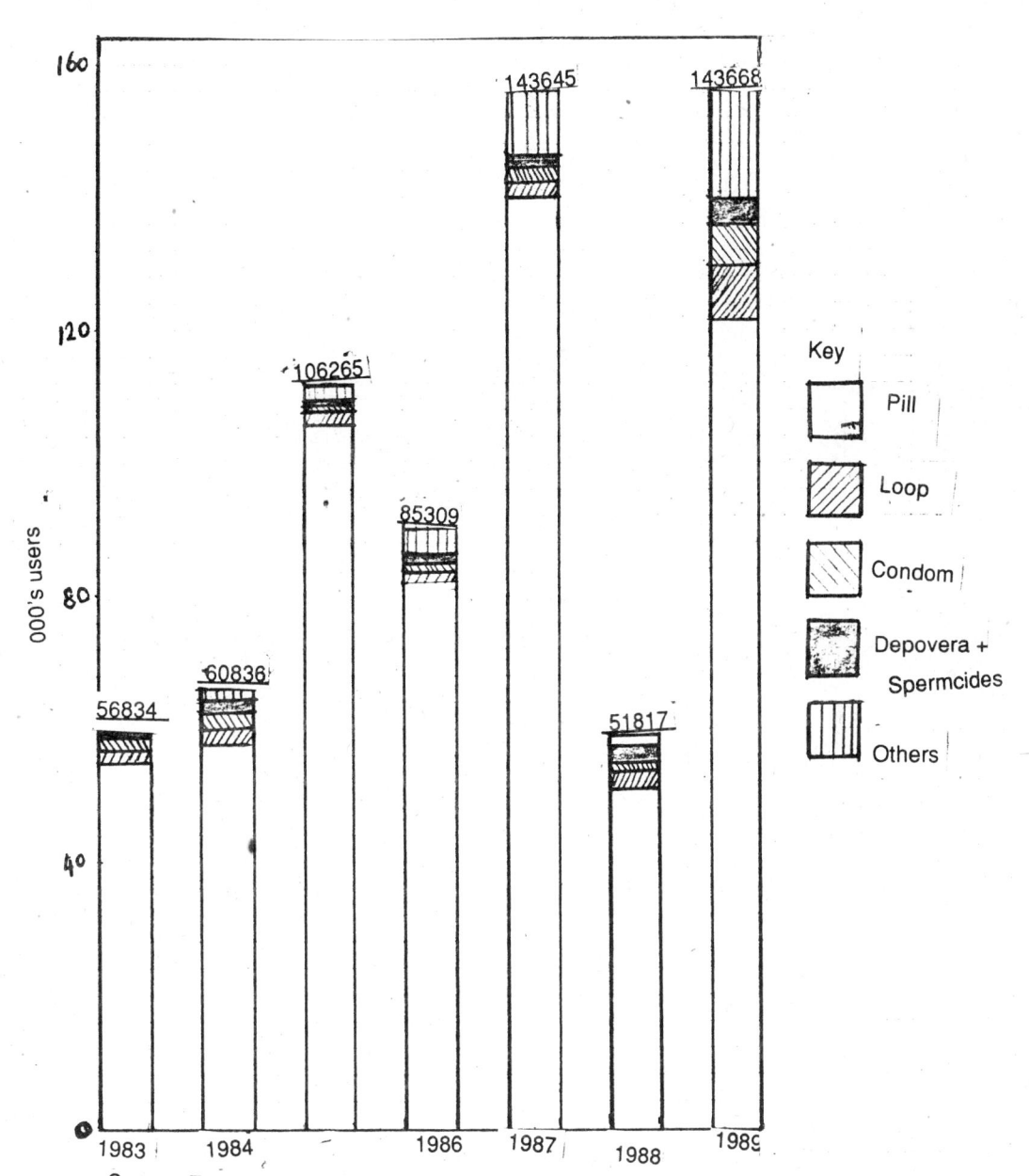

Source: Tanzania 1992 *Health Statistics; 1990* Bureau of Statistics President's Office, Planning Commission Dar-Es-Salaam Tanzania

Fig. 2
Regional Distribution in % of Tanzania Mainland of Continuing User's of Family Planning

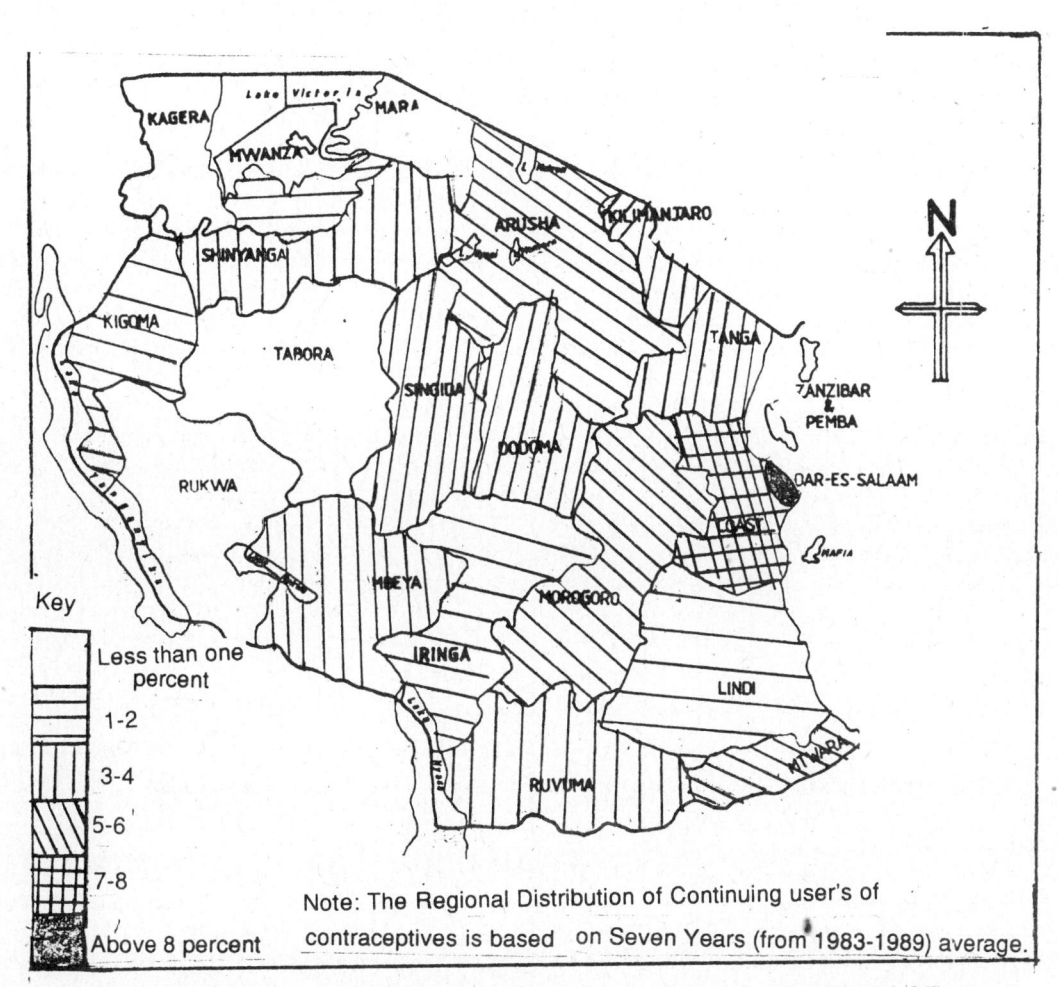

Key:
- Less than one percent
- 1-2
- 3-4
- 5-6
- 7-8
- Above 8 percent

Note: The Regional Distribution of Continuing user's of contraceptives is based on Seven Years (from 1983-1989) average.

Source: Tanzania 1992. *Health Statistics; 1990* Bureau of Statistics President's Office Planning Commission Dar-Es-Salaam Tanzania

Health Definitions of Women in a Low-Standard Settlement of Dar Es Salaam, Tanzania
Gesundheitsdefinitionen von Frauen in einem ärmeren Stadtquartier von Dar es Salaam, Tansania

Brigit Obrist van Eeuwijk

Abstract: Concepts of health are a neglected research issue in medical anthropology. Drawing on ideas developed in sociological studies in France and in the United Kingdom, this paper examines health concepts of middle-aged women in a low-standard, high-density settlement in Dar es Salaam, Tanzania. The present study uses an ethnographic approach and analyzes women's statements about health on two levels: as public discourse and as idiosyncratic beliefs of individual women. On the first level the respondents' statements can be broadly grouped into health concepts referring to „the physical and mental state„ and others relating to „the living conditions„. Individual women draw on these concepts and combine them in packages of ideas, no two of which are identical. Further research is needed to examine whether women with different views of health have different ways of maintaining and promoting health in this particular social and physical environment.

Zusammenfassung: In der Medizinethnologie sind Gesundheitskonzepte ein vernachlässigter Forschungsgegenstand. Dieser Aufsatz nimmt Ideen, die in soziologischen Studien in Frankreich und in England entwickelt wurden, auf und untersucht Gesundheitskonzepte von Frauen mittleren Alters in einem Quartier von Dar es Salaam, Tansania, das einen tiefen Wohnstandard und hohe Dichte aufweist. Die vorliegende Studie verwendet einen ethnographischen Ansatz und analysiert die Aussagen der Frauen bezüglich Gesundheit auf zwei Ebenen: als öffentlicher Diskurs und als je eigene Vorstellungen individueller Frauen. Auf der ersten Ebene können die Aussagen der Befragten grob eingeteilt werden in Gesundheitskonzepte, die sich auf den „physischen und mentalen Zustand„ beziehen, und in andere, die auf „die Lebensumstände„ Bezug nehmen. Individuelle Frauen nehmen diese Konzepte auf und kombinieren sie in „Ideenpaketen„, von denen nicht zwei identisch sind. Weitere Forschungen sind nötig, um zu untersuchen, ob Frauen mit unterschiedlicher Sicht von Gesundheit unterschiedliche Verhaltensweisen aufweisen, um die Gesundheit in dieser sozialen und physischen Umwelt zu erhalten und zu fördern.

Keywords: Health Concepts, Women, Urban Health, Gesundheitskonzepte, Frauen, Städtische Gesundheit.

Introduction

Concepts of health are a neglected research issue in medical anthropology. Although the word „health„ often appears in titles and texts, anthropologists tend to pay more attention to illness. In the widely known textbook „Culture, Health and Illness„ Cecil Helman, for instance, wrote only one paragraph on people's definitions of health (HELMAN 1990:92). Arthur Kleinman, one of the most prominent medical anthropologists, noticed this research gap some time ago: „[...] in Chinese culture we know much less about beliefs regarding health [...] and health maintenance [...] practices than we know about sickness beliefs and treatment practices [...]„ (KLEINMAN 1980:53). To my best knowledge this gap in anthropological research is still very wide.

In sociology, research on people's definition of health has a longer tradition. This type of research considers health and illness as two distinct fields of equal importance. It began, in many respects, with the work of CLAUDINE HERZLICH (1969). This classic study was based on lengthy conversations with eighty people of predominantly middle-class backgrounds in Paris and in the Normandy and a content analysis of these accounts. Herzlich analyzed the health and illness concepts of her respondents as social representations operating both as discourses within the public domain and as explanations used by individuals. She convincingly demonstrated that people drew on multiple conceptions of „healths„ which are co-existing formulations of different aspects.

„Health in a vacuum„ was the term Herzlich coined for the notion of health as the absence of disease. It refers to a state in which the body is silent, so to speak. What she calls „Reserve of Health„ is a concept which regards health as an asset rather than a state. Physical robustness or strength and resistance to attacks, fatigue and illness are emphasized. The third notion Herzlich identified is „Equilibrium„. It refers to „real health„, to a notion of positive well-being which her respondents mentioned frequently but found difficult to explain. On one level they seemed to refer to a substratum of essential harmony and balance in bodily, psychological and spiritual life, on the other to what follows in a functional sense: self-confidence, happiness, having good relations, alertness, energy, and even freedom. Herzlich came to the conclusion that different understandings and explanations for health and illness are not polar opposites to each other, but quite discrete conceptions. Health, so her argument, was seen as coming from within the individual, while illness was conceived of as something external that was produced by the way of life.

Following on from the work of Herzlich, several researchers carried out studies on the British Isles. The best known British research is the ethnographic study of Blaxter and Paterson on health attributes and behaviour of mothers and grandmothers from a working-class background in Aberdeen (1982). More recently, Mildred Paterson carried out a large-scale survey of beliefs about health and illness and links between health and lifestyles (BLAXTER 1990). Much of her work is based on in-depth interviews and content analysis. The overall picture which emerges from her data on older women's understanding of health and illness was one of low expectations. „Good health„ was mainly portrayed as the capacity to function „normally„. Their own behaviour may have a negative effect on health and thus be a reason for ill-health but not its cause. The cause of illness, as the women saw it, lay in the conditions in which they were forced to live. The younger generation had a similar concept of health as the older women. In her second study, MILDRED BLAXTER (1990) found that the majority of people expressed multiple concepts of health. Their definitions varied by stage in life-cycle, by gender and by social differences. Younger men tended to explain health in terms of physical strength and fitness, older men focused more on being still able to do things, and younger women emphasized energy, vitality and being able to cope. People of middle age expressed more complex ideas and put greater emphasis on total mental and physical well-being. Multi-dimensional concepts were expressed in particular by better off and better- educated women

Pill & Stott conducted a number of linked studies from 1981 to 1987 about beliefs on health and illness of Welsh mothers of the lower working class. They found a number of different definitions of health (PILL & STOTT 1982). A negative definition, that is health as the absence of disease, was also commonly used in terms of having the capacity to function as expected and being able to cope. Like Herzlich, they also identified a positive definition, although it was formulated in a different way. The important association here was with being cheerful, enthusiastic, and effervescent. Overall, Pill and Stott came to the conclusion that people see a link between behavior and lifestyle, and health and illness. But they do not consider health as a matter of personal responsibility but rather as a result of the conditions in which they live. Rory Williams explored older peoples beliefs about health and illness in Aberdeen. In his recent book he summarizes the results of his research (WILLIAMS 1990).

In open-ended interviews with seventy elderly people WILLIAMS (1983) came up with a similar classification as the one identified by HERZLICH (1969) in France, namely with three dimensions of health:
1) health as the absence of illness and disease,
2) health as a dimension of strength, weakness, and exhaustion, and
3) health as functional fitness. The relationships between these categories were complex. For instance, health was considered as the „strength„ to overcome a disease that was already present, but health was also described as a loss of strength that heightened the vulnerability to diseases not yet present. In other words, health as strength was seen as logically distinct from health as „an absence„ of disease. It was also viewed as being distinct from functional fitness. Fitness had a simple relationship to sickness and disease: to be disabled was to be unfit for normal roles. However, its relationship to health was more complicated. Having a weakness or vulnerability in one's constitution did not on its own imply being unfit.

This paper builds on some of the ideas developed in these studies and uses them to examine concepts of health in a very different setting, namely in an urban community of Dar es Salaam, the biggest city and de facto capital of Tanzania in East Africa. The data presented here form part of a larger anthropological study on the relationship between gender and health decision making on the household level. Ethnographic field research was conducted from March 1995 to August 1997.

Study setting

The site of this study is Ilala, a residential area near the city center which was assigned to Africans under British colonial rule (LESLIE 1963:22). Under the Slum Clearance Project of President Nyerere's socialist government (LUGALLA 1995:54) the National Housing Corporation demolished the old houses of mud and wattle walls, mud floor and thatched roof, re-built the settlement in a planned, grid-like pattern and supplied each house with basic facilities, such as a septic tank, water tap and electricity. Today, most of these houses are dilapidated, and the city services like the provision of electricity and water as well as garbage and human waste collection no longer reach the area. Following the general thrust towards a free market economy and political pluralism which mark the latest developments in Tanzania, a few private entrepreneurs as well as immigrants from the island Pemba have started to buy and renovate houses in Ilala.

For the present study we chose an administrative unit on the level of a neighbourhood as the study unit. It is called Ilala and forms part of the Ward Ilala in the Ilala District. It is a low-standard, high density settlement and has a population of almost 10,000 people living in 2385 households (AMMP 1995). Within this population we conducted several sub-studies. One of them was a household study in which we interviewed one hundred women aged thirty to forty years with at least one child under five. All of the selected women had lived in this area for more than five years. We decided to focus on women because in Tanzania, as in most other countries, women have day-to-day responsibility for the care of their children, as well as a range of other tasks in maintaining household health (UNICEF 1992:115). Two Tanzanian junior researchers visited these households and conducted semi-structured interviews in Swahili, the national language of Tanzania.

The inhabitants of this settlement are predominantly Swahili, „People of the Coast„. Historically, the Swahili are an African „mercantile civilization„ (MIDDLETON 1992) with cultural ties across the Indian Ocean, to Arabia, Persia and India. This is also reflected in our sample. In the majority of the households, both woman and spouse were Moslem (73 percent) and came originally from an ethnic group along the coast or along the old trade routes. According to the classification of the Tanzanian sociologist JOE LUGALLA (1995:126-129) the people in our sample belong to the very low level of the urban middle class. 19 percent of the women respondents and 60 percent of the spouses are low income wage earners. Others are self-employed and work as petty traders, small-scale entrepreneurs and long-distance traders. Half of the households in our sample have more than seven members, and many of them live as tenants in a single room (53 percent) or two rooms (29 percent). The daily food budget in many households (59 percent) was under Tsh 2000 (Sfr. 4), and in none of the cases more than Tsh 4000. For a household of seven members, Tsh 2000 covered the costs for one meal of rice and meat per day.

Women's definitions of health

During the semi-structured interviews, each of the women was asked about her view of „good health„. Many women found this abstract question difficult to answer; it was necessary to probe to elicit their views. If we look at the responses of all one hundred women, we can get an idea of the scope of public discourse on health in this community. In the next section we shall then look at the idiosyncratic beliefs of individual women.

The public discourse on health

It is possible to identify certain recurrent elements in women's definitions of health (see Table 1). The first set of answers relate to the physical and mental state *(hali ya kiwili, kifikiri)*, as one woman put it. For the purpose of analysis I grouped the answers of this set into the following categories: Body, „looks„, absence of sickness, well being, ability. The answers of the second group relate to living conditions *(hali ya maisha)*. The categories here are: basic necessities, cleanliness, taking care and no problems. These categories are not always clear cut; there are overlappings, for instance, between looks and „cleanliness„ or between „looks„ and „well-being„.

Table 1: Definitions of health: Good health is ...

Type of explanation	No.
Physical and mental state	
Body	75
Looks	34
Absence of sickness	29
Well-being	25
Ability	19
Living conditions	
Basic necessities	30
Cleanliness	25
Care	19
No problems	13
Total answers	269

The most frequently mentioned element was the body. A person who is healthy has a nice body *(ana mwili mzuri)*, a body that feels good and better *(mwili uwe unajisikia nafue)*. She is chubby *(mnene)*, the body is soft and „fleshy„, *(mwili unakuwa sopu sopu)* or firm *(mwili unakuwa imara)*, one has strength *(ana nguvu)*. A healthy person is not slim *(hajakonda, siyo mwembemba)* or weak *(siyo mnyonge, hajanyongea, siyo mdhaifu, asiye mdhoofu, hajadhoofika)*, her body is not „dried out„ *(hajanyauka)*. The quality of the skin receives particular attention: A healthy person has soft skin *(ngozi laini laini, nyoro)*; when you put oil on it, it stays *(unapaka mafuta yanakaa)*. She does not have scabies *(hana mapele)*, and the skin is not flabby *(ngozi haikusinyaa)*. One women referred to a concept which clearly derives from the biomedical culture: The weight of the child progresses well *(uzito wa mtoto unaendelea vizuri)*.

The second category of answers also refer to the body, but more to the way a person looks *(jinsi anaonekanavyo)* than to her physical state. A healthy person looks nice *(anapendeza)*, her face shines *(amenawiri)*, one can see the „light on the face„ *(nuvu usoni)* or the „light of the body„ *(nuvu ya mwili)*. The appearance is satisfactory *(muonekano wa kuridisha)*. The person is clean *(msafi)*, and her clothes should be clean *(mavazi yake yawe safi)*, she is attractive *(anavutia)* and has white teeth *(meno meupe)*.

The third category „absence of sickness„ includes the following range of answers: He/she is not sick *(haumwi)*, not to be sick *(kutokuumwa)* he/she has no sickness *(hana maradhi)*, he/she is not bothered by sickness *(hasumbuliwi na maradhi)*, he/she has not got a sickness now and then *(hapati maradhi mara kwa mara)*, to be without sickness *(bila maradhi)*, there should not be sickness *(kusiwe na maradhi)*, not to have signs of illness *(bila kuwa na dalili za maradhi)*.

Many women mentioned psycho-social dimensions of health which I subsumed under the heading „well-being„. Good health means that a person has life energy *(awe mzima)*, fulfillment in all she does *(utekelezaji wa yote yale ambayo atamfanya)*. She is full of life *(mchangamfu)* and does her activities with eagerness *(shughuli zake anafanya kwa bidii)*. She has joy *(mwenye furaha)* and is satisfied with life in general *(watu waridhike na maisha kwa ujumla)*. Here it is not the skin but the eyes which give a clue: the eyes of a person are lively *(macho ya mtu ni machangamfu)*. Some women stressed social relations: to have peace in the heart *(kuwa na amani moyoni)*, understanding in the family *(kuwa na uelewano katika familia)* and good collaboration *(ushirikiano)*.

The fourth category „ability„ includes more functional definitions. Good health means to be able to work every day *(kuweza kufanya kazi kila siku)* or to do activities *(kushughulika)*. A healthy person is someone who has responsibility, who works *(mtu anaye wajibu, anaye fanye kazi)*, who has strength to be able to do your activities *(ana nguvu za kuweza kufanya shughuli zako)*, who is fit *(yuko fit)* and active *(anakuwa active)*. It is a sign of health, if a child plays well *(mtoto anacheza vizuri)* or if an adult person eats well *(anayekula vizuri)* and walks well *(anatembea vizuri)*.

In the second set of answers which relate to general living conditions women most frequently mentioned the item „basic necessities„ *(mahitaji)*. A healthy person should get the basic necessities like food, clothes and a place to sleep *(awe anapata yale mahitaji muhimu kama chakula, mavazi na mahali pa kulala)*. One woman mentioned education together with other basic necessities: children should get to eat, to shower well and you can take them to school so that you give them the education to know the matters of health *(watoto wapate kula, wakoge vizuri na uweze kuwapeleka shule ili uwape elimu ya kujua mambo ya afya)*. Other women listed only one or the other of these basic necessities. Among these, food featured most frequently: to have enough food *(kuna shibe ya kutosha)* is foremost in the mind of many people. As some women put it: The children sleep without hunger *(watoto hawalai na njaa)*. Some statements about food reflect teachings of health promotion programs: to eat good food *(kula chakula kizuri; vyakula bora)*; to eat food that builds the body *(kula chakula cha kuimarisha)*; to get food three times *(kupata chakula mara tatu)* a day. Many women explained health in terms of cleanliness. Good health is cleanliness of the body, the clothes, the house and the kitchen utensils *(usafi wa mwili, nguo, nyumba pamoja na vyombo)*. Variations of this statement were made by many women. Others mentioned just one or the other element, for instance to live in a clean place *(kukaa sehemu safi)* or a clean environment *(mazingira safi)*. Many women agreed that the clothes have to be clean *(mavazi yake yawe safi)*, and the children should wash themselves *(watoto wakuoge)*. Again, what seems obvious to us is often a luxury in a settlement like this one: water, like food, is a scarce resource.

Another category are statements about care *(matunza)*. Good health means to take care of yourself *(kujitunza wewe mwenjewe)* and taking care of the body *(utunzaji wa mwili)*. Under this category I also subsumed statements about health care services *(huduma ya afya)*, people's use of them, for instance to follow family planning *(kuzaa kwa mpangilio)*, and references to health care messages such as to prevent sickness *(kujilinde na maradhi)*, to avoid infectious diseases by ensuring cleanliness *(kuepekana na magonjwa ya kuambukiza kwa njia ya kufe na usafi)* and to know cleanliness and eating well *(kujua usafi na kula vizuri)*. Several women mentioned that health can be learnt by good upbringing *(ulezi mzuri, malezi mazuri)*.

The last category refers to problems, usually phrased as a negative sentences. Healthy people do not have small, small problems *(hawana matatizo madogo madogo)*, they live without problems *(bila matatizo)*.

Idiosyncratic beliefs of individual women

If we look at all the responses and count the frequency in which these themes or categories were mentioned, we find that statements about the state of the body and mind rank higher (68%) than references to living conditions. However, this picture distorts the reality because most women gave multi-dimensional definitions that incorporated a range of elements. In fact, a refined analysis of the answers of all one hundred women reveals that the concepts of individual women are idiosyncratic, like packages of ideas, no two of which are exactly alike. They are made by assembling components of the shared social discourse on health. With reference to the two broad sets of answers „physical and mental state„ and „living conditions„, we find that 36% of the women mentioned components only of the first set, 43% of both sets and 21% only of the second set.

Many of the statements recorded in this low-income urban area of Dar es Salaam are similar to the three main themes which HERZLICH (1969) identified in Paris and in the Normandy, as the following examples illustrate: *Body-in-a-vacuum:* „Good health is not to be ill and not to have problems of illness and food.„ Or: „Good health is when a person does his or her activities without being bothered by frequent illnesses.„ *Reserve of health:* „Good health is to have life energy and to be able to work every day.„ Or: „To be healthy means to have a strong body, to have the strength to do one's work.„ *Equilibrium:* „To be in good health is to have fulfillment in everything you do, to have life energy.„ Or: „Good health is to have peace in your heart, resting time, and then, if there is enough food, there is good health.„

The middle-class women Herzlich interviewed saw health as something inside the individual, as a matter of bodily strength and/or a product of self-fulfillment. Those women in our sample who explained health in terms of the state of the body and the mind seem to share this view, but a larger number of women understood health also as a product of living conditions. Their views of health share more similarities with those of the lower working class women in the British studies of (BLAXTER & PATERSON 1982, PILL & STOTT 1982). What comes out very strongly is that many women in this low-standard, high-density settlement associate health with the fulfillment of basic needs, such as food, shelter, clothes and education.

Some of their statements show that they see a link between life style, health and illness (see also PILL & STOTT 1982):„Good health is the way a person lives, and where she lives and the food she eats; that's what gives a person a good condition.„ Or:„Cleanliness and food that builds the body and that life plan in the household bring about good health.„ But several women made it clear that one needs financial means to improve one's life style, and consequently, one's health. As one woman put it: „I see that good health means that you or any other member of the family should not get ill. If you have the basic necessities in your home and especially food, then that is good health. The way I know it you cannot get a good environment or health if you do not have the financial ability.„

The health concepts of the women in our sample did not only differ in terms of whether they emphasize the physical and mental state or the living conditions. In their statements they also expressed contradictory views on the interpretations of certain components of health or the relationship between these components. Let us look at just one example. Many women agreed that a healthy body should be chubby and strong. These concepts were sometimes gender-specific: chubbiness was associated with the female body, firmness and strength with the male body. But a number of women questioned whether „being chubby„ is an important sign of health: „Even if one is slim but not weak means good health.„ Or: „You look at the body of the person. She may be chubby, but if she is weak - weakness is a sign of illness.„ Or: „Good health is for a person to have a strong body; even if she is slim but active that person has good health.„ Or: „Good health is not chubbiness. Even a slim person can be in good health, if only she gets food, lives in a clean environment and keeps her body clean.„

In every society, the body has a social as well as a physical reality (SCHEPER-HUGHES & LOCK 1987). Ideas about what a good or healthy body should look like is culturally and socially defined. In this Swahili settlement, it is considered polite to greet a (female) person by saying „you have gained weight„ *(umenenepa);* but from casual conversations and mutual teasing I also learnt that there are both men and women who believe that „being big„ is not always healthy. It seems that the „body image„ is gradually changing, at least among some of the people in this community. Both for women and men strength as a sign for health and weakness as a sign for ill-health seem to become more important. This may partly reflect the fact that the economic crisis in Tanzania forced an increasing number of women also in this settlement to find a way to generate income for the family. An alternative explanation is that the dominant „body image„ (FISHER 1968) of contemporary Euro-American culture which is embedded in and spread by biomedical knowledge and care becomes increasingly accepted also among lower middle class people in Tanzania.

Discussion

This paper shows that the approach developed in sociological studies on health concepts in France and in the United Kingdom provide a useful starting point for anthropological studies in very different cultural settings. BLAXTER (1990) has shown that people's health definition may vary according to gender, stage in the life cycle and social class differences. We concentrated our study on middle-aged women in a low-standard, high-density settlement of Dar es Salaam. Following the lead of HERZLICH (1969) we analyzed their accounts in terms of a public discourse and in terms of idiosyncratic individual beliefs. We found that the components of the public discourse can be broadly grouped into two sets of beliefs: those referring to the physical and mental state and those referring to the living conditions. Concepts relating to the state of the body and mind include images of a healthy body, judgments by appearances, absence of disease, psycho-social well-being and ability to function normally. The second set of concepts include the fulfillment of basic needs, the importance of cleanliness, good care including health care services and absence of problems. The three main themes which HERZLICH (1969) identified among middle-class people in Paris and the Normandy could also be traced in Dar es Salaam: „Health as a vacuum„ in the sense of „absence of disease„, „health as a reserve„ understood as strength to do work, and „equilibrium„ in terms of total well-being.

But the majority of the women in our sample also emphasized living conditions. In this respect the views of the women belonging to the lowest Tanzanian middle-class were similar to those of lower working class women in the United Kingdom (BLAXTER &PATERSON 1982, PILL & STOTT 1982). However, it is important to stress the diversity of accounts offered by women of this particular social class. These women cannot be regarded as a single group who see health in a similar fashion. The women mentioned different dimensions of health and interpreted them in a number of distinct ways. Individual women drew on these concepts and assembled them in different packages. Some women, for instance, emphasized links between behavior, life style and health, others associated health with a particular body image, and this body image seems to be contested by still another group of women. From an anthropological point of view it will be of particular interest to follow up on these diverse accounts and to examine whether they can be linked with different ways of maintaining and promoting health in a basically similar physical and social environment.

References

AMMP. 1995. *Adult Mortality and Morbidity Programm Census Data.* Dar es Salaam.
BLAXTER, M. 1990. *Health and lifestyles.* London.
BLAXTER, M. and L. PATERSON. 1982. *Mothers and daughters. A three generational study of health attributes and behaviour.* London.
FISHER, S. 1968. Body image. In: *International Encyclopadia of the Social Sciences.* Edited by D. SILLS. New York. Pp. 113-116.
HELMAN, C. G. 1990. *Culture, health and illness.* Oxford.
HERZLICH, C. 1969. *Santé et maladie. Analyse d'une représentation sociale.* Paris.
KLEINMAN, A. 1980. *Patients and healers in the context of culture. An exploration of the borderland between anthropology, medicine and psychiatry.* Berkeley, Los Angeles, London.
LESLIE, J. A. 1963. *A survey of Dar es Salaam.* Oxford.
LUGALLA, J. 1995. *Crisis, urbanization and urban poverty in Tanzania. A study of urban poverty and survival politics.* Lanham, New York, London.
MIDDLETON, J. 1992. *The world of the Swahili. An African mercantile civilization.* New Haven, London.
PILL, R. and N. STOTT. 1982. Concepts of illness causation and responsibility: Some preliminary data from a sample of working class mothers. *Social Science and Medicine* 16.1:43-52.
SCHEPER-HUGES, N. and M. LOCK. 1987. The mindful body: A prolegomenon to future work in medical anthropology. *Medical Anthropology Quarterly* 1:6-41.
UNICEF. 1990. *Women and Children in Tanzania: A situational analysis.* Dar es Salaam
WILLIAMS, R. 1983. Concepts on health: An analysis of lay logic. *Sociology* 17.2:185-205.
WILLIAMS, R. 1990. *A protestant legacy. Attitudes to death and illness among older Aberdonians.* Oxford.

ARBEITSGEMEINSCHAFT ETHNOMEDIZIN
SOCIETY FOR ETHNOMEDICINE

curare Zeitschrift für Ethnomedizin

Interdisziplinär
Interkulturell
International

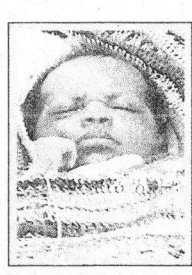

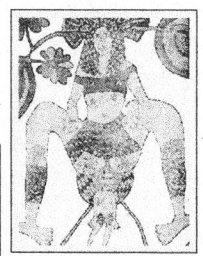

Ihr Mitglieder-Service:
- Bezug der Zeitschrift **curare**
- Vergünstigungen für Publikationen
- Subskriptionsangebote
- ermäßigte Tagungsteilnahmen
- Informations- und Beratungsservice

Gesundheit, Krankheit und Heilung im Kulturvergleich

AGEM-MITGLIEDSCHAFT

Die **Arbeitsgemeinschaft Ethnomedizin (AGEM)** ist eine gemeinnützige, interdisziplinäre Gesellschaft. Ethnomedizin vergleicht verschiedene Heilweisen, Heilmittel und -konzepte.
Aktuelle Schwerpunkte bilden die Integration kulturfremder Krankheitsvorstellungen und Behandlungskonzepte (Migranten) und die Neubewertung von Heilkundigen und Volksmedizin (z.B. Naturheilkunde).
Ethnomedizinische Betrachtungen halten uns einen Spiegel vor, in dem wir die Vorzüge und Nachteile unserer eigenen Kultur besser erkennen. Wissen aus anderen medizinischen Systemen kann auch in einer Zeit der Besinnung auf die Grundbedürfnisse des Menschen und seiner Gesundheit, die von der naturwissenschaftlichen Medizin nicht mehr abgedeckt werden, neue Lösungsmöglichkeiten aufzeigen.

JÄHRLICHE MITGLIEDSBEITRÄGE:
Deutschland & Europa: DM 150.-
Reduziert (Studenten gegen Nachweis): DM 90.-
Außereuropäische Länder: DM 190.-

ARBEITSGEMEINSCHAFT ETHNOMEDIZIN (AGEM)
Forschungsstelle für Humanethologie
C.E. Gottschalk-Batschkus
Von-der-Tann Str. 3-5, D-82346 Andechs,
Deutschland

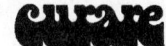

Socio-Cultural and Environmental Factors in Maternal Health in Nigeria
Soziokulturelle und Umweltfaktoren mütterlicher Gesundheit in Nigeria

Josephine Nkiru Alumanah

Abstract: Every society has its own peculiar forms of customary behavior, its own particular systme of social relationships and its own distinctive culture. Available studies show that sociocultural and environmental factors in no small measure affect not just the illnesses of complications which afflict maternal health, but also the womenís behaviour and perception of such illnesses or complications. Decision to seek help may be affected by pesonal and social enrironment as well as family backround. Access to quality care as well as the provision of quality care are also incorporated.
There are many ethnic and cultural groups in Nigeria, however, the assessment will be based on the three dominalt groups which are the Hausa, Ibo and Yoruba. The social should match the clinical for appropriate maternal health in our societies.

Zusammenfassung: Jede Gesellschaft hat ihren besonderen Verhaltenskodex, ihr besonderes System gesellschaftlicher Beziehungen und ihre unverwechselbare Kultur. Die verfügbaren Studien zeigen, dass soziokulturelle und Umweltfaktoren in nicht geringem Maße nicht nur die Krankheiten und die Komplikationen beeinflussen, welche die Gesundheit der Mütter beeinträchtigen, sondern auch das Verhalten der Frauen und ihre Wahrnehmung solcher Erkrankungen oder Komplikationen. Der Entschluss, Hilfe zu suchen, kann durch die persönliche und gesellschaftliche Umgebung wie auch durch den familiären Hintergrund beinflusst werden. Der Zugang zu qualitativ guter medizinischer Betreuung wie auch die Möglichkeit, dieselbe zu ehalten, spielen ebenfalls eine Rolle. In Nigeria gibt es viele ethnische und kulturelle Gruppen, jedoch stützt sich die Beurteilung auf die drei dominierenden Gruppen - die Hausa, die Ibo und die Yoruba. Der soziale und der klìnische Bereich sollten im Interesse der Müttergesundheit in unseren Gesellschaften einander entsprechen.

Keywords: Africa, Nigeria, maternal health, obstetrics, Afrika, Nigeria, mütterliche Gesundheit, Geburtshilfe.

Introduction

The rhetoric „Health for all by the year 2000" has been ambodied in principle by the United Nations agencies and member nations like Nigeria. Yet it is not being addressed to its logical conclusion. The source of producing an offspring could be said to be a gamble because of the hazards and the high rates of morbidity and mortality associeted with pregnancy and childbirth.

There is and estimated 5000,000 deaths every year, and nearly all of these death occur in developing countries where women´s health in poor and maternal care scarce (UNICEF 1993). The UNICEF progress of Nations Report (1993) graded Nigeria as one of the most unsafe places in teh world for women to have babies.

It should be acknowledged that what pregnant women do of fail to do for their health are influenced by many forces which include various aspects of socio-cultural aswell as environmental factors. Environment should reflect not just ecology but social as well. Social environment includes actual living conditions such as poverty or crowding, and the norms, values and attitudes that reflect a particular social and cultural context. Thus family care international (FCI 1995:2) confirms that addressing maternal health „involves incorporating and understanding the inter-relationship that exist wit hsocio-cultural, economic, gender and plotical factors".

A variety of theoretical perspectives could be used to articulate the analysis of health problems. Critical theory as a generic term that includes several specific theoretical perspectives, including marxism and neo-Marxism of various theoretical perspectives will involve a critical stance toward the existing social order, and committed to making the health of mothers better. Inequalities in the distributon of scare resources is a major problem. Critical theory is often linked to the overall society , but the same logic is being applied to typical social systems, for example, family dynamics where power reltions in the families could be found (JOHNSON 1985). To be explored then is theSocio-Behavioural perspective. This perspective believes that social and cultural factors influence behaviour which in turn influences the health of molters and their infants. The perspective focusses on local attitudes and practices.

Apart from the ill health caused by the people's socio-economic standing, cultural views, poverty and illiteracy, there are other impendiments. Getting halp may also be impeded and may depend as well on the culture of obtaining permission from the husband of a senior member of the household before seeking help, the availability and affordability of transport and health care, and the availability of adequate health facilitie. Some maternal comlplications will then be viewed, taking into congnizance the decision making regarding care, access to quality care and the question of qualitiy care itself.

Maternal Complications

SMYKE (1991) identified anaemia as being a particularly worrisone problem for wome nin the developing world as nearly two-thirds of pregnant women and on-half of all other women are estimated to be suffering from anaemia. As there is a dangerous interaction between malaria and anaemia, the rampant cases of malaria which abound in Nigeria put women at great risk.

In Nigeria, obstructed labour was also identified as a grave complication in pregnancy. According to Dr. Altire Tongo (WOMEN'S WORLD, No. 21-22, 1989) „early marriage wit hconsequent prolonged, obstructed labour is associated with abour 80 per cent of visico-vaginal fistulae (VVF) casese seen in Northern Nigeriaì (cited in SMYKE 1991: 72). Tongo added that the causes of VVF in Nigeria are almost entirely social and preventable. Dr. Tahzib also in his assessment of VVF referred to its the most dreaded conditions among the women of Northern Nigeria, and described the typical VVF patiens as frequently malnourished, anaemic and rejected, and often gas to travel long distances to seek modern treatments (cited in SMYKE 1991:71).

Anaemia which is an example of an indirect obstetrec morbidity could be caused by lack of iron, folic acid, or the lack of vital elements in the diet. It could also be caused ofr heightened by malaria, hook worm and infections. The importance of nutrition to maternal health should therefore be recognised. SMYKES (1991: 17) states that: „Between 20 and 45 per cent of women of child bearing age in the developing world do not eat the World Health Organization (WHO) recommended 2,250 calories a day under normal circumstances, let alone the extra 285 a day they need when they are pregnantì. The nutritional requirement of a woman increases during pregnancy in order to meet the needs of the growing baby and the changes which occur in the body. the woman's body at this point needs energy foods, proteins, vitamins and minerals. The increased food intake is necessary as the women's body burns energy at increased rate, and there is increase in her volume of blood. For the growth of the woman's breast and uterine tissues, good and adequate nutrition is vital. According to the WORLD BANK (1993: 76), iron deficiency anaemia „affects 458 million adult women but 238 million menì. Also as observed by SMYKE (1991: 17) „nearly two-thirds of pregnant women and one-half of all other women are estimated to be suffering from anaemiaì. This condition of undernourished anaemic women could affect thier babies by having low-birth weight, which could result to undernourished infants and stunted childten. Very serious anaemia could also result in heart failure, miscarriage of premature labour, as well as cause infection of bleeding.

Nutritional anaemia which was found to be common among the women in Bangladesh, a developing country like Nigeria, was believed to be made worse by increased requirement of nutrition following pregnancy, lactation and blood soll at delivery, which was not supplemented (SAFE MOTHERHOOD NEWSLETTER, No 13, Nov. 1993-Feb. 1994). According to GRIFTITHS et al (1991), WHO identified anaemia as one of the main illnesses that causes maternal morbitity, and was linded to poverty and low education.

Food consumption is and example of factors that give rise to anaemia and also example of effects working directly through income. Using standard indicatorssuch as infant Mortality Rate (IMR) or Life Expectancy at Birth (LEB) about two-thirds of the international variance in health status can be connected with income differences. The World Bank's 1993 World Development Report contains the fact that household income is the major determinant of the state of health of a nation. The distribution of income and the number of people inpoverty is equally important for consideration particularly in industrialised countries. The WORLD HEALTH ORGANIZATION (1993: 40), stated that „In industrialised countries life expectancy depends much more on income distribution than onincome per capitaì.

Apart from lack of income to purchase needed nutritioal diet, tradition also imposes certain food restrictions on women during pregnancy and the post partum period. In Nigeria for instance, among the Ibos, tradition abhors women taking certain types of meat. These are Nchi (Grasscutter) and Eyi (Bush Rat). Nchi is believed to be responsible for lon labour and unless the women affected is able to get the bone of any Nchi in her month, normal delivery could be impossible. As for Eyi, it is believed that tie offspring of such pregnancy must turn out to be a thief. The Irony of it is that the two sources of meat are the main ones readily available in the rural areas and among the rural folks.

Rumptured uterus will be assessed in the case of direct obstetric morbidity resulting from complications of pregnancy, labour and the puerperium. This could be cause by interventions, omissions and/or incorrect reatment. With the underaged, it could result in Vesico Vaginal Fistula (VVF). Rupture ofthe uterus occurs in one in 1,500 deliveries in the United States of America (EDEN et al 1986). In contrast, it si a fairly friquent and fatal conpliaation of labour and delivery in developing countries. Reports from hospitals in Africa have recorded rates as high as 11 cases of uterine rupture per 1000 deliveries (ELKINS 1985; RENDLE-SHORT 1960). Uterine rupture often inbolves other injuries to pelvic organs, particularly the bladder. In a survey of 129 cases of uterine rupture by LACHMAN et al (1985), 15 percent experienced rupture of the bladder. Vesico vaginal fistula (VVF), which is an opening between the bladder and results also from rupture of the bladder. After surgical of the uterus, infection and other complications often worsen the patient's state of health.

Most uterine ruptures are caused by cephalopelvic disproportion and/or obstructed labour. It has been noted taht about 3 to 23 per cent of ruptures are caused by interventions of health workers or traditional birth attendants, for example, use of forceps (SAFE MOTHERHOOD 1990). Some traditional practices do contribute to uterine rupture. In some cultures, Nigeria and Uganda for example, herbal medicine with oxytoxic properties are used by traditional birth attendants with serous consequences for uterine rupture (RENDLE-SHORT 1960). ELKINS (1985), has also drawn attention to the idea of packing the vagina with herbs which often cause severe swellilng of the cervix and increase the risk of rupture. Prolonged or obstructed labour which also causes uterine rupture is a major cause of maternal death, particilarly in Africa. In developing countries, the three major causes of obstructed labour are: cephalopelvic disproportion, pelvic contraction from rickets, infection, or malnutrition: and abnormalities of the cervix or vagina, which are sometimes due to female circumcision (LAWSON 1967).

In order to reduce the incidence of uterine rupture, fistulae and other diseases, access to and better use of health services was recommended. In a study carried out by TAHUZIB (1983) in Zaria, Nigeria, it was found that as the obstetric services of the major hospitals in the area became better known and more women came for antenatal care and delivery, the incidence of fistulae declined. The study showed that between 1970 and 1978 the number of patients delivering in the hospital increased four fold and this decreased the number of fistula cases. In 1978 no case of fistula patient came from Zaria while the cases of areas further off from the hospital increased.

Decision to seek care
Culture and women's status were identified as important impediments inhibiting women from seeking health services. African Regional Workshop on Reproductive Health organised by the WHO at Nairobi, Kenya, in November 1983 concluded that women who need health care often fail to seek it, may be treated with a little respect, or may simply find that health services just do not meet their needs (SAFE MOTHERHOOD NEWSLETTER, No. 17, March-June 1985:8). The modern medical facilities were diescovered to often clash with the tradition of the people. Some of the reasons are lack of emotional support, privacy in the hospital setting and the disruption of household responsibility as a result of hopital confinement (AVERBACH 1982, WEDDERBURN & MOORE 1990). Though embedded also in the decision to sek care is the perceived severity and etiology of the disorder. A disorder like odema is considered by the people as normal in pregnancy and should not be bothered about even when severe.

Where women's mobility is severely restrictd because of cultural prescriptions, there may be delay in seeking care. In Nigeria however, studies have shown that in certain places and within certain ethnic groups women do not decide on their own to seek care and that the decision belongs to a spouse or to an elder in the family (STOCK 1983, ABASIEKONG 1981, SHEHU 1992).

Due to the culture of certain ethnic groups as well as the low status accorded to women, young girls are given out in marriage against their will. Such young girls, without adequate care often end up as Vesico vaginal fistulae (VVF) patients. Cases sould be found mainly in the northern part of Nigeria, though cases still abound in other parts of the country. According to HARRISON (1983:385), in Zaria,

Nigeria, no matter how obvious the need for hospital management becomes for the girl who develops obstructed labour, permission to leave home for hospital can usually be given oly by the husband. This confirms how culture and status of women intertwine to deny them health care. SHEHU (1992) in Sokoto, Nigeria, also studied the socio-cultural factors in the causation of maternal mortality & morbidity. He emphasized that the status of women and the associated powerlessness exerted an influence on age at which girls marry, the average age at marriage being 13 years or less, death from severe complications do occur.

Access to quality care
To be descussed under access to adequate health services will be the existence of facilities, information to use the facilities, the facilities being within reach, as well as reasonable cost.

The Existence of Facilities:
The prescience of qualified personnel os often lacking in rural areas. Of the 200 obstetricians in Nigeria in 1980, more than 90 per cent were located in the national and state capitals (Omu, 1981).
   Ironically, the proportion of the population living in urban areas was estimated to be 11 per cent. Full range of services as well as rapid referral system is expected to minimized cases of ruptured uterus in prolonged or obstructed labour, particularly if complications set in.

Access to Information:
On access to information, most of the studies reviewed show that utilization of medical services increases with icreasing levels of education services (CALDWELL 1979; CALDWELL & CALDWELL 1985; CLELAND & VAN GINNECEN 1988). However, some of the survey results indicate a significant positive association between use of prenatal care services and level of women's education (ABBAS & WALKER 1986). Consistency is more with the use of child health services according to OKAFOR (1983). Generally, however, education increases knowledge and awareness, increases access to information, and of couse self confidence.

Financial Accessibility:
Finanacial cost is an important variable in health care utilization a cost does not only involve the pyment of medical bills but transportation costs as well (YOUNG 1981). Financial constraints are major reasons for not seeking medical care, or for seeking ine form of care rather than another. Some studies have assessed of changes in the fee structure on utilization levels. Data on Nigeria show a drastic decline in hospital births, probably due to the country's deepening economic crisis and high cost of hospital treatment. Researchers at the Ahmadu Bello University Teaching Hospital (ABUTH) in Zaria, Nigeria discovered that obstetric admissions declined sharply between 1983 and 1985, the year that the government introduced fees for prenatal care and delivery (EKWEMPU 1990). The report also found that obstetric admissions in ABUTH decreased further in 1988, when patients were required to pay for some of the essential items.
   EGUNJOBI (1983) indicated, however, that compared to other factors, the financial cost of receiving care if often not a major determinant of the decision to seek care. A survey that was conducted among a sample of 680 Ibo, Yoruba and Hausa people in Nigeria revealed five factors influencing decision to seek traditional or western medical care. These are afordability of care, accessibility, acceptability quality of care as well as the tradition and culture of avoiding of care as well as the tradition and culture of avoiding male doctors and having the permission of the husband of and elder before seeking help. With some of the researches however, cost was ranked fourth, and distance fifth (NNADI 1985).

Physical Accessibility:
The distance between potential patients and the nearest health facility has been shown as an important barrier to seeking health care, especially in rural areas (ROGHMANN & ZASTOWNY 1979; STOCK 1983). Unavailability of transport, bad roads and long distances are impediments, especially under emergency conditions.
   In the interviews carried out in Oyo State, Nigeria, EGUNJOBI (1983) discoverd that distance governed the choice of facilities. In another study in Nigeria, STOCK (1983) showed that the percentage of

individuals seeking treatments within one week of the onset of illness declined as distance from the treatment facility increased. He however added that there are differences in the size of the effect according to illness and the perceived effectiveness of the health care perlonnel.

Quality of care

The quality of care will take into consideration reasonable care, well equipped and acceptable services. An important consideration in the decision to seek care is the quality. This is related to people's own assessment of service delivery, which largely depends on their experiences with the health system and the experiences of others. In a study carried out in the city of Ibadan, Nigeria, where potential patients had access to more than one family, their perception of the quality of care took precedence over distance (IYUN 1983). STOCK (1983) and NNADI (1984) identified what the patients consideredin terms of qualtiy as qualified personnel, staff attitudes, hospital procedures, efficiency, and availability of supplies. These factors are particularly important for pregnant and nursing mothers.

The presence of qualified personnel is often lacking in rural areas. Of the 200 obstetricians in Nigeria in 1980, more than 90 per cent were located in the national and state capitals (OMU 1981) as earlier stated.

Conclusion

In Nigeria, socio-cultural andenvironmental factors do tremendously affect maternal health. This is more so, given the country's vast rural areas characterised by poverty, illiteracy and other forms of sociocultural deprivations. With the ill-health caused by the people's social, economic and the low cultural standing for the women, poverty and illiteracy; it is also difficult for the women to get help. This is by the reason of the above as well as the unavailability of adequate health facilities, unavailability of transport facilities, and the culture of being decided by others to take advantage of a facility. A survey conducted among the three main ethnic groups in Nigeria (Ibo, Hausa and Yoruba) revealed five factor that influence people's decision to seek care - either western medical care or traditional. These were also given as the severity of illness, perceived effectivness, cause, cost and distance (NNADI & KABAT 1984).

Such fingings on maternal health should be linked to the clinical, and the essential knowledge used for the development of interventions, and to encourage policies and practises that more closely match women's needs.

References

ABASIEKONG, E.M. 1982. Familism Hospital Admission in Rural Nigeria: A case Study, *Sc. S.i.Med.*, 15-45.
ABBAS, A.A. and WALKER, G.J.A. 1986. Determinants of the Utilization of Maternal and Child health Services'. Jordan, *Int. J. Epidemoil*, 15 404.
ADETOKUNBO, O.L. and ROSENFIELD, A.C. 1993. *Safe motherhood Programs: Options and issues.* Center for Population and Family Health, Columbia University New York.
AVERBACH, L.S. 1982. Childbirth in tunisia: Implication of a Decision Making Model, *Soc. Sci. Med.* 16 1499.
CALDWELL, J.C. 1979. Education as s factor in Mirtality declined: An examination of Nigerian data, *Popul. Stud.* 33, 395.
CALDWELL, J.C. and CALDWELL, P. 1985. Education and Literacy as Factors in Health. In *Good Health and Low Cost.* Edited by HALSTEAD, S.B., WARREN, J.A. and WALSH, K.S. The Rockefeller Foundation, New York.
EDEN, R.D., PARKER, R.T., and GALL, S.A. 1986. Rupture of the Pregnant Uterus, *Obstetrics and Gynaecology* 68(5), 67-674.
EGUNJOBI, L. 1983. Factors Influencing Choice of Hospitals: A Case Study of the Northern Part of Oyo State, Nigeria. *Soc. Sci. Med.* 17, 585.
EKWEMPU, C.C. 1990. Structural Adjustment and Health In Africa. *The Lancet,* 336, 56-57.
Elkins, T., Onwuka, E., Stovall, T., Hagood, M. and Osborn, D. 1985. Uterine Rupture in Nigeria", Journal of Reproductive Medicine 30(3): 195-199 (March).
FAMILY HEALTH INTERNATIONAL 1991. Net Focuses on Maternal Health, *Quarterly Journal,* Vol. 14, No.3 FHI.
FAMILY HEALTH INTERNATIONAL 1995. *Commitments to Sexual and Reproductive Health and Rights for All: Framework for Action:* FCI, New York.
GRIFFITHS, M., MOORE, M., and FAVIN, M. 1991. Mother care / The Manoff Group, Communicating Safe Motherhood: Using Communication to Improve Maternal Health in the Developing World", *Working paper* 14 (November).

GWATKIN, D.R. WILCOX R.J. and WRAY, J.D. 1981. Can Health and Nutrition Interventions Make a Difference? *World Health Forum,* 2(1), pp. 119-128.
HARRISON, K.A. 1983. Obstetric Fistula: One Social Calamity Too Many, (Commentary). *Br. J. Obstetrics and Gynaecol.* 90. 385.
-----1985. Child-bearing, Health an Social Priorities: A Survey of 22, 77 Consecutive Hospital births in Zaria, Northern Nigeria, *British Journal of Obstetrics and Gynecology* 92 (Suppl. 5.): 1-119 (Oct.).
IYUN, F. 1983. Hospital Service Areas in Ibadan City, *Soc. Sci. Med.,* 17 601.
JOHNSON, D.J. 1985. *Using Sociology to Analyse Human and Organisational Problems: A Humanistic perspectic to link Theory and Practice,* Paper given at the Clinical Sociology Co-operative Conference, Orlando, Florida, March 31- April 2, 1985
MAINE, D. (ed) 1993. *Safe Motherhood,* Programs: Options and Issues, Centre for Population and Family Health, New York.
NNADI, E.E. and KABAT, H.F. 1984. Choosing Healath Care Services in Nigeria: A Developing Nation. *J.Trop. Med. Hyg.,* 87, 47.
OKAFOR, S.I. 1983. Factors Affecting the Frequency of Hospital Trips Among a Predominantly Rural Population, *Soc. Sci. Med.* 17, 591.
OMU, A. E. 1981. Frafitional Midwives in Nigeria", *Lancet,* 1: 620-621 (March).
ROGHMANN, K.J. and ZASTOWNY, T.R. 1979. Proximity as a factor in the Selection of Health Care Providers: Emergency Room Visits Compared to Obstetric admissions and abortions, *Soc. Sci. Med.* 13, 61.
RIYSTON, E. and ARMSTRONG, S. (ed.) 1994. *Maternal Health and Safe Motherhood*: Progess Report, 1991-1992, WHO, Geneva.
SHEHU, D.J. 1992. *Women's Health Issues in Nigeria,* in MERE NAKATEREGGA KISEKKA (ed.).Taniza publishing Co., Zaria, pp 203-214.
SMYKE, P. 1991. *Women and Health,* Zed Press, London.
STOCK, R. 1983. Distance and Utilization of Health Facilities in Rural Nigeria, *Soc. Sci. Med.* 17(9), pp. 563-570.
THADDEUS, S. and MAINE, D. 1990. *Too Far to Walk: Maternal Mortiality in Context,* Centre for Population and Family Health Prevention of Maternal Mortality Programme, Columbia University, New York.
UNITED NATIONS INTERNATIONAL CHILDREN'S FUND (UNICEF) 1993. *Progess of Nations Report, World Development Report: Investing in Health,* Oxford University Press, UNICEF<.
WORLD BANK 1994. *Trends in Developing Economics 1994* Washington D.C.
WORLD HEALTH ORGANISATION (WHO) 1991. *Social and Cultural Issues in Human Resources Development for Maternal Health and Safe Motherhood,* Report of a Working Group Meeting, WHO, Geneva..
WORLD HEALTH ORGANISATION (WHO) 1992. *The Prevalence of Anaemia in Women: A Tabulation of Available Information,* WHO, Geneva, 2nd ed.
YOUNG J.C. 1981. Non-use of Physicians: Methodological Approaches, Policy Implications, and the Utility of Decision Models, *Soc. Sci.* 15, 499.

The Precarious Health Situation of African Women South of the Sahara
Die schwierige gesundheitliche Situation afrikanischer Frauen südlich der Sahara

Martin W. Bangha

Abstract: This paper gives a brief overview on current trends or evolution of health conditions of African women living South of the Sahara desert as well as some of the key problems impeding their health. It is important to recognise that there has been substantial improvement in the health situation of these women. This improvement though not exhaustively impressive, is quite appreciable. However, the situation is still considerably disturbing and can be attributed to many obstacles. The most powerful are those imposed by the weakness of the rural infrastucture and the deep-rooted traditional beliefs about the role and status of women in most African societies (confersing prestige on women and/or couples with many offsprings). This situation is further compounded by the often passive attitudes of these women, either for reasons of fear, fatalism or simply because of their ignorance of viable alternatives. Low educational attainment, large numbers of children, time-consuming domestic chores coupled with other back-breaking tasks and cultural norms among other things, all infringe on these women's health and subsequently that of the society at large.

Zusammenfassung: Dieser Beitrag gibt eine kurze Übersicht über die derzeitigen Entwicklungstrends bei den gesundheitlichen Bedingungen afrikanischer Frauen, die südlich der Sahara leben, und über einige Schlüsselprobleme, die ihrer Gesundheit entgegenstehen. Es muss anerkannt werden, dass sich die gesundheitliche Situation dieser Frauen deutlich gebessert hat. Diese Verbesserung ist zwar längst nicht ausreichend, aber doch recht beachtlich. Gleichwohl ist die Situation dieser Frauen noch ziemlich besorgniserregend und lässt sich auf viele Hindernisse zurückführen, von denen diejenigen am schlimmsten sind, die ihnen die schwache ländliche Infrastruktur und die tief verwurzelten traditionellen Auffassungen über den Status der Frau in den meisten afrikanischen Gesellschaften (wonach Frauen und/oder Paare mit möglichst viel Nachwuchs höheres Ansehen genießen) aufzwingen. Diese Situation wird noch verschärft durch die oft paasive Haltung dieser Frauen, sei es aus Furcht, Fatalismus oder einfach aus Unkenntnis brauchbarer Alternativen. Niedriges Bildungsniveau, große Kinderzahl, zeitraubende häusliche Arbeiten sowie eine Reihe anderer anstrengender Aufgaben und kultureller Normen beeinträchtigen die Gesundheit dieser Frauen und in der Folge auch die der Gesellschaft insgesamt.

Keywords: Health, Women, Poverty, Mortality, Fertility, Educational Attainment, Roles and Status of Women, AIDS, Early Motherhood, Female Headed Households, Sub-Sahara Africa, Gesundheit, Frauen, Armut, Sterblichkeit, Fertilität, Bildungsniveau, Aufgaben und Status der Frauen, Aids, frühe Mutterschaft, weiblicher Haushaltsvorstand, Afrika südlich der Sahara.

1. INTRODUCTION

The health situation of a population, since it provides the major condition for productive efforts, has been recognized as the main determining factor for socio-economic development of any country. In Sub-Saharan Africa, the health situation of the population had for long been a pressing issue and thus at the forefront of all development strategies both by the local governments and the international community. Indeed, the reduction of the high mortality levels within the sub continent had been the main subject of concern to scholars, policy makers and the general public at large; from the early days of independence up to the late 1970s, the development of health amenities in most of these countries to facilitate this lowering of mortality was one of the first priorities. A substantial part of general budgets during this period was allocated to the Ministries of Public Health leading to heavy investments in the health sector. As a result of these efforts, the situation globally is known to have improved quite well. The sanitary coverage has improved substantially along with the appreciable decline in mortality levels. Several years have been gained in the expectation of live at birth (from an average of about 40 around 1965, to over 50 years in the 1990s (see WORLD BANK 1992) while several endemic diseases have been eradicated. However, in spite of these improvements that have occurred in the health sector, the situation is still one that calls for concern. The improvement has been relatively slow compared to the other developing regions. Coverage remains imbalanced, while the health care systems have not been able to satisfy the needs of the populations especially in the rural areas. Besides, there are the persistent difficulties of meeting up with the rapidly increasing demands particularly in the urban areas. As such, there are numerous persons with inadequate or complete absence of health care.

Besides, the global economic situation since the mid 1980s has also witness changes that have wide repercussions on the health situation. This has brought along widespread poverty. The most alarming issue, has been the disparity between population growth in the sub-continent and the declining level of government's investments in the health sector. As a result, the quality of services has been even difficult to maintain let alone to improve coupled with the constant deterioration of the existing equipment. In this paper, we tried to give a brief overview of the health situation of African women living south of the Sahara desert as well as some conditions impeding on their health.

2. THE HEALTH SITUATION OF WOMEN

The position of women in the developing world has claimed worldwide attention in recent times. Women are recognized as an essential component for the attainment of sustainable development. In other words women are not only fundamental in the development process but they are also equally indispensable for the success of population programmes. In addition to other roles women provide a vast majority of the labour force involved in agricultural and food production. African women are well known for their untiring self-giving and service. They are mothers; the first educators; wives and companions, etc. Generally, they perform the dual role of producers and reproducers. This makes their participation and partnership are indispensable in productive and reproductive life. Thus the importance of their health in any society.

Indeed, women occupy a special place in Africa. Women in Sub Saharan Africa constitute well over half (approximately 51%) of the total population of about 600 million, according to UN estimates for 1995. About three-quarters of them live essentially in rural areas. They participate in, and often manage many activities that affect the health and well-being of their families.

Turning to the evolution of their health situation, demographic figures are perhaps the most revealing indicators of the sweeping changes that have transformed women's lives over the last two decades. These show that, although there are yet very profound variations between the individual countries and intra-countries, Sub-Saharan Africa is under-going a health transition characterized by a decline in mortality and "isolated" indications of declines in fertility, and little or no indications of any decline in adolescent fertility rate (UN 1989; NRC 1993). Again, in reviewing the health status of women, life expectancy rates increased substantially in most Sub-Sahara African countries, if not all, during the last decade. As such, an average girl born today can expect to live for at least a decade longer than her mother (see Table 1). Taken globally, the average life expectancy at birth stood at 45 years in 1965 but estimates as at 1990 show an average increase of about 10 years.

However, life expectancy rates for an average woman are still relatively low - below 60. The disparity between the developed or other developing countries and those in the Sub-Saharan region is most blatant. Poverty, hard manual work, endemic diseases, inadequate public health facilities and difficult deliveries in rural areas and poor nutrition, all have detrimental effects on these women's health. In the developed countries, maternal mortality has declined rapidly over the past decades and maternal deaths have become rare events. In contrast, in the developing countries, complication of pregnancy and childbirth still constitute a major problem.

Pregnancy related complications actually poses some of the greatest hazards to the health and well-being of women within the sub-continent. Even with the advancement in technology towards enhancing safer motherhood, pregnancy related complications continue to result in severe illnesses and even death. Unfortunately however, little is known about the exact of women who die during pregnancy or what actually goes wrong with their pregnancies.

Though precise data on the various causes of death are difficult to come by, it is worth mentioning here that this is in fact one of the leading causes of death (if not the leading cause) among women of procreative age in most of Sub-Saharan Africa. Official statistics are often difficult to find on this topic and where available, do not often reflect its importance because in such areas where it is so high, most of the deaths do go unregistered due to the low utilisation of health facilities. Nevertheless, at a rough estimate (WHO 1990), over 150.000 women die as a result of pregnancy each year; most of them occurring in Sub-Saharan Africa.

But in the few countries of the region where their DHS surveys included questions on maternal mortality, it is estimated that over 500 women do die per every 100.000 births. This heavy toll seems to be associated with the fact that most childbearing take places under very poor and unhealthy conditions as a result of the limited access to maternity care facilities. Consequently, the greatest risk to a woman's health in Sub-Saharan Africa seems to be related to her role as a reproducer.

Table 1
Female Life Expectancy and changes (years) for Selected African Countries between 1965 and 1990

Country	Life expectancy e_0		Gain in Years
	1965	1990	
Botswana	49	69	20
Burundi	44	48	4
Cameroon	47	59	12
Côte d'Ivoire	44	57	13
Ghana	49	57	8
Kenya	50	61	11
Lesotho	50	57	7
Malawi	40	47	7
Mali	39	50	11
Nigeria	43	54	11
Senegal	42	49	7
Togo	44	55	11
Zambia	46	52	6

Sources: World Bank, 1992.

The importance of health in promoting human resource development and enhancing women's productivity as well as well-being need not be over-emphasized. But it is worth noting that women's health is also determined by their socio-economic situation, biological factors and other aspects related to their status and role in society.

3. THE TRADITIONAL LIFE OF THESE AFRICAN WOMEN

The traditional life of most African women living in the Sub-Saharan region is a hard one. In fact, Africa is characterized by traditions and beliefs that adversely affects women's health. Though in the world today there is growing recognition of women's rights to control their bodies and fertility. In most traditional African cultures of the region, social stratification places the woman in a subservient position vis-a-vis the man both within the household or family and the society as a whole. In matrilineal societies, although the woman is crucial for lineage membership conferment, the males still make most of the decisions. In patrilineal groups, she is not a member of her husband's lineage. For the most part, she is the main producer of food. She hauls the water; she tills the soil, plants the seeds, harvests the crops and keeps watch over the children as well as soothes the husband. Food preparation is an important concern especially to the rural woman. Culturally, the bride-wealth system in most African cultures transfers the fertility rights to the husband. Sociologically, she does not control her body. She becomes the property of the husband's lineage that paid the bride-wealth.

In fact, women's status and roles in Africa have been regarded as multiple or complex, comprising an array of different components, and capable in any society of being high in one aspect and medium or low in others (OPPONG & ABU 1985). In their renown work on the role of women using role theory, Oppong and Abu have identified seven roles of the African woman: parental, occupational, conjugal, domestic, kin, community and individual roles. Besides, CHRISTINE OPPONG (1989) asserts that life for most African Women has generally been an energetic combination of childbearing, child-rearing and the generation of scarce income (see also UNECA 1989). The vast majority of women "work" in agriculture; with less than one in five in other sectors. Only a tiny percent are employed in industry. They work mainly in physically taxing activities with few labour-saving tools or machines, in low skilled wage work and the informal sector. Access to better paid jobs, higher status jobs, educational standards had been relatively limited for Sub-Sahara African women. This has further reinforced the existing cultural female subordination.

Indeed, the arduous tasks such as the domestic work, the collection of water and the gathering of fuel wood, food processing and long hours of cooking and other back-breaking tasks, ensure the survival of the household (CELCALSKI 1987). Many women had and may still have few choices or opportunities in life outside marriage and childbearing. For most of these women, the primary function of marriage is procreation. Childbearing is the very essence of it. It is a source of personal satisfaction and social status. Thus, in many parts of the sub-continent, a woman's status was measured in terms of her ability to procreate. Many offsprings guaranteed her social status and respect that extends far beyond her position in the conjugal home. Her social standing among her own groups and in the community at large was enhanced by her reproductive prowess.

One writer remarks (HANDWERKER 1989) that childbearing in Africa was a singular important mechanism that women use to gain access to the resources on which their material welfare depended. In a woman's youth or early years of reproduction, her children legitimizes her claims for income from men. In her middle age, children provide the financial support required to make her independent of spousal support that usually require much of her subservience. In her late or old age, financial support and security from children makes the difference between abject poverty, a moderate and even a comfortable level of living (HANDWERKER 1989). In any case, women feel a greater need for old age security than men (NUGENT & ANKER 1990). Consequently, an average African woman tends to continue childbearing throughout her procreative life span irrespective of whether she is happily married or not, often starting relatively early. Very few women voluntarily terminate childbearing before menopause except when compelled to do so by secondary sterility. In fact, a majority of them have large families not only because they want them but they also do need them. Given the limited opportunities, the status conferred on them by childbearing becomes more important.

It should be recalled that infertility on the contrary constitutes a major health problem for women of this region, partly because of the belief that 'no woman is healthy unless she has children'. It is actually a matter of deep and intimate concern both to the individuals and the families or society at large.

They struggle to maintain this except when forced by other circumstances. Traditional roles and the weakness of rural infrastructure further encourages childbearing. But unfortunately, these many offsprings take a heavy toll of the lives of these women through maternal mortality.

4. THE WORKING CONDITIONS OF THE WOMEN

It is often said and known that women's work or employment influences not only their childbearing behaviour, but gives them autonomy, boost their self-esteem, affords them financial independence as well as provide them with a sense of self-esteem and control over their own bodies which tends to affect their health and its management.

It is perhaps in this light that both public and private organizations over the last years have continuously attempted to favour and encourage the recruitment of female staff. Consequently, most recent studies seem to suggest that women's participation in formal sector or gainful employment is on an upward rise. However, women's participation in professional life is still very low though far better than in the past. Available data from few African countries (STEADY 1990) show that the situation has improved in countries like Botswana and Mauritius where female participation in the labour force has been substantial in the professional and technical fields.

Nonetheless, women's formal or gainful employment in most African countries is primarily concentrated in the semi-skilled and unskilled jobs in the manufacturing and services sectors or what we may term informal sector. For instance in Congo it has been estimated that approximately 54% of the individuals active in the informal sector are women (ZEGERS 1992). Most women in this sector are there because of economic need, not out of an entrepreneurial spirit (though few might be), as they are unable to obtain jobs in the formal sector for obvious reasons. The activities of this informal sector include food processing and home industry, petty trading, buying and selling food crops in urban centres. In effect, women currently control food markets in all the major towns of Cameroon.

We are not by any means trying to ignore the existence in certain areas of West Africa of a strata of both urban and rural women that control a substantial fraction of business transactions within their national territories; the "Nana Benz" as they are popularly known in Lome, Togo.

Such women commonly called (locally) the 'buyam-sellams' buy and retail foodstuffs in the markets. By this, some of these women travel long distances into the hinterland under very difficult conditions to buy the foodstuffs that have to be retailed in the urban markets. Needless to add that trading over long distances and even in local market contains some element of risk.

The concentration of women within particular sectors of the economy is apparent in the calculations of the female share of the economically active population in the total labour force and within each sector (DIXON-MUELLER & ANKER 1988). Majority of the women in the Sub-Saharan region (roughly about 75%) live in rural areas and as agriculture is the sole source of livelihood for the rural dwellers, most are involved in agriculture. In effect, women have been noted to be playing a paramount role in agricultural production in these rural economies. They produce more than 75% of the locally grown agricultural products. A number of studies have actually confirmed "that women perform between sixty and eighty per cent of agricultural work in most African countries (BOSERUP 1970). Furthermore, data from Kenya reveal that women constitute eighty per cent of all self-help labour in such activities as construction and trade (UNECA 1975:65).

Furthermore, according to ILO estimates and projections more than half of the world's working women are in agriculture and most of them in Africa, where generally the proportions are in the neighborhood of three-quarters (75%). The situation has not changed dramatically and substantially over the last two decades. This concentration of women in these sectors may not be so much the problem but rather the condition under which they carry out their numerous responsibilities.

Agricultural work is difficult and tedious. The tools are still rudimentary rendering labour time consuming. The use of improved agricultural inputs is still very elusive for most rural African women. Besides, the development of rural infrastructure to back up agriculture by African governments has progressed deliberately slow and the existing infrastructure is highly inadequate. These problems and many others are often exacerbated by the fact that most of the women carrying out agricultural work have to travel long distances from the village to the fields. Indeed, in many Sub-Saharan countries large areas of land closer to the villages are being exploited with either motorized equipment for export or cash crop production or for construction. Thus, when one considers that women must carry their tools to and from the fields and even more burdensome - the carrying of the produce back, it becomes very clear that these women are in for an arduous task.

As already mentioned, throughout Sub-Saharan Africa, foodstuffs are cultivated almost exclusively by women while men are basically involved in cash crop farming. The women in Cameroon for instance farm a few parcels of land and allocate part, if not all of the harvest, for the family. But they do not even produce enough to eat, not to talk of reserving some for planting or as seedlings. Besides, work is carried out with rudimentary tools, hence is exhausting; the farms are usually far off the village and the women may spend more energy to and from these farms than they actually do in the farms.

This notwithstanding, in most sub Saharan African cultures, the woman has undoubtedly a right to the use of land under the control of her partner/husband so long as they remain together. She enjoys the usufruct rights. But she cannot own land. Marital instability often leads to the lost of such a right. In most cases the rural women are hardly owners of the land and worse still they have no right to inheritance of the land of their deceased husbands. Their access and control of resources is very limited as their position remains relatively that of subordination. Indeed, it is common occurrence in most parts of the region for the deceased husband's extended family to "chase her off" her homestead, grabbing all the household property (OWEN 1994) or keep her with little access to the property. Such practices tends to aggravate the already poor health situation of these women.

5. EDUCATIONAL ATTAINMENT

Education and health go together. In the modern world of today, one cannot be enjoyed without the other. It is and will remain a critical and key factor in the emancipation process of the African woman. It has a very strong influence not only on demographic trends but is also closely associated with health. Indeed, educated women/mothers tend to have the power of decision on health issues and have less fatalistic attitudes towards illness than their uneducated counterparts. They are more likely and able to make use of the medical resources at their disposal.

Table 2
Educational Attainment: Proportion of Females per 100 Males for Selected African Countries between 1965 and 1989

Country	Primary Level 1965	Primary Level 1989	Secondary Level 1965	Secondary Level 1989	Adult illiteracy % Females 1990
Botswana	129	106	77	109	35
Burundi	42	80	10	57	60
Cameroon	66	85	28	68	57
Côte d'Ivoire	51	-	19	44	60
Ghana	71	81	34	65	49
Kenya	57	94	38	70	42
Lesotho	157	122	100	147	-
Malawi	59	81	40	54	-
Mali	49	58	30	48	76
Nigeria	63	82	43	75	61
Senegal	57	72	35	51	75
Togo	42	63	26	31	69
Zambia	78	91	39	59	35

- Not available.
Sources: World Bank, 1992.

In Sub-Saharan Africa female education, just like many other variables, currently present some contradictions (STEADY 1990). On the positive side, the gender gap has narrowed in terms of basic education. Vocational education for girls and schemes designed to train girls in new technical fields have increased. According to UNESCO'S statistics and projections, girl's education quadrupled between 1950 and 1985. At the primary level, it rose from 24% in 1960 to about 61% in 1990 (WORLD BANK 1994; 1992) and respectively at the secondary level from 1% to 16%. In Botswana for instance, the proportion of educated women is higher than that of men. Consequently, it can be said that the education of women both at the primary and secondary levels has improved significantly in Africa over the past three decades, though wide disparities in achievements do exist between the countries.

On a negative note, despite these gains, there is still a long way to go in order to achieve respectable standards. More boys than girls still go to school in most African countries. Boys still outnumber the girls in this regard. Furthermore the drop out rate for girls is still higher than that of boys. The sex differences in education become most marked at the higher levels. In other words, the chances for girls to pursue higher education worsens as they progress from grade to grade. About 76% of [school age] girls on the whole start primary school compared to 86% of boys. But only 36% of the girls do complete as against 44% for boys. Again, barely 40% of girls who finish primary continue to the secondary level or are likely to do so, of whom barely 18% are likely to complete (WORLD BANK 1994). As such, a large number of girls in the region receive only the most rudimentary education and subsequently draw very little benefit from it.

Several reasons have often been advanced for this situation. Girls are often required to help their mothers with work at home and in the fields, which diverts both time and energy from school work. Teenage pregnancies and early marriages also often acts as deterrents to their educational attainment. In highly islamic societies, many of the girls do not complete primary school because they enter marriage life very early. Many others drop out because of early pregnancy or because parents want their adolescent girls to start a family which opens them to numerous lineage and family alliances. Even girls who go beyond the primary, have to battle with the problem of early pregnancy or unplanned motherhood. Consequently, a large number of African women are still illiterate which may constitute serious constraints to their performance at all level.

6. OTHER CONDITIONS IMPEDING ON THE WOMEN'S HEALTH

The health conditions on the continent did improve considerably during the 70s and early 80s. But women in Africa, south of the Sahara, still face special health needs that are sometimes influenced by both environmental and socio-economic factors. Structural adjustment cost recovery programmes of the late 1980s have aggravated the health situation of the woman. Poverty, hard manual work, endemic diseases, inadequate public health facilities and difficult deliveries in rural areas and poor nutrition, all have detrimental effects on women's health. The AIDS pandemic poses serious threats to the African woman within the context of cultural sex practices and male role in sex matters. Women often find themselves in vulnerable situations for a variety reasons. Such vulnerable situations include old age, widowhood, displaced or refugee, female heads of households as well as adolescent mothers among others. Let us examine some of these conditions.

The advent of the AIDS Pandemic

AIDS has come to constitute a major world-wide health problem that may negate all the health achievements of the post-independence Sub-Saharan Africa. The rapid propagation of the AIDS virus (the human immunodeficiency virus-HIV) is a severe subject for concern in view of the enormous losses that the disease represents to families, communities and nations at large. It is increasingly becoming a major cause of death for most groups while the HIV is now expected to result in the resurgence of other diseases like tuberculosis (UN 1991). While the actual number of living AIDS cases at any time cannot be known or estimated with certainty, WHO currently estimates that Sub-Saharan Africa accounts for a disproportionate share of the world's total.

In the particular case of women, it is apparent that the weak economic conditions or poverty situation in many of the Sub-Saharan nations severely limits both men's and women's ability to earn income sufficient to sustain themselves and their families and consequently, many of the women are bound to resort to risk-taking sexual lifestyles just to survive. The pattern of spread of the disease or prevalence in large measure, tends to reflect women's quest for some measure of economic security.

Most reports on the disease tends to suggest high prevalence among the military who are salaried and regularly paid as well as along truck roads (see for instance, ORUBULOYE, CALDWELL & CALDWELL 1993) - truckdrivers are often "cashy". It is also common knowledge that armed forces personnel, truckdrivers and tourists are more prone to practice indiscriminate [commercial] sexual activity. Besides, in such encounters, there are little protective measures by way of condom use. As such, these groups serve as bridges for transmission of HIV/AIDS to the poor rural women and the urban poor who may have to barter sex for survival. And subsequently, through these women an increasing number of men and children are acquiring the virus.

Indeed, most of the sexual acts that lead to HIV transmission in women may have no relation with reproduction as much as to the pursuit of pleasure. Cultural norms, together with women's social and most importantly, economic dependency, limit their ability to negotiate safer sex with their partners and often force then to barter sex for survival. Equally their dependence tends to increase her vulnerability to physical violence in sexual encounters.

Consequently, while women in the region continue to face situations that foster their vulnerability to HIV and AIDS, to believe that the HIV protection is merely a matter of education and the mounting of awareness campaigns and promotion of condom use, is to misread the realities, not only of gender politics, but also of the difficulties of surviving structural poverty and underdevelopment. We are thus, tempted to believe that prevention strategies could be more meaningful if we do well to include in our current packages vocational training programmes and assistance that can offer the poor women some possibilities of earning a living as well as providing them with at least some partial economic independence.

Malnutrition and poverty/sap

A poor nutrition compromises health and the well-being of individuals as well as their potential development. It reduces the productivity of household and its capacity to survive. Studies have suggested that malnourished persons often have an inferior capacity and low physical returns (POPKIN & DOAN, 1990; SAFILIOS-ROTHSCHILD 1986; OPPONG 1994). Thus malnutrition aggravates the economic and social difficulties of already disfavoured persons.

Though apparent sex discrimination in nutritional practices might not exist in Africa like in the Asian continent, it is very likely that nutritional status of women especially in rural areas tend to be lower. Nutritional status depends not only on available resources but also on the time and attention dedicated to the satisfaction of physical, mental and social needs. Considering the weight of certain tasks - household and agricultural, - that the women must have to accomplish, it becomes clear that many tend to have neither the time nor the energy required for them to avoid malnutrition. As such the subservient position could be a further cause of malnutrition (OPPONG 1994; POPKIN & DOAN 1990).

The rural poor woman and her children are generally the first victims of famine/malnutrition. Besides, local feeding practices leave a lot to be desired. Proper nourishment even of breastfeeding mothers is a major problem throughout the African continent with practically no attention given to a balanced diet. The consequences of such malnutrition is not only detrimental to the individual woman but for both the family and the nations at large - in terms of continuous wastage of precious human resources, - thus an obstacle to development.

The situation is further exacerbated by widespread poverty, the poor rural infrastructure and at present the constant devaluation /depreciation of local currency under IMF's structural adjustment policies. Structural Adjustment Programme (SAP) seek reduction in public sector expenditure. The cost recovery programmes demand that poor rural women pay for even basic health services. Besides, the loss of jobs in almost every sector of such economies have brought untold sufferings to thousands, especially the women. Although we cannot determine what proportions of men in relation to women is affected, there are more serious repercussions on the African woman. In effect, when the man looses his job, the greater burden is placed on the woman who has to provide for the basic family needs.

Migration/refugees
At first, migration was a well known male phenomenon. Usually men migrated in search of jobs. Today, large numbers of women are migrating to the cities and urban areas. African cities are plagued with illiterate or semi-literate female migrants who usually control small trading, marketing and other petty economic activities. Many have moved to the cities to escape from the abject poverty. Sometimes some resort to prostitution with all its deleterious consequences.

Aside from these few, several factors have unfavorable repercussions on the general migration. Natural catastrophes and civil wars that are now very common in several African countries are responsible for massive migrations and further worsens the general situation of the female migrants. In fact, civil wars, political conflicts and instability are among the major obstacles to the improvement of health. Inter- and/or intra-tribal tensions and civil conflicts do result not only in the displacement of large numbers of families but in the loss of several members or erosion of some and separation in course of fleeing. The enormous destruction of both human life and material wealth brings about untold suffering on women. They become dislocated from their homes, communities and the usual means of subsistence, which combines with the breakdown of the health supporting infrastructure among other things, to generate high risk situations which increase women's vulnerability to a wide range of health problems.

Indeed, 'health in general is the first major victim of wars'. The official number of acknowledged deaths and injured persons usually represent only a tiny fraction of health implications of such conflicts. Actually, among the officially acknowledged refugees and internally displaced persons in the world, it has been estimated (ADEPOJU 1992), that 50% are in Africa (a greater majority of whom are in the Sub Saharan region). In addition to political refugees and freedom fighters, these displaced persons in Africa include mainly women and children fleeing from war, conflicts, persecution, famine and drought. Indeed, the bulk of these unfortunate migrants is comprised mainly of women and their children (increase in the numbers of widows andd orphans) for whom survival becomes so precarious.

The problems faced by these migrant women include unplanned and teenage pregnancies, health, and poor physical conditions. Besides, violence which includes rape, abuse and harassment also permeate the lives of migrant women and endanger their physical safety on a daily basis. They are deprived of the universally recognized basic human rights to shelter, food, water, clothing, access to health care. Also, massive migrations can equally overturn the balance between the sexes in the receiving regions. Certain declining cultural practices resurface or they are further propagated such as polygyny, again with women being further placed in very vulnerable positions.

Early motherhood or adolescent mothers

Adolescent fertility in Africa, is a complex process that is influenced on the one hand by longstanding African traditions and on the other by a rapidly modernizing and urbanizing world environment (IPPF 1994). Early childbearing has several negative economic, health and social consequences with a far more heavier impact on women's status.

Health consequences of adolescent child-bearing are comprehensively documented in UN, (1989) and NRC (1993).

Firstly, they are often forced to drop out of school and thus reducing their literacy capacity. Subsequently, their lack of skills and professional experience, leaves prostitution or other menial jobs in urban areas as the only employment options. Incidentally, young women, especially the unmarried ones, are most often least supported by their parents and the community. In some cases these women are subjected to moral persecution and even rejected by their families . Besides, they are often discriminated against.

A study in Kenya in 1988 established that about 8000 teenagers were forced to drop out of school that year due to pregnancy while a similar study in Tanzania in 1984 revealed that 18766 primary and secondary school students were expelled from school due to pregnancy. Meanwhile in Rwanda, a recent study indicated that unmarried women who had been teenage mothers had been subjected to moral persecution and had been rejected by their families (IPPF 1994). In 50% of the cases, the father did not acknowledge the child.

Data from Demographic Health Survey (DHS) conducted in several countries in Sub-Saharan Africa indicates that a greater fraction of women aged 15-19 years (at least 50%) were sexually active with an appreciable proportion that had already recorded at least a birth. While age at marriage in the majority of countries in the sub-region is tending to be delayed, the risk of earlier intercourse and subsequently of unwanted pregnancy/birth seems to be on the increase. It is well known that in general, under the age of 20, the risks entailed during pregnancy for the health of the mother and child do increase proportionately the earlier the pregnancy. Besides, there are several additional hazards associated with such pregnancies. Consequently, adolescent or teenage mothers who are not very uncommon in the region make up a highly vulnerable group. They are morally and psychologically subjected to premature tensions and responsibilities for which they are not prepared. Many young women find themselves in situations they cannot handle.

Emergence and mounting female headed households/single parents

One of the justifications for the International Year of the Family is the "breakdown of the Family" in virtually every country in the world. The most visible symptom of this breakdown is the fact that one-quarter of the world's households are managed by women without the support of a man or more precisely of a male partner (TAYLOR 1994). Despite ambiguity on the term "Female Head of Household", it has been generally observed that an increasing number of households are headed by women today. Wide variations exist between countries in the proportion of female headed households. In Africa south of the Sahara, although we do not have the exact figures, the estimate asserts that one out of every three households has practically no stable couple. In Ghana for instance, the proportion increased from about 26% to 32% of the households between 1960 and 1984. Studies made in Botswana, Kenya, Lesotho and Sierra Leone show that women head over 40% of the rural households (YOUSSEF & HETLER 1984).

The problem here is not with the increase. Such households have often been identified and understood to be poorer than those depending on a man for support. Indeed, households that once survived or that should normally survive on the work of two parents have to suffice on whatever an over-stretched woman can manage to provide by herself. This increasing trend of what TAYLOR (1994) has called "the fourth world", is for a large part responsible for what many observers have identified as the "Feminization of Poverty."

In addition to the common problems faced by each individual woman trying to deal with the requirements of domestic work and child care, these women have to act as breadwinners. Because they must integrate household and child-care demands into their work schedules, their choices of jobs are limited to low wage jobs despite their desperate need for full-time income.

Table 3
Proportion of Female Headed Households for Selected African Countries between 1970 and 1980.

Country	Around 1970		Around 1980	
	First Survey	Female Heads	First Survey	Female Heads
Botswana	-	-	45.2	1981
Ghana	1970	28.7	-	-
Kenya	1969	29.5	1979	32.1
Lesotho	-	-	1980	40.0
Malawi	1970-72	28.8	-	-
Mali	1970	15.3	1976	15.1
Nigeria	-	-	1980-81	14.3
Rwanda	1970	16.5	1978	25.2
Sudan	1972	22.1	-	-
Togo	1970	19.3	-	-
Tanzania	1970	25.0	1978	25.0
Zambia	1974	26.4	-	-

- Not available.
Sources: Tables 1a and 5a; Safilios-Rothschild, 1986.

Female headed households are made up, to a large extent of single, separated, divorced, widowed (see SAFILIOS-ROTHSCHILD 1986) women. Sometimes, they are usually young women. Often, such women represent one of the most vulnerable groups and thus, experience great difficulties in fulfilling their roles as mothers or breadwinners. It is even worse for teenage and young mothers who happened to find themselves in this group. They usually have to combine the precarious position of household head with extreme youth, immaturity and poverty. Besides poverty, such women and their children suffer the risk of all the types of harassment, and discrimination as well as the relative or absolute impossibility of gaining access to education, suitable jobs or training and in most cases, of exercising their reproductive rights, if any.

7. CONCLUSION

The health situation of a population, since it provides the major condition for productive efforts, has been recognized as the main determining factor for socio-economic development of any country. In Sub-Saharan Africa, the health situation of the population has for long been a pressing issue and thus at the forefront of all development strategies both by the local governments and the international community. In this paper, we have tried to give a brief overview of the current health situation of African women living South of the Sahara desert as well as some of the key problems impeding their health. In talking about the health situation of these women, it is important to recognise that there has been substantial improvement made in this direction. This improvement though not exhaustively impressive, is quite appreciable.

Nevertheless, their situation is still considerably disturbing and can be attributed to many obstacles, of which the most powerful are those imposed by the weakness of the rural infrastructure and the deep-rooted traditional beliefs about the role and status of women in most African societies (that which confers prestige on women and/or couples with many offsprings). This situation is further compounded by the often passive attitudes of these women, either for reasons of fear, fatalism or simply because of their ignorance of viable alternatives. Low educational attainment, large numbers of children, time-consuming domestic chores coupled with other back-breaking tasks and cultural norms among other things, all infringe on these women's health and subsequently that of the society at large.

However, any discussion about the African woman must make a distinction between the different groups of African women. Those who have received a good education and aware of their rights and privileges and those who have little education and operate largely in the rural areas. The needs of these different groups differ very greatly. As such, solutions to the problems facing these groups are as varied as the solutions to underdevelopment in general. The rural woman most often requires essentially an improvement of the rural infrastructure to lighten their over-burdened life and improve her health.

References

ADEPOJU, ADERANTI. 1992. "Africa: A Continent on the move in search for the solidarity of the countries of the North" in *Solidarity in Favour of New Migrations.* Proceedings of the Third World Congress for the Pastoral Care of Migrants and Refugees. Vatican, Rome, 1991.

BOSERUP, E. 1970. *Women's Role in Economic Development,* New York, St.Martin's Press.

CELCALSKI, E. 1987. "Energy and Rural Women's Work: Crisis Response and Policy Alternatives". *International Labour Review* 26(1). ILO, Geneva.

DIXON-MUELLER, R. and R. ANKER. 1988. Assessing Women's Contribution to Development. Training, Population, *Human Resources and Development Planning* No. 6. ILO, Geneva.

HANDWERKER, W.P. 1989. Women's Power and Social Revolution: Fertility Transition in the West Indies. *Frontiers of Anthropology* Vol.2. Sage Publications.

IPPF, 1994. "Adolescents in the Family and the Development Process" in UNECA. Third Population Conference Dakar 1992, *Conference Papers,* Vol. 3:221-230.

NATIONAL RESEARCH COUNCIL (NRC). 1993. *Social Dynamics of Adolescent Fertility in Sub-Sahara Africa.* Working Group on Social Dynamics of Adolescent Fertility. National Academy Press.

NUGENT J.B. and R. ANKER. 1990. "Old Age Support and Fertility". *Population and Labour Policies Programme Working Papers* No. 172. ILO, Geneva.

POPKIN, B.M. and R.M. DOAN. 1990. "Women's Roles, Time Allocation and Health" in CALDWELL et al, What do We Know about Health Transition: *Health Transition Series.* Vol. II (2) (Proceedings of an International Workshop, Canberra, 1989 :683-706.

OPPONG, C. 1991. "Relationship between Women's Work and Demographic Behaviour: Some Research Evidence in West Africa". *Women, Employment Programme Research Working Papers* No. 175. ILO Geneva.

---, 1989. "Women's Roles and Gender Issues in Family Planning in Africa" in RIPS. *Developments in Family Planning policies and Programmes in Africa.* Proceedings of the Colloquium on the Impact of Family Planning Programmes in Sub-Sahara Africa:Current Issues and Prospects. University of Ghana, Legon :143-193.

---, 1994. "African Family Systems in the Context of Socioeconomic Development". UNECA Third Population Conference Dakar 1992, *Conference Papers* :129-143.

OPPONG, C. and C. ABU. 1985. *A Handbook for Data Collection and Analysis on Seven Roles and Statuses of Women.* ILO, Geneva.

ORUBULOYE, IO, P. CALDWELL and JC. CALDWELL. 1993. "The Role of High Risk Occupations in the Spread of AIDS: Truck Drivers and Itinerant Market Women in Nigeria". *International Family Planning Perspectives* 19(2): 43-48.

OWEN, M. 1994. "The World of the Widow". *People and Planet* 3(2): 17-19.

SAFILIOS-ROTHSCHILD, C. 1986. *Socioeconomic Indicators of Women's Status in Developing Countries,* 1970-1980. The Population council.

STEADY, F.C. 1990. "Women: The Gender factor in the African Social Situation" in ACARTSOD. The African Social Situation: Crucial Factors of Development and Transformation. *ACARTSOD Monograph Series* :155-199.

TAYLOR, DEBBIE. 1994. "Women of the Fourth World". *People and Planet* 3(2): 13-15.

---, 1991. "Economic Crisis in Africa". *Final Review and Appraisal of the Implementation of the United Nations Programme of Action for African Economic Recovery and Development 1986-1990* (UNPAAERD). Unedited Version.

---, 1989. *Adolescent Reproductive Behaviour: Evidence from Developing Countries.* Vol. II, New York.

UNECA, 1975. 'Women in National Development in African Countries' In *African Studies Review,* Los Angeles.

---, 1989. *African Women in Development. Selected Statements by* ADEBAYO A. Addis Ababa.

WORLD BANK. 1992. *World Development Report 1992: Development and the Environment.* Oxford University Press.

---, 1994. *Better Health in Africa: Experience and Lessons Learned.* Washington, D.C.

WHO. 1990. *Global Estimates for Health Situation Assessment and Projections,* 1990. Geneva.

YOUSSEF, N.H. and C.B. HETLER. 1984. "Rural Households headed by Women/ A Priority Concern for Development Rural Employment Policy Research Programme. *World Employment Programme Research Working Papers.* WEP10/WP.31. ILO, Geneva.

ZEGERS, M. 1992. "Strategies for Women and Development in the Republic of Congo". *ILO Working Paper: Labour and Population Series for Sub-Saharan Africa.* No. 114. ILO, Geneva.

Zweimal jährlich auf 128 Seiten:

curare

Zeitschrift für Ethnomedizin
Hrsg. von der Arbeitsgemeinschaft Ethnomedizin (AGEM) im Verlag für Wissenschaft & Bildung, Berlin

curare - Schwerpunktbände:

1994-1: Psychiatrie im Kulturvergleich
1994-2: Heiler und Heilen im kulturellen Kontext
1995-1: Pilze, Schamanen und die Facetten des Bewußtseins
1995-2: Sucht und veränderte Bewußtseinszustände im Kulturvergleich
1996-1: Kognition, Krankheit, Kultur - Wahrnehmung von Körper und Krankheit in verschiedenen Kulturen
1996-2: Depression
1997-1: Theorie und Praxis der Ethnomedizin
1997-2: Geburtshilfe unter einfachen Bedingungen

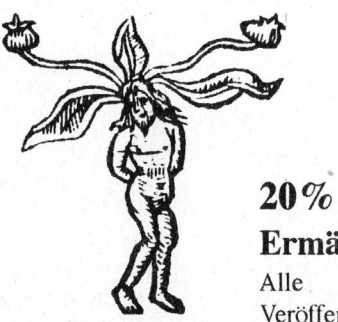

20% Ermäßigung:
Alle Veröffentlichungen der AGEM im Verlag für Wissenschaft und Bildung können von Mitgliedern der AGEM 20% ermäßigt bezogen werden.

Für Mitglieder:
Der Bezug der **curare** ist in der Mitgliedschaft bei der AGEM enthalten.

curare - Sonderbände

Sonderband 8/1995
Gebären - Ethnomedizinische Perspektiven und neue Wege
Hrsg. W. Schiefenhövel, D. Sich & C. E. Gottschalk-Batschkus. 462S., Bibliographie & Filmographie, Hardcover
ISBN 3-86135-560-4

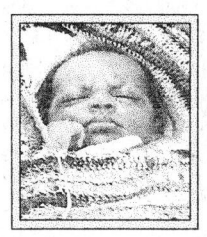

Sonderband 9/1996
Ethnomedizinische Perspektiven zur frühen Kindheit
Ethnomedical Perspectives on Early Childhood
Hrsg. C.E. Gottschalk-Batschkus & J. Schuler. 470S., zahlr. Abb., Hardcover, ISBN 3-86135-561-2

Sonderband 10/1996
Transkulturelle Pflege
Hrsg. C. Uzarewicz & G. Piechotta. 262S., Hardcover
ISBN 3-86135-564-7

Sonderband 12/1996
The medical anthropologies in Brazil
ed. by Annette Leibing on behalf of the Arbeitsgemeinschaft Ethnomedizin. ca. 250S., Hardcover

erscheint im Oktober '97

Sonderband März/1998
Therapeutische Konzepte im Kulturvergleich
Therapeutic Concepts in Transcultural Comparison
Hrsg. C.E. Gottschalk-Batschkus & C. Rätsch. 288S., zahlr. Abb. Hardcover

erscheint im März '98

Women have an Edge over Men on Traditional Medical Practice (TMPc) Knowledge: The Assumption versus the Field Situation
Frauen sind im Vorteil in Bezug auf Wissen über traditionelle Medizinpraktiken: Die Annahme und die Wirklichkeit

Musingo Tito E. Mbuvi

Abstract: The belief in some societies that men know more about Traditional Medical Practice (TMPc) than women is wrong. This belief has developed through the traditional assumption that men know more about TMPc than women. This assumption has more to do with the society's structure which tends to hide the actual functional roles of each member of the society. This has led to a situation where the roles played by women in TMPc have been hidden under her general society's obligation.
In the field, women TMPc are as competent as their male colleagues. Also, they enjoy the same status as men in all aspects of the practice from the society. The roles of women puts more responsibility on them than men. As they go about some of these duties, especially those involving TMPc and Traditional Medicines, they have unconsciously come to know more about TMPc than men contrary to what most people have been made to believe.

Zusammenfassung: Der Glaube, der in einigen Gesellschaften herrscht, dass Männer mehr über traditionelle Medizinpraktiken (tMP's) wissen als Frauen, ist falsch. Dieser Glaube wurde durch die traditionelle Annahme, dass Männer mehr über tPM's wissen als Frauen, entwickelt. Aber diese Spekulation nimmt mehr Bezug auf die gesellschaftliche Struktur, die dazu neigt, die tatsächliche funktionale Rolle jedes Mitgliedes der Gesellschaft zu verbergen. Dies führte dazu, dass die Rollen, die Frauen in der tMP's spielen, hinter ihren allgemeinen gesellschaftlichen Verpflichtungen versteckt wurden.
Im wirklichen Leben sind Frauen in der tMP's genauso kompetent wie ihre männlichen Kollegen. Weiterhin genießen sie den gleichen Status wie Männer in allen Aspekten der Praktiken innerhalb der Gesellschaft. Die Frau in ihrer Rolle hat mehr Verantwortung als Männer. Während Frauen ihre Arbeit machen, besonders solche, die in bezug auf tMP's und traditionelle Medizin, haben sie unbewusst mehr gelernt als Männer und wissen deshalb auch ihre männlichen Kollegen. Dies steht allerdings im Gegensatz zu dem, was die meisten Menschen glauben.

Keywords: Kenya, Traditional Medical Practice, Knowledge Assumptions, Society's Structure, Kenia, traditionelle Medizinpraktiken, Wissen, Annahme, gesellschaftliche Struktur.

1. INTRODUCTION

Women have played and will continue to play a major role in Traditional Medical Practice (TMPc) in different ways. The activities involve the collection, processing, consumption (treatment) and trade on these medicinal plant products. The most crucial one is the care of patients. This is the activity which has enabled them acquire more knowledge about TMPc than men. This has occurred unconsciously to both men and themselves. Their participation is increasingly providing employment and continues to generate income for thousands of rural and urban population countrywide. Their activities are of critical importance to the community as their holistic approach touches on every aspect of rural life, social, cultural and religious.

Very little specific attention has been given to the role of women in TMPc. Their critical input into family health though being appreciated it is not highlighted the way it should be. This hiding of their role is because of the society's social construction o sex roles and relations between the sexes than what is the practice. Women's knowledge about the environment is often more comprehensive because of the diversity of their tasks. Their participation can be categorized as below:

2. AS MOTHERS

The main responsibility for sustaining the family is usually assigned to the women increasingly so because of male migration to the urban centres. This is reflected in all spheres of the family life. For example, at the family level, there are more women visiting TMPrs than men not because they fall sick more but their role in the society places them at a central position in ensuring a healthy family. Among the Maasai, Croton somalensis is used to treat breathing difficulties. Where it is either smoked or the decoction drunk. For infants they inhale the smoke after it is exhaled perpendicular to their noses by a parent who smokes on behalf of the child. The mother will start going through diagnosis of the diseases, the use, preparation, the administering and the results of the medicine on the infant all through the life of that child. This definitely exposes her and puts her in close contact with the medicines/diseases more than men. Therefore as a mother, women will come across TMPc when:-

- a child is sick
- a relative is sick
- a neighbour is sick
- a husband is sick
- they meet as relatives, neighbours or friends to decide where (modern medical practice or TMPc) to take the patient
- they take a family member to the Traditional Medical Practitioner's (TMPr) clinic
- they accompany all the above when sick
- they are preparing medicines for the patients in the home
- handle/prepare/administer for/to the sick in the home
- they monitor the progress/response of the sick to Traditional Medicine
- and when they fall sick.

It should also be noted that rural households (about 70%) have women as the heads because men are in urban centres working leading to women being more experienced and knowledgeable in TMPc. Because of their overall concern over the family welfare including health, than any other member of the family, they are more conversant with TMPc than any other member of the family and the community at large.

3. AS PRACTITIONERS

Women practitioners are found in all categories of TMPc: Herbalists, Diviners, Healers, Wizards, Palmists, Psychotherapists and in some categories, they are the majority or they are the only ones in a particular category like Traditional Birth Attendants (TBAs).

The society has no control of who can become a TMPr in some categories and it has to abide by the choice of the spirits or the elders. The consequences which are believed they can befall the community if the wishes/choice of the ancestors is not adhered to has made the community to perpetuate the practice even in situations where the society may not be gender sensitive. A patient referred to a lady TMPr always goes to that TMPr with all confidence despite the gender of the TMPr. The patients have direct access to women practitioners at all times.

4. AS PATIENTS

This is discussed from the level of women patients and patients visiting women TMPrs. Though in the African society the choice of the TMPr to visit is a choice dependent on the society, friends, the family members, advice from a TMPr, fame of the TMPr or being referred to a TMPr by a former patient, In most cases it is a combination of the above. a woman patient has a right to go where she feels she will get better treatment.

A woman TMPr has no choice to decide the patients she receives/attends to. Whoever comes has a right to be attended to. This right emanates from the notion that their (TMPrs) practice is a service from God to the community through them. Refusing to do it will result in dire consequences as a punishment. The patients have no choice once they are referred to a TMPr even if it is a young girl Traditional Healer and the patient is an old man. Her role is accepted and respected and her instructions are binding, and adhered to. It should be noted that there are situations the healer may even be less than ten (10) years. This is common in cases where treatment knowledge (powers) is inherited through the ancestral line.

5. HANDLING OF THE MEDICINES
Women are found participating in all stages of the drugs preparation, use and dispensing. With established women TMPrs prescribing the drugs after diagnosis and then their assistants of both sexes doing the dispensing.

The processing is done mostly using traditional tools, mortars, pestles, grinding stones etc. The use of these tools places women at the central point as they know how to use them. Though the long necked gourds are still used, modern storage materials like plastic bottles are gaining foot.

Though some still give medicines in the form of bark or leaves tied with a string from tree bark fibres. Others are preparing and putting them in sachets while others are distilling to concentrate the active principle.

The dose issue though questioned by scientists, women are acclaimed to do it with a high degree of precision and explain the prescription more carefully and better than most men TMPrs.

6. AS HARVESTERS
High demands for plant based traditional medicines is resulting in continuos exploitation leading to shortages starting to be felt for some plants in some cases. The commercialization of the practice is placing more pressure on the already heavily used forests. Women play an active role in these activities especially the processing and the picking of some parts like flowers.

This is now being done for both domestic and commercial use by both men and women. In Nairobi, Maasai women are selling among other medicinal plant products Myrisine africana seeds and the bark of Albizia anthelmintica. In Western Kenya during market days in different village towns, there are mobile „pharmacists" (sellers) who move from one market centre to another selling their medicines to both patients and fellow TMPrs. The patients come to buy medicines known to them or prescribed by TMPr but not available locally.

7. AS FARMERS
Women make up the majority of subsistence farmers in the rural areas. It is their work which provides the family with any supplementary food. Their main responsibility for sustaining the family is increasing because of male migration to urban centres. This is a world wide situation as presented in the table below:

Tab. 1
Percentage of total agricultural production by women in several countries. (source SOUTHEMER 1991)

Country	%	Country	%
Nepal	98%	Iraq	41%
Zaire	64%	Brazil	32%
Korea	51%	Colombia	20%

Kenya's economy relies on agriculture and women form the largest percentage of the labour force. Women spend a lot of time in the farms, sowing, weeding, harvesting and accessing the status of the farm or supervising activities. This makes them come across very plants more frequently than most other people. This puts them at the forefront in deciding/influencing what medicinal plants are to be left in the farmland and also what is to be planted.

Though there are communities where women are not allowed to plant some trees, this is changing. It is even more encouraging because more and more women are acquiring land where they can decide what to plant. Women TMPr are doing this with ease because they have money.

As they weed they leave medicinal plants they know they are useful for the medication of the community. The Kalachoe spp are left in the farms and most of the people wonder what is their use. They are left because the warmed leaves are used to massage painful parts or dislocated joints. Healers will leave a herb, Evolvulus alsinoides because they use it when making good luck medicine, love potions etc.

8. AS TRAINERS

The training women offer to the society can be of two levels: to her immediate family (household) and the other members of the society. Women are the cultural guardians and the first educators. The first knowledge about TMPc on children is imparted by their mothers. In Kenya, this is likely because most of the children have to learn the mother tongue from their mothers. (ANNABEL 1991). Since the mother is the first to teach the child how to speak. Therefore, the first words uttered by a child are those he or she learned from the mother and definitely the first knowledge on Tamp a child learns is from the mother. Generally, the training or the methods of the acquisition of the knowledge to treat in the African society are varied. They range from apprenticeship, buying through a ceremony, being shown the plants through a dream/vision to being „conferred" the treatment powers by the spirits of the ancestors. The latter method has already assisted women at times and in societies where they could have/be discriminate against on gender basis.

Women TMPrs have apprentices of both sexes under their training just like their male colleagues. In spiritually acquired powers to treat in some communities like the Teso of Western Kenya, it is a senior woman healer who initiates the person chosen by the spirits to become the TMPr before he can be shown more plants, technologies by other TMPrs and through dreams/visions.

At the family level, women are the best trainers. Children spend most of their time with their mothers, this enables them to reach the children more easily then any other person. Most herbalists (men and women) learned TMPc from their mothers.

9. AS LEADERS

The number of women left behind in the rural areas to carry the burden of family survival is growing as men have gone in search o work in urban centres. In Kenya, Botswana, Ghana and Sierra Leone, almost half the households are headed by women (TAYLOR et al 1983 reprod. from SOUTHEMER 1991). This leadership is also present in TMPc. Women TMPrs have equal chances of ascending to high positions within their practice. We have senior/prominent female as well as male TMPrs within the society. Women TMPrs with strong/best medicines within a region or community are referral Institutions by Junior TMPrs of both sexes. They are famous and equally feared.

Most rainmakers among the Kamba community of Eastern Kenya are women. They lay down all the rules and regulations to be followed before and after the rains. For example, after drought, people are not supposed to plant the day after the first rains. Any member who goes against them is punished regardless of his/her gender neither the source of the authority.

Recently, associations of TMPrs have been started and ladies can vie for any post: for example, in Western Kenya, the Regional Association of TMPrs SWAVI has a lady Treasurer, Dr. Nazalina, while the local branch of the National Association for TMPrs in Kitui District is a lady Chairperson, Dr. Monica Mwikali Kaka enjoying the same respect as male TMPrs of the same calibre in the association.

10. AS CONSERVATIONIST

Women are at the forefront in conserving the environment. This is because they are the first to suffer from the environmental problems because they are so directly dependent on natural resources, often community owned for their livelihood. They have realized the period (past) when the bounty of nature could provide to their need has past SOUTHEMER 1991). This has been accompanied by a situation where their rights and access to cultivable land has decreased and the open forests, woodland and the bush from which they gather such vital necessities as fodder, fuelwood and water have grown scarce and have disappeared. All these translates to more work for women unless they conserve the resources. Women are trying to organise themselves to arrest the situation where they may lack medicine for their family by involving themselves in forestry activities.

Women are concerned with what can alleviate poverty and improve both household food and health amongst themselves. Subsistence harvesting of medicinal materials can continue sustainably. Commercialization of a product can shift the balance with devastating effects on the resource base. During the days of communal social control of use of resources, TMPrs used to harvest the plants in such a way as to allow continued regeneration of the resource through clear defined harvesting regimes. With breakdown of the traditional administrative structure the Government took over the responsibility and the approach changed to „Protection and Managing" the resources. This was to be done without the participation of the community. This approach seems to have had minimal success.

The conservation of medicinal plants continue to face problems. Because as resources become scarce, the TMPrs have to device methods of getting access to these materials by either moving to other sources, substitution (very rare) or planting. The latter option has a lot of potential but it has problems as the TMPrs have problems trying to raise these plants. Most of which are indigenous.

Women TMPrs have been collecting wildlings from the forest of medicinal plants and at the same time now they are trying to buy seedlings from the Government, NGO organisations or request from collaborating agencies. Homesteads of most female TMPrs are dotted with medicinal plants raised from the above sources. The activities have been less successful as the seedlings are not available in most cases. The maintenance of sacred sites and shrines has female members and these are actually in-situ conservation sites.

11. ACCESSIBILITY AND OWNERSHIP OF THE MEDICINES

Generally they are available/accessible to low income and socially disadvantaged groups. They are available to women from the wild and from domesticated plats like any other member of the society. Also being farmers, they are in constant contact with the useful plants and are thus the custodians. They have a right to harvest what they have planted and they can not be refused access because of their gender. They own what they plant and have overall control over their management and use. This is so even in communities like the Luhya communities where women were not traditionally allowed to plant trees. This taboo did not apply in the case of women TMPrs. Medicines from a female TMPr are hers and are accessible to all the members of the community.

12. CONTRIBUTION TO DEVELOPMENT

The contribution to development should be looked at from two levels: how it is assisting in overall development and the level of development of the practice. New technology is not penetrating the market fast enough and it is absent in the rural areas. The practice has not attained a level where they can get money from financial institutions for expansion. Despite all these, some of the practitioners are not poor by any standards and they are contributing immensely to overall national development.

Dr. Monica Kaka (mentioned above) has four assistants who assist mainly with TMPc duties: harvesting, preparation, dispensing, ceremonial treatment etc. This excludes the house servants and the farm workers. All these workers are paid salaries at the end of the month. Her major source of income is TMPc. There are several women TMPrs who are the sole breadwinners for their families. In this case, it means the woman TMPr takes care of the husband, the relatives, buys land and livestock for the family. She also pays dowry for her son's wives and takes care of her grandchildren. In some cases women TMPr assist their husbands pay dowry for them. In most African societies it is the men's responsibility to marry and take care of the wife and pay dowry. This practice is still practised especially in the rural areas. Most of the TMPrs have assistants whom they pay and are investing in property in the urban centres and have decent homes all these built with money from the practice. Majority of the TMPrs have established Guest House facilities for the comfort of their patients and the society at large. These are contributing to national development. Though lack of good education background for most of them has led to them not investing in the best business ventures.

Nationally they provide medical care to the majority of the population especially the rural poor and the urban centres where the practice is expanding rapidly. Most of them are actively training others. In Kenya, we have a formal school teaching TMPs, the School of Alternative Medicine. It provides employment both directly and indirectly and its potential is not yet fully exploited.

13. OVERALL PARTICIPATION AND EMERGING TRENDS

The participation of women TMPrs is like that of their male colleagues. They are participating fully in all spheres/aspects of the practice. They have not been disadvantaged by emerging socio-cultural changes. For example, the number of female TMPrs practicing in towns is increasing and those in the villages are constructing better treatment places just like the male TMPrs.

Therefore, all Ethnomedical survey should include women if they are to get all what that society knows about TMPc. This is so because women's knowledge about the environment is more comprehensive, because of the diversity of tasks.

References

ANNABEL, R. 1991. *Women and the Environment.* Publisher: Zed Books Ltd. London.

CLAREFIELD, G. 1996. *Articulating Indigenous Indicators. An NGO Guide for community driven project evaluation.* Environment Liaison Centre International (ELCI). Publisher: United Nations Environmental Programme, P.O. Box 30552, Nairobi.

FAO 1991. *Woman's role in dynamic forest based small scale enterprises: Case studies on uppage and lacquerware from India.* Publisher: FAO Regional Office for Asia and the Pacific.

HOMBERGH, H. 1993. *Gender, environment and development.* A guide to the literature: International Books (Utrecht, The Netherlands)

KEFRI: *Unpublished Ethnobotanical field survey reports from several Kenyan communities.* Kenya Forestry Research Institute, Information Unit, Nairobi, Kenya. P.O. Box 20412, Nairobi.

MBITI, J.S. 1968. *African religion and philosophy.* East African Educational Publishers. 1994 edition. Publisher: East African Educational Publishers Ltd. P.O. Box 45314 Nairobi

NDETI, K. 1972. *Elements of Akamba life.* East African Publishing House. Publisher The East African Publishing House, P.O. Box 30571, Nairobi.

NYAMWEYA, D. 1992. *African indigenous medicine.* African Medical and Research Foundation (AMREF) Publisher: The African Medical and Research Foundation P.O. Box 30125, Nairobi, Kenya.

SOUTHEMER, S. 1991. *Women and the Environment.* A Reader Crisis and Development in the Third World. Earthscan Publications Ltd. London.

UNDP/FAO SPFDP, 1995. *Proceedings of the 2nd Women's' Traditional Medicine Workshop.* Publisher: South Pacific Action Committee for Human Ecology and Environment, Box 1168 Suva, Fiji Islands.

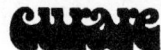

The Interrelationship between Health- and Nutritional Status for Girls, Mothers and Grandmothers
Wechselbeziehungen zwischen der Gesundheits- und Ernährungssituation von Mädchen, Frauen und Großmüttern

Veronika Scherbaum

Abstract: In many countries of Subsaharan Africa, girls and women are among the most vulnerable of the population in terms of ill-health, while their contributions as workers and managers of human welfare are central for survival. Referring to the situation of women in Ethiopia the interrelationship between health and nutrition of girls, mothers and grandmothers will be discussed. Activities to improve their health and nutritional status which takes this relationship into account will be proposed.

Zusammenfassung: In vielen Ländern Afrikas sind Mädchen und Frauen am meisten bestimmten gesundheitlichen Risiken ausgesetzt, während sie gleichzeitig einen wesentlichen Beitrag zum Überleben ihrer Familien leisten. Unter Berücksichtigung der Lebensverhältnisse in Äthiopien werden Zusammenhänge bezüglich der Gesundheits- und Ernährungssituation von Mädchen, Frauen und Großmütter aufgezeigt. Um deren Lebensbedingungen zu verbessern, werden Aktivitäten vorgeschlagen, die im besonderen auf diese Zusammenhänge eingehen.

Keywords: intra- and intergenerational health aspects, nutrition, childhood, adolescence, motherhood, aging, gender issues, culture specific factors, Ethiopia, Intra- u. Intergenerationseffekte in Bezug auf Gesundheit und Ernährung, Kindheit, Adoleszenz, Mutterschaft, Altern, Geschlechterbeziehungen, kulturspezifische Faktoren, Äthiopien.

Like in different other African countries, gender-based discrimination and subordination is deeply ingrained in Ethiopia and, unfortunately, women themselves often inculcate these cultural norms in succeeding generations. (SEN & GROWN 1988). Beside certain disappointments of the family when a girl is born (HAMMOND & DRUCE 1989), the frequency and duration of breastfeeding (KNUTSSON & MELLBIN 1969), the onset, quality and amount of supplementary food is often diminished (SCHERBAUM 1996b:50) leading to long-term effects such as chronic malnutrition (stunting) and ill-health. It is well established that stunted women are more likely to experience obstructed labour due to cephalopelvic disproportion (ROYSTON & ARMSTRONG 1986). In Ethiopia, there is evidence that the prevalence of malnutrition is higher in adult women than in adult males (UNICEF 1993:108, DEBESAI & YEMANE 1986).

Furthermore, early malnutrition might cause impaired brain development and intellectual deficits, which later - as part of a vicious cycle - can affect the level of childcare

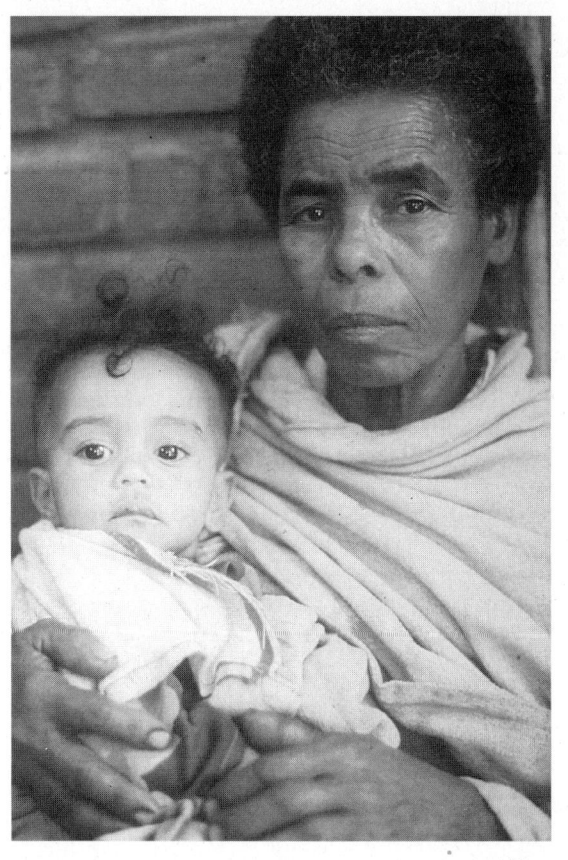

Abb. 1
Grandmother and child in Ethiopia.
Foto Veronika Scherbaum

and consequently lead again to malnutrition in the next generation (CLUGSTON 1981, MAHLER 1984).

Discrimination against female children becomes obvious in certain food taboos and cultural practises; girls are kept more often and longer inside the house and, in west Ethiopia, in order to keep them restrained in their activities, they are discouraged by pinching their arms (BULTI 1996). In some regions girls are not allowed to drink milk (SCHERBAUM 1996a:63) which together with lack of exposure to sunshine may lead to rickets (HOJER & GEBRE-MEDIN 1975) and exacerbate calcium deficiency (PARENT & KHADRAOUI 1987) contributing again to obstetric difficulties and subsequently to an increased risk of maternal death (MAHLER 1987). In this context, there is evidence that bone demineralization can be caused by multiple prolonged lactation periods, which increases also the risk of bone fractures during older age (LESLIE 1991). The average duration of breastfeeding for one child is about 25.3 months, and the estimated total fertility rate for women in Ethiopia is 7.7 children (CENTRAL STAT. AUTHORITY 1993). Moreover, other deficiencies of micronutrients, such as iodine (LAMBERG 1991), folic acid and iron (FLEMING 1989, LOZOFF et al 1987) begin before birth or during early childhood; this might affect adolescence and reproductive life and, untreated, can lead to serious sequelae or death. For example, iodine deficiency disorders (IDD) encompass a variety of life threatening conditions such as goiter, mental disorders, abortions, stillbirths and increased perinatal and infant mortality rate. According to ZEWDIE et. al. (1992) the prevalence of goiter among Ethiopian females is 27.3% versus 10.1% in males. In addition, many parents less frequently seek adequate health care for girls thus exposing them to longer periods of severe morbidity, ultimately resulting in both higher mortality and chronic disability (CHATTERJEE & LAMBERT 1989). Families general neglect of girls, lack of stimuli and encouragement often make the girls appear backward, inactive and fearful. Such neglect can also be responsible for different psychiatric disorders which are more commonly observed among females in Ethiopia (GIEL & VAN LUIJK 1969).

Because girls' labour is often essential for the whole family's existence, many parents are unable to spend resources on their daughters education (IVAN-SMITH 1990). In Ethiopia, girls and women represent only one-third of all school enrolments (UNICEF 1993:30).

Adverse, long term consequences of illiteracy and inadequate female education include: early marriage and -childbirth, higher levels of fertility and child mortality (CLELAND & VAN GINNEKEN 1988, LOVEL 1989). Clearly, continuing female illiteracy contributes to the maintenance of certain cultural beliefs about impurity during menstruation, nutritional taboos and some harmful traditional practices. (SCHERBAUM 1996a). For example, abstinence from nutritious foods during pregnancy and around child birth can have certain negative effects for both mother and child: depletion of a woman's own nutritional status so that she later might not have enough fat stores for optimal lactation. Different ethnic groups require pregnant mothers to restrain themselves from the consumption of milk-(products), fatty meat, porridge, potatoes and other foods which are white in color (YEMANE).

An average of 27% of lactating mothers have been found to be malnourished with less than 18.4 Body Mass Index (HANA 1992). Furthermore, women might deliver children of low birth weight (< 2500g) which is associated with higher morbidity (with its detrimental side effects on child growth and development) as well as a higher mortality rate. Estimates of the percentage of low-birth weight (LBW) infants are 15% (based on hospital data). The actual prevalence of LBW babies is probably higher, on the order of 20% (UNICEF 1993:108).

For wellnourished women, however, lactation may actually improve maternal health by inhibiting menses, preventing pregnancy, increasing eventual bone density and preventing cancer (ARMSTRONG 1995). The three necessary conditions for nutritional well-being - food, health and care - pose intense demands on the mother's resources, particularly on her time. Feeding the child is mainly the mother's task, but older siblings, preferably girls, are expected to take care of the younger children while the mothers work daily, approximately 15 to 18 hours in agriculture, collecting firewood, fetching water, and preparing food, marketing, washing clothes, tidying houses, beer brewing, cotton processing, basketing and other occasional activities.

Economic activities such as agriculture, animal care and marketing consume about 3 hours a day, but the time available for direct child care, mainly breast feeding, is only an hour a day (ZEWDIE & JUNGE 1990). Women have to collect wood almost every day and carry firewood equivalent to about one-fourth of their body weight (UNICEF 1993:118).

Women fetch water about two times a day, usually at the cost of an hour's walking. The traditional water pot weighs 8.9 kg and filled with water about 34 kg. Given the average body weight of 44 kilos, women carry an average 77% of their body weight for hours and uphill on many occasions (UNICEF 1993:118). Women spend an average of 4 hours a day in cooking related activities (KEBEBEW 1990).

Although a large number of Ethiopian households are chronically food insecure (ABERRA 1991), mothers often lack knowledge about the nutritional problems of their children. Many households are required to use more than 80% of their income to meet a daily average of about 1700 kcal which is less than 71% of the recommended daily calorie requirements (UNICEF 1993:116).

YEMANE (1990) found that while mothers believed their children had normal growth, 46% were actually found to be stunted. According to LATHAM (1979) the problem of malnutrition is not always so much lack of food as a lack of knowledge about healthy combinations of food and adequate feeding practices especially during illness. Further, it was found by RAMAKRISHNAN (1995) that mothers of malnourished children often suffer from depression, passivity, low self-esteem, attitudes and beliefs likely to lead to poor child care practices. A study by ABATE (1989) in five regions of Ethiopia revealed that 85% of all women are circumcised (excision or infibulation). In addition to bleeding and infection caused by the operation, obstetric complications due to scarring, problems during intercourse and psychological consequences might occur (ZENEBEWORK 1989, HUBER 1966).

The majority of girls enter the adolescence period without adequate knowledge about the reproductive system and sexuality (KEBEBEW 1990).

In addition, lack of information about family planning methods and their availability, as well as raping particularly during times of war, are major causes for teenage pregnancies. Adolescents, trying to hide their pregnancies, rarely seek prenatal care, while late induced abortions are common practice to overcome the social stigma of premarital pregnancy. Abortion, which is generally illegal in Ethiopia (but often performed under unsafe conditions), is considered to be the most common cause of maternal death (KWAST 1986).

For every women who dies as a consequence of induced abortion, many others are rendered infertile and predisposed to increased incidence of ectopic pregnancy during their subsequent life.Due to the combined effects of shorter average maternal height, poorer placental function and competition for nutrients between the mother's- and the growth needs of her fetus, adolescent mothers deliver a higher rate of low birth weight infants (FRISANCHO 1985) which perpetuates malnutrition from generation to generation (MASON 1994). This is shown in Fig. 1. In populations with chronic malnutrition maturation is usually delayed which means early child bearing is even more complicated (KURZ 1994). In Ethiopia, early childbearing is commonly associated with early marriage (ALEMU 1988), which in some areas takes place as early as eight years of age. In Ethiopia 63.6% of women marry before the age of 20 years, one of the highest rates of

Abb. 2
Women walking to fetch water about two times a day, usually need one hour. Foto: Veronika Scherbaum

early marriages in the world.

A poorly developed pelvis leads to such complications as obstructed labour, rupture of the uterus or even death (MEKONNEN 1989). Further, fistulae are common seqelae of prolonged labor with drastic physical disabilities, such as urinary incontinence and restriction of activities; abandoned by their husbands, many of these women remain socially isolated for the rest of their lives (HAILE 1983).

There is also some evidence that female infants of very young mothers are at a particular risk of death; the pressure of the husband and mother-in-law to bear a son, frequently yields to less care for girls and consequently to a shorter birth interval (ZEMED 1989). In west Ethiopia, during follow-up visits of children admitted with kwashiorkor (severe oedematous form of malnutrition) it became obvious that the case-fatality rate of girls was considerably higher as compared to boys (26.1% versus 16.7%). Lack of special care for girls recovering from severe forms of protein-energy malnutrition is a probable reason for this (SCHERBAUM 1996b:178).

Early marriage and physical abuse can alone be a source of different long term psychological problems, such as frigidity, marital disharmony and depression, which subsequently might lead to divorce (KEBEDE 1990). Wife beating after the wedding day and at least once a month is still practised in rural Ethiopia. There is a saying: „women and donkeys need a stick" (KEBEBEW 1990).

Divorced women often end up as prostitutes because they have no other financial alternative. Sexual transmitted diseases (STD's) are very common in Ethiopia and male promiscuity is the main cause. Although the men frequently infect their wives, women hesitate to seek medical care for fear of repercussions. Complications due to delayed and inappropriate therapy severely compromise women's health, productivity, fertility and pregnancy (WASSERHEIT 1989).

Infertility, always blamed on women, often results in divorce. The magnitude of physical and psycho-social consequences becomes particularly tragic with respect to AIDS, when children acquire infection in utero or are orphaned (HEYMAN 1990). The care-taking for the diseased and orphaned increases the burden and is usually carried out by young girls and grandmothers (CANTOR & HIRSHORN 1989). The high level of HIV seropositivity among young women has both a biological and a gender explanation. Biologically speaking, women are more likely exposed to the HI-Virus than men, because of the greater size of the female's genital mucus membrane. The gender issue encompasses the fact that only a few women have any say over their sexual and reproductive lives (SEIDEL 1996). Women often are unable to refuse a promiscous partner or demand safe sex. Many of the same factors that have predisposed women to ill health in the past now increase their vulnerability to AIDS, including poverty and malnutrition (ULIN 1992). In Ethiopia, many women are overworked and physically, mentally and emotionally exhausted at the end of the day, leaving them incapably of any meaningful interaction with their husbands and children (ANDREWS et al 1990). If a women has spent her entire life working beyond her physical capacities, has many pregnancies and seen some of her children die - perhaps up to an age of over 40 years-, and been undernourished and deprived since childhood, she will have accumulated all the signs and symptoms of maternal depletion resulting in severe disabilities and premature aging (KALACHE 1991). The nutritional status of older women reflects the cumulative effects of different problems such as early malnutrition, lack of child spacing, chronic anaemia, bad teeth, food of low nutritious quality and chronic digestive disturbances due to parasitic infections (BONITA 1996:35).

In Ethiopia, high priority in feeding is given to adult males rather than to children and women (YEMANE 1991). However, during old age when women are released from restrictions applying to menstruation or childbearing, their participation in life gets more accepted (FONER 1989). In rural Ethiopia, old women are valued for their traditional wisdom and expertise especially in pregnancy and birth related matters. Some elderly women are called upon to treat special illnesses like severe forms of malnutrition and certain other diseases (SCHERBAUM 1996:72).

Because of the dual system of "obbo and tschora" (BARTELS 1983:308) grandmothers play the key role in socializing their grandchildren (ROBINSON 1989). Parents and children are culturally bound to be different, they should keep respect and distance, but grandparents can be like friends with their grand children.

In addition, many older women supervise the work of young females in the household and are the main decision makers for health questions, marriage- and initiation arrangements; often they are active agents in upholding social practices that help to keep young women inferior - not only in relation to themselves but in relation to men. An older woman might even compete with her daughter-in-law for her son's allegiance and affection; her jealousy often leads her to abuse her authority. According to FONER (1989) this might be a kind of unconscious revenge for her own days as a helpless daughter-in-law. Because of the grandmother's important role in educating children (EPSTEIN 1987) and her influence on her son as the "head of the family", old women and husbands as main decision makers have to be involved in any programme (TAFERI 1990). It should also be a goal to reach the poor and most needy who are often largely excluded from existing services. Finally, "generation effects" of experienced starvation, war, and a rapidly changing society (HEISEL 1989) might affect the subsequent life of women in terms of ill-health, disabilities and mental problems (BEN-TOVIM 1987, ANDREWS et al 1990). In Ethiopia, the absence of husbands for many years, on the numerous war fronts, also left the women exposed to increased levels of abuse by undisciplined soldiers. Women suffered the anguish of having to live in the constant fear of the deaths of their husbands, sons, and their daughter too, who were conscripted in large numbers for national service. It fell to the women to bury those who died, to nurse the sick and those struggling with convalescence (UNICEF 1993:56). Demographic changes like an increasing number of old persons (KALACHE 1986), the consequences of war (leaving a greater proportion of unmarried and widowed women), urban migration, and AIDS related aspects are of importance. Noteworthy that many of the above mentioned "direct" and "indirect" interrelationships concerning health of girls and women affect children and the whole family in general.

The impact of the role of caregivers on women's health in general (DOYAL 1990) and specific consequences of certain communicable diseases (tuberculosis, leprosy, trachoma, hepatitis, scabies..) which can be transmitted during intensive care are not well researched. Under difficult circumstances (especially in times of war and AIDS) the question "who cares for the caregivers" remains unsolved. It is clear that negative consequences of these multifaceted interrelations cannot be tackled alone by selective "technical" interventions (BERMAN 1982) which are mostly concerned about mortality of mothers and children. Programmes to improve health and nutritional status during the different phases of womens' life cycles have to integrate educational, physical, mental and social as well as cultural, political, economic, agricultural and ecologic considerations. It is important to study the attitudes, beliefs and behaviour of women and link the results to health communication activities. To reach adequate acceptability, the "felt needs" of women of all age groups have to be heard and their active participation is essential for effective programmes. The following proposed programmes which are designed to consider simultaneously the different intra- and intergenerational aspects of women's health (FOGLER 1989, LEVITON 1989) therefore include education, improved nutrition and health care, social and economic policies as well as surveillance and research activities demanding a high degree of intersectoral collaboration.

Because such a programme should be integrated into the existing infrastructures, intensive information dissemination, dialog and debate at all levels is needed at the initial stage so that budget-reallocation and modifications of government- and non-governmental organisation (NGO) activities can take place."

Figure 1
Intergenerational cycle of growth Failure

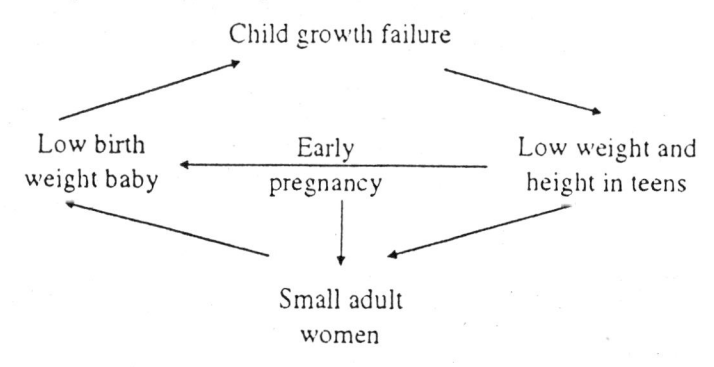

```
                Child growth failure
               ↗                    ↘
Low birth  ←  Early      Low weight and
weight baby   pregnancy   height in teens
               ↓     ↖
            Small adult
              women
```

(Source: Figure 4.9, p.56 in: ACC/SCN (1992). *Second Report on the World Nutrition Situation. Volume I: Global and Regional Results.* ACC/SCN, Geneva)

Figure 2
Interrelationship of Female Health and Nutritional Status

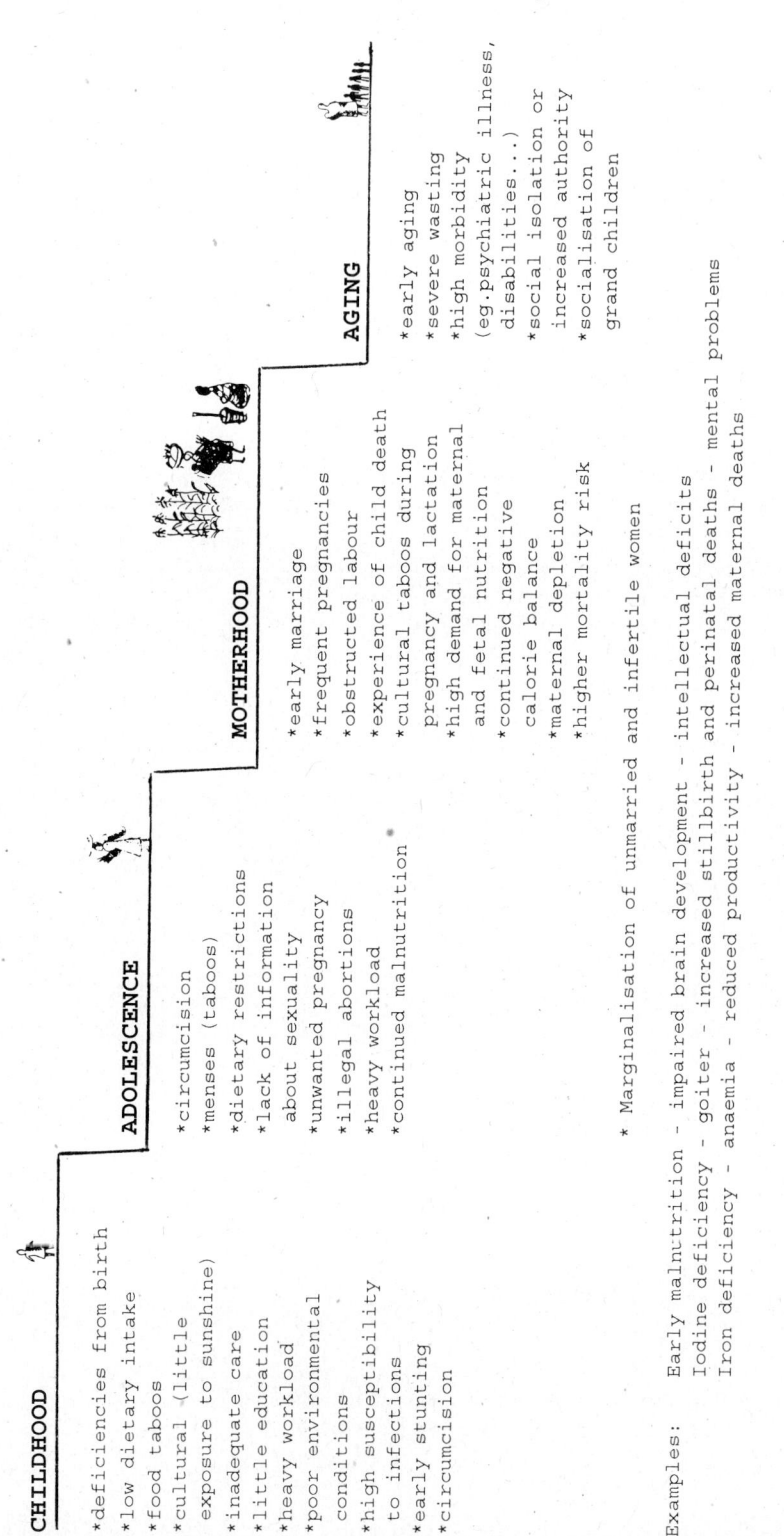

CHILDHOOD

*deficiencies from birth
*low dietary intake
*food taboos
*cultural (little exposure to sunshine)
*inadequate care
*little education
*heavy workload
*poor environmental conditions
*high susceptibility to infections
*early stunting
*circumcision

ADOLESCENCE

*circumcision
*menses (taboos)
*dietary restrictions
*lack of information about sexuality
*unwanted pregnancy
*illegal abortions
*heavy workload
*continued malnutrition

MOTHERHOOD

*early marriage
*frequent pregnancies
*obstructed labour
*experience of child death
*cultural taboos during pregnancy and lactation
*high demand for maternal and fetal nutrition
*continued negative calorie balance
*maternal depletion
*higher mortality risk

AGING

*early aging
*severe wasting
*high morbidity (eg.psychiatric illness, disabilities...)
*social isolation or increased authority
*socialisation of grand children

* Marginalisation of unmarried and infertile women

Examples: Early malnutrition - impaired brain development - intellectual deficits
Iodine deficiency - goiter - increased stillbirth and perinatal deaths - mental problems
Iron deficiency - anaemia - reduced productivity - increased maternal deaths

(adapted from: C.D.Williams et al. Mother and Child Health, 1994, p.99)

Programme Proposed to Improve Health and Nutritional Status of the Female Gender Taking Intergenerational Aspects into Account

Education
a) General education
* Emphasize importance of education also for girls, influence positive parental expectations of girls.
* Implement compulsory education, prevent "drop out of girls" by support systems for children from low socio-economic families.
* Revise curriculum (add relevant gender and generation issues, nutrition communication, sex education etc.)
* Restart improved adult literacy campaigns, add health and nutrition related messages.

b) Health and nutrition education
* Adapt health and nutrition education messages for the existing cultural context (add culture specific topics)
* Improve health and nutrition related teaching materials (including drama, role plays, flipcharts, songs, etc.).
* Extend teaching of "Mother and Child Health" (MCH) topics from health institutions to schools, local meetings, womens'groups, agricultural extension programmes, etc.
* Emphasize long-term consequences of girls and mothers health status for families, communities and the nation, promote an "intergenerational" approach.
* Discourage harmful food taboos and harmful local practices (e.g.female circumcision, massaging during delivery etc.).
* Support exclusive breastfeeding up to six months as well as the slow introduction of adequate complementary food; promote growth during early childhood, encourage good nutritional practices for the whole family, support home gardens.
* Encourage fathers'/mens'involvement in child care, work, family planning, promote birth spacing, e.g. by "satisfied users", emphasize risk of spread of STD's and AIDS and its consequences for family welfare.
* Develop strategies for the prevention of early childhood malnutrition, prevention of micronutrient malnutrition especially for pregnant women and lactating mothers.

Health Care System
* Train clinic staff, Community Health Workers (CHW's), Traditional Birth Attendants (TBA's) and women workers in the principles of the "Safe Motherhood Initiative" and about the intergenerational consequences of ill health; support their activities, approach traditional healers and pharmacies for co-operation.
* Integrate family planning services, introduce "youth clinics", promote counselling and supply of contraceptives for adolescents, unmarried women, males and risk groups, support contraceptive social marketing
* Apply latest treatment- and rehabilitation measures for severely malnourished children, include follow up visits,
* Support early recognition and treatment of nutritional disorders (e.g. vitamin A deficiencies, iodine deficiencies, anaemia, etc.) among high risk groups (children, adolescent girls, pregnant women and mothers).
* Improve access and quality of MCH services, referral systems (e.g. obstetric complications), expand services for fistula OP's, pessaries for prolaps etc.
* Set up STD clinics and -services, HIV counselling, -home based AIDS-care systems.
* Provide mental health services incl. preventive and rehabilitative measures.

Social- and Economic Policies
* Improve status of women with equal legal rights concerning education, marriage, divorce, etc.
* Guarantee equity in terms of employment, wages, maternity leave, pensions, access to resources, land, loans, etc.

* Initiate and support democratization processes in the community, intergenerational women groups etc., empower women in the decision making process.
* Organize and assist income generation projects, women cooperatives, agricultural and environmental projects.
* Improve water supply and sanitation, provide appropriate technologies (e.g. fuel saving stoves, mills etc.) to reduce women's work load and time spent on labor.
* Innovate programmes and support community care for isolated elderlies, orphans, abandoned and street children; reintegration of divorced women, unmarried mothers and teenage-prostitutes.

Surveillance / Research
* Collect essential and basic data through demographic, health-, nutrition- and socio-economic surveys.
* Explore "felt needs" of women and acceptability of programmes e.g. by focus group discussions, participatory rural appraisal, etc.
* Perform socio-and anthropolgical research about women's nutrition and health situation, including intergenerational topics and aging.
* Set up surveillance systems concerning health and nutrition issues of women and girls, carry out pilot projects focussing on intergenerational issues, intervention studies etc., health service research incl.cost-benefit analysis of programmes.
* Perform evaluations and ensure continuous modifications of the different strategies.

References

ABATE,G. 1989. *Promotive and harmful traditional practices - as related to the health of women and children in Ethiopia.* Christian Relief & Development Association (CRDA) Medical Workshop "Traditional Practices" p.10-13.

ABERRA,B. 1991. *Household food security study in Ethiopia,* Ethiopian Nutrition Institute (ENI), Addis Ababa.

ALEMU,Z. 1988. Early marriage - the silent carnage of our women. *IAC Newsletter,* March, No. 5.

ANDREWS,B. et al. 1990. Intergenerational links between psychiatric disorders in mothers and daughters: the role of parenting experiences. *J.Child Psychol. Pschiatry,* 31(7), p 1115-1129.

ARMSTRONG,H.C. 1995. Breastfeeding as the foundation of care. *Food and Nutrition Bulletin,* Vol.16 (4), p.299-312.

BARTELS,L. 1983. Oromo religion. Myths and rites of the Western Oromo of Ethiopia - an attempt to understand. *Collectanea Instituti Anthropos* 8, Berlin, Reimer, p.308.

BEN-TOVIM,D.I. 1987.*Development pychiatry: existence, prevalence and burden.* Tavistock publication Ltd, p.21-28.

BERMAN,P. 1982. Selective primary health care: is efficient sufficient? *Soc.Sci.Med.* 16: 1054-59.

BONITA,R. 1996. *Women, aging and health.* World Health Organization, p.35.

BULTI,R. 1996. *Personal communication.*

CANTOR,M.H. & HIRSHORN,B. 1989. Intergenerational transfers within the family context - Motivating factors and their implications for caregiving. In: Women in the later years: health, social and cultural perspectives. *Women and Health,* Vol. 14, 39-51.

CENTRAL STATISTICAL AUTHORITY OF THE TRANSITIONAL GOVERNMENT OF ETHIOPIA, 1993. Report on the National Rural Nutrition Survey, Core module. *Statistical Bulletin* No. 113, Addis Ababa.

CHATTERJEE,M. & LAMBERT,J. 1989. Women and nutrition: Reflections from India and Pakistan. *Food and Nutrition Bulletin,* Vol.11, 4: 13-27.

CLELAND, J.G. & VAN GINNEKEN. 1988. Maternal education and child survival in developing countries: the search for two pathways of influence. *Soc.Sci.Med.,* 27 (12): 1357-68.

CLUGSTON,G.A. 1981. The effect of malnutrition on brain growth and intellectual development. *Tropical Doctor,* 11: 32-38.

DEBESAI,H. & YEMANE,K. 1986. *Family health project.* Beneficiaries Assessment (Sociological Survey).

DOYAL,L. 1990. Health at home and in waged work:Part I Hazards of hearth and home. *Women's Studies Int.Forum,* Vol 13: (5), 501-17.

EPSTEIN,T.S. 1987. Older women as population educators. *Development Forum,* p.

FLEMING,A.F. 1989. Anaemia in pregnancy in tropical Africa. *Trans.of Roy.Soc.Trop.Med.Hyg.,* 83: 441-8.

FOGLER,J. 1989. Intergenerational women's group. *Gerontologist,* 29 (2): 268-71.y

FONER,N. 1989. Older women in nonindustrial cultures: Consequences of power and privilege. In Women in the later years: health, social and cultural perspectives. *Women and Health,* Vol. 14, 227-37.5

FRISANCHO,A.R., et al. 1985. Developmental and nutritional determinants of pregnancy outcome among teenagers. *Ameri-*

can Journal of Physical Anthropology, 66: 247-61.
GIEL,R. & VAN LUIJK,J.N. 1969. Psychiatric morbidity in a small Ethiopian town. Brit.J.Psychiatry, 115: 149-62.
HAILE,A. 1983. Fistula - a socio-medical problem. Ethiop.Med.J. 21: 71-77.
HAMMOND,J & DRUCE,N. 1989. *Sweeter than honey - Testimonies of Tigrayan women.* Links publications, Third World First.
HANA,N.T. 1992. *Prevalence of nutritional anaemia in women and children of child bearing age groups in Ethiopia*, Ethiopian Nutrition Institute, Addis Ababa.
HEISEL,M.A. 1989. Older Women in Developing Countries.In: *Women and Health,* Vol 14, 253-71.
HEYMAN,D.L. 1990. Mother to child. In: *World Health. AIDS a special threat to women.* Nov-Dec, p.13-14.
HOJER,B. & GEBRE-MEDIN,M. 1975. Rickets and exposure to sunshine. *Envirn. Child Health,* April, p. 88-89.
HUBER,A. 1966. Weibliche Zirkumzision und Infibulation in Äthiopien. *Acta Trop.,* 8(1): 87-91.
IVAN-SMITH,E. et al. 1990. *Women in Sub-Saharan Africa. The minority rights group.* Report No. 77, p 11.
KALACHE,A. 1986. Aging in developing countries: are we meeting the challenge? *Health. Pol.Planning,* 1(2): 171-75.
KALACHE,A. 1991. Aging in developing countries. In: *Principles and Practice of Geriatric Medicine.* Edited by PATHY, p 1517-28.
KEBEBEW,D. 1990. Traditional social relationships. In: *CRDA Workshop: The role of the Ethiopian family in health,* p 7-12.
KEBEDE,H. 1990. Gender Relations in Mobilizing Human Resources.I n: *Ethiopia - Rural development options.* Edited by PAUSEWANG,L. et al. Zed Ltd, London, p 58-61.
KNUTSSON,K.E. & MELLBIN,T. 1969. Breast feeding habits and cultural context - a study of three Ethiopian communities. *J. trop Ped,* p.40-49.
KURZ,K.M. 1994. Adolescent growth. United Nations Subcommittee on Nutrition, SCN News, *Maternal and Child nutrition,* p.3-6.
KWAST,B.E., et al. 1986. Maternal mortality in Addis Abeba, Ethiopia. *Stud.Fam.Plann.,* 17: 288-301.
LAMBERG,B.A. 1991. Endemic goitre - Iodine deficiency disorders. *Annals of Medicine,* 23: 367-72.
LATHAM,M.C. 1979. Human Nutrition in Tropical Africa. FAO, Rome. LESLIE,J. 1991. Women's nutrition: the key to improving family health in developing countries? *Health Policy and Planning,* 6(1): 1-19.
LEVITON,D. 1989. Intergenerational health education: The adults health and development programme. *Hygiene,* Vol 8(2): 26-29.
LOZOFF,B. et al. 1987. Iron deficiency anemia and iron therapy effects on infants developmental test performance. *Pediatrics,* 79: 981.
LOVEL,H. 1989. Targeted interventions and infant mortality. *Trans.Roy.Soc.Trop.Med.Hyg.,* 83: 10-18.
MAHLER,H. 1984. The sinister alliance. *The state of the world's children,* p 23.
MAHLER,H. 1987. The safe motherhood initiative: a call to action. *Lancet,* p. 668-71.
MASON,J. 1994. Maternal and Child Nutrition - Introduction. United Nations - Subcommittee on Nutrition, SCN News, p.1-2. Mekonnen,B. 1989. Effects of early marriage, pregnancy and abortion on women's health. *CRDA Medical Workshop,* Sept, p.6-10.
NEBIAT,T. 1990. Contribution of fathers to family health. In: The role of the Ethiopian family in health. *CRDA Medical Workshop,* Sep, p.13-16.
PARENT,M.A. & KHADRAOUI,S. 1987. Early clinical rickets and its association with malnutrition. *J. trop Ped.,* 33: 13-15.
RAMAKRISHNAN,U. 1995. UNICEF-Cornell Colloquium on Care and Nutrition of the Young Child-Planning. *Food and Nutrition Bulletin,* Vol.16 (4), p.286-292.
ROBINSON,L.H. 1989. Grandparenting: intergenerational love and hate. *J.Am.Acad.Psychoanal,* 17(3): 483-91.
ROYSTON,E. & ARMSTRONG,S. 1986. *Preventing maternal deaths.* Geneva, Switzerland: World Health Organisation.
SCHERBAUM,V. 1996a. The lifestyles of mothers and children in West-Wollega, Ethiopia with special emphasis on the nutritional situation. In: *Ethnomedical perspectives on early childhood.* Edited by C.E.GOTTSCHALK-BATSCHKUS & J.SCHULER, pp.49-66. curare Sonderband 9,Verlag für Wissenschaft u. Bildung.
SCHERBAUM,V. 1996b. Kwashiorkor: a severe form of protein-energy malnutrition in Nejo Clinic, West Wollega, Ethiopia. PhD thesis University Hohenheim, p.49.
SEIDEL,G. 1996. AIDS and Gender: a forgotten dimension. *AIDS Analysis Afika,* October, p.12-13.
SEN,G. & GROWN,C. 1988. *Development, crises and alternative visions: Third World's women's perspectives.* Earthscan publications LTD, London, p.27.
ULIN,P.R. 1992. African women and AIDS: negotiating behavioral change. *Soc.Sci.Med.* Vol.34, No.1, p.63-73.
UNICEF, 1993. *Children and Women in Ethiopia, a situation report.* Addis Ababa.
WASSERHEIT,J.N. 1989. The significance and scope of reproductive tract infections among Third World women. *Int.J.Gyn-*

ecol.Obstet., Suppl 3: 145-68.
WILLIAMS,C.D., BAUMSLAG,N., JELLIFFE,D.B. 1994. *Mother and Child Health,* Oxford University Press, p.99.
YEMANE,K. et al. 1990. *Nutritional Surveillance Pilot Study,* ENI and Central Statistical Authority, Addis Ababa.
YEMANE,K. 1991. Feeding practices among some cultural groups in Ethiopia. In: *CRDA Workshop:Nutrition and Family Health,* p.2-8.
ZEMED,A. 1989. The impact of birth spacing on the health of women and children. *CRDA Medical Workshop,* Sept., p.2.
ZENEBEWORK,B. 1989. Female Circumcision and its effects in Ethiopia. *CRDA Medical Workshop "Traditional Practices"* p.14-16.
ZEWDIE,A. & JUNGE,B. 1990. *Women, workload and time use in four peasant associations,* UNICEF, Addis Ababa.
ZEWDIE,W.G. et al. 1992. Goiter in Ethiopia. In: *Micronutrient deficiencies in Ethiopia and their inter-relationships.* PhD. thesis, University Wageningen, Netherlands.

Abb. 3
Foto: Veronika Scherbaum

"Pro Aama" - Psychosocial Situation of Women and Children in Nepal
Die psychosoziale Situation von Frauen und Kindern in Nepal

Georgia Friedrich & Murari Prasad Regmi

Abstract: This study explores the subjective well-being of Nepalese people. Subjective well-being is a composite measure of independent feelings about a variety of life concerns. The sample of this study consists of 448 Nepalese mothers from five ethnic groups: Rai, Sherpa, Tamang, Newar and Brahmin/Chhetri.
The objective of this study is to investigate about the family life, marital status and social structure, about child-rearing practices, psychosocial development of children and their psychosocial problems and psychological disorders. This study also focusses on traditional helping system of Nepalese culture.

Zusammenfassung: Diese Untersuchung hat das subjektive Wohlbefinden von Menschen in Nepal zum Thema. Das subjektive Wohlbefinden setzt sich zusammen aus voneinander unabhängigen Gefühlen bezüglich verschiedener Lebensaspekte. Die Stichprobe besteht aus 448 nepalesischen Müttern aus 5 verschiedenen ethnischen Gruppen: Rai, Sherpa, Tamang, Newar und Brahmin/Chhetri. Untersuchungsgegenstand ist Familienleben, psychosoziale Entwicklung von Kindern, ihre Probleme und Verhaltensauffälligkeiten. Außerdem berücksichtigt die Studie das traditionelle Heilungswesen in der nepalesischen Kultur.

Keywords: Nepal, psychosocial, Women's well-being, marital Discord, traditional medicine, family life, Nepal, Psychosoziale Situation, Weibliches Wohlbefinden, traditionelle Medizin, Familienleben.

Introduction

Mental health is a multi-dimensional concept. Health as „a state of complete physical, mental and social well-being and also the absence of disease or disorder." Normality in mental health is the absence of pathology (OFFER and SABSHIN 1984). Mental health is the capacity of the individual, the group and the environment to interact with one another in ways that promote subjective well-being, the optimal development and use of mental abilities (cognitive, affective and relational), the achievement of individual and collective goals consistent with justice and the attainment and preservation of conditions of fundamental equality (DENNERSTEIN et al 1993). Optimal mental health is obtained if the person can keep himself free from conflicts, and subjective distress. He should have adequate development of mental abilities, success to achieve goals and constructiveness. Women face mental health problems such as depression, stress related diseases, use of alcohol, and inequality. In a poor country like Nepal, mental health services are not adequate. Rural areas receive no proper health services. Rural women are poor, malnourished, illiterate, overworked and have no choices for pregnancy, marriage, childbirth and vocation. Women also suffer from mental distress, depression, hysteria, mental retardation and loss of self-esteem. Although women constitute a little over one half of Nepal's population, they rank lower than men in almost every social indicator in the country. Within the increasing tide of poverty in Nepal, women are the poorest of the poor, a relatively more deprived segment even from among the poor (World Bank 1991). This study also considers the assessment of risk factors in the home environment of a child. The child's normal psychosocial development is related to the mother's subjective well being. The risk factors play significant role to the well-being and life satisfaction of the mothers (CHANNABASAVANNA et al, 1994). In Nepal current child health programmes neglect „mother-child" wellness factors, environmental enrichment and primary health care. Risk factors impose detrimental effect on the mental make-up of both mother and child. Ultimately causing deficiencies in the child's personality development. Therefore, some of the fundamental questions that need to be explored in connection with the problems of mental health of mother, child and their home:
• What kind of factors restrain or obstruct women from developing the sound mental health?
• Should the conditions of mental-health development be promoted for women, and if so how?

There is not an extensive body of work in the mental health research arena in Nepal and the topic of women's mental health virtually remains unexplored, with the exception of the initial study by the authors carried out in 1995 which have scratched the surface. The need for more substantial research can be emphasized, especially in view of the fact that a fair degree of awareness has yet to be raised, particularly among the rural women folk about mental health programs and the opportunities which promote them.

Objectives of the study
The overall objective of the study, therefore, is to examine the issues involved in the mental health development for women. The factors affecting women's mental health development are to be studied as shown by the objectives below:
i) To identify families at risk for poor psychosocial development of children, and to compare these families with the no risk children.
ii) To investigate about the social structure in the villages of Solu, Chapagaon and Kathmandu urban areas.
iii) To study the subjective well-being of the mothers.
iv) To identify the behavioural problems of children as observed by their mothers.

Review of Literature
Women face dilemmas and conflict in the contexts of marriage, family relationship, reproduction, childbearing, divorce, aging, education and work. WEINER (1977) recognized that preexisting factors within and around the individual from biological, psychological and social sources all prevail to influence any condition affecting health. The work of KEMPE (1976) is significant in the area of child abuse prevention. He emphasized the right of every child to comprehensive health care. BELLE (1990) in a review of poverty and women's mental health notes that a great deal of research has been focused on depression because of the high prevalence of depressive symptoms among women compared with men. Two thirds of depressed patients are women and depression is the most commonly encountered women's health problem (CARMEN et al 1981, BENEDEK 1981; LEMPERT 1986). The researches of BRADBURN (1969), HEADEY et al (1984), DIENER (1984), LARSEN et. al (1985) and NAGPAL and SELL (1985) are very important in the field of well-being and ill-being. SPITZER et al (1981) have studied the systematic mapping of the areas associated with the overall well-being. Recent work of SELL and NAGPAL (1992) is very significant in the area of subjective well-being. The important studies done in the field of child-rearing in Nepal are by BENNETT (1974) UPRETI (1979), REGMI (1982), and THAPALIA (1987). In her study UPRETI (1979) pointed out that in general, South Asian nations like Nepal are more effectively meeting the psychosocial needs of mother and infant than technically and scientifically advanced nations. In her study on rituals related to child-rearing in Kathmandu, she argued that post partum blues or depression seemed to be less prevalent among Nepalese than among many westerners. Nepalese children suffer from varying degrees of malnutrition.

Description of the study areas
These study areas (Rural/urban) were selected on the basis of:
1. Permanence of residents to facilitate adequate follow up services.
2. Being representative of some rural and urban areas.
3. Being representative of five ethnic groups: Brahmin/Chhetri (Indo-Aryan people) and Sherpa, Tamang, Rai and Newar (Tibeto-Burman people).

Description of rural areas
1. At the base of Mount Everest, seven mountainous villages were selected from the North Eastern part of Solukhumbhu District. They are Kurima, Bagur, Harise, Sakpurna, Chandani, Mamascope and Lokhim. Their locations range from 2400 meters to 1800 meters from the sea level. The four villages (Kurima, Bagur, Harise and Sakpurna) are Sherpa villages. Sherpa people are very religious and believe in Buddhism. They do not sacrifice animals but eat meat. In most of the Sherpa houses, there is a separate place where the brass statue of Lord Buddha is kept. This particular place is kept clean where some religious books are also kept. Sherpa people mostly rely upon the traditional healing system. Their traditional healers are Lama, Dhami, and Jhankri. They go to the modern health care system only when the traditional healing system has failed to cure the disease. This might be the reason why infant mor-

tality rate in these villages is very high and life expectancy is very low. People are unaware of the modern health care facilities like immunisation and other treatment system. In Kurima village many people came to ask for help and medicine for diarrhoea. People in these areas mostly rely upon various local herbal plants for the treatment of various minor injuries and diseases. Chandani and Mamascope villages are located at the height of 2100 meters from the sea level and lived by Tamang people. They also rely upon their traditional healing system.

Their shaman healers are Lama, Dhami and Jhankri similar to Sherpa people. During our observation we found many cases of skin and urine infection. One mentally retarded male child was observed. These villagers are mostly illiterate and they have very low level of aspiration. They suffer from various diseases, and the infant mortality rate is very high and hence is a severe risk factor. Lokhim village is located at 1800 meters height from the sea level, and lived by Rai people. They rely upon the traditional healer like Dhami, and Jhankri. In the cases of wounds, injuries, the patients are taken to the health post rather than to Jhankris. There is one sub-health post in Lokhim ward no. 4 under Jubu Health Post. This has been established since two years. Pneumonia (Marki), whooping cough, and skin infections are common in this village. Rai Dhami, a traditional healer believed that people are affected by evil spirit when they have weak will-power. Recently government has started a special training for traditional healers so that they can use the modern way of treatment. The Tamang shaman spoke about good and bad spirits. When a person or a child becomes afraid of the evil spirit the part of the person's soul (Sato) becomes lost which is possessed by the ghost. The main duty of every Shaman (Dhami) is to persuade the ghost in giving back the part of the lost soul to the person whereby he becomes cured. In some cases cocks have to be sacrificed to please the ghost in giving back the soul (sato).

The Sherpa dhami uses private language while the Tamang dhami uses his mothertongue. The contents of both dhamis are same. During practice session shaman uses hymns (mantras) and rice grains were scattered. The dhami shaman goes to a trance stage and recognises the ghost. He persuades the ghost and requests to return the spirit to the child. Dhami could recognise whether the bad spirit actually had possessed the child by breaking the egg. People are not aware of mental diseases.

2. Chapagaon village is in Patan district. There is a famous temple of Bajra Barahi. The health post is situated at a quiet and clean place and is run by 13 staff members. The health workers reported about the occurrence of Psychoses, Depression and Epilepsy. In Chapagaon Newar people live. Their religion is Buddhism and Hinduism.

Description of Kathmandu's urban people
Kathmandu is urban area where both Indo-Aryan and Sino-Tibetan people live in cooperation. They follow Hinduism and Buddhism respectively. Here good hospital facilities are available. Children get proper education from nursery to university level is available to all.

Method
This study is entirely based on standardized interview and observation sources. It has good scope for primary research and in-depth examination or assessment of particular issue on mother-child relationship, home risk factors and family life. Mothers were evaluated on subjective well-being.

Selection of the sample
The target families were selected on the following criteria:
1. Presence of one child between the ages of 2 to below 8 years who was living with the parents; it was the research criterion and the sample includes 85% children of this age range.
2. Presence of caretaker who could give authentic information regarding the child and the family.
3. Presence of at least 50 mothers from each target subgroup.

Sample Structure
The total 448 families were selected from Solu, Kathmandu rural and Kathmandu urban. The distribution is given in the appendix in table no.1 a,b,c. In case of one family the mother was died due to an accident and the child was reared by his lone father. The sample of mothers was divided into six ethnic groups. The mothers followed three religions: Hindu (55.7%), Buddhist (43.9%) and Christian (.4%).

Instruments
Four instruments were used in this study: 1."Pro Aama" II (Pro Aama, stands for mother) standardized interview schedule in Nepali language was used. 2.Home Risk Card (WHO-IC MR modified) in Nepali language was filled for each subject. 3.Observation of mother was recorded on a separate sheet consisted of bipolar scales. 4.The subjective well-being inventory (SUBI) (Sell and Nagpal, 1992) in Nepali language was used to assess the well-being and ill-being of mothers.

Reliability
Alpha reliability coefficients of each item was above .88 and for 40 items alpha was .8927. Guttman Split - half reliability coefficient was .8252 for the Nepalese Version of SUBI.

Procedure
Training for The Research Workers
Six interviewers were trained in two workshops by two psychologists (authors) at the UMN (United Mission to Nepal), mental health department. During some meetings held between investigators and the research team an effort was made to understand the family in its totality. Each and every point of family functioning, its problems, and also its strengths and resources were discussed. The research instruments were administered by the research team workers by identifying the mothers individually and in one sitting itself. The interviewers read the questions and gave explanations to some questions and noted the response.

Analysis of Data
Data were coded and properly analyzed through SPSS windows, version 5. Several Pearson chi-squares, Pearson r, and multiple regressions were computed.

Results
Sociodemographic Description:
Sociodemographic characteristics of study sample are displayed in Table 2a,b,c,d,e,f,g in the appendix. All the subjects were married females with one or more children in the age group of 2-8 years. More than 42% women were illiterate. Most of the women were farmers (34%) and house wives (34%), while some of them were middle employee's (14.1%) status. The modal family size was 3 to 5 members. 55.8% families had 2 or less children. Nearly 2/3 of the mothers (65.8%) were owning land, and 43.1% mothers had cattles, of whom 45.1% mothers had no cow, 20.7% had one and only 15% had two cows. 2.5% mothers had no income. 20.3% mothers had monthly family income upto one thousand rupees. Some mothers (12.7%) lived in the rented houses. Many houses (56.9%) were in the poor condition, and some houses (20.5%) were having single room. Electric supply was not given to 32.8% houses. Similarly some houses (12.5%) had poor supply of water, 25.2% houses were having no latrine room. The care of children were provided by mothers (96.7%). From the identified children 49.6% were sons and 50.4% were daughters. The modal age at marriage for mothers (47.3%) was 15 to 19 years, followed by 33.7% mothers get married at the age of 20 to 24. Some mothers (9.4%) get married at the age of 14 or less. Interestingly many mothers (79.7%) arranged their marriages. 22.8% mothers had no son. Some mothers (8.3%) were second wife of their husband, yet husband-wife-separation problem was insignificant (1.1%). 27.9% of mothers experienced the death of one or more children. Child's mortality was caused by illness (34.4%), infection (6.4%), miscarriage (10.4%) and still birth (14.4%). 32% of the death causes were unknown. Diseases were cured by traditional healers (53.8%), vaidyas (34.8%), the herbal mediciner (34.2%) and astrologers (9.8%). Many illiterate mothers were not aware of health post. They (34.8%) had not visited to health post. Children (79%) mostly were playing with the ball, and 64.5% children were fond of role play. 74.6% mothers reported no problems of their children. Mothers identified their child's problem such as abdominal pain (4.9%), ear pain (3.1%), cough and cold (3.1%), and other problems were not so severe. When they were asked, they also identified the behavioural problems of their children such as thumb sucking (12.3%) nail biting (9.4%), bed wetting (18.5%), and stammering (4.7%). Drinking alcohol was very popular in Nepal. Many mothers (52.8%) took alcoholic drinks while their husbands (68.8%) excelled them in drinking alcohol. 15.2% mothers reported their chronic physical or mental illness and some mothers (12.3%)

reported about their not well-being. 10.3% mothers expressed their sickness, and 11.4% mothers reported their discontent with the life situation. Mothers (20.5%) expressed poverty to their life situation which they didn't change and some mothers (11.8%) were unhappy. 9.6% children were on risk. 19.2% mothers reported about their disturbance, and 41.7% mothers had feelings of sadness and depression for a long time without reasons. Discordance due to result of mutual differences in marital status was reported by 51.6% mothers. 66% mothers expressed the presence of solid reason for conflict with their husband. Physical violence was expressed by 16.1% mothers, for the differences between their husband and themselves. Nepalese women exhibited their special characteristics of tolerance that they (89.5%) reported happiness about their married life. Very few mothers (7.8%) felt unhappiness about their married life. Family planning devices were applied by 58% mothers. Responses of home risk cards revealed that 12.7% mothers expressed inadequate safe play space for their children. Some mothers (17.9%) reported that the place was full of noise. Unsanitary condition was reported by 13.2% mothers. They expressed about abject poverty (27.5%), poor housing (15.8%), and behavioural disorders (19.9%) of their children. 15% mothers neglect their children, 9.8% mothers exhibited problematic traits and 54% mothers reported about their severe marital discord.

The subjective well-being factors.

Pearson r was undertaken to correlate the results of subjective well-being (SUBI) on each factor separately with home risk card (HRC). Total score of mothers' subjective well-being correlates significantly with housing conditions * (.383), mother disturbance ** (.464), child on risk *** (.286), solve problems (.330), feeling about married life (.425), and life satisfaction of mother (.312). Thus mothers' subjective well-being is positively related with these questions. Similarly mothers subjective well-being is negatively correlated with area of settlement (-.362), family income (-.354), mothers education (-.336), fathers education (-.263), mother takes alcohol (-.317), husband takes alcohol (-.305), and problems with husband (-.367). The resulting correlations displayed in Table 3 also revealed positive relations with mothers disturbance (.197), mother confident to solve problems (.273), feeling about married life (.297), and life satisfaction of mother (.242) to their total positive score of mother's subjective well-being. Problems with husband (-.186) correlates negatively to total positive score of mother's subjective well-being. Mothers general well-being positive affect (factor 1) correlates significantly with the housing conditions, mothers disturbance, child on risk, mother confident to solve problems, feeling about married life, and life satisfaction of mother. The same factor 1 negatively correlates with area of settlement, family income, mother's education, father's education, mother takes alcohol, husband takes alcohol, and problems with husband. Perceived ill-health of mothers (factor 9) correlates significantly with housing conditions, mother disturbance, children on risk, number of problems with child, mother confident to solve problems, feeling about married life, and life satisfaction of mother. The same factor 9 negatively correlates with area of settlement, family income, father's education, mother takes alcohol, husband takes alcohol and problems with husband. General well-being negative affect (factor 11) correlates significantly with the housing conditions, mother disturbance, child on risk, type of family, number of problems with child, mother confident to solve problems, feeling about married life and life satisfaction of mother. The same factor 11 negatively correlates with area, family income, mother's education, father's education, mother takes alcohol, husband takes alcohol and problem with husband.

The correlations of mother's subjective well-being with Home Risk Card (HRC) are as follows: Abject poverty (factor 2) correlates with total score of well-being (-.350), sum of positive items (-.142), sum of negative items (-.376), general well-being positive affect (-.293), expectation-achievement congruence (-.279), inadequate mental mastery (-.302), perceived ill-health (-.305), deficiency in social contacts (-.185), and general well-being negative affect (-.420). These correlations reveales that abject poverty is related to the well-being, and perceived ill-health of mothers. Similarly poor house keeping is correlated with total score of well-being (-.249), sum of negative items (-.261), general well-being positive affect (-.229), perceived ill-health (-.205), deficiency in social contacts (-.169), and general well-being negative affect (-.288). All these correlations show that risk factors reduces the subjective well-being of mothers. Mothers problematic traits correlates significantly with the total score of well-being (-.195), sum of negative items (-.175), general well-being positive affective (-.206), expectation achievement congruence (-.214), inadequate mental mastery, perceived ill health (-.147), and general well-being negative affect (-.264). These correlations express that mothers suffering from problematic traits are related negatively to the well-being of mothers. The fifth Home Risk Factor, i.e. severe marital discord correlates negatively with total score of well-being (-.348), sum of negative items (-.363), general well-being positive affect (-.270), expectation - achievement congruence (-.245), primary group concern (-.195), inadequate mental mastery (-.327), perceived ill-health (-.313), deficiency in social contacts (-.201), and general well-being negative affect (-.273). Marital discord has negative relationship with the score of well-being, child neglect correlates negatively with deficiency in social contacts (.189) and causes ill-being.

We created a General score for Housing by valuing and combining the following questions:

Q13	Number of rooms	Q15	Water supply
Q14	Electricity supply	Q19	Latrine

We called ist: Housing Conditions

We created a General Score for Mother by valuing and combining the following questions:

Q60	Chronic physical or mental illness of mother	Q64	Mother's feeling:	not wellbeing
Q61	Mother depressed for long periods			not healthy
Q62	Mother easily upset			not content
Q63	Mother not confident to solve problems			not wealthy
Q66	Mother takes often alcohol			not happy

We called it: Mother disturbance

We created a General Score for Child by valuing and combining the following questions:

Q50	No. of problems of the child	Q55	Difficulty for mother to provide food and clothes for the child
Q53	No. of negative cicumstances	Q56	Difficulty for mother to provide playmaterials for the child
Q54	No family support for the child	Q57	No conducive neighbourhood

We called ist: Child no risk / on risk

Differences between disturbed and not disturbed mothers:

Differences between disturbed and not disturbed mothers are significant in variables such as area, type of family, owning land, family income, housing conditions. All these attitudes constituted socio-economic status of mothers. Poor socio-economic status causes disturbances among mothers. Disturbed mothers had children on high risk. However gender difference among children didn't confirm due to mothers being disturbed or not disturbed. Similarly behavioral problems of children didn't differ with the difference in mothers being disturbed or not disturbed as Pearson chi-squares were not significant.

Mothers disturbed and not disturbed differ each other in number of child living together, age of mother, mother's education, mother's caste, age of mother at marriage and duration of married life. Similarly those mothers also differ in children's sickness, physical illness, melancholia, and witch stroken. Mothers disturbed/not disturbed differ significantly in difficulty to provide food and clothes, play material to children. Similarly they also differ in problems with husband, differences on money matters, leaving the home, facing abusive behavior, physical violence, feeling about married life, family planning, sexual satisfaction, relationship to husband, relationship to mother-in-law, mother's life satisfaction, husband's life satisfaction and alcohol abuse. Working and housewife urban mothers of Kathmandu didn't differ significantly in housing conditions, child on risk, type of family and mother's education. Mother's serious problems with husband differ significantly in area of settlement, family income, mothers education, well-being, mother taking alcohol, husband taking alcohol, feeling about married life, satisfaction about sexual life, relationship to husband, relationship to mother-in-law, life satisfaction of mother, and life satisfaction of husband. Urban-rural differences happened in housing conditions, mother taking alcohol, mother's disturbance, child at risk, mother's education and satisfaction about sexual life. Mother's serious problem with husband correlates significantly with area of settlement, housing conditions, mother's education and number of punishment by mother. The Buddhist mothers took more alcohol and differed significantly from the Hindu mothers in drinking alcohol. The Buddhist mothers were more illiterate than Hindu mothers and differed significantly from each other in education. Similarly Buddhist mothers had significantly more children than Hindu mothers. Serious problem with husband correlated significantly with mothers feeling of well-being, mothers feeling happy, mothers taking alcohol, husband taking alcohol, feeling about married life, and their satisfaction about sexual life. They also correlated with relationship to husband, to mother-in-law, to father-in-law, to identified child, life satisfaction of identified child and alcohol abuse in family. Comparing the Means of mother's subjective well-being, total score, total positive score, total negative score and SUBI's eleven factors in three settlement areas: Solu, Kathmandu rural, and Kathmandu urban showed the following results: The mean of total score of mother's well-being was the highest for Solu (71.20), lowest for Kathmandu urban (61.10), and Kathmandu rural mother's mean (63.84) was in the middle. According to scale the greater the mean the lower will be the subjective well-being. Most of the means of Solu mother's in these factors were at the top except the means of factors 4, 5 and 6. The greater mean indicated that Solu mothers had least well-being while Kathmandu urban mothers exhibited adequate well-being in factors 1,2,3,7,8,9, 10 and 11. Mean life satisfaction score of Solu mothers was greatest of all the other means of Kathmandu rural (1.92), and Kathmandu urban (1.78) mothers. This expressed that Solu mothers were relatively least satisfied in their lives. Kathmandu urban mothers were highly satisfied with themselves as well as they perceived their first son, daughter, and husband, mothers and fathers-in-law also. Observation records of mother's behavior also revealed that Solu mother's understood slowly than others. Kathmandu mother's were highly spontaneous, concentrated, cheerful and active as indicated by the lowest mean in these variables. Nepalese mothers have much better subjective well-being as compared to Indian mothers. The mean scores are lower in case of Nepalese: 61.10 Kathmandu urban, 63.84 Kathmandu rural and Solu 71.20 than the Indian mean having 90.8. The higher the mean the lower will be the subjective well-being (Channabasavanna, 1994).

Differences between on risk and no risk children:
Significant differences between on risk and no risk children were found in variables such as area of settlement, owning cattle, housing conditions, mothers education, father's education, mother's caste and father's caste. Similarly children on risk and no risk differ each other significantly in scribbling, painting, rewards by others, punishment by mothers. They also differ significantly in behavioral problems like stammering, sickness, physical illness and mothers depression for long time. Children on risk and no risk differ each other significantly in mother feels well-being, feels content, feels wealthy, feels happy, mother takes alcohol, and mother's disturbance. Similarly mothers of no risk and on risk children differ in the dispute on money matters, difference on drinking habits, physical violence, feeling about married life, and relationship to husband.

Ethnic group differences:
In order to obtain differences between depressed and not depressed mothers, 9x2 Pearson chi-square were computed for 9 ethnic group of mothers: Sherpa, Tamang, Rai, Newar rural Hindu, Newar rural Buddhist, Newar urban Hindu, Newar urban Buddhist, Brahmin/Chhetri urban mother at home and Brahmin/Chhetri mother working. Pearson chi-square value of 23.487 was significant at .001 level. This showed ethnic differences in mothers depressed or not depressed. Depression was highest in Sherpa mothers (61.5%), followed by Tamang, mothers (57.8%), and Rai mothers (50%) respectively. Newar urban mothers were least depressed. Similar ethnic group differences were obtained for mother upset (chi-square 38.778 significant at .00001 level), mother drinks alcohol (chi-square 75.813), and problems with husband (chi-square 44.350) were slightly less upset. Thus Solu mothers were maximally upset. Newar urban Buddhist mothers (48.%) were least upset. Overall 68.3% mothers were upset. This is at the higher degree and it is detrimental to subjective well-being. 98% Sherpa mothers followed by Rai (87.8%) and Tamang (77.8%) drink alcohol. This is the reason that they are careless about their children's development and upbringing. Drinking alcohol is least in case of Brahmin urban mothers (14%). Among the Rai husband (93.5%) drinking is highest, followed by Sherpa (92%) and Tamang (88.9%). Tamang, Rai and Sherpa mothers have more problems with their husband. Significant ethnic differences were found in literate and illiterate dichotomy for education of father (chi-squre 154.612), education of mothers (chi-square 244.129), risk children (chi-square 41.986), mothers' disturbance (chi-square 116.358), housing conditions (chi-square 229.739), owning cattle (chi-square 295.970), owning land (chi-square 76.689). Illiteracy was maximum among Tamang fathers' (68.9%) followed by Rai (37.5%) and Sherpa (30%) fathers. Newar urban Buddhist and Brahmin fathers were all literate. Tamang mothers (91.1%) were illiterate and they were at the top followed by Sherpa (86.3%), and Rai (82%) mothers. Newar urban Hindu mothers were the least illiterate (3.9%).

Tamang children were at the highest risk (26.7%), followed by Rai (24%) and Sherpa (15.4%). Rai mothers (55.1%) were the highest in disturbance followed by Tamang (48.9%) and Sherpa (38.5%). Newar urban Hindu mothers were not at all disturbed. Tamang and Rai mothers' housing condition was extremely poor (100%) while Sherpa mothers had 98.1% poor housing condition. Owning cattle was most popular among Sherpa (100%) followed by Rai (98%) and Tamang (97.8%). Newar urban Buddhists had no cattle. All Rai and Sherpa mothers had land while urban Brahmin working mothers (72%) and Newar urban Buddhist mothers (72%) had no land. Newar and Brahmins had joint families while Sherpa, Rai and Tamang mothers lived in nuclear families. Thus total joint families were 52.5%, nuclear were 46% and very few 1.6% families were single parent only. Sherpa, Tamang, Rai, and Newar rurals had no single parent families.

Discussion

The salient features of some of the findings in this study supported that 56.9% mothers had poor housing conditions 59.3% mothers lived in two roomed homes, and 33% mothers had no any asset. Their median age at marriage ranged between 15-19 years. 22.8% mothers were living without any son, and many mothers reported that one child (40.8%) and two children (50%) died due to illness and infection, 10.4% children died due to miscarriage and the case of still birth was 14.4%. Above all 32% death of children was unknown. Life under such scarcity and problem is stressful and difficult. Housing conditions of Solu mothers (91.2%) were poor as compared to Kathmandu rural mothers (14%) while Kathmandu urban mothers were having no poor housing conditions. In Solu 80.6% mothers were disturbed as compared to Kathmandu rural (10.5%) and Kathmandu urban (9.3%). There was statistically significant difference among mothers (chi-square 110.646). Disturbed mothers had 58.1% on risk children while undisturbed mothers had 3 times less risk children, i.e. 17.7%. Disturbed mothers had 2.3% higher on risk children as compared to not disturbed mothers (had only .3%) high risk children. Disturbed and not disturbed mothers differ significantly (chi-square 65.777) in having risk children. Mother scores indicated that Rai were highly disturbed (31.4%) followed by Tamang (25.6%), and Sherpa (22.1%). Disturbances in Newar, Chhetri and Brahmin mothers were 12.8%, 5.8% and 2.3% respectively. Disturbed mothers need support, counselling and positive feedback to boost their morale and motivate them for change. The family intervention model is proposed to facilitate the change in the child. Mothers reported that 68.8% husband took alcoholic drinks. They perceived their own children sick (8.3%), physically ill (8.3%), retarded (1.1%) light melancholic (2%), witch stroken (3.3%) and mentally ill (1.3%). Similarly 52.8% mothers took alcohol. 41.7% mothers were depressed. 44.2% mothers felt discordance with husband, some 7.4% mothers felt severe discordance. Family intervention is felt at this stage to improve in the coping behavior of mothers. Risk factors in Nepalese families were very high. Severe marital discord (54%), abject poverty (27.5%), behavioral disorder of the child (19.9%), problematic traits of mothers (9.8%), and child neglect (15%) indicated not at all conducive for child's proper growth and development. Child neglect was at the top in case of Tamang (40%), followed by Sherpa (32.7%) and Rai mothers (26%). Among the newars child neglect was 25.8% and for Brahmin/Chhetri mothers child neglect was 12% only. Solu mothers had least well-being while Kathmandu urban mothers exhibited adequate subjective well-being in factors 1,2,3,7,8,9,10 and 11. The future objective of this study should be the promotion of knowledge and awareness of illiterate mothers, i.e. to educate them so that they could solve their own problems. Education is thus an important ingredient of any intervention programme. Risk factors of the family could be reduced by mobilizing community and the resources. Using appreciation techniques child neglect can be reduced. Children should be rewarded not to be punished. They should be empathized and encouraged to improve their own achievements and well-being. Child is the concern of parents in order to make life happier. In sum, there are very interesting huge data collected in relation to this study and for the time being it is equally difficult to put all of them here. Further researches are needed to validate them.

References

BELLE D. 1990. Poverty and women's mental health. *American Psychologist*, 45, 385-9

BENEDEK, E.P. 1981, Women's issues: A new beginning. *American Journal of Psychiatry*, 138: 1317-8

BENNETTE. *Journal of Psychiatry, Birth and Early Child Rearing*. Health and Family Planning, Attitudes and Practices in a Brahmin and Chhetries Community of East Central Nepal, CNAS, Vol 1, Part 1, Tribhuvan University.

BRADBURN, N.M. 1969. *The structure of psychological well-being*, Aldine, Chicago.
CORMEN, E., RUSSO, N.F. MILLER, J.B. 1981. Inequality and women's mental health: an overview. *American Journal of Psychiatry*, 138: 1319-29.
CHANNABASAVANNA, S.M., VARGHESE, M. and CHANDRA, P.S. 1994 *Indicators of Mental Health a multi central ICMR study*. Bangalore: ICMR Project, NINHANS.
DENNERSTEIN, L, ASTBURY, J and MORSE, C. 1993. *Psychosocial and mental health aspects of women's health*. WHO Geneva.
DIENER, E. 1984. Subjective well-being, *psychological Bulletin*, 95, 542-575.
ERIKSON, E.H. 1950. *Childhood and society*. New York, Norton.
HEADEY, B. HOMSTROM, E. and WEARING, A. The impact of life events and changes in domain satisfactions on well-being, *social indicators research*, 15, 203-227.
KENPE, C.H. 1976. Approaches to preventing Child abuse: the health visitors concept. *American Journal of the disabled child*. 130:130-141.
KIRAT, J. 1971. *Child Rearing Practices in Sherpa Community*. In status of children in Nepal Child Welfare Coordination, Committee, Kathmandu.
LARSEN, R.J. DIEVER, E. and EMMONS, R.A. 1985 An evaluation of subjective well-being measures, *Social Indicators Research*, 17, 1-17.
LEMPERT, L.B. 1986. Women's health from a woman's point of view: a review of the literature. *Health care for women international*, 7: 255-75.
NAGPAL, R. and SELL, H. 1985. Subjective well-being, *SEARO Regional Health Paper* No. 7, World Health Organisation, New Delhi.
OFFER, D. & SABSHIN, M. 1984. Preface. In offer, D. SABSHIN, M. (Eds.). *Normality and the life cycle: a critical integration*. New York: Basic Books, ix-xiii.
PRADHAN, H.B. 1986. *Traditional Nepali Baby Care Practices*, Institute of Medicine, TU.
REGMI, M.P. 1982. *The Personality Structure of Nepalese Gurungs*. Ph.D. Thesis, Saugar University, India.
SELL, H. and NAGPAL, R. 1992. *Assessment of Subjective well-being*. WHO, Regional Office for South East Asia, New Delhi.
SPITZER, W.O., DOBSON, A.J., HALL, J. CHESTERMAN, E., LEVI, J. SHEPHERD, R. BATTISTA, R.N. and CATCHLOVE, B.R. 1981. Measuring the quality of life and cancer patients. A consise QL-index for use by physicians, *Journal of Chronic Diseases*, 34, 585-597.
THAPALIA, H. 1987. *Child bearing and child rearing in two castes in a village of Kathmandu*. Ph.D. Thesis, University of Delhi.
UPRETI. S.N. 1979. *Family support system child-bearing and child-rearing rituals in Kathmandu*. Ph.D. Thesis. Madison University of Wisconsin.
WEINER, H. 1977 *Psychobiology and human health disease*. New York, Elsevier.
WORLD BANK. 1991. *Nepal: Poverty and Incomes*, Washington.

Appendix

Table 1a: Sample of the families by target subgroups

Caste	f	%
Sherpa	52	11.6
Tamang	45	10.0
Rai	50	11.2
Newar, rural, Hindu	50	11.2
Newar, rural, Buddhist	50	11.2
Newar, urban, Hindu	51	11.4
Newar, urban, Buddhist	50	11.2
Brahmin/Chhetri, urban, mother at home	50	11.2
Brahmin/Chhetri, urban, mother working	50	11.2
	448	100.0

Table 1b: Sample by family type and settlement

Settlement	Family	f	%
Solu	Joint	44	29.9
	Nuclear	103	70.1
	Single parent	0	0
Kathmandu Rural	Joint	72	72
	Nuclear	28	28
	Single Parent	0	0
Kathmandu Urban	Joint	119	59.2
	Nuclear	75	37.3
	Single Parent	7	3.5
		448	100.0

Table 1c: Sample of mothers by Religion

Religion	f	%
Hindu	249	55.7
Buddhist	196	43.9
Christian	2	0.4
	447	100.0

Table 2a: Age of mothers in years

Age	f	%
– 19	9	2.0
20 – 24	67	15.0
25 – 29	143	31.9
30 – 34	108	24.1
35 – 39	66	14.7
40 – 44	20	4.5
45 – 49	17	3.8
50 – 54	9	2.0
55+	8	1.8
Mother dead	1	.2
	448	100.0

Table 2b: Education of mothers.

Education	f	%
Literate	256	57.3
Illiterate	191	42.7
	447	100.0

Table 2c: Occupation of mothers

Occupation	f	%
Farmers	152	34.0
House wives	152	34.0
Seasonal employee	1	.2
Low employee	15	3.4
Middle employee	63	14.1
High employee	11	2.5
Own business	53	11.8
	447	100.0

Table 2d: Mothers by settlement area.

Area	f	%
Solu	147	32.8
KTM Rural	100	22.3
KTM urban	201	44.9
	448	100.0

Table 2e: Mothers by Residence:

Residence	f	%
Rural	247	55.1
Urban	201	44.9
	448	100.0

Table 2f: Mothers by Family size

Family Size	f	%
2 or less	2	.4
3 – 5	206	46.0
6 – 8	165	36.8
9 – 11	54	12.1
12 – 14	17	3.8
15 +	4	.9
	448	100.0

Table 2g: Number of children in family

Number of children	f	%
2 or less	250	55.8
3 – 5	168	37.5
6 – 8	30	6.7
	448	100.0

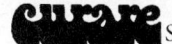

Munda Women (India) and Health Care
Munda-Frauen (Indien) und Gesundheitsversorgung
Peter Paul Hembrom

Abstract: Horopathy Ethnomedicine is the Medicine of the MUNDA Ethnic Group of India, where social medical is the culture and self medication is the practice. Taking advantage of this, if women, who are mothers, nurses and care takers of the family are trained in the scientific medicinal use of locally available herbs around their villages and on cultivable land (as they are from agricultural communities) they can take care of their primary health, as well as on that of their family, while children can make it sustained. Women would then command respect in the society.

Zusammenfassung: Horopathie nennt sich die Medizin der ethnischen Gruppe der Munda in Indien, bei denen soziale Medizin die Kultur und Selbstbehandlung die Praxis darstellt. Davon können die Frauen profitieren: wenn sie, die zugleich Mütter, Krankenpflegerinnen und Betreuerinnen der Familie sind, in der korrekten medizinischen Anwendung der in der Umgebung ihrer Dörfer und auf kultivierbarem Land (sofern sie in bäuerlichen agrarischen Gemeinden leben) verfügbaren Heilkräuter geschult werden, können sie die eigene gesundheitlichen Grundversorgung wie auch die ihrer Familie sichern, während die Kinder sie bewahren lernen können. Auf diese Weise gewinnen die Frauen den Respekt der Gesellschaft.

Keywords: India, Munda-women, horopathy ethnomedicine, health of women, training of women, respect, Indien, Munda-Frauen, horopathy Ethnomedizin, Frauen-Gesundheit, Ausbildung von Frauen, Respekt.

There are about 53 million people belonging to tribes in India. On a linguistic basis there are communities with 227 ethnic groups. The Munda speech of Central Eastern India, Nicobarese and Santhals have been placed in Australic Asiatic linguistic branch.
About 7500 wild plant species are currently recorded as being used by Mundas for medicine.

Sociomedical culture
The MUNDAs live a community health. They live in a symbiotic manner and thus maintain tribal harmony. Their medicine men render a selfless service to their own communities. Of course, they are remuncrated for their services according to their capacity. Sometimes they have to be satisfied with a leaf cup of country liquor and a handful of rice. When a member of the family is thick, the whole family is sick and when a family is the whole village is sick. Self medication is integral part of their culture. Hence men, women and even children know something. They can identify plants and make use of them when first aid is needed.

Because of this, the healing methods of Mundas have been named HOROPATHY which roughly translated means human feeling. HORO, means a human being and was used to differentiate between plant origin and animal origin. It is still being used to differentiate themselves with non-tribals.

Concept of Health and Illness
Health is considered to be a physiolgical and mental state of well-being of the body. The imbalance in this state is a disease. The causes of this imbalance are BONGAS. BONGA is a spirit. Any sudden or unusual happening which has no immediate explanation is believed to be the act of a BONGA.

The MUNDAS believe in three types of SPIRITS (1). The SINGBONGA or supreme spirit is God. Annual sacrifices are made for Him in a horea robusta . (Shorea robusta) grove, called JAHER or SARNA, set apart for observing rituals. In order to cause illnesses, other spirits must ask His permission.

(ii) The benevolent spirits are the family ancestral spirits, which take care of the family. They have first share in all new crops or festivals. They are called HAPAROM BONGAS. They are worshiped in a house especially used for this purpose. This place is called ADING. Every family has a ADING (b). The village boundary spirit e.g. SIMAN BONGA. He takes care of the village, so that it is not afflicted with diseases from neighbouring villages. The villagers observe annual rituals for this.

God and the benevolent spirits may also cause illnesses as a punishment, if there are lapses in the observations of the rituals. (iii) They are the malevolent spirits, which are called BONGA. They always try to harm people. But they can only do harm when SINGBONGA permits. In witchcraft witches use

the BONGAS power to harm people.
In the health hierarchy of MUNDAS there are various experts, but there is no general physician as such.
(i) The spiritual healers, who do not use medicine. They are generally not members of the tribe.
(ii) The soothsayers. They generally make sacrifices and administer medicine. But now as education is developing in their community they are gradually loosing their popularity.
(iii) The medicine men, who practice ethnomedicine, have received their knowledge in the form of oral history from their ancestors. Amongst them also, there are experts for nervous complaints or uterine problems or stomach complaints ect.
(iv) The traditional bone setters and some experts in accupuncture. A red-hot sickle is used for equipment.
(v) The traditional birth attendants.

The MUNDA medicine men have a different method of diagnosis. Some are experts in assessing a person's pulse, some test urine and the rest diagnose the symptoms. But for treatment, they all consider the warmness or coldness of the stomach.

Status of women in the society

MUNDA women enjoy almost equal status in the family though they are not allowed to take part in the sacrified offering and sharing of the body. They do not take part in social decision making. However they have the full power in house affairs. They are the main person to go to village weekly markets for selling or purchasing things. They are also the family treasurer. For family decisions men always seek their opinions. In the community it is the women who serve, but if the work load is very great, men share it.

The society divides labour between the sexes. Earning and hard work men do, while light work with quick and repetitive movement is done by women.

Women do not receive a share of their father's property when they marry, but they do become the mistress of their husbands. They are considered to be one man power in the family. In the society they also command respect and thus when a married woman is addressed, the plural form is always used.

Women's Role in the Health Care Delivery

Since Munda tribes are an agricultural community they are mostly marginalized or below property live, men generally work from their homes for their earnings. Thus all the responsibilty comes upon women at home, for health care services. Since they only know some of the uses of medical plants, they must consult the village medicine men. Women play an important role in sanitation and personal hygiene. If they are compowered with the knowledge of herbal medicine, the task will become much easier. They are already good nurses, but the time has come for them to be promoted by village doctors, so that they can take the burden of primary health care off of the family. A slogan has to be motivated "Health Con our Hands". The medicine men have been very effective in treating disease such as Malaria, T.B, Jaundice, Epilepsy, Asthma, Hyperrension, Diabetes, nervous uterine and stomach problems at a very low cost. The women folk can also be educated to diagnose sumptoms so that they may utilize their knowledge. The medicine men are also needed to be given an advanced and scientific knowledge.

This is neccessary because 80% of the rural tribal population has not accepted modern medicine, while the India Government has done nothing to develop the traditional technology of the tribes. For many people this may be the only available type of medicine, because of its accessibility and acceptibility. It is necessary for the government to do its part, according to the Alma Ata Declaration of 1978 for the research and development and promotion of this technology since this is the first contact most individuals have in ventorying and documenting the various medicinal plants and herbs is equally necessary. This action will build up a loosing faith on their own system, due to scale propaganda for allopathy medicine. Fortunatualy a few dedicated N.G.O.'s and many Sotholic health units have come forward to revive and promote this knowledge to tribes in the rural areas. This effort is gradually gaining momentum and becoming a movement. Women are actively participating and many places they have taken up herbal medicine practice in the village, especially in Jharkhand Area of Bihar. In the District of Sambhalpur in Orissa State, two women have ventured running a herbal dispensary in a remote part of the village. Nawadih of Gudrapara Police station with the help of Catholic Missionares.

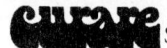

Skin Care and Herbo-Mineral Beauty Aids in India
Hautpflege und Kosmetik aus Kräutern und Mineralien in Indien
Shashi B. Vohora & Divya Vohora

Abstract: Indian systems of medicine (Ayurveda, Siddha and Unani-Tibb) envisage a perfect balance of elements, humours and temperaments. An imbalance of these causes disease states. This is true for all ailments including skin diseases. The treatment involves use of natural products: plant, animal and mineral origin drugs and cosmetics which are less `alien' to the human body vs synthetic chemical products. These measures help in „purifying" the blood and let the skin glow with natural beauty and health.

Zusammenfassung: Indische Medizinsysteme (Ayurveda, Siddha und Unan-Tibb) sorgen für eine perfekte Balance und Ausgewogenheit von Elementen, Gemütern und Temperamenten. Wenn diese Balance eines Menschen gestört ist, kann es zu Krankheiten kommen. Dies gilt für alle Arten von Krankheiten, einschließlich Hautkrankheiten. Bei der Behandlung werden auch natürliche Produkte verwendet: Drogen und Kosmetik pflanzlicher, tierischer und mineralischen Ursprungs, die dem menschlichen Körper als synthetischen, chemischen Produkten nicht unbekannt sind. Solche Behandlungsmaßnahmen helfen beim Blutreinigen und verleihen der Haut natürliche Schönheit und gesundes Aussehen.

Keywords: Indian medicine, medicinal plants, skin diseases, cosmetics, beauty aids, Indische Medizin, Heilpflanzen, Hauterkrankungen, Kosmetik, Schönheitsmittel.

1. BEAUTY IS NOT SKIN DEEP

The urge to look attractive is not new but people are becoming more beauty conscious these days. What makes a person look attractive? Pimples, black heads, blemishes, pock marks, baldness, greying of hairs, wrinkles, ravages of age etc are frequent sources of anxiety and psychological distress. Keeping the genetic makeup, racial differences and pleasing manners aside, glowing health and a vibrant youthful body are obviously the most important factors. A healthy person in the prime of youth should need no external aids to look presentable except, of course, the observance of general rules of self care and hygiene. A famous Indian dermatologist (PANJA 1985) stated: "Skin disease may be indicative of another underlying malaise. Skin is an organ, the largest one in fact, and should be handled with respect. It acts as a mirror, reflecting disease of other organs e.g. the pallor of anaemia, the yellow tinge of jaundice, the blue hue of heart disease, darkening due to chronic infections and adrenal diseases, dysmorphophobia and dermatitis artefacto due to psychological factors etc" In these cases the cause has to be looked into to restore normal health.

Abb. 1
The leaves of Lawsonia alba contain a red pigment. These are ground with water to yield a paste. This is applied on hands and feet in various decorative patterns.

2. EXTERNAL AIDS: ARE THESE SAFE?
Adverse Effects of Strong Cosmetics
External aids, are, unfortunately, a necessity for others. How do we choose these aids? What kind of soaps, shampoos and oils should we use? What is the impact of an indiscriminate use of too much cosmetics and beauty aids on ones health and personality? Let us look into these questions and problems.

According to Shahnaz Hussain, a well known expert on beauty and skin care, strong soaps and shampoos remove the natural oil from skin and hair, aggravate dryness and cause loss of lustre (HUSSAIN 1985). A simple mildly alkaline soap should be chosen. Strong medicated soaps should be avoided as these are least useful as medication, can be great sensitizers and may be toxic in certain situations. The use of soap is absolutely forbidden in acute inflammatory conditions, particularly in those that are eczematous (BEHL 1975). There are controversial reports about the dangers of hexachlorophene (a strong germicidal and deodourizer) in soaps, shampoos, talcum powders and other cosmetics and toiletries. It has even been indicted for episodes of infant mortality in France. The use of caustic materials (sodium and potassium hydroxide) in soaps may cause irritant effects, particularly in delicate skin of children, corners of eyes, mucus membranes, eroded and injured skin, burns and may cause accidental poisoning (ANONYMOUS 1955, 1979, MARTINDALE 1982). Shampoos, perfumed oils, depilatory agents and dyes may cause allergic reactions. That is why their information folders advise prior patch test (at the back of the ear or neck) for sensitivity. Vegetable dyes are usually the safest. In Europe and America, cosmetics are responsible for a great deal of contact eczema. The incidence in Asiatic countries is fortunately low but there are reports indicating a recent spurt in cosmetic induced dermatitis cases in India, particularly in urban areas (BEHL 1975).

The Vicious Cycle
Thick coats of make up with a paraphernalia of lotions, creams, powders, face packs, lipstick, rouge, mascara, eye-shadows, vermilon, perfumes etc. do not make a person attractive or desirable. On the contrary, their effect is more often repulsive. These coatings, besides looking aweful, have adverse effects. They cause blocking of numerous pores of the skin and interfere in its normal secretory and excretory functions. This interference with the physiological mechanisms takes away the normal opportunity from the skin to maintain its health. As a result it looses its smoothness and lustre necessitating more cosmetics to put up a false facade. The vicious cycle continues. How do we escape from it?

3. COSMETICS FROM NATURE
The Golden Rule
The golden rule is to avoid artificial aids to look beautiful. Health has no substitute and it can be attained only through balanced nourishing diet, proper hygiene and active habits. But this is easier said than followed in present day circumstances. Minimum use of cosmetics and toiletries with maximum safety is the next alternative. Cosmetics from Nature (e.g. plant and food-based substances) provide the answer to the problem. Obviously the body is more accustomed to these than it can ever be to synthetic chemicals. An association of centuries and generations is bound to make the system more attuned to natural products.

Ancient Heritage
Let us look back at our ancient heritage, What were the beauty aids of royal maidens, princesses, queens, lovely courtesans and dance girls? Many of these were simple items we are all familiar with. Some examples are almonds, seasame, bengal gram flour, maize flour, henna leaves, sandal wood, turmeric, rose flowers, citrus fruit juices and peels, milk, yoghurt, honey etc. The preparations included *ubtans* applied to the body before taking fragrant baths. These were meant to clear the skin of blemishes and improve its texture and complexion. Massage oils were used to tone up the system and make the skin wrinkle free and youthful. Herbal hair washes were taken to promote growth of soft, black and lusterous hair. Some of these formulae are still used in Indian households as the knowledge of recipes has been passing from mothers to daughters for generations. Readymade herbal cosmetics and toilet goods have also come into being for convenience. Fashionable beauty parlours are making extensive use of formulae and beauty aids known to ancient people.

Herbal Skin Care Products
A recent seminar organized by Central Institute of Medicinal and Aromatic Plants, Lucknow (Central Institute of Medicinal and Aromatic Plants 1994) revealed that more than 113 pharmacies are manufacturing at least 439 skin care related products in India (Table 1).

Table 1
Herbal skin care products manufactured in India.(Central Institute of Medicinal and Aromatic Plants 1994)

Category/Use	Number
Enhancement of beauty (face packs, cleansing creams)	4
Stimulating wound healing (ointments, lotions, dusting powders)	13
Care of gums and teeth (tooth powders, tooth pastes, applicants for tooth ache, bleeding gums, mouth washes).	50
Antiaging products (capsules, tablets, liquids, creams for internal and external use	41
Pain relieving agents (ointments, balms, creams, rubs, tablets, liquids, for external and internal use	66
Hair care products (oils, liquids, creams, dyes, shampoos, antidandruff agents, hair growth promoters)	88
Skin care products (creams, lotions, pastes, powders, ointments, capsules, pills for external and internal use for healthy and diseased skin)	177
Total	439

A majority of these products are intended for use in healthy state and so fall under the category of cosmetics. The number of products is obviously not exhaustive; the actual number is estimated to be much higher. It indicates the disillusionment of users with synthetic cosmetics and a growing trend of coming back to Nature for skin and hair care.

4. CONCEPT OF BLOOD PURIFICATION IN SKIN DISEASES
Skin diseases in Indian systems of medicine (Ayurveda, Siddha and Unani-Tibb) are attributed to an *impure* status of blood and the treatment is attempted with a class of natural products described as *blood purifiers*. Vohora (1985) conducted an exhaustive survey of literature on 36 medicinal plants reputed for blood purifying properties in Unani-Tibb (Greco-Arab system of medicine). The purpose was to unearth pharmacological properties relevant to the treatment of skin diseases by conventional approaches. The frequency distribution of such effects discernible after due scientific scrutiny (experimental

and/or clinical investigations) is shown in Table 2.

Table 2
Frequency distribution of pharmacological properties in 36 blood purifying plants

Activity	Number of plants
Antibacterial	24
Antifungal	11
Antiviral	9
Diuretic	11
Antiallergic/antihistaminic	4
Choleretic/hepatotonic	5
Anticancer	11
Hypoglycemic/hypocholesterolemic	15
Anti-inflammatory/antipyretic	12
Adaptogenic	12

Many polyherbal formulations are available in India intended for treatment of acne, pimples, freckles, blemishes and for clearing complexion. A famous unani formulation widely used in this sub-continent (Safi) was found to contain 17/36 *blood purifying* plants. We feel that if the unani term *Musaffi Khoon* (Blood purifying property) be equated with one or more of the 10 categories of pharmacological activities listed in Table 2 and so called blood impurities with infective agents, allergens, toxins etc. the terminology gap between Unani-Tibb and Allopathic medicine will tend to be reduced.

5. AROMATHERAPY

Edward Sagarin (KEMPANA 1973) stated, "From dawn until twilight and long into night and from the cradle of the infant to the silence of the grave, we are surrounded by the odorous materials. We take our odours for granted and little realise how much we would be affected if our lives were deprived of perfumes." Traditional medicinal systems knew the importance of such principles in human health and disease and utilized many essential oil bearing plants for therapeutic and exhilarating purposes. The philosophy behind incorporation of essential oils in perfumes, face packs, moisturizers, cleansing lotions and creams in herbal cosmetics goes beyond the effects on the skin and body to the mind and soul. This results in a general feeling of well being and mood elevation bringing out the inner glow of beauty. The latter is supported by deep penetrating, pore opening, moisturizing, soothing and emollient effects of these oil on the surface. Vohora and co-workers (VOHORA 1987) reviewed experimental and clinical studies on essential oils bearing plants used in Indian systems of medicine and Hungarian ethnomedicine. A large number of these plants were shown to possess antimicrobial and wound healing properties besides having systemic effects on cardiovascular, respiratory, digestive and central nervous systems.

6. SHORT SCIENTIFIC NOTES ON SOME SIMPLE INGREDIENTS USED IN HERBAL COSMETICS

A perusal of the ingredients of herbal consmetics used in India shows that these contain besides medicinal herbs and some mineral constituents, very simple and familiar items commonly encountered in kitchen and domestic use.

Short scientific notes on some of the ingredients used are given below:

Almonds *(Prunus amygdalis)*

Oil of almonds is reported to possess demulcent, emollient, stimulant and nervine tonic properties. Its actions are similar to that of olive oil and is used by pharmaceutical and cosmetic industry in nourishing cold creams for the skin as also in superfatted soaps. Kernels are very nutritious and calorie rich. Chemical composition of the kernels is given below (ANONYMOUS 1948-1976).

Moisture	5.2%
Protein	20.8%
Fat (Ether extract)	58.9%
Fibre	1.7%
Mineral matter	2.9%
(Ca, P, Fe, Na, K, Mg, Mn, I, Zn, As, etc.)	
Thiamine	0.24 mg/100 g
Nicotinic acid	2.5 mg/100g
Riboflavin	0.15mg/100 g

Protein concentrate of almonds contains *amandinas* as the chief protein. It is a globulin (with 19% N content) containing several essential amino acids (e.g arginine, histidine, lysine, phenyl alanine, leucine, valine, tryptophan, methionine, cystine etc.) that may be needed for nourishment of the body. It is important to note that gamma globulin fraction of the plasma contains antibodies and is credited with resistance mechanisms against infections. Poultice of kernels is reported to be useful in irritable sores and skin eruptions (ANONYMOUS 1948-1976, ANTIA 1973, CHOPRA et.al. 1956).

A crystalline compound isolated from almond shells (identitity not established) has been shown to elicit pronounced anti-bacterial action against *Pseudomonas pyocyanea*. Its minimum effective concentration is 1:500. Pure compound exerted the effect within 5 minutes but bactericidal action was seen only after 15 minutes if a dilution of 1:20 was used (GUPTA et.al. 1971).

Seasame *(Sesamum indicum)*

The oil possesses emollient properties and is claimed to be useful in piles and as a poultice in ulcers. The seasame protein concentrate forms a good protein for any *ubtan* or massage oil for nourishing and stimulating the skin. A complex cyclic ether (seasamin) isolated from the seeds is reported to elicit anti-tubercular activity. The effect was observed in 1:10 million dilution and it lasted for 3 weeks (CHOPRA et.al. 1956, RAMASWAMI et.al. 1957).

Turmeric *(Curcuma longa)*

Dried pulverised rhizomes are used. It is one of the most extensively investigated plant based drug and is reported to possess antibacterial, antifungal, antiallergic/anti-histaminic, hypocholesterolaemic and antioxidant actions due to the phenolic character of curcumin. Of its various actions, its anti-inflammatory effects are most potent. The drug is used for various inflammatory conditions and also for promoting healing process of fractures. Beneficial effects of turmeric have been reported in histamine-induced gastric ulcers in experimental animals (VOHORA 1985, ANTIA 1973, BASU 1971, BHATIA et.al. 1964, DINESCHANDRA & GUPTA 1972, PACHAURI & MUKHERJEE 1970).

Bengal Gram Flour *(Cicer arietinum)*
Dried pulverized grains are used. It is attributed with nourishing and astringent properties. Whole Bengal gram contains (per 100 g.):

Proteins	17.1 g
Fat	5.3 g
Carbohydrates	60.9 g
Calories	360
Thiamine	300 ug
Riboflavin	510 ug
Nicotinic acid	2.1 mg
Calcium	202 mg
Iron	10.2 mg
Magnesium	168 mg
Phosphorus	312 mg
Sodium	37 mg
Potassium	808 mg
Arsenic	9 ug

Presence of carotenoids and oil soluble Vitamins A, D and E has been reported (ANTIA 1973, CHOPRA et.al. 1973, MADHWAN et.al. 1973, MATHUR et.al. 1968)

Maize Flour *(Zea mays)*
Dried pulverized grains are used. It is attributed with resolvent and astringent properties. Presence of anti-bacterial substances has also been reported in maize seeds. Dried maize contains (per 100 g):

Proteins	11.1 g
Fats	3.6 g
Carbohydrates	66.2 g
Calories	342
Thiamine	420 ug
Riboflavin	10 ug
Nicotinic acid	1.4 mg
Calcium	10 mg
Iron	2 mg.
Magnesium	144 mg
Phosphorus	348 mg
Sodium	16 mg
Arsenic	30 mg

Maize flour is reported to facilitate iron absorption (ANTIA 1973, CHOPRA et.al. 1956, MOORE & DUBACH 1956).

Sandal Dust *(Santalum album)*
Dried pulverised wood is used or wood as such is ground with water to yield a paste. The paste is applied to forehead and temples for soothing effect. It is claimed to cure headache, fevers, itching and local inflammation. Oil from heart wood is said to be useful in gonorrhoeal urethritis, cystitis and skin diseases. Scientific evidence of its antibacterial and antiinflammatory effects is available in some reports (CHOPRA et.al 1956, SHENDE et.al. 1968, SRIMATI & SREENIVASAYA 1963, JAIN 1975). Sandalwood improves the normal functions of skin by influencing it at the cellular level. Its paste and scent are soothing to nerves and induce relaxation. According to Shahnaz Husain (HUSAIN 1995), a relaxed mind is a prerequisite for beauty and so it makes the cosmetic treatment more effective in acne and pimples. It is ideal for oily skin and seborrhoeic conditions. Red sandalwood protects the skin from sun damage and is therefore incorporated in sun screens and sun protective creams for use in prickly heat and rashes. Sandal dust blends well with other oils and extracts and can easily be added to various cosmetic preparations.

Citrus fruit Peels (e.g. *Citrus reticulata*)
Oil from peels contain d-limonene terpene, carene, linalool etc. The fruits are a rich source of Vitamin-C which has a significant role in increasing body resistance to diseases. Pectins, aurantin (a fully methylated flavonol), glycosides, flavonoids and anti-hyaluronidase enzyme are also reported present. Aglycone and flavonoidal principles present in citrus fruit peels are reported to possess antimicrobial properties. It is believed to exert a bleaching action which helps in clearing blemishes and improving complexion (VOHORA 1985, CHOPRA et.al. 1956, GHOSE 1958, RAMASWAMY et.al. 1972, SARIN ET.AL. 1960).

Rose Petals *(Rosa damascena)*
Besides being pleasantly fragrant, rose petals are reported to possess antibacterial and antifungal properties (DIXIT & TRIPATHI 1975, OKAZAK & OSHIMA 1953). Incorporation of the essence in lotions, creams and soaps may, therefore, have a beneficial effect in skin infections.

Honey *(Mel)*
Honey because of its highly hygroscopic nature, elicits good antimicrobial activity. It is highly nutritious and contains:

Moisture	17%
Sugars	64% (Levulose 39%, Dextrose 34%, Sucrose 1%)
Dextrin	0.5%
Proteins	2%
Wax	1%
Mineral salts	1%
(Al,Ca,Cl,Cu, Fe,I,K, Mn,Na, PO_4,S,Si etc.)	

Resins, gums, pigments, pollen grains, enzymes and vitamins (Thiamine, Ascorbic acid, Riboflavin, Pentothinic acid, Pyridoxine, Niacin, Vitamin-K etc.) are also present. The use of honey has been mentioned in face creams and lotions to remove wrinkles and blemishes, in the treatment of burns (leaving no scar), fruncles, boils and for soothing effect in irritant inflammatory conditions. An International Symposium on Apitherapy was organized in Poland wherein several papers on therapeutic effects of honey and other bee products were presented (ANONYMUS 1948-1976, APIPOL 1985, NORRIS 1969). Studies carried out at Jamia Hamdard on Polish propolis bee products, revealed good antibacterial (particularly against gram negative organisms), antifungal (against fungi responsible for superficial and dermatomycoses) and anti-inflammatory (against acute and chronic models of inflammation) effects (DOBROWOLSKI et.al. 1991).

Milk and Yoghurt *(Lactus)*
These are attributed with nourishing, cleansing and soothing effects. Traditional use of milk and yoghurt for washing hair and face before bath is not without scientific basis. These products help in restoring the natural oil of skin and hair making them soft, smooth and lusterous (VOHORA & KHAN 1978). Nature is an inexhaustible mine from which innumerable products can be unearthed for use as cosmetics. A few examples are cited above to illustrate the point.

7. CONCLUDING REMARKS
Herbo-mineral drugs and cosmetics, which are less `alien' to the human body vs synthetic products, are extensively used by women in the Indian sub-continent both for therapeutic and cosmetic purposes. The use of `blood purifying' plants for the treatment of acne, pimples, blemishes, freckles and for clearing complexion, psoralens from *Psoralea corylifolia* and *Ammi majus* for the treatment of leucoderma, Chaulmogra oil from *Gynocardia odorata* seeds for the treatment of leprosy, *Andropogon muricatus* for soothing effects and reducing `sense of heat' and itching in cases of urticaria and endogenous eczemas, *Swertia chirata* and *Azadirachta indica* internally and by local application in various types dermatitis and psoriasis, berberis sulphate from *Berberis aristata* in oriental sore, sandalwood and turmeric pastes for

pre-bath beauty application *(ubtan)* on whole body by young women in general and brides in particular, use of tender stems of *Azadirachta indica* and *Acacia arabica* as substitutes for both tooth brush and tooth paste for dental care, face packs containing maize and gram flour, yoghurt, honey, white clay, *Cucumis sativus* and citrus fruit juices/extracts, the use of *Lawsonia alba* for ornamental bridal decoration of palms and soles and as a hair dye, and of *Phyllanthus emblica* and *Sapindus trifoliatus* in hair shampoos are some striking examples of such usage.

Thus simple inexpensive natural products can be used for beauty care as also for the treatment of skin diseases. Surprisingly many beauty conscious mod women are paying exorbitant prices for these humble ingredients presented as hi-tech products in expensive colourful packs. For example alphahydroxy acids found in the so called anti-aging skin care formulations come from milk, sugar and fruit sources.

References

ANONYMOUS. 1948-1976. *The Wealth of India. vols.* I-XI, Council of Scientific and Industrial Research, New Delhi.
ANONYMOUS. 1955. *The Dispensatory of the United States of America*, Ed.25, pp. 1275-76, JP Lippincott Co, Toronto.
ANONYMOUS. 1979. *The British Pharmaceutical Codex*, Ed.11, p.828, Pharmaceutical Press, London.
ANTIA, FP. 1973. *Clinical Dietetics and Nutrition,* Oxford Press, Delhi.
APIPOL. 1985. *International Symposium on Apitherapy.* Krakow (Poland), May 23-26.
BASU, AP. 1971. *Indian J. Pharm.,* 33(6), 127.
BEHL PN. 1975. *Practice of Dermatology,* Ed.3, Thomson Press (India) Ltd., New Delhi.
BHATIA, A, SINGH, GB and KHANNA, NM. 1964. Indian J. exp. Biol., 2, 158.
CENTRAL INSTITUTE OF MEDICINAL AND AROMATIC PLANTS. 1994. *National Seminar on the Use of Traditional Medicinal Plants in Skin Care* , Lucknow, November 25-26.
CHOPRA, RN NAYAR SL and CHOPRA, IC. 1956. *Glossary of Indian Medicinal Plants,* Council of Scientific and Industrial Research, New Delhi.
DINESCHANDRA and GUPTa, SS. 1972. *Indian J. Med. Res.,* 60(1), 138.
DIXIT, SN and TRIPATHI, SC. 1975. *Indian Phytopath.,* 28(1), 141.
DOBHROWOLSKI, JW, VOHORA, SB, SHARMA, K et al. 1991. *J Ethnpharmacology,* 55, 77.
GHOSE, BP. 1958. *Indian J. Med. Sci.,* 12, 991.
GUPTA, U, BHATIA VN, VENUGOPAL, P et al. 1971. *Indian J. Med. Res.,* 59, 1002.
HUSAIN, S. 1995. Health column. *Hindustan Times,* June 28, p. 16.
HUSSAIN S. 1985. *Times of India,* Sunday Review, 25 August, p.5.
JAIN, SK. 1975. *Medicinal Plants,* Ed.2, p.125, National Book Trust, New Delhi.
KEMPANA, C. 1973. *Proc. First Workshop All India Coordinated Improvement Project on Medicinal and Aromatic Plants,* Bangalore.
MADHWAN, M, CHANDRA, K and REDDY, DJ. 1971. *Indian J.Med. Sci.,* 25, 771.
MARTINDALE. 1982. *Extra Pharmacopoeia,* Ed.28, p.45, The Pharmaceutical Press, London.
MATHUR, KS KHAN, MA and SHARMA, R. 1968. *Brit.Med. J.,* 1, 30.
MOORE, CV and DUBACH, R. 1956. *J. Amer. Med. Asso.,* 162, 197.
NORRIS, P. 1969. *About Honey,* Thornson Publications, London.
OKAZAK, K and OSHIMA, S. 1953. *J. Pharmaceut. Soc. Japan,* 73, 344.
PACHAURI, SP and MUKHERJEE, SK. 1970. *J.Res. Indian Med.,* 5(1), 27.
PANJA, RK. 1985. Miscellany, *Times of India* Sept. 1
RAMASWAMY, AS and SIRSI, M. 1957. *Die Naturwissenhscaften,* 44, 1.
RAMASWAMY, AS, JAYRAMAN, S, SIRSI, M et al . 1972. *Indian J. Exp. Biol.,* 10, 72.
SARIN, JPS, MITRA, RK, and RAY, GK. 1960. *Indian J. Pharm.,* 22(9), 234.
SHENDE, ST, BALASUNDARAM, VR and SEN, A. 1968. *Indian J. Microbiol.,* 3(2), 143.
SRIMATHI, RA and SREENIVASAYA, M. 1963.*Curr. Sci.,* 32(1), 11.
VOHORA, SB. 1985. *Hamdard Medicus* 28(1), 72.
VOHORA, SB and KHAN, MSY. 1978. *Animal Origin Drugs Used in Unani Medicine,* Ed.1, pp.32-34, 102, Institute of History of Medicine and Medical Research and Viteas Publishing House, New Delhi.
VOHORA, SB, BABULKA P, BOTZ L et al. 1987. *Curare* 10, 240.

Neue Wege in der Gesundheitsvorsorge für die weibliche Maori-Bevölkerung Neuseelands
New Initiatives from Maori Health Groups for Indigenous Women in Aotearoa, New Zealand

Christine Binder-Fritz

Zusammenfassung: Im Vergleich zur non-Maori Bevölkerung weist die weibliche Maori-Bevölkerung eine niedrigere Lebenserwartung, eine höhere Geburtenrate, aber auch höhere Kindersterblichkeitsrate, sowie niedrigeres Alter der Erstgebärenden, desweiteren eine hohe Rate an Asthma, Adipositas, Diabetes mellitus und koronaren Herzkrankheiten auf. Sowohl sozioökonomische als auch kulturrelevante Rahmenbedingungen des Lebensalltags stehen in Zusammenhang mit spezifisch weiblichen Gesundheitsproblemen: Niedrige Einkommenschicht, hohe Arbeitslosigkeit, jugendliche "Teenager-Mütter", Rauchen, Alkohol- und Drogenkonsum, Gewaltbereitschaft in der Familie, eine ungesunde Ernährung sowie der Berufs- und Alltagsstress einer ethnischen Minderheit auf der Suche nach ihrer kulturellen Identität. Das neuseeländische, monokulturelle Gesundheitssystem war in den vergangen Jahren den Bedürfnissen der indigenen Maori- Bevölkerung nicht angepasst. Nach dem Motto "Von Frauen - für Frauen" sind die indigenen Frauen nun aktiv an der Mitgestaltung im Gesundheitswesen beteiligt. Die neuen Strategien konzentrieren sich auf Health Promotion und beziehen auch auf dem Gebiet der kurativen Praktiken die physischen, psychischen, sozialen und spirituellen Dimensionen des Lebens und der Gesundheitserhaltung mit ein. Die steigende Nachfrage nach traditionellen Therapieformen (Rongoa Maori) hat dazu beigetragen, dass diese in den Maori Health Centers gemeinsam mit der modernen Westlichen Medizin angeboten werden.

Abstract: In comparison with the non-Maori population of New Zealand, the health status for Maori women is far worse and general life expectancy is still lower. Asthma deaths, stroke and heart disease among adult Maori remain 3-4 times as frequent as those for non-Maori. Risk factors for these conditions, including obesity and heavy smoking, remain much higher for some Maori groups. Law social income groups in urban areas, young "teenage-mothers" with unemployed partners in connection with alcohol and drug abuse and violence within the family are an other source of concern. Socioeconomic, cultural and self-esteem factors are among the reasons of women's health problems. Over recent years there has been a growing realisation in the health sector, that New Zealand's health services, being essentially monocultural, often failed to respond to the needs of the female Maori-population. Since Maori women themselves want to be active in developing policies for health, several initiatives for health education and health promotion from Maori health groups can be provided alongside with Western medical health care. Because the demand for traditional herbal, healing, spiritual rituals and counselling (Rongoa Maori) is steadily growing, efforts are made in creating a new synthesis of the best of traditional and modern medicine.

Keywords: Neuseeland, Maori-Frauen, Indigene Gesundheitsvorsorge, Gynäkologie und Geburtshilfe, Akkulturation, Kindersterblichkeit, New Zealand, Maori-Women, Health Promotion, Gynaecology and Obstetrics, child mortality.

Abb. 1
Junge Mütter in den urbanen Zentren vermissen das sozioökonomische Netzwerk ihrer auf dem Land lebenden Großfamilie (Foto: C. Binder-Fritz.)

Einführung und Methode

Der vorliegende Artikel basiert auf ethnografischem Datenmaterial, welches im Verlauf mehrerer Forschungsaufenthalte (1986, 1989, 1995/96, 1997) mit finanzieller Unterstützung des Bundesministeriums für Wissenschaft und Forschung, sowie des Fonds zur Förderung der wissenschaftlichen Forschung, auf der Nordinsel Neuseelands im Gebiet der Bay of Plenty gesammelt wurde. Aufgrund enger persönlicher Kontakte zu zwei Maori-Familien war es während der Forschungsaufenthalte möglich, in den Familienverbänden zu leben und Einblick in die Lebenswelt der Frauen zu gewinnen. Die Datenerhebung beruht methodisch auf qualitativen Einzelinterviews mit Heilern und Heilerinnen, Maori-Personal in Gesundheitszentren, Hebammen, Krankenschwestern, Sozialarbeiterinnen sowie anderen Verantwortlichen im staatlichen Gesundheitsdienst. Mittels der Methode der teilnehmenden Beobachtung wurde der Tagesablauf in den Community Health Centers, sowie die hier, als komplementäre Medizin praktizierten, traditionellen Heilverfahren dokumentiert. Um der Komplexität des Themas "Frauen und Gesundheit" gerecht zu werden, muss auf die soziokulturellen Rahmenbedingungen des Lebensalltags der weiblichen Maori-Bevölkerung Bedacht genommen werden. Einerseits ist es unabdingbar den Akkulturationsprozess der vergangenen hundertfünfzig Jahre in die Forschungsarbeit miteinzubeziehen, andererseits beeinflussen auch die gegenwärtigen politischen Proteste der Maori-AktivistInnen, sowie die, seit den achtziger Jahren ablaufende kulturelle Revitalisierungsbewegung, die Interpretation der Begriffe "cultural identity", "traditional culture" und "traditional Maori healing". Frauen engagieren sich zunehmend, wenn es um traditionelle Landrechte, politische Selbstbestimmung und Autonomie in sozialen und gesundheitspolitischen Belangen geht.

Zur Forschungssituation in Aotearoa (Neuseeland)

Eigene Erfahrungen während der, im Verlauf der letzten Jahre in Abständen durchgeführten ethnografischen Forschungen bestätigen die Aussagen vieler Kollegen und Kolleginnen, dass sich anthropologische Forschungstätigkeit in Aotearoa/Neuseeland immer schwieriger gestaltet. Einzelne Aktivisten-Gruppen rufen zum Boykott der Zusammenarbeit mit in- und ausländischen "weißen Forschern" auf. Medizin- und kulturanthropologische Arbeiten zur Gesundheitsversorgung der Maori-Bevökerung und zum Gebiet der traditionellen Heikunde werden als "cultural sensitive" bezeichnet, wobei viele Maori aus Sorge um den Schutz ihres "cultural and intellectual knowledge" ausländischen Forschungen gegenüber prinzipiell ablehnend eingestellt sind. Gegenwärtig folgt Neuseelands Intellectual Property Legislation der UNESCO-Erklärung aus dem Jahr 1992, wonach "intellectual property" aus drei Kategorien besteht: folklore and crafts, biodiversity und indigenious knowledge.

Im Zusammenhang mit ethnomedizinischen Fragestellungen ist auch Neuseelands Einwanderungspolitik von Interesse. Denn nicht nur die indigenen Maori, sondern auch die im letzten Jahrzehnt zahlreich eingewanderten ArbeitsmigrantInnen von den pazifischen Inseln und aus Südostasien (Cook-Inseln, Samoa, Tonga, Fiji, sowie Indien, China, Korea) verlangen eine adäquate medizinische Versorgung. Außerdem bringen die Migrantinnen lokale Heilpraktiken aus ihrer Heimat nach Neuseeland, sodass ein ausgesprochener Synkretismus der Heilkunden beobachtet werden kann.

Frauenalltag in der postkolonialen Maori-Gesellschaft

Europäische Kolonialpolitik, Fremdherrschaft und christliche Mission haben in den letzten hundertfünfzig Jahren massive Veränderungen im wirtschaftlichen Alltag und im Weltbild der autochthonen Bevölkerung Neuseelands bewirkt. Eine gezielte Besiedlungspolitik und der daraus resultierende Landverlust für die Indigenen führte in Verbindung mit einer geänderten Wirtschaftsform zu Abwanderungsbewegungen in die urbanen Zentren und zur Abhängigkeit von staatlichen Institutionen. Als Resultat der Migration in die Städte kam es zur Auflösung intakter Dorfgemeinschaften und traditioneller Familienstrukturen. Veränderte Beziehungen zwischen den Generationen und Geschlechtern, sowie eine signifikante Änderung des individuellen und sozialen Erlebens der Mutterschaft sind die Folge. Aufgrund von sozioökonomischen Veränderungen mit gestiegenen Lebenskosten und einer sehr geringen staatlichen Pension sind viele der Familien auf ein zusätzliches Einkommen angewiesen. Neben Haushalt und Familie leisten viele Frauen bis ins höhere Alter, als oftmals unqualifizierte Arbeitskraft in schlecht bezahlten Berufssparten, ihren Anteil am Familieneinkommen.

Frauenspezifische Gesundheitsprobleme
Maori weisen im Vergleich zur übrigen Bevölkerung Neuseelands eine höhere Mortalitätsrate auf. Die Altersstruktur der Maori-Bevölkerung unterscheidet sich grundlegend von der Pakeha-Bevölkerung Neuseelands (= "Die Fremden". Bezeichnung für Neuseeländer europäischen Ursprungs).

Der Anteil an Kindern und jungen Menschen ist sehr hoch, doch nur mehr 4 % der Maori-Bevölkerung erreichen das Pensionsalter, während 15% der Pakeha-Bevölkerung über sechzig Jahre alt sind (STATISTICS NEW ZEALAND 1995). Im Vergleich zur Pakeha-Bevölkerung sind eine höhere Kindersterblichkeitsrate, eine etwa sechsmal höhere Selbstmordrate, sowie etwa dreimal so viele Psychiatriefälle auffällig. Folgende Faktoren sind nach wie vor für die höhere Mortalitätsrate verantwortlich: Die deutlich schlechtere soziale und wirtschaftliche Lage eines Großteils der Bevölkerung in Verbindung mit hoher Jugendarbeitslosigkeit, erhöhter Alkohol- und Drogenkonsum, und damit im Zusammenhang eine erhöhte Unfallstatistik und Gewaltbereitschaft, sowie eine ungesunde Ernährung. Als Folge der fett- und kohlehydratreichen Ernährung leiden Maori etwa 2-3 mal häufiger an Adipositas, Diabetes mellitus und koronaren Herzkrankheiten (vgl. POMARE and DE BOER 1988). Der enorm hohe Anteil an starken Raucherinnen ist für die hohe Rate an chronischen Atemwegserkrankungen, Asthma und Lungenkrebs in der weiblichen Bevölkerung verantwortlich. Neben einer höheren Geburtenrate weist die Maori-Bevölkerung im Vergleich mit der Gesamtpopulation ein niedrigeres Alter der Erstgebärenden auf. Des weiteren ist eine erhöhte Rate an malignen Erkrankungen, vor allem des Mammakarzinoms und des Zervixkarzinoms auffällig. Anlass zur Besorgnis ist auch die seit Jahren hohe Rate am plötzlichen Kindstod (SIDS), dem etliche Präventivmaßnahmen gewidmet sind (PUBLIC HEALTH COMMISSION 1994).

Sowohl sozioökonomische als auch kulturrelevante Rahmenbedingungen des Lebensalltags stehen in direktem Zusammenhang mit den spezifischen Gesundheitsproblemen der weiblichen Maori-Bevölkerung. Folgende Faktoren sind hierbei vor allem für junge Frauen von Bedeutung:
1. Niedrige Einkommensschicht
2. Hohe Jugendarbeitslosigkeit
3. Jugendliche Erstgebärende ("Teenager-Mütter")
4. Rauchen, Alkohol und Drogenkonsum
5. Gewaltbereitschaft in Partnerschaft und Familie
6. Ungesunde Ernährung und Übergewicht
7. Berufs- und Alltagsstress

ad 1.und ad 2. Niedrige Einkommensschicht, hohe Jugendarbeitslosigkeit
Die Abwanderung vieler Jugendlicher aus den ländlichen Gemeinden in die urbanen Zentren ist nach wie vor problematisch. Auf Grund einer generell schlechteren Arbeitsqualifikation und Vorurteilen von Seiten der Weißen, erwartet junge Maori in den Städten häufig ein Leben mit niedrigem sozialen Status. Die schlechten Wohn- und Arbeitsverhältnisse, niedrige Löhne, oftmals Arbeitslosigkeit, und nicht zuletzt Verlust des sozialen Rückhaltes mit der Großfamilie auf dem Land, sind in vielen Fällen für Alkohol- und Drogenprobleme verantwortlich. Mit Besorgnis registrieren die Gesundheitsbehörden auch die steigende Zahl von jugendlichen Erstgebärenden, Schulabbrecherinnen und Sozialhilfe-Empfängerinnen. Wie auch andere Angehörige niedriger sozialer Schichten weisen viele junge Maori-Familien in den Städten vielfältige gesundheitliche Probleme auf.

ad 3. Jugendliche Erstgebärende
Der Anteil an jugendlichen Müttern (Geburtsalter 16-19) ist in der Maori-Bevölkerung (470.000) dreimal so hoch wie in der Gesamtpopulation (3,6 Mio). In der Altersgruppe der 16- bis 24jährigen Frauen werden mehr als die Hälfte aller Geburten verzeichnet (TE PUNI KOKIRI 1995). Den "Teenager-Müttern" steht aber nur selten das sozioökonomische Netzwerk ihrer auf dem Land lebenden Großfamilie zur Seite.

4. Rauchen, Alkohol und Drogenmissbrauch
In der Gruppe jugendlicher Maori-Mütter findet sich eine hohe Rate an Raucherinnen und Alkoholkonsumentinnen. Nikotin, Alkohol und Drogen sind häufige Ursache für Schwangerschafts- und Geburtskomplikationen mit Frühgeburtlichkeit und einer verminderten Lebenserwartung des Neuge-

borenen. Alkoholismus, vor allem im ersten Drittel der Schwangerschaft führt zum "fetalen Alkoholsyndrom", mit gehäuften Spontanaborten und Frühgeburten, sowie postpartal zu einer Hemmung der frühkindlichen intellektuellen und motorischen Entwicklung mit bleibenden intellektuellen Entwicklungsstörungen. Im Hinblick auf die hohe Rate am plötzlichen Kindstod (SIDS) in der Maori-Bevölkerung wird gerade das Rauchen während der Schwangerschaft als ein möglicher Risikofaktor diskutiert, da Nikotin eine plazentare Insuffizienz und damit eine erhöhte Rate an Embryopathien bewirkt. Solcherart geschädigte Kinder weisen neben einem niedrigen Geburtsgewicht auch eine erhöhte Anfälligkeit für Infektionen auf (SPIELMANN 1992; VANDENBERG 1985). Während in der Gruppe der Pakeha 33% der Mütter während der Schwangerschaft rauchen, so sind es in der Gruppe der Maori 68% der Mütter, die während der Schwangerschaft zur Zigarette greifen (ALISON et al. 1993; PUBLIC HEALTH COMMISSION 1995).

ad 5. Gewaltbereitschaft in Partnerschaft und Familie
Arbeitslosigkeit und die schwierige sozioökonomische Lebenssituation vieler junger Familien in den Städten, in Verbindung mit Alkohol und Drogen, Frustration und Depression sind jene Faktoren, die zu einer erhöhten Gewaltbereitschaft in Partnerschaft und Familie, sowie zu Bandenbildung in den Städten führen. Ein alarmierender Anstieg an körperlichen Misshandlungen der Kinder und Lebensgefährtinnen, sowie sexuellem Missbrauch, sind Zeichen für die Unfähigkeit vieler Paare zur Konfliktbewältigung und zum Krisenmanagement. Als psychosoziale Aspekte der Aggressivität und Gewaltbereitschaft können m. E. auch die akkulturationsbedingten Veränderungen der traditionellen Familienstruktur, die geänderte Wirtschafts- und Lebensweise durch Landverlust und Migration in die urbanen Zentren, sowie kulturelle Entfremdung, diskutiert werden.

ad 6. Ungesunde Ernährung und Übergewicht
Das Leben in den urbanen Zentren bedeutet für berufstätige Mütter zwangsweise auch geänderte Ernährungsgewohnheiten. Mit dem Land verloren Maori auch ihre, auf Anbau der Süßkartoffel, Jagd, Fischfang und Sammeltätigkeit beruhende Wirtschaftsgrundlage, sowie den Zugang zu einem Großteil ihrer Wälder und traditionellen Fischgründe. Die heutige Ernährung besteht vorwiegend aus billigen, hochkalorigen - und meist ungesunden - Produkten, wobei sich auch die sogenannten "fast food"-Restaurants ungemeiner Beliebtheit erfreuen. Dem gemeinsamen Essen und der Gastfreundschaft wird nach wie vor ein hoher gesellschaftlicher Stellenwert zugeschrieben, und bei jeder Zusammenkunft auf dem Marae gehört das Gemeinschaftsessen, an reichlich gedeckten Tischen, zum festlichen Zeremoniell. Es ist nicht verwunderlich, dass sich die Leidenschaft der Maori fürs Essen und der Mangel an körperlicher Bewegung in gesundheitlichen Problemen niederschlägt: Adipositas und Diabetes mellitus mit allen damit verbundenen Gesundheitsrisiken, wie Bluthochdruck, Gefäßerkrankungen und koronaren Herzkrankheiten haben in der weiblichen Maori-Bevölkerung besorgniserregend zugenommen (THE MAORI WOMEN'S WELFARE LEAGUE 1984; TE PUNI KOKIRI 1994 b).

ad 7. Berufs- und Alltagsstress
Ein hoher Prozentsatz der weiblichen Maori-Bevölkerung zählt nach wie vor zu den unqualifizierten Arbeitskräften. Bis zu den achtziger Jahren war die Zahl der Hochschulabgängerinnen sehr gering. Durch gezielte Bildungsangebote und Förderungsmaßnahmen ist allerdings eine stete Zunahme an Akademikerinnen zu verzeichnen. Migrantinnen von den benachbarten Pazifikinseln, Samoa, Fidschi, Tonga, sowie den Cook-Inseln, sind billige ausländische Arbeitskräfte und eine große Konkurrenz auf dem Arbeitsmarkt für Maori Frauen ohne Berufsausbildung. Der rege Tourismus hingegen bietet den Frauen neue Arbeitsmöglichkeiten. Im Gesundheitswesen waren die Indigenen bis vor wenigen Jahren nur spärlich vertreten, aber auch hier ist die Zahl des qualifizierten weiblichen Krankenpflegepersonals und der Hebammen in den lezten zehn Jahren deutlich gestiegen.

Familie und Verwandtschaft zählen noch immer zu den wichtigsten Lebensinhalten. Auch in einer zunehmend verwestlichten Welt existieren nach wie vor andere Wertmaßstäbe: Nicht Individualität steht im Vordergrund, sondern Gemeinschaft, und dem Interesse des Gemeinwohls wird deutlich mehr Gewicht beigemessen als dem Interesse des Einzelnen. Zu vielen Anlässen trifft sich die Verwandtschaft auf dem traditionellen Versammlungsplatz (Marae). Vor allen anderen Ereignissen verlangen aber Todesfälle umfangreiche Vorbereitungsarbeiten, um den reibungslosen Ablauf der dreitägigen Begräbnisfeierlichkeiten (tangihanga) zu gewährleisten, sowie die zahlreichen, oft mehrere hundert Gäste unterbringen und verköstigen zu können. Da viele Frauen heute berufstätig sind und in den urbanen Zentren leben, haben sich diese Zusammenkünfte in die Wochenenden verlagert. Das soziale Netz der großen Verwandtschaftsgruppe mit der Verpflichtung zur gegenseitigen Hilfeleistung bietet bei den verschiedenen Lebenskrisen einerseits Halt und Sicherheit. Andererseits bedeuten diese Zusammenkünfte auf dem Marae für die berufstätigen Frauen eine enorme zusätzliche Arbeitsbelastung, auch wenn die Vorbereitungsarbeiten dafür immer von vielen Frauen und Männern in Gemeinschaftsarbeit geleistet werden. Trotz Doppelbelastung in Familie und Beruf ist es für die Mütter und Großmütter auch selbstverständlich, zum Wohle der Gemeinschaft , unbezahlte community- und Sozialarbeit , sowie Altenpflege zu leisten. Übermäßiger Alkohol- und Nikotingenuss steht häufig in Verbindung mit dieser Mehrfachbelastung.

Neue Strategien im Gesundheitssystem
Jahrzehntelang hat die, auf westlicher Lebensweise und moderner Medizin beruhende, monokulturelle Gesundheitsversorgung den kulturspezifischen Dimensionen zur Gesundheitserhaltung in der Maori-Bevölkerung zu wenig Beachtung geschenkt. Die Kritik von seiten der Indigenen (DURIE 1994; POMARE and DE BOER 1988), sowie die Forderung einzelner, radikaler Maori-Gruppen nach politischer und kultureller Autonomie (Tino Rangatiratanga) hat unter anderem zur Reformierung der Gesundheitsdienste für Maori beigetragen. Die Gesundheitsreform des Jahres 1991 brachte wesentliche Vorteile für die indigene Bevölkerung, da der staatliche Gesundheitsdienst quasi zu einem privatisierten Unternehmen umgestaltet wurde und einzelne Maori Health Groups ihre Dienstleistungen auf der Grundlage eines zeitlich begrenzten Vertrags an die Regional Health Authorities verkaufen können. Maori betonen, dass ihre traditionellen heilkundlichen Therapien (Rongoa Maori) einen ganzheitlichen Zugang zu Gesundheit und Krankheit haben, wobei die physischen, psychischen, sozialen und spirituellen Dimensionen des Lebens und der Gesundheitserhaltung, miteinbezogen werden. Auch das Ministerium für Maori Development betont den traditionellen philosophischen Hintergrundes der Gesundheitsversorgung: "Maori want to take with them the cultural heritage of their ancestors and therefore the demand for traditional herbal, healing and spiritual rituals (Rongoa Maori) is steadily growing (TE PUNI KOKIRI 1994:15). In diesem Zusammenhang erinnert Mason Durie (1994) daran, dass wesentliche Verbesserungen der Sozial-und Gesundheitsdienste für die Indigenen seit jeher mit "strong Maori leadership" assoziiert werden. Die wichtigsten Forderungen und Prioritäten der Indigenen für eine, den Bedürfnissen der Bevölkerung angepasste, zukünftige Gesundheitsversorgung sind nach dem Maori Ministerium (TE PUNI KOKIRI 1994) die folgenden:
* Maori control, self determination and leadership in the health sector
* Promotion of health and healthy lifestyles within the Maori community
* Health must be approached from a holistic perspective, which includes cultural and philosophical dimensions
* Health care and therapy that makes sense to Maori
* Rongoa Maori (Traditional healing)

Von Frauen für Frauen: Rapua Te Mana Wahine
Mit großem persönlichem Einsatz setzen einzelne Frauen-Gruppen nun ihre eigenen Vorstellungen zu einer selbstbestimmten, und kulturelle Werte berücksichtigenden, Gesundheitsversorgung für die weibliche Bevölkerung in die Praxis um. Nach dem Motto "Von Frauen für Frauen" wird den frauenspezifischen Problemen dabei Rechnung getragen. Auf dem Gebiet der Präventivmedizin werden verstärkt Initiativen zur health promotion, Verbesserung der sozioökonomischen Lebenssituation der Familien, sowie psychologische Beratungen (counselling) und Krisenintervention, vor allem für misshandelte Frauen, gesetzt. Im Hinblick auf kurative Praktiken werden in den Community Health Centers neben der westlichen Medizin zunehmend komplementäre, heilkundliche Therapien, wie die Anwendung von Heilkräutern, Massage-Techniken, und "spirituelles Heilen" angeboten.

Im Herbst 1995 wurde vom öffentlichen Gesundheitsdienst (Public Health Commission) ein dreijähriges nationales Projekt zur Verbesserung der gesundheitlichen Situation der weiblichen Maori-Bevölkerung gestartet. Ein bereits bestehender sozialer Hilfsdienst des Whakatohea Maori Trust Board in Opotiki wurde vertraglich mit der Durchführung beauftragt. Das Arbeitskollektiv aus sechs Frauen

hat folgende wichtige Impulse gesetzt (TE WHEKE ATAWHAI 1/1995):
1. Einrichtung einer elektronischen Datenbank und Aufbau eines Netzwerks für alle an Gesundheitsfragen interessierte Frauen und Gruppen, mit Bibliothek und Adressverzeichnis.
2. Eine eigene, vierteljährlich erscheinende Informationszeitschrift (Rapua Te Mana Wahine), die an alle Gesundheitszentren versandt wird.
3. Propagierung eines "healthy lifestyle" mit folgenden Themenschwerpunkten:
    * Ernährungsberatung
    * Smokefree Kampagnen
    * Alkohol- und Drogenberatung
    * Familienberatung und Krisenintervention
    * Förderung sportlicher Aktivitäten (Netball, Basketball, Rugby, Tai Chi)
4. Unterstützung von Frauenprojekten auf dem Gebiet der Gynäkologie und Geburtshilfe, kontinuierliche Betreuung durch Maori-Hebammen während Schwangerschaft und Geburt.

Desweiteren laufen Medien-Kampagnen, um die einzelnen Projekte und Initiativen der verschiedenen Frauengruppen und Gesundheitszentren einer breiteren Öffentlichkeit vorzustellen. Anfang 1996 wurde ein nationaler Gesundheitstag für Maori Frauen veranstaltet. Bereits der Name der Zeitschrift, Rapua Te Mana Wahine ("den Blick auf Prestige und Status der Frauen lenken") zeigt, dass Hilfe zur Selbsthilfe, Krisenmanagement, sowie Stärkung des weiblichen Selbstbewusstseins, im Sinne des "empowerment for women", im Mittelpunkt der verschiedenen Maßnahmen und gesundheitsfördernden Frauenprojekte stehen.

Zielgruppe Jugendliche

Die gesundheitsfördernden Initiativen sind wegen der bereits angeführten, zahlreichen Risikofaktoren in erster Linie an die jugendliche Bevölkerung gerichtet. Um die hohe Rate an Teenager-Schwangerschaften zu senken, wurden eigene Jugendberatungsstellen (peer groups) eingerichtet. Die jugendlichen Mitarbeiterinnen haben häufig selbst die Probleme einer Teenager-Schwangerschaft erlebt und finden daher leichter Zugang zu den jungen Mädchen, um diese in Fragen der Empfängnisverhütung zu beraten. Die in Süd-Auckland neben dem Middlemore Hospital seit 1994 stationierte Beratungsstelle

Abb. 2
Sexualität und Empfängnisverhütung: Diskussion mit den Schülerinnen (Foto. C. Binder-Fritz)

konnte bereits Erfolge erzielen: Die Rate an Teenager-Schwangerschaften am benachbarten Mangere College ist von 16 auf 3 pro Jahr gefallen (TE WHEKE ATAWHAI.1/1995:8).

Mit großem persönlichen Engagement wird von Maori-Ältesten in Zusammenarbeit mit den Studenten lokaler Schauspielschulen und Theatergruppen seit kurzem mit Erfolg versucht, neue ungewöhnliche Wege auf dem Gebiet der health promotion zu gehen. Im März 1997 hatte das Tanztheater "Cher Bro" in Rotorua Premiere. Mit Finanzierung durch die regionale Gesundheitsbehörde (Eastbay Health) und mit Unterstützung von Joan Aoke konnte dieses vom Musiker Greg Tata konzipierte Projekt realisiert werden. Die zentralen Themen dieser Gesundheitskampagne sind: "Smokefree", Alkoholfreies Autofahren ("Don't drink and drive"), Sexualberatung ("Safer Sex"), Empfängnisverhütung, sowie STD+ AIDS Prävention. Die "Gesundheits-Botschaften" werden dramaturgisch aufbereitet und in einer, der Jugendkultur entsprechenden Sprache vor Schulklassen aufgeführt, um Impulse für die themenspezifische Diskussion im anschließenden Unterricht zu setzen. Einen großen Stellenwert hat dabei die Betonung von kulturspezifischen, traditionellen Werten.

Schwangerenbetreuung und Geburtshilfe

Die akkulturationsbedingten Veränderungen der Familienstruktur und Wirtschaftsweise haben zum Verlust des sozioökonomischen Netzwerks für Schwangere und Erstgebärende geführt. Durch die Medikalisierung der Geburt wurde diese ab den fünfziger Jahren sukzessive aus dem soziokulturellen Rahmen herausgelöst. Der Verlust von traditionell stützenden Ritualen in der kritischen Phase des Übergangs in den neuen Lebensabschnitt hat zu einem Bruch im Erleben der individuellen und sozialen Mutterschaft geführt. Fehlende Vertrauensbildung und fehlende soziale Fürsorge durch Familienangehörige während Schwangerschaft und Geburt, sowie eine generelle Isolation der jungen Mütter bestimmen den Alltag in den urbanen Zentren Neuseelands. Die staatlichen Institutionen konnten hier nur begrenzt Ersatz bieten (BINDER-FRITZ 1996).

Die, mit dem neuen Lebensabschnitt der Mutterschaft verbundenen Rollenerwartungen an die Frau, sowie die menschliche Reproduktion betreffende Vorstellungen und Verhaltensweisen waren ein integraler Bestandteil der voreuropäischen Sozialorganisation, der ökonomischen und politischen Verhältnisse, sowie des ideologischen Weltbildes und des Geschlechterverhältnisses. Selbstachtung und Selbstwertgefühl von Frauen und Mädchen stehen in enger Verbindung zu den soziokulturellen Rahmenbedingen des Lebensalltags. Die vielfältigen, akkulturationsbedingten Veränderungen des weiblichen Lebensalltags haben dazu geführt, dass sich viele junge indigene Frauen in der modernen neuseeländischen Gesellschaft wie Fremde fühlen, mangelndes Selbstvertrauen, sowie ein Gefühl der eigenen Wertlosigkeit empfinden. Nach wie vor ist die Rate an Schwangerschafts- und Geburtskomplikationen in der weiblichen Maori-Population deutlich höher als in der non-Maori-Population. Um den vielfältigen Problemen auf dem Gebiet der Schwangerenbetreuung und Geburtshilfe wirkungsvoll zu beggenen, kommen seit kurzem zwei neue Strategien zur Anwendung:
  1. Positive Rollenmodelle
  2. Betonung des spirituellen Aspekts der Geburt

ad 1. Positive Rollenmodelle
Ein großer Teil der jungen Maori-Generation fühlt sich weder in der modernen, westlichen Welt zu Hause, noch haben die Jugendlichen einen direkten Bezug zu den eigenen Kulturtraditionen. Die jungen Mütter, bzw. die jungen Eltern in den Städten vermissen heute die familiären, soziokulturellen Netzwerke der Maori-communities auf dem Land. Gerade in der kritischen Zeit der Umstrukturierung einer Paar-Beziehung zur Jungfamilie wirkt sich aber das Fehlen geeigneter Identifikationsmodelle und Rollenbilder für den neuen Lebensabschnitt ausgesprochen negativ aus. Die von den staatlichen Institutionen bisher angebotenen Beratungs- und Informationsdienste wurden von den Maori-Familien in der Mehrzahl der Fälle nur selten in Anspruch genommen. Daher gingen engagierte, freiberufliche Maori-Hebammen, Distriktkrankenschwestern und Sozialarbeiterinnen in den letzten fünf Jahren daran, einen Besuchs- und Betreuungsdienst aufzubauen, um den jungen Müttern kontinuierliche Fürsorge und Beratung von der Schwangerschaft bis zum Wochenbett zu ermöglichen. Die erfahrenen Betreuerinnen haben selbst Kinder geboren und verstehen sich als mütterliche Ratgeberinnen. Bei den Hausbesuchen kann Einblick in das soziale Umfeld, sowie mögliche Risikofaktoren für Mutter und Kind, gewonnen werden. Medizinische Kontrolluntersuchungen, Ernährungsberatung und Gewichtskontrolle während

der Schwangerschaft, Ermunterung zum Stillen, Krisenintervention, oder das Herstellen von Kontakten mit Smokefree-Selbsthilfegruppen für starke Raucherinnen, gehören zum Programm.

ad 2. Betonung des spirituellen Aspekts von Geburt und Mutterschaft
Nicht nur die medizinischen Kontrolluntersuchungen sind den Geburtshelferinnen ein Anliegen der Schwangerenbetreuung. Die meisten indigenen Hebammen haben es sich zum Ziel gesetzt, den Schwangeren die spirituelle Dimension der Geburt wieder bewusst zu machen. Junge Mütter erzählen, dass die Familienmitglieder sich durch die Anregungen ihrer Hebamme vor, während und nach der Geburt zu einem Gebet (karakia) versammelt haben, so wie es auch früher Brauch war. Die jungen Mütter werden auch ermuntert, die Plazenta von der Entbindungsstation mitzunehmen. Mit der rituellen Bestattung der Plazenta in der Erde wird nicht nur symbolisch an den ewigen Kreislauf von geboren werden und sterben erinnert, sondern auch die zutiefst spirituelle Bindung an das Land ihrer Ahnen, die Erde und Urmutter Papa-tu-a-nuku ausgedrückt. Einige der erfahrenenen Hebammen können den jungen Frauen auf einfühlsame Weise den philosophischen Aspekt von Gebären und geboren werden näherbringen, sodass den werdenden Müttern bewusst wird, dass mit der Geburt nicht nur der Anfangspunkt für eine einmalige menschliche Existenz gesetzt, sondern auch der Fortbestand der ethnischen Gruppe gesichert ist. Dies bedeutet, dass eine Schwangerschaft für die junge Frau, auch Verantwortung für das ungeborene Leben zu übernehmen, heißt.

Dem Thema "Rauchen während der Schwangerschaft", und den daraus resultierenden Gesundheitsrisiken für den Säugling, war das vom Künstler Hemi Toka entworfene Plakat gewidmet. Die Frauengestalt (wahine) symbolisiert "Te Whare Tangata - das erste Haus aller Menschen", eine prosaische Umschreibung der Gebärmutter. Aus Mund und Nase dieser symbolischen Frauengestalt strömt der "Atem des Lebens", die "Lebensessenz" (Tihei Mauri Ora) in den Embryo: das Kind soll in eine nikotinfreie Welt geboren werden. Ihre Hand symbolisiert Fürsorge, Schutz, Zuneigung, Ernährung und Verantwortung. Das Plakat stellt ein besonders eindrucksvolles Beispiel für die Visualiserung traditioneller Werte und Symbole im Dienste einer modernen, kulturbezogenen Gesundheitsvorsorge dar.

"Health promotion is any combination of health, education, political, spiritual or organisational initiative designed to bring about positive attitudinal, behavioural, social or environmental changes conducive to improving the health of populations" (TE PUNI KOKIRI 1994 a:15).

References
ALISON, L.H et al. 1993. Smoking during pregnancy in New Zealand. In: *Paediatrics and Perinatal Epidemiology.* 7/3 (s. 318-333).
BINDER-FRITZ, C. 1996. *Whaka Whanau. Geburt und Mutterschaft bei den Maori in Neuseeland.* Berlin. Peter Lang.
DURIE, M. 1994. *Whaiora. Maori Health Development.* Auckland. Oxford University Press.
POMARE, E. and de BOER, G. 1988. HAUORA. Maori Standards of Health. A study of the years 1970-1984. *Special Report Series* 78. Department of Health. Wellington.
PUBLIC HEALTH COMMISSION. 1994. *Our Health - Our Future. Hauora Pakari, Koiora Roa. The state of the public health in New Zealand.* Wellington.
PUBLIC HEALTH COMMISSION 1995. *Progress on Health Outcome Targets. Te haere whakamua ki nga whainga hua mo te haouora. The state of the public health in New Zealand.* Wellington.
SPIELMANN, H. et. al. 1992. *Taschenbuch der Arzneimittelverordnung in Schwangerschaft und Stillperiode.* Stuttgart. Fischer.
STATISTICS NEW ZEALAND 1995. *Facts New Zealand.* Wellington.
TE PUNI KOKIRI. MINISTRY OF MAORI DEVELOPMENT 1994. *Maori Primary Health Care Initiatives.* Wellington.
TE PUNI KOKIRI. MINISTRY OF MAORI DEVELOPMENT.1995. *Hui Whai Maramatanga. Whai Oranga. Report of the Hui on Maori Reproductive Health and HIV/ AIDS.* Wellington.
TE WHEKE ATAWHAI 1995. *Rapua Te Mana Wahine.* Panui no. 1. October 1995. Opotiki.
THE MAORI WOMEN'S WELFARE LEAGUE. 1984. *Rapuora - Health and Maori Women. Na Te Ropu Wahine Maori Toko I Te Ora.* Wellington.
VANDENBERG, M. 1985. Smoking during pregnancy and post-neonatal death. In. *N.Z. Medical Journal* 89/793

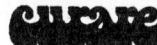

Mutterschaft und Behinderung in der matrilinearen Kultur Palaus
Motherhood and Disability in the Matrilineal Culture of Palau
Evelyn Heinemann

Zusammenfassung: Am Beispiel einer Erzählung und den Äußerungen Betroffener zeigt die Autorin wie in der traditionellen Sicht Behinderung als organisch bedingt, durch Magie verursacht oder durch einen beleidigten Gott erzeugt gesehen wird. So kann das Verhalten irgendeines Klan-Mitglieds, der längst verstorben sein kann, die Ursache für die Beleidigung des Gottes gewesen sein. Die Ursachen erkennen Baumleserinnen. Im Falle der Beleidigung eines Gottes geht der gesamte Klan zum Gottesmedium, um die Schuld durch Geldzahlung zu begleichen. Die traditionelle Sicht führt zur Entlastung der Mütter und zur Übernahme der Verantwortung durch alle Mitglieder des Klans. Die traditionelle Heilmethode versucht weniger das organische Leiden zu beheben als den psychischen Konflikt zu erkennen und für Bewältigungsmöglichkeiten zu sorgen.

Abstract: The author shows with the example of a traditional story and the expressions of disabled people and their mothers that in the traditional belief disability is caused by organic reasons, through the use of magic or through the offence against a God. The behaviour of any member of the clan, even someone who is already dead, can be the reason of the offence. The tree-readers read the causes. In the case of an offence against a God the whole clan has to go to the medium of the God to settle down the dept through paying traditional money. The traditional view leads to a relief of the mothers and to a responsibility of all members of the clan. The traditional healing is less concentrated on the disability than on the psychic conflict and offers strategies to solve the conflict.

Keywords: Palau, matrilineare Kultur, Behinderung, traditionelle Diagnosermittlung, traditionelle Heilbehandlung, Palau, matrilineal culture, disability, traditional way of diagnosis, traditional healingcure

„Der blinde Mann von Ngetmel"

Es war einmal ein altes Ehepaar, das in Ngetmel im Distrikt von Ngerchelong mit seinen zwei Söhnen lebte. Der alte Mann war blind und seine Frau verachtete ihn wegen seiner Behinderung. Die ganze Liebe der Ehefrau galt ihren Söhnen. Die Frau arbeitete auf ihrem Feld und die beiden Söhne waren gute Fischer, so dass die Familie immer zu essen hatte und etwas palauisches Geld sparen konnte. Der arme, blinde Ehemann aber genoss diesen Reichtum nicht. Wenn die Frau mit der Ernte nach Hause kam, wählte sie die guten Teile aus und gab sie sich und ihren Söhnen. Die verfaulten Teile gab sie in den Korb des alten Mannes. Wenn die Söhne mit Fisch nach Hause kamen, gaben sie dem blinden Vater die Fische, die sie nicht essen mochten. Sie und die Mutter dagegen aßen die köstlichen Fische. Eines Tages kam der Bruder des blinden Mannes, der weit entfernt von Ngetmel lebte, zu Besuch. Die Brüder hatten sich lange Zeit

Abb. 1
Eine blinde Frau, die in ihrem mütterlichen Klan lebt

nicht gesehen und der einsame, alte Mann war glücklich über den Besuch des Bruders. Er bat ihn, seinen Korb mit Essen zu holen. Der Bruder sah das verfaulte Gemüse und der blinde Mann erzählte, wie seine Frau und seine Söhne ihn behandelten, weil er nicht arbeiten könne. Der Bruder verfügte über Heilkräfte, und er ging zum Strand, um eine bestimmte Sorte Treibholz zu sammeln. Im Haus des blinden Mannes machte er damit ein Feuer und sprach einige Zauberformeln. Der Rauch zog in die Augen des blinden Mannes, und er begann zu weinen. Als er die Tränen wegwischte, konnte er ein wenig sehen, und er sagte seinem Bruder, dass ein Wunder geschehen sei. Dieser sammelte daraufhin noch mehr Treibholz, verbrannte es neben seinem blinden Bruder bis das Augenlicht völlig wiederhergestellt war. Glücklich verabschiedeten sie sich, und der Bruder versprach, auf dem Rückweg seiner Reise noch einmal vorbeizuschauen.

Als die Ehefrau und die Söhne heimkamen, verschwieg der alte Mann seine Heilung. Am nächsten Morgen schaute die Ehefrau nach ihrem Geldbeutel und zählte das Geld bevor sie aufs Feld ging. Sie gab vor, den Geldbeutel auf einem Dachbalken zu verstecken, genau über der Stelle, wo der alte Mann üblicherweise saß. Der alte Mann konnte nun sehen, dass seine Frau den Geldbeutel heimlich innerhalb einer hohlen Stelle des Bambusfußbodens an der anderen Seite des Hauses versteckte. Ihre Gier und ihr Misstrauen waren so groß, dass sie sogar ihrem blinden Mann nicht vertraute.

Als der Bruder auf dem Rückweg vorbeikam, forderte er den alten Mann auf, ihm alles Geld zu geben. Als die Ehefrau von ihrem Feld zurückkam, schaute sie als erstes nach ihrem Geld. Als sie sah, dass der Geldbeutel leer war, fragte sie ihren Mann, ob jemand in ihrer Abwesenheit im Haus war. Der alte Mann verneinte dies. Nach diesem Vorfall wurde die Ehefrau den Verdacht nicht mehr los, dass ihr Mann nicht länger blind war, und sie bekam Angst. Sie gab ihm nur noch gutes Gemüse und Fisch, und sie versteckte das Geld nicht mehr vor ihm." (BRIONES 1991:23ff.; meine Übers., E.H.)

Die obige Erzählung zeigt bereits ein völlig anderes kulturelles Verständnis von Behinderung als wir es in den USA und Europa kennen. Behinderungen betrachtet man als organisch bedingt, durch Magie oder durch eine Beleidigung der Götter verursacht. Was auch immer als Ursache der Behinderung angenommen wird, nicht die Mutter allein übernimmt die Sorge und Verantwortung für den behinderten Angehörigen, sondern der gesamte mütterliche Klan. So wurde der blinde Mann von Ngetmel nicht von seiner Ehefrau und seinen Söhnen, sondern von seinem Bruder, dem Angehörigen des mütterlichen Klans versorgt.

Die Kultur Palaus
Palau ist eine Inselrepublik im Pazifik und liegt etwa zwischen Papua Neuguinea und den Philippinen. Die Republik besteht aus 343 Inseln, von denen nur fünf bewohnt sind. 1885 wurde Palau vom Papst Spanien zugesprochen, 1899 wurden die Inseln an Deutschland verkauft und 1914 besetzten die Japaner Palau. Von 1946 an stand Palau unter der Treuhandschaft der USA, 1981 erhielt Palau seine eigene Verfassung. Die Bevölkerung bestand 1992 aus 15122 Einwohnern.

Palau ist eine matrilineare Kultur (vgl. HEINEMANN 1995). Die Kinder gehören zum Klan der Mutter, und der Bruder der Mutter (Mutterbruder) hat die Verantwortung. Nach der Heirat zieht die Ehefrau zum Ehemann und arbeitet dort für den Klan des Ehemannes. Die Ehefrau muss mit Unterstützung der Ehefrauen ihrer Brüder Essen und Dienste liefern, dafür erhält sie in regelmäßigen Tauschhandlungen von dem Ehemann palauisches Geld. Das Geld erhält der Ehemann von seinen Schwestern, diese erhalten es von ihren Ehemännern. Frauen sind der Reichtum des Klans, da sie als Ehefrauen Geld verdienen. Das traditionelle Geld ist heute noch neben dem US-Dollar gültig. Es gibt das sogenannte Männergeld und Frauengeld. Das Männergeld ist besonders wertvoll, da es vor hunderten von Jahren vermutlich aus Indonesien eingeführt wurde und kein neues hinzukommen konnte. Es existieren noch etwa 3000 Stück des Geldes. Der Wert richtet sich nach Qualität (aus Ton oder Glas), Größe und Geschichte des Stückes, welches die Geldexperten genau kennen. Frauengeld wird aus Schildpatt hergestellt und zu kleinen Tabletts geformt. Diese können noch heute hergestellt werden, die älteren Stücke sind aber die wertvolleren. Erhält eine Frau von der Seite des Ehemannes Geld, geht es an ihren Mutterbruder (daher der Name Männergeld) und dessen Schwester bewahrt das Geld auf. Frauengeld wird von Frauen der Seite des Ehemannes an die Frauen der Seite der Ehefrau für deren Dienste bei einer Feier beispielsweise gegeben.

Das Männergeld gilt als heilig und wurde nach einer Mythe den Menschen von den Göttern gegeben. Es diente als Regulativ für alle moralischen Verpflichtungen, beispielsweise zur Begleichung einer moralischen Schuld. Das gesamte soziale Leben wurde mit Hilfe des Geldes geregelt. Es gab keine Gefängnis- oder Körperstrafe. Fast jedes Vergehen, auch Mord, konnte durch eine Geldstrafe beglichen werden. Macht und Verantwortung wird in Palau über die Vergabe von Titeln geregelt. Das Land ist in zwei Hälften geteilt, die eine und die andere Hälfte des Himmels. Jedes Dorf ist in zwei Hälften geteilt, die eine und die andere Seite des Mangrovenkanals. Jeder Titel existiert zweimal, einmal auf jeder Seite. Neben dieser grundsätzlichen Dualität gibt es die Teilung in Männer- und Frauenseiten. Jeder männliche Titel hat einen komplementären weiblichen Titel. Jeder Klan hat ein männliches und weibliches Oberhaupt. Die Oberhäupter der zehn höchsten Klane eines Distriktes sind in der Männer- bzw. Frauenversammlung vertreten. Sowohl die männlichen Titelhalter als auch die weiblichen werden nur von den Frauen des Klans gewählt. Diese kontrollieren die Macht.

Traditionell war jedes Mitglied der Gemeinschaft Mitglied in einem Frauen- oder Männerklub. Jede Dorfhälfte verfügte idealerweise über drei Frauen- und drei Männerklubs, den Klub der jüngsten Männer bzw. Frauen, den Klub des mittleren Alters und den Klub für ältere Männer bzw. Frauen. Der Klub hatte, vor allem für den Knaben, wichtige Erziehungsfunktionen. Mit sechs bis zehn Jahren begann die Aufnahme in einen Klub. Der Knabe begann nun im Männerhaus zu schlafen, während die Mädchen weiter unter der Obhut der Mütter aufwuchsen. Jungen bekamen im Klub eine Ausbildung im Handwerk.

Traditionell wurde eine Mutter nach der Geburt noch etwa zehn Monate im Haus ihrer Mutter völlig versorgt, damit sie sich ganz ihrem Kind widmen konnte. Das Kind wurde gestillt, wann immer es wollte. Heute gehen die Mütter meist kurze Zeit nach der Geburt wieder zu ihren Ehemännern zurück. Das Kind erlebt eine enge Beziehung zur Mutter bis ein neues Geschwisterchen kommt. Dann wird es einem Muttersubstitut übergeben. Es gibt in jungen Jahren eine starke Verwöhnungssituation, kleine Kinder werden kaum eingeschränkt. Neben dem Abbruch der Beziehung zur Mutter durch ein neues Kind gibt es eine weitere Bedrohung in der Kindheit, die Adoption. Smith fand 1983 einen Mittelwert von 4,8 Adoptionen pro Haushalt. Es soll ein ausgewogenes Geschlechterverhältnis bei der Anzahl der Kinder entstehen: "Zuviel Söhne machen den Klan arm."

Die erste Schwangerschaft - in abgeschwächter Form auch alle weiteren - unterliegt zahlreichen Tabus. Bestimmte Nahrung ist für die Schwangere verboten und sie darf an heiligen Plätzen nicht vorbeilaufen. Sie erhält Begleiterinnen, die darauf achten, dass sie alle Tabus einhält. Etwa im fünften Monat geht sie zum Platz ihrer Geburt ins Haus ihrer Mutter zurück. Dort trägt der Mutterbruder die Verantwortung für sie und ihre Ernährung. Im sechsten Monat erhält die Schwangere vom Ehemann den "buldil", ein rundes Geldstück, das für die gesunde Entwicklung des Kindes sorgen soll. Die Geburt selbst findet im Kreise von Frauen statt.

Die bedeutendste Zeremonie ist in Palau die Zeremonie des ersten Kindes. Eine Frau, die ihr erstes Kind bekommen hat, wird hier wie eine Göttin verehrt. Die Zeremonie besteht aus einer Serie heißer Bäder, dem Dampfbad und dem öffentlichen Heraustreten. Beim öffentlichen Heraustreten wird sie von den Schwestern des Ehemannes tanzend begrüßt und erhält Geld für die Geburt des Kindes.

Auch die Rituale der Beerdigung werden nur von Frauen durchgeführt. Kranke und alte Menschen gehen zum Haus der Mutter zurück, um dort zu sterben (vgl. HEINEMANN 1995).

Die Suche nach den Ursachen von Krankheit und Behinderung

Krankheiten und Behinderungen (es gibt kein eigenes Konzept für Behinderung) können organisch bedingt sein, durch Magie hervorgerufen oder durch einen beleidigten Gott erzeugt werden.

Jeder Distrikt und jeder Klan von Palau hat in der traditionell totemistischen Religion seinen eigenen Gott, der durch zwei Tiere, meist ein Tier zu Wasser und zu Lande, repräsentiert wird. Diese Tiere dürfen von den Mitgliedern des Distriktes oder Klans nicht getötet und nicht gegessen werden.

Bei einer Krankheit ist der erste Schritt der Gang zur Baumleserin. Sie erkennt die Ursachen einer Krankheit und, falls sie die Beleidigung eines Gottes diagnostiziert, kann sie im Baum lesen, welcher Gott beleidigt wurde. Die Fähigkeit, in einer speziellen Baumsorte zu lesen - jede Baumleserin hat eine eigene Sorte - wird von der Baumleserin an ihre Tochter oder andere weibliche Verwandte weitergegeben. Erkennt die Baumleserin Magie als Ursache, verweist sie die Verwandten an eine Magierin oder einen Magier, der über Gegenmittel verfügt.

Eine Baumleserin: "Eine Frau rief an, weil sie an ihrer Arbeitsstelle krank wurde. Sie rief an, um zu erfahren, was die Ursache der Krankheit ist. Ich fand im Baum, dass Magie die Ursache ist. Jemand möchte sie aus dem Job herauswerfen. Ich sagte, dass sie kommen soll. Ich werde sie zu meiner Partnerin bringen, die für Magie zuständig ist. Ich lese nur die Ursachen, ich kann die Zukunft nicht beeinflussen" (HEINEMANN 1995:113). Die Baumleserin diagnostiziert den psychischen Konflikt. Spielt ein aggressiver Konflikt eine Rolle, diagnostiziert sie Magie. Die Mutter eines fünfjährigen behinderten Kindes erzählt: "Als K. geboren wurde, sagten meine Mutter und die Nachbarn, dass ich vom Gott der Christen gestraft wurde, weil ich meinen Ehemann einer anderen Frau weggenommen habe. Vor der Schwangerschaft mit K. hatte ich einen Kampf mit dieser Frau vor meinem Haus. Wir schlugen uns. Meine Mutter ist sehr christlich. Sie sagte, dass es Gottes Strafe für mich ist. Ich glaube nicht an Gottes Strafe, ich glaube, dass es Magie war. Die andere Frau hat Magie angewendet. Ich bleibe gerne zuhause, um mich um K. und das Baby zu kümmern. Meine Verwandten hier im Haus und auch meine Schwestern kümmern sich um K., so dass ich zu den Versammlungen meines Klans gehen kann."

Die Mutter des behinderten Kindes geht keiner bezahlten Arbeit nach und nimmt rege an den Aktivitäten des Klans teil. Sie ist durch die Behinderung ihres Kindes nicht in ihrem sozialen Leben beeinträchtigt. Irgendjemand aus dem Klan übernimmt die Versorgung des Kindes, wenn sie außer Haus gehen möchte. Sie fühlt sich nicht schuldig und reagiert nicht mit Überbehütung als Reaktionsbildung gegen Aggression aufgrund von schweren sozialen Einschränkungen und Schuldgefühlen. Die Interpretation durch den aggressiven Konflikt entlastet die Mutter und führt zur Übernahme der Verantwortung des gesamten Klans, während die Interpretation der Großmutter, beeinflusst durch Christianisierung, zu einem individuellen Schuldkomplex der Mutter führt.

Ist ein Gott die Ursache einer Krankheit, so muss mit diesem die Angelegenheit beigelegt werden. Hat die Baumleserin erkannt, um welchen Gott es sich handelt, geht der gesamte Klan zum Medium dieses Gottes.

Ein Medium: "Der am Rücken schwarz-weiß gefleckte Stachelrochen ist in unserem Distrikt Tabu. Er und auf dem Land ein spezieller Vogel repräsentieren unseren Gott. Er beschützt und unterstützt uns. Die Baumleserinnen sind Wahrsagerinnen. Ich bin ein Medium, durch das der Gott spricht. Ich erinnere mich anschließend, wenn der Gott durch mich gesprochen hat, nicht mehr an das, was ich gesagt habe. Wenn die Tat schwerwiegend war, wenn die Macht des Gottes wiederhergestellt werden muss, muss der Frager Geld bezahlen. Der Gott sagt es dann.

Es gibt eine Sektion im Dorf, wo der Quallengeist wohnt. Dorthin darf eine Schwangere nicht gehen, sonst bekommt sie ein behindertes Kind. Die Geister verletzen nur Schwangere, sie sind nur für diese gefährlich. Es ist der Meeresgott, der sich im Wasser in eine Qualle verwandelt. Deshalb haben die Babys einen Kopf wie eine Qualle, der Kopf ist ganz weich. Im Mangrovensumpf gibt es einen Stein, auf dem er seine eigenen Kinder auf die Welt bringt. Deshalb hat er eine Beziehung zu schwangeren Frauen. Zu bestimmten Zeiten sind dort viele Quallen-Babys.

Die Behinderung eines Kindes kann zwei Gründe haben. Die Schwangere ging in die Tabuzone oder ein Verwandter oder sie selbst hat einen Stachelrochen getötet. Ich kenne drei Kinder, die deformiert waren, weil die Schwangeren in die Tabuzone gingen. Wenn eine Frau ein behindertes Kind bekommt, weil sie das Tabu gebrochen hat, gehe ich hin, rede mit der Frau, tadele sie aber nicht. Die meisten Kinder sterben.

Auch die drei Kinder in unserem Ort starben. Krankheiten werden von den Göttern erzeugt, um darauf aufmerksam zu machen, dass der Gott beleidigt oder getötet wurde. Ich erinnere mich an ein blindes und körperlich schwer behindertes Kind. Der ganze Klan kam und fragte, was die Ursache ist. Der Gott kam aber nicht nieder. Deshalb war die Behinderung des Kindes nicht vom Gott gezeugt" (vgl. HEINEMANN 1995:115ff.).

Die Mutter des behinderten Kindes schildert die Suche nach der Ursache aus ihrer Sicht: "Anfangs badete ich das Kind noch im Fluss. Da er aber immer Schmerzen hatte, dachte ich, dass ich vorsichtig sein muss. Ich ließ ihn liegen und pflegte ihn zu Hause. Der Sohn der Schwester des Vaters tötete vor langer Zeit einen Stachelrochen. Es geschah aus Versehen, das kann jedem passieren. Er hatte den Gott beleidigt und wir gaben Geld beim Altar. Bei der Geburt unseres Kindes war dieser Mann schon gestorben. Wir gingen zum Medium, um zu fragen, ob es vielleicht noch etwas anderes gebe, was die Ursache sein kann. Alle Verwandten des Vaters gingen zum Medium. Der Gott kam aber nicht nieder, deshalb ist nichts falsch. Im Dorf war jeder mitfühlend; dies wird aber nicht gezeigt."

Eine andere Gesprächspartnerin: "Wenn ein Kind behindert ist oder jemand in der Familie krank wird, geht die Familie zu einer Baumleserin. Diese liest in den Blättern der Bäume, ob der Mutterbruder

Abb. 2
Ein behindertes junges Mädchen (Mitte) isst im Kreise der Frauen des mütterlichen Klans

oder Bruder oder ein Ahne etwas gemacht hat. Der Klan kommt zusammen. Die Person, die von der Baumleserin genannt wird, hat irgendetwas gegen einen anderen Klan oder Nachbar getan. Wenn dieser Klan nun einen Gott hat, der bestraft, muss dieser Gott zufriedengestellt werden. Der Klan sammelt Geld, welches dem anderen Klan gegeben wird, sonst würde wieder etwas passieren. Die Verwandten müssen diesen Gott um Vergebung bitten. Der Vater hatte zum Beispiel vor langer Zeit jemand getötet. Die Verwandten haben dies niemals, zum Beispiel durch eine Geldzahlung, beglichen. Die Behinderung des Kindes ist die Strafe für etwas, das niemals beigelegt wurde. Die Behinderung ist Sache des ganzen Klans, nicht nur der Mutter. Irgendjemand, auch ein längst verstorbener Vorfahr hat etwas unrechtes gemacht. Der ganze Klan ist verantwortlich. Es kann der Klan des Vaters aber auch der Klan der Mutter verantwortlich sein. Behinderte Kinder werden im Klan versorgt, die Nachbarn oder Nicht-Verwandten dürfen nicht belästigt werden. Meist wollen die Eltern nicht, dass diese Kinder in die Schule gehen, sie wollen das Kind in der Verwandtschaft halten" (vgl. HEINEMANN 1995:118).

Die kollektive Bewältigung von Krankheit und Behinderung

Der Tabubruch oder das Vergehen irgendeines Klanmitgliedes, welches bereits verstorben sein kann, kann einen Gott beleidigt haben. Aggression führt zur Ausübung von Magie und Gegenmagie, eine rituelle Form der Aggressionsbewältigung. Es gibt kein Konzept der individuellen Schuld, selbst dann nicht, wenn die Mutter durch Tabubruch die Behinderung hervorgerufen hat. Während der gesamten Schwangerschaft hat sie Begleiterinnen, die darauf achten müssen, dass alle Tabus eingehalten werden. Der gesamte Klan trägt die Verantwortung. Durch Geldzahlungen erhalten die Mitglieder des Klans Gelegenheit zur Wiedergutmachung, so dass der Schuld-Konflikt bewältigt werden kann.

Die Mutter ist frei von individueller Schuld. Die Mutter-Kind-Beziehung ist entlastet, die Mütter müssen nicht mit Überbehütung (als Reaktionsbildung gegen Aggression) reagieren. Sie können am sozialen Leben ohne Einschränkung teilnehmen. Eine Mutter, die eine zeitlang in den USA gelebt hatte, meinte, dass sie ihr behindertes Kind überbehüten würde. Den Begriff Überbehütung hatte sie in den USA gehört. In Palau war sie aber frei, jeden Tag zu tun, was sie tun wollte, und sie begleitete mich häufig zu Gesprächen. Die Tochter wurde im Klan liebevoll versorgt.

Durch die alleinige Verantwortung der Verwandtschaft sind die Mütter entlastet, Menschen, die sich nicht fortbewegen können, erfahren aber Einschränkungen. Sie sind auf das soziale Leben im Haus angewiesen, da Nicht-Verwandte nicht belästigt werden dürfen.

Ein zweiundzwanzigjähriger junger Mann ist durch einen Autounfall querschnittgelähmt und liegt seit fünf Jahren auf dem Bett im Haus seiner Mutter. Der Sohn des Bruders der Mutter, der in einem weit entfernten Dorf mit seiner Familie lebt und Holzschnitzer von Beruf ist, lehrte dem jungen Mann über viele Monate die traditionelle Schnitzkunst. In dieser Zeit wohnte er im Haus seiner Schwester und kehrte erst zu seiner Frau und seinen Kindern zurück, als der junge Mann die Schnitzkunst beherrschte. Unterstützung wird, wie in der Erzählung vom blinden Mann, nur von Mitgliedern des Klans angenommen (siehe Abb. 1).

Die traditionelle Sicht von Behinderung ermöglicht eine soziale Integration innerhalb des Klans. Damit einher geht jedoch nicht automatisch die Integration in die soziale Gemeinschaft. Auch birgt die völlige Verantwortung des eigenen Klans die Gefahr, Isolation und Ablehnung durch Nicht-Verwandte zu erfahren, wie dies die Erzählung vom blinden Mann zeigt. Die Erzählung ist aber gleichzeitig auch eine moralische Aufforderung, diese Impulse zu unterdrücken und mit dem behinderten Menschen zu teilen. Durch den Einfluss der USA und des Christentums ändert sich gegenwärtig die Situation für Menschen mit Behinderungen.

Eine achtunddreißigjährige Mutter lebt lediglich mit ihrem Ehemann und zwei Kindern nach westlichem Vorbild in einem Haus in der Nähe der Hauptstadt. Der fünfjährige Sohn ist körperlich behindert. Die Mutter: "Ich möchte gerne arbeiten, muss aber den ganzen Tag zu Hause bleiben wegen der Kinder. Darunter leide ich sehr. Mein Mann und ich lieben unseren Sohn sehr. Ich möchte ihn in die USA schicken, damit er eine Ausbildung bekommt. Anfangs habe ich wegen der Behinderung des Kindes viel geweint. Mit meinem Mann konnte ich nie darüber sprechen. Es war anfangs äußerst schwer für mich, mit dem Kind aus dem Haus zu gehen. Es wurde geredet, dass ich ein solches Kind habe, weil ich eine Abtreibung versucht hätte. Es gibt noch immer traditionelle Heilerinnen, die Abtreibungen mit Kräutern durchführen. Manchmal wirken die Kräuter nicht und die Frau bekommt doch ein Kind. Ich habe aber keine Abtreibung versucht." Während die Mütter, die noch im Klan leben, zufrieden sind, nicht einer bezahlten Arbeit nachgehen zu müssen, leidet diese junge Mutter darunter. Sie fühlt sich ans Haus gefesselt. Aus der traditionellen Freiheit der Frauen, Abtreibungen durchführen zu können, wird unter den Einfluss des Christentums der individuelle Schuldvorwurf den Müttern gegenüber. Sie hat jetzt die Behinderung durch unmoralisches Verhalten (einer anderen Frau den Mann wegnehmen; Abtreibung, d.h. selbstbestimmte Sexualität) selbst verursacht.

Die Beispiele zeigen, dass das Verhalten Menschen mit Behinderungen gegenüber immer durch die jeweilige Kultur bestimmt ist. Die Beziehungen zu Menschen mit Behinderungen ermöglichen ein Verstehen gerade auch der unbewussten Zusammenhänge einer Kultur. Behinderungen lösen Ängste und Schuldgefühle aus, kulturtypisch Verdrängtes wird reaktiviert. Die Blindheit des Mannes aus Ngetmel führt zum Durchbruch oraler Gier bei seiner Ehefrau und den Söhnen, ein zentraler Konflikt im ethnischen Unbewussten der Menschen Palaus (vgl. HEINEMANN 1995). Aggression zwischen Mitgliedern eines Klans oder verschiedener Klane wird durch das religiöse System kontrolliert. Behinderung löst Schuldangst aus, die wiederum kulturell bearbeitet wird, indem es die Möglichkeit des Schuldausgleichs gibt. So zeigt der andere Umgang mit Behinderung die kulturelle Geprägtheit auch des christlichen und westlichen Umgangs mit Behinderung. Die Angst vor dem Durchbruch selbstbestimmter Sexualität der Frauen wird aus den christlichen Interpretationen deutlich. Im Mittelalter bezeichnete man in Europa behinderte Kinder als Wechselbälger, d.h. als von den Dämonen zur Verbesserung der eigenen Rasse ausgetauschte Kinder, die durch Anwendung von Zauber zur Rückgabe gebracht werden konnten. Versagte der Zauber, behandelte man den ausgetauschten Balg so, wie man sich wünschte, dass das eigene Kind bei den Dämonen behandelt werden sollte. Von einer individuellen Schuldproblematik der Mütter war hier noch nichts zu erkennen. Erst in der Frühen Neuzeit, zur Zeit der Christianisierung des täglichen Lebens (Reformation) und der massiver werdenden Triebunterdrückung, wurden Wechselbälger zum Produkt des Geschlechtsverkehrs einer Hexe mit dem Teufel und liefen Gefahr, wie diese Frauen verbrannt zu werden (vgl. HEINEMANN 1998). Aus den Reaktionen auf Behinderungen können wir unsere kulturspezifischen Konflikte verstehen lernen.

References

BRIONES, R. 1991. Legends of Palau. *A Collection of Palauan Legends.* Vol.II. Koror (Palau)
HEINEMANN, E. 1995. *Die Frauen von Palau. Zur Ethnoanalyse einer mutterrechtlichen Kultur.* Frankfurt
Heinemann, E. 1996. *Aggression verstehen und bewältigen.* Heidelberg
HEINEMANN, E. 1997. *Das Erbe der Sklaverei. Eine ethnopsychoanalytische Studie in Jamaika.* Frankfurt
HEINEMANN, E. 1998. *Hexen und Hexenangst. Eine psychoanalytische Studie.* Göttingen
SMITH, D. 1983. *Palauan Social Structure,* New Brunswick (USA)

Frauen und Gesundheit im aktuellen kulturellen und sozialen Kontext Lateinamerikas
Women and Health in the Actual Sociocultural Context of Latinamerican Societies

Angelika Denzler

Zusammenfassung: Frauen werden im andinen Kulturraum (hier am Beispiel Ecuadors) aufgrund ihrer Körperlichkeit als zur Krankheit prädisponierte Wesen und deshalb als dem Mann untergeordnet betrachtet - obwohl sie andererseits als Mutter und als Heilerin für Gesundheit und Wohlergehen zuständig ist. Diese Nachordnung gegenüber dem Mann führt dazu, dass die Frau im Endeffekt tatsächlich krankheitsanfälliger ist - nämlich aufgrund der ihr kulturell zugeschriebenen Rolle und der daraus folgenden Lebensumstände, die für Frauen aus den ärmeren Schichten eine dauernde Überforderung darstellen. Die häufigsten Erkrankungen der Frauen sind damit nicht die mit den weiblichen Genitalien verbundenen, sondern „geschlechtsunspezifische" Erkrankungen, die sich aus Überlastung ergeben. Frauen entwickeln Lösungsansätze wie die Organisation in Mütter- und Nachbarschaftsinitiativen. Obwohl diese nicht zur Verbesserung der gesundheitlichen Situation gedacht sind, sondern zur Entlastung der Frauen, gewinnen die Frauen durch die Solidarität und gemeinsame Arbeit in diesen Initiativen an persönlichem Spielraum, Mut und Hoffnung. Damit werden gesundheitsfördernde Faktoren aktiviert, die dem krankmachenden Burn-Out der Überforderung entgegenwirken. Gleichzeitig bedeutet die Mitarbeit in diesen Gruppen eine zusätzliche Belastung, die frau im zunehmenden wirtschaftlichen Elend nicht unbegrenzt aufbringen kann. Wird ein gewisses Maß an Armut überschritten, brechen diese ursprünglich entlastenden Strukturen zusammen.

Abstract: In some latin-american countries women, due to their female body, are regarded as predisposed to diseases, and therefore consequently are considered to be inferior to men - although woman in the role of mother of the house and as a non-medical practioner is responsible for health and well-being. Actually this submission to man results in a poorer state of health compared to man - due to her culturally attributed role in society which leads in lower class women to a permanent over-demand. The most frequent diseases, thus, are not those of the female genitals, but "sex-unspecific" diseases, due to the over-demand. Solutions developed by women themselves are for example self-organization in comittees of mothers or neighbourhood-iniatives. These iniatives are not primarily intended to improve the health situation but to exonerate the women. Nevertheless, due to the experienced solidarity and common work in these initiatives, gain personal scope, courage and hope. So health promoting factors are raised which face the pathogenous burn-out resulting of continuous over-demand. On the other hand, the engagement in these groups is also an additional burden of time and physical energy, goods which are limited in times of increasing economic misery. If misery trespasses a certain limit, these structures cannot be maintained and will collaps.

Keywords: Südamerika/Andenraum, weibliche Armut, weibliche Krankheiten, soziokulturelle Krankheitsursachen, Nachbarschaftskomitees, Southamerica, Andean countries, female poverty, female sociocultural pathogenetic factors, neighbourhood initiatives.

Abb. 1
Kinder in Ecuador (Foto: Angelika Denzler)

> „Die Frau ist in unserer Kultur im Haus die Zuständige für das Aufrechterhalten des Wohlbefindens und damit der Gesundheit der Familie. Wir alle sind, je nach Bedarf, Ärztin, Kinderschwester, Kräuterfrau, u.U. auch Hebamme, pflegen das kranke Kind, den Mann, die Großeltern und Enkel, oder sind Ansprechpartnerinnen für Impfkampagnen. Wenn alle gesund sind, ist es gut, und keiner verliert ein Wort darüber, aber wenn jemand krank ist, dann liegt die Schuld bei uns. Außerdem arbeiten wir für das Wohlergehen unserer Familie und Gemeinschaft auch in Nachbarschaftskomitees, Müttergruppen, Initiativen für Trinkwasseranschlüsse in unserem Viertel, Schülerspeisung, Suppenküchen, Gemeinschaftssäuberungsaktionen, Gemeindeläden, Ernährungskursen, Organisation von Gesundheitstagen... Wir kümmern uns um die Gesundheit aller, nur nicht um unsere eigene. Genauso unsere Familie: Wenn die Frau krank wird, wenden weder die Frau noch die Familie vergleichbare Sorge, Zeit und Mittel auf, als wenn es sich um irgendein anderes Mitglied handeln würde. Und genauso die Gesellschaft ..."

Aus einem Referat beim internationalen Kongreß "Frauen und das Recht auf Gesundheit" in Quito, 1989, der von ecuadorianischen Frauen- und Gesundheitsorganisationen und der UNFPA organisiert wurde (CEPAM 1989: 17-18).

Die Frau scheint dem Thema Gesundheit und Krankheit, Leben und Tod, aber auch Heilen enger verbunden zu sein als der Mann, in vielfältiger Weise:

Zum einen als Handelnde; als Verantwortliche für die Gesundheit: Die Zuständigkeit für Heilung in der Familie wird zuerst bei der Mutter gesehen - daraus erwächst zum Teil im nahtlosen Übergang der Schritt zur Heilerin oder Hebamme, der "señora que sabe", der weisen Frau, der Vertrauten. Der vorliegende Artikel beschäftigt sich weniger mit der Heilerin als mit der alltäglichen Arbeit der Familienmutter).

Zum anderen als Erleidende oder als Opfer von Krankheit: als Wesen, das im andinen Kulturraum aus traditioneller Weltsicht als "zur Krankheit prädisponiert" betrachtet wird. Diese Prädisposition wird mit dem Blutverlust während der Menstruation begründet (ROESLER 1979:14 und eigene Forschung). Dadurch kämen die Lebenskräfte aus dem Gleichgewicht, und dies wiederum prädisponiert zur Krankheit. Somit wird der physiologische Zustand der Menstruation als pathologisch interpretiert: "se enferma la mujer" "die Frau wird krank", bzw. der Zustand zwischen den Menstruationen als "sano" "gesund" betrachtet (ESTRELLA 1980: 81).

Die postulierte Krankheitsdisposition der Frau wird als Beweis ihrer Unterlegenheit gegenüber dem Mann gesehen, und dient damit der Rechtfertigung ihrer sozialen Benachteiligung.

Tatsächlich kann man die Frau in der heutigen Lebensrealität in den Andenländern objektiv als krankheitsgefährdeter bezeichnen: Nicht in erster Linie aufgrund ihrer Körperlichkeit, sondern aufgrund ihrer sozialen Lebensumstände. Natürlich existieren die geschlechtsspezifischen Risikomomente, die von der Körperlichkeit der Frau herrühren: Schwangerschaft und Geburt, die körperliche und sexuelle Gewalt, denen sie als Frau ausgesetzt ist. Stärker wirkt sich aber die Tatsache aus, dass Frauen oft schlechter ernährt sind als Männer, und dass sie, um ihre Familie zu ernähren, oft ebenso hart arbeiten müssen, aber weniger Unterstützung bekommen. Es werden ihnen im Gegensatz zu den Männern deutlich weniger Erholungszeiten zugestanden. Auch im Krankheitsfall erhält eine Frau weniger Therapie als ein Mann, bzw. sie gesteht sie sich selber nicht zu.

Diese beiden Rollen, die aktive und die passive, will ich in den 3 Abschnitten dieses Artikels verdeutlichen:

Der erste Abschnitt soll pathogene Faktoren anhand einer fiktiven Lebensgeschichte einer Frau aus dem ländlichen Raum Ecuadors beschreiben, in der auch die im ländlichen Raum noch lebendigere traditionelle Kosmovision Platz findet. (Die Bezeichnung "traditionell" bezieht sich im Kontext Lateinamerikas nicht auf autochthone Kulturen, sondern auf das Produkt 500jähriger Verschmelzung präkolombinischer und europäischer Traditionen; im Gegensatz zum "modernen westlich-naturwissenschaftlichen" Weltbild). Der zweite Abschnitt beruht auf Analysen von Frauen aus dem andinen Raum bzgl. ihrer Situation; es werden verschiedene, Frauen betreffende, Krankheitsbilder und ihre sozialen und kulturellen Ursachen angesprochen. Im dritten Abschnitt werden Lösungsansätze, die von diesen Frauen befürwortet wurden, beispielhaft dargestellt und diskutiert.

Die Geschichte von Maria und José

Die gewählte sprachliche Form der Erzählung versucht sich der Ausdrucksweise der armen ländlichen und städtischen Bevölkerung anzunähern, in der für Darstellung von Emotionen sehr wenig Platz ist. Das harte Leben läßt sich nur bewältigen, indem Gefühle weitgehend unterdrückt oder an den Rand geschoben werden.

Marias Eltern, arme mestizische Kleinbauern, sind kurz vor ihrer Geburt aus dem Andenhochland in die Urwaldregion am Ostfuß der Anden eingewandert, weil es hier Land zu erwerben gab. In harter Arbeit haben sie ihr Landstück, die Finca, gerodet und bepflanzt, und eine Holzhütte am Rand des Dorfes gebaut. Die Mutter arbeitet bis kurz vor der Niederkunft. Nur selten kann sie zur Kontrolle zur Hebamme gehen, die eine Gehstunde entfernt wohnt. Die Hebamme fühlt ihr bei den Kontrollen den Puls, und sagt: "Es wird ein Junge. Sein Puls ist fast so stark wie Ihrer, Nachbarin. Ein Mädchen hätte einen schwächeren Puls!" Die Mutter ist froh. Wenn sie gleich bei der ersten Schwangerschaft einen Sohn zur Welt bringen würde, würden ihr Mann und seine Familie sie achten. Als die Wehen stärker werden, holt eine Nachbarin die Hebamme, denn der Ehemann ist nicht zuhause. Marías Geburt ist problemlos, aber beide Frauen sind bei aller Freude etwas enttäuscht, als das Neugeborenen sich als Mädchen entpuppt. "Macht nichts," sagt die Hebamme, "Sie sind ja noch jung". Auch Marías Vater ist enttäuscht, nur mit Mühe kann die Mutter ihn dazu bringen, die Hebamme zu bezahlen.

In den folgenden 3 Jahren hat Marías Mutter 4 Aborte, z.T. kurz aufeinanderfolgend - aufgrund der harten Arbeit, aufgrund Parasiteninfektionen, aber einmal auch, weil ihr der Vater im Rausch in den schwangeren Bauch getreten hatte. Die Hebamme untersucht die Abortprodukte jedesmal - einmal entscheidet sie, weil die Mutter schon wesentlich früher als bei den anderen Aborten Kindsbewegungen gespürt hatte, dass es ein Junge gewesen sei. Denn männliche Kinder entwickeln sich viel schneller im Bauch der Mutter als weibliche. Außerdem sieht der Abort aus wie ein Mäuschen, während weibliche Embryos in diesem Schwangerschaftsalter ja noch aussehen wie Schleimkugeln... Dieser Embryo wird beerdigt, damit er in den Himmel kommen kann.

Als María 4 Jahre alt ist, kommt endlich der langersehnte Stammhalter zur Welt, alle sind überglücklich. Das Kind wird José genannt und wird von der Mutter gehütet wie ihr Augapfel. Er wird den Sitten entsprechend 3 Monate länger gestillt als María, denn Jungen brauchen mehr Kraft. Wenn Mädchen zu lange gestillt werden, können sie später "mannstoll" werden - andere sagen auch, sie würden zu viele Kinder bekommen, ein kürzer gestilltes Mädchen würde nicht so leicht schwanger werden. Da Marías Mutter nach dem Wochenbett wieder auf der Finca arbeiten muss, übernimmt María die Versorgung ihres Brüderchens, und andere Pflichten im Haushalt.

Alle lieben den kleinen Prinzen, und als er mit 2 Jahren eine starke Durchfallerkrankung bekommt, wird er sofort ins Krankenhaus gebracht, obwohl das Geld kostet. Auch María hat starke Durchfälle, aber da eine Krankenhausbehandlung teuer ist, behandelt die Mutter sie mit Kräutern, und ruft schließlich die Heilerin. María überlebt, sie braucht nicht ins Krankenhaus. Die Mutter bezahlt die Heilerin mit einem Huhn - so braucht sie den Vater nicht um Geld zu bitten.

Mit 7 Jahren kommt María in die Schule, sie ist sehr stolz, schon so groß zu sein. Aber oft kann sie die Schularbeiten nicht machen, weil sie nun mit den Eltern auf die Finca zum Arbeiten muss. Diese ist weit weg, man muss weit durch Flüsse, durch Sumpf laufen. Es ist ein Malariagebiet. Beide Eltern roden und pflanzen, alle schleppen schwere Lasten nach Hause. Daheim bereiten dann die Mutter und María das Abendessen, während der Vater sich setzt und sich nach der schweren Arbeit ausruht. Die Mutter bedient die Familie beim Essen und isst im Stehen, oder wenn die anderen fertig sind. Die größten und besten Stücke bekommen der Vater und José. María findet das ungerecht, sie hat oft großen Hunger, aber Mutter erklärt, dass Männer mehr Kraft brauchen.

Am Sonntag begleitet Maria die Mutter zum Markt, wo sie die Produkte der Finca verkaufen. Das gefällt Maria, nur zu den Hausaufgaben kommt sie wieder nicht. Obwohl sie gerne und interessiert lernt, verliert sie schnell den Anschluss in der Schule. Außerdem kommen die Zwillinge zur Welt, zwei Jungen (als ob die Familie dafür entschädigt werden sollte, dass ihr Erstgeborenes ein Mädchen ist), und Maria muss einen großen Teil der Kinderbetreuung und des Haushalts übernehmen, weil die Mutter sehr schwach ist. Maria findet, dass José mit 4 Jahren jetzt alt genug ist, um auch etwas beizutragen. Sie musste im gleichen Alter auch auf den Nachwuchs aufpassen. Aber José ist ja ein Junge, er muss mit auf die Finca, sie ist seine Welt, in die er hineinwachsen soll.

Jetzt ist es auch Maria, die vor Morgengrauen als erste aufsteht, um für die Familie das Frühstück zu bereiten. Außerdem muss ja das Wasser vom 20 Minuten entfernten Fluss geholt werden, und auch die Wäsche muss dort gewaschen werden. So ist sie erleichtert, als nach 6 Jahren die Pflichtschulzeit vorbei ist. Sie hätte sowieso nicht länger zu Schule gehen dürfen, denn das bedeutet für die Eltern viele Ausgaben, und der Vater findet, dass ein Mädchen eigentlich keine Schulausbildung braucht. Anders bei José. Der muss, wenn sie von der Finca heimkommen, die Hausaufgaben machen, und wenn er mit schlechten Noten heimkommt, prügelt ihn der Vater. Für Marias Noten hatte er sich nie interessiert, so bekam sie auch keine Prügel wegen schlechter Noten.

Als Maria 14 Jahre alt wird, bemerkt sie eines Tages Blut in ihrer Unterhose. Sie fühlt keinen Schmerz, sie hat sich auch nicht verletzt. Sie denkt: "Sicher bin ich schwer krank und muss nun bald sterben." Weinend läuft sie zur Mutter. Die sagt nur: "So ist es bei den Frauen. Nimm ein Tuch und wasche es nachher". Maria ist so erschreckt, dass sie ihre Zurückhaltung vergisst: "Warum ist es so ? Was bedeutet, eine Frau sein ?" "Unsere Aufgabe ist es, für den Mann dazusein und Kinder zu empfangen," antwortet die Mutter. Und dann, leise "Ach wäre ich doch nie als Frau geboren - es ist eine Strafe Gottes." Sie schweigt, und Maria spricht nie wieder über das Thema.

Die Mutter bekommt bis zu Marias 16. Geburtstag noch 2 Kinder, von denen eines bei der Geburt stirbt, doch dann - sie ist erst 35 - wird sie nicht mehr schwanger. Erst nach einiger Zeit bringt man das mit der Operation in Zusammenhang, bei der der Mutter auf einer Reise ins Hochland notfallmäßig der Blinddarm entfernt werden musste. Offenbar hat man sie bei dieser Gelegenheit sterilisiert. Zwischen den Eltern ist jetzt oft Streit, weil der Vater im Nachbardorf eine 2. Frau genommen hat. "Du bist ja nichts mehr wert", hören ihn die Kinder zur Mutter sagen. Doch er bleibt bei ihnen. "Er ist ein guter Mann" sagt die Mutter, "er ist verantwortungsvoll, er bleibt bei den Kindern".

José ist jetzt 15, er besucht die Sekundarschule, hängt abends mit seinen Freunden auf dem Hauptplatz herum, wo sie rauchen und hinter den Mädchen herpfeifen. Als er einmal Maria dort sieht, die ein erstes Rendezvous mit einem früheren Klassenkameraden hat, schlägt er sie, als sie nach Hause kommt. Überhaupt beginnt er immer häufiger, ihr Vorschriften zu machen, obwohl er 4 Jahre jünger ist als sie. Maria findet ihn unausstehlich - bis zu dem Tag, als er das Haus verlassen muss, weil der Vater ihn totschlagen will. José hatte sich auf den Vater geworfen, als der im Suff wieder einmal die Mutter prügeln wollte. Da rastete der Vater vollends aus, denn die Autorität des Vaters darf unter keinen Umständen angetastet werden. Nun kann er nur heimkommen, wenn der Vater nicht da ist. Die Familie versorgt ihn aber weiterhin heimlich mit Essen.

Durch die Mitarbeit der jetzt 6 jährigen Schwester im Haushalt wird Maria etwas entlastet, so dass sie gelegentlich mit ihrem Freund Juan ins Kino gehen kann. Er ist Schuhmacher, und nachdem er sich überzeugt hat, dass sie noch Jungfrau ist, macht er ihr einen Heiratsantrag. Maria ist jetzt 19 Jahre alt. Es ist Zeit für sie, zu heiraten, und so nimmt sie Juan. Diese Ehe bedeutet, dass sie jetzt nicht mehr Bäuerin, sondern Frau eines Handwerkers ist; dass sie in einem Steinhaus wohnen kann, und nicht mehr auf der Finca arbeiten muss.

José heiratet zwei Jahre später die Nachbarstochter Ana. Er hat die Schule mit einem guten Abschluss beendet, aber es gibt im Dorf keine Arbeit für ihn. So arbeitet er weiter auf der Finca. Ana geht noch zur Schule, aber nach der Hochzeit bricht sie die Ausbildung auf Josés Anordnung ab, weil sie jetzt auf der Finca mitarbeiten muss. Maria ist zu dieser Zeit hochschwanger, sie lässt sich im Krankenhaus regelmäßig untersuchen - denn dort gibt es für unterernährte Schwangere Haferflockenrationen mit Trockenmilch - und Maria ist "chronisch unterernährt" und "anämisch", wie der Arzt sagt. Wegen dieser Haferflockenrationen - von denen sie die Hälfte an die kleine Schwester weitergibt - erlaubt ihr Mann ihr auch, sich im Krankenhaus von dem (männlichen) Arzt untersuchen zu lassen, und wird ihr auch erlauben, im Krankenhaus zu entbinden. Sie versteht sich gut mit Juan, außer wenn er betrunken ist, aber sie fürchtet die Nächte mit ihm, vor allem jetzt in der Hochschwangerschaft. Aber sie weiß, dass sie ihm zur Verfügung stehen muss, sonst verlässt er sie möglicherweise und sucht eine andere Frau, wie die Mutter sie warnt. Viel mehr kann die Mutter auf Marias verschämte Fragen zum Thema Sexualität auch nicht sagen. Es ist auch schwer - es gibt eigentlich gar keine richtigen Worte für "das von den Frauen". Maria fürchtet sich vor der Geburt - es gibt viele Erzählungen über Frauen, die bei der Geburt starben, und sie hat die schweren Geburten ihrer Mutter, die sie aus nächster Nähe miterlebte, in lebhafter Erinnerung. Bei der Entbindung im Krankenhaus erhofft sie sich mehr Schutz. In der Schwangerschaft hat sie häufig Nieren- und Blaseninfekte. Der Arzt sagt, sie müsse sich regelmäßig zwischen den Beinen waschen, dann gebe es nicht so leicht Infektionen. Maria ist es peinlich, dass der Arzt diesen intimen Bereich anspricht. So häufige Waschungen, wie der Arzt sie verlangt, ist sie nicht gewöhnt. Im kleinen Holzhaus ihrer Eltern war nie ein privater Rahmen da, es gab auch weder Dusche noch Toilette. Und sich vor den anderen in dieser Körperregion zu waschen - undenkbar. Außerdem befürchtet sie, dass ihr gerade in der Schwangerschaft kaltes Wasser Schaden zufügen könnte, sie eine "Kältekrankheit" bekommen könnte. Lieber holt sie sich für billiges Geld Vitamin-B-Spritzen von der Heilerin. Ihre Beschwerden werden aber schlimmer, sie bekommt Wassereinlagerungen, und bei der Geburt im Krankenhaus bekommt sie plötzlich Krämpfe, so dass ein Kaiserschnitt gemacht werden muss. Ihre Tochter kommt gesund zur Welt, und während der 40 Tage Wochenbett hat Maria erstmals in ihrem Leben Urlaub. Ihre Mutter kommt, um ihr die während des Wochenbetts verbotenen Arbeiten wie Wäschewaschen abzunehmen, und die traditionelle Hühnerbrühe zu kochen.

Später geht Maria zu den Nachuntersuchungen ins Krankenhaus, obwohl sie nach dem Kaiserschnitt nicht sicher ist, ob die dort wirklich etwas von Medizin verstehen; denn sonst hätte sie doch normal entbinden können. Aber bei den Untersuchungen wird das Kind gewogen, und wenn es Untergewicht hat, bekommt sie wieder Haferflocken. Sie geht wenig aus dem Haus, hat kaum Kontakt zu den Nachbarinnen "weil die nur schlecht über einen sprechen", und weil ihr Mann es nicht gerne sieht. Sie verbringt die freie Zeit vor dem Fernseher und schaut Soap-Operas an. Nur Ana besucht sie gelegentlich, die auch gern ein Kind hätte. Sie wird 5 Jahre lang nicht schwanger, und José beschimpft und schlägt sie deshalb. Ana läuft einmal weg, zurück zu ihren Eltern, aber die schicken sie zu José zurück. "Er ist dein Mann, dein Platz ist jetzt bei ihm."

Maria hat in diesen 5 Jahren noch 2 Kinder geboren, immer mit Kaiserschnitt, da die Ärzte sagen, nach einer Operation muss immer operiert werden. Sie hat Angst vor weiteren Operationen, und versucht ihren Mann zu überreden, dass sie Verhütungsmittel anwenden müssen. Aber er beschuldigt sie, sich nur ungestört mit ihrem Geliebten treffen zu wollen. Der Gedanke setzt sich bei ihm fest, er beschuldigt sie jetzt immer, wenn er betrunken ist, sie würde ihn betrügen.

Beim nächsten, dem 4. Kaiserschnitt bittet Maria die Ärzte heimlich, eine Sterilisierung durchzuführen. Juan fällt nach einiger Zeit auf, dass sie nicht mehr schwanger wird - er verlässt sie und zieht zu einer anderen Frau ins Nachbardorf. Maria bleibt alleine mit 4 Kindern zurück. Da sie kein Einkommen hat, arbeitet sie wieder auf der Finca ihres Vaters, obwohl ihr das nach den vielen Operationen sehr schwer fällt und die weite Gehstrecke zur Finca sie zusätzlich belastet. Sie ist nun viel mit Ana zusammen, und es entsteht eine enge Freundschaft. Ana ist verzweifelt wegen ihrer Kinderlosigkeit. Außerdem hat sie merkwürdige Blutungen, von denen sie aus Schamhaftigkeit niemand außer Maria erzählt. Obwohl Maria sie beschwört, geht Ana nicht zum Arzt. Maria versteht Anas Widerstreben. Die Schamhaftigkeit einer Frau ist ihre Ehre und die ihrer Familie - welche Demütigung, sich den Blicken eines Mannes aussetzen zu müssen. Erst als Ana schon schwer krank ist, überwindet sie die Scham, und bittet José um das Geld für den Arztbesuch. Der diagnostiziert einen Gebärmutterhalskrebs in weit fortgeschrittenem Zustand. Ana stirbt im Alter von 35 Jahren. José verunglückt kurz vor ihrem Tod auf der Finca, im Rausch.

Nach dem Tod von Ana und José fühlt María sich sehr alleine. Sie zieht zur Unterstützung der Mutter zurück zu ihren Eltern, die von Josés Tod sehr getroffen sind, v.a. die Mutter. José hatte ihr immer Geld für Medikamente gegeben, sie unterstützt wo er konnte, und hatte auch dem Vater jede Gewalt gegen sie untersagt. Die Mutter arbeitet immer noch auf der Finca mit, sie freut sich, als Maria und die 4 Kinder zu ihr ziehen.

Maria fällt die Arbeit sehr schwer. Als sie sich untersuchen lässt, stellen die Ärzte im Krankenhaus eine Tuberkulose fest. Immer noch kämpft sie auch mit den Nierenproblemen. Einen Teil der Medikamente für die Tuberkulose bekommt sie über das staatliche Tb-Programm, aber die anderen und die für die Nieren kann sie nicht bezahlen. Schließlich braucht sie alles Geld, das sie verdient, für die Ausbildung ihrer Kinder. Die Familie lebt in großer Armut, so dass Marías ältere Töchter sich entschließen, als Hausangestellte "in die Stadt" zu gehen.

Eine Zeitlang schreiben sie und schicken Geld nach Hause. Aber dann lassen sie nichts mehr von sich hören, erst die eine, dann die andere. Ein Nachbar behauptet, er habe die eine der Töchter als Prostituierte arbeiten gesehen. Maria hat kein Geld, in die Stadt zu fahren und sie zu suchen, und als Frau kann sie auch nicht allein reisen. Der Schmerz um die Töchter zehrt sie auf.

Maria stirbt im Alter von 52 Jahren, als 8 fache Großmutter. Die Ärzte sagen, sie sei an der Tuberkulose gestorben.

Frauen-Krankheiten und ihre Ursachen

Im Eingangszitat ging es schon um das Engagement, das die Frau auf den drei Ebenen Familie, (Dorf-/Stadtteil-)-Gemeinschaft und Gesellschaft für das Wohlergehen der anderen aufbringt - womit sie den Staat im sozialen Bereich auch von vielen Aufgaben entlastet, und wofür sie nichts zurückbekommt, nicht einmal Anerkennung. Warum ? Dazu im weiteren Antworten aus den Beiträgen von zwei internationalen Konferenzen der Frauen- und Gesundheitsorganisationen in Quito, Ecuador, 1989 und 1991.

Die Analyse bezieht sich auf die armen Schichten der Bevölkerung. Auf die Frauen der Mittel- und Oberschicht, die in besseren materiellen und sozialen Umständen leben, gehe ich aus zwei Gründen nicht näher ein: Sie machen in den Andenländern einen geringen Anteil der Bevölkerung aus, und ihre Denkmuster bezüglich der Zuständigkeiten von Mann und Frau unterscheiden sich kaum von den im folgenden beschriebenen:

Die Frau wird sowohl von sich selber, als auch von Familie und Gesellschaft als Wesen ohne eigene Bedürfnisse betrachtet. Selbst Frauen-Gesundheitsprogramme wenden sich in erster Linie in ihrer Funktion als Mutter an sie - d.h. eigentlich an das Kind in ihrem Leib, und an sie als dessen "Umfeld" (CEPAM 1989: 18). Das zeigt sich z.B. daran, dass nach der Entbindung Gesundheitsprogramme sich fast ausschließlich dem Kind zuwenden (CEPAM 1989: 22). Programme, die sich ausschließlich an Frauen wenden, gibt es wenige, und sie werden nicht propagiert. Die Krebsvorsorge-Untersuchung durch Brustuntersuchung und Muttermunds-Abstrich z.B., erreicht gerade 2-3% der Frauen. Dabei ist der Gebärmutterhals-Krebs die häufigste maligne Erkrankung der ecuadorianischen Frau, mit 600 Todesfällen pro Jahr, was aber von der Gesellschaft nicht thematisiert wird (SACOTO, NOBOA, GOMEZ 1989: 117).

Es wäre aber sehr vereinfacht, anzunehmen, die typischen Frauenleiden seien Erkrankungen der Gebärmutter, Eierstöcke, Brüste, und Probleme im Zusammenhang mit der Schwangerschaft.
Woran erkranken Frauen?

Dazu ist es wichtig, zunächst konkret die Lebensumstände der armen Bevölkerung zu betrachten: In den meisten Städten Lateinamerikas leben die Armen am Stadtrand oder im Umland der Städte, weit entfernt von Märkten mit billigen Einkaufsmöglichkeiten, meist ohne Wasser- oder Stromversorgung, und in winzigen Notunterkünften unter dürftigen hygienischen Verhältnissen. Für die Frauen auf dem Land, die weitab der Transportwege wohnen, gilt ähnliches.

Unter diesen Umständen ist die traditionell "primäre Aufgabe" der Frauen, nämlich die Versorgung der Familie, harte Arbeit, und sie wird in der gegenwärtig sich zuspitzenden ökonomischen Krise immer härter: Frühes Aufstehen noch in der Nacht, der aufwendige Transport von Trinkwasser und Brennmaterial, die zeitaufwendige und teure Reise bis zum Markt, wo sie ihre Produkte verkaufen und wiederum einkaufen kann. Die dauernde Suche nach bezahlbaren und guten Lebensmitteln bei immer weniger verfügbarem Geld ist ein täglicher Kampf. Das heißt auch Schlangestehen für billige Nahrungsmittel, oft gedemütigt oder beschimpft von den Verkäufern oder Transporteuren. Als "Dreck der Gesellschaft" sind die Frauen der Unterschicht wehrlos auch gewalttätigen Übergriffen ausgesetzt. All dies in Begleitung der kleineren Kinder, da es keine Kinderbetreuung gibt. Beim abendlichen Heimkommen wartet der Haushalt. Kinder und Mann wollen schnell ein Essen... Erst spät in der Nacht kann die Familienmutter als letzte ins Bett gehen - bis sie wenige Stunden später als erste wieder den Kampf aufnehmen muss (CEPAM 1989: 21).

Weil das Familieneinkommen nicht reicht, müssen Frauen zusätzlich bezahlte Arbeit suchen. Das sind meist schlechte, unterbezahlte Jobs, oder die gefährliche und undankbare Arbeit im informellen Sektor, z.B. als Straßenverkäuferin. Immer mehr Frauen sind Haushaltsvorstände, d.h. sie sind allein für die Ernährung der Familie zuständig: weil der Mann arbeitslos ist, weil er sie verlassen hat, oder weil er in einer anderen Region oder in den USA arbeitet (45% der Haushalte Lateinamerikas haben weibliche Haushaltsvorstände, BREILH 1989:33).

Zu dieser Doppelbelastung kommt als Drittes hinzu, dass die Frauen immer mehr Aufgaben im Bereich der sozialen Infrastruktur übernehmen müssen, aus denen der Staat sich zurückzieht, oder für die er keine Verantwortung übernimmt: Trinkwasseranschlüsse, Gesundheitsdienste, Müllabfuhr, Kinderbetreuung, Schulen, Suppenküchen müssen erkämpft oder in Eigeninitiative organisiert werden (CEPAM 1989: 21). Denn in den Zeiten der "Strukturanpassung", wenn der gesamte Staatsetat in die Begleichung der Auslandsschulden fließt, wird in erster Linie im Sozialbereich gestrichen. Darunter fallen zuallererst Gelder für Programme, die sich in erster Linie an Frauen wenden (CEPAM 1989: 22).

Dieser dritte Job, nach Feierabend und nach Versorgung der Familie, erfordert immer mehr Zeit und Engagement, weil der Sparkurs der Regierungen sich in der wirtschaftlichen Krisensituation verschärft. Das Engagement wird aber gleichzeitig immer überlebenswichtiger, um die Basisversorgung der Familien - also die "primäre Aufgabe" der Frauen, aufrechterhalten zu können.

Diese Dreifachbelastung, zuzüglich zu der chronischen Belastungssituation der Armut, führt bei den Frauen, die im Durchschnitt schlechter ernährt sind und mit weniger Schlaf auskommen müssen, zu Erschöpfungszuständen, Stress, ernährungsbedingter Anämie, vorzeitiger Alterung, Aborten, Erkrankungen des Skelettsystems, Veneninsuffizienz, Entzündungen, Armutskrankheiten wie Tuberkulose, Infektionskrankheiten aufgrund von Abwehrschwäche, psychosomatischen Erkrankungen und depressiven Reaktionen (BREILH 1989: 37). Dies sind die "typischen" und häufigsten Erkrankungen der Frauen, obwohl sie auf den ersten Blick nicht geschlechtsspezifisch sind.

Außerdem ist hier die Gewalt zu nennen, der die Frau vor allem zuhause, aber auch bei der Arbeit ausgesetzt ist. (Straßenverkäuferinnen werden z.B. von Polizisten oft misshandelt, oder auch sexuell missbraucht.) Gewalt gegen Frauen ist gesellschaftlich und kulturell geduldet. Sie wird kaum thematisiert, obwohl Frauen z.T. bleibende Schäden davontragen. Selbst Totschlag ist keine Seltenheit (CEPAM 1989: 24).

Aber auch geschlechtsspezifische Ursachen von Gesundheitsproblemen an den "weiblichen Organen" haben einen gesellschaftlichen und kulturellen Hintergrund, der die Pathogenität bestimmt: Eine Krankheitsursache ist die sexuelle Gewalt. Sie ist kein Problem der Städte oder der modernen Zeiten: Traditionelle Dorffeste enden nicht selten mit Vergewaltigungen. In der traditionellen Geburtshilfe existiert sogar ein Konzept von der "übernatürlichen Schwangerschaft" durch den Berg oder den Regenbogen, das den Schluss nahelegt, dass hier im kulturellen Kontext die Gefahr thematisiert wird, die der Frau droht, die sich allein zu weit vom Dorf entfernt (ROSE 1984: 90, ESTRELLA 1979: 95).

Als Folge der sexuellen Verfügbarkeit der Frau, der Promiskuität der Frau und/oder des Partners sind die sexuell übertragbaren Krankheiten zu nennen. Sie können oft nicht behandelt werden, weil der Partner (wenn er keine Beschwerden hat) sich weigert, sich therapieren zu lassen, und damit die Frau wieder infiziert. In den letzten Jahren wird zunehmend AIDS zum Problem, das in den Drittweltländern aufgrund der Armutsprostitution in erster Linie eine Frauenkrankheit ist. In den katholischen lateinamerikanischen Ländern werden zum Vermeiden dieser Krankheiten statt Kondomen (die v.a. bei den Männern kulturell kaum Akzeptanz finden) gerne Keuschheit und eheliche Treue empfohlen. Auch der Gebärmutterhalskrebs - von manchen Autoren als Armutskrankheit bezeichnet (ARMIJO 1986:178) - fällt in dieses Kapitel: hier werden mangelnde Genitalhygiene bei Frau und Mann, früh einsetzender Geschlechtsverkehr mit wechselnden Partnern bzw. ein promiskuer Partner und die daraus sich ergebenden Infektionen mit Papilloma-Viren als Risikofaktoren betrachtet.

Eine genauere Betrachtung lohnt sich auch im "klassischen Bereich der weiblichen Erkrankungen", der Erkrankungen und Todesfälle im Zusammenhang mit Schwangerschaft. Die häufigsten "mütterlichen Todesursachen": Blutungen in Schwangerschaft und Geburt, Gestosen, Infektionen des Urogenitaltraktes - lassen sich auf hohe Kinderzahlen, Unter- und Mangelernährung, Anämie, Vorerkrankungen, mangelnde Hygiene, sowie fehlende Schwangerschaftsbetreuung zurückführen (SACOTO, NOBOA, GOMEZ 1989: 109) Einige Autoren benennen direkt "Arbeitslosigkeit, Armut, Sozialstatus" als Grundursachen „causas básicas" (ebd.).

In die Statistik der "mütterlichen Todesursachen" gehen auch die Komplikationen von Aborten und Abtreibungen ein. Es wird geschätzt, dass diese in Lateinamerika 50% der "mütterlichen Sterblichkeit" ausmachen (WORLD HEALTH FORUM 1986:54). Es gibt keine genauen Zahlen, da die Abtreibungen illegal durchgeführt werden - mit der Folge hoher Komplikationsraten. Das geht so weit, dass ein Vertreter einer kolumbianischen Organisation in Quito die Vermutung äußerte, dass der erfreuliche Rückgang der mütterlichen Sterblichkeit in seinem Land wahrscheinlich nicht auf eine Verbesserung der Geburtsbetreuung zurückzuführen sei, sondern auf technisch bessere und sauberere Techniken bei den illegalen Abtreibungen (MALAVER 1991:11). In Ecuador war 1989 Abtreibung die sechsthäufigste mütterliche Todesursache (RODRIGUEZ 1989:69). Die Zahl der Abtreibungen steigt mit zunehmender Verarmung. Die Frauen sitzen zwischen allen Stühlen: Die katholische Kirche verbietet Verhütung; innerhalb des kulturellen Konzepts wollen die Männer oftmals ihre Männlichkeit durch eine große Kinderzahl demonstrieren, und die Frauen brauchen Kinder, um ihren Status als Frau durch die Geburt von Kindern und Söhnen zu verbessern. Eine gewisse Zahl von Kindern ist auch zur sozialen Absicherung unablässlich. Das Wissen um Verhütungsmittel ist gering, und es kursieren Horrorvorstellungen über die Nebenwirkungen. Auf der anderen Seite behauptet die staatliche Propaganda, dass die große Kinderzahl und damit die Frauen schuld an der Armut der Familie seien. Damit ist die Frau beim Thema Verhütung in einer denkbar ambivalenten Situation, was häufig dazu führt, dass sie nicht verhütet und dann abtreiben muss - und wenn sie das Geld für die sauber durchgeführte Abtreibung in der Privatklinik nicht aufbringen kann, dann bleibt nur der Engelmacher.

Es ist mir wichtig, die Unterschiede zwischen der Analyse der lateinamerikanischen Frauen in Quito und meiner eigenen aufzuzeigen. Die Referent/innen bei beiden Konferenzen benannten die Armut als den wichtigsten pathogenen Faktor für die Frau. Als die eigentlichen Krankheitsursachen identifizierten sie die Hintergründe der Verarmung: die Wirtschaftskrise, die Liberalisierungspolitik ihrer Regierungen, die Auslandsverschuldung, die internationalen Handelsbeziehungen und die ungerechte Weltwirtschaftsordnung. Ich habe darauf verzichtet, diesen Aspekt genauer auszuführen, da ich diese Zusammenhänge als bekannt voraussetze. Die Lateinamerikanerinnen begreifen den Kampf für das Recht der Frau auf Gesundheit als Teil des Kampfes des ganzen Volkes für Gerechtigkeit und ein besseres Leben.

In den Texten kommt aber, obwohl die Rolle der Männer und der patriarchalischen Gesellschaft mit deutlichen Worten benannt wird, das Wort "machismo" kaum vor.

Ein zweiter pathogener Aspekt ist meiner Meinung nach die Überforderung der Gesundheit der Frauen durch den Anspruch, die Frau sei die Alleinverantwortliche für das Wohlergehen der Familie, was sich dann auf die Gesamtgesellschaft ausweitet.

Die kulturelle Rollenaufteilung, die den Mann als Geldbeschaffer (der pausenlos arbeitet und nie zuhause ist) und die Frau als Organisatorin des Familienlebens definiert, ist als Familienstruktur dazu geeignet, im andauernden Elend zu überleben. Wenn in der wirtschaftlichen Krise der Mann durch noch niedrigere Löhne, Arbeitslosigkeit oder Abwesenheit seine Rolle nicht mehr erfüllen kann, und die Frau beide Aufgaben übernimmt, kann es zur Dekompensation des Familiensystems kommen, und zwar mit der Folge schwerer psychischer Pathologien bei verschiedenen Familienmitgliedern (BECKER 1996:50-54).

Die Frauen sind Heldinnen, laden alles auf sich, und brechen unter der Last zusammen. Dabei wäre die Mitarbeit der Männer konkreter einzuklagen als eine gerechte Weltwirtschaftsordnung. Auch die gesellschaftliche Akzeptanz der Gewalt gegen Frauen kann nicht dem Internationalen Währungsfond angelastet werden - auch wenn es wahr ist, dass Männer gewalttätiger werden durch den Druck, der durch Armut und Arbeitslosigkeit auf ihnen lastet, und durch die Demütigung, ihrer kulturell zugeschriebenen Rolle als Ernährer der Familie nicht mehr gerecht werden zu können.

Es liegt in der Kultur Lateinamerikas und ist gleichzeitig Ausdruck des Machismo, dass ein Mann in dieser Situation, statt als Hausmann seine Frau zu entlasten, lieber vor Scham die Familie verlässt, und damit der Frau noch mehr Arbeit aufbürdet.

Selbstorganisation als Lösungsansatz ?

Die Problematik der Frauen, in der kulturelle und soziale Bilder und Rollenzuschreibungen, ökonomische Krise und ungerechte Weltordnung, Rassismus und Ökologieprobleme ineinander verschränkt sind, kann nicht in ein Schwarz-Weiß-Schema eingeordnet werden. Das zeigt sich darin, dass sich einer der Belastungsfaktoren gleichzeitig als einer der Lösungsansätze für die Frauen entpuppt: Nämlich die bereits erwähnte Organisation in Müttergruppen, Nachbarschaftskomitees, Gruppen zur Organisation von Suppenküchen, und Einkaufskooperativen. Die Mitarbeit in einer solchen Gruppe bedeutet für die Familienmutter einen großen Aufwand an Kraft und Zeit.

Nehmen wir zur Verdeutlichung das fiktive Beispiel von Marta. Sie lebt mit ihrem Mann und 3 Kindern in einem Elendsviertel am Rande der Hauptstadt, und verkauft selbstgebackene Kekse auf dem Hauptmarkt. Sie hielt zunächst nichts von der Idee, in der Müttergruppe mitzumachen. Aber ihr Mann wird arbeitslos, und sie muss allein die Familie ernähren. Die galoppierende Inflation frisst ihre geringen Einkünfte auf, und sie merkt bald, dass die einzige Möglichkeit, ihre Familie sattzumachen, in der Teilnahme an der Suppenküche besteht, zu der alle Nachbarinnen etwas beitragen - etwas Kerosin, Gemüse, Fleischreste, Öl... Und unvermittelt findet sie sich im Nachbarschaftskomitee wieder, als es darum geht, einen Trinkwasseranschluss für ihr Viertel erkämpfen. Nun muss sie nicht mehr für teures Geld Wasser vom Tankauto kaufen. Die Müttergruppe organisiert in den Räumlichkeiten der Suppenküche

Abb. 2
Nachbarschaftskooperative zum Mülltrennen und -recycling in Quito (Ecuador)
Foto: A. Denzler

eine Kinderbetreuung, so dass Maria ohne Kinderanhang zum Markt gehen kann, um ihre Produkte zu verkaufen. Und unversehens merkt sie, wie wichtig ihr das regelmäßige Treffen mit den Nachbarinnen von der Müttergruppe geworden ist, zu denen sie früher kaum Kontakt hatte. Sie sind Gefährtinnen compañeras geworden - Gefährtinnen, die mit Kochtopfdeckeln vor ihrem Haus Lärm machen, als ihr Mann sie eines Nachts schlägt. Gefährtinnen, mit denen sie ihr Leid teilt, weil der älteste Sohn drogenabhängig ist. Gefährtinnen, die ihr das Geld für den Arztbesuch leihen. Mit denen zusammen sie - immer noch in den Räumen der Suppenküche - eine Nähwerkstatt einrichtet, mit zwei echten Nähmaschinen, an denen sie umschichtig arbeiten. Mit denen sie einen regelmäßigen Gesundheitsberatungstermin für die Frauen vom Viertel organisiert, zu dem wöchentlich eine Ärztin vom Gesundheitszentrum kommt. Es kostet sie viel Kraft, aber seit sie in der Müttergruppe und im Nachbarschaftskomitee arbeitet, sieht sie wieder einen Sinn. Natürlich gibt es im Nachbarschaftskomitee auch Männer, aber die meisten und engagiertesten Mitglieder sind Frauen. "Weil wir es für unsere Kinder machen, deshalb haben wir mehr Mut und mehr Kraft als die Männer. Mein Mann z.B. ist den ganzen Tag zu Hause, aber im Komitee mitmachen will er nicht. Wenigstens verbietet er mir nicht mehr, hinzugehen". Die gemeinsame Arbeit und die Erfolge geben Mut. Früher war Marta resigniert, bitter und verzweifelt. Nun denkt sie darüber nach, was sie im Viertel noch verbessern könnten, und die meisten Ideen werden von der Gruppe begeistert aufgenommen. Darauf ist sie stolz. Auch die Idee, zur Stadtverwaltung zu gehen und einen Busanschluss für ihr Viertel zu verlangen, ist von ihr. Man denke, Frauen aus dem Armenviertel beim Bürgermeister! Und jetzt gibt es tatsächlich eine Buslinie, so dass sie nicht mehr stundenlang laufen müssen, mit allen Waren und Einkäufen... Seitdem ist sie Jemand im Viertel, und auch ihr Mann betrachtet sie anders, mit mehr Respekt. Jetzt ist ein großes Projekt geplant - in einem von der Kirche geliehenen Haus soll ein Nachbarschaftszentrum entstehen, wo z.B. eine Werkstatt zur Ausbildung von Jugendlichen eingerichtet werden soll. Wo sie sich treffen können, statt auf der Straße herumzuhängen und zu trinken oder Drogen zu nehmen. Wo die Mütter sich treffen und das Nachbarschaftskomitee, wo man Feste und Kurse veranstalten kann, wo alle etwas näher zusammenkommen - weil es alleine einfach nicht geht, und weil man zusammen viel mehr erreicht. Weil man zusammen wieder menschliche Würde bekommt.

Überall in Lateinamerika existieren solch kleine Stadtteilinitiativen (allerdings fast ausschließlich im städtischen Raum). Sie erreichen auf der Ebene ihres Stadtteils oft erstaunliche Verbesserungen. Getragen werden sie meistens von Frauen, die aus ihrer (Selbst-)Verpflichtung als Mütter eine erstaunliche Kraft zum Kampf für soziale Verbesserungen beziehen. Dieser Mut der Mütter (im krassen Gegensatz zur Frau, die für sich selbst nichts fordert) findet seinen sichtbarsten Ausdruck in Organisationen wie den Müttern der Plaza de Mayo, die gegen die argentinische Diktatur den Kopf erhoben, und im

Endeffekt zu ihrem Fall beitrugen.

Das Engagement der Frauen in diesem Kontext (Arbeit für die Kinder, für die Verbesserung ihrer Lebensumstände) steht nicht im Gegensatz zu der traditionellen Frauenrolle der Familienversorgerin, sprengt damit auch nicht die kulturellen Wertmaßstäbe (die auch nicht hinterfragt werden), und erweitert trotzdem den Spielraum der Frauen erheblich - um den Preis der genannten Dreifachbelastung und des folglich erhöhten Krankheitsrisikos. Und: Es sind Lösungen, die nur solange aufrechterhalten werden können, wie die wirtschaftliche Situation ein Minimum an Luft für Aktivitäten belässt. Wird ein gewisses Maß an Elend überschritten, brechen auch diese Strukturen zusammen.

Resumee:

In den Slums der Städte, aber auch in den entferntesten ländlichen Gebieten entsteht derzeit eine kulturelle Umbruchsituation, hin zu einer medienvermittelten westlich-geprägten Einheitskultur. Diese Entwicklung ist verbunden mit wirtschaftlicher Verelendung, mit dem Verschwinden traditioneller Wertvorstellungen, und de facto auch mit einem Verschwinden der traditionellen, in den alten Strukturen oft sinnvollen Rollenverteilung.

Dieser Umbruch führt zu einer tiefen Verunsicherung bei Frauen und Männern. Die alten Rollen- und Denkstrukturen bieten keine tragfähigen Lösungen mehr beim praktischen Überleben, neue Rollenbilder entstehen, vor allem eine neue Frauenrolle. Das moderne Weltbild bietet der Frau mehr Möglichkeiten, und sie hat in ihrer Funktion als "primäre Organisatorin des Familienlebens" auch mehr Druck, etwas zu verändern. Andererseits dienen die traditionellen Strukturen, gerade in der Familie, zu einer lebensnotwendigen psychischen Stabilisierung - für die Frauen, aber in noch stärkerem Maß für die Männer: Sie sind es, die in der Umbruchsituation ihre Privilegien, aber auch ihre Aufgaben und damit ihre Existenzberechtigung verlieren, und dann psychisch dekompensieren. Sie erfüllen weder ihre alte noch eine mögliche neue Männerrolle. Die Frauen dagegen versuchen den Spagat zwischen der traditionellen identitätsstiftenden Frauenrolle, und einer neuen, die das Überleben sichert. Es entsteht die schizophrene Situation, dass die Rolle, die sie psychisch stabilisiert, nicht fürs praktische Überleben taugt, und umgekehrt die neue Freiheit zutiefst verunsichert. Beim Versuch, die beiden gegensätzlichen Rollen zu erfüllen, entstehen überaus kreative und lebendige Lösungsansätze, aber um den Preis eines hohen Energieaufwandes.

Kommt noch eine zusätzliche Belastung hinzu, dann bricht dieses neue improvisierte System zusammen. Ganz sicher wird sich eine wirkliche Lösung mit tragfähigen neuen Rollenmustern nur finden lassen, wenn eine Situation minimaler materieller Sicherheit gegeben ist. Dies ist aber in der derzeitigen Situation der weltweiten "Strukturanpassung" nicht absehbar.

References

ARMIJO, R. 1986. *Epidemiología del Cancer.* Ed. Intermédica, Buenos Aires.

BECKER, D. 1992. *Ohne Haß keine Versöhnung.* Kore-Verlag.

BREILH, J. 1989 "La lucha por la salud de la mujer: Fetichismo y verdad" in *"Salud, Derecho de la Mujer"* Beiträge zum Workshop und Forum " Las Mujeres y el Derecho a la Salud", CEPAM - UNFPA pp. 29 - 41 (im folgenden zitiert als: "Salud,..." pp.....)

CEPAM, Guayaquil 1989 "Las Mujeres y el Derecho a la Salud" in *"Salud, ..."* pp.17-25.

DENZLER, A. 1989. *Alternativen der Geburtshilfe in einem Dorf in Südecuador.* Dissertation Med. Fak. Heidelberg.

ESTRELLA, E. 1980. *"Función Maternal y Sexualidad".* unveröff. Forschungsbericht.

MALAVER, J. 1991 "Derechos humanos y derechos de la mujer" Redebeitrag beim Seminar *"Mujeres de los Andes. Condiciones de Vida y de Salud",* Quito

RODRIGUEZ, L. 1989 "Mujer y Derechos Reproductivos" in *"Salud, ..."* pp. 59-76

ROESLER, G. 1979 *"Formen und Träger trad.Geburtshilfe im Dpt. Puno und Probleme staatlicher Gesundheitspolitik ..."* ASA-Bericht PER 79/1

ROSE, K. 1983 *"Trad. Geburtshilfe im siziokulturellen Wandel"* Dissertation Med. Fak. Bonn

SACOTO, F., NOBOA, H., GOMEZ DE LA TORRE, V. 1989 "Mujer y Políticas de Salud" in *"Salud,..."* pp. 107-113

WORLD HEALTH FORUM 1986. Forum Interview. *World Health Forum Vol.* 7: 50-55

The Role of Women in the Traditional and Modern Peigan / Blackfoot Community
Die Rolle der Frauen in der traditionellen und modernen Peigan / Blackfoot-Gemeinschaft

Sybille Manneschmidt & Reg Crowshoe

Abstract: Women's roles in traditional Peigan/Blackfoot culture were clearly defined and in regard to health practices and services as important as men's. Historically, women were equal to their male partners in sacred medicine bundle ceremonies and had the opportunity to gain knowledge as herbalists or ritual healers as much as men. These traditional ways are still alive in the modern Peigan community and reflected in the various religious ceremonies which are lived, taught and practiced by the Elders. At the same time, modern health services, as delivered by the Medical Services Branch of the Government of Canada, show a strong participation of Blackfoot women as professional practicioners. The past and present-day roles of Peigan women in traditional healing practices, as well as their contribution in the modern health care system, are a reflection of their integral part in ensuring the cultural survival and heritage preservation of their indigenous community.

Zusammenfassung: In der traditionellen Peigan/Schwarzfuß Kultur war die Frauenrolle klar definiert und in Bezug auf Gesundheitspraktiken und -dienste genauso wichtig wie die der Männer. Historisch waren Frauen gleichberechtigte Partner in den heiligen Medizinbündel-Zeremonien und hatten die Möglichkeit, genau so wie Männer, Wissen als Kräuterkundige und rituelle Heiler sich anzueignen. Diese traditionellen Wege sind immer noch in der modernen Peigan- Gemeinschaft lebendig und spiegeln sich in den verschiedenen religiösen Zeremonien wieder, die von den Stammesältesten gelebt, gelehrt und praktiziert werden. Zur gleichen Zeit nehmen Schwarzfuss-Frauen als professionelle Berufstätige an der Bereitstellung von Gesundheitsdiensten durch die Medical Service Branch der Kanadischen Regierung teil. Die Rollen der Peigan-Frauen in der Vergangenheit und Gegenwart in traditionellen Heilungspraktiken, ebenso wie ihre Beteiligung im modernen Gesundheitssystem, reflektieren ihre bedeutende Beteiligung am Ueberleben und dem Erhalt ihres kulturellen Erbes in ihrer einheimischen Gemeinschaft.

Keywords: Women, Blackfoot people, modern health services, Frauen, Blackfoot, modernes Gesundheitssystem

Abb. 1
Amalia Crowshoe, Reg & Rose´s älteste Enkelin beim Pow Wow in ihrem traditionellen Buckskin outfit.

Historical and social overview of the Peigan community

The Peigan Nation presently consists of about 2700 members, with the majority of the population living on an Indian reserve in Southern Alberta, Canada. The Peigan are part of the Blackfoot Confederacy which contains four different member nations. They are one of the Treaty 7 tribes in Canada which signed this contractual agreement with the British Crown in 1877. The four Blackfoot Nations are called Kainai (Blood), Aputosi Piikani (North Peigan or Peigan), and Siksika (Blackfoot) in Alberta, Canada, and Amaskapi Piikani (South Peigan, Piegan or Blackfeet) in Montana, USA.

Up to the beginning of this century, the members of these bands spoke the same language and followed similar social customs. The Peigan were traditionally organized in various bands, which consisted of several extended families and lived fairly autonomously. In traditional Peigan/Blackfoot culture, the important structural categories were the family, the kin, the band, the societies and military fraternities and the tribal council. Each of these group's importance or rank was symbolized by different ceremonial paraphernalia (DEMPSEY 1986, DE JONG 1912, WISSLER 1912). Like all other groups of Plains peoples, the Peigan subsisted as nomads on hunting (primarily buffalo) and gathering roots and berries.

Nowadays, family and kin still play a central role in a Peigan person's life, but membership in particular societies is a social goal for primarily traditional thinkers. Only around 15% of the Peigan speak still their own language and about the same number of individuals take on responsibilities to keep the traditional customs alive. Church groups, Canadian government agencies and other modern, mainstream social organizations have replaced many functions and activities which were once central to traditional fraternities and societies.

Presently the Peigan community has to deal not only with the erosion of traditional cultural institutions and values but also with high unemployment, lack of on-reserve skill training and housing, and above average suicide and criminal record rates. However, over the last ten years the Peigan Band has taken over their own educational administration and schools, and many members, particularly women, have completed or are in the process of finishing their post-secondary education. Some of the key administrative positions are held by women, but Chief and Council is still dominated by males.

Traditional Peigan/Blackfoot concepts of health and healing

Blackfoot world view concepts, and therefore concepts of health, are primarily communicated in Creation stories, Napi stories and practices of traditional religious ceremonies. These practices were carried out for hundreds of years and handed down through many generations. They are full of symbolic meaning, highly structured and require a specific protocol.

Most ceremonies centre around medicine bundles, large child-sized physical objects which contain a collection of articles regarded as sacred by Blackfoot traditionalists. These bundles were and remain still important religious objects which embody particular social functions and were the physical and abstract manifestation of traditional Blackfoot belief and social systems. Blackfoot world view attributes an abstract component to each living entity and object which is called a shadow. For this reason, in Blackfoot culture, anything or any being can be explained by being part of the shadow or physical world or both. But moments in time and space, when both of these worlds are brought to the fore in their absoluteness are regarded as extremely powerful and sacred. Traditional ceremonies, and especially bundle ceremonies, are regarded as one of these occasions and have thus high potential, for example, for healing and resolving inner or social conflicts for the benefit of the Peigan community and individuals who ask for help and support.

There exist a variety of categories of these sacred bundles which have particular functions and which need, in order to be used actively, and therefore correctly, a male and female custodian who will commit themselves to the proper ways of care taking.

Role of women as agents of healing in traditional Blackfoot culture

First historical records of Blackfoot women and their roles by fur traders and explorers (MAXIMILIAN ZU WIED 1834, FIDDLER 1792) describe only specific aspects of their lives. They are regarded as hard workers who are in charge of all basic chores to ensure the welfare of their camp, apart from male activities such as hunting and protection from enemy tribes. They live in polygamous marriages and are severely punished, mutilated or even killed for adultery. Only at the turn of this century did ethnographic texts (WISSLER and DUVALL 1908, WISSLER 1911, MCCLINTOCK 1910) emphasize the importance of women

Abb. 2
Head-Smashed-In, Buffalo Jump Row Wow

as gatherers and knowledge keepers of food and plant materials and as central agents in religious ceremonies. More recent discussions (KIDWELL 1979, KEHOE 1976) stress not only the importance of their roles as mothers and keepers of the home, but also their ritual role in ceremonies as well as the individual option to achieve community recognition through deeds of bravery and charity (EWERS 1955, SCHULTZ 1919) or by obtaining valued cultural knowledge (LEWIS 1941).

Because of women's gathering and collecting activities, and, therefore, their ability to identify and characterize the location and function of specific plants, women were important as herbalists curing specific diseases and assisting in childbirth and other reproductive issues (GRINNELL 1896, GOLDFRANK 1951). Women would also be recognized as medical practicioners for illnesses which demanded more than the application of herbs, but called for a ceremonial context with diagnoses and treatment (EWERS 1955, McCLINTOCK 1910). However, it is in their contribution to ceremonial rituals where women played and still play additional important roles.

As mentioned above, specific medicine bundles were and are regarded as central religious objects which bestow on the individuals who have "*transferred rights*" to these objects specific healing powers. They are regarded essential in ensuring the well-being and survival of the community and have always a female and a male caretaker who are expected to behave in proper ways to ensure the sacredness and the physical and symbolic non-pollution of these objects. The female/male pair mostly consists of a husband and wife team, but it is also acceptable to have a brother and sister team or a daughter-father team or any other combination of female-male relatives. It is the woman who carries the bundle, who opens the bundle in the ceremony and presents the individual objects to her male counterpart. It is the man's role to provide the ceremonial context for the bundle and he facilitates the ritual process when it gets opened in public ceremonies.

Another ritual role of women evolves around their equal partnership as members of age-graded fraternal societies and in their own women's society, the Women's Buffalo Society. In the former, the All-Comrades, men could and still can only join with a female partner, who was either their wife or a female relative (WISSLER 1913). The Women's Buffalo Society or Ma'toki is regarded as a parallel social institution to the Horns or Old Bulls Society, but has historical and present-day relevance only in the Kainai and Siksika tribes (WISSLER 1913). As all societies' functions were to some extent related to contribute to the well-being of their community as a whole, women's participation in these societies has to be regarded as essential.

The third ceremonial role for Blackfoot women is in the Sun Dance. Prior to the actual ceremony, a woman makes a vow to take over the sacred Sun Dance Bundle in the following summer. The woman undertakes this sacrifice for the well-being of her family and her community. A Sun Dance woman is regarded as being able to act as intermediary between any individual or group of people and Creator and can help in situations of illness or trouble in certain ways; for example through her prayers, by painting faces and leading sweats.

It is important to understand that the ceremonial roles Blackfoot women traditionally embody, are all sanctioned through public statements in clearly structured formats. The obtaining of one of these roles is characterized through the official purchase of one of the bundles or other sacred objets that are the physical manifestation of the woman's future status and through the knowledge of specific songs and face paintings. Only after the completion of such a transfer ritual in the presence of other already ordained individuals, is a Blackfoot person regarded as being able and trained to facilitate a specific aspect of a sacred ceremony. Consequently, it is this *"official"* aspect of women's participation in ceremonies that can define them as healers, but it is also their knowledge about plants which gives them a more individualized *"right"* to practice in their community. These two strands of looking at traditional forms of women as health providers are quite distinct from each other, although often a female ceremonialist will also have knowledge of herbs, poultices and other related practices. However, a woman who has not gone through the initiations of sacred ceremonies was and is not perceived as having gained a form of official *"certification"* for her healing practices.

History of medical administration and services

Since the signing of Treaty 7 in 1877, the Indian Act forced a structural reorganization upon the Peigan which is primarily characterized through an elected Chief and Council and its administration. Prior to 1960 the Indian agent and appointed *"head chiefs"* under the directive of the Department of Indian Affairs in Ottawa (now Department of Indian and Northern Affairs, DINA) had decision-making powers over all activities pertaining to Peigan individuals and groups on the reservation.

With the signing of Treaty 7, health and education were some of the programs administered and controlled by outsiders, primarily bureaucrats. But the implementation of these programs into medical practices were open to interpretations and changed permanently over the last 100 years. For example, historically since the beginning of contact with Euro-Canadians, health services were delivered on a random basis through missionaries or medical personnel who was enlisted with the Canadian military force, the Northwest Mounted Police. The first hospital in the Treaty 7 area was provided for the Blackfoot or Siksika nation in 1889 and run by Oblate missionaries.

Presently, the following model is in practice: Peigan Nation members receive medical services categorized as insured or non-insured benefits. Services in the first category pertain to payment for hospital stays, visits to medical practitioners, payment for prescription drugs and some services provided for by nurse practitioners through a community health centre. These services are non-negotiable and are regarded as cornerstones of medical service delivery for native peoples all over Canada. Non-insured benefits, on the other hand, are open to constant negotiations and interpretations between federal health bureaucrats and community health representatives, for example, Chief and Council. These services presently include dental care, eye care, medical transportation, mental health services, and home care programs. Services in regard to the latter category get changed and re-interpreted regularly and are dependent on the Canadian government's financial situation and political agenda.

In some cases a fee for services structure has been applied to native practitioners who work outside the medical model. There is no policy or framework in place in regards to traditional native healing practices and the present practice allows for random agreements with the regional Medical Service Branch of Indian Affairs.

Role of Peigan women as modern health care providers in their community

In the present modern health care system around 20 Peigan women provide services as Community Health Representatives (CHRs), Licensed Practical Nurses (LPNs), Registered Nurses (RNs) and mental health counsellors. Depending on the depth of their training and therefore the level of their responsibilities these health care providers have a more paraprofessional background (CHRs and LPNs) and their programs have a community health emphasis or a more clinical orientation and cover all health areas from health promotion to more clinical and treatment oriented interventions. As registered nurses Peigan women have received between two and four years of college or university education finishing with a Certificate (2 years) or a Bachelor's (4 years) degree in nursing and bring an extensive background in health care practice, theory and research to their community.

Several women have some training in the area of mental health counselling. Again there is a variety of levels of certification, from a paraprofessional level to a Bachelor's degree. Including child protection workers, there are about six Peigan women who are employed in this field. There is a male Peigan member who is a trained medical doctor but does not practice on the reserve and there are a couple of men who are working as alcohol prevention counsellors, but none of them has gained any form of formal training. In general, there are fewer Blackfoot men employed in health professions than women.

It is the women who are practicing in their community as professional health care providers who have to be regarded as having achieved some form of official recognition through their formal education, and thus have achieved status in the public domain. However, there are also others who work privately out of their houses and give advise to members in their community. These are individuals who have learned through books or in various other ways about herbal practices, mental health issues, etc. These are women who have gained in individual ways knowledge but are not licensed or certified to deliver these services.

Conclusion

The authors suggest that in traditional as well as modern Peigan society women had central roles as healers. Although, in the historical literature, male practicioners or medicine men are prominently displayed, it is also mentioned that women were the primary caretakers for their sick relatives in the extended families and clans. Only by looking at the ceremonial structures and their strong relevance and relationship to health beliefs and practices, does it become clear that traditionally women had many transferred rights and responsibilities ensuring health for their communities as a whole as well as individual members.

It is in these ceremonial structures that women, as equal partners to participating men, primarily obtain and get recognition for having transferred rights and therefore have clear and publicly acknowledged positions. These traditional structures have strong analogies to the present-day official medical system of health care which provides health services through the Indian Act for the Peigan community.

Abb. 3
Peigan Women / Elders

As in the traditional system, modern day health care providers go through a process of certification and receive in the end publicly recognized status which lets the community know that they have the *"transferred rights"* to practice in the community.

Also, in both the traditional and the modern system, there are ways that allow for individuals to be active and helpful as healers in their communities. If these individuals are perceived as having achieved *"successes"* in their healing practices, they will be visited by members in the community for their services. These individuals are also recognized for their contributions, but they do not have the same status in the community as the *"certified"* traditional or modern health care providers. However, through the process of "cultural confusion" and the general deterioration of cultural ways these differences between ways of health care provisions have become sometimes unclear to Peigan members and, especially, outsiders to the community. This has been particularly the case when financial contributions were and are made to *"non-certified"* traditional health care providers.

References

CROWSHOE, R. AND MANNESCHMIDT, S. 1997. *Akak'stiman: A Blackfoot Framework for Decision Making About Health Administrations and Services.* Brocket,, Alberta: Keep Our Circle Strong Project.

DE JONG, J. 1912. Social Organization of the Southern Peigans. *Internationales Archiv fur Ethnolographie,* 20, Leiden.

DEMPSEY, H. 1979. *Indian Tribes of Alberta.* Calgary: Glenbow-Alberta Institute.

DEMPSEY, H. 1986. The Blackfoot Indians. In *Native Peoples.* The Canadian Experience. Edited by MORRISON, R.B. and WILSON, C.R., pp. 404-435. Toronto: McClelland and Stewart Inc.

EWERS, J.C. 1955. The Horse in Blackfoot Indian Culture, with Comperative Material from other Western Tribes. *Bureau of American Ethnology Bulletin* 159. Washington: Bureau of American Ethnology.

FIDLER, P. 1991. *Fidler's Journal.* Lethbridge: Historical Research Centre.

GOLDFRANK, E.S. 1951. Observation on sexuality among the Blood Indians of Alberta, Canada. *Psychoanalysis and Social Science,* 3: 71-98.

GRINNELL, J.B. 1896. Childbirth Among the Blackfeet. *American Anthropologist,* 9: 286-287.

KEHOE, A.B. 1976. Old Women Had Great Power. *The Western Canadian Journal of Anthropology,* 6(3):

KIDWELL, C.S. 1979. The Power of Women in Three American Indian Societies. *The Journal of Ethnic Studies.* 6(3):113-121.

LEWIS O. 1941. Manly-Hearted Women Among the North Piegan. *American Anthropologist,* 43:173-187.

MAXIMILIAN ZU WIED, P. 1904-1907. Travels in the Interior of North America. Vol 22-24. In *Early Western Travels,* 1784-1897, 32 vols. Edited by R.G. THWAITES. Cleveland.

MCCLINTOCK, W. 1910. *The Old North Trail.* London: McMillan.

MCCLINTOCK, W. 1948. *Blackfoot Medicine Pipe Ceremony.* Los Angeles: Southwest Museum.

ROSS, M. and CROWSHOE, R. 1996. Shadows and sacred geography: Firts Nations history-making from an Alberta perspective. In *Making History in Museums.* Edited by G. KAVANAGH. London: Leicester University Press.

SCHULTZ, J.W. 1919. *Running Eagle, the Warrior Girl..* Boston.

SCHULTZ, J.W. 1988. *Recently Discovered Tales of Life Among the Indians.* Missoula: Mountain Press Publishing Company.

TANNER, A. 1983. *The Politics of Indianness. Case Studies of Native Ethnopolicies in Canada.* St.John's: Institute of Social and Economic Research, Memorial University of Newfoundland.

WISSLER, C. and DUVALL, D.C. 1908. Mythology of the Blackfoot Indians. *Anthropological Papers,* 2(1). New York: American Museum of Natural History.

WISSLER, C. 1911. Social Life of the Blackfoot Indians. *Anthropological Papers,* 7(1). New York: American Museum of Natural History.

WISSLER, C. 1912. Social Organization and Ritualistic Ceremonies of the Blackfoot Indians. *Anthropological Papers,* 7(1). New York: American Museum of Natural History.

WISSLER, C. 1913. Societies and Dance Associations of the Blackfoot Indians. *Anthropological Papers,* 2(4). New York: American Museum of Natural History.

Arbeit, Ethnizität und Gesundheit in Brasilien
-Das Beispiel der Afro-Brasilianerinnen-
Employment, Ethnicity and Health in Brazil
-The Case of Female Afro-Brazilians-

Chirly dos Santos-Stubbe

Zusammenfassung: Afro-brasilianische Frauen üben in Brasilien meist untergeordnete Tätigkeiten aus. In ihrer Mehrzahl sind sie als Hausarbeiterinnen (empregadas domésticas) beschäftigt, eine Berufsgruppe, die über 50% des Dienstleistungssektors ausmacht. Diese Frauengruppe zeigt in unterschiedlichen Statistiken sehr hohe Morbiditätsraten. Die Autorin analysiert und interpretiert die Daten einer empirischen Studie über 130 afro-brasilianische Hausarbeiterinnen in Rio de Janeiro. Ihr subjektives Allgemeinbefinden sowie spezifisch weibliche Aspekte (Sexualität, Familienplanung, etc.) ihrer Gesundheit/Krankheit werden anhand von Statistiken und Selbstzeugnissen beschrieben. Spezifische afro-brasilianische (Ethno-)Therapien und allgemeine Heilverfahren, die von ihnen benutzt werden, schließen die Darstellung ab.

Abstract: In Brazil, afro-brazilian women usually carry out inferior tasks. Most of them are employed as domestics (empregadas domésticas), an occupation that constitutes more than 50% of the service sector. In various statistical statements, this group of women is reported to have very high rates of morbidity. The author analyses and interprets the data of an empirical study on 130 afro-brazilian domestics in Rio de Janeiro. The women's subjective sense of well-being and specific feminine aspects of their health/illness (sexuality, family planning, etc.) are described by means of statistics and their own accounts. The presentation concludes with a portrayal of specific afro-brazilian (ethno-) therapies and general medical treatments which are used by them.

Keywords: Brasilien, Afrobrasilianerinnen, Hausarbeiterinnen, Ethnomedizin, medizinische Soziologie, Gesundheitssysteme, Brazil, female Afro-Brazilians, Domestics, Ethno-Medicine, Medical Sociology, Health Systems.

Einführung

Die bezahlte Hausarbeit in Brasilien wird in ca. 92% der Fälle von Frauen ausgeübt. Diese Frauen stammen in der Regel aus den unterprivilegierten ethnischen Minderheiten des Landes. Durch eine Hochrechnung konnten wir feststellen, dass ca. 70% der Hausarbeiterinnen in Brasilien, vor allem in den urbanen Zentren der Süd-Ost Region, Afrobrasilianerinnen bzw. Nicht-Weiße sind (vgl. SANTOS-STUBBE 1995). Charakteristisch für diese Frauengruppe ist das niedrige Ausbildungsniveau (häufig Analphabetismus), die Herkunft aus einer Groß-Familienkonstellation und die Migration aus ärmeren Regionen des Landes in die Großstädte, die Wohnsegregation (oft sind diese Frauen "Favela"- [Slum] Bewohnerinnen) und der Status der unverheirateten und alleinstehenden Frau bzw. Mutter von mehreren Kindern. Obwohl die Tätigkeit der bezahlten Hausarbeit als Beruf durch die brasilianische Verfassung von 1988 anerkannt ist, arbeitet die Mehrzahl dieser Berufstätigen ohne Reglementierung, was bewirkt, dass sie niedrigste Löhne erhalten, fristlos entlassen werden können und dass sie in der Regel keinen Anspruch auf feste Arbeitszeit (häufig arbeiten sie bis zu 17 Stunden am Tag), Ferien, Sozial-, Alters- und Gesundheitsversicherung haben.

Das Ergebnis dieses Beitrages entstammt einer Befragung von 130 afrobrasilianischen "Empregadas Domésticas" (Hausarbeiterinnen) der Südregion der Stadt Rio de Janeiro, wobei hier zwei spezifische Gruppen von empregadas domésticas unterschieden wurden, nämlich diejenigen, die ständig bei ihren Arbeitgebern wohnen, d.h. am Arbeitsplatz (hier internas genannt), und diejenigen, die nach ihrem Arbeitstag zu ihrem eigenen Haushalt zurückkehren, die sog. externas. Diese Berufstätigen übten in der Regel die gesamte im Haushalt anfallende Arbeit aus (SANTOS-STUBBE 1990), nämlich:

* Vorbereitung des Frühstücks, Mittagessens und Abendessens: in Brasilien wird zweimal am Tag warm gegessen. Häufig gibt es nachmittags auch noch einen Lunch;
* Kinderbetreuung: der brasilianischen Haushalt ist beträchtlich größer als der deutsche. Viele brasilianische Familien entsprechen eher dem Typ einer Großfamilie mit teilweise drei Generationen, darunter mehreren Kindern. Ein Großteil der Sozialisation dieser Kinder liegt in den Händen, nicht

nur der "Babá" (=Kindermädchen) sondern auch der empregada. Sie müssen die Kinder waschen, ihr Essen und Trinken vorbereiten und verabreichen, sie zum Kindergarten/zur Schule bringen bzw. abholen, ihnen bei den Hausaufgaben mithelfen (obwohl viele empregadas Analphabetinnen sind!), sie in der Freizeit, beim Spielen begleiten, etc.;
* Aufräumen des gesamten Hauses bzw. der ganzen Wohnung: der kleinste Familienwohntyp in Brasilien hat meistens schon vier Einheiten (Wohn- und Schlafzimmer, Küche, Bad -oft auch eine kleine Veranda). Nicht selten finden wir Wohnungen bzw. Häuser mit über 10 Zimmern. Die meisten Häuser in Brasilien besitzen auch einen Garten;
* Putzen der gesamten Wohnung bzw. des Hauses: Fußboden, Fenster, Küche und Badezimmerkacheln, Silbergeschirr, das gesamte Mobiliar, etc. (Die Fenster der Hochhäuserwohnungen werden von den empregadas gereinigt, aber diese benutzen hierbei keinerlei Sicherheitsschutz. Es ist "üblich" in den besser gelegenen Stadtteilen empregadas zu sehen, die auf dem 10. oder 15. Stockwerk draußen die Fenster putzen.);
* Bedienen: andecken, Essen und Getränke auftragen, Türen öffnen, ans Telefon gehen, etc.;
* Geschirr spülen: es muss hier hevorgehoben werden, dass der brasilianische Haushalt sich sehr stark von dem westeuropäischen unterscheidet. Auch in den ökonomisch besser gestellten Schichten findet man eher selten technische Haushaltshilfen wie Geschirrspüler und Trockner, Waschmaschine;
* Wäsche waschen und Bügeln;
* Müll wegbringen;
* Einkaufen gehen: darin sind der Metzgerei-, Supermarkt-, Bäckerrei- und Fischmarkt-Besuch u.a. enthalten;
* Auch Verpflichtungen wie Bankbesuch, kleine Rechnungen bezahlen, Hund ausführen, Bestellungen auftragen und abholen, Botschaften überbringen, usw. werden häufig den empregadas domésticas übertragen.

Die Gesundheit der afrobrasilianischen Empregadas Domésticas

Die somatische, seelische und psychosomatische Gesundheit der afrobrasilianischen empregadas domésticas darf keineswegs ausschließlich unter individuellen Persönlichkeitsfaktoren analysiert werden. Hierbei benötigen wir zusätzlich eine historische und gegenwartsbezogene gesellschaftliche Reflektion, wodurch die genannten Aspekte der Gesundheit unter den verschiedenen ökonomischen, sozialen, kulturellen, arbeitsbezogenen und religiösen Bedingungen des Empregada-Doméstica-Lebens analysiert werden sollen. Schon aus der afrikanischen Sklavereizeit, dem das heutige Empregada-System entstammt, besitzen wir zahlreiche Berichte über den (schlechten) seelischen und körperlichen Gesundheitszustand, in dem sich die afrikanische sklavisierte Bevölkerung und deren Nachkommen befanden und vor allem über den Zustand der Frauen.

Die allgemeinen schlechten Arbeits- und Lebensbedingungen, wie Unterernährung, häufige und schwere Bestrafungen, häufige Schwangerschaften und (sowohl natürliche als auch provozierte) Aborte, Entzug der ethnischen bzw. kulturellen Ausdrucksmöglichkeiten, forcierte Entwurzelung durch Trennung der Familien und Mitglieder der Ethnie, etc. sind nur einige der Faktoren die wesentlich auf die gesamte Gesundheit der afrikanischen Sklaven eingewirkt haben. Seelische und somatische Erkrankungen, die die Sklaven/innen oftmals bis zum Tod führten, liefern uns ein deutliches Bild ihres Zustandes, der in der Regel allein als "rein" körperliche Reaktion, aber weniger als psychische und/oder psychosomatische Verarbeitungsformen ihres "Ding-Daseins" interpretiert wurde. Tuberkulose, Banzo, "Bicho-de-pé", Rheumatismus, Geschlechtskrankheiten, Erkrankungen der Atemwege, "Nervenkrankheiten" und der Suizid sollen hier nur exemplarisch erwähnt werden (vgl. SIGAUD 1844; FREITAS 1935; MACHADO, LOUREIRO, LUZ & MURICY 1978; COSTA 1983; KARASCH 1987; SANTOS-STUBBE 1989; STUBBE & SANTOS-STUBBE 1990; STUBBE 1996).

Die Gesundheitsproblematik und die Gesundheitsversorgung der Afrobrasilianer/innen wurde in den letzten Jahren nicht mehr besonders hinterfragt bzw. berücksichtigt. Die Wechselwirkung multidimensionaler Faktoren wie Familienkonstellation, Arbeitsbedingungen, Einkommen, geschlechtsspezifische Gegebenheiten, Entfaltungsmöglichkeit des persönlichen Lebensstils, Freizeitgestaltung, Ethnizität, Religion und vorhandene Ätiologien und Nosologien als Einflussvariablen eines breiteren Verständnis für Gesundheit/Krankheit werden in der Regel im offiziellen Gesundheitsversorgunssystem Brasiliens nur selten berücksichtigt (vgl. VASCONCELOS 1992). Als normative Definition von Gesundheit wird hier die Begriffsbestimmung der Weltgesundheitsorganisation (WHO) zugrunde gelegt. Danach ist Gesundheit "körperliches, seelisches und soziales Wohlbefinden" (vgl. Word Health Organization 1982). Da diese Definition sehr umfassend ist, insb. für die Analyse der Versorgung in einem Land wie Brasilien, und weil sie von der Abwesenheit von Krankheit ausgeht, wollen wir hier dieses Verständnis für unsere weitere Analyse in Anlehnung an Rössler ergänzen, bei dem "Gesundheit nicht Abwesenheit von Störungen ist, sondern die Kraft mit ihnen zu leben" (apud DIESFELD 1989, S.7). Diese Definition wird hierbei als richtungsweisend für unsere Analyse von Gesundheit und Krankeit bei den afrobrasilianischen empregadas domésticas betrachtet.

Über das allgemeine Wohlbefinden der Empregadas Domésticas

Der allgemeine Gesundheitszustand wird in diesem Zusammenhang nicht ausschließlich aus allgemeingültiger biologischer Perspektive verstanden: Hierbei soll vor allem die eigene Befindlichkeit der empregadas domésticas hinsichtlich ihres Erlebens körperlich krank oder gesund zu sein dargestellt werden und dies wiederum im Rahmen ihrer Lebens- und Arbeitsgeschichte als gegenwärtige Parameter für diese beiden Zustände. Die hier untersuchten afrobrasilianischen empregadas domésticas haben bezüglich ihres allgemeinen Gesundheitszustandes eine Reihe von Beschwerden bzw. Erkrankungen aufgezählt, bei denen eine Trennung von "somatisch" oder "psychosomatisch" schwer vorzunehmen ist.

"Ich bin krank von Kopf bis Fuß" (Edmea/interna).

Obwohl der Anfang des beruflichen Lebens bei der Mehrzahl dieser empregadas domésticas bereits in ihrer Kindheit oder in ihrem Jugendalter liegt, konnten sie ihr körperliches Wohlbefinden anhand von Erkrankungen und den eingetretenen Veränderungen von Beschwerden im Laufe ihres beruflichen Lebens genau charakterisieren. In der gesamten Stichprobe waren es 93,7% aller empregadas domésticas, die zwischen ihrem 7. und 18. Lebensjahr mit der Ausübung ihres beruflichen Lebens angefangen haben. Beide Empregadas-Gruppen unterschieden sich hier nicht voneinander. Zu den speziellen statistischen Ergebnissen der Untersuchung (vgl. SANTOS-STUBBE 1995).

Eindeutig ist bei der Analyse der statistischen Ergebnisse die Erhöhung der Beschwerden nach dem Arbeitsbeginn als empregada doméstica und die geringe Anzahl der empregadas, die gegenwärtig unter keinen Beschwerden leiden. Über ihren Zustand vor dem Arbeitsbeginn gaben 79,2% aller Befragten an unter keinen Beschwerden zu leiden. Diese körperlichen Beschwerden haben sich nach ihrem subjektiven Empfinden intensiviert in dem Ausmaß seit dem Arbeitsbeginn, dass gegenwärtig nur 6,1% aller Befragten angaben unter keinen Beschwerden zu leiden. Auch die Anzahl der an bestimmten Erkrankungen Leidenden, die niedriger lag (wie z.B. an Hypertonie; vor Arbeitsbeginn fanden sich diese Beschwerden bei 1,5% der Befragten und seit dem Arbeitsbeginn sind sie auf 21,5% gestiegen. Bei der Beschwerde "physische Erschöpfung" gab es keine Angaben zu dem Zeitpunkt vor dem Arbeitsbeginn und nach Anfang dieser erhöhte sich die Anzahl auf 20,8%. Die gynäkologischen Beschwerden liegen gegenwärtig bei 13,1% im Gegensatz zu früher als nur 1,5% aller empregadas domésticas diese erwähnten), erhöht sich im Laufe der beruflichen Betätigung als Doméstica.

Hervorzuheben ist auch der Unterschied beider Gruppen hinsichtlich einiger Beschwerden in der Gegenwart: Hypertonie, physische Erschöpfung und Wirbelsäulen-Beschwerden sind hierbei typische Erkrankungen der externas, wohingegen Gastritis, Lebererkrankungen und dauerhafte Kopfschmerzen typische Erkrankungen sind, unter denen die internas stärker leiden. Auch wenn sich die gesamte Anzahl derjenigen empregadas domésticas, die früher unter keinen Beschwerden litten im Vergleich zum aktuellen Zustand extrem gesenkt hat (nämlich von 79,2% auf 6,1%, d.h. eine Zunahme der Beschwerden von 20,8% vor der Empregada-Tätigkeit auf 93,9% gegenwärtig), so sind immer noch die internas in der Mehrzahl diejenigen, die hier häufiger unter keinen Beschwerden leiden. Diese Feststellungen werden auch anhand ihrer subjektiven Beurteilung des gesamten gesundheitlichen Wohlbefindens vor dem Arbeitsbeginn als bezahlte Hausarbeiterinnen und gegenwärtig z.T. bestätigt (Tab. 1).

Tab. 1
Subjektive Beurteilung des allgemeinen Gesundheitszustandes vor dem Anfang der beruflichen Tätigkeit als Empregada Doméstica und gegenwärtig

Beurteilung	Internas %		Externas %		Total %	
	vorher	jetzt	vorher	jetzt	vorher	jetzt
sehr unwohl	4,6%	10,8%	4,7%	26,2%	4,7%	18,5%
unwohl	6,2%	18,5%	-	15,4%	3,1%	16,9%
teils,teils	15,4%	23,1%	12,5%	15,4%	14,0%	19,2%
wohl	20,0%	32,3%	15,6%	18,5%	17,8%	25,4%
sehr wohl	53,8%	15,4%	67,2%	24,6%	60,5%	20,0%

Gesamte Summe jeweils=100,0%

Die Vergangenheit wird in der Regel von den empregadas domésticas, auch wenn es sich um andere Fragen handelt, als eher positiv und besser beurteilt als die Gegenwart, dies lässt sich hierdurch noch einmal bestätigen. Sowohl internas als auch externas, obgleich die letzteren stärker, beurteilen ihren früheren Gesundheitszustand als wesentlich besser als jetzt. Dies bestätigt sich sowohl anhand der Betrachtung des Sich-"Sehr Unwohl" und des Sich-"Sehr Wohl"-Fühlens. Dafür können wir die größere "Offenheit" über Krankheiten zu sprechen, die in Brasilien vorherrscht, als Grund anführen: Krank sein ist etwas, was verstanden und in der Regel respektiert wird. Das Nicht-Gesund-Sein und die Art der Erkrankung, soweit es keine ansteckende Krankheit ist, werden mit geringerer Hemmung zugegeben, was Gesundheitsbeschwerden zum häufigen Gesprächsthema, vor allem in den unterprivilegierten sozio-ökonomischen Schichten macht. Eindeutig bei beiden Gruppen ist jedoch die gesamte Verschlechterung ihres gesundheitlichen Zustandes.

"Die Arbeit als doméstica im Familienhaus (=casa de família) vernichtet uns (physisch)" (Isabela/externa)

Die allgemeinen Veränderungen des Gesundheitszustandes aufgrund der Auswirkungen der Arbeit auf die Gesamtgesundheit der empregada können u.a. als Effekt der Expositionsdauer in dem Empregada Doméstica-Beruf interpretiert werden (vgl. FRESE 1983, S.14-21). Dies würde hinsichtlich der Gesundheit bedeuten, dass der Effekt der Arbeitssituation und Arbeitsbedingungen der empregadas domésticas auf ihren allgemeinen gesundheitlichen Zustand um so stärker einwirkt, desto länger sie unter solchen Bedingungen leben und arbeiten. Es handelt sich also um das, was man in der Umgangssprache "Berufskrankheiten" nennen würde.

Bei einer Analyse der gesamten Lebens- und Arbeitssituation der beiden Empregada Doméstica-Gruppen können wir feststellen, dass viele ihrer Beschwerden unmittelbar mit ihren Arbeitsbedingungen in Zusammenhang stehen. Hierunter können wir die hohe Anzahl von Beschwerden rechnen wie z.B. psychische und physische Erschöpfung, Muskel- und Gliederschmerzen, Wirbelsäulenschmerzen, Krampfaderentstehung und -Schmerzen, Allergien (insb. an den Händen als Hauterkrankungen werden nach KÜPPER & STOLZ-WILLIG [1988, S.65,76,78] eindeutig durch chemische Reinigungsmittel, die bei der Putzarbeit verwendet werden, verursacht), etc.. Diese Beschwerden kamen aber in den Ausführungen der domésticas über ihre frühere Gesundheit kaum vor.

"Als doméstica hast Du nur Wert, wenn Du gesund bist. Wenn wir krank werden, haben wir keinen Wert mehr" (Valéria/externa).

Ein wichtiger Bestandteil für den Einfluss der Arbeit auf Gesundheit und Krankheit stellen die sozialen Beziehungen am Arbeitsplatz dar. Auch wenn viele domésticas ihre Beziehung zu den patroes (=Arbeitgeber) und ihre gesamte Situation am Arbeitsplatz positiv beurteilt haben, spielen dennoch Ambivalenz zu und Rollenkonflikte mit den patroes sowie schlechte Behandlung am Arbeitsplatz eine wichtige Rolle in ihrer alltäglichen Arbeitswelt. Diese Merkmale können als körperlich belastende Arbeitsstressoren wirken und das Erkrankungsrisiko erhöhen. Auch das Erleben von Entfremdungsgefühlen am Arbeitsplatz, wie es von zahlreichen domésticas berichtet wird, kann als zusätzlich negativer Einfluss angeführt werden, der auf ihre Gesundheit einwirkt. Hinsichtlich der angegebenen gegenwärtigen Erkrankungen der empregadas domésticas, erkennen wir, dass viele dieser Erkrankungen in Zusammenhang mit ihrer gesamten Lebensführung stehen. Die schlechte Wohnsituation, die prekäre Ernährungslage, der intensive psychosoziale Stress, die häufigen Schwangerschaften und Abtreibungen, etc. sind wirksame Faktoren, die auf ihre somatische Gesundheit Einfluss haben und im Laufe der Zeit zu chronischen gesundheitlichen Störungen führen. Viele der Beschwerden der empregadas domésticas erlangen nach ihrer akuten Entstehung Charakteristika von chronischen Erkrankungen, wie beispielsweise im Falle der Hyper- und Hypotonie und des Rheumatismus. Trotz aller Hinweise, die statistisch anhand ihrer eigenen Beurteilungen zusammengestellt wurden, gaben die empregadas domésticas kein eigentliches Gefühl des Krankseins zu, und zwar war dies das Empfinden von 83,8% von ihnen, darunter 83,1% (N=54) internas und 84,6% (N=55) externas.

Gesundheit unter spezifisch weiblichen Aspekten

Bei den Determinanten von psychischer und somatischer Gesundheit/Krankheit der afrobrasilianischen empregadas domésticas sind die spezifischen weiblichen Gesundheitsrisiken herzuvorheben. Früh-, Spät- und häufige Schwangerschaften, Geburten, Stillzeiten, kurze Geburtsabstände, große Kinderzahl, natürliche und provozierte Aborte, Fehlgeburten, die Doppelrolle als Alleinernährerin und Alleinerzieherin ihrer eigenen und "adoptierten" Kinder, etc. sind nur einige der Risiken, denen die Frauen in ihrer Sexualität und sozialen Stellung in den unteren ökonomischen und Bildungsschichten der brasilianischen Gesellschaft ausgesetzt sind, falls nur eine schwache körperliche (physiologische) und seelische Gesundheit sowie soziale und emotionale Geborgenheit vorhanden sind (vgl. hierzu DIESFELD 1989, S.31F; CARNEIRO & ROLAND 1990).

Sexualität und Familienplanung

Sexuelle Aufklärung auf einer demokratischen und breiten Basis, die für alle Bildungs- und Sozialschichten in der Gesundheitserziehung förderlich ist, existiert in Brasilien kaum. Über Sexualität wird in den unterpriviligierten Schichten kaum gesprochen, obwohl dieses Thema in den Familien der anderen Schichten zum Teil ebenfalls als Tabu behandelt wird, worum sich dann viele Mythen und "stories" ranken (vgl. QUINTAS 1986). Im Falle der afrobrasilianischen empregadas domésticas finden wir bei 63,1% (N=82) eine völlig fehlende sexuelle Aufklärung (darunter 55,4% [N=36] internas und 70,7% [N=46] externas), was insb. im Leben von Frauen viele negative Konsequenzen mit sich bringt. Die fast vollkommene Unkenntnis über ihren eigenen Körper und dessen biologische Funktionen bewirkt eine psycho-sexuelle Entwicklung voller ungewollter Schwangerschaften, Abtreibungen, Fehlen an sexueller Befriedigung, Schuldgefühle wegen ihres sexuellen Verhaltens und wegen ihrer Unwissenheit. Diese negativen Gefühle hinsichtlich ihrer eigenen weiblichen Sexualität werden oftmals über Generationen fortgepflanzt, was u.a. auch eine widersprüchliche Beziehung zu der einerseits "armen, liebevollen Mutter" und andererseits "schuldigen, ignoranten Mutter" hervorruft.

"Über Sexualität hat meine Mutter nie mit mir gesprochen. Sie mochte solche Themen nicht. Du weißt, es ist diese Ignoranz in der "roça (Im Hinterland)" (Marlise/interna).

Das Schuldgefühl und die Ablehnung dieser Frauen gegenüber den verschiedenen Gegebenheiten ihrer weiblichen Sexualität wie Menstruation, Schwangerschaft, Menopause und sexueller Befriedigung umfasst ihr ganzes Leben und bewirkt u.a. eine große Unzufriedenheit mit ihrem eigenen Körper und mit sich selbst, was auch mit Problemen wie Aborten, unregelmäßiger Menstruation, Periodenschmerzen, dauerhaften Blutungen, etc. verbunden ist.

"Ah, ich bete zu Gott, damit er diese ekelhafte Sache (die Menstruation) von mir wegnimmt. An diesem Tag werde ich froh sein" (Ana Maria/externa).

"Ich glaube, dass ich keine Befriedigung mit Männern finde, weil ich schon seit Kind so häufig vergewaltigt wurde. Ich kann nur mit mir selbst... Ich weiß, dass es schlecht ist... Meistens weine ich nachher" (Lucineide/interna).

Sexuelle Erfahrungen und Kenntnisse werden nach ihren Worten später durch die Welt oder durch den männlichen Partner erworben, der anhand seiner Wünsche und Vorstellungen diese Frauen über das 'korrekte" weibliche sexuelle Verhalten belehrt.

"Über Sex habe ich etwas mit meinem Mann gelernt, nachdem ich geheiratet habe" (Eliane/interna).

"Mit 18 Jahren wusste ich immer noch nicht, wie man ein Kind bekommt. Ich glaubte noch an den Storch. Ich bin eben zu blöd" (Eunice/externa).

Im diesem Kontext werden diese afrobrasilianischen empregadas domésticas häufig ungewollt und/oder ungeplant schwanger. Die sexuelle Gewalt entweder seitens des Arbeitgebers oder des eigenen Ehemannes/Partners, die ihre Sexualität ohne Einschränkungen ausüben und häufig gegen den Wunsch der Frau, ihr schlechter gesundheitlicher Zustand, die von Vorurteilen geladene soziale Umgebung der Frauen und insgesamt die schlechten sozialen Bedingungen für Alleinerziehende, zwingen sie häufig eine Abtreibung zu vollziehen, was 42,3% (N=55) aller empregadas domésticas, darunter 38,5% (N=25) internas und 46,1% (N=30) externas, betraf.

"Bei meiner ersten sexuellen Beziehung wurde ich gleich schwanger. Ich wollte es nicht, aber..." (Betinha/interna).

"... Dann wurde ich schwanger und meine Familie hat mich gezwungen eine Abtreibung zu machen..." (Marineide/interna).

Obwohl die Anzahl der zugegebenen Abtreibungen extrem hoch ist, nämlich 42,3% aller Fälle, muss man hier trotzdem mit einer hohen Dunkelziffer rechnen. Die Wahrheit zu sagen über ein Problem wie Abtreibung in einem Land, wo dies gesetzlich verboten ist und auch sozial, moralisch und insb. von der Kirche (Brasilien ist das größte katholische Land der Erde!) verurteilt wird, bedeutet für diese Frauen in jeder Hinsicht ein großes Risiko auch für ihre psychische Gesundheit. Aufgrund der bereits angesprochenen Einschränkungen für eine freiwillige Abtreibung in Brasilien wurde dieser Akt von vielen anderen empregadas zugegeben, aber nicht im Sinne einer bewussten Entscheidung sondern als "biologischer natürlicher Zufall". Durch die harten Lebensbedingungen dieser Frauen (Wasser tragen, kiloweise Wäsche mit den Händen stundenlang waschen, große Arbeitsbelastung, schlechte Ernährung, etc.) kann nicht verneint werden, dass einige von ihnen "natürlich" abtreiben. Dennoch nutzen viele Frauen diese Lebensbedingungen auch manchmal bewusst, um eine "natürliche" Abtreibung zu provozieren ohne deshalb beschuldigt werden zu können oder sich schuldig fühlen zu müssen (vgl. QUINTAS 1986; SCAVONE 1989; REDLICH & FREEDMAN 1970, S.645).

Obwohl es in Brasilien kaum Schätzungen über durchgeführte Abtreibungen gibt, entspricht die Anzahl der angegebenen Abtreibungen unserer Studie einem noch höheren Niveau als in den anderen wenigen Studien. Im Jahre 1980 wurden in den Hospitälern des INAMPS ca. 12,7% Frauen aufgenommen, die unter Post-Abtreibungsbeschwerden litten. Die "Fundaçao Oswaldo Cruz" hat im Jahre 1981 eine kleine Studie mit 50 Favela-Bewohnerinnen von Manguinhos (RJ) durchgeführt und kam zu dem Ergebnis, dass 38% (N=19) der Frauen bereits eine provozierte Abtreibung vollgezogen hatten (vgl. LABRA 1987, S.80f). Die Häufigkeit von Abtreibungen ist aus der Tab. 2 zu ersehen.

Tab. 2
Häufigkeit der Abtreibungen

Häufigkeit	Internas % (N)	Externas % (N)	Total % (N)
1	48,0% (12)	43,3% (13)	45,5% (25)
2-3	44,0% (11)	44,0% (11)	40,0% (22)
4-6	4,0% (1)	10,0% (3)	7,2% (4)
9-11	4,0% (1)	10,0% (3)	7,2% (4)
	100,0% (25)	100,0% (30)	100,0% (55)

Anzahl der Missing= 75

Das finanzielle Hindernis, da die (verbotenen) Abtreibungskliniken sehr teuer sind, bewirkt bei diesen Frauen, dass sie meistens entweder alleine oder unter sehr schlechten hygienischen Verhältnissen bei "curiosas" (=Engelmacherinnen) ihre Abtreibung durchführen. Der Besuch von traditionellen Heiler/innen, die mit Gebeten, "garrafadas" (=Pflanzenabsuden. Vgl. CASCUDO 1979, S.357f) etc. arbeiten, sowie das Aufsuchen eines Apothekers, der meistens Abtreibungen mit Hilfe von Spritzen einleitet, sind einige der zur Verfügung stehenden "Lösungen" dieser Frauen. Eine große Anzahl der empregadas, die bereits abgetrieben haben, nämlich 36,4% (N=20), davon 36% (N=9) internas und 36,6% (N=11) externas, haben ihre Abtreibung allein vollzogen. SZWARCWALD & CASTILHO (1989) zeigen, dass die Hypertonie, die Hämorrhagien, Wochenbettinfektionen und Abtreibungen die vier Hauptfaktoren für die Sterblichkeit der brasilianischen gebärenden Frauen sind (op. cit., S.141). Über die allein durchgeführten Abtreibungen vgl. die eindrucksvolle Beschreibung der Abtreibung bei der afrobrasilianischen empregada doméstica SILVA (1983); siehe auch LABRA 1987, S.72f; SCAVONE 1989, S.286,290.

Brasilianische Frauen, die eine Abtreibung allein vollziehen, verwenden eine Vielzahl von sehr gefährlichen Mitteln. Es sind meistens verschiedene Tees (z.B. "cabacinho", "fedegoso", "parreira", "alfazema", etc.; häufig gemischt mit Zuckerrohrschnaps oder Alkohol) oder die Einführung von spitzen Gegenständen in den Uterus (wie z.B. Stricknadeln, Kleiderbügel, Stücke vom Wasserschlauch und auch unterschiedliche Pflanzenwurzeln). Diese Abtreibungsgebräuche verursachen oft Hämorrhagien, starke Infektionen und sogar den Tod, obwohl keine diesbezüglichen offiziellen Sterblichkeitsraten bekannt sind, was das Fehlen an Interesse auf der politischen und medizinischen Ebene deutlich macht.

Zu den Hauptmotiven einer provozierten Abtreibung können hier folgende Faktoren gerechnet werden: die schon große Anzahl eigener Kinder, beide Altersextreme der Frau, prekäre Gesundheit, Fehlen eines Partners, Familienstand (69,2% unserer Stichprobe war ledig), schlechte Wohn- und Ernährungssituation, prekäre finanzielle Lage, Angst eine "verbotene" Schwangerschaft auszutragen und Angst vor einer fristlosen Entlassung. Viele empregadas domésticas verstecken sich und ihre Schwangerschaft monatelang vor ihren patroes voller Angst entlassen zu werden, obgleich solche Entlassungen gesetzlich verboten sind. Während der Feldforschung begegnete die Verfasserin einer Schwangeren (im siebten Monat) mit noch zwei kleinen Kindern, die in Ipanema auf der Straße wohnte. Diese afrobrasilianische ex-empregada doméstica wurde fristlos entlassen als bekannt wurde, dass sie schwanger war. Ein paar Wochen später wurde ihr Partner tödlich angefahren und sie war, von heute auf morgen, obdachlos. Sie hätte das Kind abgetrieben, wenn die Schwangerschaft nicht so weit fortgeschritten gewesen wäre. Sie fand ihre "Lösung" in der Abgabe des Kindes gleich nach der Geburt.

In diesem Zusammenhang muss betont werden, dass Abtreibung bei diesen Frauen als ein letzter extremer Ausweg gesucht wird, aber dennoch als ein sehr traumatisierendes Erlebnis zurückbleibt und von ihnen häufig bewusst oder unbewusst als Kindesmord empfunden wird. In einer katholischen Gesellschaft, in der von den Frauen mindestens die Geburt eines Kindes erwartet wird, bedeuten Aborte eine tiefgreifende psychosoziale und gesundheitliche Belastung, die zu einer Senkung des Selbstwertgefühls und zu innerpsychischen Konflikten und Ängsten führt.

Familienplanung wurde in beiden Empregadas Domésticas-Gruppen meistens in Form der Tubenligatur durchgeführt, was für viele Frauen zu einer Verschlechterung ihres gesundheitlichen Allgemeinzustandes geführt hat. Diese Art der Sterilisierung ist in Brasilien stark verbreitet, wo schon 14% der Frauen auf diese Art sterilisiert wurden, und dies auch im Falle von relativ jungen Frauen. In diesem Zusammenhang zeigen SZWARCWALD & CASTILHO (1989), dass 48% der Frauen aus einer Favela in Rio de Janeiro sterilisiert wurden, bevor sie 30 Jahre alt waren (op. cit., S.138). Insgesamt sind bereits 27% der brasilianischen Frauen sterilisiert worden (vgl. SANTOS-STUBBE 1993; CEAP, 1990). Eindeutig ist u.a. auch, dass ca. 85% der sterilisierten Brasilianerinnen Afro-Frauen und Indianerinnen bzw. Mestizinnen sind. Auch das Experiment mit dem neuen Verhütungsmittel Norplant, das für 5 Jahre im Körper der Frau wirken soll, wurde in der Regel (wie in den USA) mit armen aus diesen ethnischen Gruppen stammenden Frauen durchgeführt (vgl. Taz, 2.07.1993, S.13; CEAP, 1990). Die Verwendung der Pille als Verhütungsmittel wurde von vielen verneint, entweder aufgrund der körperlichen Unverträglichkeit oder wegen eines Verbots des Ehemannes/Partners oder auch wegen der hohen Kosten. Meistens greifen sie auf die verschiedenen traditionellen Empfängnisverhütungsmittel zurück, was dann häufig in der Fachliteratur und von den Familienplanungsexperten dahingehend interpretiert wird, als ob sie überhaupt keine Empfängnismittel benutzen würden und diese Verhütungstechniken deshalb als unbedeutend und unwirksam unterschätzt werden (vgl. DIESFELD 1989, S.36).

Ätiologische Krankheitsvorstellungen der afrobrasilianischen Empregadas Domésticas
In Brasilien gibt es eine Vielzahl von ätiologischen Krankeitsvorstellungen, die je nach ethnischer Gruppenbindung bevorzugt werden. Im Falle der afrobrasilianischen empregadas domésticas, finden wir eine Reihe von angegebenen Gründen wie psychologische, magisch/spirituelle, physikalisch-chemische und somatische für ihren verschlechterten Gesundheitszustand, wie wir aus der folgenden Tab. 3 ersehen können, obgleich häufig auch mehrere Erklärungen angegeben bzw. kombiniert wurden.

Die Hauptursachen für die Krankheitsentstehung der empregadas können wir nach PFEIFFER (1971) unter die natürlichen Ursachen einordnen. Der physikalisch-chemische Teilaspekt 'Reinigungsmittel' oder der häufige Wechsel zwischen warm (in der Küche beim Kochen) und kalt (Wäsche waschen) sind in einer Wechselwirkung mit Ursachen wie familiären Problemen, körperlichen und physischen Anstrengungen, etc. verbunden. Bei diesen natürlichen Ursachen können wir feststellen, dass die Arbeit von den empregadas als die wichtigste Ursache für ihre Krankheiten angesehen wird, und, dass deren Bedingungen ebenfalls Ursache für Erkrankungen sind.

Unter diesen natürlichen Ursachen werden auch somatisch-gesundheitliche und psychologische Aspekte verstanden, die für sie sowohl symbolisch/magische als auch psychische Bedeutung haben wobei beispielsweise die Tubenligatur, Depression, "zerrüttete Nerven" oder die "schwierige Persönlichkeit" als entscheidend für die Krankheitsentstehung angesehen werden. Ortsveränderung oder Verlust von Körperbestandteilen werden nach BARTELS (1893) auch als natürliche Ursachen für Krankheiten gedeutet (apud STUBBE 1979, S.22). Diese ätiologischen Vorstellungen gelten in vielerlei Hinsicht für die Erklärung körperlicher und psychischer Erkrankungen sowie für psychosomatische.

Tab. 3
Ätiologische Krankheitsvorstellungen

Krankheitsätiologie[a]	Internas % (N)	Externas % (N)	Total % (N)
wegen der Arbeit[b]	23,1% (15)	38,5% (25)	30,7% (40)
wegen der Ernährung[c]	18,5% (12)	16,9% (11)	17,7% (23)
wegen der alltäglichen Anstrengungen[d]	12,3% (8)	16,9% (11)	14,6% (19)
wegen spiritueller Probleme	9,2% (6)	15,4% (10)	12,3% (16)
wegen der zerrütteten Nerven	12,3% (8)	10,7% (7)	11,5% (15)
Anhäufung und Kontrast von/zwischen Hitze und Kälte	10,7% (7)	12,3% (8)	11,5% (15)
weiß nicht	10,7% (7)	3,1% (2)	6,9% (9)
wegen der chemischen Reinigungsmittel	9,2% (6)	1,5% (1)	5,4% (7)
wegen der familiären Probleme	1,5% (1)	9,2% (6)	5,4% (7)
viele Sorgen und Ärger	6,1% (4)	4,6% (3)	5,4% (7)
Erkrankungen sind hereditär	3,1% (2)	4,6% (3)	3,8% (5)
wegen der Tubenligatur	3,1% (2)	4,6% (3)	3,8% (5)
Stress	6,1% (4)	-	3,1% (4)
wegen des Rauchens und Trinkens	4,6% (3)	1,5% (1)	3,1% (4)
eigene schwierige Persönlichkeit bzw. Charakter	4,6% (3)	-	3,1% (4)
wegen emotionaler Probleme[e]	3,1% (2)	1,5% (1)	3,1% (4)

a Darunter wurden noch finanzielle Probleme (von einer externa) und das Fehlen an körperlicher Bewegung (von einer interna) als Krankheitsursache angegeben.
b Zuviel Arbeit, Probleme mit den patroes und wenig Schlaf aufgrund der Arbeitszeitregelung waren hier die Gründe.
c Schlechte, irreguläre und wenige Ernährung, übermäßiger Kaffeekonsum und die Aufnahme von kalter Nahrung wurden in diesem Zusammenhang als Krankheitserklärung genannt.
d Hierbei wurden sowohl geistige als auch physische Anstrengungen genannt.
e Depression, das Alleinsein und Probleme in der Liebe wurden hier erwähnt.

12,3% aller empregadas deuteten in einer direkten Form die Entstehung ihrer Erkrankungen aus einer solchen spirituellen/magischen Vorstellung heraus. In der Aussage "wegen spiriritueller Probleme" ist hauptsächlich ein Glauben enthalten, der eng mit den afrobrasilianischen Vorstellungen von Seele, Besessenheit, Opfer und Opfergabe, Geister, Zauber, schwarzer Magie und religiösen Pflichten verbunden ist. Diese Aspekte wirken auf die Individuen sowohl von außen nach innen sowie umgekehrt ein. Die Vernachlässigung der Opfergaben, luzide Besessenheit aufgrund von Verpflichtungen gegenüber jeweiligen Geistern (=cobrança dos santos), sowie schadende Besessenheit, "encosto" (=von einem Geist berührt zu werden), Rachezauber (=coisa feita, macumba, ebó) und böser Blick (vgl. CASCUDO 1979), die von anderen gegen die empregadas gerichtet waren, wurden u.a. angegeben als Gründe für die Krankheiten (vgl. LOYOLA 1984). Viele empregadas sahen in ihrer Krankheitsentstehung ihre eigene Schuld nämlich die Forderungen bestimmter Geister nicht erfüllt zu haben. Im o.g. Fall leiden sie vor allem unter den "negativen" Persönlichkeitsmerkmalen des Geistes, wobei diese Charaktere unvereinbar mit ihrer eigenen Persönlichkeit bleiben, was dann der Grund für die Entstehung zahlreicher Probleme und auch Erkrankungen bzw. Störungen sei. Eine Verbesserung des Krankheitszustandes tritt erst dann ein, sobald sie, auf der religiösen Ebene -hierbei können Fachärzte nicht helfen- den/die Heiler/in oder Pastor aufsuchen und die von ihnen geforderten Aufgaben erfüllen (z.B. sich gesundbeten zu lassen, ein Opfer zu geben, etc.). Im Hinblick auf die magischen und natürlichen Krankheitsvorstellungen können wir feststellen, dass die Krankheitskonzepte stark miteinander verflochten und deshalb von großer Komplexität sind. Die Verflechtung dieser ätiologischen Vorstellungen verändert und begründet ihren Krankheitszustand in einer sehr breiten Form, da von ihnen alle Lebensbereiche berücksichtigt werden sowie verschiedene Erklärungsmöglichkeiten, die von der biologischen bis hin zur religiösen Sphäre reichen, und zwar ohne große Konflikte zwischen den verschiedenen Erklärungsformen. Pragmatisch gesehen geben die o.g. aus verschiedenen Ursprüngen stammenden ätiologischen Krankheitsvorstellungen den empregadas einen größeren Spielraum bei ihrer Suche nach therapeutischen Maßnahmen, da diese sich ebenfalls an verschiedenen Heilungssystemen orientieren (naturwissenschaftliche Sicht, religiöse, etc.) und sie flexibler für die Akzeptanz der zugänglichen Heilungsverfahren macht.

Therapien und Heilungssysteme
Aufgrund der prekären Gesundheitsversorgung in den städtischen und staatlichen Krankenhäusern Brasiliens, die für die breite Bevölkerung offenstehen, sehen sich die unterprivilegierten Bevölkerungsgruppen gezwungen verschiedene Wege für die Heilung ihrer Erkrankungen oder für die Erhaltung ihres Gesundheitszustandes auszuwählen. Dadurch entstehen unterschiedliche Gesundheits- bzw. Krankheitsversorgungssyteme, die parallel zu dem offiziellen System koexistieren und je nach Bedarf und Möglichkeit der Patienten gleichzeitig oder nacheinander aufgesucht werden. Wir können hier auch Analogien zum Versorgungssystem, das De Jong (1987) für Guinea-Bissau beschrieben hat, für die städtische ökonomische Randbevölkerung Brasiliens herstellen. Es handelt sich hierbei um die Koexistenz eines offiziellen Gesundheitssystems der westlichen wissenschaftlichen Medizin (professional sector), eines "popular sector", bei dem die Behandlungen durch Laien, Eltern, Großeltern und Dorfälteste erfolgen und eines "folk sector", in dem die Versorgung durch spezialisierte traditionelle Heiler/innen durchgeführt wird. Diese neben dem offiziellen parallel laufenden Systeme entsprechen im wesentlichen Teil einer "traditionellen" Medizin, die in ihrem Kern nicht den naturwissenschaftlichen Charakter der westlichen Medizin besitzt. Es handelt sich um eine Art von Versorgung, die aus dem ursprünglichen Kulturgut der indigenen und afrobrasilianischen Bevölkerung Brasiliens stammt, und in der Regel als komplementär oder alternativ zu der mangelhaften offiziellen Versorgung im westlichen Sinne verwendet wird. Die Empregadas domésticas, die in die populären Versorgungtraditionen eingebunden sind, versuchen in der Regel vorerst ihren Gesundheitszustand selbst zu verbessern indem sie sich "Medikamente" selbst verschreiben. Da Heilung in Brasilien auf allen diesen Ebenen hauptsächlich im kurativen und kaum im präventiven Sinne betrieben wird, greifen die afrobrasilianischen empregadas domésticas um sich zu kurieren in 69,5% auf Selbstbehandlung vor allem auf phytotherapeutischer Basis zurück: Die Selbstheilungsversuche der empregadas sind in allen ihren Formen ein wesentlicher Bestandteil der Volks- bzw. traditionellen Medizin, die mit einem eigenen Verständnis der Heilung anfängt und erst dann andere Spezialisten für die Weiterbehandlung aufsucht, wenn sich der erste eigene Versuch als nicht erfolgreich erweist. In dieser Weise versuchen die domésticas hauptsächlich ihren somatischen Zustand zu verbessern, aber auch den psychischen. Es werden, nach ihren Angaben, Kräutertees (=chás

caseiros), Salben oder eigene Hauspräparate (z.B. Sirup, Spülungen, etc.) für die Behandlung von Leberbeschwerden, Allergien, Nerven, Grippe oder gynäkologischen Beschwerden etc. vorbereitet und angewendet. Wie bereits oben dargestellt, werden "seelische Probleme" bzw. Erkrankungen von den empregadas domésticas oftmal als "problemas espirituais" (=spirituelle Probleme) interpretiert, bei denen eine Selbstbehandlung schwerfällt. Aufgrunddessen greifen die empregadas in diesen Fällen dann auf Gebete, auf Anzünden von Kerzen, Kräuterbäder (=banhos de ervas. Vgl. CAMARGO 1988) aber hauptsächlich auf Räucherungen (=defumadores) zurück, dies betrifft 33,1% (N=43) aller afrobrasilianischen empregadas domésticas, darunter 24,6% (N=16) internas und 41,5% (N=27) externas. Diese Handlung ist entscheidend für die Entfernung von bösen Geistern und negativen Energien, die sich im Hause der Patientin ausgebreitet haben oder sich in ihrem Körper bzw. ihrer Seele befinden.

Bei diesen Formen von Selbstbehandlung bzw. Selbstheilungsversuchen der empregadas spielt das traditionelle Wissen der eigenen Familie, Verwandten und Nachbarn eine wichtige Rolle sowohl für die Diagnoseerstellung als auch für die Art der therapeutischen Maßnahme (vgl. DUARTE 1988, S.147). Da ca. 70% der empregadas domésticas dieser Studie nicht aus der Stadt Rio stammen, bringen sie eine Reihe von volksmedizinischen Kenntnissen mit, die sie aus ihrer ursprünglichen Region mitgebracht und unter Anleitung in der Regel der Mutter oder Großmutter und seltener durch männliche Familienmitglieder erworben haben. Dieses ethnomedizinische Wissen ist von grundlegender Bedeutung für die Bewohner des Landesinneren, wo es oftmals kaum eine Möglichkeit gibt nach der offiziellen wissenschaftlichen ("westlichen") Medizin behandelt zu werden. Vorher oder während des Aufsuchens des offiziellen Gesundheitssystems bemühen sich die empregadas domésticas noch bei verschiedenen anderen Instanzen um ihre Heilung. Diese synkretistischen bzw. dualen therapeutischen Versorgungssysteme funktionieren in einer Erfolgsabhängigkeit voneinander, da das Hauptziel die Heilung oder die Verringerung des Leidens ist, und es weniger wesentlich ist in welchem dieser Systeme dies erreicht wird. In den "evangelischen" Sekten us-amerikanischer Herkunft, die sich in der Regel in Brasilien als Kirchen konstituieren, und von den empregadas domésticas häufig besucht werden, werden andere Religionsbekenntnisse stark abgelehnt und bekämpft, vor allem die afrobrasilianischen Religionen mit ihren Inkorporations- und Besessenheitsritualen. Nichtsdestotrotz praktizieren diese evangelischen Pastoren "Heilungen" (vor allem bei den "Pentecostais" =Pfingstbewegung), insb. von seelischen Erkrankungen (durch Exorzismus, Entfernung von Geistern und sogar Inkorporation), mit Hilfe von Techniken, die oftmals an die in den Afro-Kulten bekannten, erinnern. Ebenfalls fungieren diese Pastoren als (Psycho-)Therapeuten, indem sie oftmals mit den Mitgliedern ihrer Gemeinde Gespräche und Beratungen durchführen. Indirekt berichteten einige wenige domésticas, dass sie bei "Problemen" (in gesundheitlicher oder privater Hinsicht) diese dem Pastor mitteilen und um seine Hilfe und Ratschläge bitten. Loyola (1984) berichtet in ihrem Buch von Pastoren, die bei der Kirche eine eigene Praxis betreiben und bei somatischen und psychischen Fragen konsultiert werden, obgleich "psychische Probleme" von ihnen oftmals auf das Religiöse hingelenkt werden. Ein wesentlicher Weg im spezifischen sozio-kulturellen Support-System der afrobrasilianischen empregadas domésticas besteht aber in den "magischen" traditionellen Konsultationen, wobei dabei hauptsächlich der religiöse Charakter der Behandlung im Vordergrund steht. In 49,2% (N=64) aller Fälle, darunter 43,1% (N=28) internas und 55,4% (N=36) externas, suchen die empregadas domésticas solche religiösen Heiler/innen, "maes ou pais de santo" (=Oberpriester/innen afrobrasilianischer Kulte), "erveiros e erveiras" (=Pflanzenhändler/innen und Pflanzendoktor), "rezadeiras" (=Gesundbeterinnen), Wahrsagerinnen oder Kartenlegerinnen als Spezialisten/innen für die Lösung bzw. Behandlung ihrer persönlichen und gesundheitlichen Beschwerden auf. Bei diesen Spezialisten/innen handelt es sich um Sachverständige, die anhand unterschiedlicher Mittel sowohl somatische als auch psychische Erkrankungen diagnostizieren, erklären und behandeln können. In der Regel wird diese Versorgung anhand von Naturheilkunde, Opfergaben, Gebeten oder Besessenheitsritualen vollzogen. Empregadas domésticas gehören im Rahmen der berufstätigen weiblichen Bevölkerung populärer Schichten zum Hauptklientel dieses Versorgungssystems wie schon viele Studien über traditionelle Religionen und Gesundheitsversorgung in Brasilien gezeigt haben (LOYOLA 1984; SPINU & THORAU 1994; MONTEIRO 1985). Die traditionelle Gesundheitsversorgung unterscheidet sich von der offiziellen naturwissenschaftlich orientierten medizinischen Versorgung nicht nur hinsichtlich ihres wissenschaftlichen Charakters, sondern auch hinsichtlich ihrer Zugänglichkeit für die empregadas. Die traditionellen Versorgungsdienste funktionieren in der Regel im Hause bzw. in dafür geeigneten Räumen im Garten der Spezialistin, die oftmals in der Nordregion, in den "favelas"

(=Slums) der Südregion und in der Peripherie Rios wohnen, also im geographischen Umkreis der empregadas. Diese Konsultationen sind ökonomisch unvergleichlich günstiger (der Preis wird nach der finanziellen Möglichkeit der Patientin entrichtet), und die Vertrautheit mit dem System, mit den Therapiemitteln, mit der Sprache und kulturellen Eingebundenheit des/der Spezialist/in sind vorhanden im Gegensatz zu der Behandlung nach westlichem Muster. Dies ist einer der Gründe für das häufige Aufsuchen dieses Systems durch die empregadas externas, die in einer Umwelt wohnen, in der dieses Gesundheits-System ein konstitutiver Teil der Versorgungsrealität der Armen ist. Ebenfalls wichtig bei diesen Konsultationen ist die zur Verfügung stehende Zeit für eine Diagnoseerstellung, Untersuchung und Therapie. Hierbei lassen sich die Spezialist/innen viel Zeit, die zu persönlichen Gesprächen und Nachfragen zu der Entstehung des Zustandes genutzt wird. Von großer Wichtigkeit für die kurative Behandlung der Erkrankungen, unter denen die empregadas leiden, ist der Apothekenbesuch. Pharmazeuten bzw. Apothekenpersonal spielen in den großen Zentren Brasiliens eine wesentliche Rolle im Rahmen eines quasi-offiziellen Gesundheitssystems. Ein Apothekenbesuch kann interpretiert werden als ein Versorgungsdienst, der zwischen dem traditionellen und dem offiziellen Versorgungssystem für die empregadas domésticas fungiert, obgleich dieses System für die armen Bevölkerungsschichten der großen Zentren dieselbe Wichtigkeit hat (KROEGER 1992, S.437f).

Der Apothekenbesuch (sowie Arztbesuch) dient in der Regel einer kurativen Behandlung mittels allopathischer Medikamente. Dies lässt sich anhand der aktuellen hohen regelmäßigen allopathischen Medikamentaufnahme der empregadas belegen, die bei 57,7% (N=75) der Fälle liegt, d.h. bei 53,8% (N=35) internas und 61,5% (N=40) externas, und worunter keine Antibabypillen gerechnet werden. Die gegenwärtige Medikamentenaufnahme der empregadas domésticas ist in der Tat noch höher als oben angegeben, wenn wir nach der Art des Arzneimittels fragen, wie z.B. im Falle der Analgetika, die von 51,2% der Befragten regelmäßig eingenommen werden sowie die Herz- und Kreislaufmittel von 20,7% und die Beruhigungsmitteln im Falle von 19,5% von ihnen. Der traditionelle und informelle Weg zu einer Krankheitsbehandlung wird von den empregadas domésticas oftmals gegenüber dem offiziellen Weg aus vielerlei Gründen bevorzugt: Es sind die höheren Kosten des offiziellen Gesundheitssystems, es sind die formellen Schwierigkeiten (z.B. lange Wartezeiten in den langen Schlangen, lange Wartezeiten auf die Termine, wenig Zeit bei den Konsultationen aufgrund des Personalmangels oder des Desinteresses der Ärzte, die ihre Stellung im öffentlichen Gesundheitssystem für die eigene Sicherheit behalten, obgleich sie die meiste Zeit in ihrer eigenen Privatpraxis verbringen, etc.), es sind in vielen Fällen die langen und mühevollen Anfahrtwege und vor allem der Kulturschock, der sich zwischen einer afrobrasilianischen empregada doméstica als Patientin und einem/einer weißen Arzt/in, der im Rahmen einer westlich orientierten Psychologie/Medizin ausgebildet ist und aus den oberen ökonomischen und Bildungsschichten stammt, entwickelt. Sprachbarrieren, unterschiedliche ätiologische und nosologische Erklärungsmodelle, unterschiedliche Weltanschauungen, etc., kurzum interkulturelle Kommunikationsbarrieren, sind nur einige der Faktoren, die das Aufsuchen dieses offiziellen Systems für die empregadas domésticas stark behindern. Das traditionelle, das "inoffizielle" und das offizielle Gesundheitssystem nach dem westlich-naturwissenschaftlichen Muster sind nur Teilsysteme eines breiten Angebots an Gesundheits-/Krankheitsversorgungsdiensten, die den empregadas domésticas zur Verfügung stehen, aber je nach Verfügbarkeit, Akzeptanz der eigenen Vorstellungen von Krankheit, Gesundheit und Heilung, Qualität, Preis, etc. bevorzugt werden. Nicht nur das Arbeitsverhältnis und die persönliche Lebensführung der afrobrasilianischen empregadas domésticas als marginalisierte Frauen in einer klassen- und rassenbezogenen Gesellschaft wie der brasilianischen sind die einzigen Faktoren für ihre Erkrankungen, sondern auch das Fehlen an präventiver Versorgung, die vor allem in den Ländern der sog. Dritten Welt und Schwellen-Ländern für Frauen und ihre Kinder von entscheidender Wichtigkeit ist. Mit sprachlicher Barriere ist hier nicht das allgemeine Verständnis der brasilianisch-portugiesischen Sprache gemeint, sondern der Sinn der fachmedizinisch/psychologischen Termini und insb. die Symbolsprache der Patientinnen, die stark sozio-kulturell und bildungsbedingt konzipiert ist, was für das offizielle System nicht begreifbar ist genausowenig wie umgekehrt.

References

CAMARGO, MARIA THEREZA L. DE A. 1988. *Plantas medicinais e rituais afro-brasilieros*. Sao Paulo.
CARNEIRO, SUELI & ROLAND, EDNA. 1990. A saúde da mulher no Brasil; a perspectiva da mulher negra. *Revista de Cultura Vozes*, 84 (2), mar./abr.:204-210.

CASCUDO,LUIS DA CAMARA. 1958. *Influência africana na lúdica infantil brasiliera*. Rio de Janeiro.
ders., 1979. *Dicionário do folclore brasileiro* (5.ed.). Sao Paulo.
COSTA,JURANDIR F. 1983. *Ordem médica e norma Familiar* (2.ed.). Rio de Janeiro.
CUNHA,BRUNO CARLOS DE A. 1987. *Saúde: A prioridade esquecida*. Petrópolis.
DE JONG,JOOP T.V.M. 1987. *A descent into African psychiatry*. Amsterdam.
DIESFELD,HANS J. 1989. *Gesundheitsproblematik der Dritten Welt*. Darmstadt.
DUARTE,LUIZ FERNANDO D. 1988. *Da vida nervosa nas classes trabalhadoras urbanas* (2. ed.). Rio de Janeiro.
FRESE,MICHAEL. 1983. Der Einfluß der Arbeit auf die Persönlichkeit. Zum Konzept des Handlungsstils in der beruflichen Sozialisation. *Zeitschrift für Sozialisations-forschung und Erziehungssoziologie*, 3.Jg., Hefte 1:11-28.
FREITAS,OCTAVIO. 1935. *Doenças africanas no Brasil*. Sao Paulo.
JORNAL DO BRASIL. 30.9.1990. *Medicamentos populares sao prejudicados*.
KARASCH,MARY C. 1987. *Slave Life in Rio de Janeiro 1808-1850*. New Jersey.
KROEGER,AXEL. 1992. Medizin. WERZ,NIKOLAUS (Hrsg.), *Handbuch der deutschsprachigen Lateinamerikakunde*, pp.429-444. Arnold Bergstraesser Institut Freiburg i.Br.
KÜPPER,BETTINA & STOLZ-WILLIG,BRIGITTE. 1988. *Das bißchen Putzen. Arbeitsbedingungen und Gesundheitsrisiken im Reinigungsgewerbe*. Düsseldorf
LABRA,MARIA ELIANA. 1987. A interrupçao voluntária da gravidez ou aborto induzido. *Controle da natalidade X Planejamento familiar no Brasil*, pp.71-92. Rio de Janeiro.
LOYOLA,MARIA A. 1984. *Médicos e curandeiros. Conflito social e saúde*. Sao Paulo.
MACHADO,ROBERTO, LOUREIRO,ANGELA, LUZ,ROGERIO & KATIA MURICY. 1978. *Danaçao da Norma. Medicina social e constitutiçao da psiquiatria no Brasil*. Rio de Janeiro.
MONTERO,PAULA. 1985. *Da doença a desordem: a magia na umbanda*. Rio de Janeiro.
MURDOCK,GEORGES PETER. 1980. *Theories of illness. A world survey*. Pittsburgh.
PFEIFFER,WOLFGANG. 1971. *Trankulturelle Psychiatrie*. Stuttgart.
ders., 1994. Transkulturelle Psychiatrie. *Ergebnisse und Probleme* (2.Aufl.). Stuttgart.
PFLEIDERER,BEATRIX & BICHMANN,WOLFGANG. 1985. *Krankheit und Kultur. Eine Einführung in die Ethnomedizin*. Berlin.
QUINTAS,FATIMA. 1986. *Sexo e marginalidade. Um estudo sobre a sexualidade feminina em camadas de baixa renda*. Petrópolis.
REDLICH,FREDRICK C. & FREEDMAN,DANIEL X. 1970. *Theorie und Praxis der Psychiatrie*. Frankfurt/M..
SANTOS-STUBBE,CHIRLY DOS & STUBBE, HANNES. 1988. Afrobrazilian culture and clinical psychology. Edited by PELTZER,KARL & EBIGBO,PETER O., *Clinical Psychology in Africa: South of the Sahara, the Caribbean and Afro-Latin American. A Text Book for Universities and Paramedical Schools*, pp.68-79. Chuka Printing Enugu.
SANTOS-STUBBE,CHIRLY DOS. 1989. Banzo: uma nostalgia afro-brasileira. *Journal of African Psychology*, Vol. 1, N°2:8-14.
dies., 1990. Zur Geschichte der "empregadas". *Zeitschrift für Lateinamerika-Wien*, N°38/39:83-92.
dies., 1992. Afrikanische Sklaverei und ihre Auswirkungen auf Gesellschaft und Psychologie in Brasilien. *Psychologie und Geschichte*, 1/2:101-119.
dies., 1995. *Arbeit, Gesundheit und Lebenssituation afrobrasilianischer empregadas domésticas (Hausarbeiterinnen): eine empirische sozialpsychologische Untersuchung*. Frankfurt/M..
dies., 1995. Psychosoziale Probleme afro-brasilianischer Frauen. In PETERS,UWE H., SCHIFFERDECKER,M. & KRAHL,A. (Hrsg.), *150 Jahre Psychiatrie. Eine vielgestaltige Psychiatrie für die Welt von morgen*, pp.190-195. Martini Verlag Köln.
SCAVONE,LUCILA. 1989. Mulheres pesquisando mulheres: uma experiência na área de saúde. Edited by LABRA,MARIA ELIANA, *MULHER, Saúde e Sociedade no Brasil*, pp.277-295. Petrópolis.
SIGAUD,J.F.X. 1844. *Du Climat et des Maladies du Brésil ou Statistique médicale de cet empire*. Paris.
SILVA,FRANCISCA S. DA. 1983. *Ai de vós! Diário de uma doméstica* (2.ed.). Rio de Janeiro.
SPINU,MARINA & THORAU,HENRY. 1994. *Indirekte Trancetherapie in Brasilien. Eine Ethnopsychologische Studie*. Berlin.
STUBBE,HANNES & SANTOS-STUBBE,CHIRLY DOS. 1990. Banzo - eine afrobrasilianische Nostalgie? *Curare*, 13:123-132.
STUBBE,HANNES. 1996. Suizidforschung im Kulturvergleich. *Kölner Beiträge zur Ethnopsychologie u. Transkulturellen Psychologie*, 1:57-77.
ders., 1987. *Geschichte der Psychologie in Brasilien. Von den indianischen und afrobrasi-lianischen Kulturen bis in die Gegenwart*. Berlin.
ders., 1989. Verwitwung und Trauerreaktionen in Brasilien. *Zeitschrift für Psychoso-matische Medizin und Psychoanalyse*, 35, 3:277-288.
ders., 1979. Wie Naturvölker Krankheiten erklären. *Die Medizinische Welt*, 30:342-349.
SZWARCWALD,CÉLIA L. & CASTILHO,EUCLIDES A. DE. 1989. Características da mortalidade da mulher brasileira. Edited by LABRA,MARIA ELIANA, MULHER, *Saúde e Sociedade no Brasil*, pp.135-161. Petrópolis.
VASCONCELOS,EDUARDO M. 1992. Contribuiçao à avaliaçao da estratégia de integraçao do programa de saúde mental no sistema único de saúde no Brasil recente. *Jornal Brasileiro de Psiquiatria*, 41 (6):283-286.
World Health Organization. 1982. *Basic Document*. Genf.

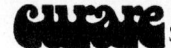

The Two Sides of the Moon. Fertility of Wayana Indian Women and their Crops in the Guyana Amazon
Die beiden Seiten des Mondes. Fertilität der Indianischen Wayana Frauen und die Gewächse im Guyanischen Amazonengebiet

Britta Veth

Abstract: In this article I would like to describe the factors influencing the fertility of Wayana women. The Wayana are Carib Indians living in Brazil, French Guiana and Surinam. In the Wayana view fertility and infertility are temporary phases, that can be manipulated by women themselves, their family and certain specialists. However, manipulation of fertility involves a risk with regard to the children, that are born as a result. The main tasks of the Wayana women are raising the children and practicing agriculture. In order to be fertile and to have fertile gardens women enter into relations with the Moon. The Moon causes menstruation as well as pregnancy. There are two sides to this though: the personification of the moon can also cause infertility in women. In the article the emphasis will be upon fertility in relation to the moon and agriculture. The other factors influencing fertility will be only mentioned shortly.

Zusammenfassung: In diesem Artikel möchte ich die Faktoren, die die Fertilität der Wayana Frauen beeinflussen, beschreiben. Die Wayana sind Karaibische Indiäner, die in Brasilien, im Französischen Guyana und Surinam leben. Die Wayana betrachten Fertilität und Infertilität wie zeitlichen Phasen, die durch die Frauen selbst, ihre Familien und bestimmte Spezialisten manipuliert werden können. Diese Manipulation der Fertilität enthält jedoch ein Risiko in Bezug auf die Kinder, die daraus geboren werden. Die wichtigste Aufgaben der Wayana Frauen sind die Erziehung der Kinder und Gartenbau. Um fruchtbar zu sein und fruchtbare Gärten zu haben gehen die Frauen Beziehungen ein mit dem Mond. Der Mond verursacht einerseits Menstruation und Schwangerschaft; anderseits kann er auch Unfruchtbarkeit bei Frauen verursachen. In diesem Artikel liegt der Nachdruck auf die Fertilität in Beziehung zum Mond und zum Gartenbau. Die andere Faktoren, die Fruchtbarkeit beeinflussen können, werden nur kurz erwähnt.

Keywords: Fertility, Wayana Indian Women, Moon, Horticulture, Guyana Amazon, Cultural Anthropology, Fertilität, Wayana Indianischen Frauen, Mond, Hortikultur, Guyanisches Amazonengebiet, Ethnologie.

Introduction

This research was financed by the 'National Research Assistent Network' and accomodated at the Department of Cultural Anthropology, Utrecht University, The Netherlands.

Even in our western, be it popular, belief the mooncycle has a certain influence on women's menstruation. According to western science the movement of the moon generates the movement of the

Abb. 1
Young Apalai woman taking manioc tubers from her garden to the village.

water on earth, causing the movement of the tides. In popular belief this includes the water in our bodies, influencing the menstrual cycle of women with menstruation taking place at full moon. In this article I would like to describe the special way in which the Wayana Indians have connected the mooncyle to the fertility cycle of women. The principal objective is to present unpublished ethnographic data concerning the Wayana perception of fertility and infertility (During different fieldwork periods in 1986-1987, 1990-1992, 1995 the data presented were collected in the villages Antécume pata and Kutaka in French Guiana, and in Kawem hakan in Surinam.). At the same time the question: to which extent women can control their own fertility, will be our guideline. As in other societies, in the Wayana view only women can be infertile. The Wayana are Carib Indians and inhabit the tropical rainforest of the Amazon. At this moment the population is approximately 1.000 people in total (Boven & Molendijk 1995:47). They live in small villages along the main rivers in the interior of Brazil, French Guiana and Surinam. They provide for their subsistence by practicing agriculture, fishing, hunting and gathering, in this order of importance. Additionally, mainly men work in temporary jobs in mining and construction, and a few women and men hold permanent employment in the schools and clinics. Nowadays their culture shows a mixture of traditional and modern customs, food and products. Our subject, female (in)fertility, will be placed in the larger context of the cosmological relations the Wayana have to maintain. The different tasks and responsibilities in their society are divided along gender. Concisely, men hunt and fish and women rear children and practice agriculture. Accordingly, the Wayana concept of fertility combines procreation with the propagation of plants. Women enter into relations with the Moon in order to be fertile and in order to have prolific gardens (see also MAGAÑA 1988:366,367). There are two sides to this though: the personification of the moon can cause fertility as well as infertility in women. In the article the emphasis will be upon fertility in relation to the moon and agriculture. The other (less important) factors influencing fertility will be only mentioned shortly, for the sake of completeness.

Women's Own Influence on their Fertility

We will start with a woman's own influence on her fertility, which are the many restrictions she has to keep to during menstruation, after an abortion or partition and during pregnancy. In the past, a girl was initiated immediately at her first menstruation, upon which she had to undergo a period of seclusion for about two weeks. Today, girls still are initiated as soon as possible after their first menstruation, but they are no longer kept in seclusion, unless they go through the same large initiation ritual together with the boys. The most remarkable feature of a Wayana initiation ritual is the ant ordeal, during which the initiates are stung all over their body. The numerous food and other restrictions before, during and after the initiation are even more difficult to endure. Each time a girl or woman menstruates, she has to keep to certain restrictions. After an abortion, the same restrictions are applied. The initiation for girls as well as boys marks their social entry in Wayana society. After they have been initiated they are considered marriagable women and men, who can fullfill their respective tasks. When a woman is pregnant, she also has to keep to certain restrictions, as demonstrated in the diagram above. Moreover, she and her family have to keep to many food and other restrictions during pregnancy and even more so after giving birth. These restrictions concern many different kinds of animals and fish, that are not supposed to be consumed, killed or sometimes even looked at during the restriction periods. If a close relative would break such a restriction, the animal concerned would give the baby a disease, because it is the most vulnerable member of the family. According to the Wayana the (shadow)soul of a newborn is not well attached to its physical body yet (see also AHLBRINK 1931). The restrictions a woman has to keep to after she has given birth are exactly the same as the ones she had to keep to after her first menstruation. Only after her first menstruation there are even more. The restrictions after birth also apply to the father of the newborn, its siblings and grandparents and other close relatives. The restrictions mentioned above last from about two weeks till one month. The dietary restrictions might last for several months, depending on the kind of animal or fish. Finally, a woman can influence her own fertility by practicing abortion. There are many different ways to abort. This knowledge women pass on among themselves, along family lines. One way is to cut off all the tubers of a certain (wild) plant at once. As we will see later on, the Wayana conceptualize tubers as babies. One of the plants used to abort like this is a winding herb, that only grows on bitter manioc (Manihot esculenta), the main crop the Wayana cultivate. Women do not use cultivated plants to abort, but only wild plants.

Tab. 1

Taboo for a woman during menstruation & after abortion	Effect
to bathe in the river	attraction of the anaconda spirit
to touch hot peppers	the receiver dies + the tree would die
to touch or feed young pet birds	the birds would not eat anymore + die
to touch a newborn baby	the baby would not eat or grow
to touch wood that is used to burn the deceased	-

(not taboo) to work in the garden	*alïhpe*: black speckles on manioc tubers

Tab. 2

Taboo for a pregnant woman	Effect
to touch hot peppers	the receiver dies + the tree makes tiny fruits without seeds
presence at fish poisoning trip	neutralization of the poison
to touch watermelons	} miscarriage
to touch pottery during fabrication	
to look at wounds	
to drink beer made by someone who has wounds	

Tab. 3

Restrictions for a woman after partition
seclusion to the house
not bathe in or come near the river (but bathe near the house)
not work, only with cotton
not touch hot peppers (on the tree)
not eat any kind of game or fish
diet of tiny fish (*opt*), normally used as bait

The Moon and the Fertility Cycle of Women

In the village Antécume pata, where I lived most of the time, there was only one woman, who had stayed infertile her whole life. By now she had passed the age of fertility and was a widow. According to one shaman she never had conceived any children, because supposedly the moon did not like her. Perhaps because she did not have sweet, but bitter or sour blood. Another informant concluded the moon has never payed her a visit, since she has never menstruated. The Wayana have connected the lunar cycle to the fertility cycle of women, with two different outcomes: menstruation or pregnancy. According to women as well as shamans the moon causes women to menstruate by visiting them the night before in their dreams. This takes place according to one shaman when the moon is a sickle, and according to another shaman, when there is a red halo around the moon. Women as well as shamans described the moon in their dreams as a beautiful young man, his body painted with red dye (The red paint is made of the fruit of the tree Bixa orellana mixed with kalapa (Carapa guianensis) oil as the main ingredients.) and adorned with feather ornaments, including a feathercrown called pumali. Wayana men adorn themselves like this, when they go dancing at a feast. One old woman said the moon also appears as an older man, and according to several young people the moon looks like your lover when he calls on you in your dream. He only pays a visit and asks how you are doing. Among the Wayana when a (young) man wants to declare his love and invite a woman to make love, he does so by visiting her in her camp, to ask how she is doing and for example drink some cassava beer. In the dream the woman just knows it is the moon and that the next day her menstruation will start. When a woman is very old, the moon does not visit her anymore. The moon is also indispensable for making a woman pregnant. This can occur, whether the moon is full or a crescent according to one shaman, or when there is a red halo around the moon for the second time, according to the other shaman. After the moon has impregnated a woman, he visits her husband or lover in his dream and encourages him to make love to the woman. This happens towards the end of the woman's menstruation. When subsequently a woman turns out to be pregnant, then who was it, her husband or the moon, the shaman asks me. It is interesting that the moon addresses the man as his kin in the dream, by saying 'Let us visit that woman, my son'. Babies, that are crying are diverted by pointing at the (full) moon and saying: 'look, your father'. In accordance with MAGAÑA (1988) this seems to implicate the Wayana conceptualize the Moon as the husband of all the women and as the father of all the men and children. I certainly would not like to characterize the moon as all the women's lover rather than husband, since if a woman would make love to the moon in her dream, she would catch a disease and eventually die. According to de Goeje among the Kaliña (Carib Indians on the coast) it is believed the moon 'deflowers' a girl at her first menstruation without her noticing it (DE GOEJE in MAGAÑA 1988).

The Moon and Rejuvenation
Each moon- or menstruation cycle entails rejuvenation for the moon as well as women. In the Wayana belief the personification of the moon grows older depending on its phase or position in the lunar orbit. When the moon is a sickle he is a very young man, at crescent or half moon he is about 25 years old, and at full moon he is an old(er) man, which is about 35 years old. Between new moon and full moon he visits the women. When the moon is waning he grows even older. At new moon this process starts all over again. No wonder that when the moon is a sickle (young) and thus most beautiful, he visits the women. In general, the Wayana equal 'young' with beautiful' and 'old' with 'ugly'. The Wayana consider a young woman, who has never had a child, as very attractive and beautiful and they consider a woman, who has been pregnant and given birth, old and not as attractive as before. After each menstrual period, a woman carries out the following ritual. She rubs her body with red dye made of Bixa orellana, and goes to the river to wash it off. The family of a newborn, initiates, and the family of a deceased, perform the same ritual after their period of seclusion or of mourning in the latter case.

Red paint is the equivalent of blood and also stands for consanguinity (see also BROWN 1986, MAGAÑA 1988). In this case the red dye represents menstrual blood, that gets washed away in the river. Secondly, the red dye symbolizes a tie of consanguinity between the woman and the moon. Thirdly, red paint used in rituals is to imitate skin-changing (HUGH-JONES 1979).

Although the Barasana are Tukano Indians living in Colombia and with a very different social system from the Carib Indians, their use of corporal paints is comparable to that of the Wayana. The Barasana as well as the Wayana utilize two kinds of corporal paints: a red dye made of the fruit of the tree Bixa orellana and black paint made of the fruit of the tree Genipa americana. Red dye is a metaphor for new life and black dye a metaphor for death. According to Christine HUGH-JONES (1979) the Barasana conceptualize menstruation as the skin-changing of a woman. Skin-changing leads to renewal and rejuvenation. This rejuvenation is depicted by rubbing red paint on the body or face and washing it off in the river. The female creator god of the Barasana, who lives in the air, is old and ugly in the evening. In the morning, after she has bathed, she becomes young and beautiful again. She rubs red paint (menstrual blood) on her face, but later removes this together with a thin layer of skin (skin-changing). In this manner the female creator god of the Barasana is comparable with the Moon (god) of the Wayana. Whereas the Barasana god rejuvenates on a daily basis, the Wayana Moon rejuvenates on a monthly basis. After each menstruation, a Wayana woman is young again, like before. However, as one informant told me, menstruation weakens a woman, because she looses blood. This is in accordance with the Wayana idea that people's bodies contain a certain amount of blood. When you loose some, it is not replaced. Whereas the Moon rejuvenates at the beginning of each cycle, women are still young after they have menstruated, but little by little they weaken.

The Origin of the Moon in Mythology

In the Amazonian Indian mythology, the moon stands for periodicity and the continuation of life (LÉVI-STRAUSS 1985:179,224). For the Wayana the moon is connected to procreation, rejuvenation and growth. In Wayana mythology there are several stories about the origin of the moon. In one of them the moon used to be an old, blind man, who had a very young wife, who did not bear children yet. Because his wife wanted to marry someone else, she abandoned her husband in the forest. The blind man was lost, but since it was the rainy season, he met many frogs. The frogs were dancing and singing just like Wayana. Because the man could not see them, he thought they were people. The frogs healed the man of his blindness by pulling out) the prickles, that he had contracted all over his body while wandering through the forest, and by taking off his feathercrown (pumali) or blindness, also referred to as mist in his eyes. The frogs accompanied the man back to his village and advised him to take revenge on his wife. The man took his wife with him on a hunting trip, pretending he had seen a fat tapir, but roasted his wife instead! Back in the village, he gave his mother-in-law the meat and fat of her own daughter to eat. After this, his father-in-law discovered the grinning head of his daughter and her family went after the man. He had fleed the village. All the family found was a deserted village, where the man had been dancing and playing the flute with the inhabitants (frogs), before they all disappeared through a passage under the old dancing wood (ehpatpë) in the center of the communal roundhouse. In the evening there was a loud noise: the man ascended into the sky and changed into the moon. His wife was at his side. This is the reason women menstruate here on earth. Since the man ascended and became the moon, he visits the women in their dreams, after which they menstruate. Apalai-story called Nunuwë (moon) narrated by Kutaka, Feb. 4, 1991. I will only analyze this myth for its significance in relation to fertility. First of all, we have as a couple, an old blind man and a young wife that did not have any children (yet). Since the man is blind, he misses his aim in hunting and therefore cannot fulfill his (male) tasks properly. Since it is mentioned that his wife is still childless, this seems to imply the man is also incapable of impregnating his wife. In the eyes of a Wayana, a correlation exists between capacity to hunt and to impregnate. When boy's reach the age of puberty they are initiated into manhood by being submitted to an antordeal after a night of dancing and drinking. Through their initiation they become hunters and capable of impregnating a woman (see also MAGAÑA 1988). The encounter of the blind man with the frogs in the myth shows parallels with the initiation of a boy into manhood. The man sings and dances with the frogs, like the initiates have to dance and sing all night long, while constantly drinking manioc beer. The prickles that have stung the man all over his body remind us of the ant ordeal the initiates have to undergo. Possibly the fog in the man's eyes refers to the intoxicated condition of the initiates. After the frogs have removed the prickles and the blindness (alias feathercrown or mist), the man is said to be beautiful and attractive to his wife again. He has become a hunter. In addition, the dancing and singing of the frogs in the rain refers to their spawning season. In the rainy season all the different kind of frogs come out in the evening to sing and dance together in the rain, while they are laying eggs! Here fertility is clearly related to initiation and capacity to hunt.

The moon as a hunter we find back in the mythology of several other Amazonian Indian tribes. Magaña describes a Kaliña (Carib) myth in which a man barbecues his wife in revenge and after this becomes the constellation Orion. The constellation Orion announces the beginning of the rainy season. In slightly different versions we also come across this same myth among the Arawak, Taulipang, Akawai, Warao, Panaré, Wapisiana and other Amazonian and Guyanese groups resulting in the origin of the constellation Orion. The moon, on the contrary, arises from an incestuous relationship between a brother and sister (MAGAÑA 1992:115-116). Among the Wayana both stories, about the incestuous brother as well as about the man who roasts his wife, are told with regard to the moon. The Waiwai Indians, who are Caribs too, relate a myth about the moon who, as a result of having sexual intercourse with his sister, lost his aimap in the hunt (FOCK 1963:54-56 in MORTON 1983-84:242,243). Note that the moon in the myth has the same attributes as the moon, who visits the Wayana women in their dreams: corporal decoration with red paint, a feathercrown, pumali, and other feather ornaments. The man in the myth treats his wife as a prey and kills and roasts her. After they die - the man by passing through the underworld - they both continue to live, side by side, in the sky. Before, people did not die and lived forever. The moon causes menstruation, in other words procreation or the continuation of life.

The Moon and the Fertility of Crops

According to one shaman the moon makes the manioc grow as well as the foetus in the womb. In other words the fertility of women has been related to the fertility of the fields. Also in former European (Dutch, German, French & other) customs around the feast of Saint Nicholas (December 5th) and New Years Eve, the fertility of the fields was combined with the fertility and honour of young women. The masked processions then held originally were fertility rites (VETH 1996:27). The Wayana have connected the fertility of women with the fertility of the fields through the moon. First of all, as mentioned earlier, the plants that are cultivated in the garden fall under the responsibility of the women. The main crop the women cultivate is bitter manioc, of which they process the tubers into beer and bread. Other crops are different varieties of sweet potatoe, banana, corn, watermelon, sugarcane, pineapple, pumpkin, papaya and hot pepper (Ipomoea batatas, Zea mays, Saccharum officinarum, Ananas comosus, Cucurbita pepo, Caryca papaya and Capsicum sp.).

The crops are planted while the moon is waxing. It is believed that if the crops would be planted while the moon is waning, they would not grow well. Watermelon, cotton and banana (Citrullus vulgaris, Gossypium barbadense and Musa sp.) are planted when the moon is full, so that their fruits will become big and full like it. Tobacco (Nicotiana tabacum) and kulaiwat (Bromelia alta, resembling pineapple), of which the men fabricate rope, belong to the male category and are mostly planted and only harvested by men. The Wayana consider the plant world analogous to the human world. Plants are, whether they are cultivated or wild, conceptualized as people and tubers as babies. Referring to the garden, the plants are claimed to be sleeping at night, while the tubers on the other hand are said to cry. The terminology the Wayana use for the anatomy of plants is similar to the one they use for people, and grammatically in the third singular person. For example, bark is named ipitpï, meaning 'his' or 'her skin' (skin is pitpï); and the stem is called ipun, 'his' or 'her body' (body is punu). There are several directives, that are only known to shamans, for whether a plant is male, female or a child. A tuber is called 'imun' and imunku signifies 'child' in Wayana. In the stories about the origin of sweet potatoe, the manioc guardian spirits (and also about the origin of charmplants and tobacco), the shaman actually sees a large baby instead of a tuber. The other way around, plants are used as a metaphor with regard to human procreation. Boy's are considered plants of their fathers and girls of their mothers. According to a shaman, 'if you cannot get any children, your plant dies out'. The way in which the women have planted the crops in the garden is called 'intercropping'. Symbolically, the Wayana garden reflects the geographical, social and political organization of a Wayana village (VETH 1994:7). Women have organized the plants in the garden according to 'family', that is with each 'species' in its own plot. Each manioc variety (the Wayana know more than seventy) has its own plot with the largest cutting in the middle. In the same way the Wayana live per family together around the eldest couple or grandparents. Manioc varieties that are used for the same kind of bread or beer are planted next to one another. In a Wayana village families, that are related to one another, live next to one another. By organizing the plants in the garden according to kinship, the women have applied the social, geographical and political system to the crops they cultivate. Moreover, according to Magaña (1988) women feed the manioc with red paint (Bixa orellana), the equivalent of blood, and in this manner manioc plants become consanguines of a woman. BROWN (1985:106) mentions with regard to the Aguaruna (Jïvaro in Ecuador), that young manioc plants are dangerous and bloodthirsty the first months after they are planted. If they are not fed in the right way by the women, they can drink the blood of people passing through the garden. In other words, women have incorporated the plants they cultivate into their own family.

Concludingly, women take care of their own children as well as of their 'children in the garden'. Now it has become understandable why the tubers and fruits in the garden fall under the care of women rather than of men. Also the homology between babies in the womb and tubers alias babies in the garden becomes clear. The moon makes the babies in the womb as well as the 'babies' in the garden grow. The moon as husband of the women, is at the same time the father of their own babies and of the babies in the garden. Depending on the context, plants are analogous or homologous to people. Finally it is striking, that for consumption only the tubers and fruits of the garden crops are used. 'Wild' fruits are also gathered for consumption. Other parts of wild as well as cultivated plants, such as the leaves, but also the resin, bark, and fruits are used for medicines or utensils rather than for consumption. Women process the (poisonous) manioc tubers into bread and beer, to feed their own children or relatives. Consumption of manioc makes blood and consumption of manioc from the same garden produces consanguinity (MAGAÑA 1988). With this the circle closes: the manioc tubers, that are conceptualized as the babies of the women and the moon, are used to produce consanguinity in humans. By cultivating and processing manioc and feeding it to their family, women are continuously (re)producing consanguinity.

Sweet blood
Blood' as well as 'menstrual blood' are called 'müu' in the Wayana language and are considered the same. This is surprising, since for example menstrual blood washed in the river is believed to attract the anaconda spirit near the village, and all kinds of water spirits in the pristine forest far away from the village. 'Normal' blood does not have this effect. As mentioned, a woman's blood has to be sweet in order for the moon to make her fertile. In the Wayana belief blood tastes and smells of what you consume. The basic food of the Wayana is bread and beer made of bitter manioc tubers. The standard meal, which is at the same time considered the only 'true' meal by the Wayana, consists of meat or fish cooked in manioc sauce, with the adding of hot peppers (see also SCHOEPF 1979). This so called 'pepre watra' is consumed with manioc bread. Besides this, the Wayana eat sweet potatoe, corn, watermelon, sugarcane, mango and other sweet and sour fruits. I have not heard of any diet that would make someone's blood sweet. The Warao Indians in Guyana associate sweet blood with being ill and with menstruation. People eat bitter manioc in order to get bitter blood (REINDERS 1993). According to MAGAÑA (1988) consumption of bitter manioc makes blood. In addition, consuming manioc from the same garden produces a tie of consanguinity between people. According to my informants consanguinity is determined first of all by birth, and secondly by consumption of the same food. Children share the same blood with both parents, although in the womb only blood of the woman is mixed with sperm, according to one of my informants. She actually compared the womb to a cooking pot. The plant analogy, according to which boy's are plants of their fathers and girls of their mothers, apparently does not hold where blood is concerned. People share the same blood with disregard to a person's sex. For example, siblings, that are born in succession, share more blood with each other than with the other siblings. Secondly, people, that eat the same food, start sharing the same blood, such as a husband and wife. It is not clear however, if this is because they consume food coming from the same garden or food coming from the same cooking pot.

Fertility chants
Female fertility is also related to the blood circulation. When a woman remains childless her blood is not running correctly through her body according to one informant. This is the doing of a malevolent shaman, who has turned the woman's blood by fastening it on top of her head. The shaman does this by blowing smoke on the woman's crown with his cigarette. The woman still has her menstruation, but it is not 'real blood'. In order to undo this, the woman has to see an ëlemi specialist. The Wayana (Apalai-The Wayana have mixed with other Caribs, such as Upului, Apalai and Tirio. In Surinam and French Guiana, Wayana is their common language.) know different kinds of healers. There are shamans, that are usually men, and ëlemi specialists, that are women as well as men. Whereas a shaman leaves his body to travel in the spiritual world himself, an ëlemi specialists addresses her or himself to the spirits of plants and animals by reciting certain chants, that are called ëlemi's. Literally, ëlemi means 'sound of a source'. Elemi's are sung in the Apalai language. Besides chants against infections, stomach and other diseases, there are chants invoking and revoking fertility in women. By singing fertility chants the ëlemi specialist can fasten or open the blood on someone's crown. On the one hand, women, who to their taste loose too much blood during their menstruation, can have their blood fixed on top of their head, in order to stop menstruating gradually. This process is irreversible. On the other hand women, who cannot get pregnant, can ask an ëlemi specialist to 'open' their blood. The latter therapy involves a risk: the children might have a physical defect. To make a woman fertile (again), the ëlemi specialist has to chant on her crown, with the use of tobacco. This means the specialist smokes a cigarette and blows smoke on the woman's crown, while chanting. The specialist calls all the plants that grow very well: the different kinds of banana's [Satume (small banana), palankuta (green banana + bitter when unripe), paluluimë (to make baked banana's), maikaman (to make cooked banana juice and baked banana's),

kuhupotkan (consumed raw only), alamapokan (red banana for consumption), kajan (coloured yellow when unripe & a little orange when ripe), pëli (yellow banana, also to make cooked banana juice)], pineapple, and the different kinds of sweet potatoe. There are two different types of sweet potatoe: napi (Ipomoea batatas) and napëk (Ipomoea batatas). There are many varieties of napi each having a different colour, such as napi taliliman ('brown napi'), kaikuiwet ('dog shit', a white sweet napi), kopeta (with pink skin and white on the inside, that you can buy in the Surinamese shops in Holland), imalijale, napi tapilem ('red napi' used in kasiri manioc beer), hapalakapumo ('egg of hapalaka = varan/monitor', a white napi). Of napëk there are only two varieties: one white and one dark purple.

Note the specialist does not call the manioc tubercules. After this the specialist recites 'banana, that grows very well'. My informant explained, that when you cut banana trees, they continue to grow and in addition make many babies. 'Why do I want a special, very large ëlemi, I also want to see children, and it is me truly ëlemi, I want to see many children, why am I going to heal so and so (chanting the woman's name)'. When the specialist has finished chanting, he alternately blows cigarette smoke on and sucks the woman's crown, her navel and going down (on top of her skirt) and her back and going down, starting at the height of the navel. The specialist blows and sucks the woman's crown to make the blood run again, that a malevolent shaman has attached there with his cigarette. This way the ëlemi specialist undoes what the shaman has caused. The ëlemi specialist blows and sucks on the woman's back to open the place for the baby, and on the woman's belly in order for it to hold it. The ëlemi specialist treats a woman for the duration of one month, starting the ëlemi every morning at 8.00, again at 9.00 and again at 10.00 o'clock, after which she leaves and returns to chant again in the evening. Chanting an ëlemi takes about 5-10 minutes. One day he might chant every hour of the day. After three weeks, he starts chanting using a small calabash, which is the final treatment. The calabash contains some water from the river. First, the specialist blows smoke with his cigarette on the water and chants 'yoooooh'. Then he chants: 'I am finished. It is me and I am real. She is going to make children.' Next the specialist names all the plants (not the banana's, for he is finished with them), and all kinds of animals that get many young, such as the dog, the cat, the collared peccary [Tayassu(/Dicotyles) tajacu (Dicotylidae)] and the black spider monkey [Ateles paniscus (Cebidae)]. After this the woman has to drink some water from the calabash. The specialist puts a bit of the water on her crown, on her navel and going down, and on her back and going down. The specialist only chants once using a calabash with water, and only with water he calls the animals. He calls the plants, because when you cut them, after one month there are two of them, after two months there are three and so on. In other words, because they multiply very well. The animals are called so that the baby will not die, after it has been born. However, there is a risk at stake, when calling the plants to make a woman pregnant. One older woman asked an ëlemi specialist to chant for her, because she wanted children with her new young husband. She was older than him. The specialist refused, because the woman is Apalai and would understand the ëlemi language. He only sings fertility chants for young girls, that do not understand Apalai. According to my informant, because the specialist is going to call 'bad' things. When the banana's grow, for example, two of them might glue together. Also the sweet potatoe kind napëk grows two by two and is flat, like four fingers affixed together two by two. Because of this the children eventually born, might 'not be good', that is have a flat nose, one deaf ear, etcetera. When an ëlemi specialist calls certain plants to invoke fertility in a woman, there is a danger that the baby shows the same pecularity as the tubers or fruits of the plants. In case of ëlemi's, babies are homologous (or equal) to the tubers or fruits, that are called upon.

When the treatment is succesful, the woman continues to get pregnant and make babies, because her blood has been turned. Hereafter she has to turn to a shaman, who will ask how many children she wants, in order to put it right. The shaman treats the woman in a shamanistic hut. In the hut or rather in the body of the shaman, who is a medium, a special baby spirit comes, for example ölukö, the caterpillar, or for example all things that grow in the forest. Because the spirit is going to cry, the people attending the shamanistic session know it is a baby. The leaves of a small liana, called mölewa, are put in a cigarette to be smoked by the shaman, in order to open the blood. The shaman is going to blow smoke and suck the crown of the woman down to her navel and again from the crown down to her back, just like the ëlemi specialist has done. During pregnancy, a woman stays under control of a shaman also. He checks if the baby is normal and he will tell you when there is something wrong with the baby, so that you can abort if you want to. After two months of pregnancy, the shaman can see whether the baby is a boy or a girl. In short, the shaman functions as a midwife among the Wayana.

Chants Provoking Infertility
When a woman does not want to get pregnant, she asks an ëlemi specialist to fix her blood on top of her head. In this case the specialist calls something that putrefies, or falls, or does not ripen, for example whatever fruit. He also calls things that are hard, such as a rock or shell, or dead leaves. A certain kind of liana, that stops growing after you cut it. Trees or herbs, that stop growing after they have been cut. He closes the blood with cigarette smoke by blowing circles on the woman's crown. This time he chants all the time over a calabash filled with water. Then the woman drinks a little of the water from the calabash, and the specialist alternately blows smoke on and sucks her crown, navel and back. This time the specialist moves in the opposite direction of when opening the blood. One time he gives the woman two pieces of tëhpa to drink in a small pan with water. Tëhpa is made by putting fresh kutuli which is a certain kind of manioc bread, between banana leaves on top of a cooking plate and baking it, after which it is put in a small pan with water. Kutuli is bread made of the sediment of rasped manioc juice. That is, when the manioc tubercules are rasped in a trough, the juice that seeps from the rasped manioc is caught in a bucket placed under the trough. Kutuli bread is considered a treat and especially liked by children. After the treatment a woman's menstruation gradually ceases. Women use this treatment as birth control, when they do not want anymore children. If the ëlemi specialist would chant every day during one month, a woman's menstruation would stop right away. In this case the specialist would call everything that does not have blood or sap (resin), like the awala palmtree, a rock, a giant tree, a liana. Five day's of chanting ëlemi's causes less menstruation. Three day's of ëlemi's causes your menstruation to stop after three years. This way you do not grow old right away, since menstruation weakens women.

Skin-Changing Spirits Causing Infertility
Menstrual blood attracts certain spirits, that can be described as skin-changing spirits. These are the Moon spirit, the Anaconda spirit and many different kinds of Caterpillar spirits. They are dangerous, because they can cause infertility in a woman. Usually they do not cause this by themselves though. They are sent by malevolent shamans, who want to make the woman concerned infertile, ill or even dead. It is beyond the scope of this article to discuss the Anaconda and Caterpillar spirits thoroughly, so I will only touch upon them. The Moon spirit will be described in the next paragraph. The Anaconda spirit visits a woman in her dreams in the guise of a beautiful young man, adorned for dancing at a feast. In contrast with the Moon spirit his body is decorated with black and (dark) red paint. If the woman would make love to the Anaconda spirit in her dream, she would start loosing blood from her vagina till eventually she would die. This disease is called mïuimë. The Anaconda spirit visits a woman in her dream, because a shaman sent him or because the woman has bathed in the river during her menstrual period. Her blood attracts him. Because of this, one of the restrictions a woman has to keep to during her period is to stay away from the river. The Caterpillar spirit only causes infertility in a woman when sent by a shaman. The caterpillar takes the place of the embryo in the womb and feeds on the placenta, menstrual blood or sperm (according to different informants). If the caterpillar is not sucked out of the womb by a shaman, the baby that is born in reality is a caterpillar spirit. After a woman has been healed of an anaconda or caterpillar spirit, she has to keep to certain restrictions or customs for many years thereafter in order to stay healthy and to restore her fertility.

The Other Side of the Moon
Whereas on the one hand the Moon is indispensable for a woman's fertility, on the other hand a hostile shaman may send a moon spirit to a woman or man in their dream in order to make them ill. According to one informant here it concerns the son or a relative of the moon. In case of a man, a female moon spirit is sent to seduce him and in case of a woman a male moon spirit. If a person would make love to the moon spirit he or she would contract the same disease as caused by the anaconda spirit, namely the loss of blood from the vagina or penis. The blood a man or woman would loose from their genital organs (when made ill by the anaconda or moon spirit) is called möuimö, meaning 'large blood' or 'father of blood'. Mïuimë is red (takpilem) and darker coloured than normal blood and comes in large lumps. Whereas normal (menstrual) blood or möu is coloured orange (tawaman) according to the Wayana. Note that the disease is named after the kind of blood you loose when ill (mïuimë). If the ill person would continue to make love to the moon (or anaconda) spirit in the dream, eventually he or she would die. In case a person has been made ill by any kind of spirit and when all other remedies (inclu-

ding ëlemi's) fail, the only one left to heal is a shaman, being the intermediary between the spiritual world and humans. Shamans usually heal in a shamanistic hut especially made for the occasion and after the night has fallen. Different spirits come in the body of the shaman, each with his or her own song. The last spirit to come heals the 'patient'. The healing is done with the use of cigarettes in which certain parts of plants or other items, that are used as medicine, are mixed with the tobacco. A plant that is used to heal the loss of blood caused by the moon spirit, (is an epiphyte (Aechmaea?, Bromeliaceae), that resembles pineapple, but grows high on a tree. The epiphyte has two names, nanaimö, which means 'father of pineapple', and sisi meaning 'sun'. Curiously enough a disease, that has been caused by the moon, is healed with a plant named after its opposite: the sun.

Conclusions

First of all, fertility as well as infertility are considered temporary phases, that can be influenced. Because of this, the reproductive qualities of women, that are essential for the continuation of society, are at the same time their most vulnerable properties. Especially concerning their fertility, women are vulnerable to hostile shamans and spirits that are attracted to menstrual blood. From a western point of view, we could explain this as the men wanting to have control over women's fertility. On the other hand, men are urged to protect the fertility of their own wife and kins-women against 'outsiders'. In addition, women rely first of all on themselves to protect their fertility.

If they keep to all the restrictions, that hold during menstruation or pregnancy and after an abortion or partition, they are not very likely to get into trouble. Also, women can count on the different specialists, such as shamans and ëlemi specialists, to help and protect them. The most important fertility agent is the moon, who is necessary to make a woman pregnant or menstruate. Only, as in one case, when the moon does not visit a woman at all, even a shaman might not be able to do something about it. Through an intricate system women's most important tasks, raising children and practicing agriculture, are combined in producing consanguinity. The Wayana women enter into relations with the moon in order to be fertile and to have fertile gardens. The Wayana consider the spiritual, animal and plant world as analogous to the human world. The moon is conceptualized as the husband of all the women and as the father of all the children and men. The tubers and fruits women cultivate are conceptualized as babies that are put under the women's care. The moon makes babies in the womb as well as 'babies' in the garden grow. The Wayana women process manioc tubers into beer and bread to feed their family, in this manner producing consanguinity. Since fertility is considered a temporary phase, manipulation becomes possible. Manipulation involves danger, because there are always two sides to something. The moon spirit causes fertility as well as infertility in women. Cultivated plants that multiply very well may on the one hand be called upon to invoke fertility in women, but on the other hand they may cause a woman to have a child with a physical disability, because of the way their tubers or fruits grow. Tubers of wild plants may be cut off all at once, to induce abortion. Not everything may be manipulable, also when it concerns fertility. But everything is explainable according to the Wayana theories.

References

AHLBRINCK, W. 1931. Encyclopaedie der Karaiben. Verhandelingen der Koninklijke Akademie der Wetenschappen te Amsterdam. *Afd. Letteren*, nr. 27 (1).

BOVEN, KARIN & MATHILDE MOLENDIJK. 1995. *Arowakse, Karaibse en Wayana vrouwen in het Surinaamse binnenland. Surinaamse Verkenningen.* Leo Victor. Paramaribo.

BROWN, MICHAEL F. 1985. *Tsewa's gift: magic and meaning in an Amazonian society.* Smithsonian Institution Press. Washington D.C.

HUGH-JONES, CHRISTINE. 1979. From the Milk River: Spatial and temporal processes in *Northwest Amazonia*. Cambridge University Press. Cambridge.

LÉVI-STRAUSS, Claude. 1985. La potiöre jalouse. Librairie Plon. Paris.

MAGAÑA, EDMUNDO. 1988. Orión y la mujer Pléyades. Simbolismo astronómico de los indios kaliña de Surinam. *CEDLA Latin American Studies* No. 44. FORIS. Amsterdam.

MAGAÑA, EDMUNDO. 1992. Literatura de los pueblos del Amazonas: una introducción wayana. *Collecciones MAPFRE* 1492. Madrid

MORTON, ELISABETH. 1983-84. ---

REINDERS, MARILEEN. 1993. *Bitter-zoet. Een Verhandeling over de Warao in Guyana.* (manuscript)

SCHOEPF, DANIEL. 1979. *La marmite Wayana. Cuisine et société d'une tribu d'Amazonie. Musée d'ethnographie.* Gengève.

VETH, BRITTA. 1994. Kinderen van de maniok. De betekenis van Manihot esculenta voor de Wayana Indianen in Suriname en Frans Guyana. in *Promotieonderzoek aan de Faculteit der Sociale Wetenschappen: Jaargroep 1991*. Edited by E. HITTERS & W. VOS, pp. 163-188. ISOR. Utrecht.

VETH, BRITTA. 1996. De herkomst van Zwarte Piet. in *Dunya-krant, 3e jaargang,* 4: 26-27

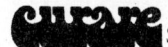

Was verstehen spanische und deutsche Frauen unter ‚Gesundheit'?
Subjektive Gesundheitskonzepte im internationalen Vergleich
How do Spanish and German Women interpretHealth?
Lay Health Concepts in Transcultural Comparison

Petra Scheibler

Zusammenfassung: Die derzeitigen Europäischen Entwicklungen wie Binnenmarkt und zunehmende Internationalisierung der Lebenswelt stellen sowohl die Gesundheitsforschung und -förderung als auch die Medizin vor neue Aufgaben. Ein Blick über die Grenzen offenbart entgegen vielfach propagierter Internationalität der Medizin zahlreiche ‚Spielarten' gesundheits- und krankheitsbezogenen Handelns von Experten und Laien, um die wir unseren Blick erweitern müssen. Der Artikel ist ein erster Schritt zum Verständnis interkultureller Unterschiede am Beispiel subjektiver Theorien über Gesundheit von spanischen und deutschen Frauen.

Abstract: Recent European developments such as the European Economic Union and increasing internationalisation have been accompanied by new tasks for health research, the promotion of ‚good health', and other areas of medicine. However, when looking across borders, it is found that the assertion of the internationalisation of medicine does not necessarily hold true: field research has shown that there are significant differences even within the European community. The paper makes a preliminary examination of the cultural differences between perceptions of ‚health' between Spanish and German women.

Keywords: Subjektive Theorien, Gesundheit, Frauen, interkultureller Vergleich, Spanien, Deutschland, Lay theories, Health, Women, intercultural comparison, Spain, Germany.

Einleitung: Subjektive Gesundheitskonzepte im internationalen Vergleich

Aktuelle medizinpsychologische Forschungsstudien haben verdeutlicht, dass das Laienverständnis von Gesundheit und Krankheit sowohl auf Gesundheitsverhalten als auch Krankheitsverhalten einen wesentlichen Einfluss hat (FALLER 1990; SCHWARZER 1992; FALTERMAIER 1994; STRITTMATTER 1995). Dies gilt insbesondere für die Akzeptanz und Wirksamkeit vorbeugender Maßnahmen und Behandlungsempfehlungen von ärztlicher bzw. psychologischer Seite. Obwohl die Erforschung subjektiver Theorien über Gesundheit und Krankheit in den letzten Jahren zunehmend an Bedeutung gewann, gibt es vergleichsweise wenig Untersuchungen, die subjektive Theorien gesunder Personen über Gesundheit, gesundheitsbezogenen Verhaltensweisen etc. zum Thema haben (FLICK 1991; FALTERMAIER 1994; STRITTMATTER 1995).

Der größte Teil der theoretischen und empirischen Arbeiten konzentriert sich auf die Erforschung von Laientheorien bereits erkrankter Personen (vgl. VERRES 1986; BISCHOFF / ZENZ 1989; MUTHNY / BECHTEL / SPÄTE 1992; KRAMER / LERCH / MUTHNY 1993). In Anbetracht der Tatsache, dass subjektive Theorien und Wissensbestände von Laien wesentlich durch den kulturellen und gesellschaftlichen Hintergrund bestimmt sind (vgl. HUI & TRIANDIS 1983; MUTHNY / BERMEJO / HECKL 1993; PFEIFFER 1993), ist davon auszugehen, dass interkulturelle Unterschiede nicht zu unterschätzende Auswirkungen auf die Inanspruchnahme und Effektivität medizinischer Versorgung haben. Zahlreiche Studien belegen den Einfluss interkultureller Unterschiede auf Behandlungszufriedenheit und Compliance bzw. Non-Compliance ausländischer Patienten in der Bundesrepublik (KENTENICH / REEG / WEHKAMP 1990; JAEDE / PORTERA 1993; ROHNER / KÖPP 1993; KOCH/ ÖZEK / PFEIFFER 1995). In diesen Studien konnte nicht nur eindrucksvoll belegt werden, dass Migration vielfältige Auswirkungen auf den Gesundheitszustand von Migranten hat, sie lassen auch den Schluss zu, dass zwischen den Kulturen wesentliche Unterschiede im Laienverständnis über Gesundheit und Krankheit bestehen, die Einfluss auf die Inanspruchnahme und Wirksamkeit medizinischer Versorgung haben. Die Relevanz interkultureller Vergleichsstudien für Gesundheitssysteme jeder multikulturellen Gesellschaft gewinnt daher zunehmend an Bedeutung (THOMAS 1993, BERMEJO 1996). Speziell für Unterschiede im Gesundheits- und Krankheitsverständnis innerhalb der europäischen Union gibt es bisher vergleichsweise wenig internationale Vergleichsstudien (SCHÄFER / HERNANDEZ 1985; MATTES 1991; BERMEJO /

MUTHNY 1994), obwohl allein 1,5 Millionen Bürger in der BRD aus den EU-Staaten stammen. Mit einem Ausländeranteil von fast 10% liegt die Bundesrepublik innerhalb der Europäischen Union an dritter Stelle (LÜTZEL 1997). Im Zuge des europäischen Binnenmarktes ist mit einer zunehmenden Anzahl europäischer Bürger zu rechnen, die aus beruflichen oder privaten Gründen ihr Heimatland verlassen um z.B. in der Bundesrepublik zu leben.

„Das Zusammenwachsen Europas und die zunehmende Internationalisierung auf den verschiedensten Ebenen der Gesellschaften und ihrer Industrien und Volkswirtschaften bis hin zur internationalen Verflechtung der Verwaltungen und die grenzüberschreitende Zusammenarbeit mit dem Nachbarland schaffen neue Bedingungen für die Gestaltung des Zusammenlebens und beinhalten andere Anforderungen an den einzelnen, sich unter diesen veränderten Bedingungen zurechtzufinden," (BIZEUL / BLIESENER / PRAWDA 1997, 9ff.)

Neue Anforderungen erwachsen nicht nur für die betroffenen Laien, die in der BRD gesundheits- und krankheitsbezogene Angebote wahrnehmen, sondern auch für den Umgang mit Gesundheit und Krankheit auf Expertenebene. Die Beschäftigung mit dieser Thematik ist auch deshalb von Bedeutung, damit Bürger anderer Nationalitäten - und möglicherweise anderen Gesundheits- und Krankheitsverständnissen - in unserem Gesundheitssystem nicht mehr nur ‚am Rande mitversorgt' werden. Diese Überlegungen waren Ausgangspunkt unserer Studie über Gesundheitswissen und Gesundheitshandeln im europäischen Vergleich.

Ziele, Aufbau und Methodik der Untersuchung

Die in diesem Artikel dargestellten Ergebnisse sind Teil einer interkulturellen Vergleichsstudie, in der Männer und Frauen aus Spanien, Deutschland, Großbritannien und Frankreich zu verschiedenen gesundheits- und krankheitsbezogenen Themenbereichen befragt wurden. Für den vorliegenden Artikel wurden die Ergebnisse einer Teilstichprobe - spanische und deutsche Frauen - gesondert ausgewertet:

Tab. 1

N=50	Spanierinnen n = 25	Deutsche Frauen n = 25
Alter : range: 30-50 J. Standardabw.:	M = 37 2,1	M = 42 2,4
Beruf:	Lehrerinnen	Lehrerinnen
Subj. Wohlbefinden:	psych. 1,8 (= gut) phys. 2 (= gut)	psych. 1,8 (= gut) phys. 2,3 (= gut)

Die Zielsetzung der Studie bestand darin, Laienvorstellungen Gesunder zu Gesundheitsverständnis und -verhalten, zum Krankheitsverständnis und -verhalten im internationalen Vergleich zu erforschen. Die Studie wurde in Anlehnung an aktuelle gesundheitspsychologische Theorien konzipiert. Gesundheit wird dabei als multidimensionales Konstrukt betrachtet, für das es gesundheitspsychologischen Erkenntnissen gemäß keine einheitliche Definition gibt. Dies ist u.a. auch der Fall, weil ‚Gesundheit' als eine soziale und kulturelle Konstruktion der Wirklichkeit verstanden werden muss, die sich in Abhängigkeit von zeitgeschichtlichen Veränderungen und kulturellen Wissensbeständen schon innerhalb einer Gesellschaft unterscheiden kann (z.B. zwischen Experten und Laien, Alter und Bildungsgrad, Erziehung und individuellen Lebenserfahrungen). Allerdings gibt es zahlreiche Bestimmungsfaktoren zur Erforschung interkultureller Gesundheitskonzepte, über die kulturelle Unterschiede und Gemeinsamkeiten auf Wissens- und Einstellungsebene erschlossen werden können. In der vorliegenden Studie wurden anhand subjektiver Gesundheitstheorien kulturelle Wissensbestände über Gesundheit und Krankheit in vergleichender Perspektive erforscht. Da bei der Wahl einer der Untersuchung angemessenen Forschungsmethode der Tatsache Rechnung getragen werden musste, dass sich die Erforschung von Alltagswissen über Gesundheit und Krankheit im europäischen Vergleich im Anfangsstadium des Wissenschaftsprozesses befindet, wurde ein exploratives, hypothesengenerierendes Vorgehen gewählt. Der Untersuchung liegt daher eine qualitative Befragung mittels Fragebogen zugrunde. Bei der nachfolgenden Ergebnisdarstellung wurde der Schwerpunkt auf die qualitative Ausprägung kultureller Wissensbestände und Handlungsmuster im interkulturellen Vergleich gelegt.

Welche Assoziationen haben deutsche und spanische Frauen zu Gesundheit?
Als einleitendes Thema wurden spanische und deutsche Frauen gebeten, alles aufzuschreiben, was ihnen spontan zum Stichwort ‚Gesundheit' einfiel. Alle Assoziationen zu diesem Begriff wurden in inhaltsanalytischen Kategorien zusammengefasst. Dabei konnten zehn Hauptkategorien von Assoziationen unterschieden werden:
1. Assoziationen zu unterschiedlichen Arten des Wohlbefindens (phys. / psych. bzw. beide Aspekte),
2. zu Medikation und ärztlicher Behandlung,
3. Assoziationen hinsichtlich einer gesunden Lebensweise,
4. zu Lebensfreude/Glück,
5. zu Abwesenheit von Krankheit und Beschwerden,
6. zu Ausdrucksformen körperlicher Fitness,
7. zu Umweltfaktoren (z.B. Natur, Klima),
8. zur Beschreibung von Krankheit und subjektiven Beschwerden,
9. zum körperlichen Erscheinungsbild von Gesundheit,
10. zu gesundheitsbezogenen Vorsorgemaßnahmen.

Insgesamt wurden von den spanischen Frauen 65 Assoziationen gegeben, von den deutschen Frauen 69. Die sechs Kategorien, die die meisten Assoziationen beinhalteten (< 5), sind im folgenden Schaubild dargestellt (angegeben sind jeweils die absoluten Häufigkeiten, Abb. 1 und 2)

Unterschiede zeigen sich vor allem bei der Assoziation ‚Wohlbefinden' (bienestar). ‚Wohlbefinden' wurde vor allem in der spanischen Stichprobe sehr häufig mit Gesundheit assoziiert. Besonders spanische Frauen nannten gleichermaßen psychische und physische Komponenten des Wohlbefindens im Zusammenhang, was auf ein ganzheitliches Konzept von Gesundheit hindeuten könnte. Deutsche Frauen thematisierten häufiger körperlich-funktionale Aspekte wie ‚körperliche Fitness' und die ‚Abwesenheit von Krankheit' zur Beschreibung für subjektives Wohlbefinden. Hierzu einige exemplarische Beispiele (die Zahlen geben dabei jeweils das Alter der befragten Frauen an):
„*Physisches und psychisches Wohlbefinden, obwohl sich beides nicht immer miteinander vereinbaren lässt,*" (Spanierin, 44)
„*Bewegungsfähig sein, einen Körper haben, der funktioniert, schmerzfrei leben, sich fit fühlen und das Leben lustvoll gestalten zu können, ohne mit körperlichen Einschränkungen konfrontiert zu sein,*" (Deutsche, 32)
Die Ausführungen der Befragten zur Assoziation ‚Wohlbefinden' enthielten z.T. sehr un-

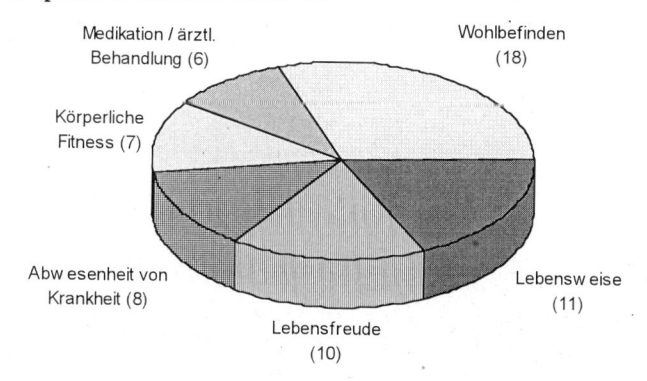

Abb. 1: Assoziationen spanischer Frauen zu Gesundheit

- Medikation / ärztl. Behandlung (6)
- Wohlbefinden (18)
- Körperliche Fitness (7)
- Abwesenheit von Krankheit (8)
- Lebensfreude (10)
- Lebensweise (11)

Abb. 2: Assoziationen deutscher Frauen zu Gesundheit

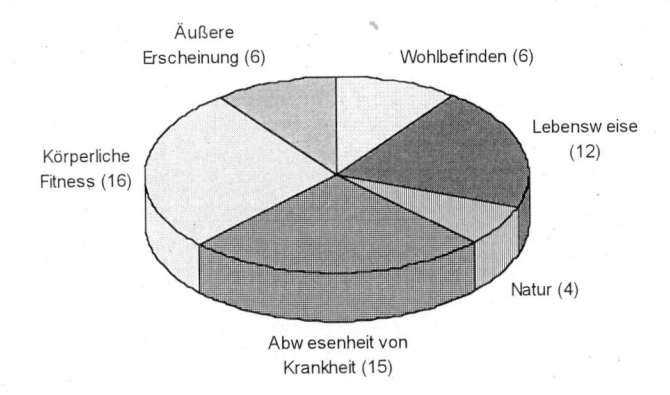

- Äußere Erscheinung (6)
- Wohlbefinden (6)
- Lebensweise (12)
- Natur (4)
- Abwesenheit von Krankheit (15)
- Körperliche Fitness (16)

terschiedliche Beschreibungen und Ausdrucksformen. Spanische Frauen thematisierten vielfach umweltbezogene Aspekte wie Natur, Klima, etc., während deutsche Frauen subjektives Wohlbefinden im Zusammenhang mit funktionellen Aspekten assoziierten. Hier einige exemplarische Beispiele:

„*Wohlbefinden, auf der Spitze eines Berges sein und klare saubere Luft atmen bei strahlend blauem Himmel„* (Spanierin, 32).

„*Wohlbefinden, Stabilität, Konfrontationen sicher ausführen und aushalten zu können„* (Deutsche, 34).

Auch innerhalb der Kategorien gab es unterschiedliche Antwortausprägungen. Während spanische Frauen unter einer gesunden Lebensweise vor allem sportliche Aktivitäten und Hygienemaßnahmen aufführten, nannten die deutschen Frauen überwiegend ernährungsbedingte Verhaltensweisen. Die Nennung vorsorgebedingter Verhaltensweisen (z.B. regelmäßige Teilnahme an Vorsorgeuntersuchungen, Nutzung von Informationsangeboten über Vorsorge und Krankheitsprävention) wurde nur von spanischen Frauen thematisiert.

In der neueren Diskussion zur Erforschung von Gesundheit und Krankheit wird immer wieder auf die enge Verflechtung von Gesundheit und Krankheit hingewiesen (ANTONOVSKY 1979; 1987). Gesundheit und Krankheit sind nicht als komplementäre Alltagsbegriffe und deshalb nicht als Gegensätze zu verstehen; Vielmehr müssen sie aus salutogenetischer Perspektive auf dem Hintergrund eines zusammenhängenden Gesundheits-Krankheits-Kontinuums interpretiert werden. Dies spiegelt sich auch in den Antworten der befragten Frauen deutlich wieder: Viele Antworten zum Thema Gesundheit enthielten auch krankheitsbezogene Anteile, die sich meistens auf die Abwesenheit von Schmerzen, Beschwerden oder Krankheit selbst bezogen. Die enge Verpflechtung von Gesundheit und Krankheit kommt u.a. auch bei den Definitionen zu Gesundheit zum Ausdruck. Die befragten Frauen gaben im Rahmen ihrer Assoziationen zu Gesundheit auch an, was sie unter ‚Gesundheit' verstehen. Es konnten fünf unterschiedliche Gesundheitsdefinitionen durch Kategorisierung unterschieden werden:

1. Gesundheit als Ausdruck psychischen und physischen Wohlbefindens (W), 2. Gesundheit als funktionale Fitness (FF), 3. körperliche Fitness (KF), 4. Gesundheit als Abwesenheit von Krankheit (AK), 5. Gesundheit als Gleichgewichtsprozess (GG). Diese Kategorien entsprechen weitgehend den Gesundheitsdefinitionen, die in deutschen und britischen Forschungsstudien erhoben wurden (vgl. BLAXTER 1990; FALTERMAIER 1994).

An erster Stelle finden sich bei den befragten spanischen Frauen Antworten, die Gesundheit durch physisches und psychisches Wohlbefinden beschreiben. Bei diesem Typus werden körperliche und psychische Komponenten als gleichwertig zur Bestimmung von Gesundheit angesehen. Dies kommt auch in den angeführten Beispielen der Befragten zum Ausdruck: Gesundheit und Wohlbefinden werden durch das Zusammenspiel körperlicher und geistiger Aktivitäten beeinflusst und aufrechterhalten. Aktivität und Lebensfreude sind hierbei häufig thematisierte Aspekte. Bei den deutschen Frauen steht die Abwesenheit von Krankheit an erster Stelle, wenn auch mit weitaus weniger Nennungen. Dieser Antworttypus zeichnet sich durch eine negative Bestimmung von Gesundheit aus und wird durch das

Abb. 3: Definitionen von Gesundheit

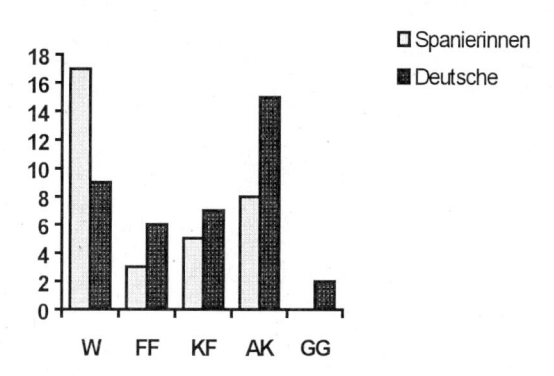

[Bar chart: Spanierinnen vs. Deutsche across categories W, FF, KF, AK, GG]

Nicht-Vorhandensein körperlicher Beschwerden oder Leiden beschrieben.
  „Physisches und psychisches Wohlbefinden, Kräfte haben, zufrieden und glücklich sein (Spanierin, 40).
  „Das Gegenteil von Krankheit, schmerzfrei sein, keine Befunde bei Vorsorgeuntersuchungen, Arbeitsfreude" (Deutsche, 33).

Subjektive Theorien über Gesundheit
In einem weiteren Schritt wurden deutsche und spanische Frauen befragt, welche Bedingungen notwendig sind, um sich gesund fühlen zu können. Aus dem breiten Antwortspektrum ließen sich auch Hinweise auf subjektive Theorien über Gesundheit erschließen. Die Antworten konnten in 7 Kategorien zusammengefasst werden:
1. Aktivitäten und Verhaltensweisen, die auf eine gesundheitsbewusste Lebensweise hindeuteten (GL),
2. Gesundheit durch Umweltfaktoren (UF),
3. Gesundheit durch funktionierenden Organismus (FO),
4. Gesundheit durch Arbeit (A),
5. Gesundheit durch Individuelle Freiräume (IF),
6. Gesundheit durch soziale Beziehungen (SB),
7. Gesundheit durch die Berücksichtigung psychosomatischer Zusammenhänge (PS).

Auffällig ist bei beiden Stichproben die Beschreibung einer gesundheitsbezogenen Lebensweise als Bedingung für Gesundheit. Jedoch scheinen spanische und deutsche Frauen im Vergleich unterschiedliche Vorstellungen über eine gesundheitsförderliche Lebensweise zu besitzen: Spanische Frauen thematisieren überwiegend hygienische Maßnahmen (z.B. in bezug auf Ernährung) und sportliche Aktivitäten; ernährungsbezogene Verhaltensweisen und die Vermeidung von gesundheitsschädigenden Einflussfaktoren wie Rauchen und Alkoholgenuss wurden an dritter Stelle genannt. Für deutsche Frauen war

Abb. 4: Subjektive Theorien über Gesundheit

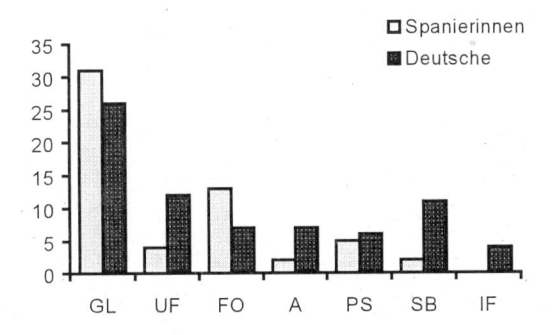

[Bar chart: Spanierinnen vs. Deutsche across categories GL, UF, FO, A, PS, SB, IF]

,Hygiene' im Kontext dieser Befragung scheinbar kein Thema. Sie erwähnten am häufigsten Ernährungsfaktoren, die sie sehr ausführlich beschreiben und umweltbezogene Faktoren wie z.B. gute Wohnbedingungen, saubere Luft und Faktoren, die sich auf das Klima bezogen wie Licht, Sonne und Wärme. Hierzu einige Beispiele:

„... sich gesund ernähren zu können und dass die Luft, die ich atme, nicht allzu verschmutzt ist ... sportliche Aktivitäten, das Laufen im Wald, frische Luft einatmen„ (Deutsche, 37).

„Sport, Hygiene, gesunde Ernährung. Ein gesundes Leben führen, ohne Drogen und Alkohol„ (Spanierin, 33).

Unter die Kategorie ‚gesundheitsbewusste Lebensweise' fielen auch Aktivitäten der Befragten, die sich auf Vorsorgemaßnahmen bezogen. Allerdings wurden diese Aktivitäten nur von spanischen Frauen angesprochen. ‚Vorsorge' bezog sich nach Angaben der befragten Spanierinnen sowohl auf selbstinitiierte, vorbeugende Handlungsweisen wie Mundhygiene und hygienische Ernährung als auch auf experteninitiierte Vorsorgemaßnahmen wie Impfungen und Vorsorgeuntersuchungen. ‚Vorsorge' war in der deutschen Stichprobe ein eher vernachlässigtes Thema. Hier wurde das Thema ‚Selbstbestimmung' häufiger angesprochen. Die meisten der befragten Frauen thematisierten die subjektive Bedeutung individuell gestalteter Freiräume in ihrem Leben, die ursächlich in Zusammenhang mit Gesundheit genannt wurden:

„Ich muss genügend Zeit für mich selbst neben der Arbeit mit Beruf, Haushalt und Kindern haben und eine Wohnung, die mich nicht einengt; genügend Selbstbestimmtheit„ (Deutsche, 40).

Was tun deutsche und spanische Frauen für ihre Gesundheit?
Die im vorangehenden Abschnitt dargestellten subjektiven Theorien über Gesundheit haben z.T. schon darüber Aufschluss gegeben, welche Verhaltensweisen deutsche und spanische Frauen als gesundheitsförderlich ansehen. Um zu erfahren, was Frauen beider Stichproben zur Aufrechterhaltung ihrer Gesundheit unternehmen, wurde die Fage gestellt: ‚Gibt es etwas, was Sie für Ihre Gesundheit tun?' Es wurden überwiegend Verhaltensweisen genannt, die auf eine gesundheitsbewusste Lebensweise (GL) hindeuteten. Darüberhinaus konnten folgende Kategorien unterschieden werden: Vorsorgemaßnahmen (V), Arztbesuche (A), die Pflege sozialer Kontakte (SK) und Maßnahmen zur Stressvermeidung (SV).

Im interkulturellen Vergleich unterscheiden sich diese Verhaltensweisen deutlich: Spanierinnen nannten Vorsorgemaßnahmen und regelmäßige Arztbesuche als gesundheitsförderliche Maßnahmen.

„Ein bisschen auf sich achten, besonders auf die Hygiene. Sport treiben und sich von Zeit zu Zeit ‚durchchecken' zu lassen. Bei jeder Art von Krankheitsanzeichen einen Arzt zu Rate ziehen„ (Spanierin, 47).

„Ich versuche auf meine Gesundheit durch Vorsorgemaßnahmen zu achten„ (Spanierin, 40).

Beide Aspekte wurden von den deutschen Frauen nicht thematisiert. Sie nannten an erster Stelle gesundheitsbewusste Ernährung, Ausgleichstechniken (Yoga, Meditation) und Sport. Besonders das Ernährungsverhalten wurde sehr ausführlich von den Befragten beschrieben.

„Ich ernähre mich gesund, zumindest meine ich das. Ich kaufe Lebensmittel im Naturkostladen oder auf dem Wochenmarkt beim BioLand-Stand. Ich verwende selten aufbereitete Nahrungsmittel. Ich gehe wöchentlich einmal zur Gymnastik und fahre oft mit dem Fahrrad„ (Deutsche, 44).

Abb. 5: Was tun deutsche und spanische Frauen für ihre Gesundheit?

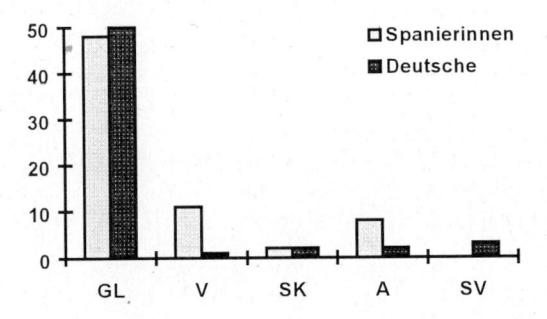

„Ich achte auf meine Ernährung; wenig Zucker, wenig Fleisch, keine Fertigprodukte, Yoga und Entspannung, Klavierspielen" (Deutsche, 32).

Insgesamt weisen die Ausführungen der befragten deutschen Frauen auf eine individualistische Umgangsweise mit Gesundheit: Im Vordergrund stehen Ansätze zur Gesunderhaltung, die auf individuelle Handlungsinitiativen der befragten Frauen schließen lassen und damit auf eine stärkere Eigenverantwortung für die individuelle Gesundheit hinweisen. Maßnahmen wie Vorsorgeuntersuchungen, die auf gesundheitspolitische Initiativen zurückgehen sowie Arztbesuche wurden von den spanischen Frauen thematisiert.

Résumé
Die hier vorgestellten Ergebnisse der Befragung spanischer und deutscher Frauen weisen insgesamt auf einen bewussten Umgang mit der eigenen Gesundheit hin. Dabei lassen sich jedoch Unterschiede in Abhängigkeit vom subjektiven Gesundheitsverständnis feststellen: Während deutsche Frauen häufiger körperlich-funktionale Aspekte thematisierten und Gesundheit als ‚Abwesenheit von Krankheit' definierten, weisen die Antworten der spanischen Frauen auf ein ganzheitlicheres Verständnis von Gesundheit hin. Auch im Hinblick auf gesundheitsbezogene Aktivitäten unterscheiden sich die Ergebnisse: Während deutsche Frauen Eigenaktivitäten wie gesundheitsbewusste Ernährung, Sport und Ausgleichstechniken nannten, sprachen die spanischen Frauen in erster Linie Aktivitäten an, die dem Bereich staatlich initiierter Präventionsmaßnahmen zuzuordnen sind. Diese Unterschiede müssen vor dem kulturellen und gesundheitspolitischen Hintergrund beider Länder interpretiert werden. Gesundheitspolitische Eigeninitiativen von Laien sowie die Übernahme der Verantwortung für die eigene Gesundheit, wie sie sich in den Antworten der befragten deutschen Frauen darstellen, sind in der Bundesrepublik Deutschland angesichts gesundheitspolitischer Entwicklungen (speziell: Kürzungen im Gesundheitssektor) eine zwangsläufige Folgeerscheinung. Parallel dazu zeichnet sich in der BRD ein Umbruch im Laienverständnis von Gesundheit und Krankheit ab. Entgegen Annahmen des biomedizinschen Krankheitsmodells, in denen Personen lange Zeit als passive Opfer von ‚Noxen' galten, versuchen immer mehr Menschen ihre Gesundheit selbst in die Hand zu nehmen. Eine Stärkung des Einzelnen in der Verantwortung für seine eigene Gesundheit ist zwar einerseits - nicht nur aus gesundheitspolitischer Perspektive - wünschenswert, andererseits birgt sie u.U. die Gefahr einer Überbelastung für die betreffenden Personen in sich. Frauen stellen hierbei eine besondere Risikogruppe dar, da sie i.d.R. nicht nur die Verantwortung für ihre eigene Gesundheit übernehmen, sondern auch im Rahmen der alltäglichen Gesundheitsselbsthilfe die Verantwortung für die Gesundheit ihrer Angehörigen übernehmen. Gesundheitsvorsorge wird von der spanischen Stichprobe stärker dem Verantwortungsbereich von Experten zugeschrieben und an diese delegiert: Die Antworten der befragten Spanierinnen weisen u.a. auf die besondere Rolle hin, die spanischen Ärzten nach wie vor in gesundheitlichen Fragestellungen zuerkannt wird. Hierfür spricht auch, dass Spanier/innen im Vergleich zu Deutschen ein größeres Vertrauen in medizinische Möglichkeiten setzen (vgl. BERMEJO / MUTHNY 1994). Die vorgestellten Ergebnisse können z.B. Aufschluß darüber geben, warum SpanierInnen, die in der BRD leben, andere Anforderungen und Erwartungen an die Gesundheitsversorgung und besonders an deutsche Ärzte stellen als z.B. deutsche Patienten. Für eine zufriedenstellende Arzt-Patient-Interaktion ist das interkulturelle Verständnis subjektiver Theorien über Gesundheit und Krankheit eine wesentliche Voraussetzung. Die Ergebnisse geben einen ersten Einblick in diese Thematik und verdeutlichen vor allem auch die Notwendigkeit, interkulturelle Unterschiede innerhalb Europas in Gesundheitspolitik und - praxis zu berücksichtigen. Angesichts der Tatsache, dass es sich um eine Pilotstudie handelt, die eine vergleichsweise geringe Stichprobengröße aufweist, möchte ich darauf hinweisen, dass die dargestellten Ergebnisse keineswegs als repräsentativ gelten können. Allerdings sollen sie als Ausgangspunkt und Anregung für weitere Forschung zu diesem Thema verstanden werden. Sowohl präventions- als auch rehabilitationsbezogene Maßnahmen können nur dann erfolgreich durchgeführt werden, wenn subjektive Theorien über die Aufrechterhaltung bzw. Wiederherstellung von Gesundheit in ihrer kulturellen Vielfältigkeit angemessene Berücksichtigung finden und auf die Anforderungen einer multikulturellen Gesellschaft ausgerichtet sind.

References

Antonovsky, A. 1979. *Health, stress, an coping.* San Francisco
Antonovsky, A. 1987. *Unraveling the mystery of health.* London
Bermejo, I. and F.A. Muthny. 1994. Krankheitsverständnis und Kontrollüberzeugungen Gesunder zu Krebs und Herzinfarkt - eine transkulturelle Vergleichsstudie. in *Zeitschrift für Medizinische Psychologie,* 3: 119-130
Bermejo, I. 1996. *Kultur, Migration und das Verständnis von Krebs und Herzinfarkt. Ein transkultureller Vergleich von Spaniern und Deutschen.* Münster.
Bischoff, C. and H. Zenz. 1989. *Patientenkonzepte von Körper und Krankheit.* Bern
Bizeul, Y., U. Bliesener and M. Prawda. 1997. *Vom Umgang mit dem Fremden. Hintergrund, Definitionen, Vorschläge.* Weinheim
Blaxter, M. 1990. *Health and lifestyle.* London
Faller, H. 1990. *Subjektive Krankheitstheorie und Krankheitsverarbeitung bei Herzinfarktrehabilitanden.* Frankfurt a.M.
Faltermaier, T. 1994. *Gesundheitsbewusstsein und Gesundheitshandeln.* Weinheim
Flick, U. 1991. *Alltagswissen über Gesundheit und Krankheit.* Heidelberg
Hui, C.H. and H.C. Triandis. 1983. Multistrategy approach to cross-cultural research. in *Journal of Cross-Cultural Psychology,* 14: 65-83
Jaede, W. and A. Portera. 1993. *Begegnung mit dem Fremden. Interkulturelle Beratung, Therapie und Pädagogik in der Praxis.* Köln.
Kentenich, H., P. Reeg and K.-H. Wehkamp. 1990. *Zwischen zwei Kulturen. Was macht Ausländer krank?* Frankfurt.
Koch, E., M. Özek and W.M. Pfeiffer. 1995. *Psychologie und Pathologie der Migration.* Freiburg.
Kramer, P., J. Lerch and F.A. Muthny. 1993. Subjektive Krankheitstheorien, Einstellungen und Phantasien zum Herzinfarkt. in *Herzkreislauf, Zeitschrift für Kardiologie und Angiologie in Klinik und Praxis,* 25: 218-224.
Lützel, Ch. 1997. Die Migration in Deutschland, Frankreich und der Europäischen Union. in *Vom Umgang mit dem Fremden.* Edited by Y. Bizeul, U. Bliesener and M. Prawda, pp. 20-59. Beltz Verlag Weinheim
Mattes, P. 1991. Gesundheit und Krankheit im internationalen Vergleich. in *Alltagswissen über Gesundheit und Krankheit. Subjektive Theorien und soziale Repräsentationen.* Edited by U. Flick, pp. 87-98. Asanger Verlag Heidelberg
Muthny, F.A., Bermejo, I. and U. Heckl. 1993. Verarbeitungswege und Bewältigungskompetenzen im interkulturellen Vergleich. in *Begegnung mit dem Fremden: Interkulturelle Beratung, Therapie und Pädagogik in der Praxis.* Edited by W. Jaede and A. Portera, pp. 147-173. GwG-Verlag Köln
Muthny, F. A., M. Bechtel and M. Spaete. 1992. Laienätiologie und Krankheitsverarbeitung bei schweren körperlichen Erkrankungen. Eine empirische Vergleichsstudie mit Herzinfarkt-, Krebs-, Dialyse- und MS-Patientinnen. in *Psychotherapie, Psychosomatik, Medizinische Psychologie,* 42: 41-53
Pfeiffer, W.M. 1993. Begegnung mit dem Fremden in Psychotherapie und Beratung. in *Begegnung mit dem Fremden: Interkulturelle Beratung, Therapie und Pädagogik in der Praxis.* Edited by W. Jaede and A. Portera, pp. 15-26. GwG-Verlag Köln
Rohner, R. and W. Köpp. 1993. *Das Fremde in uns, die Fremden bei uns.* Heidelberg
Schaefer, G. 1988. ‚Leben' und ‚Gesundheit' - begriffliche Dimensionen einer positiven Gesundheitserziehung. in *Gesundheit für alle - alles für die Gesundheit.* Edited by Bundesvereinigung für Gesundheitserziehung, pp. 18 - 29. Bonn
Schaefer, G. and D. Hernandez. 1985. *Health Education through Biological Teaching.* Edited by ISMED, University of the Philippines.
Schwarzer, R. 1992. *Psychologie des Gesundheitsverhaltens.* Göttingen
Strittmatter, R. 1995. *Alltagswissen über Gesundheit und gesundheitliche Protektivfaktoren.* Frankfurt a.M.
Thomas, A. 1993. *Kulturvergleichende Psychologie. Eine Einführung.* Göttingen
Verres, R. 1986. *Krebs und Angst. Subjektive Theorien von Laien über Entstehung, Vorsorge, Früherkennung, Behandlung und die psychosoziale Folgen von Krebserkrankungen.* Berlin

Ein Schlüssel zur Frauengesundheit: Hebammenbetreuung in acht europäischen Ländern
A Key to Women's Health: Midwivery Care in Eight European Countries

Beate Schücking

Zusammenfassung: Berufsbild und Ausbildung, Tätigkeit und Ansehen der Hebamme in acht europäischen Ländern werden beschrieben und miteinander verglichen. Besonderes Augenmerk gilt der Perspektive der Klientin auf die sie betreuende Hebamme. Basis der Darstellung ist ein Forschungsprojekt zur Geburtshilfe in Deutschland (Ost und West), Schweden, Norwegen, Tschechien, Österreich, Luxemburg, Frankreich und den Niederlanden. Trotz der geographischen Nähe existieren große Unterschiede für den Hebammenberuf in den einzelnen Ländern, analog zu sehr unterschiedlichen geburtshilflichen Traditionen. Abschließend stellt sich die Frage, zu welchen Veränderungen der europäische Angleichungsprozess im Rahmen der EU führen wird.

Abstract: The training, practice and status of midwives in eight European countries are described and compared, with special focus on the client's view of her midwife. This paper is based on a research project concerning obstretical care in Germany (East and West), Sweden, Norway, Czech Republic, Austria, Luxembourg, France and the Netherlands. In spite of their geographical proximity, the countries reflect major differences in midwifery care, corresponding to very different obstretical traditions. In conclusion, the paper poses the question as to what extent the European Community will equalize these differences.

Keywords: Hebammenausbildung und -tätigkeit, europäischer Vergleich, Frauensicht, soziale Rolle, Midwifery training, midwifery care, European differences, client's view, social status.

„Midwives? Do we still live in medieval times?„ Als ich 1993 ein Forschungsprojekt zur Geburtshilfe in Europa, speziell zu den Geburtserfahrungen der Frauen im Kontext ihrer Betreuung durch Hebammen und FrauenärztInnen (SCHÜCKING 1995) begann, kommentierte eine amerikanische Kollegin die Kurzdarstellung meines Vorhabens mit dem hier angeführten Satz: Hebammen? Aus der Perspektive eines normalen amerikanischen Frauenlebens in der zweiten Hälfte dieses Jahrhunderts werden sie mit vergangenen Zeiten assoziiert. So krass ist die europäische Einschätzung nicht; aber auch hierzulande antworten junge Frauen auf die Frage nach Hebammen u. U.: „Gibt es die noch? Ich dachte eher, früher hätte es die gegeben.„ (v. WELSER 1994)

Im folgenden soll, ausgehend von den Ergebnissen und Erfahrungen aus dem eigenen Forschungsprojekt, versucht werden zu skizzieren, wie einerseits zentral, andererseits doch je nach Gesundheitssystem recht unterschiedlich die Rolle der Hebamme von Frauen in acht europäischen Ländern in der Gegenwart ist und gesehen wird.

Die von mir untersuchten Länder sind: Deutschland, Frankreich, Luxemburg, Österreich, Tschechien, Schweden, Norwegen, Niederlande. In den Gesundheitssystemen dieser Länder gibt es zwei Modelle: Die Trennung bzw. Vermischung von Geburtshilfe und Geburtsmedizin. Norwegen und Schweden (wie auch die anderen skandinavischen Länder) sowie die Niederlande praktizieren die klare Trennung von Geburtshilfe und Geburtsmedizin. Das heißt, in diesen Ländern werden alle physiologisch verlaufenden Schwangerschaften und Geburten und Wochenbetten nicht durch Ärzte, sondern durch Hebammen betreut; die Erkennung von Pathologie bzw. Verdachtsmomenten hierzu obliegt der eigens hierzu sorgfältig ausgebildeten Hebamme.

In Deutschland, Luxemburg und Österreich ist eine solche Trennung nicht üblich, obwohl sie bei uns juristisch möglich ist: Für die Hebamme besteht die „Hinzuziehungspflicht„, d. h., sie muss bei der Geburt dabei sein; die Anwesenheit des Arztes ist im Prinzip fakultativ, hat sich aber im Zuge der Verlagerung der Geburt in die Klinik genauso eingebürgert wie die Schwangerenvorsorge durch die gynäkologische Praxis. De facto wird so für alle Frauen Geburtsmedizin angeboten und häufig auch angewendet.

Ähnlich, mit einigen Abweichungen im Detail, sieht es in Frankreich aus: Hier erfolgt die Schwangerenvorsorge und Geburtsbetreuung im von der Frau frühzeitig gewählten Krankenhaus, häufig durch die dort angestellten Hebammen gemeinsam mit Gynäkologen und Anästhesisten - Rückenmarksbetäubung (PDA) ist weit verbreitet und führt zu einem besonders hohen Interventionsrisiko für die in Frankreich gebärende Frau.

In Tschechien schließlich wird vor allem die Erstgebärende als Fall für die Geburtsmedizin betrachtet, die, wie Risikopatientinnen auch, intensiver ärztlicher Behandlung bedarf. Je nach Krankenhaus und Ort ist es der Zweitgebärenden u.U. möglich, mit Hebamme, ohne ärztliche Hilfe zu entbinden. Der Geburtsmedizin wird jedoch immer größere Bedeutung zugesprochen, v. a. seitdem „westlicher Fortschritt „ mit den entsprechenden Geräten in die Kreißsäle eingezogen ist.

Diese hier grob skizzierten Unterschiede in der Betreuung Schwangerer und Gebärender mögen die unbefangene Beobachterin verblüffen und den Schluss nahelegen, dass so unterschiedliche Betreuung zu sehr unterschiedlichen Ergebnissen führen musste.

Erstaunlicherweise ist dies im quantitativen, also statistisch erfassbaren Bereich sogenannter Geburtsergebnisse nicht eindeutig der Fall: Die am häufigsten angeführten Zahlen, nämlich die perinatale Mortalität (= Kindersterblichkeit unter der Geburt und in den ersten sieben Tagen) liegt in allen Ländern niedrig, in der Größenordnung zwischen 5 und knapp 10 Promille. Gerade die skandinavischen Länder haben schon seit langem besonders gute Ergebnisse vorzuweisen, während die deutschen Zahlen erst seit wenigen Jahren Spitzenpositionen erreichen können.

Aus gesundheitswissenschaftlicher Perspektive sind jedoch weniger die geringen Unterschiede in den Ergebnissen interessant, als die so unterschiedlichen Wege, die zu diesen ähnlichen Resultaten führen. „Mutter und Kind gesund„ heißt es in den meisten Fällen, glücklicherweise; was braucht es nun wirklich, um zu diesem guten Ausgang von Schwangerschaft und Geburt zu kommen? Ohne an dieser Stelle ökonomische Detailberechnungen aufzustellen ist z. B. schon auf den ersten Blick deutlich, dass die verschiedenen Wege sich gerade im Bereich Kosten und Aufwand sehr unterscheiden. Das geburtshilfliche Modell à la Skandinavien oder Niederlande benötigt viele Hebammen; diese müssen besonders gut ausgebildet sein. Tatsächlich sind diese Länder sowohl was die Anzahl (relativ zur Geburtenzahl) wie was die Ausbildungsdauer angeht führend. Sie weisen aber auch große Unterschiede auf: im skandinavischen Modell hat die Hebamme eine Grundausbildung in Krankenpflege gemacht und sich erst nach dieser Qualifikation und entsprechender pflegerischer Tätigkeit für die Hebammenausbildung beworben. Ihre spätere Tätigkeit als Hebamme kennt drei Einsatzmöglichkeiten: Im Kreißsaal, auf der Wochenstation, und im nur ambulant zugänglichen Gesundheitszentrum des Stadtteils. Häufig entwickelt sich ihre Berufskarriere so, dass sie zunächst im Krankenhaus arbeitet, und später - vielleicht nach eigener Familiengründung - nur noch in der Ambulanz, ohne Nachtdienste und Bereitschaften. Für die Frauen hat dies zum einen den Nachteil, dass sie von der ihre Schwangerschaft betreuende Hebamme nie zur Geburt begleitet werden können. Zum anderen erleben sie häufig die Hebammen in zwei Lager gespalten: Die Klinikhebammen als diejenigen, die nah sind am „eigentlichen„ Geschehen, der Geburt, und sich deshalb besonders kompetent fühlen; die Ambulanzhebammen als die älteren, die zwar viel Berufserfahrung haben, aber mit dem Abschied vom Kreißsaal auch Einblick verloren haben; oder sich nicht mehr an das „Eigentliche„ herantrauen, weil sie sich auf Vor- und Nachsorge beschränken.

Ganz anders die ebenfalls hebammenzentrierte Geburtshilfe in Holland: Hier wird zum Beruf ausgebildet in einem neuerdings vierjährigen Curriculum, das ganz auf den selbständigen Beruf ausgerichtet ist, in dem die Hebamme immer alle drei Tätigkeitsbereiche: Vorsorge, Geburtenbetreuung, Nachsorge - nebeneinander ausübt. Geburten finden in der Klinik wie auch zu Hause statt - als reine Klinikhebamme tätig zu sein, wird aber nur als vorübergehende, zeitlich begrenzte Möglichkeit (etwa: in der Familienphase!) gesehen. Für die Frauen bietet sich so die Chance, zur ganzheitlichen Betreuung von Schwangerschaft, Geburt und Wochenbett die eigene Hebamme zu wählen. So entsteht häufig eine intensive und vertrauensvolle Beziehung, die manchmal über mehrere Kinder hinweg, v. a. im ländlichen Raum sogar bis zur nächsten Generation führen kann. Entsprechend gut etabliert ist auch das soziale Ansehen der Hebamme, deren Praxis man kennt, und die ihre Sprechstunde in anderen Stadtteilen oder Dörfern im gleichen Raum abhält wie der Arzt.

Sowohl in Skandinavien wie in Holland ist es den Frauen selbstverständlich, dass für Schwangerschaft, Geburt und Wochenbett im Normalfall die Hebamme die einzige Expertin ist, die hilft, berät und begleitet. Eine schwedische Frau berichtete beispielsweise: „Ich hatte mit den Wehen zu kämpfen, es ging nur langsam voran. Plötzlich blickte ich auf und sah den Arzt in den Kreißsaal treten; ich erschrak, und verdoppelte meine Bemühungen. Tatsächlich war das Baby ein paar Minuten später da - später erzählte mir der Arzt, er sei nur zufällig dagewesen, habe sich Kaffee holen wollen von den Hebammen.„

Für die Schwedin bedeutet der Auftritt des Arztes die Wende zur Geburtsmedizin. Berechtigterweise hat sie Angst vor Komplikationen; dass sie grundsätzlich das Vorhandensein von Geburtsmedizin wünscht und schätzt, drückt sich z. B. darin aus, dass Risikopatientinnen eher ins Perinatalzentrum kommen als in Deutschland. Auch ist der Prozentsatz und die Akzeptanz „alternativer„ Geburtshilfe in Schweden im internationalen Vergleich eher gering.

Die durchschnittliche deutsche Frau kennt und beurteilt die Situation der Schwangerschaft und Geburt deutlich anders: Für sie ist die ärztliche Betreuung, oder zumindest Präsenz, Normalsituation geworden. Entsprechend wird bei jeder Geburt der Arzt im Kreißsaal erwartet; so manche Hebamme hört von gebärenden Frauen oder häufig auch von den Partnern, den Satz: „Gibt es hier denn keinen Arzt? Hier muss doch endlich der Arzt kommen„ - und manche Frau ist nach der Geburt etwas enttäuscht: „Also, der Arzt kam ja nur ab und zu vorbei, erst am Schluss, als ihn die Hebamme anrief, da ist er dann geblieben, hat den Dammschnitt gemacht und genäht. Das hatte ich mir anders vorgestellt - also ich hatte ihn ja vorher gefragt, ob er dabei wäre, und da sagte er „selbstverständlich! ich komme zu jeder Geburt!„ und darauf hatte ich mich verlassen„. (eine 30jährige, 1. Kind, in Oberschwaben). Eine andere Frau schätzt die Situation auch in Deutschland von vornherein realistisch ein: „Für die Geburt war mir die Hebamme wichtig - bei der habe ich mich sehr gut aufgehoben gefühlt, sie hatte 25 Jahre Berufserfahrung. Mein Mann fragte immer nach dem Arzt - ich habe ihn nicht vermisst, und als er dann kam, der Professor - ich bin privatversichert - so ein Aufstand! Wange getätschelt, geht's gut, geht's gut gefragt, und dann war er wieder weg. Ich habe doch gewusst, dass der mir nicht helfen kann, sondern hier nur seine Show abzieht, so'nen Quickie. Aber es war alles ganz in Ordnung - ich hab's ja gut hingekriegt. (Eine 32jährige, 1. Kind, in München). Obwohl diese Frau ihre Prioritäten ganz klar und deutlich formuliert: die Hebamme ist ihr wichtig, der Arzt nicht - kann sie auch als privilegierte Privatpatientin nur den Arzt wählen - die Hebamme nicht. In fast allen Kliniken werden die Frauen mit den Hebammen konfrontiert, die gerade Dienst haben; in aller Regel fremde Gesichter. So muss eine vertrauensvolle Beziehung in kurzer Zeit aufgebaut werden; wenige, wenn auch für die einzelne Frau sehr bedeutsame Stunden wird sie in der äußerst intensiven und intimen Situation des Gebärens von einer Kreißsaalhebamme (bei Schichtwechsel evtl. auch zweien oder dreien) betreut und begleitet, die sich nach der Geburt meist auf Nimmerwiedersehen verabschiedet. Das stationäre Wochenbett fällt in Deutschland in den Zuständigkeitsbereich der Pflege. Nur in den „alternativen„ Angeboten der Hausgeburtshilfe, der Geburtshäuser und teilweise im Belegsystem ist eine kontinuierliche Hebammenbetreuung möglich.

Viele Frauen bedauern dies inzwischen, und zunehmend entsteht Nachfrage nach Angeboten, wenigstens eine Hebamme für die Nachsorge zu Hause zu finden, die schon vorher (z. B. vom Geburtsvorbereitungskurs) bekannt war.

Vor allem im Vergleich zum Nachbarland Holland werden die Unterschiede deutlich: Einer holländischen Frau ist es selbstverständlich durch normale Schwangerschaft, Geburt und Wochenbett von einer selbst gewählten Hebamme begleitet zu werden; hier entstehen oft enge Beziehungen: „So gemütlich war es immer, in dieser Hebammenpraxis. Richtig schade, dass das nun vorbei ist - bis zur nächsten Schwangerschaft.„ berichtete eine 29jährige in Harlem. Aber auch eine Norwegerin erzählte: „ Vor allem als Schwangere Fühlte ich mich bei den Hebammen sehr wohl. Es gibt so ein sicheres Gefühl, bei jemand zu sein, der sich nur um's Kinderkriegen kümmert, sich nur konzentriert. Bei den Ärzten weißt du doch immer, dass du nur ein Fall unter vielen bist.„

Kontinuierliche Hebammenbetreuung scheint in den Geburtssystemen der von mir untersuchten Länder nur einen geringen Stellenwert zu haben: weder in Luxemburg, noch in Frankreich, Österreich oder Tschechien wird sie eingeplant, obwohl die Kreißsaalteams überall um ihren Wert wissen. So wurden mir z. B. in Luxemburg die Häufigkeit präpartaler CTG (Herzton-Wehenschreibung) so erklärt, dass auf diese Weise viele Frauen eine Möglichkeit hätten, den Kreißsaal und die Hebammen kennenzulernen. So muss eine (medizinisch nicht unbedingt gerechtfertigte) apparative Untersuchung eingesetzt werden, um etwas anderenorts so selbstverständliches wie den Kontakt zwischen Schwangeren und

Hebammen herzustellen! Ob das ökonomisch sein kann?

Merkwürdigerweise entdeckte ich solche und ähnliche Phänomene in allen 5 Ländern, in denen Geburtsmedizin und Geburtshilfe nicht voneinander getrennt sind. Diese Länder (BRD, A, C, F ,L) haben ähnlich ausgebildete Hebammen - ein 3jähriges Curriculum mit mehr oder weniger intensiver Praxiseinbindung an oft traditionsreichen Hebammenschulen, die allerdings auch innerhalb der Länder unterschiedliche Lehrschwerpunkte und -Qualitäten aufweisen. Aufgabe der Hebamme ist es überall, vor allem im Kreißsaal tätig zu sein - Frauen unter der Geburt zu betreuen, zu versorgen, zu beobachten und ggf. auch einzugreifen bzw. spätestens im letzten Moment der Austreibungsphase Arzt oder Ärztin hinzuzuholen. Die Variationen in dieser Funktion sind national und regional, und zumeist sicherlich historisch gewachsen: So ist in Tschechien die Hebamme bei der Erstgebärenden weit weniger aktiv als bei der mehrgebärenden Frau, die weniger ärztlicher Kontrolle unterliegt. In Frankreich übernehmen Hebammen in einer hochtechnisierten Geburtshilfe viele Funktionen, die anderswo Ärzten vorbehalten sind (Medikation, Dammschnitt, Naht), und in Deutschland waren Hebammen in den neuen Bundesländern aus der Tradition der DDR ein selbstständigeres Arbeiten gewöhnt als in Westdeutschland.

In ähnlicher Weise ist aber in allen Ländern die Hebammenarbeit unter ärztliche Weisungsbefugnis gestellt: Ärztliche Anordnungen müssen - Vorschläge der Hebammen können befolgt werden im Kreißsaalteam. Da die Hebammen auf professioneller Seite die zeitaufwendigere Betreuung der Gebärenden leistet, wird ihre Arbeit zur „Schattenarbeit„ (Iwan Illich). Sie taucht auch z. B. in gesundheitswissenschaftlichen Analysen kaum auf - Leben und Gesundheit von Müttern und Kindern wird in ärztlich definierten Erfolgsziffern wie der perinatalen Mortalitätsrate benannt. Hebammentätigkeit wird öffentlich wie professionell selten benannt. So ist z. B. in Deutschland erst im Rahmen von Gebührenverhandlungen für die selbstständige Hebammenarbeit in einer Kommission des Gesundheitsministeriums das Tätigkeitsspektrum der Hebamme durch die beiden Berufsverbände insgesamt aufgelistet und damit aktenkundig gemacht worden. Bis zu diesem Zeitpunkt (1996) war selbst das Gesundheitsministerium nicht über die gesamte Palette der Beratungs- und Betreuungsmöglichkeiten durch Hebammen informiert, erfuhr ich nicht ohne Staunen als beratendes Kommissionsmitglied.'

Nun heißt die Überschrift dieses Beitrages: Ein Schlüssel zur Frauengesundheit; es stellt sich spätestens an diesem Punkt des Überblicks über Hebammen in Europa die Frage, was denn mit diesem Schlüssel in der Mehrzahl der (geburtsmedizinisch arbeitenden) Länder geschieht - ist er verloren? vergessen? passt er nicht mehr?

Die Weltgesundheitsorganisation (WHO) ist in älteren (1985) und jüngsten Publikationen (CHALMERS 1992, OAKLEY 1990, WHO 1985A, WHO 1985B, WHO 1993, WHO 1996) unverändert der Auffassung, dass Hebammenarbeit in allen, auch den industrialisierten Ländern diese Bedeutung zukommt. M. Wagner, der langjährige Ressortleiter „Health for Women and Children„ im europäischen Regionalbüro der WHO, hat wissenschaftliche Auseinandersetzung und Entscheidungsfindung für die geburtshilflichen Empfehlungen der WHO und ihre Resonanz sorgfältig dokumentiert. (WAGNER 1994) Er beschreibt auch einige der zahlreichen Gründe, weshalb die WHO-Empfehlungen in vielen Ländern nur zögerlich umgesetzt werden: Mangelnde Selbstkontrolle auf der Basis wissenschaftlicher Evidenz auf Seiten der Medizin - Hierarchische Traditionen innerhalb von Krankenhäusern - mangelnde Information der Öffentlichkeit. Hinzuzufügen ist für den Bereich der Hebammenarbeit: Mangelnde Lobby - denn in den meisten Ländern machen Hebammen eine der kleinsten Gruppen des Gesundheitswesens aus, und selbst bei der WHO werden sie häufig der Pflege zugeordnet trotz der eindeutigen Unterschiede im Tätigkeitsprofil.

Die Forderung nach einem quantitativ wie qualitativ guten Angebot an Hebammenhilfe für alle Schwangeren steht schließlich auch in Übereinstimmung mit der Resolution der Weltfrauenkonferenz Peking, die ausdrücklich eine Gesundheitsversorgung fordert, die „available, accessible, affordable, appropiate and accessable„sein soll, und die Geburtshilfe als spezielles Problemfeld benennt. (UNITED NATIONS 1995, GIJSBEERS VAN WIJK 1996)

Aufgegriffen wird die Debatte im Sinne wirklich veränderter Praxis bisher nur in Großbritannien. Dort haben umfangreiche und in den Fachzeitschriften auf höchstem Niveau präsentierte Studien mehrfach die Gleichwertigkeit der Hebammenbetreuung im Vergleich zum herkömmlichen setting für Niedrig-Risiko-Frauen nachgewiesen - bei meist auch hier größerer Zufriedenheit der Frauen und eher niedrigeren Interventionsraten. (TUCKER et.al. 1996, TURNBULL et.al. 1996) Vorausgegangen waren gesundheitspolitische Diskussionen und Untersuchungen, die ebenfalls eine Veränderung hin zu mehr intensiverer Hebammenbetreuung forderten (WINTERTON-REPORT 1992). Inzwischen gibt es in England neue Programme der Gesundheitsversorgung, die die oben beschriebenen Erkenntnisse umsetzen: „Choose your Midwife - one to one„ beispielsweise will den Frauen ermöglichen, kontinuierlich von einer selbstgewählten Hebamme betreut zu werden.

In Deutschland und in Österreich wurden und werden in den letzten Jahren die Rahmenbedingungen für die selbstständige Hebammenarbeit verändert: Die Möglichkeiten, freiberuflich zu arbeiten, auch neben einer Festeinstellung, und eine höhere Vergütung dieser Leistungen ermöglichen ein breiteres Tätigkeitsfeld - und damit ist den Frauen ein größeres Spektrum von Betreuungsangeboten gegeben. Es bleibt abzuwarten, ob - im derzeitigen Sparkurs des Gesundheitswesens - wirklich veränderte Betreuungsformen und Projekte wie in England eingerichtet werden können. Im Zuge des Europäisierungsprozesses ist langfristig eine Angleichung der verschiedenen geburtshilflichen Modelle aneinander zu erwarten. Es bleibt zu hoffen, dass hier die Gesundheit der Frauen, ihre Bedürfnisse und Wünsche zumindest im Sinne der Pekinger Resolution, Leitlinie werden kann. Dann müssten Hebammen in allen EU-Ländern den zentralen Platz in der Geburtshilfe erhalten, den sie jetzt in einigen wenigen schon einnehmen.

References

CHALMERS, B. 1992 WHO Appropriate Technology for Birth rivisited *British Journal for Obstet. and Gynaec.*, vol 99, 709 - 710

GIJSBEERS VAN WIJK, C. M. et al 1996 Gender Perspectives and Quality of Care: Towards appropriate and adequate health care for women. *Soc. Sci. Med.* Vol 43, No 5, 707 - 720

OAKLEY, A. v. HOUD, S. 1990 *Helpers in Childbirth. Midwifery* Today Hemishere Publ. New York

SCHÜCKING, B. 1995. Frauen in Europa. Unterschiedliche und ähnliche Erfahrungen mit der ersten Schwangerschaft und Geburt. In: SCHIEVENHÖVEL, W., D. SICH, C.E. GOTTSCHALK-BATSCHKUS. *Gebären-Ethnomedizinische Perspektiven und neue Wege.* VWB Berlin

TUCKER, JS et al. 1996. Should obstetricicians see women with normal pregnancies? *British Medical Journal* 312, 554-559

TURNBULL, D. et al. 1996. Randomised, controlled trial of efficay of Midwife-managed Care. *The Lancet* Vol 348, July 27, 1996, 213-218

UNITED NATIONS 1995. *Platform for Action Report of the Main Committee of the Thourth.* World Conference on Women. A/Conf. 177/L. 5/Add 7, Beijing 13. Sept.

WAGNER, M. 1994. *Pursuing the Birth Machine.* Camperdown (Australia)

WELSER, M. v. 1994. (Moderatorin) zitierte Passantinnen-Interviews in der Sendung: *Mona Lisa,* ZDF, 13. 10. 94

WHO. 1985a. *Having a Baby in Europe. Report on a study.* Regional Office for Europe, Copenhagen.

WHO. 1985b. Appropriate technology for birth. *Lancet*, vol 2, 436-7

WHO. 1993. *Investing in women's Health. Guidelines for the Women's Health Profile,* Copenhagen.

WHO. 1996. *Safe Motherhood.* Geneva

Grundlagen der Ethnomedizin

Medizinanthropologie und Medizinethnologie

Gesundheit, Krankheit und Heilung im Kulturvergleich

Herausgeber:
Christine E. Gottschalk-Batschkus, Armin Prinz
& Judith Schuler

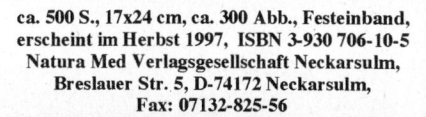

ca. 500 S., 17x24 cm, ca. 300 Abb., Festeinband, erscheint im Herbst 1997, ISBN 3-930 706-10-5
Natura Med Verlagsgesellschaft Neckarsulm,
Breslauer Str. 5, D-74172 Neckarsulm,
Fax: 07132-825-56

Das Standardwerk zum Thema Ethnomedizin, Medizinanthropologie und Medizinethnologie mit Beiträgen führender Wissenschaftler der ethnomedizinischen Lehre im deutschsprachigen Raum.

Inhalt:
- Geschichte der Ethnomedizin bis 1900 und neuere Entwicklungen
- zahlreiche zentrale ethnomedizinische Wissenschaftsbereiche und Forschungsrichtungen
- Grundlagen ethnomedizinischer Feldforschung, Auswertung, Analyse und Anleitung zum wissenschaftlichen Arbeiten
- Einblick in ethnomedizinische Fragestellungen in Gesundheitspolitik, Entwicklungshilfe und Tropenmedizin
- Diskussion ethischer Probleme mit der modernen Medizin und kulturfremden Systemen.

Ein fundamentales, interdisziplinäres Werk mit dem Anspruch eines Lehrbuchs für Studierende, Fachleute und Praktiker.

Unter Mitarbeit von:
CHRISTINE BINDER-FRITZ, Wien, ALEXANDER BOROFFKA, Kiel, DORIS BURTSCHER, Wien, IGOR DE GARINE, Gan, Frankreich, HANS-JOCHEN DIESFELD, Neckargemünd, PETER EBIGBO, Enugu Anambra, Nigeria, DAGMAR EIGNER, Wien, ELFRIEDE GRABNER, Graz, HELMUT GRÖGER, Wien, BERNHARD HADOLT, Wien, THOMAS HEISE, PAUL HIEPKO, Berlin, ELISABETH LEE HSU, Zürich, ECKHARDT KOCH, NORBERT KOHNEN, Köln, GERHARD KUBIK, Wien, LISELOTTE KUNTNER, Küttigen, RUTH KUTALEK, Wien, THOMAS LUX, Frankfurt, WOLFGANG MASTNAK, München, GUY MAZARS, Strasbourg, BRIGIT OBRIST VAN EEUWIJK, Basel, ISTVAN ORMOS, Budapest, WOLFGANG PFEIFFER, Erlangen, RENAUD VAN QUEKELBERGHE, Düsseldorf, VOLKER ROELCKE, Bonn, UWE SIEBERT, München, JOHANNES SOMMERFELD, Heidelberg, GERHARD K. TUCEK, CHRISTINE TUSCHINSKY, Hamburg, ULRIKE UNSCHULD, München, LUIS ALBERTO VARGAS, Ciudad de Mexico, Mexico, MARTINE VERWEY, Zürich, PETER WEIGL, Graz.

Die Rolle der Frau als Heilerin und Hexe in Europa zwischen 1100 und 1800
The Role of Women as Healers and Witches in Europe between 1100 and 1800

Doris Iding

Zusammenfassung: In allen Kulturen spielt die Frau als Heilerin eine große Rolle, aber nirgends erfuhr sie ein so trauriges Schicksal wie in großen Teilen Europas und der Neuen Welt. Mit der Verbreitung des Christentums wurde sie von der Heilerin zur Hexe degradiert, zu Unrecht verurteilt und verbrannt. Noch um das Jahr 1100 konnten Frauen, meistens im Schutze der Kirche, als Heilerinnen arbeiten und hohes Ansehen erlangt. Zu den bekanntesten Heilerinnen dieser Zeit zählt Hildegard von Bingen, die in einem eigenen Kloster lebte und lehrte. Die Hexenverfolgung, der ca. 1200 begann, ihren Höhepunkt im 15./16. Jahrhundert erlebte und erst 1775 endete, ist neben der Judenverfolgung eines der traurigsten Kapitel der Menschenvernichtung außerhalb einer Kriegssituation. Nicht nur mussten hunderttausende von Heilerinnen auch einen qualvollen Tod auf dem Scheiterhaufen erleiden, durch ihren Tod erlagen auch unzählige Menschen Krankheiten, gegen die ihnen von diesen weisen Frauen hätte geholfen werden können. Mit den Heilerinnen wurden uraltes Wissen, eine umfassende Kräuterkunde und zahlreiche Anweisungen für rituelle Handlungen zu Asche und Rauch. Erst langsam erholt man sich von den Wunden jener Zeit, und erst langsam erkennt man die Frau wieder als eine dem Arzt ebenbürtige Heilerin an.

Abstract: Women play a significant role as healers in all cultures, but nowhere did they experience such a deplorable fate as in large parts of Europe and the New World. With the spread of Christianity these women were degrated from healers to witches, unjustly condemned and burned. In 1100 A.D. women were still able to work as healers, usually under the protection of the church, and to achieve a high standing. Hildegard von Bingen was one of the most well-known healers of this time. She lived and taught in her own convent. Following the persecution of the Jews, the persecution of witches, which began around 1200 A.D., reached ist climax in the 15th and 16th centuries and only ended in 1775 is one of the saddest chapters of human destruction during a time of peace. Not only were hundreds of thousands of healers forced to suffer a painful death by burning at the stake, but due to the death of these wise women innumerable people died of illness which could have otherwise been treated. Along with the healers ancient knowledge, extensive herbal lore and considerable information on ritual treatment were reduced to smoke and ashes. Only slowly has it possible for the human race to recover rom the wounds inflicted during this period an to once again recognize women healers as having a rank equal to that of doctors.

Keywords: Heilerinnen, Hexe, Hexenverfolgung, Mittelalter, Hildegard von Bingen, maleus maleficarum , female healer, witches, persecution of witches, middle age, Hildegard von Bingen, maleus maleficarum

Europa und die Stellung der Heilerin im Hochmittelalter

Im Hochmittelalter befand sich Europa im Umbruch. Städte und Stände (Adel, Patrizier, Handwerker, Klerus, Bauern und Leibeigene) entstanden, neue Agrartechnologien sicherten Nahrungsmittel für eine gesündere Bevölkerung. Durch den Bergbau kam Geld auf und brachte den Handel in Schwung. Die Rolle der Frau war nicht an starre Regeln gebunden und an Beispielen wie Eleonore von Aquitanien, Blanca von Kastilien oder Kaiserin Mathilde von England zeigt sich, dass die Frauen des Adels mit regem Interesse am politischen und kulturellen Leben teilnahmen. Sie brachten sich in die Arbeitswelt ein, waren im Familiengewerbe tätig und standen in ihren Leistungen den Männern als Brauerinnen, Lehrerinnen, Ziegelbrennerinnen, Hebammen und in anderen Berufen nicht nach. Immer noch schlechter bezahlt als Männer, ging es ihnen doch besser als in den Jahrhunderten zuvor und auch danach.

Während sich das Leben für die Leibeigenen nicht wesentlich änderte, bekamen Körperpflege, Hygiene und Luxus bei Klerus und Adel mehr Bedeutung. Räume wurden in kleine, gemütliche Zimmer unterteilt und boten größere Privatsphäre. Stinkende Feuerstellen wurden durch riesige Herde ersetzt, durch die der Qualm nach außen abzog. Nachdem die entspannende und gesundheitsfördernde Wirkung des Badens entdeckt worden war, waren Badezuber in jedem reichen Haushalt zu finden. Trotzdem kann noch nicht von Sauberkeit die Rede sein, denn Abfall gab es genug.Aborte, an Senkgruben oder Abwassergräben angeschlossen, wurden nur in Abständen entleert. Welche Rolle Bakterien bei Krankheiten spielten, wusste man noch nicht, bemühte sich aber intuitiv in Wohngebieten um mehr Hygiene, um das Zusammenleben erträglicher zu gestalten. Trotzdem grassierten unzählige Krankheiten, gegen die die Menschen machtlos waren. Klerus und Aristokratie erkrankten durch maßlose Völlerei an Verdauungsproblemen, Herz-Kreislaufbeschwerden und Fettsucht. Die Bauern litten an Erschöpfungskrankheiten und anderen Auswirkungen der harten, zermürbe Arbeit. Bei guten Ernten jedoch war ihre Ernährung gesünder als die der oberen Schichten.

Aber es gab auch genug Erkrankungen, die keine Klassenschranken kannte. Bei Geburten, die oftmals sehr schwierig waren, kam es zu Deformationen der Neugeborenen, und viele Babys wurden nicht älter als 2 Jahre. Die meisten Menschen wurden von Augenkrankheiten, Ruhr, Typhus, Diphtherie, Grippe, Malaria und Epilepsie heimgesucht. Begünstigt wurde deren Verbreitung durch verseuchte Wasserreservoire und Epidemien. Das "Antoniusfeuer", ausgelöst durch mutterkornverseuchtes Getreide, grassierte und streckte selbst den gesündesten Menschen nieder. Der Brand befiel primär Hände und Füße vom Brand. Das Fleisch wurde schwarz und fiel von den Knochen. Überlebten Menschen, waren sie verstümmelt. Leichtere Hautkrankheiten wie Krätze, ausgelöst durch schlechte Hygiene, schmutzige Kleidung und rauhes Gewebe waren gang und gäbe. Auch von der Lepra und den Pocken blieb Mitteleuropa im 12. und 13. Jahrhundert nicht verschont.

Die Bedeutung der Medizin

Bei all diesen Krankheiten und Epidemien war die medizinische Entwicklung in alten Strukturen festgefahren, und es gab nur wenige qualifizierte Ärzte. Überhaupt waren Mediziner - nicht nur die weiblichen - gesellschaftlich nicht besonders hoch angesehen, und gute gesundheitliche Versorgung konnten sich nur wenige leisten. "Dem Volk blieb nichts weiter übrig, als sich zur Kirchenpforte zu drängen und mit Weihwasser besprengen zu lassen"(vgl. SZACZ 1974:133) . Frauen hatten kleine Kräuterapotheken zu Hause und kurierten Krankheiten im Rahmen ihrer Möglichkeiten weitgehend selbst. Ansonsten suchte man weise Frauen auf, die nicht nur als Ärztin, sondern auch als Zauberin, Astrologin und Prophetin arbeiteten (SZACZ 1974: 74). Sie dienten den leidenden Menschen und unterstützten sie im Rahmen ihrer Möglichkeiten. Als Hebammen verfügten sie zwar über einige Fertigkeiten, arbeiteten mit Kräutern und Zauberformeln, aber die Kunst, einen Kaiserschnitt durchzuführen, eine Embryotomie vorzunehmen oder ein Kind im Mutterleib zu drehen, war in Vergessenheit geraten. Neugeborene taufte man, wenn möglich, am Tag der Entbindung, damit sie wenigstens in den Himmel kamen, sollten sie die ersten Tage nicht überleben. Außerdem hatten Hebammen eine wichtige Funktion, nämlich die der Geburtenregulation (HEINSOHN 1985).

Medizin für das Volk

Dem Volk war es kaum möglich, sich medizinisches Wissen anzueignen. In England kursierte das Buch eines anonymen Autors "Leech Book of Bald". Für Laien geschrieben, half es mit primär nichttoxischen, milden Kräutermixturen und jeder Menge christlicher Stoßgebete bei der Selbstmedikation. Bei einem Furunkel empfahl es:"Ampfer (Rumex) auszugraben, dabei ein Vaterunser anzustimmen, dann fünf Teile davon mit sieben Pfefferkörnern zu vermischen und dabei zwölfmal das Misere, Gloria und Vaterunser zu singen, schließlich alles mit Wein zu übergießen, das Gebräu um Mitternacht zu trinken und sich warm einzupacken."(vgl. ACHTERBERG 1994:72). Medizinische Texte von Aristoteles, Hippokrates und Galen, die im 11. Jahrhundert im Nahen Osten übersetzt worden waren und über Umwege, angereichert mit arabischem Wissen, zurück nach Europa gelangten, waren nur den oberen Schichten zugänglich. Bei ihnen wurde durch diese Schriften das Interesse an der Medizin geweckt und führte zur Gründung medizinischer Schulen. Die berühmteste ist die Schule in Salerno. Sie wurde 1000 n. Chr. gegründet und durch eine Verfügung Napoleons 1811 geschlossen. Dort lehrten und lernten Männer und Frauen der unterschiedlichsten Nationen. Trotula, eine renommierte Medizinerin ihrer Zeit, hatte dort zahlreiche Schüler und Schülerinnen. Ihre Abhandlung über Gynäkologie und Geburtshilfe, sowie andere Manuskripte befinden sich heute in verschiedenen Museen Europas. Immer wieder wurde Trotulas Existenz angezweifelt, nicht zuletzt von Christian Godfred, einem Historiker aus dem 18. Jahrhundert. Er wollte nicht glauben, dass im 11. Jahrhundert eine Frau soviel medizinisches Wissen besitzen konnte. Urin- und Pulsproben waren ihr bei der ganzheitlichen Diagnosenstellung genauso wichtig wie der Charakter und das Verhalten des Patienten. Sie schrieb eine Abhandlung über die dermatologischen Phänomene der Syphilis und verwies immer wieder auf die Bedeutung der Hygiene sowohl bei chirurgischen als bei anderen Eingriffen. Bei all den Seuchen und Epidemien, die grassierten, war ihre Arbeit allerdings nur ein Tropfen auf dem heißen Stein. Neben ihr war es nur einer kleinen Gruppe von Frauen möglich, unangefochten eine geachtete Stellung als Medizinerinnen in der Gesellschaft einzunehmen. Für sie war es am einfachsten, heilerischen Fähigkeiten innerhalb eines Klosters nachzugehen. Dort genossen sie ein relativ freies und abwechslungsreiches Leben mit Reisen, Lesen, Lehren und der Heilkunst.

Das Leben der Hildegard von Bingen

Zu den bekanntesten Äbtissinnen zählt Hildegard von Bingen. Im Jahre 1106 kam sie im Alter von 8 Jahren in das aufstrebende Benediktinerkloster im Nahetal. Dort wurde sie Jutta von Spanheim anvertraut, die Hildegards visionäre Fähigkeiten schnell erkannte und unterstützte. Nach Juttas Tod im Jahre 1136 wurde Hildegard zur Äbtissin des Adelskonventes gewählt. Durch ihre charismatische Ausstrahlung gewann sie viele Anhängerinnen und gründete später ihr eigenes Kloster. Im Jahre 1141 erhielt sie in einer Erleuchtung den Auftrag, ihre Visionen niederzuschreiben. Sie begann damit im Alter von 42 Jahren und schrieb ihre drei größten Werke, ein medizinisches und zwei theologische. Vier Visionswellen ergriffen sie, und bis zu ihrem 74. Lebensjahr war sie mit den Aufzeichnungen beschäftigt. Sie starb im Jahre 1179 im 82. Lebensjahr in ihrem Kloster Rupertsberg bei Bingen am Rhein. Die Kirche, die sie kritisch beobachtete, ging davon aus, dass ihre Werke durch die Stimme Gottes diktiert wurden. Durch diese kirchliche Einschätzung war sie vor Verfolgung geschützt.

Die Äbtissin sah eine unauflösliche Verbindung zwischen Kosmos und Mensch. In Krankheiten sah sie einen Wink des Schicksals, ein neues Leben zu beginnen und deshalb hielt sie Heilung für einen holistischen Akt. Die Basis für eine Gesundung sah sie im Fasten. Aber nicht nur kranken, sondern auch gesunden Menschen empfahl sie zu fasten. Depressiven Menschen, Patienten mit Geistes- und Infektionskrankheiten, sowie Krebs- und TBC-Kranken riet sie jedoch davon ab. Fasten führt zur inneren Reinigung und Ausscheidung von Gift- und Schlackenstoffen. Eine prophylaktische Fastenkur dauerte bis zu zehn Tage. Hildegard erkannte die gesteigerte Wirksamkeit von Heilmitteln nach Fastenkuren, da der Körper frei von Schlacken- und Giftstoffen ist und Stoffwechsel, Blutdruck und Cholesterinspiegel regeneriert wurden. Ihrer Zeit in vielen Dingen voraus, riet sie z.B. Patienten mit Diabetes, weder Süßigkeiten noch Nüsse zu essen. Eine wichtige Rolle spielten bei ihrer Behandlung die Einflüsse sichtbarer und unsichtbarer Naturkräfte und - geister. Im positiven wie im negativen Sinne konnten Steine, Metalle und Pflanzen von übernatürlichen Gestalten, Dämonen und Teufeln besessen sein. Eine Anschauung, wie sie auch heute noch bei vielen Naturvölkern angetroffen wird. Auch Astrologie, Hellsicht in Träumen und Gemmologie nahmen Teil der Behandlung ein. Sie stellte Rezepte für spezielle Ernährungstherapien zusammen. Weit über 300 Rezepte zur Heilung von Erkrankung wie Darmleiden, Leberschwäche, Lungenleiden, Bluthochdruck u.v.m sind von ihr erhalten. Viele Krankheiten hatten seelische Ursachen, und spirituelle Übungen und Meditationen für jeden Tag halfen den Kranken, eigene Heilfähigkeiten zu entwickeln. Gerade in den letzten Jahren finden Hildegard von Bingens Werke wieder große Beachtung:

Ihr heilkundliches Wissen umfasste die Wirkungsweise von 485 Pflanzen, ihrer Meinung nach alle von Gott gegebene Heilpflanzen. Zu den bekanntesten zählen: Aloe, Beifuß, Fenchel, Gewürznelken, Ingwer, Krappwurzel, Lavendel, Muskat, Ringelblume, Salbei, Thymian, Weißdorn und Wermut. (HERTZKA 1988). Sie empfahl geringe, homöopathische Mengen. Sie war eine der letzten Heilerinnen ihrer Zeit, die ihre Heilkünste ausüben konnte, ohne dafür mit dem Leben zahlen zu müssen. Danach bahnte sich ein dunkles Zeitalter an, in dem die Kirche den Frauen heilerische Fähigkeiten absprach und sie zu Hexen degradierte. Je mehr sich das Christentum verbreitete, desto mehr wurde die Heilerin angeprangert und als Verbündete des Teufels dargestellt.

Die Kirche und Heilerinnen

Die kirchlichen Dogmen der folgenden Jahrhunderte stützten sich auf die Philosophie des heiligen Augustinus, wonach nur die Kirche von Sünden freisprechen konnte. Mit solchen Bestimmungen bestrafte man Hebammen, die Gebärenden bei der Geburt schmerzlindernde Mittel geben wollten, da die Wehen die Frau an ihre ursprünglich begangene Sünde erinnern sollten: "Viel Mühsal bereite ich dir, sooft du schwanger wirst. Unter Schmerzen gebierst du Kinder. Du hast Verlangen nach deinem

Mann, er aber wird über dich herrschen" (Gen 3.16). Die Kirche entschied nicht nur darüber, wer Sühne zu leisten hatte, sondern auch, wer ein Sündenbock war. Sie war medizinischen Verbesserungen gegenüber feindlich eingestellt, da sie darin einen Machtverlust sah: "Selbst die Schule von Salerno erregte den Abscheu vieler strenggläubiger Kleriker, weil sie Ernährungsregeln vorschrieb und damit den Glauben andeutete, Krankheit gehe auf natürliche Ursachen zurück und nicht auf die Tücken des Teufels." (vgl. SZCZ 1974:139)

Die Kirche richtete die Heilige Inquisition ein, die mit dem Ketzerprozess in Orléans im Jahre 1022 begründet wurde und 700 Jahre lang in Europa und Südamerika wütete. Hauptanklagepunkte bildeten hierbei: Geschlechtsverkehr mit dem Teufel, orgiastische und blutige Rituale oder okkulte Kenntnisse sowie das Töten und Verspeisen von Kleinkindern. Als Ketzer galten Templer, Katharer, Waldenser, der Orden der Armen Ritter Christi sowie Paulicianer. Bis zum 15. Jahrhundert beschränkte sich die Verfolgung primär auf diese Ordensmitglieder. Dann begann man, Juden, Heilerinnen und Hexen im Namen Gottes für alles mögliche Unheil, das über die Menschen und die Natur hereinbrach - von Epidemien bis zu Missernten - verantwortlich zu machen. Während die Kirche Juden hauptsächlich des Ritualmordes und der Gotteslästerung bezichtigte und zum Scheiterhaufen schleifte, wurden auf angrenzenden Marktplätzen Christen als vermeintliche Hexen verbrannt. (SZASZ 1974).

Krisen und Krankheiten

Diese Jahrhunderte waren angefüllt mit Epidemien und Naturkatastrophen. Klimaveränderungen brachten strengere Winter, schlechtere Ernten und Hungersnöte mit sich, die zwischen 1308 und 1317 zu einer verheerenden Situation führte. (ACHTERBERG 1994). Dazu kam im Jahr 1347 die Pest, die über Europa hineinbrach und sich in drei Krankheitsbildern zeigte: als Lungenpest mit tödlicher Lungenentzündung, als Beulenpest mit eitriger Lymphdrüsenentzündung und als Blutvergiftung. Die Krankheit raffte ihre Opfer innerhalb von 3 Tagen dahin. Vom Franziskanerorden fielen alleine 124 434 Menschen dem Schwarzen Tod zum Opfer. Da Frauen gegen diese Krankheit resistenter waren als Männer, beschuldigte man sie, sich durch Magie zu schützen und diese sogar gegen Männer einzusetzen. Neben der Pest, die immer wieder aufflackerte und besonders 1478 grassierte, wurden Menschen von einer tödlichen Form der Syphilis, von Wundrose, Pocken, von Masern und dem Veitstanz betroffen.

Trotz der Krankheiten und einem großen Mangel an guten, qualifizierten Ärzten wehrten sich die Mediziner gegen die Aufnahme von Frauen. Guy de Chauliac, der anerkannteste Chirurg des Mittelalters, wandte sich massiv gegen ihre Aufnahme in die Ärzteschaft. Er bezeichnete sie als "Idiotinnen, die Kräuter sammelten und religiösen Unsinn betrieben". Sie durften lediglich als Hebamme arbeiten, der nicht sonderlich viel Ansehen entgegengebracht wurde und die sich hervorragend als Sündenbock eignete. Kam das Kind eines reichen Patienten krank oder tot zur Welt, wurde sie genauso zur Verantwortung gezogen, wie für den Tod einer Mutter an Kinderbettbfieber. Setzten Heilerinnen ihr Wissen ein, wurden sie der Hexerei beschuldigt. Da sie nur noch in seltenen Fällen Medizin studieren durfte, konnte sie ihre Kenntnisse nur vom Teufel haben. Die Kirche behauptete, "daß, wenn eine Frau, ohne studiert zu haben, zu kurieren wagt, sie eine Hexe ist und sterben muß."

Hexenverfolgung

Mit dem Buchdruck, der um 1450 erfunden wurde, verschärfte die Verbreitung von Schriften gegen Hexen und Ketzer die Verfolgung und schürte das Feuer für die Hexenverfolgung. Eingeleitet wurde dies durch die "Summis desiderantes", eine Hexen-Ketzerbulle des Papstes Innozenz VIII im Jahre 1484, die sich gegen den Abfall vom katholischen Glauben richtete. Darin wurden Männer und Frauen gleichermaßen des Schadenszaubers beschuldigt, der angeblich zur Unfruchtbarkeit bei Menschen und Tieren führte. Der „Hexenhammer„ (maleus maleficarum), den die beiden dominikanischen Inquisitoren Jakob Sprenger und Heinrich Krämer (Institoris) 1487 veröffentlichten, war ein weiteres Werk, das zur Verfolgung von Heilerinnen führte. Dieses Handbuch bestand aus drei Teilen:

1. Hier ging man systematisch auf Zauberei und die Rolle von Hexen und Teufeln ein
2. Fälle von Schadenszauber, die Hexen begangen haben
3. die Prozessführung bzw. "auf die Arten der Ausrottung"

wie es im Untertitel heißt (vgl. SCHORMANN 1981:31).

In verschiedenen Sprachen veröffentlicht, diente es als Kompendium, um Frauen anzuklagen und Foltermethoden festzulegen. Die korrekte Identifizierung von Hexen erschien schwierig, aber mit dem „Hexenhammer„ gab man Inquisitoren und weltlichen Behörden Kriterien zur Hexenbestimmung und genaue Anweisungen für Hexenprozesse an die Hand (SZASZ 1974, HAUSCHILD 1987). Der "Hexenhammer" war das einflussreichste Buch jener Zeit und erreichte bereits vor 1669 die dreißigste Auflage. Äußerst sexistisch, weckte es jene Urangst des Mannes der Frau gegenüber. Sprenger ging gegen Frauen vor und versuchte besonders Hebammen als das Übel der Menschheit darzustellen: "Von den Frauen wiederum übertreffen Hebammen alle anderen an Verruchtheit". Man beschuldigte sie, Kinder bewusst kurz vor oder nach der Geburt zu töten, um sie dann dem Teufel zu opfern. Im „Malleus Maleficarum„ führte Sprenger an, dass "Hexen-Hebammen das Kind in utero töteten und so einen Abort herbeiführten, oder dass sie das Neugeborene in einem unbewachten Augenblick dem Satan darbrächten." (SZACZ 1974:135). Eine der größten Ängste des Mannes war, von Hexen unfruchtbar gemacht zu werden. Sogar ein Gelehrter wie Thomas von Aquin behauptete, dass wahrscheinlich eine Hexe dahinter stünde, wenn das Zeugungsorgan eines Mannes versagte (ACHTERBERG 1994).

Europa brennt
Hexenprozesse wurden in weiten Teilen Europas geführt. Es gibt nur wenige Regionen unter der lateinischen Kirche, die von den Massakern verschont blieben. Dazu zählen die spanische Halbinsel und Süditalien. In Irland, England, Skandinavien und Polen sowie Böhmen und Ungarn waren die Opfer geringer als in den Kernländern Frankreich, Norditalien, den Alpenländern, Deutschland, den Beneluxländern und Schottland. (SCHORMANN 1981). Zwischen 1580 und 1653 wurden von den ca. 100.000 Einwohnern Schottlands allein über 1600 der Hexerei beschuldigt und verbrannt. (KAMBER 1995). Im deutschen Würzburg und Bamberg richtete man Verbrennungsöfen ein. Unzählige Frauen und Kinder wurden beschuldigt, mit dem Teufel Geschlechtsverkehr zu haben.

Die Kirche beschuldigte qualifizierte Heilerinnen, "Heilungen" herbeizuzaubern und Krankheiten von einem Menschen auf einen anderen zu übertragen. Die Weise Frau, die als Geburtshelferin und Therapeutin Kranken half und bei Behandlungen Beachtliches schaffte, schien der Kirche ein Affront gegen die Obergewalt des Klerus zu sein. Die Inquisitoren verkündeten, dass Heilung von Körper und Seele nur von Gott und seinen rechtmäßigen Stellvertretern auf Erden vollbracht werden könne und dürfe (SZASZ 1974). Einer der führenden Hexenjäger, William Perkins, ein schottischer Geistlicher, sprach für viele Protestanten seiner Zeit: "Die "gute" Hexe ist ein größeres Ungeheuer als die schlechte ... Wenn irgendeine den Tod verdient, dann verdient die gute Hexe den tausendfachen Tod" (PERKINS 1610). Trotzdem handelte man sehr inkonsequent, denn wenn ein Arzt kranken Adeligen oder Geistlichen nicht helfen konnte, wurde nach eine Heilerin gerufen. Alison Peirsoun, eine gute und zuverlässige Heilerin, wurde vom Erzbischof von St. Andrew, den verschiedene Leiden quälten, gerufen. Nach erfolgreicher Behandlung verweigerte er ihr nicht nur ihren Lohn, sondern ließ sie hinrichten. Besonders pervers erscheint hier das Verhalten von Papst Innozenz VII, der das Schlüsseldokument zur Hexenverfolgung herausgab. Aus Angst, der Inquisition würde nicht genug Folge geleistet, drohte er bei Nichtbeachtung der Hexenjagd mit dem Zorn Gottes. Als er jedoch selbst auf dem Sterbebett lag, versuchte er durch Muttermilch und Knabenblut wieder gesund zu werden.

Behandlungsweisen der Hexen
Wie gingen die Heilerinnen eigentlich bei ihren Behandlungen vor? Neben magischen Beschwörungen, den unterschiedlichsten Ingredienzen sowie Wahrsagerei verwendeten viele Heilerinnen toxische und alkaloide Heilpflanzen. Die pharmakologische Bedeutung und Wirkung dieser Pflanzen war noch weitgehend unbekannt. Die Kirche glaubte nicht, dass die Pflanzen heilende Wirkstoffe beinhalten könnten, sondern ging davon aus, dass Frauen, die Pflanzen einsetzten, ihre Heilwirkung durch Anrufungen des Teufels oder Gottes beeinflussten. Bewusstseinsverändernde Pflanzen wurden dem Teufel zugeordnet. Trotzdem blieben Heilpflanzen bei Hexenprozessen weitgehend unberücksichtigt, was am mangelnden pharmazeutischen Interesse der Kirche gelegen haben kann. Die halluzinogene Wirkung dieser Pflanzen wurde vielleicht auch bewusst heruntergespielt.

Wissenschaftler, Ärzte und Astrologen waren eher an Wirkstoffen der Salben und Öle interessiert, die von Heilerinnen benutzt wurden, selbst wenn es sich um Utensilien handelte, die bei Apothekern und in jeder Hausapotheke zu finden waren. In ihnen sah man weitere Beweise für Hexerei. Salben waren aus Pflanzensaftmixturen und einer Fettsubstanz zusammengesetzt, die über die Haut aufgenommen wurde. Angaben über die Bestandteile variieren. Die meisten der aufgeführten Pflanzenanteile sind Alkaloide mit heilenden und halluzinogenen Wirkungen. Während sie in geringen Dosen Erregungszustände bewirken, kann eine hohe Dosis zum Koma oder Tod führen. Bestandteile der Salben waren unter anderem: Belladonna, Stechapfel, Eisenhut, Bilsenkraut und Alraune. Die meisten Mischungen waren starke psychedelische Drogen. Auch über die Haut aufgenommen wirkten diese Pflanzen und riefen einen Zustand hervor, der schamanischen Trancezuständen ähnlich ist. Heilerinnen wussten, wie sie die Pflanzen dosieren mussten, um Bewusstseinsveränderungen, Schmerzlinderung, Trancereisen oder Vergiftungen hervorzurufen.

Eisenhut (Herba Verbenae) wird in heutigen Kräuterbüchern kaum erwähnt. 1555 wurde es von einem Heilkundigen folgendermaßen beschrieben: "Kraut Verbena noch heutigs tags mehr in der Zauberein dann in der artznei gesamlet wird." (HAUSCHILD 1987). In homöopathischen Dosen kann es bei Epilepsie und Tremor angewandt werden. Es ruft ein Taubheitsgefühl mit anschließender Lähmung der unteren Extremitäten bei klarem Bewusstsein hervor. Diese kann ein Hinweis für Berichte sein, in denen Frauen, wahrscheinlich paralysiert, über lange Zeiträume mit offenen Augen bewegungslos dalagen.

Pflanzen, die Scopolamin, Hyoscyamin und Atropin enthalten, sind Bilsenkraut, Belladonna und Alraune. Stark dosiert weisen sie toxische Wirkung auf, werden aber medizinisch angewendet. Bilsenkraut ist schon seit der Antike als Heilmittel verwendet worden. Das Öl, aus Samen gewonnen, wird als Schlaf- und Beruhigungsmittel und bei Zahnschmerzen eingesetzt. Äußerlich angewendet wirkt es bei rheumatischen Beschwerden, Gicht und Gelenkschmerzen schmerzlindernd und heilend. Es ist dem Stechapfel in seiner Wirkung ähnlich (RÄTSCH 1987). Alraune (Radix Mandragorae) ist eine der ersten Heilpflanzen, die in medizinischen Schriften erwähnt wurde. Als Nervenberuhigungs- und Betäubungsmittel benutzte man sie bei chirurgischen Eingriffen und als Schlafmittel. Sie besitzt die Drogenwirkung aller Nachtschattengewächse und ist als Schlafmittel und seit langen Zeiten als Aphrodisiakum bekannt. In Rauschträumen werden alle Hemmungen ausgeschaltet. (HAUSCHILD 1989) Die Wurzel, ihrer Form nach einem Penis ähnelnd, wurde bei Potenzstörungen und bei Frauenleiden angewendet. Extrakte aus der Alraune, Opium und anderen Sedativa setzte man als Narkotikum ein. Die Methoden waren recht vage und führen auch immer wieder zum Tod während einer Behandlung. Belladonna fand vielseitige Anwendung, z.B. bei Herzrhythmusstörungen und Asthma. Die Pflanze, die jedoch am meisten mit Hellseherei in Verbindung gebracht wurde, war das Bilsenkraut. Sie galt als "Wahrheitsdroge". Scopolamin und Hyoscyamin sind Mittel, die krampflösend wirken.

Die von den Frauen angewandten Pflanzen waren auf jeden Fall wirkungsvoller und heilender als die astrologischen Diagnosen der Ärzte und ihre Aderlässe und Abführmittel.

Ein weiterer Anklagepunkt war die Haltung von Haustieren, insbesondere Katzen. Meistens wurde die Tiere bei Verhören gefoltert und kamen mit den Angeklagten auf den Scheiterhaufen. Da Katzen natürliche Feinde von Ratten sind, kann ihre Vernichtung zum erneuten Ausbruch der Pest geführt haben. Überhaupt war Folterung ein wesentlicher Bestandteil der Hexenverfolgung: "Das Gericht hielt Indizien für ausreichend, um in der Verhafteten eine überführte Hexe zu sehen, zu deren Verurteilung nach dem Strafgesetzbuch nur noch das Geständnis fehlt. Dieses herbeizuführen ist Aufgabe der Folter. Die Art der hier angewandten Tortur kann jedoch bei der lakonischen Kürze des Protokolls nur aus anderen Bürener Hexenprotokollen erschlossen werden. Durchgeführt wurde die Folter in diesen Verhören zuerst mit Bein- und/oder Daumenschrauben, gefolgt vom Aufzug an den auf dem Rücken gefesselten Händen - allgemein die verbreitetste Folterpraxis in Deutschland." (SCHORMANN 1981:19). Hunderttausende mussten einen qualvollen Tod sterben. Schätzungen belaufen sich zwischen 200 000 und 9 Millionen Menschen. In ganz Europa brannten Scheiterhaufen. So beschreibt es ein Zeitgenosse: Deutschland ist fast ausschließlich damit beschäftigt, Scheiterhaufen für die Hexen zu errichten. ..". Es zog sich über fast 200 Jahre hin, bis sich diese Vernichtungswelle in Europa legte. So waren die letzten Hexenhinrichtungen in folgenden Jahren: Holland - 1610; England - 1684; Frankreich - 1745; Deutschland - 1775; Schweiz - 1782; Polen - 1792. (HAUSCHILD 1987). Hexenprozesse sind die nach der Judenverfolgung größte nicht kriegsbedingte Massentötung durch Menschen bewirkt. (SCHORMANN 1981) Es gibt die verschiedensten Theorien, die den Hexenwahn erklären wollen. Sei es, dass die Hexenverfolgung vom Klerus initiiert wurde, um eine Rebellion der aufständischen Bauern zu verhindern. Oder dass die Frauen alten Religionen angehörten und somit Götter verehrten, die vom Christentum zu Teufeln erklärt worden waren. Klar ist, dass die Stellung der Frau in den alten Religionen wesentlich mächtiger war als es im Christentum der Fall war.

Dass sie nach Einführung des Christentums Amulette trugen, die römische Gottheiten symbolisierten, ist bekannt. Wie verbreitet diese Kulte waren, ist jedoch unklar. Eine weitere These berücksichtigt die sozialökonomischen Aspekte des Problems. Die Seuchen, die im 13. und 14. Jahrhundert in der Bevölkerung wüteten, töteten viele Menschen. Kirche und Staat wollten Arbeitskräfte und Steuervolumen gesichert sehen und wünschten ein Bevölkerungswachstum. Bis zu dieser Zeit hatten Frauen, mit Unterstützung von Hebammen und Heilerinnen, Anzahl und Zeitpunkt der Geburten selbst bestimmt. Um beim selbstbestimmenden Umgang mit der Fruchtbarkeit einzugreifen, riefen Staat und Kirche schlimmste Gerüchte über Hebammen und Heilerinnen ins Leben, schürten Unmut und schritten schließlich zur Vernichtung der weisen Frau. (HEINSOHN & STEIGER 1985, HAUSCHILD 1987)

Desweiteren sahen die Kirche und später auch führende Ärzte in den Handlungen der Heilerinnen nicht dämonische, sondern neurotische und psychotische Akte. Besonders führende französische Psychiater wie Esquirol und Charcot trugen dazu bei, dass die Frauen als Geisteskranke deklariert wurden. Jean-Martin Charcot (1825 - 1893) sah in der Hexerei ein Problem der Neuropathologie und versuchte die hysterischen Erscheinungen mit denen der Hexerei gleichzusetzen. Sigmund Freud, Schüler von J.M. Charcot, sah in der Hexerei kein neuropathologisches, sondern ein psychopathologisches Problem. (SZASZ 1974). Aber auch G. Zilboorg schloss sich der Meinung Freuds an: "Kurz gesagt, der „malleus maleficarum„ könnte, mit ein wenig Überarbeitung zur Beschreibung der klinischen Psychiatrie des 15. Jahrhunderts dienen, wenn das Wort Hexe durch das Wort Patientin ersetzt und der Teufel daraus gestrichen würden„ (ACHTERBERG 1994; SCACZ 1974) Weiter schrieb er: "Darüber hinaus finden sich in der medizinischen Literatur des 19. Jahrhunderts eine so große Anzahl von sorgfältig recherchierten Daten, dass wir ohne Zweifel davon ausgehen können, dass es sich bei den Millionen von besessenen Hexen und Zauberern um eine enorme Massierung von Fällen schwerer Neurosen, Psychose und weit fortgeschrittenem organischen Delirium handelt". (ZILBOORG 1969).

Das Ende des Hexenwahns

Der ganze Hexenwahn legte sich vollends erst, als das Christentum seine uneingeschränkte Herrschaft verlor. Durch die Aufklärung kam es zur Befreiung aus dieser religiösen Befangenheit. Erst langsam kam man auf die Idee, dass der Hexenwahn selbst das Ergebnis von Aberglauben ist, der an Wahnsinn grenzt. In den Jahren der Hexenverfolgung waren Heilerinnen von Ärzten, Apothekern und Chirurgen verdrängt worden. Mit all dem Heilwissen ist auch ein Teil der Riten und Traditionen verloren gegangen. "Erst mit der physischen Vernichtung der sog. "Hexen" und Volksheiler durch die Inquisition verschwanden auch die zahlreichen Varianten der Wahrsagerei, die noch im "Hexenhammer", dem Leitfaden für die Abwicklung der Hexenprozesse, erwähnt wurden. Bis heute mit dem "Betrugsstigma" der Inquisition belegt, blieb die Wahrsagerei auch vom Interessenfeld der akademischen Psychologie ausgeschlossen." (ANDRITZKY 1988).

Was Dr. W. Andritzky hier auf Wahrsagerei bezieht, kann man ohne Bedenken auf viele andere Bereiche der Heilkünste und Kräuterkunde beziehen. Dabei ist darauf zu hoffen, dass sich die akademischen Wissenschaften wieder mehr für diese Bereiche und das darin vorhandene Wissen öffnet.

References

ACHTERBERG, J. 1994. *Die Frau als Heilerin, Die schöpferische Rolle der heilkundigen Frau in Geschichte und Gegenwart.* Goldmann Verlag.

ANDRITZKY, W. 1988. *Ethnologia Americana, Coquera,* 24. Jahrgang, Düsseldorf

BINGEN, VON H. 1991. *Heilwissen, Von den Ursachen und der Behandlung von Krankheiten,* Herder Verlag, Freiburg im Breisgau

EWEN, C. 1933. *Witchcraft and Demonism,* Heath Cranton. Limited, London.

HAUSCHILD, T. 1987. *Die alten und die neuen Hexen.* Heyne Report. München.

HEINSOHN, G. 1985. *Die Vernichtung der weisen Frauen.* März Verlag. Herbstein

HERTZKA, G. 1988. *Handbuch der Hildegard Medizin.* Verlag Hermann Bauer. Freiburg im Breisgau.

GRIFFIN, S. 1970. *Women and Nature. New York.* Harper & Row

KAMBER, P. 1995. Hexen, Heilerinnen und sündiger Lebenswandel im Waadtland - 16./17. Jahrhundert. In *Krank warum?.* Cantz Verlag, Osterfildern

PERKINS, W. 1610. *A Discourse on the Damned Art of Witchcraft.* Cambridge.

RÄTSCH, C. 1987. *Indianische Heilkräuter. Tradition und Anwendung. Ein Pflanzenlexikon.* Diederichs Verlag. Köln

SCHORNMANN, G. 1981. *Hexenprozesse in Deutschland.* Vandenoeck & Ruprecht in Göttingen.

STONE, M. 1989. *Als Gott eine Frau war.* München

SZASZ, T. 1974. *Fabrikation des Wahnsinns.* Walter-Verlag. Olten und Freiburg im Breisgau

UNGER, HELGA. *Der Berg der Liebe. Europäische Frauenmystik.* Herder Verlag. Freiburg im Breisgau.

ZILBOORG, G. 1969. *The Medical Man and the Witch During the Renaissance* (1935) New York. Cooper Square

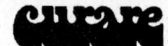

Women and Suicidal Behaviour in the Context of a Psychiatric Hospital Ward
Frauen und Suizidverhalten im Kontext einer psychiatrischen Einrichtung

David Aldridge

Abstract: The basic premise is that self-mutilating behaviour is part of an interactional pattern. Women patients are forced to adopt a position of compliance in a situation of psychiatric treatment where distress is localised. Those women who do not comply with treatment are quickly labelled as deviant, illegitimate in their claim to the sick role, and as uncooperative patients. Women admitted to hospital because they are suicidal become even more suicidal throughout the course of the therapeutic regime.
Suicidal behaviour is considered a strategy for maintaining systemic coherence, reducing conflict and clarifying a systemic hierarchy. Conflict is seen as residing in the way the system is organised rather than located in one individual. Once a system labels one of its members as illegitimate and deviant as a person, rather than a person exhibiting deviant behaviour, then distress escalates.

Zusammenfassung: Die Grundannahme besteht darin, das selbstzerstörerisches Verhalten ein Teil eines Interaktionsmusters ist. Frauen werden dahingehend gedrängt eine Position aktiver Teilnahme an einem psychiatrischen Behandlungsprogramm einzunehmen, in welchem ihr Kummer lokalisiert wird. Diejenigen Frauen, welche nicht an der Behandlung teilnehmen wollen, werden schnell als abweichend stigmatisiert, als illegitim in ihrem Anspruch auf die Rolle des kranken Menschen und als unkooperative Patienten. Frauen, welche in dem Krankenhaus aufgenommen worden sind weil sie selbstmordgefährdet sind, werden durch das angebotene therapeutische Regime so letztendlich noch stärker gefährdet.
Selbstmörderisches Verhalten wird als eine Strategie angesehen Systemkohärenz aufrechtzuerhalten, Konflikte zu reduzieren und die Systemhierarchie zu klären. Konflikte wurzeln so betrachtet eher in der Organisationsweise des Systems als in der Einzelperson. Der Kummer eskaliert dementsprechend, wenn ein System einmal begonnen hat eines ihrer Mitglieder als abweichend und als illegitim zu bezeichnen, unabhängig davon ob ein Mensch abweichendes Verhalten zeigt.

Keywords: Suicidal behaviour, family systems therapy, interaction, psychiatry, England, Suizidverhalten, Familientherapie, Interaktion, Psychiatrie, England.

This chapter is concerned with describing suicidal behaviour in the context of a psychiatric hospital ward. The basic premise is that self-mutilating behaviour is part of an interactional pattern. However, women patients are forced to adopt a position of compliance in a situation of psychiatric treatment where distress is localised. Those women who do not comply with treatment are quickly labelled as deviant, illegitimate in their claim to the sick role, and as uncooperative patients. Thus, women that are admitted because they are suicidal become even more suicidal throughout the course of the therapeutic regime.

The political context of the ward

The ward described in this chapter was in the setting of the acute admissions ward of a psychiatric hospital. At the time there were a number of women on the ward who were engaged in self-harming behaviours involving cutting their wrists, lacerating their bodies, breaking windows and over-dosing with medication. FAGERHAUGH and STRAUSS (FAGERHAUGH & STRAUSS 1977) argue that when pain is managed in a hospital setting then *"political processes are likely to occur. Patients and staff members wheedle, argue,. persuade, bargain, negotiate, holler at, shriek at command, manipulate relevant contingencies, and attempt to deceive"* (p.8).

In any area where groups of individuals co-ordinate their collective behaviour there will be differing philosophies about consensus. There will also be cultural differences between patients and staff, between patient and patient, and between staff member and staff member, about illness, health, the expression of distress and how people are expected to behave in hospital. The same arguments apply to the psychiatric hospital where the expression of distress and the management of distress are part of a politicised arena. The collective behaviour is a coping dialogue where all parties are actively striving to meet their various responsibilities, to control their environment and to make everyday circumstances more tolerable and certain. Patients do, however, expect to gain some relief from their suffering.

The presence of conflict

A number of authors (BURSTEN & D'ESCOPO 1965; CAUDILL et al. 1952; FAGERHAUGH & STRAUSS 1977) describe how outbreaks of problematic behaviour occur on hospital wards when there is a discrepancy between two warring staff authorities who define their overall position as benevolent and attempt to conceal their differences. HAWTON (HAWTON 1978) reports that ward staff frequently indicate a conflict between the desire to withhold attention, to manage the physical consequences and to try and understand the act through discussion when dealing with suicidal behaviour.

HALEY (HALEY 1980) hypothesizes that symptoms such as self-mutilation reflect an organisation with a confused hierarchy where no clear lines of authority are present. When the hierarchy of an organisation becomes confused then symptomatic behaviour becomes adaptive and stabilises such confusion. BURSTEN and D'ESOPO (1965) reiterate this position. They suggest that it is tempting to see patients who "refuse" to get well as in conflict with society or their family. This 'refusal' may be seen as resistance to social norms, defiance or seeking an aggressive control of others in the same situation. However, what appears as deviant or defiant behaviour may really be compliant. By such behaviour the organisational hierarchy is clarified, and symptomatic behaviour becomes appropriate.

It is these patterns of behaviour constituting conflict that SLUZKI (SLUZKI 1981) pursues. He suggests that the presence of a 'conflict' or a 'crisis' does not mean there is a 'pathology' preceding or underlying the conflict, rather that the current management and systemic organisation of behaviour is the conflict. Such collective behaviour occurs when people have common shared understandings and expectations. Behaviour is co-ordinated by expectations about relationships. These expectations are governed by rules and constructs designating what a behaviour counts as, and how it is to be handled. The construing of self-mutilation is critical for its management (ALDRIDGE 1984; ALDRIDGE & ROSSITER 1983; ALDRIDGE & ROSSITER 1984).

How behaviour is construed

In a paper about deviant patients in casualty departments JEFFREY (JEFFREY 1979) suggests that the moral evaluation of patients is an important feature of their treatment. Two principal categories are used for describing patients in hospital casualty departments
(a) the good, interesting patient who is legitimately ill, who will give the staff a chance to practice their skills and will test their competence and maturity,
(b) the bad, rubbish who present trivial, irrational, insoluble problems, who are illegitimately seeking the status of sick, who offer little chance of therapeutic success and who are emotionally blackmailing their significant others.

The negative connotation of behaviour is described by GARFINKEL (GARFINKEL 1956) as part of a degradation ceremony. Degradation ceremonies are communicative acts where the public identity of a person is transformed into something seen as lower in the scheme of social types. Such a process depends upon the social rules about suicidal behaviour and how the person is seen in the context of his primary reference group. In the process of degradation a person becomes construed as 'out-of-the-ordinary', deviant. Added to this further negative labels are ascribed e.g. 'abnormal', 'illegitimate' and 'un co-operative'. Garfinkel emphasises that when a negative construing of behaviour occurs it emphasises that the person is choosing such a behaviour in contrast to the positive poles which exist e.g. legitimate, co-operative and normal. In the following pages we will see how this process of degradation escalates whereby women in an apparent context of therapeutic care are systematically marginalised.

Four Women
Four women were harming themselves repeatedly on the ward of a psychiatric hospital.

1. *Sally* (aged 24)
Sally was admitted to a psychiatric hospital after an overdose of medication. Her parents were unwilling to have her at home as they said that they could not cope with her continual abuse of medication. Although the admission was to have been a short stay, the stay lengthened and Sally's behaviour became more and more damaging to herself. It is interesting to note here that Sally's parents were unwilling to have Sally home. Sally's daughter (aged 5) was living with Sally's parents and Sally returned home at weekends. During her visits home she mutilated herself, or overdosed, and was promptly returned to the hospital by her father.

Sally described an adolescence characterised by sexual adventures and disasters. At fourteen she was engaged to a soldier who drank and beat her up. She broke off this engagement at the age of seventeen. Following this she was involved in a liaison which produced her daughter, Jane. Eighteen months later she was pregnant again by another man and this pregnancy was terminated surgically. Sally was nineteen. During her first pregnancy Sally was described as a difficult and defensive patient. Her gynaecologist describes her as resentful and unhelpful. Following an interlude abroad, and return home, she sought medical help for abdominal pains, diarrhoea, loss of weight, eventually leading to a diagnosis of Crohn's disease. She was started on steroids and a high protein diet. By March she had put on weight and by August was described as in static remission. It was suggested that all medication be left off completely. However, by February 1980 there was a relapse of the Crohn's disease, followed by remission, followed by relapse in the following August.

The following period was characterised by increasing tension and irritability, difficulties with her parents and her friends. She was abusing codeine phosphate, and using alcohol to relieve tension. She had asked her general practitioner for sleeping tablets and further psychotropic drugs which were prescribed on the grounds that she inevitably abused them. It was indicated by her general practitioner. that it was difficult to establish a working relationship with her. Numerous attempts were made, after a referral to a consultant psychiatrist, to engage Sally in therapy but all proved to be fruitless.

She was admitted after an incident of self-poisoning using paracetemol and codeine phosphate to the general hospital and discharged home after 3 days. Three weeks later she had poisoned herself again and this was the episode which precipitated her admission to the psychiatric hospital.

Sally was seen as a difficult, un co-operative patient who had attempted to solve her physical health problems by a variety of previous solutions. These solutions had failed. Finally, her physical symptoms were questioned and she was seen as illegitimate in her claims to the status 'sick'. One of the criteria for occupying the status 'sick' is to co-operate with treatment and not to be seen as responsible for the state of disease. In Sally's case she was seen by her general practitioner as contributing to her own demise.

2. *Kelly*
Kelly had been a regular in-patient at the psychiatric hospital for two and a half years when she was first interviewed. She had repeatedly mutilated herself. She was first admitted, age 17, to the adolescent unit at the psychiatric hospital in June 1979 after an overdose of medication. There was a question raised at the time that she may have been three months pregnant. There was concern, too, about her mental state.

Throughout her case conference in the September of that same year, Kelly cried continuously. Even then the idea was being raised by Kelly that her mother wanted her transferred to the psychiatric hospital proper. Kelly had been staying with an aunt but this relationship deteriorated as the aunt blamed Kelly for a poor relationship with her daughter. Her mother had shown no interest in Kelly since she arrived at the hospital and there were continued outbursts of aggression and self-mutilation. This young woman was considered to be aggressive, maladjusted and deviant. Her physical symptoms, like Sally in Case 1, were seen as illegitimate, and 'hysterical' in origin. Although described as having personal problems, much of her difficulties were blamed on her familial antecedents. Her mother too was seen as aggressive and her father was a criminal. Kelly had undergone numerous attempted solutions to physical problems which had failed. The inference was made that the symptoms were illegitimate attempts to enter the 'status sick' and that when faced with life's difficulties she would escape her responsibilities by overdosing or mutilating herself.

3. Kath

This woman, aged 28, voluntarily sought admission to the psychiatric hospital as she feared for her own safety. She had been discharged, two days before admission, from the general hospital after an overdose of vodka, lager and aspirin.

Leaving home at the age of 17, and already pregnant, she lived with her husband-to-be. Her mother and step-father were moving to the South West and she did not want to move with them. The parting was difficult and she had no further contact with her parents until her daughter was born. Following the birth of her daughter, she suffered an infection of the pelvis and a hysterectomy was performed. She was 18 years old. Her parents rallied round to help her and throughout her marriage she would turn to her parents in times of stress. The marriage had many areas of conflict. Her husband was unemployed and played in a rock band. She worked full-time and in the evenings. There were recurrent depressive interludes and a twelve week stay in a psychiatric hospital. She says that she stayed in the marriage for security and to be with her daughter. During these depressive interludes she would return to her mother.

However, her husband eventually petitioned for divorce and she became involved with a young man of 18. Her former husband was awarded custody of the child, which she did not contest as her new boyfriend said that he would not live with her and her daughter.

There had been a previous episode of suicidal behaviour in the spring when she had lacerated her wrists and been admitted for a day at the psychiatric hospital. Her boyfriend had heard about this and subsequently 'rescued her' (her terminology). He had moved to the south west with her so that they could make a new start but had since returned to his old job in the Midlands.

Kath voluntarily sought admission to the hospital and initially received sympathetic treatment by the staff who saw her as being emotionally disturbed by a disruption in a key relationship. This sympathetic understanding was dispelled by her subsequent actions when she repeatedly mutilated herself. Increasingly she was seen as illegitimate and un co-operative, aggressive and uncontrollable. It is perhaps ironic that she was admitted to a psychiatric hospital at her own request because she felt suicidal, yet during her stay she engaged in behaviours of self-harm which caused increasingly greater physical injuries to herself. In a family interview her father told me that she had never had been any good and that if she were a dog he would have had her put down.

4. June

June was the eldest of the four women described here. She was aged fifty-one, married, and had four children. She was admitted to hospital after an overdose of alcohol and medication. She had been involved in an argument with her husband before her admission to hospital.

There was a history of psychiatric admissions. She had been diagnosed as manic-depressive. This psychosis, she said, had been precipitated twenty years previously by an incident abroad whilst she was in the women's navy service. In the past five years she had repeatedly been admitted for episodes of mania and episodes of overdosing. During the previous years she had complained of gynaecological problems until eventually she was sterilized, an ovary removed and a hysterectomy performed.

June was seen by the ward staff as a chronic patient, who was 'crazy' but 'likeable and harmless'. When she first engaged in self-mutilatory behaviour she was not regarded as manipulative or hostile as were the other women. However, as her stay lengthened and the number of episodes increased, becoming part of a number of collective incidents of suicidal behaviour, she was seen as 'difficult'. Sometimes on the ward she would be seen laughing with the other patients and she was construed as making no effort to leave. If pressed to make a decision about leaving, or challenged in a meeting" an episode of manic behaviour would follow. This led the staff to conclude that she was manipulating the staff and making no effort to get better.

The staff perspective on the women

The staff of the hospital ward, both medical and nursing, saw these women as difficult patients who presented a management problem. They were unresponsive to treatment, hostile, manipulative, aggressive, illegitimate in their claims, difficult, un co-operative, and seeking control. They were not accorded a legitimate place in the order of being mentally ill, but as deviants even within the context of mental illness. In fact, they were not seen as 'mentally ill' but 'disorderly', that is 'bad women' not 'mad women'. Once the staff had implemented treatment strategies to manage such behaviour, and the patients had not responded as the staff expected, their behaviour was not regarded as legitimate .

A profile of these women was constructed by the staff which saw them as illegitimate in their claims to illness although they had gained admission to a hospital on the grounds of a fear for their own safety. Despite this admission for asylum they had repeatedly harmed themselves. When the staff had introduced strategies to help these women they had not co-operated with these strategies and were, therefore, illegitimate in the eyes of the staff. Not only were they seen as illegitimate but as responsible for their own condition when they continually harmed themselves. Mutilation was seen as a direct result of their own action, and these actions came to be seen as hostile acts against the staff.

The Construing of Suicidal Behaviour.

The staff as a collective body considered this group of women in the context of the psychiatric patients on the ward using five core constructs concerning individuality, legitimacy, rersponsibility, cooperation,and permissiveness.

These women were considered by their actions as women with emotional problems precipitated by personal crises. Yet despite this understanding they were considered as a cohort of 'slashers' who set out to disrupt the smooth working of the ward, who failed to be reasonable in their demands and who provoked each other to upset the staff.

Their behaviour on the ward was seen as illegitimate in that specific treatment strategies had been formulated to combat their self-mutilation. Although initially seen as legitimate by some of the staff (because the women were either suicidally distressed through emotional loss or just plain 'crazy') the women came to be seen as illegitimate in their claims to be sick. Once seen as illegitimate, all suicidal behaviour was seen as manipulative. The questioning of medication, answering back, getting up late, demanding psychotherapy, also came to be seen as illegitimate. These women were seen as contributing to their demise by active participation in defiant behaviour, making choices that deliberately exposed them to further pain and rejection and for deliberately harming themselves. Any event which indicated a deterioration in the patient's mental health status became seen as evidence of the patient's lack of co-operation with the treatment strategy. The staff spent time working out what to do with the women, what medication to give them and what ward programme they should pursue after hours of talking, reassurance and nursing concern. When an incident of self-mutilation occurred it was seen as non-co-operation with these efforts, and taken by some staff as a rejection of their personal help and nursing skill.

The ward staff were caught in a bind about treatment. Some staff considered that a punitive line should be taken where non co-operation by patients would result in a lack of privileges. However, some other staff thought that this treatment of patients as a collective was unjust and that punitive measures should only be taken against certain mutilating women, and not against other patients. Some staff believed that although the behaviour was illegitimate, it was to be expected in the context of a mental hospital where people are 'crazy'. It was, in their view, possible to follow a permissive regime.

Of all these considerations the discussions returned eventually to how the behaviour could be controlled, and how this control by staff over patients could be implemented. This control, however, had to fit in with the beliefs of members of staff about what degree of control one human being could have over another. Eventually both sets of behaviour, the strategies of the staff and the acts of mutilation by the patients, were seen as mutual steps in the dance of maintaining control over ward life. This symmetrical escalation of mutual control seeking, with more and more extreme attempts to exhibit power tactics meant that all members of the ward experienced continuing distress. The threatening of distress thresholds to a limit where the system's viability itself is threatened means that those thresholds must be negotiated to maintain systemic viability and coherence.

The Staff Hierarchy

Haley suggests that disturbed behaviour occurs when there is a covert hierarchical conflict. The staff were divided into two hierarchical structures. There was a nursing hierarchy where staff were involved in the day-to-day routines of handling patients, handing out pills, supervising meals, changing beds and some psychotherapy. Psychotherapy was seen as an important part of mental health nursing, and an activity that nurses pursued and enjoyed.

The other hierarchical structure was that of the medical staff who were responsible for diagnosing the patient's illness, and formulating treatment strategies. The medical staff, apart from the consultant psychiatrist, were not trained in psychiatry and were only resident on the ward for six months. As the practitioners themselves said, they had no previous experience of psychiatry and were initially unused to the terms and the strategies of treatment used. What was significant was the emphasis by these medical practitioners on an epistemology that saw events in linear terms of cause and effect, and that illness could be cured by finding the appropriate strategy. The bio-medical model pervaded the strategies for controlling patient behaviour. Failure to respond to a treatment strategy, or a repeated strategy, meant that the patient's responsibility was questioned. As patients were seen to deliberately harm themselves then they violated the primary maxims of the bio-medical status of sickness; co-operation with treatment and non-responsibility for their condition

Both sets of staff changed at regular intervals. The nursing staff were rotated on a shift system within the ward. Any formulations of strategies had to be made when all staff were present. However, some nursing staff had differing perspectives on how patients were to be treated, particularly those patients who mutilated themselves. The discussions between all staff centred around a permissive approach, or an approach based on a restriction of privileges. The medical staff favoured a perspective which formulated strategies for dealing with individual patients. The nursing staff believed a policy towards the patients as a collective should be pursued.

The episodes of self-mutilation effectively thwarted any co-ordinated, planned attempt to implement either of the two policies. Once a patient mutilated herself then a recognised course of action began which resolved the crisis temporarily by staff physically treating the patient. There was no need for a negotiation of crisis procedure, the staff occupied their learned and traditional roles of 'nurse' and 'doctor'.

The circularity was a regularly repeated pattern of confusion and lengthy debate over policy, followed by attempted strategies, followed by episodes of self mutilation (see Fig. 1)

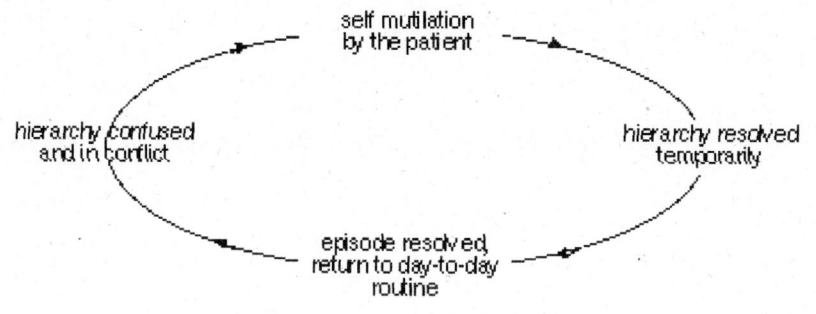

Figure 1
The cycle of conflict management in a hospital ward organisation

The Ward Situation

The ward situation was exacerbated by the reputation of the ward as a difficult place to work on (it was labelled an 'acute admissions' ward). Not only were the patients 'difficult' but a charge nurse on the same ward had himself recently taken an overdose. The staff morale was low and the nursing staff confessed anxiety about their own futures by working on such a ward. The general impression was that there were not enough nurses to actively nurse the patients and that nursing attention had to be given 'on demand'. The nursing staff saw this as a reason for their colleague overdosing coupled with an unsympathetic nursing hierarchy unwilling to listen to their claims. As one nurse said of the patients 'the squeaky wheels get oiled first'.

Both nursing staff and patients complained of a lack of continuity of medical and nursing staff to maintain some therapeutic stability. As HALEY (HALEY 1976) suggests when persons from two differing hierarchical levels conspire against a third, in this case nurses and patients against the doctors, or doctors and patients against nurses, then distress is likely to occur. In this way when conflict gets out of hand then symptoms take over, when symptoms become out of hand then conflict takes over.

When violent suicidal behaviour was used then the search for long term causal explanations was abandoned by the staff group. These four women, when behaving in a violent manner breaking windows or mutilating themselves, were deemed to be illegitimate in their demands by the ward staff. Any former legitimating factors associated with loss, depression, age or gender were abandoned in favour of immediate contextual demands. There was a circularity built into this process. Once a former set of legitimating grounds were abandoned for an immediate causal explanation then those former events became reframed negatively and previous episodes of violence 'discovered' in the patient's biography.

As an organised ward system policy disagreements between the staff were associated with rising distress throughout the patient body. Once certain threshold levels of distress were reached an episode of self-mutilation occurred which precipitated concerted action, relieved collective tensions and temporarily co-ordinated action. What became apparent was that both patients and staff had begun to place an increasing number of negative connotations on each other's behaviour. No matter how ambiguous behaviours were, each faction saw such behaviours as being against them, as examples of non-co-operation and as further evidence of illegitimacy.

There appeared to be mutual interlocking roles for describing self-mutilatory behaviour (see Figure 2).

ward staff construing

new female patient

act of wrist cutting ⊃ attempted suicide → *legitimate: example of depression and overwhelming distress

patients being treated in psychotherapy

act of wrist cutting ⊃ attempted suicide → *illegitimate: example of manipulation and non co-operation

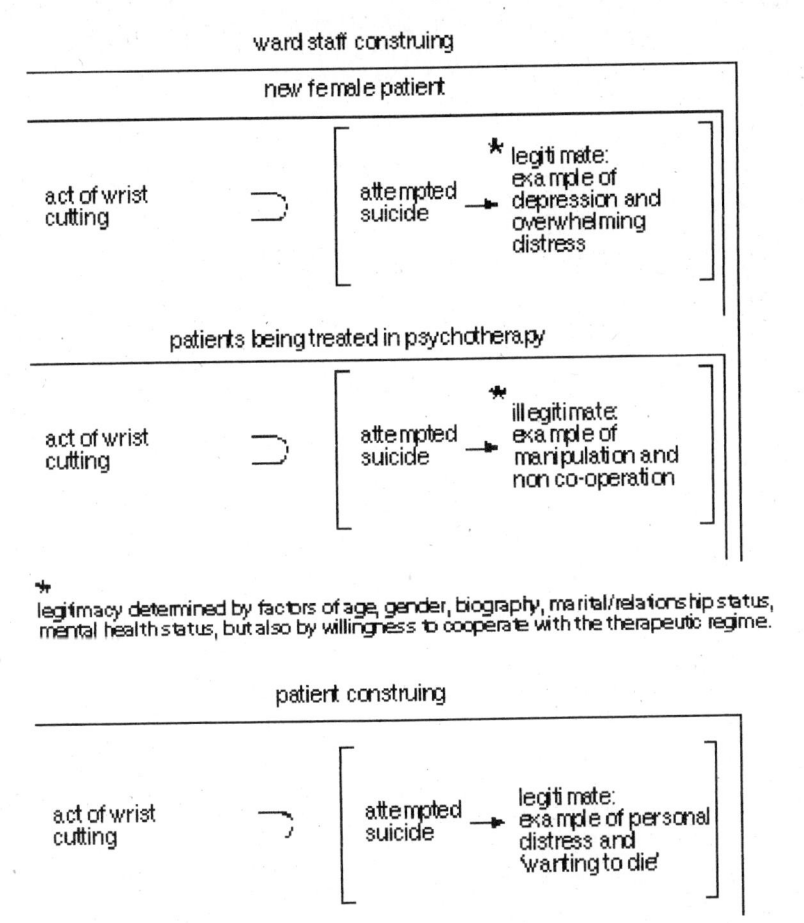

*legitimacy determined by factors of age, gender, biography, marital/relationship status, mental health status, but also by willingness to cooperate with the therapeutic regime.

patient construing

act of wrist cutting → attempted suicide → legitimate: example of personal distress and 'wanting to die'

Figure 2
Differences in the construing of the same act of wrist cutting

The core construing of legitimation was validated by the ward staff. Although the women believed themselves to be legitimate, the ward staff would only validate suicidal behaviour if certain factors were present. Eventually this process of withdrawing validation escalated until any act by the women became construed as deviant, illegitimate and un co-operative. In the same way the women became hostile towards the staff who were seen as unsympathetic, uncaring and unable to help which negated their professional skills. Hostility in this sense is the continued effort to extort validational evidence from others to support our own expectations (BANNISTER & FRANSELLA 1971). Both the women and the staff had expectations of each other that were not met. Both groups interacted in a cycle of mutual negation (see Figure 3).

In terms of regulative rules (ALDRIDGE 1992a), acts that-constituted treatment i.e. acts by patients on a hospital ward, and which did not respond to professional treatment strategies were seen as further acts of deviancy. The staff would alter their perception of the patient rather than alter their treatment strategies. They construed the patients in a way that elaborated the construing of deviancy. There became more ways of construing the patients as deviant than normal. Likewise, in a circular process of mutual escalation, there became more ways for the patients to construe the staff as failing and fewer ways to construe the staff as successful (see Figure 4). This same cycle of mutual negation appears to be a characteristic of the process of becoming suicidal (ALDRIDGE 1992b; ALDRIDGE 1992c).

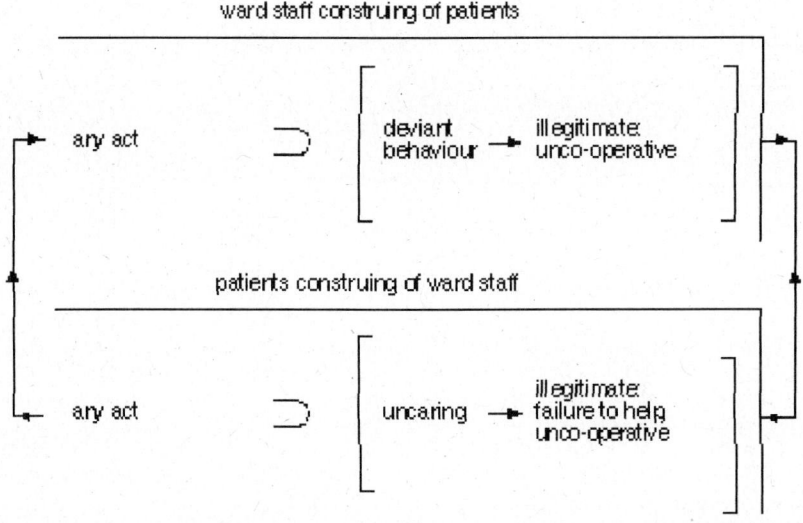

Figure 3
The cycle of mutual negation

Conclusion

The previous literature about suicidal behaviour stresses that such behaviour is not homogenous, that there are many varied paths to suicidal behaviour (ALDRIDGE 1992b; ALDRIDGE 1992c). Previous researchers have concentrated on considering past experiences and identifying particular individual characteristics. However, if current interactive behaviour is considered as maintaining systemic organisation then a different picture emerges. Suicidal behaviour becomes a strategy for maintaining systemic coherence, reducing conflict and clarifying the systemic hierarchy, albeit temporarily. The conflict is seen as residing in the way the system is organised rather than located in any one individual. Once the system labels one of its members as illegitimate and deviant as a person, rather than a person exhibiting deviant behaviour, then systemic distress will escalate. This escalation of distress threatens the future viability of such a system. Tragically this viabilty is materialised in the life of the women involved. What is an organisational problem, a hierarchical conflict between staff members, becomes a personal life and death issue for the woman herself. As these women have entered hospital seeking relief from their suffering, it seems perverse that it is they who should suffer further in a context or therapeutic care.

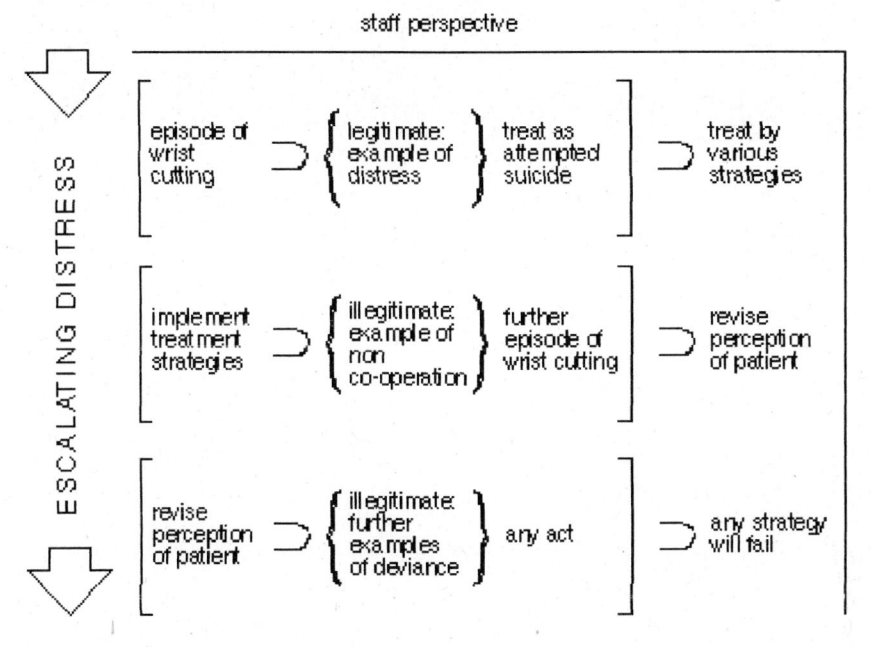

Figure 4
The escalation of distress

References

ALDRIDGE, D. 1984. Family interaction and suicidal behavior: A brief review. *Journal of Family Therapy.* 6:309-322.
ALDRIDGE, D. 1992a. Suicidal behavior 1: a search for methods in an ecosystemic research paradigm. *Complementary Medical Research.* 6:25-35.
ALDRIDGE, D. 1992b. Suicidal behavior: a continuing cause for concern. *British Journal of General Practice.* 42:482-485.
ALDRIDGE, D. 1992c. Suicidal behaviour 2: the results of applying an ecosystemic research paradigm. *Complementary Medical Research.* 6:36-45.
ALDRIDGE, D. & ROSSITER, J. 1983. A strategic approach to suicidal behaviour. *Journal of Systemic and Strategic Therapies.* 2:49-62.
ALDRIDGE, D. & ROSSITER, J. 1984. A strategic assessment of deliberate self harm. *Journal of Family Therapy.* 6:113-125.
BANNISTER, D. & FRANSELLA, F. 1971. *Inquiring Man.* Harmondsworth: Penguin.
Bursten, B. & D'Escopo, R. 1965. The obligation to remain sick. *Archives of General Psychiatry.* 12:402 407.
CAUDILL, W., REDLICH, F., GILMORE, H. & BRODY, G. 1952. Special structure and interaction processes on a psychiatric ward. *American Journal of Orthopsychiatry.* 22:314-334.
FAGERHAUGH, S. & STRAUSS, A. 1977. *The politics of pain management.* Chicago: Addison Wellesley Publishing Co.
GARFINKEL, H. 1956. Conditions of successful degradation ceremonies. *American Journal of Sociology.* 61:420-424.
HALEY, J. 1976. *Problem Solving Therapy.* San Francisco: Jossey Bass.
HALEY, J. 1980. *Leaving home.* New York: McGraw Hill.
HAWTON, K. 1978. Deliberate self-poisoning and self-injury in the psychiatric hospital. *British Journal of Medical Psychology.* 51:253-259.
JEFFREY, R. 1979. Deviant patients in casualty departments. *Sociology of Health and Illness.* 1:90-108.
SLUZKI, C. 1981. Process of symptom production and patterns of symptom maintenance. *Journal of Marital Therapy.* 7:273-280.

Die Bedeutung der melodischen Improvisation für Brustkrebspatientinnen während ihrer frühen rehabilitativen Phase nach einer Mastektomie
The Meaning of Melodic Improvisation for Beast-Cancer Patients During Early Rehabilitation after a Mastectomy

Gudrun Aldridge

Zusammenfassung: Brustkrebs ist unter den rund 200 verschiedenen Krebsarten die verbreiteste unter Frauen mit steigender Tendenz. Gleichwohl werden bei ihr die höchsten Überlebensraten festgestellt. Die Diagnose Krebs ist ein traumatisches Ereignis mit signifikantem Impakt auf Patienten und ihre Familien. Der besonders hohe, stressvolle Charakter der Krebserfahrung ist in der psychoonkologischen Literatur umfassend dokumentiert. Resultate dieser Studien weisen auf die Notwendigkeit einer adäquaten, adjuvanten Krebsbehandlung hin, die sich besonders auf die emotionalen Belastungsfaktoren und die körperlichen Beschwernisse konzentriert. Bezugnehmend auf die emotionalen Stressfaktoren wird anhand eines Fallbeispiels dargestellt, wie eine Mammakarzinompatientin ihre eigene Melodie entwickelt und damit Zugang zu ihren individuellen Ausdrucksmöglichkeiten findet.
Expressivität lässt sich infolgedessen am deutlichsten durch die Melodie ausdrücken.
Das Fallbeispiel legt dar, auf welche Art und Weise die Patientin durch das Angebot der melodischen Improvisation die Elemente Rhythmus, Tonspannung, Harmonie, Phrase und Form miteinander kombiniert und sich durch sie expressiv zum Ausdruck bringt. Ihre melodische Entwicklung zeigt nicht nur die Formung einer sinnvollen, melodischen Gestalt, sondern verdeutlicht insbesondere den ganzheitlichen Sinn dieser therapeutischen Maßnahme, indem die Patientin eine Möglichkeit fand, ihrer Expressivität Form zu geben. Für Brustkrebspatientinnen, die sich nach der Operation im Prozess neuer Orientierung und Identitätsfindung finden, ist dieses besonders wertvoll.

Abstract: Breast-cancer, one of almost 200 forms of cancer commonly found in women, is escalating in occurence. A diagnosis of cancer is a traumatic experience that has a significant impact on both the patient and her family. The particularly highly stressful character of the cancer experience is thoroughly documented in the psycho-oncology literature. These studies demonstrate the necessity for an adequate, adjuvant treatment form for cancer, that concentrates particularly on relieving emotional and bodily strain.
With reference to emotional stress factors, a case study will exemplify the melodic development of a patient with breast-cancer and the relevant nuances of her emotional expressivity. Expressivity is shown perhaps most clearly through melody. This case study presents the elements of rythm, interval, harmony, phrasing and form and brings these into expression. Her melodic development shows not only a melodic form that makes musical sense, but also how the therapeutic activity in a complete sense offers the patient a possibility in which she can find an expressive form. For patients with breast-cancer, who are seeking a new orientation and identity after the operation for the removal of a breast, this possibility for expression is especially of value.

Keywords: Expressivität, Musiktherapie, Deutschland, Mammakarzinom, expressivity, music therapy, Germany, mamma carcinom, Coping, Melodie.

Einleitung

Der vorliegende Artikel befasst sich mit der Frage, welchen Beitrag die Musiktherapie und insbesondere die melodische Improvisation für Brustkrebspatientinnen während ihrer frühen rehabilitativen Phase nach einer Mastektomie leisten kann. Insbesondere wird der musikalische Aspekt der Melodie diskutiert, in der Rolle, die er spielt, um Expressivität zu ermöglichen und zu erleichtern.

- Aus der Literatur ist bekannt, dass es insbesondere für Brustkrebspatientinnen wichtig ist, sich ausdrücken zu können.
- Es ist bekannt, dass der Aspekt der Melodie in unserer modernen Gesellschaft und Kultur eine wichtige Form der Ausdrucksmöglichkeit darstellt.
- Wenn Expressivität ein wichtiger Faktor für Brustkrebspatientinnen und Melodie eine wichtige Form musikalischen Ausdrucks ist macht es einen Sinn, in der Musiktherapie das melodische Spiel

von Brustkrebspatientinnen zu entwickeln.
Die Autorin arbeitet auf einer onkologischen Station eines Allgemeinkrankenhauses, das neben den heute üblichen allopathischen und schulmedizinischen Verfahrensweisen auch die anthroposophische Medizin einbezieht.

Die von ihr angewandte therapeutisch-kreative Kunstform ist auf der von NORDOFF und ROBBINS (1977), ursprünglich für geistig, emotional und physisch behinderte Kinder, initiierten Methode gegründet, die später an der Privaten Universität Witten/Herdecke für die Arbeit mit erwachsenen Patienten weiterentwickelt wurde. Mittelpunkt des musiktherapeutischen Geschehens ist die von Patient und Therapeut gemeinsam ausgeführte Improvisation auf unterschiedlichen rhythmisch-melodischen Instrumenten. Der ausgesprochen individuelle Charakter jeder Improvisation macht das transpersonale Ereignis dieser therapeutischen Situation deutlich, bei der jede Aktivität unlösbar von der des Therapeuten ist (ALDRIDGE 1993).

Die musiktherapeutische Behandlungsphase spielte sich für die Patientinnen während der relativ kurzen zwei bis drei Wochen umfassenden postoperativen, stationären Phase ab und erstreckte sich im Durchschnitt auf sieben Sitzungen, die zwei- bis dreimal wöchentlich für jeweils 30 Minuten stattfanden. Einige dieser Patientinnen erhielten während dieses Zeitraums Bestrahlungs - oder Chemotherapie.

Trotz der geringen Anzahl von Musiktherapiesitzungen, die einigen Patientinnen zur Verfügung stand, wurde der Therapeutin deutlich, welchen Stellenwert die Musiktherapie einnahm in der Zeit unmittelbar nach der Operation, d. h. nach erfolgter Mastektomie oder Teilresektion. Heftige, gemischte Gefühle traten während der Sitzungen auf, häufig begleitet durch Weinen. Vieles drängte zum Ausdruck und äußerte sich teilweise in heftiger Art und Weise während des Spielens auf verschiedenen Instrumenten. Die Autorin gewann den Eindruck, dass über das Verlangen nach Ausdruck hinaus bei allen Patientinnen ein Suchen und Ringen nach einer neuen Identität zu spüren war.

Brustkrebs und Coping
Die psychologische Auswirkung von lebensbedrohenden Krankheiten, wie Krebs, bildete den thematischen Schwerpunkt vieler verschiedener psychoonkologischer Forschungsstudien und wurde dort mit unterschiedlichen Schwerpunkten (psychologisch, psychosozial, Copingforschung) intensiv untersucht (BERTI, HOFFMANN & MÖBUS 1993; CARTER 1993; CARTER & CARTER 1993; CARTER, CARTER & PROSEN 1992; CUNNINGHAM, LOCKWOOD & EDMONDS 1993; GEYER 1993; HEIM, AUGUSTINY, SCHAFFNER & VALACH 1993; HÜRNY ET AL. 1993; NELSON, FRIEDMAN, BAER, LANE & SMITH 1994; RAWNSLEY 1994; SHAPIRO, RODRIGUE, BOGGS & ROBINSON 1994; STANTON & SNIDER 1993; WONG & BRAMWELL 1992). Ziel dieser Forschungsarbeiten war unter anderem die Erkundung valider psychodynamisch und psychosozial wirksamer Indikatoren, die aufgrund gewonnener Daten Aufschlüsse über den Verlauf einer Karzinomerkrankung geben konnten. Dabei vermehrten sich Vermutungen, die einen direkten Zusammenhang zwischen mentalen Ereignissen und der Verbreitung und progressiven Entwicklung von Krebs für möglich hielten. Tatsächlich konnten, wie SPIEGEL (SPIEGEL 1991) recherchierte, viele dieser Studien nachweisen, dass die Unfähigkeit, Ärger auszudrücken in verschiedener Weise mit Krebs assoziiert war, obwohl generell diesem Unvermögen keine ursächliche Bedeutung für den Krebs zugeschrieben werden kann. Einige Studien erbrachten den Nachweis, dass das Überleben der Krankheit, sowie die Krankheitsprogression durch psychosoziale Interventionen beeinflusst werden konnten. SPIEGEL selbst (ebd.) untersuchte in seiner Studie mit Brustkrebspatientinnen den Effekt von psychosozialer Intervention auf die Stimmung und das Schmerzempfinden seiner Klientinnen und stellte eine positive Wirkung auf diese Variablen fest, die sich nicht nur in einer Reduzierung von Stimmungsschwankungen und geringerem Schmerz äußerten sondern ebenso durch verminderte Phobie und bessere Copingreaktionen. Die Anwendung dieser psychosozialen Interventionen in Form von Gruppensitzungen hatten für ihn den Vorteil, dass sie den Klientinnen eine grundsätzliche Verbesserung der Lebensqualität brachten.

Subjektives Wohlbefinden bildet den Hauptaspekt der Lebensqualität und wird besonders beeinflusst durch den komplexen Copingprozess mit der Krankheit und ihrer Behandlung (HÜRNY et al. 1993). Im Rahmen der Copingforschung wurden die mit der Krankheit verbundenen Konfliktbewältigungsstrategien zunehmend Gegenstand von Untersuchungen. Abwehr wurde nicht nur als intrapsychischer Vorgang, sondern auch in Beziehung zum sozialen Kontext gesehen, als Auseinandersetzung

mit der Gesamtproblematik der belastenden Lebenssituation (BERTI et al., 1993) .
Ein Aspekt, der in der Literatur zu den Pflegewissenschaften häufig wiederkehrte, war die Forderung nach emotionaler Unterstützung der Patientinnen während der belastenden Zeitphasen ihrer Krankheit (CARTER 1993; CARTER 1994; WONG & BRAMWELL 1992)

Psychologische Variablen und Personalität
In Ergänzung zum Interesse an Copingfaktoren hat sich die Bedeutung der psychologischen Reaktionen auf die Krebserkrankung als eine prognostische Variable entwickelt, die von einigen Autoren aufmerksam verfolgt wurde (WATSON et al. 1994) . Harrison und Maguire (HARRISON & MAGUIRE 1994) identifizierten z.B. eine Anzahl von Risikofaktoren, die auf psychische Morbidität hinwiesen und empfahlen, dass bei frühzeitiger Entdeckung dieser Faktoren differenziertere und geeignetere Behandlungsmaßnahmen getroffen werden könnten, die ein rechtzeitiges und damit effektiveres Eingehen auf psychische Morbidität ermöglichen könnten.

In Verbindung mit der Diskussion über die Typ C Personalität, die eine Korrelation zwischen der Persönlichkeitsstruktur und dem Auftreten von Krebs vermutete, schien es, dass sich charakteristische Tendenzen bestimmter Eigenschaften in den Persönlichkeitsprofilen der Krebspatienten bestätigten würden (EYSENCK 1994) . Diese Vermutung war nicht neu. Schon 1906 äußerte Sir William Osler, *"Es ist oft viel wichtiger zu wissen, welcher Patient die Krankheit hat, als welche Art von Krankheit der Patient besitzt"* (EYSENCK 1994, S.167) und wies damit darauf hin, dass bereits zu Anfang dieses Jahrhunderts ein Zusammenhang zwischen Persönlichkeitsmerkmalen und dem Krankheitsbild für möglich gehalten wurde. Diese Tatsache hat einige Autoren dazu veranlasst anzunehmen, dass es Personalitätstypen gibt, die, ähnlich der Typ A Personalität für Herzkrankheiten, für eine Krebserkrankung prädisponiert ist.

Aufgrund klinischer Beobachtungen entstanden grob zusammengefasst die Personalitätstypen: Typ A (Herzkrankheiten), Typ B (das gesunde Gegenteil von Typ A) und der Typ C (Krebserkrankungen). Die für Eysenck akzeptierbaren Anhaltspunkte, die auf eine Korrelation zwischen Persönlichkeitsmerkmalen und dem Auftreten von Krebs hinwiesen, äußerten sich in den Merkmalen:
   Unterdrückung von Gefühlen, Verleugnen von Problemen, Schwierigkeiten im Umgang mit äußeren Stresssituationen, physische Inaktivität, Aggressivität statt Bestimmtheit, Rigidität statt Flexibilität und das Unvermögen, Verhaltensweisen im Hinblick auf die Befriedigung wichtiger Lebensziele zu ändern.
Die beobachteten Eigenschaften ordnete er in zwei Kategorien:
1. Die Unterdrückung der Gefühle von Furcht und Ärger, sowie die auf sie bezogenen Verhaltensweisen, wie Aggression, Dominanz oder Egoismus.
2. Ungeeignete und fehlschlagende Copingmechanismen, Gefühle der Hoffnungs - und Hilflosigkeit und schließlich Depression und Verzweiflung.

Musiktherapie und Krebsbehandlung
Im Zusammenhang mit der Forderung nach einer komplexen Behandlungsmethode, die über das rein Medizinische hinaus psychologische, psychosoziale und soziale Aspekte mit einbezieht, hat auch die Musiktherapie an Bedeutung gewonnen.

Im "Supportive Care Program of the Pain Service" der Neurologischen Station des Sloan-Kettering Cancer Center New York, ist der(die) Musiktherapeut(In) Teil des gesamten Teams, bestehend aus Psychiatern, Krankenschwestern, Neuro-Onkologen, einem Kaplan und Sozialarbeitern (BAILEY 1983; COYLE 1987) . In diesem Programm wird die Musiktherapie eingesetzt, um Entspannung zu begünstigen, Angst zu verringern, Methoden der Schmerzlinderung zu unterstützen und die Kommunikation zwischen dem Patienten und seiner Familie zu fördern (BAILEY 1985; BAILEY 1986; BAILEY 1983; COYLE 1987) . Innerhalb dieses Programms erscheint die Depression als häufig auftretender Parameter. Es kann somit hypothetisch behauptet werden, dass besonders auf ihn die Musiktherapie einen Einfluss haben wird und dadurch die Lebensqualität zu verbessern vermag.

HEYDE und von LANGSDORFF (HEYDE & v.LANGSDORFF 1983) heben hervor, wie wertvoll ein Therapieprogramm sein kann, das gleichzeitig aktiv und perzepierend ist. Im Erlebnis der Entdeckung neuer Fähigkeiten sehen sie eine Chance für die Entwicklung neuer Kräfte. Erfolgserlebnisse im schöpferisch-künstlerischen Handeln könnten ihrer Meinung nach zum Abbau der individuellen und völlig unterschiedlichen psychosozialen Probleme führen. Allerdings fehlen hier noch die Beweise. Anhaltspunkte für die positive Wirkung der Musik - und anderen Kunsttherapien sind meistens subjektiv. Bailey entdeckte bei Krebspatienten eine signifikante Stimmungsverbesserung, wenn ihnen statt Tonbandkassetten Live-Musik vorgespielt wurde. Dieses führten sie auf das menschliche Attribut des stärkeren Involviertseins zurück (BAILEY 1983) .

McCaffery (MCCAFFERY 1990) setzte Musiktherapie bei einer pharmakologischen und nichtpharmakologischen Methode der Schmerzbehandlung von Krebspatienten mit chronischen Schmerzen ein. Als rezeptiver Einsatz lenkte sie im Rahmen einer Entspannungstherapie vom Schmerz ab (MCCAFFERY 1990) .

In Ergänzung zum Einsatz der Musik als linderndes Mittel in Schmerzkliniken (FOLEY 1986) wurde die Musik auch als Mittel zur Entspannung und Ablenkung während der Chemotherapie eingesetzt (KAMMRATH 1989) . Insgesamt brachte sie vielen Krebspatient(Inn)en allgemeine Linderung (KERKVLIET 1990) und reduzierte Übelkeit sowie Erbrechen (FRANK 1985) . In der Frankstudie fühlten die Probanden Erleichterung; dieses wurde als ein ermutigendes Zeichen gesehen, Musiktherapie als Behandlungsart einzusetzen.

In einer Studie von Zimmermann (ZIMMERMANN, POZEHL, DUNCAN & SCHMITZ 1989) wurde einer Kontrollgruppe von chronischen Schmerzpatienten selbstgewählte Musik in Verbindung mit Suggestion vorgespielt. Man versuchte den Einfluss dieser Art der Musikeinwirkung auf die Kontrollgruppe zu untersuchen und stellte fest, dass sich nicht nur das emotionelle Leiden sondern auch die aktuellen physischen Schmerzen verringert hatten. Dieses würde bedeuten, dass der Einsatz von Musiktherapie einen direkten Einfluss auf die Sinnesparameter hätte.

Trotz dieser verschiedenen Forschungsstudien ist bisher wenig über den Einsatz von Musiktherapie speziell mit Mammakarzinompatientinnen veröffentlicht worden.

Die wachsende Anzahl von Langzeitstudien verdeutlichten, wie ernst der Aspekt der Integration der Krankheit in den individuellen biographischen Lebenszusammenhang genommen wurde und wie sich der Schwerpunkt der Untersuchungen immer stärker auf die Sichtweise der Betroffenen selbst verlagerte, indem versucht wurde, von der Perspektive der Betroffenen aus, Empfehlungen für unterstützende Nachbehandlungen zu geben. Hier zeigt sich die Möglichkeit eines wertvollen Beitrags durch die kreative Musiktherapie, die indiviuell auf die jeweiligen Bedürfnisse der Patientinnen einzugehen vermag. Sie trifft mit ihrer individuell angelegten Methode auf die Ergebnisse NELSONS und Kollegen (NELSON et al. 1994) , die demonstrierten, dass auch weniger emotional leidende Patientinnen mit sehr unterschiedlichen Einstellungsprofilen ihrer Krebserkerankung besonders von individuell gemessenen psychosozialen Interventionen profitieren konnten.

Die im Zusammenhang mit der Diagnose meist zitierten affektiven Probleme sind Angst und *Depression*. Patientinnen sind durch ihre Krankheit gezwungen, mit ihren eigenen emotionalen Reaktionen umzugehen. Einige schaffen es entsprechend ihrer Veranlagung besser als andere. Musik hat nichts mit *Angst, Depression* oder *Agression* zu tun. Sie ist mit keinem Etikett verbunden, das zu Einschränkungen im Ausdruck von Gefühlen führt. Musiktherapie könnte gerade in dieser Situation den Patientinnen den Raum und die Möglichkeiten bieten, sich ohne Etikett und belastende Normen aus ihrer augenblicklichen Lage und Betroffenheit heraus auszudrücken, ohne Angst zu haben, dass es gewertet wird (SONTAG 1993) . Die Musik bildet innerhalb der Therapie einen nonverbalen und wertfreien Boden, von dem aus die inneren Emotionen der Patientinnen g

Auch kann für die Patientinnen durch die Möglichkeit der kreativen Selbstäußerung die Chance bestehen, negative Gefühle, wie Angst, Anspannung und Depression in positive umzuwandeln, d.h.eine Transformation vom negativen zum positiven Gefühlspol zu bewirken. Positive Emotionen, die die qualitativen Aspekte des Lebens beinhalten, wie Hoffnung, Freude, Schönheit und bedingungslose Liebe sind dafür bekannt, dass sie den Copingprozess günstig beeinflussen (ALDRIDGE 1995; EYSENCK 1994) . Aldridge sieht im Bereich der positiven Emotionen genau den Boden, auf dem auch die Künste ihr eigenes Dasein haben. Patientinnen könnten mithilfe der aktiven Musiktherapie einen Weg zu ihren eigenen Ausdrucksquellen finden, der kreativ und nicht durch eine Krankheit begrenzt ist. Dieser Betrachtungsweise indiziert die Erwartung, Indikatoren zu finden, die, trotz einer Verschlechterung der physischen Parameter, auf eine Verbesserung der Lebensqualität hinweisen. Für Krebspatieninnen wäre dieses besonders wertvoll.

Aldridge (ALDRIDGE 1989b) bietet durch die Benutzung einer musikalischen Metapher eine Sichtweise an, die vorschlägt, die menschliche Identität wie ein Stück sinfonischer Musik zu betrachten, die kontinuierlich im Moment komponiert ist. Diese steht im Gegensatz zu einer mechanistischen Sichtweise des Menschseins, die auf den Körper fixiert ist und ihn als etwas betrachtet, das repariert werden muss. Diese Betrachtungsweise eröffnet neue Möglichkeiten für den Einsatz der kreativen Musiktherapie, in der die Patientinnen die Gelegenheit haben, sich im aktiven musikalischen Spiel selber wahrzunehmen und zu erleben. Als nonverbale Therapieform, die sich der Improvisation bedient, erleichtert sie den Zugang zur eigenen Gefühlswelt und zur Aufhebung der Unterdrückung von Gefühlen, besonders der von Furcht und Ärger führen kann.

Im Wahrnehmen und Erleben des ganzheitlichen Selbst erleben die Patientinnen nicht nur ihre körperlichen Schwächen und Gebrechen sondern auch ihre individuellen Potentiale, die unverwechselbar aus dem Moment heraus zum Ausdruck kommen können. Damit wird es ihnen möglich sein, sich im Moment des musikalischen Äußerns nicht nur als körperlich begrenzt zu erleben, sondern als ein Wesen, das seine Grenzen in der musikalischen Äußerung transzendiert (ALDRIDGE 1995).

Auch im Hinblick auf ihren wohltuenden Nutzen für den Copingprozess lässt sich die Einbeziehung der Musiktherapie in eine ganzheitliche Behandlungsform begründen. Der Literatur ist zu entnehmen, dass psychologischer und sozialer Stress die Copingaktivität beeinflussen können und infolgedessen einen Einfluss auf das Immunsystem ausüben. Es wäre durchaus zu spekulieren, dass die, durch die kreative Musiktherapie stimulierten postiven Gefühle die Copingaktivitäten erhöhen und dadurch einen positiven Einfluss auf die Erhöhung der Immunfunktion ausüben könnten.

Die Anwendung der musikalischen Metapher auf das menschliche Individuum macht es möglich, dieses in dynamischer Art und Weise als ein ganzheitliches Selbst zu hören und zwar nicht nur während der eigenen musikaischen Gestaltung sondern auch in der Beziehung zu einem anderen Menschen, wie der Therapeutin. Mit der Form des musikalischen Dialogs wäre es für Patientientinnen möglich, z.B. mit Hilfe eines rhythmischen Motivs, in einen gegenseitigen Austausch von Emotionen zu kommen und diese im musikalischen Spiel zu regulieren. Diese Überlegungen stützen ein Hauptargument, das die musikalischen Komponenten als die fundamentalen Bestandteile der Kommunikation herausstellt und insbesondere den Rhythmus als den entscheidenden musikalischen Aspekt der Kommunikation betrachtet. Dieser ist für die Art und Weise, in der wir zu uns selbst und zu anderen in Beziehung treten, von zentraler Bedeutung (ALDRIDGE 1989a). Da die musikalische Zeitstruktur, innerhalb derer der musikalische Austausch rhythmisch-melodischer Motive stattfindet, nicht statisch ist, kann mit Hilfe dieser Form, die zugleich kohärent ist, auf ein flexibles Reagieren seitens der Patientinnen eingewirkt werden. Somit erhält die Form des musikalischen Dialogs auch im Hinblick auf den in der Literatur hervorgehobenen Aspekt der Isolation eine Bedeutung, um den interpersonellen Kontakt aufrechtzuerhalten.

Zusammenfassend kann festgestellt werden, dass die Musiktherapie von einer holistischen Perspektive aus einen Beitrag leisten kann, den Bedürfnissen der Patientinnen während der verschiedenen Krankheitsphasen zu begenen. Im Sinne der Forderungen mehrerer Langzeitstudien könnte sie als rezeptive und aktive Intervention
1. physische Entlastung bringen (Reduzierung von Müdigkeit und Kraftlosigkeit, Ablenkung von Schmerzen),
2. psychologisch auf emotionale Stressfaktoren eingehen und impulshaft auf innerliche Beweglichkeit einwirken, im Sinne einer Transformation der Gefühlspole vom negativen zum positiven und
3. durch den Dialog in der Musik die kommunikativen Ausdrucksmöglichkeiten erweitern und soziale Schwierigkeiten, bzw. Hemmnisse abmildern.
4. soziale Schwierigkeiten durch die Anregung interpersonellen Kontakts verringern und Isolation reduzieren.

Mit ihren Möglichkeiten zur Intervention, Unterstützung, Affirmation, Ablenkung, Konfrontation und Kommunikation stellt sie eine sinnvolle Therapieform dar, die den medizinischen Behandlungsprozess in Form einer adjuvanten Therapie begleiten und ergänzen kann.

Expressivität

Trotz der vielseitigen Studien über einen sinnvollen Einsatz der Musiktherapie in der Krebsbehandlung gibt es im einzelnen kaum Hinweise darauf, wie die Expressivität der Patient(inn)en in der musikalischen Improvisation, in Bezug auf den Rhythmus, die Melodie und Harmonie zum Ausdruck kommt und wie sich ihre Expressivität im musikalischen Spiel innerhalb der musiktherapeutischen Situation in

Beziehung zum Therapeuten zu äußern vermag.
In unserer westlichen Kultur spielt der Aspekt der Melodie innerhalb der persönlichen Ausdrucksfähigkeit eine wichtige Rolle. Wenn man also davon ausgeht, dass mit der Methode der kreativen Musiktherapie, die den Patienten aktiv in den therapeutischen Gestaltungs- und Formungsprozess mit einbezieht, besonders Einfluss auf die Ausdrucksmöglichkeiten des Klienten genommen werden kann lässt sich nunmehr als konkrete Hypothese formulieren, dass die melodische Improvisation eine Möglichkeit bieten kann, den in der Literatur hervorgehobenen problematischen Aspekt der Ausdrucksfähigkeit, in einen anderen, d.h. künstlerischen Kontext zu bringen, indem den Patientinnen die Möglichkeit geboten wird, sich mit Hilfe der melodischen Improvisation ihre eigenen individuellen Ausdrucksformen zu erschaffen. Dass die Musik ein besonders geeignetes Medium ist, dieses zu ermöglichen, bedarf keiner weiteren Begründung.

Entscheidend ist jedoch, dass die Bedeutung der Musik nicht allein in ihrer Eigenschaft als emotionales Reizmittel zu sehen ist sondern weit darüber hinausreicht:"Musik ist ebensowenig die Ursache von Gefühlen wie deren Heilmittel. Sie ist ihr logischer Ausdruck" (LANGER 1992, S.216) . Gefühle im Menschen suchen in ihrer Dynamik und Beweglichkeit eine Form des Ausdrucks. Diese lässt sich durch die unendlichen Möglichkeiten, die in der tonalen dynamischen Vielfalt der Musik gegeben sind, realisieren.

Es ist hier wichtig, zu betonen, dass, wenn wir über eine Kunsttherapie sprechen, uns immer einige Schritte von der eigentlichen künstlerischen Tätigkeit des Patienten und Therapeuten wegbewegen (ALDRIDGE, BRANDT & WOHLER 1990) . Wenn wir über die Therapie berichten müssen wir drei verschiedene Ebenen berücksichtigen, die sich von der aktiven Ebene der künstlerischen Aufführung entfernen:

Ebene 1 Erfahrung auf der das Phänomen erlebt wird. Es lebt und existiert in dem Moment, wird aber nur teilweise verstanden. Diese individuellen, expressiven Handlungen werden in den modernen Sprachwissenschaften als *parole* bezeichnet (BURGIN 1989).

Ebene 2 Beschreibung auf der wir über die therapeutische Situation, unter Einbeziehung der jeweiligen Terminologien, z.B. Rhythmus, Melodie, Polyphonie der verschiedenen künstlerischen Disziplinen, sprechen. Die Beschreibungen sind relativ sachlich und auch überprüfbar (Tonbandaufzeichnungen). Diese entsprechen dem gemeinsamen Element der Sprache, den *usage,* der für systematisches Studium zur Verfügung steht und zu unserem normalen täglichen Diskurs gehört.

Ebene 3 Interpretation auf der wir die abstrakte Basis innerhalb der Sprache: *langue* artikulieren. Um erklären zu können was in der Musiktherapie passiert, oder das Verhältnis zwischen Handlung und Heilung zu erläutern ist es notwendig, musikalische Veränderungen in Begriffe der akademischen Disziplinen Psychologie, Psychotherapie, oder in ein medizinisches System zu übertragen. Auf dieser Ebene betreibt der Therapeut Interpretation, die ihn einen Schritt ferner dessen, was geschehen ist, abkommen lässt.

Eine Therapeutin, die auf diesen drei Ebenen agiert, findet sich in dem Dilemma, eine valide Beschreibung des aktuellen Heilungsprozesses darzustellen. Es ist ausgeschlossen, den eigentlichen therapeutischen Heilungsprozess zu verstehen und zu beschreiben, denn Heilung findet auf der Vortragsebene in der therapeutischen Situation statt (Ebene 1), und diese existiert für sich. Alles andere ist Interpretation und hängt von Sprache ab; mit anderen Worten, einer dynamischen Handlung wird eine Subjekt-Prädikat-Grammatik auferlegt. Der therapeutische Prozess wird allzuoft auf der Ebene 3 beschrieben, d.h. interpretierend und schlussfolgernd, auf der es trotz eines einheitlichen grammatikalischen verbalen Diskurses, oder langue, einen Verlust an begrifflicher Geschlossenheit gibt (ALDRIDGE et al. 1990) .

Expressivität ist ein wichtiger Aspekt der musikalischen Improvisation und kann sich in ganz unterschiedlicher Formgebung der musikalischen Parameter äußern. Um möglichst genau und exakt beschreiben zu können was in der therapeutischen Situation passiert, wird hier der Schwerpunkt auf die Ebene 2 (usage) gelegt, die sich auf die konkrete Beschreibung des künstlerischen Prozesses stützt und sich somit nicht zu weit von der eigentlichen therapeutischen Aktivität (parole) entfernt.

Zur Bedeutung von Melodie

Es lässt sich behaupten, dass die *Melodie* als wichtiger Teilaspekt der Musik für viele Menschen eine Bedeutung hat. Sie ist mit inneren Erlebnissen und dem Erinnerungsvermögen verbunden und kann als intimer Begleiter der verchiedenen Lebensstadien und - situationen fungieren. Mit Melodien vermag man sich zu identifizieren. Es ist weiter anzunehmen, dass die Melodie, in welcher Erscheinungsform auch immer, der geläufigste und verbreiteste Aspekt der Musik während aller Zeiten und Kulturen war und heute noch ist. Sie ist das Element der Musik, an dem die allgemeine Qualität der Musik gemessen wird und sich die künstlerische Qualität des Komponisten offenbart. Die Frage, warum uns die eine Melodie mehr anspricht als die andere, sie in uns weiter lebt und unter Umständen auch zu einem quälenden Ohrwurm werden kann, ist generell kaum möglich zu beantworten. Ähnliche Unklarheiten und Zweifel bezüglich grundsätzlicher Aussagen zur Bedeutung und Funktion der Melodie lassen sich nachweisen, wenn man einen Blick auf die historische Entwicklung der Melodie wirft. Diese offenbart, dass wir es mit einer paradoxen Disziplin zu tun haben, " denn das einzig Unveränderliche in ihrer Entwicklung, die Jahrtausende zurückrreicht, scheint die Klage darüber zu sein, dass es sie nicht oder noch nicht gebe" (ABRAHAM & DAHLHAUS 1982, S.10) . Johann MATTHESON beschreibt diese Tatsache mit folgenden Worten:

"Diese Kunst, eine gute Melodie zu machen, begreifft das wesentlichste in der Music. Es ist dannenhero höchstens zu verwundern, dass ein socher Haupt-Punct, an welchem doch das größeste gelegen ist, bis diese Stunde fast von jedem Lehrer hintangesetzet wird. Ja man hat so gar wenig darauf gedacht, dass auch die vornehmsten Meister, und unter denselben die weitläufigsten und neuesten, gestehen müssen: es sey fast unmöglich, gewisse Regeln davon zu geben, unter dem Vorwande, weil das meiste auf den guten Geschmack ankäme; da doch auch von diesem selbst die gründlichsten Regeln gegeben werden können und müssen."
(MATTHESON 1739, S.133) .

Unser Verständnis des heutigen Melodiebegriffs, das von unserem allgemeinen Musikverständnis der Musik des 18./19.Jh. geprägt ist, trägt auch die Merkmale des älteren und weitgespannten Melodiebegriffs der Antike, der drei Momente beinhaltet: *Harmonia* (das Zusammenstimmen der Töne), *Rhythmos* (die Zeitgliederung) und *Logos* (die Sprache, der Text) (BLUME 1989) . Bis ins 18.Jh. war der Vorrang des Vokalen ungebrochen, rückte jedoch durch die im 18./19. Jh. an Bedeutung gewinnende Instrumentalmusik in den Hintergrund. Dabei übertrugen sich die strukturellen Merkmale der gesungenen Melodie auf die der Instumentalmelodie, und zwar entsprechend der technischen Voraussetzungen (größerer Tonumfang, größere Beweglichkeit) der Instrumente.

Wie in der Antike erscheint im 19.Jh. und auch heute die Harmonie als Moment der Melodie. Rousseau und Herder räumen der Melodie, dem Neuen, Charakteristischen und Typischen die Priorität vor der Harmonie ein und wenden sich mit dieser Anschauung gegen die Auffassung Rameaus, der in dem Generellen, im System der Harmonik, die Substanz der Melodie erblickt (BLUME 1989) . Mit dem Neuen, Charakteristischen und Typischen ist der Einfall einer linearen Tonfolge gemeint (Melos=Tonfolge).

Heute werden neben der Melodik die Parameter Harmonik und Rhythmik als selbständige Größen betrachtet, die bei der Melodiebildung eine bedeutende Rolle spielen. Für eine melodische Analyse, die auch auf die Erhellung des musikalischen Zusammenhangs ausgerichtet ist, wird es somit wichtig sein, nicht nur die Diastematie, d. h. den Tonhöhenverlauf in seinen Tonabständen nach Höhe und Tiefe zu betrachten, sondern ebenso eine getrennte Betrachtungsweise der Elemente Rhythmus und Harmonie vorzunehmen.

Was sind aber nun die Merkmale unseres heutigen Melodiebegriffs im einzelnen?

Bei RIEMANN ist zu lesen (DAHLHAUS & EGGEBRECHT 1979)

"Melodie ist die in der Zeit sich entfaltende selbständige Tonbewegung, die sich gegenüber weniger selbständigen Tonfolgen (Neben -, Begleit -, Füllstimmen) auszeichnet durch innere Folgerichtigkeit oder Gesanglichkeit oder leichtere Fasslichkeit oder durch Festigkeit und Geschlossenheit ihrer Gestalt und die als konkrete Erscheinung auch das rhythmische Element in sich enthält".

Dieses Zitat hebt den Aspekt der Formhaftigkeit und Gestalt hervor und lässt sich durch die Attribute wie *selbständig, geschlossen, gegliedert, sangbar, einstimmig* und *einprägsam* ergänzen, die im alltäglichen Sprachgebrauch in Verbindung mit den Adjektiva *melodisch, melodiös* und *unmelodisch* eine Wertung erlangen können.

Desweiteren erwartet man von einer Melodie *Originalität* und *Expressivität* , d.h. neben dem Moment des Gleichmaßes und der Konvention einen Anteil von Neuheit und Außergewöhnlichkeit (ABRAHAM & DAHLHAUS 1982) .

Ästhetische Voraussetzungen

Diese Vorstellungen und Erwartungen über das, was Melodie beinhalten soll sind wiederum Auswirkungen einer Ästhetik, die den Faktor Melodie im 18./19. Jahrhundert besonders hervorhob. Der Gedanke der *Originalität* lässt sich auf die Inspirationsästhetik des 19.Jh. zurückführen, die schroff zwischen dem melodischen Einfall (der Inspiration) , der nicht lehrbar ist, und der kunstverständigen, satztechnisch - formalen Ausarbeitung unterschied.

Desgleichen lässt sich das Merkmal der *Expressivität* auf ästhetische Vorstellungen des 19.Jahrhunderts zurückbeziehen, die die musikalische Expressivität am deutlichsten in der Melodie ausgedrückt sahen. Beeiflusst wurde dieser Gedanke durch Hegels Musikästhetik, die hervorhob, dass der Mensch in der Melodie sein Inneres, seine Seele auszudrücken vermag und dadurch auch gleichzeitig in der Lage ist, sich von einem möglichen Freudens - oder Leidensdruck zu befreien (ABRAHAM & DAHLHAUS 1982) . Für Hegel ist das Innere des Menschen nicht nur in sich selbst versunken, sondern steht gleichsam neben sich. Indem ein Gefühl zugleich gegenwärtig und ferngerückt erlebt wird kann es befreiend wirken. Diesen Doppelcharakter des Gefühls (zugleich emphatisch und distanziert) sieht Hegel in der bestimmbaren Beziehung der Melodie zur Taktrhythmik und tonalen Harmonik des 17. bis 19. Jahrhunderts begründet. Auch er hebt in Verbindung mit Expressivität die für die Melodie wesentlichen Elemente: Rhythmik und Harmonik hervor. In den Regeln und Strukturen dieser beiden Elemente sieht er weniger einen Zwang, als einen Halt, auf den sich die Melodie stützen kann, um nicht ins Gestaltlose zu zerfließen. Dieser von Hegel formulierte Doppelcharakter des melodischen Gefühlsausdrucks, die Gleichzeitigkeit von Versunkensein und Darüberstehen hängt mit einem Grundzug des Musikempfindens im 19. Jahrhundert zusammen.

Kulturelle Voraussetzungen

Auch Benzon (BENZON 1993) greift die heute übliche Trennung der Musik in die Parameter: Rhythmus, Melodie und Harmonie auf, die wir generell heranziehen, wenn wir Musik analysieren. Allerdings begründet er dieses von einer kulturgeschichtlichen Perspektive aus, in dem er kulturelle Gegebenheiten artikuliert. Benzon behauptet, und er stützt sich dabei auf vorangegangene Studien, dass unsere Grunderfahrungen von Musik, wie auch alle unsere Elementarerfahrungen, holistisch sind. Auf die Musik bezogen bedeutet dieses, dass wir sie zunächst undifferenziert als Ganzheit wahrnehmen und erst allmählich in der Lage sind, unseren musikalischen Gesamteindruck in Rhythmus, Melodie und Harmonie zu differenzieren. Er argumentiert weiter, dass sich nur durch den langen Prozess der kulturellen Entwicklung die Elemente Rhythmus, Melodie und Harmonie klar unterscheiden konnten und schlägt folgende Entwicklungsstadien vor, die hier nur verkürzt wiedergegeben werden:

- "Rank 1" : *Rhythmus,* Entwicklung zur *Phrase*
- "Rank 2" : *Melodie,* Entwicklung zur *Führung,*bzw. *führenden Stimme*
- "Rank 3" : *Harmonie,* Entwicklung zur *Architektonik*

Jeder "Rank" hat seine eigenen charakteristischen Wege der Entwicklung einer besonderen Aufführungspraxis, die aus dem jeweiligen, speziellen Material (Rhytmus,Melodie oder Harmonie) hervorgeht. Festzuhalten ist, dass diese Ordnung in der Sache selbst begründet ist (BENZON 1993)

Dieses von Benzon vorgeschlagene Entwicklungsmodell ist insofern von Bedeutung, da es von einer übergeordneten kulturellen Position aus Erklärungen für den Prozess der melodischen Entwicklung im musikalischen Spiel von Patientinnen, im Verlauf der musiktherapeutischen Behandlungsphase anzubieten vermag.

Als sinnvolle Größe für eine musikalische Analyse betrachtet Benzon das Motiv, das als grundlegende Einheit für Analysen fungieren und als rhythmisches, melodisches und harmonisches Motiv erscheinen kann. Erkennbar und definierbar wird das Motiv durch seine Wiederholung. Darüberhinaus sind die musikalischen Termini *Zelle, Thema, Phrase, Periode, Satz* von Bedeutung für die melodische Analyse (NATTIEZ 1990) .

Wichtige Aspekte für die Musiktherapie

Bei der hier angewendeten Form der kreativen Musiktherapie ist das Individuum nicht nur als wahrnehmende und erlebende, sondern auch als handelnde Person beteiligt. Zwischen dem Wahrnehmen und dem Ausüben, also der Produktion von Musik, liegt das "Was", der Inhalt des musikalischenMaterials, wie z.B. dasMotiv. Für Nattiez ist dieses "Was", das produziert ist, wichtig und verdient Aufmerk-

samkeit. Bei der Betrachtung und Erfassung des melodisch Typischen oder melodisch Wesenhaften kann es nicht darauf ankommen, nach regelhaften, genormten melodischen Gebilden zu suchen. Es kommt vielmehr darauf an, losgelöst von etwaigen normhaften Vorstellungen, das Zusammenwirken der beteiligten musikalischen Einzelelemente wie rhythmisches, melodisches Motiv oder Zelle, harmonische Struktur, oder dynamische Vielfalt zu erkennen und das zu beschreiben, was durch den kreativen Prozess der Patientinnen als neu Geschaffenes hervorgebracht worden ist. Für die Analyse des musikalischen Materials einer melodischen Improvisation in der Musiktherapie sind also (gemäß NATTIEZ) folgende Punkte wichtig:
- Das Vorhandensein eines rhythmischen Motivs, das stabilitätsfördernd wirken könnte.
- Das Vorhandensein eines melodischen Motivs.
- Die weitere Entwicklung und Gestaltung des rhythmisch-melodischen Motivs.
- Die Ausbildung von Phrasen und Perioden in Beziehung zur Harmonie, d.h. zur qualitativen Ordnung der Intervalle.
- Die Artikulation und der musikalische Ausdruck, der alle dynamischen - und Temponuancen einbezieht.

Therapeutisch bedeutet dieses, immer wieder neu zu sehen, auf welche Art und Weise sich die Patientinnen mit der melodischen Improvisation individuell ausdrücken können und ihren Ausdruck in eine für sie gemäße Form bringen.

Für die melodische Improvisation stehen Instrumente, wie Metallophon, Xylophon, Klangstäbe, Glockenspiel, Marimbaphon und Vibraphon zur Verfügung, die perkussiv gehandhabt werden. Bedingt durch die horizontale Anordnung der einzelnen Tonplatten (Klangkörper) ist eine Spielbewegung vorgegeben, die mit den Tonabständen klein und groß korreliert. Die somit gegebenen Möglichkeiten der unterschiedlichen Anordnung von Tönen können verschiedene Erfahrungen von Tonspannungen und melodische Formen ermöglichen.

Aus dieser Sichtweise heraus sind die folgenden Aspekte einer Melodie wichtig für die Musiktherapie:
- Der Ausdruck von Bewegung, die in jedem Moment entsteht und wieder zerfällt; die von einem Ton wegstrebt und auf den nächsten zustrebt und die damit verbundene rhythmische Bewegungsordnung.
- Die je nach Intervallgröße ungeheure melodische Spannung, die ihre eigene dynamische Kraft besitzt.
- Das Formerlebnis: mit dem Anfang einer Melodie haben wir sofort das Ganze im Sinn.
- Das ästhetische Vergnügen, neue individuelle Formen zu entdecken, die von den eigenen Hörerwartungen abweichen (Auswirkungen der Inspirationsästhetik).
- Die Aktivierung des gefühlsmäßigen und kognitiven Bereichs (der unmittelbare Ausdruck melodischer Figuren und die Fähigkeit, sich an Motive und Melodien zu erinnern).

Anhand des Beispiels einer melodischen Improvisation soll hier demonstriert werden, dass die Melodie Möglichkeiten für die Patientin bereithält, ihre eigene individuelle Ausdrucksform zu finden.
Drei Fragen sind für die vorliegende Fallstudie relevant:
- Wie entwickelt die Patientin ihr melodisches Spiel im Kontext der melodischen Improvisation?
- Welches sind die relevanten Nuancen ihrer emotionalen Expressivität?
- Was bedeutet es für die Patientin, sich durch das Wesen der Melodie ausdrücken zu können?

Das Beispiel stammt aus der sechsten Sitzung mit einer Mammakarzinompatientin, die sich nach dem chirurgischen Eingriff einer Mastektomie während ihrer kurzen nachoperativen Rehabilitationsphase im Krankenhaus aufhielt.

Takte 1 - 9
Patientin: Metallophon, harmonische Skala c-moll, Tonumfang c^1 - as^2
Therapeutin: Klavier.
Das Beispiel beginnt mit einem Auftakt. Ein rhythmisches Motiv ist erkennbar, das, man könnte es mit einem kleinen Keim vergleichen, in sich die Möglichkeit zur Entwicklung birgt. In der Verslehre der hellenistischen Zeit (Aristoxenos "Rhythmik-Fragmente") ist es ein Jambus.
Diese rhythmische Zelle ist in zweifacher Hinsicht von Bedeutung:
1. Sie gibt der Patientin innerhalb ihrer Spielaktivität Halt und Stabilität, um die melodische Seite der Musik zu entdecken.

2. Gleichzeitig ist sie ein Bewegungsimpuls, der ihr ermöglicht, den harmonischen Tonraum von c-moll zu erfahren.

Meiner Erfahrung nach ist für die Entdeckung und Entwicklung des melodischen Sinns das Vorhandensein eines Gefühls für den Rhythmus ausschlaggebend. Der von der Patientin formulierte "Klangfuß" ist die von ihr eingeschlagene "Gangart", die sie durch die Improvisation führt und die für alles Folgende den Maßstab abgibt.

Zusammenfassend kann der erste Beginn ihres Spiels als klangliche Orientierung im harmonischen Bereich von c-moll bezeichnet werden. Die Patientin beginnt auf dem Grundton, findet ganz natürlich ihren Weg über die höher gelegene Quinte, Oktave und Quarte. Nach den ersten vier Takten führe ich ein melodisches Element ein.

Takte 9 - 20

Hier geht es nicht mehr länger um eine Orientierung im tonalen Raum, sondern um bewusstere Wahrnehmung und bewussteres Einhören in die Tonbeziehungen, was hörbar wird durch die differenzierte Anschlagsart der Patientin. Ihre Wahrnehmung des harmonischen Tonraums wird durch die Hervorhebung der zentralen Töne: Grundton und Quinte deutlich. Es sind für sie harmonische Orientierungspunkte, von denen sie ausgehen und wieder zurückkehren kann. Gegenüber der melodisch hervortretenden Stimme des Klaviers sucht sie sich als Kontrast eine harmonische Mittelstimme. Im letzten Takt des Beispiels entwickelt sie eine auftaktige Figur, die zur nächstfolgenden Entwicklung führt.

Takte 20 - 33

In diesem Abschnitt beginnt die Patientin ihr Spiel melodisch zu formen. Die Tonhöhenstruktur (Diastematik) steht im Vordergrund, sie ist nicht nur geformt, sondern zeigt gleichzeitig rhythmische Vielfalt. Beide Elemente, das melodische und rhythmische korrespondieren miteinander und gehen eine Symbiose ein. Jeder Ton steht in Beziehung zu den nächst folgenden, wie es sich anhand der Phrasierungsbögen darstellen lässt.

In diesem Beispiel sehen wir die Entwicklung formaler Prinzipien der Musik:
- die Entfaltung eines Taktmotivs zu 2-Takt-Phrasen.
- die Entfaltung der melodischen Struktur, der Diastematik.
- die Entwicklung von tonaler Einheit durch Rückkehr zu harmonisch zentralen Tönen.
- die experimentelle Erfahrung im unmittelbaren, gegenwärtigen Spiel, Musik in Form zu bringen.

Takte 33 - 44

In diesem Beispiel ist die Melodie stärker ausgeformt: nach dem auftaktigen Oktavsprung aszendiert und deszendiert sie in Zwei-Takteinheiten, wobei sie konsequent den Grundton hörbar macht.

Betrachtet man die Bewegung im Detail so entdeckt man, ausgehend von der ursprünglichen rhythmischen Zelle, typische Motivbildungen.

Im **8.-9. Takt** sequenziert sie ihr Motiv in Aufwärtsrichtung. In den **Takten 40-42** gibt sie ihm durch seine Wiederholung mehr Bedeutung. Erkennbar wird die Korrespondenz ihrer Melodieteile, die häufig 4 Takte umfassen. Das von mir angebotene harmonische Gerüst übernimmt die tektonische Funktion, über der sich die melodische Inspiration der Patientin frei variierend entfalten kann.

Dieses Beispiel verdeutlicht, dass die Patientin in der Lage war, sich als Person in einer melodischen Form auszudrücken. *Ihre Bemerkung nach dieser melodischen Improvisation war, dass sie sich in einem wunderbaren Spaziergang durch die sonnigen Straßen von Paris erlebt hätte.*

Wenn wir insgesamt nach den Ausdrucksmöglichkeiten fragen, die der Patientin durch das Angebot einer melodischen Improvisation gegeben sind, dann liegen diese in der Art und Weise, wie sie die Elemente Rhythmus, Tonspannung, Harmonie, Phrase und Form miteinander kombiniert und sich durch sie expressiv zum Ausdruck bringen kann.

Das Zusammenwirken dieser Elemente in ihrem Spiel, mit der sich allmählich entwickelnden, fließenden Melodiebewegung von immer neu entstehenden Tonfolgen weist auf eine Flexibilität hin, die zugleich in der harmonischen Struktur der Musik, die von der Therapeutin übernommen wurde, enthalten ist. Die harmonische Struktur trägt mit ihrer starken Ausdruckskraft, die aus dem Wechsel der funktionellen Bezüge von Spannung und Entspannung besteht, zu einem tieferen Erlebnis des melodischen Spiels bei.

Indem das harmonische Gerüst, insbesondere ab Takt 20 zunehmend von der Therapeutin übernommen und beibehalten wird und in seiner Struktur vorwiegend gleich bleibt, kann es als ein "Urmuster" tonaler Bestätigung angesehen werden, das das melodische Spiel der Patientin stützt und hält.

Es ist gut möglich, dass die vorgegebene C-Moll Skala mit den in ihr enthaltenen drei Halbtonschritten (wobei der wichtigste der durch die Erhöhung des 7. Tons entstandene ist, mit dem übermäßigen Sekundabstand zwischen dem 6. und 7. Ton) ein möglicher Auslöser für die sich frei entfaltende Spielweise der Patientin ist. Die der Skala immanente Tonspannung könnte die, sich in ihrem Spiel zeigende Bewegungsenergie hervorgerufen haben, die jeden Ton in ein bestimmtes Kräfteverhältnis zu den übrigen einordnet und ihm somit eine funktionelle Bedeutung für den Gesamtverlauf gibt (s. Takte 33-44).

Die emotionale Qualität, die hörbar ist im Spiel der Patientin, lässt sich nicht vom musikalischen Material, das die Patientin entwickelt hat, eliminieren, da es aktiv und lebendig ist. Dieses einzigartige Gefühl von Stimmung und musikalischem Material erhebt sich über das flüchtige, vergängliche und zufällig wirkende Klangereignis. Das, was zufällig erscheint, wird bedeutungsvoll.

Es wird hier deutlich, dass das Erlebnis einer sich auf diese Weise entfaltenden Melodie ein Erlebnis einer sinnvollen Ganzheit ist. Die deskriptive Psychologie zieht für diesen Tatbestand den Begriff der Gestalt heran (BLUME 1989), ein Gebilde, das mehr Eigenschaften besitzt als die Summe ihrer einzelnen Elemente ausmachen würde. Die Gestaltqualitäten lassen sich am vorliegenden Beispiel anhand der Anschaulichkeit seiner Form, der Synthese seiner Einzelelemente und der Möglichkeit seiner Transponierbarkeit nachweisen.

Der im Spiel der Patientin hörbar werdende harmonische Bezug, insbesondere der zum Grundton, lässt vermuten, dass sie einen Weg des Ausdrucks gefunden hat, der sie zum einen zentriert und zum anderen ihr eine Neuorientierung finden lässt.

Therapeutisch bedeutet dies für mich, dass die Patientin für sich eine Möglichkeit fand, ihrer inneren Expressivität Form zu geben. Für Brustkrebspatientinnen, die sich nach der Operation im Prozess neuer Orientierung und Identitätsfindung befinden, ist dieses besonders wertvoll.

Vielleicht kann der Wert des Grundtons darin gesehen werden, dass er diese neue Identitätssuche verankert und eine Basis für neue Orientierungsmöglichkeiten bereitzuhalten vermag. So könnte der von dieser Patientin häufiger aufgesuchte Grundton mit einer neuen Identitätsfindung verbunden sein.

Schlussfolgerungen

Wir wissen, dass Krebs eine komplexe Krankheit ist und dass die Problematik dieses Krankheitsbildes deutlich auf die Notwendigkeit einer verstärkten physischen, emotionalen und sozialen Unterstützung hinweist. Eine einseitige medizinische Behandlung der Symptome reduziert die Frauen zu passiven medizinischen Objekten. Wie wichtig und zentral dieser Tatbestand angesehen wird lässt sich anhand eines in der Literatur geforderten multisystematischen Modells mehrerer Faktoren ablesen, das versucht, die umfassenden Variablen, wie demographische, intrapersonelle, familiäre und soziökologische einzubeziehen, um ein tieferes und vollständigeres Bild über die Einstellung der Patientinnen zu ihrer Krebserkrankung zu erhalten.

Psychosoziale Interventionen, die sich auf das breite Spektrum der gemessenen Variablen bezogen, konnten signifikante Verbesserungen nachweisen, die die Wirksamkeit dieser Maßnahmen verdeutlichten.

Das gleiche trifft für die Einbeziehung der Musiktherapie als rezeptive und aktive Maßnahme zu, die zu Verbesserungen, insbesondere im affektiven Bereich führte, und sich durch eine Reduzierung von Angst, Depression, Müdigkeit und Verwirrtheit äußerte.

Durch ihren direkten Einfluss auf die Sinnesparameter konnte sie von den aktuellen physischen Schmerzen ablenken, allgemeine Linderung der chemotherapeutisch bedingten Nebeneffekte bringen, das emotionelle Leiden verringern, die Kommunikation mit der Familie fördern und eine signifikante Stimmungsverbesserung herbeiführen.

Die melodische Improvisation bietet eine besondere Möglichkeit, um einen positiven Einfluss auf den in der Literatur zentral hervorgehobenen Aspekt der Ausdrucksfähigkeit auszuüben, der bei diesen Patientinnen eine besondere Rolle spielt. Mithilfe des melodischen Aspekts der Musik konnte sich die Patientin dieser Fallstudie ihren "Weg" in der Therapie fühlend erspielen, einen Weg, den sie selber von innen heraus melodisch formte und gestaltete. Die Ausdrucksmöglichkeiten, die sie durch ihre melodische Gestaltung in dynamischer Art und Weise nutzte, offenbarten ihre kreative Energie. Es könnte möglich sein, dass diese ihren emotionalen Gesundungsprozess reflektiert und ihr den Weg zu einer neuen Identität weist.

Da diese Patientinnen sich mit überwältigenden Gefühlen konfrontiert sehen und sie herausgefordert sind, sich an eine neue radikal veränderte Zukunft anzupassen, kann dieser musikalisch-melodische Prozess, der die eigenen Gefühle in eine bewusste Form bringt, und zwar ohne unmittelbares verbales Etikett, ein signifikanter Schritt auf dem Weg zur Besserung sein.

Da der kreative Prozess immer selbstorientiert und auf die Erfahrung der eigenen Situation fokussiert ist, kann davon ausgegangen werden, dass es sinnvoll ist, diese Art der musiktherapeutischen Maßnahme auch für andere Brustkrebspatientinnen anzubieten.

Die mit der Melodie zur Verfügung stehenden Aspekte von Zeit, Raum und Harmonie könnten Patientinnen die Möglichkeit bieten, sich ihren eigenen inspiratorisch-melodischen Weg, in ihrer individuellen Zeitstruktur zu erspielen.

Jede Frau ist inspiriert, ihre eigenen Ausdrucksweisen in ihrer individuellen Zeit hervorzubringen. Ihr ist die Möglichkeit gegeben, sich selber auf einem spontanen, authentischen Weg zu akzeptieren. Sie erschafft sich eine Identität, die ästhetisch ist. In der therapeutischen Beziehung wird diese Beziehung in einer Form gepflegt, die ästhetisch und nicht moralisch ist. Das Spiel der Patientin wird nicht beurteilt. Ihre inneren Realitäten werden als schön erfahren (ALDRIDGE et al. 1990).

Die aktive, kreative Musiktherapie ist eine Intervention, die den Patientinnen die Chance bietet, der eigenen Krise schöpferisch entgegenzutreten und die eigene kreative Kraft zu nutzen, um innerlich "heil" zu bleiben auf dem Weg durch die Krankheit. In diesem Sinne würde die Musiktherapie einen Beitrag leisten, der die Lebensqualität, trotz eventueller physischer Verschlechterung, verbessern könnte. Auf diese Weise ist es möglich, verschiedene musikalische Formen zu finden, die den unterschiedlichen Krankheitsstadien entsprechen, sei es zur Unterstützung der Genesung, oder durch die Begleitung im Sterbensprozess.

Abb. 1

Das Beispiel einer melodischen Improvisation

References

ABRAHAM, L.U., & DAHLHAUS, C. 1982. *Melodielehre.* Laaber-Verlag Dr.Henning Müller-Buscher.
ALDRIDGE, D. 1989a. Music, Communication and Medicine. *Journal of the Royal Society of Medicine,* 82:743-746.
Aldridge, D. 1989b. A phenomenological comparison of the organization of music and the self. *The Arts in Psychotherapy,* 16:91-97.
ALDRIDGE, D. 1993. Music therapy research: II. Research methods suitable for music therapy. *The Arts in Psychotherapy,* 20:117-131.
ALDRIDGE, D. 1995. Spirituality, Hope and Music Therapy in Palliative Care. *The Arts in Psychotherapy,* 22:103-109.
ALDRIDGE, D., BRANDT, G., & WOHLER, D. 1990. Toward a common language among the creative art therapies. *The Arts in Psychotherapy,* 17:89-195.
BAILEY, L. 1983. The effects of live music versus tape-recorded music on hospitalized cancer patients. *Music Therapy,* 3:17-28.
BAILEY, L. 1985. Music`s soothing charms. *American Journal of Nursing,* 85:1280.
BAILEY, L. 1986. Music therapy in pain management. *J-ournal of Pain Symptom Management* , 1: 25-28.
BENZON, W.L. 1993. Stages in the Evolution of Music. *Journal of Social and Evolutionary Systems,* 16:273-296.
BERTI, L.A., HOFFMANN, S.O., & MÖBUS, V. 1993. "Traditioneller"vs."modifizierter"Forschungsansatz im Rahmen psychoonkologischer Studien. *PPmP Psychother. Psychosom. med. Psychol.,* 43:151-158.
BLUME, F. 1989. *Die Musik in Geschichte und Gegenwart: Allgemeine Enzyklopädie der Musik.* Kassel: Deutscher Taschenbuch Verlag Bärenreiter-Verlag.
CARTER, B. 1993. Long-term survivors of breast cancer. A qualitative descriptive study. *Cancer Nursing,* 16:354-361.

CARTER, B.J. 1994. Surviving breast cancer. A problematic Work Re-entry. *Cancer Practice*, 2:135-140.

CARTER, R.E., & CARTER, C.A. 1993. Individual and marital adjustment in spouse pairs subsequent to mastectomy. *American Journal of Family Therapy,* 21:291-300.

CARTER, R.E., CARTER, C.A., & PROSEN, H.A. 1992. Emotional and personality types of breast cancer patients and spouses. *The American Journal of Family Therapy,* 20: 300 - 308.

COYLE, N. 1987. A model of continuity of care for cancer patients with chronic pain. *Medical Clinics of North America,* 71: 259-70.

CUNNINGHAM, A.J., LOCKWOOD, G.A., & EDMONDS, C.V. 1993. Which Cancer patients benefit most from a brief, group, coping skills program? *The International Journal of Psychiatry in Medcine,* 23:383-398.

DAHLHAUS, C., & EGGEBRECHT, H.H. 1979. *Brockhaus Riemann Musik Lexikon 2.* Wiesbaden - Mainz: F.A.Brockhaus , B.Schott`s Söhne.

EYSENCK, H.J. 1994. Cancer, Personality and Stress: Prediction and Prevention. *Behaviour Research & Therapy,* 16:67-215.

FOLEY, K. 1986. The treatment of pain in the patient with cancer. *Cancer*, 36:194-215.

FRANK, J. 1985. The effects of music therapy and guided visual imagery on chemotherapy induced nausea and vomiting. *Oncol-ogical Nursing Forum,* 12:47-52.

GEYER, S. 1993. Life events, chronic difficulties and vulnerability factors preceding breast cancer. *Social Science and Medicine* , 37:1545-1555.

HARRISON, J., & MAGUIRE, P. 1994. Predictors of Psychiatric Morbidity in Cancer Patients. *British Journal of Psychiatry,* 165:593-598.

HEIM, E., AUGUSTINY, K., SCHAFFNER, L., & VALACH, L. 1993. Coping with breastcancer over time and situation. *Journal of Psychosomatic Research,* 37:523-542.

HEYDE, P., & v.LANGSDORFF, P. 1983. Rehabilitation Krebskranker unter Einschluß schöpferischer Therapien. *Rehabilitation,* 22:25-27.

HÜRNY, C., BERNHARD, J., BACCHI, M., VAN WEGBERG, B., TOMAMICHEL, M., SPEK, U., COATES, A., CASTIGLIONE, M., GOLDHIRSCH, A., & SENN, -.J. 1993. The Perceived Adjustment to Chronic Illness Scale (PACIS: a global indicator of coping for operable breast cancer patients in clinical trials. *Support Care Cancer,* 1:200-208.

KAMMRATH, I. 1989. Musiktherapie während der Chemotherapie. *Krankenpflege,* 6:282-283.

KERKVLIET, G. 1990. Music therapy may help control cancer pain [news]. *Journal of the National Cancer Institute,* 82:350-2.

LANGER, S., K. 1992. *Philosophie auf neuem Wege.Das Symbol im Denken,im Ritus und in der Kunst.* Frankfurt am Main:Fischer Taschenbuch Verlag GmbH.

MATTHESON, J. 1739. *Der vollkommene Capellmeister.* Kassel, Facsimile-Nachdruck 1954.

McCAFFERY, M. 1990. Nursing approaches to nonpharmacological pain control. International *Journal of Nursing Studies* , 27:1-5.

NATTIEZ, J.-J. 1990. *Music and Discourse:Toward a Semiology of Music.* Princeton,New Jersey:Princeton Univesity Press.

NELSON, D.V., FRIEDMAN, L.C., BAER, P.E., LANE, M., & SMITH, F.E. 1994. Subtypes of Psychosocial Adjustment to Breast Cancer. *Journal of Behavioral Medicine,* 17:127-141.

RAWNSLEY, M.M. 1994. Recurrence of cancer:A crisis of courage. *Cancer Nursing,* 17:342-347.

SHAPIRO, D.E., RODRIGUE, J.R., BOGGS, S.R., & ROBINSON, M.E. 1994. Cluster Analysis of the Medical Coping Modes Questionnaire - Evidence for Coping with Cancer Styles. *Journal of Psychosomatic Research,* 38:151-159.

SONTAG, S. 1993. *Krankheit als Metapher.* New York:Fischer.

SPIEGEL, D. 1991. A Psychosocial Intervention and Survival Time of Patients with Metastatic Breast Cancer. Advances,The *Journal of Mind-Body Health,* 7,:10-19.

STANTON, A.L., & SNIDER, P.R. 1993. Coping with a Breast Cancer Diagnosis:A Prospective Study. *Health Psychology,* 12:16-23.

WATSON, M., LAW, M., DOS SANTOS, M., GREER, S., BARUSCH, J., & BLISS, J. 1994. The Mini-MAC:Further Development of the Mental Adjustment to Cancer Scale. *Journal of Psychosocial Oncology,* 12,:33-46.

WONG, C.A., & BRAMWELL, L. 1992. Uncertainty and anxiety after mastectomy for breast cancer. *Cancer Nursing,* 15:363-371.

ZIMMERMANN, L., POZEHL, B., DUNCAN, K., & SCHMITZ, R. 1989. Effects of music in patients who had chronic cancer pain. *Western Journal of Nursing Research,* 11:298-309.

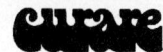

Einschneidende Maßnahmen - Schönheitschirurgie und Geschlechterverhältnisse in der westlichen Medizin
Cutting in Measures - Cosmetic Surgery and the Relationship Between the Sexes in Western Medicine

Angelica Ensel

Zusammenfassung: Schönheitschirurgie ist nicht nur eine Variante kulturspezifischer Körperformung und eine Entwicklungsstufe der westlichen Medizin. Die Erforschung des Phänomens Schönheitschirurgie aus medizinethnologischer und feministischer Perspektive zeigt: Die schönheitschirurgische Praxis spiegelt in besonderer Weise spezifische Aspekte der Machtverhältnisse zwischen den Geschlechtern in unserer Kultur. Eine zunehmende Zahl von Frauen, die sich nicht „richtig" fühlen, wird von überwiegend männlichen Ärzten neu geformt. Die schönheitschirurgische Schöpfung der Frau kann als ein dialektischer Prozess interpretiert werden. Die „Erschaffung" des anderen Geschlechts bedeutet gleichzeitig die Selbstschöpfung und Inszenierung des Arztes. Sie findet ihren Ausdruck in verschiedenen Rollenbildern. Der Schönheitschirurg agiert als Künstler, Psychologe, Magier, Priester, als Richter und als Menschenfreund. Alle diese Aspekte verbinden sich in der Rolle des Arztes als Schöpfer. Hier zeigen sich nicht nur Traditionen ärztlicher Selbstdarstellung sondern auch besondere Ausformungen einer kulturellen Geschlechterordnung.

Abstract: Cosmetic Surgery is not only a variant of culture-specific shaping of the body and a stage in the developement of western medicine. The research of Cosmetic Surgery as a phenomenon from a medical anthropological and feminist perspective points out: The practise of Cosmetic Surgery in a particularly way reflects culture-specific aspects of the balance of power referring to gender: an increasing number of women, who don't feel „right", is newly shaped by predominantly male doctors. The „creation" of women by Cosmetic Surgery can be interpreted as a dialectical process. The „creation" of the alternate gender at the same time means the doctor's selfcreation and his staging which find its expression in a variety of roles. The Cosmetic Surgeon acts as an artist, psychologist, magician, priest, judge and philanthropist. All these aspects unite in the role of the doctor as a creator. The different roles not only present a tradition of medical self-staging but simultaneously specific formations of a culturally transmitted sexual order.

Keywords: Schönheitschirurgie, Körperformung, Machtverhältnisse, Arzt-Patientin-Beziehung, ärztliches Selbstbild. Cosmetic Surgery, shaping of the body, balance of power, doctor-patient-relationship, medical self-portrayel.

Schönheitschirurgie boomt. Pro Jahr werden in Deutschland schätzungsweise 300000 Schönheitsoperationen durchgeführt und die Tendenz ist weiter steigend. Innerhalb der Medizin ist die Schönheitschirurgie auf dem Weg, sich zu etablieren und zu professionalisieren. In den Medien, besonders in TV-Talkshows und in Frauenmagazinen sind Schönheitsoperationen ein beliebtes Thema, das in regelmäßigen Abständen und immer neuen Variationen abgehandelt wird. Gleichzeitig ist die Debatte über Schönheitschirurgie mit einer Reihe von Tabuisierungen verbunden. Während Presse und Fernsehen ausführlich über das Spektrum der möglichen Operationen und über einzelne schönheitsoperierte Personen berichten, wird im privaten Bereich kaum über erfolgte Schönheitsoperationen am eigenen Körper geredet. Auch über die Ärzte, die diese Eingriffe durchführen, wird nur begrenzt gesprochen.

Die verschiedenen Auffälligkeiten und die Tabuisierungen dieser besonderen Körperformung wurden zum Ausgangspunkt eines dreijährigen Dissertationsprojekts, in dessen Mittelpunkt die schönheitschirurgische Arzt-Patientin-Beziehung stand.

Schönheitschirurgie aus medizinethnologischer Sicht

Aus medizinethnologischer Sicht ist das Phänomen Schönheitschirurgie aus drei verschiedenen Perspektiven interessant.

Zunächst können Schönheitsoperationen als eine Variante kulturspezifischer Körperformung interpretiert werden. Sie ist Ausdruck von Einstellung und Umgang mit dem Körper in unserer westlichen Gesellschaft, in der das Alter und die Spuren am Körper zunehmend diskriminiert werden und in der die Grenzen dessen, was als normaler Körper akzeptiert wird, immer enger werden. Die Möglichkeit, den eigenen Körper mittels Schönheitsoperationen total zu verändern, verstärkt den Mythos von der

Machbarkeit. Entsprechend wird der Druck, einen fitten, spurenlosen Körper zur Schau zu stellen, besonders im Berufsleben immer größer, denn: „das Gekonnte ist das Gesollte", wie es der Sozialphilosoph GÜNTER ANDERS (1988:17 ff) formuliert.

Als neues Fachgebiet, das sich zunehmend innerhalb der Medizin etabliert, weist das Phänomen Schönheitschirurgie außerdem auf die kulturelle Formung beziehungsweise Deformation der Medizin und des ärztlichen Berufsstandes hin. Als schönheitschirurgisch behandlungsbedürftig gelten Unebenheiten und Unregelmäßigkeiten am gesunden und unbearbeiteten Körper. Bei Schönheitsoperationen wird die Integrität des Körpers von Ärzten ohne medizinische Notwendigkeit verletzt. Hierbei werden von Ärzten und PatientInnen Risiken und Schmerzen in Kauf genommen, die sonst nur bei schwerer Krankheit oder Lebensgefahr eingegangen werden. Die 1992 erfolgte Ernennung der Plastischen Chirurgie zu einem Facharztgebiet spiegelt die zunehmende Professionalisierung der Schönheitschirurgie, denn die beiden Gebiete sind nicht klar voneinander abzugrenzen. „Einschneidende Maßnahmen" am gesunden Körper werden immer mehr zu alltäglichen Eingriffen. Das neue Fachgebiet trägt mit dazu bei, Bedarf und Notwendigkeit von Operationen zu schaffen und neue kulturelle Körpermodelle zu erzeugen.

Die dritte, für die Frauengesundheitsforschung wichtigste Perspektive weist auf die in der schönheitschirurgischen Praxis wirksamen Machtverhältnisse zwischen den Geschlechtern. Das „Berufseignungskriterium Schönheit" von dem NAOMI WOLF (1991:34 ff) spricht, gilt für beide Geschlechter. Frauen sind ihm jedoch in erheblich stärkerem Maße ausgesetzt als Männer. Während die Maßstäbe für den männlichen Körper erst in höheren Berufspositionen wirksam werden, wird für Frauen in fast allen Berufen und Positionen die Präsentation eines perfekten Körpers gefordert. Weitere Unterschiede zwischen den Geschlechtern finden sich in bezug auf Quantität und Qualität der angebotenen Maßnahmen. Für Männer gilt es, in erster Linie im angezogenen Zustand (für Geschäftsleute im Anzug) eine gute Figur zu präsentieren. Die für Frauen angelegten Maßstäbe gelten dagegen für den gesamten und für den nackten Körper. Entsprechend betreffen die hauptsächlich von Männern gewünschten Schönheitsoperationen nur bestimmte Körperpartien wie Gesicht, Bauch und Kopfhaar während die Palette der für Frauen angebotenen und von ihnen gewünschten Operationen den ganzen Körper vom Face-Lifting bis zum Modellieren der Beine umfasst.

Ein weiterer wesentlicher Unterschied zwischen Männern und Frauen ist das auffällig ungleiche Verhältnis der Geschlechter in bezug auf Operateure und PatientInnen. Etwa 70-80% der Operierten sind Frauen, die überwiegende Zahl der Schönheitschirurgen hingegen sind männliche Ärzte. Mit anderen Worten: Eine stetig zunehmende Zahl von Frauen, die sich nicht „richtig" fühlen, wird von überwiegend männlichen Ärzten neu geformt. Während Frauen sich - trotz beruflicher Erfolge und gesellschaftlicher Anerkennung - als „mangelhaft" empfinden, präsentieren sich männliche Ärzte als Schöpfer weiblicher Schönheit.

Arzt und Patientin
Im Mittelpunkt meiner Forschung stand die Frage nach dem „Spiel der Kräfte" (FOUCAULT 1987:256 ff) zwischen der Frau, die die Neuformung ihres Körpers wünscht und dem Arzt, der diesen Körper formt. Wie gestaltet sich diese Beziehung? Welches professionelle Selbstverständnis zeichnet Schönheitschirurgen aus? Wie sprechen diese Ärzte über sich selbst, über ihre berufliche Motivation und über den zu formenden Frauenkörper? Und wie gestaltet sich die Beziehung zwischen Arzt und Patientin? Was bedeutet es, wenn Arzt und Frau von der Operation als einer „Wiedergeburt" sprechen?

Für die Erforschung der schönheitschirurgischen Arzt-Patientin-Beziehung und des professionellen schönheitschirurgischen Selbstbildes wurden verschiedene Methoden kombiniert. Zunächst waren es teilnehmende Beobachtung des schönheitschirurgischen Beratungssettings, die Beobachtung einzelner Operationen und Interviews mit Schönheitschirurgen und Frauen, die Schönheitsoperationen an sich durchführen ließen. Dazu kam die Analyse der von Ärzten verfassten populären schönheitschirurgischen Ratgeberliteratur und der Selbstdarstellung von Schönheitschirurgen in den Medien. Hierbei standen die ärztliche Sprache über den Frauenkörper, das professionelle Selbstbild des Schönheitschirurgen und die Darstellung der Arzt-Patientin-Beziehung im Mittelpunkt des Interesses. Das gesamte aus den verschiedenen Quellen stammende Material wurde anhand von interpretativen Verfahren analysiert, unter anderem auf dem Hintergrund des von GOFFMAN (1983) geprägten Begriffs der Inszenierung sowie des FOUCAULT'schen Machtbegriffs (1987). Im folgenden werden die zentralen Themen und Ergebnisse der Forschung in Kurzform vorgestellt.

Die schönheitschirurgische Konstruktion von Weiblichkeit offenbart sich in der Sprache des Arztes über den zu bearbeitenden Frauenkörper. Hier finden sich immer wiederkehrende Topoi. Sie beinhalten kulturelle Bilder von Weiblichkeit, die Bewertungen und Zuweisungen spiegeln (siehe u.a. KOSTEK 1983, VON MALINCKRODT 1988, SCHNEIDRZIK 1970). In der von Ärzten verfassten Ratgeberliteratur erscheint der weibliche Körper grundsätzlich als bedroht. Er ist in Gefahr, alt, hässlich, tierähnlich zu werden, aus der Form zu geraten und lächerlich zu wirken. Zur populären schönheitschirurgischen Fachsprache gehören Begriffe wie „Hamsterbacken", „Fledermausarme", „Truthahnhals", „Hängebrüste" und „Fettschürzen". Sie beschreiben in erster Linie die schönheitschirurgischen Mängel am weiblichen Körper. Der ärztliche Diskurs reproduziert hier alte, kulturell tradierte Bilder von Weiblichkeit, die auch in anderen medizinischen Fachgebieten verbreitet sind. Ihnen zugrunde liegt das Modell eines labilen und mangelhaften Frauenkörpers, der aufgrund seiner Konstitution der Formung durch den Mann/Arzt bedarf.

Ärztliche Selbstinszenierung

Schönheitschirurgie ist eine Arbeit an Grenzen, die Identitäten formt. Bei Schönheitsoperationen wird ständig an und unter der Haut gearbeitet. Es sind Prozesse, bei denen Körper und damit auch Identitäten neu geformt werden. In der überwiegenden Zahl der Fälle wird hier der weibliche Körper und damit auch weibliches Selbst-Bewusstsein von männlichen Ärzten geformt. Dabei geht es jedoch nicht nur um Identität und Selbstbewusstsein der operierten Frau. Die Analyse der Selbstdarstellung von Schönheitschirurgen im Interview, in der Fachliteratur und in den Medien zeigt: Die Operation, die der Schönheitschirurg an einer Frau durchführt, ist ein Akt, in dem sich auch die ärztliche Identität bildet und bestätigt. Es ist die Selbstinszenierung des Schönheitschirurgen und die Inszenierung eines Geschlechter-Verhältnisses. Der Arzt inszeniert sich als Schöpfer der Frau, die sich als „mangelhaft" bewertet, und zwecks Neuformung in seine Hände begibt. Bei der schönheitschirurgischen Arzt-Patientin-Beziehung handelt es sich also um ein dialektisches Verhältnis, in dem beide Seiten einander brauchen.

Als Schöpfer inszenieren sich Schönheitschirurgen in unterschiedlichen Rollen. Die verschiedenen Selbstbilder werden transparent, wenn Schönheitschirurgen über ihre Arbeit sprechen.

Schönheitschirurgen sehen sich als Künstler, als „Bildhauer am lebenden Gewebe" (MÜHLBAUER 1990:31), die „Meisterwerke" (KOSTEK 1983:88) vollbringen. Im Interview wird die eigene Arbeit oft als Kombination von Hand- und Kunstwerk beschrieben und es wird betont, wie wichtig die Sensibilität für Ästhetik und Gestaltung für diesen Beruf sei (ENSEL 1996:123). Als „Psychotherapeuten mit dem Skalpell" (KOSTEK 1983) sehen viele Schönheitschirurgen die Operation als die bessere Therapie an, die oft wesentlich effektiver sei als hunderte von Therapiestunden. Schönheitschirurgen agieren als Priester, die ein Opfer- und Reinigungsritual zelebrieren, bei dem die Frau Zeit, Blut, Geld und Narben auf dem Altar der Schönheit anbietet. Oft geschieht die Entscheidung zu einer Schönheitsoperation in Lebenssituationen, denen einschneidende Veränderungen vorausgegangen sind wie Scheidung, Tod des Partners oder ein Berufswechsel. Als grenzüberschreitende Maßnahme soll die Operation den Übergang in eine neue Lebensphase markieren. So bezeichnen viele Frauen diesen Akt als eigene Aktivität - als Entscheidung zu neuen Formen (siehe GROULT 1984:419). Hier hat die Schönheitsoperation die Funktion eines Übergangsrituals, das der Arzt in der Rolle des Priesters leitet.

Wie ein Magier verwandelt der Schönheitschirurg seine PatientInnen. Dabei erzeugt er verblüffende Veränderungen. Sein genaues Vorgehen ist für Laien nur begrenzt durchschaubar und in vielen Fällen erleben die PatientInnen den Verwandlungsakt nicht bewusst, da sie narkotisiert sind. Auch die Wünsche, die mit der Veränderung durch eine Schönheitsoperation verbunden sind, haben magische Anteile, da die Operation oft als Allheilmittel für ein neues, glücklicheres Leben erscheint.

Als Richter begutachtet der Schönheitschirurg den weiblichen Körper nach seinen Maßstäben und fällt ein Urteil. Bei der Inspektion des Körpers werden oft weitere „Mängel" entdeckt, zu deren Beseitigung der Arzt auffordert, nach dem Motto: „Wenn Sie ihr Gesicht liften lassen, dürfen Sie den Hals nicht vergessen". Der körperlichen Bestandsaufnahme folgt die photographische Dokumentation der Mängel, die durch das Auge der Kamera gleichsam objektiviert werden.

Die Rolle des Arztes als Menschenfreund ist eine der beliebtesten Selbstinszenierungen von Schönheitschirurgen. Hier wird die Schönheitsoperation als humanitärer Akt und als eine sehr befriedigende

Arbeit dargestellt, die dazu beitrage, das Leben einzelner Menschen - in einer narzisstischen Gesellschaft - glücklicher zu machen (siehe KOSTEK 1983:19).

In der Rolle des Arztes als Schöpfer der Frau vereinigen sich diese - hier sehr verkürzt dargestellten - Modelle der schönheitschirurgischen Selbstinszenierung. Hier wird vom „Menschenformen" und vom „Modellieren des Körpers" (SPIEGEL 41/1979) gesprochen. Schönheitschirurgen „drehen die Lebensuhren zurück" und „verjüngen die Menschheit um einige Tausend Jahre" (KOSTEK 1983:117). Die erfolgreiche Operation wird von Ärzten und von Patientinnen als „Metamorphose", „Verjüngung" und „Wiedergeburt" (u.a. KOSTEK 1983:49) bezeichnet. In diesem Zusammenspiel von Arzt und Patientin als Schöpfer und Geschöpf wird die Schönheitsoperation zu einer Reinkarnation von Körper und Seele der Frau, während der Arzt sich als Schöpfer inkarniert, der gleichzeitig Gebärender ist: unter seinen Händen geschieht die Wiedergeburt der Frau.

Die verschiedenen schönheitschirurgischen Rollen verweisen auf eine Tradition ärztlicher Selbstdarstellung, auf angestammte ärztliche Rollenbilder, die aus Literatur, Medizingeschichte und aus den Medien bekannt sind. In der schönheitschirurgischen Inszenierung spiegeln diese Rollen unterschiedliche Konstellationen zwischen Arzt und Patientin ebenso wie bestimmte Aspekte des geschlechtsspezifischen Machtverhältnisses.

Speculum und Spiegel - Die schönheitschirurgische Geschlechterordnung
Die in der schönheitschirurgischen Praxis zum Ausdruck kommenden Schöpfungsphantasien haben eine lange Tradition in der Geschichte der westlichen Medizin. So zeigen sowohl die hier propagierten Bilder von der Frau und ihrem Körper als auch die Dramaturgie der Arzt-Patientin-Beziehung eine Reihe von Parallelen zu anderen medizinischen Fachgebieten, in der die „Krankheit Frau" (FISCHER-HOMBERGER 1979) behandelt wurde und wird. Die Praxis der Schönheitschirurgie steht in einer engen Verbindung zu Geschichte und Diskurs über die weibliche „Krankheit" Hysterie (siehe VON BRAUN 1990) und zur Geschichte und Praxis der Gynäkologie.

In diesem Sinn erscheint die heutige Schönheitschirurgie in einer Tradition der „Wissenschaften von der Frau", in der die „Ordnung der Geschlechter" (Honnegger 1991) im medizinischen Diskurs hergestellt wird. Seit der Professionalisierung der Gynäkologie wird die Frau durch den Gynäkologen auf der Grundlage einer „Natur" ihres Körpers erschaffen. Mit zunehmender Entwicklung der Gynäkologie dringt der ärztliche Blick immer mehr ins Innere des Frauenkörpers und erzeugt Normalitätskonzepte und Therapieverordnungen für die Abweichungen. Nachdem dieses Innere enteignet ist, tritt die Schönheitschirurgie auf den Plan. Nun wird auch der Schönheitschirurg Spezialist für Weiblichkeit. Während die Hysterietheorien die „Erschaffung der Frau" im Diskurs gestalteten und die Gynäkologie die Kontrolle der weiblichen Reproduktivität übernahm, macht die Schönheitschirurgie es möglich, die diskursiven Entwürfe einer imaginären Weiblichkeit dem Frauenkörper sichtbar aufzuprägen - wenn Frauen es zulassen.

References
ANDERS, GÜNTHER. 1987. *Die Antiquiertheit des Menschen*. Bd.2. München.
VON BRAUN, CHRISTINA. 1990. *Nicht ich: Logik, Lüge, Libido*. Frankfurt/M.
DREYFUß, HUBERT/RABINOW, PAUL. 1987. *Michel Foucault - Jenseits von Strukturalismus und Hermeneutik*. Frankfurt/M.
ENSEL, ANGELICA. 1996. *Nach seinem Bilde. Schönheitschirurgie und Schöpfungsphantasien in der westlichen Medizin*. Bern.
FOUCAULT, MICHEL. 1987. Das Subjekt und die Macht. In: DREYFUß, HUBERT/RABINOW, PAUL. 1987. *Michel Foucault - Jenseits von Strukturalismus und Hermeneutik*. Frankfurt/M.
GOFFMAN, ERVING. 1983. *Wir alle spielen Theater*. München; Zürich.
GROULT; BENOITE. 1984. *Leben will ich*. München.
HONEGGER, CLAUDIA. 1991. *Die Ordnung der Geschlecher*. Frankfurt/M.; New York.
KOSTEK, THADDÄUS. 1983. *Das neue Gesicht. Möglichkeiten und Grenzen der kosmetischen Chirurgie*. München.
VON MALLINCKRODT, GOSWIN. 1988. *Moderne Schönheitschirurgie. Möglichkeiten und Grenzen*. München.
MÜHLBAUER, WOLFGANG. 1990. „Die Menschen wollen lieber unauffällig als strahlend schön sein." in: *Psychologie Heute* Heft 6/1990. Weinheim.
SCHNEIDRZIK, W.E. J. 1970. *Kosmetische Chirurgie. Sinn und Unsinn von Schönheitsoperationen*. Düsseldorf; Wien.
DER SPIEGEL. 41/1979. *Hier sitze ich und forme Menschen*.
WOLF, NAOMI. 1991. *Der Mythos von der Schönheit*. Hamburg.

Körperlichkeit von Frauen in der Konsum- und Leistungsgesellschaft und der Zusammenhang zu Essstörungen
Corporeality of Women in a Consumer- and Achievement Oriented Society and its Correlations Towards Eating Disorders

Tine Eschertzhuber

Zusammenfassung: Essstörungen (besonders Anorexie und Bulimie) haben in den letzten 20 Jahren ständig zugenommen. Neben medizinischen und psychischen Ursachen lässt sich auch ein auffallender Zusammenhang zu bestimmten soziokulturellen Merkmalen feststellen. So sind fast ausschließlich Frauen aus der Mittel- und Oberschicht der westlichen Industriegesellschaften betroffen. Es ist daher anzunehmen, dass einerseits bestimmte Muster im weiblichen Lebenszusammenhang, andererseits eine spezifische Form der Körperlichkeit in der Konsum- und Leistungsgesellschaft der westlichen Industrieländer für die Entstehung von Essstörungen eine Rolle spielen. Es lassen sich hier verschiedenen Muster finden, die bei der Entwicklung weiblicher Körperlichkeit zusammentreffen: Zum einen sind dies verschiedene patriarchalische Strukturen, die den Körper der Frau kontrollieren und dabei zum Objekt machen. Zusätzlich führen das Leistungsprinzip und bestimmte in der Konsumkultur verankerte Faktoren zu einer Instrumentalisierung und weiteren Objektivierung von Körperlichkeit. Diese Strukturen spiegeln sich letztlich auch in bestimmten Essstörungen wider, wobei besonders auch die Widersprüche sichtbar werden, die in diesen Mustern von Körperlichkeit enthalten sind.

Abstract: Eating disorders (especially anorexia nervosa and bulimia) have constantly increased over the last 20 years. Apart from medical and psychological causes sociocultural factors play an important role. Especially women from the middle and upper classes are afflicted by these disorders. Therefore it can be supossed that specific patterns in a womans lifecourse play an essential part as well the specific kind of body image, which is dictated by competitive consumer society ideals.
Certain patterns can be established, which coinides during the developement of the female body. On the one hand there are certain patriarchal structures, which control a womans body and convert it into an object. On the other hand the competitive principle and certain factors which predominate in our consumer society led to an instrumentalization of the human body. These structures are especially reflected in certain eating disorders, which particulary demonstrate the contradictiones in these perceptions of the human body.

Keywords: Essstörungen, westliche Industriegesellschaft, Konsum- und Leistungsgesellschaft, eating disorders, western industrial societies, consum- and archievment oriented society.

1. Einleitung: Auffällige soziokulturelle Merkmale bei Essstörungen

Das Phänomen der Essstörungen - insbesondere der Anorexie (Magersucht) und der Bulimie (Ess-Brech-Sucht) - hat in den letzten 20 Jahren zunehmend Aufmerksamkeit auf sich gezogen. Das hängt sowohl mit der tatsächlichen Zunahme der Problematik, aber auch mit einem verstärkten Interesse der Öffentlichkeit an dieser Thematik zusammen. Das liegt meines Erachtens an den besonderen Umständen des Auftretens dieser Störungen: Anders als bei vielen anderen Erkrankungen sind nicht in erster Linie ältere oder arme Menschen, sondern gerade junge wohlhabende Menschen betroffen. Es fällt außerdem auf, dass die Problematik nur in den westlichen Industrienationen auftritt und auch dort nur nach Erreichen eines bestimmten Wohlstandsniveaus. Bruch schreibt dazu: „Neue Krankheiten sind selten, und von einem Leiden, das mit Vorliebe junge, reiche und schöne Menschen befällt, hat man bisher so gut wie nichts gehört. Doch eine solche Krankheit sucht die Töchter wohlhabender, gebildeter und erfolgreicher Familien heim, nicht nur in den Vereinigten Staaten, sondern auch in vielen anderen mit Wohlstand und Reichtum gesegneten Ländern." (BRUCH 1982, S.13)

Bruch weist hier auf die wesentlichen soziokulturellen Charakteristika der von Anorexie oder Bulimie Betroffenen hin. Hier lässt sich als erstes das Merkmal „Geschlecht" nennen: 90 - 95% der Erkrankten sind Mädchen oder Frauen (vgl. BRUMBERG 1994, S.19) . Dies legt die Vermutung nahe, dass für die Entstehung der Problematik bestimmte Faktoren des weiblichen Lebenszusammenhangs von entscheidender Bedeutung sind. Aber auch die Schichtzugehörigkeit scheint von Bedeutung zu sein. So treten Essstörungen fast ausschließlich in der Mittel- und Oberschicht auf. In den unteren sozialen Schichten, aber auch in ärmeren Ländern kommen Anorexie und Bulimie nicht vor. Joan

Brumberg führt hier eine interessante Beobachtung an: So sind in den USA Schwarze und Einwandererfamilien (zumindest in der ersten und zweiten Generation) nicht von Essstörungen betroffen (vgl. BRUMBERG 1994, S. 19). Ich sehe auch hier einen Zusammenhang mit dem (tendenziell eher niedrigen) Lebensstandard dieser Bevölkerungsschichten.

Es wird also deutlich, dass der Entstehungszusammenhang von Essstörungen eng an bestimmte soziokulturelle Faktoren gekoppelt zu sein scheint. Bordo spricht hier davon, dass jede Kultur ihre eigene Pathologie hat, die sich aus ihrer kulturellen Anordnung ergibt (vgl. BORDO 1983, S.139) Die Anorexie und die Bulimie lassen sich als typische Pathologien der Konsum- und Leistungsgesellschaften der westlichen Industrienationen bezeichnen. Ich will nun im folgenden versuchen, die kulturellen Grundmuster nachzuzeichnen, die für die Entstehung dieser Essstörungen mitverantwortlich sind. Dabei sehe ich zwei grundsätzliche Strukturzusammenhänge, die sich gegenseitig ergänzend, zusammenlaufen. Als erstes ist hier die Entwicklung einer spezifischen Körperlichkeit von Frauen in patriarchalischen Gesellschaftstrukturen zu nennen (Mit dieser Thematik haben sich besonders feministische Theoretikerinnen auseinandergesetzt; vgl. z. B. HORSTKOTTE-HÖCKER 1987 oder GAST 1989). Hinzu kommt jedoch die Bedeutung, die die Konsum- und Leistungskultur moderner Gesellschaften für die Entwicklung von Körperlichkeit hat. Durch das Zusammentreffen verschiedener Aspekte aus beiden Bereichen entsteht nun das, was ich als soziokulturelle Disposition für die Zunahme von Essstörungen bezeichnen möchte. Ich werde mich im folgenden hauptsächlich auf das Erscheinungsbild der Anorexie beziehen, obwohl ich glaube, dass viele der von mir beschriebenen Zusammenhänge auch auf die Bulimie zutreffen. Ich denke aber, dass es dennoch wichtig ist, hier zu differenzieren und zwar sowohl in der Symptomatik (Nahrungsverweigerung und starker Gewichtsverlust bei der Anorexie vs. Heißhungerattacken / Erbrechen und relativ normales Körpergewicht bei der Bulimie) als auch im Grad des Problembewusstseins (mangelnde Problemeinsicht / gestörte Realitätswahrnehmung bei der Anorexie vs. ausgeprägtes Problembewusstsein / Scham bei der Bulimie) (vgl. STAHR u.a.1995, S.21 ff).

Im übrigen glaube ich, dass ein kulturtheoretischer Ansatz, wie ich ihn darstellen werde, nur ein Bestandteil des multifaktoriellen Entstehungszusammenhangs von Essstörungen ist. Medizinische und individual- und familienpsychologisch orientierte Ansätze können bei der Erklärung von Anorexie und Bulimie ebenso hilfreiche Beiträge leisten wie auch die Frage nach dem Suchtcharakter von Essstörungen. Ich möchte mich hier jedoch auf die Analyse der - häufig eher vernachlässigten- soziokulturellen Grundbedingungen beschränken. Dabei möchte ich nun zunächst mein Augenmerk auf die spezifischen Bedingungen legen, unter denen Frauen in patriarchalischen Gesellschaftstrukturen Körperlichkeit entwickeln. Körperlichkeit soll hier und im weiteren sowohl die gesellschaftlichen Vorstellungen oder „Bilder" vom Körper als auch das daraus resultierende Körperbewusstsein bedeuten.

2. Körperlichkeit von Frauen in patriarchalischen Gesellschaftstrukturen

Um zu verstehen, wie die Körperlichkeit von Frauen durch bestimmte Strukturen der patriarchalisch organisierten Gesellschaft beeinflusst wird, ist es zunächst einmal wichtig, sich mit bestimmten Grundmustern des zugrundeliegenden abendländischen Denkens auseinanderzusetzen. Wesentliches Merkmal ist dabei das Denken in Dichotomien, wobei in diesen, wie Grosz darstellt, bereits die Tendenz zur Hierarchisierung angelegt ist: Der einen als positiv definierten Seite wird stets ein negativer und /oder untergeordneter Gegenpart zugeordnet wird (vgl. GROSZ 1994, S.3). Die der patriarchalischen Gesellschaft zugrundeliegende Dichotomie ist dabei „Mann vs. Frau". Daraus entwickelt sich das, was Hageman-White als „kulturelles System der Zweigeschlechtlichkeit" bezeichnet (vgl. HAGEMAN-WHITE 1984, S.78). Darin werden nun der Dichotomie „Mann vs. Frau" verschiedene andere Kategorien und Attribuierungen zugeordnet: Zu nennen wäre hier zunächst einmal „Geist vs. Körper„, woraus sich die für das abendländische Denken typische Trennung von Geist und Körper entwickelt. Es kommt dabei zu einer Unterordnung des Körpers unter den Geist. Gleichzeitig wird die Kategorie „Geist" dem Mann, die Kategorie „Körper" der Frau zugeordnet. Das Gleiche geschieht mit den Dichotomien " Kultur vs. Natur" und „aktiv vs. passiv" (vgl. HEKMAN 1992, S. 111 ff.). Griffin weist in diesem Zusammenhang auch auf die Parallelität der Unterdrückung der Frau, der Unterwerfung der Natur und der Disziplinierung von Körperlichkeit hin (vgl. GRIFFIN 1992, S.141).

Für die Körperlichkeit des jeweiligen Geschlechts ergibt sich daraus folgendes: Während für den Mann der Körper, da dieser der geistigen Aktivität untergeordnet ist, nur von zweitrangiger Bedeutung ist, ist er für die Identität von Frauen zentral. Dabei wird der männliche Körper als „maschinenhaft" funktionierend und damit unproblematisch gesehen. Der Körper der Frau dagegen gilt in diesen Denkstrukturen als unberechenbar und von einer der Natur innewohnenden Irrationalität bestimmt, was dem (männlichen) Rationalismus des abendländischen Denkens diametral gegenübersteht. Sobiech schreibt dazu: „Aufgrund des herrschenden cartesianischen Weltbildes wird dem Körper von Männern quasi eine ‚maschinenhafte' Existenz zugeschrieben, nach ihrem Willen formbar und beherrschbar. Frauen bleiben hingegen mit ihrer (sexuellen) Natur verwoben, ihr Körper scheint als ‚gefährlicher', dessen ‚Unbezähmbarkeit' besonderer Normalisierungsstrategien bedarf" (SOBIECH 1994, S. 13).

Der Körper des Mannes gilt also als das Normale, Unproblematische, das keiner besonderen Beachtung bedarf, während der der Frau in unterschiedlicher Art und Weise problematisiert wird und dabei auch bestimmten - von Sobiech „Normalisierungsstrategien" genannten - Kontrollstrukturen unterworfen wird. Zu nennen sind hier die Ästhetisierung und Sexualisierung des Frauenkörpers, die Tendenz, ihn auf seine reproduktiven Funktionen zu reduzieren und die Pathologisierung weiblicher Körperlichkeit. Ich werde im folgenden mich näher mit diesen Strukturen auseinandersetzen, da sie meiner Meinung nach wichtige Elemente für den Enstehungszusammenhang von Essstörungen beinhalten. Hier sei aber darauf hingewiesen, dass bereits die Grundannahme, der Körper der Frau sei unberechenbar, gefährlich und schwer zu kontrollieren, der Wahrnehmung vieler Anorektikerinnen entspricht und wichtig für deren Kampf um Unterwerfung des Körpers ist.

Die Ästhetisierung beinhaltet auch die Sichtweise des Frauenkörpers als „Abweichung,", nur dass diese hier positiv gewendet wird. Der Körper der Frau wird das „Besondere,", das sich durch seine Schönheit auszeichnet (vgl. SOBIECH 1994, S.25). Es entsteht aber gleichzeitig der Zwang für Frauen, sich an bestimmte Schönheitsnormen anzupassen. Dabei fällt auf, dass sich diese häufig aus der traditionellen Frauenrolle ableiten lassen und mit einer Einschränkung (im wörtlichen wie im übertragenen Sinn) der Bewegungsfreiheit von Frauen einhergehen. So gelten etwa raumgreifende Bewegungen von Frauen (wie z. B. große Schritte) als „unweiblich". Eine wesentliche Rolle spielt dabei auch das Ideal der Schlankheit, auf das ich an anderer Stelle noch genauer eingehen werde. Da, wie Bordo darlegt (vgl. BORDO 1993, S. 154), die Identität von Frauen in einem weitaus größerem Maße als die von Männern, über das Aussehen gebildet wird, führt die bedeutende Rolle, die Schönheitsideale dabei spielen, zu einer ständigen Beschäftigung vieler Frauen mit ihrem Körper, womit auch häufig eine große Unzufriedenheit einhergeht (vgl. HAUG 1988, S.70 ff.). Im Zusammenhang mit der Magersucht lässt sich hier ein Paradoxon feststellen: Einerseits kann in dem Versuch, keinen weiblich wirkenden Körper zu bekommen - eine Deutung die besonders im Zusammenhang mit der Pubertätsmagersucht häufig gemacht wird - eine Weigerung gesehen werden, sich weiblichen Schönheitsnormen und damit der traditionenllen Frauenrolle zu unterwerfen. Auf der anderen Seite, wird die Nahrungsverweigerung - zumindest zu Beginn der Störung - häufig mit Anpassung an Schönheitsnormen (insbesondere dem Schlankheitsideal) begründet und führt auch zur typisch „weiblichen" Besorgtheit um den Körper und sein Gewicht. Eng mit der Ästhetisierung zusammenhängend ist die Sexualisierung des weiblichen Körpers. Dabei kommt es zu folgenden Vorstellungen: Einerseits wird die Frau als von ihrer sexuellen Natur bestimmt und durchdrungen gesehen. Es entstehen Bilder des „unersättlichen Vamps,", der für Männer in seiner sexuellen Unberechenbarkeit eine Bedrohung darstellt (vgl. BORDO 1993, S. 160 ff.). Es gibt aber auch - quasi als Kontrollmechanismus - die gegenteilige Vorstellung, die der „guten" Frau jede eigenständige Sexualität abspricht, sie sozusagen zum asexuellen Wesen macht (vgl. HAUG 1988, S. 46). Für Frauen stehen also nur die Wahlmöglichkeiten zwischen den Bildern der „Heiligen" (ohne Sexualität) auf der einen Seite oder der „Hure" (von unberechenbarer Sexualitat durchdrungen) andererseits zu Verfügung. Wesentlich ist dabei, dass das Frauenbild stets über die Sexualität bestimmt ist.

Dieses rigide Schema hat nun mit der sexuellen „Befreiung" in den 60er Jahren eine gewisse Aufweichung erfahren, auch wenn es meiner Ansicht nach in den Grundstrukturen noch vorhanden ist. Dafür entwickelte sich hier eine neue Problematik: Durch den freieren Umgang mit Sexualität gewinnt die Forderung nach sexueller „Verfügbarkeit" besonders für Frauen an Bedeutung. Dies hat eine zusätzliche Sexualisierung und damit einhergehend Objektivierung des Frauenkörpers zur Folge. Baudrillard schreibt dazu: „Seiner Lebendigkeit enthoben erscheint der Körper der Frau auf dem Sexualitätsmarkt." (BAUDRILLARD zitiert nach SOBIECH 1994, S.47)

Sobiech sieht daher in der Magersucht einen unbewussten Widerstand gegen diese Vorgänge. Dies erscheint auch deshalb schlüssig, weil der Beginn der rapide Zunahme der Anorexie mit dem gesellschaftlichen Umbruch der „sexuellen Revolution" zusammenfällt (vgl. SOBIECH 1994, S.46). Aber auch sonst scheint die Sexualisierung des Frauenkörpers mit Essstörungen (insbesondere der Magersucht) im Zusammenhang zu stehen. So fällt die Parallele zwischen der „Unersättlichkeit" auf sexuellem Gebiet, die mit der weiblichen Sexualität verbunden wird, und der Gier nach Nahrung auf (vgl. BORDO 1994, S. 139ff.). Beides wird von vielen Magersüchtigen als beschämend und bedrohlich erfahren, so dass es unterdrückt und kontrolliert werden muss (vgl. WURMSER 1993, S. 28ff.). Auf der anderen Seite steht häufig eine Vorstellung von „Reinheit,", die durch sexuelle Enthaltsamkeit und Fasten zu erreichen ist. In diesem Zusammenhang ist übrigens, die hohe Korrelation auffallend, die zwischen sexuellem Missbrauch und den sich daraus ergebenden psychischen Problemen und dem Auftreten von Essstörungen besteht (vgl. STAHR u.a. 1995, S.72f.). Als weitere „Normalisierungsstrategie" lässt sich die Tendenz der Reduzierung des Frauenkörpers auf seine reproduktiven Funktionen sehen. Die Beschränkung der Frau auf die Rolle der Gebärenden und Mutter hat eine lange historische Tradition. Bereits bei Aristoteles lässt sich das Bild des Frauenkörpers als „Gefäß" für das neu entstehende Leben finden. Allerdings verschwindet im modernen Denken zunehmend die mystische Komponente, die zuvor mit dem Vorgang des Gebärens verknüpft war. Statt dessen gewinnt auch hier die Vorstellung vom „Körper-als-Maschine" - hier eben als „Produktionsstätte" neuen Lebens - an Bedeutung (vgl. MARTIN 1989, S.88). Diese Sichtweise führte unter anderem dazu, dass die Geburt immer stärker zum medizinischen Problem wurde, was auch zur Folge hatte, dass der Gebärenden zunehmend die Kompetenz in diesem Bereich entzogen wurde. Viele Frauen erleben dies als Gefühl der Ohnmacht gegenüber Vorgängen im eigenen Körper. Insgesamt geht die Vorstellung, auf den Bereich der Fortpflanzung beschränkt zu werden, für viele Frauen mit einem Gefühl der Einschränkung einher, besonders wenn auch diesem Bereich seine ursprünglich eher machtvolle Komponente entzogen wird.

Auch hier lässt sich ein Bezug zur Magersucht herstellen. So lässt sich die Nahrungsverweigerung auch als Ablehnung der auf Fortpflanzungsfähigkeit verweisenden Funktionen weiblicher Körperlichkeit sehen. In diesem Kontext lässt sich auch das Ausbleiben der Menstruation einordnen, das eines der Symptome einer anorektischen Störung darstellt.

Als letzte der hier angeführten Kontrollstrukturen möchte ich nun noch die Pathologisierung weiblicher Körperlichkeit erwähnen. Diese hat ihren Ursprung auch in einer Sichtweise, die den Körper des Mannes als Norm und den der Frau als „Abweichung" betrachtet. Mit dem Entstehen der neuzeitlichen Medizin wurde diese „Abweichung" in immer stärkeren Maße als Krankheit definiert. Dies betrifft besonders Vorgänge, die mit dem weiblichen Zyklus zu tun haben

(prämenstruelles Syndrom, Menstruation, Schwangerschaft). Diese Pathologisierung erweist sich für viele Frauen als widersprüchlich: Auf der einen Seite kann die Definition bestimmter körperlicher Zustände als Krankheit eine gewisse Erleichterung bedeuten, da damit auch Rücksichtnahme eingefordert werden kann. Andererseits verstärkt dies aber das Bild von der „von Natur aus" kranken und schwachen Frau, was wiederum zu Minderwertigkeitsgefühlen, aber auch zu ganz realen Einschränkungen z. B. im Bezug auf Berufstätigkeit führen kann. Nicht vergessen werden sollte hier, dass viele Frauen durch Doppel- und Mehrfachbelastung und häufig widersprüchlichen Anforderungen in Familie und Beruf ganz real in stärkerem Ausmaß krankmachenden Bedingungen ausgesetzt sind. Hier kann die Krankheit allerdings auch zu einer - wenn auch letztlich oft paradoxen, da selbstzerstörerischen - Form der Konfliktbewältigung werden (vgl. SOBIECH 1994, S. 85). Gerade auch Essstörungen werden von etlichen TheoretikerInnen in diesem Zusammenhang gesehen. So schreibt z. B. Orbach: „Als Feministinnen haben wir gelernt, dass Handlungen, die selbstzerstörerisch zu sein scheinen, sich fast immer als eine Art der Anpassung erweisen, als ein Versuch mit der Welt zurechtzukommen." (ORBACH 1991, S. 8). Zusammenfassend lässt sich nun folgendes festhalten: In patriarchalischen Gesellschaftstrukturen ist der Körper für Frauen bedeutsamer als für Männer. Dabei entstehen bestimmte Kontrollmechanismen gegenüber Frauen, die über deren Körperlichkeit laufen. Neben den von mir erwähnten eher indirekten Strukturen sollten hier auch die direkt den Körper von Frauen betreffenden Machtstrukturen wie etwa alle Formen von (sexueller) Gewalt gegen Frauen nicht vergessen werden. Essstörungen - insbesondere die Magersucht - lassen sich auch als eine Form des Protests gegen diese Strukturen und die damit einhergehenden Normen von Weiblichkeit sehen. Sobiech meint in diesem Zusammenhang, dass der Versuch „weniger an Körper" zu sein, als Widerstand gegen die Objektivierung des weiblichen Körpers verstanden werden kann (vgl. SOBIECH 1994, S.48). Allerdings kann dieser „Widerstand" letztlich selbstzerstörerisch sein: Zwischen 10 und 15 % der Anorektikerinnen hungern sich zu Tode. Aber auch auf abstrakterer Ebene ist er, wie Bordo darstellt, eher kontraproduktiv, da die Energien der betroffenen

Frauen einzig in der Beschäftigung mit dem eigenen Körper und damit in einem für die patriarchalische Kultur typischen Grundmuster gebunden sind (vgl. BORDO 1993, S.160).

Ich denke jedoch, wie bereits oben erwähnt, dass sich das Auftreten von Essstörungen nicht nur an den geschlechtsspezifischen Bedingungen für den Umgang mit Körperlichkeit festmachen lässt. Darüber hinaus spielen meines Erachtens die Auswirkungen, die die Konsum- und Leistungsgesellschaft allgemein auf die Entwicklung von Körperlichkeit hat, eine große Rolle. Diese überschneiden sich durchaus mit dem geschlechtsspezifischen Ansatz und haben auch in sich für die Frauen und Männer unterschiedliche Bedeutung.

3. Körperlichkeit in der Konsum- und Leistungsgesellschaft

In den westlichen Industriegesellschaften, die sich auch als fortgeschrittene kapitalistische Gesellschaften bezeichnen lassen, lassen sich zwei kulturelle Grundprinzipien finden, das der Leistung und das des Konsums (vgl. ESCHERTZHUBER 1996). Beide haben nun auch ihre spezifischen Auswirkungen auf die Körperlichkeit der in diesen Gesellschaften lebenden Menschen.

Ich möchte hier zunächst das Leistungsprinzip und seine Auswirkungen auf die Körperlichkeit näher betrachten. Als wesentliche Merkmale des Leistungsprinzips lassen sich die Forderung nach ständigem Wachstum und das die Marktwirtschaft prägende Konkurrenzprinzip nennen (vgl. HECKHAUSEN u.a. 1974). Dies bedeutet auch für den / die Einzelne(n) die Forderung stets zu „funktionieren" und für immer höhere Anforderungen bereit zu sein (und das mittlerweile nicht nur im Arbeitsprozess, wenn auch dort in besonderem Maße). Dabei wird der Körper als Mittel eingesetzt, so dass es zur Instrumentalisierung von Körperlichkeit kommt (vgl. Chatterjee 1989, S.46). Dieser Instrumentalisierung liegt ein bestimmtes Körperbild zugrunde, bei dem der Körper als ein vom Geist getrenntes manipulierbares Objekt gesehen wird. Dieses Körperbild, das ich als „Körper-als-Maschine" Metapher bezeichnen möchte, lässt sich auf Descartes zurückführe und ist, wie bereits erwähnt, charakteristisch für das abendländische Denken. Es lässt sich besonders in der modernen Medizin finden, ist aber auch ganz allgemein bestimmend für das Körperverhältnis in der Moderne.

Eine wesentliche Rolle für die Entwicklung von Körperlichkeit unter dem Leistungsaspekt spielen dabei die Auswirkungen, die die Ökonomie und damit zusammenhängende Produktionsprozess auf diese haben. Dabei wird eine möglichst optimale Anpassung an die Bedingungen des Arbeitsprozesses gefordert. Der dabei objektivierte Körper soll ständig „funktionstüchtig" und leistungsbereit sein. Das bedeutet, dass häufig Signale, die auf bestimmte Bedürfnisse oder Probleme des Körpers hinweisen, ignoriert werden (müssen) (vgl. CHATTERJEE 1989, S. 61).

Dies wiederum erfordert einen hohen Grad der Kontrolle über den Körper. Diese Kontrolle ist dabei im historischen Prozess zunehmend zur Verinnerlichung von äußeren Zwängen, zur Selbstkontrolle geworden. Ottomeyer und Anhalt schreiben dazu: „Die Selbstinstrumentalisierung, der Selbstzwang, ist für die kapitalistische Epoche der Menschheitsgeschichte spezifisch und hat sich nur über schmerzhaftes Umlernen den Lohnarbeiter-Generationen eingepflanzt." (Ottomeyer/Anhalt 1985, S. 247). Auch Foucault beschäftigt sich mit der Disziplinierung von Körperlichkeit in diesem Zusammenhang. Er zeigt auf, wie der Körper immer mehr „Zielscheibe der Macht" (FOUCAULT 1976, S.40) wird, indem er durch immer präziser werdende Disziplinartechniken, die sich in Institutionen wie der Schule, der Fabrik und dem Militär entwickeln, vereinnahmt wird. Ziel ist der „der nützliche und dabei gefügige Körper" (FOUCAULT 1976, S. 177).

Wichtig ist dabei auch die disziplinierende Funktion von Normen, die bestimmte Maßstäbe darstellen, an denen die Abweichung oder Übereinstimmung des Individuums gemessen werden kann. Insgesamt kommt es auch nach Foucault zu einer Abnahme äußeren Zwangs bei gleichzeitiger Internalisierung der Kontrolle. Sobiech weist nun darauf hin, dass die durch die Disziplinarmacht geschaffene Individualität und die damit einhergehende Körperlichkeit zunächst einmal „männlich" ist, da sie sich auf die quasi mechanistische Ausnutzung der Kräfte des individuellen Körpers im Produktionsprozess bezieht (vgl. SOBIECH 1994, S. 20). Diese „Funktion" des Körpers war (und ist) mit der Vorstellung von der männlichen Arbeitskraft verbunden, während Frauen traditionell der Reproduktionssphäre zugeordnet werden. Hier sind andere Machtstrategien von Bedeutung, die Foucault in den Bereich der „Bio-Politik" einordnet (vgl. FOUCAULT 1992, S.52). Diese zielen auf eine Regulation und Normierung der Bevölkerung als solche ab, haben aber dabei indirekt starke Auswirkungen auf die Körperlichkeit von Frauen, die, wie bereits dargestellt, verknüpft mit Sexualität und Fortpflanzung gesehen wird. Dies hat zur Folge, dass hier andere „Normalisierungsstrategien" wichtig sind (siehe oben).

Dadurch aber, dass auch Frauen in zunehmenden Maße direkt am Produktionsprozess beteiligt sind und/oder sonst an der vom Leistungsprinzip geprägten öffentlichen Sphäre teilhaben, kann es zur „doppelten Disziplinierung des Frauenkörpers„(SOBIECH 1994, S. 48) kommen. Das bedeutet, dass Frauen zusätzlich zu den immer noch geltenden „weiblichen Normalisierungsstrategien" den Anforderungen der Disziplinarmacht ausgesetzt sind. Das führt zu die Körperlichkeit betreffenden Widersprüchen (mechanistisches „Funktionieren" vs. „Naturhaftigkeit„, Kraft vs. Schwäche, Verleugnung der Sexualität vs. Sexualisierung). Dies zeigt, dass sich widersprüchliche Rollenanforderungen (beruflicher Erfolg vs. „gute Mutter„), die in feministischen Ansätzen (vgl. GAST 1989, S. 106) im Zusammenhang mit der Entstehung von Essstörungen gesehen werden, auch direkt auf der Ebene der Körperlichkeit widerspiegeln.

Ich denke aber auch, dass der für die Leistungsgesellschaft typische Hang zu ständiger Selbstkontrolle im Zusammenhang mit Essstörungen (besonders der Anorexie) zu sehen ist. So erleben viele Anorektikerinnen, die gleichzeitig oft das Gefühl haben, keine Kontrolle über ihre Lebensumstände zu haben, die (scheinbare) Kontrolle über den Körper als Triumph. Eine von Bruch zitierte magersüchtige Frau beschreibt dies so: „Man macht aus seinem Körper ein ganz eigenes Königreich, in dem man als Tyrann, als absoluter Diktator herrscht." (Bruch 1982, S.82). Aber auch die Forderung nach permanenter Leistungssteigerung, der „Rekordgedanke" (vgl. EICHBERG 1986, S.138) findet seine Parallele in der Magersucht: Viele Magersüchtige versuchen ständig unter großer Mühe, ihr eigenes Körpergewicht zu „unterbieten„, wobei dies durch ständiges Wiegen detailliert überprüft wird. Als weitere Parallele lassen sich hier Bereiche des Fitnesssports anführen, in denen auch unter großer Anstrengung die eigenen Rekorde gebrochen werden. Bordo weist hier darauf hin, dass auch extremes sportliches Training (Marathonlauf, Krafttraining) ähnliche Strukturen und „Funktionen" aufweist wie die Magersucht: Überwindung körperlicher Grenzen, Demonstration von Willensstärke und geistiger Perfektion (vgl. BORDO 1993, S. 150). Es verwundert daher nicht, dass viele Anorektikerinnen gleichzeitig zu ihrer Nahrungsverweigerung sich extremen sportlichen Belastungen aussetzen. Insgesamt passt die in der Leistungsgesellschaft vorherrschende Instrumentalisierung von Körperlichkeit gut in den Entstehungszusammenhang von Essstörungen, bei denen der Körper auch häufig zum „Instrument" zur (scheinbaren) Lösung anderer (z. B. psychischer und/oder innerfamiliärer) Konflikte eingesetzt wird.

Doch auch die Konsumkultur der westlichen Industriegesellschaften hat Auswirkungen auf die Entwicklung von Körperlichkeit, die nach mit die Entstehung von Essstörungen begünstigen. Wichtiges Kennzeichen der Konsumkultur, die mit ihrer Förderung des (Massen)konsums als unentbehrlicher Gegenpart zur kapitalistischen Produktion gesehen werden kann (vgl. FEATHERSTONE 1991, S.193), ist die Ausbreitung des Prinzips der Warenförmigkeit in immer mehr Bereichen. Auch der Körper bleibt davon nicht verschont, sondern wird, wie es Baudrillard ausdrückt, zum Konsumgegenstand. Baudrillard spricht in diesem Zusammenhang auch von der Verwendung des Körpers als Fetisch. Dabei wird dieser zum Objekt, das mit symbolischem Wert besetzt wird, um seinen „Tauschwert" zu erhöhen. In dieser Funktion rückt er immer mehr ins Zentrum der gesellschaftlichen Aufmerksamkeit. Er wird - soweit er den Idealvorstellungen von Körperlichkeit entspricht - zum „Götzen„, der Bewunderung und Verehrung erfährt (vgl. BAUDRILLARD 1981, S.97). Auch das führt zu einem entfremdeten und instrumentellen Verhältnis gegenüber dem Körper. Besonders deutlich wird dies bei verschiedenen Praktiken, bei denen der Körper zwar im Mittelpunkt steht, seine „Verwertung" zu repräsentativen Zwecken jedoch seine Bedürfnisse völlig ignoriert, was letztlich sogar zu seiner Zerstörung führen kann. Zu nennen wären hier z. B. exzessives Bodybuilding, Schönheitsoperationen oder der eng mit der Magersucht in Verbindung stehende Schlankheitswahn. Der Körper wird also Mittel der Selbstdarstellung. Dabei wird das Selbst immer stärker durch das Aussehen „verkörpert" (vgl. FEATHERSTONE 1991, S.187). Nicht den allgemein anerkannten Schönheitsidealen zu entsprechen, wird damit als persönliches Versagen erlebt. Insgesamt wird deutlich, dass es Vorstellungen vom „idealen" Körper gibt, die - auch um den Preis der Gesundheit - angestrebt werden. Als wesentliche Körperideale lassen sich dabei jugendliches Aussehen, Schlankheit und Fitness nennen.

Der Trend zur Jugendlichkeit, der auf der anderen Seite mit einer großen Angst vor Alter, körperlichem „Verfall" und dem Tod einhergeht, zeigt sich unter anderem in jugendlich wirkender Kleidung und der (kosmetischen) Bekämpfung aller auf das Älterwerden hinweisenden Merkmale (z. B. Fältchen). Besonders bei Frauen betrifft es aber auch das gesamte Körperschema: Bordo weist hier darauf hin, dass seit den 60er Jahren das Ideal des teenagerhaften Aussehens vorherrschend ist (vgl. BORDO 1993, S.63) und auch Ebert-Rohlshagen, die eine große Zahl von Frauen- und Modemagazinen auf das Körperbild von Frauen hin auswertete, fand heraus, dass das Bild des „präpubertären Mädchenkörpers" dominiert. Etwas ironisch meint sie in einem Interview: „Vom Körperbild kann man nur sagen, es bekommt jedem Mädchen, das einen modischen Körper haben will, schlecht, älter als 13 Jahre zu werden." (EBERT-ROHLSHAGEN in PÖLCHER 1996). Dieses Bild des androgynen Mädchenkörpers, dem alle fraulichen Formen fehlen, weist eine große Übereinstimmung mit dem von vielen Magersüchtigen angestrebtem Körperbild auf.

Auch das zweite in der Konsumkultur wesentliche Körperideal, das der Schlankheit, steht - ganz offensichtlich - in einem Zusammenhang zur Magersucht. Anders als in Kulturen , in denen eine ausreichende Ernährung nicht unbedingt gesichert war oder ist, stellt „Wohlbeleibtsein" in der Wohlstandsgesellschaft kein Privileg dar, sondern wird zum mit allen Mitteln zu bekämpfenden Problem. Gerade für viele - auch nicht essgestörte - Frauen nimmt die Angst davor, dick zu werden, viel Raum ein. In einer Umfrage der Zeitschrift „Glamour",,bei der 33.000 Frauen unterschiedlichen Alters befragt wurden, waren 75% der Befragten der Ansicht, zu dick zu sein, obwohl nur 25% tatsächlich (nach Maßstäben der Krankenversicherungen) „Übergewicht" hatten (vgl. BORDO 1993, S. 154). Während also Dicksein überaus verpönt ist, wird Schlankheit mit Attributen wie „Schönheit",, „Gesundheit",, „Aktivität" und „Erfolg" verbunden. Baudrillard bietet allerdings, auf die Frage, warum gerade Schlanksein zum erstrangigen Schönheitsideal wurde, noch eine völlig andere, sehr interessante Deutungsweise an. Er meint, dass hier - im Gegensatz zu der ideologischen Verknüpfung von Schlankheit mit „Leichtigkeit" und „Freiheit" - ein sehr repressives, auto-aggressives Körperverhältnis von Bedeutung ist. Dies lässt sich dadurch erklären, dass der Körper dadurch, dass er einerseits soviel Bedeutung als Symbolträger erlangt, andererseits aber durch seine letztlich nicht abwendbare Vergänglichkeit eine ständige Bedrohung darstellt, als etwas Machtvolles erlebt wird, dass es zu unterwerfen gilt. Baudrillard schreibt dazu: „Der Körper wird [...] zu diesem bedrohlichen Objekt, das man aus ‚ästhetischen' Gründen überwachen, unterwerfen und demütigen muss; und dabei muss man die Augen auf die ausgemergelten, abgemagerten Modelle der VOGUE richten, wo man die ganze umgepolte Aggressivität einer Wohlstandsgesellschaft gegenüber ihrem eigenen Triumphalismus des Körpers, die ganze heftige Verneinung ihrer eigenen Prinzipien ablesen kann." (BAUDRILLARD 1981, S.116).

Hier treffen nun verschiedene die Körperlichkeit betreffende Muster zusammen, die sich alle auch in kulturtheoretischen Erklärungsansätzen der Magersucht wiederfinden lassen: Der zentrale Stellenwert, den der Körper als Mittel der Selbstdarstellung in der Konsumkultur einnimmt, die „Bedrohlichkeit" des Körpers durch seine Naturhaftigkeit, wie sie besonders dem weiblichen Körper zugeschrieben wird und die Bedeutung, die damit zusammenhängend der Unterwerfung und Kontrolle des Körpers zukommt. Essstörungen - insbesondere die Magersucht - sind dabei von verschiedenen Paradoxien, die sich den drei Bereichen „patriarchalische Struktur",, „Leistungsprinzip" und „Konsumkultur" zuordnen lassen, geprägt:

So kann die Magersucht und auch die Bulimie als Protest gegen geltende Normen der Weiblichkeit gesehen werden. Gleichzeitig bleibt dieser Protest am Körper verhaftet, also innerhalb „typisch weiblicher" Strukturen gefangen.

Zudem spielt das Gefühl, den Körper absolut unter Kontrolle zu haben, eine wichtige Rolle für Magersüchtige. Dabei gehen aber gleichzeitig mit Voranschreiten der Störung die Möglichkeiten einer realistischen Selbstwahrnehmung und der Veränderung des Essverhaltens verloren. Die Störung „verselbständigt" sich.

Schließlich kommt es zu einer sehr starken Orientierung am Äußeren des Körpers und an geltenden Schönheitsidealen wie Schlankheit und Androgynität. Gleichzeitig wird der eigene Körper abgelehnt, was letztlich zu einem selbstzerstörerischen Umgang mit diesem führt.

4. Zusammenfassung: Magersucht als Pathologie der Kultur westlicher Industriegesellschaften

Es ist deutlich geworden, dass die meisten Muster, die für die Körperlichkeit von Frauen in der Konsum- und Leistungsgesellschaft bestehen, einen engen Zusammenhang zu den soziokulturellen Ursachen von Essstörungen, insbesondere zur Magersucht, aufweisen. Auch wenn sich diese Muster analytisch in verschiedene Bestandteile (Normierung des Frauenkörpers im Patriarchat, Beeinflussung von Körperlichkeit durch das Leistungsprinzip, Körperlichkeit in der Konsumkultur) trennen lassen, so ist es wichtig zu sehen, dass sie sich in der Realität überschneiden und gegenseitig beeinflussen.

Insgesamt lässt sich dabei eine starke Instrumentalisierung des menschlichen Körpers feststellen. Dieser wird dadurch zu einem manipulierbaren, vom Selbst getrennten Objekt. Gerade für Frauen ist nun diese Objektivierung besonders stark, da sie - zusätzlich zur allgemeinen „Funktionalisierung" des Körpers in der Konsum- und Leistungsgesellschaft - einer geschlechtsspezifischen Normierung von Körperlichkeit ausgesetzt sind, deren „Maßstäbe" durch die vorherrschende patriarchalische Kultur bestimmt werden. Stahr schreibt dazu: „Für Frauen bedeutet dies konkret, dass sie in dem permanenten Zwang stehen, sich einer Weiblichkeitskultur anpassen zu müssen, die vom dominant männlichen Geschlecht bestimmt wird." (STAHR u.a. 1995, S.70)

Da also die Körperlichkeit - insbesondere die von Frauen - in der patriarchalischen Konsum- und Leistungsgesellschaft von großer Bedeutung ist, dabei aber in unterschiedlicher Weise instrumentalisiert, diszipliniert und funktionalisiert wird, verwundert es nicht, dass sich auch die dieser Kultur charakteristischen psychischen Störungen (Anorexie und Bulimie) auf der Ebene des Körpers abspielen.

Danksagung
An dieser Stelle möchte ich mich bei Anna Maria Forstner und Dipl. Psych. Esther Burkert bedanken, die mir durch vielfältige Anregungen und (computertechnische) Unterstützung sehr geholfen haben.

References
BAUDRILLARD, J. 1981. Der schönste Konsumgegenstand: Der Körper. In *Ich habe einen Körper*. Edited by GEHRKE, C. München, pp. 92 - 126.
BORDO, S. 1983. *Unbearable Weight. Feminism, Western Culture and the Body*. Berkeley / Los Angeles.
BRUCH, H. 1992. *Der goldenen Käfig*. Frankfurt a. M..
BRUMBERG, J. 1994. *Todeshunger. Die Geschichte der Anorexia nervosa vom Mittelalter bis heute*. Frankfurt a M..
CHATTERJEE, A. 1989. *Körperlichkeit und Körperbewußtsein in Medizin, psychosozialer Therapie und Erwachsenenbildung*. Mainz.
EICHBERG, H. 1986. Der Beginn des modernen Leistens. In *Die Veränderung des Sports ist gesellschaftlich*. Edited by EICHBERG, H. Münster.
ESCHERTZHUBER, T. 1996. *Körperlichkeit in der Konsum- und Leistungsgesellschaft unter besonderer Berücksichtigung des geschlechtsspezifischen Aspekts. Beitrag zur Analyse von Bedingungen pädagogischen Denken und Handelns*.(Unveröffentlichte Diplomarbeit) Universität Regensburg.
FEATHERSTONE, M. 1991. The Body in Consumer Culture. In *The Body. Social Process and Cultural Theory*. Edited by FEATHERSTONE, M., HEPWORTH, M. and TURNER, B. London, pp. 171 - 195.
FOUCAULT, M. 1976.*Überwachen und Strafen*. Frankfurt. a.M..
FOUCAULT, M. 1992. Leben machen und sterben lassen. Die Geburt des Rassismus (Auszüge aus einer Vorlesung im März 1976). In *diskus*, Februar 1992, pp.51 - 58.
GAST, L. 1989. *Magersucht: Der Gang durch den Spiegel. Zur Dialektik der individuellen Magersuchtentwicklung und patriarchal-gesellschaftlicher Strukturzusammenhänge*. Pfaffenweiler.
GRIFFIN, S. 1992. *Woman and Nature: The roaring inside*. London.
GROSZ, E. 1994. *Volatile Bodies. Torward a Corporeal Feminism*. Bloomington / Indianapolis.
HAGEMAN-WHITE, C. 1984. *Sozialisation: Weiblich - männlich?* Leverkusen.
HAUG, F. (Ed.) 1988. *Frauenformen 2. Sexualisierung der Körper*, Berlin / Hamburg.
HECKHAUSEN, H., KROCKOW and C.v., SCHLAFKE, W. 1974. *Das Leistungsprinzip in der Industriegesellschaft*. Köln.
HEKMAN, S. 1992. *Gender and Knowlegde*. Cambridge.
HORSTKOTTE-HÖCKER, E. 1987. *Eß-Brech-Sucht und weiblicher Lebenszusammenhang im Patriarchat*. Pfaffenweiler.
MARTIN, E. 1989. *Die Frau im Körper. Weibliches Bewußtsein, Gynäkologie und die Reproduktion des Lebens*. Frankfurt a. M..
ORBACH, S. 1991. *Anti-Diät-Buch. Über die Psychologie der Dickleibigkeit, die Ursachen von Eßsucht*. München.
OTTOMEYER, K and ANHALT, P. 1985. Leib, Sinnlichkeit und Körperverhältnis im Kontext der Marxschen Theorie. In *Leiblichkeit. Philosophische, gesellschaftliche und therapeutische Perspektiven*. Edited by PETZOLD, H., Paderborn.
PÖLCHER, S. 1996. *Schönheit nach Maß. Radiosendung in der Reihe " Forum der Wissenschaft"*, Bayer. Rundfunk 13.6.1996.
SOBIECH, G. 1994. *Grenzüberschreitungen. Körperstrategien von Frauen in modernen Gesellschaften*. Frankfurt a. M. / NewYork.
STAHR, I. BARB-PRIEBE, I. and SCHULZ, E. 1995. *Eßstörungen und die Suche nach Identität*. Weinheim / München.
WURMSER, L. 1993. „Grausame Rächerin" und „gefügige Sklavin" - Sadomasochismus, Scham und Ressentiment bei

Frauen und umweltbedingtes Krankheitsgeschehen.
Ergebnisse einer Sozialökologischen Untersuchung
Women and Environmentally Induced Development of Diseases

Gerhard Grossmann

Zusammenfassung: Die Auswirkungen der noch immer zunehmenden Umweltbelastungen auf die Gesundheit bzw. auf das akute Krankheitsgeschehen der Frau wurden erstmals, aufgrund einer genauen Analyse der Notarzteinsätze in einer Großstadt, epidemiologisch nachgewiesen. Die Ergebnisse zeigen deutliche Unterschiede bezüglich des umweltinduzierten Krankheitsgeschehens zwischen der exponierten und der nicht-exponierten Bevölkerung. Mittels der vorliegenden Ergebnisse ist es nun möglich, speziell auf die Beschwerdebilder der Frauen hin ausgerichtete Präventionskonzepte zu erstellen.

Abstract: The effects of the still increasing ecological damage on the health of or on the acute development of diseases (pathological processes) in women have for the first time been epidemiologically proven on the basis of a thorough analysis of calls of emergency doctors in a city. The results show marked differences regarding the environmentally induced development of diseases (pathological processes) between the exposed and the non-exposed population. By means of the results we have to hand it is now possible to create preventive measures especially directed at women's medical complaints.

Keywords: Medizinsoziologie, Umweltverschmutzung, Frauen, Europa, Österreich, Medicine sociology, environmental pollution research, woman, Europe, Austria

1. FORSCHUNGSINNOVATION IN DER MEDIZINSOZIOLOGIE ALS TREIBENDE KRAFT FÜR DEN ERKENNTNISGEWINN

Medizinsoziologie als Wissenschaft, Prävention als deren praktisches Ziel und das Gesundheitswesen als politischen und gesellschaftlichen Ort des Handelns: dies sind die drei Grundfesten der vorliegenden Untersuchung. Deklariertes Ziel dieser Arbeit ist das Einbringen der Forschungsergebnisse in die schon längst überfällige Umgestaltung des traditionellen Gesundheitswesens in ein präventivmedizinisch orientiertes Gesundheitswesen.

Wissenschaft bedeutet demnach auch Verantwortung einer Gesellschaft gegenüber, deren Gesundheit und Wohlbefinden durch eine verfehlte und einfallslose Umweltpolitik auf das Äußerste gefährdet ist. Nun, da die noch immer viel zu leise geführten Diskussionen über die möglichen Folgen unserer vorrangig von ökonomischen Interessen getragenen Umweltzerstörung auf das Wohlbefinden und die Gesundheit von exponiert lebenden Menschen sehr oft im Keime erstickt werden, weil es an sogenannten griffigen objektiven Daten fehlt, werden in der vorliegenden Untersuchung objektive Befindlichkeitskriterien in Form von „umweltbedingten Krankheitssensationen bei Frauen„ sozusagen nachgeliefert.

Wohnumfeld und Lebensqualität

Zu den unbestritten wichtigsten Voraussetzungen zur Anhebung der urbanen Lebensqualität zählt zweifellos eine Verbesserung des Wohnumfeldes.

Gerade für Frauen trifft dies insbesondere zu, als dass sie ja einen nicht unbeträchtlichen Teil der zur Verfügung stehenden Tageszeit im direkten Einflussbereich des Wohnumfeldes verbringen. So hat sich beispielsweise gezeigt, dass Mütter mit Kleinkindern bis zu 95% der gesamten Tageszeit in der Wohnung verbringen. Aber auch ältere und daher sehr oft weniger mobile Frauen verbringen weit über 90% der Tageszeit im Wohnbereich. Es erscheint daher wenig verwunderlich, dass gerade der Minimierung negativer Einflussgrößen auf die Wohnumfeldqualität (Reduktion der gefährlichen Luftschadstoffbelastungen, Verkehrsberuhigung, Zurücknahme der Verbauungsdichten, Erhöhung des Grünflächenanteiles etc.) besonderes Augenmerk beigemessen werden muss.

Dass Wohnwert und Wohnumfeld konkrete Auswirkungen auf das Wohlbefinden von Menschen zeigen, ist schon seit über 30 Jahren in sozialwissenschaftlich-empirischen Wohnwertuntersuchungen zu Tage getreten (EIBEL-EIBELSFELDT u.a. 1985). Gerade hier knüpft die vorliegende Untersuchung an. Während bislang das subjektive Befinden der Betroffenen im Mittelpunkt des wissenschaftlichen Interesses stand, werden nun die medizinsoziologischen und ökologischen Prüfkriterien in Anwendung gebracht. Zu diesem Zwecke wurde die Zentralisation der anthropogenen Belastungen (Lärmbelastung, Luftverschmutzung, hohe Verbauungsdichte etc.) in bestimmten urbanen Regionen dokumentiert und mit dem jeweilig akuten Notfallgeschehen in Beziehung gesetzt.

Reagibilität als Bioindikator
Im Schrifttum finden sich immer wieder vereinzelte Hinweise auf die Auswirkungen schlechter Umweltqualitäten auf soziale, epidemiologische und immunbiologische Probleme (GSELL 1977). So weisen beispielsweise einige namhafte Autoren auf das Urbanisierungstrauma hin, das seine Auswirkungen im Bereich der Spätmanifestation von Kinderkrankheiten, in einer erhöhten Tumorhäufigkeit, mit einer permanenten Zunahme von Her- und Kreislauferkrankungen, Atembeschwerden sowie in einer gestörten „Paraimmunität„ (Beeinträchtigung der immunologischen Homöostase des Organismus) beobachtbar macht (SCHLEMMER 1960; HOLLAND/REID 1965; SCHAEFER 1970; EIFF 1976).

Es erweckt den Anschein, als hätte man bislang der ökologischen Rolle des Immunsystems, seiner Reagibilität gegenüber Umwelteinflüssen als Bioindikator zuwenig Aufmerksamkeit entgegengebracht.

In der sozialmedizinisch orientierten Ökologie hat man schon vor geraumer Zeit erkannt, dass Umweltveränderungen ihren Niederschlag im Gesundheitszustand des Individuums finden, wenn auch die Latenzzeiten zumindest bei bestimmten umweltinduzierten Krankheitssensationen sehr lang sein können. Aus dem bisher Gesagten lässt sich unschwer die unabdingbare Notwendigkeit einer grundsätzlichen Reform des staatlichen Gesundheitswesens in Richtung Lebensraumüberwachung und Lebensraumschutz erkennen.

Der Stellenwert der Medizinsoziologie bei epidemiologischen Fragestellungen
Gerade bei der Fragestellung, inwieweit den Umweltnoxen eine krankheitsinduzierende Wirkung nachgewiesen werden kann, hat sich gezeigt, dass die monokausale Zuordnung von krankmachenden Faktoren unzureichend ist. *Die Polyätiologie von Krankheiten verlangt nach neuen Forschungsmustern und gerade bei umweltepidemiologischen Untersuchungen müssen sehr oft von Fall zu Fall neue Untersuchungs- und Auswertungsstrategien gefunden werden.* So werden etwa häufig Ergebnisse umweltepidemiologischer Untersuchungen angezweifelt, weil spezifische Faktoren nicht kontrolliert wurden.

Kritiker solcher Studien beginnen dann die Umwelteinwirkungen verschiedener Quellen gegeneinander auszuspielen mit dem Ziel, die negativen Folgen der Umweltbeeinträchtigungen auf die Gesundheit der Betroffenen zu bagatellisieren.

Hier muss mit aller Deutlichkeit festgestellt werden, dass die schädliche Wirkung der Luftverschmutzung nicht deshalb angezweifelt werden kann, weil schlechte Ernährung und hohe Verbauungsdichte oder ein starkes Verkehrsaufkommen häufig gleichzeitig auftreten und daher nicht isoliert betrachtet werden können (HOLZKAMP 1972).

Eine kritische Überprüfung des Zusammenwirkens von verschiedenen Umweltbelastungsfaktoren und dem Auftreten von bestimmten Krankheiten ist demnach nur durch die Berechnung des Synergismus-Index (SYN-I) möglich. Mittels dieses Indexes kann festgestellt werden, ob das Zusammenwirken von z.B. zwei Einflussfaktoren E und F den additiven Effekt der Wirkung eines Faktors allein übertrifft.

Die Komplexität umweltepidemiologischer Zusammenhänge bedingt eine Krankheitsursachenforschung direkt im Lebensraum der jeweils exponierten Bevölkerung.

Abschließend muss noch hinzugefügt werden, dass die Bewertung der Aussagekraft umweltepidemiologischer Untersuchungen immer nur unter Berücksichtigung des aktuellen Wissenstandes vorgenommen werden kann (LANGMANN 1975; MARBURGER 1986; MARTH 1990).

2. DATENGRUNDLAGE UND ERGEBNISSE DER UNTERSUCHUNG
Morphologie des Untersuchungsgebietes
Die Untersuchung erstreckte sich über einen Zeitraum von 1986 bis 1994 und wurde in Graz, der zweitgrößten Stadt Österreichs, durchgeführt. Im Untersuchungsgebiet leben über 237.000 Einwohner, die Bevölkerungsdichte (Einwohner pro Quadratkilometer) beträgt umgelegt auf die Gesamtfläche 1.907 Einwohner, die Arealitätszahl (Quadratmeter pro Einwohner) beläuft sich auf 524. Wenn man nun die Arealitätszahl spezifiziert und auf den Dauerbesiedlungsraum umlegt, so zeigt sich hier eine recht deutliche Abnahme von 524 auf nur mehr 392 Quadratmeter.

Graz wirkt aufgrund seiner geographischen Lage (EU-Außengrenznähe nach Slowenien) wirtschaftlich und kulturell auf die Nachfolgestaaten des ehemaligen Jugoslawiens.

Im gesamten Stadtgebiet befinden sich 30.000 Wohnhäuser mit 110.000 Haushalten, wobei der Trend zu den Singlehaushalten in den letzten Jahren beträchtlich zugenommen hat. Graz ist von seiner Infrastruktur eine klassische Verwaltungs- und Hochschulstadt mit rund 40.000 Studenten (KUBINZKY 1966).

Der Luftverschmutzungsgrad und die Verunreinigung der fließenden und stehenden Gewässer in Graz haben bereits besorgniserregende Ausmaße erreicht. Da Graz auch direkt an der Nord-Süd-Transitroute liegt, muss dem Straßenverkehr zweifellos eine starke Umweltbelastungskomponente zugesprochen werden.

Auch durch die Masse von Einkaufszentren und Wirtschaftsbetrieben im Süden von Graz kommt es zu einem schwer kontrollierbaren Verkehrsaufkommen und den damit unweigerlich verbundenen starken Belastungen für die dort lebende Bevölkerung. Die Belastungseffekte werden auch noch durch die sehr ungünstige Beckenlage der Stadt mit wenig Durchlüftung besonders im Winterhalbjahr gesteigert.

Die Häufigkeit von Inversionslagen, die bekanntlich sehr negative Auswirkungen auf das Wohlbefinden und die Gesundheit zeigen, liegen z.B. im Winterhalbjahr bei bis zu 95% (im Jänner 1997 konnten nur 30 Sonnenstunden registriert werden!).

Den klimatischen bzw. bioklimatischen Besonderheiten kommt deswegen eine so große Bedeutung zu, weil schwere Wohlbefindlichkeitsbeeinträchtigungen oder auch bedrohliche Erkrankungen durch die angeführten Meteopathien ausgelöst bzw. begünstigt werden (KÜGLER 1975; RANSCHT-FROEMSDORFF 1976). In den siebzehn Grazer Stadtbezirken leben 107.414 männliche und 130.114 weibliche Bewohner.

Untersuchungskonzept
In diesem Abschnitt wird nun mittels komplexer statistischer Prüfverfahren der Frage nachgegangen, inwieweit sich die akute Erkrankungsdynamik in „wenig„ belasteten Wohngebieten von denen in „stark„ belasteten Wohnarealen signifikant unterscheidet.

Zu diesem Zwecke wurde das gesamte Stadtgebiet in 705 Zählsprengel (kleinste Zähleinheit) unterteilt und jedem Zählsprengel wurde ein Belastungsprofil (Luftverschmutzungsgrad, Lärmbelastung, Verbauungsdichte, Kleinklimata, Verkehrsbelastung, Grünraum) zugeordnet.

Weiters wurden alle im Untersuchungszeitraum anfallenden akuten Erkrankungen (die Daten entstammen aus den Rettungs- und Notarzteinsätzen im gesamten Stadtgebiet) den jeweiligen Untersuchungsregionen zugeordnet.

Zur Auswertung kam der gesamte Erkrankungskomplex der kardiovaskulären Notfälle (Herz-Kreislauf-Stillstand, Myokardinfarkt, Lungenödem, Angina Pectoris, Kammertachykardie, Lungenembolie, Synkope, Hypertensiver Notfall etc.), pulmonale Notfälle (Asthma bronchiale, Bronchitis, Pneumonie, respiratorische Insuffizienz, Lungenemphysem), neurologische Notfälle (Neuralgien, Migräne, epileptische Anfälle, Meningitis, Lumbago, Apoplexie), Suizid und Suizidversuch, sowie die regionalen Übersterblichkeiten (Todesfälle über dem Durchschnitt). Insgesamt gelangten 10.500 Notfalleinsätze zur Auswertung. In den nachfolgenden Abschnitten wird nun geprüft, inwieweit sich eine Koinzidenz zwischen ökologischen Belastungsmustern (Wohnumfeldqualität) und der Häufigkeit von vital bedrohlichen Krankheiten nachweisen lässt.

Kardiovaskuläre Notfälle bei der Frau unter Berücksichtigung der Wohnumfeldqualität
Bei der Betrachtung der nachstehenden Tabelle lassen sich bereits eindeutige Unterschiede zwischen den Belastungsgebieten und den Vergleichsgebieten feststellen.

Altersklasse	Notfallinterventionen auf 1.000 Einwohnerinnen	
	„schwach„ belastete Region	„stark„ belastete Region
0-15 Jahre	18,7	23,8
16-59 Jahre	20,1	36,9
60 u.m. Jahre	99,5	129,6

Die höchsten Notfallinterventionsraten finden sich in der Altersklasse der über 60jährigen Frauen. Hier zeigt sich einmal mehr die erhöhte Sensibilität dieser Personengruppe auf Umweltnoxen, die noch durch das teilweise Unvermögen verstärkt wird, umweltinduzierten Belastungen durch Kompensation (z.B. mehrmaliges Verlassen der Wohnung, Ausgleichssport etc.) zu begegnen (WICHMANN/MÜLLER/ALLHOFF 1986).

Unter Zuhilfenahme der Werte des Relativen Risikos (RR) ist es nun möglich, die perzentuelle Steigerung der Notfallinterventionen bei den kardiovaskulären Erkrankungen für jede Altersklasse der exponierten bzw. nicht-exponierten weiblichen Bevölkerung zu eruieren.

Steigerungsraten der Notfallinterventionen und Attributables Risiko (AR) bei kardiovaskulären Erkrankungen in „stark„ belasteten Gebieten:

Altersklasse/Frauen	Relatives Risiko (RR)	Attributables Risiko (AR)
0-15 Jahre	27%	17%
16-59 Jahre	100% !!	44%
60 u.m. Jahre	33%	41%

Hier zeigen sich erstmals doch recht herausragende Unterschiede bei den einzelnen Steigerungsraten der Notfallinterventionen in den „stark„ belasteten Wohnregionen.

Eine weitere wichtige epidemiologische Maßzahl findet sich in Form des Attributablen Risikos (AR), einer Maßzahl, die zur Definition jenes Anteiles dient, der zusätzlich zur normalen Krankheitshäufigkeit (= 1,0) aufgrund eines Risikofaktors bzw. von Risikofaktoren (Akkordsystem der Umweltbelastungen) auftritt.

Die Werte des Attributablen Risikos vermitteln einen quantifizierbaren Eindruck von den sogenannten Vermeidungsgrößen, d.h., würde man die „stark„ belasteten Wohnregionen auf das gleiche minimierte Belastungsniveau der „schwach„ belasteten Wohnregionen bringen (z.B. durch Rücknahme der gesamten Umweltbelastungen), so könnte man die Erkrankungszahl (Notfallinterventionen) um die oben erwähnten Prozentpunkte senken.

Für die Diagnosegruppe der kardiovaskulären Erkrankungen bei der Frau kann aufgrund der vorliegenden statistischen Datenauswertung davon ausgegangen werden, dass eine Koinzidenz von Umweltbelastungsfaktoren und dem vermehrten Auftreten kardiovaskulärer Krankheiten als gegeben anzunehmen ist. Selbst unter Berücksichtigung der Störvariablen Alter, Berufstätigkeit und Familienstand lassen sich signifikante Unterschiede bei der Erkrankungsfrequenz zwischen den „stark„ belasteten und den „schwach„ belasteten Wohngebieten feststellen.

Verteilungspanorama der Notfallinterventionen bei pulmonalen Erkrankungen unter Berücksichtigung der Wohnumfeldqualität
Durch die Wirkung des Akkordsystems (Wohnqualität, Luft- und Lärmbelastung) steigt die Anzahl der Notfallinterventionen bei pulmonalen Erkrankungen in den „stark„ umweltbelasteten Gebieten um 76%; dieser Wert versteht sich als Mittelwert für den gesamten Untersuchungszeitraum.

Für die Diagnosegruppe der pulmonalen Erkrankungen der Frau beträgt das Attributable Risiko (Vermeidungsgröße) AR = 41%, d.h. 41% der registrierten Interventionen könnten bei einer Reduktion der umweltinduzierten Belastungen auf das Niveau der Minimalbelastung in den „schwach„ belasteten Regionen gebracht werden.

In Absolutzahlen ausgedrückt würde dies eine tatsächliche Verminderung der Notfallfrequenz bei den pulmonalen Erkrankungen um 903 Interventionen bedeuten.

Die vorliegenden Ergebnisse liefern eine Reihe aufschlussreicher Hinweise auf das akute Krankheitsgeschehen in den Regionen, wobei sich gleichzeitig weitere Untersuchungsperspektiven eröffnen. So wäre es z.B. von Interesse, welche Verlaufsformen die chronisch pulmonalen Erkrankungen in den Belastungs- bzw. in den Vergleichsgebieten zeigen.

An dieser Stelle sollte man sich auch an die Kritik von MISFELD (1986) erinnern, der schon vor über 10 Jahren anhand einer Literaturstudie zum Schluss kam, dass führende Epidemiologen dem Thema „Luftverschmutzung und Krankheitsgeschehen„ eigentlich nur wenig Interesse beimessen.

Gerade dieser Umstand der „Interessenlosigkeit„ sollte Grund genug sein, sich gerade in Zukunft vermehrt den Fragen über den Zusammenhang von Umweltqualität und Wohlbefinden zu widmen.

Verteilungspanorama der Notfallinterventionen bei neurologischen Erkrankungen unter Berücksichtigung der Wohnumfeldqualität

Auch hier gilt vorerst das Interesse den Notfallinterventionen bei neurologischen Erkrankungen der Frau und zwar im Vergleich zwischen der exponierten und der nicht-exponierten Bevölkerung. Bei der näheren Betrachtung der Notfallinterventionen auf 1.000 Einwohner zeigt sich wiederum ein signifikanter Unterschied zwischen den „stark„ belasteten und den „schwach„ belasteten Regionen.

Altersklasse	Notfallinterventionen auf 1.000 Einwohnerinnen	
	„stark„ belastete Region	„schwach„ belastete Region
0-15 Jahre	8,1	5,1
16-59 Jahre	14,7	7,1
60 u.m. Jahre	29,3	14,1

Unter Zuhilfenahme des Relativen Risikos lassen sich nun auch die prozentuellen Steigerungsraten der umweltbelastungsinduzierten Notfallinterventionen errechnen.

Altersklasse/Frauen	Steigerungsraten
0-15 Jahre	15%
16-59 Jahre	107%
60 u.m. Jahre	107%

Die Anfälligkeit der weiblichen Bevölkerung für neurologische Erkrankungen in umweltbelasteten Wohnregionen ist eine auffallend ausgeprägte.

Aufgrund der vorliegenden Erkenntnisse lassen sich z.B. völlig neue, speziell für die Frau adaptierte Präventionsprogramme erstellen, wobei natürlich auf politischer Ebene gleichzeitig ein vorrangiges Sanierungskonzept für die Reduktion der Umweltbelastungsmomente erstellt werden muss.

Da ja die gesamten Untersuchungsergebnisse auch auf der Zählsprengelebene (kleinste verfügbare Untersuchungseinheit) vorliegen, kann eine ganz auf die lokalspezifischen Bedürfnisse abgestimmte Regional-, Umwelt- und Gesundheitsplanung erfolgen.

Mit der Ausweisung des Attributablen Risikos (AR) lässt sich wiederum eine Einsicht in das Ausmass der möglichen Reduktion der Erkrankungsraten erzielen.

Altersklasse	AR weibliche Bevölkerung
0-15 Jahre	9%
16-59 Jahre	52%
60 u.m. Jahre	52%

Damit können sozusagen Erfolgsquoten zur Erkrankungsvermeidung bei einer wirkungsvollen Umweltqualitätsverbesserung quantifiziert werden.

Die Aussagekraft des Attributablen Risikos besitzt demnach auch besondere Bedeutung bei der Konzeption möglicher Sanierungsprogramme.

3. LÖSUNGSANSÄTZE UND MAßNAHMENPLANUNG

Da Stadtentwicklung nur bis zu einem bestimmten Teil auf der lokalen Ebene stattfinden kann und zu einem nicht unbeträchtlichen Teil vom Umland geprägt wird, wird man sich in Zukunft zu sogenannten „Aktionsgemeinschaften„ zusammenschließen müssen, um damit auch die überregionalen Aspekte (wie etwa überregionale Verkehrsplanung, Industriestandortbestimmung etc.) in den jeweiligen lokalen Planungsvorhaben mitberücksichtigen zu können. Die Vorgaben der Primärprävention werden also über den Weg einer umfassend angelegten Umweltplanung zu erfüllen sein, wobei aber der Umstand der falschen Problemsicht, dass nämlich die Umweltkrise eine Krise der Umwelt und nicht eine der Gesellschaft sei, gerade bei der Konzeption umweltplanerischer Maßnahmen nicht aus den Augen verloren werden darf.

Gerade für die Konzeption betroffenen orientierter präventivmedizinischer Konzepte scheint es notwendig, jene Gruppenegoismen zu erkennen, die eine gezielte Umweltplanung und damit auch eine Lebensqualitätssicherung unterbinden.

Im Grunde kommen dafür drei Gruppierungen in Frage:
- Ökonomen, Unternehmer und Aktionäre verschließen sich im wesentlichen gegenüber den Emissionsfolgen auf die betroffene Bevölkerung und auf das Ökosystem. In diesem Zusammenhang wird immer wieder gerne das Argument der „Arbeitsplatzsicherung„ ins Treffen geführt.
- Ökologen, Mediziner und Umweltplaner lassen ihrerseits wiederum nur sehr zögernd ökonomische Ursachen von Emissionen (z.B. internationaler Preisverfall, Exportbeschränkungen, Konkurrenzfähigkeit etc.) als Argument zu.
- Umwelthygienisch planende Politiker setzen primär auf die Befriedigung sektoraler Interessen, meistens nur mittels eher einfallsloser technisch-funktionaler Korrekturen (Stichwort: Grünraumplanung im urbanen Bereich, Baulückenverbauung, ungeeignete Verkehrskonzepte etc.).

Auch wenn immer damit zu rechnen ist, dass präventivmedizinische Forderungen fast automatisch den Widerspruch einer potenten Interessengrupe wecken, darf keineswegs von den vorgegebenen Zielen einer menschengerechten Umweltpolitik abgerückt werden. Denn eines scheint auch klar geworden zu sein, wenn unsere Politik es nicht schafft, eine Umweltqualitätssicherung in kürzester Zeit zu bewerkstelligen, so nimmt es kaum Wunder, dass die Demokratieverdrossenheit auch ein Produkt stetigen Nichthandelns sein kann.

References

EIBEL-EIBELSFELDT, I., HAAS, H., FREISITZER, K., GEHMACHER, E., GLÜCK, H. 1985. *Stadt- und Lebensqualität*, Stuttgart/Wien

EIFF, A.W. 1976. *Seelische und körperliche Störungen durch Streß*, Stuttgart

GSELL, O. 1977. Tumoren: Sozialmedizinische Bedeutung und Epidemiologie des Krebses, in: BLOHMKE, M., FERBER, CHR. V., KISKER, K.P., SCHAEFER, H., *Handbuch der Sozialmedizin*, Band II:44-56, Stuttgart

HOLLAND, W.W., REID, D.D. 1965. *The urban factor in chronic bronchitis*, Lancet

HOLZKAMP, K. 1972. *Kritische Psychologie*, Hamburg

KUBINZKY, K.A. 1966. *Die Entwicklung des Grazer Stadtbildes von der Mitte des 19. Jh. bis zur Entstehung von Groß-Graz*, Historische Hausarbeit der Phil. Fakultät der Universität Graz, Graz

KÜGLER, H. 1975. *Medizin-Meteorologie nach den Wetterphasen. Eine ärztliche Wetterkunde*, München

LANGMANN, R. 1975. *Luftverschmutzung und Atemwegserkrankungen*, Stuttgart

MARBURGER, E.A. 1986. *Zur ökonomischen Bewertung gesundheitlicher Schäden durch Luftverschmutzung*, Berichte des Umweltbundesamtes, Berlin

MARTH, E. 1990. Abwehrschwäche durch Schadstoffbelastung aus der Luft, in: *Der praktische Arzt, Österr. Zeitschrift für Allgemeinmedizin* 45:77ff.

MISFELD, S. 1986. Mathematisch-statistische Untersuchungen zur Epidemiologie des Lungenkrebses, *Umweltbundesamt, Forschungsbericht* Nr. UBA-FB 86-004, Berlin

RANSCHT-FROEMSDORFF, W. 1976. Diagnostik von Wetterfühligkeit und Wetterschmerz, in: *Zeitschrift für Allgemeinmedizin* 52:37-41

SCHAEFER, H. 1970. *Die Folgen der Zivilisation*, Frankfurt a.M.

SCHLEMMER, I. 1960. *Der Mensch in der Großstadt*, Stuttgart

WICHMANN, H.E./MÜLLER, W./ALLHOFF, P. 1986. *Untersuchung der gesundheitlichen Auswirkungen der Smogsituation im Jänner 1985 in Nordrhein-Westfalen*, Bericht für das Ministerium für Arbeit, Gesundheit und Soziales

The Impact of Religion on Women's Mental Health
Religion und die psychische Gesundheit von Frauen
Annie Imbens-Fransen

I always had to ask God's forgiveness for defying my father. Sometimes I asked my father why he kept making me do this. Then he said, „All women are the same as that first woman, Eve. You tempt me. In your heart, this is what you want, just like Eve." I used to pray „God, let it stop." But God didn't intervene, so I thought, either it really was God's will, or I really was as bad as they said, and this was my punishment. Nell, a survivor of incest. (IMBENS & JONKER 1985/1992:66).

Abstract: After an introduction about the meaning and function of religion questions are raised about the role of religions in stimulating women's self-esteem and promoting their human rights. The view in the three monotheistic world religions and its spirituality are based on a male, androcentric, and patriarchal view of reality, which is presented as God's view. This view deprives women of the opportunity to voice a religious view based on their own lives and insights and adds meaning and value to women's lives. The impact of an androcentric religious upbringing on women's lives and mental health is illustrated by research based on interviews and counselling with Dutch, white women who have been educated as Christians. Finally this article highlights crucial aspects in counselling women with religious problems.

Zusammenfassung: Nach einer Beschreibung der Bedeutung und Funktion von Religion stellt das Artikel Fragen in wieweit Religionen die Selbstachung von Frauen und ihre Menschenrechte fördern. In die drei monotheistiche Welt Religionen beruht sich die Sicht auf die Wirklichkeit und die Spiritualität auf androzentrische und patriarchale Wahrnehmungen und Denkweisen von Männer die ihre Sicht presentieren als göttlicher Weisheit. Damit wird Frauen die Möglichkeit enzogen eine Religiose Sicht zu entwickelen und zu verworten die sich beruht auf Erfahrungen und Einsichten von Frauen. Die androcentrische religiose Betrachtungsweise blockiert die Möglichkeit für Frauen um ihr Leben als bedeutungs- und wertful zu erfahren. Die auswirkung der androzentrischen religiose Erziehung auf das Leben von Frauen und ihre psychische Gesundheit werden illustriert an Studiën und Analysen von Interviews und Beratungen/Therapieen mit Niederlandischen Frauen mit katholischer und reformatorischer Provenienz. Schiesslich werden entscheidende Aspekten für Beratungen mit Frauen mit religiosen Problemen beleuchtet.

Keywords: Theology, Androcentrism in Religions, Women, Mental Health, Theologie, Androzentrismus in Religionen, Frauen, Psychische Gesundheit.

Introduction

Preparation of this article was founded by the *Wetenschappelijk Onderwijsfonds Radboudstichting*.

My view of the impact of religion on women's mental health is based mainly on research, interviews and courses with Dutch, white women who have been raised as Christians and on counselling and contacts with sexually abused women with religious conflicts. While exchanging my research results with people from different religious and cultural backgrounds, women and men from all over the world started telling me stories about their traditions. Exchanging our stories allowed us to identify basic themes in our assorted traditions. Women and men of colour repeatedly stressed the importance of my expertise for people of colour. Similar responses came from women and some men from different cultures. These contacts enriched my view of religion. Exchanging our different views and experiences increases our awareness of religious aspects that affect women's mental health.

When reflecting on the impact of religion on women's mental health in the culture, tradition or community we are living in, it is useful to keep in mind questions like: Which religious concepts within my culture *stimulate* women's self-esteem? Which religious concepts within my culture interfere with women's self-esteem? How does religion in my community contribute to the prevention of mental, physical and sexual violence against women and children within and outside the family? How does religion in my community stimulate respect for women's human rights?

In religion people express their view of a reality comprising God, themselves, human relations, and the cosmos. Religious people do not necessarily believe in God; they may neglect or deny God. Armstrong defines Humanism as one of the religions without God. (1993, p. xix). People's religious views give them a sense of meaning and purpose in life and affect the way people think, feel, and act. Religious views are expressed through laws, values, symbols, stories, myths, and rituals. We may expect religions to contain stimulating sources of strength and insight and to support a good life for all beings. We need spiritual and inner strength to open our eyes to the structures, mechanisms, and limitations in our society that support unjust practices and relations and to the suffering they cause. Given the space and freedom, people will choose a religion that is based on spirituality, which cultivates our insight, self-esteem, strength, courage, creativity, and sensitivity to truth, justice, beauty, and love. These instruments and attributes allow us to transform ourselves and our societies to create a better life for all beings. This quality is conveyed inside and outside religions through words, attitudes, and gestures, paintings and sculptures, music and dance, and poems and stories. Biographical stories express how and where people find hope, strength, perseverance, vitality, and joy in daily life, even in difficult circumstances. (IMBENS-FRANSEN 1995/1997, pp. 15-17; 1997).

Women's voices and the God of our fathers
Creating a good life for women, and a new history in which gender-justice and equity can become a reality requires awareness that religious ideas and attitudes constitute the matrix in which women's lives are rooted (HASSAN 1995, p. ii). Christianity is one of the monotheistic world religions, besides Judaism and Islam. Their religious books repeatedly refer to God as „the One True God" and as „the God of your fathers, the God of Abraham, the God of Isaac, and the God of Jacob" (Exodus 3:14-15, The Acts 3:13) . The Qur'an refers to Abraham, Ismail, Isaac, and the Prophets who were given the revelation from their Lord. (Surah 2:135). Though these religions stress the importance of justice and truth, they have a long tradition of domination by exclusively male, androcentric, patriarchal leaders, who have based their religious views on male perceptions of reality. It means that the views and the spirituality in these religions are based on experiences, problems, questions, feelings, insights, and interests of men and on men's desires, fears, dreams, and fantasies. In the age-old practice of male domination in these world religions, men with androcentric patriarchal views claim exclusive authority to interpret reality and to present their ideas about God and about the world's creation and ideal arrangement according to God's will. They claim exclusive authority to determine what is human, male, and female and to identify God's allocation of roles and responsibilities among men and women. In doing so, they have looked after their own interests and silenced women. They have issued laws, commandments, and bans that reinforce the world order they have conceived, as well as their own position of power, while rendering women powerless (IMBENS & JONKER 1985/1992, p. 189).

HASSAN points out that in the Islamic, as well as in the Jewish and Christian traditions the alleged male superiority over women is based on three theological assumptions. Firstly it is assumed that God primarily created man, not woman, as woman is believed to have been created from man's rib. Secondly woman and not man was the primary agent of „Man's Fall". Hence „all daughters of Eve" are to be regarded with hatred, suspicion, and contempt. Thirdly woman was created not only from man but also for man (1995, pp. 4). Up to now these theological assumptions have defined woman's place in church and society. *Through Genesis, the man stands before us as the „radiance of God's glory", procreator of life in His name; the woman stands before us as the perfect answer to this, as the one who completes this gift, as the preserver of life. Catholic theological teachings on woman's specific, unique nature are not „myths", as is often claimed today, but the deepest interpretation of what is revealed to us by God's word* (CARDINAL SIMONIS 1982).

Androcentric religions present women's social role and responsibilities, dictated by men, as representative of the order created by God. This spirituality deprives women of the space and freedom to advance and express a religious view based on women's lives and insights that might add meaning and value to women's lives. Androcentric spirituality is disempowering and oppressive as it excludes women from religious discourse and deprives them of the opportunity to rectify, modify, question, or elaborate on its dominant view.

Moreover, women were excluded from many elite academic institutions until recently - at many western universities and faculties until the late 1960s or early 1970s. For centuries men have thus been able to research, concur on, and determine what is human, male, and female; what needs to be researched and what does not; what is relevant and what is not. Mainstream androcentric theology traditionally marginalizes and ignores women and children and their experiences, problems, feelings, interests, insights, and talents and imposes androcentric and patriarchal views about God and the world's creation and ideal order on women and children. Mainstream theology continues to interpret reality from the perspective of androcentric, patriarchal men who consider themselves superior to women and children (IMBENS-FRANSEN 1992, pp. 202-209). The mechanisms and problems described here are not exclusive to Christian, Dutch, white women, as women and men from different disciplines and religious and cultural backgrounds have clearly indicated. Rather, they characterize research on and by all other groups of people that became „outsiders" in mainstream academic, religious, and theological discourse, dominated by white, western, upper-middle class male scholars and spiritual and religious leaders.

Women's unheard stories
Women live in a world where women's stories rarely have been told from their own perspectives. The stories celebrated in culture are told by men. Thus men have actively shaped their experiences of self and world, and their most profound stories orient them to what they perceive as the great powers of the universe. But since women have not told their own stories, they have not actively shaped their experiences of self and world nor named the great powers from their own perspectives (CHRIST 1980, p. 4) Christ uses the word story to „all articulations of experience that have a narrative element" (180:1).

When women appear in androcentric stories they rarely function as wise, or strong, ambitious, efficient, intelligent, pioneering, persistent, vital, and loveable women. In androcentric stories women function, feel, act, and think in accordance with men's fantasies about them. In these stories women function as weak women; as ideal self-sacrificing mothers, wives, sisters, lovers, nurses, assistants, saints, and virgins; or as despicable, dominant, tempting and egoistic women, as witches and whores. The spiritual contents of androcentric stories thus becomes alienating and disempowering for women.

In recent decades - when women started telling their stories from their own perspective - they revealed that mental, physical, and sexual abuse against women and children is a worldwide phenomenon (BROWNMILLER 1975; DALY 1973; DRAIJER 1988; HERMAN 1981; FORTUNE 1983; IMBENS & JONKER, 1985/1992; MILLER 1983; MORRISON 1970; WALKER 1983, 1993). Previously mentally, physically and sexually abused women thought they were alone in the world with their unheard experiences.

In the 1980s - when teaching about *Women, religion and society* and *Reading the bible with women's eyes* - women started telling me their stories about rape and incest. At first I wondered about the subjects' correlation with the contents of my lectures and courses and the women's reasons for sharing these experiences with me. Later on I began to understand the connection between my approach to theological themes and these stories of sexually abused women. As a feminist theologian, I stimulated women to view reality and to interpret biblical texts from our own perspective and with our insights, based on our questions, experiences, feelings, interests, and desires.

It appeared that these women learned to interpret their experiences with sexual violence from their own perspective for the first time. They started to realize they did not bring the assault on themselves because of their tempting female behaviour - as the androcentric view alleges - but that they had been confronted with sexual violence because of male aggression toward women and children. Becoming conscious of this fact changed these survivors' attitude toward their experience with sexual violence: their silence out of a sense of guilt imposed by others made way for expression out of a sense that they had been wronged. Hearing these women's stories raised my awareness of the negative and harmful spiritual contents for women of mainstream androcentric theology and religion.

Before women started telling me their stories about rape and incest I truly believed I did not know any woman with this kind of experience. Now I am not sure whether I still know any women who have not experienced sexual violence. No wonder, when we look at the statistics of sexual assault against women in countries on three different continents. In the Netherlands thirty four percent of the women has been sexually abused within the family or by someone outside the family prior to their sixteenth birthdays (DRAIJER 1988, pp. 96-97). In the United States of America one in three female children is sexually abused before reaching eighteen years of age (FORTUNE 1984). In South Africa one in two women is raped at least once in her lifetime (HEESEN 1995, pp. I-III).

These statistics and those from other countries where data on the nature and magnitude of sexual violence are available reveal that: *Sexual violence is a cultural phenomenon in our society which can befall any woman at any place and at any time, regardless of her age and regardless of her relationship to the offender.* Many people continue to believe that sexual violence does not occur within their class or culture or religious circle or country due to the high sexual moral prevailing there (IMBENS-FRANSEN 1991, pp. 171-175). Sexual abuse of girls and women, however, occurs in all social milieus, both in religious and non-religious settings. Incest survivors revealed to me that the professions of their offenders included a physician, corporate executive, minister, professor in theology, director of a large social work institution, real estate agent, tradesman, unskilled worker, farmer, head nurse, school principal, government administrator, technician, staff member/diplomat. The majority of these offenders still attend church. Half of them still occupy an official church position. The majority of the survivors, however, have turned their backs on their church.

Christian androcentrism and its impact on the mental health of incest survivors
Several qualitative and explorative research projects revealed how destructive and oppressive the androcentric, patriarchal Christian view can be to women. The incest survivors interviewed for the study *Christianity and Incest* (IMBENS & JONKER 1985/1992) indicated that their religious upbringing was a contributing factor to the incest and the surrounding conspiracy of silence surrounding and caused problems in their recovery from incest. In their responses these women demonstrate main factors in Christianity that caused the incest and complicated dealing with the effects. These are: the inequity in the power dynamics between men and women in the church and in society; the view of women, men, children, and the family; prevailing views of God and of forgiveness, love, marriage, and sexuality.

All survivors had problems with the negative images of women in the bible and Christianity. On the one hand they were taught in church, at school, and at home that women were supposed to be humble, self-sacrificing, dutiful, pure, loving, and subservient, like women Saints and Mary the mother of Jesus. On the other hand they were labelled as sinful, seductive, and evil like Eve, who tempted Adam. In Christian culture many androcentric texts express such a negative view of women. Heinrich Kramer and James Sprenger, two Dominican Inquisitors, explain their belief that women are more infected by witchcraft than men. They write that women have slippery tongues, are intellectually like children, are imperfect animals, are always deceiving; are very impressionable, and are imitators of Eve, the first temptress. They describe women as more perfidious than men because they are physically and emotionally weaker, more carnal than men as is clear from their many carnal abominations and less able to retain the faith, like Eve; they incline the minds of men to inordinate passion and change men into beasts by their magic art (YOUNG 1993, p. 79).

Margaret, a survivor of incest, verbalizes the impact of this negative view of women.
Religion was being scared to death. It seemed to me that women were always to blame: They were either bad, or diseased, or possessed by the devil. (...) The woman is always the symbol of evil and of weakness. The snake is a she and a witch is a she. In those days, you weren't allowed to think that, because thinking is a sin too. And it is a mortal sin to think that way. That tormented me every night when I was confessing to God in bed before I went to sleep. (...) they kept telling you that sex was the girl's responsibility. If the girl had preserved her chastity like she should, the boy wouldn't have gotten out of control. (IMBENS & JONKER 1985/1992, p. 54-55).

Though ninety percent of these survivors had turned their backs on the church, these religious factors still complicated recovery from the incest experiences. Two aspects especially compromise the ability to overcome the effects of incest: the image of God and the attitude toward forgiveness. God was always seen as male by these survivors and mostly as a father. Sometimes as an ideal father, as opposed to the woman's own father. Many of them identified God with their own father: „My father could have been God"; „Father knew how God punished, he heard that directly from God„; „Father wanted to be worshipped too". These incest survivors sought to earn God's favour so that God would end the sexual abuse. They tried increasingly to fulfil God's expectations of women, according to their educators. They loved their neighbours and did so increasingly at their own expense. They honoured their fathers and mothers, despite the sexual abuse by their fathers. They granted the offender forgiveness, although he never gave them cause to do so. The next step was to do penance for the offenders and to pray even more. When the incest continued, they began to doubt themselves: they assumed that they had given cause for the abuse. They felt they had no rights whatsoever and were simply bad. For this reason God did not intervene but let the incest happen to them. It was also possible that God had specific reasons for it and that the incest served a purpose. Therefore, they simply had to learn to accept it and to forgive the offenders (IMBENS & JONKER 1985/1992, pp. 189-284).

The image of the androcentric patriarchal God, his characteristics and his expectations of people - but especially of women and girls - strengthens the power of the offenders. The victims are rendered powerless and deprived of all rights. Moreover, they are held responsible for the abuse that has befallen them and which they are powerless to stop. The destructive impact of incest in combination with this oppressive view of God is expressed in the fear and confusion aroused by this image. God is good, almighty, all-seeing, and just - and nevertheless allows incest to happen. Consequently, these women doubted themselves and experienced God as terrifying. They were afraid of God's almightiness in combination with the divine all-seeing eye. They recognized these characteristics in their own fathers who committed incest. They considered adversity and unjust treatment, no matter what the source, as confirmation of their guilt and proof of their own evil. They thought that they must resign themselves to this humiliation because this was God's will. They experienced that God sided with the sexual abusers. All these women experienced self-destructive urges combined with an intense fear of God, of hell, and of death. „But that fear of hell does have its upside," one of these women said, „It keeps me from committing suicide." The study *Christianity and Incest* and pastoral counselling of sexually abused women with religious problems led to the conclusion that the way these women experienced God greatly affected their chances of recovering from the traumatic aftermath of the abuse. These women were burdened with a destructive image of God. During their childhood, they internalized the male-constructed patriarchal image of God that reinforces male power and aggression over women and children. They suppose that the God of their childhood can no longer trouble them, once they have turned their back on the church or on the beliefs of their upbringing. Subconsciously, however, they go on living with this destructive, unchanged image of the God of their childhood. Many women, whether they have been abused or not, recognize their own religious experiences and feelings in the analysis in *Christianity and Incest*. The stories of these women raised as Christians motivate my thesis: *Sexual and other physical violence against women and girls is a physical violation of women's self-identities. Patriarchal Christian theology and evangelism signify a religious violation of women's identities.*

People from different religious and cultural backgrounds acknowledged the destructiveness of androcentric patriarchal thought processes and spirituality in their religions and illustrated their views with stories and literature. This exchange convinced me that in all male-dominated religions, men use religion to affirm their power and control over women. The effects of this male religious and spiritual abuse of power over women are neglect, mutilation, and rape of women's and children's minds and bodies, spirits, and talents, as well as denial and concealment of this violence against women and children.

Images of God and women's vitality

Further qualitative research enabled me to answer the following questions: How do images of God develop during women's lives? Does a correlation exist between the way women experience God, their self-consciousness, and their perceptions of other individuals? The study explored the possibility for women raised as Christians to love God *with all thy heart, and with all thy soul, and with all thy strength, and with all thy mind, and thy neighbour as thyself.* (Luke 10:27). Such is Jesus' advice for achieving eternal life or enjoying the fullest possible existence (IMBENS-FRANSEN 1995/1997, p.21).

The interviews revealed that, when perceived as a person, God was predominantly viewed as male and as the Father. However, there were some striking differences in the way women learned to believe in God as a Father. The women who progressively idealized their fathers and associated their idealized fathers with God increasingly learned to suppress and deny their own and other women's experiences, feelings, insights, and abilities. The more they idealized their father, the more they expressed a lack of respect for their mothers. These women still believed in God the way they had been taught at home, at school, and in church. This way of believing conflicted with their hearts, their souls, their strengths, and their minds. They lost both their space and their freedom to interpret reality and their own experiences and to learn from other women's perceptions and interpretations of reality. They stated that they did not experience their lives as meaningful.

It was easier for women who associated their fathers less with God to develop a more supportive image of God. They expressed greater respect for and confidence in themselves and in others, and also in women (especially two women, who associated God with their mothers). Contrary to the women who idealized their fathers and associated their idealized fathers with God, these women had greater respect for and confidence in themselves and in both their mothers and their fathers. Their images of God stimulated them to support women and children, to care for their well-being, and to struggle for their rights. (IMBENS-FRANSEN 1995/1997, pp. 139-210). The interviews both confirm and complement Mary Daly's statement: „If God is male, then the male is God." (DALY 1981, p.19).

These interviews and analyses of five samples from contemporary literature (BEGEMAN 1988; DUNBAR 1986; HILLESUM 1981; FRENCH 1987; MANDELA 1984) revealed a correlation between these women's images of God, their self-consciousness, their perceptions of others, and their vitality. Besides that the analyses revealed five moments in the course of their social and spiritual development.

Also see CHRIST, who describes women's spiritual and social quest as two dimensions of a single struggle to gain respect, equality, and freedom that include different moments (1980:1-12)

At each moment the women asked themselves different questions. The literature revealed common elements throughout the five stages of this quest. In the *first moment, or the moment of doubt and discord,* the individual doubts the purpose of her life and raises questions that reflect her way of life and the way she views God. In the *second moment or moment of introspection,* individuals explore their identity and try to find ways to cope with their present situation. In this moment a person can view herself as fully dependant on God to change her situation or may question her relation with God. The *third moment is the critical moment of insight and faith or of doubt regarding others and one's own abilities and opportunities.* While this stage may be a turning point in a woman's life, it may also strengthen her resolve to pursue her original course of life. At this critical point in her spiritual and social quest other individuals (both people close to the woman and strangers and outsiders) help her acquire new insights or reinforce old ones. Here, the woman discovers her deepest motivations and sources of strength and insight. At this point, women experience God in different ways. A woman may feel helpless and depend on approval from others - especially from men and fathers - and from God the Almighty Father. The second possibility is that a woman no longer wants to believe in God, as she has never sensed that God was on her side. Alternatively, a woman may find a faith in God and sense that God is her ally after all. This third experience gives the woman strength and self-confidence.

The *fourth moment or moment of hope or of despair* is another moment of introspection. Individuals wonder about reality and coping strategies, given their options and limitations. They ask themselves how they can be at peace with their feelings, their conscience and insight, and their abilities. In the *fifth moment or moment of being or of not being,* women define their purpose in life. This answer determines their subsequent approach to life, as well as their actions until they begin to question the meaning of their lives again. The outcome of this stage is determined by whether these individuals base the continuation of their lives on actual daily circumstances - such as being a black or Jewish woman in a society permeated with racism, colourism, fascism, and sexism - or whether they focus on fantasies and desired ideal conditions. In the first case, women can devote their energies to depicting and abolishing such injustice and oppression and may take pleasure in improving or changing these circumstances. In the second case, their lives are consumed by their utter helplessness and their sadness about the misfortune and injustice afflicting them. (IMBENS-FRANSEN 1995/1997, pp. 60-95).

Crucial aspects in counselling women with religious problems
Several factors complicate counselling for religious problems. Survivors indicated that counsellors and pastors minimized or overlooked such spiritual conflicts. They had difficulty understanding that a religious upbringing remained problematic for women. Other professionals indicated that they were hampered by their own frustration with religion, which they had so far managed to repress. On the other hand, survivors seeking counselling for these problems were reluctant to talk about their religious upbringing and particularly about God. Sexual abuse of girls within the family is the ultimate consequence of the androcentric and patriarchal view and spirituality in Christianity. The harmful impact of an androcentric religious upbringing as revealed by survivors of incest is familiar to many women from a Christian background. The drastic experiences of survivors of incest enables them to vocalize the humiliation and denial of all women in the androcentric view in Christianity.

It is crucial that women with religious problems become aware that they sometimes view reality and speak about themselves and their experiences from the perspective of others. Survivors of incest have learned to view reality through the eyes of their offenders and educators. They have internalized their offender's ideas, emotions, and desires. They adopt an image of themselves imposed by the offenders. They have internalized their offender's perspective on incest, religion, and God; they have internalized his view of themselves and of their mothers, of women and of women's roles, and of values like forgiveness. Counselling women requires unveiling these men's views by asking whose view the women express and their feelings about this view. The next step is to ask them about their own current or preferred views of different religious aspects.

The way in which women have learned to view God is the single most important aspect to be considered in counselling women with religious problems. Even women who have left the church and reject everything related to religion and God can suffer from the destructive image of God imposed on them in their childhood. When women ask for counselling they have serious problems and often a strong urge to commit suicide. In times of change, crisis, illness, misfortune, or death, their inner conflict about God can suddenly surface. Asking questions about their religious upbringing, about God, and about their feelings related to these subjects, enables them to become aware of their internalized view about God and its impact on their lives. The response from a counsellor or pastor is crucial in that process. The response „Well, God is not like that. You are looking at this all wrong. You are describing a false image of God." shows that a woman is not taken seriously and is not being allowed to escape from her oppressive image of God. When creating the space women need to express their feelings about God, it is tempting to provide our own image of God. However, women need the opportunity to seek out their own image of God.

Survivors of incest frequently mentioned that they saw God as a terrifying and all-powerful ruler who always kept an eye on them and who was always looking for a reason to punish them. They had the feeling they were bad and had no right to an enjoyable and meaningful life. Women express such a problematic image of God through statements like: „Finally I no longer believe in God. How can you believe in God, who …?" That God burdens them, frightens them, and inspires increasing self-doubt. A woman who suffers from such a destructive image of God needs room to express her emotions about God. She needs encouragement to acknowledge her fear and anger and affirmation that her emotions are acceptable and understandable.

The next step is to let her express which place God has in her life. It is helpful to name the offender who abused her, and one or both parents, and to ask who is on whose side. It appeared that survivors of incest mostly associated God with the offender's side and often even identified with the offender. When this becomes apparent it is revealing to ask: „Whom are you talking about now, God or the offender?" This approach helps trace the causes of her fear of God and another way of thinking about God. One woman who said that she had the feeling that God always let her down was asked to write down how she felt about that. She wrote:

> *God is the Father in heaven, who does everything for His children because He loves them. That's what some people say. Well, I'm going to tell God exactly what I think of Him.*
> *God gave me a mother who didn't want me. She always told me I ruined her life.*
> *God gave me a father who raped and abused me for 30 years.*
> *God gave me a husband who constantly abused me and my children. God gave my little girl a father who wanted to rape her when she was three and a half.*
> *Well thank you very much, God, that you wanted to give me all of this and that you loved me so very much. But God, I need nothing more from you, do you hear me? I want absolutely nothing from you; just leave me alone, please.*
> *Let me live my own life, goddamit. …* Nell, a survivor of incest (IMBENS & JONKER 1985/1992, p. 209).

After she had written this down she was asked to express how she wished to view God. After a few sessions her attitude toward God changed considerably. Her new view of God finally enabled her to prevent her father from continuing to abuse her. She explained that she would never have had the courage to oppose her father had she not felt that God was behind her.

To invite women to draw is another effective way to enable mentally, physically, or sexually abused women to become aware and to talk about the way they view and experience God. When counselling these women we may ask them: „What are your emotions when you think about God during the abuse? Please draw your perception of God with respect to yourself, the abuser, your parents, and the other members of your family or individuals who were influential at the moment that the abuse happened?" Abused women frequently draw God far above themselves and larger. The offender is mostly drawn in between God and themselves, larger than they are but smaller than God. A drawing enables a woman to take a step back from her experience; to talk about the drawing with the counsellor, and to analyse the drawing and her perception of God. To analyse the drawing, ask questions like: „Why did you draw God here? Why do your father and God stay so close to each other? How does that make you feel?"

In a second drawing they may be asked to express how they would like to view God. Women may ask whether they are permitted to omit God from the drawing. Clearly, if a woman needs to leave God out of her life she should express that sense in her drawing. Enabling women with religious problems to share their feelings about the image of God others have imposed on them lets them think about God in a way that gives them the freedom to interpret reality according to their own feelings, insights, interests, and desires and adds meaning and value to their lives. (IMBENS-FRANSEN 1995/1997, pp. 24-59).

References

ALI, A.Y. 1989. *The Meaning of the Holy Qur'an.* USA.
ARMSTRONG, K. 1993. *A History of God. The 4,000-Year Quest of Judaism, Christianity and Islam.* New York Times Best-seller.
BEGEMAN, N. 1988. *Victorine.* Bert Bakker, Amsterdam.
BROWNMILLER, S. 1975. *Against Our Will. Men, Women and Rape. Bantam Books.* Toronto/New York/London.
CHRIST, C.P. 1980. *Diving Deep and Surfacing. Women Writers on Spiritual Quest.* Beacon Press, Boston.
DALY, M. 1973. *Beyond God the Father. Toward a Philosophy of Women's Liberation.* Beacon Press, Boston.
DRAIJER, N. 1988. *Seksueel misbruik van meisjes door verwanten.* Den Haag.
DUNBAR, M. 1986. *Catherine - The Story of a Young Girl Who Died of Anorexia.* Penguin Books Ltd, Harmondsworth.
FRENCH, M. 1987. *Her Mother's Daughter.* USA.
FORTUNE, M.M. 1983. *Sexual Violence. The Unmentionable Sin.* The Pilgrim Press, New York.
FORTUNE, M.M. 1984. *Pamphlet Did you know that.* Seattle.
HASSAN, R. 1995. *Women's rights and Islam: From the I.C.P.D. to Beijing.* (unpublished paper) USA.
HEESEN, E. 1995. Vrouwenbeweging Zuid-Afrika op zoek naar samenwerking. in *Amandla, tijdschrift over zuidelijk afrika.* 4:I-III.
HERMAN, J.L. 1981. *Father-Daughter Incest.* Harvard University Press. Cambridge, USA/London, UK.
Hillesum, E. 1981. *Het verstoorde leven. Dagboek van Etty Hillesum 1941-1943.* De Haan, Haarlem.
IMBENS-FRANSEN, A. 1991. Women - Health - Religion. in *Women, Health & Urban Policies.* Edited by Dr. E. ROTH. pp. 171-175.
IMBENS-FRANSEN, A. 1992. Research on Women and Health. in The Netherlands. in *Information in a Healthy Society. Health in the Information Society.* Edited by: A. van BERLO, Y. KIWITZ-DE RUIJTER. pp. 202-209. Akontes publishing, Knegsel.
IMBENS-FRANSEN, 1997. Digging up women's sources of wisdom and strength in the quest for women's true spirituality. in *Revisioning Our Sources. Women's Spirituality in European Perspectives.* Edited by A. ESSER, A. HUNT OVERZEE, S.K. ROLL. Kok, Kampen.
IMBENS, A. and I. JONKER. 1985. *Godsdienst en incest.* De Horstink, Amersfoort/1992. *Christianity and Incest.* Fortress Press, Minneapolis USA/Burn & Oates. Tunbridge Wells, UK.
IMBENS-FRANSEN, A. 1995. *God in de beleving van vrouwen.* Kok, Kampen/1997. *Befreiende Gottesbilder für Frauen. Datim frühe Wunden heilen.* Kösel, München.
MANDELA, W. 1984. *Ein Stück meiner Seele ging mit ihm.* Rowohlt, Reinbek.
MILLER, A. 1983. *Du sollst nicht merken. Variationen über das Paradies-Thema.* Frankfurt am Main.
MORRISON, T. 1970. *The Bluest Eye.* New York.
PARSONS TECHNOLOGY. 1990. King James Version. *New Revised Standard Version. Hebrew and Greek Transliterated Bible,* based on Strong's Exhaustive Concordance of the Bible. USA.
SIMONIS, A.J. 1982. *Thoughts on Woman's Place in Society and Church.* Speech to the Catholic Women's Guild. (unpublished) The Netherlands.
THE BIBLE. 1989. *New Revised Standard Version.* USA.
THE HOLY BIBLE. 1974. *King James Version.* USA.
THE JEWISH BIBLE. 1985. *Tanakh The Holy Scriptures.* The New JPS Translation According to the Traditional Hebrew Text.
WALKER, A. 1983. *The Color Purple.* London.
WALKER, A. and P. PARMAR. 1993. *Warrior Marks. Female Genital Mutilation and the Sexual Blinding of Women.* New York/San Diego/London.
YOUNG, S. 1993. *An Anthology of Sacred Texts By and About Women.* Crossroad, New York.

Hidden Carers -
Die besondere Rolle der Frau in der Gesundheitsselbsthilfe
Hidden carers - The Central Role of Women in Lay Health Care
Petra Scheibler & Annette Schmitt

Zusammenfassung: Forschungsergebnisse belegen, dass die Aufgaben der Gesundheitsselbsthilfe vor allem von Frauen übernommen werden. Gesundheitsselbsthilfe umfass t alle alltäglichen Tätigkeiten, die der Bereitstellung, Aufrechterhaltung und Wiederherstellung von Gesundheit dienen. In diesem Beitrag stellen wir die Rolle von Frauen als informelle Versorgerinnen oder ‚hidden carers', wie sie von britischen Forschern genannt werden, dar und diskutieren die Konsequenzen der Rollenbelastung sowohl für das Wohlbefinden von Frauen als auch die Gesundheitspolitik in westlichen Gesellschaften.

Abstract: Research has clearly demonstrated that providing informal health care is women's work. Lay health care includes all those everyday activities which are concerned with the production, maintenance and restoration of health. In this paper we evaluate women's role as informal caregivers or ‚hidden carers' as they are called by british scholars. We discuss the consequences of these role strains for women's well-being and health policy in Western Societies.

Keywords: Gesundheitsselbsthilfe, Rolle der Frau, soziale Unterstützung, westliche Gesellschaften, Gesundheitspsychologie, Lay health care, women's role, social support, Western Societies, Health Psychology

Einleitung

Beschäftigt man sich mit dem Thema ‚Frauen und Gesundheit', stößt man auf ein Gebiet, das lange Zeit vernachlässigt und erst in den 80er Jahren in der Bundesrepublik Deutschland vermehrt zum Thema erhoben wurde: Die ‚versteckte' Gesundheitsarbeit von Frauen in der alltäglichen Gesundheitsselbsthilfe. Gesundheitsselbsthilfe ist - wie alle Formen des Gesundheitshandelns - eng mit der Sozialisation von Individuen in allen Gesellschaften verknüpft und gehört nicht nur in europäischen Gesellschaften zu einem zentralen Lebensinhalt von Frauen. Gesundheit und Krankheit sind als historisch und kulturell gewachsene, über die Sozialisation vermittelte soziale Konstrukte zu verstehen, die in der Rolle, die Frauen in der Gesundheitsselbsthilfe übernehmen, ihre besondere Ausprägung erfahren. Wir möchten diese Rolle in unserem Beitrag näher beleuchten, da aus dieser Rolle besonders unter gegenwärtigen gesellschaftlichen Veränderungen Konsequenzen für die Gesundheit von Frauen resultieren.

Frauen als ‚provider', ‚negotiator' und ‚mediator of health'

Gesundheitsselbsthilfe umfass t eine große Bandbreite von in das Alltagsleben eingebundenen Aktivitäten: den Umgang mit alltäglichen Beschwerden, die Weitergabe von Wissen über Gesundheit und Krankheit, Selbstdiagnosen, und -behandlungsmaßnahmen, Präventivmaßnahmen sowie die Betreuung erkrankter und älterer pflegebedürftiger Personen. Zahlreiche Studien belegen, dass ein Großteil der Gesundheitsarbeit von Frauen im Rahmen der unbezahlten Familienarbeit übernommen wird. Es sind vor allem Frauen, die Gesundheitswissen weitergeben und auf einen gesundheitsbewuss ten Lebensstil ihrer Familie achten (vgl. UMBERSON 1987), Gesundheitsprobleme anderer besprechen (vgl. DEAN 1986), Interpretationen für Symptome anbieten (vgl. ZOLA 1983) und weitere Behandlungsmaßnahmen vorschlagen (vgl. BIRKEL & REPPUCCI 1983, NORCROSS, RAMIREZ & PALINKAS 1996). Darüber hinaus nehmen Frauen eine wichtige Funktion in Selbsthilfegruppen und -organisationen ein (vgl. KRAUSE-GIRTH 1989). Auch leisten Frauen als Ehefrauen, Töchter und Schwiegertöchter den Großteil der pflegerischen Versorgung älterer Familienmitglieder (vgl. SOLDO & MYLLYLUOMA 1983) und stehen als Ratgeberinnen älterer Personen zur Verfügung (vgl. STOLLER 1993).

Die alltägliche Gesundheitsselbsthilfe gilt somit als geschlechtsspezifisch organisiertes Handlungsfeld, in dem Frauen als ‚hidden carers' (GRAHAM 1985) maßgeblich zur Aufrechterhaltung des Laienversorgungssystems beitragen. Nach GRAHAM übernehmen Frauen dabei vor allem drei zentrale Rollen:

- Als *provider of health* fühlen sich Frauen verantwortlich für die Bereitstellung der häuslichen Bedingungen, welche zum Erhalt der Gesundheit und zu einer schnellen Genesung von Erkrankungen der Familienmitglieder beitragen. Hierzu zählen z. B. die Sorge um ausreichende und

gesunde Ernährung der Familie und die Schaffung eines positiven sozialen Klimas, das als Unterstützung viele Belastungen vermeiden bzw. kompensieren kann.
- Als ‚*negotiators of health*‘ vermitteln Frauen in der Familie Einstellungen und Verhaltensweisen zur Gesunderhaltung und zum Umgang mit Krankheit. Sie ‚sozialisieren‘ ihre Angehörigen für eine gesunde Lebensweise und fungieren als Modelle und Wissensquellen, indem sie z. B. überlieferte Heilverfahren für den Umgang mit Körper und Krankheit vermitteln.
- In ihrer Rolle als ‚*mediators of health*‘ stellen sie die Verbindung zum professionellen Gesundheitssystem her, d.h. sie vermitteln den Kontakt der Familienmitglieder zu medizinischen Experten.

Die Sorge für andere als Teil der weiblichen Geschlechterrolle
Es ist sicherlich unbestreitbar, dass die Sorge um das Wohlergehen anderer und die Bereitstellung alltäglicher Hilfen positive, belohnende Aspekte hat und zu den grundlegenden Merkmalen enger Beziehungen gehört. Andererseits jedoch erfordert die Gesundheitsselbsthilfe, etwa bei der Pflege älterer oder kranker Angehöriger, mitunter einen sehr hohen Einsatz an zeitlichen und emotionalen Ressourcen, der finanziell nicht oder nicht vollständig vergütet wird. Die Tatsache, dass diese zumeist unbezahlte Arbeit überwiegend von Frauen übernommen wird, läss t sich nur unzureichend durch die Beschränkung der Frau auf ihre traditionelle Rolle als "Familienfrau" erklären. So hat bspw. die Berufstätigkeit von Frauen nur geringe Auswirkungen auf den Aufwand bei der Pflege und Betreuung älterwerdender Eltern (MATTHEWS & ROSER 1988) und die Ehemänner berufstätiger Frauen übernehmen auch nicht mehr Hausarbeit als die Ehemänner nichtberufstätiger Frauen (HARTMAN 1981). Zudem konnte FINLEY (1989) die Geschlechtsunterschiede bei der Erfüllung von Pflegeaufgaben nicht auf die zur Verfügung stehende Zeit und die Übernahme konfligierender Rollen zurückführen. Frauen übernehmen den Großteil der Aufgaben in der Gesundheitshilfe also nicht nur dann, wenn sie einen Aspekt ihrer zentralen Berufsrolle als Familienfrau darstellen, sondern auch zusätzlich zu anderen beruflichen Aufgaben außerhalb der Familie.

Wir sehen den Grund für die Übernahme dieser Funktionen nicht in einem gegebenen unveränderlichem "Sozialcharakter" der Frau, der sie für die Rolle der Helferin und Pflegerin prädestiniert. Wir verteten aber die Auffassung, dass Frauen mit dem Erwerb ihrer Geschlechterrolle geschlechtsstereotype Vorstellungen übernehmen, die ihnen die Erfüllung dieser Rolle nahelegen (SCHEIBLER 1995) und stimmen mit ALFERMANN (1996) überein, dass Geschlechtsstereotype in zweifacher Hinsicht in Beziehung zu traditionellen Geschlechtsrollen stehen: *Zum einen spiegeln sie Eigenschaften und Kompetenzen, die die Geschlechter in ihren jeweiligen Rollen zeigen, zum anderen stützen sie die bestehende Rollenverteilung.*

Geschlechtsstereotypen folgend wird von Frauen ein größere Fürsorglichkeit, Einfühlsamkeit, Emotionalität und Rücksichtnahme auf die Bedürfnisse und Befindlichkeit anderer erwartet (vgl. ALFERMANN 1996; EISENBERG & LENNON 1983; SHIELDS 1987). Gleichzeitig gestehen Geschlechtsrollenstereotype Frauen eher zu, sozialer Unterstützung **anzunehmen** - bspw. wird Frauen stärker der Ausdruck von Emotionen der Schwäche zugebilligt und sie gelten als hilfsbedürftiger als Männer (vgl. ALFERMANN 1996; FISCHER 1993).

Im Laufe des Erwerbs der weiblichen Geschlechtsrolle eignen sich Frauen solche Kompetenzen an, die der Erfüllung der zugeschriebenen Aufgabe als "Beziehungspflegerin" dienen. So gehen bereits Mädchen tiefere emotionale Bindungen mit Personen gleichen Alters ein, verbringen mehr Zeit in der Familie, bauen stärkere emotionale Bindungen zu Familienangehörigen auf als Jungen und tendieren eher dazu, ihren Gefühlen und Erwartungen gegenüber anderen Ausdruck zu verleihen (vgl. FISCHER, SOLLIE & MORROW 1986; BENENSON 1990). Entsprechend pflegen erwachsene Frauen stärker als Männer einen unterstützenden, expressiven und kooperativen Kommunikationsstil, der die Aufrechterhaltung und Vertiefung persönlicher Beziehungen fördert (vgl. ARIES 1987).

‚Support gap‘: Frauen im Widerspruch zwischen Helfen und Hilfe empfangen
Als ein wichtiger Aspekt der Gesundheitsselbsthilfe gilt die Bereitstellung sozialer Unterstützung in sozialen Netzwerken. Zum einen stellt die Einbindung in soziale Netzwerke einen sicheren Hintergrund für die Bewältigung alltäglicher Rollenanforderungen dar (vgl. KAHN & ANTONUCCI 1980). Zum anderen bieten soziale Netzwerke in Zeiten besonderer Belastungen, z. B. durch Krankheit, Arbeitslosigkeit oder Verwitwung, eine Vielzahl von praktischen und emotionalen Hilfen an, die die Überwin-

dung von Krisen und Adaptation an neue Situationen erleichtern. Obgleich auch paradoxe Wirkungen sozialer Unterstützung bekannt sind und enge, kontrollierende Netze bei der Neuanpassung nach Überwindung eines kritischen Lebensereignisses behindern können, so wird doch die Einbindung in ein Netz unterstützender Beziehungen vor allem als Schutz vor Beeinträchtigungen und psychischen Störungen nach Belastungen gesehen (vgl. RÖHRLE 1994).

Obwohl die Datenlage nicht ohne Widersprüche ist (vgl. MAYR-KLEFFEL 1991), gibt es zahlreiche Hinweise darauf, dass Frauen in umfangreichere, intimere und vielfältigere soziale Netzwerke eingebunden sind als Männer und insbesondere von Personen außerhalb der Familie mehr Unterstützung erhalten als Männer (vgl. Überblick bei MAYR-KLEFFEL 1991; NESTMANN & SCHMERL 1991).

Betrachtet man lediglich die Ergebnisse von Studien, die die **erhaltene** soziale Unterstützung quantifizieren, und betrachtet man die Einbindung in enge soziale Beziehungen als salutogen, dann schneiden Frauen offenbar besser ab als Männer. So kommen BUTLER, GIORDANO & NEREN (1985) zu dem Schluss :

The results of several studies of help-seeking, readiness to participate in intimate communication, and self-disclosure to others show women of all ages, from childhood on, in better positions than men of the same age (523).

Paradox allerdings ist, dass Frauen, obwohl sie in stärkerem Maße über unterstützende Beziehungen verfügen als Männer und diese auch nutzen, nicht von den salutogenen Wirkungen dieser Unterstützung zu profitieren scheinen: Zumindest stellt sich die gesundheitliche Situation von Frauen epidemiologisch nicht günstiger dar als die Situation von Männern. Vielmehr gibt es Hinweise darauf, dass Frauen bei psychischen und psychosomatischen Erkrankungen sogar höhere Belastungsquoten aufweisen (vgl. VOGT 1983).

Eine Erklärung für dieses Paradox zeichnet sich ab, wenn man nicht ausschließlich den Betrag der erhaltenen sozialen Unterstützung, sondern den "Nettobetrag" an sozialer Unterstützung betrachtet. Bezieht man so die "Kosten" enger sozialer Beziehungen ein, dann ergibt sich ein weniger positives Bild der Situation von Frauen: Frauen stellen mehr soziale Unterstützung bereit als Männer (GRUNOW et al. 1983; NESTMANN & SCHMERL 1991), und sie leisten mehr soziale Unterstützung als sie selbst zurückbekommen. Die Verantwortung für die Gesundheit der Familie, das Bereitstellen von Unterstützung und das Sicherstellen von Versorgungsleistungen verursacht nach BELLE (1982) bestimmte Kosten: Die Belastungen der Familienarbeit sind teilweise hoch, wie z.B. die Pflege kranker Angehöriger in der Familie (SCHRÖPPEL 1991), und gehen damit zu Lasten der eigenen Gesundheit. Das Paradoxe dabei ist, dass Frauen bei eigenen gesundheitlichen Problemen weniger mit Unterstützung und Hilfeleistung innerhalb der Familie rechnen können. Sie sind deshalb nicht nur eher geneigt, Hilfe außerhalb der Familie zu suchen, sondern auch vermehrt darauf angewiesen (vgl. SCHMERL & NESTMANN 1990). In diesem ‚support gap' (BELLE 1982) von Frauen wird ein besonderes Gesundheitsrisiko für Frauen gesehen:

The fact that they receive less social support than they permanently provide for others, and get back less than they need to complete their own tasks and burdens, represents a permanent source of stress for women that has immediate consequences for their physical and mental health. (NESTMANN & SCHMERL 1991: 224)

Zu diesen Belastungen durch die eigene Bereitstellung von sozialer Unterstützung kommt die sog. Ansteckung durch Stress (‚contagion of stress'):

Women experience, together with their own and direct stress, the burdens and negative life events of their loved ones as additional stress (NESTMANN & SCHMERL 1991: 225).

Zudem übernehmen Frauen auch deshalb einen größeren Anteil der "costs of caring", weil sie sich in stärkerem Maße als Männer auch dann betroffen und verantwortlich fühlen, wenn krisenhafte Ereignisse Personen treffen, die nicht zu den engsten Vertrauten oder Familienangehörigen zählen (vgl. KESSLER, MCLEOD & WETHINGTON 1985).

Die Einseitigkeit sozialer Unterstützung, die vielfach zu Lasten der Gesundheit von Frauen geht, zeigt sich auch darin, dass Männer von der sozialen Einbindung in Ehe und Partnerschaft gesundheitlich profitieren, Frauen hingegen eher zusätzlich belastet werden: MARACEK & BALLOU (1981) kommen in ihren Studien zu dem Ergebnis, dass bei Ehemännern eine höhere psychische Gesundheit und geringere Selbstmordraten zu verzeichnen sind als bei alleinlebenden Männern oder verheirateten Frauen. Gegenüber unverheirateten Frauen scheinen verheiratete Frauen in bezug auf ihr Gesundheitsbefinden sogar benachteiligt zu sein. Verheiratete Frauen mit kleinen Kindern oder kranken Angehörigen scheinen besonders für psychische Störungen und Depressionen anfällig zu sein (BROWN, BHROLCHAIN & HARRIS 1975; PEARLIN & JOHNSON 1977).

Fazit und Ausblick
Ein Blick auf die Rolle der Frau in der alltäglichen Gesundheitsselbsthilfe verdeutlicht neben positiven Aspekten auch die Schattenseiten des Helfens und die Gefahr negativer Auswirkungen auf die Gesundheit von Frauen. Besonders brisant wird die Thematik angesichts zeitgeschichtlicher Veränderungen in westlichen Industriegesellschaften. Wir können in diesem Kontext nur auf einige gravierende Auswirkungen aufmerksam machen, die uns besonders relevant erscheinen. Dazu zählen u.a. familiäre und gesundheitspolitische Veränderungen, die sich auf die traditionellen Aufgaben und Verantwortungsbereiche der Familie auswirken und Einfluss speziell auf die Rollenausübung von Frauen in der Gesundheitsselbsthilfe haben: Neben einer erhöhten Lebenserwartung in westlichen Industriestaaten ist eine Zunahme der Häufigkeit chronischer körperlicher und psychischer Erkrankungen und Pflegebedürftigkeit zu verzeichnen (v. FERBER 1989; WALLER 1996). Die Zunahme dieser Belastungen geht mit der Abnahme der Dichte und Belastbarkeit primärer Netzwerke einher, u.a. durch die Veränderung der Haushaltsgröße zu mehr Einfamilien-Haushalten, den Anstieg der Scheidungsraten und die Zunahme der Berufstätigkeit von Frauen. Durch Familienarbeit und Berufstätigkeit entstehen multiple Rollenbelastungen, die sich nachteilig auf die Gesundheit von Fauen auswirken können (zum Thema ‚Doppelbelastung durch Beruf und Pflege' liegen allerdings widersprüchliche empirische Ergebnisse vor; vgl. dazu DALLINGER 1996). Parallel zu diesen Entwicklungen wirkt sich in Deutschland derzeit der Abbau sozialer Leistungen im Gesundheitssektor erschwerend auf die Versorgung und Pflege kranker Menschen aus. Diese Veränderungen machen vor allem eines deutlich: Die Erfüllung der Aufgaben in der Gesundheitselbsthilfe, die Frauen in westlichen Gesellschaften traditionell übernommen haben, wird zunehmend erschwert. Gleichzeitig gewinnt die Gesundheitsselbsthilfe angesichts sozialpolitischer und epidemiologischer Veränderungen an besonderer Bedeutung. Dies gilt gleichermaßen für andere westliche Staaten:

> *Changing patterns of family life, ageing populations, the increasing participation of women in paid employment and economic recession have, along with other factors, highlighted a key question for many countries today: who will care for dependent members of the society? The assumption that women will care, on an unpaid and often unrecognized basis, can no longer be taken for granted* (CLULOW 1995: 63).

Diese Entwicklungen verdeutlichen die Notwendigkeit, gesundheitspolitische Maßnahmen zu etablieren, die stärker auf die Gesundheitsförderung von Frauen ausgerichtet sind. Zu denken wäre hierbei z.B. an die Errichtung bzw. Ausweitung professioneller Stützsysteme für Frauen in Belastungssituationen. In den letzten Jahren wurde in Deutschland vermehrt die Forderung nach frauenspezifischer Gesundheitsförderung erhoben, die auf der Basis eines neuen, sozialen Krankheits- und Gesundheitsverständnisses Zusammenhänge zwischen krankheitsverursachenden Lebensbedingungen und psychosomatischen Verarbeitungsformen berücksichtigt (z. B. STAHR, JUNG & SCHULZ 1991). Für Frauen stellt sich vor allem die Aufgabe, ihre Helferrolle neu zu überdenken, Grenzen eigener Handlungsfähigkeit zu erkennen und ihren Anspruch auf Gesundheit und Wohlbefinden stärker durchzusetzen. Eine Vernachlässigung dieser Problematik birgt sonst für die betroffenen Frauen die Gefahr, dass ihre Suche nach Lösungen, die heutzutage aus den Konflikten der weiblichen Helferrolle resultieren, zwangsläufig in Krankheit enden.

References

ALFERMANN, D. 1996. *Geschlechterrolle und geschlechtstypisches Verhalten.* Stuttgart.
ARIES, E. 1987. Gender and communication. in *Review of Personality and Social Psychology,* Vol. 7, Sex and Gender. Edited by P. SHAVER and C. HENDRICK, pp. 149-176. Sage Publications Newbury Park.
BELLE, D. 1982. The stress of caring: Women as providers of social support. in *Handbook of stress.* Edited by L. GOLDBERGER and S. BREZNITZ, pp. 496-505. New York.
   deutsch: dies. 1990: Der Stress des Versorgens: Frauen als Spenderinnen sozialer Unterstützung. In: *Ist geben seliger als Nehmen? Frauen und social support.* Edited by C. SCHMERL and F. NESTMANN, pp.36-52. Frankfurt/M.
BENENSON, J. F. 1990. Gender differences in social networks. in *Journal of Early Adolescense,* 10: 472-495.
BIRKEL, R. and N. REPPUCCI. 1983. Social networks, information-seeking, and utilization of services. *American Journal of Community Psychology,* 11: 185-205.
BÖHM, N. 1987. Frauen - das kranke Geschlecht? Zur Epidemiologie psychischer Erkrankungen bei Frauen. in *Weibliche Beziehungsmuster, Psychologie und Therapie von Frauen.* Edited by B. ROMMELSBACHER, pp. 71-101. Campus Verlag Frankfurt a. M.
BROWN, G. W., M. BHROLHAIN, and T. HARRIS. 1975. Social class and psychiatric disturbance among women in an urban population. *Sociology,* 9: 225-254.
BUTLER, T., S. GIORDANO, and S. NEREN. 1985. Gender and sex role attributes as predictors of utilization of natural support systems during personal stress events. *Sex Roles,* 13: 515-524.
CARTER, C.O and J. PEEL. 1976. *Equalities and inequalities in health.* New York.
CLULOW, Ch. 1995. Who cares? Implications for caring responsibilities for couples and families. *Sexual and Marital Therapy,* 10: 63-68.
DALLINGER, U. 1996. Pflege und Beruf - ein neuer Vereinbarungskonflikt in der späten Familienphase. *Zeitschrift für Familienforschung,* 8: 6-42.
DEAN, K. 1986. Lay care in illness. *Social Science and Medicine,* 22: 275-284.
EISENBERG, N. and R. LENNON. 1983. Sex differences in empathy and related capacities. *Psychological Bulletin,* 94: 100-131.
FINLEY, N. 1989. Theories of family labor as applied to gender differences in caregiving for elderly parents. *Journal of Marriage and the Family,* 51: 79-86.
FISCHER, A. 1993. Sex differences in emotionality: Fact or stereotype? *Feminism and Psychology,* 3: 303-318.
FISCHER, J., D. SOLLIE and K. MORROW. 1986. Social networks in male and female adolescents. *Journal of Adolescent Research,* 6: 1-14.
FRANKE, A. 1991. Die Gesundheitsversorgung als krankmachender Faktor. in FRAUENGESUNDHEITSBILDUNG: GRUNDLAGEN UND KONZEPTE. Edited by I. STAHR, S. JUNGK, and E. SCHULZ, pp. 36-42. Juventa Weinheim.
GRAHAM, H. 1985. Providers, negotiators, and mediators: Women as the hidden carers. In *Women, health, and healing.* Edited by E. LEWIN and V. OLESEN, pp. 25-52. Tavistock New York.
GRUNOW, D., K. BREITKOPF, H.-J. DAHME, R. ENGFER, V. GRUNOW-LUTTER and W. PAULUS. 1983. *Gesundheitsselbsthilfe im Alltag.* Stuttgart.
HARTMAN, H. 1981. The family as the locus of gender, class, and political struggle: The example of housework. *Signs,* 6: 366-394.
KAHN, R. L. and T. L. ANTONUCCI. 1980. Convoys of social support: A life course approach. in *Aging.* Edited by I. B. KIESLER, J. N. MORGAN, and V. K. OPPENHEIMER, pp. 383-405. Academic Press New York.
KESSLER, R. C., J. D. MCLEOD, and E. WETHINGTON. 1985. The costs of caring: A perspective on the relationship between sex and psychological distress. in *Social support: Theory, research and applications.* Edited by I. G. SARASON and B. R. SARASON, pp. 491-506. Martinus Nijhoff Dordrecht.
KRAUSE-GIRTH, C. 1989. Frauen, Medizin und Gesundheit. in *Frankfurter Beiträge zur psychosozialen Medizin,* Bd. 1. Edited by J. JORDAN and C. KRAUSE-GIRTH, pp. 86-104. Frankfurt.
MATTHEWS, S. and T. ROSNER. 1988. Shared filial responsibility and the family as the primary caregiver. *Journal of Marriage and the Family,* 50: 185-195.
MARACEK, J. and D. BALLOU. 1981. Family roles and women's mental health. *Professional Psychology,* 12: 39-46.
MAYR-KLEFFEL, V. 1991. *Frauen und ihre sozialen Netzwerke. Auf der Suche nach einer verlorenen Ressource.* Opladen.
MECHANIC, D. and P. D. CLEARY. 1980. Factors associated with the maintenance of positive health behaviour. *Preventive Medicine,* 9: 805-814.
MECHANIC, D. 1986. *From advocacy to allocation.* New York.

NESTMANN, F. and C. SCHMERL. 1991. The lady is not for burning - The gender paradox in prevention and social support. in *Social prevention and the social sciences*. Edited by G. ALBRECHT and H.-U. OTTO, pp. 217 - 234. Wiley New York.

NESTMANN, F. and C. SCHMERL. 1992. Wer hilft im Alltag? *Gruppendynamik*, 2: 161-179.

NORCROSS, W. A., C. RAMIREZ, and L. A. PALINKAS. 1996. The influence of women on the health care-seeking behavior of men. *Journal of Family Practices*, 43: 475-480.

PEARLIN, L. and L. JOHNSON. 1977. Marital status, life strains, and depression. *American Sociological Review*, 42: 704-715.

RÖHRLE, B. 1994. *Soziale Netzwerke und soziale Unterstützung*. Weinheim.

SCHEIBLER, P. 1995. Geschlechtsspezifische Sozialisation. In *Handbuch des Kinder- und Jugendschutzes*. Edited by G. BIENEMANN, B. W. NIKLES, M. HASENBRINK, and H.-W. CARLHOFF, pp. 41-45. Votum Münster.

SCHMERL, C. and F. NESTMANN. 1990. *Ist Geben seliger als Nehmen? Frauen und Social Support*. Frankfurt/M.

SHIELDS, S. A. 1987. Women, men, and the dilemma of emotion. in *Review of Personality and Social Psychology*, Vol. 7. Sex and gender. Edited by P. SHAVER and K. HENDRICK, pp. 229-251. Sage Publications New York.

SOLDO, B. and J. MYLLYLUOMA. 1983. Caregivers who live with dependent elderly. *The Gerontologist*, 23: 605-611.

SCHRÖPPEL, H. 1991. *Von wegen Rabentöchter! Der Pflegenotstand in Familien mit verwirrten alten Menschen*. Friedberg.

STAHR, I., S. JUNGK, and E. SCHULZ. 1991. *Frauengesundheitsbildung - Grundlagen und Konzepte*. Weinheim.

STOller, E. P. 1993. Gender and the organization of lay health care: A socialist-feminist perspective. *Journal of Aging Studies*, 7: 151-170.

UMBERSON, D. 1987. Family status and health behaviors: Social control as a dimension of social integration. *Journal of Health and Social Behavior*, 28: 306-319.

VOGT, I. 1993. Psychologische Grundlagen der Gesundheitswissenschaften. in *Gesundheitswissenschaften*. Edited by K. HURRELMANN and U. LAASER, pp. 46-62. Beltz Verlag Weinheim.

VOGT, I. 1985. *Für alle Leiden gibt es eine Pille. Über Psychopharmakakonsum und das geschlechtsrollenspezifische Gesundheitskonzept bei Frauen und Mädchen*. Opladen.

VOGT, I. 1983. Frauen als Objekte der Medizin. Das Frauensyndrom. *Leviathan*, 11: 161-199.

VON FERBER, C. 1989. Hilfebedürftigkeit im Niemandsland: Überforderung primär-sozialer Hilfen - ‚Selbstbeschränkung' professioneller Gesundheitshilfen. in *Kommunale Gesundheitsförderung. Aktuelle Entwicklungen, Konzepte, Perspektiven*. Edited by A. LABISCH, pp. 61-68. Deutsche Zentrale für Volksgesundheitspflege Frankfurt a.M.

WALLER, H. 1996. *Gesundheitswissenschaft*. Stuttgart.

ZOLA, I. K. 1983. *Socio-medical inquiries*. Philadelphia.

Übergänge im Frauenleben - Medikalisierung und Stigmatisierung durch die westliche Medizin
Rites of Passages in Female Sexuality: Medicalization and Stigmazitation in Western Medicine

Eva Schindele

Zusammenfassung: Frauen leben in Monats- und Lebenszyklen. Vor allem Pubertät, Schwangerschaft und Wechseljahre sind solche Lebensübergänge, in denen ungewohnte Bewegung ins Leben der Mädchen und Frauen kommt. Diese Zeiten brauchen besonderen Schutz, aber auch Begleitung und Ermutigung. In traditionellen Kulturen gibt es eine Vielzahl von Ritualen, die Frauen helfen, den neuen Lebensabschnitt zu integrieren. Bei uns dient der Gang zu Frauenärztin oder - arzt als Ersatz für fehlende komplexe Rituale. GynäkologInnen gelten in unserer Kultur als die ExpertInnen für Weiblichkeit. Innerhalb der letzten 20 Jahre hat sich die Gynäkologie immer mehr der gesunden Frau bemächtigt. Vor allem durch die Bewertung der Lebensübergänge als riskante, fast krankhafte Zustände ist es gelungen, die Frauen an sich sich zu binden. Beispiele aus Pubertät, Schwangerschaft, und Wechseljahre zeigen, wie die medizinische Lesart die Selbstwahrnehmung der Frauen prägt.

Abstract: In traditional cultures, a complex series of communal rituals mark a woman's entry into puberty, pregnancy, and menopause. In modern culture, however, the increasing medicalization of female sexuality, particularly in the last twenty years, has meant that regular visits to the gynecologist's office now replace the function of communal rites of sexual passage. But rather than recognizing women's sexuality as a healthy part of the collective life of the community, the culture of medical gynecology interprets women's sexuality according to a model of illness, offering women little encouragement or support during the critical phases of their sexual lives. Moreover, the increasingly medicalized view of female sexuality has bound women more tightly to a medical system that offers interventions that contribute to negative self-images for women, and detract from their physical and psychological health.

Keywords: Medikalisierung von Schwangerschaft, Pubertät, Wechseljahre, moderne Übergangsrituale, Frauenärzte als Experten, Einfluss auf weibliche Selbstwahrnehmung, medicalisation of puberty, pregnancy, menopause, negative female self-images

Frauen leben in Monats- und Lebenszyklen. Pubertät, Schwangerschaft und Wechseljahre sind solche Umstellungszeiten, die mit körperlichen Attraktionen verbunden sind: So fängt das Mädchen an, aus der Scheide zu bluten und ihre Brust wächst, die Frau, die zur Mutter wird, bekommt einen dicken Bauch, ihre Brüste spannen. Die älter werdende Frau verliert langsam wieder ihre Blutungen, sie entwickelt vielleicht Hitze und ihre Schleimhäute werden trockener. Das, was sich auf der körperlichen Ebene so offensichtlich vollzieht, hat eine seelisch-geistige Entsprechung, aber auch eine soziale Komponente. Die Frau wird Mitglied einer anderen sozialen Gruppe und die gesellschaftlichen Erwartungen an sie verändern sich. Ungewohnte Bewegung kommt so ins Leben der Mädchen oder Frauen. Viele Frauen fühlen sich in diesen Übergangszeiten verunsichert, denn sie spüren, dass eine Phase des Lebens zu Ende geht und die zukünftige noch nicht greifbar ist. Manche Frauen sind erschrocken über ihre körperlich-seelischen Veränderungen und sie sind oft verletzbarer, aber auch sensibler als sonst.

Vor allem vorindustrielle Kulturen kennen für diese Übergangszeiten im Leben der Frau bestimmte Rituale, die diese Phasen begleiten. Rituale sind in diesem kulturellen Kontext meist komplexe Systeme, die religiöse, ethische und soziale Regeln der jeweiligen Gesellschaft integrieren. Sie werden vom Kollektiv als verbindlich anerkannt und helfen der einzelnen Frau, die psychische Umstellung zu vollziehen. Zumindest "im Idealfall", so die Ethnopsychoanalytikerin Maya Nadig, "nehmen Rituale auch Rücksicht auf die individuellen Bedürfnisse und Nöte ihrer Mitglieder, indem sie ihnen die zur Erhaltung der psychischen Integrität notwendigen Schutz- und Abwehrmechanismen zur Verfügung stellen." (NADIG 1994). Oft erstreckt sich der Vollzug von Ritualen über längere Zeiträume, die sich in drei Phasen gliedern lassen: der alte Zustand wird durch "Trennungsrituale" verabschiedet, den Höhepunkt des Übergangs leiten "Schwellen- oder Umwandlungsrituale" ein und in der letzten Phase helfen "Angliederungsrituale", den neuen Zustand zu akzeptieren. Dabei spielen Vermittler wie Medizinmänner, Hebammen oder Schamanen eine wichtige Rolle. Sie fungieren als ÜbergangsmentorInnen und sind gleichzeitig Verbindungsglied zwischen der Gemeinschaft und dem Einzelnen. Sie ermöglichen so die Veränderungen zu er(leben), *ohne dass es zu so heftigen sozialen oder individuellen Erschütterungen kommt, dass der "Fluß des Lebens stillsteht."* (GENNEP 1986). Die Rituale haben also integrative Funktionen. Sie sollen sowohl den neuen Zu- oder Umstand in die Persönlichkeit integrieren, als auch die Statusveränderung von der einen in eine andere soziale Gruppe vollziehen helfen.

Diese Funktionen von Ritualen in vorindustriellen Gesellschaften im Hinterkopf, drängt sich die Frage auf, wie in unserer Gesellschaft die weiblichen Übergangsphasen wahrgenommen und gestaltet werden, welche kulturellen Hilfsangebote den Frauen zur Verfügung stehen, wie diese die weibliche Selbstwahrnehmung prägen und welcher individuelle Gestaltungsspielraum den Frauen dabei bleibt?

In unserer Kultur hat sich in den letzten 20 Jahren ein bestimmter Umgang mit weiblichen Lebensübergängen eingebürgert: das Ritual, in diesen Zeiten der Veränderung einen Arzt - in der Regel eine(n) GynäkologIn - mehr oder minder regelmäßig aufzusuchen. Dabei übernimmt der Frauenarztärztin oft die Rolle der ÜbergangsmentorIn (HENZE 1995). Denn sie sind es, die in unserer Kultur als die ExpertInnen für weibliche Übergangsphasen gelten. Dabei hat er (oder sie) sich seine Qualifikation für diese Aufgabe nicht durch eigene körperliche -lebensgeschichtliche Erfahrungen (wie z.B. eine Geburt oder die Wechseljahre) erworben, sondern durch ein naturwissenschaftlich-technische Ausbildung, die auf der Grundlage statistischer Durchschnittswerte bestimmte medizinische Normen festschreibt, unabhängig von der einzelnen Persönlichkeit der Frau (SCHINDELE 1993).

Gleichzeitig hat sich ein medizinischer Blick auf die weiblichen Lebenübergänge durchgesetzt. Sie werden als körperliches Geschehen definiert, das die Medizin verspricht im Griff zu behalten. Ein „privater„ *Mädchen- oder Mutterpass, ausgegeben vom Frauenarzt, dokumentieren diese Übergangsphasen.* Ihre Bedeutung im weiblichen Lebenslauf wird ebenso ausgeblendet wie die kollektive und geistig-spirituelle Dimension. Anders als in vorindustriellen Gesellschaften in denen die Statusveränderung des einzelnen Mitgliedes begleitet und kollektiv verarbeitet wird, hat das moderne Ritual, einen Frauenarzt oder - ärztin aufzusuchen, den Charakter der Individualisierung und Vereinzelung. Im Mittelpunkt tritt die scheinbar hilfsbedürftige Patientin einem oft männlichen Vertreter einer machtvollen Profession gegenüber, der vorgibt zu wissen, wo es lang geht. So ist es gelungen, gesunde weibliche Lebensereignisse in Krankheiten oder zumindest in höchst riskante Lebensereignisse umzudeuten, die dringend der Beaufsichtigung und Behandlung durch den Gynäkologen bedürfen.

So sucht die GynäkologIn nach der Abweichung, dem Pathologischem und dem noch-normalen Befund, der aber oft schon vorsichtshalber bereits im Vorfeld als krankheitsverdächtig eingestuft wird - um ihn „unter Kontrolle zu halten„ . In diesem Kontext proflierte sich die Gynäkologie immer mehr als Managerin weiblicher Übergangsphasen. Vor allem durch die Einführung des Risikobegriffes in die Gynäkologie ist es gelungen, die Frauen an sich zu binden. Denn wen schüchtert die Vielzahl von Risiken, der angeblich wir Frauen schon allein durch unsere Geschlechtlichkeit ausgesetzt sind, nicht ein? Dabei sind ja Risiken nichts weiter als Wahrscheinlichkeitsberechnungen für ein Ereignis, das eintreten kann, oder auch nicht. Die Gynäkologie bietet an, diese statistischen Risiken nun durch ständige Überwachung bei der individuellen Frau zu bändigen, nicht selten, ohne dass mit wissenschaftlichen Studien wirklich belegt wäre, dass diese oder jene medizinische Maßnahme auch wirklich sinnvoll ist.

Was bedeutet das für Frauen?
Sich ständig der eigenen Intaktheit versichern zu müssen, verunsichert und es verstärkt das Gefühl, fremd zu sein in der eigenen Haut. Es unterstützt die ohnehin schon vorhandene Tendenz bei Frauen, sich von außen betrachten und beurteilen zu lassen. Eine Neigung, die in einer Phase, in der körperliche und psycho-soziale Umstellungen die Frau erfassen, tendenziell noch zunimmt. Frauen suchen Ermutigung, *Hilfe und Halt beim Gynäkologen. Doch was sie im Regelfall bekommen, sind vor allem medizi*nische Interpretationen der eigenen Befindlichkeit und Erklärungen für unbekannte oder überraschend erlebte körperliche und seelische Phänomene. Dies strukturiert die eigene Selbstwahrnehmung im Sinne der medizinischen Weltsicht. Auf diesem Hintergrund haben es Frauen schwer, ein Gefühl für sich selbst in ihrer gerade spezifischen psycho-sozialen Situation zu entwickeln. Damit wird das Angebot der Medizin, die Unberechenbarkeit des eigenen Körpers zu bändigen, umso attraktiver.

Pubertät

Bereits junge Mädchen lernen inzwischen, dass zum Erwachsenwerden der Gang zu Frauenarzt oder -ärztin gehört. Häufig sind es die Mütter die ihre pubertierenden Töchter zum Frauenarzt mitnehmen, eine Fürsorglichkeit, bei der die Frage erlaubt sein muss, inwieweit sie damit sich selbst die Töchter mit ihrem aufkommenden sexuellen Begehren vom Leib halten wollen, in dem sie den Fachmann dazwischenschalten. Außerdem gibt es mittlerweile eine regelrechte Kampagne, gesponsert vor allem von Pillenherstellern und unterstützt von den Standesorganisationen der Gynäkologen, die den heranwachsenden Mädchen den Gang zum Frauenarzt schmackhaft machen soll. Aus einem solchen Ratgeber für Mädchen: "Irgendwann kommt für dich der Zeitpunkt, wo Du zum Frauenarzt gehen solltest. Dein Körper zeigt es Dir. Du wirst etwachsen. Man sieht es dir deutlich an, dass aus dir eine Frau wird."

Mädchen beschreiben zum Teil ihre Erfahrungen bei Frauenärztin oder - arzt wie einen Intitiationsritus, eine Einführung in eine Kultur, in der ihre Weiblichkeit von Fach-Männern (und auch Frauen) definiert und geprüft wird. Sie lernen, dass sie zukünftig ihre Normalität von Experten- und Expertin regelmäßig bestätigen lassen müssen. Dabei stehen nicht nur ihre Sexualorgane zur Disposition, sondern ihr Selbstbild als Frau mit den verschiedenen Rollen, die sie in dieser Gesellschaft inne hat: z.B. als Frau, Geliebte, Mutter.

Nach der organmedizinischen Untersuchung beim Frauenarzt entwickeln manche Mädchen mitunter plötzlich andere, auch deformierte Bilder von ihrem Körperinneren. Viele beschreiben die Untersuchung als unangenehm, angstvoll und zudringlich (RAFFAUF 1990). (Später stellt sich übrigens deutlich ein Gewöhnungseffekt ein) Dabei wird von ihnen erwartet, dass sie ihre Schamgefühle, die auch Wächter der eigenen Intimität sind, überwinden. Schließlich passe Scham nicht zum selbstbewussten "Girlie." In einer poppig aufgemachten Broschüre namens "Gynnie", die mit den "Schauermärchen vom Frauenarzt" aufräumen will und in allen österreichischen Schulen an Mädchen ab 12 kostenlos verteilt wird, sagt dann auch eine kesse 15 jährige: "Ich gehe lieber fünf mal zum Frauenarzt als einmal zum Zahnarzt." Solche Erfahrungen prägen das Selbstverständnis und die Selbstachtung der Mädchen. Mit Eintritt in ihre körperlich fruchtbare Phase der Weiblichkeit, wird ihnen der Besuch beim Frauenarzt wohlwollend als "Service" für den Körper nahegebracht. "Gynnie" schreibt: "Bei der jährlichen Generalüberholung kann der Frauenarzt Erkrankungen an den inneren oder äußeren Geschlechtsorganen erkennen und behandeln." Gleichzeitig implizit die Drohung an die Mädchen: Wenn Du Dich nicht überprüfen lässt, könntest Du möglicherweise keine Kinder oder auch Krebs bekommen. Die weiblichen Sexualorgane als tickende Zeitbombe, die angeblich die Integrität der Frau bedrohen könnte, wovor sie der Gynäkologe schützt. Dem Mädchen wird dadurch schon früh vermittelt, dass ihre Geschlechtlichkeit kontrollbedürftig ist und ihre Geschlechtsorgane besonders krankheitsanfällig sind. So werden Mädchen wenig motiviert, die eigenen körperlichen Impulse wahrzunehmen oder gar ihnen zu trauen. Ihr Körper (und ihre Sexualität) wird zur Sache des Fachmanns(oder der Fachfrau) Hier wird die Basis für die abhängige Patientin gelegt, die ihr Leben lang regelmäßig den Gynäkologen aufsucht, um sich bestätigen zu lassen, dass sie gesund oder in "Ordnung" ist.

Schwangerschaft

Eine Vorbemerkung: Wie keine andere weibliche Lebensphase wurde Schwangerschaft und Geburt in den letzten Jahren medikalisisiert. Die "anderen Umstände" sind zu einem riskanten, wenn nicht gar krankhaften Ereignis umgedeutet worden, das der permanenten Überwachung durch den Gynäkologen bedarf. Die Schwangerenvorsorge wurde zu einem Check-up der Schwangeren und des Fotus ausgebaut. Die Zahl der medizinischen Untersuchungen hat sich in den letzten 15 Jahren verfünffacht, die Zahl der Frauen, die als Risikoschwangere eingestuft werden, ist gleichzeitig drastisch gestiegen, ebenso die Rate der Kaiserschnitte (1995:17,5%) (COLLATZ 1993). Gerechtfertigt wird diese "Hochrüstung" mit den angeblich guten Ergebnissen in der perinatalen Sterblichkeit. Zwar ist die perinatale Sterblichkeit zurückgegangen, gleichzeitig ist aber z.B. die Anzahl der zu Frühgeborenen drastisch gestiegen. Laut bayerischer Perinatalaerhebung von 1982 - 1992 um 50% (THIEME 1992. Außerdem klagen viele Frauen nach dem ersten Kind über einen Baby-Schock und die Anzahl der Trennungen ist in den ersten Jahren nach der Geburt des 1. bzw. 2. Kindes auffallend hoch.

Der kulturelle Blick auf die Schwangerschaft hat sich in den vergangenen zwei Jahrzehnten drastisch verändert (SCHINDELE 1995). Der Gynäkologe Erich Saling, der die Geburtshilfe in Deutschland nach dem Krieg wesentlich mitgeprägt hat, freut sich 1989: "Der intra-uterine Raum ist seit Ende der

60er Jahre auf damals unvorstellbare Weise erobert worden" (SALING 1989). Durch die Möglichkeiten ein Bild des Ungeborenen auf einen Monitor zu projizieren hat sich die An-Sicht von Schwangerschaft revolutionär verändert (DUDEN 1991). Aus einem kraftvollen weiblichen Leib wurde ein nackter Embryo, von dem sich die Medizin berufen fühlt, ihn (mitunter sogar vor der Mutter) zu beschützen. So interessiert sich heute die Gynäkologie weniger für die Beziehung zwischen schwangerer Frau und ihrem Kind im Leib, sondern das Kind als "Produkt" steht im Mittelpunkt der Aufmerksamkeit.

Gleichzeitig werden FrauenärztInnen in unserer Kultur als *die* Instanz anerkannt, die Macht hat, für ein gesundes, möglichst vielleicht sogar für ein perfektes "Baby" zu sorgen. Und die Gynäkologie als medizinisches Fach tut alles, um diesen "Mythos der Machbarkeit" aufrechtzuerhalten und so die Patientin an sich zu binden. Natürlich gelänge das nicht, wenn sich Frauen (und Paare) an dieser Konstruktion nicht beteiligen würden: Während die eine Seite immer mehr technisches Gerät auffährt, um den lebendigen Prozess zu kontrollieren, muss die andere Seite sich als Lieferantin von Labordaten, Bildern und Kardiogrammen zur Verfügung stellen. Stillschweigend wird dabei von beiden Seiten davon ausgegangen, dass bereits die Überwachung der körperlichen Parameter einen positiven Verlauf der Schwangerschaft und Geburt garantiert. Dies hat den Charakter eines Beschwörungsrituals: Das Kind wird gesund, *weil* die Frau zum Arzt geht oder anders ausgedrückt: Der Ultraschall wird gemacht, nicht um zu schauen, *ob* alles in Ordnung ist, sondern *damit* alles in Ordnung ist (ENSEL 1994).

Immer mehr Informationen über das "Ungewisse", vor allem über den Zustand des Föten, werden mit Hilfe immer neuer diagnostischer Methoden erhoben. All dies wird, selbst von psycho-somatisch orientierten Ärzten, als eine Möglichkeit angeboten, den Frauen Ängste zu nehmen (STAUBER 1995). Schließlich passt diese Info-anhäufung in unser Zeitalter, in der die Information zu einem Wert an sich wurde, ohne dass die Konsequenzen der Informationen zum Thema gemacht würden. Auf die Schwangerschaft bezogen heißt das, dass zwar die Diagnostik boomt, doch die Möglichkeiten der Therapie eher gering sind, so dass sich die so oft beschworene Machbarkeit des gesunden Nachwuchses häufig in der Beseitigung des nicht in die medizinisch-definierte Norm passenden Fötus erschöpft.

Unter diesem Vorzeichen der Machbarkeit von gesundem Nachwuchs konnte sich die vorgeburtliche Auslese in den letzten 15 Jahren als Standard der Schwangerenvorsorge immer mehr etablieren - und zwar weitgehend unbemerkt von der Öffentlichkeit. Die neun Monate der Schwangerschaft gerieten parallel dazu immer mehr unter Produktivitäts- und Rationalisierungsdruck - ein Trend, der in unsere Zeit passt. Maßstäbe der Warenproduktion werden auf natürliche Lebensprozesse ausgeweitet und setzen sie unter das Diktat der Rationalität. Dies bekommen vor allem schwangere Frauen zu spüren, die (in Grenzen) diesen Prozess gestalten können und gleichzeitig symbiotisch mit diesem Wachstumsprozess verbunden sind. Sie - so die gesellschaftliche Erwartung und auch oft die Haltung, die Frauen sich selbst abverlangen - sollen handeln wie der „homo oeconomicus„ - kühl, vernunftbetont und berechnend. Nicht wenige Frauen fühlen sich hin- und hergerissen zwischen ihrem Gefühl zu dem in ihnen heranwachsenden Kind und dem, was gesellschaftlich als vernünftig gilt. Dieser Konflikt kann zu schwerwiegenden oft unbewussten Konflikten führen, die sich dann in körperlichen Problemen niederschlagen. Die „gute Hoffnung„ ist in den letzten Jahren immer mehr von einem medizinischen Risikoblick verdrängt worden. Frauen gehen, heute mehr denn je, nicht mehr mit einem Kind sondern mit dem Risiko schwanger. Dieses Bewusstsein prägt die neun Monate einer Schwangerschaft und prägt auch die Wahrnehmung dieses Prozesses. Viele schwangere Frauen haben inzwischen weitgehend die Bilder und Definitionen der Medizin übernommen. In diesem permanenten Prozess des Sich-Versichern-Müssens übersehen viele Frauen, dass nicht sie, sondern die Dynamik der Technik (der übrigens auch der Arzt unterworfen ist) den Ablauf der Schwangerschaft bestimmt. Zwischen die schwangere Frau und ihr Kind im Leib drängt sich die Technologie und bestimmt mehr und mehr die Gefühle, die die Frau zu ihrem Kind im Leib entwickelt. Dies ist ein subtiler Prozess, den viele Frauen oft selbst garnicht realisieren. Erste wissenschaftliche Untersuchungen deuten daraufhin, dass durch diese Form des Schwangerencheck-ups Frauen häufig nicht weniger, sondern mehr Ängste entwickeln. Zunehmend fühlen sich Frauen in ihrem wachsenden Leib fremd und können den Takt ihrer eigenen inneren Uhr nicht mehr wahrnehmen. Es gelingt ihnen nicht, die seelischen und körperlichen Veränderungen in diesen Zeiten des Übergangs in ihr Selbstbild zu integrieren. Immer mehr Frauen verirren sich im Gestrüpp von angeblichen Risiken, Komplikationen und medizinischen Untersuchungen. Auch wenn Frauen versuchen, sich von diesem Risikoblick zu distanzieren, so sind sie doch in ihn verwickelt und ständig gezwungen sich innerlich von dem kulturellen Ansinnen, aus Schwangerschaft und Geburt einen möglichst fehlerfrei ablaufenden Produktionsprozess zu machen, oder besser gesagt machen zu lassen, zu distanzieren. FrauenärztInnen erheben in unserer Kultur den Anspruch, den Prozess des Schwangergehens und des Gebärens zu gestalten. Dabei treten sie sogar in Konkurrenz zum Partner. "Idealerweise haben heutige Schwangere nicht nur einen Partner, sondern mindestens zwei: den Vater des Kindes und ihren Arzt bzw. ihre Ärztin,"(VORSORGE INITIATIVE 1993) heißt es in einer Broschüre die Aktion Sorgenkind mit dem Berufsverband der Frauenärzte herausgegeben hat. Anders als es die Werbekampagne verspricht, versagen Ärzte gerade in der Rolle des gleichberechtigten Partners. Untersuchungen zeigen, dass sich Frauen eher bevormundet, kontrolliert und durchgecheckt fühlen, als unterstützt und begleitet. Und die FrauenärztInnen selbst schätzen die psycho-soziale Begleitung der Frauen als nebensächlich, als „eine Banalität„ ein (BERLINER FORSCHUNGSVERBUND PUBLIC HEALTH 1996). Dabei ist es nicht das supertolle Ultraschallgerät, was Frauen einfordern, sondern sie beurteilen die Qualität der Vorsorge in Abhängigkeit von der Beziehung und dem Vertrauensverhältnis, dass sie zum GynäkologIn aufbauen konnten (SCHÜCKING 1994). Dabei wünschen sie sich vor allem eine kontinuierliche Begleitung, die sich nicht nur auf die Zeit der Schwangerschaft, sondern auch auf Geburt und Wochenbett erstreckt. Doch statt die vorhandenen Kompetenzen der Frauen und die Ressourcen der Familien zu fördern, übernehmen Mediziner die Regie im Prozess des Elternwerdens und beanspruchen mit ihrer naturwissenschaftlichen Interpretation viel Raum im Beziehungsgefüge, in dass das Kind einmal hineingeboren werden wird. Dabei wird verkannt, dass der Familien- und Freundeskreis für die Interaktion mit dem Kind auf Dauer von unvergleichlich größerer Bedeutung als das Medizinsystem ist." (GEIBEL-NEUBERGER 1995)

Wechseljahre
Wie sich Mädchen in der Pubertät von der Kinderrolle verabschieden müssen, so erleben Frauen in späteren Jahren das Verschwinden ihrer körperlichen Fruchtbarkeit. Wechseljahre sind eine Zeit des Abschiednehmens und der Neuorientierung, die alle Frauen mehr oder weniger trifft. Das Versiegen der Menstruation und die hormonelle Umstellung sind dabei nur die körperlichen Aspekte, das Auseinandersetzen mit dem Älterwerden, das Bilanzziehen und die Frage, auf welchen Fundamenten das eigene Leben gebaut ist, bestimmen die seelisch-geistige Dimension. Für die amerikanische Feministin German Greer ist das Klimakterium eine wichtige Lebensphase, keine Zeit, durch die man hindurchhastet, die man verschweigt oder sogar abstreitet, sondern der Grundstein für einen Neubeginn (GREER 1991). Doch alle diese Facetten des Älterwerdens interessieren die Medizin wenig. Überhaupt zeigt die Gynäkologie wenig Achtung vor der älteren Frau. Ihre Gebärmutter wird als "morsch", "zersetzt", "schwerverknorpelt" oder als "überflüssig" bezeichnet. Damit wird der Frau vermittelt, dass ihre Sexualorgane und letzten Endes sie selbst nicht mehr viel wert sind. So kommt es, dass die viele Gebärmütter vor oder während der Wechseljahre ohne handfeste medizinische Indikation entfernt werden und dass jede 2. Frau in Deutschland, die älter als 50 ist, keine Gebärmutter mehr hat. Manche Mediziner in den Kliniken sprechen dann auch zynisch vom "40er-Service", denn Frauen ohne Gebärmutter können einfacher mit Hormonen substituiert werden.

Gerade dieser Lebensphase hat sich die Gynäkologie in den letzten Jahren bemächtigt. Frauen lernten neue Begriffe wie "Hormonsubstitution" und und "Osteoporose" hinter denen sich für viele das Schreckgespenst des Alterns per se verbirgt. (Auf diesen Hintergrund lässt sich der Jungbrunnen "Hormone" gut verkaufen.) Frauen lernten von Menopausenexperten, übrigens meist männlichen Geschlechts, dass die Menopause ein zur Krankheit führender Prozess sei. Der Grund: Die Frauen seien biologisch auf die heutige hohe Lebenserwartung garnicht eingerichtet (HESCH et.al. 1987). Also auch hier liegt angeblich die Krankheit im biologischen Prozess des Frauseins begründet und deshalb erklärt der Hormonexperte Rolf Dieter Hesch, die "Östrogensubstitution zu einem *Grundrecht* der Frau in unserer Gesellschaft (FOCUS 7/1993). Hinter der Forderung nach dem *Recht auf Hormonsubstitution* versteckt sich die *Drohung:* Wer nicht mitzieht, wird früher oder später an Knochenschwund oder am Herzinfarkt sterben. Die Propaganda wirkt bereits: Fast jede Frau fragt sich inzwischen, inwieweit sie gegenüber sich selbst oder ihrer Familie verantwortungslos ist, wenn sie dem natürlichen Versickern der Geschlechtshormone nicht mit dem lebenslangen Schlucken von Hormonen entgegensteuert. Viele Frauen geraten unter einem Entscheidungsdruck, der sie inzwischen mehr beschäfigt als ihre Hitzewallungen oder Schlafstörungen (RÖRING 1994). All dies verunsichert und treibt weiter in die Arme der medizinischen ExpertInnen. Dabei gelingt es nur selten, die Wechseljahre mit Hilfe der Hormone zu nivellieren. Oft sind ÄrztInnen wenig hilfreich, wenn es darum geht, Möglichkeiten der geistigen Umorientierung und des inneren Wachstums aufzuzeigen. Das Älterwerden kann nicht als Chance begriffen werden. Dabei werden Frauen heute durchschnittlich 80 Jahre alt, d.h. die Frauen sind für 1/3 ihres Lebens gefordert, Vorstellungen zu entwickeln, die dem Rollenbild der Ehefrau und Mutter nicht mehr entsprechen. Das macht Angst, vor allem in einer Kultur, in der jugendliche Attraktivität und Geschlechtsreife höchste Ideale sind und die älter werdende Frau als altes Eisen abgestempelt wird. So verwundert es nicht, dass in Kulturen, in denen Frauen nach der Menopause hochgeschätzt werden, Wechseljahrsbeschwerden unbekannt sind. Nordamerikanische Wissenschaftlerinnen fanden kürzlich heraus, dass sich, obwohl sich Knochendichte und Hormonspiegel mexikanisch-indianischer und nordamerikanischer Frauen gleichen, die indianischen Frauen trotzdem weder an Wechseljahrsbeschwerden noch an Knochenbrüchen leiden. Das legt den Schluss nahe, dass weniger die fehlenden Hormone für die Befindlichkeitsstörungen verantwortlich sind. Vielmehr ist eine körperlich - aktive Lebensart, gekoppelt mit zunehmender gesellschaftlichen Wertschätzung der Schlüssel für ein erfülltes Leben im und nach dem "Wechsel" (MARTIN 1993).

References:
BERLINER FORSCHUNGSVERBUND PUBLIC HEALTH (Hrsg). 1996. *Integration gesundheitsördernder und medizinischer Maßnahmen in der Schwangerschaft*, S.27
COLLATZ, JÜRGEN. 1993. Entspricht die derzeitige Versorgung den Betreuungs- und Beratungsbedarf schwangerer Frauen in *GFG-Rundbrief* 1
DUDEN, BARBARA. 1991. *Der Frauenleib als öffentlicher Ort. Vom Mißbrauch des Begriffs Leben*, Hamburg
ELKELES THOMAS. 1992. Die Bedeutung risikospezifischer Versorgungsangebote bei der Säuglingssterblichkeit. In: *Forum Gesundheitswissenschaften* 1, Bielefeld
ENSEL, ANGELICA. 1994. Bedeutung und Wandel des Geburtsterrritoriums, Zur Veränderung der Einstellung zu Geburt und Schwangerschaft in unserer Kultur, Aspekte aus einer medizinethnologischen Analyse. In: *Deutsche Hebammenzeitschrift* 6
GEIBEL-NEUBERGER, ULRICH. 1995. Die soziokulturelle Einbettung von sechs sich entwickelnden Elternschaften bei der Geburt des ersten Kindes in der BRD aus ethnomedizinischer Sicht. In: SCHIEFENHÖFEL, WULF et. al *Gebären - ethnomedizinische Perspektiven und neue Wege*, Berlin
GREER, GERMAINE. *Wechseljahre*. 1991. Düsseldorf
HENZE, KARL-HEINZ & STEMANN-ACHEAMPONG, SUSANNE. 1995. Medizintechnologie und ihre Folgen. In ARBEITSGEMEINSCHAFT SOZIALWISSENSCHAFTLICHE TECHNIKFORSCHUNG NIEDERSACHSEN, *Zwischenergebnisse und neue Projekte*, Göttingen
HESCH, ERNST - RUDOLF et. al. 1987. Ostrogensubstitution bei Frauen nach der Menopause. *Niedersächsisches Ärzteblatt*, 60, 17:5-10
MARTIN, MARY C. 1993. Menopause without symptoms: The endocrinology of menopause among rural Mayan Indians. *Am J Obstet Gynecol* 168:1839-45.
NADIG, MAYA. 1994. Die archaische Kunst des Übergangs - Geburtsrituale bei den Cuna, Magar und Maya. *Neue Züricher Zeitung* vom 24.12.
RAFFAUF, ELISABETH. 1990. Strategien der Frauen zu Bewältigung ihrer Ängste. In: *Gyne* 6
RÖRING, REGINA. 1994. Die Formierung eines Frauenideals für die Wechseljahre. In: *Gesundheitskult und Krankheitswirklichkeit, Jahrbuch für Kritische Medizin* 23, Berlin
SALING, ERICH. 1989. An einer Subspezialisierung führt kein Weg vorbei. In: *Deutsches Ärzteblatt* v. 8.6.
SCHINDELE, EVA. 1993. *Pfusch an der Frau, Krankmachende Normen, Überflüssige Operationen, Lukrative Geschäfte*, Hamburg
SCHINDELE, EVA.1995. *Schwangerschaft - Zwischen guter Hoffnung und medizinischem Risiko*, Hamburg
SCHÜCKING, BEATE. 1994. Schwangerschaft - (k) eine Krankheit? In: *Zeitschrift für Frauenforschung*, Bielefeld 4
STAUBER, MANFRED; FREUD, ERNEST W.; KÄSTNER R., Psychosomatische Forderungen an die moderne Geburtshilfe. In: SCHIEFENHÖFEL, WULF et. al. *Gebären - ethnomedizinische Perspektiven und neue Wege*, Berlin
THIEME, CH. 1992. Geburtshilfe in Bayern. Frühgeburt: Ergebnisse der BPE. In: Der Frauenarzt 33: 877-882, zitiert nach RAUCHFUß, MARTINA, Psychosomatische Aspekte von Schwangerschaftskomplikationen in RAUCHFUß, M. et al. (Hrsg) *Frauen in Gesundheit und Krankheit, Die neue frauenheilkundliche Perspektive*, Berlin 1996
VAN GENNEP, ARNOLD. 1986. *Übergangsriten - Les rites de passage*. Frankfurt
VORSORGE INITIATIVE (Hrsg). 1993. *Schwangerschaft heute*.

Geburt als Initiation der Frau oder wie ging es zu, dass Athene dem Zeus aus dem Kopf entsprang?
Birth as Rite of Passage for Women or how Athene came out of Zeus′ Head.

Sigrid Weiß

Zusammenfassung: Geburt ist ein Ereignis im Leben der Frau, das neben biologischen und soziokulturellen auch spirituelle Dimensionen hat. Körperliche, symbolische und spirituelle Ebenen der Geburt sollen in einen ursprünglichen, weiblichen Lebenszusammenhang gebracht werden. Das Muster der Initiation liegt in den physiologischen Notwendigkeiten der Geburt begründet, und bildet die Grundlage für das Initiationsritual, das so oft und deutlich die Geburtssymbolik verwendet. Aber nicht nur die Strukturen und Symbole sind entscheidend. Geburt ist Initiation für die Frau, sie ist mit dem veränderten Bewusstseinszustand und dem religiösen Bewusstsein in vielfältiger Weise verbunden. Geburt/Wiedergeburt als verbreitetes religiöses Phänomen ist keine zufällige Metapher sondern in der Körperlichkeit und Spiritualität der Frau verankert. Geburt ist das Geheimnis des Lebens und die Konfrontation mit (Körper-)grenzen und Todesangst zugleich.
Auch die Hebamme zeigt den ursprünglichen Zusammenhang von Geburt und sakraler Sphäre klar. Sie wird gleich dem Schamanen berufen und erhält ihre Ausbildung auch aus übernatürlichen Quellen. Sie ist medizinische und spirituelle Begleiterin der Frau, und vielleicht die ursprüngliche Schamanin.

Abstract: Birth, as a significant event in female life, has besides its biological and sociocultural meaning, highly spiritual dimensions. Sensual, symbolic and spiritual aspects of childbirth should be seen in a wider context of female life. The pattern of initiation lies within physiological requirements of childbirth. Childbirth forms the basic structure for transforming rituals, that often use symbols drawn from this female experience, to express the idea of rebirth into a new social or spiritual role. Childbirth does not only form this universal pattern, childbirth is initiation for woman, and it has several connections to religious consciousness. Birth as religious symbol is not abstract but lies within female experience and power to create and give birth. It is the secret of life, an encounter with death, and at the same time it can be rebirth.
The traditional midwife is clearly linked into spiritual realms, besides her supporting and medical care for pregnant woman. Like the shaman she has a supernatural call and receives advise from there. The midwife has the shamanic power to conduce the souls of the unborn into life.

Keywords: Geburt, Initiation, religiöses Bewusstsein, matriarchale Religion, birth, rite of passage, religous consciousness, matrimarchial religion.

Einleitung

Das ethnomedizinische Wissen um die Geburt hat die westliche Geburtshilfe sehr bereichert. Engagierte Forschung über die Geburtsvorgänge in anderen Kulturen haben wesentlich dazu beigetragen, die technische Geburtshilfe zu kritisieren, zu überdenken, und neue Ansätze zu entwickeln. Das zeichnet die ethnologische und ethnomedizinische Geburtsforschung aus, denn nicht alle Gebiete der Ethnologie, bzw. Etnomedizin finden gleichermaßen Eingang in die gesellschaftspolitische Diskussion. (vgl.: SCHIEVENHÖFEL et.al. 1995) Allerdings ist eine wesentliche Komponente der Geburt in traditionellen Gesellschaften bislang sehr wenig berücksichtigt worden, obwohl gerade darin ein wesentlicher Unterschied zur westlichen Geburtshilfe liegt: Die spirituelle Dimension. Diese Ebene der Geburt begegnet dem Beobachter primär in den Ritualen, die die Geburt begleiten. Die „rites de passage" sind im Zusammenhang mit Geburt ein geflügeltes Wort.

Diese Übergangsriten, erstmals von Van Gennep formuliert, und bis heute ein oft gebrauchtes Konzept, begleiten alle Übergänge oder Krisen im Leben, also Hochzeiten, Geburt, Todesfälle und der Übergang vom Jugendlichen zum Erwchsenen Oft werden diese Übergangsrituale nur auf der sozialen Ebene interpretiert. So gesehen, begleiten sie diese Veränderungen im Leben, um das Individuum zu stabilisieren, und die gesellschaftlichen Rollen zu vermitteln. In jeder Kultur ist die Geburt auch in den jeweiligen soziokulturellen Kontext eigebettet. Die Einstellung zu Schwangerschaft, Geburt und Wochenbett, die Vorschriften und Tabus, die damit verbunden sind, sind so unterschiedlich wie die

Kulturen selbst. Dadurch wird auch der Geburtsverlauf und die Handlungen und Empfindungen der Frau maßgeblich beeinflusst. (vgl. KUNTNER 1995)

Und doch ist Geburt auch ein Ereignis, das Frauen aller Kulturen in einem tiegreifenden Ereignis miteinander verbindet. Viele Verbindungen, die im folgenden zu zeigen sind, verweisen uns auf einen Kern des Geburtserlebnisses, der grenzüberschreitend ist, sowohl individuell als auch kulturell. Geburt ist das Urgeheimnis des Lebens, das sichtbar wird. Geburt wird nicht nur als Übergang gefeiert, sondern ist Initiation für die Frau, da Geburt bewusstseinsveränderndes Potential hat, das alle Ebenen des Individuums berührt. Ähnlich der Schamanismusforschung gehe ich davon aus, dass hinter den kulturspezifischen Erscheinungen eine universelle Erfahrung steht.

Geburt als Grundlage des Rituals
Mehrere Autoren bearbeiten Geburt unter dem Blickwinkel eines Übergangsritus:

„If we view birth as a rite of passage, the patterns of interaction between individuals and social groups comes clearly into focus. Transitional rites define and regulate the passage from one social status to another. They guard the treshold between social categories of beeing. The individual on the journey between two kinds of social identity is controlled and protected and the behaviour of everyone involved carefully circumscribed to achieve an orderly transition." (KITZINGER 1982)

Mit diesen Worten charakterisiert Sheila Kitzinger die soziale Ebene der Geburt als Übergangsritus. Diese soziale Interpretation ist eine sehr gebräuchliche. Sie fokussiert die Anpassung an neue soziale Rollen und die Erwartungen die damit an das Individuum verbunden sind.

Andere Autoren betrachten dies unter einem etwas anderen Blickwinkel. Rita Gross sieht in der Geburt die ursächliche Struktur des Übergangsrituals:

*„Physiological birth is the occasion for rituals in almost all small-scale societies. The well-known pattern for transition rituals - withdrawal, seclusion and return - is evident in the activities surrounding physiological childbirth. In this case there is an especially close connection between physiological requirements and ritual elaboration. Other transition rituals do not carry the same physiological necessity for withdrawal and seclusion, which strengthens the hypothesis that the **experience of giving birth is the model upon which other transition rituals are based.**"* (GROSS 1993, S.227)

Separation - Transition - Reintegration, diese dreiphasige Struktur ist ursächlich mit dem physiologischen Ablauf der Geburt verwandt. Da man aber kaum annehmen kann, dass die Geburt diesem Schema folgt, kann man schließen, dass van Gennep Strukturen entdeckt hat, die dem Muster der Geburt ähneln.

Die kulturellen Phänomene, die als rites de passage bezeichnet werden, sind also von der Gesellschaft und ihrem Weltbild geprägte Formen der Verarbeitung der Geburt. Bei genauerer Betrachtung des Ablaufes von Schwangerschaft, Geburt und Wochenbett ist es unwahrscheinlich, dass Geburt ein Übergang ist, oder als solcher gefeiert wird. Genau genommen ist Geburt der Übergangsritus, die Grundlage für alle anderen Übergangsriten, die analog dieser Struktur entwickelt und gefeiert werden.

Felicitas Goodman ist eine der wenigen, die diesen Zusammenhang formuliert hat. Auf der Suche nach der Tiefenstruktur von Ritualen, die für sie noch nicht befriedigend analysiert waren, stieß sie auf jenen Zusammenhang:

„Bei der Dekonstruktion der Rituale (Anm.: mit Hilfe der generativen Semantik) und der Reihung ihrer Elemente zu logischen Abfolgen gab sich die gesuchte Tiefenstruktur plötzlich zu erkennen. Es ist gut möglich, daß sie deshalb noch niemandem aufgefallen ist, weil Ritualstrukturen bisher ausschließlich von Männern analysiert worden sind. Was mir als Frau äußerst sinnvoll erscheint, sobald ich es einmal erkannt hatte, war die Tatsache, daß es sich bei dem verborgenen Muster um das ergreifende Drama der Geburt handelte. Klar und deutlich stellen die Rituale eine Transformation der Geburtsvorgänge ins Rituelle dar: angefangen bei den Wehen der Mutter über das Ausstoßen der Frucht aus dem Schoß bis hin zum Willkommenheißen des Neugeborenen, zu seiner Versorgung und schließlich dem Anlegen an die Mutterbrust zur ersten Nahrungsaufnahme." (GOODMAN 1994)

Neben dieser Tiefenstruktur betont Felicitas Goodman die Bedeutung der religiösen Trance und des damit verbundenen ekstatischen Erlebnisses. Menschen die in Trance fallen, nehmen eine gänzlich anderen Aspekt der Wirklichkeit wahr. (GOODMAN, ebenda).

regressus ad uterum als Initiationssymbolik

Mircea Eliade beschreibt einen Initiationsritus, der sich auf wunderbar explizite Weise auf die Geburt bezieht. Obwohl die meisten Zeremonien des *kunapipi*-Geheimkultes, der im australischen Arnhemland, im Nordterritorium, sowie im Zentrum dokumentiert ist, den Männern vorbehalten sind, ist die Ideologie des *kunapipi* von weiblichen religiösen Symbolen geprägt insbesondere der Gestalt der großen Mutter. Die Einweihung in den *kunapipi*-Kult ist nur für Jugendliche zugänglich, die die Pubertätsweihe schon hinter sich haben. Die Kernsymbolik ist ein *regressus ad uterum*, eine symbolische Rückkehr in die Gebärmutter, um dort neu ausgetragen und wieder geboren zu werden. Die Neophyten werden im heiligen Bezirk von der Schlange Lu`ningu verschlungen. Sie werden mit Ocker und dem Blut ihrer Armvenen bestrichen, was das Blut der beiden mythischen Schwestern symbolisiert. Der Tanzplatz ist ein Dreieck, der den Uterus selbst symbolisiert.

Das Verlassen des heiligen Platzes geschieht durch zwei Pfosten, die durch eine darüberliegende Stange zu einem Tor verbunden sind, das Ganze wird mit Zweigen bedeckt, und die Neophyten darunter versteckt. Auf dieses Gerüst klettern zwei Männer, die wie Neugeborene schreien.

Die Überlieferung dieser Gesellschaft berichtet, dass am Anfang die Frauen alle Geheimnisse des Kultes und alle heiligen Gegenstände besaßen und dass die Männer ihnen diese später geraubt hätten.

„Man ist beeindruckt von der Eindringlichkeit, mit der man die Rückkehr in den Schoß der Urmutter wiederholt. Die sexuelle Pantomime und besonders der rituelle Austausch der Frauen - eine orgiastische Zeremonie, die im kunapipi-Kult eine große Rolle spielt - betonen noch die heilige Atmosphäre des Mysteriums von Zeugung und Geburt. In der Tat hat man bei dieser ganzen Zeremonie den Eindruck, daß es sich weniger um einen rituellen Tod handelt, dem eine Auferstehung folgt, als vielmehr um eine totale Erneuerung des Initianden dadurch, daß er von der großen Mutter ausgetragen und geboren wird. Das soll natürlich nicht heißen, daß die Symbolik des Todes völlig fehlt: denn von der Schlange verschlungen werden und sogar in den mütterlichen Schoß zurückkehren heißt notwendig, daß man der profanen Seinsweise abstirbt. Die Symbolik des regressus ad uterum ist immer ambivalent. Dennoch sind es die spezifischen Merkmale der Zeugung und Schwangerschaft, die den kunapipi-Kult beherrschen. Wir haben hier also ein vollkommenes Beispiel eines Initiationsthemas vor uns, das um die Vorstellung einer neuen Geburt kreist und nicht mehr um die Vorstellung des symbolischen Todes und der symbolischen Auferstehung." (ELIADE 1989, S. 97)

Die Symbolik des regressus ad uterum wird allgemein durch den Wald, die Hütte, ein Gefäß, oder durch das Eindringen in den Schoß der Großen Mutter oder in den eines Ungeheuers, einer Schlange oder auch eines Fisches, Haustieres oder Gefäßes dargestellt.

Weibliche Einweihunswege

„Das fundamentale Erleben der Geburt bildet im Lebenszyklus der Frau in den Stammeskulturen bzw. in den traditionell verankerten Gesellschaftsformen eine bestimmende Konstante, und zwar im Sinne eines Übergangs vom Mädchen zur Frau, von der Frau zur Mutter. Zugleich gilt die Geburt allgemein in den kulturellen Riten als Symbol für die Vermittlung von Tod und Neugeburt. Die Gebärmutter erscheint als der Ort, aus dem das Leben kommt und zu dem es in den Schoß zurückkehrt" (HAMPE 1995)

Die Initiationen der Frau sind mit ihren sexuellen Zyklen verbunden. Der traditionelle Einweihungsweg verläuft über die erste Menstruation, Schwangerschaft, Geburt und Menopause. So sind diese Einweihungen auch eng mit dem Blut verknüpft. Stellt man sich vor, dass Frauen, bevor sie sich mit saugendem Material behalfen, in die Erde menstruiert haben, könnte dies als ein freiwilles Blutopfer gedeutet worden sein, das ohne Verletzung oder Tod von den Frauen kam. Weit verbreitet ist auch die Vorstellung, der Fötus würde aus dem ausbleibenden Menstruationsblut gebildet werden. Nach dem Blutverlust der Geburt ist die Wandlung von Blut zu Milch das nächste Blutmysterium. Die Verhaftung mit dem Blut geht mit der Menopause zu Ende.

ERICH NEUMANN (1981) bezeichnet dies als „Blutmysterien",. MIRCEA ELIADE (1989) hingegen hat diesen spezifisch weiblichen Einweihungsweg aus ethnologischer Sicht beschrieben. Eliade charakterisiert die Initiation der Mädchen als 1) weniger verbreitet als die der Knaben, obwohl sie schon auf einer frühen Kulturstufe bezeugt sind, 2) weniger ausgearbeitet im Ritus und 3) individuell, da die erste Menstruation den Zeitpunkt der Absonderung bestimmt.

Die weiblichen Pubertätsriten beginnen also mit dem Zeichen der ersten Menstruation, das ist der

Zeitpunkt der Absonderung aus der Gemeinschaft. Zum Zeitpunkt der Abschlussfeiern kann sich eine Gruppe von Mädchen gebildet haben, die gemeinsam unter der Leitung älterer Frauen (in Afrika), oder weiblicher Verwandter den Abschluss feiert. Die Wissensvermittlung bezieht sich laut Eliade auf die Sexualität, die Stammesbräuche, die Überlieferungen, die den Frauen zugänglich ist, und als wesentlichen Kern die Offenbarung der weiblichen Sakralität. Die besondere Seinsweise der Frauen liegt in ihrer Aufgabe Schöpferin zu sein. Weiters betrifft die Unterweisung die Verpflichtungen gegenüber Gesellschaft und Kosmos, die religiöser Natur sind. Die Absonderung findet meist im Wald oder einer abgelegenen Hütte statt. Wie auch bei den Knabeninitiationen sind der Wald und die Hütte Symbole des Jenseits, also des Todes, aber auch der Schwangerschaft im mütterlichen Schoß. Während dieser Phase der Absonderung unterliegen die Initiandinnen strengen Auflagen. Sie müssen im Dunkel verharren, dürfen den Erdboden nicht berühren, müssen Nahrungsvorschriften einhalten, die Sonne vemeiden und besondere Kleidung tragen. Die Abschlusszeremonie beschreibt Eliade anhand eine Stammes der australischen Nordküste. Nach drei Tagen der Isolation wird das Mädchen mit Ocker bemalt und geschmückt. In der Morgendämmerung begleiten die Frauen die Neophytin zum Bach oder einer Lagune, wo sie ein rituelles Bad nimmt. Danach wird es unter Beifall und Jubel ins Dorf begleitet und als Frau vorgestellt. Der ursprüngliche Ritus enthielt auch Lieder und Tänze.

„Die Grunderfahrung - die allein uns über die Entstehung der Riten Aufschluss geben kann - ist eine weibliche Erfahrung und sie kristallisiert sich um das Geheimnis des Blutes." (ELIADE 1989, S. 87)

Die Yao - ein altes Matriarchat

Eliade beschrieb die mehrstufige Einweihung der Frauen ebenfalls für die Yao. Bei den Yao beginnt sie mit der ersten Menstruation, wird während der Schwangerschaft wiederholt und vertieft und kommt erst nach der Geburt des ersten Kindes zum Abschluss.

> „Das Mysterium des Blutes findet bei der Entbindung seine Krönung. Die Offenbarung, daß sie auf der Ebene des Lebens Schöpferin ist, stellt für die Frau eine religiöse Erfahrung dar, die nicht in Begriffe männlicher Erfahrung übersetzt werden kann." (ELIADE 1989, S. 88)

Gerade für diesen Stamm der Yao, kommt Göttner-Abendroth in ihrer Analyse zu interessanten und neuen Schlussfolgerungen bezüglich der Religiosität. Das Volk der Yao bewohnt gemeinsam mit den Miao-Gruppen Regionen in Südwestchina. Die Matriarchatsforscherin HEIDE GÖTTNER-ABENDROTH (1991) beschreibt die Yao als ursprünglich matriarchale Gesellschaft. Die Tracht der Frauen ist schwarz, rot und weiß, die Farben der dreigestaltigen Göttin. Ahnenverehrung, Ahnenopfer und feierliche Begräbnisriten sind starke religiöse Elemente. Überreste matrilokaler Familien- und Sippenstrukturen lassen auf die ursprüngliche Gesellschaftsordnung vor der chinesischen Verdrängung schließen. Aus vielen Merkmalen schließt die Autorin, dass es sich dabei um eine klassisch-matriarchale Kultur gehandelt habe. Weltbild und Religion äußern sich in Natur- und Ahnenverehrung, und einem ausgeprägten Schlangen- und Drachenkult, der sich später mit dem Taoismus verband.

Die Ahnenverehrung war mit den großen Megalithbauten dieser Region verknüpft. Erdaltare und Ahnentempel wurden erbaut, wo Feste zu Ehren der Toten gefeiert wurden. Der Wu-Kult ist noch heute lebendig, und ein altes Element der Kultur. Hinter dieser Bezeichnung verbirgt sich Schamanismus als medizinische und priesterliche Tätigkeit, verbunden mit ekstatischen Tänzen und Jenseitsfahrten in Trance. Das chinesische Bildzeichen für Wu stellt eine weibliche Person dar, und der Beginn des Schamanismus liegt in dieser Kultur bei den Frauen. Diese verkörperten die Ahnin in diesem sippenorientiertem Totenkult. Der Glaube an die Wiedergeburt war ein sehr konkreter, denn die Enkelin war dafür zuständig, die Totenseele der Ahnin aus dem Jenseits zu holen. Da diese Totenfeste ausgelassene Feiern waren, bei denen auch die Erotik eine große Rolle spielte, verband sich mit dem Eingehen der Seelen in die Schamanin eine ganz konkrete Hoffnung auf Wiedergeburt in Form eines Kindes. Gerade diese Fähigkeit, die Ahnen auch tatsächlich wiederzugebären, war die ursprüngliche schamanische Fähigkeit. Das spiegelt sich noch heute in der Erzählung von der jungen Schamanin Nisan, die im Gegensatz zu den männlichen Schamanen als einzige einen Toten wieder zum Leben erwecken konnten.

Geburt gilt den Yao als die konkrete Fähigkeit von Frauen, die Seele eines Ahnen wiederzugebären. Dies gilt als schamanische Kunst. Wiedergeburt ist im Rahmen dieses Weltbildes kein abstraktes Konzept der geistigen Erneuerung, das mit den biologischen Tatsachen nichts zu tun hat, sondern tief im Lebenszyklus der Frau, ihrer Sexualität und Spiritualität auf profaner und sakraler Ebene verankert.

Heide Göttner-Abendroth stellt die Geburt, und die damit verbundene Konzeption einer Wiedergeburt der Ahnen in einen matriarchalen Rahmen. Diese Fähigkeit ist auch mit der weiblichen schamanischen Kunst verbunden.

Hebammen und weiblicher Schamanismus

Ähnliche Hinweise finden sich bei der Betrachtung der Hebammen. Die traditionelle Hebamme ist sowohl geburtshilfliche als auch rituelle Begleiterin bei Geburten, und unterscheidet sich gerade dadurch von Hebammen unserer Kultur. Auch der Hebammenstand der Quiché in Guatemala beinhaltet sowohl geburtshilfliche als auch spirituellschamanistische Komponenten.

Hebammen sind den Heilern dieser Volksgruppe sowohl in der Art der Berufung als auch in Teilen der Berufsausübung ähnlich.

Schon ihr Name drückt ihre Sonderstellung im Dorf aus. Ratit ak'al werden sie genant, was „Großmutter" bedeutet. Die Berufung steht im Spannungsfeld zwischen destino, "die Bestimmung" und castigos, „Strafen". Castigo ist das Leid, das man im Falle eines unerfüllten destinos erleiden muss.

Destino, die Berufung, ist am Tag der Geburt bereits festgeschrieben. Im tzolkin, dem Maya Kalender ist der Tag kawuq, der „Nahual der Frauen" bedeutet, bestimmend. Die castigos, die sich in Krankheit, Alpträumen und leidvollen Schicksalsschlägen äußern, sind die Berufung, der sie sich wie der Schamane nicht ohne Schaden zu nehmen, verweigern kann. Andere Träume sind instruktiver Natur. Das Wissen, das hier vermittelt wird, bildet einen wesentlichen, wenn nicht sogar den einzigen Teil des Wissenserwerbes.

Die Initiation und Bestätigung als Hebamme erfolgt bei der ersten Geburt. Ihr erfogreicher Abschluss ist unbedingt nötig. Nun ist für die Frau auch die Zeit des Leidens und der Krankheit beendet. Das destino ist erfüllt. (vgl. GIRRBACH 1995)

Lois Paul und Benjmin D. Paul berichten über die Berufung einer Hebamme in San Pedro, Guatemala.

„*The way Rosa came to activate her calling, as she and her community reconstructd the sequence of events, followed the classic Pedrano pattern for a person who becomes a sacred practitioner, wheter shaman or midwife: birth signs, premonitory dreams, delicate health, a long illness leading to revelation by a shaman of her true destiny, show of reluctance, discovery of magic objects, dream instruction, an opportune case that demonstrates her competence, the growth of a clientele.*" (PAUL & PAUL 1975)

Die Verwandtschaft von Schamanen und Hebammen erstreckt sich also auf die Berufung, die Hilfe aus dem Jenseits, die heilenden Qualitäten, die diese Personen besitzen, ihre rituelle Funktion und ihre Vermittlerrolle zwischen den Welten.

Eine Vermutung die sich aufdrängt, ist, dass eine der wichtigen Wurzeln des Schamanismus, das Hebammentum ist, da Hebammen sich wohl sehr früh in der Menschheitsgeschichte auf diese Aufgaben spezialisiert haben. Die Notwendigkeit zur Geburtsbegleitung war vom Anfang der Menschheitsgeschichte an gegeben. Mag sein, dass die Figur der Hebamme sich aus der Mutter über die Stammesälteste zur eigenen Spezialistin entwickelt hat. Jede Frau, die Geburten begleitet, hat die eigene Initiation der Geburt bereits hinter sich, ist also eine Eingeweihte. Jede Frau ist in der Lage, Leben zu schaffen und so die Seelen ins Leben zu holen. Dies mag eine ursprüngliche Aufgabe der Schamanin gewesen sein, eine Fähigkeit die zutiefst im Geburtswissen verankert ist.

Das veränderte Bewusstsein der Gebärenden - initiatorische Potentiale

Der veränderte Bewusstseinszustand ist jene Möglichkeit der menschlichen Wahrnehmung, die über das Materielle, mit den körperlichen Sinnesorganen und dem Intellekt Wahrnehmbare hinausgeht. Die Herbeiführung dieser Bewusstseinsveränderung wird in traditionellen Kulturen bewusst gesucht, wobei sich die Menschen verschiedener Methoden bedienen. So vielfältig die Erfahrungsmöglichkeiten in diesem Bereich auch sind, eines haben sie gemeinsam, die Verbindung zur anderen Dimension, zum Jenseits, zum Mystischen. Ein gänzlich anderer Aspekt der Wirklichkeit zeigt sich, der das Individuum verändert.

Geburten haben dieses Potential zur Bewusstseinsveränderung, zum Wechsel der Wahrnehmungsebene. Nach der sozialen und emotionalen Destabilisierung der Schwangerschaft ist Geburt eine Extremsituation auf körperlicher Ebene, - die im wörtlichen Sinn - Grenzen sprengt. Intensivster Schmerz und die Begegnung mit der Todesgefahr, der Angst. Atmung ist ein wesentlicher Teil der

Geburtsarbeit und verändert sich im Laufe des Geburtsvorgangs. Kein anderes Erlebnis kommt der Ich-Auflösung des Schamanen so nahe wie die Geburt. Alte Gehirnregionen werden aktiviert, die jenseits kultureller Kontrolle liegen (siehe unten). So können Frauen auch ungehemmt schreien, Agressionen freisetzen und Todesmut, sowie ungeheure Kräfte aktivieren.

*Diese Erfahrung kann spontan auftreten und ist im weiblichen Leben, in der weiblichen Körper*lichkeit verankert, ohne dass eine Methode der Bewusstseinsveränderung diesen Zutritt verschaffen müsste.

Michel Odent hat in seinen salle sauvage Frauen beobachtet, die unter Wahrung von privacy entbinden konnten. All den Vorteilen einer beweglichen und aufrechten Geburtshaltung sieht Odent etwas Wesentliches zugrundegelegt: den Wechsel der Bewusstseinsebene, der es der Gebärenden erlaubt, das relativ junge kulturelle Gedächtnis zu verlassen und auf weit ältere Bereiche des menschlichen Gehirns zuzugreifen. Dieses ältere Gedächtnis ist im viscero-affektiven Gehirnbereich eingeschrieben, der als vorkulturell, phylogenetisch alt und dem Körper am nächsten stehenden Gehirnregion beschrieben wird. Dieser Wechsel der Bewusstseinsebene kommt einer Regression gleich, die sich durch einen charakteristischen Schrei während der Wehen ausdrückt. Mit dieser Regression gehen eine veränderte Zeitwahrnehmung, ein besseres Annehmen der Öffnung der Schließmuskeln und einer Lockerung der Dammuskulatur einher. Auch die kulturelle Scham, die Frauen besonders beim Ablassen von Urin und Fäkalien während der Geburt zu schaffen macht, ist ausgeschaltet. Schmerz kann besser verarbeitet werden, und die Körperhaltung während der Wehen und beim Austritt des Kindes werden individuell und von kulturellen Konventionen unabhängig erprobt und gefunden. Umgekehrt können gewisse Körperhaltungen diesen Wechsel der Bewusstseinsebenen erleichtern und anregen. Das Knien mit vorgebeugtem Oberkörper (Gebetshaltung) oder eine Seitenlage mit gebeugten Beinen (Fötalhaltung) tragen dazu bei. Auch der Aufenthalt in warmem Wasser, ein halbdunkler Raum, die Anwesenheit einer Frau, der Hebamme oder Mutter fördern die Aktivierung jenes uralten Wissens. Die Kommunikation mit der Gebärenden läuft im Optimalfall über die Haut, die Körperberührung, denn Worte würden zu sehr im Logisch-Rationalen verhaftet bleiben. Die Freiheit und Beweglichkeit des Körpers geht einher mit der Freiheit und Intensität der Emotionen, und dies ist auch in den Momenten nach der Geburt noch überaus wichtig. Der Zeitpunkt der ersten Begegnung von Mutter und Kind stellt die Beziehung her und sichert das Überleben des Kindes. Das erste Stillen ist im veränderten Bewusstseinszustand auch von der Seite der Mutter eine instinktive, reflexartige Handlung, die keiner Unterweisung bedarf.

> *„Das Ausschütten der für den Geburtsvorgang notwendigen Hormone ist begleitet von einer Reduzierung der Aktivität des neuen Gehirns; und das ist der Grund, warum sich Frauen ab einem bestimmten Stadium bei einer normalen physiologischen Geburt scheinbar von allem, was sie umgibt und auch von ihren Helfern lösen, um sich auf einen anderen Planeten zu begeben. Ihre Bewußtseinsebene verändert sich, und das muß auch so sein, wenn der richtige Hormonspiegel erreicht werden soll."* (ODENT 1994)

Die Suche nach dem Auslöser des „Fötus-Auscheide-Reflexes" führte Odent zur Angst als Auslöser eines Adrenalinaustoßes. Tatsächlich entspricht dies dem Erfahrungsschatz von Hebammen, dass ein Schreck das Ende der Geburt herbeiführen kann. Viele Frauen berichten aber auch von einer Angst, die sie auch ohne äußeren Anlass kurz vor dem Austreten des Kindes empfanden. Diese Angst kann durch ein fremdes, bedrohliches Gefühl ausgelöst werden, oder aber duch die konkrete Angst zu sterben. Meist setzt kurz darauf besagter „Fötus-Ausscheide-Reflex" ein, der mit ungeheurer Kraft die Geburt so schnell und effizient wie möglich beendet. Zudem treten Dammrisse bei diesen Geburten äußerst selten auf.

Odent selbst zieht nun eine interessante Schlussfolgerung aus diesen Beobachtungen, die den Bewusstseinswechsel, die Angst und die darauffolgende Beendigung der Geburt betreffen. Während das „neue Hirn" die Konzepte von Zeit, Raum und Begrenzung ermöglicht, was uns als Individuum definiert, *als Identität mit Grenzen in Raum und in der Lebenszeit und auch das Konzept von Tod* ermöglicht, beziehen sich die alten Gehirnstrukturen auf ein Gefühl für das Ganze. Das Bewusstsein, das mit dem alten Gehirn verknüpft ist, fördert eine spirituelle Weltsicht, welche das Konzept von Raum und Zeit transzendiert. Auch der Wille zum Überleben gehört in diesen Bereich.

Es ist daher bezeichnend, dass Frauen während der Geburt mit einer Todesangst konfrontiert sind, die sie überschreiten müssen.

„Es ist, als ob das Wissen vom Tod und die Angst davor, die im neuen Hirn enthalten ist, sich auflösen, sobald ein bestimmter Bewußtseinszustand erreicht ist. Es ist, als ob der Frau während der Geburt ein physiologischer Mechanismus zur Verfügung stünde, der ihr hilft, dieses Wissen und diese Angst, die charakteristisch für den Menschen sind, im richtigen Moment zu vergessen. Und dieser Mechanismus besteht in der Reduzierung der Kontrolle, die das neue Hirn ausübt". (ODENT 1994)

Die Geburt bringt Frauen an die Schwelle, an die Grenze der physischen Existenz, was sich in jenem Angstzustand ausdrückt. Das Überwinden dieser Existenzkrise ist der entscheidende Auslöser für jene Kraft, die das Kind letztendlich in die Welt setzt. Und er stellt selbst die Verbindung zwischen jenem Bewusstseinszustand, der bei Geburten eintritt und einer spirituellen Wahrnehmung, die die Grenzen von Zeit und Raum transzendiert, her.

Diese Sichtweise bringt uns sehr nahe an ethnologische Konzepte der Initiation. Erst die Konfrontation mit dem Tod, bringt den Initianden und den Schamanen zu seinem Wissen. Dies ist ein weiterer Zusammenhang zwischen körperlichem und spirituellem Geburtsbegriff. Geburt muss nicht erst als symbolisches Konzept verwendet werden, um reale Erfahrungen im veränderten Bewusstseinszustand zu machen. Die körperliche Geburt der Frau ist die Wurzel jener Erfahrung, die Initianden aller Kulturen nachvollziehen. Geburt führt zur Todesangst und zu ihrer Überwindung, und ist damit eine Möglichkeit zur Initiation.

Der Schrei der Schwestern

Die „Schwesternschaften" der „hill congregations" Jamaicas bestehen hauptsächlich aus Frauen, deren Ziel die Besessenheitstrance und Glossolalie ist. Sie erreichen diesen veränderten Bewusstseinszustand durch singen und tanzen. Die Erfahrung, die man damit machen will, ist die der Wiedergeburt. Am Weg in die Besessenheit, stöhnen und schreien die Frauen und nennen es selber „in den Wehen liegen". Sheila Kitzinger verglich die Tonbandaufnahme einer solchen rituellen Zusammenkunft mit Aufnahmen aus einem Kreißsaal in Kingston. Sie waren kaum zu unterscheiden. Nicht nur dieselben Laute wurden gemacht, sondern auch die gleichen Wörter und Phrasen benutzt. Frauen in den Wehen, zitieren Passagen aus der Bibel oder verwenden religiöse Symbole sprachlicher Art spontan zum Ausdruck ihrer Empfindungen bei der Geburt.

Bei der Geburt werden also religiöse Symbole verwendet, um das Ereignis fassbar zu machen und zum Ausdruck zu bringen. Zugleich wird die psychische Erfahrung der spirituellen Wiedergeburt durch die sprachliche Identifizierung mit der physischen Geburt ausgedrückt. Diese beiden Ebenen sind also untrennbar miteinander verknüpft und erfahren ständigen Austausch. In Symbolik, Ablauf und Bedeutung als Übergang sind sie verwandt.

„The frightening experience of giving birth in the hospital is given meaning and significance by use of powerful symbols drawn from religion, just as the experience of psychic rebirth sought in revivalist services is enhanced by actions associated with the physical sensation of parturition. Symbols of birth and spiritual rebirth are indissolubly linked, metaphorically transformed from one mode into the other and back again." (KITZINGER 1982)

Niederschlag in frauenorientierten Religionen

Diese schöpferische und lebenspendende Kraft der Frau fand ihren Niederschlag in den frühen matriarchalen Kulturen. Der erste greifbare Ausdruck davon, sind die unzähligen altsteinzeitlichen Frauenfigurinen, von denen auch viele in Gebärhaltung oder mit einem Kind an der Brust dargestellt sind. (vgl. GIMBUTAS 1982)

„Statues of pregnant women dating from the paleolithic period are important as indicators of the earliest attachment of religious significance to birth. .. Although the exact use and significance of these figures cannot be determined, it seems undeniable that they reflect and express concern with birth specifically and with feminine energy in general as central existential and religious symbols. (GROSS 1993, S. 227)

Eine andere interessante Deutung für diese Figuren, die meist keine ausgeprägte Standfläche haben, stammt von Hans Biedermann.

Sie *„sind in die Hand geschäftet wie der Faustkeil noch älterer Epochen, und sie wurden vielleicht wirklich dazu hergestellt, um umklammert zu werden. Es gibt zweifellos Augenblicke im Leben jedes Men-*

schen, in welchen er den festen Halt sucht, in welchen er darauf angewiesen ist, sich festzukrallen: Momente der restlosen Forderung durch innere oder äußere Lebensumstände - der Verwundung, des Schmerzes und Todes, eher aber noch durch die Wehen der Geburt." (BIEDERMANN 1987, S. 13).

In Catal Hüyük, in der heutigen Türkei fand James Mellaart eine stadtähnliche Siedlung (sie wird oft mit den nordamerikanischen Pueblosiedlungen verglichen), die auf 6.500 bis 5.700 v. Ch. datiert wird.

Das weitaus bedeutendste Thema künstlerischer Darstellung sind die Abbildungen der Muttergöttin. In den vielen Sanktuarien ist sie mit gespreizten Beinen gemeinsam mit den Stierhörnern als Symbol des Männlichen dargestellt. Sie scheint in Gebärhaltung abgebildet zu sein. Die Reliefs der Göttin wurden mit Händen berührt, die zuvor mit rotem Ocker gefärbt wurden. Roter Ocker ist das Symbol des Blutes und des fruchtbaren Lebens schlechthin.

Auch die ersten plastischen Darstellungen von Geburten sind dort zu finden. Religion und Geburt erscheinen in Catal Hüyük in ihrem ursprünglichen Zusammenhang. Man fand auch etwa 50 Plastiken aus Stein, die hauptsächlich Frauen darstellen, und eine Lehmplastik einer Gebärenden auf einem Thron/Gebärsessel, die Unterarme auf die Lehnen gestützt, die als Löwenköpfe gestaltet sind. Diese Göttin-Figur wurde im Getreidebehälter des Heiligtums gefunden.(vgl. GIMBUTAS 1982, GÖTTNER-ABENDROTH 1989, BIEDERMANN 1987, DUERR 1990)

Hans Peter Duerr sieht in den Kulträumen, auch Sanktuarien genannt, direkte Nachempfindungen der ursprünglichen heiligen Höhle.

„Offenbar wird der Stier auch in Catal Hüyük ein chthonisches Tier, das aus der Erde kam, und da vieles darauf hindeutet, daß die Gebirgshöhlen des Taurus einst die Gebärmutter der Göttin waren, wird die Geburt des Stiers in zweierlei Weise dargestellt.: Wie wir gesehen haben, wird er zum einen von der Göttin als Frau geboren; zum anderen aber wird er gezeigt, wie er aus der „Mutter Erde" kommt. So sieht man in einem der Heiligtümer die Göttin mit gespreizten Beinen und Armen - höchstwahrscheinlich in Geburtsstellung - über drei Stierköpfen, wobei der unterste der Stiere aus der Erde auftaucht. An beiden Seiten der Szene öffnen sich an der Wand tiefe Höhlen." (DUERR 1990, S. 101)

Abgesehen davon, dass die Darstellung der Göttin jene der Stierhörner bei weitem an Größe und Eindringlichkeit überragt, ist dies eine bedeutende Beobachtung.

„Es scheint, als handelte es sich auch hier nicht um eine todbringende, vielmehr um eine mütterliche, das Leben bergende und regenerierende Göttin, aus deren Schoß das Leben - die Menschen, die Tiere und die Vegetation - hervorkam und in den es wieder zurückkehrte.

Vermutlich sollen die ausgebreiteten Arme und die gespreizten Beine der Göttin zweierlei zum Ausdruck bringen: Einerseits gebiert sie das Leben, andererseits nimmt sie das Leben in ihren Schoß zurück, wobei vorerst offenbleiben kann, ob man im neolithischen Catal Hüyük den Tod als „ein Sterben in die Göttin", als einen Beischlaf mit ihr auffaßte, ihre Haltung an der Wand also auch eine Beischlafhaltung ist." (DUERR 1990, S. 104)

Waren also die Kulträume Catal Hüyüks die Weiterentwicklung der Höhle, so ist es auch wahrscheinlich, dass in jenen Kulträumen, deren Atmosphäre die Gebärende Göttin prägte, sowohl religiöse Handlungen als auch Geburten stattfanden. Die Göttin könnte bei einer Geburt nicht präsenter sein als in diesen Räumen, die Geburt und Religion in einem sehr ursprünglichen Zusammenhang zeigen.

Zusammenfassung

Geburt ist ein sozialer und individueller Übergang, der durch Rituale, die die jenseitige Welt miteinbeziehen, begleitet wird. Durch das bewusstseinsverändernde Potential und die Begegnung mit dem Tod ist Geburt aber auch eine Einweihung im schamanischen Sinn. Die Geburt in ihren Phasen ist ein Urmuster der Initiation, und die Hebamme ist die Urbegleiterin dieses Vorgangs. Die traditionelle, weil spirituelle Hebamme ist eine Heilerin, die in die weiblichen Mysterien eingeweiht ist, und Vermittlerin zwischen der Welt der Menschen und dem Ursprungsort der Seelen sein kann.

Das religiöse Konzept von Tod und Wiedergeburt, das auch in den Hochreligionen noch existiert, stammt aus dem weiblichen Bereich der Geburt und Geburtshilfe, und wurde von patriarchalen Religionen übernommen, da es für die geistige Reife des Menschen offensichtlich unerlässlich ist, in den Urgrund, die Gebärmutterhöhle zurückzukehren, um wiedergeboren zu werden.

Geburt ist ein Teil des traditionellen Einweihungsweges von Frauen, der mit ihrer Sexualität und dem Blut korrespondiert. Nicht umsonst sind Gebärmutter, Vagina und Brüste sowohl Sexual- als auch

Geburtsorgane. Matriarchale Religionen gaben diesen Zusammenhängen Raum. Das dreifache Konzept der Göttin etwa ist mit den drei großen Zyklen der Frau verbunden, und Geburt ein Urmysterium.

ELIADE (1989) unterscheidet zwei Arten der Initiation, die sich des Themas regressus ad uterum bedienen:

1) solche, die eine Rückkehr in die Gebärmutter als geheimnisvollen, aber nicht lebensgefährlichen Akt darstellen. Die Betonung liegt dabei auf dem Akt der Wiedergeburt. Der Tod ist bezogen auf das Absterben der profanen Seinsweise.

2) die Rückkehr in den Uterus unter Lebensgefahr.
Dazu gehören jene Mythen, in denen der Held von einem Meerungeheuer verschlungen wird und nach einer gewaltsamen Öffnung des Bauches siegreich zurückkehrt. Die mythischen Erzählungen einer vagina dentata, oder die Themen eines paradoxen Durchganges, wie es zwei ständig in Bewegung befindliche Mahlsteine darstellen. Eine Aufgabe, die nur unter Aufgabe des physischen Körpers gelöst werden kann. In diesem Kontext manifestiert sich die Große chthonische Mutter als Göttin des Todes und der Unterwelt. Das Unternehmen ist deswegen besonders gefährlich, weil der Held nicht in den embryonalen Zustand versetzt wird.

Dies könnte im Kontext der Matriarchatsdebatte eine Verdrängungsprozess durch patriarchale Religionen bedeuten, in denen die Große Mutter bereits als Feindbild wahrgenommen wird, und sich daher die Erlebnisse mit ihrem Symbol, ihrer Energie langsam verändern.

So kam es beispielsweise in Griechenland, wo die kretische Zivilisation die letzte Blüte matriarchaler Kulturen war, dazu, dass die Göttin Athene dem Zeus aus dem Kopf entsprang. Zeus fand also einen Weg, sich die Macht der Frauen Leben zu schenken, anzueignen.

Frauen und Gesundheit
Die Vorstellungen die wir über unseren Körper haben sind sehr wesentlich in einem umfassenden Gesundheitsbild. Die Beschäftigung mit diesen Vorstellungen und Alternativen dazu können unsere Beziehung zu körperlichen Vorgängen ändern. So kann es auch im konkreten Geburtsverlauf einen Unterschied machen,ob eine Frau die Konzeption des Wehenschmerzes als Strafe für die Sünden Evas in sich trägt, oder Geburt als kraftvolles, initiatorisches Erlebnis betrachtet, das in anderen Zeiten und Kulturen als Mysterium geehrt wurde.

References
BIEDERMANN, H. 1987. *Die großen Mütter*. Bern und München.
DUERR, H. P. 1990. *Sedna oder Die Liebe zum Leben*. Frankfurt am Main.
ELIADE, M. 1989. *Das Mysterium der Wiedergeburt. Versuch über einige Initiationstypen*. Frankfurt/Main.
GIMBUTAS, M. 1982. *The Goddesses and Gods of Old Europe*. London.
GIRRBACH, E. 1995. Geburtshilfe als Beruf und Berufung: QuichéHebammen in Guatemala. In *Gebären -*
GOODMAN, F. 1994. *Die andere Wirklichkeit. Über das Religiöse in den Kulturen der Welt*. München.
GÖTTNER-ABENDROTH, H. 1989. *Das Matriarchat I. Geschichte seiner Erforschung*. StuttgartBerlin Köln. 1991.
GROSS, R. 1993. Birth. In *The Encyclopedia of Religion*. Edited by M. ELIADE. New York.
HAMPE, R. 1995. Frau und Geburt im Kulturvergleich: eine kunst- und kulturanalytische Studie. *Europäische Hochschulschriften*/ 19/B. Frankfurt am Main.
KITZINGER, S. 1982. The Social Context of Birth: Some Comparisons between Childbirth in *Jamaica and Britain*. In *Ethnography of Fertility and Birth*. Edited by MACCORMACK, C. P. New York.
KUNTNER, L. 1995. Geburtshilfe außerhalb des Krankenhauses in traditionellen Gesellschaften. In *Gebären - Ethnomedizinische Perspektiven und neue Wege*. Edited by W. SCHIEVENHÖFEL, D. SICH & C. E. GOTTSCHALK-BATSCHKUS. Berlin.
NEUMANN, E. 1981. Die Blutmysterien. In *Birth. An Anthology of Ancient Texts, Songs, Prayers, and Stories*. Edited by MELTZER, D. San Francisco.
ODENT, M. 1994. *Geburt und Stillen: Über die Natur elementarer Erfahrungen*. München.
PAUL L. and PAUL. B. 1975. The Maya midwife as a sacred specialist: a Guatemalan case. In *American Ethnologist*, Vol. 2, number 4. Washington.
SCHIEVENHÖFEL W., D. SICH and C. E. GOTTSCHALK-BATSCHKUS. 1995. *Gebären Ethnomedizinische Perspektiven und neue Wege*. Berlin.

Folk Customs, Beliefs and Traditional Curing Methods of the Period between Conception and Weaning in Hungarian Peasant Communities

Volksbräuche und traditionelle Heilverfahren von der Empfängnis bis zum Abstillen in ungarischen bäuerlichen Gemeinschaften

Peter Babulka & Ágnes Pataki

Abstract: The authors examined, based mainly on literature data, the traditional practices and beliefs which influence the health of women and their children during pregnancy, child delivery and infant care. This study focuses on the traditional beliefs pertaining to conception, pregnancy, childbirth, women in confinement, brestfeeding and weaning. Following these episodes nutritional and behavourial restrictions, protective measures and traditional treatments of illnesses afflicting both mothers and their babies are discussed in details. Special attention is payed to the (nutritional and medicinal) plants, which have important roles both in nourishment and in herbal treatment during pregnancy, childbirth, early motherhood, brestfeeding and infant care. The results of this research might be interesting and useful not only for experts of modern obstetrics and infant welfare but for mothers who are planning to deliver their babies at home.

Zusammenfassung: Die Verfasser untersuchen das Leben der Mütter der Kinder beeinflussende Vermutungen und traditionelle Heilverfahren an Hand literarischer Angaben. Sie verfolgen in ihrer Studie die mit der besagten Periode in Zusammenhang stehende traditionelle Denkmuster (Empfängnis, Schwangerschaft, Geburt, Wochenbett, Stillen, Abstillen). Ausführlich werden die in den einzelnen Perioden gebräuchlichen Ernährungsgewohnheiten, die verbotenen und empfohlenen Bräuche und die traditionellen Behandlungsmethoden während dieser Perioden erörtert. Die Autoren schenken ihre Aufmerksamkeit der Bekanntmachung der gebräuchlichen Ernährungsmethoden und der Anwendung der Heilpflanzen, weil diese während der Schwangerschaft, der Geburt, des Kinderbettes, des Stillens und der Säuglingspflege eine besonders große Rolle spielen, sowohl in der Ernährung, als auch in den traditionellen Therapieverfahren. Die in der Studie veröffentlichten Angaben können nicht nur für die praktizierenden Gynäkologen und Säulingspfleger, sondern für alle Mütter, die ihre Kinder zu Hause zur Welt bringen wollen, wertvoll sein.

Keywords: Perinatal Health, folk beliefs, medicinal plants, ethnomedicine, Hungary, Gesundheit in der perinatalen Periode, Volksglauben und Meinungen, Heilpflanzen, Volksmedizin, Ungarn.

Introduction

Actuality and necessity of the analysis of folk customs, beliefs and curing methods concerning the period between conception and weaning have been supported by the following facts:
- more than 2/3, at some areas even now 90 % of deliveries in the world are conducted by traditionally trained midwives and elderly women (COSMINSKY 1983). Knowledge of these midwives and elderly women concerning pregnancy, delivery or child-care represent such a value, that can offer information for obstetricians and midwives supporting natural way of delivery or people interested in natural or home delivery.
- There have been enlisted among the others in WHO's recommendations in connection with delivery, being in effect since 1985, as follows:
  a) Training of professionally educated midwives and helpers at delivery should be promoted. In case of healthy delivery let them the preparation of the mother, conduct of delivery and aftercare.
  b) Well-being of the mother should be ensured by participation of the person in delivery, chosen by her and

Abb. 1
Baby in a swing-cot hanged on a peach-treein the vineyard for the time the mother works. (Photo: Dr. Sándor Ébner 1928, Sióbogárd, Tolna County, Hungary - courtesy of the Ethnographic Museum, Budapest, Hungary)

ensuring their connection during post delivery period.
c) It is not recommended to keep pregnant woman laying on her back during labour or delivery, and each woman should decide which is the proper position for her to give birth.
d) The healthy neonate, as far as possible, should remain with the mother all the time.
e) Critical point of view of obstetricians regarding technical centred care and honouring emotional, psychological and social relations of delivery, should be supported.
- There has been an increasing interest in Hungary towards deliveries in presence of the father, the 24 hours 'rooming in' delivery and child care system and recently towards home delivery. To promote, propagate and ensure necessary professional background for the latter the Alternatal Foundation has been found recently (MARKOCZI 1993).

In the present study the authors attempt to give a general view, based on source material of the last hundred years, concerning folk customs, beliefs and curing methods of one of the most beautiful period of human life.

Marriage and Wedding

In olden times, children gave the reason of life for the village people who considered them as an unavoidable and natural concomitant of the marriage. Therefore, infertility was explained not as a disease but the punishment of God for the delicts, mostly committed by the wife. The mother was blamed also for giving birth to a physically or mentally ill child. Thus they tried to influence, in many ways, the normal delivery and the birth of a healthy child with defined sex of kind. The expectant mother tried to influence the number of children to be born in such a way e.g. that she took as much dishes of soup at the wedding table as the wanted number of children. In order to have an easy delivery the bride had to kick a bucket or to broke a jar into pieces (Note: as the water flows out of the bucket, based on the analogy, so easy will the foetus come out from the womb).

Pregnancy

Not only the family, but the whole village was anxious to make the life of the pregnant woman easier. She was not obliged to make hard work and was allowed to take desired food without offer. In the rational knowledge concerning pregnancy she was not allowed to lift hard things, to jump, to be jolted, she had to avoid sexual intercourse during the first and last third of the pregnancy, however, she was advised to move as much as she could to attain easy labour. They tried to cause spontaneous abortion by the violation of the above prohibitions, the pregnant woman was carrying heavy sack, she jumped off the ladder or the garret, or she was riding horse carriage. They tried to avoid abortion by magical methods, or baths made of different plants, or smoking by different herbs, respectively. To have only one child was a family model to be followed in some parts of the country. In many families, to deliver more children was not an honour for a woman but a curse, thus the pregnant mother tried to keep her newer pregnancy in secret, as long as it was possible. When her pregnancy become known it was she who was blamed not to be careful in avoiding to get pregnant. In those families where there were more than one child, the pregnant mother had to continue her work and to do housekeeping. Thus she had much less time to have a rest. To get rid of the unwanted pregnancy and the birth-control came into practice at the end of the last century. Procured abortions were carried out by trained or untrained traditional midwives and the old women of peasant communities, as well. The latter ones also dealt with the treatment of gynaecological complaints. The embryo was regarded as a human being from "half time of the pregnancy", "from the 4th or 5th month on" or "from the first time the baby moves". The real importance of this idea is that up to this time limit abortion can be procured without any legal consequences, while afterwards it is considered a sin to be punished. The popular ways of birth-control (procured abortion) in Hungary in the 19th and 20th centuries were, based on the ethnographical documents concerning this subjects and collection of GÉMES (1987), as follows:
1. Positive ways of birth-control (e.g. magic performances for fertility), 2. Negative ways of birth-control a) infanticide, b) effective birth-control: procured abortion and contraception.

Among the different ways of birth-control the (medicinal) plants have of great importance. Besides different implements and objects (e.g. pencil, stick used for making shell shaped pastry, hairpin made of bone, hairclip, wire, wooden spoon, wheelarm of a bicycle, needle), roots, twigs or stems of plants were also used for "poking", "pricking" or "pushing up". Besides inserting washed and disinfected parts of plants into the vagina or the womb, irrigation with herbal extracts and steambath were also used to cause abortion. Different parts of the following plants were most frequently used for this purpose:

yarrow (Achillea millefolium L.), sweet-flag (Acorus calamus L.), pheasant's eye (Adonis sp.), lyme-grass (Agropyron repens [L.]Beauv.), marsh mallow (Althaea officinalis L.), hollyhock (Althaea rosea [L.] Cav.), horse radish (Armoracia lapathifolia Usteri), wormwood (Artemisia absinthium L.), mugwort (Artemisia vulgaris L.), belladonna (Atropa belladonna L.), Chinese thuja (Biota orientalis [L.] Endl., Thuja orientalis L.), common centaury (Centaurium umbellatum Gilib.), greater celandine (Chelidonium majus L.), wild chicory (Cichorium intybus L.), water-hemlock (Cicuta virosa L.), hemlock (Conium maculatum L.), carrot (Daucus carota L.), ground ivy (Glechoma hederacea L.), licorice (Glycyrrhiza glabra L.), hellebores (Helleborus sp.), privet (Ligustrum vulgare L.), dwarf mallow (Malva neglecta Wallr.), oleander (Nerium oleander L.), tobacco (Nicotiana sp.), peony (Paeonia officinalis L.), wild parsnip (Pastinaca sativa L.), pelargonium (Pelargonium zonale [L.] Ait.), parsley (Petroselinum hortense Hoffm.), tormentil (Potentilla erecta [L.] Rausch.), radish (Raphanus sativus L.), soapwort (Saponaria officinalis L.), common comfrey (Symphytum officinale L.), black bryony (Tamus communis L.), eastern white cedar (Thuja occidentalis L.), vervain (Verbena officinalis L.).

Indisposition, vomiting, dizziness occurring during the first months of pregnancy were, in many places, considered as normal. They used to draw conclusions on the sex of the baby, so did not do anything against it. Complaints, in some places, were treated by consumption of different food (walnuts, almonds, crab-apples, fried apples, lemon, unripe fruits, prunes, bread-crust), drinks (spiced spirits, milk, vinegar, cabbage juice) or material (chalk, alum, salt, lime, white clay), or compacts on stomach (warmed salt, artemisia boiled in vinegar). Taking care of pregnant woman was not an obligatory thing. Carefulness and forbearance were practised rather towards mothers with their first child, several prohibitions, however, referred to all women. Since they could not treat neither foetal nor partial anomalies, they tried to avoid these dangers by strict observance of prohibitions concerning the period of pregnancy. From among the periods examined, most prohibitions refer to pregnancy, of which will be mentioned here only a few of the most known, or the ones referring to positive or negative character of the health condition of the baby to be born. (Note: prohibitions, suggested actions or predictions may refer to the sex, outlook, conditions of life - financial situation, occupation, etc. - of the baby to be born, however, due to the space limit, we cannot deal with them in this paper.) Almost all prohibitions concerning pregnant women or others (e.g. visitors, member of her family), are based on some analogies. For example, the mother should not look at a corpse, because stillbirth can happen. The mother should avoid eating double fruit, due to the danger of giving birth twins. There are, however, suggested actions, besides prohibitions, targeting to give birth a healthy child without any complications (BERDE 1940, BONDAR 1982, BOSNYAK 1980, 1982, 1984, FÜGEDI 1982, GRYNAEUS 1974, HOPPAL 1982, KAPROS 1986, 1990, KARA 1973, MORVAY 1956, ORTUTAY 1977-1982, TIMAFFY 1980, ZENTAI 1983).

Prohibitions concerning the mother can be classified, as follows:
1. Prohibited deeds - for the sake of the normal delivery and the newborn baby, or the work performed by a pregnant woman and considered as unclean (for example cabbage pickling, home-canning, etc.) will not be successful, respectively.
2. Gazing at something - This was a basic prohibition of central importance. There are several stories of beliefs on causing some kind of physical abnormalities of the baby, e.g. harelip, pilosity and malformed face were caused by gazing at some kind of unusual phenomena, such as an animal, mask, travelling circus show, either in reality or in movie.
3. Prohibited foods - It was a basic rule in the circumstance of a pregnant woman to offer her all sort of foods, not to deny any desired thing, since these things were desired by the foetus, and having not received them, miscarriage or premature delivery will take place. For the sake of the newborn baby the eating of certain kind of foods, mainly of plant origin, or collecting and stealing of certain food plants were also prohibited for the mothers.

Delivery
Delivery was conducted by officially trained midwife or so called peasant midwife, having practical experience. The father usually did not participate in the process but in case of difficult deliveries the woman was seated on her husbands knee, thus partly held by him, partly assisting her in expulsion embracing her waist.

Prohibitions and suggested deeds concerning delivery were directed to avoid difficult delivery, to defend actions by supernatural powers or to give birth a healthy child (BERDE 1940, BONDAR 1982,

BOSNYAK 1980, 1982, 1984, FÜGEDI 1982, GRYNAEUS 1974, HOPPAL 1982, KAPROS 1986, 1990, KARA 1973, MORVAY 1956, ORTUTAY 1977-1982, TIMAFFY 1980, ZENTAI 1983).

Positions during delivery are varied from area to area. They sometimes gave birth in a standing or kneeling position, sitting on two chairs fixed to each other in V shape, laying on earth or in bed. Parturient woman was obliged to walk until the expulsive stage, her pain was released by hot water or medicinal steaming, massage, compress containing herbal extracts, onion juice inunction, drinking spicy wine or spirit or different herbal teas (ergot, garden rue, rose flower, caraway). In case of extremely strong pain magical process were performed. Umbilical cord represented an important role in the popular belief, since real life starts when the cord was cut. After birth midwives tied knots on the umbilical cord of the newborn, then strangulates it several centimeters from the body. The strangulated part withered within a few days. It was kept, in some places, on the cross-beam of the peasant home and when the child reached his seventh years, he was asked to untie it. The untying of the knot symbolized (as a matter of analogy) *the resolution of the tasks of life. They also used to discharge much blood from the cord*, attributing cleaning and preventive effect to it. To promote expression of placenta the woman had to blow into an empty bottle of narrow neck or a process based on some kind of thermal effect was practised (steaming, smoking, sitting bath, compress). Womb was fixed after delivery by midwives using massage. After-pains, besides magic rituals were reduced by unction of lard, warm compress or drinking spirit with rye leaves. In case of strong bleeding compress of alum, vinegar or parsley decoction was applied, or the woman had to drink hot drinks or spicy spirits. According to our preliminary examinations in Hungarian ethnomedicine there were - and still there are - at least 30 kind of herbs used internally or externally in hemostasis during delivery, irregular menstruation and bleeding after abortion. Bleeding was reduced internally by medicinal teas or alcoholic herbal extracts, while externally by compress on pudendum, baths, steaming or smoking were applied until the seize of bleeding (HALASZNÉ ZELNIK 1981, KESZEG 1978, KOCZIAN 1985, 1988, KOCZIAN et al.1977, OLAH 1987, PÉNTEK & SZABO 1985, RAB 1991). After delivery mother and the baby were taken care by the midwife. She visited them for a certain period of time, usually for a week, to wash the baby, to take care of the mother and to make laundry. If the baby seemed to be weak, he or she was baptized by the midwife immediately after delivery to avoid him or her frightening the human beings as an unbaptized spirit. The circumstance of delivery was considered as an important mark. Most wide-spread belief in a great part of Europe, that baby born with teeth, with a sixth finger or delivered in mantle will have supernatural power.

Puerperium

Puerperal period of time were 6 weeks at most places, while mothers theoretically should not perform any work, mothers, however, of more children were not able to keep it. Even they were not permitted, however, to leave the house until the short church ceremony, representing the end of puerperal period. Mothers usually spent puerperal period in the same bed with their babies, or in some areas in a bed covered by a sheet specially prepared for this occasion. Data relating to the nourishment of woman in confinement show us that it differed depending on places, ethnic communities and in time. However, to take foods/dishes to woman in confinement (komatál, radina, posztrik) was a wide-spread and well-known custom in all over the country. (Note: literal translation of komatál is a dish from a friend). It means that the childhood-friend of the mother, who became the god-mother of the newborn baby, took different foods to the mother for 1 or 2 weeks after delivery. These were festive, rich in calories and enough for the whole family (Note: the mother was not allowed to make dishes during this time). On the day of delivery the mother was not allowed to eat anything else but warm milk, warm tea or thick brown soup, therefore, the

Abb. 2
Delivery Chair. Reconstruction. West Transdanubia, Hungary - courtesy of the Ethnographic Museum, Budapest, Hungary

god-mother of the newborn and her women relatives began to take her different dishes on the day after delivery.

The komatál consisted of the different festive foods of a certain geographical area. These were as follow:
1. Soups: chicken-broth, beef-broth; in olden times and on fasting days potato soup or caraway-seed soup were eaten in places of catholic religion
2. Meat dishes: fried meat, meat fried in breadcrumbs, stuffed meat, meat stewed with paprika
3. Vegetable dishes and sauces: made of carrot and different kind of fruits
4. Sweet pastries/cakes: pie, strudel, fancy-cake, plain-cake, doughnut
5. Drinks: wine or brandy.

The solemnity of the komatál was stressed e.g. by wrapping the foods/dishes with beautifully embroidered covering. According to folk beliefs, in some places, mother had to eat as much food as it would be enough to fill the place of the foetus in the womb. The custom of komatál derives mainly from necessity and it also has some other functions. The most important aims of taking foods to woman in confinement were to give help the mother to recover, as shortest time as possible, and to supply her family with enough foods during this period of time. The komatál was a matter of prestige and of high social value. The person who made the dishes was frequently beyond her means and took dishes to the mother in confinement and her family when they had no need to get them. It seems from the data collected that till the first half of the 20th century the custom of komatál met the health requirements in families of average property status and different foods considered to promote lactation were given to the mother. These were e.g. milk, caraway seed-soup, boiled cubed carrot, dishes made of potato and corn. According to the beliefs they did not take, however, bean, poppy and sour dishes because these were considered as harmful for the newborn. The consumption of great amount of alcohol, which was and is now condemned by phyicians, is mentioned in both older and newer literature sources. They tried to prevent or treat any kind of after pains, inflammations and infections by giving the mother wine or brandy seasoned mainly with spices, like pepper, caraway, laurel and ginger. Since both puerpera and unbaptized baby were representatives of a transitional stage, most important targets of certain evil forces - e.g. witch, evil-"bába", devil - they used to defend themselves by objects of magic power or religious relics. Largest danger was the change of the baby - that is to place a sick child with mental or physical abnormality on the place of the healthy baby, or taking the mother's milk away or spoil it. Therefore there are several prohibitions or suggested deeds concerning puerperal period, as well. Examples are, as follows: the mother must not leave the house during the time of puerperium (2-6 weeks) otherwise her child will be ill. Nobody should sit on the bed of the puerpera to avoid taking mother's milk away. The mother's milk must not drop on the ground because the ants will take it away. In order that the mother should have sufficient milk, she must not give away anything from the house for six weeks. (BERDE 1940, BONDAR 1982, BOSNYAK 1980, 1982, 1984, FÜGEDI 1982, GRYNAEUS 1974, HOPPAL 1982, KAPROS 1986, 1990, KARA 1973, MORVAY 1956, ORTUTAY 1977-1982, TIMAFFY 1980, ZENTAI 1983).

Nursing - Taking Care of the Baby

In opposition to the colloquial medical practice colostrum was considered as harmful, thus it was milked out, and the baby was fed by tea or another woman's milk until the start of milk secretion.

Abundant quantity of milk was ensured by performance of magic practice and consumption of certain food or drink including herbal ones (RAB 1991, ORTUTAY 1981). Some food, first of all leguminous plants were prohibited due to their harmful character for the baby. In case of lacteal fever, the mother was offered to drink spirit with centaury extract, boiled wine, her breasts were steamed, smeared or they put a compress on them with different plants or material. Babies usually were breastfed until the age one, however, this process lasted for two-three years, taking special care of the circumstances of weaning.

There are several beliefs known concerning milk and suckling or concerning the prohibitions and suggested deeds of the period in question (BERDE 1940, BONDAR 1982, BOSNYAK 1980, 1982, 1984, FÜGEDI 1982, GRYNAEUS 1974, HOPPAL 1982, KAPROS 1986, 1990, KARA 1973, MORVAY 1956, ORTUTAY 1977-1982, TIMAFFY 1980, ZENTAI 1983). When the baby signalled hunger, he or she was always suckled. The baby was kept continuously beside the mother during the night to be able to suckle at any time. In spite of this, they started to feed him very early, from the 2-5 month, with mushy food masticated by the mother or grandmother, since women were obliged to return to the usual household and agricultural work, by which they had to be away from the child for a longer period of time. Where there was a chance for that, the baby was fed by another nursing mother of the family by her own milk. It was a generally used practice to give "dummy" (a piece of soft linen cloth containing sugar and crumb of bread) for the babies to make them calm. In many places of the country, decoction made of poppy-head and a piece of bread soaked in spirit were given to crying and fidget babies. It was a frequent problem during lactation, that the mother's nipple injured, ruptured or excoriated. There were more than 20 kind of plants, and material of plant (plum jam, wine, oil, honey, flour), animal (egg, lard, butter, tallow, wool) or mineral origin (lime collected from yellow coloured wall, wax) used mostly in the forms of compress or plaster (BERDE 1940, OLAH 1987, ORTUTAY 1981, PÉNTEK & SZABO 1985, VASAS 1985). There are much less prohibitions referring to the new-born babies or young children than to the pregnant woman, there are, however, much more suggested actions. Prohibitions, first of all are to prevent from exchange, bewitching or the evil eye, and are based rather on contagious magic than analogy, like in case of pregnancy. Therefore it was prohibited to put diaper contacting the baby's body or the bath water out after sunset, since evil powers in the possession of these things can do harm for the child.(BERDE 1940, BONDAR 1982, BOSNYAK 1980, 1982, 1984, FÜGEDI 1982, HOPPAL 1982, KAPROS 1986, 1990, KARA 1973, MORVAY 1956, ORTUTAY 1977-1982, TIMAFFY 1980, ZENTAI 1983).

Abb. 3
Mother suckling her child (Photo: Gábor Lükö 1932, Moldva, Roumania, Hungary - courtesy of the Ethnographic Museum, Budapest, Hungary

From among suggested deeds concerning new-born babies first of all different kinds of stimulation were used, actions based on a similarity or contact would have an influence on the life of the child further on. For example, the baby was placed onto a pillow to become a nice and fat one. They put a coin in the bath of the baby to cause richness and luck. Prevention of evil powers is also characteristic by placing special objects into or near the cradle. After all, beliefs and customs of this age are concentrating under these two topics, having an effect on the baby's external and internal characteristics and his prevention from the evil.

Infant and Young Child Age

Majority of suggested actions during infant age served as prevention from the evil eye or cure of the child suffering in an unknown disease, respectively. Since most diseases of the young children were considered as results of the evil eye, they were protecting against it most. Serious problems of this age besides evil eye, were attributed to the agosság or ebag. Children casted an evil eye on will become colicky, will not sleep, cries a lot and will suffer of diarrhoea. Most usual way to cure such children takes place by coaly water (that is a certain number of glowing embers are thrown into the water, then the child will be washed by this water or drink it). They consider about this method to go beyond cure. It also reveals the person casted an evil eye on the child, so treatment will be easier, often with the help of this person.

It is a well-spread method to cure children with an evil eye on to bath him in water prepared with different plants (melilot, thyme, types of mint, wild marjoram, agrimony, betony, artemisia, walnut) and other material, or to smoke them using different plants and other material. Most of baths were considered as of strengthening power, however, collection of water and other material according to specialised circumstances, method, time and other factors of taking bath represented greater importance, than the material itself placed in the water. Agosság or ebagosság covers different diseases: premature birth, atrophy, rachitis, hypertrichosis, TBC. It is characterised by the hairiness (lanugo or hairy mole) of the baby, or he is thin, or his skin is wrinkled, having oldish outlook. According to the belief, the disease has been caused either by the mother, who kicked a hairy animal during the pregnancy, or the other reason can be the presence of "szőrférgek", some hairy worms, living in his navel, grudging the nutriments away. Cure took place by magic methods, or by filtering the hairy worms by bathing, or by symbolical boiling or baking of the baby according to strictly regulated circumstances. The exchanged child has physical and/or mental deficiencies. According to folk beliefs, his or her mother is a supernatural being of negativ character who exchanged her handicapped child for a healthy one. Thus, the child which seemed to be healthy in the beginning, and his or her health problems became evident later, was considered as exchanged. Exchanged child, like his or her real mother, was considered of supernatural power, thus he was able to talk for example at the "kis csupor, nagy kanál" test (The exchanged child is given a task impossible to solve - he is given a small jar and a large spoon, he has got to take milk out of the jar with the spoon too big for the hole of the jar. The exchanged child should say: "small jar and large spoon, how come!"). Cure itself took place by the assassination of the child, hoping that the real mother of the exchanged child, due to her worry about the life of her baby, will change the healthy child back. Not only the obviously invalid child was considered as exchanged one, but those who learned to walk or speak later than the others, or who were underdeveloped. This circle of belief coincides in the way of treatment with that of the agos child belief (BERDE 1940, BONDAR 1982, BOSNYAK 1980, 1982, 1984, FÜGEDI 1982, HOPPAL 1982, KAPROS 1986, 1990, KARA 1973, MORVAY 1956, ORTUTAY 1977-1982, TIMAFFY 1980, ZENTAI 1983). There have been several medicinal herbs used in the treatment of more frequent complaints and diseases of the infant and young child age (for example insomnia, gastric spasm, colic, diarrhoea, constipation, skin diseases, thrush, helminthiasis, diseases of the respiratory tract, dentition, otalgia, opthalmopathies). It is, unfortunately hardly indicated obviously in the ethnopharmacobotanical data referring to the diseases or symptoms above mentioned, that the herbal medicine in question was used in treatment of babies or children. There is data of several hundreds of ethnomedicinal application - herbs and their fields of application only, with obvious reference to the ethnomedicinal use in the treatment of children or neonates (BERDE 1940, HALASZNÉ ZELNIK 1981, KESZEG 1978, KOCZIAN 1985, 1988, 1990, KOCZIAN et al 1975, 1977, OLAH 1987, PÉNTEK & SZABO 1985, SZABO & PÉNTEK 1976, RAB 1982, 1991, RAB et al 1981, VAJKAI 1943, VASAS 1985).

When looking through Hungarian ethnopharmacobotanical data - similarly to the ethnopharmacobotanical collections in other countries - we often encounter mentions of the application of herbs/herbal medicines, without notes of their application in children's diseases. In spite of this, many herbs out of them are widely used in recent phytotherapeutical practice for the treatment of children's diseases. It is needed to specialise and confirm data concerning the application of individual plants, and to perform further targeted collecting and data evaluation for the sake of recording new data to reveal ethnomedicinal treatment of infant and young children's diseases.

Weaning
Beginning of the summer, start of the ripening of fruits was considered as the most favourable period for weaning. Weaning - based on the beliefs - had less problems, than the other mentioned periods. There can hardly be found any prohibition, while suggested actions promoted mostly the seize of milk secretion based on an analogical way. For example some drops of milk should be put on a hot coal or iron for as soon the milk evaporates from the hot object so quickly will the mother go dry (BERDE 1940, BONDAR 1982, BOSNYAK 1980, 1982, 1984, FÜGEDI 1982, GRYNAEUS 1974, HOPPAL 1982, KAPROS 1986, 1990, KARA 1973, MORVAY 1956, ORTUTAY 1977-1982, TIMAFFY 1980, ZENTAI 1983). Other, rational group of suggested actions aimed to generate disgust in the child, feeling some bad taste on the breast, causing disgust towards milk. Thus they were compressed or inuncted by garlic or some other kind of plant materials with bad smell or taste (hemlock, red pepper, walnut leaves, cabbage leafs). They frightened the child away sometimes putting a pricky brush in the mother's clothe or a black cloth on her breast. To cause the mother go dry was promoted by cold compress, placing Camphor on the breasts or reduced food and liquid intake.

Discussion
Knowledge in Hungarian peasant communities concerning pregnancy, delivery and child-care contains many elements, based on rational knowledge and their practice are supported by scientific explanation. By the questionnaire prepared in the possession of the above material, projected assess of data in the future and further reviews on the special literature will promote to define methods useful for pregnant woman, mothers to deliver or caring their children, thus they are obviously to be followed.

References

BERDE, K. 1940. *A magyar nép dermatológiája. (Dermatology of the Hungarians.)*, Budapest: Magyar Orvosi Társulat.

BONDAR, F. 1982. Sarkadkeresztúr néphite. (Folk beliefs in Sarkadkeresztúr.), in *Folklore Archivum* 14, Budapest: MTA Néprajzi Kutató Csoport., pp. 34-37, 47.

BOSNYAK, S. 1980. A moldvai magyarok hitvilága. (Folk Beliefs of the Moldavian Hungarians. - [South of Hungary]), *Folklore Archivum* 12, Budapest: MTA Néprajzi Kutató Csoport, pp. 186-195.

BOSNYAK, F. 1982. A gyimesvölgyi magyarok hitvilága (Folk Beliefs of Ghymes-Valley Changos [Rumania])., *Folklore Archivum* 14, Budapest: MTA Néprajzi Kutatócsoport, pp.133-136.

BOSNYAK, F. 1984. A bukovinai magyarok hitvilága II. [Orvoslás, a születéstől a halálig, történelmi emlékek] (Folk belief systems of Hungarians living in Bukovina. II. [Curing between birth and death, historical memories]) *Folklore Archivum* 16, Budapest: MTA Néprajzi Kutató Csoport, pp. 84-97.

COSMINSKY, S. 1983. Traditional midwifery and contraception., in Bannerman, R.H., Burton, J., Wen-Chieh, Ch'en (eds.): *Traditional medicine and health care coverage.*, Geneva: World Health Organisation., pp. 142-162.

FEHÉR, Z. 1975. Bátya néphite (Folk beliefs from Bátya)., *Folklore Archivum* 3, Budapest: MTA Néprajzi Kutatócsoport.

FÜGEDI, M. 1982. Emberfeletti hatalmú lények Mátraderecske faluközösségeinek hiedelmeiben. (Supernatural Beings in the Beliefs System of Mátraderecske [North-East of Hungary]), *Folklore Archivum* 14, Budapest: MTA Néprajzi Kutatócsoport, pp. 182-183, 188-199.

GÉMES, B. 1987. A népi születésszabályozás (magzatelhajtás) Magyarországon a XIX.-XX. században. I. (Popular ways of birth-control [procured abortion] in the 19th and 20th centuries. Volume I.), *Documentatio Ethmographica* 12., Budapest: MTA Néprajzi Kutató Csoport. 1-296.

GRYNAEUS, T. 1974. *Cumania* 229-236.

HALASZNÉ ZELNIK, K. 1981. *Gyógyszerészet (Pharmacy)* 25:361-367.

HOPPAL, M. 1982. Varsányi hiedelmek (Folk Belief Stories from Varsány)., *Folklore Archivum* 14, Budapest: MTA Néprajzi Kutatócsoport, pp. 231-238.

KAPROS, M. 1986. *A születés szokásai és hiedelmei az Ipoly mentén. (Folk customs and beliefs of birth at Ipoly.)*, Debrecen.

KAPROS, M. 1990. A születés és a kisgyermekkor népszokásai (Folk customs of birth and young child age.)., in Dömötör, T, and Hoppál, M (eds.): *Magyar Néprajz (Hungarian Ethnography)*. VII., Népszokás, néphit, népi vallásosság. (Folk custom, folk belief, folk religiousness.), Budapest: Akadémiai Kiadó., pp. 9-31.

KESZEG, V. 1978. A mezőségi Detrehemtelep népi gyógyászata (Ethnomedicine of settlement 'Detrehem' in Mezőség), in Kos, K., FARAGO, J. (eds.) *Népismereti dolgozatok. (Composition on Popular Knowledge)*, pp. 97-117., Bukarest: Kriterion Könyvkiadó.

KOCZIAN, G., PINTÉR, I., GAL, M., SZABO, I., SZABO, L.GY. 1975. *Botanikai közlemények (Botanical Reviews)* 63:29-35.

KOCZIAN, G., SZABO, I., SZABO, L. GY. 1977. *Gyógyszerészet (Pharmacy)* 25 (1):5-17.

KOCZIAN, G. 1985. *A hagyományos parasztgazdálkodás termesztett, a gyűjtögető gazdálkodás vad növényfajainak ethnobotanikai értékelése. (Ethnobotanical evaluation of the cultivated plants of traditional agriculture, and that of wild plant species of gathering livelihood.)* Ph. D. dissertation, Mosonmagyaróvár: ATE Mezőgazdasági Kar.

KOCZIAN, G. 1988. *Gyógyszerészet (Pharmacy)* 32 (8):417-421.

KOCZIAN, G. 1990. *Gyógyszerészet (Pharmacy)* 34 (7):371-377.

KARA, J. 1973. Nagydobronyi szokások és hiedelmek (Folk customs and beliefs from Nagydobrony)., *Folklore Archivum* 1, Budapest: MTA Néprajzi Kutató Csoport., pp. 40-63.

MARKOCZI, M. 1993. *Természetgyógyászat (Natural medicine)* 3 (12):15.

MORVAY, J. 1956. *Asszonyok a nagycsaládban. (Women in great families)*, Budapest.

OLAH, A. 1985. *Fűbe-fába az orvosság! [Békés megyei népi orvoslás.]. (Medicines in grass and trees [Ethnomedicine in Békés-county])*, Békéscsaba., pp. 21-29.

OLAH, A. 1987. *Zöld varázslók, virág-orvosok. [Népi gyógynövényismeret Békés-megyében.] (Green-magicians, flower-doctors. [Popular knowledge on medicinal plants at Békés-County.])*, Békéscsaba.

ORTUTAY, GY. ed. in chief 1977-1982. *Magyar Néprajzi Lexikon I.-V. (Hungarian Ethnographical Lexicon Volume I-V.)*, Budapest: Akadémiai Könyvkiadó.

PÉNTEK, J., SZABO, A. 1985. *Ember és növényvilág. Kalotaszeg növényzete és népi növényismerete. (Plant Kingdom and Traditional Human Life in the Calata Area [Kalotaszeg]).*, Bukarest: Kriterion Könyvkiadó. pp. 197-308.

RAB, J. 1982. *Gyógyszerészet* 26 (9):325-333.

RAB, J. 1991. *Gyógyszerészet* 37 (7):373-380.

RAB, J., TANKO, P., TANKO, M. 1981. Népi növényismeret Gyimesbükkön (Popular knowledge on plants at Gyimesbükk)., in Kos, K., FARAGO, J.(ed.): *Népismereti Dolgozatok (Composition on Popular knowledge).*, pp. 28-38.

SZABO, A., PÉNTEK, J. 1976. *Ezerjófű. Etnobotanikai útmutató. (Centaury. An Ethnobotanical Guide.)*, Bukarest: Kriterion Könyvkiadó.

SZABO, L. GY. 1978. *Herba Hungarica* 17 (3):81-96.

TIMAFFY, L. 1980. *Szigetköz.*, Budapest: Gondolat.,

VAJKAI, A. 1943. *Népi orvoslás a Borsa-völgyében. (Ethnomedicine in Borsa-valley.)*, Kolozsvár.

VASAS, S. 1985. *Népi gyógyászat. Kalotaszeg. (Ethnomedicine - Kalotaszeg.)*, Bukarest: Kriterion Könyvkiadó.

ZENTAI, T. 1983. Ormánsági hiedelmek (Folk Beliefs in the Ormányság Region)., *Folklore Archivum* 15., Budapest: MTA Néprajzi Kutatócsoport, pp. 79-89, 92-96, 152-155, 158-159, 163-165.

Schwangerschaft als Risiko - Zur Entwicklung der Schwangerenvorsorge in Ost- und West-bezirken Berlins
Pregnancy as Risk - The Development of Prenatal Care in Districts of East- and Westberlin

Elke Barbian & Inez Werth

Zusammenfassung: Die medizinische Schwangerenvorsorge ist von einer stetig wachsenden Verfeinerung des technischen Instrumentariums zur Erkennung von Unregelmäßigkeiten und einer Risikoorientierung geprägt. Sie zielt darauf ab, aufgrund anamnestischer Befunden oder Auffälligkeiten während der Schwangerschaft Aussagen über ihren Verlauf und die Geburt sowie über die Gesundheit des Kindes zu machen. Diese Ausrichtung spiegelt sich wieder in einer ständigen Erweiterung des Risikokatalogs in den Mutterschaftsrichtlinien und immer intensiverem Einsatz von Ultra-Schall und anderen Methoden der pränatalen Diagnostik. Die technischen Möglichkeiten kommen zwar einerseits dem Sicherheitsbedürfnis der Frauen entgegen, andererseits verursachen sie neue Verunsicherungen und schwächen das Vertrauen der Frauen in ihren eigenen Körper. Während die Ambivalenz dieser Entwicklung durchaus von einer Reihe von Akteuren erkannt wird, scheint es für alle Beteiligten schwierig, sich der inneren Dynamik dieses Prozesses zu entziehen.
In den noch durch den Übergang in ein anderes Gesundheitssystem geprägten Ostbezirken Berlins ist eine größere Akzeptanz der medizin-technischen Dignostik anzutreffen sowie eine höhere Bereitschaft, dem Arzt Entscheidungskompetenz zuzubilligen.

Abstract: Prenatal care is presently determined by an increasing refinement of technical instruments to recognize irregularities and by a certain emphasis on risk factors in order to improve the capacity to anticipate the course of both pregnancy and birth and to achieve more secure statements about the child's health. This orientation is reflected in a growing expansion of the risk-catalogue in the maternity regulations („Mutterschaftsrichtlinien") as well as in intense sonographing and the employment of other methods of prenatal diagnosis. On the one hand these technical facilities meet women's need for security, on the other hand they cause new insecurities and weaken women's confidence in their own body. While some of the professionals are aware of the ambivalence of this development, it seems difficult for anybody involved to escape its inner dynamics.
In the boroughs of East Berlin where the impact of the former socialist health system is still existent one finds a higher acceptance of diagnoses based on medical technics as well as a greater willingness to allow doctors the competence of decision making.

Keywords: Bundesrepublik Deutschland/DDR; Medizinsoziologie; Schwangerenbetreuung; Medizintechnik; Schwangerschaftserleben, Federal Republic of Germany /GDR; prenatal care; sociology of medicine; medical technics; perception of pregnancy

Schwangerschaft, ein natürlicher und an sich gesunder körperlicher Vorgang im Leben einer Frau, wird heute mehr und mehr als ein Zustand begriffen, der professioneller Betreuung bedarf, die mittlerweile überwiegend von der Medizin besetzt wird. Während die Beachtung des lebensweltlichen Bereichs der Schwangeren in den Hintergrund getreten ist, konzentriert sich die medizinische Vorsorge immer stärker auf die Abwendung von Gefahren und auf Risikofrüherkennung. So wurde der Begriff der Risikoschwangerschaft entscheidend erweitert (vgl. TIETZE 1992) und das diagnostische Instrumentarium (HOFF 1995:47) immer stärker differenziert. Dies hat zu einer stetigen Verfeinerung der Vorsorgeprogramme (vgl. WULF 1992a) geführt, wobei aber die Aussagekraft der Befunde manchmal überschätzt wird. Die Konsequenzen daraus werden auf unterschiedlichen Ebenen sichtbar, für die Frauen vor allem in einem veränderten Erleben von Schwangerschaft.

Eine Untersuchung des Berliner Forschungsverbundes Public Health (BARBIAN et al 1996) ist der Frage nachgegangen, inwieweit die Vorsorgeangebote der Schwangerenbetreuung mit dem Bedarf, d.h. den Wünschen und Vorstellungen der schwangeren Frauen, übereinstimmen. Dabei wurde dem Einfluss der Technik innerhalb der Schwangerenvorsorge - vor allem auf das Erleben der Frauen -gezielte Aufmerksamkeit geschenkt.

Um regionale Bedingungen als auch den Wandel, der sich im Gesundheitswesen durch die Anpassung des Ostberliner an das Westberliner Versorgungssystem vollzogen hat, mit zu erfassen, wurden die Interviews in jeweils zwei Ost - und zwei Westberliner Bezirken durchgeführt.

Während in der Bundesrepublik Deutschland die medizinische Schwangerenvorsorge in der Regel von niedergelassenen GynäkologInnen und unter bestimmten Bedingungen auch von Hebammen durchgeführt wird und die nichtmedizinische Betreuung wie z.B. Beratungsangebote oder Geburtsvorbereitungskurse anderen Berufsgruppen in unterschiedlichen organisatorischen Zusammenhängen überlassen bleibt, war sie in der DDR in zentralen Schwangerenberatungsstellen (angegliedert an Kreiskrankenhäusern oder Polikliniken) integriert, wo Gynäkologen, Hebammen und Fürsorgerinnen für alle möglichen Belange der Schwangerschaft zuständig waren.

Der Wegfall dieser Schwangerenberatungsstellen bzw. ihr Übergang in das dezentrale Versorgungssytem westdeutscher Prägung ist nicht nur für die professionellen Akteure eine erhebliche Umstellung, sondern bringt auch für die Frauen veränderte Bedingungen mit sich, die auf das Erleben der Schwangerschaft nicht ohne Einfluss bleiben.

Die technische Weiterentwicklung in der Schwangerenvorsorge bedeutet für viele Frauen mehr Sicherheit, andererseits entstehen neue Verunsicherungen. So beobachten besonders Hebammen bei den Frauen ein abnehmendes Vertrauen in den eigenen Körper. „Frauen verlassen sich weniger auf ihre körperlichen Gefühle und konzentrieren sich mehr auf die Aussagen des Arztes", fasst es eine von ihnen in Worte. Auf ärztlicher Seite entspricht dieser Entwicklung das sukzessive Verschwinden manueller Untersuchungskompetenzen und eine zunehmende Fixierung auf die Apparate. Eine ältere Gynäkologin bedauert, „dass viele junge Kollegen ihre Hände vergessen, und... ihre Augen vergessen und das, was die Patientin sagt, vergessen".

Auch wenn nicht alle MedizinerInnen den technischen Neuerungen nur positiv gegenüber stehen und sich durchaus distanziert äußern: „Die diagnostischen Möglichkeiten, von denen wir sicher viele haben, sicher werden auch viele verworfen werden", setzt die Existenz dieser Verfahren jedoch eine innere Dynamik in Gang, der sich zu entziehen nicht einfach ist. Die generelle Schwierigkeit, unter einem einmal erreichten technischen Niveau freiwillig zurückzubleiben, hat hier ebenso Einfluss wie die Erwartungen der Frauen, die ein weniger an Diagnostik nicht selten als Vernachlässigung werten.

1. Der Umgang mit der Risikoschwangerschaft

Als Ergebnis einer längeren Entwicklung sind mittlerweile im Mutterpass 49 Risikomerkmale dokumentiert, so dass der Anteil der diagnostizierten Risikoschwangerschaften sich heute zwischen 50 und 63 % bewegt (LINK/KÜNZEL 1989:140; GROßPIETSCH 1994:189; HOFF 1995: 46). Dabei darf nicht übersehen werden, dass eine Risikoschwangerschaft u.U. eine negativ wirkende Etikettierung eines an sich gesunden Zustandes bedeuten kann, die die Frauen erheblich verunsichert. Bereits das Wort „Risiko" ist negativ besetzt (WULF 1992 b:127) und hat, wie folgende Zitate illustrieren, eine angstauslösende Wirkung: „Am Anfang hat mich das bestürzt", „ dieses Wort Risikoschwangerschaft ist einfach so furchtbar, es ist, dass man wirklich gleich graue Haare davon bekommt". Das wird auch von GynäkologInnen und Hebammen erkannt, „die Frauen sind so mit Angst besetzt, das ist eine Katastrophe" und „sie kommen immer schon zaghaft an". Auch gilt es zu bedenken, dass es sich hier teilweise um nicht objektivierbare Größen des möglichen Risikos handelt und der Umgang wesentlich vom subjektiven Vorverständnis und dem Erfahrungshorizont der jeweils betreuenden GynäkologIn abhängt (vgl. WULF 1992b). Das spielt auch dann eine Rolle, wenn z.B. neu niedergelassene GynäkologInnen in den Ostbezirken nun auch schwangere Frauen betreuen, nachdem sie zuvor als spezialisierte Klinikärzte keine Erfahrung in der Geburtshilfe gemacht hatten.

Die Ambivalenz der Ärzte hinsichtlich des Umgangs mit dem Begriff der Risikoschwangerschaft kam auch in der Untersuchung zum Ausdruck, „... was früher als normal eingestuft wurde, ist nicht mehr normal... die richtigen medizinischen Risiken sind die wenigsten, das andere ist durch die Gesellschaft hervorgebracht" oder aus der entgegengesetzten Position Aussagen wie „jede Schwangerschaft ist ein Risiko". Um Verunsicherungen zu vermeiden, verwenden manche GynäkologInnen den Begriff nur noch eingeschränkt, auch wenn die Kriterien entsprechend dem Mutterpass erfüllt sind.

Auch die Einstellung zur Altersindikation als Risikokriterium ist sehr unterschiedlich. Während manche GynäkologInnen es ablehnen, Frauen jenseits des 35. Lebensjahres als Risikoschwangere zu behandeln und eine Neudefinition des Risikokatalogs fordern, sehen andere hingegen die Altersindikation als „fließende Grenze" oder aber als selbstverständlich an. Ungeachtet der Einsicht in die Vielschichtigkeit dieses Begriffs darf nicht übersehen werden, dass für die MedizinerInnen weitere Aspekte hinzukommen. Neben der Haftung bezüglich der Beratungspflicht (vgl. SCHLUND 1992; SCHLUND 1995:203f) gehören dazu vor allem ökonomische Anreize, da eine diagnostizierte Risikoschwangerschaft die Vorsorge hinsichtlich Frequenz und Technikeinsatz erweitert. Gerade bei den GynäkologInnen in den Ostberliner Bezirken ist der wirtschaftliche Druck, der aus den Investitionskosten für die Niederlassung erwächst, unverkennbar. Ein weiteres Problem, auf das von allen Untersuchungsgruppen hingewiesen wird, sind die sozialen Bedingungen als Ursache medizinischer Risiken, die allerdings in der ärztlichen Beratung oft nicht erkannt werden, so dass ihnen nicht mit adäquaten Mitteln begegnet wird. Stattdessen werden die Frauen häufig in die Klinik überwiesen, „ab und zu Wehen sind normal, beim Gynäkologen geht aber gleich die Maschinerie los". Im Osten der Stadt wird an dieser Stelle gern auf die Vorteile der verlorengegangenen Schwangerenberatungsstellen hingewiesen, die, da man die häuslichen Bedingungen der Frauen kannte, eher in der Lage waren, entsprechend zu intervenieren.

2. Ultraschall
Die Untersuchungsergebnisse lassen erkennen, dass in der Praxis sehr viel häufiger Ultraschalluntersuchungen stattfinden als es die jüngste Regelung der Mutterschaftsrichtlinien mit drei Sonographien für eine normal verlaufende Schwangerschaft vorsieht (vgl. Mutterschaftsrichtlinien Novellierung vom 1.4.95). Die Mehrzahl der Frauen und Hebammen, aber auch der GynäkologInnen berichten von einem deutlich umfangreicheren Einsatz dieser Technik, wobei die Angaben von „viermal" bis zu „öfter", „alle 14 Tage" oder gar „jedes Mal" reichen.

Die Ursachen hierfür liegen auf verschiedenen Ebenen: So sind eine Reihe von MedizinerInnen davon überzeugt, dass nur durch regelmäßige Ultraschalluntersuchungen eine effektive Überwachung der Schwangerschaft und des Wachstums des Foeten möglich ist - wie auch folgende Äußerung belegt: „jeden Monat gibt es Besonderheiten, die zu beobachten sind... Ich weiß, dass die anderen auch nachgucken". Dazu kommt die rechtliche Absicherung, „wenn man etwas übersieht, steht man ja immer mit einem Bein so'n bisschen im Knast". In diesem Zusammenhang sollte nicht vergessen werden, dass ein Teil dieses auf Absicherung bedachten Vorgehens aus dem Verlust konservativer Untersuchungsmethoden resultiert. In den neuen Bundesländern kommt erschwerend hinzu, dass die GynäkologInnen, die nicht aus der Schwangerenbetreuung kommen und über wenig Praxis mit dem U-Schall verfügen, dazu neigen, diesen expansiv einzusetzen, um Erfahrungen in seiner Anwendung zu gewinnen und die notwendigen Qualifikationen zu erwerben. Ein anderer Aspekt, der nicht unerwähnt bleiben darf, ist der immer drängender vorgebrachte Wunsch der Schwangeren nach regelmäßigen Ultraschall-Untersuchungen. Folgende Zitate illustrieren diese Situation aus ärztlicher Perspektive: „jeden Tag können die das machen" oder Ultraschall wird „knallhart gefordert". Mancher Gynäkologe fühlt sich gar als „Service-Unternehmen" für die Visualisierungswünsche der Familien: „...und dann kommt die ganze Sippe ...und die wünschen sich das ständig". Die werdenden Mütter untermauern mit positiven Schilderungen die Wahrnehmung der ÄrztInnen: Ultraschall ist „schön" oder „toll".

Eine Erklärung für diese positive Resonanz mag sein, dass die frühzeitige Visualisierung vielen Frauen den Kontakt zum Ungeborenen eröffnet. So kommt dem Ultraschall, vor allem solange keine Kindsbewegungen zu spüren sind, ein hoher Stellenwert für die emotionale Bindung zu. Aussagen wie „das Baby winkt" oder gar, „es war gut zu sehen, wie es sich bewegt, da glaubt man erst so richtig, dass man schwanger ist" machen deutlich, in welchem Maße die Wahrnehmung der Schwangerschaft von der „Sichtbarmachung" beeinflusst wird (vgl. DUDEN 1991; SCHINDELE 1990). Besonders Frauen in den Ostbezirken der Stadt nehmen dieses Babyfernsehen, das es in der DDR in dieser Form nicht gab, mit Begeisterung auf. Die vorrangige Funktion des Ultraschalls ist die Vermittlung von Sicherheit, dass es „dem Kind gut geht", dass „die Schwangerschaft intakt ist". Gleichzeitig kann er aber zu einer Quelle der Verunsicherung werden, wenn Befunde wie „der Kopf ist zu klein" oder „zu wenig Fruchtwasser" nicht der Norm entsprechen. Die Frauen werden „total verunsichert...und können sich gar nicht auf ihr eigenes Körpergefühl verlassen, sind total fixiert auf dieses Ergebnis,". Die Freude an der Schwangerschaft ist so nicht selten von Ängsten überschattet. Ein weiteres Thema sind die möglichen Risiken der Ultraschall-Diagnostik (vgl. BLEECH/ROBINSON 1990). Sie werden von den GynäkologInnen ganz unterschiedlich eingeschätzt. Während manche Ärzte die Diskussion um die Schädlichkeit des Ultraschall „übertrieben" finden, sind andere vorsichtiger und bevorzugen einen zurückhaltenden Umgang:

„Ich achte immer darauf, nicht so lange und oft zu gucken...es könnte in den ersten vier Monaten durch die Wellen eine kleine Störung geben". Die Frauen selbst werden durch immer wieder erscheinende Presseberichte über eine mögliche Schädlichkeit des Ultraschalls aufgeschreckt. In der ärztlichen Beratung erhalten Frauen vorwiegend den Hinweis, dass Ultraschall unschädlich ist bzw. keine eindeutigen Forschungsergebnisse vorliegen. Dies gilt ganz besonders für die Ostberliner Bezirke, wo Frauen sich ihre Bedenken rasch durch die GynäkologInnen zerstreuen lassen. Hebammen hingegen berichten, dass die Frauen trotz ihrer Begeisterung für das Babyfernsehen bei längeren Untersuchungen spüren, wie das Kind unruhig wird und sie sich danach „total schlecht fühlen".

Durch die Verfeinerung der Ultraschalltechnik in den vergangenen zehn Jahren ist inzwischen ein erweiterter Fehlbildungsausschluss des Foeten möglich (vgl. Mutterschaftsrichtlinien Novellierung vom 1.4.1995). Wie die Untersuchungsergebnisse zeigen, weisen Westberliner ÄrztInnen diese Maßnahme überwiegend im Fall bestimmter Risiken oder Verdachtsmomente an, während sie für viele Ostberliner GynäkologInnen zu der aus DDR-Zeiten beibehaltenen Routine gehört. Hier ist - was auch für sonstige Maßnahmen der Pränataldiagnostik gilt - ein weniger kritischer Umgang mit dem Einsatz von Technik anzutreffen als in den Westberliner Bezirken. Ebenso scheint die Norm des gesunden Kindes stark ver*innerlicht, und es wird - neben dem individuellen Wunsch - eine gesamtgesellschaftliche Verpflichtung miteinbezogen*. So argumentiert eine Ärztin „Feindiagnostik ist eine weitere Sicherheit für die Frau und letztendlich ja auch für die Gesellschaft...denn ein missgebildetes Kind kann die Gesellschaft doch sehr teuer kommen". Andere betonen, dass gerade vor dem Hintergrund der niedrigen Geburtenrate „es wichtig ist, dass alles in Ordnung ist". Von den Schwangeren erwarten GynäkologInnen ein Sich-Einfügen in einen für richtig erachteten Maßnahmekatalog oder lassen ihr Bedauern erkennen, dass man die Frauen nicht „wie früher" - ob sie wollen oder nicht - zur Feindiagnostik „schicken" kann.

2.2. Die genetische Diagnostik

Neben der feindiagnostischen Sonographie umfasst die Pränataldiagnostik Methoden wie Amniozentese (vgl. MURKEN 1987) oder Chorionzottenbiopsie (FUHRMANN/RAUSKOLB/JOVANOVICH 1992: 287), bei denen fetale Zellen entnommen und labortechnisch auf eine mögliche Behinderung des Ungeborenen überprüft werden. Mitunter gehen diesen Verfahren serologische Tests zur Wahrscheinlichkeitsbestimmung - z.B. der Alpha-Fetoprotein-Test (AFP) (vgl. FUHRMANN/WEITZEL 1985) oder die sog. Triple-Diagnostik (GROTH/SCHULZE 1993:29) - voraus. Von der Triple-Diagnostik halten aufgrund ihrer weitgefassten Wahrscheinlichkeitsvarianzen und den damit verbundenen Verunsicherungen der Frau allerdings viele GynäkologInnen wenig oder „gar nichts" oder befürchten, dass die Ergebnisse nur Anlass „zu vielen unnötig durchgeführten Amniozentesen bei völlig gesundem Kind" geben. Der AFP-Test wird - ähnlich wie die Feindiagnostik oder das Toxoplasmosescreening - in den Ostberliner Bezirken routinemäßig durchgeführt, während er im Westen bislang noch nicht zum Regelkatalog gehört.

Die Aussicht, durch Amniozentese oder Chorionzottenbiopsie eine Behinderung frühzeitig zu erkennen, hat tief in die Vorstellungen der Frauen eingegriffen und den Bedarf enorm ansteigen lassen, auch über die ursprüngliche Indikation wie familiäre Vorbelastungen oder Alter (35 Jahre und älter) hinaus. Die Initiative für die Anwendung geht häufig von den Frauen selbst aus, wie es eine Gynäkologin beschreibt, „das ist schon sehr geschient und gebahnt, dass sie mit diesen Themen kommen". Durch die Auffindungsmöglichkeit bestimmter Behinderungen geht der Wunsch nach einem gesunden Kind zunehmend in den Anspruch über, von der Medizin die Garantie für ein gesundes Kind zu erhalten. „Es muss ein gesundes Kind sein", fasst dies eine Beraterin zusammen, „die Schwangerschaft, die Geburt, alles muss perfekt sein." Bei den Ostberliner InterviewpartnerInnen wird weniger die Anspruchshaltung als eine - ähnlich wie bei der Feindiagnostik - selbstverständliche Befolgung ärztlichen Rates sichtbar. Gemeinsam ist allen Frauen jedoch die Sorge, durch eine Amniozentese oder eine Chorionzottenbiopsie einen Abort zu induzieren (MURKEN 1994: 152) oder den Foetus zu schädigen.

Eine zusätzliche Belastung besteht darin, dass viele Frauen sich bis zum Erhalt des Ergebnisses der Untersuchung nicht wirklich auf die Schwangerschaft einlassen können. „Erst als man mir gesagt hat, dass alles in Ordnung ist, habe ich mich so richtig gefreut auf das Kind", beschreibt es eine Schwangere, die Zeit zwischen Untersuchung und Mitteilung sitzt sie „natürlich wie auf Kohlen", „es ist die schlimmste Zeit". Die Konsequenzen wirken sich nicht selten negativ auf den gesamten Verlauf der Schwangerschaft aus. Hinzu kommt, dass sich viele ÄrztInnen in einem Dilemma fühlen, ihrer Aufklärungspflicht nachzukommen, denn sie fürchten, die Schwangere „mit diesem Quatsch" zu belasten.

Nicht alle GynäkologInnen sind sich der Notwendigkeit eines ausführlichen Gesprächs bewusst. So bleibt es häufig bei knappen Informationen über die medizinischen Risiken dieser Diagnostik und die Treffsicherheit ihrer Aussagen, während eine qualifizierte, auch psychosoziale Beratung, die die Frauen in ihrer Entscheidungsfindung unterstützt, fehlt. Dies gilt in verstärktem Maße für die Ostberliner Praxen. Viele Frauen fühlen sich allein gelassen, wie Äußerungen belegen: „ich meine, es sind nicht sehr viele menschliche Dinge da" oder „als ich mich noch ein bisschen beraten lassen wollte, hieß es, da gibt es nichts weiter zu beraten, entweder Sie lassen das machen oder nicht". Auch mangelt es an Aufklärung im Falle eines positiven Befunds. „Die Schwangeren sind sich nicht bewusst, was hinterher kommt", wird übereinstimmend beobachtet. Sie wissen selten, dass es keine therapeutischen Maßnahmen im Falle einer diagnostizierten Schädigung gibt und was eine in der 20. bis 22. Woche eingeleitete Geburt bedeutet. Der schwierige Umgang mit dieser Situation lässt manche GynäkologInnen von einem ausführlichen Gespräch über die Konsequenzen zurückscheuen. So ist nur wenigen Frauen bewusst, dass bei positivem Befund in der Regel ein Schwangerschaftsabbruch folgt. „Nur akademisches Abklären ist kein Grund" , „sonst ist es nur ein unnötiges zusätzliches Risiko". Im Fall einer realistischen Beratung treten Frauen nicht selten von der geplanten Untersuchung zurück.

Abschließend wäre festzustellen, dass, obwohl die ambivalente Wirkung des medizin-technischen Einsatzes während der Schwangerschaft von einigen Akteuren gesehen wird, es für die einzelnen - sei es GynäkologIn oder Schwangere selbst - schwierig scheint, sich der Dynamik dieser Entwicklung zu entziehen. Gleichzeitig mehren sich die Stimmen, die für einen behutsamen Einsatz plädieren, da nicht nur Sicherheit gewonnen wird, sondern auch erhebliche Verunsicherungen in Kauf genommen werden müssen. Ein Ende der Technisierung lässt sich jedoch nicht absehen, wobei in den neuen Bundesländern die Akzeptanz der technischen Hilfsmittel besonders hoch erscheint.

References
BLEECH, B.A.L.; J. ROBINSON. 1990. Risk of antenatal ultrasound. *The Lancet* 336 [6]: 871-875
DUDEN, B. 1991. *Der Frauenleib als öffentlicher Ort. Vom Missbrauch des Begriffs Leben.* Hamburg, Zürich
FUHRMANN, W.; R. RAUSKOLB; V. JOVANOVIC. 1992. Pränatale Diagnostik. Aufgaben und Methoden. In (1992^3): *Schwangerschaft I. Klinik der Frauenheilkunde und Geburtshilfe.* Bd. 4. Edited by W.KÜNZEL, K.-H. WULF, pp.285-314. München, Wien, Baltimore
FUHRMANN, W., H.K. WEITZEL. 1985. Maternal serum alpha-fetoprotein screening for neutral tube defects. Hum Genet 69: 47-61
GROßPIETSCH, G. 1995. Prägravide Vorsorge - Schwangerenvorsorge. in: Hebammenlehrbuch. Edited by G. Martius and W. Heidenreich, pp 163-196. Stuttgart
GROTH, S., C.SCHULZE. 1993: Ethische Überlegungen zur Triple-Diagnostik. Pro Familia Magazin. Sexualpädagogik und Familienplanung 1: 5-6
HOFF, B. 1995. Vertragsärztliche Versorgung. Ärztliche Betreuung bei Schwangerschaft und Entbindung. Neue Ergebnisse. DOK 1-2: 44-48
LINK, G., W. KÜNZEL. 1989. Häufigkeit von Risikoschwangerschaften. Eine Analyse der Perinatalstatistiken der Bundesländer. Gynäkologe 22: 140-144
MURKEN, J. (Hrsg.) 1987. Pränatale Diagnostik und Therapie. Stuttgart
[Mutterschaftsrichtlinien]. Richtlinien über die ärztliche Betreuung während der Schwangerschaft und nach der Entbindung. In der Fassung vom 10. Dez. 1985, geändert 1987, 1989, 1990 (zweimal), 1991, 1992, 1994, 1995 RVO 246
SCHINDELE E.1990. *Gläserne Gebärmutter.* Frankfurt/Main
SCHLUND, G.H. 1992. Sorgfaltspflichtverletzung des Geburtshelfers und Schaden des Kindes aus juristischer Sicht. *Gynäkologe* 25: 192-195
SCHLUND, G.H. 1995. Haftungsfragen in Frauenheilkunde und Geburtshilfe. *Gynäkologische Praxis* 19: 203-204
TIETZE, K.W. 1992. *Gesetzliche und soziale Grundlagen der Schwangerenvorsorge. Qualitätskontrolle.* in *Schwangerschaft I. Die normale Schwangerschaft. Klinik der Frauenheilkunde und Geburtshilfe,* Band 4. Edited by KÜNZEL, W., K.-H.WULF. (1992^3) pp 87-105 München, Wien, Baltimore
WULF, K.-H. 1992a. Schwangerenvorsorge - Inanspruchnahme und Effektivität. Dtsch. Ärztebl. 89 [40]: 1803-1807
WULF, K.H. 1992b. Untersuchungen während der Schwangerschaft. Risikoschwangerschaft. in Schwangerschaft I. *Klinik der Frauenheilkunde und Geburtshilfe.* Bd. 4, Edited by KÜNZEL, W., K.-H.WULF. (1992^3) pp 107-132. München, Wien, Baltimore

Wendepunkt Geburt - Unvereinbarkeit von Frau- und Muttersein als Gesundheitsrisiko in westlichen Industrieländern
Turning Point Birth - The Incompatibility of Being a Mother and a Woman as a Health Risk in Western Industrial Countries

Joachim Bensel & Gabriele Haug-Schnabel

Zusammenfassung: Der Übergang zur Mutterschaft gehört zu den kritischen Lebensereignissen. Er kann in westlichen Ländern mit dem Wechsel von einer gesellschaftlich akzeptierten und integrierten Position der Frau hin zu einer zweitklassigen Stellung, verbunden mit sozialer Desintegration und persönlicher Verunsicherung, einhergehen. Übergangsriten, die in traditionalen Gesellschaften noch anzutreffen sind, fehlen weit gehend. Die mütterliche Kompetenz, die ererbten intuitiven Geburts- und Betreuungskompetenzen werden von Spezialisten mit erlernter Berufskompetenz nicht beachtet oder in Frage gestellt. „Kranken"häuser regeln Geburtszeitpunkt und verlauf, Rhythmusfindung und Nahrungsbedarf für das gesunde Mutter-Kind-Paar. Der Erfolg der gesellschaftlichen Wiedereingliederung nach der Geburt eines Kindes hängt fast ausschließlich von den persönlichen Anstrengungen der Mutter ab.
Verschiedene psychosomatische Reaktionen, die mit der Überlastung durch diese anspruchsvolle Aufgabe zusammenhängen, zeigen sich u. a. in Phänomenen wie Heultage, Wochenbettdepression oder Überforderungsreaktionen, auch als Konsequenz einer alleinigen und somit unbiologischen 24-Stunden-rund-um-die-Uhr-Betreuung des Säuglings. Kommen zusätzliche Probleme in der Nachgeburtsphase seitens des Säuglings hinzu, wie z. B. die berüchtigte 3-Monats-Kolik, kann das mütterliche Ressourcensystem endgültig zusammenbrechen. Diskutiert werden in diesem Zusammenhang Prävention und Intervention, um die intuitiven Fähigkeiten der Frau im Übergang zu stützen, die intuitiven Fähigkeiten des Vaters zu erkennen und zuzulassen, das soziale Netz der Eltern zu stabilisieren und psychische und physische Folgereaktionen einer fehlenden Passung zwischen elterlichen bzw. kindlichen psychobiologischen Bedürfnissen einerseits und angebotener Kulturwelt andererseits zu vermeiden.

Abstract: The transition to motherhood is one of the most critical events in the life of a woman. In western countries it can be accompanied by a shift from a socially accepted and integrated position as a woman to a second-class status associated with social disintegration and personal insecurity. Transition rituals, or rites of passage, as still to be found in traditional societies, are for the most part missing. The maternal competence, the inherited intuitive birth and nurturing abilities, are either ignored or viewed sceptically by specialists with their skills learned in professional training.
Hospitals determine the time of birth, the course of labour, the establishment of sleep rhythms and feeding regimens for the healthy mother-baby pair. The success of social reintegration after the birth of a child depends almost exclusively on the personal efforts of the mother. Various psychosomatic reactions arise as a consequence of this demanding task, which often proves overwhelming. These manifest themselves in the form of phenomena such as maternity blues, post-partum depression or "overload"-reactions, in part due to the mother having sole responsibility for the newborn around the clock - a totally unbiological demand. When additional problems arise on the part of the baby in the period after birth, such as the notorious 3-month colic, the mother's resource system may be overtaxed to the breaking point. In this context, prevention and intervention are discussed, with the goals of supporting the intuitive capabilities of the woman in transition, recognizing the intuitive abilities of the father and giving them a chance for meaningful expression, stabilizing the social network of the parents, and avoiding possible psychic and physical reactions resulting from inadequate matching between the parental and child's psychobiological needs on the one hand and opportunities provided by the cultural world on the other.

Keywords: Kulturenvergleich, Geburt, Wochenbett, Humanethologie, Übergangsriten, angeborenes Elternprogramm, Frau und Mutter, Vereinbarkeit von Familie und Beruf, crosscultural comparison, birth, puerperium, human ethology, rites of passage, intuitive parental care, woman and mother, compatibility of family and work

Mutter (Eltern) werden ohne Rituale

Einschneidende Veränderungen in der Lebensbiographie eines Menschen werden bei traditionalen Gesellschaften von kulturell genau festgelegten Riten begleitet. Deren Lebensweisen erleichtern uns die Vorstellung über unsere Vergangenheit, dienen uns als evolutionäres Modell. Obwohl traditionale Gesellschaften - wie wir - Angehörige der Spezies Homo sapiens mit allen intellektuellen Potentialen dieser Entwicklungsstufe und deshalb nicht mit unseren stammesgeschichtlichen Urahnen identisch sind. Doch ihre Lebensweisen und sozialen Strukturen, wie sie etwa bei traditionalen Gesellschaften in Südamerika, Südafrika und in Neuguinea zu finden sind, ähneln nach unserem heutigen Kenntnisstand dem Leben unserer Vorfahren mehr, als dies unser Leben in den industrialisierten Großgesellschaften der Jetztzeit tut. Ein Vergleich zeigt, dass beispielsweise zur Pubertät gehörende Initiationsriten bei den traditionalen Gesellschaften den Übergang vom Adoleszenten zum Erwachsenen erleichtern, während dieser Entwicklungsabschnitt bei uns nahezu ohne Initiationsäquivalente zu einer Krisenperiode geworden ist (KLOSINSKI 1991, HAUG-SCHNABEL 1993).

Noch interessanter und aussagekräftiger erscheint ein Vergleich, der die soziale Einbettung der beginnenden Mutterschaft in beiden Lebenswelten vorstellt. Der Begriff „rites de passage" (GENNEP 1960) kennzeichnet die Zeit der Schwangerschaft, Geburt und Elternschaft als eine Übergangszeit, in der die Frau in den meisten Kulturen durch präzise Vorschriften, familiäre Unterstützung und Kulthandlungen auf ihren neuen Status als Mutter vorbereitet wird. Eine kurzfristige Separation aus ihrem gewohnten Lebensbereich, kombiniert mit Riten der Reinigung und Säuberung, gehören dazu. Der alte Status wird aufgehoben, deutlich gemacht an der Konfrontation mit speziellen neuen Anforderungen sowie mit einer den Umstellungsprozess symbolisierenden Warteperiode. Vor allem aber ist hier eine mit Feierlichkeiten vollzogene Wiedereingliederung in die Gesellschaft zu finden, die mit Hilfe von Privilegien den neuen Status bewusst werden lässt (SEEL 1986).

Selbst für den Vater gibt es in manchen Kulturen eine so genannte „Couvade", eine Geburtsvorbereitungsphase speziell für Männer, die eine Kindstötung unwahrscheinlicher macht (ELWOOD & MASON 1994).

In den Industrienationen fehlen solche Übergangsriten weit gehend. Zwar sind einige Autoren der Ansicht, dass zumindest die Rituale der ersten 2 Übergangsabschnitte, Separation und Aufhebung des alten Status, auch in veränderter Form bei uns noch existieren (KUMAR 1994). Aber die eine moderne Geburt begleitenden rituellen Handlungen im Krankenhaus, wie das Rasieren der Schamhaare, der Einlauf, das Bad sowie die Gratulation nach der Geburt (KITZINGER 1980), aber auch schon zuvor die Geburtsvorbereitungskurse bzw. Selbsthilfegruppen (ALBRECHT-ENGEL 1995) sind wohl nur ein schwacher Ersatz für die eine Frau im Übergang aufrüttelnden, stützenden und nachhaltig beeinflussenden Stammesriten. Die Geburtsvorbereitungskurse haben sich in den letzten Jahren weiter entwickelt von reinen Gymnastik- und Atemtechnikübungsstunden hin zu einer auch psychologischen Vorbereitung auf das Geburtsgeschehen. Aber sie bleiben dennoch vorrangig ein Programm für die Mittelschicht und bieten wenigen Frauen Hilfe für die postpartale Zeit.

Neu ist, dass die Schwangerschaft zeitlich primär durch die zum Geburtstermin hin immer häufiger werdenden medizinischen Vorsorgetermine gegliedert wird. Ab dem Bekanntwerden der Befruchtung liegt das Schwangerschaftmanagement - nahezu unabhängig vom Gesundheitszustand von Mutter und Kind - in medizinischer Hand. Es steht nicht zur Diskussion, dass die medizinische präventive Versorgung eine wichtige, Menschenleben rettende und somit humanitäre Errungenschaft zunehmenden Wissens und immer weiter entwickelter Technologie ist. Und dennoch sollte die Risikokomponente nicht automatisch, nahezu „naturgemäß" das Werden eines Kindes dominieren. „Wird auch alles gut gehen?" „Mach' ich die Geburt richtig?" „Ist unser Kind gesund?" Neben einer durchorganisierten Schwangerschaft bleibt die Einstimmung auf das Kind individuelle Privatsache, sehr oft sogar allein Sache der Frau. Ist sie aufgeschlossen, kontaktfreudig und wohnt sie zudem günstig, so trifft sie sich mit Frauen, die ihr bislang unbekannt waren, und deren einzige Gemeinsamkeit mit ihr der in etwa zum gleichen Zeitpunkt bevorstehende Geburtstermin ist. Die Gemeinsamkeiten nehmen zu, der wachsende Bauch, die Kurzatmigkeit, das Sodbrennen und die Gespräche über die Geburt. Über die Zeit danach wird weit weniger gesprochen. Der Geburtstermin bildet gedanklich eine Zäsur, zumindest beim ersten Kind, die Zeit danach ist noch außerhalb der Vorstellungsmöglichkeiten. Außerdem wird man sich danach in dieser Gruppenkonstellation kaum mehr wiedersehen; man wird sich wieder fremd. Dennoch kommt es in der etwa dreimonatigen Kontaktzeit - ermöglicht durch den allen gemeinsamen besonderen Zustand - zu vertraulichen Gesprächen über höchst Intimes, bis hin zu offen ausgesprochenen Ängsten. Im Gespräch wird nach Gemeinsamkeiten gesucht und Unterschiede werden zumindest anfangs mit Erschrecken wahrgenommen. Die wenige Erfahrung, nicht das wenige Wissen, verstärkt wie in allen Verunsicherungsmomenten des Erlebens den Wunsch nach Übereinstimmung, nach sozialer Ratifizierung durch die Mehrheit.

Schwangerschaft und Geburt sind aus dem Normalleben ausgegliedert. Erst für Betroffene werden sie zum Thema, doch der Betroffenenstatus lässt sie dann nicht mehr angstfrei erleben und erfahren.

Gerade jetzt wären Übergangshilfen wichtig für eine Neuorientierung der werdenden Eltern in der Gesellschaft, für die Einstimmung auf eine völlig neue Lebenssituation, nämlich die eines Paares mit Kind oder Kindern. Das Sicherheitsnetz einer Großfamilie existiert kaum noch. Selbst auf dem Land sind Flexibilität und Mobilität mit ihren Folgen der räumlichen Aufgliederung der Familien und der Distanzierung der Angehörigen gang und gäbe, und selbst wenn noch mehrere Generationen zusammenleben, ist die Weitergabe von Wissen und Erfahrung über die Grundregeln der Familienentstehung nicht gewährleistet (ALBRECHT-ENGEL 1995: 32). Der sich hieraus ergebende Traditionsbruch hat auch positive Seiten, könnte er doch die Chance einer Neudefinition des Umgangs und Lebens mit dem Neugeborenen bedeuten sowie eine individuelle Gestaltung des Erziehungsstils und der Familienprägung. Unsere westliche, körperdistanzierte, von Verwöhnungsängsten bestimmte Tradition reicht kulturgeschichtlich weit zurück (DEMAUSE 1980), und es scheint notwendig, mit ihr immer mehr zu brechen.

Geburtssituation
Werfen wir doch einmal einen Blick auf die eigentliche Geburtssituation. Ohne Vorerfahrung durch frühere Teilnahme an einem Geburtsvorgang befreundeter oder verwandter Frauen oder stützende Hilfe durch eine intime Begleitperson ist vor allem die Erstgebärende oft in einer Situation der Hilflosigkeit und gibt die Geburtsverantwortung an das ihr zumeist gänzlich unbekannte medizinische Personal ab. Es ist noch nicht einmal gewährleistet, dass dieselbe Hebamme vor, während und nach der Geburt die Schwangere begleitet. Ist diese Verantwortungsübergabe aus situativer Not heraus erst einmal erfolgt, so ist es „... offensichtlich, daß Schwangere und Gebärende nicht als aktive, kraftvolle Frauen gesehen werden, die „von Natur aus" die Fähigkeit haben, Kinder auszutragen und zu gebären, sondern daß der Ansatz der Medizin ist, einen potentiell Frau und Kind gefährdenden Vorgang zu überwachen und zu optimieren" (ALBRECHT-ENGEL 1995: 37). Und auch in Bezug auf den Säugling, den zweiten am Geschehen beteiligten Akteur, schreibt SCHLEIDT (1989: 15) angebracht provokant: „Beim Umgang von ‚Fachleuten' ... mit dem Säugling bekommt man manchmal den Eindruck, daß ein Neugeborenes als eine sehr unvollkommene Konstruktion eines Lebewesens angesehen wird, das unbedingt auf ein ‚verbesserndes' Eingreifen von außen angewiesen ist. Daß ein Säugling im Laufe der Evolution alles mitbekommen hat, um erfolgreich zu überleben, wird oft übersehen."

Anonymer Geburtsbeistand ist an die Stelle einer vertrauten Person getreten, eine medizinisch funktionelle horizontale Gebärposition („Steinschnittlage") an die Stelle selbst gewählter vertikaler sitzender, kniender oder stehender Geburtsstellungen. Risikominimierung steht im Vordergrund, mit dieser Begründung ist die Anzahl der mitunter auch unnötigen Kaiserschnitt-Entbindungen gestiegen (z. Z. ca. 15 %, ALBRECHT-ENGEL 1995). Sectiogeburten bergen jedoch eigene Gefahren: Es wird auf eine erhöhte psychosomatische Anfälligkeit der Mütter im 1. Jahr hingewiesen (GAREL et al. 1988). Langzeitfolgen zeigten sich noch nach 4 Jahren, durch Sectio entbundene Mütter hatten seltener weitere Kinder, häufiger Empfängnisschwierigkeiten, sie waren erschöpfter und ihre Kinder waren häufiger im Hospital (GAREL et al. 1990). Auch waren Säuglinge, die mit einem ungeplanten Kaiserschnitt auf die Welt kamen, in der von uns durchgeführten „Freiburger Säuglingsstudie" vorübergehend einige Wochen lang unruhiger als normal entbundene Babys. In Bezug auf weitere Verhaltens- oder Entwicklungsvariablen entsprechen die Ergebnisse von Kaiserschnittkindern unterschiedslos den bei normal entbundenen Kindern gewonnenen Werten.

Eine frühe postpartale Kontaktaufnahme zwischen Mutter und Säugling mit erstem Anlegen kurz nach der Geburt ist mit ihrer positiven Wirkung bereits auf die frühe Mutter-Kind-Interaktion durch verschiedene Studien gut belegt. Sie scheint jedoch weder eine essentielle Voraussetzung für den Start des Bindungsprozesses noch des Stillgeschehens zu sein, vergleichbar einer sensiblen Phase, in der nur in einem begrenzten Zeitrahmen spezielle Erfahrungen und deren Verarbeitung möglich sind. So nutzen keineswegs alle traditionalen Gesellschaften die Kontaktmöglichkeiten in den ersten Stunden nach der Geburt intensiv aus (LOZOFF 1983), und auch für westliche Mutter-Kind-Paare, bei denen einer der beiden Beteiligten zuerst medizinisch notfallmäßig versorgt werden muss, besteht nicht die Gefahr, aufgrund fehlenden Frühkontaktes keine enge und liebevolle Beziehungen aufbauen und nicht stillen zu können. Die körperliche Nähe zwischen Mutter und Neugeborenem bietet eine durch wechselseitige Signalgebung gestützte Möglichkeit der Natur, den Bindungsprozess einzuleiten (HAUG-SCHNABEL

1984, 1987).

Die Beziehungsaufnahme wird nicht allein durch frühes Anlegen in Gang gebracht, sie geschieht en passant, von allein, wenn die Schwangerschaft und Geburt begleitenden Umstände stimmen. Es könnte sein, dass ein positiver Effekt eines möglichst sofortigen Kontakts dann besonders zum Tragen kommt, wenn es darum geht, Folgen bevorstehender Trennungen zwischen Mutter und Säugling in der Wochenbettzeit aufzufangen (LOZOFF 1983). Diese messbare Bedeutung käme frühem postpartalem Kontakt mit Anlegen in Industrieländern zu, da hier die bei traditionalen Gesellschaften überall anzutreffenden postnatalen Rooming-in Bedingungen noch nicht selbstverständlich sind, vor allem aber die mütterliche Einweisung in das neue Leben und mütterliches Selbstbewusstsein in dieser Übergangsphase noch nichts Selbstverständliches sind.

Rooming-in findet in fast 98 % von 123 untersuchten nonindustriellen Gesellschaften statt. 81 % dieser Kulturen stillen mindestens 2 Jahre lang (Lozoff 1983). Nach einigen Rooming-in-Studien der 70er Jahre und dem Aufgreifen des Begriffs an vielen Kliniken ist allgemein der Anschein erweckt worden, Rooming-in wäre an deutschen Kliniken gang und gäbe. Es handelt sich jedoch in Wahrheit um eine Inflationierung des Begriffs, da es sich in den allermeisten Fällen nur um ein Teil-Rooming-in mit nur zeitweisem Zusammensein von Mutter und Kind handelt. Zitat BARTOSZYK (1984: 95): „... leider führt der starke Konkurrenzkampf zwischen den Geburtskliniken dazu, daß häufig fortschrittliche Methoden wie ‚sanfte Geburt' und ‚Rooming-in' versprochen werden, die dann in der Praxis nicht konsequent durchgehalten werden ...". In einer Osnabrücker-Studie waren es gerade mal 5 % der Mutter-Kind-Paare mit „echtem", d. h. Voll-Rooming-in, bei dem Kind und Mutter tags wie nachts zusammen waren (SCHIEMANN 1993).

Die Belege des positiven Einflusses von echtem Rooming-in mehren sich: Es hat einen fördernden Einfluss auf Stillrate und -erfolg und damit auf die körperliche Entwicklung, führt zu einer geringeren Infektionsgefahr des Kindes und hat eine stabilisierende Wirkung auf das Befinden der Mutter (s. hierzu Übersicht in Schiemann 1993). Auch unterstützt es den Aufbau der Mutter-Kind-Interaktion (MARX 1981). Babys, die unter Rooming-in Bedingungen im Krankenhaus untergebracht sind, schreien dort weniger (KEEFE 1987, WOLKE 1991) und dieser Effekt zeigte sich in unserer Studie auch noch in den Wochen nach der Entlassung.

Wir gebären in Krankenhäusern. Krankenhausgeburten haben sich in Deutschland erst seit etwa 40 Jahren durchgesetzt. Sie sind somit eine Erscheinung der neuesten Zeit (SCHIEMANN 1993). Ein verunsichernder Wechsel vom heimischen in ein fremdes Territorium - und das alles unter den Extrembedingungen einer beginnenden Geburt - ist jedoch sicher nicht nur bei Säugetier-Verwandten problematisch (NAAKTGEBOREN & SLIJPER 1970). Trotz des damit verbundenen Heimvorteils ist die Hausgeburt mehrheitlich mit Angst verbunden, weniger als 1 % aller Geburten in Deutschland finden zu Hause statt. Eine generelle Angst bezüglich der nicht direkt vor Ort präsenten High-Tech-Medizin ist sicher unbegründet. Hausgeburt ist eine verantwortbare Alternative für einen Teil der Schwangeren (SACK & SCHIEFENHÖVEL 1995), da sie in viel stärkerem Maße unsere Jahrmillionen erprobte biologische Ausstattung, aber auch psychologische Aspekte beim Ablauf einer Extremsituation berücksichtigt und auf die prinzipiell gegebene Eigensteuerung des Geburtsgeschehens setzt (SCHIEFENHÖVEL 1988). Fehlt eine eher ideologische Angstschürung, so werden heute noch ein Drittel aller Kinder, wie z. B. in den Niederlanden, mit fachkundiger Hilfe zu Hause entbunden und dies ohne erhöhte Mortalitätsrate (POP et al. 1995).

Ambulante Geburten scheinen ein akzeptabler Kompromiss zwischen Krankenhausgeburt mit stationärem Aufenthalt während der Wochenbettzeit und einer Hausgeburt für all diejenigen Mütter zu sein, die während der Entbindung das gesamte technische Inventar in Griffnähe und das fachmedizinische Risiko-Know-how aus Sicherheitsgründen nicht missen wollen oder dürfen, aber bei unbedenklichem Befinden von Mutter und Kind möglichst schnell wieder in ihre vertraute Umgebung zurückkehren möchten.

Das Wochenbett
Ambulante Entbindungen und Hausgeburten zeigten in der Freiburger Säuglingsstudie wie auch in einer holländischen Studie (POP et al. 1995) keine erhöhte Inzidenz von Heultagen und Wochenbettdepression. Aufhorchen lassen im Gegensatz dazu die hohen Werte kurz- oder längerfristig depressiv gestimmter Mütter im stationären Wochenbett nach einer Krankenhausentbindung (in manchen Indu-

strienationen bis zu 85 %, KUMAR 1994, KAPFHAMMER 1994). Die häufig zitierten hormonellen Ursachen der sog. Heultage sind umstritten, es liegt bis heute kein eindeutiger Kausalnachweis für den direkten Zusammenhang zwischen Hormonumstellungen und Stimmungsveränderungen vor (BÖLTER et al. 1986). Die als Heultage oder Baby-Blues benannte Phase ist gekennzeichnet durch Weinerlichkeit, Ängstlichkeit und Erschöpfung als Begleitphänomene einer instabilen Stimmungslage, die nach wenigen Tagen von selbst und ohne Folgewirkung abklingt (RINGLER 1991). Vor allem Erstgebärende zeigen diese vorübergehende Gestimmtheit nach der Geburt (BÖLTER et al. 1986, POP et al. 1995). Diese Daten konnten von uns bestätigt werden. Auch dieser Umstand passt nicht in das Bild der Hormonhypothese. Vor dem Hintergrund einer deutlich erhöhten Anfälligkeit für depressive Gestimmtheit bei stationär untergebrachten Wöchnerinnen sollten mögliche Ursachen auch in den eher unbiologischen prä, peri- und postnatalen Geburtsbedingungen, die in den Industrienationen überwiegen, gesucht werden.

Bei der gravierenderen und länger anhaltenden Wochenbettdepression, Inzidenz 10 -14 % (RINGLER 1991), fanden sich Hinweise auf die Bedeutung sozialer Unterstützung durch Kindsvater, Familie und Freunde. Langzeitfolgen auf die sozioemotionale Entwicklung des Kindes wie auch der partnerschaftlichen Beziehung sind bekannt (KAPFHAMMER 1994). Die wichtigsten auslösenden Faktoren werden in Problemen, die mit der Elternschaft einhergehen, gesehen (CHALMERS & CHALMERS 1986) sowie in negativen Lebensereignissen während Schwangerschaft und Wochenbett (KAPFHAMMER 1994, KUMAR 1994). STERN und KRUCKMAN (1983) fanden nur vereinzelt Hinweise von Wochenbettdepression in Nigeria, Nepal, China und Südostasien, dort sind allerdings auch bedeutsame Übergangsrituale für die werdende Mutter die Regel. Jedoch gibt es bislang noch methodische Probleme beim Vergleich der Befragungsergebnisse zur postnatalen Depression über verschiedene Kulturen hinweg, und häufig sind auch nur anekdotenhafte Hinweise vorhanden (KUMAR 1994). SCHIEFENHÖVEL (1991) interpretiert Wochenbettdepression als eine iatrogene Pathologie: die Trauerreaktion auf das weggenommene Kind. Dies könnte für einen Teil der Mütter zutreffen, aber auch ambulant oder zu Hause Gebärende zeigen - ohne institutionell bedingte Trennung vom Kind - depressive Gestimmtheit, die wohl eher auf Umstellungsschwierigkeiten oder Überforderungs- und vorübergehende Ohnmachtsgefühle zurückzuführen sind.

In Deutschland ist die Geburtsteilnahme der Väter inzwischen obligatorisch (90 %, ALBRECHT-ENGEL 1995). Dies ist im Kulturenvergleich eher ungewöhnlich. Nur in 27 % der untersuchten traditionalen Gesellschaften sind die Väter bei der Geburt anwesend (LOZOFF 1983), jedoch zeigen sie in der Zeit danach ein verstärktes Engagement bei der Versorgung von Mutter und Kind. In westlichen Ländern ist das Engagement während der postnatalen Säuglingsphase jedoch nahezu unverändert im Verantwortungs- und Organisationsbereich der Mütter verblieben. Väter wurden zwar Geburtsväter, blieben dann aber meist wie gewohnt Feierabend- und Feiertagsväter. Deutsche Väter gehen meist wenige Tage nach der Geburt wieder zur Arbeit. Auch wenn in unserer Studie sich 48 % aller Wöchnerinnen eine stärkere Präsenz des Vaters und anderer familiärer Stützen wünschen würden, kamen die Väter durchschnittlich erst nach 18 Uhr nach Hause und hatten weniger als 1 Stunde Zeit mit ihrem Baby, bis dieses wieder schlief. LEYENDECKER-SCHÖLMERICH (1991) fand etwas höhere väterliche Präsenz-Zeiten für die gesamte Wachzeit (2 Stunden 35 Minuten), die Zeiten betrugen jedoch nur ein Drittel der mütterlichen. Es wäre angemessen, eine mindestens dreimonatige „Triadenkennenlernzeit" nach der Geburt einzuführen, bei der sich Mutter und Kind, Vater und Kind, aber auch Vater und Mutter in ihrer neuen Rolle und jedes Elternteil für sich mit der neuen Situation intensiv vertraut machen könnten. Wäre das die Forderung nach etwas ganz Neuem oder gab es schon einmal Ähnliches?

Vergleichen wir doch den Mutter-Säugling-Alltag in den traditionalen Gesellschaften und bei uns.

In den *traditionalen Gesellschaften wird die junge Mutter bei ihren Haushaltstätigkeiten entlastet.* Anfangs, direkt nach der Geburt eines Kindes, übernehmen ihre Mutter, Geschwister und andere Verwandte einen Großteil der Alltagsaufgaben, damit sie sich weit gehend ungestört dem Kind widmen kann (HERZOG-SCHRÖDER 1995). Nach dieser speziellen Art des Wochenbetts erhält sie dann Hilfe bei der Betreuung des Kindes. Das sog. Allo-mothering, d. h. die Situation, dass mit Mutter und Kind zusammenlebende und beiden vertraute Personen des Sozialverbandes das Baby mitbetreuen, entlastet die Mutter, trennt jedoch Mutter und Kind nicht. Sobald das Kind Zeichen gibt, zur Mutter zu wollen, Hunger hat, sich erschreckt, müde wird oder aus anderen Gründen weint, wird es sofort der Mutter zurückgegeben. Die Hälfte der Wachzeit verbringt das Kind in Körperkontakt mit seiner Mutter. Die andere Hälfte übernehmen andere Bezugspersonen, von denen der Vater nach der Mutter die zweitwichtigste Rolle spielt (SCHIEFENHÖVEL 1984).

Ganz wichtig: die Frau verbleibt auch als junge Mutter in ihrem Lebens- und Aktivitätsbereich, anstehende Veränderungen werden traditionsgemäß eingeführt, die gesellschaftliche Wiedereingliederung geschieht in einer feierlichen, die Mutter ästimierenden Form. Kinder erhöhen die Attraktivität ihrer Eltern im Sozialverband, speziell auch in der Altersgruppe der jungen Erwachsenen zu der die neuen Eltern gehören. Das Kind wird zur „sozialen Drehscheibe" (SCHIEFENHÖVEL 1984). Es gibt keine Fremdbetreuung für Säuglinge und Kleinkinder, ein risikoreicher Einflussfaktor auf die Eltern-Kind-Beziehung entfällt (BENSEL 1994), es gibt nur eine Mitbetreuung durch sowohl der Mutter als auch dem Kind vertraute Personen in „häuslicher" Umgebung und - vor allem - in schnell erreichbarer Nähe der Mutter.

Betrachtet man den Mutter-Säugling-Alltag in unserer Zivilisationsform, bringt die Geburt eines Kindes und der Start in die Mutterschaft zumindest für die Frau oft einschneidende Veränderungen mit sich. Ein neuer Lebensabschnitt beginnt, vor allem für die bislang berufstätige Frau, der erschreckend wenig mit dem bisherigen Leben gemeinsam, kaum Anknüpfungspunkte an die Zeit zuvor haben kann. Der häusliche Beruf Mutter und Hausfrau muss bewusst vorbereitet werden, da sich vieles durch den Übergang von der Berufstätigkeit zur Familientätigkeit ändert. Ist dieser Übergang erwünscht, ja ersehnt, wird die Umstellung einfacher werden. Dennoch bleibt es eine Umstellung, die allein schon so Fundamentales wie die Strukturierung des Tagesablaufs betrifft. Einige wenige Sätze, zusammengestellt aus Artikeln in Eltern- und Frauenzeitschriften der Jahre 1995 und 1996, sollen Einzelpunkte des neuen Szenarios verdeutlichen:

- Eine größere Familie braucht eine größere Wohnung, die geräumiger, aber günstig sein sollte, da zumindest zeitweilig ein Gehalt entfällt. Der Umzug aufs Land kann anstehen. Das bedeutet ein Wechsel der bisherigen Lebensumwelt.
- Falls Bekannte bisher fast ausschließlich über die Ausbildung oder die Arbeit gefunden worden sind, müssen neue Wege zur Kontaktaufnahme eingeschlagen werden.
- Die Erfahrung zeigt, dass jungen Müttern aus dem Berufsleben kommend die regelmäßige Ansprache und der Kollegenkreis fehlen können.
- Ohne eigenes Einkommen, ohne finanzielle Selbstständigkeit, vom Gehalt des Mannes zu leben, bedeutet eine Umstellung, vor allem einen nötig werdenden Einstellungswandel.
- Und eine ganz wichtige Frage zum Schluss. Wie schätzt die junge Mutter selbst den Wert von Erziehungs- und Familienarbeit ein? Von der Antwort auf diese Frage hängt ihr Bedürfnis nach Anerkennung ihres Opfers oder nach Bestätigung für ihre Überzeugung ab.

Mutter-Säugling-Alltag kann Alleinsein mit dem Kind bedeuten, wenn nicht ein engagierter Eigeneinsatz und die bewusste Unterstützung durch den Vater diese sich zuerst einmal fast automatisch ergebende Situation grundlegend verändern. Ohne Eigenmotivation und väterlichen Einsatz wird aus der Mutter-Kind-Beziehung die gemeinsame Mutter-Kind-Isolation (HAUG-SCHNABEL 1992, 1993b). Spätestens dann wird Mutterschaft als „ausgegliedert aus dem Normalleben" empfunden.

Wir haben erfreulicherweise den Mutterschutz und den 3jährigen Erziehungsurlaub, doch viele Mütter hängen mit ihren Kindern gerade in dieser Zeit am Rande des sozialen Netzes. Frauen können allein erziehend sein, aus Überzeugung oder weil der Partner und Kindsvater fehlt. Zwar ist ihr finanzielles Existenzminimum gesichert, regional erkämpfte Mutter-Kind-Projekte (HASSENSTEIN 1990) erlauben das so wichtige Zusammensein zwischen Mutter und Kind, doch vor sozialer Isolation, gesellschaftlichem Außenseitertum können sie allein eigene Energie und Kontaktfreudigkeit retten. Zudem bekommen diese Mütter die soziale Kontrolle ihrer Umgebung bei typischem, Erwachsene jedoch oft störendem Kinderverhalten ungedämpft und nicht „geteilt durch zwei" zu spüren. Hier sind „Übermütter" gefordert, und das 24-Stunden-rund-um-die-Uhr.

Kinder erhöhen die Attraktivität ihrer Eltern im Sozialverband. Das hatten wir für die traditionalen Gesellschaften gesagt. Mit Kind oder Kindern zu leben und aufzutreten, hebt bei uns nicht mehr automatisch den sozialen Anerkennungsstatus der Eltern, schon gar nicht in der Gruppe der gleichaltrigen jungen Erwachsenen. Im Gegenteil, Kinder werden oft als störend erlebt - und dies wird auch ihren Eltern nahe gebracht.

Bei diesen Konflikten sind die Mütter immer in exponierter Angriffsstellung. Ob allein erziehend oder verheiratet haben sie oft durchaus vergleichbare Probleme: Die Überbewertung der außerhäuslichen Erwerbstätigkeit und die strikte Trennung zwischen Arbeitsleben und Familienleben schufen die

Voraussetzungen für einen weit gehend kinderfreien Berufsalltag - zumeist für den die Familie finanzierenden Vater. Die Überbewertung der außerhäuslichen Erwerbstätigkeit und die strikte Trennung zwischen Arbeitsleben und Familienleben schufen aber ebenso die Voraussetzungen für einen weit gehend anerkennungsfreien Familienkinderalltag der im häuslichen Bereich managenden Mutter. Unsere Frauen können zumeist nur zwischen der bereits genannten 24-Stunden-rund-um-die-Uhr-Betreuung oder einer Berufstätigkeit, kombiniert mit einer stundenlangen völligen Trennung vom Kind wählen. Das Kind wird dann in vielen Fällen nicht zu Hause von vertrauten Personen betreut, sondern in fremder Umgebung von Menschen, deren Vertrauen Kind und Mutter erst noch gewinnen müssen. Und umgeben von vielen Gleichaltrigen mit gleichen Bedürfnissen und in gleichen Nöten! Die Situation der Fremdbetreuung muss als reine Kulturerscheinung gewertet werden. Jedoch aus der Situation der Mütter und Familien in unseren heutigen Lebensbedingungen wird der Wunsch nach Fremdbetreuungsmöglichkeiten schnell verständlich. Bei weitem nicht alle Familien fangen die Säuglings- und Kleinstkindzeit durch Betreuung des Kindes im bezüglich Emotionen, Erziehungsstil und Lebensumfeld „nahen" Familienkreis auf. Es ist noch eine kleine Gruppe von Idealisten, in der sich Vater und Mutter Familienarbeit und Erwerbsarbeit während der Zeit der Kindheitsjahre teilen, um sowohl am Familienleben als auch am Erwerbsleben teilnehmen zu können. Die biologische Ausstattung für Väter als aktive Miterzieher ihrer Kinder ist durchaus vorhanden, wie uns die langsam vermehrt zur Verfügung stehenden Ergebnisse über intuitive Elternkompetenz der Väter zeigen. Vieles, was eine „gute Mutter" ausmacht, haben Väter auch in ihrem Verhaltensinventar (EIBL-EIBESFELDT & HERZOG 1987, PARKE et al. 1972, PARKE & O'LEARY 1976).

Realisieren lassen sich väterliche Potenzen am besten, wenn Mann selbst das Glück hatte, seinen eigenen Vater als präsenten Vater erlebt zu haben. Wenn seine Partnerin den aktiven Vater neben sich duldet, ja gut heißt (weil sie auch nach der Geburt eines Kindes in verschiedensten Bereichen Anerkennung erfährt, nicht nur als Mutter, ein Zustand, der fast zwingend zur Folge hätte, einen Alleinanspruch auf die Mutterposition zu erheben). Und - nicht zuletzt - unsere Gesellschaft anerkennt, wie wichtig die häusliche Erziehungsarbeit ist. Eine gesellschaftliche Aufwertung der Familienarbeit gegenüber der Berufstätigkeit würde jedem Vater und jeder Mutter den Umdenkprozess in diese Richtung erleichtern.

Allein mit den ersten Problemen - Fachinstruktionen versus angeborenem Elternprogramm
Häufig allein gelassen von erfahrenen Helfern und mit Gefühlen der Unsicherheit, ob des Umgangs mit ihrem jüngsten Familienmitglied, sind es auch hier wieder vor allem Erstgebärende, die sich in der Not an den Kinderarzt wenden oder Ratgeberjournale oder -bücher in Anspruch nehmen, wenn sie mit den ersten anstehenden und zu lösenden Alltagsproblemen mit ihrem Kind konfrontiert werden. Anstatt den eigenen angeborenen intuitiven Fähigkeiten zu vertrauen (PAPOUSEK & PAPOUSEK 1987), werden häufig starre Schemata aufgegriffen, die, vergleichbar einem erprobten Rezept, Sicherheit im Umgang mit dem Baby geben sollen. Die in den 70er Jahren eingeführte goldene Regel des 4-Stunden-Mahlzeiten-Intervalls (LOZOFF et al. 1977) hat sich in den Köpfen vor allem des Krankenhauspersonals festgesetzt, und es braucht einer gesunden Portion Selbstbewusstseins, um statt dessen ein biologisches „Füttern-nach-Bedarf" mit seinen interindividuell höchst unterschiedlichen Intervallen zu praktizieren. Die Stillrate nahm in den letzten Jahren leicht zu, nach einem situativ bedingten Anstieg während der beiden Weltkriege auf über 95 %, einem anschließenden starken Abstieg und einem leichten Wiederanstieg seit den letzten 20 Jahren ist sie momentan wieder auf dem Niveau von 1869, d. h. etwa 20 % der Mütter stillen noch mit 3 Monaten (ENDE 1979, KORFMANN 1992).

Herauszufinden, was dem Baby fehlt, wenn es als mehrdeutiges Unwohlsignal nur Schreien zur Verfügung hat, ist eine Herausforderung für jedes junge Elternpaar. Auch hier sind es wiederum die Erstgebärenden, die deswegen häufiger den Kinderarzt konsultieren. Und die weniger belastbaren und unstrukturierten Familien, die ihr Kind fälschlicherweise als exzessiven Schreier einstufen (RÄIHÄ et al. 1995). Das Schreien in seiner Bedeutung zu entschlüsseln, ist eine anspruchsvolle Lernleistung, die von den primären Bezugspersonen mühsam in den ersten Monaten gelernt werden muss und bei vielen zunehmend besser klappt. Wird das Schreien zu einem täglich mehrstündigen Problem, fallen viele Eltern in ein soziales Loch. Sie bilden unter dem zunehmenden Gefühl fehlender Elternkompetenz private Theorien über die möglichen Ursachen und bedienen sich aus einem bunten Strauß von Familienhausmittelchen und Therapieempfehlungen des Kinderarztes. Die Empfehlungen der Ärzte selbst haben wenig mit den von diesen vermuteten Ursachen zu tun (KELLER et al. 1990). Die meisten Therapieversuche haben lediglich Placebowirkung, da Schreien nach dem 2. Monat jedoch spontan zu remittieren pflegt, glaubt man an einen Therapieerfolg, und die Eltern haben das beruhigende Gefühl, endlich etwas Effektives beitragen zu können, das Elend zu beenden. Anhaltendes exzessives Schreien kann die Bindung zwischen Säugling und Eltern stark belasten und kann im schlimmsten Fall bei Kindesmisshandlung enden (vgl. Übersicht in BENSEL & HAUG-SCHNABEL 1997). Langzeitfolgen werden diskutiert, ein ehemaliges Schreikind, auch wenn es in der späteren Entwicklung nicht mehr besonders unruhig ist, kann in der Wahrnehmung der Eltern zu einem besonders anfälligen Kind werden. Gerade in diesem Fall, der sog. „3-Monats-Kolik", spielen vielfältige psychosoziale Faktoren, gerade in der Übergangszeit und Anfangszeit als junge Familie eine große Rolle. RAUTAVA et al. (1993) fanden in einer großangelegten finnischen Studie folgende, die Babyunruhe vermindernden Faktoren: Eine positive sexuelle Beziehung der Partner, ein positives Selbstbild als Frau, ein verständnisvoller Partner, wenig Stress während der Schwangerschaft, keine soziale Isolation beider Eltern während der Schwangerschaft, keine Unsicherheit bei der Geburt und beim Gedanken an danach, keine körperlichen Schwierigkeiten während der Schwangerschaft, ein positives Geburtserlebnis, kein feindliches Krankenhauspersonal und kein enttäuschter Vater über den Geburtsverlauf und über sein reales Baby. Es scheint uns interessant, dass vieles davon Faktoren sind, auf die traditionale Übergangsriten einen förderlichen und entspannenden Einfluss haben können.

Wie sehr unsere westliche Kultur, mit ihren künstlich geschürten „Verwöhn-Ängsten" dem Säugling und Kleinkind gegenüber den biologisch sinnvollen Betreuungskonzepten enteilt ist, lässt sich auch gut am Beispiel Körperkontakt aufzeigen. Der menschliche Säugling gehört zum Jungentypus Tragling (HASSENSTEIN 1970, KIRKILIONIS 1992, LOZOFF & BRITTENHAM 1979), der darauf angelegt ist, nahezu ständigen Sicherheit gebenden Körperkontakt zu seinen Bezugspersonen zu halten, mitgenommen zu werden und reichhaltige Stimulation zu erfahren. Während Säuglinge auch heute noch in traditionalen Gesellschaften wie den Hochland-Papua 60 % und mehr der Tageszeit und nahezu 100 % der Nacht im Haut-zu-Haut-Kontakt mit ihren Bezugspersonen verbringen (SCHIEFENHÖVEL 1992), liegen die Werte in westlichen Nationen bei ca. 10 %. Gerade das gemeinsame Schlafen im Bett der Mutter (Eltern), co-sleeping genannt, wird von weniger als 10 % der deutschen Familien selbst im ersten Trimenon praktiziert (NOLTING et al. 1993). Gerade aber das co-sleeping wird ganz aktuell als Präventionsmaßnahme gegen plötzlichen Kindstod diskutiert (KONNER & SUPER 1987, MCKENNA 1990) und führt zu einer hohen Synchronisation des Aktivitätsrhythmus von Mutter und Kind (SIEGMUND et al. 1994). Anders und TAYLOR (1994) zeigen am Beispiel co-sleeping auf, wie im Laufe der westlichen Kulturgeschichte die Säuglinge erst aus dem Elternbett und dann aus dem Elternschlafzimmer vertrieben wurden. Parallel mit dem Getrenntschlafen von Bezugsperson und Kind entstand auch der elterliche Anspruch auf ein selbstständiges Ein- und Durchschlafenkönnen des Säuglings und Kleinkindes. Säuglinge, die nachts wiederholt aufwachen und nicht von selbst wieder einschlafen können, werden als „night-waker" tituliert, ihr Verhalten als Nachtterror bezeichnet. Unsere Zeit verlangt nach verhaltenstherapeutischen Maßnahmen, um den natürlichen Wunsch nach elterlichen Anwesenheitssignalen abzudressieren (KAST-ZAHN & MORGENROTH 1995).

Der Blick auf unsere Stammesgeschichte und der Kulturenvergleich offenbaren eklatante Mängel der westlichen Industrieländer beim Umgang mit werdenden und gewordenen Müttern einerseits und den Neugeborenen andererseits. Dank der menscheneigenen Plastizität und Anpassungsfähigkeit an die unterschiedlichsten Lebensbedingungen und immer wieder neu entwickelter zivilisatorischer Kompensationsmechanismen bedeutet dies nicht zwangsläufig eine existenzielle Gefährdung für Mutter und Kind. Aber Zivilisation in dieser Form kostet etwas. KENT BAILEY (1996: 8) schreibt dazu lakonisch: „Es ist keine Frage, ob der moderne Mensch fehlangepasst ist oder nicht, aber es ist die Frage, ob eine ausreichende Zahl von Passungen erreicht und pathologische Fehlpassungen vermieden werden oder nicht, um seelisch gesund und glücklich zu sein".

References
ALBRECHT-ENGEL, I. 1995. Geburt in der Bundesrepublik Deutschland. In: *Gebären - Ethnomedizinische Perspektiven und neue Wege.* Hrsg. W. SCHIEFENHÖVEL, D. SICH UND C. E. GOTTSCHALK-BATSCHKUS, S. 31-42. Curare Sonderband 8. VWB Berlin.
ANDERS, T. F. & T. R. TAYLOR. 1994. Babys and Their Sleep Environment. *Children's Environment* 11,2: 123-134.
BAILEY, K. 1996. Mismatch Theory 1: Basic Principles. Across Species Comparison and Psychopathology *(ASCAP) Newslet-*

ter 9,2: 7-9.
BARTOSZYK, J. 1984. *Vorbereitung auf die Elternschaft und die ersten drei Lebensmonate des Kindes: Eine empirische Untersuchung unter besonderer Berücksichtigung des Vaters.* Dissertation, Universität Düsseldorf.
BENSEL, J. & G. HAUG-SCHNABEL. 1997. Primär exzessives Schreien in den ersten 3 Lebensmonaten. In: *Handbuch der Kleinkindforschung,* 2. rev. Aufl. Hrsg. H. KELLER. Huber Verlag Bern, im Druck.
BENSEL, J. 1994. Ist die Tagesbetreuung in Krippen ein Risiko? Eine kritische Beurteilung der internationalen Krippenforschung. *Zeitschrift für Pädagogik* 40,2: 303-326.
BÖLTER, D., M. KIRSCHBAUM and D. BECKMANN. 1986. Eine Verlaufsuntersuchung über Stimmungsschwankungen in den ersten fünf Tagen nach der Entbindung. *Psychotherapie Psychosomatik Medizinische Psychologie* 36,2: 75-82.
CHALMERS, B. E. & B. M. CHALMERS. 1986. Post-Partum Depression: A Revised Perspective. *Journal of Psychosomatic Obstetrics & Gynaecology* 5: 93-105.
DEMAUSE, L. 1980. *Hört ihr die Kinder weinen. Eine psychogenetische Geschichte der Kindheit.* Suhrkamp Frankfurt.
EIBL-EIBESFELDT, I. & H. HERZOG 1987. *Yanomami, Patanoetheri (Venezuela, Oberer Orinoko). Männer im Umgang mit Säuglingen.* Publikationen zu wissenschaftlichen Filmen. Sektion Biologie. Serie 19,8.
ELWOOD, R. W. & C. MASON. 1994. The Couvade and the Onset of Paternal Care: A Biological Perspective. *Ethology and Sociobiology* 15: 145-156.
ENDE, A. 1979. Zur Geschichte der Stillfeindlichkeit in Deutschland 1850-1978. *Kindheit* 1: 203-214.
FIELD, T. M. & S. M. WIDMAYER. 1980. Developmental Follow-Up of Infants Delivered by Caesarean Section and General Anesthesia. *Infant Behavior & Development* 3,3: 253-264.
GAREL, M., N. LELONG and M. KAMINSKI. 1988. Follow-Up Study of Psychological Consequences of Caesarean Childbirth. *Early Human Development* 16,2-3: 271-282.
GAREL, M., N. LELONG and M. KAMINSKI. 1990. Psychological Consequences of Caesarean Childbirth in Primiparas. *Journal of Psychosomatic Obstetrics & Gynaecology* 6,3: 197-209.
GENNEP VAN, A. 1960. *The Rites of Passage.* Routledge and Kegan Pauls Press London.
HASSENSTEIN, B. 1970. *Tierjunges und Menschenkind im Blick der vergleichenden Verhaltensforschung.* A. W. Gentner Stuttgart.
HASSENSTEIN, H. 1990. Das Programm „Mutter und Kind„ Baden-Württemberg. Eine Hilfe für die alleinerziehende Mutter und ihr Kind. *Der Kinderarzt* 21: 37-41.
HAUG-SCHNABEL, G. 1984. Kindgemäßes Angebot? - Verhaltensbiologische Überlegungen zur Pflege und Erziehung von Säuglingen und Kleinkindern. *Das öffentliche Gesundheitswesen* 46,1: 34-40
HAUG-SCHNABEL, G. 1987. Neues zur Mutter-Kind-Beziehung. *Der Kinderarzt* 18,1: 46-50.
HAUG-SCHNABEL, G. 1993. Verunsichernde Zeit der Reife. *Psychologie Heute* 20, August: 36-40.
HERZOG-SCHRÖDER, G. 1995. *Zeitzuteilung im Alltag der Yanomami Frauen. Eine ethnographische Analyse.* Vortrag auf dem Workshop „Biologische und kulturelle Aspekte der Zei" der Arbeitsgemeinschaft Humanethologie in der GfA, Andechs.
KAPFHAMMER, H.-P. 1994. Psychische Störungen im Zusammenhang von Geburt und Wochenbett. In: *Psychiatrie für die Praxis* 19. Hrsg. H. HELMCHEN, H. HIPPIUS, W. M. GREIL, M. M. HAMBRECHT, M. M. LINDEN und J. M. TEGLER. S. 45-53. MMV Medizin Verlag München.
KAST-ZAHN, A. & H. MORGENROTH. 1995. *Jedes Kind kann schlafen lernen.* O & P Ratingen.
KEEFE, M. R. 1987. Comparison of Neonatal Nighttime Sleep-Wake Patterns in Nursery versus Rooming-In Environments. *Nursing Research* 36,3: 140-144.
KELLER, H., C. UBOZAK and J. RISAU. 1990. The Concept of Colic and Infant Crying in Pediatrics: An Exploratory Study. *Early Child Development and Care* 65: 71-76.
KIRKILIONIS, E. 1992. Das Tragen des Säuglings im Hüftsitz - eine spezielle Anpassung des menschlichen Traglings. *Zoologische Jahrbücher - Abteilung Allgemeine Zoologie und Physiologie der Tiere* 96: 395-415.
KITZINGER, S. 1980. *Frauen als Mütter. Mutterschaft in verschiedenen Kulturen.* München.
KLOSINSKI, G. 1991. *Pubertätsriten - Äquivalente und Defizite in unserer Gesellschaft.* Huber Verlag Bern.
KONNER, M. J. & C. M. SUPER 1987. Sudden Infant Death Syndrome: An Anthropological Hypothesis. In: *The Role of Culture in Developmental Disorder.* Edited by C. M. SUPER. pp. 95-108. Academic Press San Diego.
KORFMANN, A. 1992. *Dortmunder Längsschnittstudie zur Ernährung von Säuglingen: Auswertungen zu Art, Mengen und Einführungszeitpunkten der einzelnen Nahrungskomponenten sowie zur Energie- und Nährstoffzufuhr und zum Wachstum vom 1. - 12. Lebensmonat.* Dissertation, Universität Kiel.
KUMAR, R. 1994. Postnatal Mental Illness: A Transcultural Perspective. *Social Psychiatry & Psychiatric Epidemiology* 29,6: 250-264.

Leyendecker-Schölmerich, B. 1991. *Alltagsumwelten von Säuglingen.* Dissertation, Fachbereich Psychologie, Universität Osnabrück.
Lozoff, B. & Brittenham, G. 1979. Infant Care: Cache or Carry. *Journal of Pediatrics* 95,3: 478-483.
Lozoff, B. 1983. Birth and ‚Bonding' in Non-Industrial Societies. *Developmental Medicine and Child Neurology* 25,5: 595-600.
Lozoff, B., G. M. Brittenham, M. A. Trause, J. H. Kennell and M. H. Klaus. 1979. The Mother-Newborn Relationship: Limits of Adaptability. *Journal of Pediatrics* 91,1: 1-12.
Marx, G. 1981. *Die Sprache der Mutter zum Neugeborenen und Säugling. Eine Analyse von Umfang, Inhalt und Form.* Dissertation, Naturwissenschaftliche Fakultät, Universität Salzburg.
McKenna, J. J. 1990. Evolution and Sudden Infant Death Syndrome (SIDS); Part 1: Infant Responsivity to Parental Contact. *Human Nature* 1,2: 145-177.
Naaktgeboren, C. & E. Slijper 1970. *Biologie der Geburt. Einführung in die vergleichende Geburtskunde.* Parey Verlag Hamburg.
Nolting, H.-D., S. Schlegelmilch, B. Trumann and K. W. Tietze. 1993. *Schlaflagen, Schlafumgebung und Schlafverhalten von Säuglingen.* MMV Medizin Verlag München.
Papousek, H. & M. Papousek. 1987. Intuitive Parenting: A Dialectic Counterpart to the Infant's Integrative Competence. In: *Handbook of Infant Development* (2nd ed.). Edited by J. Osofsky. pp. 669-720. Wiley New York.
Parke, R. D. & S. E. O'Leary. 1976. Father-Mother Infant Interaction in the Newborn Period: Some Findings, Some Observations and Some Unresolved Issues. In: *The Developing Individual in a Changing World.* Eds. K. Riegel & J. Meacham. Mouton The Hague.
Parke, R. D., S. E. O'Leary and S. West. 1972. Mother-Father-Newborn Interaction: Effects of Maternal Medication, Labor and Sex of Infant. *Proceedings of the American Psychological Association:* 85-86.
Pop, V. J., H. A. Wijnen, M. van Montfort, G. G. Essed, C. A. de Geus, M. M. van Son and I. H. Komproe. 1995. Blues and Depression During Early Puerperium: Home versus Hospital Deliveries. *Journal of Obstetrics and Gynaecology* 102: 701-706.
Räihä, H., L. Lehtonen and H. Korvenranta. 1995. Family Context of Infant Colic. *Infant Mental Health Journal,* in press.
Rautava, P., H. Helenius and L. Lehtonen. 1993. Psychosocial Predisposing Factors for Infantile Colic. *British Medical Journal* 307: 600-604.
Ringler, M. 1991. Psychosexualität und Geburt. In: *Patient Frau. Psychosomatik im weiblichen Lebenszyklus.* Hrsg. M. Springer-Kremser, M. Ringler und A. Eder. S. 185-203. Springer Verlag Wien.
Sack, A. & W. Schiefenhövel 1995. Analyse von 855 Hausgeburten im Münchner Raum. In: *Gebären - Ethnomedizinische Perspektiven und neue Wege.* Hrsg. W. Schiefenhövel, D. Sich und C. E. Gottschalk-Batschkus. S. 271-286. Curare Sonderband 8. VWB Berlin.
Schiefenhövel, W. 1984. Bindung und Lösung - Sozialisationspraktiken im Hochland von Neuguinea. In: *Bindung und Besitzdenken beim Kleinkind.* Hrsg. C. Eggers. S. 51-80. Urban & Schwarzenberg München.
Schiefenhövel, W. 1988. *Geburtsverhalten und reproduktive Strategien der Eipo.* Reimer Verlag Berlin.
Schiefenhövel, W. 1991. Ethnomedizinische und verhaltensbiologische Beiträge zur pädiatrischen Versorgung. *Curare* 14: 195-204.
Schiefenhövel, W. 1992. Kultur und biologische Rhythmen: Stillpraktiken und Behandlung von Säuglingen in Melanesien. Wissenschaftliche Zeitschrift der Humboldt-Universität zu Berlin, *Reihe Medizin* 41,2: 77-80.
Schiemann, D. 1993. *Postnatales Rooming-in. Eine empirische Untersuchung - Konsequenzen für die Praxis.* Hans Huber Verlag Bern.
Schleidt, M. 1989. Die humanethologische Perspektive: Die menschliche Frühentwicklung aus ethologischer Sicht. In: *Handbuch der Kleinkindforschung.* Hrsg. H. Keller. S. 15-29. Springer Heidelberg.
Seel, R. M. 1986. Birth Rite. *Health Visitor* 59: 182-184.
Siegmund, R., M. Tittel and W. Schiefenhövel 1994. Time Patterns in Parent-Child Interactions in a Trobriand Village (Papua New Guinea). *Biological Rhythm Research* 25,3: 241-251.
Stern, G. & L. Kruckman. 1983. Multidisciplinary Perspectives on Postpartum Depression: An Anthropological Critique. *Social Science and Medicine* 17: 1027-1041.
Wolke, D. 1991. Psycho-biologische Aspekte der Pflege von Frühgeborenen. *Deutsche Krankenpflegezeitschrift* 44: 478-483.

Hebammenwesen im Andenraum.
Eine Form des weiblichen Schamanismus?
Midwives in the Andean Communities, A Form of Female Shamanism?

María Ofelia Burgos Lingán

Zusammenfassung: Die Hebammen sind eine bedeutende und konstante Präsenz im Leben der Frauen im reproduktiven Alter. Eine Analyse ihrer Funktion zeigt, wie sie aus einer emisch kulturellen Sicht anderes zu verstehen sind als bisher. Die Berufung, rituelle Initiation, ihre Unterweisung und Spezialisierung, die Qualität der Beziehung zu den Gebärenden, die Rollenaufteilung mit ihren kultischen Partners, die Dualität ihrer Fuktionen, ihr Heilungsinstrumente und der Stigma der Verfolgung etc., zeigen eher das Profil einer Priesterin, Heilerin und Hebamme.

Ihre charismatische Persönlichkeit, ihre besondere Aufgabe in der Tradierung des weibliches indigenen Wissens und Erhaltung des Lebens in den Dorfgemeinden entsteht aus ihrer besonderen Fähigkeit die Prinzipien ihrer Kultur als eine untrennbare Einheit zwischen Frau-Weiblichkeit-Erde-Kultur-Kosmos lebendig zu verkörpern.

Abstract: Acquiring an understanding of Andean midwives and their funtions under consideration of their cultural background is seen as a challenge. From the viewpoint of village inhabitants, midwives are regerded as recognized menbers of the community, and are honored and respected because of their healing function.

For this reason they are also of interest to public health institutions, who attemt to integrate them as potential representatives of basic public health care services. However, these efforts have not remained unchallenged, and they present the basis for a cultural conflict, which has contributed to misunderstandings concerning the true dimesion of their personality, role and function as a representave element and as a symbol of cultural life in the indigenous Andean commnity.

Keywords: Perú, Andenraum, Frauen, Hebammen, Traditionelle Therapie, Symbolisches Heilen, Schamanismus, Peru, Andean region, midwives, traditional treatment, healing with symbols, shamanism.

Eine Vorstellung von den Hebammen und ihren Funktionen aus dem inneren Zusammenhang ihres kulturellen Hintegrundes zu bekommen, ist eine Herausforderung. Aus der Sicht der Dorfbewohner sind sie anerkannte Gemeindemitglieder und werden wegen ihrer heilenden Funktion geehrt und respektiert. Aus diesem Grund sind sie für die Gesundheitsinstitutionen attraktiv, die sie als potentielle Trägerinnen der offiziellen Basisgesundheitsversorgung zu integrieren versuchen. Dieser Versuch ist nicht widerspruchsfrei und bildet die Grundlage für einen Kulturkonflikt, der dazu beigetragen hat, dass die reale Dimension ihrer Persönlichkeit, Rolle und Funktionen als repräsentativer Teil und als Symbol des kulturellen Lebens der indigenen andinen Gemeinde nicht verstanden wird. Der folgende Beitrag ist

Abb. 1
Die Hebamme prüft den Puls der Gebärenden.

ein Versuch, sich mit diesem Kulturkonflikt auseinanderzusetzen und ein neues Bild der Hebammen aus ihrem eigenen kulturellen Kontext zu gewinnen. Der Artikel ist Teil einer umfassenden Analyse des reproduktiven Zyklus im südlichen Andenraum Perus (vgl. BURGOS 1995). Während der Inkazeit berichtet der Chronist GUAMAN POMA (1956,1:137), dass die Heiler oder Medizinmänner, "hampicamayoc" genannt wurden und die Hebammen "weise Frauen", "Gevatterin", oder "Patin", hießen (in Quechua: "uauauachachic vicza allichac hampicamayoq"), "die den Unterbauch befreit, heilt und bei der Geburt hilft". Die Ammen der Waisenkinder hießen "uaccha rurocha ñuñochic". Sie waren von jeglicher Arbeit oder Verpflichtung befreit. Einige heilten auch Verrenkungen und andere Krankheiten (GUAMAN POMA 1966, III:72, 135); d.h. sie wirkten auch als Heilerinnen oder Medizinfrauen. Diese vierfache Bezeichnung als "weise Frauen, Gevatterinnen, Heilerinnen oder Medizinfrauen und Hebammen" definiert deutlich ihre vielseitige Funktion als Frauen, die durch ihre Fähigkeit, das Göttliche und die Menschen bezüglich der Fruchtbarkeit zu verbinden, einen speziellen Status haben.

Es sind Frauen, die sich in den Angelegenheiten des weiblichen Kultes spezialisiert haben und die medizinischen Kenntnisse haben, die Frauen bei der Geburt zu behandeln. Da die Geburt eng mit der Göttin "Pachamama" (Muttererde) verbunden ist, besitzen die Hebammen auch die Fähigkeit, sich mit den okkulten Kräften der Unterwelt in Verbindung zu setzen. Die Fähigkeit und die Macht in den unterschiedlichen Ebenen des Kosmos zu agieren ist ein spezielles Merkmal der Heilerinnen und Heiler in den Anden.

Die Hebammen und ihre besondere Verbindung mit der Muttererde (Pachamama)
SILVERBLATT (1990:23) bezieht sich auf die spezielle Rolle der Hebammen im religiösen Leben der andinen Dorfgemeinde. Die Mutter- erde Pachamama beschützte die Hebammen und übermittelte ihnen die heiligen Kräfte der Fruchtbarkeit für die menschliche Reproduktion. Diese besondere Funktion wurde von den Chronisten mit ihren Vorurteilen übersehen, die sie mit Heilern und anderen Pflanzenkundigen des einheimischen Gesundheitssystems in einen Topf warfen. Nach SILVERBLATT (1990:23) werden heute die Hebammen "Pacha comadres" (Gevaterrin der Erde) genannt. Nach GAMARRA (1967:46) werden sie in Huaylas von den Eltern des Kindes "zweite Mutter" oder "Gevatterin des Bodens" genannt. Die Bezeichnung "Gevatterin des Bodens" weist auf die verschiedenen Ebenen der spirituellen Verbindung hin, - mit dem Boden, der Muttererde, der Göttin Pachamama. Als Patin ist sie Beschützerin des Kindes und gleichzeitig Verwandte der Eltern. Sie ist zentrales Verbindungsglied einer Lebenstrilogie. Sie begleitet die Dorfgemeindebewohner in den entscheidenden Momenten der Reproduktion, Erhaltung und Wiederherstellung ihrer Gesundheit und - speziell die Frauen- bei der Geburt. Für SILVERBLATT (1990:23) stellen die Hebammen eine heilige Verbindung zwischen der Göttin Pachamama (Muttererde) und der menschlichen Reproduktion her. Als weise Frau, bzw. Gevatterin" sind sie heilige Opferbringerinnen der Geburten. Sie begünstigen die Familien gegenüber der mächtigen Göttin der Fruchtbarkeit und stellen eine Verbindung zwischen ihr und der menschliche Genese her.

Verfolgung und Verurteilung der Hebammen
Seit der Eroberung und der Kolonialzeit wurden die Hebammen durch die Eroberer ständig wegen ihrer Ausdauer in der Ausübung und Erhaltung ihrer Religion gewaltsam verfolgt und gemartert, genauso wie die männlichen Vertreter des Kultes an die andinen Götter.
Der Chronist GUAMAN POMA DE AYALA (1966, III:72, 135) berichtet:
"Die Priester, die Statthalter, oder Kommendeinhaber (Encomendero), und die Landrichter (Corregidor) verwickeln diese Indianer ständig in Streit und bezeichnen sie als Hexer, was nicht wahr ist... Sie sind gute Christen und es wäre angebracht, daß sie ihren Beruf weiter ausübten zum Wohl Gottes, der Majestät und der armen Indianer, die sie von Krankheit des Schreckens heilen".
Nach SILVERBLATT (1990:23) verfolgten und verurteilten die Spanier mit ihrem von der Krone diktierten Katholizismus und unter dem Einfluss der Verfolgung der Heilkundigen im Mittelalter, alle Heiler und Heilerinnen als Hexer. Die Chronisten lassen jedoch ungewollt und zu ihrem Nachteil, durchblicken, dass die Einheimischen die Hebammen in einer besonders ehrwürdigen Stellung hielten.

EHRENREICH, ENGLISH (1984:11-37) und HUIZER (1991:5) analysieren die Bedeutung des Geschlechts und der Klasse in den Kämpfen der Heilkundigen und ihren Zusammenhang mit den Befreiungsbewegungen. SILVERBLATT (1990) demonstriert in ihrer Analyse über die geschlechtlichen Strukturen in den Anden, wie gerade die Verfolgung die Flucht der Priesterinnen und die Artikulation des weiblichen Widerstandes bedingte. Später fanden sie Zuflucht im Untergrund und der Ausübung der Zauberei. HUIZER (1990:28-58) hat auch die Bedeutung der Zauberei im Widerstand der Unterdrückten Lateinamerikas untersucht. Diese historische kollektive Erfahrung prägt die Persönlichkeit der Hebammen. Sie sind zwar freundlich, können aber genauso schweigsam, reserviert, misstrauisch und distanziert sein. Sie sind eben ein wichtiger Bestandteil des passiven Widerstandes.

Ihre Verfolgung ist nicht beendet; im Gegenteil hat sie im Laufe der Zeit, der Epochen und Regierungen verschiedene Formen angenommen und sie besteht immer noch unter dem Deckmantel sogenannter "entwicklungsfördender" Projekte für verarmte Gebiete, die die Hebammen als Träger von Geburtenkontrollprogrammen zu instrumentalisieren versuchen. Dies ist einer der Faktoren, die dazu beigetragen haben, dass ihr Wissen verdrängt wird. Im folgenden behandele ich die wesentliche Aspekte die zur Ausübung der Funktion als Hebamme begleiten.

Die Berufung der Hebammen

In der gleichen Art und Weise wie alle anderen Auserwählten für den Kult der andinen Götter erhielten die Hebammen ihre Berufung in Träumen. In den Anden wurde die religiöse Vorbestimmung durch Träume offenbart. Die Chronisten und Priester ARRIAGA 1968, COBO 1964, GUAMAN POMA 1956, MURUA 1946 (in: SILVERBLATT 1990:56) bestätigen, dass die Frauen für bestimmte Verantwortungspositionen innerhalb des einheimischen religiösen Systems auserwählt werden konnten, indem die Gottheit Illapa (der Blitz) sie in Träumen ansprach oder mit ihnen kopulierte, wenn sie als Hirtinnen die Tiere auf die weitabgelegenen Weiden der Hochebene führten. In gleicher Weise waren "außergewöhnliche Geburten", Wunderzeichen der Muttererde für die Menschen, ähnlich wie der Maisstengel mit mehreren Maiskolben oder die Zwillingskartoffel, Ausdruck der Kraft der Fruchtbarkeit, mit der die Saramama (Muttermais) und die Axomama (Mutterkartoffeln) gesegnet wurden (SILVERBLATT 1990:23). Es muss hier erwähnt werden, dass Pachamama eine Gottheit ist, die verschiedene Gottheitsformen annimmt, wie Saramama (Mais), Axomama (Kartoffel), Cocamama (Koka) und Quinuamama (Quinoa). Wegen der speziellen Identifikation der Frauen und Hebammen mit Pachamama und ihren Gottheiten, wurden abnorme Geburten als Wunderzeichen, Macht und Berufung der Göttin interpretiert. Der Chronist POLO (1916:33) berichtet, dass die Kinder, die während eines Gewitters auf dem Feld geboren wurden, oder die Kinder des Donners vorbestimmt waren, sich in höherem Alter dem Kult zu widmen, weil man annahm, dass ihre Opfergaben von den Göttern lieber angenommen würden.(in: SILVERBLATT 1990:57). MARISCOTTI (1978:130) bemerkt, dass die Berufung als Fruchtbarkeitspriesterin in Verbindung mit dem Blitz dadurch entsteht, dass der Blitz von den Einheimischen als ein großartiges Kennzeichen der Gottheit der atmosphärischen Phänomene angesehen wurde. Dieser Gott hatte eine hervorgehobene Stellung in den lokalen und inkaischen göttlichen Pantheons und war ein aktiver Förderer der menschlichen, tierischen und pflanzlichen Fruchtbarkeit. Nach TOMASO und anderen (1985:206) nehmen Frauen im heutigen Apurímac den Beruf der Hebamme durch übernatürliche Berufung an, weil sie vom Blitz getroffen sind oder weil die Mutter oder Verwandte den gleichen Beruf ausgeübt haben. Die 80jährige Ignacia fing sehr jung als Hebamme an. Sie wurde vom Blitz getroffen. Sie wachte eines Nachts auf und fand eine kleine Alpakadecke mit sechs Muscheln, ein kleines Messer und Glas. Ihr Vater sagte: "Sicher wirst Du im Leben etwas lernen". Sie wurde Hebamme. Genauso in Cusco schreibt ZAMALLOA (1972:23), dass die Hebammen ihre Berufung durch Offenbarung erhalten und sie über tiefe Kenntnisse über die Heilpflanzen, die sie bei den Geburten verwenden, verfügen.

Rituelle Einweihung

Es gibt nur wenige marginale Hinweise über den Inhalt der Rituale bei der Einsetzung der Hebammen. Nach dem Chronisten COBO, "musste man um Hebamme zu werden, viele Zeremonien, Fasten und Opfergaben machen", um in Kontakt mit der übernatürlichen Welt zu treten. Andererseits verteidigt der Chronist Garcilazo die traditionellen Heilkundigen gegen die Zaubereibeschuldigungen der Spanier, erwähnt aber, dass eine Frau, die Hebamme ist, mehr Hexe als Hebamme sei, da sie spezielle Rituale zelebrieren müsste, um das Hebammentum ausüben zu können. (vgl. SILVERBLATT 1990:23)
Um eine Annäherung an den Charakter und die Struktur der Spezialisierung der Hebammen zu erreichen, gehe ich von folgenden unterschiedlichen Ansätze aus:
1. die Studie von SILVERBLATT (1990) über den Parallelismus in der andinen Geschlechtertrennung,
2. die Studien von BASTIEN (1977:61-62), en Kaata, Bolivia, über die Rituale und weiblichen Symbole,

3. die Analyse der Rituale der männlichen Schamanen, die MARISCOTTI (1978:121-148) sehr ausführlich untersucht hat.

Von dieser Grundlage ausgehend ist es möglich anzunehmen:

1. dass die Hebammen ihre Rolle über die Linie der weiblichen Abstammung übernommen haben, die sie mit ihren weiblichen mythischen Ahnen verbindet.
2. dass die rituelle Einsetzung der Hebammen und Schamanen sowohl parallele Strukturen, wie eine kultische geschlechtliche Teilung aufweist.

D.h. die Matrix der Berufung, Einsetzung und Unterweisung von Frauen wie Männern richtet sich nach den gleichen kosmologischen Prinzipen, nur die Funktionen und Symbole sind geschlechtlich differenziert aber gleichzeitig komplementär. Ein bedeutendes Zeichen der andinen Kultur ist die hoch spezialisierte Rolle der Ritualisten. Die andine Religion ist in Heiligtum, Rituale und Ritualisten von Staat, Territorium, Dorfgemeinde, "Linajes" (Sippe) und Familie eingeteilt. Jedes System hat seine eigenen Symbole, Rituale und Ritualisten, die sich nicht miteinander vermischen. Jedes Territorium hat weibliche und männliche heilige Orte. Wenn die Menschen in differenzierten ökologischen Zonen leben, nutzen sie diese Ressourcen und haben entsprechende einzigartige Rituale für jede Ebene.

Die Viehzüchter der Hochebenen haben Riten für Alpaka, Lama und Schafe, während die Bewohner der mittleren Ebene Riten für Kartoffeln haben, und die Bewohner der unteren Ebenen Rituale mit Getreiden praktizieren. Die Familien und "Linajes" (Sippen) haben weibliche Symbole und Rituale.

Die Spezialisierung richtet sich nach den gesellschaftlichen Schichten, daher die Vielfalt von Ritualisten und Riten. Seit der Eroberung war die Spezialisierung der Ritualisten teilweise durch das Geschlecht vorbestimmt.

Nach Rowe (in: BASTIEN 1977:62), übernahmen früher mehr Frauen als Männer die Rollen von:
- *huacavillac* (Pflege der "Huacas"= Heilige Orte)
- *mallquivillac* (Pflege der Mumien der Ahnen)
- *libiacpavillac* (Vermittlerin des Blitzes)
- *punchauvillac* (Vermittlerin der Sonne)

In der Regel hatten die Frauen eher untergeordnete Aufgaben als Assistentin, oder bei der Behandlung, Beichte, Zubereitung der kultischen Getränke (Maisbier) und der Wahrsagung. Anscheinend besteht diese Norm bis heute. BASTIEN (1977:61) hat in Kaata, Bolivien beobachtet, dass die Männer "Mesarituale" für das Glück machen, um die Heiligen Orte der Erde zu nähren und gute Ereignisse, wie eine gute Ernte, die Genesung eines Kranken etc., zu begünstigen. Die Frauen demgegenüber führen "Mesarituale" gegen Pech und Unglück aus, um den Fluss zu nähren. In diesem System haben die Frauen die primäre Rolle von "warmi yachaq" (wissender Frau) oder Wahrsagerin angenommen. Ihre Rituale sind darauf gerichtet, die körperliche oder soziale Ursache der Desintegration symbolisch zu verändern.

Aufgrund der bisherigen Informationen könnte man vermuten, dass der weibliche Götterkult - ähnlich wie beim männlichen Schamanen- in Ebenen von Wahrsagerinnen, Hebammen und anderen Ritualistinnen aufgeteilt war; aber das ganze System funktionierte gleichzeitig nach der Komplementarität und dem Parallelismus der geschlechtlich-kultischen Teilung. BASTIEN (1977:63) beobachtet hierzu, dass die rituellen weiblichen und männlichen Funktionen bis heute mit dem lokalen symbolischen System der Metaphern des Körpers verbunden geblieben ist. Während des jährlichen Zyklus der rituellen Darstellung opfern die männlichen Wahrsager Symbole der Hochebene, wie Lamafett und Föten, an alle vierzehn Heiligtümer der Erde des Berges Kaata. Sie nähren alle Höhenlagen des Berges, die nicht nur die Einheit der Gemeinde symbolisieren, sondern auch die körperliche Einheit. Die weiblichen Wahrsagerinnen präsentieren als ergänzendes Gegenstück Symbole der unteren Ebene, wie Schweinefett, tote Ratten für den Wind, den Fluss und den Erdrutsch; die Erosionselemente des Berges Kaata. Die Opfergaben werden flussabwärts gestreut, von "Oben" nach "Unten" (im symbolischen und ökologischen Sinn), von der Hochebene in Richtung Urwald, um beide Ebenen zu verbinden und zu integrieren. Während des Rituals opfert die warmi yachaq (wissende Frau) nicht nur symbolische Objekte der Erde, des Körpers und der Sippe, sondern ersetzt zugleich das, was entfernt oder aufgerüttelt wurde. Ihre Rolle ist durch ihre strukturelle Stellung innerhalb der Gesellschaft, speziell durch ihre biliniale Erbschaft und die Virilokalität bestimmt. BASTIEN (1977:63,64) assoziiert dieses Prinzip mit der Vorstellung der männlichen permanencia (Beständigkeit) und des weiblichen zyklischen Geschehens (ciclicidad) d.h. die weibliche Macht und ihre Fähigkeit das Böse zu vertreiben liegen in ihrer menstruellen, ausscheidenden Fähigkeit. Sie sind sozial und physiologisch fähiger, die Symbole der Verluste des Körpers und der Erde wiederherzustellen. Man kann das Männliche als Zentrum, als Achse, als Element des Fortbestehens und das Weibliche als die zyklische Peripherie, wie das Mondsymbol des ewigen Werdens und Schwindens, wie Ebbe und Flut verstehen. BASTIEN (1977:64) betont, dass trotz der symbolischen und örtlichen Unterschiede zwischen den Geschlechtern beide, sowohl männliche wie weibliche Wahrsager, zur Aufrechterhaltung, zur Beständigkeit und zum Erhalt des Kaata-Körper-Bergs beitragen. Die Männer machen Opfergaben für den ganzen Berg und beeinflussen damit zukünftige Ereignisse, während die Frauen, die das Böse und das Unglück löschen, helfen, die Person, die Gemeinde und die Gesellschaft wieder zu integrieren. Diese Rollen als Wahrsager und Wahrsagerinnen gehen über die Linien der männlichen und weiblichen Abstammung.

Wissenserwerb
Nach Lira in Quispicanchis, Cusco, (in: MARISCOTTI 1978:131-133), schließt sich der Schamane nach der Berufung und der initiatischen Erfahrung ein und fastet drei Tage lang. Damit tritt er in eine lange Periode der Unterweisung ein, die "karpachikuy" genannt wird. Man weiss nicht viel darüber, was diese Unterweisung bedeutet, es wird vermutet, dass sie breite esoterische Zeremonien beinhaltet, wie rituelle nächtliche Bäder in hohen Seen oder Flusseinmündungen, ekstatischen Erfahrungen im Inneren der Berge, der Residenz des Blitzes und der Toten. Dadurch tritt der Schaman in Kontakt mit den Geistern der Berge. Die Macht eines Schamanen ist von der Zahl der "Suyaq" (Ahnengeister) abhängig, die ihm in Form von Raubvögeln erscheinen. Die Sagen und Traditionen der mittleren Anden berichten über die Verwandlung der Schamanen in Vögel und über ihre Fähigkeit, zum Land der Toten zu wandern und dort mystische Kämpfe zu führen. Nach MARISCOTTI (1978:138-140) sind die ekstatischen Erfahrungen mit dem Glauben an Schutzgeister assoziert und dürften von früheren kosmologischen Mythen inspiriert worden sein. Der Ahnengeist könnte der Gott der meteorologischen Phänomene, eine komplexe mythische Figur, halb Gott, halb Kulturheld (héroe civilizador) mit schamanistischen Zügen gewesen sein. Die "Suyaq" (Ahnengeister) waren mythologisch verwandte Gottheiten dieses außerordentlich polymorphen Gottes. Nach den noch erhaltenen historischen Berichten aus Quispicanchis, Cusco, handelt es sich um ein mythologisches legendäres Katzenwesen, das jährlich Hagel mit sich bringend erscheint und das mit den Geister der Berge den "Apu" und "Auki", verwandt ist. Dieses Katzenwesen könnte das alter ego einiger Professioneller des Kultes gewesen sein. Diese Erfahrungen waren mit dem Gebrauch halluzinogener Substanzen verbunden, wie die archäologischen Entdeckungen von zeremonieller Keramik und Textilien aus Chavín zeigen.

Bezüglich der weiblichen Unterweisung berichtet Polo de Ondegardo (in: MARISCOTTI 1978:133), dass sowohl Frauen wie Männer sich diesem Beruf gewidmet haben, dessen Vertreter nicht nur in Guarochirí, in Cusco, bei den Collas, Guancas, in den Ebenen waren, sondern auch im Land von Guánuco, im Land der Chachapoyas und in vielen anderen Provinzen. Wenn es Evidenzen gibt, dass beide Geschlechter den schamanischen Beruf ausgeübt haben, könnte man vermuten, dass die Hebammen ähnliche Zeremonien erfahren haben, die wahrscheinlich speziell mit den weiblichen Gottheiten verbunden waren und innerhalb der kultischen Hierarchie auf ihre spezifische Funktion als Weise, Heilige und Hebamme ausgerichtet waren. Die Tatsache, dass die Hebammen in ihren Heilungstätigkeiten Abführ-, Fasten- und Reinigungskuren anwendeten und bis heute noch gute Pflanzenkundige sind, deutet darauf hin, dass sie diese Methoden kennengelernt und selbst erlebt haben mussten, bevor sie sie praktizieren konnten. Das Wochenbettritual ist ein Beispiel dafür. Es ist noch zu erklären, ob die initiatische Erfahrung und Unterweisung der Frauen die gleichen Rituale verlangt wie die der Männer oder ihre Wissenserwerb über den Gebrauch von anderen rituellen Drogen oder Erfahrungen geht, die nur mit den weiblichen Gottheiten verbunden ist.

BASTIEN (1977:64) berichtet, dass in Kaata, Bolivia, die Wahrsager Hellseher sind, weil sie Koka kauen, und Kokaín ist auch die Droge, die den weiblichen Wahrsagerinnen eine religiöse Trance ermöglicht, durch die sie die Zukunft visualisieren können. Nach dem Mythos der Entstehung der Kokapflanze aus Cajatambo (DUVIOLS 1973:34) war die Koka ursprunglich nur Nahrung des Sonnengottes. Die Huacas beneideten ihm und entsendeten Urau, der geschickt an den Samen drankommt und mit ihnen in anderen Gebiete flieht. Urau war ein Heiler und hinterließ mehrere Töchter auf seinem Weg, die als Huacas (heilige Orte) von den Bewohnern geehrt wurden. Nach ROSTWOROWSKI (1985:35) entsteht die Kokapflanze aus den zerstückelten Körper einer schönen Frau, die wegen ihren leichten Verhältnissen von der Älterrat des Dorfes zur Tode verurteilt wurde. Die Koka ist eine der wichtigste rituelle und Heilpflanzen der andinen Kultur und insbesondere das Wahrsagemedium par excelenz der andinen Schamanen, Heiler und Hebammen. Bezüglich der Vermittlung des Wissens bei Hebammen wird auch wenig berichtet. Nach den Untersuchungen von GUTMANN (1988:1-24) über die orale Tradition in Pomacanchi, Cusco, wird deutlich, dass es eine weibliche Form gibt die Welt zu verstehen, die eng verbunden ist mit der Art und Weise, wie sie es auch vermitteln. Im Rhythmus, der gramatikalischen Struktur und im Symbolismus ihrer Erzählungen und Märchen befindet sich schon die Essenz und Matrix ihrer Lebensprinzipien kodifiziert. Diese wird über die mündliche Überlieferung weiter tradiert. Eine weitere Vermittlung des Wissens geschieht meistens über die Familie und durch die direkte Erfahrung.

Das Verhältnis der Hebammen zu ihren Schutzgeistern
Nach TOMASO u.a.(1985:210) beten die Hebammen aus Apurímac generell zu den "Apus" (den Schutzgeistern der Berge) um Hilfe während der Geburt, wobei jede Hebamme ihren bevorzugten Apu anbetet. Wenn eine Familie nach der Hilfe einer Hebamme verlangt, bringen sie unter anderem Schnaps als Opfergabe für die Schutzgeister mit. Damit zelebriert die Hebamme die Zeremonie der "tinkasqa" (Opfer an die Apus). Die Hebamme Timotea sagt darüber: "Ich trinke sehr wenig. Alles gebe ich den Apus, damit sie nicht denken, dass ich geizig bin, und mir helfen." Ohne diese Opfergaben kann ein Unheil geschehen. Dieser Akt des Glaubens ist in der andinen Rationalität tief verwurzelt und auf den zentralen Prinzipien der Reziprozität und der Bewahrung des Gleichgewichts der Kräfte begründet.

Die Wahrsagung
Eine der speziellen Fähigkeiten der Professionellen des Kultes ist nach MARISCOTTI (1978:124) ihre Hellsichtigkeit, um die Ursache des Böses zu erahnen. In der Regel wird dies durch die mediale Kraft der Kokablätter unterstützt, liegt aber eher in der Fähigkeit der Schamanen, mit den Schutzgeistern zu kommunizieren. Diese werden konsultiert, um eine Diagnose des Leidens, der Krankheiten, des Verlorenen zu führen, oder darüber ob das Übel durch Hexerei, Raub oder Strafe der Götter verursacht ist.

Die Hebammen besitzen speziell diese Fähigkeit und machen sehr viel Gebrauch von den Kokablättern, um in die Zukunft sehen, die Ursache der Probleme zu finden und vor allem für die Geburtsangelegenheiten, um das Geschlecht des Kindes, den gesundheitlichen Zustand der Gebärenden und den Ausgang der Geburt zu erfahren. D.h. die Fähigkeit der Hebammen mit der Koka umzugehen bedeutet eine spezielle Verbindung mit der Gottheit Kokamama (Mutter Koka), eine Version der allumfassenden Pachamama. Außerdem ist der Mythos der Entstehung der Koka eng mit der Vorstellung der Macht des Eros und der Fruchtbarkeit verbunden. MORE (1990:84) fasst zusammen, wie die Hebammen der Dorfgemeinde San Juan de Catacaos, Piura, die Ursachen der Krankheiten einordnen. Sie sind:
- Kosmisch, wenn die Agenzien die natürlichen Phänomene sind (Finsternis, Erdbeben, Wind).
- Menschlich, wenn der Mensch z.B. Agens des bösen Blicks ist.
- Mythisch, wenn die Agenzien die bösen Ahnen oder die heilige Orte sind, die Deformationen und Aborte verursachen.
- Religiös, wenn Gelübde an die Götter und Heiligen nicht erfüllt worden sind.

Die Dualität der Funktionen
Bei den andinen HeilerInnen ist oft zu beobachten, dass sie in sich zwei antagonistische Rollen - der weißen und schwarzen Magie - in einer Person vereinen. In der Regel praktizieren manche nur die weiße Magie, andere nur die Schwarze, aber es gibt auch solche, die einer weiß-schwarzen Tradition angehören. (MARISCOTTI 1978:125) Diese Eigenschaft leitet sich aus der Dualität der andinen Götter ab, die gleichzeitig wohltätig und gütig wie auch zerstörerisch sind. Pachamama kann zerstörend sein, wenn man sie nicht respektiert. BASTIEN (1977: 64) berichtet, dass der mächtige und zu fürchtende Blick der Wahrsagerin Rosita schon sieben Todesfälle verursacht habe. Die Polizei von Charazani in Bolivia fürchtete sich vor ihr. Die Hebammen verkörpern in ihrer Person antagonistische Funktionen, da ihr Wissen ihnen erlaubt, beide Bereiche des Lebens zu berühren, und die Mittel, speziell die Pflanzen und Rituale verfügen, die die Fruchtbarkeit fördern oder unterbinden. Wenn sie in der Lage sind, kosmische, menschliche, mythische und religiöse Agenzien von Unheil zu beseitigen, müssen sie auch fähig sein, sich und ihre Patienten gegen das Böse zu schützen. Da ist dann die Grenzlinie schwer zu ziehen. Trotz aller Anklagen, dass sie "mehr Zauberei als das Hebammentum" ausgeübt hätte, bezieht sich

die Bezeichnung "uauauachachic hampicamayoq" mehr auf den Gebrauch ihrer besonderen Fähigkeiten für Heilung, Schutz, Förderung des Lebens und die Wiederherstellung der Ordnung.

Das Instrumentarium der Hebammen
Die Chronisten berichten, dass die Zauberer und "Ministranten" Steine für verschiedene Zwecke angewendet haben. Cobo sagt: ihnen oder ihren Vorfahren hat es der Donner gegeben, andere haben es von einer Huaca (heiliger Ort), andere haben sie durch eine im Traum erschienene Tote; einige Frauen gaben zu verstehen, dass sie während eines Gewitters vom Donner befruchtet worden seien, ... und neun Monate später hätten sie mit intensiven Schmerzen geboren, und im Traum sei ihnen gesagt worden, dass alles, was sie mit ihnen machen würden, wahr würde" (in: MARISCOTTI 1978:144).

Nach MARISCOTTI (1978:142-144) führten die Heiler Talismane und kultische Objekte mit sich, und zwar als Erinnerung an ihre ekstatischen Erfahrungen und als Symbole ihrer Macht (wie wilde einbalsamierte Katzen, getrocknete Pumapfoten oder Bronzesphären, - in Chucuito "kaxya" "Blitz" genannt) - für ihre Sitzungen mit den übernatürlichen Wesen. In Cusco werden sie cuya (kuya, khuya), qhaqya mesa, mésay-rumi genannt, kommen aus dem "Haus des Blitzes" und sind Gaben der Geister der Berge. Manchmal sind es nur archäologische Reste, die sie mit höchster Ehrfurcht und Vorliebe aufbewahren. In der Hochebene von Moquegua benutzen die Heiler Quarzkristalle für die Diagnose, die "Stern" "Magnetnadel" oder "largavista" genannt werden und von denen sie sagen, sie hätten sie in den Bergen gefunden, als sie ihre Berufung erhielten und ihre Aufgabe übernahmen.

Die Hebammen benutzen genauso wie ihre männlichen Counterparts auch Steine während der Geburt oder für das Ritual des Wochenbettes, um den Uterus der Mutter in die richtige Stellung zu bringen. VALDIZAN (1922, 1985:I,339) berichtet über den Bezirk von Hualgayoc, Cajamarca, dass die "Empfangsfrauen" (eine andere Bezeichnung für Hebamme) Magnetsteine anwenden, und zwar wegen ihrer effektiven Wirkung auf das zur Welt kommende Kind, das sie nach außen "ziehen".

In Lima, (id.1922,1985:I,338) werden die Magnetsteine auf die Füße der Gebärenden gelegt, um den Fötus "anzuziehen". Von dem Magnetstein, der sich fest an den Unterleib der Frau heftet, meinen die Hebammen, dass er arbeitet" damit der Uterus in seine normale Stellung zurückkommt. Wenn der Stein sich lockert, ist dies ein Zeichen, dass er "ermüdet ist, da er seinen Zweck erfüllt hat". Es besteht die Vorstellung, dass der Uterus ("die Mutter") durch den ganzen Körper weit verstreut ist, daher muss man die "Mutter sammeln und festigen". VALDIZAN (1922)(1985: I,337) fügt hinzu, dass die Magnetsteine sich nähren, wenn sie mit Eisensplittern gedeckt werden. Je stärker und wilder sie sind, desto mehr Eisenpartikel haften an ihnen. Wenn die Adhäsion der Partikel größer ist, werden sie als männlich identifiziert, wenn sie schwächer ist, als weiblich. Die Hebamme besitzt eine respektable Zahl solcher Steine und benennt sie mit speziellen Namen, die ihre besonderen Eigenschaften beschreiben: "großer Teufel", "Dicke", "Mächtige Dicke" etc. POLIA (1989:32) berichtet, dass der "Dicke Stein" oder Andesita für körperliche Reinigungsreibungen angewendet wird, um die negative Einflüsse löschen, da sie die Fähigkeit haben, das Böse zu absorbieren. Ein anderer "Magnetstein", der Magnetit, der für die Liebesmagie sehr geschätzt ist aber auch magisch- therapeutische Eigenschaften aufweist, wird von Meister Francisco Guarnizo von Huancabamba für die weiblichen Blutungen verschrieben. Die Frauen müssen ein Stück Magnetit am Hals tragen, nachdem dieses durch ein "Mesa-Ritual" aktiviert worden ist, um die Blutung zu unterbrechen und die Gebärmutter "aufzuheben".

In Cusco beobachtete SUSUKI (1982:115), dass die Hebammen Öle, Lamafett, Muskatnuss, Kork, nach links gedrehten Faden und Pulver aus gemahlenen Steinen mit sich führen. Die Kokatasche ist unabdingbar. Über Huaylas berichtet Gamarra (1967:42) über ähnliche Utensilien und zusätzliche Pflanzen zur Beschleunigung der Geburt. MARISCOTTI (1978:87-110) beschreibt und analysiert ausführlich die kultischen Objekte, die für die Opfergaben an Pachamama verwendet werden: Amulette, Talismane, zeremonielle Gefäße, Muscheln, einbalsamierte Tiere und Föten, Spiegel, Bronzesphären, Mais, Stroh, Blumen, Mineralien, Maisbier, Fett, Koka, Weihrauch, Tabak, Federn, eisenhaltige Ockerfarben, eingeschnürte Muschelreste, Glasperlen, kleine Haushaltsobjekte, Tier- und Gestirnefiguren aus Zinn, rotgefärbte Wolle, Meerschweinchen etc. Nach VAN DEN BERG (1989:43) unterliegen die Riten einer ähnlich grundlegenden Struktur, wie die Art und Weise in der man um Hilfe oder Teilnahme bittet, die so charakteristisch ist bei den andinen Völkern. Die rituellen Instrumente sind in der Regel die gleichen: Opfergaben, Tiere, Essen, Koka, Getränke, Musik und Tänze. Innerhalb der gegebenen Struktur und beim Gebrauch von traditionellen rituellen Instrumenten herrscht eine große Vielfalt und

Kreativität bei der Gestaltung jeden Ritus. Ich liste hier die Objekte auf, die "Mama Panchita", eine Hebamme aus Cusco, als Opfergaben der Mutterde zum Wohl ihrer Patienten darbringt:
> Eine kleine Decke, wo die Opfergaben eingerichtet werden
> In vier geteiltes Papier
> Kleine Glöckchen, um die Geister zusammenzurufen
> Rote Nelken.
> Kleine Engelchen aus Brotmehl
> Eine Muschel in der Mitte des Opferrechtecks
> Samen von Mais, Koka, Huayruros, Bohnen,
> Sorgfältig ausgewählte Kokablätter, je fünf pro Bündel
> Schafs - oder Lamafett.
> Zinnfiguren
> winzig kleine Bonbons
> Farbiger Faden
> Schafswolle
> goldene oder silberne Streifen
> kleine bunte Zettelchen

Alles wird unter Gebeten sorgfältig geordnet, mit Schnaps besprengt und liebevoll geschlossen. Anschließend wird es mit einem Kreuz bezeichnet und durch Verbrennung geopfert. Wenn die Asche weiß ist, so bedeutet dies, dass die Opfergaben von Pachamama mit Wohlwollen empfangen worden sind. Die Verteilung der Opfer gaben ist eine symbolische Rekonstruktion der kosmischen Matrix.

Die Unterweisung der Hebammen

Nachdem wir nun die speziellen Fähigkeiten der Hebammen untersucht haben, stellen wir fest, dass die Professionellen des Kultes, sowohl Männer als auch Frauen einen zwar nicht identischen Werdegang aufweisen, aber doch sehr ähnliche Prozesse durchlaufen, die man als schamanistisch bezeichnen kann. Für beide Geschlechter ist folgendes festzustellen:
- die Berufung als Auserwählte für die Funktionen des Kultes durch dieselbe übernatürliche Gottheit, Illapa, der Blitz.
- die Notwendigkeit einer tiefen und langjährigen Internalisierung der Prinzipien, Traditionen, Mythen und Ahnen ihrer eigenen Kosmologie und Religion.
- das Charisma und die Entwicklung ihrer Fähigkeiten als Wahrsager/innen und Hellseher/innen,
- die Fähigkeit, mit den Göttern ihres Pantheons zu kommunizieren und sie für ihre Heilungstätigkeiten aufrufen zu können und als Vermittler zwischen Menschen und Göttern zu wirken,
- die Fähigkeit, zwischen guten und negativen Kräften differenzieren zu können.
- die Fähigkeit, die entsprechenden Rituale nach Status und Geschlecht ausführen zu können,
- fundiertes Wissen über Kräuter Heilpflanzen, halluzinogene Pflanzen, ihre Wirkung und Anwendung.
- sehr genaue Kenntnisse über ihr eigenes medizinisches System, Körper, Gesundheit und Krankheit.
- das Wissen über den Zusammenhang zwischen Astronomie und agraischem Zyklus.

Die Spezialisierung der Hebammen bedeutet dann, dass sie die obenerwähnten Fähigkeiten speziell auf die weiblichen Funktionen anwenden, insbesondere auf die Betreuung des gesamten reproduktiven Zyklus von der Zeugung über Schwangerschaft, Geburt, Wochenbett, Behandlung des Neugeborenen, die rituelle Behandlung der Plazenta und der Nabelschnur, Krankheiten bis zur Wiedereingliederung von Mutter und Kind in die Gemeinde. Die Heilungsressourcen einer Hebamme sind vielfältig, da sie in ihrer Funktion religiöse, magisch-rituelle, medizinische und psychosomatische Methoden anwendet. D.h. sie verfügt über ein integrales Konzept von Gesundheit und Krankheit. Ihre Handlungsmethoden bezwecken die Wiederherstellung des Gleichgewichtes und der Harmonie der weiblichen Funktionen, da sie für die Fruchtbarkeit des gesamten Kosmos verantwortlich sind. GAMARRA in Huaylas (1967), BOLIVAR DE COLCHADO in Ayacucho (1968), ZAMALLOA (1972) u. SUSUKI (1982) in Cusco und TOMASO (1985) in Apurímac bestätigen, dass die magisch-religiöse und heilende Funktion der Hebammen in den Dorfgemeinden weiter besteht und ausgeübt wird, vor allem in den Gebieten, wo eine starke kulturelle Identität besteht. Selbst dort, wo es offizielle medizinische Einrichtungen und Dienstleistungen gibt, werden die Hebammen bevorzugt, da die Bevölkerung ihnen eher vertraut.

Der Selbstbild der Hebammen

Während der Projektarbeit mit Hebammen im Landesbezirk Apurímac, zur Systematisierung und Wiedergewinn ihres Wissens, war es möglich ein Selbstbild von ihnen als Frauen zu gewinnen.

Die Hebammen sind in der Regel die älteste Frauen der Dorfgemeinde. Dies entspricht das mythische Bild von Pachamama (nach den Sagen, eine alte Frau, die unter der Erde lebt).

Sie leben als Subsistenzbäuerinnen von ihrem Acker, Tiere und der Vermarktung ihrer Produkte, genauso wie die andere Frauen der Dorfgemeinde. Daher sind sie keine fremde Körper im Leben der Gemeinde. Das Besondere an ihnen ist die Qualität ihres Lebens und die Symbolik, die in ihrer Biographie impliziert ist. Aus der Analyse ihrer Zeichnungen ergibt sich das Bild einer erdegebundene Frau, die aus einem stärken körperlichen Bewusstsein ausgeht. Sie haben die besondere Eigenschaft und Fähigkeit in ihren alltäglichen Leben die verschiedene Ebenen und Lebensräume des Kosmos zu durchwandern und lebendig zu integrieren. Sie erleben diese Welten durch ihre täglichen Aktivitäten, in dem sie ihre Tiere in ihren "hoheren" Lebensraum weiden, ihre Familien in ihrem "Zentrum und Mitte" (Haus) durch Hausarbeit versorgen. Ihr Ackerarbeit mit Kartoffeln ("oben") und Mais ("unten",im Tal) ist die wesentliche Verbindung zu Pachamama und ihren anderen Numens, Axomama und Saramama. Dadurch erlangt sie ihr Wissen, innige Identität und Reziprozität mit der Pflanzenwelt und auch die der Heilpflanzen. Ihre besondere Aufgabe ist die Verwandlung der Produkte der Erde in Nahrung, Kleidung, Heilung, Opfergaben und zeremoniellen Getränke, wie das Maisbier zu Begleitung der rituellen Festen und Ackerarbeit. Das andine Konzept der vertikale Nutzung des Bodens ist hier impliziert. (MURRA 1975:79-115). Die Göttin Zañumama (Tonerde) ihrer Gefäße ist das wichtigste und immer wiederkehrendes weibliches Symbol in ihren Zeichnungen.

Durch das Weben verwandeln sie die Wolle in Kleidung, Farbe und Symbole. Der Weg ist das verbindende Symbol zwischen den Ebenen des Kosmos, der Fluss und die Forelle deuten ihre Verbindung zum Wasser. Der Mann ist die Brücke zum parallelen männlichen Welt um die Kontinuität des Lebens zu sichern. Gleichzeitig steht ihr alltägliches Leben in Übereinstimmung mit dem gesamt Zyklus ihrer Existenz. In ihrer Kindheit und Pubertät weidete sie die Tieren in der Hochebenen ("oben"), wo sie ihre Berufung empfängt. Danach als Frau und Mutter in ihrem Haus ("Mitte") (auch ein Statussymbol) ernährt sie ihre Familie und lernt die Planzenwelt kennen und anwenden. Das Feuer und das Acker sind ihre wichtigste Lebensräume in diesem Lebensabschnitt. Mit den gesammelten Lebenerfahrungen und -wissen, - als ältere und weise Frau,- widmet sie sich der Heilung der Geburten in ihrer Dorfgemeinde. Ihre Leben ist eine Wanderung durch alle diese weibliche Sphären im Alltag und als gesammte Lebenzyklus und bewahren damit das Gleichgewicht der Reproduktion zwischen den menschlichen, ökologischen und kosmischen Ebenen. Ihre weibliche Existenz bildet eine integrale Einheit zwischen Mikrokosmos und Makrokosmos. Diese lebensweltliche Erfahrung und Wissen verbunden mit dem Charisma des Religiösität und Widerstand ist die "vitale Kraft" (HUIZER 1991:11-13), die diese besondere Frauen und Hebammen trägt. In den Untersuchungen von VAN QUEKELBERGHE (1994,3(1)) über schamanistische Therapie und symbolisches Heilen findet sich eine deutliche Bestätigung dafür, dass auf die Hebammen im andinen Raum, wie wir sie bis hier dargestellt haben, alle schamanistischen Charakterisierungen zutreffen, wie:

1. die Fähigkeit zu verbinden, zu vermitteln, zu beschützen und zu vereinen::
    - zwischen drei Welten
        (d.s. die Obere Welt = Hanan Pacha, die Welt Hier = Kay Pacha und die Unterwelt= Ukhu Pacha)
    - zwischen Menschen und Ahnengeistern (der Gott Illapa)
    - zwischen Menschen und Göttinnen (Pachamama, Saramama, Cocamama, Zañumama, Mama cocha)
    - zwischen Toten - (Tieren und Menschen)
    - zwischen Leben und Tod (Geburt als Übergang)
2. im Besitz einer kosmozentrischen, integralen und harmonischen Sicht des Menschen zu sein,
3. die Anwendung von ganzheitlichen Methoden, die eine Vielfalt von physiologischen, psychologischen, sozialen, religiösen, mythischen etc. Aspekten zu vereinen versuchen,
4. die Fähigkeit zum Wahrsagen und Hellsehen, und zwar in Verbindung mit der Fähigkeit, veränderte Bewusstseinszustände zu erleben.
5. die Einbeziehung der Gemeinschaft
6. den gebärenden Frauen alle Voraussetzungen zu schaffen, die die notwendigen Prozesse der Regres-

sion bei der Geburt ermöglichen.

7. vor allem der intensive Rekurs auf traditionsgebundene Erzählungen, Mythen und Handlungsrituale. Die folgende Feststellung, *"dass der Schamanismus bestrebt ist, harmonische, friedvolle, erlebnisintensive Kommunikation im gesamten kosmobiologischen Lebenszusammenhang aufrechtzuerhalten oder (wieder-) herzustellen... im Sinne einer "Synchronisierung" der Energien entlang der Weltachse zu bewirken... und beschützend und vereinend zu handeln."* trifft sehr genau die Rolle und Funktion der Hebammen im andinen Raum.

Schlussfolgerung

Eine Intervention dieser weiblichen Gruppe durch Hebammenausbildungs- und Entwicklungs programmen für Mutter-Kind-Versorgung oder Familienplanung ohne Rücksicht auf ihre besondere religiöse, *therapeutische und rituelle Funktion ist eine Form der kulturellen Agression durch Machtentzug,* deren Reichweite noch nicht untersucht worden ist.

Danksagung

Ich danke Holger C. von Rauch für die einfühlsame und genaue Korrektur des Manuskripts.

References

BASTIEN, JOSEPH W. 1977. Femenine ritualist and symbols in the Andes. in: *Boletín bibliográfico de antropología americana.*Vol.40, n. 49, s. 61-77. Texas

BASTIEN, JOSEPH W. 1978. Mountain/Body Methaphor in the Andes. in: *Boletín del Instituto Francés de Estudios Andinos*, VII, n. 1-2, pp 87-103.

BOLIVAR DE COLCHADO, FANNY. 1968. Actitud de los Campesinos ante el Personal Auxiliar de Salud. in: *Dos estudios en la zona de Cangallo.*1-31, Ayacucho. Instituto Indigenista del Perú.

BOLIVAR DE COLCHADO, FANNY. 1969. Algunos aspectos de la salud en Cangallo. in: *Cuatro estudios de problemas.* 1-42, Ayacucho. Instituto Indigenista del Perú.(mimeo).

BURGOS LINGAN, MARIA OFELIA. 1995. El Ritual del Parto en los Andes. Nijmegen: *Derde Wereld Centrum Ontwikkelungsstudien,* Katholieke Universiteit. Niederlande.

DUVIOLS, PIERRE. 1973. Un mythe de l'origine de la coca. (Cajatambo). in: *Boletín Francés de Estudios Andinos.* Lima. Tomo II n.1.pp.34

HUIZER, G. 1991. Indigenous Knwoledge and Popular Spirituality: a Challenge to developmentalists. in: Proceedings of the inter- national Workshop *"Agricultural Knowledge Systems and Role of Extension".* Hohenheim. pp 51-71.

MARISCOTTI DE GORLITZ, ANA MARIA. 1978. Pachamama Santa Tierra. Contribución al estudio de la religión autóctona en los andes centro-meridionales. *Indiana Beiheft* n.8. Iberoamerikanisches Institut Preußischer Kulturbesitz. Berlin.

MUGUIRO IBARRA, FRANCISCO; MORE LOPEZ,JOSÉ Y COLABORADORES. 1990. *Nuestra experiencia en salud.* CIPCA. Centro de investigación y promoción del campesinado. Comunidad Campesina de San Juan de Catacaos. Piura, Perú.

MURRA, JOHN V. 1975. *Formaciones económicas y políticas del mundo andino.* Ediciones IEP:Instituto de Estudios Peruanos. pp 339. Lima. Perú.

POLIA M., MARIO. 1989. *Las lagunas de los encantos. Medicina tradicional andina del Perú septentrional.* CEPESER: Central Peruana de Servicios. Piura, Perú.

ROSTWOROWSKI DE DIEZ CANSECO, MARIA. 1985. Mitos andinos relacionados con el origen de las subsistencias. in: "*Boletín de Lima*", Año 7. n. 37, pp. 33-37. Lima. Perú.

SILVERBLATT, IRENE. 1990. Luna, sol y brujas. Género y clases en los andes prehispánicos y coloniales. *Archivos de historia andina./*10. Centro Bartolomé de las Casas. Cusco, Perú.

SUSUKI LOPEZ, LEONCIO. 1982. *Historia de la atención primaria en Cusco, Apurímac y Madre de Dios.* XI Región de Salud. pp.6-10 y 17-18. Anexo I. Cusco, Perú.

TOMASO, D.DE; CAPRARA, A.; CHIESA, E. 1985 . Equipo sociosanitario de la prelatura de Chuquibambilla. Trabajo con parteras tradicionales en la provincia de Grau, Apurímac. in: SARAVIA, L.M.; SUEIRO, R. (Editores): *Experiencias de desarrollo popular en el campo de la medicina tradicional y moderna. Centro amazónico de antropología y aplicación práctica.* DESCO. Lima. Perú.

VALDIZAN, H. MALDONADO, A. 1922. La Obstetricia en el Folklore Peruano. in: *Rev. de Psiquiatría y Discusiones Conexas.* Vol. IV:1 Lima, Perú.

ZAMALLOA G.; ZULMA. 1972. Ciclo vital en Sayllapata. Estudio de la cultura campesina del distrito de Sayllapata, Provincia de Paucartambo, Cusco. in: *Allpanchis* n. 4 pp. 21-32. Cusco. Perú.

VAN QUEKELBERGHE, R. 1994. Schamanistische Therapie: Vorwärts zum Ursprung symbolischen Heilens. in: *Ethnopsychologische Mitteilungen.* Band 3, Heft 1, Vol.3, n.1.

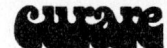

Teenage Pregnancy as an Issue of Gender Violence:
The Case of Zimbabwe
Schwangerschaften von Jungendlichen als ein Thema der Gewalt zwischen Geschlechtern: Der Kasus Zimbabwe

Caroline Hof & Annemiek Richters

Abstract: A qualitative study on teenage pregnancy was conducted in the period from July till Septemberœ1996 in Bulawayo, Zimbabwe. The results of the interviews with teenage mothers and fathers gaveœreason to analyse to what extent teenage pregnancy may be regarded as an issue of genderœviolence. Gender violence is looked at as a violation of basic human rights for women reflectingœpower imbalances inherent in patriarchal societies. It includes physical, sexual, and psychologicalœviolence which is likely to have negative effects on women's health. While acknowledging thatœwhat should be considered as gender violence according to international standards is notœuniversally recognized as such, it is argued that awareness must be raised concerning theœidentification of gender violence and its possible causal relationships with teenage pregnancy.œParticular emphasis is given to women's right to bodily integrity, and freedom and equality inœsexual and reproductive matters.

Zusammenfassung: Von Juli bis September 1996 wurde in Bulawayo, Zimbabwe eine Studie zum Thema Schwangerschaft von Jugendlichen durchgeführt. Auf Grund der Befragungen der jungen Mütter und Väter wurde untersucht, inwiefern diese Schwangerschaften als Teil von Gender Gewalt betrachtet werden sollen. Die Autorinnen sind der Meinung, dass Gender Gewalt als Verletzung der Menschenrechte die Machtunterschiede in einer patriarchalen Gesellschaft entblößt. Die körperliche, sexuelle und psychische Gewalt, die an den Frauen ausgeübt wird, hat gesundheitliche Folgen. Obwohl es noch keine eindeutige internationale Maßstäbe für Gender Gewalt gibt, soll das Bewusstsein bezüglich der Gender Gewalt und dem möglichen Zusammenhang mit Schwangerschaften von Jugendlichen gefördert werden. Es wird insbesondere das Recht der Frauen auf ihre körperliche Integrität und ihre Entscheidungsfreiheit in Bezug auf die Sexualität und Fortpflanzung betont.

Keywords: Teenage pregnancy, gender violence, human rights, qualitative research, Zimbabwe, Schwangerschaften von Jugendlichen, Qualitative Untersuchung, Zimbabwe, Menschenrechte, Gender Gewalt.

1. Introduction

Various studies on fertility in Sub-Saharan countries have revealed that sexual activity amongœteenagers starts at young ages (AGYEI 1992:14; GAGE-BRANDON 1993:15). This activity can haveœsevere consequences for many youngsters, especially females. Unprotected sexual intercourse mayœresult in sexual transmitted diseases like infection with HIV and premariÇtal pregnancies oftenœleading to dismissal from school (CAMPBELL 1994:249; COKER 1990; KELLER 1992:133). Theseœpregnancies are not always wanted.

Through the years, a considerable amount of studies have stated that insufficient knowledgeœconcerning reproductivity, sexuality and contraceptives, and inadequate family planning facilitiesœare reasons for non-use of contraceptives (AGYEI & EPEMA 1992:15; BARKER 1992:202-3; KELLERœ1992:134; MAKINWA-ADEBUSOYE 1992:70). The decision of adolescents to use contraceptives is, however, not solely based on knowledge and availability of contraceptives, but is also influenced by the social and cultural context in which particular beliefs are embedded. Programmes geared towards prevention of teenage pregnancies are likely to fail if they do not take into account ideas and behaviour concerning gender relations, sexuality and contraception.

One way to approach and analyze unwanted teenage pregnancy and its causes is through the concept of gender violence. Sexuality and contraception are pre-eminently aspects of life in which inequality between men and women is reproduced and in which women's rights are violated (MSAKY 1992:11; SHALLAT 1993:32). Focusing on the gender imbalance and the concomitant violence against women may add to our understanding of the complexity of factors which induce teenage pregnancy. Thus far this focus has been missing in the literature on teenage pregnancy. Our field work taughts us the relevance of this approach. Gender violence is not only a cause of teenage pregnancy, it may also be a source for continuous violations of women's rights.

2. Gender violence defined
In 1993 a Declaration on the Elimination of Violence against Women was adopted at the 48th session of the UN General Assembly. This declaration was developed in order to stress that violence against women occurring across the world should finally be acknowledged and addressed as an issue of human rights (RICHTERS 1994:107-12). Violence can be defined as an assault on a person's physical and mental integrity. Violence directed against women or affecting women disproportionally *because* they are women is known as gender violence. It encompasses physical, sexual and psychological violence, whether occuring in private or public life. All these forms of violence may severely affect the life, bodily integrity, physical, sexual and psychological health, and freedom of women (RICHTERS 1994:1-4).

In this article gender violence will be emphatically conceptualized as an act embedded in the socio-economic, political and ideological context of power relations between men and women. It may subsequently be defined as violence which reflects power imbalances inherent in patriarchal society.

Investigating teenage pregnancy and its relationship with gender violence demands an analysis of social and cultural conditions which promote, facilitate or prevent violence against adolescent girls.

Given the above definition of gender violence, there are several problems to be dealt with in identifying precisely which effects of gender inequality on women's lives can be considered as a violation of women's mental and physical integrity. A particular problematic point is that there may be a discrepancy between an outsider's judgement in this respect and the judgement of the woman concerned. What is at stake here is the problem of the universality versus cultural relativity of individual human rights. Is, for example, `exclusion from decision making in matters of sexuality and contraceptive use' an assault of women's mental integrity, if a woman does not suffer from it herself? These and other problems will be discussed after the presentation of a number of themes which to us as outsiders need to be be included in the examination of teenage pregnancy as an issue of gender violence. The themes which will be explored in this study are African teenage relationship, sexuality and contraceptive use.

3. Field study of teenage pregnancy in Zimbabwe: its approach
During three months qualitative research was carried out in and around of Bulawayo, Zimbabwe's second largest city. Twenty-five teenage mothers were interviewed and fifteen males who had impregnated teenage girls. Most males were no teenagers themselves at the time of the pregnancy, but were in their mid-twenties. Most females became a teenage mother during the last two years. However, some girls had delivered their baby a few days before the interview and a few had become a teenage mother more than two years ago. Similar differences in time passed since the birth of their child were found among the group of teenage fathers. The themes of the interviews were also subject of various group discussions. In this article merely one direct reference is made to the outcome of these groupsdiscussions.

The interviews were conducted by the first author with the help of two Zimbawean, highly qualified nurses. They had experience as assistants in other research about sex-related issues, and felt comfortable in discussing the topics addressed in this article. Their mother tongue was Ndebele, the language primarily used in the interview process. The responses of the interviewees cited are the translations made by the two Zimbabwean research associates.

The interviews were arranged by key-informants who introduced the interviewers into different kinds of communities. A drawback of this method is that it may have led to an unrepresentative selection of teenage mothers and fathers. Our assumption is, however, that the possible selection bias has not necessarily debilitated our research, since its purpose was not directed at obtaining statistics, but in the first instance to acquire a deeper insight into the embeddedness of teenage pregnancy and related issues in a particular socio-cultural context. The approach chosen was therefore a qualitative and exploratory one. This entails obviously that the resulting data and the conclusions drawn from it, must be validated in further research.

4. African teenage relationships
The African dating system differs from that of most Western countries. The majority of teenagers dates secretly and meet each other in public places. It is considered to be inappropriate if older people see

boys and girls showing any affection to each other. That's why many teenagers do not bring their dating partners to their parents' homes: the boyfriend is not known at the girl's place and his family does not know about the existence of his girlfriend. Secret dating facilitates the non-°acceptance by males of resulting pregnancies and their denial of previous involvement with the teenage girls concerned (HAILONGA 1993:19; HENDERSON 1994:35-6).

Women's problems in their interaction with men about sexual issues originate from attitudes shaped during childhood and adolescence (KIAI 1994:5). GOSSA (1990:93) indicates that boys and girls are treated differently from early ages onwards. Girls face discrimination in terms of food, education and workload and are considered to be a poor investment. Being brought up to feel weaker, less useful for their family and society, does not leave women's psychological health unaffected. They experience a loss in self-esteem which slowly restricts them in their potential to decisional power. These literature findings were confirmed by most of our informants:

„ I think that men are taking the decisions in a relationship. It was taught in my upbringing that women are lower than men and that they are subordinated to them. I think it is oke and I do not really want to change it „ (17 year old female)

The age difference characteristic for African relationships can be a forced way of maintaining authority over women. In Zimbabwean culture women are culturally bound to obey older men (MEURSING 1995:1697). In our study both boys/men and girls mention that females are believed to mature much faster than males. They think that females of the same age as their male partners will finally end up with an older appearance than these partners and that this appearance can form a threat to male's authority. The following two responses clearly indicate the anxiety males would experience when having a girlfriend of the same age.

„I want to have a younger girlfriend because younger girlfriends do not challenge older boyfriends. So the communication will be better. If my girlfriend would be of the same age, she will not accept things so easily from me. Then she will also have the power to challenge me" (26 year old male).
„I think that women should have limited opportunities of decision making. I will be scared of women who have power" (22 year old male)

This preference for an age differential also applies to girls. Their choice for older men is based on the fact that they consider school boys too immature for them. Girls think that they can not communicate very well with boys of the same age. Additionally, they also feel that they cannot accept any directions given by boyfriends of the same age, whereas they will accept decisions made by older boys because of their authority. Some girls reported to be seduced by older working men who are able to give gifts and money to them. Their motivation to date these older men could be one of economic reasons since their living circumstances are of a poor standard. Even though not all teenagers considered age difference to be very important to them, societal pressures made males feel obliged choosing a younger girlfriend whereas girls felt forced into choosing an older boyfriend.

According to most teenagers males are regarded as the future head of the family which gives them the right of decision making. Little opportunity is left for a woman to disagree with them. One girl mentioned that women are sometimes allowed to take decisions, but that men have the final saying. According to her women just have to follow the lead. She would like to change it, but she does not believe that there are any possibilities to do so, since it is tradition.

Not every teenage relationship is characterised by male authority. Some males and females responded that they were both making decisions in their relationship and that they not necessarily wanted an age difference in order to keep authority among men.

„My mother told me not to have a girlfriend of the same age, because she will challenge me. But, I did not want to lead my girlfriend and to be the only decision maker" (30 year old male)

Preference for a partner of the same age was based on the fact that both partners can have the same level of thinking and that decisions can be made in consultation with each other.

Refusing decisions made by a male partner can lead, however, to negative consequences which can make a woman refrain from disagreeing with him. A substantial amount of girls reported fear of physical abuse when they would argue against his decision. Loss of respect is mentioned as another problem which a girl can be subjected to when she disagrees with her boyfriend. The following remark reflects the acceptance of violence:

„In my relationship, my boyfriend takes the decisions because he is older. I accept these decisions out of fear; it has already become an automatic reaction. If I would argue against him, then he may become aggressive. I rather prefer participating in the decision process, but it makes life easier if I do not argue against him„ (16 year old female)

From the above we venture to conclude that girls' exclusion from decision making in teenage relationships can be identified as a form of psychological gender violence. Girls may have conformed to traditional norms and rules, but they don't seem to do so wholeheartedly. As we will see in the next two sections, lack of decision power may lead to other kinds of gender violence, such as violence in the form of fear for or occurrence of rape and violence in the form of unprotected sex.

5. Beliefs and attitudes concerning sexuality

In order to understand why teenagers fall pregnant and whether they are willing to use contraceptives, teenage sexuality should be explored in more detail. The willingness of using contraceptives may be dependent on how positive or negative sexuality is experienced. The difficulty with researching sex-related issues is the chance of receiving social desirable answers. However, even social desirable answers inform us about the experience of sexuality in premarital relations in a particular society: they reflect what society is expecting from teenagers in this particular respect.

The origin of beliefs and attitudes concerning sexuality can also be traced back to the upbringing of African boys and girls. Many African females are still brought up to be socially and sexually passive and have not been able to develop assertiveness skills relating to matters of sex (MSAKY 1992:10). They have hardly any say in sexual issues (MWORIA 1994:83). Unmarried women are trained to always *"say no"* and married women to *"never say no"* and to be obedient (KIAI 1994:7; PAIVA 1993:100). In sexual relationships women are unequal partners who have to satisy men's sexual needs at the expense of their own pleasure (MSAKY 1992:11). Their sexuality is seen as the fulfillment of male sexuality (KAMAU 1995:43).

In our study many girls reported that it is the men who are enjoying sex and that sexuality on average is not very enjoyable for themselves:

„I think men are physically made to enjoy sex. Sex for women is just part of life and is not important to them. However, I think that women also need to enjoy it „ (18 year old female)

Additionally, males are expected by both males and females to take the initiative in sexual matters. A few males thought that women who take initiatives are suffering from a mental disease:

„I think that women who initiate sex are crazy and disturbed, it should be the man who takes the first steps" (24 year old male)

6. The refusal of sex

Zimbabwean girls don't only experience difficulty in bargaining on pleasurable sex, they also report problems with refusing sex. There are several reasons underlying these problems.

One of them is the girl's lack of negotiating power due to the age differential.

„I knew that my boyfriend was cheating on me, but because he was older, I could not refuse sex to him" (16 year old girl).

Some girls said that they would have liked being in the position to refuse, however they reported not having reached that position. Not being able to refuse is sometimes accepted as part of their life:

„*A woman can refuse, but then this woman will run the risk that she will be forced into sex. I would like to change it, but it can not be done, because a woman needs to follow the man*" (16 year old girl)

This latter statement refers to the fact that refusing sex may lead to sexual violence. Out of fear for sexual or physical abuse several girls decided to give in to the sexual demands of their partner. One girl told us that she had many times feared physical abuse when she was refusing sex to her boyfriend. This boyfriend did not respect her refusals and finally raped her. Other girls from our study reported that they would not fear sexual abuse by their own partners, but thought that other men could force their girlfriends into sex. Women are socialised such that they accept the occurrence of violence. Already from early age, they are taught that particular behaviours may provoke violence by men. Therefore they learn to adapt their behaviour to what will be expected from them (EL-BUSHRA 1993:2):

„*I told my sisters-in-law that my husband had forced me into sex, but they told me that this is part of life*" (22 year old girl)

Several females told us that they were forced into sexual intercourse by their boyfriends or relatives. Hardly any of these girls had spoken about this incidence with anyone. During the interview it was the first time they had opened up. They reported that it was a new experience being able to talk about these issues confidentially. After the interview a few girls had decided to take somebody in confidence and to inform that person about their sexual abuse.

A further reason why refusing sex is problematic mentioned by girls is that refusal may lead to separation from their boyfriends. A boyfriend may reject a girlfriend because he suspects her having other boyfriends or because he thinks that she lacks love for him. This fear to be rejected is also expected to be related to the fact that some girls may be dependent on money or gifts from their boyfriends. This dependency may make these girls more vulnerable to sexual violence in the form of sexual exploitation by men:

„*Some girls sleep with boys because they feel pressurised into sex because they have received presents and money from them*" (25 year old male)

7. The use of contraceptives

Contraceptive use among our teenage informants was reported to be almost non-existent. Fears for side effects, lack of knowledge, and inaccessibility to family planning services were often cited as the causes of non-use. These causes are also mentioned in other studies (AGYEI 1992:15; HAILONGA 1993:27; KELLER 1989:128). It is questionable whether the removal of the obstacles mentioned will lead to a drastic increase of contraceptive use. The decision to practice family planning is not solely based on a rational decision outside a socio-cultural context. Personal and societal attitudes towards sexuality and contraceptives are exercising influence over the use of family planning. If a person feels ashamed that one is sexually active, then it is not very likely that this person will go out and look for contraceptives. In fact with buying contraceptives, one admits both to the outer world and to oneself that one is sexually active.

The use of contraceptives is found to be associated with promiscuity and loose morals (HAILONGA 1993:29; HENDERSON 1997:38). This was confirmed by our teenagers. Whether they gave a social desirable answer is, however, unclear. Certain is that the remarks made relating to contraceptive use indicate that premarital sex in Zimbabwe is regarded in a very negative way. Some adolescents considered contraceptive use by a girl to be more loose than contraceptive use by a boy. According to BERGLUND (1997:3) the cultural stereotype that *"nice girls do not enjoy sex"* will restrict girls in their choice of using family planning.

Also health workers of family planning clinics have been mentioned to show negative attitudes towards adolescents who want to buy contraceptives. Their negative approach to teenagers eventually drives them away (KAMAU 1995:49). Family planning clinics seem to have different approaches to boys or girls:

„*A boy should buy contraceptives, because he has authority and nobody will question him. But if a woman will do it, family planning people become suspicious*" (24 year old girl)

Many teenagers believed that contraceptives only are for married couples and not for teenagers. The fact that family planning clinics in Zimbabwe mainly focus on married couples and hardly pay any attention to young people also indicates an ignorance or disapproval of teenage sexuality.

8. Decisionmaking about the use of contraceptives

What has become clear in the interviews is that women find it difficult to insist on pleasurable sex and to undertake any initiative. It is therefore likely that they also face difficulties in proposing the use of contraceptives and to be assertive about safe sex. Some girls reported that they had talked about contraceptives with their male partner, but that he was the one who would finally decide about it. However, most girls said that they have not suggested the use of contraceptives to their boyfriends. They were of the opinion that in case they would have proposed contraceptive use, it would be the boy who would decide about it in the end anyhow. If he refuses, then there is nothing they can do about introducing contraceptives in their relationship. The only way of protecting themselves would be through using the pill secretly.

In our study it was difficult to assess why teenagers had not used contraceptives. During the interviews a substantial percentage of teenagers reported that they hardly knew about contraceptives. However, when we asked questions to other teenagers about contraceptives during group discussions, most teenagers seemed to be well informed about them. This made us wonder whether our group of teenage mothers and fathers really knew so little about contraceptives or whether they had given us a social desirable answer.

The denial of women's right to regulate their own fertility is generally not considered to be a form of violence. It is only of late that some authors have struck a different note. According to TOUBIA (1995:18), for instance, the most damaging type of sexual violence is that women lack control over their own fertility and need male's consent to protect themselves. Considering the consequences of the inability to protect oneself against sexual transmitted diseases, gynecological complications and unplanned pregnancies sometimes resulting in unsafe abortions, we should conceptualize the exclusion of decision making on fertility issues as a form of gender violence. By insisting on safe sex or refusing unsafe sex with their partners, women are likely to face all kind of negative consequences which can ultimately make them accept unsafe intercourse. As one girl said:

„*If my boyfriend would refuse me using contraceptives, then I want to refuse having sex with him. However if I refuse sex, I will be accused of wanting other boys and he will leave me. I will feel powerless because I know I will be in a no-win situation*" (16 year old female)

9. Discussion

In this contribution an attempt has been made to analyze teenage pregnancy in Zimbabwe through the concept of gender violence. The main forms of violence related to teenage pregnancy were found to be exclusion of decision making concerning sexual and reproductive issues, restriction of expression of female sexuality, fear of sexual abuse, or the actual occurrence of sexual abuse. They are all violations of women's right to bodily integrity; and freedom and equality in sexual and reproductive matters.

Although most pregnancies were not planned for, we estimate that about one third of them were wanted. Girls who were happy with their pregnancy, had often left primary or secondary school at young ages mainly because of money problems. They worked in their parents home or in other households. The coming of a child was seen as as a positive change in their lives. Most of these girls were also married to their former boyfriends. In contrast, teenage pregnancy was experienced to be problematic by girls who did not feel ready yet for motherhood, wanted to finish their education and look for a good job, or were rejected by their boyfriends.

Since girls are exempted from school, they will have limited opportunities of becoming economically independent. After birth of the child they can face increased poverty, especially if the father of the child refuses to take financial responsibilty for the child. Through their lack of resources they will become dependent on other people, especially on men. Some women start having relationships with men merely for economic reasons or finally end up in prostitution. These are both circumstances in which they can become easily targets for more forms of gender violence such as sexual exploitation.

It is one thing to identify as outsiders issues of gender violence relating tot teenage pregnancy, but it

is another thing to find ways to change this state of affairs
. Analysing teenage relationships informed us about the assumptions society and teenagers hold concerning gender roles and decision making in Zimbabwe. These assumptions underly all the different forms of gender violence identified in this article. Efforts to prevent gender violence should take these ascribed gender roles and the internalization of societal and cultural expectations of teenagers into account. Preventing programs should also raise the question of how much suffering experienced by the girls is actually caused by gender violence. Before any intervention one should carefully and critically listen to what women have to say about their needs and wishes.

Some girls in our study said that they did not mind not being able to exercise more influence over their own lives since culturally it has never been that way. It could be that these girls honestly do not long for more participation in decision making processes. Regarding them to be deprived of their rights and being subjected to gender violence may then be seen as an inappropriate judgment. However, this lack of interest in persuing their basic human rights may have been caused by anxiety for changes and its consequences. It is therefore that any attempts to change the situation should be handled with much care.

The ultimate cause of many unwanted teenage pregnancies is the power imbalance between men and women at both societal and personal levels. Preventing teenage pregnancies therefore demands changes in attitudes towards these imbalances also in society as a whole. As long as women can not fully participate in the decision making process to control their own sexuality and reproductivity a substantial percentage of teenage pregnancies may remain to be the symptoms of patriarchy.

Elimination of gender violence will mean that: relationships between men and women will be based on equality, they both make decisions on reproductive and sexual issues, assertive women who want to negotiate on pleasurable and safe sex are accepted as normal human beings, women do not have to fear for or experience sexual abuse, double standards have lost its function of oppressing women and poverty as a result of gender discrimination and a source for further exploitation by men is non-existent. Our expectation is that the amount of unwanted teenage pregnancies will be drastically reduced.

Acknowledgment

Hereby we would like to thank the two Zimbabwean nurses Flora Sibindi and Tendai Maruta for their great support and quidance of this research.

References

AGYEI, W.A., E.J. EPEMA. 1992. Sexual behavior and contraceptive use among 15-24 year olds in Uganda. *International Family Planning Perspectives* 18:13-17.

BARKER, G.K. and S. RICH. 1992. Influences on adolescent sexuality in Nigeria and Kenya: findings from recent focus group discussions. *Studies in Family Planning* 23, 3: 199-210.

BERGLUND, S., J. LILJESTRAND, F. DE MARIA MARIN, N. SALGADO and ZELAYA. 1997. The background of adolescent pregnancies in Nicaragua: a qualitative approach. *Social Science and Medicine* 44, 1:1-12.

CAMPBELL, B. and M.T. MBIZVO. 1994. Sexual behaviour and HIV knowledge among adolescent boys in Zimbabwe. *Central African Journal of Medicine* 40, 9: 245-250.

CARILLO, R. 1991. *Violence against women: an obstacle to development. in A development and human rights issue.* Center for Women's Global Leadership. pp. 19-41. Plowshares Press, Higland Park, New Jersey.

COKER, O. 1990. *Early childbirth: a risk to safe motherhood.* Report on the IAC-Regional Conference on Traditional Practices Affecting the Health of Women and Children in Africa. 19-24 November, Addis Ababa, Ethiopia, pp 107-108.

EL-BUSHRA, J. and E.P. LOPEZ. 1993. Gender-related violence: it's scope and relevance. *Focus on Gender* 1, 2 June:1-9

GOSSA, A. 1990. *Early childhood marriage and early pregnancy as a risk to safe motherhood.* Report on the IAC-Regional Conference on Traditional Practices Affecting the Health of Women and Children in Africa. 19-24 November, Addis Ababa, Ethiopia, pp. 93-98.

GAGE-BRANDON, J., D. MEEKERS. 1993. Sex, contraception and childbearing before marriage in Sub-Saharan Africa. *International Family Planning Perspectives,* 19:14-18.

HAILONGA, P. 1993. *A study to identify adolescents knowledge, attitudes and beliefs towards teenage pregnancy.* Ministry of Health & Social Services, Namibia.

HENDERSON, P. 1994. Silence, sex and authority. The contradictions of young girl's sexuality in New Crossroads, Cape Town. *VENA Journal* 2:33-39.

KAMAU, J.N. 1995. Issues in Gender Violence: a review of current research and writing. in *The gendered politics of land*. Edited by P. MC. FADDEN, pp. 38-56. Harare: Sapes Books.

KELLER, A., P. SEVERYNS, A. KHAN and N. DODD. 1989. Toward Family Planning in the 1990s: A review and assessment. *International Family Planning Perspectives* 15, 4: 127-135.

KIAI W. 1994. Act now on teen pregnancies. *Gender Review* 1, 3: 5-8

KWARAMBA, R. 1995. *Femicide: gender violence as a neglected public health issue and a major cause of death among women.* The international Family Therapy Conference, 31 July- 3 August, pp. 120-130

MAKINWA-ADEBUSOYE, P. 1992. Sexual behavior, reproductive knowledge and contraceptive use among young urban Nigerians. *International Family Planning Perspectives* 18: 66-70.

MEURSING, K., T. VOS, O. COUTINHO, M. MOYO, S. MPOFU, O. ONEKO, V. MUNDY, S. DUBE, T. MAHLANGU and F. SIBINDI. 1995. Child sexual abuse in Matabeleland, Zimbabwe. *Social Science and Medicine* 41, 12: 1693-1704.

MSAKY, H.I. 1992. Women, AIDS and sexual violence in Africa. *VENA journal* 2:10-12

MWORIA, K. 1994. Gender issues and reproductive health. *The courier* 147:80-83.

PAIVA, V. 1993. Sexuality, condom use and gender norms among Brazilian teenagers. *Reproductive Health Matters* 2, 98-109.

RICHTERS. A. 1994. *Women, culture and violence. A development, health and human rights issue.* Women and Autonomy Centre (VENA), Leiden University.

SHALLAT, L. 1993. Sexuality and reproduction. Rights of life. *Women's Health Journal* 3:31-37.

TOUBIA, N. 1994. Women's reproductive and sexual rights. in Gender *Violence and women's human rights in Africa.* pp 15-20. Center for Women's Global Leadership. Plowshares Press, Highland Park, New Jersey.

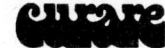

Frauengesundheit und Geburtssysteme
Women and Health and Birth Systems
Liselotte Kuntner

Zusammenfassung: Weltweit wird „Gesundheit für alle im Jahre 2000„ postuliert. Man hat sich dabei die Verbesserung der Gesundheitsversorgung in den sich in Entwicklung befindenden Ländern zum Ziel gesetzt. Man darf annehmen, dass diese Verbesserung auf die Biomedizin, auf ihre Techniken und Praktiken abstellt, wie auch auf die moderne Pharmakologie. Es ist eine Tatsache, dass solche Behandlungsformen und Medikamente heute für den größten Teil der Weltbevölkerung unerreichbar und unerschwinglich sind. Dazu kommt, dass bei der Verbreitung der Biomedizin oft unangepasste Methoden und Verfahren eingesetzt werden, auch im Bereich der Frauengesundheit. Es wird oft übersehen, dass in vielen Ländern wirksame lokale Heilverfahren phytotherapeutischer und physiotherapeutischer Art bekannt sind.

In dieser Arbeit wird auf sinnvolle Strategien zur Gesunderhaltung und Krankheitsverhütung in der Geburtshilfe die Rede sein. Es werden vor allem traditionelle Verfahren im Unterschied zu modernen Praktiken dargestellt, der Umgang mit der Wöchnerin und dem Kind, sowie die Phase Postpartum und der Laktationszeit. Für die letztere wird auf den hohen Wert traditioneller Stillmittel im westafrikanischen Raum hingewiesen. Diskutiert wird auch die Problematik übertragbarer Krankheiten unter Berücksichtigung traditioneller Hygienevorstellungen und der etablierten westlichen Geburtsmethoden - auch im Zusammenhang mit den Geburtspositionen.

Abstract: The concept of „Health for Everybody in 2000„ has been postulated worldwide. Improvement of health care in developing countries is the main aim of these efforts. It is thought that they will be based on biomedicine, its techniques and practices as well modern pharmacology. Unfortunately it is a fact that those kind of treatment and drugs are unobtainable and unaffordable for most of the world's population. What's more, biomedicine will often use unsuitable methods and procedures. It is often overlooked that in many countries local treatments of phytotherapeutic or physiotherapeutic kinds are known. In this paper efficient strategies for health care and prevention of illness in obstetrics will be discussed. Traditional procedures, as opposed to modern practices, will be described, including the care for women postpartum and their children, as well as the lactation period. The high value of traditional lactation remedies of Western Africa will be pointed out. The problems of transferable diseases will be discussed, referring to traditional views of hygiene and well established Western methods of birth - also in connection with positions in labour.

Keywords: Frauengesundheit, Traditionelle Geburtssysteme, Westliche Geburtssysteme, Gebärhaltung, Mutter- u. Kind-Gesundheit, Traditionelle Laktationsmittel, Women´s Health, Traditional Birth Systems, Western Birth Systems, Position in Labour, Health of Mother and Child, Traditional Means and Substances for Lactation.

Abb.1
Mid-Wife bei den
MAFA
(Foto: Godula Kosack)

Einleitung

Von zunehmender Bedeutung für Gesundheitsprogramme wird in armen Ländern die Unterstützung der lokalen traditionellen Heilkunde, des traditionellen Geburtssystems und der Hausmedizin sein, ebenso wie die Unterstützung ihrer Vertreterinnen und Vertreter, das heißt der Heilerinnen und Heiler, der Hebammen und der heilkräuterkundigen Frauen. Das Ziel wäre eine breite, angepasste Gesundheitsversorgung insbesondere in den Dörfern.

Dies setzt allerdings Kenntnisse der lokalen Heilmethoden und eine ernsthafte Auseinandersetzung mit ihnen voraus. Auf Grund eigener Erfahrung möchte ich hervorheben, dass die Kommunikation mit den Heilkundigen sowohl einen gewissen Zeitaufwand und ein subtiles Vorgehen erfordert, wie auch Kenntnisse von deren Weltbild, etwa ihren religiösen Anschauungen, von ihren Vorstellungen von Gesundheit, Krankheit und Tod, und schließlich ein Einfühlen in ihre Lebensform und Arbeitsweise.

Eine der wichtigsten Voraussetzungen zur möglichen Zusammenarbeit ist die Anerkennung des traditionellen Heilsystems und des lokalen Geburtssystems. Nur unter diesen Bedingungen kann eine Bereitschaft der Heilkundigen zum Wissensaustausch erwartet werden.

Traditionelle Geburtssysteme

Durch die weltweite Verbreitung biomedizinischer Vorstellungen über die Geburt sind heute Geburtssysteme traditioneller Art grundlegenden Veränderungen unterworfen. Zum Verständnis der Geburtshilfe außerhalb des Krankenhauses ist es von Nutzen, das lokale traditionelle Geburts- und Schutzsystem zu erfassen. Es gibt viele verschiedene Faktoren, die dabei in Betracht gezogen und untersucht werden sollten. Ich verweise hier auf meine ethnomedizinische Publikation "Geburtshilfe außerhalb des Krankenhauses in traditionellen Gesellschaften" (KUNTNER 1995), in welcher diese Faktoren dargestellt wurden. Zudem wurde meine Forschung mit der Geburt eines Mafakindes im Mandara-Gebirge in Nordkamerun dokumentiert.

Gebärverhalten und Gebärhaltung

In allen traditionellen Geburtssystemen gibt es für die Geburt selber unter anderem Maßnahmen für die schwangere Frau, die den physiologischen Ablauf unterstützen und den Schmerz erleichtern sollen. Die Frauen lernen, sich dem Geburtsvorgang angepasst zu verhalten. Das aktive Gebärverhalten der Frau wird als sehr wichtig betrachtet. Mit "aktivem Gebärverhalten" meinen wir Umhergehen und Bewegen, das Einnehmen von bestimmten Körperstellungen zur Förderung und Erleichterung des Geburtsvorgangs, entsprechend den Bedürfnissen der Gebärenden. Zum physiologischen, das heißt wehengerechten Verhalten zählen wir auch die Wahl einer aufrechten Gebärhaltung: die Frauen gebären in kauernder, kniender, stehender oder sitzender Stellung, gestützt von einer Betreuerin oder vom Mann, auf einem Hocker oder auf einem Gebärstuhl, aber auch in Knieellenbogenlage. Durch schmerzgesteuerte Verhaltensänderungen sind die Gebärenden in der Lage, selbständig günstige Gebärpositionen zu finden. Wir beobachten, dass bei der Geburt bei den Frauen ein großes Bedürfnis entsteht, sich während der Wehen festzuhalten und zu stützen. Dazu braucht sie Hilfsmittel wie Balken, Stangen oder Seilschlingen und Tücher, die an der Decke befestigt sind oder eine Hilfsperson, von der sie gestützt und gehalten wird. (Abb.1)

Die in zahlreichen Publikationen dargestellten Ergebnisse bestätigen die Vorteile der vertikalen Gebärhaltung (CROWLEY P. ET AL. 1991, GARDOSI 1992, KUNTNER 1994a, KUNTNER 1994b). Für die Praxis heißt das: die Fixierung der Gebärenden an das Bett, die Geburt in Rückenlage, wirkt sich ohne Frage nachteilig auf das Geburtsgeschehen aus und bietet keine Vorteile für das Wohlergehen und die Gesundheit von Mutter und Kind; sie sollte deshalb vermieden werden.

Dazu zitieren wir Punkt 17 aus den "Allgemeinen Empfehlungen" der WHO: "Die Gebärenden sollten während der Wehen und der Entbindung nicht in eine Lithotomieposition gebracht werden. Vielmehr sollten sie ermutigt werden, während der Wehen umherzugehen, und jede Frau muss frei entscheiden können, welche Stellung sie während der Entbindung einnehmen will." (WHO KONGRESSBERICHT 1985)

Hygienische Aspekte der vertikalen Gebärhaltung und der traditionellen Geburtshilfe

Bei der Geburt in vertikaler Körperhaltung - welcher Form auch immer - fließen das Fruchtwasser, das Blut und die Exkremente auf den Boden. Die Flüssigkeiten werden von der Erde aufgesogen oder

Abb. 2
Geburt eines MAFA-Kindes (Foto: Godula Kosack)

mischen sich mit dem Staub des gestampften Bodens. Nach der Geburt werden diese, zum Beispiel bei den Mafa, als "unrein" betrachteten Auscheidungen mit einer Hacke fein säuberlich zusammengekehrt und zusammen mit der Plazenta in einem Gefäß - einem Tontopf - versorgt, ohne dass mit dem Inhalt in Berührung gekommen wird. Das Gefäß wird am Ort der Geburt bestattet, innerhalb oder außerhalb des Gehöftes. Meistens übernimmt die Hebamme diese Arbeit.

Bei dieser Art der Geburtshilfe bzw. der Geburt im Sitzen auf Steinen oder ähnlichem kommen weder die Mutter und das Kind, noch die Hebamme mit den Helferinnen, und schon gar nicht Familienangehörige mit den Ausscheidungen der Geburt direkt in Berührung. (Abb.2 + 3) Normalerweise wird in der traditionellen Geburtshilfe auch nicht vaginal untersucht, so auch nicht bei den Mafa. Dies dürfte ebenfalls, bei ungünstigen hygienischen Verhältnissen, die Gefahr einer Infektion verringern. Im weiteren ist zu erwähnen, dass bei der Geburt außerhalb des Krankenhauses die Gebärende an die hauseigenen Keime angepasst ist.

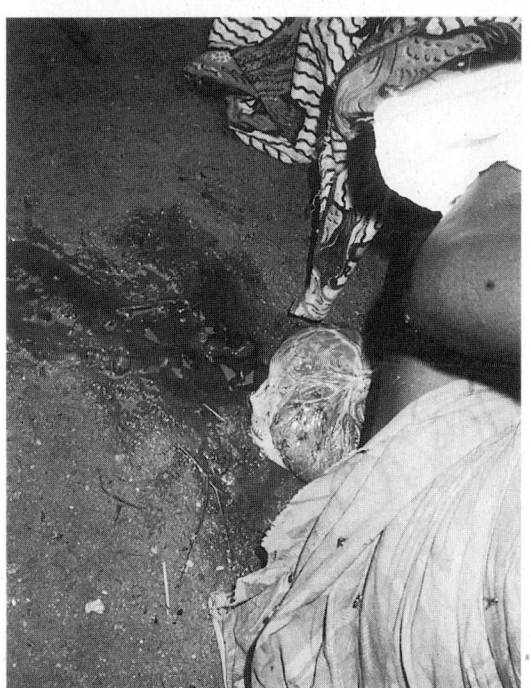

Die Gefahren und möglichen Komplikationen, die Mutter und Kind sowohl bei der Geburt wie auch ganz besonders in der Zeit danach, im Puerperium, bedrohen können, sind aber bekannt und es wird alles Erdenkliche unternommen, sie zu vermeiden. So sind

Abb. 3
Placentarphase - die Placentar erscheint rasch und vollständig. Das Kind wird erst nach der Geburt der Placenta abgenabelt. (Foto: Liselotte Kuntner)

zum Teil auch die Isolation und die Abschirmung der Wöchnerin und des Neugeborenen vor Familienangehörigen oder fremden Personen zu verstehen. Die Isolation ist in traditionellen Gesellschaften als Schutzmaßnahme sehr verbreitet.

Alle geschilderten hygienischen Maßnahmen sind meines Erachtens sinnvolle, empirisch gewonnene Verhaltensweisen, die dem traditionellen Schutzsystem für Mutter und Kind zuzuordnen sind.

Aus früheren Auseinandersetzungen mit der traditionellen europäischen Geburtshilfe ist bekannt, dass die Puerperalinfektion bei der Hausgeburt selten oder nie auftrat, auch nicht unter sehr einfachen hygienischen und geburtshilflichen Bedingungen (MÜLLER 19969). Hierzu möchte ich auch Erfahrungen von G. und W. Schiefenhövel darstellen, welche diese während Forschungen bei den Eipo im Hochland von Irian Jaya (Papua Neuguinea) sammelten. Wir zitieren im Folgenden aus (SCHIEFENHÖVEL 1988). Beim Geburtsgeschehen der Eipofrauen fehlten hygienische Vorstellungen, wie sie sich europäische Betrachter gewohnt sind. Das führte bei den Forschern unwillkürlich zu Fragen, ob dieser Umstand nicht zu schwerwiegenden Konsequenzen, Puerperal- und Nabelinfektionen, führen müsste. Offenbar ist das aber im Hochland von West-Neuguinea nicht der Fall, denn die Forscher haben in den erfassten 79 Fällen keine fieberhaften oder andere, auf Infektionen hinweisende, Symptome gesehen. Im Gegenteil, die Frauen verließen nach einigen Tagen das Frauenhaus und nahmen ihre übliche Arbeit wieder auf. Vergleicht man das Geburtsverhalten der Bergpapua-Frauen nicht mit unserer, auf Asepsis zielenden Krankenhausroutine, sondern mit der früher üblichen Hausgeburtssituation, so ist der Unterschied schon weniger gravierend. Bei den Eipo-Geburten werden meist frische, keimfreie Blätter als Unter- und Vorlage verwendet, so dass von daher gesehen kaum eine aufsteigende Infektion bei der Wöchnerin befürchtet werden muss. (Bekanntlich werden nach Geburt diese Blätter weggeworfen. Die Verf.) Die Geburtsbetreuerin und die Schwangeren selbst verzichten nicht nur auf vaginale Untersuchung, sondern auch auf jede Berührung der Vulva. Erstgebärende werden sogar davon abgehalten, die Hand auch nur in die Gegend des äußeren Genitale zu bringen. Der Geburtsfortschritt wird ganz offenbar an äußerlich festzustellenden Kriterien und den Auskünften der Gebärenden selbst abgelesen. Vaginale oder rektale Untersuchungen wären auch gar nicht indiziert, denn therapeutische Konsequenzen würden sie ohnehin kaum haben können.

Die weise Beschränkung der Eipo-Frauen auf konservative, non-invasive Formen der Geburtsbetreuung wiegt also, bei Verzicht auf Diagnose und Therapie eventuell auftretender Pathologien, das Fehlen von Sauberkeit oder gar auf Asepsis zielender Vorbereitungen offenbar auf. Auch mit Blick auf hygienische Maßnahmen kann man also die Hypothese aufstellen, dass die Geburt ein Vorgang ohne primären Krankheitswert ist. Er dürfte so gut an die normalen Lebensbedingungen des Menschen angepasst sein, dass sowohl die meisten Neugeborenen als auch die Mütter überleben, ohne die in anderen Kulturen übliche peinliche Sauberkeit. (Ende Zitat.)

Die guten geburtshilflichen Ergebnisse - die Gesundheit von Mutter und Kind unter den geschilderten Bedingungen - die W. Schiefenhövel schilderte, sollen noch durch eine Bemerkung ergänzt werden: Meines Erachtens sollte dabei der Geburtsmodus der Eipofrauen in seiner Ganzheit betrachtet werden, auch im Zusammenhang mit denen bei Ihnen üblichen vertikalen Geburtspositionen.

Frauengesundheit und Modelle der westlichen Geburtshilfe

Auf Grund vieler Gespräche mit Frauen - auch Geburtshelferinnen - in traditionellen Gesellschaften möchte ich vorerst die Sichtweise der Gebärenden wiedergeben.

Aus verschiedenen Gründen lehnen die Frauen die Rückenlage mit aufgestellten oder in Metallhaltern aufgehängten Beinen ab, einmal weil sie diese Stellung als unbequem und schmerzhaft empfinden, zum andern weil sie dabei dem Anblick ihrer Genitalien ausgesetzt sind.

Im weiteren entsprechen solche geburtshilflichen Praktiken selten dem kulturell geprägten traditionellen Gebärverhalten und den psycho-hygienischen Vorstellungen der Frauen was sowohl Schwangerschaft und Geburt als auch das Wochenbett und die Zeit danach (Puerperium) betrifft. Die Frauen sind aber fast überall den herrschenden Bedingungen in einer nach westlichem Modell geleiteten Geburtshilfe völlig ausgeliefert, ganz besonders bezüglich der Gebärhaltung.

Es sei vermerkt, dass zum Beispiel in Afrika die Tendenz zunimmt, männliche, nicht ärztlich ausgebildete Geburtshelfer einzusetzen. (Im französisch-afrikanischen Raum heißen sie "accoucheurs" oder auch "gardiens", Bezeichnungen aus der Kolonialzeit). In Burkina Faso werden bereits sogenannte "Sages-hommes" ausgebildet, die allerdings nicht auf große Akzeptanz bei den Frauen stoßen. Es wiederholt sich also hier anscheinend die geschichtliche Entwicklung, wie wir sie aus unserer Gesellschaft kennen, nämlich der Übergang von der weiblichen zur männlichen Geburtshilfe und damit deren Vorherrschaft.

Viele Frauen wollen nicht von männlichem Pflegepersonal entbunden werden; so verweigern sich insbesondere beschnittene Frauen, die oft an Genitalinfektionen leiden. Untersuchungen oder Geburtshilfe durch männliches Gedundheitspersonal stellen einen zu starken Eingriff in ihre Intimsphäre dar. Es ist daher nicht verwunderlich, dass aus den geschilderten Gründen geburtshilfliche Einrichtungen, zum Beispiel in ländlichen Gegenden, ungern oder überhaupt nicht frequentiert werden (ROTES KREUZ 1995). Die medizinische Versorgung könnte jedoch in vielen Fällen für Mutter und Kind von großem Nutzen sein.

Hygienische Aspekte der Geburt in Rückenlage

Der Export der Geburt in Rückenlage, mit oder ohne Episiotomie, erfolgte von Beginn des Medizintransfers an (Kolonial- und Missionsmedizin), ohne Zugabe der uns bekannten, notwendigen, der Hygiene dienenden Materialien wie Leintücher, Unterlagen usw.

Es ist anzunehmen, dass dem medizinischen Personal in armen Ländern die Einrichtung von Entbindungsräumen bekannt ist. Diese besteht zumeist aus einem flachen Holzgestell, überzogen mit einem Chromstahlblech, oder aus einem sogenannten Entbindungstisch mit Kunstlederüberzug, der intakt sein kann, oft aber halb defekt oder zerschlissen ist. Bei der Geburt wird das Material bekanntlich beschmutzt; bei defektem Überzug fließen die Ausscheidungen auch ins Polster. Trotz Reinigung, mit welcher Sorgfalt auch immer, bleiben defekte Stellen schmutzig und feucht und werden in den Tropen eine Brutstätte für Bakterien. Jedem Hygieniker dürfte es vor einer solchen Vorstellung schaudern.

Mangels Material - Leintüchern, Vorlagen, von Wegwerfmaterial gar nicht zu reden, die bei uns eine gewisse Hygiene gewährleisten - liegt die Gebärende in ihren Ausscheidungen und möglicherweise mit ihr auch das Neugeborene. Es muss damit gerechnet werden, dass das Fruchtwasser, der Urin, das Blut (alle drei im Normalfall steril) und der Stuhl infiziert sind. Nicht unberücksichtigt dürfen dabei auch Frauen bleiben, die mit Gonorrhoe oder HIV infiziert sind. Nach Köhler (WACKER et. al. 1994) ist bei intensivem Kontakt des Kindes während der Geburt mit blutigen Sekreten die Übertragung einer HIV-Infektion möglich.

Weiter ist bekannt, dass in armen Ländern über die Hälfte der mütterlichen Sterbefälle im Puerperium auftreten. Bei der kurzen Verweildauer (nur wenige Stunden oder einen Tag) post partum in Krankenhäusern in der dritten Welt treten die Komplikationen nicht selten auf, nachdem die Mutter wieder nach Hause zurückgekehrt ist (Hospitalinfektion) (WACKER et.al. 1994). Dort kann die traditionelle Hebamme die Puerperalsepsis weder mit den uns bekannten medizinischen Maßnahmen noch mit den traditionellen Heilmitteln angehen, nicht zuletzt weil durch die Geburt im Krankenhaus oder ähnlichem ein Einbruch in die Praktiken der traditionellen Geburts- und Schutzsystems erfolgt ist.

Zur Puerperalsepsis in Krankenhäusern von Entwicklungsländern

Da die Puerperalsepsis nach Wacker (WACKER 1995) in den Entwicklungsländern eine überragende Bedeutung hat, sei hier nochmals kurz auf sie eingegangen.

Die häufigste Ursache von Fieber nach der Geburt ist die Endometritis puerperalis. Sie wird definiert als ein "fieberhafter Krankheitsprozess im Wochenbett,,, der durch das Eindringen von pathogenen Keimen in eine der Geburtswunden entstanden ist. Es handelt sich dabei fast immer um die Aszension von Keimen aus der Scheide. Die Faktoren, die eine Aszension begünstigen, sind wohl allgemein bekannt.

Dazu schreiben P. Reitmeier, R. Unkels und B. Utz (WACKER et.al. 1994): "Die Endometritis puerperalis lässt sich besonders unter den Bedingungen eines Distriktkrankenhauses nicht immer verhindern." Sie weisen auf die bekannten vorbeugenden Maßnahmen hin.

Soweit mir bekannt ist, wurde aber bis jetzt der hygienischen Situation bei der Geburt in Rückenlage unter den geschilderten Bedingungen in Krankenhäusern von Entwicklungsländern keine besondere Aufmerksamkeit geschenkt. Meines Erachtens werden hier hygienische Regeln, die wir bei uns als selbstverständlich voraussetzen, zum Teil auf krasse Weise missachtet. Ich wage die ketzerische Frage, ob es sich bei der so weit verbreiteten gravierenden Puerperalsepsis mit hoher mütterlicher Sterblichkeitsrate nicht zum Teil um "hausgemachte Pathologie" handelt. Diese ist ja bekanntlich in der Geschichte der Geburtshilfe nicht neu. Tatsache ist, dass in Entwicklungsländern zunehmend auch nicht-pathologische Geburten ins Krankenhaus, Dispensarium, maternity ward (maternité) verlegt werden. Geburt und Mutterschaft werden also zunehmend institutionalisiert und damit normiert.

In Anbetracht dieser Entwicklung und der geschilderten Verhältnisse muss man sich fragen, ob Mutter und Kind in traditionellen Gesellschaften außerhalb medizinischer Einrichtungen nicht besser aufgehoben wären, solange die Frauen auf ein noch einigermaßen intaktes Geburts- und Schutzsystem mit sinnvollen Praktiken zurückgreifen können.

Einbezug von traditionellem Wissen
Anderseits möchte ich betonen, dass sich sinnvolle traditionelle Geburtspraktiken ohne Zweifel in das medizinische Konzept eines Krankenhauses oder ähnlichem integrieren lassen, zum Beispiel vertikale und andere Gebärpositionen oder der Gebrauch eines Gebärhockers, wie es in der heutigen wissenschaftlichen Geburtshilfe in Europa zunehmend der Fall ist. Solche Hocker werden aber bereits in Krankenhäusern oder ähnlichen Einrichtungen in Entwicklungsländern benützt, wobei auch dort - mit wenigen Ausnahmen - die bei uns bekannten Schwierigkeiten von Seiten des Personals bei ihrer Einführung aufzutreten pflegen.

Ich möchte als positives Beispiel ein vielbeachtetes Projekt für die Geburtshilfe zitieren, das 1975 nahe bei Fortaleza (Nordostbrasilien, Bundesstaat Ceará) unter der Aufsicht der Universität von Ceará aufgebaut wurde. A. Denzler stellt in ihrer Dissertation (DENZLER 1989) das Projekt und die Organisation dar und weist auf den Schulungsmodus der traditionellen Hebammen hin, wie auch auf deren Arbeitsmethoden und ihre eindrückliche Mitarbeit im Projekt. Dazu schreibt sie: "Die Hebammen erhalten eine regelmäßige Supervision. In 5000 Geburten verloren sie keine einzige Patientin! Nach 6 Jahren wurde beschlossen, das Projekt auf den ganzen Bundesstaat auszudehnen. Auch innerhalb der Universitätsklinik wurden Veränderungen vorgenommen: dank freundlicherer Atmosphäre und Einsatz der traditionellen Geburts-Schemelchen konnten die Kaiserschnittzahlen um bis zu 50% gesenkt werden."

Voraussetzung zur Veränderung der üblichen Praktiken ist daher die Akzeptierung der traditionellen Methoden durch die Mitarbeiterinnen und Mitarbeiter der Gesundheitsdienste in Entwicklungsländern. Von Bedeutung ist die Vermittlung von neuen Erkenntnissen über traditionelle Gebärpositionen sowie über die psychisch-emotionalen als auch über die physischen Bedürfnisse der Gebärenden (KUNTNER 1991, SICH 1993). Ich möchte erwähnen, dass ich für Ärzte, Hebammen und weiteres, im geburtshilflichen Bereich tätigem Personal, wie auch für traditionelle Geburtsbetreuerinnen, didaktisches Material entwickelte, das heißt Faltblätter in deutscher, englischer, französischer und spanischer Sprache, mit Text und Zeichnungen. Sie sind zur Weiterbildung, als Information und zur Verwendung in medizinischen Ausbildungsprogrammen gedacht (KUNTNER 1994b). Dank persönlicher Kontakte sind solche Faltblätter bereits in einigen Ländern (in Europa, Afrika, Lateinamerika und Asien) im Umlauf.

Die Erweiterung des biomedizinischen Wissens durch vermehrte Kenntnisse über die traditionellen geburtshilflichen Praktiken könnte die allgemeine Anerkennung der traditionellen Hebamme fördern und, im Sinne einer Wechselwirkung, zu einer sinnvollen Zusammenarbeit mit ihr führen. Gesichert wären damit auch lokal besser angepasste Strukturen in der Geburtshilfe der Entwicklungsländer.

Andere ethnomedizinische Traditionen
In der traditionellen Geburtshilfe gibt es für den Bereich Schwangerschaft, Geburt, Wochenbett und Laktationszeit viele angepasste gesundheitserhaltende und therapeutische Maßnahmen z.B. phytotherapeutischer und physiotherapeutischer Art. In dieser Abhandlung kann nicht auf die Ethnobotanik, d.h. auf die Anwendung von Heilpflanzen sowie auf traditionelle Heilmittel eingegangen werden. Einige Angaben dazu finden sich im Band „ Schwangerschaft und Geburt„ in der Reihe Ethnomedizin (ALBRECHT-ENGEL 1997) und im Band „ Grundlagen der Ethnomedizin„ (GOTTSCHALK-BATSCHKUS et.al. 1997). Für die Gesundheit von Mutter und Kind, insbesondere für stillende Frauen, kennt die traditionelle Geburtshilfe weltweit bewährte Essensvorschriften für das Wochenbett und die Stillzeit. Bekanntlich hat ein ausreichend gestilltes Kind einer gesunden Mutter - insbesondere in armen Ländern - bessere Chancen vor Krankheiten geschützt zu werden und zu überleben. Wegen des hohen Stellenwerts und des beeindruckenden Einflusses von Nahrungsmitteln und Heilpflanzen auf die Laktation werden abschließend traditionelle Laktationsmittel der Mafafrauen in den Mandarabergen in Nordka-

merun dargestellt. Eine besondere Essensempfehlung für die Wöchnerin bei den Mafa ist die Suppe aus den Früchten und vor allem aus den Blättern eines Feigenbaumes. Feigen enthalten wertvolle Fruchtzucker. Der Inhaltsstoff „Ficin„ ist vor allem in den Blättern vorhanden (Milchsaft) und wirkt auf die Verdauung und auf Entzündungen durch Steigerung des Enzymflusses, was besonders wichtig für das Stillen ist.

Der afrikanische Säugling und das Kleinkind ist von Anfang an voll in das Familienleben integriert. Im Panje - einem traditionellen afrikanischen Kleidungsstück - ist es auf dem Rücken der Mutter sowohl zu Hause, auf dem Feld, auf dem Markt und anderswo überall dabei. Die Brust wird ihm gereicht, wann es will und nicht, wenn gerade „Stillzeit„ ist. Die Milchsekretion wird bei der jungen Mutter meistens durch traditionelle Stillmittel stimuliert.

Tab. 1
DIE BEIDEN LAKTATIONSMITTEL DER MAFA

1) - Hirsemehl	2) - Madzaf Wa, Kraut für die
- eine Tasse Erdnussöl	Brust, eine laktagoge Pflanze,
- Chiendang oder Menda,	an der Sonne getrocknet
Paste von Erdmandeln	- Chiendang oder Menda,
- Mbrom, 3-4 Bohnenfrüchte der	Paste von Erdmandeln
Tamarinde - Hirsemehl	- kochendes Wasser
- Zitronensaft und Zucker	

Die empirisch gewonnene Wirkungsweise der Inhaltsstoffe dieser Laktationsmittel wurde überprüft und chemisch-pharmakologisch analysiert. In der nun folgenden Zusammenstellung wurde nur die Analyse der Hauptinhaltsstoffe mit ihren möglichen Wirkungen berücksichtigt.

Analyse der Hauptinhaltsstoffe

Tab. 2
TRADITIONELLE LAKTATIONSMITTEL DER MAFA

Hirsemehl (Digitalia exilis)
4% Fett
10% Eiweiß
Vit. B1 u. B2
Wirkung: Eiweiß- u.
Kohlenhydratlieferant

Erdnussöl (Arachis hypogaeae)
50% Fett (hoher Anteil an mehrf. unges. Fettsäuren)
24-30% Eiweiß
3-8% Kohlenhydrate
Vit. B u. E
Wirkung: auf Keimdrüsen, Aufbau von Hormonen, z.B. Prolaktin

Erdmandeln (Cyperus esculentus)
Öl (ungesättigte Fettsäuren)
Stärke
Proteine, Alkaloide
Zucker (hoher Anteil)
Wirkung: Kohlenhydrat- u.
Proteinlieferant

Tamarindenfrüchte (Tamarindus indica)
in der Pulpa der Bohnenfrüchte:
Invertzucker, Pektine, Eisen, Gerbstoffe
Wirkung: Blutbildung, Kohlenhydratlieferant, Geschmacks korrigens, mildes Laxans, in großen Mengen abortive Eigenschaften

Zitronensaft (Citrus sp.)
Vit. C
Wirkung: desinfizierend (Speise u. Magen)

Madzaf Wa (Euphorbia hirta)
Lektine, Alkaloide, Latex (Milchsaft), Terpene, Polyphenole
Wirkung: Immunstimulans (Lektine)

Wenn die Mafafrau finanziell in der Lage ist, sich die Zutaten zu diesen Mitteln - die nicht nur Still-, sondern auch Nahrungsmittel sind - zu besorgen, darf man annehmen, dass sie für die Stillzeit gut ernährt ist. Für arme Frauen wäre die finanzielle Unterstützung zur Beschaffung von laktationsfördernden Mitteln aus ethnomedizinischer und gesundheitspolitischer Sicht zu begrüßen.

Zur Gesundheit von Mutter und Kind wäre zu wünschen, dass die dargestellte Problematik in der Geburtshilfe von Gesundheitseinrichtungen in den Ländern der dritten Welt zur Kenntnis genommen würde. Die Auseinandersetzung mit dem Thema zielt auch darauf ab, dass Entwicklungshilfeorganisationen ihre Strategien im Bereich Medizin - Frauen - und Gesundheit überprüfen und gegebenenfalls anpassen.

Danksagung

Bei den Laktationsmitteln verdanke ich die Zusammenstellung der Hauptinhaltsstoffe mit der Analyse Dr. sc.nat. Barbara Frei, Apothekerin, Dept. Pharmazie, ETH, Zürich. Prof. Dr. Godula Kosack, den Frauen Aissatou, Bédékwa, Dabagi und Tawasa bin ich zu großem Dank dafür verpflichtet, dass sie mich an den geburtshilflichen Traditionen der Mafa teilnehmen ließen.

References

ALBRECHT-ENGEL, INES. 1997. *In Wellen zur Welt. Das traditionelle Wissen über Schwangerschaft und Geburt.* In der Reihe: Ethnomedizin. Neue Perspektiven für unsere Gesundheit. CHRISTINE E. GOTTSCHALK-BATSCHKUS (Hrsg.) NaturaMed Verlagsgesellschaft, Neckarsulm.

CROWLEY P., CROWLEY, P., ELBOURNE, D., ASHURST, H. GARCIA, I., MURPHY, D. AND N. DUIGHAM. 1991. Delivery in an Obstetric Birth Chair: a Randomized Controlled Trial. Brit. J. Obstet. Gynecol. 98: 667-674.

DENZLER ANGELIKA. 1989. *Alternativen der Geburtshilfe in einem Dorf in Südecuador.* Diss. Ruprecht-Karls-Universität, Heidelberg.

GARDOSI J. 1992. The Physiology of Squatting During Labor. Am. J. Obstet. Gynecol. 166: 341.

GOTTSCHALK-BATSCHKUS, PRINZ, SCHIEFENHÖVEL, SCHULER (Hrsg.). 1997. *Grundlagen der Ethnomedizin. Gesundheit, Krankheit und Heilung im Kulturvergleich.* NaturaMed Verlagsgesellschaft, Neckarsulm.

KUNTNER LISELOTTE. 1991. *Neue Erkenntnisse und Ansichten über die Gebärhaltung. Der Gebärhocker Maia.* Hans Marseille Verlag, München. 2. Auflage.

KUNTNER LISELOTTE. 1994a. Die Gebärhaltung der Frau. Schwangerschaft und Geburt aus geschichtlicher, völkerkundlicher und medizinischer Sicht. Hans Marseille Verlag, München. 4. Auflage.

KUNTNER LISELOTTE. 1994b. *Faltblätter: Das Gebärverhalten der Frau.* (Franz. Version: Participation active de la femme durant son accouchement. Engl. Version: Birth Behaviour of Woman. Span. Version: La participatión activa de la mujer durante el parto.) 1994/5 (Erhältlich bei L. Kuntner, Kornweg 6, CH-5024 Küttigen. Preise pro Exemplar sFr. 2.50 bei mindestens 10 Exemplare, sFr. 2.- pro Exemplar bei 25 Exemplaren, sFr. 1.50 pro Exemplar bei 100 Exemplaren.)

KUNTNER, LISELOTTE. 1995. Geburtshilfe außerhalb des Krankenhauses in traditionellen Gesellschaften. Curare, Sonderband 8: *Gebären - Ethnomedizinische Perspektiven und neue Wege.* Kleine Reihe 3. VWB - Verlag für Wissenschaft und Bildung 1995 (Ein Sonderdruck der Arbeit ist erhältlich für DM 6.- beim Verlag, Postfach 110368, D-10833 Berlin.)

MÜLLER, C.. 1969. *Volksmedizinisch-geburtshilfliche Aufzeichnungen aus dem Lötschental.* Verlag Huber, Bern (vergriffen).

ROTES KREUZ. SCHWEIZ. 1995. Tschad-Gegensätze überwinden. *Zeitschrift International,* August 1995.

SCHIEFENHÖVEL, WULF. 1988. *Geburtverhalten und reproduktive Strategien der Eipo.* Dietrich Reimer Verlag, Berlin

SICH, DOROTHEA (Hrsg.). 1993. *Medizin in Entwicklungsländern 34.* Medizin und Kultur. Eine Propädeutik für Studierende der Medizin und der Ethnologie. (H.J. DIESFELD) Verlag Peter Lang, Frankfurt a.M.

WACKER.1995. Chirurgische Klinik der Universität des Saarlandes. Script: 5. *Workshop für angepasste chirurgische Versorgung in Entwicklungsländern.* Oscar-Orth-Straße. 66421 Homburg/Saar.

WACKER, J., M.D. BALDE, G. BASTERT. 1994. *Geburtshilfe unter einfachen Bedingungen.* Springer-Verlag, Heidelberg

WHO KONGRESSBERICHT. 1985. "Gemeinsamen interregionalen Konferenz über bedarfsgerechte Geburtstechnologie". Fortaleza, Brasilien.

Die Veränderung des Körperbildes in der Schwangerschaft
Body Image Changes during Pregnancy
Claudia Offermann

Zusammenfassung: Ein zentrales Ereignis in den meisten weiblichen Biographien ist die Schwangerschaft und die zahlreichen damit verbundenen physischen und psychischen Prozesse. Im Mittelpunkt des vorliegenden Beitrages steht die Frage, wie schwangere Frauen ihren veränderten und sich verändernden Körper erleben und empfinden und wie sich diese Veränderungen vor dem Hintergrund eines soziokulturell gegebenen Attraktivitätsstereotyps, das in erster Linie Schlankheit vorschreibt, auf ihre Einstellungen und ihr Verhalten auswirken. Auch wenn die Schwangerschaft nicht mit Übergewicht gleichgesetzt werden darf, so zeigt sich doch, dass viele schwangere Frauen sich erhebliche Sorgen über ihre Gewichtszunahme machen und spätestens für die Zeit nach der Entbindung sportliche und diätetische Maßnahmen planen, um ihr ursprüngliches Gewicht und ihre Figur wieder zu erreichen.

Abstract: One important event in female life cycle is pregnancy including numerous physical and psychological processes. The focus of this essay is to examine how pregnant women experience their changed and changing body on the basis of an attractiveness stereotype prescribing slimness and which effects these changes have on attitudes and behavior. Athough pregnancy must not be compared to obesity, it is a known fact, that a lot of pregnant women are very concerned about their weight gain and therefore are taking steps - dietary restraint and sports - to loose weight already during pregnancy or immediately after childbirth.

Keywords: Körperbild, Body Image, Schwangerschaft, Pregnancy, Klinische Psychologie, clinical psychology.

1. Einleitung
Innerhalb der klinisch-psychologischen Forschung gibt es eine Vielzahl von Untersuchungen zum Körperbild (Body Image) und Körpererleben von Frauen, die sich jedoch überwiegend auf den Bereich der Essstörungen (Anorexie, Bulimie und Adipositas) und die damit einhergehenden Verzerrungen des Körperschemas beschränken. Die vielfältigen Veränderungen des Körperbildes und -erlebens, die sich im Verlaufe der Schwangerschaft einstellen sowie der Umgang der schwangeren Frauen mit diesen Veränderungen wurden bis zum Beginn der neunziger Jahre weitgehend vernachlässigt. In jüngerer Zeit haben sich jedoch einige Studien mit verschiedenen Aspekten dieses Themenbereiches beschäftigt. Neben Versuchen, die schwangerschaftsbezogenen Veränderungen des Körperbildes deskriptiv zu erfassen und in einen bestimmten Phasenverlauf zu untergliedern (z.B. RICHARDSON 1990) gehen verschiedene Untersuchungen der Frage nach, wie die wahrgenom-menen Veränderungen - insbesondere die Gewichtszunahme - von den werdenden Müttern bewertet werden und sich auf ihr Ernährungsverhalten sowie die Einschätzung der eigenen physischen Attraktivität auswirken (FAIRBURN & WELCH 1990; DAVIES & WARDLE 1994; OFFERMANN 1995). In diesem Zusammenhang wird immer wieder darauf hingewiesen, dass das kulturell verankerte Schönheitsideal, das in unserer Gesellschaft vor allem Schlankheit vorschreibt, eine entscheidende Rolle spielt (z.B. SUMNER et al. 1993) (Alle folgenden Aussagen und Angaben beziehen sich auf den mitteleuropäischen und angloamerikanischen Raum, sofern nicht anders gekennzeichnet).

Der vorliegende Beitrag gibt einen Überblick über den aktuellen Forschungsstand, geht den möglichen soziokulturell geprägten Ursachen dafür nach, warum in unserer Gesellschaft ein weibliches Attraktivitätsstereotyp existiert, in dem für den schwangeren Körper nur wenig Raum bleibt und analysiert, welche Konsequenzen dies für das Körpererleben in der Schwangerschaft nach sich zieht.

2. Die Veränderung des Körperbildes in der Schwangerschaft
Die Schwangerschaft bringt ein breites Spektrum an körperlichen Vorgängen und Veränderungen mit sich, die jedoch nicht ohne weiteres vergleichbar sind. Manche Prozesse vollziehen sich kontinuierlich über den gesamten Schwangerschaftsverlauf hinweg, z.B. das Wachstum des Bauches, andere sind in der Regel auf bestimmte Perioden beschränkt wie etwa die Schwangerschaftsübelkeit.

Darüber hinaus gibt es bezüglich dieser Vorgänge und ihrer Bewertung bzw. des Umgangs mit ihnen erhebliche interindividuelle Unterschiede. Diese lassen sich auf konstitutionelle Ursachen, aber auch auf psychische Faktoren und situative Bedingungen zurückführen. Daher wird die Beschreibung der schwangerschaftsbedingten körperlichen Veränderungen im allgemeinen anhand eines Phasenmodells vorgenommen.

RICHARDSON (1990) unterscheidet beispielsweise vier Phasen der Veränderung des Körperbildes in der Schwangerschaft. Die *reduction phase* (1.-20. Schwangerschaftswoche) ist vor allem durch das Ausbleiben der Menstruation, Gewichtsverlust und ein verringertes Aktivitätsniveau gekennzeichnet. Die *expansion phase* (21.-26. Woche) lässt sich in erster Linie durch die Wahrnehmung der ersten Kindsbewegungen charakterisieren. Appetit und Aktivitätsniveau nehmen wieder zu, die Gewichtszunahme wird positiv empfunden, weil sie das Wachstum und damit die Realität des Kindes bestätigt. In der *tension phase* (27.-32. Woche) treten Sorgen über die körperlichen Veränderungen - besonders über die Gewichtszunahme - in den Vordergrund. Das Kind wird allmählich als „eigenständiges Individuum„ wahrgenommen, die Gewichtszunahme wieder stärker als körperliche Veränderung im eigentlichen Sinne angesehen. In der *stabilization phase* (33. Woche - Entbindung) nehmen schließlich die Sorgen bezüglich der körperlichen Veränderungen wieder etwas ab. Die jetzt noch erfolgende Gewichtszunahme wird wieder positiver empfunden, die Einschränkung der körperlichen Beweglichkeit allerdings als unangenehm erlebt.

Andere Autoren nehmen andere Phasenunterteilungen vor. Die Ergebnisse über Art, Umfang und zeitliche Verteilung der körperlichen Veränderungen sind - stichproben- und methodenabhängig - zum Teil uneinheitlich. Zusammenfassend kann jedoch festgehalten werden, dass der Gewichtszunahme und dem veränderten Körperbild eine herausragende Bedeutung zukommen. Die durchschnittliche Gewichtszunahme während der Schwangerschaft beträgt etwa 12-13 kg, wobei es eine erhebliche interindividuelle Varianz gibt. Es treten Sorgen über den Verlust der körperlichen und sexuellen Attraktivität und Ängste vor dem Zurückbleiben irreversibler physischer Veränderungen nach der Entbindung auf.

Neben den körperlichen Veränderungen im engeren Sinne kommt es im Laufe der Schwangerschaft auch zu signifikanten Veränderungen im Ernährungsverhalten, die sich teilweise physiologisch erklären lassen, zum Teil aber auch auf psychologische Faktoren zurückzuführen sind. Allgemein wird über eine veränderte Hungerwahrnehmung berichtet, die jedoch keinem einheitlichen Muster folgt. Etwa 70% der Schwangeren leiden unter Schwangerschaftsübelkeit. Es werden meistens mehr Mahlzeiten pro Tag eingenommen als vor der Schwangerschaft. Dies lässt sich einerseits darauf zurückführen, dass das Essen die Übelkeit reduziert, andererseits aber auch darauf, dass jetzt ‚für zwei' gegessen wird. Auch die Zusammensetzung der konsumierten Lebensmittel verändert sich, wobei eine möglichst gesunde Ernährung angestrebt wird. Ferner kommt es zu gelegentlichem Heißhunger auf bestimmte Speisen, aber auch zu spezifischen Aversionen gegen manche Nahrungsmittel. Ein geringer Teil der schwangeren Frauen hält Diät, um die Gewichtszunahme zu kontrollieren, manche Frauen berichten über gelegentliche Episoden von ungezügeltem Essen, weil sie nicht so streng auf ihr Gewicht achten müssen wie sonst.

3. Soziokulturelle Aspekte des Körpererlebens in der Schwangerschaft

Da die Schwangerschaft ein natürlicher biologischer Vorgang ist und die damit einhergehende Gewichtszunahme nichts mit Übergewicht oder ‚Dicksein' zu tun hat, stellt sich die Frage, warum die zusätzlichen Pfunde von vielen betroffenen Frauen als problematisch empfunden werden. Als Erklärung lässt sich das soziokulturell geprägte Attraktivitätsstereotyp heranziehen. Über alle historischen Epochen hinweg gab es ideale Frauengestalten mit einer Variationsbreite von knabenhaft bis üppig, die für die natürlichen Varianten des Körperbaus in der Regel nur wenig Raum ließen (Vgl. BROWNMILLER 1984). Eine mehr oder weniger große Menge an Fettgewebe im weiblichen Körper gilt jedoch aus evolutionsbiologischen Gründen als genetisch determiniert. Von Anorektikerinnen oder Leistungssportlerinnen ist bekannt, dass der Ovulationszyklus aussetzt, wenn ein bestimmtes Maß an Körperfett unterschritten wird.

Das aktuelle Attraktivitätsstereotyp wurde seit den fünfziger Jahren kontinuierlich magerer und schreibt für Mädchen und Frauen in unserer Gesellschaft neben Schlankheit auch körperliche Fitness vor. ROSE (1994) hebt hervor, dass diese beiden Eigenschaften zu einem Synonym für die junge, erfolgreiche Frau geworden sind, auf deren Gesicht und Körper die Doppelbelastung durch Erwerbs- und

Familienarbeit und das Austragen von Schwangerschaften keine Spuren hinterlassen. Der knabenhafte, vorpubertäre Mädchenkörper wird zum ästhetischen Ideal erhoben. Unter diesen Voraussetzungen muss eine Schwangerschaft fast zwangsläufig zum kritischen Ereignis werden.

Obwohl bekannt ist, dass Frauen allgemein dazu neigen, ihren Körperumfang zu überschätzen (CASH & HICKS 1990), konnte gezeigt werden, dass schwangere Frauen - ähnlich wie etwa essgestörte Frauen - zu einer noch stärkeren Verzerrung ihres Body Image im Sinne einer Überschätzung tendieren (SLADE 1977). SUMNER et al. (1993) führen dies darauf zurück, dass schwangere Frauen aufgrund der vielfältigen und starken körperlichen Veränderungen, die mit der Schwangerschaft einhergehen, ihre Aufmerksamkeit verstärkt diesen körperlichen Prozessen zuwenden und daher besonders sensibel auf sie reagieren. In einer von SUMNER et al. (1993) durchgeführten Studie fand sich in einem frühen Schwangerschaftsstadium (16. Woche) jedoch eine stärkere Überschätzung des Körperumfangs als in einem relativ späten (32. Woche). Dies führen die Autoren darauf zurück, dass die körperlichen Veränderungen am Anfang der Schwangerschaft, wenn ihr Verlauf von der betroffenen Frau noch nicht abzusehen ist, als bedrohlicher empfunden werden.

Aus dem bisher Dargestellten ergibt sich die Frage, welche Auswirkungen ein verzerrtes Körperbild, d.h. meistens die Einschätzung des eigenen Körpers als ‚zu dick' auf Selbstbild und Verhalten einer schwangeren Frau hat.

4. Empirische Ergebnisse zum Körperbild und Essverhalten schwangerer Frauen
Drei klinisch-psychologische Untersuchungen zum Körperbild und zum Essverhalten schwangerer Frauen in Abhängigkeit vom soziokulturell gegebenen Schlankheitsideal erbrachten interessante, wenn auch teilweise widersprüchliche Ergebnisse und sollen deshalb kurz gegenübergestellt und diskutiert werden.

FAIRBURN & WELCH (1990) konzentrierten sich auf die Einstellungen schwangerer Frauen zu Figur und Gewicht und deren Auswirkungen auf die Ernährungsgewohnheiten während der Schwangerschaft. Die Stichprobe setzte sich jeweils zur Hälfte aus Frauen zusammen, die bereits vor dem Eintreten der Schwangerschaft regelmäßig Schlankheitsdiäten durchführten und aus Frauen, für die das nicht zutraf. Insgesamt kamen Diäten und andere Methoden der Gewichtskontrolle in der Schwangerschaft relativ selten vor (6%), allerdings berichteten einige Frauen (26%) über regelmäßiges ‚overeating', das mit einer überdurchschnittlichen Gewichtszunahme, z.T. bis zu 20 kg, einherging. Es zeigte sich, dass diejenigen Frauen, die auch während der Schwangerschaft eine Diät hielten, aus der Gruppe der ehemaligen ‚dieters' stammten, ebenso wie die ‚overeaters'. Innerhalb der ehemaligen Diät-Gruppe ergab sich jedoch ein interessanter Unterschied: Obwohl alle Frauen dieser Gruppe ihren Körper insgesamt als auch einzelne Körperregionen negativer einschätzten als die nicht-diätende Vergleichsgruppe und sich im Hinblick auf die Zeit nach der Entbindung erhebliche Sorgen um Gewicht und Figur machten, behielt doch nur ein Teil während der Schwangerschaft Diätmaßnahmen bei. Die anderen setzten ihre Methoden der Gewichtskontrolle vorübergehend aus, weil sie die Schwangerschaft als „license not to worry about weight„ (FAIRBURN & WELCH 1990:158) erlebten. Möglicherweise hatten diese Frauen aufgrund vergangener Diäterfolge auch so viel Vertrauen in ihre Fähigkeit, später wieder abnehmen zu können, dass sie sich eine Diätpause erlauben konnten. Für die Zeit nach der Geburt planten jedoch alle ehemaligen ‚dieters' diätetische und sportliche Maßnahmen zur Gewichtsreduktion. Die Gruppe der vor der Schwangerschaft nicht-diätenden Frauen äußerte sich über die Gewichtszunahme nur wenig besorgt, die meisten fanden ihren ‚dicken' Bauch schön.

DAVIES & WARDLE (1994) gehen davon aus, dass die ‚normalerweise' geltenden Attraktivitätsnormen während der Schwangerschaft mehr oder weniger außer Kraft gesetzt werden, weil in diesem Zeitraum weniger die gewichtsmäßige Abweichung vom Idealtyp im Vordergrund steht als vielmehr der reproduktive Aspekt. Tatsächlich zeigte sich in ihrer Untersuchung, dass die schwangeren Frauen im Unterschied zu einer nicht-schwangeren Kontrollgruppe mit ihrem Körper und ihrem Gewicht weniger unzufrieden waren und zum Befragungszeitpunkt keine bedeutsame Gewichtsreduktion anstrebten. Im Unterschied zu früheren Untersuchungen (z.B. SLADE 1977) fand sich bei den schwangeren Frauen eine realistischere Einschätzung des eigenen Körperumfangs als bei der Kontrollgruppe. Die allgemeine Idealfigur - genauso schlank wie in der Kontrollgruppe - veränderte sich jedoch durch die Schwangerschaft nicht. Zwei Drittel der schwangeren Frauen standen der Gewichtszunahme mit positiven oder gemischten Gefühlen gegenüber, ein Drittel mit neutraler bis negativer Einstellung. Veränderungen in den

Ernährungsgewohnheiten wurden hauptsächlich auf Übelkeit oder Sodbrennen zurückgeführt und standen nicht mit dem Versuch der Gewichtsreduktion in Zusammenhang. Trotz der ‚Erlaubnis zum Zunehmen' machten sich auch in dieser Stichprobe viele schwangere Frauen Sorgen darüber, wie sie ihr zusätzliches Gewicht nach der Schwangerschaft wieder würden reduzieren können. Ein Einfluss der Diätorientierung vor der Schwangerschaft ließ sich in der von FAIRBURN & WELCH (1990) aufgefundenen Richtung auch hier nachweisen.

OFFERMANN (1995) untersuchte ebenfalls die Veränderungen des Körpererlebens und des Essverhaltens während der Schwangerschaft in Abhängigkeit von der jeweiligen Gewichtszunahme und Attraktivitätsorientierung (d.h. dem Versuch, dem gängigen Schönheitsideal nachzukommen). Es zeigte sich, dass die Unzufriedenheit mit dem eigenen Körpergewicht proportional zur schwangerschaftsbedingten Gewichtszunahme anstieg und zwar unabhängig von der jeweiligen Attraktivitätsorientierung der einzelnen Frauen. Den Wunsch nach Gewichtskontrolle äußerten jedoch nur diejenigen Frauen, die über eine stark ausgeprägte Attraktivitätsorientierung verfügten. Diese Frauen können vermutlich mit den ‚dieters' von FAIRBURN & WELCH (1990) verglichen werden, während für die anderen möglicherweise gelockerte Attraktivitätsnormen wie von DAVIES & WARDLE (1994) angenommen, gelten.

Zusammenfassend lässt sich festhalten, dass die Verbindlichkeit des allgemeingültigen Schlankheits-ideals für den Zeitraum der Schwangerschaft zwar reduziert oder sogar aufgehoben wird, was sich im Nachlassen von ‚Figur-Sorgen' und Diätbemühungen zeigt. Gleichzeitig bestehen jedoch auch Sorgen wegen der erfolgten Gewichtszunahme und die Befürchtung, zusätzliches Gewicht nach der Entbindung nicht wieder loswerden zu können, so dass spätestens für diese Zeit Maßnahmen zur Gewichtsreduktion geplant werden. In welche dieser beiden Richtungen eine Frau stärker tendiert, hängt wesentlich von ihrer allgemeinen Attraktivitätsorientierung ab.

5. Diskussion

Diese Ergebnisse spiegeln einen Großteil der von ROSE (1994) vertretenen Position wieder, die hinter der Herausbildung des schlanken und sportlichen Schönheitsideals für Frauen einen „Zwang zur ‚Vermännlichung'„ (ROSE 1994:33) sieht, die Produktion eines scheinbar androgynen Körpers, der sich aber doch am männlichen Körperschema orientiert. Dies beinhaltet auch die Tabuisierung der spezifischen Zyklen und Funktionen des Frauenkörpers. Rose betont weiter, dass es neben der Anpassung des weiblichen Körperideals an das männliche Modell auch zu einer Anpassung des weiblichen Körpers an männliche - d.h. lineare - Zeitstrukturen kommt. Sie führt diese historische Entwicklung darauf zurück, dass Frauen nicht mehr auf ihre traditionelle Rolle beschränkt nun auch vom „Zwang zum selbstbestimmten Leben„ (ROSE 1994:34) erfasst und damit den Gesetzen des Männerkörpers unterworfen werden, „jenes Körpers, der sich in der Industriegesellschaft als funktional erwiesen hat„ (ROSE 1994:34). In der modernen Frauenbiographie westlicher Prägung bleibt Mutterschaft zwar als Bestandteil vorhanden, stellt aber - im Gegensatz zu früher oder auch zu anderen Gesellschaften - keine eigenständige soziale Rolle mehr dar, die möglicherweise mit einer Statuserhöhung der Frau und gesellschaftlicher Würdigung einhergeht. Rose kommt zu dem Schluss, dass die solchermaßen veränderte Frauenrolle zwar den Zugang zu mehr gesellschaftlicher Macht eröffnet, „doch nur unter der Bedingung, dass sich die Frau den männlichen ‚Spielregeln' unterwirft„ (ROSE 1994:37).

Ob es nun als ‚Fortschritt' anzusehen ist, dass Frauen sich wenigstens in der Zeit der Schwangerschaft ein Stück weit vom Schlankheitsideal und den damit einhergehenden Diät- und Trainingsplänen emanzipieren, oder ob es als besorgniserregend eingeschätzt werden muss, dass sogar noch während der Schwangerschaft Pläne zur Gewichtsreduktion für ‚die Zeit danach' geschmiedet werden, ist eine Frage der Perspektive. In diesem Zusammenhang muss auch der Tatsache Rechnung getragen werden, dass es für schwangere Frauen zumindest in der Bundesrepublik angesichts der Einbettung des gesamten Schwangerschafts- und Geburtsgeschehens in einen institutionalisierten medizinischen Rahmen äußerst schwierig ist, nicht über ihr Gewicht und ihre Figur nachzudenken. Bei jeder Vorsorgeuntersuchung findet eine Gewichtskontrolle statt, und die werdende Mutter wird - auch von den entsprechenden Medien - mit einer Unmenge von Ernährungsanweisungen und kosmetischen Tips zur Prävention von bleibenden Schönheitsfehlern eingedeckt. Kaum ist die Entbindung überstanden, kommt schon die Krankengymnastin ans Bett der frisch Entbundenen, um mit der Rückbildungsgymnastik zu beginnen. Auch hierin zeigt sich also die Tendenz, den weiblichen Körper wieder in seinen ‚Normalzustand' zu versetzen, und es wird weiterhin deutlich, dass die schwangere Frau selber für die entsprechenden Aktivitäten verantwortlich gemacht wird. Sicher gibt es - wie auch aus den oben zitierten Untersuchungen hervorgeht - viele Frauen, die ihren schwangeren Körper selbstbewusst genießen und schön finden. Andererseits ist zumindest von ehemals essgestörten Frauen bekannt, dass viele in der Schwangerschaft wieder auf extreme Mechanismen der Gewichtskontrolle zurückgreifen und damit ihre eigene Gesundheit und die ihres Kindes erheblich gefährden.

Viele Aspekte, die mit der Schwangerschaft als komplexem physischen, psychischen und sozialen Prozess einhergehen und ihren Verlauf mitbeeinflussen wie etwa die Geplant- und Erwünschtheit der Schwangerschaft, die Unterstützung durch den Partner, die berufliche Situation der Frau, aber auch medizinische und gesellschaftliche Faktoren, mussten in diesem Beitrag unberücksichtigt bleiben. Es ist jedoch zu hoffen, dass sich - auch im Hinblick auf eine verstärkte Interdisziplinarität - die sozialwissenschaftliche und medizinische Forschung weiterhin mit diesem für die psychische und körperliche Gesundheit von Frauen zentralen Themenbereich beschäftigen wird.

References
BROWNMILLER, S. 1984. *Weiblichkeit*. Frankfurt/M.:Fischer.
CASH, TH. & HICKS, K. 1990. Being Fat versus Thinking Fat: Relationships with Body Image, Eating Behaviors, and Well-Being. *Cognitive Therapy and Research,* Vol. 14(3) 1990: 327-341.
DAVIES, K. & WARDLE, J. 1994. Body Image and Dieting in Pregnancy. *Journal of Psychosomatic Research,* Vol. 38(8) 1994:787-799.
FAIRBURN, CH. & WELCH, S. 1990. The Impact of Pregnancy on Eating Habits and Attitudes to Shape and Weight. *International Journal of Eating Disorders,* Vol. 9(2) 1990:153-160.
OFFERMANN, C. 1995. *Das Erleben des Körpergewichts bei schwangeren und bei dicken Frauen. Eine Vergleichsstudie*. Psychologisches Institut der Universität Heidelberg: Unveröffentlichte Diplomarbeit.
RICHARDSON, P. 1990. Women's Experiences of Body Change During Normal Pregnancy. *Maternal-Child Nursing Journal,* Vol. 19(2) 1990:93-111.
ROSE, L. 1994. „Ich bin stolz auf meinen durchtrainierten Körper". *Psychologie Heute,* 6/1994:32-37.
SLADE, P.D. 1977. Awareness of body dimensions during pregnancy: an analogue study. *Psychological Medicine,* 7/1977:245-252.
SUMNER, A., WALLER, G., KILLICK, S. & ELSTEIN, M. 1993. Body image distortion in pregnancy: a pilot study of the effects of media images. *Journal of Reproductive and Infant Psychology,* Vol. 11/1993:203-208.

Blutspuren. Das Tabu Menstruation im westlichen Kulturkreis
Traces of Blood. Menstruation as a Taboo in Western Cultures

Marie-Therese Karlen

Zusammenfassung: Im vorliegenden Beitrag wird nach den Wurzeln eines Tabus gesucht, das heute noch wirksam ist: das Tabu Menstruation. Die Spurensuche erfolgt doppelstrangig. Einerseits wird dargestellt, wie das Tabu Menstruation historisch gewachsen ist und sich bis heute erhalten hat. Angefangen mit antiken Körperkonzepten über das im Mittelalter vorherrschende Frauenbild und die Hexenverfolgung in der Neuzeit bis zum Umgang mit der Menstruation in der Gegenwart, wird der Weg aufgezeigt, den die Menstruation als - vordergründig aus männlicher Sicht - "typisches Frauenleiden" und mit ihr die Frauen bis heute gegangen sind.
Andererseits werden, in einem zweiten Teil, aktuelle Interpretationen aus Ethnologie und Psychologie präsentiert, die dazu dienen, hinter die Fassade historischer Begebenheiten zu blicken und das mit der Menstruation gekoppelte Tabu in seinen Ursprüngen aufzudecken. Die Verknüpfung zwischen historischem Rückblick und aktuellen Thesen lässt Schlussfolgerungen zu, die zeigen, wieso sich Frauen bis heute nicht vom oftmals krankmachenden Tabu Menstruation befreit haben.

Abstract: The present paper is an attempt to discover the roots of a still existing phenomena: menstruation as a taboo. The first part of the paper shows how this taboo has been risen throughout history. Classical body concepts, the predominate perception of the female gender during Middle Ages, the witch-hunt of modern times and the way how to deal with menstruation in present days - every single of this epochs reflects the difficult part that menstruation as a "specifically female suffering" has played upon today - according to male interpretation.
In a second part, recent anthropological and psychological theories are presented to find out the origins that underlie the taboo entangled with menstruation. The act of connecting historical review and recent theories explains why women haven't succeeded up to present days in breaking free from this often sickening taboo.

Keywords: Geschlechterbeziehungen, Menstruation, Tabu, westlicher Kulturkreis, Geschichte, gender relations, menstruation, taboo, Western cultures, history

1. WAS IST EIN TABU?

- Im Fremdwörterbuch steht unter "Tabu": "etwas, das sich dem (sprachlichen) Zugriff aus Gründen moralischer, religiöser oder konventioneller Scheu entzieht; sittlich konventionelle Schranke." Unter Tabuisierung ist zu lesen: "das Totschweigen, das Zu-einem-Tabu-Erklären eines Bereichs od. eines Problems" (DROSDOWSKI 1992: 437).
- Andernorts wird Tabu als Umgehung bestimmter Personen, Orte oder Objekte definiert, was die Annahme einer Kombination von ritueller Kraft und ritueller Gefahr nahelegt. Rituelle Verbote sind gemäß der Anthropologin Mary Douglas Produkte eines Klassifikationssystems, das soziale, psychologische und intellektuelle Antworten auf Phänomene bietet, die die klassifikatorische Ordnung bedrohen. In neueren Studien über Symbol und Ritual wird das Tabu nicht mehr als universell einheitliches Konzept gesehen. Vielmehr gehen diese Studien davon aus, dass jede Form von Umgehen oder Verbot als Bedingung des jeweiligen symbolischen oder soziokulturellen Zusammenhangs zu betrachten ist (SEYMOUR-SMITH 1986: 276).
- Eine weitere Definition: GEORG WINTERER (1992) betont die durch Tabuisierung ermöglichte Trennung eines Objektes vom Allgemeinen. Er spricht von den Antipoden Idealisierung, Abwertung und Objektspaltung als Charakteristika des Tabus im freudschen Sinne. Das Augenmerk ist allerdings auch hier auf das Tabu als Orientierungshilfe im Dschungel ungeschriebener Gesetze von Moralvorstellungen und gesellschaftlichen Normen gerichtet (WINTERER 1992: 13ff).

Die Verknüpfung dieser Definitionen meint: Durch Totschweigen gelingt es dem Menschen, bestimmte Dinge unter Kontrolle zu bringen. So entstehen konventionelle Schranken, die helfen, explosive Mischungen aus Anziehung und Abstoßung in den Griff zu bekommen. Tabus dienen dazu, um die Lebenswelt bedrohende Elemente zu klassifizieren und die Umwelt zu strukturieren. Der Mensch schafft diese Orientierungshilfen zum Teil aus Angst vor eigener Unzulänglichkeit, zum Teil aus Furcht vor Fremdem und Unbekanntem.

2. GESCHICHTE DER MENSTRUATION
Die Antike

In der Antike nahmen Frauen weder an Schlachten noch an gefährlichen Sportarten teil. Sie boten den Wissenschaftlern im Vergleich zum männlichen Geschlecht wenig Gelegenheit, ihre Körper zu erforschen. Die Gelehrten mussten sich zur Interpretation des weiblichen Körpers mit dessen Ausscheidungen begnügen. Menstrualblut lieferte den Anlass zu vielschichtigen Theorien. Die regelmäßig wiederkehrende Blutung wurde mit höchstem Interesse beobachtet. Schon damals brachte man die Menstruation wie die Gezeiten des Meeres mit dem Monats- oder Mondzyklus in Verbindung (GRUHN/KAZER 1989: 11). Das Mysterium Menstruation gab Anlass zu Spekulationen und Versuchen, das Geheimnis durch "wissenschaftliche" Erklärungen zu lüften. Hier liegt der Herd vieler Irrtümer, die sich seit Jahrtausenden um die Menstruation ranken.

Zwei Beispiele, die das Menstruationsverständnis der Antike illustrieren:
HIPPOKRATES (460 - 377 v. Chr.) vertrat die Auffassung, die Menstruation sei der Beweis für die Verschiedenheit zwischen Mann und Frau. Die Monatsblutung war für ihn ein Abtropfen von Überflüssigem (DEAN-JONES 1994: 226).

ARISTOTELES (384 - 322 v.Chr.) sah "die Frau [als] eine Art zeugungsunfähigen Mann. Denn Weibchen sein bedeutet eine gewisse Schwäche, weil etwas nicht imstande ist, aus der letzten Nahrungsstufe Samen ausreifen zu lassen. Diese Stufe ist das Blut" (VOSS 1988: 36). Den Ursprung des Menstrualbluts ortete Aristoteles im Überschuss ungebrauchter Nahrung.

Für beide Wissenschaftler war die Menstruation das Hauptunterscheidungsmerkmal zwischen Mann und Frau. Zudem glaubten sie an die Giftigkeit des Menstrualblutes. Auch über den menschlichen Ursprung waren sie einer Meinung: "In both theories, however, even the bodies of men were originally constituted from menstrual blood, [...]" (DEAN-JONES 1994: 225ff).

Das Mittelalter

Im 11. Jahrhundert entwickelte der arabische Philosoph und Arzt Avicenna (980 - 1037) eine weitere Theorie. Der Ursprung des Menstrualblutes war für ihn ein Überschuss an Blut im weiblichen Körper. Thomas von Aquins (1224 - 1274) Auffassung über die Frau gleicht jener von Aristoteles aufs Haar: "Hinsichtlich der Einzelnatur ist das Weib etwas Mangelhaftes und eine Zufallserscheinung" (VOSS 1988: 36).

Im 14. Jahrhundert verbreitete die Kirche unter dem stark in Mythologie und Aberglauben verhafteten Volk die aus der Antike übernommene These, die Frau, das Naturprinzip, sei ihren Trieben ausgeliefert.

Die Ausschlusstaktik wurde wieder aufgenommen, obwohl Papst Gregor im Jahre 735 den menstruierenden Frauen den Gang zur Kirche und sogar das Empfangen der Kommunion erlaubt hatte. Der Grundstein dieser "christlichen" Sanktionen liegt in der Schöpfungsgeschichte. Darin wird Eva die Schuld für die Beschwerlichkeit des Lebens angelastet. Sie ist "die Brecherin des göttlichen Gesetzes, die Verführerin des Mannes. Davon abgeleitet, war die Ursache allen Übels das Weib. Von da an waren Sexualität und Sündenfall miteinander verknüpft" (RUEB 1995: 120).

Die Kirche setzte in dieser Zeit alles daran, die Kritik, die sie über Jahrhunderte hinweg von Seiten sich ständig neu formierender Glaubensgemeinschaften hatte erdulden müssen, zu sühnen. Eine gezielte kirchliche Maßnahme war die Inquisition, die im 12. und 13. Jahrhundert in Spanien, Frankreich und Italien, als Instrument zur Verfolgung Andersdenkender eingesetzt wurde. Ab dem 15. Jahrhundert fand diese "Säuberung" ihren nahtlosen Übergang in der Hexenverfolgung.

Die Neuzeit
Hexenjagd!

Die humanistischen Ärzte der frühen Neuzeit waren davon überzeugt, dass "[...] die Frau, mit ihrem ewig hungrigen Schoß wie ein Tier, durch Geschlechtsverkehr und Schwängerung gefüttert werden müsse, weil sie sonst dem Wahnsinn verfalle" (BECKMANN/BECKMANN 1990: 102). Der berühmte Arzt Paracelsus vertrat noch im Jahre 1566 voller Überzeugung die These, es gebe kein Gift in der Welt, das schädlicher sei als das Menstrualblut. Inwieweit diese Überzeugung die Wahl der zu "Hexen" Gestempelten beeinflusst hat, wird heute unterschiedlich interpretiert. Einerseits wird behauptet, die Hexenjagd habe die Ausrottung einer ganzen Frauenkultur zum Ziel gehabt: "Die Hexenverfolgung stand in der Tradition der gleichen Tabus, die Frauen zu allen Zeiten aufgezwungen worden sind. Der mittelalterliche Hexenpogrom war höchstwahrscheinlich eine einzige riesige Tabuisierung der Menstruation. Wie sonderbar und makaber mutet es an, dass die Hexenverfolger trotz aller sonst angewandten Hinrichtungsmethoden ein Gesetz immer einhielten, nämlich: "Du sollst nicht das Blut einer Hexe vergießen." Warum? Im Blut der Frau, so meinte man, lag ihre Macht" (SHUTTLE/REDGROVE 1982: 222ff.). Hier ist von 9 Millionen verbrannter "Hexen" die Rede, was sich jedoch bei der Konsultation historischer Quellen als reine Spekulation erweist. Diese Quellen sprechen andrerseits von 100'000 Menschen, die dem Hexenwahn in Europa zum Opfer gefallen sind. Die Hexenverfolgung wird in Historikerkreisen nicht als reine Frauenverfolgung, sondern als Sündenbockdenken der damaligen Volkskultur - jemand musste für Naturkatastrophen, Epidemien und dergleichen den Kopf hinhalten - und als politische Ambitionen der Kirche, die keine Andersdenkenden neben sich duldete, verstanden.

"So zeigt sich schließlich, dass [...] von einer "intentionalen", geplanten und über ganz Europa hinweg systematisch ausgebreiteten Frauenverfolgung nicht die Rede sein kann, trotz der über 80% weiblichen Opfer. Es wird zugleich auch deutlich, wie zahlreiche Projektionen, Spekulationen und Fehlinformationen die Hexenforschung in frauengeschichtlicher Perspektive verfälscht haben" (OPPITZ 1995: 264).

18. Jahrhundert bis heute
Die weitere Entwicklung des Menstruationsbildes ist geprägt von der Etablierung der "neuen" Religionen. Sowohl Katholizismus als auch Protestantismus blieben Dogmen verhaftet, die den Bereich der Sexualität zunehmend tabuisierten. Obwohl 1840 in Frankreich auf wissenschaftlicher Ebene die Zusammenhänge der weiblichen Monatsblutung aufgedeckt worden waren, änderte sich die vorherrschende Einstellung kaum: "Fünf Tage im Monat - so die Forscher - menstruiert die Frau, ist sie siech und psychisch erregt. Sie ist "periodisch irre!" (HERING/MAIERHOF 1991: 44). Die aufkeimende Psychoanalyse gegen Ende des 19. Jahrhunderts führte zu einer verstärkten Konzentration auf die menschliche Sexualität. Mit Sinnlichkeit hatte aber die aus der Aufklärung hervorgegangene Wissenschaft - wie zuvor die Kirche - wenig am Hut. Anfangs des 20. Jahrhunderts nahmen die Frauen allmählich ihren Körper selbst in die Hand. Ärztinnen, wie Anna Fischer Dückelmann schrieben gegen die männliche Vorstellung an, die Menstruation sei eine Krankheit. "(...) ist die monatliche Blutung nicht als ein Zustand der Krankheit aufzufassen; sie steht in Verbindung mit einem physiologischen Vorgang und ist daher bei gesunden Frauen auch mit keinerlei nennenswerten Beschwerden verbunden" (ibid. 58). Die Mythen um die Krankheit "Menstruation" verblassten zwar, nicht aber jene die an der Giftigkeit des Menstrualblutes festhielten. Bis in die 50er-Jahre wurde unter Wissenschaftlern über die Existenz von Menotoxin (Menstruationsgift) debattiert. Der negative Beweis erfolgte im Jahre 1958.

Die sexuelle Revolution der 60er-Jahre und das durch die weibliche Emanzipation entstandene neue Bewusstsein haben es bis heute nicht geschafft, das negativ belegte Tabu Menstruation in ein positives zu verwandeln. Blütenweiße Binden, von selbstbewussten, jungen und dynamischen Frauen präsentiert, beweisen, dass die Mehrheit es immer noch vorzieht, "die Klappe zu halten, Tabletten zu schlucken und die Binden möglichst unauffällig verschwinden zu lassen" (HERING/MAIERHOF 1991: 143). Nur so kann verhindert werden, dass erneut Assoziationen von Krankheit, Schwäche und Hysterie aufsteigen. Reinheit, Normalität und Verfügbarkeit: diese Dreieinigkeit ist historisch gewachsen und prägt das weibliche Bewusstsein heute noch. Immerhin liefert die Menstruation der Frau - wenn schon nicht Gelegenheit, sich in ihre Weiblichkeit zurückzuziehen - die Möglichkeit, ihre sexuelle Verfügbarkeit durch die Ausrede "Menstruation" zu limitieren. Dies mag allerdings für jene, deren sexuelle Lust gerade während dieser Zeit am größten ist, ein schwacher Trost sein.

3. AKTUELLE THEORIEN DER MENSTRUATION
In diesem Kapitel werden aktuelle Theorien aus Anthropologie und Psychologie vorgestellt, die auf der Suche nach einer Erklärung für die bis heute anhaltende Tabuisierung der Menstruation sind.

Anthropologische Konzepte
Mary Douglas: Menstruation als Indikator für Machtverteilung
Mary Douglas vertritt die Ansicht, die Menstruation - das Symbol weiblicher Andersartigkeit - werde vom Mann als Bedrohung seiner Rollenidentität empfunden, vor allem dann, wenn die männliche

Machtdominanz nicht gesichert sei. Die Anthropologin untermauert ihre These mit Untersuchungergebnissen aus drei Kulturen.

Im australischen Volk der Walbiri sind die Männer die Machthaber. Ihnen ist "die Vorstellung einer Verunreinigung durch das andere Geschlecht fremd. Selbst Menstruationsblut wird nicht gemieden, und dem Kontakt damit werden keine Gefahren nachgesagt" (DOUGLAS 1988: 185ff).

Der Umgang der Geschlechter im afrikanischen Volk der Nuer ist geprägt von Liberalität. Der Mann fühlt sich auf keine Art und Weise in seinem Status bedroht. Ausgeprägte Reinheitsvorschriften fehlen auch in diesem Stamm fast vollständig (DOUGLAS 1988: 187ff).

Bei den afrikanischen Lele hingegen ist das Geschlechterverhältnis ambivalent, die Macht in der Geschlechterbeziehung umkämpft. Nach Douglas' Aussage entsehen in diesem Volk vielfältige Bedrohungen durch den Kontakt, die Berührung mit dem anderen Geschlecht, was sich in zahlreichen Vermeidungsstrategien gegenüber Körperausscheidungen des anderen Geschlechts, insbesondere gegenüber Menstrualblut ausdrückt (DOUGLAS 1988: 195ff).

Die Resultate aus der Verknüpfung zwischen Machtverteilung und Menstruationskonzepten führt zu Douglas' Schlussfolgerung: Glaubt der Mann seine Dominanz in der Geschlechterbeziehung gefährdet, benützt er die Menstruation als typisch weibliches Phänomen, um das andere Geschlecht für unrein zu erklären, auszugrenzen und in dessen Autonomie einzuschränken.

Chris Knight: No meat - no sex!
Um seine These zu konstruieren, greift CHRIS KNIGHT (1991) das marxistische Geschichtsbild - die klassenlose Urgemeinschaft - auf: "[...] traditional hunter-gatherer societies [...] were strongly egalitarian, based on a sharing way of life, and at their heart were rules or taboos which ensured that values such as sexual access and food were not nakedly fought over, with the strongest monopolising the most, but distributed fairly" (KNIGHT 1991: 23). Knight geht aber noch einen Schritt hinter die Jäger- und Sammlergesellschaft zurück, auf die Stufe der Primaten, die er mit der kapitalistischen Zweiklassengesellschaft gleichsetzt. Die Weibchen bilden die Arbeiterklasse innerhalb der sie für die Reproduktion der Gattung verantwortlich sind. Die Männchen sind die Kapitalisten, die die Arbeiterklasse unterdrücken. Den Sprung von dieser männlich dominierten Klassengesellschaft zur klassenlosen Gemeinschaft der Sammler- und Jägerkultur bezeichnet Knight als die große Revolution in der Menschheitsgeschichte. Der Anthropologe ist überzeugt, dass diese soziale, politische und sexuelle Revolution von der weiblichen Art, der unterdrückten revolutionären Klasse, initiiert wurde. Der Ausbeutung müde, verlangte die untergeordnete Klasse nach Gleichberechtigung. Auch die männlichen Artgenossen sollten ihren Teil zum Überleben beitragen, auf die Jagd gehen und so die Frauen bei der Ernährung der Kinder unterstützen. Um die Männer zu dieser Aktivität zu bringen, setzten die physisch unterlegenen Frauen ihr einziges Machtinstrument, die Sexualität, ein. "(...) any male who approached seeking sex without first joining his comrades in the hunt would have had to be met with refusal. No meat: no sex (ibid. 25). Das weibliche Machtinstrument verlangte nebst absoluter Solidarität selbst auferlegte Bescheidenheit und Moral. Individuelle sexuelle Wünsche mussten unterdrückt, der Körper in den Dienst der Frauengruppe gestellt werden. Diese Gruppensolidarität führte zur synchronen Menstruation und erlaubte den gleichzeitig stattfindenden Sex-Streik. Der Mond diente als Uhr, so dass die Frauen bei Vollmond menstruierten und die Männer das Mondlicht zur Jagd nutzen konnten (ibid. 37).

In der sozialen Synchronisation - die Frau menstruiert, der Mann jagt - sieht Knight den Ursprung des Tabus Menstruation. Um jeglichem Verdacht zu entgehen, vermieden es die Männer mit Blut in Kontakt zu geraten. Diese Erklärung gilt auch für das Tabu um rohes Fleisch. "It would have remaind taboo for as long as it remained uncooked - just as women remain 'taboo' whilst menstruating" (KNIGHT 1991: 39).

Psychologische Konzepte
Jutta Voss: Negative Tabuisierung durch männliche Machtapparate
JUTTA VOSS (1988) vertritt die These, die Menstruation stelle in der Evolutionsgeschichte den Übergang vom Tier zum Menschen dar. "Die Wahrnehmung dieser ungeheuren Körpersensationen, die Regelmäßigkeiten des erscheinenden Blutes, hat menschliche Evolution ermöglicht und religiöse Kulte und die menschliche Kultur eingeleitet" (VOSS 1988: 56). In die Zeit des Matriarchats (100'000 v. Chr. bis etwa 2'000 v. Chr.) siedelt sie die Entwicklung des psychisch-mythischen Bewusstseins an. Die Zeit

danach bezeichnet sie als Patriarchalisierung und geistig-rationale Bewusstseinsphase (ibid: 13).

Der Umschwung von Matriarchat zu Patriarchat schaltet die Psychologin gleich mit dem Übergang der Jäger- und Sammlergesellschaft zur Ackerbaukultur. Durch "Domestizierung" wurde der Mann aggressiv in seinem Sexverhalten, unterdrückte durch physische Überlegenheit die autonome weibliche Sexualität und wies der Frau minderwertige soziale Rollen zu. Diese Unterdrückung fand ihren Niederschlag im patriarchalen Menstruationstabu (VOSS 1988: 68ff). Im Zusammenhang mit der negativen Tabuisierung prangert Jutta Voss die katholische Kirche an: "Die Ordination wird verweigert, weil Frauen in sich, in ihrem Leib, das wirkliche Blutwandlungsmysterium tragen, den nie endenden Zyklus des Lebens. Das männliche Blut, auch das Blut Jesu, ist und bleibt Tötungsblut und kann daher als Wandlungsmysterium nur symbolisch verstanden werden. Das Wandlungsmysterium des weiblichen Blutes ist immer real" (VOSS 1988: 50).

Georg Winterer: Männliche Angst vor weiblichen Attributen
GEORG WINTERER (1992) kommt nach eingehender Auseinandersetzung mit dem Verhältnis des Mannes zur menstruierenden Frau zum Schluss, dass das Hauptmotiv der Tabuisierung die Angst der Männer vor der Frau mit ihrem Verwandlungspotential und ihrer Fähigkeit zur Reproduktion ist. Durch ihr Verwandlungspotential entzieht sich die Frau männlicher Kontrolle und Berechenbarkeit. "Ihre Macht ergibt sich dabei nicht zuletzt daraus, dass sie es ist, die die Art hervorbringt, den Prozessen des Lebens damit unmittelbarer verbunden ist, als dies für den Mann gelten mag" (WINTERER 1992: 206). Menstruation ist etwas, das dem Mann fremd und bedrohlich erscheint. Um dieses Bedrohliche zu "bändigen" erklärt er die Menstruation zum Tabu. Dies wiederum hat negative Auswirkungen auf das Menstruationserleben der Frau. Dass sogar emanzipierte Frauen gute Miene zum bösen Spiel machen, liegt gemäß Winterer darin, dass nur die Unterdrückung der Menstruation mit all ihren Begleiterscheinungen ein Weiterkommen in der immer noch männlich dominierten Berufswelt ermöglicht.

"Erkauft wird dieses "Weiterkommen" jedoch allzuoft mit der Aufgabe der alten Kunst der Verwandlung, verkümmert zum Rudiment der Anpassung an männliche Normen bis hin zur Selbstaufgabe" (WINTERER 1992: 207).

Zusammenfassung
Die kurz umrissenen Konzepte haben eines gemeinsam: alle Erklärungsansätze für das Tabu Menstruation gründen in der Angst des Mannes; in den meisten Fällen vor der Frau oder - so bei Chris Knight - vor sozialen und gesellschaftlichen Sanktionen. In Mary Douglas ist es die Angst vor Machtverlust, Jutta Voss und Georg Winterer sprechen beide von männlicher Furcht vor dem weiblichen Verwandlungspotential, das in der Menstruation seinen Ausdruck findet und die Andersartigkeit der Frau symbolisiert.

4. SCHLUSSFOLGERUNG
Bevor Schlussfolgerungen gezogen werden, eine grundsätzliche Frage: Was haben Tabus für einen Sinn? Der Versuch einer Begriffsdefinition in Kapitel 1 hat gezeigt, dass es sich um Orientierungshilfen handelt, die dem Menschen helfen, die Komplexität seiner Umwelt zu reduzieren. Dies zeigt, wie wichtig Tabus gerade in der heutigen Zeit sind. Dabei gilt es aber zwischen positiv und negativ zu unterscheiden. Das Tabu Menstruation ist - auch in seiner heutigen Ausprägung - ein negatives. Das Aufrollen der verschiedenen Epochen bis zurück in die Antike macht klar: Der negative "Beigeschmack" der Menstruation resultiert primär aus männlichem, nicht weiblichem, Willen. Er hat sich - wenn auch in der heutigen Generation nicht mehr als solcher manifestiert - bis in die Gegenwart gehalten. Eigentlich, so möchte man meinen, sollte das weibliche Selbstwertgefühl heute alles daran setzen, diesem negativen Tabu den Garaus zu machen. Dem ist nicht so. Allein zu sehen, wie Wissenschaftlerinnen das Thema "Tabu Menstruation" oft angehen, ist alarmierend. Die entscheidende Frage, warum sich Frauen die "männliche" Interpretation eines so typisch weiblichen Phänomens immer noch gefallen lassen, wird nicht gestellt. Es ist bezeichnend, dass wiederum männliche Kollegen die Antworten auf weibliche Verhaltensmuster suchen und dabei zwar zu interessanten, teilweise aber gewagten, Schlüssen kommen. Die eher spekulative Theorie des Anthropologen Chris Knight, sieht das Tabu Menstruation gar von Frauen selbst -aus äußerst pragmatischen, nämlich ernährungspolitischen Gründen - geschaffen. Georg Winterer zieht den Schluss, dass die männlich dominierte Berufswelt die Frauen davon abhält, das ihnen auferlegte Tabu abzustreifen.

Jutta Voss hingegen argumentiert mit männlicher Überlegenheit auf physischer Ebene argumentiert, die den Sturz des Matriarchats - dessen Existenz wissenschaftlich widerlegt ist - plausibel machen soll. Nicht nur scheint dies fadenscheinig und spekulativ, auch werden keine zukunftsweisenden Antworten gesucht. Mary Douglas bleibt im Deskriptiven haften, ohne den geringsten Versuch zu unternehmen, dem Wieso und Warum des passiven Verhaltens der Frau auf die Spur zu kommen.

Frauen scheinen von der Thematik derart betroffen, dass sie die Existenz männlicher Unterdrückungsmechanismen einzig durch Unterlegenheit und Ausgeliefertsein erklären können. Oft sind diese Erklärungsversuche von Frustration und Bitterkeit gekennzeichnet. Beides ist wohl kaum dazu angetan, einen objektiven Blickwinkel zu schärfen. Solange aber Frauen in Frustration verharren und ihr Unterlegenheitsgefühl weiter "pflegen", wird es ihnen nicht gelingen, sich vom negativen, einengenden, oft sogar krankmachenden Tabu zu befreien. Frau Dr. Müller-Landgraf vom Medizinhistorischen Institut der Universität Bern meint dazu: "Bis wir aufhören, die Monatsblutung als Fluch zu betrachten, bleibt die Tabuisierung bestehen. Es liegt an uns Frauen, etwas zu verändern!" Sie hat recht. Wir haben es in der Hand, die Menstruation zu einem positiven, einem "heiligen, spirituellen" Tabu werden zu lassen. Dazu müssen wir zuerst einen besseren Zugang zu diesem so typisch weiblichen Phänomen finden, die Menstruation mit schönen Dingen verbinden, sie zu etwas Wertvollem werden lassen. Möglichkeiten gibt es viele, ohne dass wir gleich an einen allmonatlichen Rückzug in die unserer Kultur fremde Menstruationshütte denken. Wieso nicht ein junges Mädchen, das zum ersten Mal menstruiert, mit einem Fest in den Kreis der Frauen aufnehmen? Wieso nicht sich selber Blumen schenken, und so "die Tage" verschönern? Wieso nicht die Zeit der Monatsblutung allem Kopfschütteln zum Trotz mit Freude und Festlichkeit gestalten? Das alles wäre ein erster Schritt, um das Bewusstsein in eine andere Richtung zu lenken - weg vom negativen hin zum positiven Tabu Menstruation.

References

BECKMANN, D. and B. BECKMANN. 1990. *Beifuß und andere Hexenkräuter.*Campus Verlag.

DEAN-JONES, L. 1994. *Women's Bodies in Classical GreekScience.* Clarendon Press.

DOUGLAS, M. 1985. *Reinheit und Gefährdung.* Dieter Reimer Verlag.

DROSDOWSKI, G., D. BERGER and F.WURMS (Hrsg.). 1992. *Schülerduden. Fremdwörterbuch.* Duden-Verlag. 437.

GRUHN, J.G. and R.R. KAZER. 1989. *Hormonal Regulation of the Menstrual Cycle. The Evolution of Concepts.* PlenumMedical Book Company.

HERING, S. and G. MAIERHOF. 1991. *Die unpässliche Frau.Sozialgeschichteder Menstruation und Hygiene1860 -1985.* Centaurus- Verlagsgesellschaft.

KNIGHT, C. 1991. *Blood relations. Menstruation and the origins of culture.* Yale University Press.

OPPITZ, C. 1995. *Der Hexenstreit. Frauen in der frühneuzeitlichen Hexenverfolgung.*Herder Verlag.

RUEB, F. 1995. Hexenbrände. *Die Schweizergeschichte des Teufelswahns.*Weltwoche-ABC-Verlag.

SEYMOUR-SMITH, C. 1986. *Macmillan Dictionary ofAnthropology.*The Macmillan Press.

SHUTTLE P. and P. REDGROVE. 1982. *Die weise Wunde Menstruation.* Fischer Taschenbuch Verlag.

VOSS J. 1988. *Das Schwarzmondtabu. Die kulturelle Bedeutung desweiblichen Zyklus.* KreuzVerlag.

WINTERER G. 1992. *Menstruation als Tabu. Eine theoretisch-empirische Untersuchung über das Verhältnis des Mannes zur menstruierenden Frau.* Roland Asanger Verlag.

Female Genital Mutilitation in the North of Burkina Faso
Genitalverstümmelung von Frauen im Norden Burkina Fasos

Karl L. Dehne, Jürgen Wacker, Jean Nadembega & Roselyne Ira

Abstract: In a collaborative effort between an international NGO and provincial health authorities, a study of attitudes, beliefs and practices related to Female Genital Mutilation was conducted among 70 women in a remote and ethnically heterogeneous area in northwestern Burkina Faso. With basic training and close supervision, locally recruited "peer interviewers" proved capable to collect information that appeared both scientifically valid and useful for policy planning. Study data were supplemented with evidence from the training of village birth attendants, findings from obstetrical practice at the provincial hospital and published anthropological reports on the two main ethnic groups that live in the area. Female Genital Mutilation is still universally practised in the study area, but its meaning and practice has changed. During the course of half a century, initiation rites have been abandoned and excision as an inherited profession performed by persons of caste replaced by an acquired occupation. The age at excision has significantly dropped and its importance and meaning profoundly changed under the parallel onslaught of progressing and deepening islamisation and modernisation. Differences in the age at excision and in the motivation for the operation between the main ethnic groups remain distinguishable, and will have to be taken into account when designing programmes to eradicate Female Genital Mutilation. Basic maternity and child health services should be provided and combined with educational interventions targeting not only the concerned women and the excisers, but also husbands and religious and community leaders.

Zusammenfassung: Vertreter einer internationalen Nichtregierungsorganisation und der Gesundheitsdienste einer Provinz führten gemeinsam in einer ablegenen und ethnisch heterogenen Gegend im Nordwesten Burkinas bei 70 Frauen eine Befragung über ihre Einstellungen und Praktiken bezüglich Genitalverstümmelung durch. Die Interviewer wurden lokal rekrutiert und waren dank einer kurzen Ausbildung und enger Aufsicht in der Lage, wissenschaftlich valide und für die weitere Programmplanung nützliche Informationen zu sammeln. Die Ergebnisse der Befragung wurden mit Erfahrungen während der Ausbildung von Dorfhebammen und geburtshilflicher Praxis am Provinzkrankenhaus und mit anthropologischer Literatur über die zwei wichtigsten Ethnien die in dieser Gegend leben verglichen. Genitalverstümmelungen bei Frauen sind weiterhin die Regel in dieser Region, aber ihre Bedeutung und Praxis haben sich im Laufe der zweiten Hälfte dieses Jahrhunderts geändert. Initiationsriten sind verschwunden und das Durchführen von Beschneidungen scheint nicht mehr ein ererbter Beruf bestimmter Kasten zu sein, sondern eine Beschäftigung, die anderwitig erlernt wird. Die Beschneidungen werden nun wesentlich früher durchgeführt, und haben durch fortschreitende Islamisierung und Modernisierung Änderungen in ihrem Bedeutungsinhalt erfahren. Zwischen den veschiedenen ethnischen Gruppen sind Unterschiede bezüglich des Alters, bei dem die Beschneidungen vorgenommen werden, und bezüglich der Gründe für die Beschneidungen weiterhin feststellbar. Diese Unterschiede müssen beachtet werden, wenn Programme mit dem Ziele entwickelt werden sollen, diese Vestümmelungspraktiken abzuschaffen. Es wird empfohlen, Basisgesundheitsdienste für Mutter und Kind einzurichten und Aufklärungsmaßnahmen zu treffen, die nicht nur auf die betroffenen Frauen selbst, sondern auch auf jene Frauen die die Verstümmelungen durchführen, die Maenner der betroffenen Frauen und die Dorfältesten und Religionsführer ausgerichtet sind.

Keywords: Burkina Faso, femal genital mutilation, Fulani, Gurmance, Islamisiation, rites of passage, Genitalverstümmelung bei Frauen, Fulbe, Gulmance, Islamisierung, Initiationsriten.

Introduction

Female Genital Mutilation (FGM), is defined as the removal, for ritual or religious reasons, of some or all of the external female genitalia. It is routinely practised by ethnic groups in more than 20 countries across the north African savannah as well as in Egypt, the southern part of the arab peninsula, Malaysia and Indonesia. The total number of women mutilated has been estimated at 85 to 115 million (WHO 1994, HEDLEY & DORKENOO 1992). However, the evidence is patchy. In a few countries, such as Sierra Leone, Djibouti and the Sudan, studies have determined the magnitude of the problem (the number of women mutilated), and even the prevalence and range of medical complications (HOSKEN 1982, EL DAREER 1982, KOSO-THOMAS 1987, IDLEY et.al. 1984). In most others including Burkina Faso documented knowledge of FGM is scarce. The often quoted estimate of 70% of women mutilated in that country, is based on one interview with an expert in the capital Ougadougou (WHO 1994, HOSKEN

1987). Except for some scattered anthropological reports, FGM in rural areas has not been studied.

Two main types of mutilations have been described: Excision, meaning the removal of the clitoris and, possibly, of adjacent parts or the whole of the labia minora, and infibulation, the removal of the clitoris, parts or all of the labia minora and sections of the labia majora. In infibulation, the two sides of the vulva are stitched together to leave only a small opening for the passage of menstrual blood and urine. In addition, types of genital operations and manipulations have been recorded by anthropologists, which do not qualify as FGM in the strict sense of "removal of external female genital organ tissue". These include incisions around the clitoris, its artificial lengthening and the insertion of rings through the labia. Some authors see excision and infibulation in the context of a even larger and more general set of practices which could superficially be called "marking of the body", to include scarifications, ritual ear piercing, uvulectomy, the insertion of rings through the lips, etc (BOURREL 1983, DELUZ 1987). Neighbouring ethnic groups, even those belonging to the same cultural stock, can have totally different modes of operations (DELUZ 1987). Although the magnitude of excision and infibulation is difficult to estimate, their harmfulness is not in doubt. Severe immediate and long-term complications have been described, such as haemorrhage, shock, infection, urine retention, keloid formation, problems during pregnancy and childbirth, and sexual dysfunctions (WHO 1994, VERZIN 1975). The latter is the result of painful intercourse and reduced sexual sensitivity, especially following infibulation. Penetration can be difficult or even impossible, and at times re-cutting is required (SHANDALL 1967). There is an increased risk of infertility due to ascending infections, and of HIV-infection, as scar tissue and the small vaginal opening are prone to laceration during sexual intercourse (Carballo 1988). FGM is believed to have serious psychological consequences, too, although little further research has been carried out to substantiate this assumption (BASHER 1979). Such severe consequences can hardly go unnoticed by the girls' parents and the women that perform the operations. Nevertheless FGM continues presumably because the rationale underlying it so entrenched in the societies that the operation is integral part of the socio-cultural fabric. In many societies, the benefits gained by recipients and their families in terms of social recognition (or avoidance of sanctions) seem to outweigh any potential danger. Moreover, in many instances, the excisers, often high status opinion-leaders, tend to have a vested interest in that the practice continues. The operations are usually well paid (KOUBA & MUASHER 1985).

In-depth knowledge of the societal structures and the underlying local belief systems that sustain FGM is therefore essential when designing educational interventions and to eradicate it. Unfortunately, for many geographical areas and ethnic groups not even basic knowledge of FGM has documented. "

Objectives
This study aims to fill the existing gap in the understanding of FGM insofar as it provides insight into its cultural context in one geographically and culturally distinct area in Burkina Faso, the department of Sebba in the province of Seno. The study was timely and opportune, as Burkina Faso is one of those African countries that has not only consistently condemned FGM, but also taken concrete steps to address the problem. A radio campaign against excision launched as early as 1975 had to be discontinued because of hostile reactions by the public (TIENDREGEOGON 1982). Nevertheless senior politicians including the late President, Captain Thomas Sankara continued to speak out against FGM (DORKENOO). The constitution of 1991, adopted by a general referendum, upholds equal rights between men and women and provides for the prohibition of FGM (18). In 1990, a National Committee to Combat the Practice of Female Circumcision was created, and two years later this was followed by the creation of similar committees at provincial level. These committees aim to collect relevant data on FGM, to formulate action plans to combat the practice and to implement appropriate information and education activities (KITI 1990, COMITÉ PROVINCIAL DE LUTTE CONTRE LA PRATIQUE DE LÉXCISION 1992). This study constituted the first step taken towards the achievement of these objectives in the study area. It was carried out in a collaborative effort between an international NGO (Save the Children Fund/ UK) and the health authorities of Seno province.

Geographic and cultural background
The department of Sebba is located in the northeastern corner of Burkina Faso, one of the world's remotest and most deprived areas. Its borders being virtually identical with those of a 19th century Fulani emirate, the Yagha, it constitutes a distinct geographical and cultural space. Today's population

of approximately 80,000 is mainly composed of Fulani and Rimaibe, former Fulani slaves, and of a few thousand Gurmances. Ethnic minorities include the Mossi, Sonrai, Haussas and Bellas, most of them immigrants that have settled in the Yagha during colonial times when slavery was officially abolished. Gurmances and Fulani/Rimaibes have basic ethnographic similarities, such as patrilinearity, patrilocality and polygyny, but differ on many determinants of social organisation, including modes of production, settlement and land use patterns, and religion. The Fulani are traditionally pastoralists, with their life revolving around their herd. Numerous myths give vivid proof of the importance of cattle in Fulani society. Transhumance, the seasonal migration of adolescent boys with the cattle, pre-inheritance, the building-up of a herd from a son's (and often a daughter's) birth on and throughout his adolescent's period so to allow the young person on the day of his or her marriage to lead an economically and geographically independent life, and the relative ease with which marriages can be dissolved (this involves the reimbursing of bridewealth) and new unions formed, are only but a few of the characteristics of Fulani culture that have made anthropologists describe it in terms of individualism and personal freedom (RIESMAN 1974). As in other pastoralist societies, the social and economic status of women has often been characterized as involving greater autonomy as compared to that of women in the surrounding agriculturist societies. A strong behavioural code expressed in the concept of Puulako (Fulani-ness), prescribes self-discipline and forbids the overt expression of emotion or physical need, both for men and women. (KIRK-GREEN 1979). In Sebba, as much as in other parts of the Sahel, a combination of ecologic disaster (repeated droughts) and socio-political changes which included the weakening of the traditional chief system and the emancipation of slaves, have eroded the traditional life style and modes of production. Many Fulani families, for whom agriculture used to be shameful, were forced to start millet and sorghum farming, to herd cattle for their former servants or to migrate to the cities (Bovin & Manger 1989). Seasonal migration of many young men to coastal countries such as Ivory Coast and Ghana, a long standing demographic feature of other regions of Burkina Faso (INSD 1990), has also become important in the northern sahel provinces, including the Yagha. In contrast, transhumance, migration with the herds, is now practised by a small minority only (PIQUEMAL 1993).

Wherever Fulani groups have been studied in the West African savannah (RIESMAN 1974), adherence to Islam had almost become a trait of their ethnicity. Hardly any traces of an independent religious belief system or collective ancestor or spirit cult have been found (DUPIRE 1970). In Sebba, the influence of islam on daily life appears to have gradually increased, especially since the 30s and 40s, when the Yagha became a centre of an islam reform movement, the hamallism. Although there is no clear evidence of a difference in the ideology of the so called "moderate" muslims and of the hamallists (MOREAU 1964), the existence of several muslim sects competing for the right interpretation of the Koran, has probably accelerated the erosion of non-islamic traditions. Religious leaders are now consulted for all major life events and ceremonies such as name-giving and marriage, and prayers and Koranic schools are well attended. In some villages up to a dozen inhabitants have accomplished the hadj, the pilgrimage to the holy sites in Saudi Arabia prescribed in the Koran (DEHNE 1992, unpublished data).

Knowledge of and adherence to islamic principles, have always been inconsistent and unevenly spread within Fulani populations (MONTEIL 1963). In present-day Sebba, non-islamic features of Fulani society persist, including frequent divorce and widespread sexual relations before and out of marriage (of both males and females). Islamic inheritance laws seem to be known by most, but are not always strictly followed. Where pre-inheritance has been abolished, this appears to have been due to convenience end economic reasoning (the small size of the herds) rather than religious consideration (DEHNE, unpublished data). Since the 1970s a brand of sunnit fundamentalism (wahabiya) has started spreading in the area. In a few villages, women go veiled and, in open conflict with long standing traditions, efforts are made to seclude them in their compounds. Rimaibes, former Fulani slaves, form the largest "ethnic group" in Sebba. Up to 50% of the population are believed to be either Rimaibes, mostly of Gurmance or Mossi descent, or immigrants that have settled in Rimaibe villages and sub-villages and have been assimilated (PIQUEMAL 1993). Differences in appearance, lifestyle and production patterns between Rimaibes and Fulani nobles, but even more so between Rimaibes and second and third generation Mossi and other settlers have increasingly become blurred. Several generations of intermarriage - according to both islamic law and Fulani tradition, marriage of a Fulani man with a slave/Rimaibe woman is not prohibited - have left no visible difference between the originally lighter skinned Fulanis and the Rimaibes. Differences in clothing and hairstyle, reportedly almost categorical in the past (DE

COUTOULY 1923), have largely disappeared, too. A recent survey attempted to classify the population by residence in Fulani or Rimaibe subvillages, but when compared with self-reported ethnicity, between 15 and 20% of the sample proved to have been misclassified (UNSO 1991).

The Rimaibe and the other assimilated non-Fulani groups (see below) are traditionally agriculturalists, but production systems are converging, and agro-pastoralism, practised by all groups (including the Gurmance), has become the typical economic feature of the area (PIQUEMAL 1993). During the great droughts of the mid-70s and mid-80s, many Rimaibe bought lifestock from their former Fulani masters in exchange against basic foods such as millet and sorghum. Rimaibe villages and subvillages were founded in several waves from the 1960s onwards as satellites of the original Fulani villages resemble the latter. Rimaibe values and behavioural norms are dominated by Fulani culture and islam, presumably in very much the same way as those of the Fulani aristocracy. However, the extent and depth to which the Rimaibe actually identify with a value and belief system so closely linked to pastoralism, and with a behavioural code that describes any deviation as non-Fulani remains to be studied (DUPIRE 1970). During colonial times, many Rimaibes converted to the hamallist brand of islam, which had an emancipatory appeal to them. Development workers have sometimes experienced Rimaibe villages as more homogeneous and collaborative as compared to the Fulani ones usually dominated by reservedness and individualism. While most Yagha villages are dominated by Fulani/Rimaibe language, customs and settling patterns, a handful Gurmance villages located on the south eastern border of the department with the Gurmance heartland, have resisted assimilation. In these villages, Gurmancema remains the only spoken language. Very few persons have converted to islam. The Gurmances are subsistence agriculturists (sorghum, millet). Traditionally they live in large family clans, cultivate their land collectively and share what has been produced (INSTITUT NATIONAL DE LA STATISTIQUE ET DE LA DEMOGRAPHIE 1979). However, in recent years there has been a tendency to more individualised cultivation and to diversification in work arrangements. Animal husbandry is now generally practised along with millet farming (PIQUEMAL 1993). As with the Fulanis and Rimaibes, an increasing number of young men engage in seasonal migration to the cities and neighbouring countries in the search of remunerated work. The Gurmances have their own original and coherent religion and cosmology, distinct even from that of closely related neighbours, such as the Mossis. They believe in tienu, the creator, who gives children, food, medicine, among all other things, and in calibi, one's personal destiny. Fortune and misfortune are also affected by ancestors and ancestresses who act upon their own destiny and with the approval of tienu, god. These ancestors need to be honoured, and at crucial junctions of life the gurmances sacrifice to their altars. Buli, powerful spirits mediate between god and man (SWANSON 1985).

The Gurmances are a typically gerontocratic society in the sense of Meillassoux (Meissalloux). The authority and power of the patrilineal extended family and his virtually absolute control over women's marriage, fertility and sexuality were still standing during colonial times and even thereafter (SWANSON 1985), are only now slowly changing. The strong ancestor belief has tended to consolidate these power structures and control mechanisms. The Yagha has had very little intervention from development programmes. NGOs have been running a primary health care programme and a water scheme (SCF, UK) and have contributed to the organisation of women's cooperatives (ACORD). Recently UNSO has embarked on an integrated rural development scheme. School enrolment in the province is very low and the literacy rate (5,4%) the lowest in the country (but Koranic schools are well attended). Only three clinics and one medical centre served the Yagha at the time of the survey. The provincial hospital, where basic surgery can be performed, is between 70 and 100 km away. The area is far from the main transport routes and inaccessible during the rainy season (3-4 months).

Methods

Direct observation and in-depth ethnographic interviews had to be ruled out, as none of the investigators was proficient in Fulani or Gurmancema and only one was female (two were expatriates). Given the sensitivity of the subject, interviews with the help of interpreters had to be excluded, too. They would probably have resulted in the rejection of the investigators by the women themselves, by their husbands or the village elders, and in an eventual failure of the study. The FGM study was therefore combined with a health and vaccination questionnaire sample survey, for which local female interviewers had already been recruited and were being trained. The survey took place during the cold season 1992/1993.

A convenience subsample of roughly a quarter of the total of 320 women included in the main health survey were to be interviewed, with preference given to women that had been cooperative and informative during the longer health interview. The field supervisor (R.Ira) ensured that women from ethnically mixed villages, assumed to be a good ground for studies of cultural change, were included in the sample. Attention was given to keeping the questions and hence the conversations as factual and inoffensive as possible. The questionnaire was structured with a few core questions, taking into account that the locally recruited interviewers had little experience with conducting explorative interviews or eliciting sensitive information. Any reference to the potential harmfulness of FGM or its illegality was carefully avoided. The interviewers were instructed to record answers to the few open questions as faithfully as possible and not to offer any personal comments or judgements. Except for a few non-Fulani speaking Gurmances, all women were interviewed in Fulfulde.

The questionnaires were examined by the principal investigator the evening of the interview, to resolve any issues related to unclear Fulfulde-French or Gurmancema-French translation or incomplete notes, and to obtain background information on the interviewees. In a few exceptional cases, additional information was sought through re-interviewing the next day, when the survey team re-visited the same village. During these evening meetings the four interviewers were encouraged to compare their own views about FGM and their experiences at the provincial capital Dori where all of them resided with those of the women they had interviewed. To obtain an as comprehensive as possible idea of FGM in the study area, the survey data were supplemented and compared with anedoctal evidence from the training of village birth attendants (COWLEY 1992) and with findings during the obstetrical practice of one of the authors at the provincial hospital (J.Wacker). The hospital serves a large area and different ethnic groups including a few Fulanis/Rimaibes of the Sebba area. Very few Gurmances attend, as their settlement in the south east of the department areas are too far away. Finally, the findings from the Yagha were compared with published anthropological reports about Fulani and Gurmance populations in other geographical areas.

Findings

Characteristics of the interviewed women

A total of 70 women from 12 villages were interviewed, more than half (Hosken 1982b) of them living in three villages in the northcentral part of the department. Another 12 women were from one ethnically mixed village in the southeastern corner of the Yagha. The village has several subvillages inhabited by Gurmances, Rimaibes, Fulanis and minority groups such as Haussas. Between 2 and 6 women were interviewed in each of the other 8 villages. The age of the women varied between 19 and 58 years, with most of them between 25 and 49 years old. Both the mean and medium age were 37 years. 23 women identified themselves as Rimaibe and an equal number as Gurmances, 14 women were Fulanis and 10 Mossis. All of them had been born in the Yagha, and most had lived in the same or a neighbouring village since birth. All but 15 Gurmance women spoke Fulfulde. The close association between ethnicity and religion was confirmed. While all Fulanis, Rimaibes and assimilated Mossis were muslims, most of the Gurmances were animists. Only a few gurmance women residing in Rimaibe or ethnically mixed villages had converted to islam.

Answers to core questions - concerning reasons for excision (as the practice is universally called in French in the study area), the age at which it was practised, and by whom and where, whether girls were excised in groups and, if not, whether this had happened some time in the past - were obtained from between 39 and 60 out of the 70 women interviewed. Prompted by open questions, most women explained what they knew and thought about the operation itself and about past excision ceremonies. One woman reportedly expressed her reservations with regards to the illegal context of FGM in Burkina Faso, while several more did not respond to the questions for reasons they did not disclose. Discussions with the four interviewers provided further information on practices at the provincial capital.

Prevalence of FGM

All respondents stated that their own children, except for a few very young ones (see below), had been excised. They also mentioned that all adults in their village or "quartier" with no exception (males and females) were "excised". Many women were reluctant, however, to discuss or unable to recall their own operation. They simply indicated that "they themselves had of course been excised, too, when they were young". Two years before the survey, Cowley (UNSO 1991) had examined 20 women from various parts of the department whilst training birth attendants. All women had been mutilated. At the regional hospital, one of the authors (J.Wacker) found that the majority of Fulani speaking women giving birth (mostly Fulani and Rimaibe, but also Bellas and Haussas) had been excised. No exact statistics were kept. The four interviewers confirmed that, in contrast to the (surveyed) villages (in Yagha) where female-excision was universal, some parents in town had stopped excising their children.

Age at operation
Most Fulani and Rimaibe women had their daughters excised before the age of 2, with those arguing from a religious point of view tending to have it done earlier, at a few months or even weeks. In contrast, the Gurmance women had their daughters excised between the ages of 2 and 5.

> *Interviewer L. Among the Gurmance in this area, excision is universally practised. Nowadays excisions are carried out at the age of 2 to 4 years, individually and without any ceremonies. In former times, they were done at the age of 12 to 14, just before marriage. All the girls of the same paternal ligneage were gathered for one or two weeks. Sexual relationships were forbidden before excision.*

Excisers
When asked who had carried out the operations, 39 out of the 70 women responded by referring to the ethnicity of the excising woman ('exciseuse' in French). Most Rimaibe women, all Mossis and a few Gurmances had their daughters excised by a Rimaibe, whereas three others mentioned that is had been a Haussa or Bella woman. Most Gurmance women in the multi-ethnic village in the southeast of the department stated that their daughters had been excised by a Fulani. The few Fulanis that responded also indicated that a Fulani woman had carried out the operation. Some women pointed out that their (Rimaibe, Haussa or Bella) excisers had inherited their occupation from their mothers and grandmothers. Other excisers were reported to have acquired the skills from peers. As for the circumcision of boys, several women mentioned that itinerary old men, Fulani or a Bella, had circumcised their sons or that they were expected to perform the operation during their next round. The following account by one of the interviewers confirms the presence of specialist circumciser (and 'exciseuses') at the provincial capital Dori.

> *Interviewer F: Circumciser is an inherited profession here in Dori, but there are also people who learn how do circumcise on their own initiative or for curiosity. Foreigners from Niger and Nigeria perform the circumcision of our boys. One or two hospital nurses also carry out the operations, at double the price. Traditionally, circumcisers have a small knife (called pembourki in Fulfulde), which is exclusively used for the operations. Excision is similar to the circumcision of boys in that there is a special knife, too. (Except for the nurses mentioned above), there are currently only two men in Dori that perform circumcisions, both of them foreigners, and only one woman to excise girls. She is from the neighbouring province of Oudalan, more precisely from a village called Saonga. The other women that knew how to do excisions have died. But there are some Rimaibes living in the villages around Dori that can perform excisions. Many women from Dori town are known to have taken their daughters there.*

In Yagha villages, an about equal number of excisions take place in the village where the young girl and her family reside and in a neighbouring village, with women from between two to four neighbouring villages calling upon the same 'exciseuse'. One woman asserted that "there could never be a lack of an exciseuse in a village". The interviewer interpreted this to say that excisions were imperative, regardless of the presence or absence of a trained or skilled person in a particular village. Excisions are carried out at the excisee's or the exciser's home. None of the women in the sample reported that temporary huts would be built or used specifically for the occasion. Boys' initiation (circumcision) camps reportedly continue to operate in some of the Gurmance villages and sub-villages.

The remuneration for the operation at the time of the survey reportedly varied between 100 CFA, "100 CFA plus millet", 200 or 250 CFA in the Yagha to 500 CFA in (not surveyed) villages around Dori. A (male) circumcision performed by a nurse in Dori town cost 1000 CFA.

The operation
The questionnaire did not include any questions on the operation itself and its medical complications, but several women elaborated on these issues spontaneously. There was little variation in what they

reported. Excisions are usually carried out during the cold dry season, when there is less work in the fields (and the mothers can therefore look after the girls) and when the wounds tend to heal better. Before the actual cutting, the exciseuse speaks some Koranic verses, which are believed to facilitate the healing process. The operation is usually carried out with a razor blade. Severe bleeding occasionally occurs, mentioned by two of the interviewed women, one of them an exciseuse herself. (None of the the women elaborated on measures to stop such bleeding). A black powder made of medicinal plants (wansame) may be applied in order to prevent infection. After the operation, the exciseuse regularly washes the wound with a tepid herbal tea/infusion (gawudi until it heals. Members of all ethnic groups referred to this plant. The wound usually heals within one or two, occasionally within three or four weeks.

Type of FGM.
Cowley, whilst training traditional birth attendants in the region, had found various degrees of mutilation (COWLEY 1992). Either the clitoris had been removed or the clitoris (or part of it) and the labia minora. Similarly at the provincial hospital, where one of the co-authors (J.Wacker) had found various degrees of mutilations, but neither infibulations, which involve suturing, nor serious accidental cicatrization or narrowing of the vaginal introitus, nor indeed any obvious consequences in terms of prolonged labour or increased need for caesarean section. Only very few women were treated at for acute consequences of FGM, such as haemorrhage or infection.

Past practices
Knowledge of and willingness to recall and explain past and abandoned rituals and ceremonies considerably varied among the interviewed women. About half provided details of such ceremonies in their villages, while the others limited themselves to stating that such practices had been abandoned and/or that they did not know anything about them. Fulani and Rimaibe women admitting to the existence of excision ceremonies in the past, stressed that such practices had been abandoned long ago, well before their time, and even before that of their mothers. They claimed that little they knew was due to their mothers' or other older relatives' tradition. One 44 old Rimaibe suggested that the abolition of group excisions dated back about 40 years ago. Another Rimaibe, 40 year old, remembered to be excised together with her mates at the age of 8.
> *Djénéba M. 40: Many years ago, during our time, excisions were done in groups. 6 or 8 of us were gathered in one hut. Every morning an old women would come to give us water and food. We all slept on the same mat. Three weeks later each of us joint our mothers.*

Reports by Gurmance women were very similar in content, but generally more detailed. However, the age at which groups of girls used to be excised, differed. While the Rimaibes mentioned the age of 6 to 9, several Gurmance women remembered that excisions had been carried out among 8-14 year old girls.

The following common elements recurred in virtually all reports. Groups of 6 to 10 girls of the same age would be gathered and taken to a special place or a hut outside the village. Relatives would bring food to the camp, but were not allowed to visit the girls. On the day of excision, for an animal was slaughtered for each girl. After the excision, two old women from the village would look after them until the wounds healed. On the day of their return into the village, the girls would wear a special uniform, and led by the old woman, pass from door to door to collect some cash or kind (millet). A feast involving eating, drinking, singing and dancing would then be held in honour of the newly excised, in which the whole village participated. From this moment on the girls were considered women. They could start attending prayers and/or get married.

Only a handful of women explicitly referred to excision as a time of instruction and preparation for adult life and transition from adolescence to full membership in society. They mentioned that the newly excised received advice concerning marriage and married life during their seclusion in the excision camp and the new role the girl would be able to assume thereafter. "Once the excision (ceremony) was over, it was the wedding day they awaited", one woman stated. One Rimaibe woman stressed the importance of the excisees' dancing and singing on the final day of the excision ceremony. The rest of the village would wish them success for their future homes and families. Muslim women in general did not refer l-13/3/ââ to the girls' newly acquired marriageability, but to the fact that they were now clean and could take part in the prayers. For them, the new clothes worn on the day of excision symbolised the newly acquired state of cleanliness or purity.

Reasons for abandoning excision ceremonies
Few women gave reasons why group excisions and ceremonies had been abandoned. For muslim women the main reason appeared to lie in their religion, in the need for girls, even at young age, "to be clean" and to be able to attend prayers. A delegate (political leader) of a Rimaibe village who had been helping with the study, confirmed this:

> Abderrhaman A. Excision ceremonies have been abandoned in the villages in this area, mainly for religious reasons. Nowadays people here pray a lot, much more than in former times. They used to be animists. Our religion demands that our children pray (attend prayers). If a child is not circumcised (excised), he/she is not allowed to do so.

For the animist Gurmances the abandoning of excisions ceremonies had more do with the fact that people had learnt about excisions being forbidden and with the need to hide the practice.

Male circumcision was not included in the questionnaire, but was frequently brought up by the interviewees themselves. The circumcision of groups of 7-9 year old boys persists in some villages in central Yagha. Little was reported about ceremonies, except for the boys' return from the camp during which they would collect money and chase chicken and other animals, as was reported for the girls.

> Fatima B. Circumcison ceremonies take place in our village. Each year the boys of a certain age are gathered, and their circumcision takes place in the bush, in a hut built by the feticheurs (gurmances).

Reasons for present-day excision
53 out of the 70 women interviewed answered this question. The responses can be divided into three main groups, those referring to islamic faith and to health reasons, and statements concerning excision as a custom or tradition without any specific belief contents. Almost half of the respondents gave two or more explanations for why they thought excision was imperative. Table 3 summarises their answers.

By far the most common reason stated was the need to prevent (or cure) a disease of the genital organs called bourouwel, which was believed to be caused by "worms" of the clitoris (and the prepuce in boys). It was described as causing localized symptoms including the swelling or itching of the genitalia, small wounds and discharge. "Illnesses of sexual organs are very common among our young children" was a frequent response. Some women stressed the general symptoms of bourowel rather than its cause, the genital affection. Due to the worms, the girls were believed to be permanently ill, or fall frequently sick from diarrhoea, high temperature or general malaise. They might also suffer from abdominal pain as a result of bourouwel . The illness was considered life threatening. "If a child ends up passing blood, people will say it is bourouwel ; and if the diarrhoea has already exhausted the child, he/she will die", one woman reported. There was no obvious difference between Fulfulde or Gurmancema speakers. Gurmances, too, believed that little girls often suffer from disease of the sexual organs, which excision would cure. The Gurmancema word used, jembiyiani, translated into "sore clitoris" or "sores of the clitoris" (SWANSON 1985).

When asked as whether the worms were visible during excision, the only exciseuse interviewed, a 48 old Rimaibe, justified her belief in bourouwel as follows:

> Aissatou: Immediately after incision one can see pus, white tissue, coming out of the wound. Others bleed a lot. So that's why I can somehow say it is the worms (that cause bourouwel

Most interviewed women had no clear idea of how the affection was acquired. For some, young children just "have worms" around the clitoris, and its removal of the clitoris (assumingly together with the worms) would cure them. For others, excision constituted a preventive measure. A girl would be at risk of the worms entering her genital organs, as long as she was not excised. Independently of bourouwel, two Gurmance and Rimaibe women expressed their view that being excised facilitated birth-giving.

The second most frequent set of answers referred to religion. Either islamic teaching was believed to demand excision or the severe consequences in an islamic society such as the Yagha of not being excised were elicited, or both. Religious reasons were frequently combined with the motivation to reduce the girls and women's sexual desire. Excision was believed to prevent them from being sexually too active or from looking for men. Those who referred to the Koran as demanding excision, more often associated female excision with male circumcision than those who did not. "Our religion demands that everybody, boy or girl, be circumcised", these women said. Examples of the consequences women would suffer if they were not excised included the impossibility to get married, the prohibition to attend prayers and that to participate in work in public. A substantial minority of women did not seem to feel strongly about either belief or argument. Even when prompted by the interviewers, did they not know why girls were or should be excised, or could provide no reason other than that excision was a long-standing custom. Others referred to excision as imperative merely because of the severe sanctions that would be inflicted on a woman that was not excised, linking it to existing norms rather than specific religious beliefs they held themselves.

> *Interviewer: Why do you think girls are (should be) being excised?Kadidja B: Because it's our custom to do so. We already found this custom established when we were born. Moreover, people say that girls would be sickly all the time if they were not excised. And the muslims don't accept it (if someone is not excised). Such a person would not be allowed to take part in the daily work. They would not even allow her to fetch water for them.*

Most women mentioned either health reasons (bourouwel) or religion. Kadidja's response which included both was therefore untypical in this respect. Only one woman attempted to bridge the health and the religious beliefs by describing the worms as proof that the girls were not clean/pure. Excision, she pointed out, would purify them and therefore was a prerequisite for attending prayers. Several women made an explicate difference between boys' circumcision as being imperative for muslims and the reasons for which excision of girls was practised (to prevent bourouwel).

For most Gurmances and Mossis and some Rimaibes bourouwel was the primary reason for excision - with some of them qualifying their responses with statements such as "that's what people say" or "really, I do not know why this practice exists". For a large proportion of Rimaibes and Fulanis, and some Mossis and Gurmances (mostly muslims of the hamallist brand), the main reason was religion. Those who felt most strongly about the sanctions which would be imposed on those who were not excised, all belonged to wahabiya (sunnit) fundamentalist families.

The reasons for excision proved to be of particular interest for the interviewers, three of them having young daughters themselves. They reported that in contrast to the villages surveyed, at the provincial capital Dori, the religious type of argument was predominant and had largely superseded the belief into bourouwel . One of them was surprised by the Yagha women's responses and did not seem to know about bourouwel . The others suggested that bourouwel in the Yagha was identical with guldjis (=worms) in Dori. Lively debates resulted from reports on a young Dori woman who having being ridiculed by her mates had attempted to excise herself, and had suffered severe injuries. On the other hand, some men in town were reported to prefer sexual relations with unexcised women, as intercourse was experienced as more pleasurable. The interviewers had also learnt about accounts that unexcised women had easier deliveries, in contrast to traditionally held beliefs.

Discussion
Methodological lessons
The belt of countries across the African continent where FGM is practised strikingly corresponds with the pattern of countries with high infant mortality rates, resulting from very low levels of female education and poor infrastructure, among other factors (DORKENOO 1992). The encountered methodological and logistical difficulties, unexperienced local interviewers, reserved respondents, and hard-to-access terrain, were therefore hardly surprising, as they are inherent to virtually all studies of FGM. In the Yagha, one of the World's least developed areas, the closest researchers had come to the study of FGM, was a questionnaire sent to the maternity at the provincial hospital in Dori and the collection of anthropological data in one nearby village as part of a national study of folk-demography in the late 1970 (INSTITUT NATIONAL DE LA STATISTIQUE ET DE LA DEMOGRAPHIE 1979).

In this study, most of the logistical constraints were overcome by combining the FGM study with a larger health survey, for which transport arrangements had already been made and interviewers from the provincial capital had been identified. The provincial capital Dori has to a large extent kept its essentially rural character, so that the interviewers, although better educated than most women in the area, and proficient in French, experienced little social distance from the interviewed women. The fact that the Fulfulde dialect spoken in the Yagha noticeably differs from that in Dori also proved to be an advantage. Realizing that their visitors were not from the area, the interviewed women felt at no risk with regards to breaches of confidentiality. During the interviewers' training two key principles of the study of FGM had been stressed: listening to and respecting the community's own perception before embarking on sensitization activities and exercising discretion and tact in referring to locally held beliefs (WHO 1994). These principles were largely abided by, although on a few occasions the interviewers experienced difficulties in containing their astonishment and excitement with regards to the beliefs expressed by the women they were interviewing. Nevertheless, the study design had severe limitations, including the small size and uncertain representativeness of the sample, the inability to discuss and to explore in depth the women's beliefs and their rationale for excision, and inevitable losses from imperfect translation. The last two constraints could have been overcome, if it had been possible to employ a trained anthropologist, to use a geographically more focused qualitative design and to extend the study over a period longer than one cold season. Under the given circumstances, however, and with the given objectives, a different design would most likely have had no advantage. Present-day excision practices, characterised by the loss of initiation ceremonies, and by operations performed at low age, performed by Rimaibes or persons belonging to minority groups, cannot be understood without referring to Islam, and to a lesser degree, to modernisation. Where ages at excision become younger, the practice is having less and less to do with its original meaning of initiation (DORKENOO 1992).

In the Yagha, the youngest age at which the interviewed women still associated excision with ceremonies was 6-8 years. Most girls are now excised well before that age. The growing influence of Islam has undoubtedly been the main reason for the decline in age at excision. It works through various societal mechanisms, including the requirement to be "pure" before given permission to attend prayers, the increasing association of female excision with male circumcision and, possibly, among those Gurmances converted to islam, through increasingly earlier marriage. Economic reasons should not be ruled out, however, although none of the women interviewed mentioned them. Prolonged economic crises (and an increasing number of live children per family) have severely affected parents' capacity to make the economic transfers traditionally associated with the passage from adolescence into adulthood. Many young men are now forced to engage in seasonal labour in the cities and neighbouring countries to cover the costs for bridewealth and marriage, previously the responsibility of parents. Pre-inheritance has largely disappeared. In a similar context of economic constraints and excision in Sierra Leone, KHOSO-THOMAS (1987) pointed out: "A younger girl is more easily controlled and cannot refuse; neither can she demand expensive gifts and jewelry from her parents" (KOSO-THOMAS 1987). Where ideology and religion dominate the discourse, such reasons might not easily be reported.

Among the Gurmances (male circumcision and) female excision used to be either equivalent to or associated with a rite of initiation into adulthood in the past. The finding that it was practised at puberty and just before marriage until one or two generations ago, the persistence of excisions ceremonies until very recently in the neighbouring Gurma (ASSAAD 1980) and the fertility rites reported by anthropologist Cartry during the 1960 and 1970s (GEIS-TRONICH 1991), all suggest its likely role as a passage rite. Most present-day Gurmance clans still practice excision (CARTRY 1968), although no longer at puberty. Among the Yagha Gurmances studied FGM is still universal. The age at which Gurmance girls are now excised, two to five years, is consistent with so-called "black" excision, black because it does not involve purification ceremonies (INSTITUT NATIONAL DE LA STATISTIQUE ET DE LA DEMOGRAPHIE 1979). "White" excisions of 12-15 year old girls just before marriage, characterised by ceremonies that involve the wearing of belts of white cowries and fibres to symbolize purity, appear to have been abandoned, although in the villages surveyed memories of group excisions and initiations are still fresh among study participants. Reports from adjacent areas in the (southern) Gurma show that black excision, performed hidden from neighbours and friends, out of fear to be considered backwards or old-fashioned, has become the norm there, too (GEIS-TRONICH 1991). Although falling short of stopping excision, the national publicity campaigns may therefore have had at least partial success in that awareness of alternative norms was introduced, even in such remote rural areas as the Yagha. On the other hand, as with the Fulanis, economic constraints might well have contributed to the disappearance of excision ceremonies and fertility rites, without necessarily eroding the underlying rationale. The costs for the initiation used to be enormous, including expenses for sacrificed animals and cowries, as well as the remuneration of the exciseuse (INSTITUT NATIONAL DE LA STATISTIQUE ET DE LA DEMOGRAPHIE 1979). In the stratified societies of West Africa such as the Fulanis, endogamic castes exist, specialised occupational groups including blacksmiths, leatherworkers and bards. They form intermediate societal layers between the aristocracy and the (ex-) slaves (TAMARI 1991). DE COUTOULY (1923) gives evidence that the wives of blacksmiths might have performed excisions among the Yagha Fulanis in the past. "The Fulanis of the Cercle de Dori like those of the Futa Djallon, practice the circumcision of boys and the excision of girls. These two operations are carried out by members of the blacksmith caste: men for boys and women for the girls" (DE COUTOULY 1923). Today's descendants of bards and blacksmith castes are few in the Yagha, with their residence limited to a few villages around Sebba town (IDRISSA 1992), and excisions among the Fulanis and Rimaibes are nowadays performed by Rimaibes. As for those Gurmances that reported to have had their daughters excised by a Fulani exciser, the most plausible explanation is that, in reality, these were Rimaibes, too. Many Gurmances in that part of the Yagha do not distinguish between the various Fulfulde speaking groups, and Fulani women are unlikely to do this kind of work. Ironically, many Fulanis in the area now speak of Rimaibes as Fulanis, while Rimaibes who wish to stress their difference of descent call themselves as such. In reality, the vast majority of excisions is therefore probably nowadays performed by Rimaibes. Nevertheless in Dori, and to lesser extent in the Yagha as well, a pattern seems to be developing by which excision is performed by "foreigners", or the occupation is not passed on to the next generation at all.

The meaning of FGM
For some of the women interviewed, especially those not or only superficially islamised, the meaning of excision has largely been reduced to a vague notion or requirement of their tradition or religion. The specific contents and educational function these customs might have had in the past, seem to have been lost, without any new and coherent belief system replacing them. In Gurmance mythology, clitoridectomy was performed upon the belief that unless the clitoris, seen to resemble and called a "small penis", jembili, was removed, the young woman would not be able to bear children. Swanson (SWANSON 1985) reported that "with the major trend away from excision today, it is now rationalized by many that an unexcised woman will at least have a harder time in labour". To the young man interviewed by this author, whom he thought to represent the general opinion of the young in that area, even such thinking seemed foolish (SWANSON 1985). Only two Yagha women mentioned that excision was being practised "to facilitate childbirth", but the inability of women to report such rites might not necessarily mean their inexistence in nearby areas or their complete lack of significance. Knowledge of the rites or their meaning may only be possessed by a few older men, or the rites themselves might continue in a much simplified or modified form, while still representing the same collective worldview (SWANSON 1985). To what extent bourouwel, the worm disease, represents an adaptation or reinterpretation of this traditional belief can only be speculated. Bourouwel was mentioned by all ethnic groups in the study area, and a similar belief may exist among the Mossis as well (DORKENOO 1992, BARRY 1991). But bourouwel is also intriguingly similar to a myth found among women in the Western Sudan: In El Dareer's description of FGM in Sudan figures a midwife who described the main characteristic of El Duda, the worm, as discharge, causing the vulva to stick together. Children are believed to acquire it while crawling on the ground, while others were thought to have been born with it. Relatives often notice the child ailing or not gaining weight. The midwife claimed to see a white worm jump out each time she held and cut the clitoris and vulva. Releasing the worm assumingly cured the complaints (EPELBOIN & EPELBOIN 1979). Could these beliefs be of the same origine? Hosken, trying to explain why barbers perform excisions among the Haussas of Nigeria, pointed to Egypt as the only other place where barbers had been recorded to do the operating and to the fact that many devout muslims take part in the pilgrimage to Mecca and are thus familiar with the practices of the middle east (DAREER 1982a). The belief in the worm disease in the Yagha might have been imported in a similar way. Oddly however, the most islamised women in the Yagha were not concerned.

One of the interviewers suggested another explanation for bourouwel. The belief could be indigenous, originating from times when excision was still a rite of initiation into adulthood. As part of this function, excision could have been believed to protect against real STDs, currently reportedly very common in the study area. With the age at excision decreasing, bourouwel would then have been re-interpreted as being protective against diseases common during childhood such as diarrhoea. Unfortunately, this theory could not be substantiated. It is uncertain as whether STDs such as syphilis or gonorrhoea were already prevalent in Africa before and during the early stages of colonization (BARTON 1991).

For many muslim (boys and) girls, excision has attained a new meaning of "initiation", that into the community of believers. Although there is no clear reference to it in the Koran and in confirmed traditions of the prophet (SAHIB 1984), FGM is now widely associated with Islamic teaching in the Yagha.

In many villages, not being excised means exclusion from essential functions and roles in family and community. The benefits gained by the recipient girl and her parents include the ability to socialise with peers (e.g. when fetching water) and to get engaged and married. Not surprisingly, such considerations were most often quoted by women from 'fundamentalist' families and villages. Few women, however, seemed to have internalised the religious rationale for excision. The statement of the nominally muslim woman quoted above is only the most explicit expression of this fact. Some women even explained that their religion only demanded the circumcision of boys, and that excision was being practised to avoid bourouwel or for no known reason at all. If not for the severe sanctions they risked to suffer, these women would probably require little persuasion to abandon the practice. At the provincial capital excision has started to be abandoned, despite the steadily increasing influence of islam, and despite the almost complete lack of educational interventions.

Policy implications
In agreement with other authors who have written about FGM in West Africa (THIAM 1978), we feel, that they are probably only two groups of people in the Yagha who categorically wish these mutilations to continue: certain muslim 'fundamentalists' (wahabiya sunnits) and those who absolutely hold to the continuation of FGM in the name of ancestral values (THIAM 1978). The two influences may currently still be of similar importance in the Yagha, but they show opposite trends. While traditional animist beliefs and, to some degree, the old collective structures that have sustained excision among the Gurmances, are fading, the influence of the wahabiya version of Islam continuous to grow.

In Gurmance villages, a combination of basic maternity and child health service provision and education on reproductive and child health might therefore well result in the rapid further erosion of the practice within a decade or two. Information and education activities should perhaps initially be targeted at the most modern sectors of Gurmance society, such as young men that have lived in urban areas or neighbouring countries. However, in ethnically mixed villages and perhaps even in those still dominated by traditional animist beliefs, increasing assimilation ("Fulanisation") might slow down this process in the medium term, as islamic teaching creates new pressures to continue the practice.In Fulani/Rimaibe villages the strengthening of health services and the provision of basic health information, will not suffice to make the population abandon FGM, as the poor uptake of already existing health education services in the area shows, but such measures will still be important. Detailed questions on complications of the operations had been deliberately omitted during the interviews, but the harmfulness of FGM will inevitably have to be addressed when discussing FGM with the concerned women. This should be done in an objective manner which avoids blaming either the parents or the excisers. In contrast to reports from the national capital Ouagadougou in the early 1980s (HOSKEN 1982b), intentional infibulation and unintentional narrowing of the vagina appear to be uncommon or non-existent in the study area. This will have to be further investigated. The risk of HIV-transmission through the use of unsterile instruments can also be assumed to be very small, as group excisions have been abandoned and renewable razor blades are now being used. Other acute and long-term consequences, however, including the ever prevalent psychological consequences of the operations undoubtedly occur. Unlike in Sierra Leone, where excisers are experienced, trained health personnel that can successfully deal with complications such as bleeding, fainting attacks and infections and who refer complications beyond their competence to the next hospital (KOSO-THOMAS 1987), excisers in the Yagha have acquired their knowledge and skills entirely from mothers and peers. Few, if any complications are referred and treated at the hospital, be it for lack of access or because of shame and fear of stigmatization. The effectiveness of the herbs used to stop infections and to clean the wounds could be investigated. There was little secrecy about the operations during the interviews, and the names of the exciseuses were freely mentioned, giving rise to the opportunity to reach this important group with specifically designed education and training interventions. The interviews showed that each exciser served up to four villages or sub-villages. Even if some of the interviewed women had preferred practitioners in neighbouring villages for reasons other than the unavailability of an 'exciseuse' in their home village, would the total number of excisers in the Yagha hardly exceed 40. These practitioners might have a vested interest in that the operations continue. Unless they are wives of imams or otherwise wish FGM to continue for ideological reasons, however, they might well accept alternative sources of income. In most Yagha villages, no traditional birth attendants exist (DEHNE et.al. 1995). Most women give birth assisted by an older female relative or an old woman living in the same compound, or completely unattended (Thiam 1978). The re-training of 'exciseuses' as village midwives would therefore achieve a double objective. They could better use their knives or razors to hygienically cut the umbilical cord. At the same time, a series of messages and interventions should be designed to start creating alternative norms. Young people from the provincial capital, especially those who have not had their daughters excised, could open the discussion in the villages, where the subject has so far been a taboo, and could build on the experience made by the interviewers. To identify and involve religious leaders will also be crucial, to start dispelling misconceptions about the religious origin of FGM. For example, so-called "muslim fundamentalists" in Egypt hold that FGM is not an Islamic practice, and try to enforce this view and promote eradication. In any case, this study among a small sample of women in the Yagha, should only be seen as the first step towards a more participatory assessment of FGM in the area. Ultimately, the process of abandoning FGM will have to be undertaken by the concerned women themselves, although they might continue to benefit from national and international technical support, advocacy and finance (SWANSON 1985).

Conclusion

With basic training and close supervision, and by concentrating only on women that had proven to be cooperative and communicative in an on-going health survey, "peer interviewers" proved capable to collect information on a sensitive subject such as FGM. The objective to obtain a comprehensive view of current and past FGM practices and of the ever evolving societal structures and belief systems in this particular geographical and administrative area was at least partially achieved. Future educational interventions will be able to build on the friendly human relations formed during the study.Although an ancient and deep-rooted practice, FGM is far from inert to cultural and socioeconomic change. In the study area, during the course of perhaps less than half a century, initiation rites have been abandoned and excision as an inherited profession performed by persons of caste partially replaced by an acquired occupation. The age at excision has significantly dropped and its importance and meaning profoundly changed under the parallel onslaught of progressing and deepening islamisation and modernisation. Despite converging production patterns and increasing cultural assimilation of Gurmances and minority groups to the dominant Fulanis/Rimaibes customs and norms, differences in the age at excision and in the motivation for the operation remain distinguishable. Any programme to convince the population to abandon FGM will have to take these differences into account. Basic maternity and child health services should be provided and combined with educational interventions targeting the concerned women, their husbands, excisers and religious and community leaders.

References

ANONYMOUS, 1991. *Monographie du Yagha (undated), Préfeture du Département de Sebba,* transcribed in 1991 by: Projet de Développement Intégré de ma Province du Séno, UNSO

ASSAAD, M.B. 1980. *Female Circumcision in Egypt: Current Research and Social Implications.* WHO/EMRO Technical Publication: Seminar on Traditional Practice Affecting the Health of Women and Children in Africa, 229, Alexandria

Ba, A.H. and DIETERLEN, G. 1961. *Koumen: Texte initiatique des pasteurs peul,* Paris-The Hague: Mouton

BARRY, K. 1991. *Introduction à l'Histoire de Yagha,* Report perpared for: Projet de développement Intégré de la Province du Séno, UNSO, unpublished

BARTON, T.G. 1991. *Sexuality and Health,* An Annotated Bibliography, AMREF, Nairobi

BASHER, T.A. 1979. *Psychological Aspects of Female Circumcision,* Report on a Seminar in Khartoum. WHO/EMRO Technical Publication, 2, 71-105

BOURREL, P. 1983 Complications des coutumes et mutilations rituelles chez l'Africain, *Contraception, Fertilité, Sexualité,* Dec; 11(12): 1351-8

BOVIN, M. and MANGER, L. 1989. *Adaptive strategies in African arid lands,* Proceedings from a Seminar at the Scandinavian Institute of African Studies, Uppsala, Sweden, April

CARBALLO, M. 1988. AIDS and female circumcision, *Inter-African Committee on Traditional Practices Affecting the Health of Women and Children Newsletter,* Mar (5):8

CARTRY, M. 1968. La Calebasse de l'excision en Pays Gourmantché, *Journal de la Societé des Africanistes,* XXXVIII, 2:189-225

CHI-BONNARDEL, R. 1965. *The Atlas of Africa,* Editions Jeune Afrique, p127

COMITÉ PROVINCIAL DE LUTTE CONTRE LA PRATIQUE DE L'EXCISION, 1992. *Province du Séno, Dori,* Programme d'Activités

COWLEY, J. 1992. *Save the Children Fund,* BP 615 Ouagadougou, Burkina Faso, in a letter to the first author

DE COUTOULY, F. 1923. Les populations du Cercle de Dori, *Bulletin du Comité d'Etudes Historiques et Scientifiques de l'Afrique Occidentale Francaise,* p 269-301

DEHNE, K.L., WACKER, J. and COWLEY, J. 1995. Training birth attendants in the sahel, *World Health Forum,* Vol. 16, No.4, 1995

DELAFOSSE, M. 1931. *The Negroes of Africa*, Associated Publishers, Washington,

DELUZ, A. 1987. Social and symbolic values of feminine kne initiation among the Guro of the Ivory Coast, in: PARKIN D, NYAMWAYA D (eds), *Transformation of African Marriage*, Manchester University Press

DIALLO, T. 1971. *Origine et migration des peuls avant le XIXe siècle*, Annales de la Faculté des Lettres et des Sciences Humaines, Universtité de Dakar, No 1-3, pp. 123-193

DIALLO, K. 1984. *Excision or Female Circumcision: Mali's Experience*, WHO/EMRO Technical publication: seminar on Trdational Practices Affecting the Health of Women and Children in Africa, 96. Senegal

DIRIE, M.A, and LINDMARK, G. 1991. Female circumcision on Somalia and women's motives, *Acta Obstetrica et Gynecologica Scandinavia*, 70(7-8: 581-5)

DORKENOO, E. and ELWORTHY, S. 1992. *Female Genital Mutilations: proposals for change. The Minority Rights Group*, 379/381 Brixton Road, London SW9 7DE UK

DUPIRE, M. 1970. *Organisation sociale des peul, Etude d'ethnographique comparée*, Librairie Plon, Paris

EL DAREER, A. 1982. *A Study on Prevalence and Epidemiology of Female Circumcision to Date*. WHO/EMRO Technical Publication: Seminar on Traditional Practices Affecting The Health of Women and Children in Africa, 312 Alexandria

EL DAREER, A. 1982. *Woman Why Do You Weep?* London: Zed Press

EPELBOIN, S. and EPELBOIN, A. 1979. Special Report: Female Circumcision, *People*, 6(1), 24-29

GEIS-TRONICH, G. 1991. *Materielle Kultur der Gulmance in Burkina Faso*, Studien zur Kulturkunde, Band 98, Franz-Steiner Verlag, Stuttgart

HEDLEY, R. and DORKENOO, E. 1992. *Child Protection and Female Genital Mutilation*, Advice for Health, Education and Social Work Professionals, FORWARD, 38 King Street, London WC2E 8JT

HOSKEN, F.P.M 1978. The epidemiology of Female Genital Mutilation. *Tropical Doctor*, 8, 150-156

HOSKEN, F.P. 1982. *Female Circumcision in the World Today, A Global review*. WHO/EMRO Technical Publication: Seminar on Traditional Practices Affecting the Health of Women and Children in Africa, Alexandria

HOSKEN, F.P. 1982b. *The Hosken Report, Genital and Sexual Mutilation of Females*, Lexington: International Network News.

IDLEH, A., ABDILLAH, R. and DAVID, A. 1984. Traditional practices affecting the health of women and children in DJIBOUTI, in: *Report on a seminar on traditional prcatices affecting the health of women and children in Africa*, organized by the Senegal Ministry of Public Health and NGO Working group on traditional practices affecting the health of women and children Dakar, Senegal; Ministry of Public Health and NGO Working Group on traditional practices affecting the health of women and children, 196-206

IDRISSA, B. 1992, Expose sur les castes dans le departement de Sebba, *Save the Children Fund*, BP 615, Ougadougou, unpublished

INSD, DIRECTION DE LA RECHERCHE DEMOGRAPHIQUE, 1979. *Rapport Final provisoire*, Etude de „Folk-Demography" comme base d'une politique de population en Haute Volta, ORSTOM

INSD, 1990. *Recensement general de la population*, Burkina Faso 1985, Ouagadougou

KIRK-GREEN, A.H.M. 1979. Maudu Laawol Pullako: survival and symbiosis, in: ADAMU M, KIRK-GREENE M (eds), *Pastoralists of the West African Savanna*, Manchester University Press

KITI No AN VII - 0318/FP/SAN-AS, 18 May, 1990. *Haut Commissariat de Dori*, Province de Dori, 15 April 1992

KOSO-THOMAS, O. 1987. *The Circumcision of Women: A Strategy for Eradication*. London: Zed Press

KOUBA, L. and MUASHER, J. 1985. Female Circumcisison in Africa: An Overview. *African Studies Review*, 28(1), 95-110 (20)

MEISSALLOUX, C. 1975. *Femmes, Greniers et Capitaux*, Paris: Maspero

MONTEIL, V. 1963. Contributions à la sociologie des peul, *Bulletin de l'IFAN*, serie B , 25, p3-4,

MOREAU, R.L. 1964. Les marabouts de Dori, *Archives de sociologie des religions*, 17, pp 113-134,

PIQUEMAL, D. 1993. *Dynamique agraire et approche gestion de terroirs: L'agro-pastoralism du departement de Sebba*, PhD thesis, University of Aix-en Provence

RIESMAN, P. 1974. *Freedom in Fulani Life*, University of Chicago Press

SAHIB, H.A.A. 1984. *Islam's Attitude to Female Circiumcision*. WHO/EMRO Technical Publication: Seminar on Trdational Prcatices Affecting the Health of Women and Children in Africa, 69, Senegal

SANANKOUA, B. 1990. *Un empire peul au XIXe siècle, La Diina du Maasina*, Karthala, 1990

SHANDALL, A. 1967. Circumcision and Infibulation of Females, *Sudanese Medical Journal*, Vol 5, No 4

SWANSON, R.A. 1985, *Gourmantche Ethnoanthropology*, University of America Press

TAMARI, T. 1991. The Development of Caste Systems in West Africa, *Journal of African History*, 32, pp.221-250

TIENDREGEOGON, A. 1982. Female Circumcision in Upper Volta, in: *Traditional practices affecting the health of women and children*, WHO/EMRO, Technical Publication No. 2, Vol 2, Alexandria

THIAM, A. 1978. *La parole aux Négresses*, Editions, Denoel/Gonthier, Paris, 1978 quoted in minority groups, page 28

UNSO, 1991. *Programme Sahel Burkinabe, Situation socio-economique du departement de Sebba*, domument préliminaire 1991, Dori

VERZIN, J.A., 1975. The sequelae of female circumcision, *Tropical Doctor*, Vol.5, p163-169

WHO, 1994, *Division of Family Health, Geneva, Female Genital Mutilation*, 31 July, Working sheet G1: Actions for eradication.

WHO, 1994, *Division of Family Health, Geneva, Female Genital Mutilation*, 31 July, Working sheet G1: Health Consequences.

WHO, 1994, *Division of Family Health, Geneva, Female Genital Mutilation: Prevalence and Distribution*, 31 July

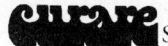

Beschneidung von Mädchen und Frauen -
Über die Schwierigkeit, Traditionen zu verändern
Female Genital Mutilation -
About the Difficulty to Change Traditions

Friederike Schneider

Zusammenfassung: Von der Beschneidung bzw. genitalen Mutilation, die in ihrer extremsten (und sehr häufigen) Form in der fast vollständigen Entfernung der äußeren weiblichen Geschlechtsorgane besteht, sind weltweit über 100 Millionen Frauen betroffen, die meisten davon in Afrika. Die Auswirkungen auf die physische und psychische Gesundheit sind beträchtlich. Trotz des offiziellen Verbots der Praxis durch die Gesetzgeber und langjähriger Aufklärungsarbeit internationaler und ortsansässiger Organisationen hält sich der Brauch hartnäckig; im Zuge der wachsenden internationalen Migration müssen sich auch europäische Länder und die USA zunehmend mit der Problematik auseinandersetzen. In dem Artikel werden die Beweggründe, Rechtfertigungen und Motivationen der Befürworter der Beschneidung im Kontext der Bedeutung von Traditionen für Identitätsbildung und Perpetuierung von Machtstrukturen dargestellt und analysiert. Aus diesen Einsichten ergeben sich wichtige Anhaltspunkte für effektive Strategien zur Realisierung gesellschaftlicher Veränderungen.

Abstract: Over 100 million women worldwide, most of them in Africa, suffer the consequences of female cirumcision, an operation that consists in the removal of part or all of the external female genitalia. The detrimental effects on physical and psychological health can be considerable. Even though the practice is illegal in many African countries, and there have been many years of tireless campaigning by international and local groups, the practice continues. Because of the increasing international migration, many western societies have to find ways of dealing with this problem as the immigrants are taking their traditions with them. The article analyses the reasons, justifications and motivations of the advocates of Female Genital Mutilation within the context of the importance of traditions for cultural identity and the perpetuation of power structures. These insights may indicate effective strategies towards societal changes.

Keywords: Weibliche Beschneidung, Afrika, Tradition, Frauenrechte, Female Genital Mutilation, Circumcision, Africa, Tradition, Women's Rights.

Einleitung

Noch vor 20 Jahren wusste in westlichen Ländern kaum jemand von der Existenz der „weiblichen Beschneidung„, des vor allem in Afrika verbreiteten Brauches der teilweisen oder vollständigen Entfernung des äußeren weiblichen Genitales als kulturelle Praxis. Die Reaktionen der wenigen Personen, die damit in Berührung kamen oder davon hörten, schwankten zwischen ungläubigem Staunen, Entsetzen, Schock, Wut und Trauer; Mary Daly sprach von „unaussprechlichen Greueln„ (DALY 1981:175); die Diskussion um das Thema war, vor allem in feministischen Publikationen, geprägt von einer fast atemlosen Emotionalität (z.B. BRAUN et. al 1979). Inzwischen ist der Diskurs sachlicher geworden; man spricht über das „Unaussprechliche„, und ist übereingekommen, anstatt der irreführenden Bezeichnung „weibliche Beschneidung„ den korrekteren Begriff „Female Genital Mutilation„ (FGM) zu verwenden. Neben den schon seit längerer Zeit aktiven Organisationen, wie *Terres des Femmes*, Fran Hoskens *Women's International Network WIN*, die *Minority Rights Group* und *FORWARD* (Foundation for Women's Health, Research and Development) in Großbritannien und dem *Inter African Committee IAC* gibt es weltweit zusehends mehr Aktivitäten, Symposien, Gruppierungen, Projekte und Vereine, die sich um eine Abschaffung dieses barbarischen Rituals bemühen, zu denen auch die 1996 ins Leben gerufene (I)NTACT (Internationale Aktion gegen die Beschneidung von Mädchen und Frauen) in Deutschland gehört. Nicht zuletzt haben auch Romane, wie Alice Walkers *Possessing the Secret of Joy*, und Filme, wie *Warrior Marks. Female Sexual Mutilation and the Sexual Blinding of Women* von Alice Walker und Pratibha Parmar oder *Fire Eyes* von Soraya Mire dazu beigetragen, die Problematik einem größeren Publikum zugänglich zu machen.

Unglücklicherweise ändert dies kaum etwas an der Situation in Afrika und im Nahen Osten. Entgegen aller Erwartungen und Hoffnungen hält sich der Brauch der genitalen Verstümmelung hartnäckig, und die verfügbaren Zahlen geben keinen Anlass zu Optimismus: Während 1980 die Zahl der beschnittenen Frauen auf 70 Millionen geschätzt wurde (LEVIN 1980:197), waren es 1995 bereits über 127 Millionen (HOSKENS 1995:27).

Die Operation in ihren verschiedenen Formen und Ausprägungen wird in 26 afrikanischen Ländern praktiziert, die sich in einem breiten Streifen parallel zum Äquator ziehen, von Ägypten, Äthiopien, Somalia, Kenia und Tansania im Osten über Kamerun und Nigeria bis zu Senegal und Mauretanien im Westen. Im Sudan, in Somalia und in Ägypten wird die Infibulation, die drastischste Beschneidungsform, an fast allen Mädchen im Alter von vier bis acht Jahren durchgeführt, und es gibt so gut wie kein begleitendes Ritual. In den anderen Ländern herrschen Exzision bzw. Klitoridektomie vor, die auch von Beduinen, koptischen Christen in Ägypten und den christlichen Amhara in Äthiopien praktiziert wird. Außerhalb Afrikas existiert die Beschneidung in Syrien, Jordanien, Süd-Jemen und bei einigen mittel- und südamerikanischen Ethnien, z.B. in Peru und in Mexiko sowie unter islamischen Gruppen in Malaysien und Indonesien.

In Afrika ist neben dem allgemeinen Bevölkerungswachstum die Islamisierung für die Verbreitung des Brauchs verantwortlich, wie Hanny Ligthfoot-Klein es im südlichen und westlichen Sudan beobachten konnte: Die Einheimischen, die die Praxis von den islamischen Einwanderern übernehmen, führen in ihrem Eifer, „modern und hygienisch„ zu sein, die extremste Form der Beschneidung durch; sie nennen das „die Mädchen sauberkratzen„, und lassen nicht einmal ein Stück Haut übrig (LIGHTFOOT-KLEIN 1993:66-67).

Auch in Uganda, wo Frauen traditionell nicht beschnitten wurden, ist die Praxis inzwischen, wiederum von einer islamischen Elite, eingeführt worden. (LIGHTFOOT-KLEIN 1993:68). Dabei besteht die Tendenz zu einem immer jüngeren Beschneidungsalter, manchmal bereits als Säugling, und der Reduzierung von Ritualen parallel zu einer zunehmenden Medikalisierung, d.h. die Operation wird im Krankenhaus durchgeführt. Die einzigen, die der Tortur entgehen, sind körperlich oder geistig Behinderte, die ohnehin keinen Ehemann finden werden, und Kinder von Prostituierten. Diese Personengruppen haben jedoch einen außerordentlich niedrigen sozialen Status, und in islamischen Ländern ist „Sohn einer unbeschnittenen Frau„ die schlimmste Beleidigung.

Die Beharrlichkeit, mit der an der weiblichen Beschneidung festgehalten wird, ist wirklich ein erstaunliches Phänomen. In Gegenden, wo sämtliche anderen Traditionen verschwunden sind, in modernen Metropolen, unter Gebildeten und Analphabeten, Reichen und Armen, unter Fundamentalisten und glühenden Verfechtern der „Modernisierung„ wird die Beschneidung als absolute Notwendigkeit verteidigt. Selbst Migranten in Europa und den USA, die die meisten Sitten und Bräuche ihres Gastlandes übernommen haben und sich mit dessen Werten identifizieren, praktizieren die genitale Mutilation weiter, auch wenn sie wissen, dass sie damit gegen Gesetze verstoßen. Die westlichen Länder, die afrikanische Immigranten aufnehmen, kommen nicht umhin, sich mit der Problematik der weiblichen Beschneidung auseinanderzusetzen, sowohl in medizinischer als auch in rechtlicher und sozialer Beziehung. Davon später mehr.

Zur Phänomenologie der Beschneidung

Die Beschneidung von Frauen und Mädchen muss zunächst im umfassenderen Kontext von Körperveränderungen gesehen und interpretiert werden. Bewusst herbeigeführte Veränderungen am Körper sind wahrscheinlich so alt wie die Menschheit selbst und stellen kulturelle Leistungen dar; weltweit (und historisch) ist dabei die Vielfalt der Eingriffe beträchtlich. Man unterscheidet zwischen reinen Deformationen, zu denen u. a. Tätowierungen, Einschnitte mit künstlich hervorgebrachter dekorativer Narbenbildung, Ausweitung von Lippen (Tellerlippen) und Ohren, künstliche Verlängerung des Halses durch Metallspiralen sowie die Veränderung der Kopfform durch Aufschnallen von Brettchen im Kindesalter gehören, aber auch das früher in China übliche Verkrüppeln der Füße durch Einschnüren und Verengen der Taille durch Korsetts im Europa des 18. Jahrhunderts.

Von der Deformation unterscheidet sich die Mutilation oder Verstümmelung dadurch, dass bei letzterer Körpersubstanz entfernt wird; die Folgen für den Organismus sind meistens, aber nicht immer, gravierender. Beliebt sind Modifikationen an den Zähnen, die von Abfeilen bis Ausschlagen bzw. Herausschneiden (bei Säuglingen) reichen. Andere Verstümmelungen betreffen die Uvula, die aus angeblich medizinischen Indikationen bei Neugeborenen herausgerissen wird; auch Fingerverstümmelungen, d.

h. Abhacken eines oder mehrerer Finger, sind zum Beispiel in Melanesien oder Australien weit verbreitet, oft bei Trauerfällen als äußeres Zeichen des erlittenen Verlustes.

Auch die vielen verschiedenen Operationen an den Geschlechtsteilen fallen unter die Kategorie Mutilation. Am häufigsten ist dabei die Beschneidung der Vorhaut beim Mann, die im Islam und im Judentum aus religiösen Gründen vorgeschrieben ist. Eine besonders drastische Form der männlichen Beschneidung ist die bei einer Reihe von australischen Stämmen praktizierte Subinzision, bei der auf der Penisunterseite die Harnröhre der ganzen Länge nach aufgeschnitten und die Wunde anschließend offengehalten wird, was zu einer Formveränderung führt und funktionale Beeinträchtigungen nach sich zieht; bei einigen südafrikanischen Stämmen wird eine einseitige Hodenextirpation durchgeführt. Die Variationsbreite und der Einfallsreichtum in der chirurgischen Ausformung des menschlichen Körpers ließen van GENNEP schon 1909 feststellen „dass der Körper wie ein simples Stück Holz behandelt wurde, das jeder nach seiner Vorstellung geschnitten und gestaltet hat„ (VAN GENNEP 1981:103-104).

Körperveränderungen werden nicht ohne Grund vorgenommen: Sie haben eine semiotische Dimension, sie stellen kulturelle Ausdrucksformen dar. Oft sind (oder waren) die physischen Modifikationen ein integraler Teil von Übergangsriten; sie markieren den Eintritt in eine neue Lebensphase, und der permanent veränderte Körper ist eine dauerhafte Erinnerung und zugleich eine lebenslange Bestätigung des neu gewonnenen Status, als Erwachsener, Amtsträger etc. Schmucknarben und Tätowierungen haben oft rein dekorative Funktionen, machen damit jedoch - wie Schmuck, der am Körper getragen wird - ihren Besitzer wertvoller und imposanter. „Was Außenstehenden als unheimliche Entstellung vorkommen kann, erscheint in der kulturspezifischen Innenperspektive als kunstvolle Gestaltung des richtigen, des schönen und des ausgezeichneten Menschen„ (STRECK 1989:104). In dem Maße, wie sich die traditionellen Kulturen wandeln, ändern sich auch Ansichten und Praxis von Körperveränderungen: Was früher als schön oder auch nützlich galt, z.B. Gesichtsnarben als Zeichen der Stammeszugehörigkeit, oder Tätowierungen als Statussymbol, gerät in Misskredit, wird als unzeitgemäß und altmodisch empfunden. Dies trifft, wie bereits angedeutet, auf die weibliche Beschneidung nicht zu, woraus sich schließen lässt, dass ihre kulturelle Bedeutung ungebrochen ist, dass die Mitglieder der Gesellschaft die Botschaft, die durch die Praxis der Beschneidung vermittelt wird, verstehen und befürworten. „Was dem menschlichen Fleisch eingeschnitten wird, ist ein Bild der Gesellschaft„ (DOUGLAS 1988:153).

Es gibt verschiedene Formen weiblicher genitaler Beschneidung: die sog. Sunna-Beschneidung, Klitoridektomie, Exzision und Infibulation, die sich letztlich darin unterscheiden, wie viel Körpersubstanz abgeschnitten wird. Bei der echten Sunna-Beschneidung, die irrtümlicherweise auf den Propheten Mohammed zurückgeführt wird, wird die Vorhaut der Klitoris abgetrennt, oft aber auch die Klitorisspitze. Diese Form der Beschneidung ist selten, sie wird als zu mild und daher uneffektiv erachtet. Klitoridektomie und Exzision bestehen im teilweisen oder vollständigen Herausschneiden der Klitoris, der Labia minora und der Labia majora, wobei die Übergänge fließend sind, in Abhängigkeit von der Geschicklichkeit der Operateurin und dem Widerstand des Kindes. Die Infibulation folgt auf die gründliche Exzsion und ist ein operatives Verschließen der Vulva um den Vaginaleingang, wobei die vaginale Öffnung auf ein Minimum reduziert wird, die nur den Abfluß von Urin und Menstruationsblut erlaubt. Die Infibulation wird auch als pharaonische oder sudanesische Beschneidung bezeichnet. Die Operationen finden gewöhnlich ohne Betäubungsmittel statt, unter unhygienischen Bedingungen; als Instrument dienen heute meist Rasierklingen oder kleine Messer. Wenn es nach der Operation zu Komplikationen kommt, ist dies Allahs Wille; nie wird die Ungeschicklichkeit der Hebamme bzw. Operateurin dafür verantwortlich gemacht. In vielen Ländern Afrikas ist die Beschneidung jedoch gesetzlich verboten, so daß die Beteiligten zögern, ärztliche Hilfe in Anspruch zu nehmen und unter Umständen den Tod des Kindes in Kauf nehmen. Die physischen und psychischen Auswirkungen der genitalen Mutilation sind erheblich (siehe BAHIR TIBEB i.d.B.).

Begründungen, Erklärungen, Rationalisierungen
Die zahlreichen Befürworter und Befürworterinnen der Beschneidung haben eine ganze Reihe von Begründungen auf Lager, mit denen sie den Brauch energisch verteidigen; es ist nicht einfach, sich durch das dichte Gewebe aus Überzeugungen, Annahmen, Aberglauben, Mythen, Märchen und Rationalisierungen hindurchzukämpfen, die oft miteinander zusammenhängen, und sich gelegentlich auch widersprechen. Fest steht, dass die Beschneidung dauerhaft im Weltbild der sie praktizierenden Menschen verankert ist, und von ihnen selbst als Teil ihrer kulturellen Identität interpretiert wird. Als einen

Hauptgrund für das Weiterbestehen des Brauches wird mehrheitlich die *Tradition* genannt; so z.B. in der umfangreichen Studie von ASMA EL DAREER im Sudan (1982). Ältere Frauen bzw. Großmütter sind besonders am Erhalt der Praxis interessiert, da sie die gesellschaftliche Rolle der Bewahrerinnen von Traditionen erfüllen; ihr Alter verleiht ihnen einen höheren Status, Autorität und die Möglichkeit, Einfluss auszuüben. Auf diesen Aspekt werde ich später noch näher eingehen.

Im Zusammenhang mit dem traditionellen Wert der Beschneidung wird Jomo KENYATTA gerne und oft zitiert: „Kein richtiger Kikuyu würde ein Mädchen heiraten, das nicht beschnitten ist..."(KENYATTA 1965:127). KENYATTA, selbst ein Kikuyu, der in London bei Malinowski studiert hatte und der erste Präsident des unabhängigen Kenia war, nutzte die Kontroverse um die Beschneidung in Kenia für politische Zwecke aus, indem er die genitale Verstümmelung als einen essentiellen Teil des afrikanischen Stammeslebens und die Basis der Moral deklarierte und sie zum wesentlichen Faktor des nationalen Kampfes um Unabhängigkeit erhob.

Auch in gebildeten Kreisen rechtfertigt die Tradition den Brauch, wie der Kommentar einer afrikanischen Soziologin zeigt: „Es ist ein afrikanischer Brauch...Es ist gewiss kein Gesundheitsproblem und afrikanische Frauen haben wichtigere Probleme„ (Zit. in HOSKEN 1993:147). Auch Personen aus gebildeten Schichten, die theoretisch gegen den Brauch sind, können sich in der Praxis dem sozialen Druck nicht widersetzen und lassen ihre Töchter beschneiden oder gar infibulieren (LIGHTFOOT-KLEIN 1993:27-28). Es gibt einige schriftliche und archäologische Hinweise auf die Existenz der Beschneidung lange vor dem Islam, wobei die ältesten Quellen Ägypten, den Sudan und die Küsten des Roten Meeres betreffen; man kann vermuten, dass die Beschneidung dort ihren Ursprung hatte (FRANKENBERGER 1987). In einigen Ethnien in Westafrika existieren auch Mythen, die den Ursprung der Beschneidung erklären (BECK KARRER 1992:31-34).

Ein weiterer bedeutender Faktor in der Rechtfertigung der Beschneidung ist die *Religionszugehörig- keit,* wobei Moslems, Animisten und Christen dieses Argument gleichermaßen ins Feld führen. Die Beziehung zwischen dem Islam und der genitalen Mutilation ist besonders interessant, und gibt Anlass zu allerhand Kontroversen. Unbestritten ist die Tatsache, dass die Beschneidung sich mit dem Islam ausbreitet (LIGHTFOOT-KLEIN 1993:66), und in vielen Gebieten nur von dem islamischen Anteil der Bevölkerung praktiziert wird. Auch sind es ausschließlich Moslems, die die Infibulation durchführen, z.B. im Sudan, in Somalia und in Ägypten, und die Praxis als religiöse Verordnung verteidigen (GLAUBRECHT 1995:59).

In Wirklichkeit wird die Beschneidung von Frauen im Koran mit keinem Wort erwähnt. Es gibt jedoch Überlieferungen; demnach soll der Prophet zu einer Beschneiderin gesagt haben: „Berühre nur die Oberfläche und schneide nicht zu tief; so wird ihr Gesicht schön werden und ihr Ehemann wird sich freuen„. Eine andere Überlieferung besagt: „Die Beschneidung ist für Männer Pflicht, für Frauen ist sie nur ehrenvoll„ (SCHÄDELI 1992:50). Demnach gibt es also weder eine Vorschrift, noch ein explizites Verbot für die Praxis, und die dem Propheten zugesprochenen Äußerungen sind offen für Interpretationen in alle Richtungen. Fest steht, dass die Beschneidung und ihr - tatsächlicher und gewünschter - Effekt auf Frauen den islamischen Vorstellungen von Moral und Sexualität entgegenkommt; so erklärt sich die reibungslose und dauerhafte Allianz zwischen dem Brauch und der Religion.

Der Einfluss auf die *weibliche Sexualität* ist der offensichtlichste Aspekt der genitalen Mutilation, und das Ziel der Eindämmung oder Unterdrückung sexueller Gefühle wird von den Befürwortern offen zugegeben. Dies basiert auf der Vorstellung, dass der weibliche Sexualtrieb um ein vielfaches stärker als der männliche ist, so stark, dass die Frau ihn nicht kontrollieren kann und er folglich durch soziale Intervention in Schranken gehalten werden muss, da die Frau sonst sexuell einfach unersättlich und zwanghaft promisk wäre. Dies ist für Moslems eine Schreckensvision, und an der Kontrolle der Sexualität ist in islamischen Gesellschaften die ausgeprägte Furcht vor der „fitna„ (eigentlich „Anfechtung„ oder „schöne Frau„), Unordnung oder Chaos; maßgeblich beteiligt. Wenn man den Verlockungen der Sexualität nachgibt, kommt es zu Aufstand, Krise und Anarchie (SAADAWI 1980:121).

Man tut den Frauen und Mädchen also einen Gefallen, indem man sie durch die Beschneidung vor ihrer eigenen Sexualität und ihren zerstörerischen Folgen bewahrt. Eng damit zusammen hängt auch die hohe Wertschätzung der Jungfräulichkeit und das Konzept von Ehre im Islam; Würde und Ehre einer Familie sind aufs engste mit dem sexuellen Verhalten der weiblichen Mitglieder. Die Frauen tragen damit eine immense Verantwortung, denn wenn sie sich etwas zuschulden kommen lassen, oder auch nur den Anschein erwecken, ist die Ehre der Männer ebenfalls vernichtet. Dies rechtfertigt nicht nur die

Absonderung der Frau im Haus und ihre Verschleierung, sondern auch ihre Tötung im Falle illegitimer, d.h. vor- oder außerehelicher sexueller Kontakte.

Die Verknüpfung der genitalen Mutilation mit der Geschlechtsidentität ist einer der Hauptfaktoren, der die Abschaffung des Brauches so schwierig macht. In allen Gesellschaften ist das Geschlecht eine soziale Konstruktion, aber die Kriterien, die die Zugehörigkeit zu dem einen oder anderen Geschlecht ausmachen, können beträchtlich variieren. Nichtsdestoweniger ist die sichere und unanfechtbare Geschlechtsidentität, getragen und gefestigt durch das entsprechende Rollenverhalten, von fundamentaler Bedeutung für die Positionierung des Menschen in der Gesellschaft, für sein Selbstverständnis und sein Selbstwertgefühl. Je traditioneller eine Gesellschaft ist, desto eindeutiger pflegen auch die Rollenzuschreibungen zu sein. Gerade im Islam wird der Unterschied zwischen den Geschlechtern rein physisch durch ihre Segregation betont; männliche und weibliche Sphären bleiben im Idealfall gänzlich getrennt, die Aktivitäten sollten sich nicht überschneiden und nicht geteilt werden, und die Geschlechter sollten in jeder Beziehung deutlich voneinander zu unterscheiden sein. Für eine Frau ist es unerlässlich, wenn sie soziale Anerkennung erreichen will, gemäß der Geschlechtsrolle „ganz Frau„ zu sein; gelingt ihr dies nicht, wird sie verachtet, im schlimmsten Falle verstoßen. Die geschlechtsspezifische Sozialisation verhindert jedoch ein nonkonformes Verhalten von Frauen fast immer erfolgreich.

Die symbolische Kategorie „Frau„ beinhaltet in beschneidenden Ländern sowohl die Mutilation der Genitalien als auch „weibliche„ Verhaltensweisen und Wesensmerkmale in Abgrenzung von „männlichen„. So ist sexuelle Lust ein ausschließlich männliches Privileg; für eine Frau schickt es sich nicht, sich am Geschlechtsakt in irgendeiner Form zu beteiligen; sie muss wie ein „Holzblock„ daliegen und eine „unnatürliche Unbeweglichkeit„ an den Tag legen, um den Regeln des Anstandes zu gehorchen. Eigeninitiative oder das Zeigen von Leidenschaft werden als Scheidungsgrund betrachtet (LIGHTFOOT-KLEIN 113-115). Da mit der Beschneidung (angeblich) die Libido weitgehend zerstört wird, befreit dies die Frau von einer entwürdigenden, unweiblichen Eigenschaft. „Eine unbeschnittene Frau ist wie ein Mann„ (HOSKEN 1995:74), d. h. sie hat keine eindeutige geschlechtliche Identität, sie ist nicht begehrenswert und nicht „gut: „Die Exzision ist wichtig für alle Frauen, damit es keine Verwechslung zwischen den Geschlechtern gibt. Um eine wirkliche Frau zu sein, muss jede Frau beschnitten werden. Glauben Sie mir, ein Mann hat viel mehr Spaß mit einer Frau, die keine Klitoris hat„ (Eine siebenfache Mutter aus Ägypten, zit. in HOSKEN 1995:57).

Neben der felsenfesten Überzeugung, dass Beschneidung und Infibulation der sexuellen Lusterhöhung beim Mann dienen, die eheliche Treue der Frau garantieren, und auch ihren eigenen sexuellen Genuss erhöhen - sie darf nämlich durchaus sexuelle Gefühle haben, so lange diese durch ihren legitimen Ehemann hervorgerufen, gemäßigt und nicht erkennbar sind - gibt es noch einen ganzen Katalog anderer Argumente für die genitale Mutilation und ihre Nützlichkeit. So werden oft ästhetische Gründe angegeben, denn die unbeschnittenen Geschlechtsorgane der Frau werden als abstoßend hässlich, widerwärtig und ekelerregend angesehen, so sehr, dass der Anblick Blindheit verursachen kann (EL DAREER 1982:73). Die Vulva wird mit einem Pferdemaul verglichen (EL DAREER 1982:59). Im Zusammenhang damit stehen auch die Ideen von der inhärenten Unreinheit weiblicher Genitalien, sowohl in physischer als auch symbolischer Beziehung. Man nimmt an, dass die Operation „übelriechenden Ausfluss verhindern und die Geschlechtsorgane sauberhalten„ würde (LIGHTFOOT-KLEIN 1993:18). Im Sudan wird ein unbeschnittenes Mädchen als „nigsa„ (unrein) bezeichnet, und die Beschneidungsprozedur heißt „tahara„ (oder tahur), Reinigung oder Säuberung (HOSKEN 1993:90). Bei den Kikuyu heißt es, dass die Klitoris Schmutz und Krankheiten anzieht, oder einfach stinkt (HOSKEN 1993:176). In weiten Teilen Westafrikas hingegen wird die Klitoris als gefährlich angesehen, weil sie ein Kind bei der Geburt töten würde; außerdem kann sie die Geschlechtsteile des Mannes schädigen und ihn sterilisieren (HOSKEN 1993:40).

Verbreitet ist die Überzeugung, dass die Beschneidung eine gesundheitsfördernde und krankheitsverhindernde Wirkung hat, und Melancholie, Nymphomanie, Irrsinn, Hysterie, Epilepsie und die Neigung zum Schuleschwänzen kurieren kann (LIGHTFOOT-KLEIN 1993:56). Besonders infam scheinen die Thesen, die sich auf die weibliche Fruchtbarkeit und deren Förderung durch die Beschneidung beziehen, denn in ganz Afrika ist die Mutterschaft Hauptfunktion, Sinn und Erfüllung einer Frau. In einigen Ethnien, z.B. bei den Tagouana an der Elfenbeinküste, wird geglaubt, eine unbeschnittene Frau könne überhaupt nicht empfangen; die Klitoris verhindert Menstruation, Empfängnis und Geburt (LIGHTFOOT-KLEIN 1993:56). Die Kikuyu glauben, dass die Beschneidung den „Weg ebnet und den Geburtskanal erweitert für eine gefahrlose Geburt„ (HOSKEN 1993:176). (Nach Schätzungen von Ärzten sind ca. 30 Prozent der Fälle von Unfruchtbarkeit direkt auf die genitalen Mutationen zurückzuführen (LIGHTFOOT-KLEIN 1993:102)). Manche Ideen bezüglich der heilenden und ordnenden Kraft der Beschneidung sind recht originell: „Alle müssen beschnitten werden...es macht sie dicker„ (HOSKEN 1993:140); „Mädchen, die nicht beschnitten sind, verwildern....unbeschnittene Frauen sind vergesslich und zerbrechen Gegenstände, sie haben einen widerlichen Geruch, sie wollen sich scheiden lassen...„ (HOSKEN 1993:151). Oder die Beschneidung verhindert, dass die Gebärmutter herausfällt und dass Würmer die Vagina eindringen (LIGTHFOOT-KLEIN 1993:22). Jenseits aller Rationalisierungen, und der traurigen Wahrheit wohl recht nahe, steht ein Sprichwort aus Kordofan: „Die Frau ist eine „Qirba„ (Ledersack für Wasser), wir nähen sie zu, öffnen und füllen sie, wie es uns gefällt„ (Zit. in BECK-KARRER 1992:27).

Mutterschaft, Macht und Ökonomie

Um die wirklichen Gründe für das Fortbestehen der genitalen Mutilation zu verstehen, ist es notwendig, die soziale Position der Frau in Afrika und eine Reihe von damit in Beziehung stehenden sozio-ökonomischen Faktoren in Betracht zu ziehen. Dabei muss immer bedacht werden, dass Afrika ein riesiges Land ist, mit unzähligen Ethnien, deren ethnische Grenzen sich nicht mit den Ländergrenzen decken. Um einen Überblick über soziale Verhältnisse und Geschlechterrelationen zu erhalten, lassen sich gewisse Verallgemeinerungen nicht vermeiden.

Grundsätzlich kann jedoch festgestellt werden, dass afrikanische Gesellschaften patriarchal strukturiert sind, d.h. hierarchisch geordnet mit Frauen am unteren Ende der Hierarchie. Ihre benachteiligte Position wird damit gerechtfertigt, dass sie physisch, intellektuell und moralisch unterlegen sind, hilflos und schutzbedürftig. Im Islam stellt die Unterordnung der Frau ein religiöses Gebot dar: eine gottgefällige Frau ist ihrem Ehemann untertan, sie ist schweigsam, regungslos, keusch und rein.

Die schlechte soziale Stellung der Frau ermöglicht auch ihre Ausnutzung als Arbeitstier; in fast ganz Afrika leisten die Frauen den Großteil der Arbeit und sind für die Versorgung der Familie verantwortlich. Aber sie dürfen kein Eigentum besitzen, sie sind Eigentum, entweder der Familie des Vaters oder des Ehemannes. Dabei muss bedacht werden, dass in afrikanischen und islamischen Gesellschaften das Individuum an sich bedeutungslos ist; was zählt, ist die Gemeinschaft, und das Wohl des einzelnen wird dem Wohl der Allgemeinheit untergeordnet. Hier kommt die Beschneidung ins Spiel; vor der Beschneidung ist das Mädchen kein vollwertiges Mitglied der Gesellschaft, es ist kaum mehr als ein Gegenstand; erst mit der Beschneidung wird es zu einem Menschen. Die Frau wird im wahrsten Sinne des Wortes „zugerichtet„, damit sie sich - symbolisch - in die Gesellschaft einfügen kann. Die Beschneidung wird zum äußeren Zeichen für die Integration, die die Aufgabe der körperlichen Integrität verlangt; als Gegenleistung dafür wird die soziale Integration gegeben. Viele Frauen sagen daher auch: „Meine Familie hat dies *für* mich getan, nicht mir *an*getan„ (LIGHTFOOT-KLEIN 1993:92). So können die Verteidiger der Beschneidung selbstgerecht und im Brustton der Überzeugung behaupten: „Es ist keine Misshandlung. Es ist ein Akt der Liebe„ (Zit. in LEVIN 1996 b:6).

Patriarchale Verhältnisse sind Abhängigkeits- und Machtverhältnisse; in afrikanischen bzw. islamischen Gesellschaften stellt die Ehe für die meisten Frauen den einzigen Weg zu ökonomischer und sozialer Sicherheit bzw. Versorgung dar, eine Sicherheit, die dauernd bedroht ist durch die Möglichkeit der Verstoßung durch den Ehemann, wenn sie beispielsweise keine Kinder gebären kann. Die Mutterschaft ist die eigentliche Bestimmung der Frau, ihr „Universum„ beschränkt sich auf Sexualität und Familie. Die Beschneidung ermöglicht erst die Heirat, die ihrerseits Bedingung ist für die Mutterschaft, die Manifestation der wertvollsten Eigenschaft einer Frau, ihrer Fruchtbarkeit. Mit der Heirat wird das Mädchen in die Familie des Ehemannes aufgenommen, wo sie zunächst eine Fremde ist und auf der untersten sozialen Stufe steht. Ihre Position verbessert sich erst mit der Geburt eines Kindes, vorzugsweise eines Sohnes; ein Sohn stellt zugleich Existenzberechtigung und Alterssicherung der Frau dar; die Bindung zwischen Müttern und Söhnen ist zeitlebens sehr eng und der starke Einfluss der Mutter auf das Privatleben des Sohnes eine Selbstverständlichkeit. Auch sehr gebildete Mütter respektieren (oder fürchten) ihre Mütter und wagen es nicht, ihnen zu widersprechen (LIGHTFOOT-KLEIN 1993:91).

Je älter die Frau wird, und je mehr Kinder sie geboren hat, um so mehr steigt ihr Ansehen; in ihrer ureigentlichen Sphäre, der Familie, verfügt sie über beträchtliche Macht, die sich auf einen stets anwachsenden Personenkreis erstreckt. Es ist beobachtet worden, dass Großmütter die unerbittlichsten

Befürworterinnen der Beschneidung sind, in ihrer Rolle als „Hüterinnen der Traditionen„ und in ihrer Verantwortung für die Kontinuität der patrilinearen Erbfolge, die „ihre unmittelbare und vorrangige Quelle für Identität und Sicherheit„ (HAYES 1975:624) ist. Die Frauen identifizieren sich vollständig mit den Zielen der patriarchalen Gesellschaft, die in ihren Augen Schutz vor einer feindlichen, gefährlichen Welt bietet und die ihnen das Überleben erst ermöglicht. Davon zutiefst überzeugt, möchten die Frauen verständlicherweise nichts tun (oder unterlassen), was ihre weiblichen Nachkommen um diese existentiellen Sicherheiten bringen könnte. Die Mädchen werden entsprechend sozialisiert, zu Ruhe, Freundlichkeit, Zurückhaltung, als unterlegenes Geschöpf, das keine Forderungen stellt und abhängig ist vom Wohlgefallen der Männer.

Eng mit der Beschneidung verbunden ist ein anderer sozio-ökonomisch relevanter Brauch, der die weibliche Lebenswelt mitbestimmt: die Institution des Brautpreises. Der zukünftige Ehemann zahlt der Familie der Braut eine angemessene Summe - die sich bei infibulierten Frauen unter anderem nach der Größe der verbleibenden Vaginalöffnung richtet. Je kleiner die Öffnung, desto höher kann der Brautpreis angesetzt werden. Eltern sind daher bestrebt, bei der Mutilation der Tochter den gewünschten Effekt zu erreichen, um wenigstens finanziell einen Vorteil aus dem ansonsten nutzlosen Nachwuchs zu schlagen. Sollte sich in der Hochzeitsnacht herausstellen, dass die Braut keine Jungfrau mehr ist, kann sie auf der Stelle heimgeschickt und der Brautpreis zurückverlangt werden, was eine Schande für die Familie darstellt. Auch um dies zu vermeiden, wird das Kind so eng wie möglich zugenäht, da man annimmt, dass dies die beste Garantie für ihre Keuschheit ist und sie vor Vergewaltigungen schützt (was nicht der Fall ist, aber die Folgen einer Vergewaltigung können durch Refibulation unkenntlich gemacht werden). Die Vermittlung von Ehen ist wiederum Frauensache: Die Mütter suchen die Bräute für ihre Söhne aus und stellen sicher, manchmal zusammen mit anderen weiblichen Familienmitgliedern, dass sie den Anforderungen entsprechen und exzisiert bzw. infibuliert sind: „Die Narben der Infibulationsoperation sind ein Siegel, das ein unberührbares, vitales Eigentum der sozialen Gruppe kennzeichnet - und damit die Ehre der Familie und die patrilineare Vererbung sicherstellt. Dieses Siegel muß intakt in die Ehe eingebracht werden und dort in eine andere Vererbungslinie übergehen. Wäre sie nicht intakt, würde diese Vererbungslinie, diese Familie also, sie nicht akzeptieren„ (LIGHTFOOT-KLEIN 1993:86).

Eine Personengruppe profitiert mehr als alle anderen von der Institution der Beschneidung: Die Beschneiderinnen, die oft zugleich auch als Hebammen fungieren. Sie werden hoch geachtet, und können, im Gegensatz zu den meisten anderen Frauen, ihr eigenes Geld verdienen. Ihre Einkünfte stammen aus einer nie versiegenden Quelle - sämtlichen weiblichen Mitgliedern der Gesellschaft zu verschiedenen Zeiten ihres Lebens. Defibulationen, das Aufschneiden für den Geschlechtsverkehr und die Geburt, und Refibulationen bringen mehr ein als die ursprüngliche Beschneidung. BeschneiderInnen (in einigen wenigen Ethnien erfüllen auch Männer diese Funktion) sind im allgemeinen sehr selbstbewusst und überzeugt von ihrer gesellschaftlichen Bedeutung, und nicht geneigt, ihre Position aufzugeben, wie Madame Fatou, eine Bambara und Beschneiderin in Senegal: „Ich werde für meine Dienste bezahlt und habe ein gutes Einkommen, und die Eltern schätzen meine Arbeit„ (Zit. in HOSKEN 1995:89); ein Beschneider aus Nigeria:„Beschneidung ist der Beruf meiner Familie. Ich habe zwei Häuser mit den Einnahmen aus der Beschneidung gebaut und habe mehrere Kinder in verschiedenen Schulen...Was für ein Schaden am weiblichen Organ soll daraus schon entstehen? Meiner Meinung nach schadet es nichts„(Zit. in HOSKEN 1995:64); Madame Yassin aus Mali: „Heutzutage bezahlen die Eltern tausend Francs für die Operation...Ich bin bekannt und verdiene gut„ (Zit. in HOSKEN 1995:90). In Städten werden, wie erwähnt, die Mädchen zunehmend häufiger in Krankenhäusern beschnitten, entweder von Ärzten oder medizinisch geschultem Personal, aber immer gegen Bezahlung.

Bei der Untersuchung der ökonomischen Faktoren im Umfeld der Beschneidung drängt sich einem unweigerlich die Erkenntnis auf, dass diese maßgeblich an der Perpetuierung des Brauches beteiligt sind: „Mit den Operationen werden Vermögen gemacht„ (HOSKEN 1993:103). Es wird auch deutlich, dass die Beschneiderinnen, obwohl sie gewaltig davon profitieren, lediglich die Exekutoren sind; der eigentliche „Motor„, die treibende Kraft, ist die Mutter-Sohn-Dyade, vor allem in islamischen Gesellschaften. Zwar sind es die Männer, die den Brautpreis und die Kosten für die Beschneidung zahlen, aber sie wählen die Braut nicht selbst aus - das tut ihre Mutter, die auch für die „Qualitätskontrolle„ zuständig ist und darauf achtet, dass ihr Sohn keine Fehlinvestition tätigt.

Ethnologie, Menschenrechte und Kulturrelativismus: Genitale Mutilation und die westliche Welt
Genitale Mutilationen sind Menschenrechtsverletzungen und stellen eine besonders grauenhafte Form von Kindesmisshandlung dar, mit unabsehbaren Folgen für die psychosoziale Entwicklung, da dem Kind das Recht auf seinen eigenen Körper abgesprochen wird. „For the self-identity of individuals in all cultures, the body holds intense emotional power. The existential seat of personhood is the body„ (OHNUKI-TIERNEY 1994:240). Genau das ist es, was die Beschneidung angreift; sie verhindert das Enstehen des Bewusstseins für das Zusammenspiel von Körper, Geist und Emotionen. „Körperliche Integrität bedeutet Selbstachtung„ (LEVIN 1996 b:9), und genitale Mutilationen sind „nicht nur eine Verletzung der Menschenrechte, sondern ich glaube, dass sie die Würde und den Wert jeder Frau, in der Tat jedes menschlichen Wesens, auf direkte und persönliche Art verletzen...Diese Verstümmelungen werden kleinen Kindern angetan aus keinem anderen Grund als dass sie weiblich sind, mit dem Zweck, auf ihre normalen, natürlichen Funktionen und ihre Persönlichkeit Einfluss zu nehmen. Wie kann man für Gerechtigkeit, für Menschen- und Frauenrechte arbeiten, für Gleichheit und Demokratie und gleichzeitig diese sinnlosen gewalttätigen Angriffe auf Millionen wehrloser Kinder ignorieren, mit dem Ziel, ihr Verhalten zu kontrollieren und die männliche Überlegenheit durchzusetzen„ (HOSKEN 1993:6).

Diese Erkenntnisse finden keine ungeteilte Zustimmung. Die ersten Anti-Beschneidungs-Aktivistinnen in den siebziger Jahren hatten enorme Probleme, überhaupt ernst genommen zu werden. Man war fest davon überzeugt, dass die genitale Mutilation von Frauen entweder gar nicht existierte, oder auf kleinste Regionen beschränkt und ohnehin im Verschwinden begriffen war, bezeichnete die Behauptungen der Frauen als „irrational„ und machte sich über sie lustig (BRAUN et al. 1979:9). Auch heute noch ist diese Meinung verbreitet: Der Antrag auf Asyl von Fauziya Kassindja, einer jungen Frau aus Togo, die 1996 nach Amerika flüchtete, um der drohenden Mutilation zu entgegen, wurde in erster Instanz abgelehnt, da der Richter ihre Geschichte als „irrational und unglaubwürdig„ bezeichnete (DUGGER 1996:4).

Oft ist die Reaktion auf die bloße Erwähnung der weiblichen Beschneidung ein gequältes „überlass das doch den Afrikanerinnen„, und selbst die Uninformiertesten fühlen sich plötzlich berufen, den „kulturellen Imperialismus„ zu entdecken. Kein Wunder: Im Neuen Wörterbuch der Völkerkunde wird, unter dem Stichwort Beschneidung, kategorisch erklärt: „Die verschiedenen Formen der Mädchenbeschneidung sind durchweg streng in die komplexen Initiationsriten eingebunden, die vom Symbolgehalt und der Auswirkung her für die betroffenen Frauen von entscheidender Bedeutung sind und auf die wichtigsten Lebensaufgaben als Ehefrau und Gebärerin hinführen (z.B. S. DINSLAGE, 1981). Mögliche radikale Veränderungen oder geforderte Verbote solcher blutiger Rituale stellen derzeit unangemessene Eingriffe in traditionelle Weltbilder und Wertvorstellungen dar„...(HIRSCHBERG 1988:52).

Tatsächlich sind in den meisten Ländern Afrikas, in denen die Beschneidung praktiziert wird, die „blutigen Rituale„ gesetzlich bereits seit langem verboten. Der Autor erwähnt Sabine DINSLAGE, die anhand von sechs westafrikanischen Ethnien den Nachweis zu erbringen versuchte, dass die Beschneidung in mythischen Ursprüngen begründet und „Teil eines ganzen rituellen Komplexes„ ist (DINSLAGE 1981:8). Und was ist mit Kopfjagd, Kannibalismus und Sklaverei? Auch diese Institutionen waren kulturell bedeutsam, identitätsstiftend und in rituelle Komplexe eingebettet, aber niemand weint ihnen eine Träne nach. Aber heutzutage „haben wir keine - außer zynisch, wenn es um Angelegenheiten der Frauen geht - sogenannte postkoloniale Gesellschaft in Afrika die von „westlichen Standards„ noch unberührt ist„ (LEVIN 1996 b:6-7).

Die internationale Migration gibt der Beschneidungsproblematik eine weitere Dimension. Erste Fälle von genitaler Mutilation, durchgeführt von afrikanischen ImmigrantInnen, wurden in Europa bereits in den späten siebziger und frühen achtziger Jahren bekannt - wobei zu bedenken ist, dass die Amputation der Klitoris bis Mitte des 20. Jahrhunderts auch im Westen als ein probates, wenn auch nicht allzu häufig angewandtes, Mittel angesehen wurde, spezifisch weibliche Beschwerden, wie Hysterie, zu kurieren. Eine Reihe von westlichen Ländern haben spezielle Gesetze gegen die Beschneidung erlassen, z. B. Großbritannien, Schweden, Norwegen und Kanada, was nicht bedeutet, dass in Ländern ohne spezielle Gesetzgebung, wie Deutschland oder den USA, die Beschneidung deshalb legal ist, wie es gelegentlich in Zeitungsartikeln suggeriert wird.

Aber die Erfahrung hat gezeigt, dass Immigranten beharrlich an dem Brauch festhalten: In Frankreich machte 1982 der Fall eines drei Monate alten Mädchens Schlagzeilen, das an den Folgen der Beschneidung verblutet war. Die Eltern lebten bereits seit 10 Jahren in Paris, und hatten die Beschneiderin aus Mali einfliegen lassen (HOSKEN 1993:300). Ein anderer Mann aus Mali, der seine Tochter mit einem Taschenmesser operierte, „schien keine Vorstellung von der damit verbunden Gefahr zu haben...er sah nichts Falsches in dem, was er getan hatte„ (HOSKEN 1993:301). Es gibt keine empirischen Untersuchungen, wie viele Kinder von Immigranten in der westlichen Welt von der Beschneidung bedroht sind; Schätzungen für Frankreich allein beliefen sich 1991 auf 20 000 (HOSKEN 1993:301). Zunächst scheint es vollkommen unverständlich und schockierend, dass Immigranten, die jeder anderen Beziehung weitgehend in das Gastland integriert sind, auf dieser so anachronistisch erscheinenden Praxis bestehen, aber bei näherem Hinsehen erweist sich dies als durchaus erklärlich. Zum einen wird über die genitale Mutilation nicht gesprochen, weder im Heimatland noch im Gastland; die Prozedur ist Privatangelegenheit. Zum anderen sind auch die Aufnahmegesellschaften, trotz verbesserter Gleichberechtigung von Frauen, patriarchal strukturiert und die offensichtliche „Aufmüpfigkeit„ der westlichen Frauen, die Geschlechterkämpfe, die offen thematisiert werden und der freizügige Umgang mit Sexualität können von den überwiegend islamischen Einwanderern leicht als Indiz verstanden werden, dass die Gesellschaft bei der Kontrolle der Frauen versagt hat. Ein Mann aus San Jose, der seine dreijährige Tochter selbst beschnitt, rechtfertigte sich damit, dass das Kind „zu wild„ war, zu gerne draußen spielte und Jungen als Freunde hatte. Er sagte, die Operation würde sie „zähmen„ (BURSTYN 1995:30).

Während es letztlich unbedingt notwendig ist, die genitale Mutilation aus der privaten Sphäre an die Öffentlichkeit zu bringen, verstärkt die Sensationslust der Medien oft das Leiden der Opfer:„ Vor zehn Jahren war die Debatte um die weibliche Beschneidung begrenzt auf Gesundheitsbeamte, Missionare und andere mit einem speziellen Interesse an Afrika. Heute kann es sein, dass wir irgendeine große Frauenzeitschrift in die Hand nehmen und auf die Nahaufnahme einer jungen afrikanischen Frau stoßen, mit ausgebreiteten Beinen, ihre entblößte, vernähte Vagina für alle Welt sichtbar,„(FUAMBAI AHMADU, zit. in LEVIN 1996 b:6). Diese entwürdigende Vermarktung ruft in den Betroffenen Gefühle von Scham und Minderwertigkeit hervor. Die heftige Kritik von seiten der Vertreter westlicher Gesellschaften an der genitalen Mutilation wird von vielen AfrikanerInnen als rassistischer und diskriminierender Angriff auf ihre eigene Kultur aufgefasst; auch sehr wohlmeinenden Feministinnen wie Alice WALKER ist vorgeworfen worden, die genitale Mutilation als den Gipfel der Unterdrückung von Frauen darzustellen, und damit die Überlegenheit des Westens zu bestätigen (LEVIN 1996 b:5). Hinzu kommt, dass viele beschnittene Frauen (und ihre Männer), in einem logischen Zirkelschluss, weiße unbeschnittene Frauen nicht ernst nehmen (können), da sie keine „richtigen„ Frauen sind.

Wege aus dem Labyrinth
Da die zahlreichen Faktoren, die das Fortbestehen der Beschneidung ermöglichen, auf sozialer und ökonomischer Ebene unauflöslich miteinander verbunden sind, kann es auch keine einfache, wirksame Strategie gegen den Brauch geben. Staatliche Verbote haben sich in der Vergangenheit als uneffektiv erwiesen, oder schlimmer, hatten einen genau entgegengesetzten Effekt, einen konservativen „backlash„ wie 1994 in Ägypten (EL-GAWHARY 1996:13). Zweifellos ist akuter Mangel an finanziellen Ressourcen einer der Hauptgründe für die langsamen Fortschritte bei der Aufklärungsarbeit in Ländern, wo die Beschneidung praktiziert wird. Inzwischen gibt es überall Organisationen und Gruppierungen, die sich gegen den Brauch aussprechen (HOSKEN 1993:101 ff.), allen voran das Inter-African Committee (IAC) mit angegliederten Gruppen in 24 afrikanischen Ländern. Aber diese können sich eine „gut geplante, gut organisierte Kampagne gegen FGM, mit der entsprechenden technischen Expertise und adäqatem Finanzierungsniveau„ (WHO 1996:10) nicht leisten. Statt dessen müssen sie mit bescheidensten Mitteln und großem Kräfteeinsatz versuchen, ihre Zielgruppe, vorwiegend traditionell geprägte AnalphabetInnen in entlegenen Dörfern, von den gesundheitlichen Folgen der genitalen Mutilation zu überzeugen.

Dies ist nicht einfach, auch nicht für die „Zielgruppe„; eine Hebamme aus Somalia beschreibt das Dilemma: „Ich kann mein Kind nicht opfern. Sie leidet, so oder so. Was kann ich tun...Als Hebamme kenne ich die schrecklichen Folgen für die Gesundheit. Als Mutter weiß ich, wie das Kind darunter leidet, gehänselt, beleidigt und von ihren Freunden gemieden zu werden. Später wird sie noch schlimmere Probleme bekommen, wenn die Familie des Mannes, den sie heiraten soll, sie als „untauglich„ abweist.

Wie können wir die Operationen stoppen, wenn wir wissen, dass unsere Mädchen, wenn sie nicht beschnitten sind, keine Ehemänner finden, und ihren Müttern die Schuld dafür geben: Ihre Leben sind in jedem Fall ruiniert!„ (Zit. in HOSKEN 1993:123).

Nur Menschen mit einer starken Persönlichkeit und einem hohen Maß an Individualität sind in der Lage, in dieser problematischen Situation Prioritäten zu setzen und das Wohl des Kindes vor die Forderungen der Gemeinschaft zu stellen. Es kristallisiert sich deutlich heraus, dass eine zunehmende Individualisierung entscheidend zu der Eliminierung der genitalen Mutilation beitragen wird:

„Als meine älteste Tochter sechs Jahre alt war, begann sie mir wegen der Initiation Fragen zu stellen. Sie hatte von ihren Schulfreunden von den Geschenken und Feierlichkeiten gehört. „Ich will wie meine Freunde sein; ich will beschnitten werden„, sagte sie. Sie fragte wieder und wieder, und zweifellos hatte ihre Großmutter auch etwas damit zu tun. Mir wurde klar, dass ich etwas unternehmen musste, und so sagte ich ihr, dass ich alles vorbereiten würde. Am nächsten Tag, als wir allein waren, setzte ich sie auf einen Stuhl und forderte sie auf, die Beine weit zu spreizen. Ich befahl ihr, sich die Augen zuzuhalten und nicht hinzuschauen, sondern mutig zu sein und nicht zu weinen. Dann presste ich ihre Klitoris mit meinen Fingern und nahm ein Küchenmesser und berührte damit ihre Klitoris, so dass sie das kalte Metall an ihrer warmen Haut fühlen konnte. Schließlich sagte ich: „So, das war's, jetzt bist du beschnitten wie alle anderen, und gab ihr ein Geschenk, wie es üblich ist, damit sie es ihren Freunden zeigen konnte„ (HOSKEN 1995:87). Man liest diese Worte nicht ohne Erleichterung: So benimmt sich eine Mutter, die ihr Kind liebt und es vor Leid bewahren will. Diese Frau ist in der Lage, selbständig und eigenwillig zu handeln, ohne Bezug auf Traditionen oder einen Ehemann, der ihr Vorschriften macht; sie hat die Sicherheit der Gemeinschaft ersetzt durch individueller Identität und Eigenverantwortung, die die Voraussetzung sind für Empathie, für Mitgefühl und Verantwortungsbewusstsein für ein anderes Individuum. Neben der Betonung der Gemeinschaftsidentität vor dem Recht des einzelnen spielt die Geschlechtersegregation eine bedeutende Rolle in der Aufrechterhaltung des Brauchs, denn die Kommunikation zwischen den Geschlechtern bzw. den Ehepartnern wird damit effektiv unterbunden. Je höher der Bildungsstand, desto eher lösen sich diese Strukturen auf zugunsten eines Miteinanders von Frauen und Männern, wie der folgende Bericht eines Gynäkologen aus Khartoum zeigt:

„...meine Frau und ich trafen alle Vorbereitungen für die traditionelle Feier und luden unsere Familien und Freunde ein. Die traditionelle Beschneiderin, die wir engagiert hatten, wurde instruiert, nur so zu tun, als führe sie die Operation durch, die heutzutage in einem Zimmer stattfindet, und nicht wie früher vor den Gästen im Hof. Die Beschneiderin wurde gut bezahlt für ihre Gefälligkeit und ihr Schweigen. Wir gaben unseren Töchtern etwas Äther zu riechen, damit sie nicht wussten, was vorging, denn Mädchen in dem Alter können kein Geheimnis für sich behalten. Sie glaubten, sie wären operiert worden. Das war der einzige Weg, wie wir sie schützen konnten, als sie Kinder waren. Natürlich erzählten wir ihnen alles, als sie älter wurden„ (HOSKEN 1995: 54). Man beachte das „wir„. Die Entscheidungen werden gemeinsam gegen die Familien und gegen die bestehenden gesellschaftlichen Normen getroffen, die Mutter-Sohn-Dyade wird durch die Mann-Frau-Dyade ersetzt. Man könnte einwenden, wie es auch geschehen ist, dass offensichtlich einflussreiche und wohlhabende Personen, wie die vorgenannten, einen klaren Standpunkt gegen die genitale Mutilation beziehen und auf Konfrontationskurs gehen sollten; aber, wie der erwähnte Arzt selbst bemerkte, würde ein derartiges Verhalten ihn selbst und seine Familie ruinieren. Sie würden zu Außenseitern der Gesellschaft - und Außenseiter haben keinen Einfluss; es ist zu überlegen, ob die „subversiven„ Aktionen auf lange Sicht gesehen nicht sehr wirkungsvoll sein könnten. Schließlich sind die Mädchen nicht beschnitten; aufgrund ihres hohen sozialen Status werden sie zweifellos Ehemänner finden, und erfahrungsgemäß ist damit das Ende des Brauches etabliert: Töchter von unbeschnittenen Frauen werden nicht beschnitten, und die Mütter verlangen es auch nicht von ihren Schwiegertöchtern.

Hieraus ergibt sich unter anderem, dass bei der Bekämpfung der genitalen Mutilation die gebildeten, sozial hochstehenden Bevölkerungsschichten strategisch viel besser eingesetzt werden könnten, als dies in der Vergangenheit geschehen ist; eine Abschaffung des Brauches von „oben nach unten„ ist leichter zu realisieren als umgekehrt, da die sozial schwächeren Verhaltensweisen der als privilegiert angesehen Gruppen kopieren. Bei diesem Prozess könnte auch, wie SCHÄDELI (1992) feststellte, paradoxerweise der Islam, der zur Zeit noch eine erhaltende Wirkung auf die Frauenbeschneidung ausübt, als ein Instrument zu ihrer Abschaffung dienen (SCHÄDELI 1992:66). Schließlich praktiziert die überwältigende Mehrheit von Moslems auf der Welt keine genitale Mutilation; obwohl die Sunna-Beschneidung in den Überlieferungen erwähnt wird, läuft eine so massive Verstümmelung wie die Infibulation den islamischen Vorstellungen von der Vollkommenheit der Schöpfung gänzlich zuwider; im Koranvers 32/8 heißt es: „Der alles vollkommen gemacht hat, was Er schuf„. Eine auf religiösen Argumentationen beruhende Kampagne im Sudan in den achtziger Jahren brachte zwar nur einen bescheidenen Erfolg, aber ein Zusammenschließen der Kräfte von gesellschaftlicher Oberschicht und religiösen Führern würde eine Veränderung sicher beschleunigen. Überhaupt sind Koordination und Kooperation die Schlüsselworte für die Eliminierung der genitalen Mutilation, auf nationaler und internationaler Ebene; hierzu gehört auch die finanzielle, administrative und moralische Unterstützung von Kampagnen und Organisationen durch die Industrienationen.

Danksagung

Mein besonderer Dank gilt Sabine Frankenberger von (I)NTACT für das Überlassen von wichtigen Materialien.

References

BECK-KARRER, C. 1992. Frauenbeschneidung in Afrika. *Arbeitsblätter des Instituts für Ethnologie der Universität Bern* Nr. 5. Bern.
BRAUN, I.; LEVIN, T.; SCHWARZBAUER (Hg.) 1979. *Materialien zur Unterstützung von Aktionsgruppen gegen Klitorisbeschneidung*. München: Frauenoffensive.
BURSTYN, L. 1995. Female Circumcision Comes to America. *The Atlantic Monthly;* October 1995, Volume 276, No. 4: 28-35.
DALY, M. 1981. *Gyn/Ökologie*. München.
EL DAREER, A. 1982. *Woman, Why Do You Weep? Circumcision And Its Consequences*. London.
DINSLAGE, S. 1981. *Mädchenbeschneidung in Westafrika*. München.
DUGGER, C. 1996. Roots of Exile. A Special Report. A Refugees Body Is Intact but Her Family Is Torn. *The New York Times Metro*, September 11, 1996.
EL-GAWHARY, K. 1995. 90 Prozent Frauen amputiert. Ägypten will die Klitorisbeschneidung bestrafen. Ob das diesmal wirkt, hängt von den islamischen Rechtsgelehrten ab. *die tageszeitung*, 25.07.1996, S. 13.
FRANKENBERGER, S. 1987. *Die weibliche Beschneidung im Sudan und in Ägypten: Einheimische Überzeugungen als Faktoren für das Fortbestehen der Praktik*. Unveröff. Magisterarbeit. Köln
VAN GENNEP, A. 1981/1909. *Les Rites de Passage*. Paris.
GLAUBRECHT, S. 1995. *Mädchenbeschneidung im östlichen Afrika*. Unveröff. Magisterarbeit. Freiburg.
HAYES, R.O. 1975. Female genital mutilation, fertility control, women's roles, and the patrilineage in modern Sudan. *American Ethnologist* 2 (4):617-633.
HIRSCHBERG, W. (Ed.) 1988. *Neues Wörterbuch der Völkerkunde*. Berlin.
HOSKEN, F.P. 1993. *The Hosken Report. Genital and Sexual Mutilation of Women*. Fourth revised Edition. Lexington: Women's International Network News.
HOSKEN, F.P. 1995. *Stop Female Genital Mutilation. Women Speak: Facts and Actions*. Lexington: Women's International Network News.
KENYATTA, J. 1965/1938. *Facing Mount Kenya*. New York: Vintage Books.
LEVIN, T. 1980. „Unspeakable Atrocities„: The Psycho-sexual Etiology of Female Genital Mutilation. *The Journal of Mind and Behaviour*, Autumn Vol. 1, No. 2:197-210.
LEVIN, T. 1996 a. (Rezension). Efua Dorkenoo. Cutting the Rose. Female Genital Mutilation: The Practice and its Prevention. London 1994. *The European Journal of Women's Studies*, Vol. 3:315-328.
LEVIN, T. 1996 b. *Alice Walker, Matron of FORWARD: Toward the Abolition of FGM*. Unveröff. Manuskript. Frankfurt.
LIGHTFOOT-KLEIN, H. 1993. *Das grausame Ritual. Sexuelle Verstümmelung afrikanischer Frauen*. Frankfurt.
OHNUKI-TIERNEY, E. 1994. Brain Death and Organ Transplantation. Cultural Bases of Medical Technology. *Current Anthropology*, Vol. 35, No. 3:233-242.
EL SAADAWI, N. 1980. *Tschador. Frauen im Islam*. Bremen.
SANDERSON, L.P. 1981. *Against the Mutilation of Women: The Struggle To End Unnecessary Suffering*. London.
SCHÄDELI, S. 1992. Frauenbeschneidung im Islam. *Arbeitsblätter des Instituts für Ethnologie der Universität Bern* Nr. 5. Bern.
STRECK, B. 1987. *Wörterbuch der Ethnologie*. Köln.
WORLD HEALTH ORGANIZATION (Hg.) 1996. *Female Genital Mutilation*. A Joint WHO/UNICEF/UNFPA Statement. Final Draft. Genf.

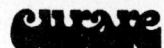

Arbeitsmigrantinnen in der Bundesrepublik - Kulturspezifische Gesundheits-/Krankheitskonzepte
Female Labour Migrants in Germany. Culture Specific Concepts of Health and Illness.

Giselind Berg

Zusammenfassung: Obwohl Arbeitsmigration kein neues Thema ist, hat das Gesundheitssystem bisher darauf kaum reagiert. Deutlich wird dies u.a in der geringen Wahrnehmung der kulturspezifischen Dimension von Krankheit, obwohl diese sowohl für die Kommunikation wie für die Inanspruchnahme bedeutsam ist. Auf der Basis einer Studie über Frauen aus der Türkei werden unterschiedliche Interpretationen vorgestellt, wobei zu berücksichtigen ist, dass auch dort verschiedene Krankheitserklärungen nebeneinander existieren. Nach volksmedizinischen Vorstellungen südosteuropäischer Länder - wie beispielsweise der Türkei - gilt Krankheit als etwas, das ‚von außen' kommt. Für den Kranken heißt dies, dass er für die Entstehung der Krankheit keine Verantwortung trägt. So gelten etwa der ‚böse Blick', schwarze Magie, die Besessenheit von Geistern als Verursacher unterschiedlicher neurologischer oder psychiatrischer Krankheitsbilder. Chiffren wie die der ‚fallenden Organe', oder dass der ‚ganze Körper' schmerzt, sind ein Hinweis auf humoralpathologische Vorstellungen. Solche und andere Ausdrucksformen deuten auf ein ganzheitliches Körpergefühl hin, das jedoch in der hiesigen medizinischen Praxis meist auf Missverständnis stößt.

Abstract: Although labour migration is quite an established phenomenon, our health system has up to now hardly responded. Among other things, this can be seen in the fact that little attention is given to culturally different concepts of disease, despite their importance for communication in as well as for utilization of our health system. Based on a study on Turkish women the essay attempts to interprete a number of concepts taking into account that in the Turkish cultural context there, too, are different explanations of disease at the same time. According to folk-medicine ideas in South-East-European countries - as for example Turkey - disease is something which comes „from outside„. That means for sick people that they are not responsible for the development of their disease. In this way, for example, the „evil eye„, black magic or being obsessed with ghosts are seen to be the cause of different neurologic or psychiatric clinical pictures. Ciphers like „falling organs„ or the „entire body aches„ are indications of humoral-pathological ideas. These and other images show a holistic body concept and are up to now seldom adaequately understood in our medical practice.

Keywords: Kulturspezifische Krankheitskonzepte; Arbeitsmigrantinnen; Frauen aus der Türkei, Bundesrepublik Deutschland, Medizinsoziologie; Culturalspecific concepts of disease; female labour migrants; Turkish women; Federal Republic of Germany, medical sociology.

Einleitung

Auch nach mehr als drei Jahrzehnten Arbeitsmigration ist der Gesundheitszustand der ehedem als 'Gastarbeiter' begrüßten ausländischen Bürger in einer schlechteren Verfassung als bei Deutschen einer vergleichbaren Schicht. Obwohl für diese Gruppe - anders als etwa für Flüchtlinge oder Asylbewerber - der allgemeine Krankenversicherungsschutz den formalen Zugang zum Gesundheitssystem gewährleistet, gibt es noch immer Schwierigkeiten mit der gesundheitlichen Versorgung. Ablesbar ist dies u.a. an der nach wie vor geringeren Inanspruchnahme von Vorsorgeuntersuchungen in der Schwangerschaft bzw. von Früherkennungsangeboten für Kleinkinder durch ausländische, insbesondere türkische Frauen, obwohl epidemiologische Studien diese im Hinblick auf Säuglings-, wie Müttersterblichkeit als besondere Risikogruppe ausweisen. (ELKELES/KORPORAL 1993)

Doppelt so häufig wie bei deutschen Patientinnen sind bei Ausländerinnen Schmerzsymptome Anlass, einen Arzt aufzusuchen (ZENTRALINSTITUT 1989). Neben Rücken- und Magenschmerzen nehmen Kopfschmerzen eine besondere Stellung (GROTTIAN 1991). Verglichen mit deutschen Frauen sind psychische/psychiatrische Diagnosen häufiger Anlass einer Krankschreibung (ZENTRALINSTITUT 1989). Bemerkenswert sind auch jene Frauen, die an mehrfachen Krankheiten leiden, was sie als „alles kaput„ umschreiben, in der medizinischenTerminologie als Multimorbidität bekannt ist.

Bei der Betrachtung ihrer Krankeitsbiographien zeigt sich, dass sich zunächst für ihre zahlreichen, mitunter dramatischen Krankheitsbilder zunächst kein Befund ermitteln lässt. (GROTTIAN 1991). Mit der Zeit entwickeln sie vielfältige, schwere Krankheitbilder (LEYER 1991). Ihr häufig erfolgloser Versuch vom Arzt eine Erklärung sowie eine Besserung ihres Leidens zu erlangen, veranlasst sie zu mehrfachem Arztwechsel (` doctor shopping`) in der Hoffnung, beim nächsten Mal mehr Glück zu haben.

Bei der hier lediglich skizzierten Übersicht des Krankheitspanoramas werden nicht zuletzt Schwierigkeiten der kulturellen Verständigung deutlich

Betrachtet man türkische Migrantinnen, resümieren es sich. dass es die türkische, ebensowenig wie die deutsche Frau gibt. Auch wenn ihre Beweggründe und Erwartungen im Hinblick auf das Aufnahmeland ähnlich gewesen sein mögen, können jedoch ihre subjektiven Motive, ihre persönlichen Voraussetzungen, hinsichtlich regionaler Herkunft, Familienstand, schulischer oder beruflicher Bildung, Schichtzugehörigkeit etc. durchaus erheblich variieren (GROTTIAN 1991). Auch für den Umgang mir Gesundheit und Krankheit wirken die kulturelle wie soziale Umgebunge prägend, wobei festzustellen ist, dass unterschiedliche Krankheitserklärungen nebeneinander existieren können. Dies gilt auch für die subjektiven Krankheitskonzepte, wobei unübersehbar ist, dass die Ausbildung darauf einen zentralen Einfluss hat.

Hinzukommt, dass diese Konzepte, sowohl im individuellen Lebenslauf wie innerhalb der sozialen Umgebung Wandlungen unterworfen sein können, etwa durch Veränderungen der sozialen Verhältnisse, der medizinischen Infrastruktur oder auch individueller Heilerfahrungen.

Kulturspezifische Krankheitskonzepte
In der Arztpraxis treffen unter Umständen westliche Medizin und volksmedizinische Konzepte bzw. Laienvorstellungen aufeinander. Das in den Industrieländern vorherrschende naturwissenschaftlichmedizinische Paradigma begreift Krankheit als eine regelwidrige und überprüfbare Abweichung von einer festgelegten Norm (SEIDLER 1979), die sich an objektivierbaren Fakten, wie biochemischen oder pysikalischen Messwerten orientiert. Individuelle Voraussetzungen, wie sozialer Status oder kultureller Hintergrund einer Person werden nicht berücksichtigt. Das subjektive Befinden hat im Vergleich zum medizinischen Befund kaum Bedeutung, im Vordergrund steht die Krankheit, nicht das persönliche Erleben, das Kranksein (KLEINMAN/EISENBERG/GOOD 1987).

In volksmedizinischen Vorstellungen südosteuropäischer Länder (z.B. Italiens oder der Türkei) gilt Krankheit als etwas, das „ von von außen„ kommt. Dabei spielen Wasser /Luft ebenso eine Rolle wie etwa der sog. „böse Blick„ (malocchio oder nazar) oder magische Einflüsse wie Geister (RUHKOPF et al. 1993). Der „böse Blick„ - erkennbar an plötzlichen Kopfschmerzen und Übelkeit - war bereits in vorislamischer wie vorchristlicher Zeit bekannt. Er wird, wie auch die schwarze Magie u.a. für allgemeines Unwohlsein oder Depressionen veranwortlich gemacht. Neurologische oder psychiatrische Krankheitsblder sollen durch Besessensein von Geistern entstehen können, das gilt z.B. für Epilepsie, Meningitis, Fieberkrämpfe, Lähmungen aber auch Psychosen, einschließlch von Schwangerschafts- und Wochenbettpsychosen. (ZARIFOGLU 1992)

Die Volksmedizin hält für diese Krankheiten verschiedene Methoden bereit. Das Tragen eines blauen Steins (`Fatma´s Auge `) soll gegen den „bösen Blick„ schützen. Bei Krankheiten, die durch den „bösen Blick„ oder Geister entstanden sind, wird der hoca aufgesucht, der verschiedenen Möglichkeiten der Behandlung hat. Er schreibt einen Koranvers auf ein Papier, liest die Sure vor und befestigt dieses Papier an der Schulter des Betroffenen. Das Papier kann auch in Wasser gelegt werden und dann vom Kranken getrunken werden. Daneben gibt es weitere Heilpersonen, die sich z.B. auf Erkrankungen des Skelettsystems und Brüche (Knochenheiler) oder die Behandlung von Infektionskrankheiten (Ocak) spezialisiert haben. Darüberhinaus werden neben dem hoca bei chronischen Beschwerden oder wenn die westliche Medizin nicht die erhoffte Wirkung gebracht hat, Wallfahrtstätten (Grabstätten, Heilquellen) aufgesucht. Welches Erklärungsmodell und welche Methode auch immer zur Anwendung kommen, wichtig ist dabei vor allem die soziale Akzeptanz (KOEN 1986).

Das Erkennen von Krankheiten ist an Krankheitszeichen gebunden, wie äußere Veränderungen oder Schmerzen. Schmerzintensität und Dauer sind bei der Unterscheidung, ob eine Krankheit als leicht oder schwer eingeschätzt wird von großer Bedeutung. Nicht langandauernde Schmerzen , auch wenn sie periodisch immer wieder auftreten, werden als leicht eingestuft. Dabei sind Symptom und Krankheit eng miteinander verknüpft, verschwindet das Symptom gilt die Krankheit als geheilt (BERG 1992) . Daraus kann dann die irrtümliche Schlussfolgerung gezogen werden, dass nun der Zeitpunkt zum Absetzten der Therapie gekommen ist, was beispielweise für die Medikamenteneinnahme sehr problematisch werden kann.

In jüngster Zeit wird auch außerhalb ethnomedizinischer Zusamenhänge die Bedeutung des Schmerzes als einer Erfahrung hervorgehoben, die in den individuellen wie den soziokulturellen Kontext eingebunden ist (BENDELOW 1993)

Kranksein ist identisch mit 'Nicht-Wohlbefinden', erst dann beginnt die Wahrnehmung der Krankheit, unabhängig davon, ob eventuell 'öbjektive' Krankheitszeichen durch Laboruntersuchungen oder bildgebende Verfahren (Röntgen, Ultraschall etc.) erkennbar sind.

Wenn das Auftreten von gesundheitlichen Störungen so eindeutig an bereits Wahrnehmbares wie körperliche Veränderungen oder Schmerzzustände gebunden ist, könnte dies ein Anhaltspunkt zur Erklärung der geringen Teilnahme von Türkinnen an Maßnahmen der Krankheitsprävention bzw. der Früherkennung. sein.

Traditionell geprägte Vorstellungen haben dort insbesondere einen wichtigen Platz, wo aus spezifischen Verhaltenweisen Sicherheit für bedrohlich eingeschätze Lebensphasen, sog. transitorische Krise, wie Schwangerschaft, Geburt und Wochenbett gewonnen werden soll. Für diese Phasen gelten verschiedene Regeln, so nehmen beispielweise Wöchnerinnen nach 40 Tagen ein Reinigungsbad, bei vorheriger sexueller Enthaltsamkeit. Gleichzeitig lassen sich auch in diesem Kontext erhebliche Änderungen traditioneller Verhaltensweisen erkennen. Während traditionsgemäß Dinge, die den Körper der Frau betreffen, nicht zwischen den Geschlechtern kommuniziert werden, die Geburt - ob in der Klinik oder zu Hause - unter Auschluss des Mannes stattfindet, nehmen hier mittlerweile junge türkische Männer in zunehmendem Maße an der Geburt ihrerer Kinder teil (GROTTIAN 1984).

Befragt man Frauen aus der Türkei zu ihren persönlichen Anschauungen über Gesundheit, tritt ein Spektrum an Vorstellungen zutage, die von einem funktionalen bis zu einem biopsychosozialen Konzept im Sinn der WHO reichen (GROTTIAN 1991). Aus ihren Äußerungen über Entstehungsbedingungen und Behandlungsformen von Krankheit, lassen sich verschiedene Krankheitsvorstellungen erkennen. Es finden sich psychologische und biomedizinische Modelle neben vornehmlich traditionellen Konzepten. Zu nennen ist das Kalt-Warm -Schema, bzw. das Konzept der Körpersäfte Blut, Speichel, Urin und Sperma (TÜRKDOGAN 1974). Das auch in anderen Regionen, etwa der mexikanischen Volksheikunde bekannte Kalt-Warm-Schema basiert auf einer Zuordnung von Nahrungsmitteln und Heilpflanzen von heiß bis kalt. Durch komplementär ausgewählte Speisen soll die gestörte Wärmbalance wieder ausgeglichen werden (TÜRKDOGAN 1974; GROTTIAN 1991). Es besteht eine Verbindung zu der Galen'schen Humoralpathologie, in seiner Terminologe handelt es sich allerdings um Blut, Schleim, gelbe und schwarze Galle. Beim gesunden Menschen befindet sich das Ensemble der Säfte im Gleichgewicht. Kommt es durch Krankheit zu einer Verschiebung, besteht die Therapie in Austreiben oder Ablassen der pathogenen Säfte durch Ausschwitzen, Aderlass oder Abführen (FISCHER-HOMBERGER 1984). Dieses Modell würde über Byzanz ins arabische Weltreich übernommen und in der ` Medizin des Propheten ` popularisiert (KOEN 1986). Eine besondere Rolle kommt dem Blut als einer das physiche wie psychische Sein tragenden Kraft zu. Da Blut als nicht regenerierbar gilt sind z.B. Blutentnahmen angstbesetzt, weil eine weitere Schwächung des Kranken befürchtet wird (Zimmermann 1994).

Ein wichtiger gesundheitlicher Indikator für Frauen ist ihre Regel. Menstruatiosblut gilt als unrein, wenn es also nicht frei fließen kann, verunreinigt es den Körper und kann Kopfschmerzen auslösen (Del VECCIO-GOOD 1980) .„Schmutziges Blut„ gilt außerdem als Ursache weiterer Beschwerden wie Juckreiz, Frühjahrsmüdigkeit und übermäßige Gewichtszunahme (TÜRKDOGAN 1974).

Vor diesem Hintergrund wird deutlich, dass ausländische PatientInnen ihre Beschwerden auch mitunter in einer Art und Weise darstellen, die aus medizinischer Sicht ncht nachvollziehbar ist. Selbst wenn die sprachliche Verständigung gewährleistet ist, was ja häufig genug ein Problem darstellt, so kommunizieren unter diesen Umständen Arzt und Patientin auf unterschiedlichen Ebenen. Werden Schmerzen überwältigend erlebt, besteht eine Form dies auszudrücken darin, dass „der ganze Körper wehtut„. Damit soll artikuliert werden, dass Kummer und Schmerz, den ganzen Menschen, den gesamten Körper erfasst haben. Andere Umschreibungen, wie etwa „meine Leber tut mir weh„ oder „meine Moral ist kaputt,„ sind nicht primär als anatomische Angabe zu vertstehen, sondern eher als Hinweis auf die Zuschreibung, die diese dies Organe im humoralpathologischen Kontext haben. So gilt die Leber ein zentraler Ort der Selbstrepräsentanz, im westlichen Medizinsystem dem Herzen vergleichbar. Veränderungen der Leber - wenn sie zum Beispiel „groß wird„ - stehen für schmerzhafte Ereignisse und

Unglück. „Die Leber, die fällt„, soll anzeigen, dass das Leben aus dem Lot geraten ist (THEILEN 1985). Sprechen Frauen von ihrer „kaputten Moral„, ist darin ein Ausdruck von Bedrückung und tiefer Traurigkeit zu sehen.

Die Beobachtung, dass Patienten aus dem Mittelmeerraum Krankheiten, auch solche mit psychischem/psychosomatischem Hintergrund, meist auf ein spezifisches Organ bezogen darstellen - und dementsprechend auch eine körperliche Untersuchung erwarten - hat dazu geführt ihnen eineNeigung zum Somatisieren zuzuschreiben. Die „Somatisierungstendenz der Migranten„ ist jedoch eine Fehlinterpretation, da die cartesiansche Trennung von Leib und Seele ist in den Krankheitsvorstellungen des Südens nicht vorhanden ist. So ist das Erleben sehr körperbezogen, Konflikte oder Leiden werden als leibliches Missbefinden wahrgenommen (PFEIFFER 1992).

Darüberhinaus sind auch bei einheimschen Patienten mit geringenm Bildungsniveau und sozialem Status Verhaltensweisen erkennbar, psychische Probleme auf die Ebene des Körpers zu verlegen. Mit dieser Haltung der Patienten korrespondiert nicht selten auf Seiten der Ärzte eine symptomatisch orientierte Diagnoe und Therapie, die es beiden Seiten ermöglicht, die Konfrontation mit sozialem wie psychischem Leid zu vermeiden (BRUCKS 1987).

Kommunikation
Diese Ebene der Kommunikation ist besonders bedeutsam im Bereich psychischer bzw. psychiatrischer Störungen. da gerade hier die kulturelle Gebundenheit der Definitionen wie der Symptomatik besonders deutlich zutage tritt. Zwar liegen in der Bundesrepublik kaum epidemiologische Studien vor, es werden jedoch bei Migranten aus dem Mittelmeerraum vornehmlich depressiv/hypochondrische Reaktionen und Wahnvostellungen beobachtet (ZARIFOGLU 1992), wobei ethnopsychiatrische Erfahrungen auf kulturelle Deutungsschemata magischen Bewusstseins verweisen. Diese Deutungsschematata schließen auch symptomimmanent festgelegte Symptome wie Lähmungsempfindungen, Hilf-und Willenlosigkeit, Schluckbschwerden oder Störungen des Magen/Darmbereichs ein. Es handelt sich dabei um kulturell vorgegebene Reaktionsmuster verschiedener magischer Beeinträchtigungsformen (ZIMMERMANN 1988:81). Ist eine Erkrankung nicht orgamedizinisch erklärbar, kann dies als Zeichen für eine Verhexung (fattura) genommen werden (POTERA 1988). Dass diese Erklärungsmodelle auch im Umfeld hochentwickelter Medizin durchaus noch eine eine Realität besitzen, wurde in einer Universitätsklinik deutlich, wo beinahe ein Drittel der Eltern die Krankheit ihres Kindes als magisch verursacht einschätzten (ZIMMERMANN 1995).

Ärzte und Therapeuten stehen in diesen Fällen ohne sprachliche und soziokulturelle Kenntnisse vor Schwierigkeiten für Anamnese und Therapie . Die Fehlinterpretation psychischer Symptome, kann zu häufigen stationären Aufnahmen und erfolglosen - überwiegend medikamentösen - Behandlungen, bzw. zu Behandlungsabbrüchen durch die Patienten führen. Die Versorgungsmängel in diesem Bereich sind vielfach belegt (LEYER 1991; LAJIOS 1993). Auch der Lagebericht ser WHO über die seelische Gesundheit von Migranten in Europa 1991 weist darauf hin, dass Migranten viel häufiger als einheimische Patienten mit hochdosierten Psychpharmaka behandelt und in psychiatrische Einrichtungen zwangseingewiesen werden.

Führt man sich vor Augen, dass Wahrnehmung und Erleben von Krankheiten soziokulturell geprägt sind, ist es angezeigt, bessere Voraussetzungen für eine erfolgreiche Kommunikaion zu schaffen. Sowohl im Hinblick auf größere Effektivität wie auf mehr Versorgungsgerechtigkeit ist es nötig, muttersprachliches Personal in Gesundheitseinrichtungen zu beschäftigen, sowie neben der sprachlichen Verständigung die ethomedizinische Dimension in die Aus-, Fort- und Weiterbildung gesundheitbezogener Berufe zu integrieren. Eine größere Berücksichtigung `des Fremden`, käme letztlich allen zugute.

References

BENDELOW, G.A. 1993. Pain perception, emotions and gender. *Sociology of Health & Illness* 15: 273-294

BERG, G. 1992. Gesundheit und Kranksein in der Migration. *Informationsdienst zur Ausländerarbeit* 3/4:14-118.

BERG, G. 1995. Ausländische Frauen und Gesundheit. Migration und Gesundheit. *Bundesgesundheitsblatt* 2:46-51.

BRUCKS, U., E. V. SALISCH and W.-B. WAHL. 1987. Soziale Lage und ärztliche Sprechstunde. Deutsche und ausländische Patienten in der ambulanten Versogung. *Beiträge zur sozialen Entwicklung im Gesundheitswesen.* Hamburg

DEL VECCHIO-GOOD, M.: OF BLOOD and BABIES. 1980. The Relationship of Popular Islamic Physiology to Fertility. *Social Science & Medicine* 14B : 147-156

ELKELES, F. TH., M. FRANK and J. KOPORAL. 1993. Frühgeburtlichkeit und Schwangerenvorsorge. *Zeitschrift für Geburtshilfe und Perinatalogie* 194 :22-28.

FISCHER-HOMBERGER, E. 1984. *Krankheit Frau.* Darmstadt

GROTTIAN, G. 1984. Schwangerschaft und Geburt als sich wandelnder Erwartungs- und Erfahrungsprozeß von Frauen aus der Türkei, in : *Frauenforschung. Beiträge zum 22. Deutschen Soziologentag.* Edited by Sektion Frauenforschung in den Sozialwissenschaften in der DGS. Campus Verlag Frankfurt/New York

GROTTIAN, G. 1991. *Gesundheit und Kranksein in der Migration. Sozialisations- und Lebensbedingungen bei Frauen aus der Türkei.* Frankfurt am Main

KLEINMAN, A.; EISENBERG, L.; GOOD, B. 1978. Culture, Illness and Care. Clinical Lessons from Anthropologic and Crosscultural Research. *Annals of internal Medicine* 88:251- 258,

KOEN, E. 1986. Krankheitskonzepte und Krankheitsverhalten in der Türkei und bei Migrantinnen in Deutschland : ein Vergleich. *Curare* 9:129-136

LAIJOS, K. 1993. *Die psychosoziale Situation von Ausländern in der Bundesrepublik: Integrationsprobleme ausländischer Familien und die seelischen Folgen.* Leske + Buderich Opladen

LEYER, E. M. 1991. *Migration, Kulturkonflikt und Krankheit. Zur Praxis der transkulturellen Psychotherapie.* Opladen

PFEIFFER, W. M. 1992. Probleme der Arbeitsmigranten in psychotherapeutischer Sicht. *Interkulturell* 1/2:113-126.

POTERA, A . 1988. Gesundheitliche Lage italienischer Migranten in der BRD. Versorgungssituation und psychosoziale/therapeutische Möglichkeiten. In *Vom heimatlosen Seelenleben.* Edited by A. MORTEN, pp. 84-97. Psychiatrie Verlag Bonn

RUHKOPF, H., E. ZIMMERMANN, S. BARTELS. 1993. Das Krankheits- und Therapieverständnis türkischer Migranten in der Bundesrepublik Deutschland. In *Beratung von Migranten.* Edited by F. NESTMANN, N. NIEPEL, pp. 233-251. VWB Berlin

THEILEN, I. 1985. Überwindung der Sprachlosigkeit türkischer Patienten in der Bundesrepublik Deutschland: Versuch einer ganzheitlichen Medizin als Beitrag zur transkulturellen Therapie. In *Gesundheit für alle. Die medizinische Versorgung türkischer Familien in der Bundesrepublik.* Edited by J. COLLATZ, E. KÜRSAT-AHLERS and J. KORPORAL. E.B.-Verlag Rissen Hamburg

SEIDLER, E. 1979. Krankheit und Gesundheit. In *Wörterbuch der medizinischen Grundlagen.* Edited by E. SEIDLER. Freiburg

TÜRKDOGAN, O. 1974. *Bir Kasabada Geleneksel Tip ve modern Tip Süreklinigi.* 1.Uluslararrasi Türk Folklor Semineri. Ankara

ZARIFOGLU, F. 1992. Soziokulturelle und migrationsspezifische Aspekte von psychischer Erkrankung bei Flüchtlingen aus dem nahen und mittleren Osten. In Was macht Migranten in Deutschland krank? Zur Problematik von Rassismus und Ausländerfeindlichkeit und von Armutsdiskriminierung in psychosozialer und medizinischer Versorgung. Edited by J. COLLATZ, pp. 113-123. E.B.-Verlag Rissen Hamburg

ZENTRALINSTITUT FÜR DIE KASSENÄRZTLICHE VERSORGUNG IN DEUTSCHLAND. 1989. *Die EVaS-Studie. Eine Erhebung über die ambulante medizinische Versorgung in der Bundesrepublik Deutschland.* Deutscher Ärzte-Verlag Köln

ZIMMERMANN, E. 1994. :Ausländische Patienten und klinische Praxis. In *Kränkung und Krankheit. Psychische und psychosomatische Folgen der Migration.* Edited by D. KIESEL, S. KRIECHHAMMER-YAGMUR and H. VON LÜPKE, pp. 25-38. Haag und Herchen Verlag Frankfurt am Main

ZIMMERMANN, E. 1995. Gesundheitliche Lage und psychosoziale Probleme ausländischer Kinder in der Bundesrepublik Deutschland. *In Psychologie und Pathologie der Migration. Deutsch-türkische Perspektiven.* Edited by E. KOCH, M. ÖZEK and W. M. PFEIFFER, pp. 246-256. Lambertus Verlag Freiburg im Breisgau

ZIMMERMANN, E. 1998. Kulturspezifische Probleme des psychiatrischen Krankheitsverständnisses. In *Vom heimatlosen Seelenleben.* Edited by A. MORTEN, pp. 73-97. Psychiatrie Verlag Bonn

Aspekte der gesundheitlichen Versorgung türkischer Migrantinnen in Deutschland
Aspects of the Health Care Situation of Turkish Migrants in Germany

Matthias David, Theda Borde, Emine Yüksel & Heribert Kentenich

Zusammenfassung: Betrachtet man die Präsenz von (türkischen) Migrantinnen in medizinischen Versorgungsstrukturen deutscher Großstädte und Ballungsräume, zeigt sich deutlich, dass diese Patientinnengruppe keine kleine Minderheit ist. Die Türkinnen bleiben jedoch offenbar durch mangelnde Sprachkenntnisse, Schichtzugehörigkeit und niedrigen Bildungsgrad häufig von gesundheitsfördernden Informationen und Maßnahmen des deutschen Gesundheitssystems ausgeschlossen. Spezifische Bedürfnisse von Migrantinnen (qualifizierte Dolmetscherdienste, gezielte Fortbildung für Medizinpersonal, Akzeptanz und Einbeziehung kulturspezifischer Krankheits- und Behandlungskonzepte) werden in den verschiedenen Strukturen des Gesundheitssystems in Deutschland nur ungenügend berücksichtigt. Das Klinikpersonal als auch die ausländischen Patientinnen gehen ein für beide Seiten unbefriedigendes Arrangement mit dieser Situation ein. Wir untersuchen in diesem Zusammenhang zwei problematische Teilaspekte des Fachgebietes Frauenheilkunde, nämlich die Sterilitätstherapie und die Geburtsbegleitung. Hier werden die Besonderheiten und Defizite in der Versorgung türkischer Migrantinnen besonders deutlich. Da die Krankheitsbewältigung durch Nachvollziehbarkeit von Entscheidungen und das Erkennen eigener Handlungsmöglichkeiten entscheidend positiv beeinflusst wird, sollten in den Kliniken neben gezielter Fortbildung für Ärzte und Schwestern psycho-soziale Betreuungsmaßnahmen in der jeweiligen Muttersprache und eine zielgruppenorientierte Gesundheitsförderung für (türkische) Migrantinnen angeboten werden.

Abstract. The presence of (Turkish) migrants in the health care structures of German cities indicates that this group of patients is not a small minority. Obviously due to language problems, their educational and social status, Turkish women, however, are often excluded from health promoting information and measures. As migrant-specific institutional regulations (like qualified interpreters, specific intercultural training for medical staff members, acceptance and inclusion of cultur-specific concepts of illness and treatments) are lacking in German health care services, intercultural interaction in the clinic context is usually solved by ad-hoc arrangements, that stay unsatisfying for both sides. We regard two problematic aspects in gynecology and obstetrics: sterility treatment and birthing coach, as here particularities and deficiencies in the health care for migrants become distincty visible. Regarding the positive impact of understanding and perceptibility of decisions, actions and options on coping with illness, specific health promotion programs for migrants need installation. To ensure equal efficiency of health care and health promotion for all patients, health services should realize the multi-ethnic reality and implement culture sensitive strategies to improve access and services.

Keywords: Türkische Migrantinnen, Gynäkologie, Geburtshilfe, Sterilitätstherapie, Geburtsbegleitung Versorgungsforschung, Turkish Migrants, Gynecology, Obstetrics, Sterility Treatment, Birthing Coach, Health Care Services.

Die Ethnizität prägt das Denken, Fühlen und Handeln von Menschen. Das betrifft auch Gesundheitsstörungen, deren angenommene Ursachen und die Erwartungen an eine Therapie.

Um Migranten medizinisch effektiv versorgen und um sinnvolle Maßnahmen der Prävention und Gesundheitssicherung installieren zu können, muss man deren Lebenssituation und kulturelle Hintergründe verstehen. Notwendig sind auch immer wieder Bestandsaufnahmen der aktuellen Versorgungssituation und Analysen der vielfältigen interkulturellen Probleme, die sich zwischen deutschen Medizinssystem auf der einen und ausländischen Patientinnen und Patienten auf der anderen Seite ergeben.

Türkische Patientinnen und Frauenheilkunde in Deutschland

Derzeit leben in Berlin ca. 12% Ausländer, hauptsächlich in den westlichen Bezirken Kreuzberg (Anteil der Ausländer an der Wohnbevölkerung (31,7%), Wedding (26,5%), Tiergarten (23,5%) und Schöneberg (20,8%) (STATISTISCHES LANDESAMT BERLIN 1996). Diese multikulturelle Realität spiegelt sich in der Gesundheitsversorgung wider. Je nach Standort und Einzugsgebiet eines Krankenhauses oder einer Praxis ergibt sich ein unterschiedlich hoher Migrantenanteil unter den Patientinnen.

Die größte ethnische Minderheit in der Bundesrepublik ist türkischer Herkunft, über 2 Millionen türkische Migranten leben z.Zt. in Deutschland, davon etwa 140 000 in Berlin.

Betrachtet man die Präsenz von (türkischen) Migrantinnen in medizinischen Versorgungsstrukturen, insbesondere den Frauenkliniken, zeigt sich deutlich, dass diese Patientinnengruppe keine kleine Minderheit ist: So gab es 1994 in Berlin 28 5031 Geburten, 22% von ausländischen Eltern. Beim Vergleich der Entbindungszahlen letzten Jahre in Berlin zeigt sich ein Rückgang der Geburtenrate bei den deutschen Frauen und eine leichte Zunahme bei den Ausländerinnen. Dies wird auch im Kreißsaal der Frauenklinik des Virchow-Klinikum im Berliner Wedding deutlich: Von 2 045 Kindern wurden 1994 38 % von deutschen und über 40% von türkischen Frauen geboren. Im gynäkologischen Bereich derselben Klinik machen türkische Frauen bis zu einem Fünftel aller behandelten Kranken aus.

Neben den rein quantitativen Angaben wissen wir wenig über die Qualität der Versorgung ausländischer bzw. türkischer Patientinnen im deutschen Gesundheitswesen.

Die Türkinnen bleiben offenbar durch mangelnde Sprachkenntnisse, Schichtzugehörigkeit und niedrigen Bildungsgrad häufig von gesundheitsfördernden Informationen und Maßnahmen des deutschen Gesundheitssystems ausgeschlossen (KENTENICH et. al. 1984).

Die Migrationsproblematik mit ihren vielfältigen, eben auch gesundheitlichen Belastungen für die Betroffenen, wird in den nächsten Jahren weiter zunehmen. Wegen der politisch-rechtlichen Unsicherheit der Migranten (die Türkei ist kein EU-Mitglied, deshalb eingeschränkte Bleibe- und Nachzugsrechte) kann eine dauerhafte Erkrankung zur Bedrohung werden, indem sie den aufenthaltsrechtlichen Status u.U. gefährdet oder durch Arbeitsunfähigkeit die mit der Migration verbundenen Ziele der Familie in Frage stellt.

Im Rahmen von Fragebogenuntersuchungen berichteten türkische Frauen über eine höhere Zahl von Krankheitssymptomen und morbiden Episoden als deutsche Frauen. Sie fühlten sich durch diese auch stärker beeinträchtigt. Weil ihnen aber geringere materielle und soziale Ressourcen zur Verfügung stehen und sie nur begrenzte Möglichkeiten sehen, von den familiären Verpflichtungen freigestellt zu werden, konsultieren sie den Arzt häufig verzögert oder gar nicht (DIETZEL-PAPAKYRIAKOU 1985). Dies gilt besonders für die weniger stark akkulturierten Frauen.

Weitere Ursachen sind wahrscheinlich in Sprachbarrieren, allgemeinen Kommunikationsproblemen, kulturellen Missdeutungen und ethnischen Aspekten in der Arzt-Patientin-Beziehung zu suchen. Berichte türkischer Frauen deuten darauf hin, dass die Mitteilungen, Empfehlungen und Anordnungen, wie auch die durchgeführten Untersuchungen des Arztes häufig nicht genau verstanden werden (DIETZEL-PAPAKYRIAKOU 1985). Ausländische Patientinnen sind häufiger unzufrieden mit Diagnostik und Therapie in Praxen und Klinikambulanzen (WIMMER-PUCHINGER 1994). Vorsorgeuntersuchungen (Schwangerschaft, Zervixabstrich) werden kaum bzw. seltener als bei deutschen Frauen in Anspruch genommen. Dies resultiert z.T aus mangelndem Gesundheitswissen oder aus Unkenntnis der Versorgungsstrukturen im deutschen Gesundheitssystem (GROTTIAN 1991, ZINK & KORPORAL 1984).

Folge der mangelnden Nutzung von Präventionsmaßnahmen, der verspäteten Arztkonsultationen und der Kommunikationsprobleme ist ein z.T. verspätetes Erkennen gravierender Erkrankungen und damit eine verspätete Krankenhauseinweisung.

Aktuellere Arbeiten zur Versorgungssituation von Türkinnen im Bereich Frauenheilkunde/Geburtshilfe liegen kaum vor.

Zink und Korporal fassten 1984 die sozialmedizinisch-epidemiologischen Probleme von Ausländerinnen im Vergleich zu deutschen Frauen bezogen auf Schwangerschaft, Geburt und Wochenbett zusammen: häufigere Multiparität, schlechtere Schwangerschaftsüberwachung, höhere perinatale Mortalität (ZINK & KORPORAL 1984).

Die Entbindung bei ausländischen Frauen wird häufiger operativ beendet (LAND et. al. 1982, ZINK & KORPORAL 1984), soziale Faktoren beeinflussen bei Ausländerinnen die erhöhte Frühgeburtenrate zusätzlich negativ (ELKELES et. al. 1988).

Günay und Haag untersuchten 1990 das Auftreten psychosomatischer Symptome bei deutschen und türkischen Frauen und stellten fest, dass Türkinnen deutlich häufiger (offenbar als Ausdruck einer stärkeren psychosozialen Belastung) über solche Beschwerden klagten (GÜNAY & HAAG 1990).

Teilweise werden Gesundheitsstörungen aber auch als "normal" akzeptiert, der psychische und physische Verschleiß durch die Arbeitsbelastung wird als Teil der objektiven Lebensbedingungen im Aufnahmeland und als nicht therapierbar hingenommen (BAYMAK-SCHULDT 1982).

Insbesondere ausländische Frauen aus ländlichen Regionen der Herkunftsländer haben nicht selten ein nur diffuses Wissen über Aufbau und Funktion des eigenen Körpers. Sie sind nicht darüber informiert, welche Störungen der Körperfunktionen auftreten können. Ihr Wissen über Ursachen dieser Beschwerden bzw. deren Verhinderung ist sehr begrenzt (MEYER-EHLERT & WOHLFAHRT-SCHNEIDER 1986).

Wir werden nun nach diesen allgemeinen Ausführungen nachfolgend auf zwei problematische Teilaspekte des Fachgebietes Frauenheilkunde, nämlich die Sterilitätstherapie und die Geburtsbegleitung eingehen. Hier werden die Besonderheiten und Defizite in der Versorgung türkischer Migrantinnen besonders deutlich. Die Diskussion eigener Untersuchungsergebnisse erlaubt damit auch Vorschläge zur Verbesserung dieser Situation.

Probleme der Sterilitätstherapie bei türkischen Paaren

Die Bedeutung der Fruchtbarkeit für die gesellschaftliche Stellung türkischer Paare verliert auch in der Migration nicht an Bedeutung. Kinderlosigkeit wird in der türkischen Gesellschaft wie auch in der türkischen Gemeinschaft in Deutschland als „unnatürlicher Zustand" nur schwer akzeptiert. Die meisten türkischen Frauen werten Kinderlosigkeit als ein grundsätzliches, wenn nicht gar existentielles Problem. Der soziale Status der muslimischen Frau, ihre Würde und ihre Selbstachtung sind eng mit dem Fortpflanzungspotential in der Familie verbunden. Geburt und Kindererziehung gelten als Familienverpflichtung und nicht nur als biologische Funktionen. Eine Adoption fremder Kinder kommt aus religiösen und gesellschaftlichen Gründen kaum in Frage, sie wird nicht als Lösung des Unfruchtbarkeitsproblems betrachtet.

Die künstliche Befruchtung erscheint natürlich in den Lehren des Islam nicht. Da alle Wege, die zu einer erfolgreichen Schwangerschaft und einem eigenen Kind führen, erlaubt sind, gibt es aber gegen die neuen reproduktionsmedizinischen Behandlungsmöglichkeiten keine Vorbehalte (SEROUR 1995).

Zwischen Januar 1992 und August 1994 kamen 1 250 Paare in die Kinderwunschsprechstunde der Frauenklinik Berlin-Charlottenburg des Virchow-Klinikums. Von diesen Neuaufnahmen waren 60% Deutsche, 9,6% gemischter Nationalität und 30,4 % ausländische Paare, davon über zwei Drittel türkische. Die Besonderheiten in der Sterilitätdiagnostik und- therapie bei türkischen sterilen Paaren waren bisher nicht untersucht worden, obwohl türkische Patientientinnengruppe z.B. in der Sterilitätssprechstunde unserer Klinik im Verhältnis zur Wohnbevölkerung deutlich überrepäsentiert war. Um dieses Forschungsdefizit auszugleichen, haben wir 1993 bis 1996 im Rahmen eines vom Bundesministerium für Forschung und Technik geförderten Projekts Untersuchungen zum Problemkreis „Sterilitätstherapie bei türkischen Paaren" durchgeführt (YÜKSEL 1997).

Hauptziel war die Entwicklung eines psychosomatischen Betreuungskonzeptes in Landessprache, was zum einen wegen der unzureichenden Verständigungsmöglichkeiten zwischen deutschem Medizinpersonal und türkischen Frauen/ Paaren zum anderen aber auch wegen der Quanität dieser Patientinnengruppe notwendig erschien.

Im klinischen Alltag würde eine landessprachliche Betreuung der Paare zu einem besseren Verständnis der besonderen psychosozialen Dimension des Kinderwunsches türkischer Paare durch das medizinische Personal beitragen. Es bietet ferner bessere Informationsmöglichkeiten für die betroffenen Paare bezüglich Körperwissen und Verständnis der verschiedenen Maßnahmen der Sterilitätstherapie. Wiederholungen unnötiger diagnostischer Schritte auf Grund von Kommunikationsproblemen werden vermieden und die Therapie kann auf ein vertretbares und notwendiges Maß beschränkt werden. Gleichzeitig lassen sich Möglichkeiten der Lösung der Sterilitätskrise des Paares z.B. durch die Erörterung von Alternativen (Leben ohne Kind, Adoption, Pflegekind) verbessern.

Es wurde eine Kinderwunschsprechstunde mit einer türkischen Ärztin eingerichtet. Zu dem wurden Einzel- und Gruppenberatungen in türkischer Sprache angeboten. Begleitend erfolgten halbstandardisierte leitfadenorietierte Interviews mit über 200 türkischen Paaren sowie Fragebogenuntersuchungen zum Gesundheits- und Körperwissen, Migrations- und Akkulturationsstatus sowie psychosomatischen Aspekten.

Im Ergebnis zeigte sich, dass sich die türkischen Paare im Vergleich mit den deutschen Paaren einer Kontrollgruppe hinsichtlich ihres Umgang mit den verschiedenen diagnostischen und therapeutischen Aspekten der in vitro-Fertilisation deutlich unterscheiden: Sie haben eine stärkere Intensität des momentanen Kinderwunsches, sind am Beginn der Sterilitätstherapie deutlich jünger, haben eine geringere Bereitschaft zu operativen Eingriffen, aber eine höhere Bereitschaft zu invasiven Therapiemethoden. Sie sind deutlich weniger bereit, eine Adoption als Alternative bei nicht erfülltem Kinderwunsch zu akzeptieren und sind stärker bestrebt, die Behandlungsdauer nicht zu begrenzen („grenzenlose Therapiebereitschaft").

Nur etwa 11% der türkischen Paare wiesen recht genaue Kenntnisse biologischer Gundlagen auf, 21% hatten mäßige, 68 % gar keine Vorstellungen hierzu. Auch über das, was mit ihnen während einer In vitro-Fertilisations ("Retorten-Befruchtung")-Behandlung geschieht, wussten 80% der in der Sterilitätssprechstunde befragten Türkinnen und Türken nichts. Sie sind offenbar in die modernen Therapieverfahren des deutschen Geunsdheitssystems eingebunden, ohne dieses kognitiv erfassen zu können. Dass die jungen türkischen Paare die Möglichkeiten einer solchen Spezialsprechstunde trotz der soziokulturellen Barrieren überhaupt nutzen, ist ein Zeichen für den hohen Leidensdruck bei ungewollter Kinderlosigkeit, der durch den Druck von Eltern- und Schwiegereltern, mit bzw. bei denen die jungen Paare z.T. im gemeinsamen Haushalt leben, verstärkt wird. Daraus ergibt sich dann der Zwang zur frühen aktiven Therapie (YÜKSEL 1997).

Die Ergebnisse unserer Studie machen deutlich, dass eine Beratung und Therapiebegleitung der türkischen sterilen Paare in Landessprache zur Lösung der Sterilitätskrise betragen und dabei helfen kann, den Kinderwunsch neu in die individuelle Lebensperspektive einzuordnen.

Soziokultureller Umbruch - türkische Väter als Geburtsbegleiter
Die hier lebenden Türken befinden sich in einer Situation des soziokulturellen Umbruchs. Traditionen aus dem Heimatland treffen z.B. auf Vorstellungen und Abläufe des modernen deutschen Medizinbetriebs. Diese Konfrontation kann zum einen zu einem verstärkten Beharren auf tradiontenellen Werten und Verhaltensweisen führen, zum anderen aber auch zu einer Anpassung an die neuen Verhältnisse (KENTENICH et.al. 1995).

In deutschen Entbindungskliniken ist die Anwesenheit des Vaters bei der Entbindung als Bestandteil des Konzepts der individuellen familienorientierten Geburtshilfe seit Beginn der 80er Jahre fest etabliert. In der Türkei ist dagegen die Vaterteilnahme bei der Geburt bis heute weder üblich noch erwünscht. Wir konnten jedoch in den letzten Jahren beobachten, dass türkische Schwangere während der Entbindung zunehmend von ihren Männern und nicht mehr ausschließlich von weiblichen Familienangehörigen begleitet werden. Die Geburtsteilnahme ist offenbar Ergebnis eines Akkulturationsprozesses, wobei sich Phänomene des totalen soziokulturellen Umbruchs (Männerbegleitung bei der Geburt) und Tradierung von Bekanntem (Begleitung durch Frauen) miteinander vermischen, denn nur in knapp 40% war der Ehemann allein im Kreißsaal dabei, häufiger gab es gemeinsam oder alternierend eine Geburtsbegleitung mit der Schwiegermutter, der Schwägerin oder anderen weiblichen Familienmitgliedern.

Eine systematische Befragung von 80 türkischen Männern vor und nach der Geburtsbegleitung ergab, dass der Entschluss, die Frau in den Kreißsaal zu begleiten, relativ kurzfristig und spontan und somit auch ohne größere Vorbereitung erfolgte, während bei deutschen Männern die Entscheidung meist schon früh in der Schwangerschaft fällt und häufig mit einer intensiveren Vorbereitung auf das Ereignis verbunden ist (DAVID et.al. 1995).

Die meisten türkischen Männer zogen ein insgesamt positives Resümee, was dazu Anlass geben sollte, dass Hebammen und Ärzte türkische Väter auch kurzfristig, u.U auch „auf Probe", zur Geburtsteilnahme motivieren. Insbesondere wenn keine anderen Verwandten oder Bekannten anwesend sind, wird dadurch das Gefühl des Alleinseins in doppelt fremder Umgebung für die Kreißende sicher gemildert. Andererseits empfanden sich die befragten türkischen Männer häufiger als die deutschen als Ersatz für die Hebammen. Ursache sind wahrscheinlich Sprachschwierigkeiten der Partnerin, so dass der Mann als „Dolmetscher und Bote" fungieren muss, oder die kulturelle oder soziale Distanz zum medizinischen Personal (DAVID et.al. 1995).

Beachtenswert, aber bisher nicht untersucht, sind die Probleme, die sich aus der mangelhaften Nachbereitung des gemeinsamen Geburtserlebnisses mit den türkischen Vätern/ Paaren ergeben können und die möglichen sozialen Folgen des veränderten Umgangs mit Schwangerschaft und Geburt für die Beziehung des Ehepaares. Hier könnten im Vorfeld muttersprachliche Informationsmaterialen Abhilfe schaffen. Bei den befragten türkischen Männern lag das Informationsdefizit erwartungsgemäß im Bereich der allgemeinen sexuellen Aufklärung (Schwangerschaft-, Geburtsvorgänge usw.). Daraus ergibt sich die Frage, ob die üblichen Geburtsvorbereitungskurse diese Art Aufklärungsarbeit überhaupt leisten können und sollen. Die etablierten „abendländisch-mitteleuropäischen", mittelschichtorientierten Geburtsvorbereitungs- und Betreuungskonzepte sind demnach bei Türkinnen bzw. türkischen Paaren nicht oder nur eingeschränkt anwendbar.

Besonderheiten der Versorgungssituation türkischer Frauen im Krankenhaus
Nicht nur bei der Betreuung vor und während der Entbindung ergeben sich für Türkinnen in einer deutschen Klinik besondere Probleme, die nachfolgend thesenhaft dargestellt werden sollen. Eine größere zweijährige Untersuchung im Rahmen eines Public Health- Projekts, die der Analyse der Versorgungssituation gynäkologischer erkrankter türkischer Frauen im Krankenhaus dient, wird weitere Details zur Beschreibung der Situation liefern. Es wird sich zeigen, ob sich die aus der empirischen Untersuchung einer kleinen Stichprobe ergebenden Hypothesen bestätigen lassen.

- Spezifische Bedürfnisse von Migrantinnen (qualifizierte Dolmetscherdienste, gezielte Fortbildung für Medizinpersonal, Akzeptanz und Einbeziehung kulturspezifischer Krankheits- und Behandlungskonzepte) werden in den verschiedenen Strukturen des Krankenhauses nur ungenügend berücksichtigt. Das Klinikpersonal als auch die ausländischen Patientinnen gehen ein für beide Seiten unbefriedigendes Arrangement mit dieser Situation ein. So erfolgt in der Regel die Sprachvermittlung immer noch durch Angehörige oder Zufallspersonen. Über die Qualität der Übersetzung besteht keine Kontrolle. Zusätzlich verkompliziert wird die Situation insbesondere in der Gynäkologie dadurch, dass aufgrund des Schamgefühls der Patientin oder des Sprachvermittlers wichtige Aussagen oder Fragen, die Tabubereiche berühren, nicht angesprochen oder weitergegeben werden. U.U. werden wichtige Informationen nicht übermittelt.
- Die durch die Erkrankung und den daraus resultierenden Krankenhausaufenthalt aus ihrer gewohnten Umgebung herausgenommenen Türkinnen sind in einer deutschen Institution häufig auf sich allein gestellt. Da Laienwissen und subjektive Krankheitstheorie in der Klinik nicht zählen, nehmen sie hier in besonderem Maße ihre eigene Unwissenheit wahr. Sie erleben sich verstärkt als Fremde, fühlen sich abhängig und verhalten sich schicksals- und arztergeben. Diese für den Behandler durchaus bequeme Compliance ist aber wenig hilfreich für die Krankheitsbewältigung, die durch Nachvollziehbarkeit von Entscheidungen, Durchschaubarkeit von Ereignissen und das Erkennen eigener Handlungsmöglichkeiten entscheidend positiv beeinflusst wird.
- Das in den Augen türkischer Migrantinnen - vor allem im Vergleich zur medizinischen Versorgung im Herkunftsland - positive Bild des deutschen Medizinsystem hinsichtlich der Kompetenz der Ärzte, der technischen Ausstattung, der Professionalität der Pflege usw. wird z.T. durch Benachteiligungsängste „als Ausländerin in einer deutschen Institution" gebrochen.

Perspektiven
Die zukünftige Relevanz des Problems ergibt sich aus drei Aspekten:

1) bezüglich Wohnbevölkerung und insbesondere durch den Anteil der Patientinnen in ambulanten und stationären Versorgungsstrukturen sind Türkinnen (und andere Ausländer/innen) in Berlin und anderen deutschen Großstädten keine Randgruppe;

2) die ausländischen Bevölkerungsgruppen weisen besondere sozio-ökonomische Arbeits- und Lebensbedingungen auf

3) eine Zunahme der Probleme in den nächsten Jahren ist zu erwarten durch
   - ein zunehmende Anzahl von Migrantinnen
   - eine zunehmende Geburtenzahl bei Türkinnen/Migrantinnen
   - ein höheres Lebensalter (Zunahme gynäkologischer Erkrankungen, z.B. Karzinome).

Die multikulturelle Wirklichkeit in den Kliniken deutscher Großstädte und Ballungsräume und der Anspruch der Krankenhäuser als medizinscher Dientsleistungsbetrieb erfordert deshalb aus unserer Sicht Verbesserungen in der Versorgung von Migranten wie z.B. den Einsatz qualifizierter Dolmetscher in ausreichender Zahl, ein Angebot psycho-sozialer Betreuungsmaßnahmen in der jeweiligen Muttersprache, gezielte Fortbildung für Ärzte und Schwestern, zielgruppenorientierte Gesundheitsförderung und spezifische Angebote zur Krankheitsbewältigung.

References

BAYMAK-SCHULDT, M.1982. *Ausländische Frauen in Hamburg. Gesundheitswissen - Gesundheitsverhalten.* Eine empirische Untersuchung im Auftrag der Senatskanzlei. Senatsverwaltung Hamburg.

DAVID, M., A. REICH, E. YÜKSEL and H. KENTENICH. 1995. Geburtsbegleitung durch türkische Männer in Deutschland - eine transkulturelle Anpassung. in: *Psychosomatische Gynäkologie und Geburtshilfe* 1994/1995. Edited by V. FRICK-BRUDER, H. KENTENICH, M SCHEELE, pp. 189-194. Psychosozial-Verlag Gießen.

DIETZEL-PAPAKYRIAKOU, M. 1985. Krankheitsverhalten türkischer Arbeiterfrauen - Ergebnisse einer Intervallbefragung. in: *Gesundheit für alle. Die medizinische Versorgung türkischer Familien in der BRD.* Edited by J. COLLATZ, E. KÜRSAT-AHLERS, J. CORPORAL, pp. 323-337. EBV-Rissen Hamburg.

ELKELES, T., M. FRANK and J. KOPORAL 1988. Säuglingssterblichkeit und Jugendgesundheitsdienst. *Soziale Arbeit* 4: 122-129.

GROTTIAN, G.1991. *Gesundheit und Kranksein in der Migration. Sozialisations- und Lebensbedingungen bei Frauen aus der Türkei.* Frankfurt/M..

GÜNAY, E. and A. HAAG. 1990. Krankheit in der Emigration - Eine Studie an türkischen Patientinnen in der Allgemeinpraxis aus psychosomatischer Sicht. *Psychother. Psychosom. med. Psychol.* 40: 417-422.

KENTENICH, H., P. REEG and K.H. WEHKAMP. 1984. *Zwischen zwei Kulturen - Was macht Ausländer krank?* Verlag Gesundheit Berlin.

KENTENICH, H., E. YÜKSEL and M. DAVID 1995. Soziale Konflikte und gynäkologische Erkrankungen, *Sexuologie* 3: 235-249

LAND, F.-J., B. HÖVELMANN, H. NEUMANN and M. DIETZEL-PAPAKYRIAKOU 1982. *Gesundheit und medizinische Versorgung ausländischer Arbeiterfamilien.* Bochum

MEYER-EHLERT, B. and U. WOHLFAHRT-SCHNEIDER 1986. *Gesundheitsbildung und -beratung mit Ausländerinnen.* Express-Edition Berlin.

SEROUR, I. 1995. Bioethik bei künstlicher Befruchtung in der muslimischen Welt. *Der Frauenarzt* 12: 1433-1437.

STATISTISCHES LANDESAMT BERLIN. 1996. *Berlin Statistik* 1995. Landeszentrale für politische Bildung Berlin.

WIMMER-PUCHINGER, B.1994. Erwartungen an die Geburtshilfe aus der Sicht der Frauen. *Gynäkol. Geburtshilfl. Rundsch.* 34: 117-122.

YÜKSEL, E. 1997. *Psychosomatisches Betreuungskonzept steriler türkischer Paare in der Migration.* Inauguraldissertation, Freie Universität Berlin.

ZINK, A. and J. KORPORAL 1984: Soziale Epidemiologie von Ausländern in der Bundesrepublik Deutschland. in: *Zwischen zwei Kulturen - Was macht Ausländer krank?* Edited by H. KENTENICH, P. REEG, K.H. WEHKAMP, Verlag Gesundheit Berlin.

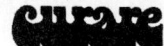

There will Always be Sadness in Our Home The Consequences of Sexual Violence Towards Female Refugees, Identification and Treatment
Die Konsequenzen sexueller Gewalt an weiblichen Flüchtlingen, Identifikation und Behandlung

Mia Groenenberg

Abstract: In situations of war, repression and forced migration, women are at risk to become a victim of sexual violence. Besides that, they can be victim of other kinds of violence and losses. Because of prejudices and taboos, the victims, their families as well as the careproviders, tend to repress the facts concerning sexual violence. The victim than does not get the support she needs. This can have far reaching consequences for the physical, mental and social functioning of the victim. At the other hand, too much emphasize on sexual violence and neglecting the effects of other violence, can be stigmatising. In my article, that is based on my experience as a psychotherapist for refugees and as a trainer for careproviders in former Yugoslavia, I will discuss the ways to deal with the consequences of sexual violence, in a context that does justice to the complex reality of multy traumatized women. I will pay attention to individual, relational as well as community aspects that play a role. Case material will illustrate the paper.

Zusammenfassung: In Zeiten des Krieges, der Unterdrückung und der erzwungenen Migration, sind besonders Frauen in der Gefahr, Opfer von sexueller Gewalt zu werden. Desweitern werden sie oft Opfer anderer Formen von Gewalt und Verlusten. Aufgrund von Vorurteilen und Tabus neigen die Opfer, ihre Familien und auch die Hilfsorganisationen dazu, Fakten und Hintergründe über sexuelle Gewalt zu verschweigen. In diesem Fall bekommt das Opfer nicht die Unterstützung, die es benötigt. Weitreichende Konsequenzen für die physische, mentale und soziale Disposition des Opfers können die Folge sein. Andererseits können die Überbetonung der sexuellen Gewalt unter gleichzeitiger Nichtbeachtung der Folgen anderer Formen von Gewalt für das Opfer stigmatisierend wirken. Ich werde in meinem Artikel, der sich auf meine Erfahrungen als Psychotherapeutin von Flüchtlingen und als Betreuerin von Hilfsorganisationen in Ex-Jugoslawien gründet, verschieden Formen des Umgangs mit den Folgen sexueller Gewalt diskutierten und dabei auf den gesamten Kontext eingehen, der der komplexen Lebensrealität multitraumatisierter Frauen Rechnung tragen soll. Meine Aufmerksamkeit richtet sich sowohl auf die individuellen, als auch auf die Beziehungs- und Gemeinschaftsaspekte, die dabei eine Rolle spielen. Fallstudien werden den Artikel illustrieren.

Keywords: Female refugees, sexual violence, secrets, psychotherapeutic treatment, weibliche Flüchtlinge, sexuelle Gewalt, Geheimnisse, psychotherapeutische Behandlung.

Introduction

There are many myths and prejudices about sexual violence. In the Netherlands, too, the subject was taboo until recently. The idea that it is the woman's fault if she is sexually assaulted still exists. Denial and ignorance are encountered at a number of different levels: in the society, the community, the family, and in the victim of sexual violence herself. In my work as a psychotherapist in an outpatient mental healthcare center for refugees I am confronted more and more with the damaging effects of sexual violence. This could also be because over the years I have become more open to the problem. Sexual violence can be directed towards women as well as towards men, in this paper I will limit myself to the consequences sexual violence has for women. The provision of mental healthcare to female refugees who are victims of sexual violence is from the outset complicated by the multiplicity and the complexity of the problem. Traumatization, uprooting and acculturation all play a role in it. In addition, the view of sexual violence that exists within a particular culture or tradition has a strong influence on the process of coming to terms with the experience. I would like to consider this view in more detail in order to focus on some areas of attention for treatment.

The occurrence of sexual violence

The occurrence of sexual violence is always in a situation of power inequality. It is found on a large scale in situations of war or where there is repression for political, ethnic or religious reasons. Sexual violence towards women and men can be used here as an explicit means of intimidating and making ineffective certain population groups. Sexual violence towards women involves not only the woman herself, but also the husband and family. As a consequence of rape the woman is humiliated and made ashamed in the inner circle of partner and family. In addition the family is made ashamed in the eyes of the outer world.

In all these situations the ultimate goal of the sexual violence is: keeping the opponent or repressed group down, making it ineffective and finally, destroying it. Sexual violence also takes place in daily life, in a society that has become violent as a result of war and repression. Thus, for example, healthcare workers in the former Yugoslavia have noticed an increase in domestic violence. Tensions are worked off in this manner; at the same time, norms have become blurred and the offenders are possibly emotionally numbed. What also may play a role here is that men feel threatened by the autonomy women gained while their husbands were in the war. I have heard similar stories from South Africa. The longterm oppression of blacks here has resulted in an increase in violence in both the society and the family. The victims are mostly women. (GROENINK E. 1995: IV-VI) In the Netherlands we have to deal with refugees from situations of war and repression, who during their flight and the first period of their stay in the Netherlands are forced into a dependent position, and as a result are vulnerable. Women in particular can be exploited in such a situation.

The specific character of sexual violence

In all cases of sexual violence the victim is reduced to an object that the aggressor uses to vent his lust of power on. The victim is thus ignored as a person, is in a way stripped of her personality. Sexual violence generally occurs in combination with other violence. However, more than with other forms of violence incompatible feelings are called up. This is because sexuality becomes associated with aggression. Besides pain, feelings of lust can be experienced during the violence as a result of certain physical and physiological processes. (AGGER.I.1989: 309) This is a deeply wounding situation which can scar a person for a long time afterwards. The ability to enjoy a sexual relationship can be seriously damaged and this can effect the relational aspects of the victim's life. The experience has even more impact when the woman gets pregnant, has to take a decision about an abortion, or a decision if she will keep the baby or give it for adoption. If she decides to keep the baby she will have to face specific emotional problems during the upbringing of the child. Besides that she has to face the opinion of her partner, family and society.

An unspeakable experience
From the viewpoint of society

Because of its painful nature for the victim and the taboos that often surround sexuality, sexual violence is a subject that is difficult to talk about. As a result, victims can live for a long time in isolation. In the Netherlands this became evident, once again, not so long ago when women, 50 years after world war II, broke their silence and came forth with their experiences as 'comfort women' for the Japanese. They had been forced in the then occupied Dutch East Indies to work in brothels for the Japanese soldiers. One of them, Jan O'Herne, said in an interview, that she had never talked to her daughters about it. She had kept her problems with the sexual relation and her sleep problems hidden, also from her husband. Influenced by the testimonies of Korean women she decided to make public her experiences. This was an enormous relief. She received support and recognition. The prejudice she had so dreaded did not occur. (SOEST M.v.1994:49-54)

At a government level, it has been long known from official documents that European, as well as Asian women were forced to work in the Japanese brothels. This was not regarded as rape but merely as something that can happen in war, and at the time no attention was paid to the consequences for the women.(CAPTAIN E.1994: 41 -42) Since 1992 it has been known that in the former Yugoslavia women and girls were, on a large scale, systematically assaulted and raped. At the beginning, this received a lot of publicity. The topic was exploited in a political battle which was waged over the heads of the women. The above-mentioned events illustrate that there is a tendency in society to trivialize or to deny sexual violence. Women, when they bring their experiences out into the open, are often met with disbelief and a lack of understanding. There are doubts about the truth of their story. One reason for this could be that people often find it difficult to face up to the fact that their fellow man is capable of such atrocities. Another factor playing a role is that the victims often describe their experiences in a confused, contradictory and fragmented way when they bring them out into the open. This can detract from their credibility. It has to do with a conflict in the women between denying the events and putting them into words, and leads to 'double thinking': revealing and keeping secret at the same time. (HERMAN J.L.1993: 12,118) This phenomenon also applies to the listeners, the society, who listen to the story in a concerned way and at the same time keep silent about it, or stigmatizes it. (CAPTAIN E. 1994: 37-38)

From the viewpoint of the cultural tradition
For the woman, denial does not help, nor is it really possible. Talking can be an enormous relief and, to a certain extent, is necessary for the healing process . However this can only occur if there is someone willing to listen and if recognition is offered. Even then, guilt and shame hinder communication about sexual violence. Often a person is unwilling to talk about the experiences out of the fear of lack of understanding, prejudice, rejection or acts of revenge. From the viewpoint of the cultural tradition this attitude has to do with the image of woman that exists in the community that the woman was raised in. In many cultures virginity is holy and a woman is ostracized if she has extramarital or premarital sexual contact, whether or not it is forced. The husband is put under pressure to repudiate his wife and/or to take revenge on the offender. The woman is seen as a 'whore' and through her internalizing of the prevailing norms and values will see herself as damaged, dirty and worthless and an unworthy wife and mother. The accepted norms and values of the community the woman was raised in are reflected in the way she experiences and perceives herself. I would like to illustrate this with a case.

Vlora is a 35 year old Albanian woman from Kosovo. One day the police came, looking for her husband. He was not home. Vlora was raped by them. A week later they returned and the same thing happened. Her youngest children were home, and they discovered their mother unconscious. The incident caused her, her husband and her family great shame. They could no longer remain living there. A relative helped them escape.

She was referred to us by the Refugee Council. She was suffering from different sorts of physical complaints, in particular headaches, nausea, vomiting and diarrhea. She was very nervous and was afraid of walking on the street and as a result avoided walking alone on the street. She had the feeling that people were looking at her and that they could see what had happened to her. She was very ashamed. She slept fitfully and had nightmares. She was extremely depressed and was not able to adequately carry out tasks related to her 4 children. She could no longer see any point in her life. She felt that she was carrying a burden that she would never be free of. In addition, she felt guilty because her family had to flee because of her. This was how she experienced it. A quote from her: "life will never be the same again. I'll never be able to be independent again and free like I was before. There is always sadness in our home and it will always be there." The husband is extremely grieved by what happened to his wife. His pride has been hurt. According to custom he should have cast his wife out. He could not do this because of the children. He feels the shame acutely, and says: " I'd rather that she had chopped off her hands than this." He is a kind man, he has sympathy for his wife. He tries to do as many household chores as possible for her.

The relationship appears to be good. She thinks her husband is right. She has brought shame on them. She only lives for her 4 children who are respectively 14, 10, 6 and 3 years old. The family is not allowed to talk about what happened.

Secrets
Family secrets
We often see that there is a family secret when there has been sexual violence. Sometimes the woman does not tell her husband, and shares the secret only with her mother. Sometimes there is no-one she can share the secret with. In the literature on family therapy it is put forward that family secrets often involve sexuality, birth and death (PINCUS L. and DARE C. 1978). Secrets can have a binding effect: when the secret is shared by the whole family it can distinguish the family from the "outside world". When family members keep important secrets for each other they become estranged from each other,

and this can have a destructive effect on the family bond. Strangely enough, one reason for keeping the secret is precisely the fear that the family will fall apart if the secret becomes known among its members. For example: the woman is afraid that her husband will send her away, or that he will walk away himself, and that she will be left alone with the children, if the fact that she was violated becomes known between them.

Another reason for keeping secrets is that in this way people try to avoid the strong and confusing feelings of guilt, shame and anger that memories of the violence call up. The woman wants to forget, banish what happened as if it had never occurred. It also occurs that parents decide not to burden their children with these severe problems. This can sometimes be viewed as a protective measure. A detrimental effect of secrets is that the fantasy of vulnerable children can be stimulated by them and the children can become anxious.

> Vlora's youngest daughter had suffered from enuresis since the rape. The youngest son became anxious if he saw men in uniform on the street.

On the other hand a secret can be so dominantly present in the minds of the parents that they unconsciously project it onto their children. This can lead to communication problems.

> When her oldest daughter, who is now 14, sits quietly staring ahead of her, Vlora thinks that she is thinking about the rape and that she is imagining her mother in this degrading situation. Vlora feels guilty.

Sometimes the secret about an event becomes more important than the event itself. In such a case all communication in the family seems to be organized around it. The content of the secret seems less important than the effect it causes.

The victim and her secret
Keeping the secret is most difficult for the victim herself. It places her in isolation. The burden of the traumatic memory, which is often expressed in disturbing symptoms, rests on her alone. Her negative self-image, caused by feelings of being damaged, guilt and shame does not get the chance to be corrected, as would happen if she were in an equal relationship. She remains a victim and becomes a patient.

Symptoms resulting from sexual violence
At an individual level the problems caused by sexual violence can be expressed in a combination of the following symptoms:
* symptoms of a post traumatic stress disorder such as flashbacks, nightmares, mental withdrawal, psychic numbing.
* depressive feelings like feeling dejected, apathetic and having no appetite. The depression is related to the loss of trust in oneself and others.
* a low self-esteem caused by feelings of worthlessness, shame and guilt. A negative self-image reflects the negative attitudes of the society. Guilt feelings are related to the infringement of internalized norms and values learned in the society in which the victim was reared.
* various physical symptoms and a preoccupation with physical functioning. Such symptoms are generally for women an acceptable way of expressing problem.
* relationship problems, which on closer examination are seen to be related to sexual problems. Especially when the woman has kept the violence she experienced secret from her partner, a vicious circle of violence can arise. The woman can become anxious when her partner makes sexual approaches, and is disturbed by flashbacks. The partner can feel rejected and this can lead to physical abuse.
* social isolation, due to shame, and often also due to stigmatization and rejection by the social environment.

Areas of attention for mental health care
The woman as patient
It is our experience that refugees who are referred to us are in a crisis situation, for which direct assistance is necessary. In such cases we prefer to begin treatment simultaneous with the collection of diagnostic information. Initially, the emphasis of the treatment is on more adequate functioning in the short term. Supportive techniques are used and symptoms are treated by a combination of cognitive

behaviorally oriented interventions, sometimes combined with medication (VEER G.v.d. 1992:125-147).In the work with victims of sexual violence body-work is important. We use exercises for relaxation, breathing, concentration, grounding etc. When the patient has got some control over the symptoms than more attention can be devoted to dealing with emotions related to the traumatic experiences, and to reinterpreting the violence suffered in order to place it in a meaningful context. The client's own strength and potential are central during the treatment. The main aim is to try to break through her helplessness and to help her regain power over her own situation. In the light of the silence surrounding sexual violence I would like to mention some points of attention for treatment.

* In the first place, the development of a *good working alliance* is of vital importance. An atmosphere needs to be created in which confidentiality is emphasized and difficult subjects are able to be discussed. The therapist should be aware of, besides her own prejudices and taboos, the cultural differences between her and her client. Regarding the sexe of the therapist there is often a preference for a female therapist. The reason behind it can be that men can be associated with the offenders. Besides that it is possible that shame can be better tolerated in front of a woman.
* If the therapist thinks that sexual violence is an important factor in the problem then she can try to *bring it up for discussion* under the right conditions. The conditions are that the patient has some control over her symptoms and that she has a kind of social support system. This can help her to manage strong affects like rage and helplessness that may come up.

My experience is that the signals can be easily missed or interpreted differently. On the other hand, the therapist should avoid placing the emphasis too much on the sexual violence. In view of the complexity and the multiplicity of the problems of refugees there may be many more problems disturbing the client or other problems that are more urgent, for example the woman can be more concerned about a possible negative answer in the asylumprocedure and be afraid to be sent back to her home country, or be worried about familymembers in the homecountry.

A difficulty for the therapy can be when there are indications of sexual violence and the woman sends out signals to this effect, but she does not talk about it. It can be helpful if the therapist lets it be known that she is familiar with the fact that refugees can be victims of sexual violence. Sometimes talking about "something that is impossible to talk about" can be helpful. Also symbolic communication through poems or drawings can help to break the silence.

* If the client is able to share her experiences with the therapist it can have a liberating effect. It can be the beginning of a sometimes long and painful process in which the violence the client has experienced is given *meaning*.

Emotions that are difficult to accept and that were originally directed against herself, such as anger, can be made conscious and a suitable form of expression found for them. Making an official complaint against the offenders, for example to the war crimes tribunal in the Hague, could be one form. Also, writing down the story, with the aim of using this during the asylum procedure and bringing the injustice to public knowledge, can also help. This is the so called testimony method. (VEER G.v.d.1992:149-153)

In looking for a meaning it is important to look at the personal history of the woman. Also important here is the culture in which the woman was socialized and the norms and values which she has internalized. The influence of these norms and values on how she sees herself in a negative light can be talked about. In addition, the relative nature of norms and values can be discussed. When possible, it is important to involve the partner here. By placing the violence in a political-historical framework it is possible for it to be seen as directed towards a group and not against the woman herself.

The partner, the family
The woman's individual development cannot be seen separate from the people in her immediate surroundings with whom she has close relationships. Whether the woman can share the experiences with her husband depends on the nature of the relationship and the degree of autonomy that the partners allow each other. If they do not have secrets from each other then the pressure to talk about it will be greater than when little is shared. If the woman decides not to tell her partner, the guilt feelings can sometimes be unbearable. They can remain with her for a long time. Another important aspect is the moral pressure the husband feels to take action, for example to send his wife away or to take revenge, if he hears that his wife has been raped. One sometimes suspects that the husband actually knows what has hap-

pened but that he would prefer not to know it officially so that he does not have to do anything. It is useful to talk about the norms and values held by the client and her husband and to treat the problems they give rise to as a common problem. The situation can sometimes be made more straightforward if talks can be had with the couple together about an experience the woman has been unable to discuss and which is a cause of symptoms. The husband can be asked to assist in bringing the symptoms under control.

In the literature it is put forward that the sharing of a secret with other family members is often a relief. The problem becomes a shared one, and is no longer born by only one person. As a result, the symptoms decline; the bond between the family members is strengthened. The often feared destructive consequences do not occur. At the other hand, it is sometimes more important to look at the function of the secret instead of at the content, and discuss with the familymembers what having the secret means to them and what it does to the familydynamics.

The group
We have had positive experiences with group work with women who have been raped. The aim of the group was to break through the isolation of the women. We worked with exercises focusing on the body and with games; daily problems were talked about. Information was also provided. The emphasis was on the problem-solving capabilities of the women themselves, their own strength and the giving and receiving of support from each other. This seemed to be a valuable experience. The traumatic events were not necessarily discussed in the group. All women got the possibility for individual treatment besides the group.

The community
Since support from the immediate social environment is essential in overcoming the effects of rape, the social network of the victim should be strengthened. Acceptance and support are central in the assistance given to victims of sexual violence. The immediate environment plays an important role here.

At the community level it is important to break through the silence surrounding sexual violence and to spread information, via mass media, about how it occurs and the consequences for victims. Stigmatization, blaming and rejection of victims should be fought against. Maybe here is as well a task for the spiritual leaders in a community. Of course people who play a role in the socialization of children, like parents and schoolteachers, should be conscious about the way they transmit values and norms about gender issues.

Closing remark
I still have contact with Vlora. In our talks I sought contact with the strong woman she used to be and in fact still is. I tried to bring out her strength and fighting spirit. She can now feel more anger and can say that she is actually not guilty and that it happened as a result of the political situation. I did breathing and active relaxation exercises with her. In addition I gave her small tasks to carry out to help her to go on to the street alone. She is doing much better. A problem, though, is that according to the traditional view this is not possible. A woman who has undergone such a thing can never be happy again. I hope that we can work this through in the group that Vlora is going to join. In addition, we are trying to work with her husband.

The last time I saw her she told me, at the end of the talk, that recently a friend made a joke, and to her surprise she had laughed a lot. This was the first time in years. There is thus hope.

References
AGGER I.1989. Sexual torture of political prisoners: an overview. *Journal of Traumatic Stress* 2, 305-318.
CAPTAIN E. 1994. Spreken over gedwongen prostitutie en zwijgen over verkrachtingen. *ICODO info* 94-1,37-48.
GROENING E. 1995. Op geslagen vrouwen kun je geen samenleving bouwen. *Amandla, tijdschrift over Zuidelijk Afrika*, sept.1995, IV-VI.
HERMAN J.L.1993. *Trauma en Herstel*. Wereldbibliotheek.
PINCUS L. and DARE C.,1978. *Secrets in the family*. London.
SOEST M.V.1994. Gedwongen in een Japans legerbordeel, *ICODO info*, 94-1,49-54.
VEER G.V.D.1992. *Counselling and Therapy with Refugees*. John Wiley and Sons, Chichester.

The Health of Refugees: Are Traditional Medicines an Answer?
Gesundheit von Flüchtlingen: Ist traditionelle Medizin eine Lösung??

Barbara E. Harrell-Bond & Wim Van Damme

*Witchdoctors...are not the peculiar heritage of the African. They are rather the unsurprising accompaniment of poor social conditions, of fear, of ignorance and despair, and as such they are found, even today, in every civilisation earth. The witchdoctor is certainly an integral part of African cultures; he stands between man and spirits; he offers, and sometimes provides peace of mind to the distraught and anxious....He may be unhygienic, unskilled and avaricious - so is the back street abortionist....(*GERMAN IN ORLEY 1970*).*

Abstract: Based on a wide range of data on refugees in East Africa, the essay discusses the roles of traditional medicine and healers within the context of displaced populations and the limits of humanitarian health intervention and of modern medicine. A combination of a number of cultural, geographical, financial and social barriers and the limited scope of humanitarian emergency health services leaves space for the practice of traditional medicine in displaced populations. In a refugee situation, it is not uncommon to see this role taken up by opportunist traditional healers, sometimes unqualified, who engage in this lucrative activity to benefit from the situation of chaos. The official rejection of traditional medicine in many parts of Africa has contributed to emergence of competing and conflicting relations between traditional medicine strongly supported by indigenous cultural practices and beliefs and modern medicine. Drawing from the experience in many parts of East Africa, the article challenges the tendency by many foreign observers to romanticise the role of traditional medicine and the powers and influence of the healers in the loght of the social changes that takes place after forced migration. The article points to the dearth of research on the use of traditional medicine by refugees and calls for more research into the potential role traditional medicine and healers can play in providing therapeutic medicinal and societal service.

Zusammenfassung: Dieser Beitrag erläutert, gestützt auf eine breite Datenbasis über Flüchtlinge in Ostafrika, die Rolle der traditionellen Medizin und der Heiler im Zusammenhang mit vertriebenen Bevölkerngsgruppen und die Grenzen humanitärer Gesundheitsinterventionen und der modernen Medizin. Eine Kombination zahlreicher kultureller, geographischer, finanzieller und gesellschaftlicher Schranken und die begrenzte Reichweite humanitärer gesundheitlicher Hilfsdienste lassen Raum für die Ausübung der traditionellen Medizin bei vertriebenen Populationen. In der Situation von Flüchtlingen wird nicht selten beobachtet, dass diese Aufgabe von opportunistischen - mitunter nicht qualifizierten - traditionellen Heilern übernommen wird, die sich in diesem lukrativen Gewerbe engagieren, um von der chaotischen Situation zu profitieren. Die offizielle Ablehnung der traditionellen Medizin in vielen Teilen Afrikas hat dazu beigetragen, dass viele konkurrierende und konfliktreiche Beziehungen zwischen der traditionellen Medizin, die durch heimische kulturelle Praktiken und Glauben stark gestützt wird, und der modernen Medizin entstanden. Angesichts der Erfahrungen in vielen Teilen Ostafrikas kritisiert der Beitrag die Tendenz gar mancher ausländischer Beobachter, die Rolle der traditionellen Medizin und die Macht und den Einfluss der Heiler im Licht der gesellschaftlichen Veränderungen, die nach erzwungener Migration stattfinden, romantisch zu verklären. Der Beitrag weist auf die mangelnde Erforschung der Anwendung traditioneller Medizin durch Flüchtlinge hin und fordert eine vertiefte Untersuchung der möglichen Funktion, welche die traditionelle Medizin und die Heiler bei der therapeutisch medizinischen und sozialen Betreuung übernehmen könnten.

Keywords: Africa, Culture, Modern Medicine, Traditional Medicine, Healers, Refugees, Afrika, Kultur, Moderne Medizin, Traditionelle Medizin, Heiler, Flüchtlinge.

Introduction

We live in a world which is marked by increasing levels of poverty, violence and political instability. One of the major symptoms of these ills are the millions of refugees and internally displaced. Since most refugees tend to avoid the camps and settlements established by humanitarian agencies, preferring to settle themselves among their hosts, many of these people do not have access to adequate ‚modern‘ (allopathic) medicine. Moreover, even the availability of adequate health services to refugees in camps is contingent on the flow of international aid, which is itself dependent on the vagaries of media attention and the political interests of the donors.

This essay is being written during the course of a fieldtrip to Kenya where a research programme to compare the health and welfare of refugees living in camps with those who are settled amongst their hosts is beginning in this country and in Uganda. The discussion is drawn from data collected in the course of research conducted amongst Ugandan refugees living in the Sudan in 1983-4 (HARRELL-BOND 1986), 20 person days of observations and interviews in Kakuma Refugee Camp, Turkana District, Rift Valley Province, north-western Kenya, a report of an evaluation of health services conducted in Hagadera, one of three camps located in the north-east region of Kenya (BOELAERT 1996), and research concerning the global refugee phenomenon conducted over the past 15 years in many countries around the world. The discussion concerning the use of traditional medicine by refugees is, however, limited to examples of its practice from research in Africa.

There are some northern humanitarian organisations which see this situation as an ideal time to promote the practise of traditional medicine as an answer to the unmet health needs of such populations. In this paper, we use the term, traditional, with considerable misgivings when referring to medical practitioners who operate outside the boundaries of modern medicine. The use of the term, traditional, as an adjective to describe local healers in Africa or elsewhere is problematic, especially when used in an article in which the emphasis is on culture as a process and which is in disagreement with those who believe that what is ‚traditional' equates to some unchanged primordial past before the impact of outside influences from the West.

While acknowledging that both traditional and modern medicine have a part to play in health care for the forcibly displaced, this essay aims to caution those who tend to uncritically idealise traditional medicine and its practitioners. Laying aside the contested issue of the effectiveness of their treatments, refugees and others who are living in situations of instability in Africa are particularly vulnerable to the opportunism of some traditional healers whose interventions may actually contribute to increased conflict and further social disruption. A ‚human rights' approach to humanitarian interventions requires all those involved to equip themselves to be able to distinguish between those aspects of a culture which are functional and those that are dysfunctional, especially those which are at variance with international standards. This must be especially the case for those concerned with the rights and welfare of women.

With the intrusion of IMF and World Bank policies which insist on cost recovery health programmes, which most of the poor cannot afford, one may expect more of the world's population to be thrown back on alternative therapies as access to modern medicine becomes even more difficult. As such, it becomes even more important that the activities of traditional healers and the therapies which they administer are subjected to research in order that those who are able to provide useful therapies are distinguished from those whose interventions are iatrogenic. The term, iatrogenic, is usually employed to describe the negative effects of modern medicine, but the dictionary meaning, ‚caused by the process of medical examination or treatment', allows us to apply it to the interventions of traditional healers.

The Successes and Limits of Modern Medicine
Over the past fifty years modern medicine has developed powerful drugs to combat many infectious diseases, for example, anti-biotics, other anti-infectious drugs as well as vaccines for many childhood diseases. Even before that, life saving surgical interventions had been in practice, such as caesarean sections and other abdominal operations, but these became much more effective with the advent of antibiotics.

Thanks to these developments, such killers as pneumonia, diarrhoea, malaria, meningitis, and tuberculosis all became easily curable with modern medicine. However, there are still many diseases for which modern medicine has no effective treatment, such as AIDS, most forms of cancer, mental disorders and many psychological and psychiatric problems. At the same time, some bacteria and parasites have been developing resistance to treatments, presenting serious challenges to the effectiveness of modern medicine.

Barriers to Accessing Modern Medicine
Modern medicine has undoubtedly achieved great successes, such as the eradication of smallpox throughout the world and the control of non-venereal trepanomatosis, but there are a number of barriers to accessing it. Cultural acceptance of various therapies differs widely from place to place. However, one form of medical intervention, the injection of drugs, has received almost universal acceptance. Because injections of anti-biotics and anti-malarials have been demonstrated to produce such rapid results, they

have become the preferred treatment in most parts of Africa *for any illness*. Many patients do not believe they have received proper medical attention unless they have received an injection. Similarly, the acceptance of surgical interventions varies widely from one area to another and for different types of ailment, but it is remarkable how willingly many people undergo major surgery for certain indications, while objecting to a life-saving caesarean section for a blocked labour.

In Kakuma refugee camp in Kenya this was a particular problem for those working in the health services. Because many of the southern Sudanese women had been raised on a sub-nutritional diet, they developed pelvises too small to deliver the babies whose birth weight had been improved by the prenatal care provided in the camp. Their husbands, however, often refused to allow their wives to be delivered through a caesarean section. One Kenyan health worker hit upon the idea of employing 'male motivators' to educate the men which was successful in at least reducing resistance. It is unfortunate to reflect on the fact that the diet fed to the refugees in Kakuma who are not targets of special feeding programmes like the pregnant women are, continues to fail to meet the nutritional requirements of this population. Hence another generation of girls is being raised with the same deficiencies of the adults.

Geographical barriers combine with poverty to prevent vast numbers of people, not only refugees, from accessing the services of persons competent to dispense modern medicine. In many parts of Africa the majority of people still live over ten kilometres from a health centre. Such a distance may be too far in the advent of an acute illness.

Moreover, the quality of training of medical staff and their motivations vary widely and the tendency is to staff the most remote health centres with the most junior, who then often receive inadequate supervision. In many instances, health systems have been created by outsiders without sufficient appreciation of the context in which medical personnel are expected to work. In some situations, people do not trust the health worker because s/he *is an outsider, or, because s/he is an insider whom they know to be untrustworthy.* In some African countries, for example, Burkina Faso, primary health care was interpreted as training a young person for each village through a crash course of a few weeks. This person might be able to learn to use modern drugs for a few life-threatening disorders, but s/he will never be able to know the limits of this knowledge. Once the inevitable serious mistakes occur, it will be impossible for such a health worker to regain the confidence of the community s/he is intended to serve.

Perhaps the most important barrier to accessing modern medicine is financial. The post-independence optimism that there could be free medical care for all has long evaporated. As noted above, in most countries everyone has to pay for health services, a situation which has been exacerbated by World Bank insistence on cost recovery. Practitioners of modern medicine almost always require cash payments for their services and, on the spot, while the availability of money in many rural areas is seasonal. There are even places where a monetary economy is non-existent any more, for example, in large parts of Zaire or Somalia.

The cost of treatments is related to the seriousness of the illness. In parts of rural Africa it has been found that often not less than 20 to 25 percent of a family's annual cash income is spent on direct medical expenses. People are often forced to divest themselves of land and other capital resources in order to receive treatment. For example, in Guinea it was observed that food stocks required to carry a family through the 'hungry season' were being sold off early in order to pay the doctor to save the life of one of its members. There are social or class barriers as well which discourage the adequate utilisation of modern health services. Access to education in most African societies is very limited and those who achieve some qualification often feel superior to their less-educated compatriots. At the same time, because their reference group are the elite members of their professions, who live in urban centres and earn higher salaries, qualified health workers posted in remote areas are often frustrated in their social and economic ambitions. Few training institutions pay sufficient attention to training medical workers to be culturally sensitive towards other groups in their own country, or even to understand the special problems of the extremely poor. In the course of fieldwork in Kenya in March, a district medical officer working in Turkana remarked that when a woman was admitted, before examining her, he would require an assistant to cut off her beads. Since their beads completely cover a woman's neck from chin to shoulders, and because of the desperate lack of water in this desert environment, they are usually very dirty, one can understand the doctor's wish for his examination to be unimpeded by them. However, given the significance of the elaborate beads the Turkana women wear, one could assume that the tendency would be to avoid medical care if at all possible.

These factors combine to influence the relations of health workers with their patients who may be blamed for the health problems they present. For example, in the wake of such a preventable disease as measles or diarrhoea, very often nurses or doctors will berate the parent for not having taken the necessary precautions. The same happens if people delay consulting the health services and reach the clinic with an advanced or complicated presentation of a disease. As a consequence, the anticipation of such humiliation increases the tendency for people to further delay consulting medical practitioners.

The Role of Traditional Medicines

Although modern medicine has taken a prominent place in African society, traditional forms of medicine have continued to be practised on a wide scale. Many of their practices are no doubt efficacious, for example, there are healers who specialise in bone setting, treating bites of scorpions and snakes. Many of the discoveries of ‚traditional medicines' have been the basis for the developments in modern medicine, usually with no regard to the ‚intellectual rights' of those who discovered them. The most classic example is the discovery of quinine by the Amazon Indians. For other examples, such as the Aboriginal Tea Tree remedy ′which treats everything from migraines to eczema, has not been popularised and is readily available to chemist in the west' ('The Spice of Life' in Sunday Monitor, 27 April 1997:19).

At the same time, however, some foreign observers of other societies suffer the tendency to romanticise the role of traditional medicine, and power and influence of the healers themselves. Among some humanitarian workers as well as anthropologists a kind of myth has been promulgated about the ‚harmony' between man and his environment as well as among ‚men' which supposedly reigned in African societies in which traditional medicine was an integral part. Those who hold such romantic views of ‚traditional' culture also believe that if there were only greater knowledge of, and respect for the traditions, it would be possible to return to such a harmonious past. How do those who hold such views of African traditions square them with other concerns, such as the rights of women in societies whose traditions include, for example, the practice female genital cutting?

As is common throughout the world, many patients use different combinations of modern and traditional medicine in their quest for healing. At the same time, in many parts of Africa, traditional medicine has been officially rejected and healers are unable to practice openly for fear of arrest. As a consequence of this difficult position vis-à-vis the law and modern medicine, that treatments involve as much contact with the supernatural as the use of different herbs or treatments, *and* the fact that their livelihoods depend on their knowledge, healers are understandably loathe to discuss their practices with others, especially with outsiders, or to subject them to analysis. As ROBERT CHAMBERS (1983) long ago pointed out, while the science of agriculture has long been highly developed in rural societies, medicine is not. It has always been possible, as he reminds us, for farmers to experiment with different agricultural techniques and thus employ scientific methods for improving outcomes, but attempts to learn about the causes of human illnesses and diseases involve life and death situations. Consequently, such experimentation could not be done. In every society, human life is invested with sacred connotations. In fact, all medical experimentation is faced with ethical dilemmas.

Most important, no culture is static, all are fluid; all societies are constantly adapting to influences, both external and internal. This is also the case with traditional medicine. It has already been noted that Africans, for example, believe that injections are the best treatment they can receive. This belief in injections is so strong that people reject other forms of medication. In Uganda we observed the Red Cross posters which read ‚Do not ask for injections. Tablets are just as good'. Nevertheless, in order to impress their clientele with their up-to-date skills, many traditional healers now offer their patients an ‚African injection' which entails the use of a razor blade or knife to cut the skin to facilitate the absorption of their medicines in the body. More seriously, because many commercially manufactured drugs are easily available on the market in Africa without prescription, some traditional healers - without adequate knowledge of dosages or their consequences - have also incorporated anti-biotics and other powerful drugs into their therapeutic arsenal.

Traditional healers have long engaged in surgical interventions as well (see, for example, ROLES 1966). The circumcision of males and the cutting of female genitals are perhaps the most well-known. In some countries healers remove cataracts and perform other operations on the eye. The major complications which can arise from such surgery are serious haemorrhage and bacterial infections.

Because traditional healers are operating in direct competition with those who practice modern medicine, a serious problem of competition and *territoriality* has developed between them. Patients who admit having consulted a traditional healer before resorting to the recognised health facilities will be seriously reprimanded by the nurse or doctor treating them. Similarly, traditional healers may terrorise their clients by saying that there is serious incompatibility between their medicine and the treatment which they will receive from modern medical practitioners. Because the practices of traditional healers are not limited to dispensing medicines for specific complaints, but encompass other functions which rely on their supernatural powers, they are in a much stronger position to make the claim that their ‚medicines can not be mixed‘ with modern medicine.

Cost is also a problem for those who consult traditional healers. Although the practitioner may not demand cash immediately and may be more flexible than their counterparts who dispense modern medicine in the manner and timing of payments, the user will eventually have to pay in one way or another and often the price demanded is also considerable. Unlike his modern counterpart, the traditional healer has supernatural sanctions to ensure payment!

The Consequences of Forced Migration on Social Structure
When people are forcibly uprooted from their homes they rarely flee as complete communities. Families are separated, elderly often left behind, individuals may have been killed and others are away, engaged in fighting. People do not easily leave their homes. The pattern of flight very often finds families or groups of individuals hiding for long periods of time as near as possible to their homesteads with the hope that they will be able to return. In these situations, often for prolonged periods of time, they often lack access to adequate food and water and the normal health services available to them before the conflict which caused their flight ensued. In such a situation the only services which are likely to be available are those persons who claim expertise in the use of traditional medicines.

When people settle in another place they are often forced to live among strangers or with groups with whom they are in conflict. It is not unusual for civilians loyal to different fighting factions to find themselves sharing the same living area. Many people have been bereaved and are mourning lost relatives; others are uncertain whether or not members of their families have survived. Having survived for long periods of time in remote areas where access to even food and water was severely restricted or where they may have been exposed to diseases for which they have no immunity; they may be malnourished, exhausted and ill and often severely traumatised by their experiences of violence, flight, and loss. Not only have they lost material possessions, but, most importantly, they have also lost their networks of social support. They face a future of profound uncertainty.

Often people who have been forcibly uprooted are forced to live in camps or settlements organised by humanitarian agencies and made completely dependent on charity. Their freedom of movement is curtailed and their normal day-to-day routines are profoundly disrupted. For example, the way of organising life in refugee camps, which requires people to remain on an assigned plot whether or not they have other kinsmen living in another part of the camp, actively hinders if not prevent the reconstruction of social networks. Another dimension of camp life are the relationships of competition and conflict which are exacerbated by the presence of humanitarian agencies which are themselves competing for power and influence among themselves (VOUTIRA & HARRELL-BOND 1995). Camps also expose the inhabitants to the added danger of communicable diseases which rapidly turn into epidemics (VAN DAMME 1995). Humanitarian agencies organise emergency health services which offer a limited number of services for what have been deemed as the priority needs, leaving many real and perceived needs unmet. Most notably, treatments for mental and psychosomatic disorders are not covered by these health services. In fact, most of the resources of these emergency health programmes are focused on health services and activities aimed to reduce child mortality.

As a result, there is an enormous space for traditional healers to operate, but the problem in such a disrupted society is that many of the people who formerly delivered such services are simply not there. This space is rapidly filled by opportunistic individuals who may or may not have any previous experience as healers. It has indeed been observed that in such situations, ‚new‘ traditional healers appear almost overnight. For example, during research conducted among Ugandan refugees, in one settlement of 3,000 people it was found that there were 93 individuals who claimed that they could cure various illnesses (HARRELL-BOND 1986:320).

The Social Roles of Traditional Healers in Refugee Situations

It has already been emphasised that populations which have been violently uprooted cannot be regarded as normal ‚communities'. The social chaos which is typical of refugee camps provides an ideal situation for manipulation and exploitation of people by political factions as well as by charlatans whose motives are monetary or power-seeking, whose method of encouraging compliance is articulated in terms of a return to ‚traditional values'. As GEERTZ (1973) has noted, in situations of crisis, conservatism may emerge as one way to cope with suffering, injustice and chaos. Humans ‚can adapt...somehow to anything his imagination can cope with but he cannot deal with chaos....Therefore our most important assets are always the symbols of our general orientation in nature, on earth, and in society, and in what we are doing' (as quoted by Landau nd). The way in which chiefs are regaining power by redefining ‚traditional values' in the chaos of war-torn southern Sudan is illustrated in the manner in which disputes have been resolved according to ‚customary law' which, in the absence of statutory law, is being redefined.

See ALUR (1997). Monyluok Alur, who served as a ‚magistrate' in the areas under the administration of the Sudan Peoples Liberation Alliance (SPLA), has recorded cases which he judged over a ten year period. One of the most extreme examples he has recorded which illustrates the dangers of encouraging an unchecked ‚return to traditions' involved a charismatic traditional leader who asserted that to achieve peace, his community must make a human sacrifice to appease God. Although arrested and tried for murdering his own young son before the community, the SPLA was afraid to punish him for his crime because of the support he had from his followers.

While there is a growing appreciation in medical circles of the value of traditional folk medicine, little attention has been paid to the social roles of those who claim to have such ‚traditional' healing powers. The problem is that in addition to prescribing herbs which may or may not have therapeutic value, healers also involve themselves in divining who or what is responsible for the illness (which, at times, may well have psychological value, but at others, may be seriously dysfunctional). Healers may play an apparently useful role is legal disputes, administering oaths on ‚medicines' which are believed to kill those who lie, but some are also prepared, *for a price*, to practise ‚black magic' against a client's enemy.

Among the Ugandan refugees in southern Sudan, self-proclaimed healers actively sought out patients. Finding someone ill, the usual diagnosis was that the patient had been ‚poisoned'. For example, a trained nurse/midwife who was ill was found to be receiving treatment for ‚poisoning'. She was asked how could she, a person trained in modern medicine, subject herself to a treatment which involved small incisions with an unsterilised blade in the neck? She explained that during the period they had been hiding in the bush from military attacks the only medicine that was available was from such people. In the camp she had fallen ill and had been treated for malaria, but did not recover. Three healers came to visit from a nearby camp to warn her mother that her daughter had been poisoned.

As in many African societies, illness among the Ugandans was explained as having resulted from someone else's actions, from inter-personal malevolence, and the guilty person(s) have to be found and punished Thus curing someone who has ostensibly been poisoned involves not only treating the illness through a method which in itself endangers life, but divining to determine who was guilty of the poisoning. Both activities are chargeable professional services. Once the guilty is identified, s/he, and it is most *frequently* a she, punishment must be administered. Among the Ugandans, there were cases where entire communities joined in stoning the individual identified by the healer as guilty. People who escaped death had to flee for their lives and not everyone escaped (HARRELL-BOND 1986: Chapter 7).

The cure for poisoning involved stripping and bathing the ill person (in the open, whatever the temperature) with a mixture of cold water and oil mixed with a powder made from a root which produces a foam when rubbed into the skin of the patient; the foam is the evidence that the poison is coming out! In Uganda, it was said that such healers used motor oil; in the refugee camps they used the vegetable fat that was supplied in the ration provided by the World Food Programme (WFP). Apparently, liquid vegetable oil was not a suitable vehicle for their ‚cure', but a spate of poisoning events could be predicted when the WFP food allocation included solid edible fat!

Nevertheless, an American non-governmental agency (NGO) responsible for administering some refugee camps appointed a ‚chief' herbalist to supplement the health services of the clinic. Staff of the clinic in one of these camps complained that although the ‚chief herbalist' was being paid a salary by the

NGO (paid for by UNHCR), he was also charging his patients while their services were free. They complained that among other things, co-operation with their preventative health programme was hampered because of this man had other solutions and was actively advising the residents not to comply, in fact, they were strongly advised to avoid the clinic. Their problems in delivering health services in competition with the camp's chief herbalist were exacerbated by the shortage of medical supplies in their clinic and the fact that the most senior member of their staff was a Sudanese who had less training than the Ugandan refugee staff (ibid.:322).

This ‚chief herbalist' was given a test in curative herbs by a medical anthropologist who happened to be working in the area; it was found that he lacked even a basic knowledge of standard medicinal plants (HARRELL-BOND 1986:321). Nevertheless, this humanitarian agency proudly reported to UNHCR on their appointment of the herbalist, saying that ‚the results appear satisfactory'. Moreover, they also reported that they were considering setting up a ‚laboratory' in a nearby village for the study of traditional herbs, in apparent ignorance of the enormous expense of such an undertaking and the scientific expertise such pharmaceutical studies require.

The popularity of diagnosing poison as the cause of illness has been explained by Willis as another example of the ability of traditional healers to adapt their treatments to conform to new ideas: ‚It is obvious that, alone in the whole body of sorcery beliefs, „poison" corresponds to an idea in current and accepted western belief since it has a putatively empirical basis. This fact…gives it heightened validity under the pressure of western influences…especially those in closest contact with the centres of modernisation.' See HARRELL-BOND (1978) for a discussion of the functions of such beliefs among the elite in Sierra Leone.

Whether or not as a result of the improving health of refugees in the camps in southern Sudan, or in response to the problematic social conditions which persisted among these populations, as time passed, ‚traditional healers' began to become more innovative in their efforts to secure clients. For example, one ‚divined' that a particular member of one extended family had entered into a contract with another such practitioner to ‚get rich'. This involved writing down a list of names of family members and assigning each a number. Over an unspecified time, this herbalist would arrange for each member to die. Just before death, the victim would see his ‚number' appearing somewhere on his or her body, usually on the back. (In the absence of mirrors, this would obviously require someone else to point out that yes, a number had appeared!) Once all the relatives on the list had died, the person who had paid the herbalist heavily for his services would simply wake up rich.

The diviner managed to support these allegations with a convincing story describing one of the members of the endangered family and than rattled off a long list of the potential victims, citing names so common that he could be sure that some at least would be among the extended family group. People became hysterical, but the herbalist reassured them, if they paid enough, he could arrange the ritual which would protect them. Needless to say, almost overnight the frightened family managed to collect the required payment, money, cloth, meat, sugar, and soap, and received the protective ritual. The problem did not stop there; the story circulated and within days, all over the district, Ugandan refugees began seeing numbers appearing on their bodies. As the hysteria spread, the prices for protection also rose (ibid.:322-3).

Conclusions

There is no doubt that traditional healers play significant roles in refugee situations. They have been found helpful in facilitating family tracing (BOOTHBY 1993). They have also played an important role in ‚cleansing' demobilised soldiers, allowing them to resume their place within civilian society (DOLAN & SCHAFER 1997). They also play a crucial part in helping people come to terms with bereavement, especially where deaths have occurred in the process of war and flight and it has been impossible to bury the dead or to perform the appropriate funeral rituals.

In most African societies, where proper funeral rituals have not been performed, it is believed that the living will be punished by supernatural forces - by the spirits of the deceased. Illness is often explained in these terms and in some cases it may be impossible for a health worker to convince a patient to comply with a prescribed treatment until s/he believes that these spirits have been appeased. In such cases, the role of the traditional healer will be a crucial adjunct to modern medicine.

Healers, however, have also been credited for providing the spiritual and political justifications for war and individual violent acts (for example, see RANGER 1991). ‚Healers' were also employed in the war in Mozambique to oversee cannibalistic rituals which initiated boy soldiers into accepting their new role as killers (BOOTHBY et al. 1992:5). The problem is that we are not dealing with a homogeneous ‚traditional' medical profession which has standards for the training of its members who then hold recognised credentials and who are subjected to the discipline of their profession when they depart from its standards.

In most African societies there is a broad range of practitioners whose activities range from dispensing herbs, divining, rain-making, casting out evil spirits, administering oaths, identifying those guilty and determining punishments for breaches of social norms (which are normally defined and articulated by men), selling protection against being shot in warfare, and identifying and killing the enemies of their clients. It is not unusual for one traditional healer to claim the powers to perform all of these activities. Since their practice is highly lucrative, in situations of extreme chaos and material deprivation, the temptation for individuals to exploit the hardships of their fellows may be irresistible.

Few humanitarian workers have either the skills or the time which would be required to discriminate between those traditional healers who are charlatans and those whose interventions will have genuinely therapeutic medicinal or societal effects. There is obviously a great need for research concerning this phenomenon as it is played out among uprooted populations. As ‚culture' is a process and traditions are constantly being reinterpreted and redefined by those with the power to influence others, humanitarian organisations cannot simply rely on anthropological texts - even where they do exist.

References

ALOR KUOL, MONYLUAK. 1997. *Administration of justice in the (SPLA/M) liberated Areas:Court cases in war-torn southern Sudan*', Refugee Studies Programme, University of Oxford, February.

BOELAERT, M. 1996. *Over-consumption or under-supply?*, unpublished internal report, Institute of Tropical Medicine, Antwerp.

BOOTHBY, NEIL. 1993. ‚Reuniting unaccompanied children and families in Mozambique: An effort to link networks of community volunteers to a national programme', *Journal of Social Development in Africa*, 8 (2):11-22.

BOOTHBY, B, P. UPTON and A. SULTAN. 1992. ‚*Children of Mozambique: the cost of survival*', US Committee for Refugees, Washington DC, 1992:5

CHAMBERS, ROBERT. 1983. *Rural Development: Putting the Last First*, Longman.

DOLAN, CHRIS and J. SCHAEFER. 1997. ‚The re-integration of demobilised soldiers in Mozambique: a research report to USAID, Maputo', *Refugee Studies Programme*, May.

GEERTZ, CLIFFORD. 1973. *The Intepretation of Culture: Selected Essays*, Hutchinson, Basic Books.

HARRELL-BOND, B.E. 1978. ‚The fear of poisoning and the management of urban social relations among the professional group in Sierra Leone', *Urban Anthropology*, no. 7(3).

HARRELL-BOND, B.E. 1986. *Imposing Aid: Emergency Assistance to Refugees*, Oxford University Press.

LANDAU, LOREN B. 1997. ‚*Beyond dependency: Is human development an appropriate model for refugee assistance?*', Department of Political Science, University of California - Berkeley, draft, nd (available in RSP library)

ORLEY, JOHN. 1970. *Culture and Mental Illness: a Study from Uganda*, East Africa Publishing House, Nairobi.

RANGER, T. O. 1991. ‚The meaning of violence in Zimbabwe', Paper presented at conference, ‚*Violence and Decolonisation in Africa*, April.

ROLES, N.C. 1996. ‚Tribal surgery in East Africa during the XIXth century', Part 1 - Ritual Operation', in *East African Medical Journal*. 43 (12):570-94.

SUNDAY MONITOR. 1997. ‚*The spice of life*', 27 April:19.

VAN DAMME, W. 1995. ‚Do refugees belong in camps? Experiences from Goma and Guinea', *Lancet*, 346, 579-594.:

VOUTIRA, E. and B.E. HARRELL-BOND. 1995. ‚In Search of the locus of trust: the social world of the refugee camp', in (eds.) DANIEL, E. VALENTINE and JOHN CHR. KNUDSEN, MISTRUSTING REFUGEES', University of California Press, Berkeley: 207-224.

WILLIS, R. G. 1968. ‚Changes in mystical concepts and practices among the Fipa', *Ethnology* Vol. 7, No. 2:139-157.

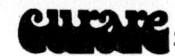

Migration to Multicultural Australia:
Its Impact on the Self-Care of Women
Übersiedlung in ein multikulturelles Australien:
Die Auswirkung auf die Selbstversorgung der Frauen

Elvia Ramirez & Shane Taylor

Abstract: The central theme guiding this research is the primary health care concept of self-care with a wholistic approach to health encompassing lifestyle and well-being and the role of empowerment as a motivating factor. This exploratory research investigates the impact of immigration on the self-care attitudes and behaviours of women in a developed, urbanised country. Those self-care attitudes and behaviours of women are studied through the perception of workers providing direct assistance to them. This research further investigates the dual perspectives of those women who are both providers of services and who themselves are immigrant women. It examines the experiences of immigrant women in pursuing and achieving self-care actions, the difficulties as well as the progress which has been made in this field. Perspectives have been gained from workers operating in greater Brisbane - Australia's third largest metropolis.

Zusammenfassung: Das zentrale Thema dieser Forschung ist das primäre Gesundheitskonzept von Selbstversorgung mit einem ganzheitlichen Ansatz zur Gesundheit, einschließlich Lebensstil und Wohl und die Rolle der Ermächtigung als motivierende Faktoren. Diese Forschung untersucht die Auswirkung der Übersiedlung in bezug auf Einstellungen und Benehmen in punkto Selbstversorgung innerhalb eines urbanen, entwickelten Landes. Diese Punkte wurden von Arbeitern untersucht, die diesen Frauen direkte Unterstützung liefern. Die Forschung untersucht weiterhin die dualen Perspektiven solcher Frauen, die sowohl unterstützende Dienste anbieten, als auch selbst übergesiedelt sind. Die Forschung untersucht die Erfahrungen von übergesiedelten Frauen, während diese Selbstversorgungsaktivitäten nachgehen und setzt sich sowohl mit den Schwierigkeiten als auch mit den Fortschritten auseinander, die in diesem Bereich gemacht werden. Die Untersuchungen wurden bei Arbeiterinnen aus der Umgebung von Brisbane - Australiens drittgrößter Metropole - durchgeführt.

Keywords: Self-Care, Empowerment, Immigration, Australia, Perceptions, Psychology, Selbstversorgung, Ermächtigung, Übersiedlung, Australien, Perspektive/Sicht, Psychologie.

Introduction

Australia is one of the most ethnically heterogeneous countries on earth. Today, some 98 per cent of the population are either migrants or descended from migrants who have come in successive waves to this country in just over the last 200 years. The vast majority of those in the initial migration waves came from Europe and they overwhelmed and displaced to a large degree, the indigenous people of Australia. With the lifting of the *White Australia Policy* in the early 1970s, arrivals have come from a much broader range of sources, from virtually every country in the world. This ethnic diversity prompted the adoption of an official policy of *multiculturalism* to ensure maximum participation and cohesion and fair treatment for all people, while being responsive to the cultural and ethnic diversity of contemporary Australia.

Into this context comes the important issue of womens' health status. This research is guided by the concept of self-care which has as its underpinnings the influence of lifestyle and wider community issues as key determinists impinging upon the health care status of an individual. The common belief is that doctors and other professionals are the 'real' experts on womens' health and that biomedicine exclusively holds the key to improving it. However the increasing realisation of the social or lifestyle origins of many health problems have led to a greater emphasis being placed on more wholistic approaches to health maintenance and improvement, including self-care.

Cultural variations in concepts of sickness and health are now well documented (BAER 1987, KLEINMAN 1988, LOCK & GORDON 1988, LUPTON 1994) however they do not imply that comparability of womens' health status in different societies is impossible. As DOYAL (1995;6) has stated, it is clear that womens' lives vary enormously and recognition of this reality must remain at the heart of any analysis of their health and welfare however we should not deny any possibility of women having beliefs, values or interests in common.

This exploratory work examines the ways by which women's empowered decisions can lead to healthy lifestyles and relationships - choices which are crucial to the self-care ethic. It focuses particularly on the social and cultural influences on their well-being and the major obstacles that can act to prevent them from optimising their health in this way.

More specifically, the perceptions of women having the dual role of being both a provider and consumer are explored in this research. Bearing in mind that women do not constitute a unified and homogeneous group, some cross-cultural similarities and differences are highlighted. Women are both the major consumers and providers of health care in Australia (SALTMAN 1991; ix) and it is this nexus of women as provider/consumer, guided by the philosophy of self care, which has provided a useful framework for this analysis. Many of these women realise that empowerment enables them as workers to assist and even role model self-care activities. Yet sometimes hindering this process are the implications of her ethnicity, the ethnicity of her clients and the many dynamic social and cultural processes and interactions taking place in multicultural Australia.

Women and Health in a Multicultural Policy Framework

The status of women is an important element of the Australian Government's *Social Justice Strategy*, in that it removes practices and structures that discriminate against women and prevent their full social and economic integration. As a major receiving country of immigrants and refugees since the late 1940s, Australia has had long experience with planning for permanent settlers and dealing with ethnic and cultural diversity. Immigrants have similar rights and benefits to the Australia-born, and identical rights following the acquisition of citizenship, available after two years residence. A key aim of Australia's *Social Justice Policy* has been the removal of barriers of race, language, religion or culture in policy formulation, program design and service delivery.

The *National Non-English Speaking Background Women's Health Strategy* gives more attention to improving health services for certain migrant women than improving their health generally. Only two of the 35 recommendations refer to community action/development, they were; "strengthening the community action component of health promotion program for NESB women", this being complemented by "resourcing community development programs for NESB women."

The discourse of self-care however, has made little head-way into public health policy in general with the notable exception of the *Goals and Targets for Australia's Health in the Year 2000 and Beyond* report which has goals relevant to people with chronic health problems and their carers. In a section on *Life Skills and Coping*, it has the goal "to enable people to cope positively with everyday life and reduce mental distress associated with significant life events" (1993; 159) and also "to enable people to participate actively in decision-making and activities to improve their health and environment" (1993;161). Yet there is growing evidence that if we are to succeed in reducing inequalities in the health of population sub-groups and improve the health of the whole population, socio-economic and environmental factors must be addressed (AIHW, 1996;2). In examining concepts of health, illness and healing, self-care is not new however the societal context of modern, urban, multicultural Australia is such that it demands to be treated seriously as a perspective with much to offer.

The two worlds of care; the world of informal, private, caring relationships arising from family, community and other social ties, and the world of professional government-financed services too often function independently of one another. However there should be an area of overlap, and in this area we attempt to explore self-care in a cross-cultural framework. The potential for activity in this area to have positive effects is huge. The intention is to illustrate what has occurred through the eyes and experiences of these workers and to point out the relevance of self-care from the varied perspectives of ethnically diverse women.

Self-Care

The concept of self-care carries with it a responsibility, according to BERNHARD (1975; 25) that one can direct one's own life as opposed to being a victim of circumstances. Self-care means consideration for self and others in a relationship while self-care is never exploitative of another as it maintains the right of independence, dependence and interdependence in a significant relationship. The concept of self-care poses significant questions "what can I do for myself? what can I do for you? to what purpose? at what cost?" However barriers can exist and many women can find it difficult to develop feelings of competence and self-worth associated with positive mental and physical health. Self-care is about the acquisition of knowledge and the confidence to participate more effectively in one's own health care. The multiculturalism of Australia brings together diverse women with different contributions and challenges to these principles of self-care.

The issue of empowerment is an important one in the self-care concept. Empowered women see themselves as meaningful, appreciated and respected individuals who are recognised for their ideas and contributions. They see their jobs and roles as stimulating, challenging and rewarding. They realise that empowerment enables them to "make a difference" by meeting personal and practical needs as well as organisational needs. The importance of these themes to the future of health care delivery to the ethnically and culturally diverse women and their communities of Australia as well as to their quality of life in general, necessitated this preliminary, exploratory research.

Methodology

Health care workers were selected from a range of roles, positions and backgrounds. The sample is in no way meant to be representative of views, rather, professional links determined the nature of the cross-section and this was intended to solely gauge a diversity of anticipated views. They were located working in their roles in the Brisbane metropolitan area (population approximately 2 million), capital of the state of Queensland, in coastal north-eastern Australia. Given that the research is a preliminary exploration, a rigorous analysis of these data or the inference to women health care workers in general cannot be made.

The research instrument was a structured interview questionnaire. This was sufficient to guide the interviewer through the discussion leaving possibilities open for responses to be further explored. The research instrument was pilot tested to highlight any problems and locate any discrepancies with the material gathered and the aims of the project.

The first set of questions constituted a profile of the worker; her ethnic background, professional background (including the issue of professional skills recognition), the migration process, recency of arrival, category of migration and resettlement experiences - these data were both factual and perceptual. A summary of her work and professional experience in Australia was compiled as well as relevant data prior to migration.

Then an indication was gathered of her main client group - the types of clients she is currently working with or has encountered in the past. Explorations of the self-care concept were made firstly as perceived and borne out by the worker and then as held by the clients. More specific questions based on these data were asked about the discrepancies or problems between self-care intentions and realising or acting them out.

Ethical issues were intrinsic to this research. Respect for the privacy of the interviewees was essential and personal information was confidential. An optional debriefing group was offered to the participants in this research, while referrals could be made to councellors of torture and trauma if emotional wounds were opened due to the sensitive nature of some questions in the research instrument.

Outcomes

The health workers and their own backgrounds of self-care

The women health-care workers came from various ethnic groups in Asia, Latin America and Eastern Europe (Privacy concerns do not allow us to identify the actual nationalities of interviewees.). They had only lived in Australia for less than 10 years. Most of them had undergone further English-language training and all had to undergo further professional training before they could work in their current positions. These workers had varied migration experiences - some were refugees and some came under the 'skilled' category. Their current positions varied considerably however all were responsible for the physical and/or emotional health of their clients, exclusively or dominated by women - some were ethno-specific, while some had client bases which were very ethnically mixed and included non-migrants.

Previous occupations were also diverse - some had worked in crisis and emergency situations, as nurses, psychologists, counsellors, stomatologists and so on, while some had little labour force experience prior to migration. Overall they described themselves as "flexible", "adaptable", "strong", "independent", "determined", "non-judgmental" and "approachable" - attributes which are not always present in members of their client groups. They all mentioned that it was important in their current positions to be constantly updating their knowledge so as to make informed decisions and monitor their services and evaluate more efficient and flexible ways of accommodating cultural and ethnic diversity in the provision of these services. All held a strong commitment to making other women more aware of health issues.

Several of the workers felt that they had a strong sense of control over life. Some had migrated from countries where this control was more difficult and challenged by warfare, more intense pressure to conform to traditions and so on. The workers indicated that this control contributed to them being responsible of their own health to a large extent, together with the fact that it was their job to be knowledgeable about health issues (though not necessarily self-care principles).

Most of the workers it was found, had taken advantage of the opportunities presented to them in Australia and this would explain why they are in their current positions. Some of the workers admitted that in their original countries they had other women to speak with and learn from about health matters and many of them role-modelled aspects of self care. They noted that depression can set in when they are cognisant of the isolation that can occur after migration but saw the possibilities for this to be changed. New networks of friends for them often centred around work, study and other interests - a situation which was not necessarily the same for their clients.

Some workers realised that self-care was central to their jobs and that they needed to be in complete control of their own mental and physical health and well-being before they could be of assistance to their clients. Although there is an official policy on promoting self care, this is not nearly as prominent as biomedical policies which have much larger funding attached. However these workers in varying degrees are aware of self-care ideas and practices which can act to mitigate many of the health problems they do encounter in their client groups.

Barriers to self-care
Domestic violence situations emerged frequently as one aspect of lifestyles which had detrimental effects on health and well-being. Several workers identified in their client communities women who remained in abusive relationships where stress, tension and fear were frequently present. For many migrant families this situation arises when pressures of change in a multicultural society cause pressures and anxieties. For one example, the status and role of women may be different from the original country and this can be compounded when women can find a position in the labour force more easily than their husbands - not an uncommon situation. Resentment and anger by males can result if traditional roles are reversed in this new society.

> "Husbands will argue that meeting with other women for recreation activities
> is not a positive influence, that by meeting others they neglect the family and
> house chores and therefore a lot of women feel very isolated and miss
> an intimate relationship with at least another woman who can understand
> them, particularly because men don't often talk about feelings which are central
> for women."

Also identified as a barrier was the view of some women that although they live under rules set by husband, religion, or other members of the community, often it is also the case that they live under the pressures they may impose upon themselves beleiving these external rules to be their own. Such rules are acted upon in the belief that they are making the decision to play traditional roles instead of confronting education or the workplace. The preference to remain isolated or remain at home rather than face the community to work, participate and recreate was a feature which was frequently identified in some communities. This form of self-imposed isolation makes these women difficult to target for self-care strategies. This area needs considerably more research. Some of them however have a number of ways for informal networks to affect their help-seeking behaviour. These networks can buffer stress and influence individuals as to when and where to seek formal services and can transmit values, attitudes and norms that facilitate or discourage the use of formal help.

Some women are brought up in the belief that their bodies, especially their reproductive systems are sinful and they find it difficult to become informed about certain health issues and the various self-care practices that can work to help them. Some of the workers noted that they see their clients as being very vulnerable to these perceptions in many cases, and the workers feel hopeless when they cannot cope with some traditions which prevent women from taking better care of themselves.

Research by PITTAWAY (1991) has highlighted how refugee women have unique experiences quite distinct from other migrant women which necessitate additional resettlement services or special provisions within the framework of existing services. Health workers interviewed for this research tended to agree that among their clients who had a refugee experience, there were several barriers present which impinged upon their self-care abilities. Some have lived for many years in refugee camps prior to being accepted for Australian resettlement where limitations are extreme and where escaping from the country of origin can be a traumatic experience that can have an impact many years later. Feelings of guilt seemed to be a prime example. Particularly for women who have family or friends they left behind in a warzone or violent society, these stresses and guilty feelings can act to prevent a women from taking care of herself - she doesn't want to be seen as "indulging" herself by participating in activities such as massage or sport, or even to eat healthy foods because of the concerns she feels about those left behind. Yet these are the very activities which can be so important to self-care.

Although many women have a great deal of control in their families and do great amounts to ensure the health and well-being of its other members, this can at times or even at all times take precedence over the importance of a woman's own care of herself. They will perceive there to be no time, money or resources to rest, meditate, play or eat healthier food etc. Ironically it may be the most functional of families where all other members are very healthy and relaxed where it is the women whose health is in a slow march to deterioration or dependence on drugs (minor tranquilizers) as that is perceived to be the easiest and quickest way of coping as other self care options are too hard. The workers interviewed mentioned many clients where this is the case and again these women come from ethnic backgrounds where the image of a strong, healthy family is very important yet the sacrifice of her own self-care practices makes them hard to identify until a health crisis occurs.

This issue centres around the predisposition of women to look after others - a role which is important in all cultures but also which is the primary role of women in many cultures. However, arrival to Australia can conflict with this role and some women will acquire new role models and in this process may even be able to role model this care for other family members. A typical response to illustrate how women can neglect themselves as they are oriented to only looking after the rest of the family is this quote by an Asian worker - "we were taught to live for others and that to live is to give". The implication here is that women are to look after themselves but only so that their health is sufficient to be able to support and encourage the health of others. Many cultures, not only those from Asia, regard it as selfish to look after oneself first and although the self-care principles are inclusive and are not promoting self-care at the expense of others, sometimes women can consider it to be that way and therefore disregard it. DOYAL (1995; 232) has highlighted how despite their active participation in promoting the well-being of others, unless womens' health needs are met, their capacity to carry out these activities will be arbitrarily constrained and they will be unable to realise their own potential as human beings.

The message of self-care can also meet barriers when cross-cultural communications break down, despite the specific training that health-care workers have to prevent this. Some women are reluctant to question health care providers (particularly mainstream health care providors) or are unsure of the proper questions to ask, this can limit their ability to work out for themselves what lifestyle choices need to be made to rectify health problems. Certain cultural barriers prevent some women from speaking about self-care issues, "many women are good at keeping things to themselves - then they become depressed - do not sleep, or eat."

Opportunities for self-care
The women workers interviewed could potentially act as disseminators of great amounts of knowledge pertaining to self-care, natural medicine, preventative measures and healthy lifestyles but in a community of change and with conflicting pressures these can be hard to enact. Nevertheless they did recognise that such a diverse mix of cultures living and interacting to various degrees was more conducive to the possibility of the adoption of new self-care practices.

Comparatively well resourced, the Australian health care system gave the workers the basic support needed in their work. "Here I have the resources to support the women I work with" (in health provision). Furthermore, some of the workers stated that they tried to act as mentors of less-experienced health-care workers.

Women may have more of a sense of community in Australia as they may have no extended family here as they did in the old country. This type of community can be seen as the best support and so belonging to that is strong. When a group of refugee women from a particular ethnic background came together to share the problems of their new lives it was health and particularly lifestyle choices and ways for them to help themselves that provided the key to breaking down barriers of communication between them. Once women understood that their distress was a rational and shared response to their situation, they were able to think more positively about how to promote their own mental and physical health and that of others.

Many of the workers noted that migrant women have remarkable survival skills, self-preservation skills and coping skills but not always can they easily transfer those to self-care skills. This is ironic, for these women often are at the forefront of establishing new lives and new roles for themselves and their families in their new country, sometimes with limited capital or assistance and frequently with language or other cultural difficulties. Nevertheless such skills may be easily transferable and many workers see this more as an opportunity given that self-care skills should be comparatively simple to learn and apply. Many of the workers shared breakthrough stories in this research, providing examples of key individuals in certain communities who made empowered decisions which had positive effects on their health and that of their families and communities.

Many of the workers found that the environment and society of Australia is more conducive in many ways to certain self-care activities than their original countries. REID and TROMPF (1990; 65) have studied how "some immigrants have considerable cultural advantages to alternative ideas about freedom and dignity." In their framework of findings, it may well be that the self-care concept has a lot more to offer particular groups of women settling in multicultural Australia. The opportunities in some societies for these types of self-care are far fewer. Fewer open spaces, less fresh food, less recreation time, more kin obligations and so on meant that many self-care practices were harder to follow in the original country. Overall, the study reflects that women can have a wholistic view of health. For example, most workers interviewed could understand the close association between mental health and lifestyle and short and long term physical health. However, it seems that for some, the more exposed they are to the 'Western world' of Australian cities, the more fragmented their vision of health becomes.

Concluding Discussion

How women maintain a state of well-being despite conflicting roles in a new, diverse and challenging environment is an interesting field of research. The dual perspectives of women health workers who not only deal with these problems in their client communities but who have also dealt with these issues at a personal level have provided many insights here. Their adaptability and flexibility in resolving their health concerns, maintaining their health, dealing with threats to it or repairing themselves from a health crisis in a multicultural health context offers a wealth of knowledge for all to share.

The migration process can cause some social or lifestyle problems to act as origins of health problems, but arrival in a multicultural city also offers numerous opportunities to share knowledge on self-care actions. Womens' active and deliberate involvement in meeting their own health care needs, encompassed under the ethic of self-care, can sometimes meet cultural resistance, stress or even conflict in some situations. Numerous barriers were identified and some of the key ones explored here. Collectively however, it is beyond doubt that the migration of women from all parts of the world to Australia, and specifically Brisbane, has had some impact upon the self-care of individuals and communities. These women are not simply passive receptors of changing notions of self-care but through complex processes of cultural and personal change are able to influence their own practices and those of others.

However, cultural change and adaptation can be a sensitive issue, this study needs to explore further the circumstances whereby self-care practices can be transformed to be more culturally appropriate in those circumstances where self-care is still denied or not given a high enough priority. Temporal changes in attitudes were found to have occurred and also generational differences in approaches to self-care services were evident in the study. There was evidence to suggest that some women realised that the successful participation in their culture depends on their own self-care and their willingness to share self-care strategies with others.

Although some aspects of self-care challenge traditional roles of women from some cultures there remain some concrete actions which all can take to improve their health status. Mutual understanding can help give migrant women of diverse backgrounds insight into ways of promoting self-care and combating common threats to it. The breadth of these actions is such that the very definition of what constitutes 'health' can be called into question. Under what conditions professional health workers/carers support or even role model self-care in the community needs further exploration although there is evidence that this is occurring to some extent. These women with their varied ethnic and personal backgrounds, often with key family members thousands of kilometres away, must be able to provide effective assistance and support to one another on the basis of their common humanity.

Women are gatekeepers of information and furthermore, through role modelling of self-care for other women they can empower them. Many of the workers interviewed also had the power to manipulate information on self-care without knowing the full cultural implications for their clients by doing so. However the way empowered decisions lead to a healthy lifestyle and the ability of women to take responsibility for much of their own health protection should still be given greater recognition as a viable perspective and an often successful solution for many health problems.

There would appear to be no single formula, pattern or set of responses - the diversity of cultures and within that, the range of individuals and personalities, means that approaches to further the pursuit of self-care must be adaptable. The activity of self-care has been around as long as humanity but its practice and reason for being have undergone many revisions. In a multicultural society where the ongoing processes of migration continue to shape the lives and experiences of women and their health, the way these health workers accept, encourage, promote, and even have the power to role-model self-care to their communities has been an interesting example of how different cultures interact.

References

ALCORSO, C SCHOFIELD, T. 1991. *The National Non-English Speaking Background Women's Health Strategy* (for the Office of the Status of Women, Department of Prime Minister and Cabinet) Canberra, Australian Government Publishing Service.

AUSTRALIAN INSTITUTE OF HEALTH AND WELFARE (AIHW). 1996. *Australia's Health* Australian Government Publishing Service Canberra.

BAER, H. (ed). 1987. *Encounters with Biomedicine: Case Studies in Medical Anthropology.* Gordon and Breach, New York.

BERNHARD, Y. 1975. *Self-Care.* Celestial Arts Millbrae, California

DOYAL, L. 1995. *What Makes Women Sick: Gender and the Political Economy of Health.* Macmillan Basingstoke.

KLEINMAN, A.. 1988. *The Illness Narratives: Suffering, Healing and the Human Condition.* New York, Basic Books.

LEWIN, E, OLESEN, V. 1985. *Women, Health and Healing; Toward a New Perspective.* Tavsitock, New York.

LOCK, M GORDON D. (eds) 1988. *Biomedicine Examined.* Dordrecht Kluwer.

LUPTON, D. 1994. *Medicine as Culture: Illness, Disease and the Body in Western Societies.* Newbury Park Sage.

NUTBEAM, D. 1993. *Goals and Targets for Australia's Health in the Year 2000 and Beyond;* Report prepared for the Commonwealth Department of Health, Housing and Community Services. Canberra, Australian Government Publishing Service.

PITTAWAY, E. 1991. *Refugee Women - Still at Risk in Australia, A study of the First Two Years of Resettlement in the Sydney Metropolitan Area.* Australian Government Publishing Service, Canberra.

PUNAMAKI, R and ASCHAN, H. 1994. Self-care and Mastery among Primary Health Care Patients *Social Science Medicine,* Vol. 39, No. 5, pp. 733-741.

REID, J and TROMPF, P. 1990. *The Health of Immigrant Australia: A Social Perspective.* Harcourt Brace Jovanovich Publications Sydney.

SALTMAN, D. 1991. *Women and Health: An Introduction to the Issues.* Harcourt Brace Jovanovich Publications Sydney.

WHELEHAN, P and Contributors. 1988. *Women and Health: Cross Cultural Perspectives.* Bergin and Garvey Publishing Inc Massachusetts.

Women and AIDS in Uganda and the Future of Ethnomedicine
Frauen und AIDS in Uganda und die Zukunft der Ethnomedizin
Kabahenda Nyakabwa

Abstract: AIDS poses enormous social, economic demographic and developmental challenges for Uganda. Mortality rates have reached such apocalyptic proportions that the government, families and communities can nof longer cope with the financial and emotional cost invvolved
in caring for the sick and the dying. Because of the gendered structures of social, economic and political inequalities, women, who are soceity's most vulnerable group, aee the most adversely affected. Massive financial assistance from the international community is necessary if the country is to deal effectively wit hthe short term and long term challenged posed by the AIDS epidemic. Africans have long relied on traditional medicines to cure various illnesses. The use of herbal remedies, particularly those reputed to improve the immune system, should be promoted and developped through research. The implications of the AIDS epidemic for the country are discussed and policy strategies proposed.

Zusammenfassung: Die Immunschwäche Aids bedeutet für Uganda eine enorme gesellschaftliche, ökonomische und demographische Belastung sowie eine enorme Belastung für die Entwicklung des Landes. Die Mortalitätsrate hat derart apokalyptische Ausmaße erreicht, dass die Regierung, die Familien und die Gemeinden nicht länger imstande sind, die finanziellen und emotionalen Kosten zu tragen, die mit der Betreuung der an der Seuche Erkrankten und Sterbenden verbunden sind. Wegen der geschlechtsgebundenen Strukturen gesellschaftlicher, wirtschaftlicher und politischer Ungleichheit sind die Frauen, die verletzlichste Gruppe der Gesellschaft, am stärksten benachteiligt. Durchgreifende finanzielle Hilfen von seiten der Völkergemeinschaft sind notwendig, wenn das Land die Herausforderungen, die die Aids-Epidemie akut und auf längere Sicht darstellt, wirklich meistern soll. Lange Zeit haben sich die Afrikaner an traditionelle Heilmittel gehalten, um verschiedene Krankheiten zu behandeln. Die Anwendung von Heilpflanzen, vor allem solchen, die im Rufe stehen, das Immunsystem zu verbessern, sollte gefördert und durch Erforschung entwickelt werden. Die Folgen der Aids-Epidemie für das Land werden erörtert und politische Strategien vorgeschlagen.

Keywords: Africa, Uganda, AIDS, traditional medicine, immune system, Afrika, Uganda, AIDS, Traditionelle Medizin, Immunsystem.

Introduction
In the 1980s when Acquired Immune Deficiency Syndrom (AIDS) first appeared in Uganda, Ugandans mused at its emaciating effect and gave it the euphemistic name of „slim",. Uganda was the first African country to openly acknowledge the existance fo this disease and to conduct and aggressive campaign towards its prevention. In spite of a phenomenal effort to fight the AIDS epidemic, Uganda is currently one of the worst AIDS-hit countries in Africa. Reportedly 1.7 Ugandans are infected wit hthe HIV virus (AFRICA REPORT May/June 1994); the total Ugandan populstion of 17 millions is directly and indirectly affected, mortality and morbidity rates have reached ominous proportions, whole communities may be decimated, and social disruption.

Many factors can account for the explosive AIDS situation in Africa and Uganda but none as dramatic as economic misery, patriarchy, culture, religion and inadequate health care resources (BARNETT and BLAIKIE 1992; LATHAM 1993; TURSHEN 1991). The purpose of this paper is to illustrate the reality of the AIDS epidemic in Uganda as a medical and social disease that poses enormous economic, social, and developmental challemges for Uganda in general, and for women in particular. The other purpose is to advocate for use of ethnomedicine as an alternative therapy to western drugs, which are not affordable by the majority of people living with AIDS (PWAs). The implications of the AIDS epidemic for the country are discussed and policy strategies proposed.

The AIDS Reality
AIDS has become Uganda`s number one killer disease and the following statistics illustrate the magnitude of the problem:
- In the period 1985-89 AIDS was responsible for one quarter of the loss years of productive life (UNAIDS Fact Sheet, March 1996, n.p.)

- In 1995-99 AIDS is expected to cause more than half of this loss (ibid.).
- 1.8 million Ugandans were allegedly infected with the HIV virus. More than 46.000 people are known to suffer from full-blown AIDS (Reuters North American Wire 1. December 1996, 8). •
  AIDS in Uganda is a plague that cuts across age, gender, sexual orientation, class, religion, tribe, social economic status, rural and urban boundaries. Young affluent urban professionals, prostitutes, school children above the age of 15 as well as people in the rural areas are equally affected (AFRICA REPORT May / June 1994; BARNETT and BLAIKIE 1992;).
- A joint study conducted by UNICEF and Makerere University in 1990 reported that eighty three per cent of all reported AIDS cases were among individuals between 15-40 years of age.
- According to the latest World Bank report on Uganda's social indicators, AIDS will lower the population growth rate from the 3.7 % it would have been without AIDS, to 3.1 % during 1995-2000. „Because of the long latency period, even if effective AIDS control practices were adopted today, the annual number of AIDS deaths will continue to inctrease for the remainder of this decade,,(1993, 9).
- The mortality rate has reached such crises proportions that the government, families and communities are beginning to feel the strain.
- The financial and emotional burdens involved in caring for HIV/AIDS patients and the millions of orphaned children are beyond the capability of the government and families.
- Although the disease seems to be on the wane, „entire communities have been wiped out, and a generation of orphans is left to fend for themselves,, (FINANCIAL TIMES 31 Dec. 1996).
- A study of orphans in Uganda revealed that 38% of the children were under the care of their grandparents, 7% were cared for by aunts, 5% by uncles, 5% by sisters/brothers, and 2% by childred under 16 years of age (UNAIDS Fact Sheet, March 1996, n.p.).
- „Figured from the World Health Organization (WHO) reveal that between 1980 and 1994 average life expectancy dropped from 52 to 42, among the lowest in the world,,. (REUTERS NORTH AMERICAN Wire 1 Dec. 1996).
- „By the year 2010, life expectancy could fass to 31 - unless the limited successes now being reported in the anti-AIDS campaign can be sustained and expanded,,, (ibid.).

The Impact of HIV/AIDS on Women's Lives The following case studies depict the situation of many women in Uganda today.

Case Study # 1

Ms Namukasa is a 45 year-old single parent of six children. Her oldest daughter, Margaret, who has just died of AIDS left her three children in Namukasa's care. Ms. Namukasa's elder brother and his wife died in the war of liberation in 1985, leaving their five children in the care of Namukasa. Margaret was a petty-trader in Kampala, the capital city. Two of Ms. Namukasa's other faughters are HIV positive and keep falling sick. Each has two very young children. Ms.Namukasa has never worked outside the home and can barely read and write. She grows all her food and was depending on her oldest daughter for money. She now has to care for her five daughters, her seven grand-children, her brother's five children (2 nieces and 3 nephews) and does not have time to grow as much food as she used to. The death of her oldest child, the sickness of the two daughters and their impending death have had an emotional toll on her. She was recently diagnosed with high blood pressure and has been advised to take bed-rest. Her thee younger kaughters have had to quit school because she cannot afford to pay their school fees. Moreover, they have to help her take care of their sisters, nephews and nieces, and cousins.

Case Study #2

Mrs. Bagonza, Mrs. Kintu, and Mrs. Okello are sisters in their thirties. Mr. Bagonza, a prominent lawyer and Mr. Kintu an Accountant with the Central Bank, were both young men under 45 years of age who died of AIDS. Mr. Kintu, in a desperate search for a cure, visited private doctors in Zaire and West Germany and the Kintu family has been left virtually penniless. Mr. Okello, a university Professor, and his wife have full-blown AIDS and are on their death-beds. Mrs. Baganza and Mrs. Kintu have persistently tested seronegative. There are twelve children involved in this case study, rangingfrom 6 years of age to 14. Mrs. Bagonza and Mrs. Kintu both gave high school education but they have never worked outside the home. Since the deaths of their husbands, they have withdrawn from society and all they do is sit in their homes and cry. Mrs. Bagonza is a relatively well-off widow but her in-laws have already expropriated some of her property and she fears they may take it all. Mr. and Mrs. okello do not have much money and their healthcare is costing their extended family a lot of money. Relations between the Okellos and their extended families are visibly strained. The three sisters claim they are victims of their marriages but are powerless against this disease. They have elderly and sickly parents.

The impact of HIV/AIDS on women in Uganda demonstrates that it is women who bear the brunt of the continent's misfortunes such as wars, famine and disease, patriarchy, gender-based oppression, lack of rights and poverty (PAULME 1963; JAMES 1992). Although men and women are both infected with the HIV virus, the latter are more adversely affected because of their specific economic, social, health and biological situations (BARNETT and BLAIKIE 1992; CALDWELL, ORUBULOYE & CALDWELL 1992). Extreme economic deprivation and lack of social status, and a patriarchal system which encourages polygamy have predisposed women to high rates of HIV infection and AIDS. It is poverty that forces poor women and young girls into prostitution, thus placing them at high risk for unwanted pregnancies, HIV infection and AIDS. The „sugar daddy„ phenomenon means that young school girls render sexual favours to urban middle class and affluent men known as „sugar daddies„ in exchange for money and other material goods. The men and the girls both become carriers and they in turn spread the virus (AFRICA REPORT BARNETT and BLAIKIE 1992; NEW YORK TIMES 22 June 1992;).

Monogamous relationships are not shields against infection because of a double sexual standard whereby women are expected to remain faithful to their husbands and boyfriends while turning a blind eye to their infidelities. Even when a woman knows or suspects that her husbands or partner has been unfaithful to her, the notion of „negotiating safer sex practice„ is out of the question because of cultural reasons, her economic dependence on the man and her lack of assertive skills (Unlin 1992). A study done in Uganda in 1990 reported that 30% of the women surveyed believed themselves at risk because they could not stop their partners from having sex with other women for reasons stipulated above (MARIASY & RADLETT 1990).

In Uganda as in the rest of Africa, devolopment has taken place on the backs of women because they perform most of the hard labour. However, in a male-dominated society, it is the men who own the property. Traditionalfemale roles are centred around domestic chores and reproductive responsibilities including raising children and care-giving (UNICEF 1989). This means that women delay seeking care for themselves because they are busy caring for children and ill family members. In addition to the burden of family care, food production also falls on their shoulders. Notwithstanding, women have limited decision making powers within the family and within society, including power to control their own sexuality, and therefore their own bodies, to challenge men's behaviour, and to negotiate the conditions under which they have sexual intercours (HUNTER 1990; UNLIN 1990). But when their husbands or partners die they are deprived of property and inheritance rights and left virtually destitute (BARNETT and BLAIKIE 1992). Their predicament is further complicated by officials of the office of the Administrator General who reportedly dfraud millions of money from the estates of widows and children that fall under their jurisdiction (UGANDA CONFIDENTIAL 29 Nov.- 6 Dec. 1993). AIDS, therefore, does not create new contexts for women, it only aggravates the problems of their existing conditions in society. Surprisingly, for unknown reasons seropositive women are reported to live longer than men (BARNETT and BLAIKIE 1992).

As Caregivers, the role of women in the fight against AIDS in Ugandan society should not be over looked; as survivors they cannot effectively participate in the country's development without an amelioration in their social conditions. By implication, therefore, women form a special category that requires special attention in terms of health delivery services and AIDS prevention programmes. Apart from maternity and ante-natal clinics, medical clinics that cater exclusively t women are scarce. Yet, AIDS symptomatology is different in women than in men and consequently, many women are misdiagnosed. The need for female-centred clinics to respond to the specific needs of all women and particularly seropositive women is urgent in Africa and Uganda.

Economic and developmental challenges
The economic and moral challenges posed by the AIDS epidemic for Uganda are frightening. In most cases, people with AIDS (PWAs) particularly in urban centres, are young educated professionals and

their death implies direct an indirect deprivation of human and financial resources necessary for Ugandas present and furture development. The economic and developmental impact is harsh. First, the country loses directly because civil servants, taxpayers, potential investors, consumers and young parents, who, at the peak of their errning and reproductive capacity, are dying in great numbers. Second, the disease may make government and companies dysfunctional through inceased deaths among the managerial, professional and skilled labour supply. According to the World Bank, such losses „can be expected to slow the growth of the modern sector of the Ugandan economy, over the medium to long term„ (1993, 10). Third, increased deaths in the rural areas could lead to a drop in coffee production which accounts for 90% of Uganda´s foreign exchange earnings. Time spent caring for the sick and dying means that less time is devoted to food production and in the long term this may cause famine. Fourth, the country also loses indirectly because government and companies accord sick-leave to those dying of AIDS, death benefits to surviving family members, time off for co-workers to attend funeral services and burial and grief-leave, all of which affect production and efficiency. In the long run, therefore, capital that could be used for development and investment purposes is being diverted to AIDS education and prevention programs thereby slowing down progess.

AIDS is and incurable and expensive disease. The cost of medical care is clearly above the means of a debt-burdened Third World nation like Uganda. Palliative drugx such as the controversial AZT, DDI (Dideuxyinosine) and DDC (Dideoxycytidine) which are prolonging the lives of PWAs in the western countries are not accessible to nor affordable by Third World countries. The implicatin is that in dess developed countries PWAs have virtually no change of survival. For example PWAs in western countries can lead healthy lives for 12 to 15 years after diagnosis while the longevity of an ordinary PWA in Uganda varies from six months to three years following diagnosis. According to a Canadian doctor, „the cost of drug therapy for the direct and indirect treatment of HIV and AIDS can range from about two thousand dollars upwards to tens of thousands of dollars annually per person. These costs usually increase as a person progresses from HIV infection to full-blown AIDS„ (Kilby Mar. 1993, 31). As the number of PWAs increases treatment costs will soar but the government has to choose between PWAs who are going to die in the long run and development projects. The moral dilemma posed by this epidemic becomes obvious. Hard-pressed families have todevote all their resources to doctors and medicines and by the time the PWA finally dies, their financial and emotional resources are severely depleted. The total effect on the country will be increased poverty at both the macro and micro levels.

It is for this reason that it is imperative for the government of Uganda to start seriously considering the promotion and development of ethnomedicine.

The Future of Ethnomedicine
Long before the advent of western medicine, Africans treated their sick and dying with herbal remedies. Due to colonialism and racism in the western world, African ethnomidicine has been denigrated. In the competion to a cure for AIDS, the western medical establishment, and some African governments reportedly sabotage the knowledge and contribution of African doctors (New African Sept. 1996, 16-17 & 21). According to the World Health Organization (WHO), herbal preparations account for 30 to 50 per cent of total medicinal consumption in China while Japanese consumption of herbal medicine is reportedly the highest in the world (WHO Fact Sheet No, 134, 24 Sept. 1996, p. 2). In North America and Europe, health food stores abound with expensive herbal remedies which grow wild in Africa and cost nothing.

In Uganda, medical doctors are in short supply, pharmaceutical products are in short supply, furthermore their cost is beyond the means of ordinary people. Most people rely mainly on taditional practitioners and local medicinal pants for primary health care. The use of traditional medicines to treat opportunistic diseases such as fever, yeast infection, diarrhoe and vomiting should be promoted and developped. A country like Uganda would benefit greatly if scarce resources could be devoted to research in ethnomedicine, particularly, herbal medicines that are reputed to improve the immue system. These would prolong the lives of PWAs and at the same time reduce their medical expenditure and future poverty.

Social Challenge
As more poeple die, increasing numbers of the elderly, spouses and children are left without adequate

financial and emotional support. One of the most visible social impacts of the AIDS epidemic on Uganda is the increasing number of orphans and their elderly grandparents (The Christian Science Monitor 16 March 1994; Toronto Star 24 Mar. 1994). By the end of 1991, it was estimated that the total number of children orphaned by AIDS ranged between 620,000 and 1,200,000 (HUNTER 1900). Forty per cent were under the care of guardians who are over 50 years of age while 25 % were under the care of individuals above the age of 60 (Uganga/UNICEF Report October 1991).

Caring for PWAs and the orphans left by them places an enormous burden on surviving families and society. Depending o the age of a child, the death of a parent can be the most catastrophic event in his or her life. The younger the child the more he or she is dependent on his or her parents. Loss of a parent in early childhood means loss of a central figure of attachment in the child's emotional life (OSTERWEIS et al. 1984). Some children may have witnessed their parent's dying of AIDS and are psychologicallly traumatized by the manner in which their parents died. Due to their tender ages, the psychological effects may not manifest themselves until late adulthood. In case where both parents die, the parental role is assumed by grandparents, uncles, aunts, or close family friends. Change of homes and guardians, especially in early childhood, creates chaos and disorganisation in the lives of children and has deleterious effects on their emotional, social, psychological and intellectual development (OSTERWEIS et al. 1984). Generally speaking, Uganda is a very poor country and many families already experience severe economic hardships. In African culture adoption is relatively unknown and an practise that is not easily acceptable. The cultural expectation is that surviving immediate and extended family members will take cae of orphans of their deceased/dying relatives. But the size of Ugandan families and the sheer numbers of children involved makes it practically impossible for Ugandans to provide adequate care for these childrens. Grandparents and the extended family are the only social support networks and welfare system available to orphans. With increasing deaths, inflation and rising costs of living, the economic effects on the families become apparent.

A study done in Uganda in 1990 found that both guardians and children were experiencing stress. Guardians report psychological stress from dividing already scarce resources among natural and orphaned children. Orphans leave home at young ages because they are continually disadvantaged in the distribution of material resources and psychological support. They may be overworked by relatives or other guardians who consciously or unconsciously wiew them a s burden. Lack of supervision, poper caretaking and school or vocational activities lead to poor scocialization, alienation from guardians and the community and possible delinquency (HUNTER 1990, 686). This ha serious implications for the country's development. Essentially, these children may be emotionally, socially, and financially incapacitated to the extent that they may become unproductive members of society. Therefore, their participation in Uganda's development process will be ineffentive.

Government Responses and Community Based Organizations Governmental, non-governmental and community groups have organises locally and the international community responded with financial and material generosity towards HIV/AIDS prevention educational programs.

AIDS support organizations (ASO) have mushroomed in Uganda. The first and internationally recognized one is The AIDS Support Organization (TASO). Although TASO provides counselling, practical support and training for people with AIDS (BARNETT and BLAIKIE 1992, 108), it does not have branches in all parts of the country. Other local initiatives include The Uganda Women's Efforts to Save Orphans (UWESO) which helps orphans with clothing and scholarships; Orphans Community Based Organization (OCBO) are run by the National Resistance Councils to register orphans (BARNETT and BLAIKIE 1992, 108); the National Council for Children (NRC) under the Ministry of Labour and Social Affairs was recently established reportedly „to coordinate a national programme of action for children.„ The NRC entrusts Restistance Council's (RCs) vice-chairpersons and members with the childrens „protection and welfare.„ (THE NEW VISION 23 May 1994). Policy Implications AIDS in Uganda should be addressed in a development context. Such a proposition would take into consideration the definition of the United Nations Declaration on the Right to Development which states that, development is a comprehensive economic, social, cultural and political process that aims at the attainment of a better life for the entire population on the basis of their ective, free and meaningful participation in development and in the fair distribution of benefits resulting therefrom (ENCYCLOPEDIA OF HUMAN RIGHTS 1991,384). Ugandans do not participate equally in the development process. The unequal status of women and marked regianal diffferences in terms of wealth distribution and healthcare infrastructure means that AIDS affects Ugandans disproportionately (World Bank 1993). Without a revision of some of the aspects of existing health, political and social institutions and a total change in individuals'world view, the fight against AIDS will be futile. In spite of alarming death rates in the whole country, health services are not equitably distributed and the seriousness of the epidimic is not readily apparent to the people at risk. For example, AIDS control is still confined largely to health ministries; health structures are grossly inadequate; churches continue to campaign against condom use; sodiers rape with impunity (AFRICA REPORT May / June 1994, 29). On the basis of the above considerations, the following policy strategies at the national, regional and international levels are proposed:

National / Regional Strategies

1. Health must take precedence over other government priorities because without a healthy society, other development efforts will be fruitless. The World Bank reports that „Uganda's aggregate health indicators are among the world's worst„ (1993, 52).
2. The use and development of herbal medicines should be promoted. AIDS Support Organizations must act as media for raising individual consciousness about herbal remedies that could prolong the lives of PWAs.
3. In the absence of a miracle cure, Uganda's salvation in terms of future development lies with its children. The care of orphans in African societies was always assumed by the extneded family based on the assumpion that the extended family was itself intact. Given the present circumstances in Uganda, extended families are also dealing with their own deaths, bereavement and orphans. Therefore, their financial and emotional resources are depleted and they are no longer in a position to cope with the situation. Instituitional care is not a viable alternative for Uganda for the follwing reasons: (a) because it is an alien concept in African culture; (b) because it would isolate children from their kin and familiar surroundings, marginalize them and expose them to the stigma of being known as „AIDS orphans„ (The Christian Science Monitor 16 March 1994); (c) because it raises issues of child sexual molestation which are becoming public concerns in Uganda today (The New Vision 12 Jan 1994); and (d) because the country does not have the necessary infrastructure and human resources necessary for institutional care. Hence, a foster care/parenting programme that helps orphans children to copr with their deprivation while simultaneously offering them an opportunity for self-development should be implemented.
4. There should be strong and effective legislation to protect women and children from seropositive men. Those who rape women and children are a menace to society and should be prosecuted and if found guilty, incarcerated.
5. Regardless of their social, economic or political status, the justice system must serve all Ugandans fairly.
6. Legal education on the rights of women and children to property and inheritance, and freedom from violence must become and integral part of all programs offered by AIDS support organizations.
7. There should be more female centred research geared to exploring women's knowledge, attitudes and practices, support systems and coping resources particularly of long surviving seropositive women.

International Strategies

1. Research done in Thrid World countries by western academics and medical personnel has tended to enhance the careers and fame of the same while obscuring the efforts and contributios of local professionals; research findings should be shared equally.
2. The availability of vaccines of any other therapeutic drug to affected countries should be mandetory.
3. More funding should be channelled towards social science research and should focus on tch effect of multiple bereavement on the elderly, children, families and communities. How are children, families and communities coping? What are the effects, if any, of multiple bereavement? How does the nation plan to cope with the psychological effects of this epidemic?
4. Fighting AIDS and its effects on Uganda requires a concerted effort of the government, local and international NGOs and the international community. Internationaldonor agencies can play a key role in providing additional resources - physical, financial and trchnical - to enable the government to meet the shelter, educational, nutritional, clothing, and health needs of the orphans.

Summary
This paper has illustrated that AIDS poses enormous social, economic, demographic and developmental challanges for Uganda. Mortality rates have reached such apocalyptic proportions that the government, families and communities can no longer cope with the financial and emotional cost involved in caring for the sick and the dying. Modern medicines on the market are beyond the finalcial capabilities of PWAs and their care-givers. It is imperative, therefore, that the government devotes time and money to the development and promotion of ethnomidicine. Because of the gendered structures of social, economic and political inequalities, women, who are society's most vulnerable group, are most adversely affected. Thus, massive financial assistance from the international community is necessary if the country is to deal effectively with the short term and long term challenges of the AIDS epidemic.

Conclusion
In conclusion, the AIDS situation in Uganda begs the following questions: Why is it that despite an open and aggressive AIDS campaign, and in spite of the knowledge acquired about this epidemic through the traumatic experience of high death rates in families and communities, the AIDS situation in Uganda has not abated? Dr. Mann, acknowledged specialist in the fight against AIDS, recently admitted that „AIDS prevention programs are losing strength and credibility and can do little to prevent the epidemic from spreading to vulnerable countries„ (Ottawa Citizen 10 August 1994). The evidence leads the author to conclude that increased knowledge is a necessary but insufficient mechanism to fight AIDS; prevention programs provide only a partial solution and therefore new strategies must be explored. The selective nature of AIDS, its direct and indirect economic and social costs portend destitiution, social and economic devastation at macro and micro levels. In order to halt the ravages of this disease in Africa, AIDS prevention education must be combined with a change in the pre-existing conditions that predispose people to HIV and AIDS. Such conditions include economic, social and gender inequaltities such as women's lack of control over their own sexuality, lack of property and inheritance rights, lack of legal and political rights, unequal access to healthcare, and cultural practices such as polygamy which relegate an inferior and powerless position to women in families and society. This calls for a developmental model which emphasizes the provision of basic human needs with a human rights component. One of the most important aspects of such a model would the involvement of women in all phases of AIDS-related planning, programme development, implementation and monitoring. The other would be the recognition of the worth of every Ugandan and women not only as agents of reprodution, but as productive members of society with equal political, social an economic rights as preconditions for a healthy society.

References
AFRICA REPORT (Denville, NJ). May/June 1994. *Julie Flint.* „*AIDS: The Plague Years*„ 27-29
CALDWELL, J.C.., ORUBULOYE, I.O. & CALDWELL, P. 1992. Undereaction to AIDS in Sub-Saharan Africa. *Social Science and Medicine* 34 (11), 1169-1182.
FINANCIAL TIMES, 31 December 1996. *Michela Wrong.* „*Openness in Tackling . AIDS Has Led to Sharp Falls in Infection Rates*„.
GOVERNMENT OF UGANDA & UNICEF PROGRAMME OF COOPERATION (October 1991). *Expanded Programme of Communication for Control of AIDS in Uganda. Plan of Action 1991-1992.*
HUNTER, S. 1990. Orphans as a window on the AIDS epidemoc in Sub-Saharan Africa: Initial Results and implications of study in Uganda. *Social Science and Medicine,* 31 (6), 681-690.
JAMES, S.N. (1992).„Transgressing Fundamental Boundaries: The Struggle for Women's Human Rights.„ *Africa Today,* Vol. 39, No. 4, 34-45.
KILBY, D. 2 March 1993. „Playing Catch-Up with Reality: The Future Challenges are Already Here, „In *AIDS; The Challenge.„* Proccedings ot the Conference on AIDS at the Westin Hotel, Ottawa, Canada.
LAWSON, E. 1991. Encyclopedia of Human Rights. „*The Declaration on the Right to Development (1986).*„ New York: Taylor and Francis Inc.
LATHAM, M.C. „AIDS in Africa: A Perspective on the Epidemic„. *Africa Today.* Vol.40, No 3, 39-53.
Mariasy, J. & Radlett, M. 1990. Women in Vulnerable Sex. *AIDS Watch.* 10 (23).
NEW AFRICAN (London). September 1996. „*AIDS-Why African Successes Are Scoffed,*„ pp.16 17&21.
THE NEW VISION (Kampala). 23 May 1994. „Our children: Our future.„ p. 12. The New Vision (Kampala). 12 May 1994.

„*We are worried about our kids*".
NEW YORK TIMES INTERNATIONAL. 22 June 1992. JANE PARLEZ. „*Briton sees AIDS halting Africa population rise.*"
OSTERWEIS, M., SOLOMON, F., & GREEN, M. 1984. *Bereavement: reactions, and care.* Washington: National Academy Press.
PAULME, DENISE, ed. 1979. *Woman of Tropical Africa.* Berkley and Los Angeles: University of California Press.
REUTERS NORTH AMERICAN WIRE. 1 December 1996. Goolnar Bradbury. „*Hard-Hit Uganda Fights Back at AIDS.*"
SAUNDERS, J. & VALENTE, S. 1987. *Bereavement in survivors of AIDS.* In M.A. MORGAN (Eds.), Proceedings of the 1987 King's College Conference, pp. 203-208. London, Ontario.
SCHOEPF, B.G.. et al. (1991). Gender, Power and Risk of AIDS in Zaire. In MEREDITH TURSHEN (Ed.). *Women and Health in Africa.* Trenton, N.J.: Africa World Press.
TORONTO STAR (Toronto). 24 March 1994. LENNOX SAMUELS. „*A Land of the Orphaned an Old*".
TURSHEN, MEREDITH, ed. 1991. *Women and Health in Africa.* TRENTON, NJ.: Africa World Press.
UGANDA CONFIDENTIAL (Kampala). 29 November - 6 December 1993. SSEZI CHEEYE. „*Women: The Death Industry.*" p. 13.
ULIN, P.R. (1992). African Women and AIDS. Negotiating Behaviour Change. *Social Science and Medicine.* 34(1), 63-73.
UNAIDS. Geneva. March 1996. Fact Sheet, n.p.
UNICEF. 1989. *Children and Women in Uganda: A Situational Analysis.* Kampala: United Nations Children's Fund.
THE WORLD BANK. 1993. *Uganda:* Social Sectors: A World Bank Country Study.
WASHINGTON, D.C.: *The International Bank for Reconstruction* / World Bank.
THE WORLD HEALTH ORGANIZATION (WHO). September 1996. Fact Sheet No. 134. „*Traditional Medicine*", p. 2.

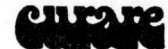

Women and Epilepsy: Psycho-Socio-Economical Problems of Female Epileptics and their Attitude towards Epilepsy
Frauen und Epilepsie: Psychologische, gesellschaftliche und wirtschaftliche Probleme von Epileptikerinnen und ihrer Einstellung zur Epilepsie

Yonas Bahire Tibeb

> *Lord have mercy on my son, for he is epileptic and he suffers terribly*
> ST. MATTHEW 17.15

Abstract: Female patients (n=280) diagnosed to have epilepsy, in one month time at Emmanuel Hospital, were interviewed using unstructured questionnaire, to determine psycho-socio-economic problems of epileptic women and their knowledge and attitudes toward epilepsy. The study was done in March and April, 1996 on a total of 280 women epileptic patients (100%) aged between 17-38 years. From the total 280 patients, 180 (64.2%) divorced after the first episode of epilepsy, 88 patients (31.4%) were single, 20 patients (7.1%) admitted being raped and twelve out of twenty patients (60%) have unlawful children. 200 patients (71.4%) are illiterate and out of the literate 75% dismissed from school because of epilepsy. Only 18 patients (6.4%) are employed, 42 patients (15%) are homeless and 220 patients (78.5%) are jobless and dependent on their parents. 248 patients (91.4%) believe that epilepsy is caused by witchcraft or evil spirit and is contagious. 280 patients (100%) use both traditional and modern medicine at the same time or intermittently. The study demonstrates that women epileptics are socially out casted, almost completely ignored, sexually abused and underprivileged because of their illness and gender.

Zusammenfassung: Weibliche Patientinnen (n= 260) mit Epilepsie, die in einem Zeitraum von einem Monat diagnostiziert wurden, wurden an Hand eines nicht strukturierten Fragebogens befragt, welche psychologischen, gesellschaftlichen und wirtschaftlichen Probleme Epilepsie mit sich bringen. Dabei versuchte man, die Probleme der Epileptikerinnen und ihr Wissen und ihre Einstellung über Epilepsie zu ermitteln. Diese Studie wurde im März und April 1996 mit 280 weiblichen Epileptikerinnen (100%) zwischen 17 und 38 Jahren durchgeführt Von den 280 Patientinnen wurden 180 (64,2%) nach dem ersten Epilespieanfall geschieden, 88 Patientinnen (31,4%) sind ledig, 20 Patientinnen (7,1%) haben zugegeben, vergewaltigt worden zu sein und 12 von 20 Patientinnen (60%) haben uneheliche Kinder. 200 Patientinnen sind analphabetisch (71, 4%) und von den Alphabeten wurden 75% wegen Epilepsie aus der Schule entlassen. Nur 18 Patientinnen (6,4%) sind berufstätig, 42 Patientinnen (15%) sind obdachlos und 220 Patientinnen (78,5%) sind arbeitslos und abhängig von ihren Eltern. 248 Patientinnen (91,4%) glauben, dass Epilepsie durch Hexerei oder böse Geister verursacht wird und ansteckend ist. 280 Patientinnen (100%) benutzen sowohl traditionelle als auch moderne Medizin. Diese Studie belegt, dass Epileptikerinnen wegen ihrer Krankheit und ihres Geschlechts aus der Gesellschaft ausgestoßen, man kann sogar sagen, ignoriert und sexuell missbraucht werden und unterprivilegiert sind.

Keywords: Epilepsy, Psycho Socio Economical Problems, Knowledge Attitude, Women, Ethiopia, Epilepsie, psychologische, gesellschaftliche, wirtschaftliche Probleme, Wissen, Einstellung, Frauen, Äthiopien

1. BACKGROUND INFORMATION ON ETHIOPIA

Ethiopia is located in the North-Eastern part of Africa, covering an area of one and a quarter million square kilometers. It extends between 3° and 18° north latitudes and between 33° and 48° east longitudes. The country borders on the Sudan in the North and West, Kenya in the South and East, and Republic of Djibouti. According to 1987 census, Ethiopia had a population of just under 46 million. Ninety per cent of the population is rural and an estimated 1% of the rural population art nomads (ETHIOPIA'S CENTRAL STATISTICS OFFICE 1987).

The people of Ethiopia are predominantly of Hamtic stock, with a mixture of Semitic and Negroid Strains. An estimated total of 70 languages and 200 dialects are spoken in the country. The official language is Amharic, with its own alphabet. Other widely spoken languages by major nationalities are Oromigna, Tigra, Tigrigna and Guragigna.

Topographically, the dominant feature of the country is central plateau, varying from 2,000 to

3,000 meters above sea level, with some mountains rising above 4, meters. There are two rainy seasons. The first and heavy one between July and September and the second (small rains) between February and March. The most important food crops are teff (Eragrostis Tef), wheat, barley, maize, millet, enset (Ensete Ventricosum) and coffee (mainly exported- is the major cash crop).

Ethiopia is still underdeveloped. The average annual income per family is about 100 US Dollars (Assefa & Zein 1986). In spite of technological backwardness and low productivity, the agricultural sector contributes a dominant share of the gross domestic product.

2. GENERAL HEALTH SERVICES

With high infant mortality, the major health problems of the country are communicable diseases and nutritional disorders. Among those under 5 years, measles, poliomyelitis, tetanus, diarrhea and malnutrition are the most important diseases. Health services are available with a radius of 12 km to only about 45% of the population (Ethiopia, Ministry of Health 1988). There are at present 2,200 doctors in Ethiopia giving a ration of one doctor to 22,500 people. Health services get only 2.5% of the government annual budget in addition to this very limited budgetary allocation for health. There is also formidable problem of under utilization of available health services due to illiteracy, geographical barriers and poverty, particularly in the rural areas. As a result, a significant proportions of the rural population resorts to traditional or local healers who use charms, spells and amulets as well as a holy water found in the vicinity of important churches and monasteries.

3. SOCIAL SERVICES OF ETHIOPIAN WOMEN

With regard to health, the situation of women is deplorable. As many as 60% of all mothers suffer due to lack of balanced diet and from various stages of malnutrition. Only five per cent of all women are assisted by trained mid-wives when giving birth. The deliveries of the remaining women are left to nature and untrained mid-wives. Of the 37 low income countries, Ethiopia maternal mortality rate is the highest at 700 per 100,000 live births.

In most parts of Ethiopia, women constitute, a minority in political and economic institutions but in agricultural sector - the largest private sector in Ethiopia - women are an essential productive force and are at the heart of development - rural women constitute 60% of the total agricultural labour force and produce about 80% of food and cash crops in Ethiopia. In Ethiopia, women in particular are full-time cultivators while most men manage live stock in traditional manner.

4. EPILEPSY IN ETHIOPIA

Public health problems in Ethiopia are responsible for the greater prevalence of Epilepsy because of a lack of primary care facilities. Increased rates of birth injury during which the infant may be deprived of oxygen (Asphyxia Neonatorum), prolonged childhood febrile convulsions, and diseases such as malaria, meningitis, sleeping sickness, syphilis and tuberculosis, as well as cerebral trauma and parasitic infections are among the conditions that can lead to epileptic seizures if left untreated. Status epileptics, a state of continuous seizures, is a common cause of death in Ethiopia.

Beside infection of central nervous system, epilepsy is the most prevalent neurological disorder in Ethiopia. The prevalence rates of the disease in Ethiopia based on a population faced studies, is 4, 8-8,/1,000 community-based study Giel 1970 and 5.3/1,000 community-based study Takele-Haimanot 1990.

The management of epilepsy is high priority for several reasons. First and for most, it is a common problem in Ethiopia. Epilepsy can occur both on idiopathic disorder unknown ethnology, and as disorder that is secondary to some kind of damage to the brain. Not only is epilepsy a common problem, but it is one which affected people of all ages, for it could begin at any age. Currently, both the traditional and modern methods of treatment are used by the people for epilepsy but the traditional healing methods are used more by most people. In the context of Africa, the situation of Ethiopia is not exceptional as far as epilepsy is concerned. At present in Ethiopia services are provided at 30 centers throughout the country. Six of these centres are in Addis Ababa and the rest are in the other region.

The management of epilepsy in developing countries require cultural knowledge and approaches beyond the usual practices of Western Medicine.

Over a 30 years period, there has been no detailed study of psycho-socio-economical impacts of epilepsy on women epileptics and their attitudes to it. This study addresses itself to this question.

This paper focuses on Ethnophysiological explanatory models of epileptic seizures among Ethiopia women epileptics.

5. MATERIAL AND METHODS

The study was performed in the only Neuro-psychiatric hospital in Addis Ababa, Ethiopia. In the hospital about 100-150 epileptic patients are seen everyday in the outpatient clinic out of which 50-70 are now patients. In the hospital there is one epilepsy clinic and this epilepsy clinic has one very old EEG machine. In the hospital phenobarbitone and phenytoin are widely available, they are effective and they are cheap to purchase.

Female patients (n-280) diagnosed to have epilepsy on one month time at Emmanuel Hospital, were interviewed using unstructured questionnaire. The questions were made as simple and straight forward as possible and translated into Amharic, the Ethiopian official language. To avoid bias and get as much information as possible, the questions were constructed to encourage open answers. The investigator and other medical doctor did the interview. The study was done in March and April 1996, and 280 women epileptic patients were interviewed.

6. RESULTS

Tab. 1

AGE IN YEARS (280)	NO.	%
17-23	25	8.9
24-30	125	44.6
30-35	100	35.7
35-38	30	10.7

As summarized in Table No. 1, 280 (100%) were aged between 17-38 years. All are in the active and productive age.

Tab. 2

MARITAL STATUS	NO.	%
Married	10	3.5
Widow	2	0.7
Single	88	31.4
Divorced	180	64.2
(After the first episode of epilepsy)		

180 (64%) patients divorced after the first episode of epilepsy out of 280 (100%) epileptics. 88 (31.14%) women epileptics were single. Only 10 (3.5%) out of 280 (100%) women epileptics married.

Tab. 3

LEVEL OF EDUCATION	NO.	%
Illiterate	200	71.4
Read and write	40	14.2
Grade 2-8	30	10.7
Grade 9 and above	10	3.5

200 (71.4%) women epileptics out of 280 (100%) women epileptics were illiterate 40 (14.2%) women epileptics only can read and write, 30 (10.7%) women they are in grade 2-8 only 10 (3.5%) women epileptics are in grade 9 and above.

Tab. 4

OCCUPATION	NO.	%
Employed	18	6.4
Jobless	220	78.5
Jobless and homeless	42	15.0

200 (78.51%) women epileptics were jobless and dependant on the family 42 (15%) women epileptics were jobless and at the same time homeless only 18 (6.4%) women epileptics were employed.

The term spinning or rotary illness was used for epilepsy among all respondents. 248 women epileptics (88.5%) sustained physical morbidity as a result of the seizure. 80 (32.2%) out of the 248 (100%) women epileptics sustained a burn as a result of falling into fire during fit. (5 (6.25%) out of 80 (100%) women epileptics who were burnt were severely disfigured or disabled as a result of their burns.

QUESTION: WHY YOU DIVORCED?

Tab. 5
RESULT (180 RESPONSES)

	NO.	%
Husband believed epilepsy is contagious	90	50.0
Economical reasons because of epilepsy	50	27.7
Husband's family couldn't tolerate me	35	19.4
Other 35-38		
Don't know	5	2.7

As shown in Table 5, 90 (50%) women epileptics out of 180 (100%) divorcee epileptics stated that they separated because of husband believed epilepsy is contagious. 50 (27.7%) out of 180 (100%) divorcee epileptics responded that they divorced because of economical problems because they are unable to earn for living. 35 (19.4%) divorcee epileptics gave the information they separated because of husband's family couldn't tolerate them. Very small number of the divorcee epileptics 5 (2.7%) they don't know the reasons of their divorce. 20 patients (7.1%) out of 280 (100%) women epileptics admitted being raped and 12 out of 20 women epileptics have unlawful children.

QUESTION: WHY YOU STOPPED GOING TO SCHOOL?

Tab. 6
RESULT (80 RESPONSES)

	NO.	%
Because of epilepsy	60	75.0
Economical problems	18	22.5
Other	2	2.5

When asked why they stopped going to school 60 (75%) of 80 (100%) interviewed stated that because of epilepsy. 18 (22.5%) out of 80 (100%) interviewed gave the information that they stopped going to school because of economical problems.

QUESTION: DO YOU THINK YOU KNOW THE CAUSE OF EPILEPSY?

Tab. 7
RESULT (280 RESPONSES)

	NO.	%
Evil spirit	183	65.3
Physical contact with	40	14.2
Punishment/curse from God	20	7.1
Born with it	15	5.3
Don't know	12	4.2
Accident	10	3.5

Nearly 65.3% of the response regarding knowledge on the course of epilepsy belonged to category „evil spirit" 14.2% believe that cause of epilepsy is physical contact with convulsing person. Seven per cent believe that epilepsy was curse or punishment from God, only 3.5% believe that accident is the cause of epilepsy.

QUESTION: DO YOU KNOW WHAT SOMEONE HAVE TO DO WHEN YOU ARE HAVING A CONVULSIVE ATTACK/FIT?

Tab. 8
RESULT (280 RESPONSES)

	NO.	%
Don't know	2	0.7
Protect/guard patient	14	5.0
Give herbal medicine	10	3.5
Give holy water	200	71.4
Hanged man's rope	4	1.4
Conventional medicine	10	3.5
Strike match near nose	40	14.2

Among the respondents, 71.4% mentioned giving holy water is possible treatment for epilepsy. 14.2% of the respondents believe that strike match near nose is a treatment of convulsive attack or fit. 1.4% gave the information that tying hanged man's rope which had been used for suicide had a therapeutic effect during the attack. Herbal medicine also mentioned as possible treatment by 3.5%.

QUESTION: HOW SHOULD SOCIETY TAKE CARE OF PERSONS WITH EPILEPSY?

Tab. 9
RESULT (280 RESPONSES)

	NO.	%
Government to take care	150	53.5
Pray for them	60	21.4
Medicine to be provided	40	14.2
Don't know	12	4.2
Let own family help	8	2.8

Regarding the question of how society should care of for the epileptic, 53.5% responded the government should take care of them. 21.4% respondents believed to pray for them. 14.2% stated that medicine to be provided to the epileptics.

7. COMMENTS AND CONCLUSION
- Women epileptics in Ethiopia suffer from social deprivation and prejudice. Epilepsy contributes to economic under productivity, marital instability and poor parenting.
- Epilepsy carries a strong social stigma for women epileptics and women afflicted by it can become ostracized by the society.
- The word spinning or rotary illness and ideas about dizziness from spinning around leading to seizures provide ethnophysiological explanations for epilepsy among Ethiopian epileptic women.
- Many of their ethnophysiological models re held in conjunction with magical beliefs including witch craft, spirit possessions and other supernatural manifestations.
- Severe burn was such a common occurrence among women epileptics in Ethiopia. Beliefs about the contagious nature of epilepsy may also put the person with epilepsy in great danger. Burns as a result of falling into the fire may occur if those nearby flee in fear.
- Herbal medicine, holy water, strike match near nose and putting hanged man's rope were the commonest ethnotherapy for epilepsy.
- We agree with (WHO) community based treatment plan for epilepsy, where patients and families have some degree of control of the management of their illness.
- Many people view the treatment of epilepsy as within the domain of traditional healers or holy water and are reluctant to seek medical help even when available. Thus, the first step should be to tell the availability of treatment at the hospital or clinic.
- Production of health educational materials about epilepsy to the public should be sustained and encouraged.

References

DADA TO and ODEKU E.L. 1966. Epilepsy in Nigerian Patient, a review of 234 cases. *West Africa. Med. J.* 15, 153-163.

DANESI M. A. 1984. Patient Perspectives of Epilepsy in a Developing Country. *Epilepsy* 25, 184-190.

DANESI M.A., ODUSOTE K.A., ROBERTS O. O. and ADU E. O. 1981. Social problems of Adolescent and Adult Epileptics in Developing Country, as seen in Lagos. *Nigeria Epilepsia* 22, 689-696.

GIEL R. 1967. The Epileptic Outcast. *East Africa Med. J.* 45, 27-31.

GIEL R. 1970. The Problem of Epilepsy in Ethipia. *Trop. Geogr. Med.* 22, 439-442.

HURST L.A., REEF H.E. and SACHS S.B. 1961. Neuro Psychiatric Disnper in the Bantu *S.Afr. Med. J.* 35, 750-761.

JILEK-AALL, JILEK W. MILLER JR. 1979. Clinical and Genetic Aspects of Seizure Disorders Prevalent in an Isolated African Population. *Epilepsyia.*Vol. 20: 613-622.

TEKLEHAIMANOT R., ABEBE M., GEBREMARIAM A., FORSGREN L., HOLMGREN G., HEIJBEL J. and EKSTEDIT I. 1990. Community-Based Study of Neurological Disorders in Rural Central Ethiopia, *Development of Screening Instrument, Ethipia, med. J.* 28: 123-137.

Challenges for Adequate Ethnomedical Contributions Towards Addressing Depression in Contemporary African Women: An Educational Psychological Perspective
Forderung nach adäquaten ethnomedizinischen Beiträgen im Hinblick auf depressive Erkrankungen bei afrikanischen Frauen heute: Eine bildungspsychologische Perspektive

Hannah I. Carew

Abstract: It is the mentally healthy people who become initiators and driving forces for their personal and national development. That African women who are the "pillars of their family lives" and "engines" of their country's economic development are experiencing poor health status and services should be a disturbing fact to women leaders and development-oriented policy-makers. This paper centres on severe depression a mental health problem common among women than men world-wide. It seems the disease is treated with triviality in some settings inspite of the "sheer size of undetected psychiatric morbidity." Some of the causes among contemporary African women are examined. Explanations are provided as to why the majority show a passivity towards seeking Western professional help for treating personal illnesses. The concern is for women not to perpetuate their passivity. The key issue is what contributions can traditional medicine offer ?. Recommendations consider research, that counselling psychology caters for appropriate handling of the ill-effects of the unfamiliar created by various changes and appropriate staff training for community health workers (CHW). Also included is the enhancement of adaptive coping styles among girls through relevant socialization experiences.

Zusammenfassung: Es sind die geistig-seelisch gesunden Menschen, die zu Initiatoren und Antriebskräften für die eigene und die nationale Entwicklung werden. Dass der Gesundheitszustand afrikanischer Frauen, welche die "Stützen des Familienlebens" und die "Motoren" der wirtschaftlichen Entwicklung ihres Landes sind, schlecht ist und sie wenig Betreuung erfahren, sollte Frauen in Führungspositionen und auf Entwicklung hin orientierte Politiker alarmieren. Der vorliegende Beitrag befasst sich mit schweren Depressionen, einer weltweit häufigen Störung der seelischen Gesundheit von Frauen wie auch von Männern. Es scheint, dass die Krankheit in manchem Umfeld "trotz der schieren Größe unentdeckter psychiatrische Morbidität" nicht recht ernst genommen wird. Einige der Ursachen bei heutigen Frauen in Afrika werden untersucht. Erklärungen werden gegeben im Hinblick darauf, warum die meisten Frauen passiv bleiben und sich scheuen, bei eigenen Krankheiten westliche professionelle therapeutische Hilfe zu suchen. Es soll erreicht werden, dass die Frauen nicht weiter in ihrer Passivität verharren. Die entscheidende Frage ist, welchen Beitrag die traditionelle Medizin leisten kann. Die Empfehlungen berücksichtigen Forschungen, dass die beratende Psychologie für einen angemessenen Umgang mit den nachteiligen Folgen der durch verschiedene Veränderungen erzeugten Entfremdung und für entsprechendes Gruppen-Training der Mitarbeiter im Gesundheitsdienst der Gemeinde (CHW) sorgt. Dazu gehört außerdem die Förderung adaptiver Bewältigungsstrategien bei den Mädchen durch entsprechende Sozialisationserfahrungen.

Keywords: African women, depression, passive help-seeking, coping styles, traditional medicine, Afrikanische Frauen, Depression, passive Hilfesuche, Bewältigungsstrategien, traditionelle Medizin.

Background

The current world view is that having good health and health knowledge are basic human needs and rights. The term health is used in this paper to refer to an attribute (ANDERSON 1985). It can also mean a resource for leading satisfying lives as suggested by the WHO (1985 p 27). Therefore, health is that which TALCOTT PARSONS (1975) says maximizes the capacity of individuals to perform the functions or activities for which men and women have been socialized. In Africa, the strong and positive health - development relationship is well known. The appointment of certain men and women into the high profile position of their communities as indigenous healers/doctors is a testimony of the Africans' value for good health and healing and their dread for the opposite, ill-health. Surely, personal experiences of pain and discomfort, immobility and dependence on other people as the opportunity costs of illness can elicit the response of fear in many people. Yet the fear of ill-health could also be learned and fostered in communities through cultural practices. Individuals are expected to conform to their cultural values by internalizing and practising the distinctive ways their ethnic groups respond to various stimuli including ill-health.

Indeed, cultural prescriptions largely determine responses to ill-health. No doubt, women are the known perpetrators and reinforcers of predominant cultural perceptions and attitudes to ill-health in particular. Many years ago among many communities including the Kalenjins of Kenya for example, it was only women who serving as herbalists enjoyed the high profile position of traditional doctors.It is common knowledge that specialist African female traditional doctors usually serve as midwives, female circumcisors, bone setters, masseurs and herbalists. But other specialist areas like mental ill-health are within men's domain. NYAMWAYA (1992) however notes the horizontal integration between male and female traditional doctors by their confering and referral of patients.

According to VLASSOFF (1994) women strongly value their role as primary health care (PHC) providers. As the bearers of culture, when performing their roles as PHC providers and educators, it becomes quite easy for women to perpetuate the dominant perceptions and attitudes about the causes of illnesses and their appropriate sources and methods of treatment. It is equally easy for women to perpetuate such negative responses as ostracism and stigmatization to patients of certain diseases as evident in cases of some skin conditions, mental illnesses and disabilities in general.

Regarding the health status of African women per se, the OAU and UNICEF state that they experience the worst in the world (OAU & UNICEF 1992 p 16). This is manifested in their sickly appearances, actual high morbidity rates, fast ageing and untimely deaths. With the awareness of this situation and the special health risks and needs of women world-wide, the world women leaders ably articulated their case at the September 1995, 4th World Women's Conference in Beijing. There was a strong request for the world leaders to urgently address the protection, promotion and sustenance of the good health of women. One health condition that deserves urgent attention among women is depression. It is a mental illness which Patricia Smyke identifies as one of the numerous mental health problems affecting women world-wide (SMYKE 1991 p 123). It is believed to show gender differences as early as adolescence (GRAHAM & RUTTER 1985 pp 351 - 367; PETERSON et al 1991 p 247 and AVISON & MCALPINE 1992 p. 77). The situation in Africa is anyone's guess in that the enormous knowledge gap about health and diseases in Africa has been noted by researchers. Existing literature according to FEACHEM & JAMISON (1991 p 25) do not even deal with certain diseases thereby negatively affecting planning efforts. Furthermore, what is available is not disaggregated according to gender.

This paper focuses on severe depression among contemporary African women irrespective of their geographical location. The illness is being addressed because it has a "female face" i.e. a high incidence among them vis-a-vis males (WEISSMAN 1977 and VINGERHOETS et al 1990). It is also an illness believed to be affecting an increasing number of people. Many patients remain untreated and are not even recognized (WHO 1996 p 77). Furthermore, African women have an unwillingness to seek professional medical help for mental illnesses particularly from Western mental health care providers (FOSU 1995 p 1079). Since the situation is the same with other ailments, such a behaviour must be stopped to avoid its perpetuation to the detriment of individuals and communities. Their behaviour of passivity creates a dilemma because women seem to worry about the health status of their significant others but not theirs. This paper therefore attempts to address the two questions below:-

1. Why is there a negative attitude towards seeking medical help among mentally unwell African women?
2. Can traditional medicine offer any contribution towards the effective management of depression among contemporary African women?

It is argued that maintaining mental well-being among African women partly depends on their perceptions and attitudes towards causes of illness and the appropriate sources and methods of treatment. Other contributing factors are how the women react to emotions involving life events as well as their perceived self-efficacy, i.e. whether they themselves believe they have a strong control over their lives or not. Given the circumstances of the women, it is further argued that sustained mental well-being is the greatest asset and one of the few avenues African women have to enjoy increased feelings of personal self-esteem in their communities. By experiencing high self-esteem, it is likely that many African women will be able to counter their long standing marginalisation and inadequacies.

The point is emphasized that individuals have the capacity for adaptation and change. An advantage must be taken of this fact by utilizing some of the time tested methods of Educational Psychology to modify the current culture based health values held by African women. Educational Psychology is a discipline which is part and parcel of man's daily life contributing to the basic activity of learning. It can therefore significantly contribute to improving women's health status in Africa. As already known, learning is an on-going exercise, these women can be made to learn how to properly adjust and live harmoniously in their environment. Indeed, this harmonious adjustment is greatly enhanced by mental well-being and the development of adaptive coping styles to undergo the uncomfortable challenges of changing circumstances.

Causes of Depression among Contemporary African Women

Observations and library search indicate that depression occurs in both emotional and physical forms and once started a vicious cycle which is difficult to break may begin. The physical manifestations include marked slowness and inactivity which lead to general poor performance, loss of appetite and possibly weight. There is deterioration in memory and concentration as well as negative thinking and self-defeating behaviours. Also reported are tiredness, headaches and pains in the chest and at the back of the neck. Persistent frustration and sadness seem to typify the emotional reactions. ROWE (1983) for instance suggests patients more or less "imprison" themselves thereby cutting themselves off from meaningful relationships. This "imprisonment" could lead to experiences of inadequacies and loss of personal control over important areas of one' life such as work, sex and hobbies.

In the light of the above the fact that health problems are more than outright medical problems, the identification of the root causes of depression could throw some light on appropriate treatment and preventive measures. A number of genetic predispositions, hormonal changes, social and personality factors seem to interact in the causation of depression. But given the trends in contemporary African communities, the biological or physical causes will not be addressed.

Regarding the social origins of depression, it should be noted that contemporary African women have not been spared the low social status and positions which their grandmothers and mothers experienced. Playwrights, health care providers and development-oriented personnel have repeatedly depicted the striving's of African women in such words as pain, burden, abuse etc.. Women are still exploited economically and only cosmetic shifts are noticed in their involvement in areas of national decision-making and politics.

These responses to women's efforts do elicit dissatisfaction, frustration and depression in many. For instance, MATHABANE (1994) recounts his mother's experiences of bouts of insanity which is typical of many women. When accorded such low social status, individuals tend to internalize and practice it culminating in the marginalization of women's physical, psychological and emotional needs (KWAWU 1994 and MANDERSON et al 1994). Besides the negative cultural practices, other social sources of African women's depression are their having had traumatic or maladaptive patterns of upbringing during childhood as in the case of emotional and physical abuse. Research studies confirm that such experiences do not provide individuals with effective coping skills to handle severe discomfort (COURT 1974). They also do not allow the development of positive self-image and self-worth (MAHER 1989).

The age-old stigmatization for not being circumcised, for natural or spouse induced infertility and being unmarried do also cause depression. Having chronically sick or troublesome drug-taking children particularly during adolescence can also cause depression in mothers. Equally important is economic insecurity at the household level resulting from long-term unemployment and or famine. The Structural Adjustment Policies (SAPs) have recently contributed to women's depression through large scale retrenchment which is presently impacting urban women. These were generally employed in such low profile jobs as telephonists, clerks, messengers and typists. Depression may also arise from physical and emotional insecurity within the home in the form of physical assaults, non-confiding unstable marital relationships and divorce. A common complaint of depressed women is that of adultery. But many lack the social support to handle the problem. If a troubled wife is aware of the existence of a network of relatives and friends and is assured of their understanding, material and financial aid, she is likely to believe her problems are not just hers but shared (CAPLAN 1974). Such awareness may reduce her worries, the feelings of helplessness and even enhance her self-worth to tolerate the threatening problem.

Perhaps the most significant current social sources of depression among African women are the plethora of crises in the continent. In addition to those cited by Adedeji formerly of the UNECA are the consequences of the problematic disease AIDS which as yet does not have a vaccine and cure. According to Newsweek of Dec. 1996, 59 percent of the infected people in the world live in sub-Saharan Africa where women are especially susceptible. In Zaire for instance, a half of the pregnant women carry the virus and therefore subjecting them to depression among other complaints. Such patients also have to face social stigmatization with its psychiatric implications. Their reactions of shame, guilt and fear make Aids patients well deserving of regular counselling services to support them come to terms and cope with the disease.

Equally discomforting have been the unprecedented physical insecurity emanating from Africa's disasters in the form of political upheavals and armed conflicts. As victims of war, women have to contend with personal loss in the form of loss by death or separation from some of their family members, the loss of property, privacy and social standing. Reliance on humanitarian rations, having irregularly treated wounds which threaten to cause disabilities and experiencing torture and rape are all depressive. The scale of these factors together with idleness and uncertainties, negatively impact the social functioning of women. They are candidates for mental disorders (HARRELL-BOND 1992). The UNHCR and some NGOs such as the Radda Barnen and Lutheran World Federation have therefore provided Western based counselling services for women in refugee and internally displaced situations. A good example is witnessed in the Kakuma Refugee Camp of North Western Kenya.

However, the above economic and social variables should not be allowed to cloud the women's personality variables. These are the factors which are within and personal to individual women. ALLPORT (1961) suggests these variables are vital in human functioning in that they determine thoughts and actions. The three which will be highlighted include their cognitive abilities to derive the meanings which they attach to issues that cause them severe discomfort. The other two are the levels of their self-esteem and the quality of coping skills, i.e. how well they respond to threatening situations.

Cognitive abilities as we know are enhanced by formal education. Consequently, educated women are expected to better understand the meanings of certain factors and their likelihood of posing threats to them. Advanced education also enables individuals to be more reflective, self-evaluative and problem-solving. They will be less evasive of problems by resorting to destructive emotions which trigger health-related problems. Greater education according to the WORLD BANK (1993 p 42) enables women to live healthier lives. As a personality variable, self-esteem refers to an individual's personal feelings of his/her worth. Whether individuals accord themselves positive or negative regard is determined largely by the messages they get from their significant others. The tendency is to internalize those messages and behave accordingly. BROCKNER & HUTTON (1978) suggest that people with positive self-esteem are less depressed, less prone to ulcers, drugs etc than those with negative self-esteem. Working with adolescents, HARTER (1990 & 1993) shows that a clear connection exists between self-esteem and social support. Individuals with low levels of support reported low self-esteem.

Regarding coping styles it is currently believed that women on the average cope less effectively with adversities than men and therefore are more likely to be depressed (VINGERHOETS et al 1990). PETERSON et al (1991) suggest that negative life events induce boys but not girls to develop effective coping strategies which protect them from depression later in life. This gender difference in resilience is the result of cultural norms and habits in the type of socialization to which both groups were exposed. Basically boys are encouraged to be brave and girls cry. In this way boys are exposed to face and solve problems and girls learn to either evade or give in to them. This seems to be a root cause of women's weak coping skills.

Why African Women do not Actively Seek Western Medical help?

Since colonial days, the Western approach to medicine has received official recognition and dominance (NYAMWAYA 1992 p 1) but indigenous medicine has been actively complementing the Western. The above question therefore baffles many and calls for a thorough analysis given that sick people are expected to willingly seek medical help and thereby avoid the opportunity costs of illness. In her report on African women's health, Patricia McFadden refers to their marginalizing the seeking of help for all other health needs except those relating to their "birthing" roles. The concerned are left to assume that women either endure pain and discomfort or practice self-medicalizaiton. This glaring unwillingness should raise social concern and encourage efforts to stop the practice on the grounds that good health is a basic human need (MASLOW 1954).

It has been known for sometime that most ailments including depression can be managed well and cost-effectively. Thus if the practice is allowed to continue, the likelihood is strong that it will be perpetuated to daughters and other womenfolk through the socialization process much to the detriment of society. Furthermore, the incapacitation of women would lead to outright poverty in many homes because many of them are currently heads of financially weak households. For instance, as many as 54 percent of women are household heads in Lesotho.

So far, among the reasons which relate to women's passivity to personal health care are inaccessibility, competing demands, the dislike for hospitalization, lack of adequate social support, the strong influence of cultural perceptions of disease causation and marked preference for traditional medical care. With the majority of the women living in rural areas (about 84 percent in Kenya by 1989), the remoteness of dwellings, and therefore long distances from health facilities is a case in point. The shortage of professionally trained medical staff in rural areas as well as the lack of financial resources to pay for the cost of treatment also encourage inaccessibility. Rural African women are known to be among those who "earn less, own less, and control less. They therefore find it difficult to pay for modern medical services. A recent study on patients' perceptions of public, voluntary and private dispensaries in rural areas in Tanzania by AHMED et al (1996 pp 370 - 374) point out that rural people have difficulty in paying for health services. The cost free government run public dispensaries were frequented by low income patients 73 percent of whom were farmers. One is thus left to imagine reactions when the government health facilities start implementing the SAPs led cost-sharing policy.

Women also have the tendency to ignore their deteriorating health status in the midst of competing demands from childcare and domestic chores in particular. A close observer is often tempted to ask whether many know the appropriate time when help is needed? The low quality of the social support which they experience is another area of concern. According to NIRAULA (1994) rural women are not likely to get encouragement from family members to seek medical help as compared to men. Social support here refers to the concern and material resources that relatives and friends are willing to provide for an individual experiencing threatening situations to realize that the problems are shared. In many instances, women are advised to perservere but in the worst of cases they are discouraged by comments to the effect that their situation is not different nor are they unique to be spared such experiences. Those responses are likely to be met by opposition from the currently empowered African women who may even be willing to utilize alternatives such as separation or divorce. However, it seems the negative interpretations given to women taking the onus of divorce or separation is a factor preventing many from moving out of their homes. Yet the continuation of the discomforting problems could lead women to develop depressive thoughts and actions.

The dislike for hospitalization can also prevent some women from reporting illness. According to NYAMWAYA (1992 p 9) African patients are never left alone to cope with illness though this is the emphasis of hospitalization in Western medicine. For many Africans, the lay relatives play an important role in the healing process. Caring is their duty. Thus by hospitalizing a mentally ill woman, she may perceive of her condition as stigmatizing leading to the worsening of her condition. She may even have difficulties in reintegrating in her community after treatment (FOSU 1995 p 1030).

As already pointed out, the perceived cause of a disease seems to be the most important factor in the help-seeking behaviour. Given that Africans strongly regard supernatural forces in the causation of disease (VAN LUIJK 1984 pp 281 - 308, NYAMWAYA 1992 p 5 and FOSU 1995 p 1030) they believe that illnesses caused by the supernatural must be treated similarly. Consequently, certain diseases will never be reported to Western medical health care practitioners. Finally, but equally important, is the preference for traditional health care which is a direct result of cultural perceptions, beliefs and attitudes. In the case of mental illnesses, it has been reported that large numbers of psychiatric problems are treated by traditional healers (FOSU 1995 p 1030). Having been socialized to value treatment from the known local doctors to whom patients and their relatives can talk in their local languages and feel free to ask many questions, the high preference in contrast to that of Western health care practices could be understood.

What can traditional medicine offer?

That the Western medical approach has been experiencing challenges from the traditional approach should not be a surprise. Traditional medicine serves and will continue to attract much more than the 80 percent of Africa's population as quoted by BANNERMAN (1982). Besides coverage, RICHMAN (1987) refers to a crisis with shifts from cure to care in the Western approach. Citing the "massive effects" of social, economic and environmental factors in people's health status, SHAPIRO (1996 p 3 & 4) calls for an emphasis on personal care. He suggests that a shift from mere emphasis on physical illnesses and therefore the technological aspects of care will enhance the full meaning of the concept of holistic health in the Western health care system.

The above is a reflection of the current perceptions of patients about healing where in addition to wanting their symptoms dealt with, they would like to have information and explanations to help them develop a sense of control over their lives. But the fulfilment of this will take time. Available evidence indicate that the Western approach does not cater for all the needs of African patients much to their disappointment. When treating the severely depressed by the Western approach for instance, there is the tendency to be attracted by the striking physical aspects at the expense of the emotional which are subtle but more devastating. Relapses among patients are likely since the emotional aspects were masked and remained untreated. Patients and their relatives are therefore, likely to lose faith in this form of health care leading to passivity and the development of a vicious cycle of the illness.

On the contrary, the traditional approach has the virtue of being holistic. TWUMASI (1986) notes that the doctors are concerned about treating not just the physical illness of patients but every other aspect. For this reason he sees them playing the combined role of physician, psychiatrist and social worker in the healing process. MBITI (1969 p. 166) therefore acknowledges traditional doctors as the greatest gift from God and the most useful source of help. According to BELL (1994 p. 158) traditional doctors will continue to command popular confidence even if they can not cure an affliction or remove the symptom because they are credible and accessible. He further says the doctors reassure patients of their anxieties and help them to cope with the psychosomatic effects of disappointment associated with failure, unemployment, witchcraft etc. These revelations therefore make the system deserving of the description of KLAUSS & ADALA (1994) that it is superior in the treatment of psychiatric and psychosomatic diseases. Notwithstanding the above strengths, one however notices that the traditional medical approach for treating depression has a major drawback. This relates to the gender disparity in the staff who deliver the service of healing. Being a disease which is cared for only by specialists, men who are mainly spiritualists provide service. In urban Ghana for instance MULLINGS (1984) observes they work mainly in the spiritualist churches. This exclusion of female doctors gives cause to doubt whether some patients get the required services. Are some cases not treated as trivial and therefore denied complete treatment? Women are known to be chided for seeking audience when they have problems. Is it not possible that because the male traditional doctors operate in a culture dominated profession and serve as opinion leaders, the same attitude comes into play now and again? If so, will this not deny some women from experiencing the WHO goal of Health for all?

The other issue concerns the persistence of the illness. So far we seem to be operating on the perceived responses of the patients to care, but what about the actual? Can we for certain say that women disclose much to the male doctors? Although this is an area for research, it is possible depression persists because some women do not really open up to the healers on the grounds that men may not actually understand their situation and therefore treat their cases lightly. With this possibility in mind it becomes necessary to have female traditional doctors who may supposedly understand the situation of the sick women working alongside the males in the healing process of depressed women as a complimentary measure. The writer sees this as a great challenge to traditional medicine that will cause a cultural revolution, but it is an achievable goal. At present, it can be achieved through partnership with donors and institutions which are interested in improving women's health as well as women's active participation in development.

The WHO and researchers such as BANNERMAN (1982) and KLAUSS & ADALA (1994 p. 142) have called for the integration of the two health care systems for the benefit of society. But evidence shows only lip service support (RAMESH & HYMA 1981). Depression is however, one illness that strongly offers this opportunity by even taking care of gender considerations. Given that African patients prefer "talk doctors" to the "needle doctors." i.e those providing mainly counselling services than those who give injections and medications, the incorporation of female traditional doctors can be an effective way of meeting the expectations of female patients. In combination with their medical skills their female attributes of good listening, talking and caring can be brought to bear.

The Way Forward
The need to reinvigorate these sick women and for that matter be proactive to reduce the incidence of the illness is challenging. It goes without saying that mental well-being is fundamental for personal happiness as well as personal and social development. BRIEGER (1981 p 578) rightly says that the lack of understanding is not the main reason why people do not accept new kinds of health behaviour. Rather the impact of having weak personality variables particularly low self-esteem seems to be the issue.

A major consideration outside the use of medicinal drugs and counselling services seems to be the provision of health education. Both formal and informal health education can offer the way out in treating severe depression. To complement the formal training of female traditional healers are efforts to increase adult awareness about the importance of certain parenting skills and the development of programmes for primary and secondary schools which aim at developing life skills in girls in particular. According to REARDON, many children have not experienced appropriate parenting culminating in their reacting negatively to other people particularly through violence (REARDON 1995 p 36 and 37). Parents therefore ought to be guided on how to rear their children so that children become aware as early as possible that individuals can differ without denying each other's self-esteem. In other words, people must treat each other as worthy human beings irrespective of their gender. Hopefully, situations which lower self-esteem such as prejudices, neglect and wife battering that emanate from negative cultural practices and cause depression in women could be significantly reduced.

That education is a socializing process is not a new idea, but MAHFOUZ's conception (1996 p 44) offers a new dimension that if accepted, provides for African women an opportunity to escape from being marginalized and having to experience servere depression. He sees it as a continuous learning process that helps to achieve self-empowerment, sustainability, equal participation in community affairs and capacity building. By emphasizing these variables, Mahfouz's view addresses the key problem of low self-esteem in African women. With African homes still waiting to modify their patriarchic practices, it means that children can not avoid internalizing their cultural practices. LAZAR (1996 p 30) claims that for children of both gender, women are central to the development of self-image, self-esteem and a sense of the possibilities in one's future. The writer joins her in asking: if women are treated as second class citizens in their own culture, what impact does this have on the messages concerning dignity and self-sufficiency that they convey to their male and female children? Fortunately, serving as social organisations which actively socialize the young, formal schools can empower school-aged girls who are the most vulnerable to indoctrination. No doubt, schools shape learners' personal and social development. This contribution can not be more useful than at adolescence when depression begins to show gender preference in girls.

So far, the trend in social relations and disease causation makes it clear that there is a strong need to develop school-based programmes which address sustained health behaviour and the development of life skills in young people. The successes of the UNICEF led child to child programs show that even primary school children can easily acquire and disseminate positive health attitudes. It seems that the crucial life skills are coping strategies, self-awareness, critical thinking and problem-solving. In the light of the dynamism of the contemporary world and the associated fear arousing unfamiliar, unpredictable and at times life-threatening stimuli, it is recommended that priority should be given to the development of adaptive coping strategies in young people. Individuals cannot avoid some threatening stimuli. They should therefore be exposed to situations where they practice and learn to tolerate or bear with them rather than get shattered through such destructive emotional responses as depression.

Having adequate and regular funding for research is another measure that can significantly assist in addressing this problem of depression in African women. If the traditional female doctors could be trained as has been done in the area of midwifery and some incorporated in research teams on depression, the better. Their inclusion and some of the questions raised during field work may stimulate public interest in the topic and possibly public action to address it. At the moment, funding to undertake certain epidemiological research is scarce but the setting up of regional health research and training centres is a way out. The African Medical Research Foundation (AMREF) in Kenya is respected for its leadership role in PHC, education and research. It has therefore attracted some funding from foreign sources. The kenya Medical Research Institute (KEMRI) is also working along similar lines. Thus promoting similar institutions in the other African sub-regions is an understatement. Favourable national government policies also support necessary health research and educational activities and should be encouraged. For instance, the Kenyan Government recently waived the Value Added Tax on all AMREF's imported equipment to hasten the construction of their new training centre.

Religious institutions have equally made their presence felt in PHC and research in Africa. Besides the laudable work of the Catholic and Methodist churches, the Bahais have been actively involved through the MENU institute in Western Kenya. Their programmes focus on training in basic health care techniques for children and families as well as running follow-up training courses. Mental health should be one of the new courses to be introduced. It is however hoped that the participation rate of female CHW will be increased in the above programmes to offer females a chance to contribute to the mental well-being of their womenfolk. They can bring hope and strength in the healing process by honest sharing from real life situations, personal circumstances and struggles to reinforce the fact that they also do care. This way, achieving one of the goals of PHC would have been assured.

Conclusion

Millions of African women are vulnerable to suffering from severe depression not so much from the overwhelming nature of the causes, as the poor quality of some of their personality variables. It was noted that the high incidence of depression in women vis-a-vis men can be attributed to the socialization process. Whereas boys were encouraged to be brave in the face of discomforting situations, girls were encouraged to evade those situations by either crying or giving in. These behaviours encouraged boys to develop problem-solving skills whilst girls never developed much of those essential skills.

That research and training of CHW are vital in disseminating to women information about having health-related behaviours is an understatement. Other long term and effective measures are having school-based programs which make girls in particular aware of the root causes of health hazards and ill-health. They may therefore make personal effort to use methods that help them overcome the factors which block their aspirations and motivations leading to depression. Though female traditional doctors have so far been excluded from the direct treatment of depression because it falls within the male domain, advantage must be taken of the current conferring and referral activities between practitioners of this system of medical care for the benefit of patients. These female doctors can offer lasting psychotherapeutic services where the known male doctors may fail thereby contributing effectively to the reinvigoration of their womenfolk to better life situations. It is now time for action over the issue of integration between the Western and traditional health care systems. However, time is ripe not just for vertical integration but also for the horizontal between the male and female practitioners themselves. This is certainly an important way of achieving the WHO Alma Ata goal of Health For All.

References

AHMED et al. 1996. Patients' Perception of Public, Voluntary and Private Dispensaries in Rural areas of Tanzania. *The East African Medical Journal.* Vol. 73 No.6 pp. 370-374 June.
ALLPORT, G.W. 1961. *Pattern and Growth in Personality,* Holt Rinehart and Winston, New York.
ANDERSON, R. 1984. *Health Promotion: An overview European Monographs in Health Education Research,* 6 pp. 4-119.
AVISON, W.R. and ALPINE, D.D. 1992. Gender Differences in Symptoms of Depression Among Adolescents *J. Health Soc. Behav* 33 pp. 77.
BANNERMAN, R.H. 1982. Traditional Medicine in Modern Health Care *World Health Forum* Vol. 3 No. II pp 8 13 Geneva.
BELL, L.W. 1991. *Mental and Social Disorder in Sub-Saharan Africa: The Case of Sierra Leone 1787 to 1990.* Greenwood Press, Westport.
BRIEGER, W. 1981 Health Education Can Help - If Properly conducted. *World Health Forum* vol. 2 p. 578. Geneva.
CAPLAN, G. 1974. *Support Systems and Community Mental Health Behaviour.* Publications. New York.
COURT, J. 1974. Characteristics of Parents and Children. In: *The Maltreated Child.* CARTER, J. (ed) Priority Press.
FEACHEM, R.C. and JAMISON, D.T. (eds) 1991. *Disease and Mortality in Sub-Saharan Africa.* A World Bank Publication. Oxford University Press.
FOSU, G.B. 1995. Women's Orientation Toward Help-seeking for Mental Disorder. *Social Science and Medicine.* Vol. 40 No. 8 pp. 1029-1040. Pergamon, Great Britain.

GRAHAM, P. and RUTTER, M. 1985 Adolescent Disorders pp. 351-367. In: RUTTER & HERSOR (eds) *Child and Adolescent Psychiatry: Modern Approaches* Blackwell Scientific. Oxford.
HANNINEN, V. and ARO HILLEVI 1996. Sex Differences in Coping and Depression among Young Adults. *Social Science and Medicine.* Vol. 43 No. 10 pp. 1453-1460. Pergamon, Great Britain.
HARRELL-BOND, B. 1992. The Refugee Experience and Culture-shock In: *Report on the National Seminar on Refugee Rights and Law,* Eldoret, Kenya.
KLAUSS, V. and ADALA, H.S. 1994 Traditional Herbal Eye Medicine in Kenya. *World Health Forum* Vol. 15 No. 2 pp 138-143 Geneva.
KWAWU, J. 1994. Gender and Household Health-Seeking Behaviour pp. 225-229. In: WIJEYARATHE P. et al (eds) *Gender, Health and Sustainable Development.* IDRC, Ottawa, Canada.
LAZAR, S.G. 1995. Gender Inequality: Self-Image and Sustainable Development pp. 29-32 In: SERAGELDIN, I & MAHFOUZ. A (eds). *The Self and the Other: Sustainability and Self-empowerment. Environmentally Sustainable Development* Proceedings Series No. 13. The World Bank Washington, D.C.
MAHER, P. 1989. Childabuse: The undetected "special need" British *Journal of Special Education* Vol. 16 No. 1 pp 11 - 13.
MANDERSON, L. JENKINS, J and TANNER, M. 1993 Women and Tropical Disease: An Introduction *Social Science and Medicine*Vol. 37 No. 4 pp. 441-443.
MASLOW, A. 1954. *Motivation and Personality.* Harper and Row, New York.
MATHABANE, M. 1994. *African Women: Three Generations.* Harper Collins.
MBITI, J.S. 1969. *African Religion and Philosophy.* Heinemann, London.
NEWSWEEK 1996. *Haves and Have Nots* December 9 pp 48 and 49.
NYAMWAYA, D. 1992. *African Traditional Medicine: An Anthropological Perspective for Policy Makers and Primary Health Care Managers.* AMREF, Nairobi.
OAU & UNICEF 1992. *Africa's Children, Africa's Future:* Background Sectoral Paper.
PARENS, H. 1995 Parenting and Child Development pp 33-35 In: SERAGELDIN, I & MAHFOUZ, A. (eds) *The Self and the Other, Sustainability and Self-Empowerment,* World Bank.
PARSONS, T. 1975. The sick role of the physician reconsidered. Millbank Memorial Fund Quarterly *Health and Society.* 53 pp 257 - 278
PETERSON, A.C., SARIGIANI, P.A. and KENNEDY, R.E. 1991. Adolescent Depression: Why More Girls? *Journ Youth Adolsc.* 20 p 247.
POLUNIN, I. 1982. Traditional Medicine in Modern Health Care (Round Table Discussant). *World Health Forum* 3 (1) pp. 19 and 20.
RAMESH, A. and HYMA, B. 1981. Traditional Medicine in an Indian City *World Health Forum*Vol. 2. No. 4 pp. 495-499 Geneva.
REARDON, B. 1995. Peace Education pp. 36-38. In: SERAGELDIN, I. & MAHFOUZ, A. (eds) *The Self and the Other, Sustainability and Self-Empowerment.* World Bank. Washington, D.C.
RICHMAN, J. 1987. *Medicine and Health,* Longman.
ROWE, D. and KEGAN PAUL. 1983. *Depression: the way out of your prison.* Routledge, London.
SERAGELDIN, I and MAHFOUZ, A. 1995. (eds) *The Self and the Other: SustainabilityandSelf-Empowerment.* Environmentally Sustainable Development Proceedings Series No. 13. The World bank. Washington, D.C.
SHAPIRO, J. 1996. Primary Care is Dead: Long Live Personal Care. *Primary Care Management* Vol. 6 No. 1 pp. 3 and 4. Pearson Professional Ltd. England.
SMYKE, P. 1991. *Women and Health.* Zed Books; Ltd UN NGO Liason Project. London.
TWUMASI, P.A. 1984. *Professionalization of Traditional Medicine in Zambia,* IDRC, Canada.
VAN-LUIJK, J.N. 1984. The Utilization of Modern and Traditional Medical Care pp. 282 - 308 In: J.K. VAN GINNERKEN & A.S. MULLER (eds) *"Maternal Child Health in Rural Kenya" An Epidemiological Study.* Croom Helm.
VINGERHOETS, A.J., J.M. and VAN HECK, G. 1990. Gender, Coping and Psychosomatic Symptons *Psychol, Med.* 20 p. 125.
VLASSOFF C. 1994. Gender inequalities in health in the Third World: Uncharted ground. *Social Science and Medicine* 39 (q) pp. 1249-1259.
WEISSMAN, M.M. and KLERMAN, G.L. 1977. Sex Differences in the Epidemiology of Depression *Arch Gen. Psycho.* 34, p.98.
WHO 1978. Report on the International Conference on Primary Health Care. *Alma Ata* 6-12 Sept. Geneva.
WHO 1985. *Targets for Health for All.* Copenhagen.
WHO 1996. *The World Health Report* 1996. Fighting disease, fostering development. Geneva.
WOMEN'S BUREAU, Ministry of Culture and Social Services 1996 *Women and Men in Kenya Facts and Figures.* Nairobi, Kenya.

ETHNOMEDIZIN – SCHÄTZE DER GESUNDHEIT
Herausgeberin: Christine E. Gottschalk-Batschkus

Diese völlig neue Buchreihe lädt ein zu einer faszinierenden Entdeckungsreise. Namhafte Forscher erschließen uns verborgenes Wissen und jahrtausendealte Geheimnisse indigener Völker zu Gesundheit und Heilung.

Erika Diallo-Ginstl (Hrsg.)
Ernährung und Gesundheit
Von anderen Kulturen (essen) lernen
Geb., 144 S.
mit ca. 35 farb. Abb.
ISBN 3-930706-11-3

Hermann Lechleitner (Hrsg.)
Selbstheilungskräfte
Die Quelle zur Stärkung und Heilung im eigenen Ich
Geb., 136 S.
mit ca. 30 farb. Abb.
ISBN 3-930706-13-X

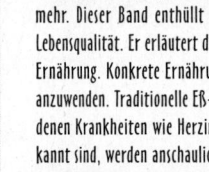

Ernährungsbedingte (Wohlstands-) Krankheiten sind heute keine Seltenheit mehr. Dieser Band enthüllt die Zusammenhänge zwischen Nahrung und Lebensqualität. Er erläutert die wesentlichen Gesichtspunkte einer gesunden Ernährung. Konkrete Ernährungstips helfen, dieses Wissen umzusetzen und anzuwenden. Traditionelle Eß- und Kochgewohnheiten anderer Kulturen, bei denen Krankheiten wie Herzinfarkt oder Arteriosklerose weitgehend unbekannt sind, werden anschaulich dargestellt.

Die Aktivierung der Selbstheilungskräfte des Körpers ist häufig fester Bestandteil von Heilungsritualen. Dieses Buch vergleicht Schamanen- und Heilbräuche verschiedener Völker und stellt eine Verbindung zwischen traditionellen Ritualen zu modernen Heilweisen her. Es eröffnet neue Perspektiven für die Bewältigung von Krankheiten und zeigt ganz konkret, mit welchen Methoden der Körper entspannt und das Immunsystem gestärkt werden kann.

Ines Albrecht-Engel (Hrsg.)
In Wellen zur Welt
Das traditionelle Wissen über Schwangerschaft und Geburt
Geb., 144 S.
mit ca. 30 farb. Abb.
ISBN 3-930706-12-1

Christian Rätsch
Medizin aus dem Regenwald
Die Weisheit der Naturvölker
Geb., 144 S.
mit ca. 60 farb. Abb.
ISBN 3-930706-14-8

Eine Geburt ist ein ganz natürlicher Vorgang, doch vielfach haben Frauen die Fähigkeit verlernt, ihrem Körper zu vertrauen. Dieses Buch zeigt, wie Frauen in anderen Kulturen Kinder ohne technische Hilfe zur Welt bringen. Es gibt Anregungen für eine aktivere Gestaltung der Geburt und erklärt, wie Komplikationen bei der Geburt vermieden werden können. Der westlichen Geburtshilfe werden Beispiele aus außereuropäischen Kulturen gegenübergestellt.

Dieser Band macht den Leser mit der faszinierenden Welt der Regenwaldmedizin vertraut. Detailliert und informativ beschreibt er die Wirkungen und den Gebrauch einzelner Pflanzen – und weiht so in das kostbare Heilpflanzenwissen ein, das die Regenwaldbewohner seit Jahrtausenden nutzen und pflegen. Ein unverzichtbarer Naturmedizin-Ratgeber mit vielen Tips und wertvollen Informationen.

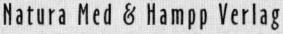

Natura Med & Hampp Verlag
Gehen Sie jetzt auf Entdeckungsreise und bestellen Sie bei:
Natura Med Verlagsgesellschaft, Breslauer Straße 5, 74172 Neckarsulm
Telefon: 0 71 32 / 9 86 41 16 • Fax: 0 71 32 / 8 25 56

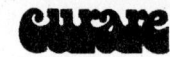

„Ukonjwa wa fikira mingi" -
Psychische Störungen, psychosozialer Kontext und subjektive Krankheitskonzepte bei ostafrikanischen Frauen
„Ukonjwa wa fikira mingi" -
Depressive Symptoms, Psycho-Social Risk Factors and Subjective Explanatory Concepts in East African Women

Heike Dech, Joyce Nato, Horst Haltenhof & Wielant Machleidt

Zusammenfassung: Die Situation von Frauen im ländlichen Afrika ist charakterisiert durch soziale Benachteiligung und hohe Arbeitsbelastung. Der schnelle soziale Wandel, der Niedergang von traditionellen sozialen Schutzmechanismen sowie ökonomische Unsicherheiten stellen insbesondere für Frauen in Afrika eine große Belastung dar. Wir untersuchten mit qualitativen und quantitativen Methoden 300 Patientinnen der Allgemeinambulanz eines Distriktkrankenhauses im ländlichen Ostafrika auf psychische Störungen, psychosoziale Belastungsfaktoren sowie subjektive Krankheitserklärungskonzepte. Es zeigte sich, daß depressive Symptome, insbesondere Somatisierungen und Hypochondrie vorherrschten. Bei den Vergleich zwischen dem Self Reporting Questionnaire (SRQ) und psychosozialen Belastungsfaktoren zeigte sich, daß das Zusammenleben mit den Angehörigen als protektiver Faktor anzusehen ist, während finanzielle Nöte und Eheprobleme sich als signifikante Belastungsfaktoren bei der Entwicklung vornehmlich depressiver Symptome erwiesen. Dies spiegelte sich auch in der Erhebung der subjektiven Krankheitserklärungskonzepte wieder.

Abstract: The general psycho-social situation of women in rural Africa is characterized by discrimination in the field of education and by the heavy demands of their everyday work. Rapid social change, accompanied by the break-down of traditional social norms and roles as well as economic insecurity is a heavy burden especially for women in Africa. All this can lead to exhaustion and result in psychiatric morbidity. 300 female adult patients at the general out-patient of a district hospital in rural East Africa were investigated with qualitative and quantitative methods in order to determine psychological disturbances and psychosocial risk factors and to understand their subjective explanations of their illness.
The study revealed that somatization and hypochondriasis prevail. The comparison between the Self Reporting Questionnaire (SRQ) and psychosocial stress factors showed that living together with relatives is a protective factor, whereas severe financial problems and marital problems were significantly contributing to the development of depressive symptoms. This is also reflected in the evaluation of explanatory concepts.

Keywords: Psychische Störungen, Depression, Frauen, Self Reporting Questionnaire, Psychosoziale Belastungsfaktoren, Kenya, Afrika, psychiatric disorders, depression, women, self reporting questionnaire, psycho-social risk factors, concepts of illness, Kenya, Africa

„Studien in Afrika und Asien, in denen viele Forschungsmittel und Aufmerksamkeit auf Entwicklungsprobleme gerichtet sind, betonen den ländlichen Zusammenhang, widmen sich teilweise den Wegen, mit denen Politik und Programme die Arbeitslast von Frauen vervielfacht haben, während gleichzeitig ihr Status in der Gesellschaft erniedrigt wurde (z.B. indem Landrechte an Männer vergeben wurden, oder durch Vernachlässigung der Bedeutung von Frauen in der Subsistenzproduktion). Es wurde deutlich, daß viele Entwicklungsprojekte scheitern, weil Wissenschaftler und Planer zu wenig die Arbeit von Frauen einbeziehen".

MONK & MOMSEN (1995)

Zur Situation von Frauen in Ostafrika

In Ostafrika ist die Erwerbstätigkeit von Frauen ein elementarer Wirtschaftsfaktor. Neben der Bewirtschaftung von Acker und Feld obliegt den Frauen Handel und Verkauf der Produkte auf dem Markt. In der Subsistenzlandwirtschaft ist der Großteil der landwirtschaftlichen Produkte für Mann und Kinder bestimmt, während die Einnahmen aus dem Verkauf der Überschüsse als privater Besitz der Frauen angesehen werden. Traditionellerweise ist es daher nicht unüblich, daß Frauen sich einen gewissen Wohlstand erwirtschaften können. Zusätzlich weist ihnen die Tradition das Recht zu, Landnutzung und Erbe in Anspruch zu nehmen. Ebenfalls sollte nicht die bedeutende Rolle vergessen werden, die der

Frau als Ehefrau und Mutter in der Familie zukommt. Nur bei Nomaden, beispielsweise bei den Massai, haben die Frauen eine untergeordnete Funktion.

Für den Schutz der Frauen haben die „lineages" eine entscheidende Rolle. Es sind dies traditionelle Tragpfeiler des sozialen Zusammenhalts, die das Verwandtschaftssystem stützen. Die Frau, die einer solchen „kin-group" angehört, hat die Sicherheit, weitgehend sozial integriert zu sein. Dies ist auch dann noch der Fall, wenn sie mit ihrem Ehemann nicht im Heimatdorf wohnt und von ihm sozial und personal abhängig ist (SACKS 1982). Falls eine Frau aber von ihrer Sippe ausgeschlossen wird und keine neue eheliche Heimat finden kann, hat sie mit großen Schwierigkeiten in ihrem privaten oder beruflichen Leben zu rechnen (GLUCKMANN 1969).

Wenn neue „lineages" entstehen, so geschieht das nicht selten durch die „Ältesten", die - in der Absicht, Machtpositionen (wieder) zu etablieren - eheliche Verbindungen einleiten. Kinderreiche Ehen genießen in Afrika insofern hohes Ansehen, als sie Verbindungen zwischen verschiedenen „lineages" festigen. Der Ehemann seinerseits sichert sich, indem er den Brautpreis zahlt, das Recht, alle Kinder, die dieser Ehe geboren werden, in seine „lineage" einzubinden. Das gilt herkömmlicherweise auch dann, wenn er eigentlich nicht selbst der biologische Vater aller Kinder ist oder wenn sich das Paar mittlerweile getrennt hat. Anzufügen ist, dass die polygamen Heiratsgepflogenheiten, die es einem reichen Kenianer erlauben, mehr als nur eine Frau zu heiraten, gelegentlich Konkurrenz unter den Frauen hervorbringen. Andererseits kommt es aber auch vor, dass Nebenfrauen durch die erste Frau sogar ermutigt werden, in die existente Ehe zu kommen (BRABIN 1984).

Diese hier für Kenia skizzierte Grundstruktur besteht in den meisten afrikanischen Ländern. Sie hat sich in diesem Jahrhundert für die Frauen jedoch erkennbar verschlechtert. Denn immer weniger Männer, die mit zunehmender Landflucht ihre Shamba (Bauernhof, Feld, Acker) verlassen haben, kehren zu ihrer Familie zurück. Zwar kann man davon ausgehen, dass etwa 70 Prozent der in den Städten arbeitenden Männer einen Teil ihres Lohnes an ihre Familien auf dem Land überweisen. Dennoch ist die finanzielle Situation der Frauen auf dem Land oftmals sehr unbefriedigend, weil diese Zahlungen nicht regelmäßig einkommen. Selbst wenn die Familien Überweisungen erhalten, belaufen sich diese zumeist nur auf recht bescheidene Größenordnungen, denn den Männern bleibt unter den Bedingungen, die Städte bieten, eigentlich nur die Möglichkeit, Hilfs- und Gelegenheitsarbeiten zu übernehmen. Studien belegen, dass demzufolge besonders die Frauen verarmen und nach neuen Wegen zum Überleben suchen müssen (OKPALA 1992, OWEI & JEV 1992).

Aus all den Komplikationen, die die räumliche Distanz mit sich bringt, folgt, dass die Beziehungen dieser zugezogenen Städter zu ihrer Großfamilie („extended family") immer häufiger abbrechen. Das hat auf der einen Seite Isolation und Vereinsamung, auf der anderen Seite weiter steigende Armut zur Folge.

Im großen und ganzen ist die Situation der Frauen in Kenia mit der der Frauen in anderen Entwicklungsländern vergleichbar. Frauen sind, wie es in dem oft zitierten UNA-Report formuliert wird, *„die Hälfte der Menschheit, leisten zwei Drittel aller Arbeitsstunden, erhalten ein Zehntel des Welteinkommens und besitzen weniger als ein Hundertstel des Eigentums"* (1980).

Die heutige Situation von Frauen in den afrikanischen Entwicklungsländern ist im wesentlichen Resultat eines Prozesses, im Verlaufe dessen die traditionellen soziopolitischen Strukturen - und damit auch die gesellschaftlichen Rollen der Individuen - in den administrativen Sog des Kolonialismus gerieten: Männliche Kolonialbeamte, die aus Kulturen kamen, in denen Frauen zu dieser Zeit abseits des öffentlichen Lebens standen, traten zumeist nur mit männlichen „chiefs" in Kontakt. Wie sehr das traditionelle System, in dem Frauen ein separater Rechtsraum eingeräumt war, der kolonialen Erosion unterlag, zeigt sich in exemplarischer Weise darin, dass das den jeweiligen „lineages" gehörende Land mit festgelegtem Nutzungsrecht für die Frauen nun in eine Eigentumsform transformiert wurde, auf die praktisch nur Männern Zugriff eingeräumt wurde (MONK & MOMSEN 1995). So kam es, dass die kolonialen und postkolonialen Landverteilungsprogramme, indem sie den Landtitel der Stämme auf - in der Regel männliche - Individuen übertrugen, Frauen ihrer traditionellen Bewirtschaftungsrechte verlustig gingen. Die „lineage" als landbesitzende Einheit hat also durch die Landenteignungen in der Kolonialzeit an Einfluss verloren.

Neben der verwandtschaftlichen Organisation in „lineages" existieren in afrikanischen Gesellschaften die Organisation in Altersklassen. Diese Altersklassen gibt es sowohl für Männer als auch für Frauen. Initiationsriten, die für Mädchen mit Beginn der Geschlechtsreife durchgeführt werden, sind

Zeugnis einer verbindenden „Kultur der Frauen" mit eigenen Ausdrucksformen. Die gesamtgesellschaftliche Bedeutung der Riten zeigt sich in der Unterweisung der Geschlechterkomplementarität, der Wiederspiegelung der Sozialordnung und in der Sicherung der weiblichen Fruchtbarkeit. Darüber hinaus sind die weiblichen Riten wichtig zur Traditionsbewahrung, denn die Frauen halten in rituellen Sequenzen bzw. Liedern die Erinnerung an historische Ereignisse lebendig.

Kategorien wie Geschlecht und Verwandtschaft müssen im wirtschaftlichen, politischen und religiösen Zusammenhang betrachtet werden; sie sind also als Verbindung zwischen privater und öffentlicher Sphäre zu sehen. Heute bestehen Wahlmöglichkeiten zwischen unterschiedlichen Formen der Eheschließung - wie traditionell, christlich oder islamisch -, die in vielen afrikanischen Gesellschaften nebeneinander existieren. Für die Fortsetzung der Polygamie sind wirtschaftliche Aspekte wie die Entlastung bei Haushaltspflichten und bei der Kinderversorgung ausschlaggebend, was eine eigenständige, wirtschaftliche Tätigkeit, z.B. im Handel, ermöglicht (SCHÄFER 1995).

Zahlreiche Studien zum Wandel von Ehe- und Familienformen befassen sich mit den sozialen Veränderungen durch die Arbeitsmigration der Männer. Tendenzen, die sich dabei im afrikanischen Gesellschaftsvergleich herausarbeiten lassen, sind das Aufbrechen der verwandtschaftlichen Kontroll- und Unterstützungsformen sowie eine Instabilisierung und Individualisierung der Eheprobleme. Die Geschlechterungleichheit wird zudem durch die Männerabwanderung verstärkt (SCHÄFER 1995).

„Der Einfluß der Frauen auf die Ressourcennutzung und auf politische Entscheidungsprozesse ist nach wie vor indirekt. Obwohl Frauenorganisationen die Verhandlungsmöglichkeiten der Frauen und ihren Lebensstandard verbessert haben, konnten sie nicht direkt zur Verbesserung ihrer Mitbestimmung in der lokalen oder nationalen Politik beitragen" (MOORE 1988).
Auch kommen ostafrikanische Frauen in kommunalen Aufgaben zusammen, z.B. in Baumanpflanzungsprojekten und Kreditgemeinschaften (HYMA & NYAMWANGE 1993, MACKENZIE 1996).

Mehrere Studien stellten die ungleich höhere Belastung für Frauen durch die Umstrukturierung der internationalem Wirtschaft in sowohl postindustriellen als auch Entwicklungsländern heraus. Sie belegen, dass besonders die Frauen verarmen und nach neuen (nach wie vor marginalen) Wegen zum Überleben suchen müssen oder gezwungen sind, sich in schlechtbezahlten Haushaltsdienstleistungen in peripheren Regionen der entwickelten Wirtschaften zu verdingen (vgl. MONK & MOMMSEN 1995).

Armut, soziale Benachteiligung und psychische Störungen

Für das Verständnis der im klinischen Alltag auftretenden psychischen Erkrankungen müssen einige soziokulturelle Überlegungen vorangestellt werden: Das subsaharische Afrika besteht aus 53 unabhängigen Staaten. Weil zudem der Kontinent eine ethnische Multitribalität aufweist, verbietet sich jede Verallgemeinerung über „den Afrikaner" (GERMAN 1987, ORLEY 1970). Hinzu kommt, dass der Kulturwandel, mit seinen unterschiedlichen Ausprägungsformen, den diversen Lebenswelten eine schwer erfassbare Komplexität verleiht. Das Spektrum der Formen der Produktion und Reproduktion des Lebens in Afrika reicht von nomadischer Subsistenzwirtschaft bis hin zur Großstadttechnologie.

In Afrika befinden sich die meisten - und gemessen am westlichen Standard - am wenigsten entwickelten Länder der Welt (vgl. DIESFELD 1989). Bei einem Bevölkerungswachstum mit Raten von über 3% (WELTENTWICKLUNGSBERICHT 1993) ist fast die Hälfte der Bevölkerung in einem Alter von unter 15 Jahren. Angesichts der Zunahme von Arbeitslosigkeit und Unterernährung ist für die meisten Afrikaner die Zukunftsperspektive entschieden ungünstig.

Die in der Klinik zu beobachtenden Erkrankungen von Menschen müssen in diesem Rahmen gesehen werden (vgl. DESJARLAIS 1995). Um ein Beispiel zu nennen: Es kann als Resultat von Armut gewertet werden, wenn Schwangere, bedingt durch ungenügende Geburtshilfe, komplizierte Verläufe ihrer Geburten erleben müssen. Der Mangel an Fürsorge in dieser entscheidenden Phase kann zu frühkindlichen Hirnschädigungen und konsekutiv zu einer höheren Häufigkeit von Epilepsien führen; eine gestiegene Anfälligkeit für psychiatrische Krankheitsbilder als Sekundärfolge kann ebenfalls nicht ausgeschlossen werden. Ebenso erhöhen Unterernährung, Vitaminmangel und die in den Entwicklungsländern häufig auftretenden Meningitiden das Risiko für das Entstehen psychiatrischer Störungen (GERMAN 1980). Ebenfalls gehen in Afrika häufig vorkommende Infektionskrankheiten wie Malaria, Typhus, Syphilis und AIDS mit neuropsychiatrischen Symptomen einher.

Neben der ökonomischen Armut ist die Auflösung traditioneller Strukturen als ein Faktor zu zu nennen, der direkt oder indirekt auf die Entstehung psychiatrischer Erkrankungen einwirkt (vgl. DECH

1996). Kriminalität und Suchtmittelmissbrauch sind weitere Erscheinungen, welche die Entwicklung psychiatrischer Störungen begünstigen (BOROFFKA 1996).

Während die Häufigkeit psychischer, insbesondere depressiver Störungen in der Kolonialzeit zumeist nicht erkannt wurde, zeigte sich in der Untersuchung von GIEL & VAN LUJIK (1969) an allgemeinmedizinischen Patienten, dass 18,5% der Patienten an psychiatrischen Störungen litten im Gegensatz zu nur 9,3% mit Infektionskrankheiten. MBANEFO (1971) fand in einer Studie in allgemeinmedizinischen Ambulanzen, dass psychiatrische Erkrankungen gleichhäufig wie Erkrankungen an Malaria waren (15%). Nachfolgende größere Studien der WHO (1975, 1978a; HARDING 1980) und anderen (BEN-TOVIM 1982, GERMAN 1987, NDETEI 1979) in Afrika zeigten, dass 20-40% der Patienten, die eine Einrichtung der Basisgesundheitsversorgung (Primary Health Care, PHC) aufsuchen, an psychiatrischen Problemen leiden, welche jedoch häufig nicht diagnostiziert werden (HARDING 1980, DEJONG 1986).

Untersuchung im Trans-Nzoia Distrikt in Westkenia
Vor diesem Hintergrund konzipierten wir unsere Untersuchung über psychische Störungen bei Frauen im ländlichen Ostafrika, wobei wir auf die Kombination von qualitativen und quantitativen Methoden großen Wert legten: Nach einer offenen, emisch, bzw. lebensweltlich orientierten Befragung schlossen wir standardisierte Methoden zur Erfassung der psychischen Symptomatik an.

Die Untersuchung erfolgte in mehreren Schritten: Zunächst wurden mittels einer Key informant Befragung Informationen zur Lebenssituation in diesem ländlichen Distrikt gesammelt. Darauf aufbauend wurde die Untersuchungsmethode konzeptioniert und durch die Entwicklung eines den dortigen Lebensverhältnissen angepassten psychosozialen Fragebogens und durch die Auswahl und Übersetzung der psychiatrischen Selbstbeurteilungsinstrumente vorbereitet. Für die Patientenerhebung verwendeten wir ein zweistufiges Vorgehen: Zuerst erfolgte ein Screening, darin auffällige Patientinnen wurden dann mit etischen und emischen psychiatrischen Verfahren eingehend untersucht.

Eine Übersicht zur standardisierten Depressionsmessung auf dem afrikanischen Kontinent findet sich bei ODEJIDE (1986). Auswahlkriterien für die Instrumente zur standardisierten Untersuchung depressiver Symptome waren, dass nur solche in unserer Studie verwendet werden sollten, die bereits in unterschiedlichen Kulturen erprobt und validiert sowie international anerkannt sind. Wie an anderer Stelle ausführlich dargelegt, bedarf es hierzu korrekter Übersetzungsprozeduren (DECH 1996). Natürlich ist ROGLER (1989) zuzustimmen, wenn er anmerkt, dass ein Bias, d.h. eine Verzerrung trotz sorgfältiger Übersetzungsmethoden vorhanden sein kann. Dies kann an den zugrundeliegenden, den Übersetzungsprozess präformierenden Forschungskonzepten der Originalversion liegen, so dass emische Elemente in der Zielkultur möglicherweise nicht ausreichend beachtet werden (vgl. KLEINMAN 1985, 1987). Ein wichtiger Bestandteil unserer Untersuchung war daher eine an dem psychosozialen Kontext der Patientin orientierte offene Exploration.

Der Trans-Nzoia Distrikt - in dem wir unsere Untersuchung durchführten - mit seiner Distrikthauptstadt Kitale liegt knapp 400 km entfernt von Nairobi im fruchtbaren Hochland an der Grenze zu Uganda. In diesem Distrikt leben 470.000 Einwohner; Haupterwerbszweig ist die Landwirtschaft in Groß- und Kleinfarmen mit Mais, Tee und Kaffee. Die Distrikthauptstadt Kitale mit 40.000 Einwohnern ist zugleich Handelszentrum (Marktflecken) für die benachbarten Distrikte bis hin zur sudanesischen Grenze, hat also einen weiten Einzugsbereich.

Im ländlichen Bereich werden psychisch kranke Menschen sowohl aufgrund der Stigmatisierung des psychiatrischen Fachgebiets und der geringen Überweisungsrate als auch aufgrund der mangelnden Kenntnisse des allgemeinmedizinischen Personals und der somatischen Präsentiersymptomatik (DECH 1995), bisher kaum in der psychiatrischen Spezialambulanz vorstellig. Deshalb rekrutierten wir die zu untersuchenden Patientinnen in der allgemeinmedizinischen Ambulanz des Distriktkrankenhauses. Eine altersgematchte gesunde Kontrollgruppe (n=50) wurde auf einem Amt und in einer Kirchengemeinde rekrutiert. Teilergebnisse dieser breiter angelegten Untersuchung sollen im folgenden vorgestellt werden.

Häufigkeit nicht-psychotischer Störungen und demographische Informationen

Von den 300 randomisiert in der Allgemeinambulanz mittels des Screeninginstruments SRQ und unseres psychosozialen Fragebogens untersuchten Frauen (18-65 Jahre) lagen 61 (20.3%) über dem cut-off point (mehr als 8 bejahte Fragen im SRQ) und wurden ausführlich (BDI, HAMD, ausführliches Interview und klinische Exploration) untersucht. Von diesen auffälligen Patientinnen erwiesen sich 10 (16.4% bzw. 3.3%) Patientinnen als falsch positiv, insofern bei ihnen eindeutig eine körperliche Erkrankung (n=6) im Vordergrund stand oder eine Psychose (n=1) bzw. andere Störungen (n=3) vorlagen; diese Patientinnen wurden von der weiteren Auswertung ausgeschlossen. Es verblieben 51 Patientinnen (17%).

Dies bestätigt im Wesentlichen die Ergebnisse lokaler Voruntersuchungen: In einer früheren, nicht mit standardisierten Methoden erhobenen Untersuchung an 140 kenianischen Ambulanzpatienten fanden NDETEI & MUHANGI (1979), dass 20% an psychiatrischen Störungen (überwiegend Depression und Angststörungen) litten, 59.3% waren körperlich erkrankt, die verbleibenden 20.3% waren nicht eindeutig zuzuordnen. DHADPHALE (1983, 1989), der ebenfalls den SRQ verwendete, fand 25.5% psychisch Auffällige in seiner kenianischen Stichprobe. In einer Gemeindestudie im benachbarten Uganda fand Orley 20% der weiblichen und 23% der männlichen Probanden an einem depressiven Syndrom leidend, gegenüber nur 10% in der Londoner Vergleichsstichprobe (ORLEY & WING 1979).

Neben der bereits angesprochenen internationalen WHO Studie über psychische Störungen in der Basisgesundheitsversorgung in Entwicklungsländern (HARDING 1980) ergab sich auch in der neueren internationalen, multizentrischen Studie der WHO über psychische Probleme im allgemeinmedizinischen Bereich, dass etwa ein Viertel der Patienten eine erkennbare, nach ICD-10 diagnostizierbare psychische Störung hatte, wobei depressive Störungen am häufigsten waren (SARTORIUS 1993).

Das mittlere Alter der Gesamtstichprobe (n = 300) war 31.2 Jahre, was in Entsprechung zu den demographischen Gegebenheiten dieses Entwicklungslandes steht, in dem fast die Hälfte der Bevölkerung nicht volljährig ist.

Bezüglich des Familienstandes der untersuchten Patientinnen waren 22.3% unverheiratet, 2.0% verlobt, 66.7% verheiratet, 4.0% waren getrennt bzw. geschieden, 3.3% waren verwitwet (missing: 1.7%). Es fanden sich keine signifikanten Unterschiede bezüglich des Familienstandes zwischen den im Screening nicht auffälligen und den auffälligen Patientinnen (p=1.177).

Die mittlere Schulbildung der untersuchten Patientinnen war 7.7 Schuljahre und ist im Vergleich mit anderen afrikanischen Ländern als relativ gut zu bewerten. Auf eine Schulausbildung wird von den Eltern und insbesondere von den Müttern großer Wert gelegt. Ob sich diese oft unter großen finanziellen Einschränkungen der Familie erreichte Qualifikation in einer besseren beruflichen Zukunft und mehr sozioökonomischer Sicherheit auszahlt, ist angesichts der demographischen Entwicklung gerade für Frauen jedoch zunehmend fraglich. Dies zeigte sich in der Auswertung der Arbeitstätigkeiten der untersuchten Frauen, in der, relativ zur Schulbildung, weniger qualifizierte Tätigkeiten überwogen.

Psychische Symptomatik - Standardisierte Erfassung mit dem SRQ

Der Self Reporting Questionnaire (SRQ) wurde in Zusammenarbeit mit der WHO als Sreeninginstrument zur Identifikation psychiatrischer Störungen (suspected psychiatric morbidity/probable psychiatric cases) von Harding et al. (1980) entwickelt und in einer internationalen Studie über psychische Erkrankungen im Bereich der Basisgesundheitsversorgung eingesetzt. Der Fragebogen ist vergleichsweise einfach in der Anwendung und hat sich als nutzliches Screeninginstrument in einigen Entwicklungsländern mit unterschiedlichstem kulturellen Background erwiesen.

Der SRQ existiert in der Form SRQ-20 und SRQ-24. Der häufiger eingesetzte SRQ-20 enthält überwiegend Fragen, die neurotische und depressive Symptome erfassen sollen . Wie bei anderen psychiatrischen Screeninginstrumenten kann man bei dem SRQ-20 von einer Sensitivität und Spezifität von 70-80% ausgehen; bei der Anwendung des SRQ in unterschiedlichen Kulturen zeigte sich, dass der cut-off jeweils zwischen den einzelnen Kulturen etwas variert (MARI & WILLIAMS 1985).

Dass er als Sreeningsinstrument in afrikanischen Ländern geeignet ist, belegt eine Reihe von Untersuchungen (DIOP 1982, DHADPHALE 1983, 1989, HALL 1987, RAHIM 1989, TAFARI 1991). Abgesehen von einer im Sudan erhobenen Studie mit sehr niedrigem cut-off-level, erwies sich im subsaharischen Afrika ein cut-off level zwischen 8/9 positiv beantworteter Fragen als angemessen [7/8 in Zimbabwe (HALL & WILLIAMS 1987); 3/4 in Sudan (RAHIM 1989); 8/9 in Kenia (DHADPHALE 1983,1989); 8/9 in

Äthiopien (KORTMANN 1987); 9/10 in Äthiopien (TAFARI 1991); im Senegal wurde der SRQ-24 verwendet (DIOP 1982)].

In Kenia wurde der SRQ bereits von Dhadphale und Kiganwa eingesetzt. Die damals erstellte Übersetzung in Kiswahili wurde in den Publikationen (DHADPHALE 1983, 1989, KIGANWA 1991) jedoch nicht veröffentlicht. Sie erschien auch der Verfasserin und ihren Mitarbeitern in einigen Punkten als missverständlich, so dass wir eine gründliche Überarbeitung vornahmen.

Für die Darstellung der Symptomverteilung wurde die Häufigkeit der im Self Reporting Questionnaire (siehe Tabelle) angegebenen Beschwerden aller untersuchter Patientinnen (n=300) im Vergleich zu den psychisch auffälligen Patientinnen (n=52) dargestellt.

Tab. 1
Self Reporting Questionnaire - Symptomhäufigkeit (in %)
Patientengruppe (n=52) und Screeninggruppe (n=300)

Item Nr.	Self Reporting Questionnaire	Pat %	Screen %
1	Do you often have headache?	83	49
2	Is your appetite poor?	88	39
3	Do you sleep badly?	92	34
4	Are you easily frightened?	73	22
5	Do your hands shake?	37	4
6	Do you feel nervous, tense or worried?	82	26
7	Is your digestion poor?	81	37
8	Do you have trouble thinking clearly?	56	9
9	Do you feel unhappy?	48	16
10	Do you cry more than usual?	31	5
11	Do you find it difficult to enjoy your daily activities?	31	4
12	Do you find it difficult to make decisions?	44	6
13	Is your daily work suffering?	21	4
14	Are you unable to play a useful part in life?	29	4
15	Have you lost interest in things?	44	6
16	Do you feel that you are a worthless person?	29	4
17	Has the thought of ending your life been in your mind?	38	11
18	Do you feel tired all the time?	40	6
19	Do you have uncomfortable feelings in your stomach?	88	46
20	Are you easily tired?	92	35

Wie aus der obigen Auswertung ersichtlich, wurden Somatisierung und Hypochondrie am häufigsten angegeben. Somatisierung ist als eine Tendenz, seelische Belastungen sowohl körperlich wahrnehmen als auch in einer körperlichen Ausdrucksweise zu kommunizieren, ausführlich beschrieben worden (ESCOBAR 1987, KIRMAYER 1984, LIPOWSKI 1988). Somatisierung ist nicht selten Ausdruck einer depressiven oder Angststörung, wird aber gerade im allgemeinmedizinischen Bereich häufig nicht als psychiatrisches Problem erkannt, (SCHULBERG 1985, GOLDBERG 1988). Dies gilt umso mehr für die medizinische Versorgungssituation in Entwicklungsländern (Harding 1980), wo psychische Störungen aufgrund mangelnder Ausbildung des Personals nicht als solche diagnostiziert und aufgrund der im Vordergrund stehenden somatischen Symptomatik falsch behandelt werden. Während der Somatisierung für die Psychopathologie depressiver Störungen in Afrika von vielen Untersuchern eine überragende Bedeutung beigemessen wird, ist diese verstärkte Somatisierungstendenz von einigen Psychiatern in Frage gestellt worden (vgl. ILECHUKWU 1991). So fand BINITIE (1975) häufig psychische Symptome bei den von ihm untersuchten nigerianischen Patienten. Möglicherweise handelt es sich also bei vielen Patienten nicht um ein rein körperliches Erleben und Ausdrücken depressiver Befindlichkeit, sondern um eine Präsentiersymptomatik (DECH 1995): Da die meisten Patienten mit der modernen Medizin ein rein körperliches Behandlungskonzept verbinden und psychische Erkrankungen zudem stark stigmatisiert sind, präsentieren sie auch in erster Linie somatische Symptome. Bemerkenswert ist bei der von uns untersuchten Stichprobe eine häufige Angabe von psychischen Symptomen, die sich deutlich von den Angaben der unauffälligen Probanden abheben.

Psychosoziale Belastungsfaktoren

Bisher gibt es kaum psychiatrische Untersuchungen in Afrika, die - abgesehen von demographischen Variablen wie Geschlecht, Alter und Schulbildung - eine differenzierte Betrachtung psychosozialer Parameter einbeziehen. Ausgehend von den Konzepten von BROWN & HARRIS (1978, 1996), deren LEDS uns jedoch für unsere explorative Untersuchung im ländlichen Afrika nicht einsetzbar erschien, entwickelten wir einen kurzen Fragebogen zur standardisierten Erhebung relevanter psychosozialer Parameter bzw. Variablen, der gleichzeitig kulturelle Gegebenheiten der Menschen in einem ländlichen Distrikt Ostafrikas berücksichtigt und zeitökonomisch bei einer großen Stichprobe ist. Über die spezifischen Lebensbedingungen der Probanden wurden zuvor sogenannte Key Informanten befragt.

Tab. 2
Psychosoziale Parameter und SRQ - Produktmomentkorrelationen (n=300)

Variable	Vorkommen %	Korrelation m. SRQ
lives with family	90.7	- 0.13 *
marital problems	15.4	0.16 *
sick children	18.4	- 0.041
bigger financial problems	36.0	0.20 *
loss of husband/children	7.6	0.08
loss of job	3.2	0.13 *
loss of house/farm	7.2	0.06
loss of animals	5.6	0.17 *

(* = Korrelationen größer 0.12 sind signifikant)

Bei dem Vergleich zwischen SRQ und den erhobenen psychosozialen Belastungsfaktoren zeigte sich, dass das Zusammenleben mit den Angehörigen als protektiver Faktor anzusehen ist (negative Korrelation mit den SRQ). Immerhin 36% gaben beträchtliche finanzielle Sorgen an, was sich als signifikanter Belastungsfaktor erwies. Unter den sozioökonomischen Gegebenheiten dieses Entwicklungslandes scheint dies durchaus plausibel; da keine Fremdanamnesen erhoben wurden, kann nicht beantwortet werden, inwieweit möglicherweise auch eine depressiv getönte Wahrnehmung zu dieser hohen Zahl beiträgt. Der Verlust von Tieren (agrarische Gesellschaft!) und damit von Besitz und materieller Sicherheit sowie der Verlust der Erwerbstätigkeit kann in einem Land, in dem es für die überwiegende Mehrheit der Bevölkerung keine sozialstaatliche Unterstützung gibt zur Bedrohung der materiellen Existenz werden. Als weitere signifikante Belastungsfaktoren ergaben sich Eheprobleme: In den einzelnen Berichten der Patientinnen wurde deutlich, dass die zentralen Probleme körperliche Gewalt von Seiten des Ehemannes, Alkoholabusus und mangelnde finanzielle Unterstützung für Frau und Kinder waren. Die als Belastungsfaktor auffälligen Eheprobleme spiegeln sich auch bei der Erhebung der Krankheitserklärungskonzepte wieder (infertility, beating by husband, marital problems). Hier wird sicherlich das Spannungsfeld der disparaten Rollenerwartungen und der finanziellen Nöte ausgetragen (vgl. Richters 1996).

Diese Belastungsfaktoren stimmen weitgehend mit den europäischen Ergebnissen von BROWN & HARRIS (1978, 1996) überein, die Kindheitstraumata, Bedrohungs- und Verlustsituationen als grundlegende Belastungsfaktoren herausarbeiteten. In der von uns untersuchten Stichprobe waren jedoch Verlustsituationen wie der Tod des Ehemannes oder eines Kindes keine signifikannten Belastungsfaktoren. Der Verlust von engen Angehörigen scheint durch die immer noch bestehenden Strukturen der Großfamilien wohl eher hingenommen zu werden.

Subjektive Krankheitserklärungskonzepte

Psychische Störungen werden kulturell unterschiedlich erlebt bewertet und verarbeitet. Krankheitskonzepte in einer jeweiligen Kultur sind untrennbar mit den ihr eigenen Denk- und Symbolstrukturen, die dem jeweiligen Handeln seinen spezifischen Sinn verleihen, verbunden. Es ist allgemein bekannt, dass Menschen in ostafrikanische Kulturen sich häufig auf übernatürliche Kräfte berufen, wenn sie Naturgegebenheiten und Lebensereignisse erklären wollen. Zumeist aber wenden sich - im Sinne eines Behandlungspluralismus - Menschen, die in dieser Kultur erkranken, nicht nur an traditionelle, sondern auch an westlich orientierte Einrichtungen der Gesundheitsversorgung. Für diese Polypragmatik gibt es vielfache Zeugnisse (vgl. DECH 1995, HIRST 1996).

Anders als in einer Untersuchung von REYNOLDS-WHYTE (1991) in Tanzania, in der mittels Fallbeschreibungen die Einstellungen der Bevölkerung zu wichtigen psychiatrischen Erkrankungen ermittelt wurden, sollte es in unserer Untersuchung darum gehen, wie die Patientinnen selbst ihre Beschwerden oder Störungen sehen, d.h. welche Konstellationen sie diesen attribuieren und welche Entstehungsursache sie hierfür als ausschlaggebend ansehen.

Um die Angaben im Rahmen des Möglichen nicht zu präformieren, wurde eine offene Frage gestellt, jeweils in derselben Formulierung: „How do you see the cause of your illness?". Die Antworten wurden, auch im Falle von mehr als einer Angabe, wörtlich notiert und in der Auswertung gruppiert.

Tab. 3
How does the patient view/attribute the cause of her illness? (n=52)

Explanatory concepts	
like any other illness	21.7 %
malaria	16.7 %
bewitchment	13.3 %
too many thoughts	10.0 %
I don't know	10.0 %
psychosocial problems (e.g. relatives)	8.3 %
problems with husband	6.7 %
infertility, no conception	6.7 %
unclean food, dirty water	5.0 %
overburdened, heavy work	1.7 %

Ganz analog der mit emischen und etischen Methoden erhobenen Symptomatik, vermuteten die Patientinnen zumeist, ihre Erkrankung habe Gründe im Somatischen, was daraus hervorgeht, dass sie ihre Erkrankung in ihrer subjektiven Ätiologie quasi mit „Krankheit überhaupt" gleichsetzten: Das am häufigsten genannte Erklärungsmuster, die Depression sei entstanden „like any other illness" impliziert ein eher somatisches Krankheitskonzept, natürlich auch die erwartete Behandlung, wenn ein Patient ein Krankenhaus aufsucht. Nur am Rande sei hier auf die fraglos vorhandenen Interdependenzen zwischen Behandlungsangebot und Therapieerwartung einerseits sowie Krankheitserklärungskonzepten andererseits hingewiesen (MACHLEIDT & PELTZER 1994). DHADPHALE (1983) und OVUGA (1986) betonen in diesem Zusammenhang, dass das Präsentieren von somatischen Symptomen mit der Erwartungshaltung der Patienten zu tun hat, auf diese Weise eher Hilfe zu bekommen. Die Kategorie „like any other illness" weist Ähnlichkeiten mit „I don't know" auf. Beide sind letztlich Äußerungsformen einer Unfähigkeit zur konkretisierbaren Kausalitätsrekonstruktion und damit sicherlich nicht untypisch für depressive Erkrankungen.

Es ist nicht von der Hand zu weisen, dass auch die Erwartung, vom Behandler die Diagnose gestellt zu bekommen und auf diese Weise eine Entlastung zu erfahren, im Falle dieser beiden Kategorien eine Rolle spielt. Wenn von Patientinnen die Vermutung ausgesprochen wird, vielleicht an Malaria erkrankt zu sein, so ist dies ein durchaus naheliegendes Erklärungsmodell, zeigt diese Infektionskrankheit doch, abgesehen von Fieber und Schüttelfrost, auch Symptome wie Erschöpfungsgefühl, Antriebstörungen und Energielosigkeit. Zugleich erfährt die Patientin durch diese Kausalattribuierung die Möglichkeit eines sekundären Krankheitsgewinns, wenn ihr als „wirklich Kranke" von der Umgebung Schonung gewährt wird. Nach den Erfahrungen der einheimischen Psychiater wird diese Malaria-Vermutung sehr häufig von depressiven Patienten angegeben (DHADPHALE 1989, NDETEI & MUHANGI 1979) und weiterhin vom allgemeinmedizinischen Personal in Unkenntnis dieser Differentialdiagnose falsch eingeschätzt. MBANEFO (1971) fand in einer Studie in allgemeinmedizinischen Ambulanzen, dass psychiatrische Erkrankungen gleichhäufig wie Erkrankungen an Malaria vorlagen (15%).

Aber keineswegs nur somatisch orientierte, körperbezogene, sondern auch psychogene, konfliktorientierte Attribuierungen der Beschwerden wurden in unserer Studie häufig genannt: Ehe- und familiäre Probleme. Hierbei handelte es sich häufig um Alkoholmissbrauch des Ehemannes und die damit verbundenen finanziellen Engpässe für Frau und Kinder, oder auch die Entfremdung bei räumlicher Trennung der Ehepartner.

Zu den Konfliktpunkten gehört auch die Angabe „no conception" bzw. „infertility", da hierfür grundsätzlich die Frau angeschuldigt wird und Schwierigkeiten bzw. einen Statusverlust in der eingeheirateten Familie erleidet. Das Ansehen der Frau bestimmte sich in traditionellen afrikanischen Gesellschaften weitgehend aus ihrer innerfamiliären Reproduktionsfunktion heraus (MEYER-MANSOUR 1985). durch die, besonders in Bezug auf männliche Nachkommen der Erhalt der patrilinear organisierten Großfamilien gesichert wurde und wird. Kinderreichtum ist, wie in allen Entwicklungsländern, zugleich die Altersversicherung. Nicht mit der Heirat, sondern erst nach der Geburt gesunder Kinder/Söhne erwirbt eine Frau soziales Ansehen in der eingeheirateten Familie. Kinderlosigkeit, aber auch geringe Kinderzahl oder ausschließliche Geburt von Mädchen, wird weiterhin als schweres Unglück angesehen und ist ein Grund für das Heiraten einer zweiten Frau oder nicht selten ein Scheidungsgrund. „Infertility/no conception" ist daher als schwerwiegender psychosozialer Stressor zu werten.

In der Kategorie „too many thoughts" verbirgt sich das Symptom des depressiven Grübelns, was hier aber als Auslöser für die Beschwerden empfunden wird. Es spiegelt ebenso die weitverbreitete Einstellung, dass Kummer krankmacht, wieder. Immer wieder wird in der Literatur referiert, dass in afrikanischen Kulturen kein Konzept über depressive Erkrankungen existiert. Dem können wir sowohl aus unserer klinischen Erfahrung als auch von Seiten dieser Studie nicht zustimmen, wird doch gerade das Nennen von „too many thoughts" als ein Synonym für Depression verstanden. Bei diesem kulturspezifischen Ausdruck handelt es sich sicherlich um depressive Störungen, bei denen kognitive Störungen im Vordergrund der Symptomatik stehen.

Die Einschätzung Marsella's von 1979, dass in vielen Kulturen kein traditionelles Konzept über depressive Störungen existiert, ist uns für den afrikanischen Raum nicht nachvollziehbar, mehren sich doch die Berichte darüber, dass eine zumindest depressionsähnliche Symptomatik sehr wohl im traditionellen System erkannt und behandelt wird (BROADHEAD 1996, DECH 1995, GATERE 1980, HALTENHOF & KRAUSE 1996, LEFF 1994). Bemerkenswerterweise wurden sozio-ökonomische Belastungen von den Patientinnen selbst nicht als Auslöser genannt, während diese in der statistischen Untersuchung depressiogener psychosozialer Belastungsfaktoren signifikant waren.

13 % gaben übernatürliche Kräfte (bewitchment) als Ursachen ihrer Erkrankung an. Dieser Anteil liegt etwas höher als in dem Bericht von REYNOLDS-WHYTE (1991) aus Tanzania. Andere Untersuchungen kommen zu ähnlichen Ergebnissen (Dhadphale 1983, Makanjoula 1987). Den Berichten aus Ostafrika von EDGERTON (1971), OTSYULA (1973) und GATERE (1980) zufolge, dass viele Patienten beide Systeme polypragmatisch in Anspruch nehmen, kann man vermuten, dass dieser Anteil noch höher liegen könnte, aber bei Untersuchern in der nach westlichem Muster organisierten Basisgesundheitsversorgung nicht angegeben wird (vgl. DECH 1995). Zwar ist das Ausüben der traditionellen Heilkunde in Kenia nicht mehr illegal, doch besteht vermutlich weiterhin eine Zurückhaltung, diese traditionellen Kausalitätsvorstellungen im staatlichen Gesundheitssystem anzusprechen.

Eine abschließende Bemerkung
Depressive Verstimmungszustände kommen vermutlich bei Menschen aller Zeiten und Kulturen vor (vgl. HALTENHOF & KRAUSE 1996). Allerdings zeigen sich kulturell unterschiedliche Ausformungen und „Veränderungen in der Gestaltung depressiver Affektivität (KRAMBECK 1996)". Nichtsdestotrotz kann davon ausgehen, dass durch die koloniale Erosion und Verarmung der afrikanischen Gesellschaften zusätzliche Belastungsfaktoren hinzugekommen sind, die zur Entwicklung psychischer Störungen beitragen.

Ob sich die soziale Situationen von Frauen in Ostafrika künftig zu ihren Gunsten ändern wird, ist also im Rückblick auf die Schilderungen und Untersuchungsbelege unserer Arbeit zumindest fragwürdig, denn zu schnell greift die Urbanisierung auch in die Lebenswelt der Landbewohner ein, wie diese wiederum letztlich auch von diesen durch die Landflucht gefördert wird. Beides zusammengenommen, scheint die Adaptionsfähigkeit aller an der Veränderung Beteiligten überholt zu haben. Frauen sind hiervon besondes betroffen, obliegt ihnen doch im Zuge der Auflösung der tradtionellen Strukturen in besonderes hohem Maße, oft als Alleinerziehende und „weiblicher Haushaltsvorstand", die Verantwortung für die Versorgung der Kinder während ihr Zugang zu Bildung, Information und Einkommen gering ist. Für das hohe Armutsrisiko von Frauen in Entwicklungsländern ist der Gegensatz von hoher Arbeitsbelastung und geringen Verdienstmöglichkeiten bestimmend.

Diese Belastungsfaktoren sollten therapeutisch aufgegriffen werden. Dass durchaus Ressoucen existieren zeigen Ansätze aus anderen Bereichen (MEYER-MANSOUR 1985, HYMA & NYAMWANGE 1993, MACKENZIE 1996), insbesondere das Konzept der Selbsthifegruppen. Angesichts der Ressourcenknappheit in der staatlichen Gesundheitsversorgung ist gerade auch im Bereich Mental Health Care eine Stärkung des ambulanten Bereichs erforderlich. Im ländlichen Bereich stellen die weitgehenden Familienbeziehungen und -verpflichtungen eine wichtige Ressource für Mental Health Care dar, sofern es Beratungsangebote über den Umgang mit psychischen Erkrankungen für die Betroffenen und ihre Angehörigen gibt. Eine weitere wichtige Ressource sind im psychosozialen Bereich tätige, nichtstaatliche Organisationen und Projekte (NGO) mit denen Kooperationen bzw. Vernetzungen etabliert oder intensiviert werden sollten.

Danksagung
Wir bedanken uns bei der GTZ, insbesondere bei Herrn Dr. Nachtigal und Frau Weyhe, für die technische Unterstützung bei dieser Untersuchung.

References
BEN-TOVIM, D., KUNDU, P., 1982. Integration of psychiatric care with PHC. *Lancet* 1982: Oct 2

BINITIE, A., 1975. A Factor-Analytical Study of Depression Across Cultures. *Brit J Psychiat* 127: 559-563.

BOROFFKA, A., 1996. Depressive Erkrankungen - Diagnostische Konzepte und therapeutische Strategien aus transkultureller Sicht. *Curare* 19: 207-218

BRABIN, L., 1984. Polygyny: An Indicator of Nutritional Stress in African Agricultural Societies? *Africa* 54: 31-45

BROADHEAD, J.C., ABAS, M.A., 1996. Depression in Zimbabwe - Investigations and community involvement in the generation of recommendations for service development. *Curare* 19: 227-232

BROWN, G.W., HARRIS, T.O., 1978. *Social origins of depression: A study of psychiatric disorders in women.* London: Tavistock.

BROWN, G.W., HARRIS, T.O., EALES, M.J. 1996. Social factors and comorbidity of depressive and anxiety disorders. *Brit J Psychiat* 168 (suppl 30): 50-57

DECH, H., 1995: Westliche und traditionelle Therapie in Ostafrika. In: QUEKELBERGHE R v (Hrsg): *Ethnopsychologie und Ethnopsychotherapie.* Landau.

DECH, H., 1996. Die Behandlung psychischer Erkrankungen im kulturellen Wandel Ostafrikas. *Ethnopsychologische Mitteilungen* 5: 21-32

DECH, H., 1996. Editorial: Transkulturelle Perspektiven depressiver Störungen. *Curare* 19: 187-192

DECH, H., 1997. Psychiatrische Basisgesundheitsversorgung in Afrika - Historische Entwicklungen und aktuelle Problemstellungen. In: HOFFMANN, K. & MACHLEIDT, W. (Hrsg): *Psychiatrie im Kulturvergleich.* Berlin: VWB (in press)

DECH, H., NATO, J., 1996. Depressive Symptomatik und psychosoziale Belastungsfaktoren bei afrikanischen Frauen. *Curare* 19: 243-254

DECH, H., RICHTER, P., SANDERMANN, S., MARIN, A., SURGULADZE, S.A., 1995. Transcultural research on depression - Some considerations. In: G. NANEISHVILI: *The Actual Problems of Psychiatry.* Georgia, Tbilisi: Asatiani Scientific Research Institute of Psychiatry Publ.

DEJONG, J.T., DEKLEIN, G.A., TENHORN, S.G., 1986. A baseline study on mental disorder in Guinea-Bissau. *Brit J Psychiat* 148: 27-32

DESJARLAIS, R., KLEINMANN, A., EISENBERG, L. and B. GOOD. 1995. *World Mental Health - Problems and Priorities in Low-Income Countries.* Oxford University Press.

DHADPHALE, M., COOPER, G., CARTWRIGHT-TAYLOR, L., 1989. Prevalence and Presentation of Depressive Illness in a Primary Health Care Setting in Kenya. *Am J Psychiatry* 146: 659-651

DHADPHALE, M., ELLISON, R.H., GRIFFIN, N. L., 1983. The frequency of psychiatric disorders among patients attending semi-urban and rural general out-patient clinics in Kenya. *Brit J Psychiat* 142:379-383
DIESFELD, H.J., 1989. *Gesundheitsproblematik der dritten Welt.* Darmstadt: Wiss. Buchgesellschaft
DIOP, COLLIGNON, 1982. Diagnosis and symptoms of mental disorders in a rural setting in Senegal. Afr *J Medicine Med Sci* 11:95-103
EDGERTON, R., 1966. Conceptions of psychosis in four East African societies. *Am Anthropologist* 68: 408-425
ESCOBAR, J.I., BURNAM, M.A., KARNO, M., FORSYTHE, A., GOLDING, J.M,. 1987. Somatization in the community. *Arch Gen Psychiat* 44: 713-718
GATERE, S.G., 1980. *Patterns of psychiatric morbidity in rural Kenya.* M.Phil. thesis; Institute of Psychiatry: London.
GERMAN, G.A., 1980. Zur psychiatrischen Bedeutung der Armut. In: PFEIFFER, SCHOENE: *Psychopathologie im Kulturvergleich.* Stuttgart: Enke
GERMAN, G.A., 1987. Mental Health in Africa. *Brit J Psychiat* 151: 435-446
GIEL, R., VAN LUJIK, J.V., 1969. Psychiatric Morbidity in a Small Ethopian Town. *Brit J Psychiat* 115: 145-62
GLUCKMANN, M., 1969. *Custom and Conflict in Africa. Kapitel 3.* New York: Barnes & Noble
GOLDBERG, D.P., BRIDGES, K., 1988. Somatic presentations of psychiatric illness in primary care setting. *J Psychosom Res* 32: 137-144
HALL, A., WILLIAMS, H., 1987. Hidden psychiaric morbidity. A study of prevalence in an out-patient population at Bindura Provincial Hospital. *Centr Afr J Med* 33:239-243
HALTENHOF, H., KRAUSE, J., 1996. Thematik wahnhafter Depressionen in westlichen Ländern. *Curare* 19: 219-226
HARDING, T.W., DE ARANGO, M.V., BALTAZAR, J., CLIMENT, C.E., IBRAHIM, H., LADRIDO, L., MURPHY, R.S., WIG, N.N., 1980. Mental disorders in PHC: a study of their frequency and diagnosis in four developing countries. *Psychol Med* 10: 231-242
HIRST, M., COOK, J., KAHN, M., 1996. Shades, witches and somatization in the narratives of illness and disorder among the Cape Nguni in the Eastern Cape, South Africa. *Curare* 19: 255-282
HYMA, B., NYAMWANGE, P., 1993 Woman's role and participation in farm and community tree-growing activities in Kiambu District, Kenya. In: MOMSEN JH, KINNAIRD V (Eds.:): *Different Places, Different Voices: Gender and Development in Asia, Africa and Latin America.* London
ILECHUKWU, S.T.C., 1991. Psychiatry in Africa: Special Problems and Unique Features. *Transcult Psychiat Res Rev* 28: 169-217
KIGANWA, A., 1991. Psychiatric morbidity and referral rate among medical in-patients at Kenyatta National Hospital. *East Afr Med J* 68: 383-388
KIRMAYER, L.J., 1984. Culture, Affect and Somatization. *Transcult Psychiat Res Rev* 21: 159-188
KLEINMAN, A.M., 1987. Anthropology and Psychiatry: The Role of Culture in Cross - Cultural Research on Illness. *Brit J Psychiat* 151: 447 - 454
KLEINMAN, A.M., GOOD, B. (Eds), 1985. *Culture and Depression.* University of California Press; Berkeley.
KORTMANN, F.,1987. Problems in communication in transcultural psychiatry - The self reporting questionnaire in Ethiopia. *Acta Psychiat Scand* 75:563-567
LEFF, J.P., 1994. Transcultural aspects.In: Paykel, E.S. (Ed): *Handbook of Affective Disorders;* 2.Edition. Edinburgh: Churchill-Livingstone
LIPOWSKI, Z.J., 1988. Somatization: the concept and ist clinical application. *Am J Psychiat* 145: 1358-1368
MACHLEIDT, W., PELTZER, K., 1994. Comparison of culturally different approaches towards the therapy of schizophrenia. *Curare* 17: 59-81
MACKENZIE, F., 1986. Local initiatives and national policy: gender and agricultural change in the Murang'a District, Kenya. *Canad J African Studies:* 377-401
MARI, J.J., WILLIAMS, P., 1985. A comparison of the validity of two psychiatric screening questionnaires (GHQ-12 and SRQ-20) in Brazil, using ROC analysis. *Psychol Med* 15: 651-659
MARSELLA, A.J., SARTORIUS, N., JABLENSKY, A., FENTON, F.R.,1985. Cross-Cultural studies of Depressive disorders: An Overview. In: KLEINMAN A, GOOD B: *Culture and Depression.* Berkeley.
MBANEFO, S.E., 1971. The general practioneer and psychiatry. In: *Psychiatry and Mental Health Care in General Practice.* Ibadan: University of Ibadan Publ.
MEYER-MANSOUR, D., 1985. *Frauenselbsthilfegruppen in Kenia.* Hamburg: Weltarchiv.
MINISTRY OF HEALTH, GOVERNMENT OF KENYA, 1986. *National guidelines for the implementation of primary health care in Kenya.* Hrsg.: BENNETT FJ, MANENO J. Nairobi.
MONK, J., MOMSEN, J., 1995. Geschlechterforschung und Geographie in einer sich verändernden Welt. *Geographische*

Rundschau: 214-221

NDETEI, D.M., 1988. Psychiatric phenomenology across countries: constitutional, cultural, or environmental?. *Acta Psychiat Scand Suppl* 344: 33-44

NDETEI, D.M., MUHANGI, J., 1979. The prevalance and clinical presentation of psychiatric illnesses in a rural setting in Kenya. *Brit J Psychiat* 135: 269-272

ODEJIDE, A.O., 1986. Standard instruments used in the assessment of depression in Africa. In: SARTORIUS N, BAN TA . *Assessment of Depression*. Berlin: Springer.

OKPALA, J., 1992. *A comparative study of teachers's and rural woman's survival strategies under the Structural Adjustment Programme (SAP) in Nigeria*. International Geographical Union Study Group and Gender Working Papers Nr. 20

ORLEY, J.H., 1970. *Culture and Mental Illness. A Study from Uganda*. East African Publishing House

ORLEY, J., WING, J., 1979. Psychiatric disorders in two African villages. *Arch Gen Psychiat* 36: 513-520

OTSYULA, W., 1973. Native and western healing: the dilemmma of East African Psychiatry. *J Nerv Ment Dis* 156: 297-299

OVUGA, E.B.L., 1986. The different faces of depression. *East Afr Med J* 63: 109-114

OWEI, O.B., JEV, M., 1993. *Coping with structural adjustment in Nigeria: Professional woman and contigent work in Port Harcourt*. International Geographical Union Study Group on Geography and Gender Working Paper Nr. 21

PFEIFFER, W.M., 1996. Das Bild der Depressionen im Kulturvergleich. *Curare* 19: 193-200

RAHIM, S I , CEDERBLAD, M,.,1989. Epidemiology of mental disorders in young adults of a newly urbanized area in Khartoum, Sudan. *Brit J Psychiat* 155: 44-47

REYNOLDS-WHYTE, S., 1991. Attitudes towards mental health problems in Tanzania. In: Schulsinger F, Jablensky A (Hrsg.): The national mental health programme in the United Republic of Tanzania - A report from WHO and DANIDA: *Acta Psychiat Scand Suppl* 364, Seite 65

RICHTERS, A., 1996. Women, emotions and depressive disorders: between adjustment and protest. *Curare* 19: 233-242

ROGLER, L.H., 1989. The meaning of culturally sensitiv research in Mental Health. *Am J Psychiat* 146: 296-303

SACKS, K., 1982. An Overview of Woman and Power in Africa. In: O'BARR JF (Eds.): *Perspectives on Power: Woman in Africa, Asia and Latin America*. Durham, N.C.: Duke University, Center for International Studies, Occasional Papers Series, Number 13: 1-10

SANDERMANN, S., Dech, H., Othieno, C.J., Kathuku, D.M., Ndetei, D.M., 1996. Die Generierung einer kulturspezifischen Symptomskala zur Depressionsmessung in Afrika. *Curare* 19: 283-294

SCHÄFER, R., 1995. *Frauenorganisationen und Entwicklungszusammenarbeit - Traditionelle und moderne afrikanische Frauenzusammenschlüsse im interethnischen Vergleich*. Centaurus-Verlagsgesellschaft: Pfaffenweiler.

SCHULBERG, H.C., SAUL, M., MCCLELLAND, M., GANGULI, M., CHRISTY, W., FRANK, R. 1985. Assessing depression in primary medical psychiatric practices. *Arch Gen Psychiat* 42: 1164-1170

TAFARI, S., ABOUD, F.E., LARSON, C.P., 1991. Determinants of mental illness in a rural Ethiopian adult population. *Soc Sci Med* 32:197-201

UNA/USA, 1980. United Nations Association of the USA: Progress for half of the world' s people: The UN decade for woman. In: UNA/USA (Ed.): *Issues of the 80s*. New York

WELTENTWICKLUNGSBERICHT, 1993. *Investitionen in die Gesundheit. Kennzahlen der Weltentwicklung*. Weltbank: Washington, D.C.

Autoren & Herausgeber dieses Bandes / Authors & Editors

K. Weldemichael Afework
(MD.) Dr., Medical Doctor working in the control of AIDS Programme of the Ministry of Health, Ethiopia. Currently he is a student of PhD at the University of Vienna in department of Medical Anthropology. His area of research is women and health with focus to Adolescents and traditional medicine.
PO Box 34 240, Addis Ababa, Ethiopia   S. 13 / 61

David Aldridge
is professor for Clinical Research Methods in the Faculty of Medicine, University of Witten Herdecke. He is currently completing a book about suicide from an ecosystemic perspective and a book about spiritual healing. His interests lie in bringing various forms of therapeutic knowledge together and in developing research strategies that can develop such knowledge. He is totally addicted to new electronic media, an aggressive advocate of bringing the social sciences into medicine, and dedictaed to bringing the arts and sciences into dialogue.
Universität Witten-Herdecke, Institut für Musiktherapie, Alfred Herrhausen Str. 50, D-58448 Witten, Germany.   S. 207

Gudrun Aldridge
Diplom Musiktherapie, arbeitet freiberuflich als Musiktherapeutin. Zur Zeit ist sie in der Universität Aalborg (Dänemark) als PH.D. Studentin eingeschrieben, um ihren Doktor in Musiktherapie zu absolvieren. Ihre Arbeitsschwerpunkte sind die Psychosomatik und Frauen und Gesundheit.
Kirchender Dorfweg 145, D-58313 Herdecke, Germany.   S. 217

Josephine Nkiru Alumanah
Lecturer / Health Sociologist.
Department of Sociology/Anthropology, University of Nigeria, St. Anthony's Villa, 4B College Road, Odenigbe, Nsukka Nigeria.   S. 79

Peter Babulka
Ph.D. • Date of birth: 4th July 1953, • Head of Regulatory Affairs, Pharmafontana Co., • Invited lecturer in ethnobotany:, Department of Folklore, Eötvös Lóránd University, Budapest, Visual and Cultural Anthropology Department, Miskolc University, Miskolc, • Fields of interest - Traditional application of medicinal plants and their effectiveness, ethnobotany
H-1213 Orsova u. 6. Budapest, Hungary.   S. 279

Martin Wultoff Bangha
Cameroonian of the English-speaking background, I am a demographer by profession trained at the United Nations Regional Institute for Population Studies (RIPS), the University of Ghana, Legon from 1989 to 1992. I hold the master of arts (M.A.) and master of philosophy (M.PHIL.) degrees of this University in Population Studies after a first degree in Economics from the University of Yaounde, Cameroon.
Union for African Population Studies, UEPA-UAPS, UAPS Secr., BP 21007, Dakar- Ponty, Dakar, Senegal   S. 85

Elke Barbian
Dipl.-Soziol., geb. 1952, Dozentin: Univ. Hamburg, Bremen; Erwachsenenbildung zu Medizinsoziologie, Bevölkerungspolitik/Familienplanung, Frauen u. Gesundheit. Forschung an der TU Berlin: Reproduktionsmedizin u. Gesundheitsförderung, -versorgung von Schwangeren u. jungen Müttern im Rahmen des Berliner Forschungsverbundes Public Health.
Univ. Berlin TU, Institut für Ökologie und Biologie, Sekr. FR 1-1, Franklinstr. 28/29, D-10587 Berlin, Germany.   S. 287

Yonas Bahire Tibeb
M.D., Trainee Psychiatrist. Emmanuel Psychiatric Hospital Addis Abeba, Ethiopia. Main Areas of Interest is Ethnopsychiatry and Transcultural Psychiatry
Emmanuel Psychiatric Hospital, P.O. Box 20 76, Addis Abeba, Ethiopia   S. 409

Joachim Bensel
Dipl.-Biol.
Albert-Ludwigs-Univ. Freiburg, Institut für Biologie I - FVM, Forschungsgruppe Verhaltensbiologie des Menschen, Trennenbacher Str. 4, 79106 Freiburg, Germany.   S. 293

Giselind Berg
Dr. phil. (Berlin) : Studium der Pharmazie und Soziologie mit Schwerpunkt Entwicklungs- und Medizinsoziologie. Arbeitsgebiete sind Migration und Gesundheit, Reproduktionsmedizin, Frauengesundheitsforschung, Public Health/Gesundheitswissenschaften.
Institut f. Ökologie u. Biologie der TU Berlin, Sekr.: FR 1-1, Franklinstraße 28/29, D-10587 Berlin, Germany.   S. 367

Christine Binder-Fritz
Geb. 1956 in Wien. Dr. phil., Ethnologin und dipl. MTA (1977-1994 Zytogenetik, Pränataldiagnostik). Seit 1994 Lehrbeauftragte an der Universität Wien. Feldforschungen in Neuseeland: 1986, 1989, 1995/96, 1997. Wissenschaftliche Schwerpunkte: Ethnomedizin (Gynäkologie und Geburtshilfe, tradit. Heilkunde der Maori), Kulturwandelphänomene, Migration und Transkulturelle Pflege.
Institut f. Geschichte der Medizin der Univ. Wien, Abt. Ethnomedizin, Währingerstr. 25, A-1090 Wien, Austria. S. 133

Theda Borde
Dipl. Polit. Humboldt-Universität zu Berlin, Universitätsklinikum Charité-Virchow, Frauenklinik / Public Health-Projekt,
Augustenburger Platz 1, D-13353 Berlin, Germany. S. 373

Maria Ofelia Burgos Lingán
Dipl. Päd. Dr. 1946 in Perú geboren. Seit 1971 Projektarbeit in Perú u. entwicklungspolitische Arbeit: Frauenförderung, ländliche Entwicklung, Basisgesundheitsversorgung u. traditionelle Medizin. Aufenthalte in Chile, México und Honduras. Moderatorin für entwicklungspolitischen Seminaren, Beraterin von Basisgesundheitsprojekten im Ausland. Mitarbeiterin des Deutschen Bundestages.
Meckenheimer Allee 82, D-53115 Bonn, Germany. S. 303

Hannah I. Carew
Lecturer in the Dept. of Educational Psychology at Moi University, Kenya. Research interests: Marginalised and disadvantaged groups in society, namely, the academically poorly performing students, refugee children, street children, the visually impaired and women.
Moi University, P.O. Box 3900, Eldoret, Kenya. S. 415

Reg Crowshoe
is a member of the Peigan Nation in Southern Alberta and acknowledged Blackfoot ceremonialist. He is presently director of the Oldman River Cultural Centre in Brocket. (Contribution with S. Manneschmidt) S. 157

Wim van Damme
Dr., is a medical doctor, specialist in Public Health and now working at the Public Health Department of the Institute of Tropical Medicine, Antwerp Belgium. He teaches Public Health in Unstable Situations. Between 1985 and 1992 he worked in Peru, Sudan, and Guinea with the internally displaced and refugees.
Institute of Tropical Medicine, Nationalstraat 155, B-2000 Antwerp, Belgium. S. 385

Matthias David
Dr.med., geb. 1961 in Brandenburg/H., Medizinstudium in Berlin, seit 1989 zunächst im Klinikum Berlin Buch, ab 1991 dann im Berliner Universitätsklinikum Rudolf Virchow Weiterbildung zum Facharzt für Geburtshilfe und Gynäkologie. Schwerpunkte der wissenschaftlichen Tätigkeit: Geburtshilfliche Themen, Medizinhistorie, Public Health/ Migration und Gesundheit.
Humboldt-Univ.Berlin , Charité-Virchow-Klinikum, Frauenklinik, Augustenburger Platz 1, D-13353 Berlin, Germany S. 373

Heike Dech
Wiss. Assistentin. 1991-1992 Dept. of Psychiatry, University of Nairobi, Kenya. Initiatorin der Seminarreihe „Transkulturelle Psychiatrie" seit an der Psychiatrischen Klinik der Univ. Heidelberg. Projekt „Transkulturelle Depressionsforschung". Mitarbeit bei dem vom BMFT geförderten Schwerpunkt Tropenmedizin der Univ. Heidelberg. Interessen: Transkulturelle Depressionsforschung, Frauenpsychiatrie, Mental Health Care Services, Gerontopsychiatrie.
Psychiatrische Universitätsklinik, Voss-Str. 4, D- 69115 Heidelberg, Germany. S. 425

Karl Lorenz Dehne
is medical doctor and public health specialist. His main interests lie in reproductive health, mother and child care and AIDS. In 1992/1993, he was Coordinator of the Save the Children Fund (UK) primary health programme in Burkina Faso. He worked for the WHO at its Regional Office for the Western Pacific in Manila, Philippines, and is now Team Leader for Eastern Europe in the Department of Country Support in UNAIDS, Geneva.
MPH. UNAIDS, c/o World Health Organization, Av. Appia, CH-1211 Genève 27, Switzerland. S. 341

Angelika Denzler
Geb. 1962. Dr. med., Assistenzärztin Gynäkologie/ Geburtshilfe in München, verheiratet, eine Tochter. Studienaufenthalte in Ecuador 1986/87, 1991 und 1993. Wissenschaftliche Schwerpunkte: Psychosomatik, Geburtshilfe im interkulturellen Vergleich, Gesundheitssituation von Frauen, Migration, Menschenrechte, soziopolitische und kulturelle Situation in Lateinamerika (Schwerpunkt Argentinien, Andenländer), Entwicklungspolitik, Bevölkerungspolitik. Terhallestr. 45, D-81545 München, Germany . S. 147

Angelica Ensel
geb. 1955, Dr.phil. Ethnologin, Hebamme, Fachzeitschriftenredakteurin. Studium der Ethnologie, Deutschen Volkskunde u. Sportwissenschaft. Feldforschung: Alternative Geburtskonzepte und ihre Einlösung, Schönheitschirurgie und die Arzt-Patientin-Beziehung. Schwerpunkte im Bereich Frau-Körper-Macht-Institutionen und in der Frauengesundheitsforschung. Veröffentlichungen über Schönheitschirurgie und über Machtstrukturen im Geburts-Raum.
Zeißstr. 51, Haus 1 , 22765 Hamburg, Germany. S. 231

Tine Eschertzhuber
Geb. 1968, Diplompädagogin, Studium der Soziologie und der Pädagogik in München und Regensburg , Studienabschluß: Herbst 1996, Forschungsschwerpunkte: geschlechtsspezifische Arbeitsteilung , Sozialisation und Geschlecht, Frauen und Körperlichkeit.
Malergasse 8, D-93047 Regensburg, Germany. S. 235

Wilhelm Föllmer
Prof. Dr. med. habil. Ärztlicher Direktor der Kurklinik Dünenhaus, Timmendorfer Strand. 14 Jahre in Libyen als Chefarzt der Re. Frauenklinik, Generaldirektor. Später Berater des libyschen Gesundheitswesens. In den letzten Jahren in Kamerun zur Vorbereitung eines Projektes. Bis 1989 Vize
Passatweg 14, D-23669 Timmendorfer Strand, Germany. S. 21

Georgia Friedrich
Clinical Psychologist, Mental Health Program, United Mission to Nepal. Trainings in behaviour therapy and psychodrama. After working more than 25 years in a counselling centre in Germany she came to Nepal 3 years ago and worked there as the first clinical psychologist in the country.
UMN-Health Services, P.O.Box 126, Kathmandu, Nepal. S. 113

Christine E. Gottschalk-Batschkus
Medizinstudium an der LMU München. Ethnomedizinische Forschung 1992-1996 in Papua Neuguinea. Veröffentlichungen (u.a.): 1990 mit Marc M. Batschkus „Unser Kind-ein Mensch ohne Fesseln". Elternratgeber. 1992: „Merkilfen zum Physikum" 1994: "ABC für Vorschulkinder". 1997: „Grundlagen der Ethnomedizin, Medizinanthropologie und Medizinethnologie" mit A. Prinz, W. Schiefenhövel u. J. Schuler (Hrsg.). curare-Sonderbände im Verlag für Wissenschaft & Bildung: 1995 mit W. Schiefenhövel u. D. Sich (Hrsg.): „Gebären-Ethnomedizinische Perspektiven und neue Wege". 1996 mit J. Schuler (Hrsg.): „Ethnomedizinische Perspektiven zur Frühen Kindheit". Seit 1995 mit J. Schuler Hrsg. der Reihe „Beiträge zur Ethnomedizin". Hrsg. der Reihe „Ethnomedizin - Neue Perspektiven für unsere Gesundheit" im NaturaMed / Hampp Verlag. Im Vorstand der Arbeitsgemeinschaft Ethnomedizin seit 1993.
Melusinenstr. 2, D-81671 München, Germany.

Mia Groenenberg
Psychologist-psychotherapist with a psychoanalytic background, trained in different methods of psychotherapy with specialization in system-oriented therapy. Since 1986 she works with refugees from many different cultural backgrounds. Since 1993 she works for Pharos, a Refugee Health Care Centre in the Netherlands. She gives consultation and participates in training-programmes for mental health care workers in the Netherlands. Since 1995 she also participates in training-programmes offered by Admira in former Yugoslavia, directed at aid to women who are victims of rape and other forms of sexual abuse. She wrote a chapter about „female victims of sexual violence" in the book: Counselling and Therapy with Refugees, by G. van der Veer (1992, Wiley, Chichester, England).
Pharos, Prins Hendrikkade 120, NL-1011 AM Amsterdam, The Netherlands. S. 379

Gerhard Grossmann
Ass.Prof. Univ.-Doz. Dr. Forschungsgebiete: Medizinsoziologie, Sozialepidemiologie, Demographie, Sozialmedizin, Menschliches Verhalten in Ausnahmefällen, Panikforschung.
Kapitän des Forschungsschiffes „MS Maasholm„ für epidemiologische Untersuchungen.
Institut für Soziologie, Karl-Franzens-Universität Graz, Universitätsstraße 15/G4, A-8010 Graz, Austria. S. 243

Horst Haltenhof
Dr. med.; Studium der Medizin in Marburg; Weiterbildung zum Psychiater an der Psychiatr. Univ.-Klinik Marburg und der Neurologischen Klinik der Städtischen Kliniken Kassel; Arbeitssschwerpunkte: depressive Störungen, Erleben und Verarbeiten psychiatrischer und neurologischer Erkrankungen, psychosoziale Probleme in der Primärversorgung; Oberarzt an der Klinik für Sozialpsychiatrie und Psychotherapie der Medizinischen Hochschule,
Medizinische Hochschule Hannover, Konstanty-Gutschow-Str. 8, D-30625 Hannover, Germany. S. 425

Barbara E. Harrell-Bond

Dr., is an anthropologist. She was the founder and director of the Refugee Studies Programme, University of Oxford, 1982-96. Her career as an anthropologist research began in 1966 with a study of an urban housing estate in the UK. She began research in Africa (Sierra Leone) in 1967 and specialised in the anthropology of law.

Refugee Studies Programme, Queen Elizabeth House, University of Oxford, 21 St Giles, Oxford, OX1 3LA, U.K. S. 385

Gabriele Haug-Schnabel

PD Dr. (haben Text schon geschickt???)

Albert-Ludwigs-Univsität Freiburg, Institut für Biologie I - FVM, Forschungsgruppe Verhaltensbiologie des Menschen, Trennenbacher Str. 4, 79106 Freiburg, Germany. S. 293

Evelyn Heinemann

Prof.Dr., geb. 1952. Sonderschullehrerin, Diplom-Pädagogin und Diplom-Psychologin mit psychoanalytischer Weiterbildung (DPV). Seit 1992 ist sie Professorin für Allgemeine Sonderpädagogik am Pädagogischen Institut der Johannes Gutenberg-Universität Mainz. Sie hat Bücher zur Ethnopsychoanalyse (Palau, Jamaika) im Fischer Verlag veröffentlicht.

Johannes Gutenberg-Universität, Pädagogisches Institut, Colonel-Kleinmann-Weg 2, D-55099 Mainz, Germany. S. 141

Peter Paul Hembrom

Dr. F.E.S., Rtd. D.F.O., Tribal Herbalist Trainer and Researcher in Ethnomedicine. Born in 1929, comes from the Munda Ethnic Group of the Australoid Asiatic Linguistic Group of India. Trainer in the grass root & national level with collaboration of N.G.O.'s.

Horopathy Ethnomedicine Research & Development Centre, Vill. & P.O. Maheshmunda-815 312, Dist. Giridih, Bihar, India S. 123

Caroline Hof

has graduated in July 1996 in Clinical and Health Psychology at the University of Leiden, the Netherlands. During her studies she completed a one year research program at the University of Exeter, United Kingdom, and developed an interest concerning „women, health and culture". After her graduation she conducted the research „Teenage pregnancy as an issue of gender violence: the case of Zimbabwe" under supervision of Prof. Annemiek Richters. At the moment she is working as a research assistant at the Women and Health Department of the Academic Hospital in Leiden.

Leiden University Medical Centte, Women and Health Department, Poortgebouw, P.O. Box 9600, NL-2300 RC Leiden, The Netherlands. S. 313

Doris Iding

Geb. 1962, Studiert an der Münchener LMU Ethnologie, Religionswissenschaft und Psychologie.Mitarbeiterin bei der AGEM seit 1996. Interessenschwerpunkte liegen auf Schamanismus, transpersonaler Psychologie, Bewusstseinsforschung, sowie Todes- und Jenseitsvorstellungen bei verschiedenen Völkern.

Walhallastr. 19, D-80639 München, Germany. S. 199

Annie Imbens-Fransen

is a theologian and established „the Foundation for Pastoral Care for Women" - after her research on the correlation between „Christianity and Incest" - to provide pastoral counselling for abused women. She publishes extensively and lectures and teaches about themes like „Christianity and Incest, Reading the Bible with Women's Eyes" for women's organizations, church groups, pastors, health care professionals, and students. She participated in Women's symposia and the „World Health Organization" symposia in Europe, as well as in exchange programmes with China, South Africa, and India. In 1996 she was a Coolidge Fellow at „The Association for Religion and Intellectual Life" research colloquium at Yale University.

Stichting Vrouw en Pastoraat, Van der Lansstraat 2, 5644 TA Eindhoven, The Netherlands S. 249

Roselyne Ira

is a sociologist who graduated from the university of Ougadougou. She has participated as a field researcher in a series of demographic studies commissioned by by the Institut National de la Statistique et de la Demographie in Ouagadougou, Burkina Faso. She was a consultant for the Save the Children Fund primary health care project and is now a self-employed business woman.

BP 650, Save-the-Children Fund, Ouagadougou, Burkina Faso. S. 341

Peter Mwangi Kagwanja

Moi Univ., School of Social Cultural Development Studies, Dept.t of History, P.O. Box 3900, Eldoret, Kenya. S. 29

Marie-Therese Karlen
Geb. 1963. Nach mehrjähriger Tätigkeit als kaufmännische Angestellte von 1993 bis 1995 Studium an der Universität in Freiburg i.Ue. (Ethnologie, Journalistik und Geschichte). 1995 Abschluss in Journalistik. Seit 1995 Studium an der Universität Zürich (Ethnologie im Hauptfach, Publizisitik und politische Wissenschaften in den Nebenfächern). Studienschwerpunkte: Geschlechterbeziehungen - Politik und Recht - Migrationsethnologie. Neben dem Studium Tätigkeit als freie Journalistin.
Wehntalerstr. 34, CH-8057 Zürich, Switzerland. S. 335

Edmund J. Kayombo
is an assistant research fellow of the institute of traditional medicine of Muhimbili University college of University of Dar-Es Salaam. Currently he is a student of PhD programme at the University of Vienna in the Department of Medical Anthropology. His area of research is traditional medicine.
Institut of Traditional Medicine, Muhimbili University College, PO Box 65 586 Dar-Es Selaam, Tanzania. S. 13 / 61

Prof. Dr. med. Heribert Kentenich
DRK-Kliniken Westend, Frauen- und Kinderklinik, Pulsstraße 4, D-14059 Berlin, Germany. S. 373

Liselotte Kuntner
diplomierte Physiotherapeutin und Ethnologin. Seit 1976 beschäftigt sie sich mit dem Thema „Gebärhaltung". Sie hat verschiedentlich zum Thema publiziert (siehe Literaturliste) und viele Vorträge und Workshops an Universitäten und Hebammenschulen gehalten. 1987 entwickelte sie zusammen mit Hebammen den Gebärhocker Maia. Sie hat in Asien, Afrika und Lateinamerika Forschungsreisen getätigt. Seit 1989 ist sie Lehrbeauftragte am Ethnologischen Seminar der Universität Zürich, wo sie Vorlesungen und Seminare zum Thema „Geburt und Mutterschaft im Kulturvergleich" hält.
Kornweg 6, CH-5024 Küttingen, Switzerland. S. 321

Kirsten Langeveld
geb. 1960, studierte kulturelle Anthropologie an der Freien Universität in Amsterdam. Im Nationalen Ethnologischen Museum in Leiden beschrieb sie die Maskenkollektion der afrikanischen Abteilung. Danach war sie hier als Registrator bei der Kollektionsverwaltung angestellt. Seit 1994 arbeitet sie als Promovenda an der Universität von Utrecht, wo sie die Untersuchungen über die 'gender'-Relationen und Masken der Diola-Gemeinschaft (Senegal) ausarbeitet (finanziert von der Niederländischen Stiftung für Tropenforschung (WOTRO).
Dept. of Cultural Anthropology, Faculty of Social Sciences, Utrecht University, Heidelberglaan 2-III, NL-3584 Utrecht, The Netherlands. S. 53

Wielant Machleidt
Prof. Dr.med; ärztlicher Direktor der Klinik für Sozialpsychiatrie und Psychotherapie im Zentrum für Psychologische Medizin der Medizinischen Hochschule Hannover. Vorsitzender der Sektion Transkulturelle Psychiatrie in der Deutschen Gesellschaft für Psychiatrie, Psychotherapie und Neurologie.
Medizinische Hochschule Hannover, Konstanty-Gutschow-Str. 8, D-30623 Hannover, Germany. S. 425

Sybille Manneschmidt
lives as a rancher, psychologist and anthropologist in the foothills of Southern Alberta. She has worked cross-culturally in Africa, Asia and Europe and has been involved over the last 10 years with the Peigan Nation.
P.O.Box 2154, Pincher Creek, AB TOK 1WO Canada. S. 157

Musingo Tito E. Mbuvi
Ethnobotanist and interested in community forestry. He has been doing research on plants that are of use/value to different communities with a bias towards indigenous medical food plants.
He is currently Officer-in-Charge of the Kenya Forestry Research Station. This is the Station doing and/or co-ordinating forestry research at the Coast. This involves co-ordinating and initiating new research activities.
Kenya Forestry Research Institute, Coast Forest Research Station - GEDE, PO Box 201, Malindi - Kenya. S. 97

Jean Nadembega
is a state registered nurse and was the technical assistant with the the SCF primary health care programme at the time of the study. He then became the coordinator of the programme and is now working in refugee health in Ruanda with CONCERN.
BP 650, Save-the-Children Fund, Ouagadougou, Burkina Faso. S. 341

Joyce Nato
M.D. (Nrb.), M.B.Ch.B. (Nrb.), FMC Psych (Nrb.);District Psychiatrist, Trans Nzoia District, Western Kenya. Special interests: mental health care services, psychiatric morbidity in women, community psychiatry. P.O.Box 727, Kitale, Kenya. S. 425

Herta Maria Nöbauer

Geb. 1959 in Oberösterreich. Neben beruflicher Tätigkeit Studium der Ethnologie, Philosophie, Zeitgeschichte und Afrikanistik in Wien. Diplomierte 1996 über die medizinisch-therapeutische Bedeutung des Bori-Kultes für Hausa-Frauen. Gründungsmitglied der ARGE Wiener Ethnologinnen. Forschungsschwerpunkte: feministische Theorien; weibliche Widerstands- und Konfliktlösungsformen; Körpervorstellungen und Leibwahrnehmungen. Derzeit Vorbereitungen zu Feldaufenthalt im Hausaland und Dissertation zu letzterem Thema.
Sachsenplatz 2/16, A-1200 Wien, Austria. S. 39

Kabahenda Nyakabwa
41 York Street, P.O. Box 52021, Ottawa, Ontario KIN 580, Canada. S. 401

Wilson Nyaoro

BSc(Hons) (Nairobi); MPhil. CEIS(Moi); CIEM(Cape Town). Lecturer in the Dept. of Environmental Planning and Management at Kenyatta University, Kenya. He is an Environmentalist who has specialised in Resource Use Planning and Management. He is the author of „Environmental Constraints to Sustainable Rural Water Supply Development in Kenya; Towards a Planning Alternative" and several scientific papers. He has long been involved in refugee issues, indigenous knowledge systems and project planning, appraisal and evaluation. He is consultant to the Global Environmental Facility - Kenya's Biodiversity Project. Recently he has shown critical interest in Ethnomedical Systems as well as their healing power and policity implications.
Kenyatta University, Dept. of Enviromental Planning, PO Box 43844, Nairobi, Kenya. S. 45

Brigit Obrist van Eeuwijk

Dr. phil., Ethnologin. Von 1984 bis 1986 Feldforschung zum Thema Kinderfehlernährung in Papua New Guinea. Während mehreren Aufenthalten von 1990 bis 1993 arbeitete sie in einem medizinethnologischen Projekt. 1992 mit Lenka Svejda Hirsch vom Schweizerischen ArbeiterInnen Hilfswerk mit einer Studie zum Krankheitsverhalten von türkischen und kurdischen Menschen in der Region Zürich beauftragt. Im Auftrag oder in Zusammenarbeit mit dem Schweizerischen Tropeninstitut begleitete sie seit 1993 mehrere Studien in Dar es Salaam, Tanzania. 1995/1997 leitete sie ein vom Schweizerischen Nationalfonds finanziertes Forschungsprojekt zum Thema "Gesundheitsbezogene Entscheidungsfindung im Haushalt" in Dar es Salaam.
Ethnologisches Seminar der Universität Basel, Münsterplatz 19, CH-4051 Basel, Switzerland. S. 71

Claudia Offermann

Geb. 1966. Diplom-Psychologin, Assistentin am Lehrstuhl für klinische Psychologie der Universität Landau. Zur Zeit Promotion zum Thema ‚Eßstörungen bei türkischen Migrantinnen'. Seit 1994 Ethnologiestudium an der Universität Heidelberg. Forschungsschwerpunkte: Eßstörungen, Körpererleben von Frauen, interkulturelle Aspekte von psychischer Gesundheit und Krankheit, Forschungsmethoden.
Universität Koblenz-Landau, Abteilung Landau, Fachbereich 8: Psychologie, Im Fort 7, D-76829 Landau, Germany. S. 329

Ágnes Pataki

• university student of ethnography at the Eötvös Lóránd University, Budapest, • main field of interest: folk beliefs
H-1103 Gergely u. 118., Budapest, Hungary. S. 279

Armin Prinz

Geb. 29.7.1945. PD Dr. phil. et med. Ethnologe und Arzt für Allgemeinmedizin. Habilitiert für Ethnomedizin am Institut für Geschichte der Medizin der Universität Wien. Leiter der Abteilung Ethnomedizin. Feldarbeiten in Afrika (Zaire, Senegal, Tansania, Äthiopien), etwa 100 wissenschaftliche Arbeiten zur Ethnomedizin allgemein und der Heilkunde der Azande und der Serer. Filmdokumente beim IWF.
Univ. Wien, Inst. f. Geschichte d. Medizin, Abteilung Ethnomedizin, Währingerstr. 25, A-1090 Wien, Austria. S. 13 / 61

Elvia Ramirez

Ethnic Health Promotion Officer, Southern Zone Public Health Unit, Queensland Health Department. Born in El Salvador, obtained a degree in psychology, practised family counselling psychology for twelve years, lectured at the Faculty of Medicine in the National University of El Salvador. Migrated to Australia in 1989 under the Special Humanitarian Program. Currently undertaking a masters degree on health science with a major in health promotion. Has published in assisting refugee survivors of torture and trauma.
AHURI, Queensland University of Technology, Faculty of Built Environment, QUT, GPO Box 2434, Brisbane, Queensland 4001, Australia. S. 393

Murari Prasad Regmi
Dr. Head of the Central Dept. of Psychology, Tribhuvan University, Kathmandu. He has received his PhD degree in Psychology from Saugar University, India, and Advanced Training in psychology from Freie Universität Berlin, Germany. He has been teaching Psychology courses in this University since more than 25 years. He is author of „Psychology Moving East", „Grurngs: Thunder of Himal", „Himalayan Mind", and „Learning in Nepal", published from USA, India and Sweden respectively. He has published many researches in the areas of cross-cultural learning and self-esteem.
Tribhuvan University, P.O. Box 3115, Kathmandu, Nepal. S. 113

Annemiek J.M. Richters
Prof. Dr., physician and anthropologist. Chair: women and health care, Leiden University Medical Centre. Books: The medical anthropologist as narrator and translator (1991, in Dutch); Women, culture and violence: A development, health and human rights issue (1994).
Psychosomatic Gnecology and Sexology, Poortgebouw, P.O. Box 9600, NL-2300 RC Leiden, The Netherlands. S. 313

Chirly dos Santos-Stubbe
Dr. phil., Dipl.Psych., geb. in Brasilien. Dipl. Psychologi, Soziologie u. Afro-Brasilianistik in Rio de Janeiro u. Mannheim. Lehrbeauftragte für med. Psychologie u. med. Soziologie an der Universität Mannheim/Heidelberg. Freie Mitarbeiterin der Deutschen Stiftung für internationale Entwicklung. Mitherausgeberin zweier internationaler Fachzeitschriften. Forschungsschwerpunkte: med. u. klinische Psychologie, med. Soziologie, Frauen (-Arbeit u. -Gesundheit), afro-brasilianische Geschichte und Kultur, brasilianische Ethno-Medizin.
Collinistr. 5, D-68161 Mannheim, Germany. S. 163

Petra Scheibler
Dr., geb. 1960, Diplompsychologin, Diplom-Sozialwissenschaftlerin, arbeitet als wissenschaftliche Angestellte an der Universität Oldenburg im Bereich Psychologie im Gesundheitswesen. Ihre Forschungsschwerpunkte sind u.a. subjektive Theorien über Gesundheit und Krankheit im interkulturellen Vergleich und interkulturelle Kommunikation. Seit 1986 ist sie Mitglied der Arbeitsgruppe des Weiterbildungsprogrammes ‚Psychologische Gesundheitsförderung für Krankenhauspflegepersonal' am Fernstudienzentrum der Universität Oldenburg.
Universität Oldenburg, Fachbereich 5, Arbeitseinheit Psychologie im Gesundheitswesen, Postfach 2503, D - 26111 Oldenburg, Germany. S. 185/257

Veronika Scherbaum
Geb. 1952. Diplom-Ernährungswissenschaftlerin, Doktorarbeit bei Prof. Fürst, Univ. Stuttgart-Hohenheim. MSc in Mother and Child Health, Universität London. 1984 sowie 1988-91 Nutrition Consultant in West-Äthiopien. 1992/93 Master of Science (MSc) in Mother and Child Health, Universiy of London. Seit 1993/94 Doktorarbeit bei Prof. Dr. Fürst, Universität Stuttgart-Hohenheim.
Dorfstr. 36, D-72074 Tübingen, Germany. S. 103

Eva Schindele
Geb. 1951. Dr. zwei Kinder. Sozialwissenschaftlerin und Publizistin, Buchveröffentlichungen u.a.: „Gläserne Gebärmütter" Frankfurt a.M. 1990; „Pfusch an der Frau" Hamburg 1993 (Taschenbuch 1996); „Schwangerschaft - zwischen guter Hoffnung und Risiko" Hamburg 1995.
Bulthauptstr. 32, D-28209 Bremen, Germany. S. 263

Annette Schmitt
Dr., geb. 1962, Diplompsychologin, arbeitet als Forschungsstipendiatin an der Universität Oldenburg. Ihre Forschungsinteressen sind enge soziale Beziehungen, soziale Emotionen und der Umgang mit belastenden Lebensereignissen.
Universität Oldenburg, Fachbereich 5, Institut zur Erforschung von Mensch-Umwelt-Beziehungen, Postfach 2503, D - 26111 Oldenburg, Germany S. 257

Friederike Schneider
Dr. phil. Ethnologin, Heilpraktikerin. Studium in Mainz; Feldforschungen in Australien und Schottland. Forschungsschwerpunkte: Symbolisches Heilen, traditionelle Heilmethoden, Geschichte der Ethnologie, Frauenforschung. 1997 erscheint ihr neues Buch „Miklouho-Maclay und die heroische Ethnologie: Die Neuguinea-Tagebücher.
Köllertalstrasse 178, D-66265 Heusweiler, Germany. S. 355

Beate A. Schücking
Prof. für Gesundheits- und Krankheitslehre, Psychosomatik an der Universität Osnabrück, Dr. med., Ärztin und Psychotherapeutin; Forschungsschwerpunkt Frauengesundheit in verschiedenen Lebensphasen, Ethnopsychosomatik.
Univ. Osnabrück, A6, Gesundheitswissenschaften, Albrechtstr. 28, D-49069 Osnabrück, Germany. S. 193

Judith Schuler
Dr. phil., Anthropologin. Freie Redakteurin, Lektorat. Chefredakteurin der Zeitschrift curare seit 1994. Reihen: „Beiträge zur Ethnomedizin" (zusammen mit Christine E. Gottschalk-Batschkus); „Medizin am Zügel der Evolution" (zusammen mit Wulf Schiefenhövel); „Das Transkulturelle Psychoforum" (zusammen mit Thomas Heise). Publikationen: 1993 „Infantizid - Biologische und soziale Aspekte"; 1996 (Hg. mit Christine E. Gottschalk-Batschkus) „Ethnomedizinische Perspektiven zur frühen Kindheit"; 1996 Videopublikation: „Muttergottheiten, Fruchtbarkeitssymbole und Mutterschaft. Prof. Dr. Heinz Kirchhoff spricht über seine Sammlung"; 1997 „Krankheit, Heilung und Kultur."
Willi-Ernst-Ring 27, D-83512 Wasserburg, Germany.

Shane Taylor
Researcher at the Australian Housing and Urban Research Institute at the Queensland University of Technology. A qualified educator and Arts graduate with honours, helped compile and draft the Australian National Report for the United Nations Habitat II Conference, Istanbul 1996. Interests include Refugee Housing and Resettlement, service provision and planning for Geographies of Inequality. Has published in Regional Economic Development and implications of economic restructuring on labour and society.
AHURI, Queensland University of Technology, Faculty of Built Environment, QUT, GPO Box 2434, Brisbane, Queensland 4001,
Australia   S. 393

Britta Veth
(Drs.) is attached to the Department of Cultural Anthropology at Utrecht University in Utrecht to finish her Ph.D. thesis. Her research concerns the relationship between Wayana Indian women, cultivated and medicinal plants, and spirits that influence fertility. The research was carried out in French Guiana and Surinam. Indigenous collective (land) rights and indigenous organization (both with special regard to Surinam), and Participatory Methods are also part of her specializations.
Dept. of Cultural Anthropology, Utrecht University, P.O.Box 80.140, NL-3508 TC Utrecht, Netherlands.   S. 175

Shashi B. Vohora
M.V.Sc., Ph.D., D.Sc., Reader in the Dept. of Medical Elementology and Toxicology, Hamdard University, New Delhi. He is the first Ph.D. in Science Policy in India. Major areas of interest: Neuro-psycho-behavioural studies, Medicinal Plants, Medical Elementology, Traditional Mineral Drugs. Participant in many National and International Conferences. Organising Secretary of the IHMMR/WHO sponsored First International Conference on Elements in Health and Disease, New Delhi (1983) and National Symposium on the Development of Indigenous Drugs in India, New Delhi (1988).
Jamia Hamdard University, Department of Medical Elementology and Toxicology, Faculty of Science, Hamdard Nagar, New Delhi 110 062,
India.   S. 125

Divya Vohora
B. Pharm. is currently pursuing her studies for M. Pharm. programme in Pharmacology at the Jamia Hamdard University, Department of Pharmacology, Faculty of Pharmacy, Hamdard Nagar, New Delhi 110 062, India.   S. 125

Jürgen Wacker
MD. was the gynaecologist at the Centre Hopitalier Regional in Dori, Burkina Faso, and is now with the University Hospital in Heidelberg, Germany. His main interest lies in safe motherhood and obstetrics and gynaecology in low cost settings. He is author and has contributed to a series of publications on mother care in developing countries.
Universitäts-Frauenklinik, Voss-Str. 9, D-69115 Heidelberg, Germany.   S. 341

Sigrid Weiß
Geb. 1970, Diplomandin der Ethnologie, Uni Wien. Titel der Diplomarbeit. „Geburt als heiliges Wissen der Frauen um Tod und Wiedergeburt,. Schwerpunkte: Geburt, matriarchale Religion, Schamanismus. Freie Journalistin, Mutter eines zweijährigen Sohnes.
Urbaniweg 12, A-7091 Breitenbrunn, Austria.   S. 269

Inez Werth
Diplom-Politologin, geb. 1947, wissenschaftliche Tätigkeit am Institut für sozialökologische Forschung, Frankfurt, zu Fragen der Abfallwirtschaft und im Rahmen des Berliner Forschungsverbundes Public Health an der TU Berlin zur Integration gesundheitsfördernder und medizinischer Maßnahmen während Schwangerschaft u. Geburt. Weiterer Schwerpunkt ist die Entwicklung der Reproduktionsmedizin unter medizinsoziologischen Aspekten.
Univ. Berlin TU, Institut für Ökologie und Biologie, Sekr. FR 1-1, Franklinstr. 28/29, D-10587 Berlin, Germany.   S. 287

Emine Yüksel
DRK-Kliniken Westend, Frauen- und Kinderklinik, Pulsstraße 4, D-14059 Berlin, Germany.   S. 373

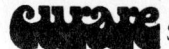

E. Keywordregister (deutsch)

Adoleszenz	13, 103	
Afrika	29, 61, 79, 355, 385, 401, 425	
Afrika südlich der Sahara	85	
Afrika, West	53	
Afrikanische Frauen	415	
Afrobrasilianerinnen	163	
AIDS	85, 401	
Akkulturation	133	
Altern	103	
Andenraum	147, 303	
Androzentrismus in Religionen	249	
angeborenes Elternprogramm	293	
Annahme	97	
arabische Länder	21	
Arbeitsmigrantinnen	367	
Armut	85, 147	
Arzt-Patientin-Beziehung	231	
ärztliches Selbstbild	231	
Äthiopien	13, 103, 409	
Aufgaben der Frauen	85	
Ausbildung von Frauen	123	
Australien	393	
Behinderung	141	
Beruf	293	
Bewältigungsstrategien	415	
Bildungsniveau	85	
Blackfoot Gruppe	157	
Bori-Frauen	39	
Brasilien	163	
Burkina Faso	341	
DDR	287	
Depression	415, 425	
Deutschland	185, 217, 287, 367	
Diagnosermittlung, traditionelle	141	
Einstellung	409	
Elternprogramm, angeborenes	293	
England	207	
Entführung	13	
Epilepsie	409	
Ermächtigung	393	
Ernährung	103	
Erziehung zum Familienleben	13	
Essstörungen	235	
Ethnologie	175	
Ethnomedizin	163	
Europa	243	
europäischer Vergleich	193	
Expressivität	217	
Familie	293	
Familie und Beruf	293	
Familienleben	113	
Familienplanung	61	
Familientherapie	207	
Fertilität	85, 175	
Flüchtlinge	379, 385	
Frauen-Gesundheit	123	
Frauenärzte als Experten	263	
Frauengesundheit	321	
Frauenrechte	355	
Frauensicht	193	
Fruchtbarkeit	53	
Fulbe	341	
Gebärhaltung	321	
Geburt	269, 293	
Geburtsbegleitung	373	
Geburtshilfe	79	
Geburtssysteme, traditionelle	321	
Geburtssysteme, westliche	321	
Geheimnisse	379	
Gender Gewalt	313	
Genitalverstuemmelung	341	
Geschichte	29, 335	
Geschlechterbeziehungen	103, 335	
gesellschaftliche Probleme	409	
gesellschaftliche Struktur	97	
Gesundheitskonzepte	71	
Gesundheitspsychologie	257	
Gesundheitsselbsthilfe	257	
Gesundheitssysteme	163	
Gesundheitswesen, modernes	157	
Gulmance	341	
Guyanisches Amazonengebiet	175	
Gynäkologie u. Geburtshilfe	133, 373	
Hausaland	39	
Hausarbeiterinnen	163	
Haushaltsvorstand, weiblicher	85	
Hauterkrankungen	125	
Hebammen	303	
Hebammenausbildung	193	
Heilbehandlung, traditionelle	141	
Heilen, Symbolisches	303	
HeilerInnen	385, 199	
Heilpflanzen	125, 279	
Hexe	199	
Hexenverfolgung	199	
Hildegard von Bingen	199	
Horopathy Ethnomedizin	123	
Hortikultur	175	
Humanethologie	293	
Immunsystem	401	
Indien	123	
Indigene Gesundheitsvorsorge	133	
Indische Medizin	125	
Industriegesellschaft, westliche	235	
Initiation	269, 341	
Interaktion	207	
interkultureller Vergleich	185	
Intra- u. Intergenerationseffekte	103	
Islam	21, 341	
Kenia	29, 45, 97, 425	
Kindersterblichkeit	133	
Kindheit	103	
Klinische Psychologie	329	
Konstenrentabilität	45	
Konsum- u. Leistungsgesellschaft	235	
Konzeptualisation	45	
Körper-Geist-Hierarchie	39	
Körperbild	329	
Körperformung	231	
Körpervorstellungen	39	
Kosmetik	125	
Krankheiten, weibliche	147	
Kultur	385	
Kulturelle Anthropologie	53	
Kulturenvergleich	293	
Kulturspez. Krankheitskonzepte	367	
kulturspezifische Faktoren	103	
Laktationsmittel, traditionelle	321	

Machtverhältnisse	231	
Mammakarzinom	217	
Maori-Frauen	133	
Masken	53	
matriarchale Religion	269	
matrilineare Kultur	141	
Medikalisierung von Schwangerschaft		263
Medizin, moderne	385	
Medizinsoziologie	163, 243, 287, 367	
Medizintechnik	287	
Melodie	217	
Menschenrechte	313	
Menstruation	13, 335	
Mittelalter	199	
Mond	175	
Munda-Frauen	123	
Musiktherapie	217	
Mutter	293	
Mutter- u. Kind-Gesundheit	321	
mütterliche Gesundheit	79	
Mutterschaft	103	
Mutterschaft, frühe	85	

Nachbarschaftskomitees 147
Nepal 113
Neuseeland 133
Nigeria 79

Österreich 243

Palau 141
passive Hilfesuche 415
Perinatalen Periode 279
Perú 303
politische Ökonomie 29
Psychiatrie 207
Psychische Gesundheit 249
Psychische Störungen 425
Psychologie 393
psychologische Probleme 409
psychosomatische Störungen 21
Psychosoziale Belastungsfaktoren 425
Psychosoziale Situation 113
psychotherapeutische Behandlung 379
Pubertät 263

Qualitative Untersuchung 313

Religiöses Bewusstsein 269
Respekt 123
rituelle Praktiken 39

Schamanismus 303
Schönheitschirurgie 231
Schönheitsmittel 125
Schwangerenbetreuung 287
Schwangerschaft 329
Schwangerschaften von Jugendlichen 313
Schwangerschaftserleben 287
Selbstversorgung 393
Selbstwahrnehmung, weibliche 263
Self Reporting Questionnaire 425
sexuelle Gewalt 379
Sicherheit 45
soziale Rolle 193
soziale Unterstützung 257
soziokulturelle Krankheitsursachen 147
Spanien 185
Städtische Gesundheit 71
Status der Frauen 85
Sterblichkeit 85
Sterilitätstherapie 373
Subjektive Theorien 185
Südamerika 147
Suizidverhalten 207

Tabu 335
Tansania 61
Theologie 249
Tradition 355
Traditionelle Medizin 385, 401
Traditionelle Therapie 303
traditionelle Medizin 29, 61, 113, 415
traditionelle Medizinpraktiken 97
Türkei 367
Türkische Migrantinnen 373

Übergangsriten 293
Übergangsrituale, moderne 263
Übersiedlung 393
Uganda 401
Umweltverschmutzung 243
Ungarn 279

Verhütungsmittel 61
Versorgungsforschung 373

Volksglauben 279
Volksmedizin 279

Wayana Indianischen Frauen 175
Wechseljahre 263
Weibliche Beschneidung 355
Weibliches Wohlbefinden 113
westliche Gesellschaften 257
westlicher Kulturkreis 335
wirtschaftliche Probleme 409
Wochenbett 293

Zimbabwe 313

F. Index of Keywords (english)

Adolescence	13, 103	
Africa	29, 79, 355, 385, 401, 425	
African women	415	
Afro-Brazilians, female	163	
aging	103	
AIDS	85, 401	
Andean countries	147	
Andean region	303	
Androcentrism in Religions	249	
arabic countries	21	
attitude	409	
Australia	393	
Austria	243	

Balance of power	231
beauty aids	125
birth	269, 293
birthing coach	373
Blackfoot people	157
Body Image	329
body-mind-hierarchy	39
Bori-women	39
Brazil	163
Burkina Faso	341

Child mortality	133
childhood	103
circumcision	355
client's view	193
clinical psychology	329
compatibility of family and work	293
conceptions of body	39
concepts of illness	425
conceptualisation	45
consum- and archievment oriented society	235
contraceptives	61
coping	217, 415
cosmetic surgery	231
cosmetics	125
cost-effectiveness	45
crosscultural comparison	293
Cultural Anthropology	53, 175
cultural component	61
culturalspecific concepts of disease	367
culture	385
culture specific factors	103

Depression	415, 425
diagnosis, traditional way of	141
disability	141
doctor-patient-relationship	231

Eating disorders	235
educational attainment	85
empowerment	393
England	207
environmental pollution research	243
epilepsy	409
Ethiopia	13, 103, 409
Ethno-Medicine	163, 279
Europe	193, 243
expressivity	217

Family	293
family life	113
family life education	13
family planning	61
family systems therapy	207
Federal Republic of Germany	287, 367
female headed households	85
fertility	53, 85, 175
folk beliefs	279
Fulani	341

GDR	287
gender issues	103
gender relations	335
gender violence	313
genital mutilation, femal	341, 355
Germany	185, 217, 367
Gurmance	341
Guyana Amazon	175
Gynaecology and Obstetrics	133
Gynecology	373

Hausaland	39
Healer	199, 385
healing with symbols	303
Health	85, 123, 185
Health Care Services	373
Health Concepts	71
Health of Mother and Child	321
Health Promotion	133
Health Psychology	257
Health Systems	163
health aspects, intra- and intergenerational	103
help-seeking, passive	415
Hildegard von Bingen	199
history	335
horopathy ethnomedicine	123
Horticulture	175
human ethology	293
human rights	313
Hungary	279

Immigration	393
immune system	401
India	123
Indian medicine	125
interaction	207
intercultural comparison	185
Islam	21
Islamisiation	341

Kenya	29, 45, 97, 425
kidnapping	13
Knowledge Assumptions	97

Lactation, substances for	321
Lay health care	257
Lay theories	185

Maleus maleficarum	199
mamma carcinom	217
Maori-Women	133
marital discord	113
masks	53
maternal health	79
matrilineal culture	141
matrimarchial religion	269
medical self-portrayel	231
medical sociology	163, 367
medical technics	287
medicalisation of puberty	263
medicinal plants	125, 279
medicine sociology	243
medicine, modern	385

melody	217	
menopause	263	
menstruation	13, 335	
mental health	249	
middle age	199	
midwifery care	193	
midwifery training	193	
midwives	303	
migrants, female labour	367	
Modern Health Services	157	
moon	175	
mortality	85	
motherhood	103	
motherhood, early	85	
Munda-women	123	
music therapy	217	
Muslemic society	21	
Neighbourhood initiatives	147	
Nepal	113	
New Zealand	133	
Nigeria	79	
nutrition	103	
Obstetrics	79, 373	
Palau	141	
parental care, intuitive	293	
perception of pregnancy	287	
perceptions	393	
perinatal health	279	
persecution of witches	199	
Perú	303	
position in labour	321	
poverty	85	
poverty, female	147	
pregnancy	263, 329	
prenatal care	287	
psychiatric disorders	425	
psychiatry	207	
psycho-social risk factors	425	
psycho-socio-economical problems	409	
psychology	393	
psychosocial	113	
psychosomatic disorders	21	
psychotherapeutic treatment	379	
puerperium	293	
Qualitative research	313	
Refugees	385	
refugees, female	379	
religous consciousness	269	
respect	123	
rite of passage	269, 293, 341	
ritual practices	39	
roles and status of women	85	
Safety	45	
secrets	379	
self reporting questionnaire	425	
Self-Care	393	
self-images, negative female	263	
sexual violence	379	
shamanism	303	
shaping of the body	231	
significance	45	
skin diseases	125	
social status	193	
social support	257	
society's structure	97	
sociocultural pathogenetic factors, female	147	
sociology of medicine	287	
somestics	163	
Southamerica	147	
Spain	185	
sterility treatment	373	
Sub-Sahara Africa	85	
suicidal behaviour	207	
Taboo	335	
Tanzania	61	
teenage pregnancy	313	
Theology	249	
tradition	355	
traditional birth systems	321	
traditional healingcure	141	
traditional means	321	
traditional medical practice	97	
traditional medicine	61, 113, 385, 401, 415	
traditional medicine systems	29	
traditional treatment	303	
training of women	123	
turkish migrants	373	
turkish women	367	
Uganda	401	
urban health	71	
Wayana Indian women	175	
West-Africa	53	
western birth systems	321	
western cultures	335	
western industrial societies	235	
western societies	257	
witches	199	
woman and mother	293	
women's rights	355	
women's role	257	
women's health	321	
women's well-being	113	
work	293	
Zimbabwe	313	